The Acts of Welsh Rulers 1120–1283

THE ACTS OF WELSH RULERS
1120–1283

edited by

HUW PRYCE

with the assistance of

CHARLES INSLEY

*Published on behalf of the History and Law Committee of
the University of Wales Board of Celtic Studies*

CARDIFF
UNIVERSITY OF WALES PRESS
2005

First published in 2005
PPC edition with corrections published in 2010

British Library Cataloguing-in-Publication Data
A catalogue record for this book is available from the British Library

ISBN 978-0-7083-2383-0
e-ISBN 978-0-7083-0-2387-8

Printed in Great Britain by CPI Antony Rowe, Chippenham, Wiltshire
Typeset by Mark Heslington, Scarborough, North Yorkshire

I Nancy

CONTENTS

THE ACTS

LIST OF MAPS

LIST OF GENEALOGICAL TABLES

LIST OF TABLES

LIST OF PLATES

ACKNOWLEDGEMENTS

When over a decade ago Rees Davies suggested that I might like to undertake an edition of the acts of Welsh rulers I had edited only two charters and was far from certain that I wanted to edit any more. That I overcame my initial hesitation owes a great deal both to his characteristically generous support and to the encouragement and help of many others, and it is a pleasure to acknowledge my debt to all the institutions and individuals without whose assistance this edition would never have seen the light of day. The foundations were laid in a project funded by the Higher Education Funding Council for Wales in 1993–4 that identified the majority of the documents, and I am grateful to Kari Maund for her efficiency and diligence in compiling the resulting *Handlist*. Work on the edition itself was supported initially by a substantial grant from the Leverhulme Trust that allowed the employment of Charles Insley as a research assistant for eighteen months from September 1995 and also paid for copies of documents and other expenses. Warm thanks are due both to the Trust for its generosity and to Charles Insley for his invaluable help, in particular for transcribing a great majority of the texts; he also shed important new light on aspects of the diplomatic of Welsh rulers' charters. As sole editor since March 1997 I checked all the transcripts passed on to me by Dr Insley, transcribed the remaining texts and collated variant readings as necessary, completed entries for documents known only from mentions in other sources, supplied English summaries of documents extant as texts, provided endnotes discussing individual points of detail and wrote the Introduction: the responsibility for errors or other deficiencies in the edition is therefore mine alone. I am indebted to the Arts and Humanities Research Board for the award of a grant under its Research Leave scheme that enabled me to take a year's sabbatical leave in 2000–1 during which the bulk of the remaining editorial work was completed. That work was also facilitated by the support of the Department of History and Welsh History at University of Wales, Bangor, and especially of Duncan Tanner during his term of office as head of department. For grants towards the publication costs of what has turned out to be a much longer volume than originally anticipated I wish to record my gratitude to the Marc Fitch Fund and the University of Wales Board of Celtic Studies for their generous support as well as to Research Centre Wales at University of Wales, Bangor. My thanks go to Susan Jenkins, Ruth Dennis-Jones and Richard Houdmont for advice on costings and other practicalities prior to submission of the final version of the work to the University of Wales Press and to Ceinwen Jones and Nia Peris as the editors responsible for seeing the work through the press. I am grateful to Aimee Pritchard for drawing the maps.

My recently retired Bangor colleague Tony (A. D.) Carr gave valued encouragement and assistance from the very beginning of this project, as did J. Beverley Smith, to whose published work the present volume owes much. I am likewise greatly indebted to Ralph Griffiths for his stalwart support. The final text of the edition was improved by the helpful corrections and suggestions of the anonymous reader appointed by the Board of Celtic Studies. I am very grateful to Tessa Webber for providing detailed comments on the palaeography of originals; to Paul Russell for answering queries on tricky points of Latinity; to David Trotter for help with documents in French; and to Julia Barrow for advice on editorial conventions. David Crook kindly informed me about two original documents held at Belton House and arranged for me to be able to publish them here. David Crouch, Jon Crump and Nicholas Vincent also brought documents to my attention I would otherwise have missed and gave other valuable help. For access to unpublished material on Welsh place-names I am indebted to Ann Daniels of the Melville Richards Place-Names Archive at the University of Wales, Bangor, and the archive's director, Hywel Wyn Owen; to Terry James and the Carmarthenshire Antiquarian Society Place-Names Survey; and to Iwan Wmffre, whose doctoral thesis proved an indispensable guide to place-names in Cardiganshire. For help with individual texts and other matters I also wish to thank Paul Brand, Pierre Chaplais, John Cottrell, Fred Cowley, Seán Duffy, Anne Duggan, R. Geraint Gruffydd, Sally Harper, David Howlett, Daniel Huws, Helen Nicholson, Robert Patterson, Paul Remfry, W. Rhys Robinson, Richard Sharpe, Fred Suppe, David Thornton and Louise Wilkinson. In addition, I benefited from feedback on papers read at seminars at the University of Liverpool and University College London and conferences at University of Wales, Lampeter, and University of Wales Swansea. Research trips to London and Oxford were made more enjoyable by the hospitality of, respectively, Jeremy Palmer and Gifford and Thomas Charles-Edwards.

I am grateful to all the librarians and archivists who facilitated access to documents and manuscripts in their care and answered my queries, particularly Claire Breay of the British Library, Ghislain Brunel of the Archives Nationales de France, Gaye Morgan of All Souls Library, Oxford, and Gordon Reid of the Powys County Archives Office. Thanks are also due to His Grace the Duke of Rutland for allowing access to his muniments at Belvoir Castle. Every effort has been made to obtain permission to publish texts of documents, and I should like to thank the following institutions and individuals for granting such permission with respect to material in their custody or ownership: the National Library of Wales; the Berkeley Will Trust; Gwynedd Archives Service; the Master and Fellows of Trinity College, Cambridge; Cardiff County and City Library; the Glamorgan Record Office; the Denbighshire Record Office; the Devon Record Office; the Bishop of Hereford and the Hereford Record Office; the Powys County Archives Office; the British Library; Lambeth Palace Library; The National Archives; the Society of Antiquaries of London; the Bodleian Library, Oxford; Shropshire Records and Research; the Countess of Sutherland; Archivio Segreto Vaticano; the Vatican Library; Mrs Vanda Wright. No. 471 is published by permission of the Provost and Fellows of Eton College. Texts from the 'Magnum Registrum Album' are reproduced by kind permission of the Chapter of Lichfield Cathedral. Derbyshire Record Office D3580/T1–3 are reproduced by permission from the Longsdon family papers. I am also grateful to the Glamorgan Record Office, the Provost and Fellows of Eton College, the British Library and The National Archives for permission to reproduce photographs of documents.

Finally, I wish to thank my wife Nancy Edwards and son Iestyn for all their support and understanding during my long preoccupation with the present work. The dedication expresses the special debt of gratitude I owe Nancy: through her advice and unstinting encouragement she has played an essential role in ensuring this volume's completion.

Huw Pryce

GENERAL ABBREVIATIONS AND CONVENTIONS

Add.	Additional
BL	British Library, London
cd.	calendared
Ch.	Charter
cmt.	commote
fo(s)	folio(s)
Lat.	Latin
m.	membrane
Mod.	Modern
MS(S)	Manuscript(s)
NLW	National Library of Wales, Aberystwyth
par.	parish
Pat.	Patent
pd.	printed
pl.	plural
R.	Roll
TNA: PRO	The National Archives: Public Record Office, London
trans.	translated
W.	Welsh

Dates of manuscripts are expressed according to established conventions: thus s. xiii in., s. xiii med. and s. xiii ex. for the early, mid- and late thirteenth century respectively, s. xiii^1 for the first half and s. xiii^2 for the second half of the thirteenth century, s. xiii/xiv for the end of the thirteenth or beginning of the fourteenth century, s. xiii–xiv for the thirteenth to fourteenth centuries.

Where they have been identified, the modern forms of Welsh place-names are generally given in the forms recommended in *A Gazetteer of Welsh Place-Names*, ed. E. Davies (Cardiff, 1957), or M. Richards, *Welsh Administrative and Territorial Units* (Cardiff, 1969), the main exceptions being commonly used English forms such as Anglesey, Cardiff, Carmarthen or Swansea. The Welsh territorial term *cantref* (pl. *cantrefi*) has been treated as an English noun and rendered as cantref (pl. cantrefs).

All secondary works are referred to in the notes in an abbreviated form: full bibliographical details of both abbreviated references and works cited by author and short title (or short title only in the case of some edited texts) are provided in the Bibliography.

MANUSCRIPT SOURCES CITED

Aberystwyth, National Library of Wales,
 Bachymbyd 217: **441**; 984: **318**
 Bodewryd MS 102D: **542**
 Llanstephan MS 156: **563**
 NLW MSS 1506C: **500, 514**; 1641B, vol. ii: **13, 283, 554**; 2020B (formerly Panton MS 52):
  260; 3075D: **391**; 3746D: **179**; 7011D: **369, 529**; 7851D (Shrewsbury Cartulary): **522**;
  9070E (formerly Panton Papers 20): **234**; 13211E: **391**; 13215E: **391**
 Peniarth MSS 208: **513**; 225B: **234**; 231B: **345, 368–9, 387, 397, 529**; 236: **601**
 Penrice and Margam Charters 45: **188**; 51: **133**; 54: p. 113; 59: **136**; 73: **177**; 85: **142**; 86:
  161; 87: **145**; 88: **163**; 89: **157**; 90: p. 113; 91: **146**; 92: p. 113; 93: p. 113; 95: p. 113; 100:
  148; 106: **153**; 107: **174**; 108: **119**; 109: **182**; 110a: **164**; 110b: **164**; 111: **163**; 112: **126**;
  115: **199**; 120: **204**; 123: **219**; 140: **272**; 212: **131, 154**; 523: **183**; 1957: **189**; 1973: p. 114;
  2017: **134**; 2019: **130**; 2020: **123**; 2021: **128**; 2022: **129**; 2023: **127**; 2024: **147**; 2025: **137**;
  2026: **153**; 2027: **157**; 2029: **162**; 2030: **165**; 2031: **159**; 2032: **161**; 2033: **172**; 2034: **171**;
  2035: **175**; 2036: **180**; 2051: **184**; 2052: **186**
 Penrice and Margam Rolls 288: **123, 133, 135, 144, 153, 160, 188**; 290: **617–18**; 292:
  127–8, 130, 139, 142–3, 145–6, 148, 157, 161, 165, 166, 169, 172, 180; 293: **181, 188,**
  189–90; 543: **131, 138, 154–5, 162, 172–3, 178**; 2089: **131**; 2090: **122, 151, 159–60, 171,**
  174–7; 2093: **122, 131–4, 136–8, 142–3, 146, 152, 154–5, 157, 162, 164, 170, 172**
 SA/MB/2: **529**
 Slebech 247: **31–2, 59, 60, 64**
 Wynnstay Estate Records, Inspeximus, Shrewsbury, 5 April 1584: **549, 565**; Transcript by
  William Jones of Dôl Hywel, Llangadfan, 18 July 1795: **5–6**; Ystrad Marchell
  Charters, nos 5: **483**; 11: **541**; 14: **544**; 15: **487**; 18: **8**; 21: **553**; 23: **555**; 33: **556**; 34: **563**;
  35: **551**; 41: **569**; 42: **9**; 50: **548**; 51: **545**; 53: **575**; 54: **10**; 58: **231**; 59: **11**; 60: **12**; 62: **577**;
  64: **16**; 65: **17**; 68: **282**; 80: **581**; 101: **496**

Belton House, Grantham,
 Charter of Llywelyn ap Iorwerth: **226**
 Letter patent of Dafydd ap Llywelyn: **304**

Belvoir Castle, Muniments of the Duke of Rutland,
 Bakewell Ch. 1438: **587–8**
 'Transcripts of Derbyshire Charters at Haddon Hall' by W. A. Carrington (1890), vol. i:
  588; vol. v: **588**; vol. vi: **587–8**

Berkeley Castle Muniments, Select Book 1 (Cartulary of St Augustine's Abbey, Bristol):
462

Caernarfon, Gwynedd Archives Service, Newborough (Rug) Estate Archives (Rug Section)
XD2/1111: **482**; XD2/1112: **488**; XD2/1113: **504**

Cambridge
  Corpus Christi College MSS 16: **111, 284, 300**; 295: **195**; 452: **191**
  Trinity College MS R. 5. 33 (Register of Glastonbury Abbey): **467, 476**

Cardiff
  Cardiff County and City Library MSS 3.11: **1, 480**; 4.83: **499**; 4.101: **197–8, 207, 225, 234**
  Glamorgan Record Office, CL/DEEDS/1/2384: **587**; CL/DEEDS/1/3250: **18**

Eton College Records, 64/1: **471**

Évreux, Archives départementales de l'Eure, H 9: **469**

Exeter, Devon Record Office, 312M/TY18: **22**

Hereford Record Office, AL 19/1 (Register of Thomas Cantilupe): **389**

Lichfield Dean and Chapter Muniments, 'Magnum Registrum Album': **586, 599**

Llandrindod Wells, Powys County Archives Office, Welshpool Borough Collection, AA1:
593

London
  British Library,
      Additional Charters 10637: **508**; 26727: **108**
      Additional MSS 4558: **307**; 14949: **260**; 21253: **500**; 50121 (Lilleshall Cartulary): **579**
      Cotton Charter 24/17: **252**
      Cotton MSS Claudius B. ii: **195**; Domitian A.iii (Leominster Priory Cartulary): **238**;
          Domitian V: **220**
      Harleian Charters 75 A 25: **181**; 75 B 28: **150**; 75 B 29: **121**; 75 B 30: **144**; 75 B 31: **141**;
          75 B 40: p. 114; 75 C 19: **190**; 75 C 21: **176**; 75 C 34: **155**; 75 C 35: **168**; 75 C 36: **151**;
          75 C 37: **170**
      Harleian MSS 696: **218–19, 229, 423, 440**; 1240 (Mortimer Cartulary): **244, 259, 317,
          424**; 2044: **252**; 2079: **252**; 3725 (Register of Aberconwy Abbey): **206, 218**; 4799
          (Cartulary of Lichfield Cathedral): **586, 599**; 6068: **35, 55, 197**; 6280: **43, 52, 57, 73**
  Lambeth Palace Library, Register of Archbishop Pecham: **77, 101–2, 428–31, 454–5, 538**
  The National Archives: Public Record Office,
      C 47 (Chancery Miscellanea), C 47/10/43: **458**; C 47/27/1: **361–2, 399**; C 47/27/2: **398**
      C 49 (Chancery and Exchequer King's Remembrancer Parliamentary and Council
          Proceedings), C 49/81 (Brevia Regis J; formerly C 49/Roll 9): **239**
      C 53 (Charter Rolls), C 53/8: **119, 156**; C 53/12: **29, 33, 47**; C 53/28: **477**; C 53/34: **284**;

Matlock, Derbyshire Record Office, D3580/T1: **583**; T2: **584**; T3: **585**

Oxford
    All Souls College MS 182: **77, 101–2, 428–31, 454–5, 538**
    Bodleian Library,
        Blakeway MS 17: p. 87
        Bodleian MS 937: **195**
        Dugdale MSS 15: **252**; 39: **1, 480**
        Rawlinson MS B.464: **500, 514**

Paris
    Archives Nationales de France, J 655, no. 14: **235**
    Bibliothèque Nationale, Nouvelles acquisitions latines 391: **113**

Ruthin, Denbighshire Record Office, Wynnstay Estate Archives DD/WY/4202: **499**

Shrewsbury, Shropshire Records and Research Centre,
    MS 6001/6869 (Haughmond Cartulary): **1–2, 197–205, 207–8, 225–7, 258, 289, 480, 546**
        212/box 385: **226**
    972 (Sutherland)/box 220: **582**
    2922/15/1: **200, 202–3, 205, 225–6**

Vatican City
    Archivio Segreto Vaticano, Reg. Vat. 11: **253**; 13: p. 77, **279**
    Biblioteca Apostolica Vaticana,
        MSS Reg. lat. 179: **193–4, 196**; 470: **192**
        MSS Vat. lat. 1220, 6027: **195**

Winchester, Hampshire Record Office, A1/1 (Register of John of Pontoise): **428**

Wright family, half of bipartite chirograph: **597**

BIBLIOGRAPHY
(INCLUDING BIBLIOGRAPHICAL ABBREVIATIONS)

AC *Annales Cambriae*, ed. J. Williams ab Ithel (Rolls Series, London, 1860).

Acta of William I Regesta Regum Anglo-Normannorum: The Acta of William I (1066–1087), ed. D. Bates (Oxford, 1998).

The Acts of William I, King of Scots 1165–1214, ed. G. W. S. Barrow with the collaboration of W. W. Scott (Regesta Regum Scottorum, 2; Edinburgh, 1971).

Adami de Domerham De Rebus Gestis Glastoniensibus, ed. T. Hearne, 2 vols (Oxford, 1727).

ALEXANDER, J. W., *Ranulf of Chester: A Relic of the Conquest* (Athens, Ga., 1983).

ALTSCHUL, M., 'The lordship of Glamorgan and Morgannwg, 1217–1317: I. Glamorgan and Morgannwg under the rule of the De Clare family', in *Glamorgan County History*, iii. 45–72.

AM Annales Monastici, ed. H. R. Luard, 5 vols (Rolls Series, London, 1864–9).

Ancient Laws and Institutes of Wales, ed. A. Owen, 2 vols (Record Commission, London, 1841).

Anglo-Scottish Relations, 1174–1328, ed. E. L. G. Stones (London, 1965).

Ann. Cestr. Annales Cestrienses, ed. R. C. Christie (Record Society of Lancashire and Cheshire, 14; London, 1887).

ANON, 'Documents illustrative of the history of the princes of upper Powis', *Arch. Camb.*, 3rd series, 13 (1867), 116–24.

—— 'Historical Records Commission', *Arch. Camb.*, 4th series, 11 (1880), 148–50.

—— 'Index to "Llyfr Coch Asaph"', *Arch. Camb.*, 3rd series, 14 (1868), 151–66, 329–40, 433–43.

—— 'Merionethshire', *Arch. Camb.*, 5th series, 2 (1885), 227–9.

—— 'Miscellanea VII', *Mont. Coll.*, 9 (1876), 418–19.

—— 'The Rhos Fynach charter', *Proc. Llandudno and District Field Club*, 11 (1924–5), 129–31.

—— 'South-west Wales and the public records', *The Caermarthenshire Miscellany* (March 1892), 30–1.

—— 'A Trefeglwys charter: charter of Gruffuth ap Cynan to the abbey of Haughmond', *Mont. Coll.*, 33 (1904), 239–42.

—— 'Valle Crucis Abbey: additional particulars', *Arch. Camb.*, 1st series, 1 (1846), 151–3.

—— 'Valle Crucis Abbey—award', *Arch. Camb.*, 3rd series, 10 (1864), 100–1.

The Antient Kalendars and Inventories of the Treasury of His Majesty's Exchequer, ed. F. Palgrave, 3 vols (Record Commission, London, 1836).

Arch. Camb.   *Archaeologia Cambrensis.*

Antiphonale Sarisburiense, ed. W. H. Frere, 6 vols (London, 1901–25; repr. Farnborough, 1966).

BANKS, R. W., 'Notes to the account of Cwmhir Abbey, Radnorshire', *Arch. Camb.*, 5th series, 5 (1888), 204–17.

BANNISTER, A. T., *The Place-Names of Herefordshire: Their Origin and Development* (n. p., 1916).

BARING-GOULD, S. and FISHER, J., *Lives of the British Saints*, 4 vols (London, 1907–13).

BARRELL, A. D. M. and DAVIES, R. R., 'Land, lineage, and revolt in north-east Wales, 1243–1441: a case study', *CMCS*, 29 (Summer 1995), 27–51.

BARROW, G. W. S., *The Kingdom of the Scots: Government, Church and Society from the Eleventh to the Fourteenth Century* (London, 1973).

—— 'Wales and Scotland in the Middle Ages', *WHR*, 10 (1980–1), 302–19.

BARTLETT, R., *Gerald of Wales 1146–1223* (Oxford, 1982).

BARTON, P. G., 'Gruffudd ap Gwenwynwyn's Trefnant market charter 1279–1282', *Mont. Coll.*, 90 (2002), 69–86.

BARTRUM, P. C., 'Plant yr Arglwydd Rhys', *NLWJ*, 14 (1965–6), 97–104.

BARTRUM, *WG*   Bartrum, P. C., *Welsh Genealogies, AD 300–1400*, 8 vols (Cardiff, 1974).

BATESON, M., 'The laws of Breteuil', *EHR*, 15 (1900), 73–8, 302–18, 496–523, 754–7.

BBCS   Bulletin of the Board of Celtic Studies.

BERGER, É., 'Les préparatifs d'une invasion anglaise et la descente de Henri III en Bretagne (1229–30)', *Bibliothèque de l'École des chartes*, 54 (1893), 5–44.

BEZANT LOWE, W., *The Heart of Northern Wales* (Llanfairfechan, 1912).

BINCHY, D. A., 'Some Celtic legal terms', *Celtica*, 3 (1956), 221–31.

BIRCH, *Catalogue*   Birch, W. de G., *A Descriptive Catalogue of the Penrice and Margam Abbey Manuscripts*, 6 vols (London, 1893–1905).

BIRCH, *Margam*   Birch, W. de G., *A History of Margam Abbey Derived from the Original Documents in the British Museum, H. M. Record Office, the Margam Muniments etc.* (London, 1897).

BIRCH, *Seals*   Birch, W. de G., *Catalogue of Seals in the Department of Manuscripts in the British Museum*, 6 vols (London, 1887–1900).

BISHOP, T. A. M., *Scriptores Regis* (Oxford, 1961).

The Black Book of St. David's, ed. J. W. Willis-Bund (Cymmrodorion Record Series, 5; London, 1902).

The Book of Fees, commonly called Testa de Nevill, 2 vols (London, 1920–3).

BRADNEY, J. A., *A History of Monmouthshire*, 4 vols (London, 1904–33).

BRADY, R., *A Complete History of England* (London, 1685).

BRAND, P., *The Origins of the English Legal Profession* (Oxford, 1992).

Breudwyt Ronabwy, ed. M. Richards (Cardiff, 1948).

BRIDGEMAN, G. T. O., *History of the Princes of South Wales* (Wigan, 1876).

—— 'The princes of upper Powys', *Mont. Coll.*, 1 (1868), 5–194.

BROWN, A. E., 'The castle, borough and park of Cefnllys', *Radnorshire Society T.*, 42 (1972), 11–22.

BRUNEL, C., 'Les actes des rois de France scellés de sceau d'or', *Mitteilungen des Instituts für österreichische Geschichtsforschung*, 62 (1954), 112–20.

BS   Brenhinedd y Saesson, or, The Kings of the Saxons, ed. T. Jones (Cardiff, 1971).

BT, Pen20   Brut y Tywysogyon, Peniarth MS. 20, ed. T. Jones (Cardiff, 1941).

BT, Pen20Tr   Brut y Tywysogyon, or, The Chronicle of the Princes, Peniarth MS. 20 Version, trans. T. Jones (Cardiff, 1952).

BT, RBH   Brut y Tywysogyon, or, The Chronicle of the Princes, Red Book of Hergest Version, ed. T. Jones (2nd edn, Cardiff, 1973).

BULLOCK-DAVIES, C., *Professional Interpreters and the Matter of Britain* (Cardiff, 1966).

CAC   Calendar of Ancient Correspondence concerning Wales, ed. J. G. Edwards (Cardiff, 1935).

Calendar of County Court, City Court and Eyre Rolls of Chester, 1259–1297, ed. R. Stewart Brown (Chetham Society, 84; Manchester, 1925).

Calendar of Documents relating to Scotland, ed. J. Bain, 4 vols (Edinburgh, 1881–8).

Calendar of the Wynn (of Gwydir) Papers, ed. J. Ballinger (Aberystwyth, 1926).

CAMARGO, M., *Ars Dictaminis, Ars Dictandi* (Typologie des sources du moyen âge occidental, 60; Turnhout, 1991).

CAMERON, K., *The Place-Names of Derbyshire*, 3 vols (EPNS, 27–9; Cambridge, 1959).

Canterbury Professions, ed. M. Richter (Canterbury and York Society, 67; Torquay, 1973).

'Canu Owain Cyfeiliog', ed. G. A. Williams, in *Gwaith Llywelyn Fardd I ac Eraill o Feirdd y Ddeuddegfed Ganrif*, ed. K. A. Bramley *et al.* (Cyfres Beirdd y Tywysogion, 2; Cardiff, 1994), 191–277.

CAP   Calendar of Ancient Petitions relating to Wales, ed. W. Rees (Cardiff, 1975).

CARPENTER, D. A., *The Minority of Henry III* (London, 1990).

CARR, A. D., 'Anglo-Welsh relations, 1066–1282', in M. Jones and M. Vale (eds), *England and her Neighbours, 1066–1453: Essays in Honour of Pierre Chaplais* (London and Ronceverte, 1989), 121–38.

——— 'An aristocracy in decline: the native Welsh lords after the Edwardian conquest', *WHR*, 5 (1970–1), 103–29.

——— 'The barons of Edeyrnion, 1282–1485 [I]', *JMHRS*, 4 (1961–4), 187–93.

——— 'A debatable land: Arwystli in the Middle Ages', *Mont. Coll.*, 80 (1992), 39–54.

——— '"The last and weakest of his line": Dafydd ap Gruffydd, the last prince of Wales', *WHR*, 19 (1998–9), 375–99.

——— 'The last days of Gwynedd', *TCHS*, 43 (1982), 7–22.

——— *Medieval Anglesey* (Llangefni, 1982).

——— *Owen of Wales: The End of the House of Gwynedd* (Cardiff, 1991).

——— 'The priory of Penmon', *J. of Welsh Ecclesiastical History*, 3 (1986), 18–30.

——— 'Prydydd y Moch: ymateb hanesydd', *THSC*, 1989, 161–80.

——— and SMITH, J. B., 'Edeirnion and Mawddwy', *History of Merioneth*, ii. 137–67.

CARRINGTON, W. A., 'Illustrations of ancient place-names in Bakewell and the vicinity, from original archives preserved at Haddon Hall, and from other sources', *J. of the Derbyshire Archaeological and Natural History Society*, 15 (1893), 31–64.

Cart. Bristol   The Cartulary of St Augustine's Abbey, Bristol, ed. D. Walker (Bristol and Gloucestershire Archaeological Society; Gloucestershire Record series, 10; 1998).

Cart. Chester   The Chartulary or Register of the Abbey of St Werburgh, Chester, i, ed. J. Tait (Chetham Society, new series, 79; Manchester, 1920).

Cart. Glouc.   Historia et Cartularium Monasterii S. Petri Gloucestriae, ed. W. H. Hart, 3 vols (Rolls Series, London, 1863–7).

Cart. Haugh.   *The Cartulary of Haughmond Abbey*, ed. U. Rees (Cardiff 1985).

Cart. Lilleshall   *The Cartulary of Lilleshall Abbey*, ed. U. Rees (Shropshire Archaeological and Historical Society, [Shrewsbury] 1997).

Cart. Shrews.   *The Cartulary of Shrewsbury Abbey*, ed. U. Rees, 2 vols (Aberystwyth, 1975).

Cartae   *Cartae et Alia Munimenta quae ad Dominium de Glamorgancia Pertinent*, ed. G. T. Clark, 6 vols (2nd edn, Cardiff, 1910).

The Cartulary of the Knights of St. John of Jerusalem in England. Part 2. Prima Camera: Essex, ed. M. Gervers (Oxford, 1996).

Cat. Anc. Deeds   *A Descriptive Catalogue of Ancient Deeds in the Public Record Office*, i (London, 1890).

CChancW   *Calendar of Chancery Warrants, 1244–1326* (London, 1927).

CChR   *Calendar of the Charter Rolls preserved in the Public Record Office* (London, 1903–27).

CCR   *Calendar of the Close Rolls preserved in the Public Record Office* (London 1900–).

CDI   *Calendar of Documents relating to Ireland*, ed. H. S. Sweetman and G. F. Handcock, 5 vols (London, 1875–86).

CFR   *Calendar of the Fine Rolls, 1272–1471* (London, 1911–).

CHAPLAIS, P., *Diplomatic Documents,* i. *1101–1272* (London, 1964).

—— 'English diplomatic documents to the end of Edward III's reign', in D. A. Bullough and R. L. Storey (eds), *The Study of Medieval Records: Essays in Honour of Kathleen Major* (Oxford, 1971), 22–56.

—— *English Royal Documents: King John–Henry VI 1199–1461* (Oxford, 1971).

—— *Essays in Medieval Diplomacy and Administration* (London, 1981).

CHARLES, B. G., 'An early charter of the abbey of Cwmhir', *Radnorshire Society T.*, 40 (1970), 68–74.

—— *The Place-Names of Pembrokeshire*, 2 vols (Aberystwyth, 1992).

—— 'The records of Slebech', *NLWJ*, 5 (1947–8), 179–98.

CHARLES-EDWARDS, T. M., *Early Irish and Welsh Kinship* (Oxford, 1993).

—— and JONES, N. A., '*Breintiau Gwŷr Powys*: the liberties of the men of Powys', in T. M. Charles-Edwards, M. E. Owen and P. Russell (eds), *The Welsh King and his Court* (Cardiff, 2000), 191–223.

Charters of the Honour of Mowbray 1107–1191, ed. D. E. Greenway (London, 1972).

Charters of the Redvers Family and the Earldom of Devon, 1090–1217, ed. R. Bearman (Devon and Cornwall Record Society, new series, 37; 1994).

CHENEY, C. R., *English Bishops' Chanceries 1100–1250* (Manchester, 1950).

—— 'The office and title of the papal chancellor, 1187–1216', *Archivum historiae pontificiae*, 22 (1984), 369–76.

Chester Charters   *The Charters of the Anglo-Norman Earls of Chester c.1071–1237*, ed. G. Barraclough (Record Society of Lancashire and Cheshire, 126; 1988).

CHIBNALL, M., 'Dating the charters of the smaller religious houses in Suffolk in the twelfth and thirteenth centuries', in M. Gervers (ed.), *Dating Undated Medieval Charters* (Woodbridge, 2000), 51–9.

—— *The Empress Matilda: Queen Consort, Queen Mother and Lady of the English* (Oxford, 1991).

—— 'Houses of Augustinian canons', in *VCH Shropshire*, ii. 59–83.

Chronica Magistri Rogeri de Houedene, ed. W. Stubbs, 4 vols (Rolls Series, London, 1868–71).

The Chronicle of John of Worcester, iii, ed. P. McGurk (Oxford, 1998).

'Chronicle of the thirteenth century. MS. Exchequer Domesday', *Arch. Camb.*, 3rd series, 8 (1862), 272–83.

CHURCH, S. D., *The Household Knights of King John* (Cambridge, 1999).

CIM Calendar of Inquisitions Miscellaneous (Chancery) preserved in the Public Record Office (London, 1916–).

CIPM Calendar of Inquisitions Post Mortem (London, 1904–).

CLANCHY, M. T., *From Memory to Written Record: England 1066–1307* (2nd edn, Oxford, 1993).

CLARK, G. T., 'Contributions toward a cartulary of Margam', *Arch. Camb.*, 3rd series, 13 (1867), 311–34; 14 (1868), 24–59, 182–96, 345–82.

—— 'The lords of Avan, of the blood of Jestyn', *Arch. Camb.*, 3rd series, 13 (1867), 1–44.

—— 'Some account of the parish of Llancarvan, Glamorganshire', *Arch. Camb.*, 3rd series, 11 (1865), 261–76, 343–60; 12 (1866), 1–29.

CLR Calendar of Liberate Rolls (London, 1917–).

CMCS Cambridge Medieval Celtic Studies; *Cambrian Medieval Celtic Studies* from no. 26, Winter 1993.

COKAYNE, G. E., *The Complete Peerage*, 13 vols in 14 (new edn, London, 1910–59).

Col Llyfr Colan, ed. D. Jenkins (Cardiff, 1963).

COLE, E. J. L., 'Elystan's line in Kerry', *Radnorshire Society T.*, 22 (1952), 49–52.

CONSTABLE, G., *Letters and Letter-Collections* (Typologie des sources du moyen âge occidental, 17; Turnhout, 1976).

COPLESTONE-CROW, B., 'The foundation of the priories of Bassaleg and Malpas in the twelfth century', *Monmouthshire Antiquary*, 14 (1998), 1–13.

CORBETT, J. S., *Glamorgan: Papers and Notes on the Lordship and its Members*, ed. D. R. Patterson (Cardiff, 1925).

—— 'Historical notes', in J. Ward (ed.), 'Our Lady of Penrhys', *Arch. Camb.*, 6th series, 14 (1914), 357–406 at 380–93.

Councils and Synods with Other Documents relating to the English Church: II. A.D. 1205–1313, ed. F. M. Powicke and C. R. Cheney, 2 vols (Oxford, 1964).

COWLEY, F. G., 'The monastic order in south Wales from the Norman Conquest to the Black Death' (unpublished Ph.D. thesis, University of Wales, 1965).

—— *The Monastic Order in South Wales 1066–1349* (Cardiff, 1977).

—— 'Neath versus Margam: some thirteenth century disputes', *T. of the Port Talbot Historical Society,* 1 (1967), 7–14.

COX, D. C., 'County government in the early Middle Ages', in *VCH Shropshire*, iii. 1–32.

COX, J. C., 'Ancient documents relating to tithes in the Peak', *J. of the Derbyshire Archaeological and Natural History Society*, 5 (1883), 129–64.

—— *Notes on the Churches of Derbyshire*, 4 vols (Chesterfield, London and Derby, 1875–9).

CPL Calendar of Entries in the Papal Registers Relating to Great Britain and Ireland: Papal Letters, i. *A.D. 1198–1304*, ed. W. H. Bliss (London, 1893).

CPR Calendar of the Patent Rolls preserved in the Public Record Office (London, 1891–).

CR Close Rolls of the Reign of Henry III preserved in the Public Record Office (London, 1902–38).

CROOK, D., *Records of the General Eyre* (Public Record Office Handbooks, 20; London, 1982).

CROUCH, D., 'The administration of the Norman earldom', in Thacker (ed.), *Earldom of Chester*, 69–95.

—— 'The earliest original charter of a Welsh king', *BBCS*, 36 (1989), 125–31.

—— *The Image of Aristocracy in Britain, 1000–1300* (London, 1992).

—— 'The March and the Welsh kings', in E. King (ed.), *The Anarchy of Stephen's Reign* (Oxford, 1994), 255–89.

—— 'Robert, earl of Gloucester, and the daughter of Zelophehad', *J. of Medieval History*, 11 (1985), 227–43.

—— 'The slow death of kingship in Glamorgan', *Morgannwg*, 29 (1985), 20–41.

—— *William Marshal: Court, Career and Chivalry in the Angevin Empire 1147–1219* (London and New York, 1990).

—— and THOMAS, G., 'Three Goldcliff charters', *NLWJ*, 24 (1985–6), 153–63.

CRR Curia Regis Rolls (London, 1923–).

CRUMP, J. J., 'The Mortimer family and the making of the March', in M. Prestwich, R. H. Britnell and R. Frame (eds), *Thirteenth Century England*, *VI* (Woodbridge, 1997), 117–26.

—— 'Repercussions of the execution of William de Braose: a letter from Llywelyn ab Iorwerth to Stephen de Segrave', *Historical Research*, 73 (2000), 197–212.

CTB The Correspondence of Thomas Becket, Archbishop of Canterbury, ed. A. Duggan, 2 vols (Oxford, 2000).

CW '"Cronica de Wallia" and other documents from Exeter Cathedral Library MS 3514', ed. T. Jones, *BBCS*, 12 (1946–8), 27–44.

CWR 'Calendar of Welsh Rolls', in *Calendar of Various Chancery Rolls, Supplementary Close Rolls, Welsh Rolls, Scutage Rolls, preserved in the Public Record Office A.D. 1277–1326* (London, 1912), 157–362.

DAMSHOLT, N., 'Kingship in the arengas of Danish royal diplomas, 1140–1223', *Mediaeval Scandinavia*, 3 (1970), 66–108.

Damweiniau Colan, ed. D. Jenkins (Aberystwyth, 1973).

DANIEL-TYSSEN, J. R., *Royal Charters and Historical Documents of the Town and County of Carmarthen, and the Abbeys of Talley and Tygwyn-ar-Daf*, ed. A. C. Evans (Carmarthen, 1878).

D'ARBOIS DE JUBAINVILLE, H., 'Charte originale du Pays de Galles', *Revue celtique*, 7 (1886), 86–7.

DAVIES, E. H. C., 'Property and landownership in Llangadfan', *Mont. Coll.*, 79 (1991), 29–112.

DAVIES, J. C., 'Giraldus Cambrensis and Powis', *Mont. Coll.*, 49 (1945–6), 179–94.

—— 'A grant by David ap Gruffydd', *NLWJ*, 3 (1943–4), 29–32.

—— 'A grant by Llewelyn ap Gruffydd', *NLWJ*, 3 (1943–4), 158–62.

—— 'A papal bull of privileges to the abbey of Ystrad Fflur', *NLWJ*, 4 (1945–6), 197–203.

—— 'The records of the abbey of Ystrad Marchell', *Mont. Coll.*, 51 (1949–50), 3–22.

—— 'Strata Marcella documents', *Mont. Coll.*, 51 (1949–50), 164–87.

DAVIES, R. R., *Conquest, Coexistence, and Change: Wales 1063–1415* (Oxford, 1987).

—— *Domination and Conquest: The Experience of Ireland, Scotland and Wales 1100–1300* (Cambridge, 1990).

—— 'Henry I and Wales', in H. Mayr-Harting and R. I. Moore (eds), *Studies in Medieval History presented to R. H. C. Davis* (London, 1985), 133–47.

—— 'Law and national identity in thirteenth-century Wales', in *idem et al.* (eds), *Welsh Society and Nationhood: Historical Essays presented to Glanmor Williams* (Cardiff, 1984), 51–69.

—— *Lordship and Society in the March of Wales, 1282–1400* (Oxford, 1978).

—— 'The lordship of Ogmore', in *Glamorgan County History*, iii. 285–311.

—— *The Revolt of Owain Glyn Dŵr* (Oxford, 1995).

—— 'The status of women and the practice of marriage in late-medieval Wales', in D. Jenkins and M. E. Owen (eds), *The Welsh Law of Women* (Cardiff, 1980), 93–114.

DAVIES, W., 'Charter-writing and its uses in early medieval Celtic societies', in H. Pryce (ed.), *Literacy in Medieval Celtic Societies* (Cambridge, 1998), 99–112.

—— 'The Latin charter-tradition in western Britain, Brittany and Ireland in the early mediaeval period', in D. Whitelock, R. McKitterick and D. Dumville (eds), *Ireland in Early Mediaeval Europe: Studies in Memory of Kathleen Hughes* (Cambridge, 1982), 258–80.

—— *The Llandaff Charters* (Aberystwyth, 1979).

DAVIES, W. S., 'Materials for the life of Bishop Bernard of St. David's', *Arch. Camb.*, 6th series, 19 (1919), 299–322.

D.B. Domesday Book [ed. A. Farley], 2 vols (London, 1783).

Decrees of the Ecumenical Councils, ed. N. P. Tanner, 2 vols (London and Washington, DC, 1990).

Dialogus de Scaccario, ed. C. Johnson (London, 1950).

Diceto *Radulphi de Diceto Decani Lundoniensis Opera Historica*, ed. W. Stubbs (Rolls series, London, 1876).

DICKINSON, J. C., *The Origins of the Austin Canons and their Introduction into England* (London, 1950).

DK Descriptio Kambriae (in *Gir. Camb. Op.*, vi).

DMLBS Dictionary of Medieval Latin from British Sources, ed. R. E. Latham *et al.* (London and Oxford, 1975–).

DNB Dictionary of National Biography, ed. L. Stephen and S. Lee, 63 vols (London, 1885–1900).

DODD, A. H., *A History of Caernarvonshire 1284–1900* ([Caernarfon] 1968).

DOUIE, D. L., *Archbishop Pecham* (Oxford, 1952).

DU CANGE Du Cange, C. du F., *Glossarium Mediae et Infimae Latinitatis*, 8 vols, ed. L. Favre (Niort, 1884–7).

DUFOUR, J., 'Peut-on parler d'une organisation de la chancellerie de Philippe Auguste?', *Archiv für Diplomatik*, 41 (1995), 249–61.

DWB The Dictionary of Welsh Biography down to 1940, ed. J. E. Lloyd and R. T. Jenkins (London, 1959).

DWNN, L., *Heraldic Visitations of Wales*, ed. S. R. Meyricke, 2 vols (Llandovery, 1846).

Eadmer, *Historia Novorum in Anglia*, ed. M. Rule (Rolls Series, London, 1884).

EASTERLING, R. C., 'The friars in Wales', *Arch. Camb.*, 6th series, 14 (1914), 323–56.

EDWARDS, A., *Letters of a Peacemaker: The Intervention of Archbishop John Peckham in the Welsh War of 1282* (Tregarth, 1998).

EDWARDS, J. G., 'Madog ap Llywelyn, the Welsh leader in 1294–5', *BBCS*, 13 (1948–50), 207–10.

—— 'The royal household and the Welsh lawbooks', *TRHS*, 5th series, 13 (1963), 163–76.

EEA, i   *English Episcopal Acta*, i. *Lincoln 1067–1185*, ed. D. M. Smith (Oxford, 1980).

EEA, v   *English Episcopal Acta*, v. *York 1070–1154*, ed. J. E. Burton (Oxford, 1988).

EEA, vii   *English Episcopal Acta*, vii. *Hereford 1079–1234*, ed. J. Barrow (Oxford, 1993).

EGC   Earldom of Gloucester Charters: The Charters and Scribes of the Earls and Countesses of Gloucester to A.D. 1217, ed. R. B. Patterson (Oxford, 1973).

EHD, iii   *English Historical Documents*, iii. *1189–1327*, ed. H. Rothwell (London, 1975).

EHR   English Historical Review.

EMANUEL, H. D., *A Catalogue of the Gwysaney Manuscripts* ([Aberystwyth] 1953).

—— 'The Gwysaney manuscripts', *NLWJ*, 7 (1951–2), 326–43.

Episc. Acts   Episcopal Acts and Cognate Documents relating to Welsh Dioceses 1066–1272, ed. J. C. Davies, 2 vols (Cardiff, 1946–8).

Epistolae et Vita Divi Thomae martyris et Archi-Episcopi Cantuariensis, 2 vols, ed. C. Lupus (Brussels, 1682).

EPNS   English Place-Names Society.

EVANS, A. L., 'The lords of Afan', *T. Port Talbot Hist. Soc.*, 2: 3 (1974), 18–40.

EVANS, D. L., 'Llyfr Coch Asaph', *NLWJ*, 4 (1945–6), 177–83.

—— 'Some notes on the history of the principality of Wales in the time of the Black Prince', *THSC*, 1925–6, 25–110.

EVANS, J. W., 'The early church in Denbighshire', *TDHS*, 35 (1986), 61–82.

—— 'The survival of the *clas* as an institution in medieval Wales: some observations on Llanbadarn Fawr', in N. Edwards and A. Lane (eds), *The Early Church in Wales and the West* (Oxford, 1992), 33–40.

EWGT   Early Welsh Genealogical Tracts, ed. P. C. Bartrum (Cardiff, 1966).

The Extent of Chirkland 1391–1393, ed. G. P. Jones (London, 1933).

EYTON, *Shropshire   Eyton R. W., Antiquities of Shropshire*, 12 vols (London, 1854–60).

Facsimiles of Early Charters from Northamptonshire Collections, ed. F. M. Stenton (Northamptonshire Record Society, 4; 1930).

Feet of Fines of the Ninth Year of the Reign of King Richard I (Pipe Roll Society, 23; 1898).

FICHTENAU, H., *Arenga. Spätantike und Mittelalter im Spiegel von Urkundenformeln* (Mitteilungen des Instituts für Oesterreichische Geschichtsforschung, Ergänzungsband 18; Graz and Cologne, 1957).

FLANAGAN, M. T., 'The context and uses of the Latin charter in twelfth-century Ireland', in H. Pryce (ed.), *Literacy in Medieval Celtic Societies* (Cambridge, 1998), 113–32.

—— *Irish Society, Anglo-Norman Settlers, Angevin Kingship: Interactions in Ireland in the Late Twelfth Century* (Oxford, 1989).

Foedera   Foedera, Conventiones, Litterae etc., ed. T. Rymer, 4 vols in 7 (revd edn, Record Commission, London, 1816–69).

FRAME, R., *Ireland and Britain, 1170–1450* (London and Rio Grande, Ohio, 1998).

GALBRAITH, V. H., 'Monastic foundation charters of the eleventh and twelfth centuries', *Cambridge Historical J.*, 4 (1932–4), 205–22.

GCBM I   Gwaith Cynddelw Brydydd Mawr I, ed. N. A. Jones and A. Parry Owen (Cyfres Beirdd y Tywysogion, 3; Cardiff, 1991).

Gesta Regis Henrici Secundi et Ricardi Primi Benedicti Abbatis, ed. W. Stubbs, 2 vols (Rolls Series, London, 1867).

Gilberti ex abbate Glocestriae episcopi primum Herefordiensis deinde Londoniensis epistolae, ed. J. A. Giles, 2 vols (Patres Ecclesiae Anglicanae; Oxford, 1845).

GILLINGHAM, J., *The English in the Twelfth Century: Imperialism, National Identity and Political Values* (Woodbridge, 2000).

Gir. Camb. Op.   Giraldi Cambrensis Opera, ed. J. S. Brewer, J. F. Dimock and G. F. Warner, 8 vols (Rolls Series, London, 1861–91).

'Giraldus Cambrensis: *De Invectionibus*', ed. W. S. Davies, *Y Cymmrodor*, 30 (1920).

GIRY, A., *Manuel de diplomatique* (Paris, 1894).

Glamorgan County History, iii   Pugh, T. B. (ed.), *Glamorgan County History*, iii. *The Middle Ages* (Cardiff, 1971).

Glanvill   Tractatus de legibus et consuetudinibus regni Anglie qui Glanvilla vocatur, ed. G. D. G. Hall (London, 1965).

GMB   Gwaith Meilyr Brydydd a'i Ddisgynyddion, ed. J. E. C. Williams with the assistance of P. I. Lynch (Cyfres Beirdd y Tywysogion, 1; Cardiff, 1994).

GPC   Geiriadur Prifysgol Cymru (Cardiff, 1950–).

GRAHAM, R., 'Letters of Cardinal Ottoboni', *EHR*, 15 (1900), 87–120.

GRAY, T., 'The hermitage of Theodoric, and the site of Pendar', *Arch. Camb.*, 6th series, 3 (1903), 121–53.

The Great Register of Lichfield Cathedral, ed. H. E. Savage (William Salt Archaeological Society, Collections for a History of Staffordshire, 1926 for 1924).

GREEN, F., *National Library of Wales, Calendar of Deeds and Documents*, ii. *The Crosswood Deeds* (Aberystwyth and Cardiff, 1927).

GRESHAM, C. A., 'The Aberconwy charter', *Arch. Camb.*, 94 (1939), 123–62.

—— 'The Aberconwy charter: further consideration', *BBCS*, 30 (1982–3), 311–47.

—— 'The Cymer Abbey charter', *BBCS*, 31 (1984), 142–57.

—— *Eifionydd: A Study in Landownership from the Medieval Period to the Present Day* (Cardiff, 1973).

GRIFFITHS, M., 'Native society on the Anglo-Norman frontier: the evidence of the Margam charters', *WHR*, 14 (1988–9), 179–216.

GRIFFITHS, *PW*   Griffiths, R. A., *The Principality of Wales in the Later Middle Ages: The Structure and Personnel of Government*, i. *South Wales, 1277–1536* (Cardiff, 1972).

GRIFFITHS, R. A., 'The authors of urban records in medieval Wales', in W. Prevenier and T. de Hemptinne (eds), *La Diplomatique urbaine en Europe au moyen âge: Actes du congrès de la Commission internationale de Diplomatique, Gand, 25–29 août 1998* (Louvain and Apeldoorn, 2000), 157–76.

—— *Conquerors and Conquered in Medieval Wales* (Stroud and New York, 1994).

GUYOTJEANNIN, O., 'L'influence pontificale sur les actes épiscopaux français (Provinces ecclésiastiques de Reims, Sens et Rouen, XIe–XIIe siècles)', in R. Grosse (ed.), *L'Eglise de France et la papauté (Xe–XIIIe siècle). Actes du colloque historique franco-allemand* (Bonn, 1993), 83–102.

——, PYCKE, J. and TOCK, B.-M., *Diplomatique médiévale* (L'atelier du médiéviste, 2; Turnhout and Paris, 1993).

'Gwaith Dafydd Benfras', ed. N. G. Costigan (Bosco), in *Gwaith Dafydd Benfras ac Eraill o Feirdd Hanner Cyntaf y Drydedd Ganrif ar Ddeg*, ed. *eadem et al.* (Cyfres Beirdd y Tywysogion, 6; Cardiff, 1995), 361–557.

'Gwaith Llygad Gŵr', ed. P. I. Lynch, in *Gwaith Bleddyn Fardd a Beirdd Eraill Ail Hanner y Drydedd Ganrif ar Ddeg*, ed. R. M. Andrews *et al.* (Cyfres Beirdd y Tywysogion, 7; Cardiff, 1996), 205–303.

Gwaith Llywarch ap Llywelyn 'Prydydd y Moch', ed. E. M. Jones assisted by N. A. Jones (Cyfres Beirdd y Tywysogion, 5; Cardiff, 1991).

'Gwaith Owain Cyfeiliog', ed. G. A. Williams, in *Gwaith Llywelyn Fardd I ac Eraill o Feirdd y Ddeuddegfed Ganrif*, ed. K. A. Bramley *et al.* (Cyfres Beirdd y Tywysogion, 2; Cardiff, 1994), 191–277.

'Gwaith Peryf ap Cedifor', ed. M. E. Owen, in *Gwaith Llywelyn Fardd I ac Eraill o Feirdd y Ddeuddegfed Ganrif*, ed. K. A. Bramley *et al.* (Cyfres Beirdd y Tywysogion, 2; Cardiff, 1994), 333–66.

H   Maund, K. L., *Handlist of the Acts of Native Welsh Rulers, 1132–1283* (Cardiff, 1996).

Haddan and Stubbs   *Councils and Ecclesiastical Documents relating to Great Britain and Ireland*, ed. A. W. Haddan and W. Stubbs, 3 vols (Oxford, 1869–78).

HAGUE, D. B. and WARHURST, C., 'Excavations at Sycharth castle, Denbigshire, 1962–63', *Arch. Camb.*, 115 (1966), 108–27.

Handbook of British Chronology, ed. E. B. Fryde *et al.* (Royal Historical Society Guides and Handbooks, no. 2; 3rd edn, London, 1986).

A Handbook of Dates for Students of British History, ed. C. R. Cheney, revd M. Jones (Royal Historical Society Guides and Handbooks, no. 4; revd edn, Cambridge, 2000).

Handlist of Manuscripts in the National Library of Wales, iii (Aberystwyth, 1961).

HARVEY, P. D. A. and McGUINNESS, A., *A Guide to British Medieval Seals* (London, 1996).

HAYS, R. W., *The History of the Abbey of Aberconway 1186–1537* (Cardiff, 1963).

—— 'Rotoland, subprior of Aberconway, and the controversy over the see of Bangor', *J. of the Historical Society of the Church in Wales*, 13 (1963), 9–19.

HECTOR, L. C., *The Handwriting of English Documents* (2nd edn, London, 1966).

HESLOP, T. A., 'The seals of the twelfth-century earls of Chester', in Thacker (ed.), *Earldom of Chester*, 179–97.

HFS   *Historiae Francorum scriptores coaetani*, ed. A. [and F.] Duchesne, 4 vols (Paris, 1636–49).

Hist. Gwydir   *The History of the Gwydir Family, Written by Sir John Wynn of Gwydir*, ed. J. Ballinger (Cardiff, 1927).

L'Histoire de Guillaume le Maréchal, ed. P. Meyer, 3 vols (Société de l'histoire de France; Paris, 1891–1901).

Historia Gruffud vab Kenan, ed. D. S. Evans (Cardiff, 1977).

History of Merioneth, ii   J. B. Smith and Ll. B. Smith (eds), *History of Merioneth*, ii. *The Middle Ages* (Cardiff, 2001).

H. L. J. J. W., 'Basingwerk Abbey', *Arch. Camb.*, 1st series, 1 (1846), 97–116.

HOLT, J. C., 'What's in a name? Family nomenclature and the Norman conquest', in *idem, Colonial England, 1066–1215* (London and Rio Grande, Ohio, 1997), 179–96.

—— 'Willoughby deeds', in *A Medieval Miscellany for Doris Mary Stenton* (Pipe Roll Society, new series, 36; 1962 for 1960), 167–87.

HUDSON, J. G. H., 'Diplomatic and legal aspects of the charters', in Thacker (ed.), *Earldom of Chester*, 153–78.

HUGHES, H. D., *Hynafiaethau Llandegai a Llanllechid* (Bethesda, 1866).

HUWS, D., *Medieval Welsh Manuscripts* (Cardiff, 2000).

HW   Lloyd, J. E., *A History of Wales from the Earliest Times to the Edwardian Conquest*, 2 vols (3rd edn, London, 1939).

IK   Itinerarium Kambriae (in *Gir. Camb. Op.*, vi).

INSLEY, C., 'Fact and fiction in thirteenth-century Gwynedd: the Aberconwy charters', *Studia Celtica*, 33 (1999), 235–50.

—— 'From *rex Wallie* to *princeps Wallie*: charters and state formation in thirteenth-century Wales', in J. R. Maddicott and D. M. Palliser (eds), *The Medieval State: Essays presented to James Campbell* (London and Rio Grande, Ohio, 2000), 179–96.

—— 'The wilderness years of Llywelyn the Great', in M. Prestwich, R. Britnell and R. Frame (eds), *Thirteenth Century England, IX* (Woodbridge, 2003), 163–73.

Inventaire sommaire des archives départementales antérieures à 1790: Eure: Archives ecclésiastiques – série H, ed. G. Bourbon (Évreux, 1893).

Ior   Llyfr Iorwerth, ed. A. R. Wiliam (Cardiff, 1960).

J.   Journal.

JACK, R. I., *Medieval Wales* (London, 1972).

—— 'Religious life in a Welsh Marcher lordship: the lordship of Dyffryn Clwyd in the later Middle Ages', in C. M. Barron and C. Harper-Bill (eds), *The Church in Pre-Reformation Society* (Woodbridge, 1985), 143–57.

JANAUSCHEK, L., *Originum Cisterciensium* (Vienna, 1877).

JEAYES, I. H., *Descriptive Catalogue of Derbyshire Charters in Public and Private Libraries and Muniment Rooms* (London, 1906).

JENKINS, D., 'A lawyer looks at Welsh land law', *THSC*, 1967, 220–48.

JMHRS   Journal of the Merioneth Historical and Record Society.

JOHNS, C. N., 'The Celtic monasteries of north Wales', *TCHS*, 21 (1960), 14–43.

—— 'Postscript to the Celtic monasteries of north Wales', *TCHS*, 23 (1962), 129–31.

JOHNSTONE, N., 'Cae Llys, Rhosyr: a court of the princes of Gwynedd', *Studia Celtica*, 33 (1999), 251–95.

—— 'An investigation into the location of the royal courts of thirteenth-century Gwynedd', in N. Edwards (ed.), *Landscape and Settlement in Medieval Wales* (Oxford, 1997), 55–69.

JONES, E. D., DAVIES, N. G. and ROBERTS, R. F., 'Five Strata Marcella charters', *NLWJ*, 5 (1947–8), 50–4.

JONES, F., 'Boundaries of the lordship of Talley, 1668', *BBCS*, 24 (1970–2), 518–26.

JONES, G. R. J., 'The defences of Gwynedd in the thirteenth century', *TCHS*, 30 (1969), 29–43.

—— 'The Llanynys quillets: a measure of landscape transformation in north Wales', *TDHS*, 13 (1964), 133–58.

—— 'The pattern of medieval settlement in the commote of Rhos Is Dulas and its antecedents', *Würzburger geographische Arbeiten*, 60 (1983), 41–50.

—— 'The tribal system in Wales: a re-assessment in the light of settlement studies', *WHR*, 1 (1960–1), 111–32.

J[ONES], H. L., 'Arvona mediaeva II: Beddgelert priory', *Arch. Camb.*, 1st series, 2 (1847), 153–66.

—— 'Cymmer Abbey, Merionethshire', *Arch. Camb.*, 1st series, 1 (1846), 445–60.

—— 'Mona mediaeva no. XII: Penmon priory', *Arch. Camb.*, 1st series, 4 (1849), 44–60.

JONES, J. (Myrddin Fardd), *Enwau Lleoedd Sir Gaernarfon* (Caernarfon [1914]).

JONES, M. C., 'The abbey of Ystrad Marchell (Strata Marcella), or Pola', *Mont. Coll.*, 4 (1871), 1–34, 293–322; 5 (1872), 109–48; 6 (1873), 347–86; 10 (1877), 397–406.

—— 'The feudal barons of Powys', *Mont. Coll.*, 1 (1868), 257–423.

—— 'Some account of Llanllugan nunnery', *Mont. Coll.*, 2 (1869), 301–10.

—— [Untitled], *Proceedings of the Society of Antiquaries of London*, 2nd series, 3 (1864–7), 384–5.

—— 'Valle Crucis Abbey: its origin and foundation charter', *Arch. Camb.*, 3rd series, 12 (1866), 400–17.

—— 'Welsh Pool materials for the history of the parish and borough', *Mont. Coll.*, 7 (1874), 267–352.

JONES, N. A. and PRYCE, H. (eds), *Yr Arglwydd Rhys* (Cardiff, 1996).

JONES, O. E., 'Llyfr Coch Asaph: a textual and historical study', 2 vols (unpublished MA thesis, University of Wales, 1968).

JONES PIERCE, T., 'Einion ap Ynyr (Anian II) Bishop of St Asaph', *Flintshire Historical Society J.*, 17 (1957), 16–33.

—— 'Lleyn ministers' accounts 1350–51', *BBCS*, 6 (1931–3), 255–75.

—— *Medieval Welsh Society: Selected Essays by T. Jones Pierce*, ed. J. B. Smith (Cardiff, 1972).

—— 'Strata Florida Abbey', *Ceredigion*, 1 (1950–1), 18–33.

—— 'Two early Caernarvonshire accounts', *BBCS*, 5 (1929–31), 142–55.

KETTLE, A. J., 'Religious houses', in *VCH Chester*, iii. 124–87.

KING, D. J. C., *Castellarium Anglicanum*, 2 vols (London, 1983).

—— 'Two castles in northern Powys: Dinas Brân and Caergwrle', *Arch. Camb.*, 123 (1974), 113–39.

KNOWLES, D., BROOKE, C. N. L. and LONDON, V., *Heads of Religious Houses: England and Wales 940–1216* (Cambridge, 1972).

LANHAM, C. D., *'Salutatio' Formulas in Latin Letters to 1200: Syntax, Style, and Theory* (Münchener Beiträge zur Mediävistik und Renaissance-Forschung, 22; Munich, 1975).

LATHAM, R. E., *Revised Medieval Latin Word-list from British and Irish Sources* (London, 1965).

LATIMER, P., 'Henry II's campaign against the Welsh in 1165', *WHR*, 14 (1988–9), 523–52.

LAWRENCE, C. H., *St Edmund of Abingdon* (Oxford, 1960).

LEACH, G. B., with appendices by A. J. Taylor and J. E. Messham, 'Excavations at Hen Blas, Coleshill Fawr, near Flint – second report', *Flintshire Historical Society J.*, 18 (1960), 13–60.

LE STRANGE, H., *Le Strange Records* (London, 1916).

The Letters and Charters of Cardinal Guala Bicchieri, Papal Legate in England, 1216–1218, ed. N. Vincent (Canterbury and York Society, 83; Woodbridge, 1996).

The Letters of John of Salisbury, ed. W. J. Millor, H. E. Butler and C. N. L. Brooke, 2 vols (London, 1955–79).

Letters of Medieval Women, ed. A. Crawford (Stroud, 2002).

The Letters of Pope Innocent III (1198–1216) concerning England and Wales: A Calendar with an Appendix of Texts, ed. C. R. Cheney and M. G. Cheney (Oxford, 1967).

LEWIS, C. P., 'Gruffudd ap Cynan and the Normans', in Maund (ed.), *Gruffudd ap Cynan*, 61–77.

LEWIS, C. W., 'The treaty of Woodstock, 1247: its background and significance', *WHR*, 2 (1964–5), 37–65.

LEWIS, E. A., 'A contribution to the commercial history of mediaeval Wales', *Y Cymmrodor*, 24 (1913), 86–188.

—— *The Mediaeval Boroughs of Snowdonia* (London, 1912).

LHUYD, *Parochialia Parochialia . . . Issued by Edward Lhwyd*, ed. R. H. Morris, *Arch. Camb.*, Supplements, 3 vols (1909–11).

The Liber Epistolaris of Richard de Bury, ed. N. Denholm-Young (Roxburghe Club, London, 1950).

Llandaff Episcopal Acta 1140–1287, ed. D. Crouch (Publications of the South Wales Record Society, 5; Cardiff, 1988).

LLOYD, *Powys Fadog* Lloyd, J. Y. W., *History of the Princes, the Lords Marcher and the Ancient Nobility of Powys Fadog*, 6 vols (London, 1881–7).

LLOYD, J. E., 'The age of the native princes', in *idem* (ed.), *A History of Carmarthenshire*, i (Cardiff, 1935), 113–200.

—— 'Border notes', *BBCS*, 11 (1941–4), 48–54.

—— 'Dolforwyn', *BBCS*, 10 (1939–41), 306–9.

—— 'Edward I and the county of Flint', *Flintshire Historical Society J.*, 6 (1916–17), 15–25.

—— 'Edward the First's commission of enquiry of 1280–1: an examination of its purpose and content', *Y Cymmrodor*, 25 (1915), 1–20.

—— 'Edward the First's commission of enquiry of 1280–1: a postscript', *Y Cymmrodor*, 26 (1916), 252.

—— 'Goleugoed', *BBCS*, 9 (1937–9), 344–5.

—— 'Gwern Feifod', *BBCS*, 2 (1923–5), 320–1.

—— 'Llywelyn ap Gruffydd and the lordship of Glamorgan', *Arch. Camb.*, 6th series, 13 (1913), 56–64.

—— *Owen Glendower* (Oxford 1931).

—— *The Story of Ceredigion* (Cardiff, 1937).

—— 'Who was Gwenllian de Lacy?', *Arch. Camb.*, 6th series, 19 (1919), 292–8.

LLOYD, S. D., *English Society and the Crusade* (Oxford, 1988).

LONG PRICE, D., 'Talley Abbey in Carmarthenshire', *Arch. Camb.*, 4th series, 10 (1879), 161–87.

LTMW Jenkins, D., *The Law of Hywel Dda: Law Texts from Medieval Wales, Translated and Edited* (Llandysul, 1986).

LTWL *The Latin Texts of the Welsh Laws*, ed. H. D. Emanuel (Cardiff, 1967).

LUCHAIRE, A., *Études sur les actes de Louis VII* (Paris, 1885).

LW *Littere Wallie preserved in Liber A in the Public Record Office*, ed. J. G. Edwards (Cardiff, 1940).

MADDICOTT, J. R., *Simon de Montfort* (Cambridge, 1994).

MALDEN, H. E., 'The possession of Cardigan Priory by Chertsey Abbey. (A study in some mediaeval forgeries)', *TRHS*, 3rd series, 5 (1911), 141–56.

Mat. Becket *Materials for the History of Thomas Becket, Archbishop of Canterbury*, ed. J. C. Robertson and J. B. Sheppard, 7 vols (Rolls Series, London, 1875–85).

Matthaei Paris Monachi Albanensis Angli Historia Major ..., ed. M. Parker (London, 1571).

Matthaei Paris Monachi Albanensis Angli Historia Major ..., ed. W. Wats (London, 1640).

MAUND, K. L., *Ireland, Wales and England in the Eleventh Century* (Woodbridge, 1991).

—— *The Welsh Kings: The Medieval Rulers of Wales* (Stroud, 2000).

—— (ed.), *Gruffudd ap Cynan: A Collaborative Biography* (Woodbridge, 1996).

The Merioneth Lay Subsidy Roll 1292–3, ed. K. Williams-Jones (Cardiff, 1976).

MEYRICK, S. R., 'On a deed of gift to the abbey of Ystrad Marchell', *Archaeologia*, 21 (1827), 445–9.

Mon. Ang. Dugdale, W., *Monasticon Anglicanum*, ed. J. Caley, H. Ellis and B. Bandinel, 6 vols in 8 (London, 1817–30).

Mon. Ang. (1st edn) Dugdale, W., *Monasticon Anglicanum*, 3 vols (London, 1655–73).

Mont. Coll. *The Montgomeryshire Collections*.

MOORE, D., 'O Rys ap Tewdwr i Rys ap Gruffudd: y frwydr am Ddeheubarth 1093–1155', in Jones and Pryce (eds), *Yr Arglwydd Rhys*, 53–75.

MORGAN, R., 'The barony of Powys, 1274–1360', *WHR*, 10 (1980–1), 1–42.

—— 'An early charter of Llanllugan nunnery', *Mont. Coll.*, 73 (1985), 116–19.

—— 'The foundation of the borough of Welshpool', *Mont. Coll.*, 65 (1977), 7–23.

—— 'The territorial divisions of medieval Montgomeryshire [I]', *Mont. Coll.*, 69 (1981), 9–44.

—— 'The territorial divisions of medieval Montgomeryshire [II]', *Mont. Coll.*, 70 (1982), 11–39.

—— 'Trewern in Gorddwr: Domesday manor and knight's fief, 1086–1311', *Mont. Coll.*, 64 (1976), 121–32.

MORRIS, J. E., *The Welsh Wars of Edward I* (Oxford, 1901).

NEVILLE, C. J., 'Charter writing and the exercise of lordship in thirteenth-century Celtic Scotland', in A. Musson (ed.), *Expectations of the Law in the Middle Ages* (Woodbridge, 2001), 67–89.

NICHOLLS, K. W., 'The Butlers of Aherlow and Owles', *J. of the Butler Society*, 2 (1969), 123–8.

NICHOLSON, H. J., 'Margaret de Lacy and the hospital of St John at Aconbury, Herefordshire', *J. of Ecclesiastical History*, 50 (1999), 629–51.

NIERMEYER, J. F., *Mediae Latinitatis lexicon minus* (Leiden, 1976).

NLWJ *National Library of Wales Journal*.

OP *The Description of Penbrokshire by George Owen of Henllys, Lord of Kemes*, ed. H. Owen, 4 vols (London, 1892–1936).

ORMEROD, G., *The History of the County Palatine and City of Chester*, ed. T. Helsby, 3 vols (London, 1882).

ORPEN, G. H., *Ireland under the Normans, 1169–1333*, 4 vols (Oxford, 1911–20).

OWEN, D. H., 'Tenurial and economic developments in north Wales in the twelfth and thirteenth centuries', *WHR*, 6 (1972–3), 117–42.

OWEN, *Catalogue* Owen, E., *A Catalogue of the Manuscripts relating to Wales in the British Museum*, 4 parts (Cymmrodorion Record Series, 4; London, 1900–22).

OWEN, E., 'A contribution to the history of the Praemonstratensian abbey of Talley', *Arch. Camb.*, 5th series, 10 (1893), 29–47, 120–8, 309–25.

OWEN, H. and BLAKEWAY, J. B., *A History of Shrewsbury*, 2 vols (London, 1825).

OWENS, B. G., 'Rûg and its muniments', *JMHRS*, 1 (1949–51), 83–8.

PAINTER, S., *William Marshal: Knight-Errant, Baron, and Regent of England* (Baltimore, Md., 1933).

PALMER, A. N., *History of the Thirteen Country Townships of the Old Parish of Wrexham, and of the Townships of Burras Riffri, Erlas, and Erddig* (Wrexham, 1903).

—— 'The portionary churches of mediaeval north Wales', *Arch. Camb.*, 5th series, 3 (1886), 175–209.

PARIS, *CM* Matthew Paris, *Chronica Majora*, ed. H. R. Luard, 7 vols (Rolls Series, London, 1872–88).

PARIS, *HA* Matthaei Parisiensis, Monachi Sancti Albani, Historia Anglorum, ed. F. Madden, 3 vols (Rolls Series, London, 1866–9).

PARKES, M. B., *English Cursive Book Hands 1250–1500* (repr., London, 1979).

PATTERSON, R. B., *The Scriptorium of Margam Abbey and the Scribes of Early Angevin Glamorgan: Secretarial Administration in a Welsh Marcher Barony, c.1150–c.1225* (Woodbridge, 2001).

'PEARMAIN', 'The vill of Llanllugan', *Bye-gones*, 1886–7, 40–1.

PEARSON, M. J., 'The creation of the Bangor cathedral chapter', *WHR*, 20 (2000–1), 167–81.

PENNANT, T., *A Tour in Wales*, 2 vols in 4 (London, 1784).

PIERCE, G. O., *Place-names in Glamorgan* (Cardiff, 2002).

—— *The Place-names of Dinas Powys Hundred* (Cardiff, 1968).

—— 'The Welsh *mystwyr*', *Nomina*, 23 (2000), 121–39.

Pipe Roll Volume in series *The Great Rolls of the Pipe, 5 Henry II–* (Pipe Roll Society, 1884–).

PL Patrologia cursus completus . . . series Latina, ed. J.-P. Migne, 221 vols (Paris, 1841–64).

Placita de Quo Warranto temporibus Edw. I. II. & III. in Curia Receptae Scaccarii Westm. Asservata (Record Commission [London], 1818).

POWEL, D., *The Historie of Cambria* (London, 1584).

POWICKE, *Henry III* Powicke, F. M., *King Henry III and the Lord Edward: The Community of the Realm in the Thirteenth Century*, 2 vols (Oxford, 1947).

PR Patent Rolls of the Reign of Henry III preserved in the Public Record Office A.D. 1216–1232, 2 vols (London, 1901–3).

PRATT, D., 'Fourteenth-century Bromfield and Yale – a gazetteer of lay and ecclesiastical territorial units', *TDHS*, 27 (1978), 89–149.

PRESTWICH, M., *Edward I* (London, 1988).

PREVENIER, W., 'La chancellerie des comtes de Flandre, dans le cadre européen, à la fin du XIIe siècle', *Bibliothèque de l'Ecole des chartes*, 125 (1967), 34–93.

PRICE, G. V., *Valle Crucis Abbey* (Liverpool, 1952).

PRITCHARD, E. M., *Cardigan Priory in the Olden Days* (London, 1904).

PRYCE, H., 'The church of Trefeglwys and the end of the "Celtic" charter tradition in twelfth-century Wales', *CMCS*, 25 (Summer 1993), 15–54.

—— 'The context and purpose of the earliest Welsh lawbooks', *CMCS*, 39 (Summer 2000), 39–63.

—— 'The dynasty of Deheubarth and the church of St Davids', in J. W. Evans and J. M. Wooding (eds), *St David: Cult, Church and Nation* (Woodbridge, forthcoming).

—— 'Esgobaeth Bangor yn oes y tywysogion', in W. P. Griffith (ed.), *'Ysbryd Dealltwrus ac Enaid Anfarwol': Ysgrifau ar Hanes Crefydd yng Ngwynedd* (Bangor, 1999), 37–57.

—— 'The household priest (*offeiriad teulu*)', in T. M. Charles-Edwards, M. E. Owen and P. Russell (eds), *The Welsh King and his Court* (Cardiff, 2000), 82–93.

—— 'Lawbooks and literacy in medieval Wales', *Speculum*, 75 (2000), 29–67.

—— 'The medieval church', in *History of Merioneth*, ii. 254–96.

—— *Native Law and the Church in Medieval Wales* (Oxford, 1993).

—— 'Negotiating Anglo-Welsh relations: Llywelyn the Great and Henry III', in B. K. U. Weiler with I. W. Rowlands (eds), *England and Europe in the Reign of Henry III (1216–1272)* (Aldershot, 2002), 13–29.

—— 'Owain Gwynedd and Louis VII: the Franco-Welsh diplomacy of the first prince of Wales', *WHR*, 19 (1998–9), 1–28.

RCAHMW, *Glamorgan I. iii*   Royal Commission on Ancient and Historical Monuments in Wales, *An Inventory of the Ancient Monuments in Glamorgan. Volume I: Pre-Norman. Part III: The Early Christian Period* (Cardiff, 1976).

RCAHMW, *Glamorgan III. 1a*   Royal Commission on Ancient and Historical Monuments in Wales, *An Inventory of the Ancient Monuments in Glamorgan. Volume III–Part 1a: Medieval Secular Monuments. The Early Castles from the Norman Conquest to 1217* (London, 1991).

RCAHMW, *Glamorgan III. ii*   Royal Commission on Ancient and Historical Monuments in Wales, *An Inventory of the Ancient Monuments in Glamorgan. Volume III: Medieval Secular Monuments. Part II: Non-defensive* (London, 1982).

RCAHMW, *Radnor*   Royal Commission on the Ancient and Historical Monuments and Constructions in Wales and Monmouthshire, *An Inventory of the Ancient Monuments in Wales and Monmouthshire. III – County of Radnor* (London, 1913).

Rec. Caern.   *Registrum vulgariter nuncupatum 'The Record of Caernarvon' e codice ms^{to} Harleiano 696 descriptum*, ed. H. Ellis (London, 1838).

Recueil des actes de Louis VI roi de France (1108–1137), i, ed. J. Dufour (Paris, 1992).

The Red Book of the Exchequer, ed. H. Hall, 3 vols (Rolls Series, London, 1896).

REES, W., *A History of the Order of St John of Jerusalem in Wales and on the Welsh Border* (Cardiff, 1947).

—— *South Wales and the March 1284–1415: A Social and Agrarian Study* (Oxford, 1924).

REES, W. J., 'Account of Cwmhir Abbey, Radnorshire', *Arch. Camb.*, 1st series, 4 (1849), 233–60.

—— *An Historical and Descriptive Account of the Ruinated Abbey of Cwmhir, in the County of Radnor* (London, 1850).

Reg. Aberconway   *Register and Chronicle of the Abbey of Aberconway from the Harleian MS. 3725,* ed. H. Ellis (Camden Miscellany, 1; 1847).

Reg. Cantilupe   *Registrum Thome de Cantilupo Episcopi Herefordensis*, ed. R. G. Griffiths and W. W. Capes (Hereford, 1906; London, 1907).

Reg. Grégoire X   *Les Registres de Grégoire X (1272–1276) et de Jean XXI (1276–1277)*, ed. J. Guiraud and E. Cadier, 4 fascicules (Paris, 1892–1906).

Reg. Hon. III   *Regesta Honorii Papae III*, ed. P. Pressutti, 2 vols (Rome, 1885–95).

Reg. Innocenz' III.   *Die Register Innocenz' III.*, ed. O. Hageneder *et al.* (Rome, 1964–).

Reg. Peckh.   *Registrum Epistolarum Fratris Johannis Peckham, Archiepiscopi Cantuariensis*, ed. C. T. Martin, 3 vols (Rolls Series, London, 1882–5).

Reg. Pontissara Registrum Johannis de Pontissara Episcopi Wyntoniensis, ed. C. Deedes, 2 vols (London, 1915–24).

Reg. Swinfield Registrum Ricardi de Swinfield, Episcopi Herefordensis MCCLXXXIII– MCCCXVII, ed. W. W. Capes (Canterbury and York Society, 6; London, 1909).

REMFRY, P. M., 'Cadwallon ap Madog rex de Delvain, 1140–1179 and the re-establishment of local autonomy in Cynllibiwg', *Radnorshire Society T.*, 65 (1995), 11–32.

—— 'The native Welsh dynasties of Rhwng Gwy a Hafren 1066–1282' (unpublished MA thesis, University of Wales, 1989).

—— *A Political History of Abbey Cwmhir and its Patrons 1176 to 1282* (Worcester, 1994).

'Report by Sir Frederick Kenyon on a collection of charters, rolls, and papers from Ashridge Park, County Buckingham, belonging to the representatives of the late Lord Brownlow', *T. of the Shropshire Archaeological Society*, 4th series, 11 (1927), 78–82.

RHF Recueil des historiens des Gaules et de la France, ed. M. Bouquet *et al.*, new edn, L. Delisle, 24 vols (Paris, 1869–1904).

RHYS, M., *Ministers' Accounts for West Wales 1277 to 1306. Part I* (London, 1936).

Rice Merrick. Morganiae Archaiographia. A Book of the Antiquities of Glamorganshire, ed. B. Ll. James (South Wales Record Society, 1; 1983).

RICHARDS, M., 'The Carmarthenshire possessions of Talyllychau', in T. Barnes and N. Yates (eds), *Carmarthenshire Studies: Essays presented to Major Francis Jones* (Carmarthen, 1974), 110–21.

—— *Welsh Administrative and Territorial Units* (Cardiff, 1969).

RICHARDS, R., 'Sycharth', *Mont. Coll.*, 50 (1947–8), 183–8.

RICHTER, M., 'David ap Llywelyn, the first prince of Wales', *WHR*, 5 (1970–1), 205–19.

—— *Giraldus Cambrensis: The Growth of the Welsh Nation* (2nd edn, Aberystwyth, 1976).

—— 'A new edition of the so-called Vita Dauidis secundi', *BBCS*, 22 (1966–8), 245–9.

—— 'The political and institutional background to national consciousness in medieval Wales', in T. W. Moody (ed.), *Nationality and the Pursuit of National Independence* (*Historical Studies*, 11; Belfast 1978), 37–55.

RIPPON, S., *Gwent Levels: The Evolution of a Wetland Landscape* (CBA Research Report 105; York, 1996).

RL Royal and Other Historical Letters Illustrative of the Reign of Henry III from the Originals in the Public Record Office, ed. W. W. Shirley, 2 vols (Rolls Series, London, 1862–6).

RMWL Evans, J. G., *Report on Manuscripts in the Welsh Language*, 2 vols (London, 1898–1910).

ROBERTS, G., 'Documents and charters connected with Strata Florida Abbey', *Arch. Camb.*, 1st series, 3 (1848), 191–213.

ROBERTS, G., *Aspects of Welsh History* (Cardiff, 1969).

ROBERTS, S. E., 'Legal practice in fifteenth-century Brycheiniog', *Studia Celtica*, 35 (2001), 307–23.

RODERICK, A. J., 'Marriage and politics in Wales, 1066–1282', *WHR*, 4 (1968–9), 3–20.

The Roll of the Shropshire Eyre of 1256, ed. A. Harding (Selden Society, 96; London, 1981).

Rot. Chart. Rotuli Chartarum in Turri Londinensi Asservati A.D. 1199–A.D. 1216, ed. T. D. Hardy (Record Commission, London, 1837).

Rot. Claus. Rotuli Litteratum Clausarum in Turri Londinensi Asservati A.D. 1204–A.D. 1227, ed. T. D. Hardy, 2 vols (Record Commission, London, 1833–44).

Rot. Fin. *Excerpta e Rotulis Finium in Turri Londinensi Asservatis, Henrico Tertio Rege, A.D. 1216–1272*, ed. C. Roberts, 2 vols (Record Commission, London, 1835–6).

Rot. Hund. *Rotuli Hundredorum temp. Hen. III & Edw. I in Turr' Lond' et in Curia Receptae Scaccarii Westm. Asservati* [ed. W. Illingworth], 2 vols (Record Commission, London, 1812–18).

Rot. Lib. *Rotuli de Liberate ac de Misis et Praestitis regnante Johanne*, ed. T. D. Hardy (Record Commission, London, 1844).

Rot. Pat. *Rotuli Litterarum Patentium in Turri Londinensi Asservati*, I.i. *A.D. 1201–A.D. 1216*, ed. T. D. Hardy (Record Commission, London, 1835).

Rotuli Parliamentorum, 7 vols (Record Commission, London, 1783–1832).

Rotuli Parliamentorum Anglie hactenus inediti MCCLXXIX–MCCCLXXIII, ed. H. G. Richardson and G. O. Sayles (Camden 3rd series, 51; London, 1935).

Rotulus Wallie, or, The Transactions between Edward I and Llewellyn, the Last Prince of Wales: Part I, ed. T. P[hillipps] (Cheltenham, 1865).

ROWLANDS, I. W., 'The 1201 peace between King John and Llywelyn ap Iorwerth', *Studia Celtica*, 34 (2000), 149–66.

—— 'King John and Wales', in S. D. Church (ed.), *King John: New Interpretations* (Woodbridge, 1999), 273–87.

—— 'The making of the March: aspects of the Norman settlement in Dyfed', in R. A. Brown (ed.), *Proceedings of the Battle Conference on Anglo-Norman Studies, III, 1980* (Woodbridge, 1980), 142–57.

RRAN, iii *Regesta Regum Anglo-Normannorum*, iii, ed. H. A. Cronne and R. H. C. Davis (Oxford, 1968).

RUELLE, P., '*A tous présents et à venir, salut.* Notes pour l'histoire d'une formule', in *Mélanges Rita Lejeune* (Gembloux, 1969), ii. 1663–73.

SAINTY, Sir J., *The Judges of England 1272–1990: A List of Judges of the Superior Courts* (Selden Society, Supplementary Series, 10; London, 1993).

SALTMAN, A., *Theobald, Archbishop of Canterbury* (London, 1956).

SANDERS, *Baronies* Sanders, I. J., *English Baronies: A Study of their Origin and Descent 1086–1327* (Oxford, 1960).

SAYERS, J., 'English Cistercian cases and their delegation in the first half of the thirteenth century', *Analecta Sacri Ordinis Cisterciensis*, 20 (1964), 85–102.

—— 'The judicial activities of the General Chapters: II', *J. of Ecclesiastical History*, 15 (1964), 168–85.

—— *Papal Government and England during the Pontificate of Honorius III (1216–1227)* (Cambridge, 1984).

SCHALLER, H. M., 'Dichtungslehren und Briefsteller', in P. Weimar (ed.), *Die Renaissance der Wissenschaften im 12. Jahrhundert* (Zurich, 1981), 249–71.

SEEBOHM, F., *The Tribal System in Wales* (London, 1895).

Select Cases in the Court of King's Bench, i, ed. G. O. Sayles (Selden Society, London, 1936).

The Seventh Report of the Deputy Keeper of the Public Records (London, 1846).

SIDDONS, M. P, *The Development of Welsh Heraldry*, i (Aberystwyth, 1991).

—— 'Welsh equestrian seals', *NLWJ*, 23 (1983–4), 292–318.

—— 'Welsh seals in Paris', *BBCS*, 29 (1980–2), 531–44.

SILVESTER, R. J., 'The Llanwddyn hospitium', *Mont. Coll.*, 85 (1997), 63–76.

The Sixth Report of the Deputy Keeper of the Public Records (London, 1845).

SMITH, A. H., *The Place-names of Gloucestershire. Part II. The North and West Cotswolds* (EPNS, 39; Cambridge, 1964).

—— *The Place-names of the West Riding of Yorkshire. Part IV* (EPNS, 33; Cambridge, 1961).

SMITH, J. B., 'The age of the princes', in *History of Merioneth*, ii. 1–59.

—— 'Castell Gwyddgrug', *BBCS*, 26 (1974–6), 74–7.

—— 'The "Cronica de Wallia" and the dynasty of Dinefwr', *BBCS*, 20 (1963–4), 261–82.

—— 'Cymer Abbey and the Welsh princes', *JMHRS* 13: 2 (1999), 101–18.

—— 'Dower in thirteenth-century Wales: a grant of the commote of Anhuniog', *BBCS*, 30 (1982–3), 348–55.

—— 'Dynastic succession in medieval Wales', *BBCS*, 33 (1986), 199–232.

—— 'Edward II and the allegiance of Wales', *WHR*, 8 (1976–7), 139–71.

—— 'England and Wales: the conflict of laws', in M. Prestwich, R. Britnell and R. Frame (eds), *Thirteenth Century England, VII* (Woodbridge, 1999), 189–205.

—— 'The kingdom of Morgannwg and the Norman conquest of Glamorgan', in *Glamorgan County History*, iii. 1–43.

—— 'Land endowments of the period of Llywelyn ap Gruffudd', *BBCS*, 34 (1987), 150–64.

—— 'Llywelyn ap Gruffudd and the March of Wales', *Brycheiniog*, 20 (1982–3), 9–22.

—— *Llywelyn ap Gruffudd, Prince of Wales* (Cardiff, 1998).

—— 'The lordship of Senghennydd', in *Glamorgan County History*, iii. 311–31, 638–40.

—— 'Magna Carta and the charters of the Welsh princes', *EHR*, 99 (1984), 344–62.

—— 'The middle March in the thirteenth century', *BBCS*, 24 (1970–2), 77–93.

—— 'Offra principis Wallie domino regi', *BBCS*, 21 (1964–6), 362–7.

—— 'The origins of the revolt of Rhys ap Maredudd', *BBCS*, 21 (1964–6), 151–63.

—— 'Owain Gwynedd', *TCHS*, 32 (1971), 8–17.

—— 'Parishes and townships in medieval Merioneth', in *History of Merioneth*, ii. 717–26.

—— 'The rebellion of Llywelyn Bren', in *Glamorgan County History*, iii. 72–86.

—— 'The treaty of Lambeth, 1217', *EHR*, 94 (1979), 562–79.

—— 'Treftadaeth Deheubarth', in Jones and Pryce (eds), *Yr Arglwydd Rhys*, 18–52.

—— and BUTLER, L. A. S., 'The Cistercian order: Cymer Abbey', in *History of Merioneth*, ii. 297–325.

—— and O'NEIL, B. H. St J., *Talley Abbey, Carmarthenshire* (London, 1967; 2nd impression 1970).

—— and PUGH, T. B., 'The lordship of Gower and Kilvey in the Middle Ages', in *Glamorgan County History*, iii. 205–65.

SMITH, Ll. B., 'Disputes and settlements in medieval Wales: the role of arbitration', *EHR*, 106 (1991), 835–60.

—— 'The gage and the land market in late medieval Wales', *Economic History Review*, 2nd series, 29 (1976), 537–50.

—— 'The *gravamina* of the community of Gwynedd against Llywelyn ap Gruffudd', *BBCS*, 31 (1984), 158–76.

SOMMER-SECKENDORFF, E., *Studies in the Life of Robert Kilwardby, O.P.* (Rome, 1937).

SPURGEON, C. J., 'Gwyddgrug Castle (Forden) and the Gorddwr dispute in the thirteenth century', *Mont. Coll.*, 57 (1961–2), 125–36.

St Davids Episcopal Acta 1085–1280, ed. J. Barrow (Publications of the South Wales Record Society, 13; Cardiff, 1998).

STACEY, R. C., *Politics, Policy, and Finance under Henry III, 1216–1245* (Oxford, 1987).

Statuta capitulorum generalium ordinis Cisterciensis ab anno 1116 usque ad annum 1786, ed. J. M. Canivez, 8 vols (Louvain, 1933–41).

Statutes of the Realm, i (London, 1810).

STEPHENSON, D., *The Governance of Gwynedd* (Cardiff, 1984).

—— 'Llywelyn ap Gruffydd and the struggle for the principality of Wales, 1258–1282', *THSC*, 1983, 36–47.

—— 'The politics of Powys Wenwynwyn in the thirteenth century', *CMCS*, 7 (Summer 1984), 39–61.

—— *Thirteenth Century Welsh Law Courts* (Pamphlets on Welsh Law; Aberystwyth, 1980).

STRINGER, K. J., 'The charters of David, earl of Huntingdon and lord of Garioch: a study in Anglo-Scottish diplomatic', in *idem* (ed.), *Essays on the Nobility of Medieval Scotland* (Edinburgh, 1985), 72–101.

—— *Earl David of Huntingdon 1152–1219* (Edinburgh, 1985).

SUPPE, F. C., *Military Institutions on the Welsh Marches: Shropshire, A.D. 1066–1300* (Woodbridge, 1994).

—— 'Roger of Powys, Henry II's Anglo-Welsh middleman, and his lineage', *WHR*, 21 (2002–3), 1–23.

Survey of the Honour of Denbigh 1334, ed. P. Vinogradoff and F. Morgan (London, 1914).

T. Transactions.

Taxatio ecclesiastica Angliae et Walliae auctoritate P. Nicolai IV circa A.D. 1291 (Record Commission, London, 1802).

TAYLOR, A. J., 'A fragment of a *dona* account of 1284', *BBCS*, 27 (1976–8), 253–62.

TCHS Transactions of the Caernarvonshire Historical Society.

TDHS Transactions of the Denbighshire Historical Society.

TESKE, G., *Die Briefsammlungen des 12. Jahrhunderts in St. Viktor/Paris: Entstehung, Überlieferung und Bedeutung für die Geschichte der Abtei* (Bonn, 1993).

Testa de Nevill sive Liber Feodorum in Curia Scaccarii temp. Hen. III & Edw. I [ed. J. Caley and W. Illingworth] ([Record Commission, London] 1807).

TEULET, A., *Layettes du Trésor des chartes*, i (Paris, 1863).

The Text of the Book of Llan Dâv, ed. J. G. Evans with J. Rhys (Oxford, 1893; repr. Aberystwyth, 1979).

THACKER, A. T. (ed.), *The Earldom of Chester and its Charters: A Tribute to Geoffrey Barraclough* (J. of the Chester Archaeological Society, 71; Chester, 1991).

THOMAS, D. R., *The History of the Diocese of St Asaph*, 3 vols (new edn, Oswestry, 1908–13).

—— 'Montgomeryshire document II', *Arch. Camb.*, 5th series, 2 (1885), 304–11.

THOMAS, R. J., *Enwau Afonydd a Nentydd Cymru* (Cardiff, 1938).

THSC Transactions of the Honourable Society of Cymmrodorion.

TIBBOTT, G., 'An Abbey Cwmhir relic abroad', *Radnorshire Society T.*, 5 (1935), 64–7.

Tours in Wales (1804–1813) by Richard Fenton, ed. J. Fisher, *Arch. Camb.*, Supplement (London, 1917).

Tours in Wales by Thomas Pennant, Esq., iii, ed. J. Rhys (Caernarfon, 1883).

Transcripts of Charters relating to the Gilbertine Houses of Sixle, Ormsby, Catley, Bullington, and Alvingham, ed. F. M. Stenton (Publications of the Lincoln Record Society, 18, for 1920; Horncastle, 1922).

Treaty Rolls, i. *1234–1325*, ed. P. Chaplais (London, 1955).

TREHARNE, R. F., *The Baronial Plan of Reform, 1258–1263* (Manchester, 1932).

—— 'The Franco-Welsh treaty of alliance in 1212', *BBCS*, 18 (1958–60), 60–75.

TRHS   Transactions of the Royal Historical Society.

TURBUTT, G., *A History of Derbyshire*, 4 vols (Cardiff, 1999).

TURVEY, R., 'The defences of twelfth-century Deheubarth and the castle strategy of the Lord Rhys', *Arch. Camb.*, 144 (1995), 103–32.

—— 'King, prince or lord? Rhys ap Gruffydd and the nomenclature of authority in twelfth-century Wales', *The Carmarthenshire Antiquary*, 30 (1994), 5–18.

—— *The Lord Rhys, Prince of Deheubarth* (Llandysul, 1997).

USHER, G. A., 'The Black Prince's *quo warranto* (1348)', *WHR*, 7 (1974–5), 1–12.

VAUGHAN, R., *Matthew Paris* (Cambridge, 1958).

VCH   Victoria History of the Counties of England, ed. H. A. Doubleday *et al.* (London, 1900–).

VINCENT, N., *Peter des Roches, Bishop of Winchester 1205–38: An Alien in English Politics* (Cambridge, 1996).

Vita Griffini Filii Conani: The Medieval Latin Life of Gruffudd ap Cynan, ed. P. Russell (Cardiff, forthcoming).

Vocabulaire international de la diplomatique, ed. M. C. Ortí (Commission international de diplomatique; Valencia, 1994).

VSB   Vitae Sanctorum Britanniae et Genealogiae, ed. A. W. Wade-Evans (Cardiff, 1944).

WALKER, R. F., 'The Anglo-Welsh Wars, 1217–1267' (unpublished D.Phil. thesis, University of Oxford, 1954).

—— 'Hubert de Burgh and Wales, 1218–1232', *EHR*, 87 (1972), 465–94.

—— 'The supporters of Richard Marshal, earl of Pembroke, in the rebellion of 1233–1234', *WHR*, 17 (1994–5), 41–65.

[——], 'The Welsh war of 1294–5', in E. B. Fryde (gen. ed.), *Book of Prests of the King's Wardrobe for 1294–5 presented to John Goronwy Edwards* (Oxford, 1962), xxvi–liii.

—— 'William de Valence and the army of west Wales, 1282–1283', *WHR*, 18 (1996–7), 407–29.

—— and SPURGEON, C. J., 'The custody of the de Clare castles in Glamorgan and Gwent, 1262–1263', *Studia Celtica*, 37 (2003), 43–73.

Walter Map, *De Nugis Curialium: Courtiers' Trifles*, ed. M. R. James, revd C. N. L. Brooke and R. A. B. Mynors (Oxford, 1983).

WALTERS, D. B., 'The renunciation of exceptions: Romano-canonical devices for limiting possible defences in thirteenth-century Welsh law suits', *BBCS*, 38 (1991), 119–28.

WAQUET, J., *Recueil des chartes de l'abbaye de Clairvaux: XIIe siècle*, fasc. 1 (Troyes, 1950).

WAR   The Welsh Assize Roll 1277–1284, ed. J. C. Davies (Cardiff, 1940).

WARREN, W. L., *King John* (2nd edn, London, 1978).

WARRINGTON, W., *The History of Wales, in Nine Books, with an Appendix* (London, 1786).

WATERS, W. H., *The Edwardian Settlement of North Wales in its Administrative and Legal Aspects (1284–1343)* (Cardiff, 1935).

WATKIN, H. R., *The History of Totnes Priory and Medieval Town*, 2 vols (Torquay, 1914–19).

W. B. J., 'Charter of Gwenwynwyn prince of Powys A.D. 1201', *Arch. Camb.*, 2nd series, 4 (1853), 205–6.

WEBBER, M. T. J., 'The scribes and handwriting of the original charters', in Thacker (ed.), *Earldom of Chester*, 137–51.

Welsh Medieval Law, ed. A. W. Wade-Evans (Oxford, 1909).

Welsh Records in Paris, ed. T. Matthews (Carmarthen, 1910).

Wendover   *The Flowers of History by Roger of Wendover*, ed. H. G. Hewlett, 3 vols (Rolls Series, London, 1886–9).

WERNER, K. F., 'Kingdom and principality in twelfth-century France', in T. Reuter (ed.), *The Medieval Nobility* (Amsterdam, New York and Oxford, 1979), 243–90.

WHR   Welsh History Review.

WILKINSON, P. F., 'Excavations at Hen Gastell, Briton Ferry, West Glamorgan, 1991–92', *Medieval Archaeology*, 39 (1995), 1–50.

William of Malmesbury, *Gesta Regum Anglorum*, ed. R. A. B. Mynors, R. M. Thomson and M. Winterbottom, 2 vols (Oxford, 1998–9).

WILLIAMS, C. R. (ed.), *The History of Flintshire. Vol. I: From Earliest Times to the Act of Union* (Denbigh, 1961).

WILLIAMS, D. H., *Atlas of Cistercian Lands in Wales* (Cardiff, 1990).

—— 'Basingwerk Abbey', *Cîteaux*, 32 (1982), 87–113.

—— *Catalogue of Seals in the National Museum of Wales, Vol. 1: Seal Dies, Welsh Seals, Papal* Bullae (Cardiff, 1993).

—— 'Catalogue of Welsh ecclesiastical seals as known down to 1600 A.D. Part I: Episcopal seals', *Arch. Camb.*, 133 (1984), 100–35.

—— 'Catalogue of Welsh ecclesiastical seals as known down to 1600 A.D. Part IV: Seals of Cistercian monasteries', *Arch. Camb.*, 136 (1987), 139–55.

—— 'Cistercian nunneries in medieval Wales', *Cîteaux*, 26 (1975), 155–74.

—— 'Fasti Cistercienses Cambrenses', *BBCS*, 24 (1970–2), 181–229.

—— 'Goldcliff priory', *The Monmouthshire Antiquary*, 3 (1970–8), 37–54.

—— *The Welsh Cistercians* (Leominster, 2001).

—— *Welsh History through Seals* (Cardiff, 1982).

—— *White Monks in Gwent and the Border* (Pontypool, 1976).

WILLIAMS, G. A., 'The succession to Gwynedd, 1238–47', *BBCS*, 20 (1962–4), 393–413.

WILLIAMS, R., 'Wynnstay MSS. – charters of Trefeglwys', *Arch. Camb.*, 3rd series, 6 (1860), 330–3.

WILLIAMS, S. W., 'The Cistercian abbey of Cwm Hir', *Mont. Coll.*, 24 (1890), 395–416.

—— *The Cistercian Abbey of Strata Florida: Its History, and an Account of the Recent Excavations on the Site* (London, 1889).

—— 'Further excavations at Strata Florida Abbey', *Arch. Camb.*, 5th series, 6 (1889), 24–58.

WILLIAMS-JONES, K., 'Llywelyn's charter to Cymer Abbey in 1209', *JMHRS*, 3 (1957–60), 45–78.

WILLIS, B., *A Survey of the Cathedral Church of St. Asaph*, 2 vols (London, 1801).

WILSHIRE, L. E., 'Boniface of Savoy, Carthusian and archbishop of Canterbury, 1207–1270', *Analecta Cartusiana*, 31 (1977), 4–90.

WMFFRE, I., 'Language and history in Cardiganshire place-names', 4 vols (unpublished Ph.D. thesis, University of Wales, 1998).

WOOD, M. A. E., *Letters of Royal and Illustrious Ladies of Great Britain*, i (London, 1846).

WYNNE, W., *The History of Wales: Comprehending the Lives and Succession of the Princes of Wales, from Cadwalader the Last King, to Lhewelyn the Last Prince, of British Blood* (London, 1697).

WYNNE, W. W. E., 'Valle Crucis Abbey: additional document A.D. 1247', *Arch. Camb.*, 1st series, 3 (1848), 228–9.

YEATMAN, J. P. *et al.*, *The Feudal History of the County of Derby*, 5 vols in 9 sections (London etc., 1886–1906).

YOUNG, A., *Robert the Bruce's Rivals: The Comyns, 1212–1314* (East Linton, 1997).

Ystrad Marchell Charters *The Charters of the Abbey of Ystrad Marchell*, ed. G. C. G. Thomas (Aberystwyth, 1997).

WEBSITES

Images and discussion of Strata Marcella charters held in the National Library of Wales: *http://www.llgc.org.uk/drych/drych_s018.htm*

Images and discussion of no. 263: *http://www.ukans.edu/carrie/ms_room/jjcrump/document.html*

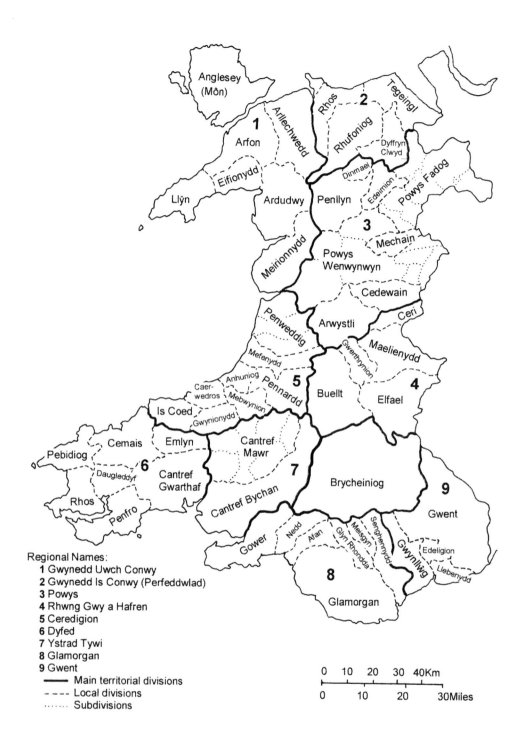

Anglesey
(Môn)

Arllechwedd

Rhos

2

Tegeingl

1

Arfon

Rhufoniog

Dyffryn
Clwyd

Eifionydd

Dinmael

Edeirnion

Powys Fadog

Llŷn

Ardudwy

Penllyn

Meirionnydd

3

Mechain

Powys
Wenwynwyn

Cedewain

Penweddig

Arwystli

Ceri

Maelienydd

Mefenydd

Gwerthrynion

Anhuniog

Pennardd

5

Caer-
wedros

Mebwynion

Buellt

Elfael

4

Is Coed

Gwynionydd

Cemais

Emlyn

Cantref
Mawr

Pebidiog

6

Daugleddyf

Cantref
Gwarthaf

7

Brycheiniog

9

Rhos

Cantref Bychan

Gwent

Penfro

Gower

Nedd

Afan

Glyn Rhondda

Meisgyn

Senghennydd

Gwynllŵg

Edeligion

Llebenydd

8

Glamorgan

Regional Names:
1 Gwynedd Uwch Conwy
2 Gwynedd Is Conwy (Perfeddwlad)
3 Powys
4 Rhwng Gwy a Hafren
5 Ceredigion
6 Dyfed
7 Ystrad Tywi
8 Glamorgan
9 Gwent
—— Main territorial divisions
- - - Local divisions
······· Subdivisions

| 0 | 10 | 20 | 30 | 40Km |

| 0 | 10 | 20 | 30Miles |

MAP 1. Territorial divisions of twelfth- and thirteenth-century Wales

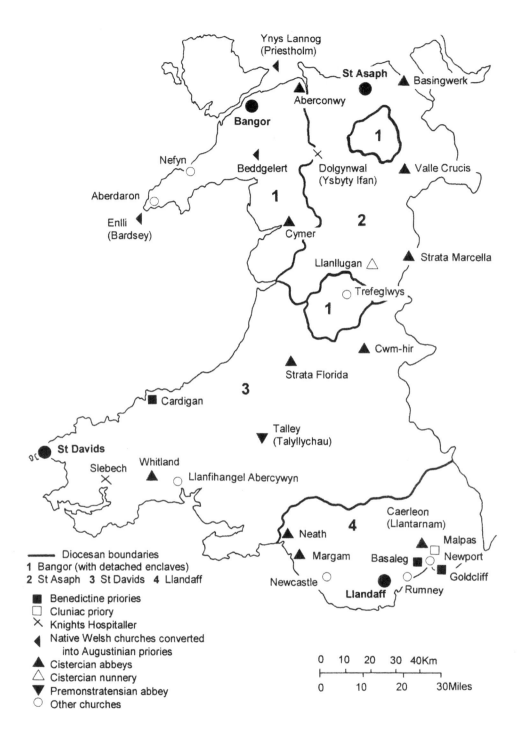

MAP 2. Religious houses and other churches in Wales which were beneficiaries of charters or parties to agreements in this edition

TABLE 1. The dynasty of Arwystli

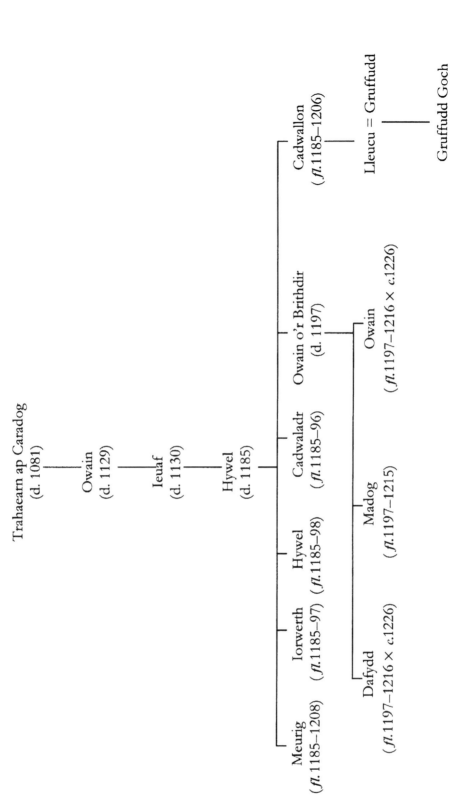

TABLE 2. The dynasty of Cedewain

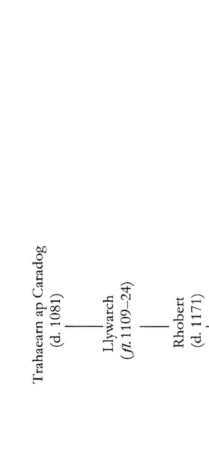

Trahaearn ap Caradog
(d. 1081)
|
Llywarch
(*fl.*1109–24)
|
Rhobert
(d. 1171)
|
Maredudd (1) = Juliana de Lacy = (2) Maredudd Sais
(d. 1244)

Owain I   Gruffudd   Hywel   Owain II
(d. 1236)   (d. 1261)

TABLE 3. The dynasty of Deheubarth

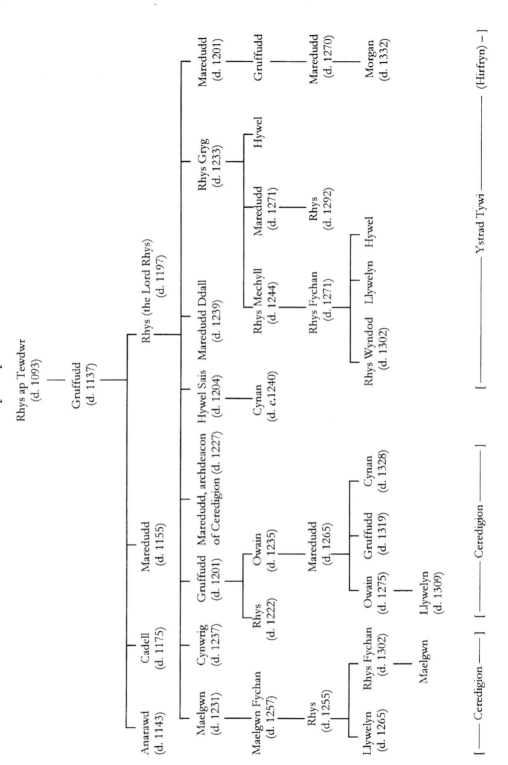

TABLE 4. The dynasty of Elfael and Maelienydd

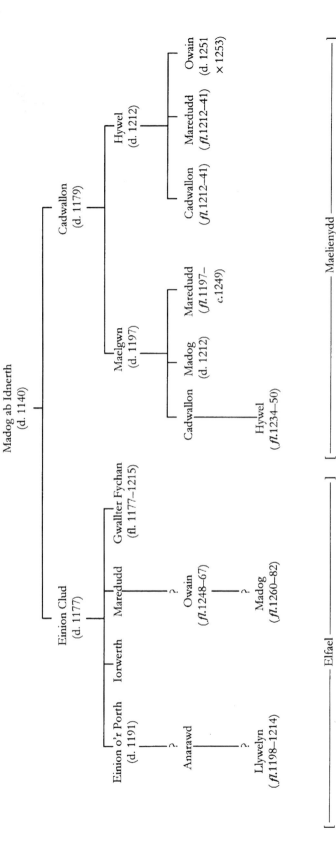

TABLE 5. The dynasty of Glamorgan

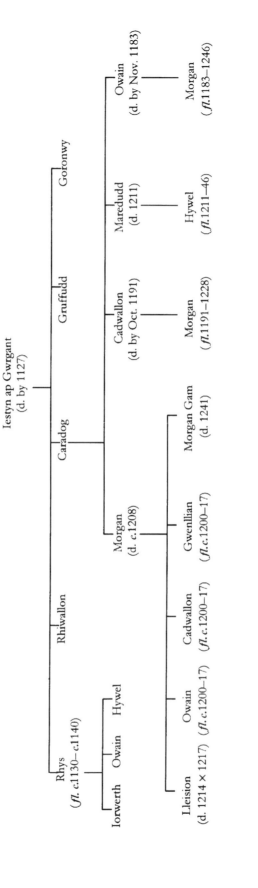

Iestyn ap Gwrgant
(d. by 1127)

Rhiwallon

Caradog

Gruffudd

Goronwy

Owain
(d. by Nov. 1183)

Morgan
(*fl.*1183–1246)

Rhys
(*fl.* c.1130– c.1140)

Iorwerth   Owain   Hywel

Morgan
(d. c.1208)

Cadwallon
(d. by Oct. 1191)

Mareudd
(d. 1211)

Morgan
(*fl.*1191–1228)

Hywel
(*fl.*1211–46)

Lleision
(d. 1214 × 1217)

Owain
(*fl.*c.1200–17)

Cadwallon
(*fl.*c.1200–17)

Gwenllian
(*fl.*c.1200–17)

Morgan Gam
(d. 1241)

TABLE 6. The dynasty of Gwynedd

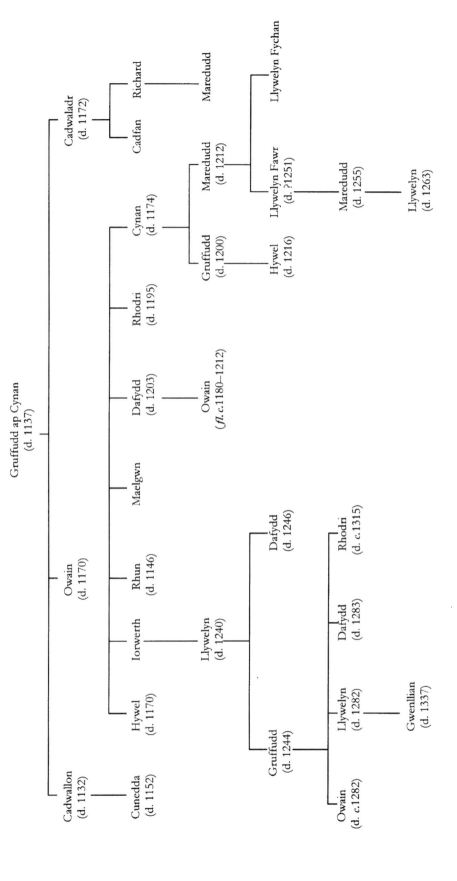

TABLE 7. The dynasty of Gwynllŵg

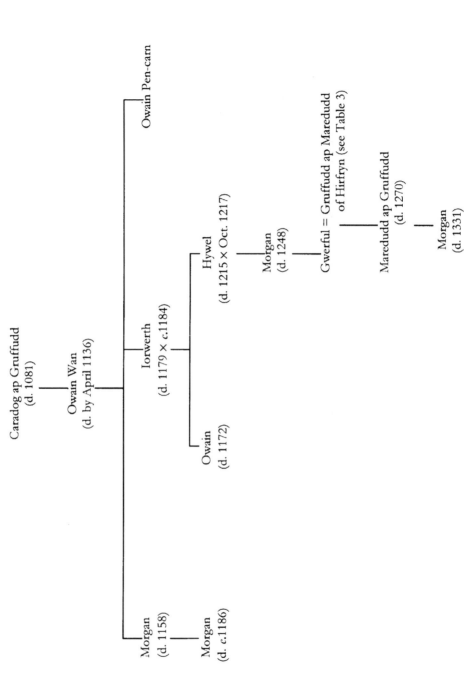

TABLE 8. The dynasty of Powys

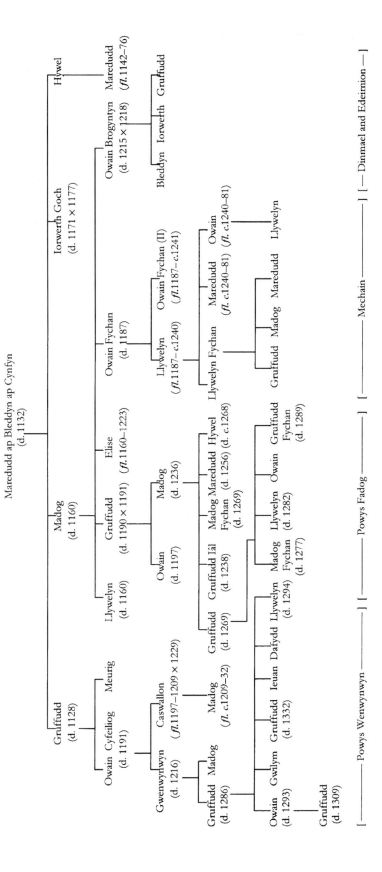

TABLE 9. The dynasty of Senghennydd

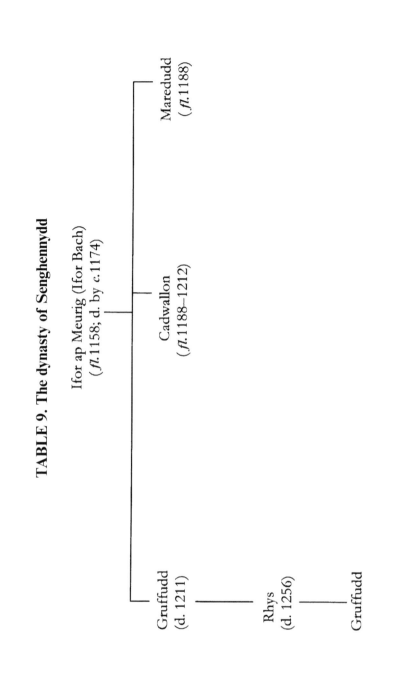

Ifor ap Meurig (Ifor Bach)
(*fl*.1158; d. by c.1174)

Cadwallon
(*fl*.1188–1212)

Maredudd
(*fl*.1188)

Gruffudd
(d. 1211)

Rhys
(d. 1256)

Gruffudd

INTRODUCTION

This edition attempts to assemble the first comprehensive collection of acts issued by native rulers of Wales from the earliest extant twelfth-century documents to the death of Dafydd ap Gruffudd in 1283 during the Edwardian conquest that extinguished independent rule.[1] It thereby aims to make more accessible than before a key body of source material for the study of medieval Wales during an era of struggles for power by native rulers both among themselves and with Marcher lords and the English crown, an era sometimes characterized as 'the age of the princes'.[2] Coverage is intentionally broad. The term 'ruler' has been applied to members not only of the dominant dynasties of Deheubarth, Powys and, above all, Gwynedd but also of minor dynasties such as those of Arwystli or Senghennydd; and, in a world where political power was often contested and fragmented, to individuals within each dynasty who exercised some measure of authority, however limited geographically or temporally. Likewise, the edition includes all known documents issued as expressions of a ruler's will – both those extant as texts and those known only from mentions in other sources – even if, as is the case with petitions or some letters, these do not conform to acts in the strict sense of instruments, particularly charters, that create, modify or confirm a juridical action or situation.[3] (Texts of agreements with the English crown and other third parties are included irrespective of whether they survive in ratifications issued by the Welsh ruler concerned, partly for the sake of completeness but also on the assumption that, where such ratifications are not extant, the terms were at least approved by the ruler, in some cases quite possibly in a written act now lost.)

Identification of the corpus of documents has been greatly facilitated by Kari Maund's compilation of a handlist of acts in a project that prepared the ground for the present edition.[4] In addition, much is owed to the efforts of previous editors of individual documents or collections of documents. As well as standard editions and calendars of royal

---

[1] The latest known acts of Welsh rulers before 1120 are charters of the later eleventh century preserved in the Book of Llandaff: *Text of the Book of Llan Dâv*, 267–75; cf. Davies, *Llandaff Charters*, 129; Crouch, 'Earliest original charter', 125–7.

[2] See Lloyd, 'Age of the native princes'; Jones Pierce, *Medieval Welsh Society*, Chap. I, 'The Age of the Princes' (admittedly this essay applies the phrase only to the century that ended with the death of Llywelyn ap Gruffudd of Gwynedd in 1282).

[3] Cf. Guyotjeannin *et al.*, *Diplomatique médiévale*, 104–5.

[4] *H*. This edition contains most of the documents listed in *H* (see the concordance, below, pp. 816–23) together with further discoveries made since *H* went to press. Errors in *H* have normally been corrected silently in the present work.

sources concerning mainly England or the monastic charters in Dugdale's *Monasticon*, these publications include important volumes of Welsh documents, namely G. T. Clark's edition of Glamorgan charters, J. Goronwy Edwards's calendar of letters concerning Wales contained among the Ancient Correspondence (SC1) in The National Archives: Public Record Office, the same scholar's edition of *Littere Wallie* and Graham Thomas's edition of Strata Marcella charters.[5] As the endnotes to individual documents make clear, the present work also draws extensively on earlier historiography of twelfth- and thirteenth-century Wales. The same is true of Part I of this Introduction, which aims to supply some historical context for the documents contained in the edition and to clarify issues bearing on their chronology. This is followed, in Part II, by an analysis of the diplomatic of the acts.

I. WELSH RULERS, 1120–1283

ARWYSTLI

The native lords of Arwystli in the twelfth century belonged to the same dynasty as those of Cedewain, sharing descent from Trahaearn ap Caradog (d. 1081), who had taken over the kingship of Gwynedd after the death of Bleddyn ap Cynfyn in 1075.[6] This connection with Gwynedd may explain why Arwystli formed a detached portion of the diocese of Bangor. All known acts of the rulers of Arwystli consist of charters issued in favour of either St Michael's church, Trefeglwys (and the Augustinian abbey of Haughmond in Shropshire to which it was granted by Hywel ab Ieuaf) or the Cistercian abbey of Strata Marcella near Welshpool. For most of the period covered by the dynasty's surviving acts Arwystli was subject at different times to the overlordship of rulers from Powys, Gwynedd and possibly also Deheubarth.

The earliest surviving charters are those of Hywel ab Ieuaf (d. 1185), whose father Ieuaf ab Owain ap Trahaearn was killed in 1130 by his first cousins, the sons of Llywarch ap Trahaearn, in the blood-bath that resulted in the blinding, castration and death of at least seven members of the family in 1129–30.[7] To judge by his earliest extant charters, Hywel claimed royal status in the 1140s or early 1150s, styling himself *rex Arguestli/Arewestil*.[8] Possibly he obtained the backing of Cadell ap Gruffudd of Deheubarth, who witnessed the first charter and also Bishop Meurig (Maurice) of Bangor's confirmation of the second, as a counterweight to the ambitions of Madog ap Maredudd (d. 1160) of Powys, who asserted overlordship over Hywel and his land by 1151.[9] Hywel joined Madog in Henry II's campaign against Owain Gwynedd in 1157 and the later medieval prose tale *Breuddwyd*

---

[5] *Cartae*; *CAC*; *LW*; *Ystrad Marchell Charters*. These examples are of course not exhaustive. Among other valuable earlier editions are Una Rees's publication of the Haughmond Cartulary (*Cart. Haugh.*) and papers by J. Beverley Smith printing previously unpublished documents.

[6] *EWGT*, 104–5. For the rulers of Arwystli see further Morgan, 'Territorial divisions [II]', 28–32; Stephenson, 'Politics of Powys Wenwynwyn', 43–4, 46; Carr, 'Debatable land', 39–45; Pryce, 'Church of Trefeglwys', esp. 15–18, 42–7.

[7] *BT, Pen20Tr*, 50; *BT, RBH*, 110–13; cf. Davies, *Conquest*, 72.

[8] Nos 1–2.

[9] No. 480.

Rhonabwy claimed that Madog's authority extended as far south as Gwanan 'in the farthest part of Arwystli'.[10] A poem by Cynddelw (fl. *c.*1155–*c.*1195) thanking Hywel for the gift of a bull associates the ruler of Arwystli with Talgarth (SH 962 902), half a mile south-west of Trefeglwys, suggesting that this was Hywel's principal court.[11] A patron of the Augustinians of Haughmond by the early 1150s, Hywel later also seems to have supported the Cistercians, as he was buried at Strata Florida Abbey on his death in 1185.[12] The choice of burial place may also indicate that Hywel had aligned himself with the Lord Rhys of Deheubarth, the most powerful Welsh ruler after the death of Owain Gwynedd in 1170, and youngest brother and eventual successor of Cadell ap Gruffudd with whom Hywel seems to have been associated earlier.[13]

Hywel had at least six sons, but the extent to which these maintained their father's authority in Arwystli is uncertain.[14] None of these sons is known to have styled himself, or been referred to, as 'king'. Lloyd, relying on the Welsh chronicles, held that Hywel was succeeded by Owain o'r Brithdir (thus named after a township in the parish of Llanidloes), and that the cantref was annexed by Gwenwynwyn ab Owain Cyfeiliog of Powys after Owain's death in 1197.[15] The sequence of events may have been the reverse, however, as all versions of the chronicle record Owain's death after stating that Gwenwynwyn seized Arwystli. More importantly, the charters issued by Owain's brothers and sons suggest that the succession to Arwystli was more complex than Lloyd suggested, and that Hywel ab Ieuaf's sons and grandsons retained significant influence in the region until at least *c.*1216. As Cadwaladr ap Hywel's grant of lands in the parish of Trefeglwys to Strata Marcella was made no later than December 1196, Owain o'r Brithdir cannot have held all his father's lands in the cantref.[16] The confirmations for Strata Marcella in 1198 by Meurig and Hywel may suggest, moreover, that the abbey considered them to be at least potentially powerful despite Gwenwynwyn's annexation the previous year.[17] Meurig also occurs as a grantor of lands in the parish of Trefeglwys in 1208.[18] It is unknown whether this charter was issued before or after Llywelyn's occupation of the lands of Gwenwynwyn (including, presumably, Arwystli) following the latter's arrest by King John in 1208. Gwenwynwyn was restored to his lands with the king's support at about the end of November 1210.[19]

Another son of Hywel ab Ieuaf, Cadwallon, confirmed lands to Strata Marcella in 1206,

---

[10] *HW*, ii. 496; *Breudwyt Ronabwy*, 1. Gwanan has not been identified, but the description of it as lying 'in the farthest part' (*yg gwarthaf*) of Arwystli suggests a location in the northern commote of Arwystli Uwchcoed: ibid., 24. See also R. G. Gruffydd, *Studia Celtica*, 38 (2004), 97.

[11] *GCBM I*, no. 22.

[12] *BT*, *Pen20Tr*, 73; *BT*, *RBH*, 168–9. The suggestion of Williams, *Cistercian Abbey of Strata Florida*, 111, followed by *HW*, ii. 598, n. 130, that Hywel may have granted the church of Llangurig to Strata Florida should be disregarded, as the church was granted to the abbey by Cadwgan, bishop of Bangor: *CPL*, i. 558–9.

[13] Carr, 'Debatable land', 41.

[14] *Ystrad Marchell Charters*, 72. 'Gruffudd Carno' should be discounted: see note to no. 10.

[15] *HW*, ii. 566, 584; *BT*, *Pen20Tr*, 79; *BT*, *RBH*, 180–1 (although the editor assigns the annals for this year to 1198, comparison with the Peniarth 20 version of the *Brut* shows that the correct year was 1197); *BS*, 144–5.

[16] No. 7.

[17] Nos 5, 8.

[18] No. 6.

[19] *BT*, *Pen20Tr*, 83–4; *BT*, *RBH*, 188–9.

a grant confirmed in turn by Gruffudd Goch ap Gruffudd Carno, very probably Cadwallon's grandson, the following year.[20] Gruffudd Goch also occurs in 1208 and among the men of Arwystli at Llandinam in, probably, 1216 × c.1226; he may also be identifiable with the *Grifut Coyc* who witnessed a charter at Llandovery in 1215.[21] Strata Marcella obtained wide-ranging confirmations from three of the sons of Owain o'r Brithdir in 1215.[22] Since the year-date in those confirmations probably signified 25 March 1215 × 24 March 1216 by modern reckoning, they may have been made in the wake of Gwenwynwyn's expulsion from his lands by Llywelyn ap Iorwerth of Gwynedd early in 1216.[23] Two of these sons of Owain o'r Brithdir, Dafydd and Owain, were probably present at Llandinam in 1216 × c.1226.[24]

That Cadwallon ap Hywel's charter of 1206 and the charters of Dafydd and Owain, sons of Owain o'r Brithdir, are dated at Llandovery in Cantref Bychan, about thirty-six miles south-west of Talgarth, could indicate that the grantors were in exile when the charters were issued.[25] Likewise, the presence of Owain Brogyntyn in the witness list of the third Strata Marcella confirmation of 1215, issued by Madog ab Owain o'r Brithdir, may show that Owain had taken refuge north of Arwystli in Owain Brogyntyn's lands of Edeirnion and Dinmael.[26] Be that as it may, it appears that the dynasty suffered a reduction in its authority and lands in the thirteenth century, being subject to the overlordship of Llywelyn ap Iorwerth and his son Gruffudd ap Llywelyn from 1216 to 1240 and to that of Gruffudd ap Gwenwynwyn and his son Owain ap Gruffudd from 1241 to 1274, when the cantref was seized by Llywelyn ap Gruffudd after the abortive assassination plot against him involving Owain.[27] Although it was recovered by Gruffudd ap Gwenwynwyn as a result of Edward I's first Welsh war of 1277, Llywelyn continued to assert his right to Arwystli in the years leading up to the conquest. The extent of the Arwystli dynasty's decline by this period is revealed by the unsuccessful, and quite possibly collusive, claims to the territory brought by several of Hywel ab Ieuaf's descendants against Gruffudd ap Gwenwynwyn and Owain ap Gruffudd in 1279–81.[28]

CEDEWAIN

Maredudd ap Rhobert (d. 1244)

Maredudd is the only ruler of Cedewain known to have issued acts.[29] According to genealogists of the late fifteenth and sixteenth centuries, he was descended from Trahaearn ap Caradog and thus shared a common ancestry with the rulers of Arwystli.[30] The same sources

---

[20] Nos 9–10.
[21] Nos 6, 11, 16; cf. *Ystrad Marchell Charters*, 81.
[22] Nos 11–13.
[23] Stephenson, 'Politics of Powys Wenwynwyn', 43.
[24] No. 17.
[25] Nos 9, 11, 13.
[26] No. 12.
[27] Davies, *Conquest*, 217, 229–31; Morgan, 'Territorial divisions [II]', 32.
[28] *WAR*, 125–30; Carr, 'Debatable land', 42–4.
[29] For the history of Cedewain in this period see Morgan, 'Territorial divisions [I]', 10–21.
[30] *EWGT*, 105.

state that his mother was Dyddgu ferch Madog ab Idnerth. If this is correct, Maredudd was also related to the dynasty of Elfael-Maelienydd, with several of whose members he was associated in a letter from Llywelyn ap Iorwerth probably written in the summer of 1212.[31] Maredudd's father Rhobert ap Llywarch ap Trahaearn has been assumed, probably correctly, to have been the same person as the Rhobert ap Llywarch who died in 1171.[32]

The earliest certain reference to Maredudd in the sources occurs in 1211, when he is named as one of the Welsh lords who joined King John's campaign against Llywelyn ap Iorwerth, and exchequer records show, contrary to the assertion of the Welsh chronicles, that he remained loyal to the king a year later, receiving payment from the crown in September 1212.[33] When Maredudd first established his authority over Cedewain is unknown. Although the two documents recording his judgement on behalf of Llywelyn ap Iorwerth at Llandinam in a dispute over lands in Arwystli, in which he is styled 'lord of Cedewain', could belong to Llywelyn's first occupation of Arwystli in 1208–10, they are far more likely to date from the prince's second period of occupation that began in 1216.[34] One reason for supposing this is that Maredudd is not attested as an ally of Llywelyn until 1215, whereas between at least August 1211 and September 1212 he was a supporter of John against Llywelyn. That the prince regarded Maredudd with suspicion at this time is shown by the letter, already mentioned, sent no later than the beginning of August 1212 in which Llywelyn urged Maredudd and other Welsh lords to protect the lands of Ratlinghope Priory in Shropshire.[35] The letter shows that at least some of the lords addressed were based in Ceri, the commote bordering immediately on Cedewain to the south. It is uncertain whether Maredudd, who is given no territorial designation in the letter, was in control of Cedewain by this time or was a refugee in Ceri together with the descendants of Madog ab Idnerth (possibly his maternal kin). However, the balance of probability is that his stature as a prominent Welsh ally of the king in 1211–12 derived from his tenure of the commote.[36] Whether, or for how long, he held the commote before 1211, we can only guess: the sources are silent about Maredudd, and indeed Cedewain, for the forty years following his father's death in 1171.[37] That the commote retained its autonomy in this period from the rulers of Powys is suggested, however, by the absence of any grants of land in it to Strata Marcella, in contrast to the situation in Arwystli.[38]

---

[31] No. 234.

[32] *BT, Pen20Tr*, 66; *BT, RBH*, 152–3; cf. *HW*, ii. 648, n. 182; Morgan, 'Territorial divisions [I]', 11.

[33] *BT, Pen20Tr*, 85, 86; *BT, RBH*, 190–1, 194–5; *HW*, ii. 638, n. 131.

[34] Nos 16–17.

[35] No. 234.

[36] Although the Welsh chronicles refer to 'Maredudd ap Rhobert of Cedewain' in their accounts of John's campaign in 1211, this territorial association could have been made with the benefit of hindsight and does not provide contemporary testimony that he held the commote at that time. That Maredudd appears with the title *dominus* among the witnesses of Madog ap Maelgwn's charter for Cwm-hir in May 1212 may imply that he held Cedewain by then: no. 113. The genealogist Lewys Dwnn (*c.*1550–*c.*1616) asserted that Maredudd bought Cedewain from his maternal uncle, Madog ap Samwel, but the basis for this assertion is unclear: Dwnn, *Heraldic Visitations*, i. 136 and n. 3.

[37] Remfry, 'Native Welsh Dynasties', 161 argues that Maredudd became lord of Cedewain only in August 1211, with royal support, and may have been landless before that.

[38] Cf. Morgan, 'Territorial divisions [II]', 35; Williams, *Atlas*, 91. Gerald of Wales implies that Cedewain had earlier been associated with Powys in an account of a threat by Bishop Adam of St Asaph in 1176 to enter Ceri *cum Powisensibus et de Keddewein*: *Gir. Camb. Op.*, i. 33 (*De rebus a se gestis*, I. 6).

From at least 1215 Maredudd was a prominent ally of Llywelyn, an alliance illustrated by several of his acts as well as by two issued by the prince.[39] However, after the prince's death he numbered among the Welsh lords who supported the claims of Gruffudd ap Llywelyn against Dafydd, Llywelyn's designated successor, in 1241.[40] By the end of his life Maredudd may have enjoyed the role of an elder statesman in Welsh politics, for the Welsh chroniclers commemorated him as the 'most eminent counsellor of Wales'.[41] Yet, if his wider influence in Wales is clear, the nature of his rule in Cedewain remains elusive. Maredudd granted land at Aber-miwl and probably also at Gelynnog to Strata Florida, the abbey at which he eventually died, having taken the monastic habit, in 1244.[42] Maredudd also founded a Cistercian nunnery at Llanllugan.[43] This patronage of the Cistercians may well have been designed in part to maintain the independence of Cedewain from Powys Wenwynwyn. In particular, Llanllugan, though apparently supervised by Strata Marcella, whose patrons were the rulers of Powys Wenwynwyn, was endowed in part with some of the lands between the Rhiw and the Helygi, along Cedewain's northern border with the Powysian commotes of Llannerch Hudol and Caereinion, which Maredudd seized from Gwenwynwyn c.1216.[44]

Maredudd married Juliana de Lacy, on whom he apparently conferred (unspecified) dower lands and who survived him to marry Maredudd Sais by 1252. She may have been a daughter of Walter de Lacy (d. 1241) of Weobley in Herefordshire.[45] The date of the marriage is unknown, but is unlikely to have occurred before c.1205, if, as is very likely, she was the mother of Maredudd's son Owain II (d. 1261), who was presumably born after the death of his eldest son Owain I in 1236.[46] If she had also borne Owain I, she probably married Maredudd no later than c.1220, as the recording of Owain's death in the Welsh chronicles suggests that he was at least a young adult by 1236; moreover, Owain I had two younger brothers.[47] Maredudd was eventually succeeded in 1248 by Owain II, after the latter had promised to pay Henry III an entry fine of 300 marks. However, royal influence over Cedewain waned following Owain II's death on c.1 November 1261, when the commote appears to have been seized by Llywelyn ap Gruffudd of Gwynedd, who had already driven Gruffudd ap Gwenwynwyn from most of the neighbouring lands of southern Powys in 1257. Though Gruffudd was restored to the district between the Rhiw and the Helygi in his agreement with Llywelyn in December 1263, he was deprived of it by the prince, who had begun building a castle at Dolforwyn in Cedewain in 1273, after the discovery of Gruffudd's plot against him in 1274. Cedewain fell to royal forces in the spring of 1277 and was granted to Roger Mortimer on 6 January 1279.[48]

---

[39] Maredudd was named, along with Gwenwynwyn and the warband of Madog ap Gruffudd, among those from Powys who joined Llywelyn's campaign in south-west Wales at the end of 1215: *BT, Pen20Tr*, 91; *BT, RBH*, 206–7. See also nos 16–17, 19–20, 239, 242.

[40] Williams, 'Succession', 400, 404–5, 408; no. 21.

[41] *BT, Pen20Tr*, 106. *BT, RBH*, 238–9, and *BS*, 234–5, refer to him respectively as 'the chief counsellor of Wales' and 'the chief counsel of all Wales'.

[42] No. 14; *BT, Pen20Tr*, 106; *BT, RBH*, 238–9; *AC*, 85.

[43] No. 18.

[44] For the seizure of these lands see no. 591.

[45] No. 15.

[46] Cf. *BT, Pen20Tr*, 104; *BT, RBH*, 232–3; Morgan, 'Territorial divisions [I]', 12.

[47] No. 18.

[48] *BT, Pen20Tr*, 108, 112; *BT, RBH*, 242–3, 252–3; Morgan, 'Territorial divisions [I]', 12–20; Smith, *Llywelyn*, 183 and n. 169; *CChR 1257–1300*, 211.

DEHEUBARTH

In the twelfth and thirteenth centuries Deheubarth signified the kingdom in the south-west restored by Gruffudd ap Rhys (d. 1137) and his sons which comprised Ystrad Tywi, Ceredigion and those areas of Dyfed seized from the Marcher lords.[49] The kingdom reached its greatest extent and power under Rhys ap Gruffudd, also known as the Lord Rhys, but after his death in 1197 its lands were fragmented as the result of struggles among his descendants, who sought support from both the princes of Gwynedd and the English crown. The dynasty, descended from Cadell ap Rhodri Mawr, achieved a remarkable recovery beginning in the generation after the death of Rhys ap Tewdwr in 1093 and the Norman conquest of Dyfed.[50] Rhys's son Gruffudd ap Rhys returned from exile in Ireland *c*.1113 and led risings against the Normans in 1115–16 and again, in alliance with the sons of Gruffudd ap Cynan of Gwynedd, in 1136–7.[51] (Gruffudd ap Rhys married Gruffudd ap Cynan's daughter Gwenllian, the mother of his younger sons Maredudd and Rhys.) Attacks on the Normans were continued by Gruffudd's sons, whose co-operation and perseverance resulted in major territorial gains and the restoration of a native kingdom in the south-west.

Cadell ap Gruffudd (d. 1175)

Cadell succeeded to the kingship of Deheubarth after his brother and predecessor Anarawd ap Gruffudd was killed by the warband of Cadwaladr ap Gruffudd ap Cynan in 1143. (Anarawd's son Einion ab Anarawd served as Rhys ap Gruffudd's *penteulu* or chief of military retinue until he was killed at the instigation of Roger de Clare in 1163; Einion's son Anarawd ab Einion was a benefactor of the Hospitallers of Slebech.)[52] Cadell's rule was marked by important military successes, often in conjunction with his younger half-brothers Maredudd and Rhys, including the capture of several castles in 1146 and the conquest of all of Ceredigion, apart from Pen-gwern in Llanfihangel, from Hywel ab Owain of Gwynedd by 1151.[53] However, later in that year Cadell was severely wounded by Normans from Tenby.[54] His injuries almost certainly incapacitated him as a ruler, since only Maredudd and Rhys are named as leading further campaigns in 1151 and 1153, and probably explain why he went on a pilgrimage to Rome, entrusting 'all his authority to Maredudd and Rhys, his brothers, until he should come back'.[55] The pilgrimage is assigned to 1153 in *Brut y Tywysogyon*, but both the B- and the C-texts of *Annales Cambriae* offer a different chronology, placing it in the year after the death of Maredudd ap Rhys in 1155,

---

[49] For Deheubarth in the twelfth and thirteenth centuries the essential narrative remains that of Lloyd in *HW*, ii. See also *idem*, 'Age of the native princes'; *idem*, *Story of Ceredigion*, 26–105; Davies, *Conquest*, esp. 34–43, 50–5, 217–27.

[50] *Gir. Camb. Op.*, vi. 166–7 (*DK* I. 2, 3); *EWGT*, 39 (no. 2), 47 (no. 24). See further Maund, *Ireland, Wales and England*, 33–8; Moore, 'O Rys ap Tewdwr'.

[51] *BT, Pen20Tr*, 39–44, 51–2; *BT, RBH*, 82–97, 112–17; *AC*, 35–6, 40–1.

[52] *BT, Pen20Tr*, 62–3; *BT, RBH*, 142–5; nos 31–2.

[53] *BT, Pen20Tr*, 53, 54, 55, 57; *BT, RBH*, 118–19, 120–3, 124–5, 128–31.

[54] *BT, Pen20Tr*, 57; *BT, RBH*, 130–1. *AC*, 45, places the wounding in the following year, in an annal which seems to cover events from February 1152 to 16 December 1153.

[55] *BT, Pen20Tr*, 58; also *BT, RBH*, 132–3.

and the year before Henry II's first Welsh campaign, that is, in 1156.[56] The account in *Brut y Tywysogyon* therefore implies that Cadell retained the kingship of Deheubarth until 1153, and then only abdicated temporarily in favour of his half-brothers. By contrast, the B-text of *Annales Cambriae* implies that Cadell had lost authority by 1155, for it states that, after the death of Maredudd, Rhys obtained his brother's 'portion'; only after Rhys had succeeded to the kingship did Cadell go to Rome. It is difficult to decide which of these accounts is likely to be more the accurate. However, the important point with respect to dating acts issued or witnessed by Cadell is that he seems to have lost his capacity to rule as 'king of Deheubarth' after he was wounded in 1151. He evidently returned from Rome, for he died at the Cistercian monastery of Strata Florida in 1175 after assuming the monastic habit.[57]

Rhys ap Gruffudd (the Lord Rhys) (d. 28 April 1197)

All the Welsh narrative sources agree that Rhys succeeded his brother Maredudd – described in *Brut y Tywysogyon* as lord or king of Ceredigion, Ystrad Tywi and Dyfed – upon the latter's death, aged twenty-four, in 1155.[58] Though himself even younger than Maredudd, Rhys had almost a decade's experience of campaigning with his brothers and was thus well prepared for the new challenge to his dynasty's conquests posed by Henry II (1154–89). In 1158 Rhys was forced to submit to the king and surrender Ceredigion to Roger de Clare, earl of Hertford (d. 1173) and Cantref Bychan with its castle of Llandovery to Walter Clifford (d. 1190).[59] However, the prince seized every opportunity to regain these lands and, despite two royal campaigns against him in 1159 and 1163 (the latter followed by a further submission at Woodstock on 1 July 1163), the Marchers' recovery proved short-lived: Rhys seized Cantref Mawr before the end of 1163 and reconquered most of Ceredigion in 1164.[60] In August 1165 he joined his uncle Owain Gwynedd and other Welsh leaders at Corwen to resist Henry II's disastrous last campaign against the Welsh, and later that year Rhys completed the conquest of Ceredigion, capturing Cardigan and Cilgerran castles.[61] Ceredigion remained in his hands for the rest of his reign, a success reflected in Rhys's surviving acts, all of which grant land in the region, and most of it continued to be held by his descendants until 1277. One consequence of the reconquest of Ceredigion was the prince's assumption of the patronage of Strata Florida, a daughter house of Whitland Abbey (another Cistercian house patronized by the prince) which had been founded in 1164 by his cousin, Robert fitz Stephen, the Clares' constable of Cardigan, and Rhys confirmed and augmented the possessions of other Marcher foundations in Ceredigion.[62]

After the death of Owain Gwynedd in November 1170 Rhys became the most powerful Welsh ruler and remained so for the rest of his life. His hegemony in south Wales was

---

[56] *AC*, 46. These texts merely state that Cadell went on pilgrimage to Rome, without implying that he had only temporarily abdicated his authority.

[57] *BT, Pen20Tr*, 71; *BT, RBH*, 166–7. The former chronicle says that he died 'of a long infirmity', perhaps a reference to the injuries of 1151.

[58] *BT, Pen20Tr*, 58; *BT, RBH*, 132–3; *AC*, 46. Both versions of *BT* say that Maredudd died 'in the twenty-fifth year of his age'. For Rhys see further Jones and Pryce (eds), *Arglwydd Rhys* (esp. Smith, 'Treftadaeth Deheubarth'), and Turvey, *Lord Rhys*.

[59] *BT, Pen20Tr*, 60; *BT, RBH*, 136–9.

[60] *BT, Pen20Tr*, 61–3; *BT, RBH*, 140–5; *HW*, ii. 510–14.

[61] *BT, Pen20Tr*, 63–4; *BT, RBH*, 144–7.

[62] Nos 23–4, 29.

recognized by Henry II, who in October 1171 confirmed Rhys in possession of Ceredigion and Ystrad Tywi, together with Emlyn, Ystlwyf and Efelffre in Dyfed, and on his return from Ireland after Easter 1172 appointed the prince 'justice in all south Wales', thereby probably delegating to him authority over the Welsh rulers of Gwynllŵg, Gwent, Glamorgan, Maelienydd, Gwerthrynion and Elfael, rulers who accompanied him to meet Henry II at the council of Gloucester in June 1175 and most of whom were related to Rhys by marriage.[63] Despite strains, especially in 1184 and 1186, the détente with Henry II lasted until the latter's death in July 1189. However, the last years of Rhys's reign were marked by a resumption of hostilities against royal and Marcher lands and castles in south Wales as well as by increasingly bitter struggles among the prince's sons, two of whom captured and briefly imprisoned their father in 1194.[64] Rhys died on 28 April 1197, aged sixty-five, and was buried in St Davids cathedral.[65]

Rhys ap Gruffudd's successors, 1197–1240

Gruffudd ap Rhys (d. 25 July 1201), eldest legitimate son of Rhys ap Gruffudd and his wife Gwenllian ferch Madog ap Maredudd of Powys, was clearly the Lord Rhys's chosen successor and was recognized by Richard I's government shortly after his father's death in 1197. However, the succession to Deheubarth was challenged by Gruffudd's elder illegitimate half-brother Maelgwn ap Rhys, with whom Gruffudd had been in conflict since 1189, and later in 1197 Maelgwn, aided by Gwenwynwyn of southern Powys, occupied Ceredigion and captured Gruffudd, who was handed over for imprisonment to the English. Gruffudd was released in July 1198 and recovered all of Ceredigion apart from the castles of Cardigan and Ystradmeurig after Gwenwynwyn's defeat at Painscastle on 13 August.[66] By December 1199 Maelgwn sought royal assistance and agreed by 11 April 1200 to surrender Cardigan and the adjacent commote of Is Hirwern to John in return for the four cantrefs of Ceredigion and Emlyn.[67] Gruffudd ap Rhys died on 25 July 1201, shortly after seizing Cantref Bychan and Llandovery following the death of his brother Maredudd ap Rhys on 2 July.[68] Gruffudd left a widow, Matilda de Braose (d. 29 December 1210),[69] with whom he had two sons, Rhys Ieuanc (d. August 1222) and Owain (d. 17 January 1235).

Maelgwn exploited the opportunity presented by Gruffudd's death to recover Cilgerran in 1201 and, with Gwenwynwyn's help, to occupy Cantref Mawr and Cantref Bychan in 1203, thereby excluding Gruffudd's sons.[70] In 1204 Hywel Sais ap Rhys, an ally of Gruffudd, died, probably from wounds inflicted by Maelgwn's men in Cemais. Later in that year Maelgwn was expelled from Ystrad Tywi by the sons of Gruffudd and their uncle Rhys Gryg ap Rhys (d. 1233): Rhys Ieuanc and Owain took Cantref Bychan, Rhys Gryg

---

[63] *BT, Pen20Tr*, 66–8, 70–1; *BT, RBH*, 154–5, 158–9, 164–5; Smith, 'Treftadaeth Deheubarth', 30–2.
[64] For the last phase of Rhys's reign see most recently Gillingham, *English in the Twelfth Century*, 59–68.
[65] *BT, Pen20Tr*, 76–7; *BT, RBH*, 178–9; *AC*, 60–1; *AM*, ii. 66. As Lloyd suggested (*HW*, ii. 475, n. 53, 582 and n. 38), Rhys was probably born *c*.1132, as he was younger than Maredudd, who died in his twenty-fifth year in 1155 and was thus born 1130 × 1131.
[66] *AC*, 61; *CW*, 31–2; *BT, Pen20Tr*, 78–80; *BT, RBH*, 178–83; *HW*, ii. 584; Smith, 'Dynastic succession', 212–13.
[67] No. 41 and note.
[68] *BT, Pen20Tr*, 81; *BT, RBH*, 184–5.
[69] *BT, Pen20Tr*, 84; *BT, RBH*, 190–1.
[70] *AC*, 63; *BT, Pen20Tr*, 82; *BT, RBH*, 186–7.

Cantref Mawr.[71] From 1208 events in Deheubarth were greatly influenced by Llywelyn ap Iorwerth of Gwynedd, who occupied Ceredigion north of the Ystwyth in that year and handed the area between the Ystwyth and the Aeron to Rhys Ieuanc and Owain sons of Gruffudd ap Rhys. However, their hold on Cantref Bychan and northern Ceredigion was interrupted, first, by Rhys Gryg's capture of Llandovery on 8 September 1210 and, second, by their expulsion from Ceredigion in the summer of 1211 by the forces of Falkes de Bréauté, Maelgwn and Rhys Gryg and their subsequent submission to John.[72] By contrast, Maelgwn and Rhys Gryg, faced by John's castle-building policy in Wales after his defeat of Llywelyn ap Iorwerth in the summer of 1211, defected from the crown and their rising was supported by Llywelyn the following summer (1212). The sons of Gruffudd ap Rhys remained loyal to the crown, however, and with its support seized Cantref Bychan and Cantref Mawr from Rhys Gryg in late January 1213; later in the year Rhys Gryg was captured and imprisoned in Carmarthen castle.[73] Rhys Ieuanc and Owain then changed sides again and allied with Maelgwn, secure in Ceredigion since 1210, in an invasion of Dyfed on 27 May 1215. The allies also sought the help of Llywelyn ap Iorwerth, who in December 1215 led a force including them and also Rhys Gryg, released from captivity on 13 June 1215, which won major victories in Deheubarth, including the capture of Carmarthen.[74]

At a council of his magnates at Aberdyfi early in 1216 Llywelyn imposed a partition on the rulers of Deheubarth that would last, with some modifications, until the prince's death in 1240.[75] Maelgwn chose the share comprising Cantref Gwarthaf (including Carmarthen), Cemais and Emlyn (including Cilgerran) in Dyfed; the commotes of Malláen in Cantref Mawr and Hirfryn (with Llandovery) in Cantref Bychan; and the commotes of Gwynionydd and Mebwynion in Ceredigion. Rhys Gryg was restored to Cantref Mawr and Cantref Bychan, apart from the commotes allocated to Maelgwn, and was also granted Cydweli and Carnwyllion in Dyfed, while the sons of Gruffudd ap Rhys were restored to Ceredigion, apart from Gwynionydd and Mebwynion. Rhys Gryg's share was reduced at the end of August 1220, after Llywelyn arrived in Ystrad Tywi with an army and forced Rhys to surrender Cydweli, Carnwyllion, Gwidigada and Gower to the Marchers, in accordance with instructions from the regency government of Henry III.[76] On the death of Rhys Ieuanc without a direct heir in August 1222, Llywelyn divided his lands between Maelgwn and Owain ap Gruffudd.[77] William Marshal II's campaign in 1223 restored Cardigan and Carmarthen to the crown,[78] and by his death at Llannerch Aeron (20 November 1230 × 14

---

[71] *BT, Pen20Tr*, 82; *BT, RBH*, 186–7; *CW*, 32. These accounts of Hywel's death are probably more reliable than *AC*, 62 (B), which states that Hywel died from an illness at Chepstow after returning from John's court, which he had visited 'around Easter', or else was killed by *Franci*: see *HW*, ii. 618, n. 37; *BT, Pen20Tr*, 193–4.

[72] *BT, Pen20Tr*, 83, 84, 85–6; *BT, RBH*, 188–9, 192–3; *CW*, 33–4.

[73] *BT, Pen20Tr*, 86–8; *BT, RBH*, 192–9; *CW*, 34–5.

[74] *BT, Pen20Tr*, 90–2; *BT, RBH*, 202–7; *CW*, 36; *AC*, 71–2.

[75] *BT, Pen20Tr*, 92; *BT, RBH*, 206–7; *CW*, 36; *HW*, ii. 649. Davies, *Conquest*, 228, has a map and notes that the division (as reported in *CW*) was made in accordance with the principles of Welsh law.

[76] No. 248; *HW*, ii. 659. However, Rhys seems to have been soon restored to Cydweli and still held it in 1222: Walker, 'Hubert de Burgh', 470–1.

[77] *BT, Pen20Tr*, 99; *BT, RBH*, 222–3; *AC*, 75 (B).

[78] *BT, Pen20Tr*, 99–100; *BT, RBH*, 222–5; *AC*, 75 (B); Carpenter, *Minority*, 307–9.

February 1231) Maelgwn's lands were largely concentrated in Ceredigion Is Aeron.[79] During the Marshal rebellion Rhys Gryg, Owain ap Gruffudd and Maelgwn Fychan ap Maelgwn (d. 1257) unsuccessfully besieged Carmarthen. Rhys Gryg was wounded when the siege was raised in March 1233 and died shortly afterwards at Llandeilo Fawr and was buried at St Davids near the grave of his father the Lord Rhys. Owain ap Gruffudd died at Strata Florida on 17 January 1235 and was buried in the chapter house near his brother Rhys Ieuanc.[80] Rhys Gryg's son Rhys Mechyll (d. 1244) and Owain's son Maredudd ab Owain (d. 1265) continued their fathers' lineages in Ystrad Tywi and Ceredigion respectively.

The lineage of Maelgwn ap Rhys, 1231–83

In the thirteenth century native lordship in Ceredigion was exercised by the lines of Maelgwn ap Rhys and his nephew Owain ap Gruffudd ap Rhys. Maelgwn's son and successor Maelgwn Fychan seems to have moved his power-base into northern Ceredigion, persuading Llywelyn ap Iorwerth to make Maredudd ab Owain grant him the commote of Mefenydd in exchange for Pennardd in 1236, allegedly with a view to despoiling the monks of Strata Florida of their lands at Ystradmeurig; he also held Creuddyn and probably gained Perfedd by the 1240s.[81] However, in April 1246 Maelgwn was driven out of Ceredigion by a royal force sent in support of his kinsmen Maredudd ap Rhys Gryg and Maredudd ab Owain, and fled to Meirionnydd; although he subsequently made peace with the crown, Maelgwn was restored to only two commotes in the northern and southern extremities of Ceredigion, namely Genau'r-glyn and Is Coed.[82] Maelgwn Fychan was predeceased by his son Rhys ap Maelgwn on c.24 June 1255 and died in 1257; both were buried at Strata Florida.[83]

Rhys ap Maelgwn left two sons, Llywelyn ap Rhys (d. 13 January 1265) and Rhys Fychan ap Rhys (d. 1302).[84] Rhys Fychan appears to have been established in Genau'r-glyn by 1260, and in 1274 he obtained the contiguous commote of Perfedd in an exchange with Cynan ap Maredudd ab Owain, to whom he gave Pennardd.[85] Rhys Fychan surrendered to

---

[79] Chancery records last refer to Maelgwn on 20 November 1230; he had been replaced by his son, Maelgwn Fychan, by 14 February 1231: *CR 1227–31*, 458; *PR 1225–32*, 424. *Annales Cambriae* (C) places Maelgwn's death in 1230: *HW*, ii. 674, n. 110. By contrast, *BT, Pen20Tr*, 102, and *BT, RBH*, 228–9, place it as the first entry under 1231 and add that Maelgwn was buried in the chapter house of Strata Florida.

[80] Owain died at Strata Florida 'on the Wednesday next after the eighth day from Epiphany' in 1235 (*BT, Pen20Tr*, 103; *BT, RBH*, 232–3; *AC*, 81; *CW*, 38). Although the year was reckoned by Welsh chroniclers to begin on 25 March, this probably refers to 17 January 1235 rather than to 15 January 1236, as the entry is followed by an account of Henry III's marriage to Eleanor of Provence, said by both the vernacular and the Latin chronicles to have occurred in the same year as Gruffudd's death. Admittedly this is not in itself conclusive, since the marriage was celebrated on 20 January 1236, but it should be noted that the versions of *Brut y Tywysogyon* are more specific, placing the marriage at Christmas, presumably in 1235 by modern reckoning; if the sequence of events given is correct, this implies that the marriage occurred well after Gruffudd's death. See *BT, Pen20Tr*, 104, 203; *Ystrad Marchell Charters*, 30. Owain's death is assigned to 1236 in *HW*, ii. 768.

[81] *AC*, 81 (B); *Rot. Claus.*, ii. 73a; *CPR 1232–47*, 488 (cited in *HW*, ii. 700, n. 39).

[82] *AC*, 86; *CPR 1232–47*, 493; *HW*, ii. 710; Smith, *Llywelyn*, 55. Maelgwn's son-in-law Maredudd ap Llywelyn (d. 1255) was lord of Meirionnydd: n. 83 below.

[83] *AC*, 89; *BT, Pen20Tr*, 109, 111; *BT, RBH*, 244–7, 248–9.

[84] *BT, Pen20Tr*, 114; *BT, RBH*, 254–5.

[85] No. 66; *BT, Pen20Tr*, 117; *BT, RBH*, 262–3.

the crown in the 1277 war, doing homage to Edward I at Worcester on 1 July, but on *c*.1 August he fled with the men of Genau'r-glyn to Llywelyn ap Gruffudd.[86] Rhys briefly recovered his lands in the next Welsh war. On 24 or 25 March 1282 he joined Gruffudd ap Maredudd in capturing the town and castle of Aberystwyth, thereby acquiring the cantref of Penweddig (comprising Genau'r-glyn, Perfedd and Creuddyn).[87] However, in January 1283 Rhys surrendered to William de Valence, whose forces had reached Aberystwyth, and he remained in royal pay from March to July, when he defected to Dafydd ap Gruffudd (who had tried to win his support with a grant of Penweddig on 2 May). Captured shortly afterwards, Rhys spent the rest of his life in royal custody and service.[88]

The lineage of Owain ap Gruffudd, 1235–83

By the 1240s Maredudd ab Owain ap Gruffudd held five commotes in Ceredigion: Genau'r-glyn, Pennardd, Mebwynion, Gwynionydd and Is Coed.[89] In April 1246, following the death of Dafydd ap Llywelyn in February, Maredudd, together with Maredudd ap Rhys Gryg, made peace with Henry III, and in August he received royal ratification of his grant of Gwynionydd in dower to his wife Elen.[90] Over ten years later, in early December 1256, Maredudd was granted Builth and the Lord Edward's lands around Llanbadarn Fawr by Llywelyn ap Gruffudd, who had occupied northern Ceredigion. Maredudd did fealty to Llywelyn on that occasion and remained a loyal and active adherent of the prince until his death at Llanbadarn Fawr in March 1265, being praised by the native chronicler as 'defender of all Deheubarth and counsellor of all Wales'.[91]

Maredudd left three sons – Owain, Gruffudd and Cynan – whose lands lay south of the Ystwyth. Owain's share of his father's lands included Anhuniog, while Gruffudd appears to have held Gwynionydd.[92] The sons continued their father's loyalty to Llywelyn ap Gruffudd.[93] Owain died on 18 July 1275.[94] His son Llywelyn ab Owain (d. 1309) was the only member of the dynasty of Deheubarth to retain lands in Ceredigion after the conquest of 1282–3.[95] Gruffudd, Cynan and their nephew Llywelyn surrendered to Payn de Chaworth, the commander of royal forces in west Wales, on 2 May 1277, quitclaiming the commotes of Mefenydd and Anhuniog to the crown, and did homage to Edward I at Worcester on 1 July. Gruffudd was allowed to return to Ceredigion, but Cynan was released only on 10 October, while Llywelyn ab Owain was detained as a ward of the king; his lands

---

[86] *BT, Pen20Tr*, 118–19; *BT, RBH*, 264–7; Griffiths, *PW*, 3–4.

[87] *CAC*, 44–5; *BT, Pen20Tr*, 120; *BT, RBH*, 268–71.

[88] Griffiths, *Conquerors*, 50–1; Smith, *Llywelyn*, 571–2 and n. 209; no. 457.

[89] *AC*, 81; *CPR 1232–47*, 487, 493; *CChR 1226–57*, 475.

[90] *CPR 1232–47*, 470, 479; no. 69.

[91] *AC*, 91; *BT, Pen20Tr*, 110 (which erroneously states that Builth was granted to Maredudd ap Rhys Gryg), 114; *BT, RBH*, 246–7, 256–7; *HW*, ii. 718, 720–2, 725, 726–7; Smith, *Llywelyn*, 93–5, 98, 108, 151–2; no. 328. Maredudd was buried in the chapter house at Strata Florida.

[92] Nos 71, 73.

[93] See nos 70, 72, 79–80, 221; Griffiths, *Conquerors*, 49–50.

[94] According to *BT, Pen20Tr*, 117, followed by *BS*, 250–1, he died 'on the fifteenth day from the Calends of August' (*y pymthecuet dyd o galan Awst*: *BT, Pen20*, 221). *BT, RBH*, 262–3, reads: 'on the fifteenth day from August' (*yn y pymthecuet tyd o Awst*). Cf. *BT, Pen20Tr*, 215. Presumably the Latin annal underlying these texts read *xv kal. Aug.*, i.e. 18 July.

[95] No. 83 and note. Llywelyn's lands were inherited by his sons Owain and Thomas after his death, which occurred in 1309, before 3 May: *CIPM*, v. 42–3 (no. 91).

were restored to him after he did homage to Edward I on 15 February 1279.[96] Cynan continued to hold lands in at least Perfedd, as he was in dispute with Strata Florida, situated in that commote, in 1279–80.[97] However, Cynan and Gruffudd increasingly resented the demands imposed by the royal administration based at Cardigan in the years after 1277, and both sided with Llywelyn ap Gruffudd in 1282. Gruffudd joined Rhys Fychan ap Rhys in capturing Aberystwyth on 24 or 25 March and recovered Mefenydd.[98] After royal forces occupied Ceredigion in January 1283 Gruffudd joined Dafydd ap Gruffudd in Gwynedd; he issued a charter at Llanberis on 2 May, and presumably surrendered once Dafydd had been captured the following month.[99] Cynan (and Rhys Fychan) surrendered to William de Valence in January 1283, serving the crown from March to July before transferring their allegiance to Dafydd ap Gruffudd.[100] Shortly afterwards they were captured and imprisoned at Bridgnorth, and later occur, together with Gruffudd, in the king's service in Flanders in 1297.[101] Gruffudd died by 24 March 1319 and Cynan by 18 June 1328; the latter ended his days in receipt of a corrody at the Augustinian house of Thornton in Lincolnshire.[102]

The lineage of Rhys Gryg, 1233–83

None of Rhys Gryg's descendants succeeded in establishing hegemony over the whole of Ystrad Tywi.[103] Rhys's eldest son Rhys Mechyll (also known as Rhys Fychan) faced a challenge from his brother Maredudd ap Rhys (d. 1271), who, supported by Gilbert Marshal, appears to have held the four western commotes of Cantref Mawr in 1240, thereby establishing a lordship based on Dryslwyn castle and leaving Rhys Mechyll with the eastern commotes and Dinefwr castle. After his death, shortly before 6 April 1244,[104] Rhys Mechyll was succeeded by his son Rhys Fychan (d. 1271). Both Rhys Fychan and his uncle Maredudd ap Rhys submitted to Henry III in 1246. However, both Welsh rulers entered a confederacy with Owain ap Gruffudd and his brother Llywelyn in October 1251, and Maredudd joined in Llywelyn's conquest of Perfeddwlad in December 1256 and was subsequently restored to his lands in Ystrad Tywi, from which he had been expelled by Rhys Fychan in alliance with the English. However, while Rhys Fychan defected from the English during the campaign that ended in the Welsh victory at Cymerau in June 1257, thereafter remaining loyal to Llywelyn, Maredudd's allegiance wavered between Llywelyn

---

[96] No. 74; *BT, RBH*, 264–7; *BT, Pen20Tr*, 118–19; *CWR*, 180; Griffiths, *Conquerors*, 50.
[97] Nos 76, 81.
[98] No. 77; *CAC*, 44–5; *BT, Pen20Tr*, 120; *BT, RBH*, 268–71.
[99] No. 78; Griffiths, *Conquerors*, 51; *idem, PW*, 5.
[100] Smith, *Llywelyn*, 572, n. 209.
[101] Griffiths, *Conquerors*, 51; Morris, *Welsh Wars*, 279–80.
[102] *CPR 1317–21*, 323; *CCR 1327–30*, 401. Cf. *CPR 1307–13*, 57; *CCR 1313–18*, 186. The records referring to Gruffudd ap Maredudd and his brother Cynan in the late thirteenth and early fourteenth centuries show that the latter was a different person from the Cynan (?ap Maredudd) named with Madog ap Llywelyn as one of the leaders of the Welsh rising in 1294 (possibly in Brecon, where he was captured), who was executed at Hereford on 14 September 1295, notwithstanding the identification of him as Cynan ap Maredudd ab Owain ap Gruffudd in *BS*, 260–3 (partially followed by Griffiths, *Conquerors*, 51). *BT, Pen20Tr*, 122, and *AM*, iv. 522 (*Ann. Wig.*), respectively refer to him as Cynan ap Maredudd and *Conan*. Cf. Walker, 'Welsh war', xxviii; Edwards, 'Madog ap Llywelyn', 207.
[103] For Ystrad Tywi in the thirteenth century see Smith, '"Cronica de Wallia"', esp. 265–74.
[104] *BT, Pen20Tr*, 106; *BT, RBH*, 238–9; *HW*, ii. 710, n. 98, citing *CPR 1232–47*, 422.

and the crown in the following years, and at the Treaty of Montgomery he was the only 'Welsh baron' whose homage was denied Llywelyn, although the latter purchased it from the crown for 5,000 marks in 1270.[105] Maredudd died at Dryslwyn in 1271, probably on 27 July, and was buried at Whitland.[106] This was followed on 17 August by the death at Dinefwr of Rhys Fychan, who was buried at Talley.[107]

Maredudd was succeeded at Dryslwyn and its appurtenant commotes of Catheiniog, Mabudrud and possibly Gwidigada by his son Rhys ap Maredudd (d. 1292), while Dinefwr and the eastern commotes of Cantref Mawr, namely Maenordeilo, Malláen, Caeo and Mabelfyw fell to Rhys Fychan's son Rhys Wyndod (d. 1302). Both lords surrendered to Payn de Chaworth in April 1277, while Hywel ap Rhys Gryg, who had been granted Mabelfyw and other lands in return for his homage by Llywelyn ap Gruffudd in August 1258 after Maredudd ap Rhys's defection to the crown, fled with Rhys Wyndod's son Llywelyn to the prince in Gwynedd.[108] Both Rhys Wyndod and Rhys ap Maredudd recovered some of their lands in Ystrad Tywi following their surrender. However, the former joined in the Welsh rising in 1282, capturing the castles of Llandovery and Carreg Cennen which he had surrendered to the crown in April 1277, and he was among the adherents of Dafydd ap Gruffudd at Dolbadarn in May 1283.[109] Rhys ap Maredudd, by contrast, remained loyal to Edward I, and was duly rewarded with royal grants of the commotes of Mebwynion and Gwynionydd in Ceredigion as well as Rhys Wyndod's commotes of Malláen and Caeo. However, although he held all of Cantref Mawr except for the commote of Gwidigada, which, with Elfed, was retained by the crown, he failed in his long-cherished ambition to recover the ancestral seat of his dynasty at Dinefwr, which he finally quitclaimed to Edward on 16 October 1283.[110] Within four years, in June 1287, an accumulation of grievances against royal officials at Carmarthen drove Rhys into a revolt which led to the seizure of his lands by the crown and to his execution at York on 2 June 1292, following his betrayal in Malláen the previous April.[111]

ELFAEL AND MAELIENYDD

The cantrefs of Elfael and Maelienydd formed part of the region known as Rhwng Gwy a Hafren (between the Wye and the Severn) or the middle March, a region that also comprised the small commotes of Ceri, Gwerthrynion and Deuddwr and, originally, the

---

[105] Nos 316, 328–9, 363, c. x, 398 and note; *CIM*, i, nos 1443, 1800; *HW*, ii. 719–22; Smith, '"Cronica de Wallia"', 269–72.

[106] The date is given as 'the sixth day from [the calends of] August' (*y chwechet dyd o Awst*) in *BT, Pen20*, 219; *BT, Pen20Tr*, 116. According to *BT, RBH*, 258–9, and *BS*, 248–9, Maredudd died on the sixth day after the calends of August (i.e. 7 August). All the versions of the chronicle almost certainly derive their date from a Latin annal that read *vi kal. Aug.*, i.e. 27 July (as suggested in *HW*, ii. 750 and n. 179).

[107] *BT, Pen20Tr*, 116; *BT, RBH*, 258–9.

[108] Nos 85–8, 92–3, 99; *BT, Pen20Tr*, 118; *BT, RBH*, 264–5. Hywel's loyalty to Llywelyn is emphasized in Smith, '"Cronica de Wallia"', 277. Hywel and his men received the king's protection on 7 January 1278: *CWR*, 161; see also no. 89.

[109] Smith, *Llywelyn*, 421, 452, 523, 572 and n. 209; nos 78, 457; cf. nos 101–2.

[110] No. 97; Smith, '"Cronica de Wallia"', 273–4.

[111] Smith, 'Origins of the revolt'; Griffiths, *Conquerors*, 67–83.

cantref of Buellt (Builth).[112] Builth was conquered by the Braose family towards the end of the eleventh century.[113] The remaining territories faced considerable pressure from the Marchers, especially the Mortimers of Wigmore, during the twelfth and thirteenth centuries, and came under the overlordship of the princes of Gwynedd for two periods in the thirteenth century. The native rulers of Elfael and Maelienydd known to have issued acts belonged to the dynasty of Elystan Glodrydd; more precisely, they represent the lines of two of the sons of Madog ab Idnerth (d. 1140), namely Einion Clud (d. 1177) of Elfael and Cadwallon ap Madog (d. 1179) of Maelienydd.

The lineage of Einion Clud (d. 1177)

Einion Clud is first mentioned in the chronicles in 1160, when he was captured by his brother Cadwallon ap Madog and sent to Owain Gwynedd, who handed him over to the 'French' (that is, the Marchers), from whom he escaped.[114] Five years later both brothers were in the Welsh force under Owain that faced Henry II.[115] Einion married a daughter of the Lord Rhys of Deheubarth, and, like Cadwallon, was one of the Welsh rulers who accompanied Rhys to the council of Gloucester in 1175. Einion was killed in 1177, though by whom is unknown.[116] Shortly before his death he granted land in Elfael Is Mynydd to the Cistercian abbey of Cwm-hir, founded in 1176 by his brother Cadwallon.[117]

Einion Clud was succeeded by his son Einion o'r Porth, whom Gerald of Wales described as *Elevemiae princeps* in his account of Archbishop Baldwin's journey to preach the Third Crusade in Wales in 1188. Einion and his first cousin Maelgwn ap Cadwallon, *princeps Maeleniae* were the only two Welsh lords to respond to Baldwin's call to take the cross.[118] Three years later, in 1191, Einion was killed by one of his brothers, probably Iorwerth, Maredudd or Gwallter Fychan.[119] Like his father, he was a benefactor of Cwm-hir.[120] Within a few years of Einion's death Elfael fell to William de Braose, lord of Brecon and Radnor, who held the castles of Colwyn and Painscastle by 1196, when these were taken by the Lord Rhys. However, despite Rhys's military success, Braose retained his hold on the cantref, and Gwenwynwyn's attempt to capture Painscastle in 1198 met with disaster. Among the Welsh killed by the English force relieving the siege on 13 August was Anarawd ab Einion, probably a son of Einion o'r Porth.[121] It is likely that the Llywelyn ab Anarawd, who by December 1214 granted lands in Elfael near the border with the commote of Llythyfnwg to Cwm-hir, was a son of this Anarawd and thus a grandson of Einion o'r Porth.[122] Whether he was the same as the Llywelyn ab Anarawd 'of Gwerthrynion' who

---

[112] *HW*, i. 252–6. For this region in the twelfth and thirteenth centuries see further Smith, 'Middle March'.

[113] *HW*, ii. 402–3.

[114] *BT, Pen20Tr*, 62; *BT, RBH*, 140–3.

[115] *BT, Pen20Tr*, 63; *BT, RBH*, 144–5.

[116] *BT, Pen20Tr*, 70, 72; *BT, RBH*, 164–5, 168–9.

[117] No. 103.

[118] *Gir. Camb. Op.*, vi. 14, 16 (*IK* I. 1).

[119] *BT, Pen20Tr*, 74; *BT, RBH*, 172–3; *CW*, 29. For the names of the three other known sons of Einion Clud see no. 234; *BT, Pen20Tr*, 90; *BT, RBH*, 202–3.

[120] No. 104.

[121] *BT, Pen20Tr*, 76, 79–80; *BT, RBH*, 176–7, 180–1; Smith, 'Middle March', 80; Remfry, *Political History of Abbey Cwmhir*, 7.

[122] Ibid.; no. 104.

quitclaimed his rights in Gwerthrynion to Ralph Mortimer in 1241 is, by contrast, doubtful.[123] There is no evidence to suggest that Einion Clud's descendants held lands in Gwerthrynion, a commote independent of Elfael and Maelienydd in the late twelfth century under its own ruler, Einion ap Rhys, and the Llywelyn ab Anarawd who patronized Cwm-hir held lands in Elfael Is Mynydd.[124]

If the identification of this Llywelyn ab Anarawd as a grandson of Einion o'r Porth is correct, he may well have died or been incapacitated by 1215, for in that year Reginald de Braose, as a result of his alliance with Llywelyn ap Iorwerth, allowed Gwallter Fychan ab Einion Clud to take Elfael with its castles of Colwyn and Painscastle.[125] It is unknown for how long Gwallter held the cantref. Possibly it was recovered by Reginald de Braose after his submission to the crown in June 1217 and, although the Welsh seem to have occupied it by October 1228, following Reginald's death the previous June, it numbered among the Braose lordships eventually held by Hubert de Burgh following the death of William Marshal II on 5 April 1231, and de Burgh was responsible for the rebuilding of the castle at Painscastle by Henry III's army in August-September 1231.[126] However, although the Tony family were established in Elfael Is Mynydd by the 1240s, the line of Einion Clud retained some authority in the cantref, for its other commote of Elfael Uwch Mynydd was held by Owain ap Maredudd ab Einion Clud in 1248.[127] Owain submitted to Llywelyn ap Gruffudd after the latter's capture of Builth castle in July 1260, and was rewarded by the release of his son Madog, who had been imprisoned by Llywelyn, together with a gift of £300.[128] Owain was alive at the end of 1267, when Llywelyn ap Gruffudd complained to the king of Earl Gilbert de Clare's occupation of Elfael Is Mynydd despite its rightfully belonging to Owain, but was dead by November 1271. His sons succeeded him as lords of Elfael Uwch Mynydd and remained subject to Llywelyn ap Gruffudd until the Marchers recovered Elfael in 1277.[129]

The lineage of Cadwallon ap Madog (d. 1179)

Cadwallon ap Madog successfully withstood pressure from the Mortimers and established a powerful lordship in Maelienydd and the adjoining commote of Ceri.[130] Although no acts of his are extant, he was probably responsible for founding – or, possibly, re-founding – the Cistercian abbey of Cwm-hir, a daughter house of Whitland, in 1176, and the grants of his sons and grandsons to the abbey may well include confirmations of lands originally donated by Cadwallon.[131] After he was killed in 1179 Cadwallon was succeeded by his eldest son Maelgwn (d. 1197), described by Gerald of Wales as being 'prince of

---

[123] Smith, 'Middle March', 89, no. 2.
[124] For Gwerthrynion see *BT, Pen20Tr*, 70; *BT, RBH*, 164–5; *Gir. Camb. Op.*, vi. 17 (*IK* I. 1); Smith, 'Middle March', 79–80, 83–4. Cf. Remfry, *Political History of Abbey Cwmhir*, 7, n. 43.
[125] *BT, Pen20Tr*, 90; *BT, RBH*, 202–3; *HW*, ii. 645.
[126] *BT, Pen20Tr*, 102; *BT, RBH*, 228–9; *PR 1225–32*, 205–6; Walker, 'Hubert de Burgh', 484, 487, 488–90; cf. *HW*, ii. 652, 666.
[127] *CR 1247–51*, 72, 113.
[128] *AC*, 98; *BT, Pen20Tr*, 112; *BT, RBH*, 250–1; Smith, *Llywelyn*, 127.
[129] Nos 106–7, 365; Smith, 'Middle March', 85–7.
[130] See Remfry, 'Cadwallon ap Madog'. His authority in Ceri is revealed in *Gir. Camb. Op.*, i. 37–8 (*De rebus a se gestis*, I. 6).
[131] Remfry, 'Cadwallon ap Madog', 16, 23–4, 28, n. 45; *idem, Political History of Abbey Cwmhir*, 1–6. Although there is no earlier authority for Cadwallon's foundation of Cwm-hir than a petition of *c.*1322 (*CAP*, 54–5), it is credible in view of the grant to the abbey by Einion Clud (d. 1177): no. 103.

Maelienydd' in 1188.[132] It is quite possible that Maelgwn ap Cadwallon died in exile in Gwynedd, as both he and his younger brother Hywel were driven from Maelienydd by Roger Mortimer in 1195 and Llywelyn ap Iorwerth later claimed that he had fostered Maelgwn's son Madog ap Maelgwn.[133]

Madog ap Maelgwn and his uncle Hywel ap Cadwallon ap Madog had re-established themselves in Maelienydd and Ceri by 1212 at the latest. Both were hanged on King John's orders at Bridgnorth in that year, almost certainly on *c*.3 August, for the murder of William de Mora.[134] However, Madog issued a charter granting lands to Cwm-hir in the south-east of Maelienydd in May 1212, and a letter from Llywelyn ap Iorwerth implies that both he and Hywel ap Cadwallon also held Ceri at about this time. These sources show, moreover, that Madog had turned against his erstwhile foster-father, as the charter contains a remarkable clause stating that Madog's nobles had sworn never to endure the dominion of any prince over them, a clear reference to Llywelyn, whose letter singled out Madog and warned him not to repay the good done to him by the prince with evil by attacking the lands of Ratlinghope Priory in Shropshire.[135] There is circumstantial evidence to suggest that Madog, together with his brothers (also addressed by Llywelyn in his letter) and uncle Hywel ap Cadwallon, were restored to at least part of their lands in Maelienydd and Ceri through an agreement with Roger Mortimer in 1210 or 1211.[136]

It may well be that the execution of Madog and Hywel in August 1212 persuaded the two surviving sons of Maelgwn ap Cadwallon, namely Cadwallon and Maredudd, to renew their dynasty's close ties with Llywelyn, who had rapidly recovered from his crushing defeat by John the previous summer. They had certainly done so by 1215, for they joined the prince in his campaign in south-west Wales at the end of that year, and in May 1220 Llywelyn upheld the brothers' right to Maelienydd when he wrote to the papal legate, Pandulf, rejecting demands by the regency government in England that the cantref should be handed over to Hugh Mortimer.[137] Maelienydd continued to be held by the brothers, together with their first cousins, the sons of Hywel ap Cadwallon, under the overlordship of Llywelyn until the latter's death in April 1240. However, pressure from Ralph Mortimer was probably mounting by February 1241, as Maredudd and his kinsmen were granted a safe conduct to travel to the king at Worcester in that month, presumably in order to assert their claim to Maelienydd against the lord of Wigmore. They were at war with Mortimer by the summer, and on 14 August 1241 Maredudd ap Maelgwn, together with three sons of Hywel ap Cadwallon and their nephew Hywel ap Cadwallon ap Hywel, submitted to the king at Shrewsbury and agreed to a truce with Ralph Mortimer to last until Michaelmas.[138] A week later the king ominously notified 'the Welsh of the land late of Owain ap Hywel in Maelienydd' that he was willing to receive any of them who came into his peace and to the fealty and service of Ralph Mortimer.[139] Despite meetings with the king on the eve of the

---

[132] *Gir. Camb. Op.*, vi. 16 (*IK* I. 1); *BT, Pen20Tr*, 79; *BT, RBH*, 180–1.
[133] *BT, Pen20Tr*, 75; *BT, RBH*, 174–5; no. 234. See further Smith, 'Middle March', 81, with the modifications in *idem*, 'Cymer', 103–4.
[134] See note to no. 234.
[135] Nos 113, 234.
[136] See note to no. 113.
[137] *BT, Pen20Tr*, 91–2; *BT, RBH*, 206–7; no. 247.
[138] Nos 110–12, 116, 118; Smith, 'Middle March', 82–3.
[139] *CPR 1232–47*, 257.

expiry of the truce (28 September 1241) and again in 1243, the lords failed to recover Maelienydd.[140]

However, Maredudd ap Maelgwn and Hywel ap Cadwallon appear to have retained half of the adjoining commote of Ceri until they were deprived of it for having broken their fealty to the king by siding with Dafydd ap Llywelyn in 1245–6. Their attempts to recover their half of the commote were unsuccessful, but their kinsman Owain ap Hywel ap Cadwallon (Maredudd's first cousin) promised an entry fine of £50 for the other half on 30 July 1248, though the grant did not become immediately effective, as on 5 November the king ordered Thomas Corbet to give Owain seisin without delay.[141] Owain seems to have died by August 1253, since before Henry III sailed for Gascony in that month Gruffudd ap Gwenwynwyn successfully petitioned him for the farm of Ceri formerly taken by Owain.[142] Yet Gruffudd's influence in Ceri was short-lived, as he was driven from most of his lands in Powys Wenwynwyn by Llywelyn ap Gruffudd in 1257, and Maelienydd fell to the prince of Gwynedd in 1262.[143] Llywelyn was confirmed in his possession of Ceri by the Treaty of Montgomery (1267), which also provided that he would be allowed to hold Maelienydd if he could prove his right to it.[144] The prince's hold on the region ended with Edward I's first Welsh war of 1276–7.[145] Thereafter, although not entirely extinguished, the lordship exercised by the native dynasty of Maelienydd was a pale reflection of what it had been under Cadwallon ap Madog or the overlordship of Llywelyn ap Iorwerth. On 7 June 1278 Edward I granted a quarter of Ceri to Maredudd ap Maelgwn's son Madog and grandson Hywel ap Llywelyn.[146] The remaining three-quarters of the commote was granted on 6 January 1279 to Roger Mortimer, who also permanently recovered Maelienydd (and Gwerthrynion) for his family.[147]

GLAMORGAN

Although nominally subject to the Anglo-Norman lords of Glamorgan, with their *caput* at Cardiff, the dynasty descended from Iestyn ap Gwrgant effectively controlled the uplands between the Taff and the Neath from the twelfth to the mid-thirteenth centuries.[148] It is

---

[140] See Smith, 'Middle March', 82–3 and note to no. 110. Only Maredudd ap Maelgwn and Owain ap Hywel ap Cadwallon were present at the latter meeting, and Owain's brothers Cadwallon and Maredudd are not attested after 1241.

[141] No. 117; *Rot. Fin.*, ii. 37–8; *CR 1247–51*, 125. See further Cole, 'Elystan's line'; Morgan, 'Territorial divisions [I]', 31–2.

[142] *CR 1253–4*, 108. (The petition has not been calendared among the lost acts of Gruffudd since the phrase *supplicavit nobis Griffinus filius Wehunwen per nuncios suos* suggests that it was made only orally, an interpretation arguably supported by the lack of any written record of the king's consent referred to retrospectively in this royal mandate of 27 December 1253.) Cf. also ibid., 20–1. Owain was still alive in May 1251: Morgan, 'Territorial divisions [I]', 33.

[143] Ibid., 42; Smith, *Llywelyn*, 139–47.

[144] No. 363, cc. iv–v; Smith, *Llywelyn*, 183.

[145] Ibid., 418 and n. 105; Morgan, 'Territorial divisions [I]', 36–7.

[146] *CWR*, 166.

[147] *CChR 1257–1300*, 211; cf. *WAR*, 236, 242.

[148] For Glamorgan in this period see Smith, 'Kingdom of Morgannwg'; Altschul, 'Lordship of Glamorgan'; Crouch, 'Slow death'; Evans, 'Lords of Afan'.

likely that Iestyn, a follower of Caradog ap Gruffudd (d. 1081), last king of Morgannwg, died by 1127.[149] According to the antiquary Rice Merrick, drawing on the lost register of Neath Abbey, four of Caradog's sons were benefactors of the abbey, founded by Richard de Granville in 1130, and the grant of Llanilid by Rhys ab Iestyn was included in King John's confirmation for Neath in 1214.[150] Merrick also states that Rhys and his brother Rhiwallon made an agreement with Richard de Granville by which they were granted lands between the Neath and the Tawe, grants almost certainly datable to 1136 which were presumably designed to prevent further attacks on Richard's lands in western Glamorgan in the Welsh rising of that year.[151] However, it was the line of Caradog ab Iestyn which came to dominate the hill country of Glamorgan, together with considerable areas of the lowlands between the Ogmore and Neath rivers, from the mid-twelfth century onwards.[152]

Caradog and his wife Gwladus, daughter of Rhys ap Tewdwr of Deheubarth, had four sons: Morgan, Cadwallon, Maredudd and Owain. According to Gerald of Wales, these shared authority over their father's lands after Caradog's death. Gerald also reports that, after killing Owain (an event that took place no later than November 1183), Cadwallon himself perished while besieging a castle.[153] Both men left sons: Morgan ab Owain, last attested in 1246,[154] and Morgan ap Cadwallon. The latter held the commote of Glynrhondda in the early thirteenth century, until it was annexed by his cousin Hywel ap Maredudd, lord of the commote of Meisgyn, in 1228.[155] Hywel presumably succeeded to Meisgyn after the death of his father Maredudd ap Caradog in 1211.[156] After the death of his cousin Morgan Gam in 1241 Hywel assumed the leadership of upland Glamorgan, but was expelled from his lands in 1246 by Richard de Clare.[157]

The lineage of Morgan ap Caradog (d. *c*.1208)

Morgan was probably Caradog ab Iestyn's eldest son, as he succeeded to his father's extensive lands in the cantref of Afan and appears to have exercised some kind of overlordship over his brothers.[158] He is named first both in Gerald of Wales's account of Caradog's sons and in a charter issued jointly with two of his brothers, granted common pasture to Neath Abbey in

---

[149] Crouch, 'Slow death', 30–1; *AM*, i. 12.

[150] *Rice Merrick*, 13; no. 119.

[151] *Rice Merrick*, 39, 54; Crouch, 'Robert, earl of Gloucester', 230; no. 120. The sons of Iestyn also attacked the lordship of Brecon: *Gir. Camb. Op.*, vi. 20–1 (*IK* I. 2).

[152] The family held lands as far east as the Llancarfan area: nos 132, 168.

[153] *Gir. Camb. Op.*, vi. 69 (*IK* I. 7). Owain died during the reign of Henry II, while Earl William (d. 23 November 1183) was lord of Glamorgan; Cadwallon's death occurred by October 1191, when Gerald completed the first recension of *IK*. Joint lordship is arguably implied by a charter in which Caradog *Uerbeis* refers to land granted by him in Meisgyn as belonging to the *feudum* of Morgan, Cadwallon and Maredudd: *Cartae*, ii. 346–7 (no. 346). However, the precedence given to Morgan both here and in the brothers' confirmation of the grant (no. 121) suggests that he enjoyed some sort of supremacy, a point developed below.

[154] No. 187.

[155] *AM*, i. 36; Smith, 'Kingdom of Morgannwg', 26.

[156] *BT, Pen20Tr*, 86. Maredudd led men in the service of Henry II in 1188, and occurs as a pledge with his brother Morgan ap Caradog in 1199: *Pipe Roll 34 Henry II*, 106; *Llandaff Episcopal Acta*, no. 44.

[157] *BT, Pen20Tr*, 107; *BT, RBH*, 240–1; Altschul, 'Lordship of Glamorgan', 50–1; Walker and Spurgeon, 'Custody of the de Clare castles', 44.

[158] Smith, 'Kingdom of Morgannwg', 36. See also RCAHMW, *Glamorgan III. 1a*, 17–19.

the mountains between the Taff and the Neath (an area including Meisgyn and Glynrhondda), and is the only member of his dynasty named as attending the council of Gloucester in 1175 with his maternal uncle the Lord Rhys.[159] It is unknown how long before this Morgan had succeeded his father, although it has been suggested, without explanation, that he may have done so *c.*1147 and his earliest extant charter, issued after Caradog's death, could be as early as 1158.[160] What is clear is that he gravitated into the political orbit of the Lord Rhys and sought to regain lands conquered by the Normans. In particular, Morgan seized the opportunity to realize his ambitions presented by the death of Earl William of Gloucester on 23 November 1183, as he must have been the leader behind the major Welsh rising in Glamorgan which erupted at the end of 1183 and continued into the following year.[161] It was presumably as a result of this rising that Morgan came to control the strategic-ally important lowlands around the Neath estuary, across whose quicksands he escorted Archbishop Baldwin in March 1188, control almost certainly secured by the building of a castle on the west bank of the river at Briton Ferry.[162] Morgan significantly extended his hold on the lowlands after he was granted the castle and lordship of Newcastle, to the east of Afan, by Prince John, probably soon after John's marriage to Earl William's heiress Isabel of Gloucester on 29 August 1189. The lord of Afan's authority in Newcastle is reflected in his grants of land there to Margam Abbey, a Cistercian house founded by Robert, earl of Gloucester in 1147.[163] Morgan's latest charter bearing a date was issued at about Michaelmas 1208, and he probably died shortly after this.[164]

Morgan was succeeded in Afan by the eldest of his four sons, Lleision ap Morgan, who led 200 troops in the service of King John in 1204 and who consented to several of his father's grants to Margam.[165] Lleision's latest dated charter was issued on Christmas Day 1213.[166] He was probably dead by the summer of 1217, when Llywelyn ap Iorwerth granted Landimôr in Gower to Lleision's brother Morgan Gam, a grant which implies that Morgan was lord of Afan.[167] If so, it is likely that by then Morgan Gam had already outlived his other two brothers, Owain and Cadwallon, both of whom were almost certainly older than him. Owain seems to have been Morgan ap Caradog's second son, for, unlike Cadwallon or Morgan Gam, he issued two charters jointly with Lleision and also confirmed grants by his father and Lleision.[168] That Cadwallon was the third son is suggested by his confirmation of grants by his father, Lleision and Owain.[169] Morgan ap Caradog also had at least one

---

[159] See n. 153 above; nos 121, 140; *BT, Pen20Tr*, 70–1; *BT, RBH*, 164–5.
[160] RCAHMW, *Glamorgan III. 1a*, 17; no. 121.
[161] Smith, 'Kingdom of Morgannwg', 34, 36–8.
[162] *Gir. Camb. Op.*, vi. 72 (*IK* I. 8); Wilkinson, 'Excavations at Hen Gastell', esp. 5–6, 35–6; RCAHMW, *Glamorgan III. 1a*, 18, 139–41. The principal stronghold of the lords of Afan in this period was probably Plas Baglan (SS 756 923), the site of a masonry castle by the thirteenth century: ibid., 38, 149–52.
[163] Smith, 'Kingdom of Morgannwg', 38–9; nos 124–30, 139, 142–3, 145–6, 148; Cowley, *Monastic Order*, 22–3.
[164] No. 148; Smith, 'Kingdom of Morgannwg', 39, 587, n. 182.
[165] *Rot. Lib.*, 88; nos 124, 136–7, 142, 146. Lleision is called Morgan ap Caradog's *primogenitus* in no. 137.
[166] No. 167.
[167] No. 239; cf. Altschul, 'Lordship of Glamorgan', 46.
[168] Nos 160–1, 170–2.
[169] No. 173.

daughter, Gwenllian, who, like Lleision and Owain, appears to have had rights in land in the fee of Newcastle.[170]

Morgan Gam lost control of Newcastle, and sought to recover it as well as to remain independent of his nominal overlord, Gilbert de Clare, earl of Gloucester and Hertford (1218–30), to the extent of confirming Gilbert's charters for Margam after his death.[171] Although he was imprisoned by Gilbert in 1228–9, Morgan resumed his attacks after his release, joining Llywelyn ap Iorwerth, an ally since 1217, in his campaigns in south Wales in 1231 and 1232, by which time the lordship of Glamorgan was in royal custody during the minority of Gilbert's heir, Richard de Clare. Morgan died in February 1241 and was buried at Margam.[172] He was succeeded by his sons Lleision and then, by 1262, Morgan Fychan (d. 1288), under whom Afan was subjected to the authority of the lord of Glamorgan and increasingly integrated into neighbouring Marcher society. The Anglicization of Morgan Gam's descendants – illustrated by the title 'lord of Avene' adopted by Morgan Fychan's son Lleision – helps to explain why, alone of the Welsh lordships of Glamorgan, Afan survived into the fourteenth century.[173]

GWYNEDD

In the twelfth and thirteenth centuries Gwynedd, the most powerful of the medieval Welsh kingdoms, was ruled by descendants of Rhodri Mawr (d. 878), son of Merfyn Frych (d. 844), founder of the kingdom's second dynasty.[174] The heartland of the rulers' power lay in Gwynedd Uwch Conwy, the districts to the west of the river Conwy protected by the mountain ranges of Snowdonia comprising the cantrefs of Arllechwedd, Arfon, Llŷn, Ardudwy and Meirionnydd, the commote of Eifionydd and the island of Anglesey, site of the rulers' principal court of Aberffraw. For much of this period the rulers also controlled the districts east of the Conwy, namely the cantrefs of Dyffryn Clwyd, Rhos, Rhufoniog and Tegeingl (Englefield) known variously as Gwynedd Is Conwy, Perfeddwlad (lit. 'Middle Country') or the Four Cantrefs. In its full extent, therefore, Gwynedd consisted of a broad arc of territory in north Wales extending from the river Dee near Chester to the river Dyfi which marked the border with Ceredigion.[175] In addition, the kingdom's rulers sought to extend their authority beyond Gwynedd, notably at the expense of Powys, and for significant periods in the thirteenth century Llywelyn ap Iorwerth (d. 1240) and his grandson Llywelyn ap Gruffudd (d. 1282) succeeded in establishing a hegemony over the other native rulers that made them the most powerful rulers in Wales. This dominance was recognized in 1267 by the Treaty of Montgomery, in which the English crown granted to Llywelyn ap Gruffudd and his successors the title of 'prince of Wales'. However, Llywelyn's hegemony was short-lived, and Edward I's conquest of Gwynedd in 1282–3 marked the extinction of native rule in Wales.

---

[170] No. 169.
[171] No. 178. For what follows see Altschul, 'Lordship of Glamorgan', 46–50.
[172] *AM*, i. 116.
[173] Evans, 'Lords of Afan', 28–31; Altschul, 'Lordship of Glamorgan', 51–2.
[174] *EWGT*, 36, 38; cf. Maund, *Welsh Kings*, 37–42.
[175] Cf. *HW*, i. 229–42; Jones, 'Defences of Gwynedd'; Stephenson, *Governance*, xiii–xvi.

Gruffudd ap Cynan (d. 1137)

Gruffudd re-established the dynasty of Rhodri Mawr, excluded from power since 1039, as rulers of Gwynedd, a position maintained by his descendants until the Edwardian conquest.[176] The son of Cynan ab Iago ab Idwal and his Hiberno-Scandinavian mother Raghnhildr, daughter of Olaf Sihtricsson, Gruffudd was born in Dublin *c.*1055. He first crossed the Irish Sea to try and seize Gwynedd in 1075 and eventually killed its king, Trahaearn ap Caradog, at the battle of Mynydd Carn in 1081. Shortly afterwards, however, Gruffudd was captured by the Normans and imprisoned for at least twelve years at Chester, and his rule in Gwynedd effectively began only after the final expulsion of the Normans from Gwynedd Uwch Conwy in 1098 and his acquisition of Anglesey the following year.[177] The dominance he subsequently achieved in Gwynedd was facilitated by a minority in the earldom of Chester from 1101 to 1114, and had grown sufficiently threatening by the latter year for Henry I to lead a campaign in Wales which secured Gruffudd's submission.[178] Thereafter Gruffudd took care not to provoke the king and concentrated on consolidating his power in north Wales. After the expulsion, probably in 1098, of the Breton Hervé, consecrated bishop of Bangor in 1092 when Robert of Rhuddlan held Gwynedd, Gruffudd kept the see vacant until April 1120, when he secured the consecration of his nominee, David the Scot (d. 1139).[179] During the remaining years of his reign Gruffudd sought to expand Gwynedd, thereby providing a channel for the ambitions of his three sons, who led campaigns into Meirionnydd (1124), Dyffryn Clwyd (1125), Powys (1132) and Ceredigion (1136).[180] Gruffudd died in 1137 aged eighty-two and was buried in Bangor cathedral.[181] He was survived by his widow Angharad (d. 1162), daughter of Owain ab Edwin of Dyffryn Clwyd, mother of his sons Cadwallon (killed in 1132), Owain and Cadwaladr, as well as five daughters, including Gwenllian (d. 1136), wife of Gruffudd ap Rhys (d. 1137) of Deheubarth, and Susanna, wife of Madog ap Maredudd (d. 1160) of Powys.[182]

Owain Gwynedd (d. (?23) November 1170)

Gruffudd ap Cynan was succeeded by his eldest surviving son Owain, who not only maintained unitary rule of Gwynedd but also, by the last decade of his life, assumed the leadership of native Wales against the English.[183] After his accession Owain completed the conquest of Ceredigion, undertaken in alliance with the dynasty of Deheubarth, and granted the southern half to his son Hywel and the northern half to his brother Cadwaladr, who also held Meirionnydd and Anglesey. (It is uncertain whether Cadwaladr possessed Nefyn in Llŷn, whose church he granted to the Augustinian abbey of Haughmond in Shropshire, before his expulsion from Gwynedd in 1152 or only after his restoration in 1157.)[184] However, in 1143 Cadwaladr was temporarily expelled from his share of

---

[176] See further Maund (ed.), *Gruffudd ap Cynan*; *Historia Gruffud vab Kenan*, ed. Evans.
[177] *BT, Pen20Tr*, 20–1; *BT, RBH*, 36–9.
[178] *BT, Pen20Tr*, 37–8; *BT, RBH*, 78–83.
[179] No. 191.
[180] *BT, Pen20Tr*, 49, 50, 51–2; *BT, RBH*, 108–11, 112–15.
[181] *BT, Pen20Tr*, 52; *BT, RBH*, 116–17; *Historia Gruffud vab Kenan*, ed. Evans, 33.
[182] *EWGT*, 47 (no. 25), 98 (no. 5a), 104 (no. 12); *BT, Pen20Tr*, 50, 62; *BT, RBH*, 112–13, 142–3; *HW*, ii. 470.
[183] See further Smith, 'Owain Gwynedd'; Pryce, 'Owain Gwynedd'.
[184] No. 197.

Ceredigion, and also possibly from Anglesey, as punishment for the murder by his warband of Anarawd ap Gruffudd ap Rhys, to whom Owain's daughter was betrothed, and in 1147 he was driven out of Meirionnydd by Hywel and Cynan sons of Owain.[185] His position became even more precarious in 1150, when Hywel seized his son Cadfan, to whom Cadwaladr had transferred northern Ceredigion the previous year, and in 1152 Cadwaladr was expelled from Anglesey and sought refuge in England, being granted the estate of Ness in Shropshire by Henry II by 1155 or 1156. In the mean time, the attempt to annex Ceredigion to the dynasty of Gwynedd had been thwarted by Cadell ap Gruffudd and his younger brothers Maredudd and Rhys, who had captured the whole region except for one castle from Hywel ab Owain by 1151.[186] The pressure on Ceredigion by the dynasty of Deheubarth helps to explain why Owain Gwynedd resumed his kingdom's expansion in the north-east, capturing the commote of Iâl in 1149 and, it seems, Tegeingl by the following year; the attempt to check his progress by Madog ap Maredudd of Powys and forces supplied by Ranulf II, earl of Chester ended in victory for Owain at the battle of Coleshill in 1150.[187]

However, Owain faced a more formidable opponent in Henry II, whose campaign against Gwynedd in the summer of 1157, supported by the exiled Cadwaladr, Madog ap Maredudd, Madog's brother Iorwerth Goch and Hywel ab Ieuaf of Arwystli, compelled him to submit and give homage to the king, surrender his conquests in Tegeingl and restore Cadwaladr to his lands.[188] After his restoration Cadwaladr remained loyal to his brother for the rest of his life. The death of Madog ap Maredudd in 1160 presented further opportunities for expansion, and Owain seems immediately to have occupied the Powysian commotes of Edeirnion and Cyfeiliog.[189] On 1 July 1163 he demonstrated his continuing submission to Henry II by giving homage to the king at Woodstock following the king's second Welsh campaign, against the Lord Rhys, who also gave homage on that occasion.[190] However, by the autumn it appears that Owain had angered the king by adopting the title 'prince', and by the end of 1164 he had assumed the leadership of the Welsh in a widespread rising against the Marchers and the crown and approached Louis VII of France in an attempt to form a Franco-Welsh alliance against Henry II. The Welsh rising provoked a major royal campaign against Owain and his allies, gathered at Corwen in August 1165, that ended in disaster for the king as his army fell victim to torrential rains on the Berwyn mountains and was forced to retreat.[191]

After Henry's defeat in 1165 Owain was at the height of his power, a dominance given expression by the adoption in his letters of the titles 'prince of the Welsh' and 'prince of Wales'.[192] In 1166–7 he recovered Tegeingl with the support, in the latter year, of his nephew Rhys ap Gruffudd of Deheubarth.[193] He also continued his negotiations with Louis VII, no doubt being one of the 'kings of Wales' who sent messengers to the French king in 1168 to forge an alliance against Henry II. The authority enjoyed by Owain in his last years is

---

[185] *BT, Pen20Tr*, 53, 56; *BT, RBH*, 118–19.
[186] *BT, Pen20Tr*, 57–8; *BT, RBH*, 128–31; *HW*, ii. 496.
[187] *BT, Pen20Tr*, 55, 57; *BT, RBH*, 124–5, 128–9; *HW*, ii. 492, 494–5; cf. Smith, 'Castell Gwyddgrug'.
[188] *BT, Pen20Tr*, 59–60; *BT, RBH*, 134–7; *HW*, ii. 496–500.
[189] Ibid., 510.
[190] Diceto, i. 311.
[191] Latimer, 'Henry II's campaign'; Pryce, 'Owain Gwynedd'; *CTB*, i, no. 12; nos 193–4 below.
[192] No. 196; *CTB*, ii, nos 202, 223; below, p. 74.
[193] *BT, Pen20Tr*, 64–5; *BT, RBH*, 148–9.

reflected in his unflinching defiance of attempts by Archbishop Thomas Becket and Pope Alexander III both to secure the election of a bishop of Bangor acceptable to the archbishop, following the death of Bishop Meurig (Maurice) in 1161, and, by 1169, to compel him to separate from his wife Cristin ferch Gronw ab Owain, on the grounds that she was his first cousin and thus related within the prohibited degrees of consanguinity.[194] This defiance of the ecclesiastical authorities led to his being excommunicated by his death in November 1170, probably on the twenty-third of that month, but the sentence was disregarded by his clergy, who buried Owain in Bangor cathedral. His brother Cadwaladr died in 1172, probably on 29 February, and was buried beside him.[195]

The struggle for Gwynedd, 1170–1201

The succession to Owain Gwynedd was contested among his sons and grandsons, resulting in a division of Gwynedd that was eventually overcome by Llywelyn ap Iorwerth, who succeeded in subduing the whole of the kingdom by 1201.[196] Owain's eldest son, and possibly his intended successor, Hywel ab Owain was killed by his half-brothers Dafydd and Rhodri at the battle of Pentraeth towards the end of 1170.[197] An attempt by Dafydd in 1173–4 to establish hegemony over all of Gwynedd was thwarted in 1175 by his brother Rhodri, with the result that Dafydd was largely confined to Gwynedd Is Conwy, though he also exercised lordship in at least part of Llŷn, granting land and tithes at Nefyn no earlier than 1177.[198] Rhodri controlled Anglesey, Arllechwedd and Arfon while Gruffudd and Maredudd, sons of Cynan ab Owain (d. 1174), held Eifionydd, Ardudwy and Meirionnydd. Despite his failure to overcome his brother and nephews, Dafydd may have remained the most powerful ruler in Gwynedd until 1194. One advantage he enjoyed was an alliance with the English crown: he married Henry II's half-sister Emma of Anjou in the summer of 1174, and was the only ruler of Gwynedd present at the council of Oxford in May 1177, when he was granted the manor of Ellesmere in Shropshire as a marriage gift.[199] However, Dafydd lost most of his lands in Gwynedd after his defeat by Gruffudd and Maredudd sons of Cynan and their cousin Llywelyn ap Iorwerth at the mouth of the Conwy in 1194. The role of Rhodri in that battle is uncertain, but after his death the following year Gruffudd ap Cynan ab Owain achieved a dominant position in Gwynedd, holding Anglesey, Arfon, Arllechwedd and Llŷn; in addition, he seems to have continued to exercise lordship in Meirionnydd while his brother Maredudd held Eifionydd and Ardudwy.[200]

After the defeat of Dafydd in 1194 most of Perfeddwlad was held by Llywelyn ap Iorwerth, the son, born in 1173, of Iorwerth Drwyndwn ab Owain Gwynedd and Marared

---

[194] *CTB*, ii, nos 190, 202; Pryce, 'Owain Gwynedd', 1–2, 9.

[195] *BT, Pen20Tr*, 65, 68 and notes at 184, 185; *BT, RBH*, 158–9; *Gir. Camb. Op.*, vi. 133 (*IK* II. 8); *HW*, ii. 522 and n. 136, 550 and n. 67.

[196] For interpretations of the events of this period see *HW*, ii. 549–53, 564–5, 587–90, 612–15; Stephenson, *Governance*, 199–200; Carr, 'Prydydd y Moch'; Insley, 'Wilderness years'.

[197] *BT, Pen20Tr*, 65; *BT, RBH*, 150–1; 'Gwaith Peryf ap Cedifor', ed. Owen; Smith, 'Dynastic succession', 213–15.

[198] Nos 198–9; Stephenson, *Governance*, xviii, n. 10.

[199] *HW*, ii. 551, 552–3; Carr, 'Prydydd y Moch', 166–7. Dafydd's special status in Gwynedd is implicit in Roger of Howden's account of the council of Oxford, in which Dafydd, termed *rex Nortwaliae*, is listed only second, after the Lord Rhys, *rex Swtwalliae*, among the Welsh rulers present: *Gesta*, ed. Stubbs, i. 162; cf. *Chronica*, ed. Stubbs, ii. 133–4.

[200] *BT, Pen20Tr*, 75; *BT, RBH*, 174–5; *AC*, 59; *HW*, ii. 588–9; Smith, 'Age of the princes', 18–21; Pryce, 'Medieval church', 276–7.

(Margaret), daughter of Madog ap Maredudd (d. 1160) of Powys. Iorwerth seems to have played little or no part in the struggle for the succession to his father, perhaps because he was prevented by a facial disfigurement, though he remained in Gwynedd, being buried in Penmachno.[201] The date of Iorwerth's death is unknown, but, according to Gerald of Wales, Llywelyn had begun staking his claim to Gwynedd in 1188 by attacking both Dafydd and Rhodri.[202] Llywelyn consolidated his grip on Perfeddwlad in 1197 by capturing Dafydd, who, after his release the following January, spent the rest of his life in English exile and died in 1203 (by 27 May).[203] Dafydd's widow Emma still held the manor of Halesowen in 1212 and their son Owain ap Dafydd remained with her in England, receiving a (speculative) grant of lands in Gwynedd from King John in October of the same year.[204]

When Llywelyn succeeded in extending his power west of the Conwy to the heartland of Gwynedd is uncertain, but there is a good case for supposing that he mounted a serious challenge to Gruffudd ap Cynan ab Owain Gwynedd's hegemony during 1199. (Llywelyn's two charters for Aberconwy Abbey, dated 7 January 1199, are spurious and therefore cannot be used as evidence in this connection.)[205] On 28 September Llywelyn was granted protection by King John and confirmed in all his lands. However, on 3 December John granted Gruffudd ap Cynan ab Owain all the lands he could win from the king's enemies, and a similar grant was made to Gwenwynwyn ab Owain of Powys the following day.[206] These grants suggest that the crown feared Llywelyn's growing power in Gwynedd; moreover, the favour shown Gruffudd may imply that he had already been displaced by Llywelyn.[207] A further indication of Llywelyn's ambitions in the autumn of 1199 is his petition to Pope Innocent III to be allowed to marry the daughter of Rognvald (Reginald), king of Man and the Isles, notwithstanding the fact that she had previously been betrothed to his uncle Rhodri ab Owain (d. 1195). It is surely significant that the pope's response, addressed to the bishop of Man, the archdeacon of Bangor and the prior of Ynys Lannog and dated 24 November 1199, refers to Llywelyn as *princeps Norwalie*, no doubt echoing the usage in the petition.[208] By the end of October it seems, then, that Llywelyn sought to revive the Manx alliance which had earlier helped to strengthen Rhodri's position and had also adopted a title asserting his right to rule the whole of Gwynedd, a title also used by Gruffudd ap Cynan ab Owain.[209]

---

[201] *HW*, ii. 550, 587.
[202] *Gir. Camb. Op.*, vi. 134 (*IK* II. 8).
[203] *HW*, ii. 589–90 and n. 76; *Rot. Lib.*, 36.
[204] *HW*, ii. 616, n. 26, 640. Dafydd and Emma had been granted Halesowen by Henry II: ibid., 590. Since this edition went to press Louise Wilkinson has drawn my attention to a legal case in 1221 in which the abbot of Halesowen claimed that Emma, after receiving Halesowen from Henry II, had granted land pertaining to the manor *in maritagium* with her niece Agnes to the defendant, Stephen of Chatley, although this was denied by Stephen's attorney: *CRR*, x. 137–8. The outcome of the dispute is unknown, and, even if the abbot's claim was correct, it is uncertain whether Emma's grant was the subject of a written act.
[205] Nos 218–19 and notes.
[206] *Rot. Chart.*, 23a, 63a; *HW*, ii. 614–15.
[207] Smith, 'Cymer', 103–4; *idem*, 'Age of the princes', 19–21; Smith and Butler, 'Cistercian order', 301–3.
[208] *Reg. Innocenz' III.*, ii. 430–1 (no. 224).
[209] No. 206. Cf. the reference in September 1199 to *petitio Gifini principis Norwaliae* to build a Cistercian abbey, presumably Cymer: *Statuta*, ed. Canivez, i. 236; Smith, 'Cymer', 104. Given the scarcity of evidence, it is, of course, possible that Llywelyn had adopted the title *princeps Norwallie* before 1199, though he is unlikely to have done so before his occupation of Perfeddwlad in 1194: cf. nos 213, 216.

If this interpretation is correct, Gruffudd ap Cynan ab Owain may well already have lost much if not all of his power in Gwynedd Uwch Conwy to Llywelyn when he retired in 1200 to die in the abbey of Aberconwy, of which he was a benefactor.[210] In any event, there can be no doubt that Llywelyn was master of Gwynedd after Gruffudd's death, a mastery consolidated by his expulsion of Maredudd ap Cynan from Llŷn in 1201. (Maredudd was expelled from Meirionnydd the following year by his nephew Hywel ap Gruffudd ap Cynan (d. 1216), who accepted Llywelyn's overlordship, and died in 1212.)[211] The prince's supremacy was further secured by obtaining the recognition and support of the crown, which began efforts to negotiate with Llywelyn in January 1201 that culminated in a peace agreement on 11 July: the prince swore fealty to the king in return for seisin of the lands in his possession and also promised to give him homage after his return to England from the continent.[212]

Llywelyn ap Iorwerth (d. 11 April 1240)

From 1201 Llywelyn's supremacy in Gwynedd appears to have been unchallenged, providing the foundation from which he eventually established a hegemony over native Wales greater than that achieved by any Welsh ruler since Gruffudd ap Llywelyn (d. 1063).[213] The *rapprochement* with John lasted until 1210. It was reinforced by the prince's marriage to the king's illegitimate daughter Joan (d. 1237), which probably took place in the spring of 1205; Llywelyn was granted Ellesmere, resumed by the crown following Dafydd ab Owain's death in 1203, as a marriage gift on 16 April 1205.[214] (Though papal approval had been given in April 1203 for the Manx marriage requested by Llywelyn in 1199, this decision was reversed on 17 February 1205 in the light of new evidence that Rhodri ab Owain had in fact consummated his marriage to Rognvald's daughter.)[215] John accepted the prince's occupation of southern Powys following Gwenwynwyn's arrest at Shrewsbury on 8 October 1208, and Llywelyn joined the royal campaign against William I of Scotland the following year.[216] However, these friendly relations broke down in 1210, a change reflected in John's restoration of Gwenwynwyn to his lands about the end of November.[217] This was followed, in the summer of 1211, by a devastating royal campaign against Gwynedd which compelled Llywelyn to accept harsh terms of surrender on 12 August, notably the quitclaim to the king of Gwynedd east of the Conwy (Perfeddwlad), a concession that the rest of Gwynedd would escheat to the crown if the prince died without an heir with Joan and the promise of a massive tribute of 10,000 cows.[218]

In August 1211 not only had Llywelyn's ambitions for wider hegemony in Wales been crushed but his control of Gwynedd had been severely curtailed and its future as a native principality put into question. Within less than a year, however, John's efforts to tighten his grip on Wales through a programme of castle building had lost him the support of several of the Welsh leaders who had joined him in 1211: in July 1212 Llywelyn recovered

---

[210] *BT, Pen20Tr*, 80; *BT, RBH*, 182–3; no. 206.
[211] *BT, Pen20Tr*, 81; *BT, RBH*, 182–3; *CW*, 32; *HW*, ii. 648, n. 181.
[212] No. 221; Rowlands, '1201 peace'.
[213] For recent assessments of Llywelyn's reign see Davies, *Conquest*, 236–51; Smith, *Llywelyn*, 11–29.
[214] *HW*, ii. 616–17 and nn. 27–8; cf. nos 225–7.
[215] *Reg. Innocenz' III.*, vi. 69–70 (no. 47); ibid., vii. 383–6 (no. 220); cf. Pryce, *Native Law*, 84–6.
[216] No. 228; *HW*, ii. 622–3.
[217] *BT, Pen20Tr*, 84; *BT, RBH*, 188–9.
[218] Davies, *Conquest*, 295–6; Smith, 'Magna Carta'; no. 233.

Perfeddwlad apart from the castles of Degannwy and Rhuddlan, forming a pact with Maelgwn and Rhys Gryg, sons of the Lord Rhys, in Deheubarth and Gwenwynwyn in southern Powys, who likewise rose against the English. Llywelyn's determination to lead the Welsh against John in the summer of 1212 is further revealed by his alliance with Philip Augustus, king of France.[219] Rumours of a plot against him forced John to call off a campaign against Gwynedd in August 1212, and by June 1213, following the lifting of the interdict and the surrender of his kingdom to the papacy, the king agreed to a truce with Llywelyn – who had completed his conquest of Perfeddwlad by capturing Degannwy and Rhuddlan earlier in the year – which lasted until May 1215. However, Llywelyn then resumed his attacks, in an alliance with the baronial opposition to the king negotiated by Giles de Braose, and captured Shrewsbury. The peace achieved by the issue on 15 June of Magna Carta, in which the king agreed to restore to the Welsh their lands and charters, including that granted by Llywelyn in 1211, soon broke down and in December 1215 Llywelyn led an army comprising the forces of nearly all the native Welsh rulers into south-west Wales, where he conquered extensive territories, including the royal strongholds of Cardigan and Carmarthen.[220] In 1216–17 the prince's hegemony was extended even further. His authority over the native rulers of the south was demonstrated at Aberdyfi early in 1216, when, with his council, he presided over a partition of Deheubarth among the sons and grandsons of the Lord Rhys. In southern Powys his intervention that year was more direct, as Llywelyn expelled Gwenwynwyn from his lands after the latter's defection to John and occupied them for the rest of his life.[221] The submission of Reginald de Braose, previously loyal to the Welsh, to the regency government of the young Henry III in June 1217 precipitated renewed campaigning by Llywelyn in the south, in Brycheiniog, Gower and Dyfed.[222] Although the Treaty of Lambeth that ended the civil war in England in September 1217 included an offer of peace to Llywelyn and his Welsh allies, a settlement was only reached six months later.[223]

The three agreements at Worcester in March 1218 negotiated by the papal legate Guala acknowledged Llywelyn's dominant position in Wales. The prince was effectively confirmed in his occupation of Powys and of the royal castles of Cardigan and Carmarthen, but at the price of asserting the king's overlordship not only over him but also, crucially, the other Welsh lords, who were required to do homage to the king.[224] That these agreements did not satisfy Llywelyn's ambitions is revealed by his subsequent claims to the homages of Welsh rulers, including an abortive attempt to have them do homage to his son and chosen successor Dafydd in 1238;[225] by renewed attacks on Marcher and royal lands and castles in the 1220s and 1230s;[226] and by his adoption, probably in 1230, of a new title, 'prince of Aberffraw and lord of Snowdon', which proclaimed his dual status as both overlord of the

---

[219] No. 235.
[220] *HW*, ii. 639–48; Smith, 'Magna Carta'; *BT, Pen20Tr*, 88, 90, 91–2; *BT, RBH*, 198–9, 202–3, 204–7.
[221] *BT, Pen20Tr*, 92; *BT, RBH*, 206–9; Davies, *Conquest*, 228.
[222] *BT, Pen20Tr*, 95–6; *BT, RBH*, 214–17.
[223] *HW*, ii. 653; Smith, 'Treaty of Lambeth', 577–8 (c. 10); cf. Painter, *William Marshal*, 252.
[224] Nos 240–2. For further consideration of Llywelyn's relations with the crown from 1218 onwards see Walker, 'Hubert de Burgh'; Pryce, 'Negotiating Anglo-Welsh relations'.
[225] No. 247; Williams, 'Succession', 395–6.
[226] *HW*, ii. 658–63, 667–9, 673–80.

whole of native Wales and ruler of his patrimonial principality of Gwynedd.[227] Yet, though Llywelyn continued to dominate Wales for the rest of his life, notwithstanding some setbacks (notably in 1223, when William Marshal II recovered Cardigan and Carmarthen and the prince was forced to submit to the king at Montgomery), he never succeeded in securing a comprehensive peace granting him royal confirmation of all his territorial gains and, above all, the homages of the other Welsh rulers.[228] The series of truces agreed after the withdrawal of Henry III's army from Painscastle in September 1231, while renewed, with some modifications, until the prince's death, were primarily concerned with procedures for securing compensation and settling disputes arising from warfare in the March rather than with a resolution of fundamental issues in Anglo-Welsh relations.[229]

Llywelyn's efforts to ensure the succession of Dafydd, his son by Joan, were integral to his aim of maintaining the supremacy of Gwynedd.[230] The designation of Dafydd, born after August 1211, as heir in preference to his elder half-brother Gruffudd, the result of an extra-marital relationship with Tangwystl, was justified by Llywelyn on the grounds of Gruffudd's illegitimacy. Dafydd's status as successor was confirmed by the crown in 1220 (and again in 1229, when the king took Dafydd's homage for 'all the rights and liberties' which would fall to him after his father's death) as well as by the pope in 1222.[231] Llywelyn also sought to elevate Dafydd's status by securing for him the hand of Isabella de Braose, daughter of William de Braose, lord of Brecon and Builth, together with a promise of Builth as her dowry, as conditions of her father's release after his capture in Henry III's Ceri campaign of 1228; the marriage went ahead in 1230 despite the execution of William on 2 May for his affair with Joan, discovered the previous Easter.[232] Not surprisingly, the designation of Dafydd as heir was resented by Gruffudd, who enjoyed considerable sympathy in Gwynedd. Llywelyn dispossessed Gruffudd of Meirionnydd and Ardudwy in 1221, but subsequently granted him southern Powys, which he was holding in 1226.[233] However, Gruffudd was imprisoned by his father from 1228 to 1234, after which he appears to have been reinstated in southern Powys and was granted, or restored to, Llŷn, until Dafydd, following his receipt of fealty from the other Welsh princes at Strata Florida on 19 October 1238 (a move designed further to secure his succession), expelled him from the lands in Powys, leaving him only Llŷn.[234]

Dafydd's mother Joan, legitimized by Pope Honorius III in April 1226, died at Aber in February 1237 and was buried across the Menai at Llan-faes on Anglesey, where Llywelyn founded a Franciscan friary in her memory.[235] Although imprisoned after the discovery of her affair with William de Braose at Easter 1230, she was released the following year and resumed her role as a negotiator with the crown on behalf of her husband; indeed, her status seems to have grown during her last years, to judge by her adoption of the new title

---

[227] See below, pp. 76–7.

[228] No. 254 and note.

[229] Nos 266–7, 269–70, 273–4.

[230] See further Smith, 'Dynastic succession', 218–20; *idem, Llywelyn*, 12–14, 25–6.

[231] No. 253; *PR 1225–32*, 269–70.

[232] *AM*, iii. 117; nos 261–3.

[233] *BT, Pen20Tr*, 98; *BT, RBH*, 220–1; nos 282–3.

[234] *BT, Pen20Tr*, 103, 104; *BT, RBH*, 232–3, 234–5.

[235] *CPL*, i. 109; *BT, Pen20Tr*, 104; *BT, RBH*, 234–5. The date of death given in *Brut y Tywysogyon* (February) and *Ann. Cestr.*, 60–1 (the Purification, i.e. 2 February) is probably preferable to that of the Tewkesbury annals (30 March 1237): *AM*, i. 101.

of 'lady of Wales'.[236] Llywelyn died three years later, on 11 April 1240, after assuming the monastic habit at Aberconwy, where he was buried.[237]

Dafydd ap Llywelyn (d. 25 February 1246)

Dafydd succeeded his father and swiftly made peace with the crown, which showed its determination to prevent him from maintaining the wide authority in Wales enjoyed by Llywelyn. Thus it was for Gwynedd only that Dafydd gave homage to the king at Gloucester on 15 May 1240. Moreover, he agreed that claims by Gruffudd ap Gwenwynwyn and other of the 'king's barons' (meaning the Marchers) to lands held by him should be subject to arbitration and explicitly conceded all the homages of the 'barons of Wales' to the king. Dafydd's readiness to submit reflected the fragility of his position in Gwynedd, where, according to Matthew Paris, his elder half-brother Gruffudd waged war against him from Llywelyn's death in April until he was captured by Dafydd around the end of September.[238] Once Gruffudd was imprisoned at Cricieth castle Dafydd had less incentive to comply with the provisions for arbitration and, after failing on several occasions to appear before the arbitrators as requested, a royal campaign was mounted against Gwynedd which forced him to surrender to the king at Gwerneigron near Rhuddlan on 29 August 1241. The terms granted threatened the integrity of Gwynedd. Dafydd was required not only to surrender Tegeingl, one of the four cantrefs of Perfeddwlad, to the crown but also, more importantly, to hand over Gruffudd and the latter's eldest son Owain to the custody of the king, who would decide whether Gruffudd was entitled to a portion of Gwynedd.[239] The agreement was confirmed in London on 24 October, when Dafydd granted Degannwy to the king to cover the expenses of the royal campaign against him and also conceded, as his father had done thirty years earlier, that Gwynedd should escheat to the crown if he died without a legitimate heir.[240] The scale of Dafydd's humiliation is reflected in the new style he adopted after his submission at Gwerneigron, namely, *David filius Lewelini quondam principis Norwallie* ('Dafydd son of Llywelyn, the former prince of North Wales').

One key to Henry's success was the support he received from other Welsh lords, including Gruffudd ap Madog of northern Powys and Maredudd ap Rhobert of Cedewain as well as the dispossessed Gruffudd ap Gwenwynwyn of southern Powys, who appear as pledges for Senana in the agreement she reached with the king at Shrewsbury on 12 August for the release of her husband Gruffudd ap Llywelyn.[241] The claims of Gruffudd and the sympathy he enjoyed in Wales enabled the king to hold Dafydd in check. However, this restraint was lifted on 1 March 1244 when Gruffudd fell to his death while trying to escape from the Tower of London, where he had been held since September 1241.[242] By June Dafydd had risen in alliance with the other Welsh rulers apart from Gruffudd ap Madog and Gruffudd ap Gwenwynwyn in Powys and Morgan ap Hywel of Caerleon and attacked the Marchers

---

[236] *HW*, ii. 685–6; nos 280–1.
[237] Paris, *CM*, iv. 8; *BT*, *Pen20Tr*, 105; *BT*, *RBH*, 236–7; *AC*, 82–3; *CW*, 38.
[238] No. 291 and note.
[239] *HW*, ii. 696–8; Smith, *Llywelyn*, 32–5; nos 300–3.
[240] Nos 304–5.
[241] No. 284.
[242] Paris, *CM*, iv. 295–6; *BT*, *Pen20Tr*, 106; *BT*, *RBH*, 238–9; *AC*, 84–5. For events between the deaths of Gruffudd and Dafydd see further *HW*, ii. 700–6; Smith, *Llywelyn*, 47–55.

and the English border. In June or July he also urged Pope Innocent IV to annul the agreements made with Henry in 1241 on the grounds that these had been extracted from Dafydd by force through an unjust war after the king had disregarded the earlier agreement to settle disputes by arbitration. Moreover, the prince sought to secure his independence of the king by claiming to hold Gwynedd as a vassal of the pope, and also adopted the title 'prince of Wales'. This bid for independence foundered in April 1245, when, in response to pressure from Henry's proctors, Innocent IV declared that Dafydd was a vassal of the king of England.[243] However, the prince and his allies – who by January 1245 included, significantly, Gruffudd ap Llywelyn's second son Llywelyn ap Gruffudd[244] – continued to wage war across Wales, eventually provoking another royal campaign against Gwynedd in August 1245. Yet, though Henry reached the Conwy estuary and built an imposing new castle at Degannwy, he failed to penetrate Gwynedd Uwch Conwy and secure Dafydd's submission and so on 26 October he withdrew to Chester, ordering an embargo on trade with Wales. Four months later, on 25 February 1246, Dafydd died, still childless, at Aber and was buried beside his father at Aberconwy.[245]

Llywelyn ap Gruffudd (d. 11 December 1282)

Llywelyn ap Gruffudd is perhaps the best known, and certainly the most studied, Welsh ruler of the twelfth and thirteenth centuries.[246] Already before the death of his father Gruffudd ap Llywelyn in March 1244, Llywelyn had established himself in the cantref of Dyffryn Clwyd and he had joined Dafydd ap Llywelyn's war against the English by the end of that year. On Dafydd's death in February 1246 he pressed his claim to share in the rule of Gwynedd, which was partitioned between him and his elder brother Owain, 'by counsel of the wise men of the land'.[247] However, Gwynedd was further weakened as Owain and Llywelyn were unable to resist the royal army which reached Degannwy in the spring of 1247, and on 30 April they were compelled in the Treaty of Woodstock to cede Perfeddwlad to the crown and hold Gwynedd Uwch Conwy from the king in return for military service.[248] Although Henry III had not invoked the terms of the Treaty of Gwerneigron and its associated agreements, he had ensured that Gwynedd would be both truncated and divided. Further division followed with the allocation, probably by Owain, of the commote of Cymydmaen in Llŷn to Gruffudd ap Llywelyn's third son Dafydd by July 1252.[249] Llywelyn sought to strengthen his position by forming an alliance (jointly with his brother Owain) with Maredudd ap Rhys Gryg and Rhys Fychan ap Rhys of Deheubarth in October 1251.[250] Yet the key to mastery of Gwynedd lay in overcoming his brothers, whose disputes with him over the partition of the territory were exploited by the crown by 1253,

---

[243] Richter, 'David ap Llywelyn'; nos 306–8.
[244] *CR 1242–7*, 347.
[245] The date is given in *Ann. Cestr.*, 64–5 (*quinto kal. Martii*) and *AM*, iv. 437 (*Ann. Wig.: prima die Quadragesimae*). *Brut y Tywysogyon* places the death in March: *BT, Pen20Tr*, 106; *BT, RBH*, 238–9. *AC*, 85 gives only the year.
[246] Smith, *Llywelyn*, provides a detailed and fully documented biography; references in the following paragraphs will therefore be largely confined to documents contained in the present edition. Llywelyn's career is also assessed in Davies, *Conquest*, chs. 12–13.
[247] No. 318; *BT, Pen20Tr*, 107; cf. *BT, RBH*, 238–41.
[248] No. 312.
[249] No. 440.
[250] No. 316; cf. also no. 323.

and in mid-June 1255 Llywelyn defeated and captured Owain and Dafydd at the battle of Bryn Derwin, near the boundary between Arfon and Eifionydd. Owain remained a prisoner for over twenty years, being eventually released as one of the terms of the Treaty of Aberconwy in November 1277, when he was granted Llŷn. He appears to have played no active political role thereafter and died before Llywelyn, probably in 1282.[251]

The victory at Bryn Derwin gave Llywelyn control of most of Gwynedd Uwch Conwy. It was followed, in November 1256, by the recovery of Perfeddwlad (apart from the castles of Diserth and Degannwy, eventually captured in 1263) and by campaigns in 1257–8 which resulted in the annexation of Meirionnydd, the restoration of northern Ceredigion to its native dynasty and of Maredudd ap Rhys, Llywelyn's ally, to Ystrad Tywi, the recovery of Builth and Gwerthrynion by the Welsh, and the prince's occupation of southern Powys. A royal campaign against Gwynedd in August–September 1257 achieved little. Llywelyn's dominance was reflected in the agreement of mutual aid reached in March 1258 with the baronial party in Scotland led by the Comyns, in which he is given the title 'prince of Wales' at the head of a list of most other native rulers.[252] Possibly the Welsh parties to the agreement gave their assent to it on the same occasion in 1258 that all the Welsh lords formed a pact in which they may well have sworn allegiance to the prince.

However, Llywelyn appreciated that, for his hegemony to endure, he needed above all to secure peace with the English crown. The first step in this direction was taken on 17 June 1258, when the king, facing baronial discontent in England, abandoned plans for another Welsh campaign and agreed a truce with Llywelyn which would last for four years.[253] There followed, in October 1259, the first of a series of attempts by Llywelyn to obtain royal recognition of his paramount status in Wales through an offer of homage and payments in return for the homages of the other Welsh rulers.[254] The prince was not inhibited by such negotiations from seizing the castle and lordship of Builth from Roger Mortimer in 1260; and, after the final collapse of the truce in November 1262, it was to the middle March that he turned in his next phase of territorial expansion. (He had also, by September 1262, adopted a new, self-confident title, 'prince of Wales and lord of Snowdon', after a period of using no title at all since his appearance as 'prince of Wales' in the Scottish agreement of March 1258.)[255] Maelienydd, held by Mortimer, was overrun; the Welsh of Brecon and Blaenllyfni rose to join Llywelyn; and by March 1263 the prince's forces threatened Abergavenny. In the north-east Diserth and Degannwy were finally captured in August and September respectively, and in December Gruffudd ap Gwenwynwyn abandoned his fealty to the king and came to terms with Llywelyn.[256]

In 1263, too, the prince began co-operating with Simon de Montfort in the baronial war against Henry III, and on 19 June 1265 secured an agreement with de Montfort, acting in the king's name, whereby Llywelyn promised to pay 30,000 marks in return for peace and the recognition that he held the principality of Wales from the king.[257] Though the agreement did not survive de Montfort's death at Evesham on 4 August 1265, it indicated the kind of

[251] Smith, *Llywelyn*, 440–1 and n. 190.
[252] No. 328.
[253] Nos 331, 336, 342.
[254] No. 338.
[255] No. 353.
[256] No. 358.
[257] Nos 361–2.

settlement Llywelyn had been seeking since at least 1259 and provided a precedent for the more comprehensive and durable peace concluded, through the arbitration of the papal legate Ottobuono, with Henry III and the Lord Edward at Montgomery on 29 September 1267.[258] By the Treaty of Montgomery Llywelyn became the first (and last) Welsh ruler to receive official recognition from the English crown as prince of Wales, ruling a principality of Wales comprising not only Gwynedd (including Perfeddwlad) but also all the territories held by the 'Welsh barons of Wales' (except for Maredudd ap Rhys of Ystrad Tywi). In return, Llywelyn was obliged to give homage and fealty to the king together with 25,000 marks, to be paid in annual instalments. Although the treaty proved to be less supportive of his position as prince of Wales than Llywelyn had hoped and failed to avert further conflict, its significance should not be underestimated: the recognition attained by Llywelyn in 1267 not only set the seal on a remarkable political ascendancy beginning with the victory at Bryn Derwin twelve years earlier but marked the realization of a goal that had eluded even his grandfather Llywelyn ap Iorwerth at the height of his power.

Over the next decade Llywelyn's authority faced challenges from several directions: the Marcher lords, especially in the south-east; the Welsh leaders of newly conquered areas, notably Maelienydd, Elfael and Brecon; the bishops of Bangor and especially St Asaph;[259] and from within his own family. Despite his destruction of Earl Gilbert de Clare's new castle at Caerphilly in 1270, the prince failed in his attempts to extend his power over the Welsh of upland Glamorgan, while Humphrey de Bohun and Roger Mortimer respectively sought to recover the lordships of Brecon and Maelienydd.[260] The most serious threat to Llywelyn came in 1274, however, when his brother, Dafydd – restored to his lands in Gwynedd by the terms of the Treaty of Montgomery following his defection to the crown in 1263 – conspired with Gruffudd ap Gwenwynwyn of southern Powys and the latter's son Owain in an abortive plot to assassinate the prince on 2 February; Dafydd was to succeed to the principality and give his daughter in marriage, together with Ceri and Cedewain, to Owain. As Llywelyn learned of the full extent of the plot Dafydd fled again to England and was followed at the end of the year by Gruffudd and Owain.[261]

In the mean time, Henry III had been succeeded, in November 1272, by Edward I, who returned to England from crusade in August 1274. Edward's return was followed by a deterioration in Llywelyn's relations with the crown. The prince not only absented himself from Edward's coronation but ignored five summonses between December 1274 and April 1276 to do homage to the new king. Llywelyn did not deny his obligation to do this, but insisted that his grievances concerning Marcher attacks and the king's harbouring of Dafydd and Gruffudd ap Gwenwynwyn should first be redressed. In addition, in January 1272 he had ceased the payments due under the terms of the Treaty of Montgomery.[262] A further bone of contention was the capture and imprisonment at the end of 1275 of Llywelyn's wife Eleanor de Montfort – whom he had married by proxy earlier in the year in fulfilment, it seems, of an agreement with her father Simon de Montfort – while she was sailing from France to Wales. The king, for his part, insisted that Llywelyn should do him

---

[258] No. 363.
[259] Nos 369, 383, 387, 397.
[260] Nos 366, 375, 377, 380, 392–3.
[261] Nos 383, 603–4.
[262] Nos 378, 380, 384–5, 390–1, 393.

fealty and homage unconditionally and on 12 November 1276 the prince was condemned as a rebel. A final attempt at negotiation by Llywelyn early in 1277 failed,[263] and a massive campaign was launched against him which resulted in a crushing defeat and the collapse of the principality recognized in 1267.

Llywelyn's humiliation was spelled out in the Treaty of Aberconwy on 9 November 1277, which, though preserving his title of 'prince of Wales', stripped it of most of its substance.[264] Gwynedd was truncated and divided in a manner reminiscent of the terms of the Treaty of Woodstock thirty years earlier: Llywelyn was obliged to cede Perfeddwlad to the king, to restore Dafydd to a share of Gwynedd (although the latter was granted the cantrefs of Rhufoniog and Dyffryn Clwyd and the lordship of Hope by the king in compensation for this share, so that Llywelyn could hold it for his life) and to acknowledge the claims of his other brothers Owain (released after over two decades of captivity) and Rhodri (who quitclaimed his share to Llywelyn for 1,000 marks).[265] In addition, the prince was only allowed to keep the homages of five, fairly minor, Welsh lords, and these only for his lifetime; the other Welsh homages fell to the king. Llywelyn himself was required to travel to London to do homage to Edward at his Christmas court.

During the following years Llywelyn remained outwardly submissive to the king, but relations nevertheless became strained as Edward sought to tighten his jurisdictional grip on Wales. True, Eleanor was released in January 1278 and celebrated her marriage to Llywelyn at Worcester cathedral on 13 October in the presence of the king, who paid for the wedding feast. However, the claim to Arwystli, held by Gruffudd ap Gwenwynwyn of southern Powys, which the prince initiated in February of that year developed into an increasing source of tension, as the king insisted on his right to exercise jurisdiction in the case and came to be seen by Llywelyn as conniving with Gruffudd's attempt to prevent it being tried by Welsh law, even though this was allowed, so the prince believed, by the provision in the Treaty of Aberconwy that disputes arising in Wales should be settled by the laws of Wales. The litigation proceeded so slowly that the case had not been resolved when war broke out in 1282.[266] In the mean time, Llywelyn had begun reconstructing alliances with other Welsh leaders, and also made an agreement of mutual aid with Roger Mortimer on 9 October 1281.[267] In addition, widespread discontent had arisen in Wales against English rule, especially in those areas such as Perfeddwlad and northern Ceredigion brought directly under English control in 1277, discontent whose causes are articulated in *gravamina* presented to Archbishop Pecham of Canterbury in late October 1282.[268] The war began when Dafydd ap Gruffudd attacked Hawarden castle on Palm Sunday (21 March) 1282. The king reacted swiftly by organizing a major campaign based on three military commands at Chester, mid-Wales and west Wales. When precisely Llywelyn assumed leadership of the rising is uncertain; a crucial catalyst may have been the death of Eleanor after giving birth to a daughter, Gwenllian, on 19 June.[269] Despite attempts at

[263] Nos 398–9, 401.
[264] No. 402; see also nos 403–5, 407.
[265] Nos 405, 458–9.
[266] Nos 409, 415, 420, 427.
[267] No. 425.
[268] Nos 77, 101–2, 429, 454, 536.
[269] Smith, *Llywelyn*, 509–10.

intervention by Archbishop Pecham in the autumn, Llywelyn refused to surrender. Instead, he made for the middle March, quite possibly in an attempt to raise support in an area which had shown loyalty to him in the 1260s, and was killed near Builth on 11 December 1282.[270]

Dafydd ap Gruffudd continued the struggle, assuming Llywelyn's title 'prince of Wales and lord of Snowdon', until his capture in late June 1283, probably the twenty-second, and was executed at Shrewsbury on 2 October.[271] Of the other two sons of Gruffudd ap Llywelyn, Owain, as already noted, had predeceased Llywelyn in 1282, while Rhodri, who supported Edward I in both 1277 and 1282, survived as a knight in England until his death c.1315.[272] Llywelyn's daughter Gwenllian was taken in her cradle from Gwynedd to the Gilbertine nunnery of Sempringham in Norfolk, where she died on 7 June 1337.[273]

GWYNLLŴG

The native lords of Gwynllŵg were descendants of Caradog ap Gruffudd (d. 1081), the last king of the pre-Norman kingdom of Morgannwg (Glamorgan).[274] Gwynllŵg, located between the Rhymni and the Usk, appears as one of the constituent cantrefs of Morgannwg in fifteenth-century lists of the cantrefs and commotes of Wales, but had almost certainly become detached from the rest of Morgannwg to its west before the Norman conquest of lowland Glamorgan, including the coastal plain of Wentloog in Gwynllŵg, by Robert fitz Hamon c.1093.[275] Caradog's son Owain Wan ('the weak') failed to maintain the extensive hegemony established by his father and seems to have been restricted to the upland commote of Machen.

Morgan ab Owain (d. 1158) and Iorwerth ab Owain (d. 1179 × c.1184)

Owain ap Caradog was killed at Carmarthen in 1116. On 15 April 1136 his sons Morgan and Iorwerth were responsible for killing Richard fitz Gilbert de Clare, lord of Ceredigion, near Abergavenny and went on to occupy the lordships of Caerleon and Usk in lowland Gwent.[276] They were also granted 300 acres of moorland by Earl Robert of Gloucester from his demesne lands in Rumney in return for their homage, a gift datable to 1136 or early 1137 that has been interpreted as an attempt to prevent the brothers attacking the lordship of Glamorgan. Morgan and Iorwerth supported Robert in the civil war of Stephen's reign and obtained confirmation of their conquests in Gwynllŵg and Gwent by Henry II.[277] Royal favour was also reflected in the grant of an annuity of 40s. to Morgan from at least 1155–6.[278]

Morgan ab Owain was killed together with his poet Gwrgant ap Rhys by the men of Ifor

---

[270] Ibid., 550–67.
[271] Ibid., 578–9; nos 456–7. For Dafydd see further Carr, '"Last and weakest of his line"'.
[272] Carr, *Owen of Wales*, 3–7.
[273] Smith, *Llywelyn*, 580, 586.
[274] For Gwynllŵg and its dynasty in the late eleventh and twelfth centuries see Smith, 'Kingdom of Morgannwg', 6–7; Crouch, 'Slow death'.
[275] Smith, 'Kingdom of Morgannwg', 10, 12–13.
[276] *BT, Pen20Tr*, 41; *BT, RBH*, 88–9; *HW*, ii. 471 and n. 34.
[277] Nos 462–3; Crouch, 'Robert, earl of Gloucester', 230, 241–2, nn. 5, 6; Crouch, 'Slow death', 33–6.
[278] See note to no. 465.

Bach of Senghennydd in 1158, and was succeeded by his brother Iorwerth, with whom he had previously co-operated.[279] However, the 40s. annuity from the English exchequer was transferred to Morgan's son Morgan ap Morgan, the grantor of two charters, who seems to have died during the year beginning at Michaelmas 1185.[280] Iorwerth ab Owain married Angharad, daughter of Uchdryd (Uthred), bishop of Llandaff (1140–8). She bore Iorwerth two sons: Owain, killed by men of Earl William of Gloucester in 1172, and Hywel, Iorwerth's successor. Caerleon was confiscated from Iorwerth by Henry II for an unspecified reason in September 1171 and only restored through the intervention of the Lord Rhys at the council of Gloucester in June 1175, which Iorwerth attended.[281] Also in 1175, without Iorwerth's knowledge, Hywel sought to strengthen his chances of succeeding his father by blinding and castrating his uncle Owain Pen-carn ab Owain.[282] Iorwerth is last attested in a charter giving consent to a grant by his son Hywel to Glastonbury Abbey almost certainly issued no earlier than 1179.[283] Since Hywel was the grantor of this charter, and since it also refers to his having established the Cistercians at Llantarnam near Caerleon, Iorwerth appears to have relinquished effective authority to him by this time, perhaps because of illness or injury. The date of Iorwerth's death is unknown, but had probably occurred by 1184, for the reference to *Hoel de Carliun* in the pipe roll for 1184–5 suggests that Hywel had succeeded to the lordship by that date.[284] It may also be significant that in the charter for Glastonbury Hywel is styled simply by his patronymic (*Hoelus filius Ioruerthi filii Oeni*), whereas his other surviving charters use the style 'Hywel of Caerleon' or 'Hywel, lord of Caerleon'. Although the latter styles appear to have been a new development for the dynasty (and thus the previous use of the patronymic did not in itself imply a lack of lordship), they are most unlikely to have been adopted while Iorwerth was alive and could still claim, however nominally, to be lord of Caerleon, and the same may well apply to the usage of the exchequer.[285]

Hywel ap Iorwerth (d. 1215 × 1217)

The scanty evidence about Hywel as lord of Caerleon allows two important conclusions. First, he continued his dynasty's policy since 1154, interrupted only in 1171–5, of loyalty to the crown, no doubt regarded as the best safeguard of the lands and authority recovered by his uncle and father in Stephen's reign. In 1184–5 he guarded castles for the king in Glamorgan and Gwynllŵg in the face of the major Welsh revolt precipitated by the death of Earl William of Gloucester in November 1183, and continued to serve the crown under Richard I.[286] Not for nothing did Gerald of Wales, in a passage added to the third recension of the *Itinerarium Kambriae* c.1214, name him with Dafydd ab Owain of Gwynedd as examples of rulers who divided their loyalties equally between the Welsh and the English.[287]

---

[279] *BT, Pen20Tr*, 60; *BT, RBH*, 136–7.

[280] See note to no. 465.

[281] *BT, Pen20Tr*, 66, 71; *BT, RBH*, 154–5, 164–5; *HW*, ii. 540, 545–6.

[282] *BT, Pen20Tr*, 70; *BT, RBH*, 162–3.

[283] No. 467.

[284] *Pipe Roll 31 Henry II*, 7.

[285] See below, p. 117.

[286] *Pipe Roll 31 Henry II*, 7; *Pipe Roll 3–4 Richard I*, 165; *Pipe Roll 9 Richard I*, 194.

[287] *Gir. Camb. Op.*, vi. 145 (*IK* II. 12). This passage occurs only in the third recension of the *IK*: ibid., xx, 145, n. 3.

Second, Hywel continued his dynasty's benefactions to religious houses. As well as confirming his relatives' grants to Glastonbury Abbey and Goldcliff Priory he made additional grants to the latter house, confirmed Robert de Candos's grants to Malpas Priory, founded a daughter house of Strata Florida at Llantarnam near Caerleon in 1179 and granted tithes from the mill of Ebbw collated to the chapter of Llandaff cathedral by Bishop Henry (1193–1218).[288]

The precise date of Hywel's death is uncertain. According to an exchequer memoranda roll for 7 Henry III, Hywel of Caerleon died 'in (the) war' (*in guerra*), and the previous roll refers to 'the war of Hywel of Caerleon'.[289] This war presumably took place during the period of attacks on royal and Marcher lands in Wales led by Llywelyn ap Iorwerth and his allies from the early summer of 1215; if so, Hywel died no earlier than 1215.[290] In any case, his death had occurred by October 1217, as it was Hywel's son and successor Morgan ap Hywel who lost Caerleon in that month to forces sent by Earl William Marshal, lord of Striguil.[291]

The successors of Hywel ap Iorwerth

The loss of Caerleon proved to be permanent, for despite various efforts, both legal and military, Morgan ap Hywel failed to recover it. At his death, shortly before 15 March 1248, Morgan held the castle of Machen (temporarily lost to Gilbert Marshal in 1236) in upland Gwynllŵg together with the commotes of Edeligion and Llebenydd in the lordship of Caerleon in Gwent.[292] He was succeeded by Maredudd ap Gruffudd (d. 1270), lord of Hirfryn in Ystrad Tywi, son of Morgan's daughter and heiress Gwerful and of Gruffudd ap Maredudd, a grandson of the Lord Rhys.[293] Maredudd was the last of his dynasty to exercise lordship in Gwynllŵg and Gwent, for in autumn 1270, probably in response to the destruction of Caerphilly castle by Maredudd's overlord Llywelyn ap Gruffudd, Machen, Edeligion and Llebenydd were seized by Earl Gilbert de Clare and permanently annexed as demesne lands of the lordship of Glamorgan. Maredudd's son Morgan ap Maredudd (d. 1331) appears as a leader in Glamorgan during the unsuccessful Welsh revolt of 1294–5, but is subsequently found in the service of the crown, to which he remained loyal during the rebellion of Llywelyn Bren in 1315–16.[294]

---

[288] Nos 468–72, 474–5; *Llandaff Episcopal Acta*, 98.

[289] TNA: PRO, E 368/5, m. 9d; E 368/4, m. 6 (*a tempore guerre Hoheli de Kaerliun qui mortuus est*). I am very grateful to David Crouch for providing me with these and other references to unpublished exchequer sources and for his helpful comments on the dating of Hywel ap Iorwerth's death.

[290] Cf. Painter, *William Marshal*, 250–2. By contrast, Lloyd held that Hywel was succeeded by his son Morgan ap Hywel *c*.1210, noting that 'Morgan of Caerleon' occurs in a charter of Countess Isabella of Gloucester for Basaleg Priory datable to January 1214 × 23 February 1216: *HW*, ii. 653, n. 213; *EGC*, 32–3 (no. 4). However, no. 476 shows that Hywel was still alive in March 1211, and a reference to pledges of Hywel being in the (lost) originalia roll of 14 John may well imply that he was alive when the latter was written at Easter(?) 1213: TNA: PRO, E 159/4 (5 Henry III), m. 19. The naming of Morgan with a toponym in the charter does not necessarily indicate that he had succeeded his father.

[291] *L'Histoire de Guillaume le Maréchal*, ed. Meyer, ii. 277–82 (lines 17748–872); cf. ibid., iii. 250–2; Painter, *William Marshal*, 252.

[292] *HW*, ii. 653, 674, 701, n. 43, 712–13 and n. 113; *Rot. Fin.*, ii. 31; *CIPM*, i. 36–7 (no. 150); nos 271, 477–8.

[293] *BT, Pen20Tr*, 115; *BT, RBH*, 258–9; *CIPM*, ii. 164 (no. 289); Smith, *Llywelyn*, 345–8, 352, n. 49.

[294] Altschul, 'Lordship of Glamorgan', 55–6; RCAHMW, *Glamorgan III. 1a*, 299; Smith, 'Edward II', 142; *idem*, 'Rebellion of Llywelyn Bren', 82; *CPR 1330–4*, 160.

POWYS

Powys, a kingdom in north-east Wales whose rulers had extended their authority westwards into Ceredigion in the early twelfth century, was exposed to the hegemonic ambitions of the princes of Gwynedd as well as to attacks from the Marchers of the Anglo-Welsh border.[295] Its native dynasty in the twelfth and thirteenth centuries was descended from Bleddyn ap Cynfyn (d. 1075), king of Powys and Gwynedd.[296] After the death of Bleddyn's grandson Madog ap Maredudd in 1160 Powys was divided among various members of the dynasty and, like Deheubarth after the death of the Lord Rhys, was never again subject to unitary rule. From the late twelfth century the two major divisions of the kingdom were northern Powys (alias Powys Fadog, after Madog ap Gruffudd (d. 1236)) and southern Powys (alias Powys Wenwynwyn, after Gwenwynwyn ab Owain Cyfeiliog (d. 1216)). Northern Powys comprised the commotes of Iâl, Maelor Gymraeg (Bromfield), Maelor Saesneg, Nanheudwy, Cynllaith and Mochnant Uwch Is Rhaeadr; its rulers were chiefly based at Overton and Dinas Brân above Llangollen. Southern Powys, whose rulers made Welshpool their principal centre by the thirteenth century, consisted of the commotes of Mochnant Uwch Rhaeadr, Caereinion and Cyfeiliog together with smaller commotes or *swyddi* (such as Swydd Llannerch Hudol) on either side of the Severn and also the cantref of Arwystli, annexed by Gwenwynwyn. Other branches of the dynasty, especially that of Owain Brogyntyn ap Madog, held the commotes of Penllyn (annexed by Llywelyn ap Iorwerth in 1202), Edeirnion and Dinmael; while the cantref of Mechain retained its independence of southern Powys under the lineage of Owain Fychan ap Madog.[297]

Madog ap Maredudd (d. *c*.9 February 1160)

Powys probably reached its greatest extent under Madog ap Maredudd, who succeeded his father Maredudd ap Bleddyn as sole ruler of the kingdom in 1132. Madog expanded the kingdom eastwards into Shropshire, seizing Oswestry in 1149, and also established overlordship over Hywel ab Ieuaf, ruler of Arwystli, by 1151.[298] Six years later Madog and Hywel, together with Madog's brother Iorwerth Goch, joined Henry II in his campaign against Owain Gwynedd, who had seized the commote of Iâl in 1149 and defeated Madog and Ranulf II, earl of Chester the following year. Later in 1157 Iorwerth Goch destroyed Owain Gwynedd's castle of Tomen y Rhodwydd in Iâl.[299] Madog died in 1160 – 'at the beginning of Lent', that is, *c*.9 February, according to the poet Gwalchmai ap Meilyr – and was buried at the church of Meifod.[300] Shortly afterwards his son, and probably his intended successor, Llywelyn ap Madog was killed, a death that marked the end of unitary rule in Powys, which was divided between Madog's three remaining sons, Elise, Gruffudd Maelor (d. 1190 × 1191) and Owain Fychan (d. 1187), his brother Iorwerth Goch and his nephew Owain Cyfeiliog (d. 1197).[301]

---

[295] For Powys in the late eleventh and earlier twelfth centuries see *HW*, ii. 411–22; Davies, 'Henry I and Wales'; Maund, *Welsh Kings*, 71–92.
[296] *EWGT*, 39 (no. 3), 47 (no. 27), 95 (nos 1b–e), 102–3 (no. 8).
[297] For the divisions of Powys see *HW*, i. 242–9; ii. 583–4; Davies, *Conquest*, 230.
[298] No. 480. For Madog see further *HW*, ii. 489, 492–4, 496, 508–9; Davies, *Conquest*, 49–50.
[299] *BT*, *Pen20Tr*, 57, 59; *BT*, *RBH*, 128–9, 134–5.
[300] *BT*, *Pen20Tr*, 61 (and note at 180–1, which rejects as inaccurate the statement, unique to this text, that Madog died at Winchester); *BT*, *RBH*, 140–1; *AC*, 48; *GMB*, no. 7, line 136.
[301] *BT*, *Pen20Tr*, 62; *BT*, *RBH*, 140–1; Smith, 'Dynastic succession', 210–12.

The medieval Welsh prose tale, *Breuddwyd Rhonabwy*, possibly composed as late as the early fourteenth century, preserves a tradition of friction between Madog and Iorwerth Goch, who received Sutton near Wenlock and other Shropshire manors in serjeanty from Henry II in 1157 in return for his services as an interpreter.[302] Iorwerth was granted custody of Chirk castle by Henry II in April 1166 and expelled from Mochnant by his nephews Owain Fychan and Owain Cyfeiliog in the same year; he continued to receive payments from the crown until 1171. The cessation of those payments after Michaelmas of that year may indicate that he had died by then, but this is uncertain.[303] Possibly Iorwerth continued to struggle for a share of Powys after 1166, and he was held in sufficient regard there for Cynddelw to compose an elegy in his memory after he was killed in an otherwise unknown battle.[304]

The lords of Penllyn, Edeirnion and Dinmael

In the years following Madog ap Maredudd's death in 1160 several members of his dynasty exercised rights of lordship in the north-western commotes of Powys. Thus in 1176 Maredudd ap Hywel, named with Owain Cyfeiliog and Owain Fychan as capturing Henry II's castle of Carreghofa in 1163 and the son of Hywel ap Maredudd ap Bleddyn (d. 1142) according to late medieval genealogists, styled himself 'lord of the province which is called Edeirnion'.[305] It is unknown when Maredudd died, but his first cousin Elise ap Madog ap Maredudd held Esgyngaenog in Edeirnion as well as lands in Penllyn by 1183, though he seems to have become lord of Penllyn only after the death of his brother Gruffudd ap Madog in 1190 × 1191.[306] Possibly Elise succeeded Maredudd ap Hywel as lord of Edeirnion; this could explain why he was named, together with Gruffudd, as one of the 'princes of Powys' who met Archbishop Baldwin at Oswestry in 1188.[307] In 1202, however, Llywelyn ap Iorwerth deprived Elise of Penllyn, apart from the castle of Crogen and seven appurtenant townships.[308] Elise's nephew Madog ap Gruffudd of northern Powys may have annexed Edeirnion at the same time, and had certainly established his lordship there by early 1207.[309] Presumably Elise retained Crogen in Penllyn, and perhaps also lands in Edeirnion, as he continued to enjoy some prominence until 1223, after which he is no longer attested.[310]

Reconstructing the position in the region is further complicated by the presence of a third son of Madog, Owain Brogyntyn, named after the village of Porkington near Oswestry, who received regular payments from Henry II in 1160–9.[311] Owain's grants to Strata Marcella and Basingwerk show that he held lands in Penllyn before its annexation by Llywelyn ap Iorwerth and in Dinmael by 1207.[312] He also seems to have held Edeirnion

---

[302] *Breudwyt Ronabwy*, 1; *HW*, ii. 520; Bullock-Davies, *Professional Interpreters*, 15–17.
[303] See note to no. 481.
[304] *GCBM I*, no. 12.
[305] No. 482; *BT*, *Pen20Tr*, 53, 62; *BT*, *RBH*, 118–19, 142–3; Bartrum, *WG*, i, Bleddyn ap Cynfyn 1; *HW*, ii. 509, n. 86.
[306] Nos 483, 487.
[307] *Gir. Camb. Op.*, vi. 142 (*IK* II. 12).
[308] *BT*, *Pen20Tr*, 82; *BT*, *RBH*, 184–5.
[309] No. 504; Stephenson, 'Politics of Powys Wenwynwyn', 42. There are no references to Elise in Edeirnion after 1198: no. 488.
[310] No. 489.
[311] *HW*, ii. 494, 566; Carr and Smith, 'Edeirnion and Mawddwy', 138–9.
[312] Nos 490–6.

in or before August 1211, when Llywelyn ap Iorwerth promised not to intervene there except to intercede for Owain, who had only ever held the land from the king: the clause does not necessarily indicate that Owain was currently in possession of Edeirnion, and could imply, rather, that he was claiming it, presumably against Madog ap Gruffudd, lord of the commote in 1207.[313] That Owain held it by his death is suggested, however, by the fact that his sons and grandsons were lords of both Edeirnion and Dinmael in the thirteenth century.[314] Owain last occurs in 1215 and was dead by May 1218, when his son Bleddyn ab Owain submitted to Henry III.[315]

Northern Powys: the lineage of Gruffudd ap Madog (d. 1190 × 1191)

Gruffudd Maelor ap Madog ap Maredudd established an extensive hegemony in northern Powys by his death.[316] Of his two sons, Owain ap Gruffudd died in 1197, thereby eliminating the danger of territorial fragmentation, and the unity of northern Powys was preserved by Madog ap Gruffudd, from whom it took the name Powys Fadog.[317] Madog founded the Cistercian abbey of Valle Crucis near Llangollen *c.*1200 and was also a benefactor of its mother house Strata Marcella.[318] Although he sided with King John in 1211–12, by 1215 Madog threw in his lot with Llywelyn ap Iorwerth of Gwynedd, with whom he had been associated at the beginning of the thirteenth century, and remained loyal to the prince until his death in 1236; he was buried at Valle Crucis.[319]

It is uncertain how far Gruffudd ap Madog, the eldest of Madog's five sons, succeeded in establishing a hegemony in northern Powys commensurate with that of his father.[320] His status as heir is implicit in the confirmation, issued in Gruffudd's name alone, of Madog's grants to Valle Crucis in 1236.[321] That disputes soon arose between at least two of Gruffudd's brothers is revealed by the murder of his namesake, Gruffudd Iâl, by Maredudd ap Madog in 1238; although deprived of his lands by Llywelyn ap Iorwerth, who maintained his overlordship of northern Powys until his death in 1240, Maredudd appears alongside his three surviving brothers in the record of a dispute settlement in favour of Valle Crucis in 1247.[322] Possibly the threat posed by his younger brothers, supported by the crown, led Gruffudd to enter into an agreement of mutual help with Llywelyn ap Gruffudd in 1250, although this is uncertain as the correct date of the document may have been 1257.[323] In any case, if it was made in 1250, the agreement did not override Gruffudd's loyalty to Henry III, to whom he had given fealty in 1241 and from whom he received a promise in July 1244 that he should hold the whole of his father's patrimony, and it was only

---

[313] No. 233.
[314] *HW*, ii. 683, 759; Carr, 'Barons of Edeyrnion', 188–9; Carr and Smith, 'Edeirnion and Mawddwy', 139–41.
[315] No. 12; *Foedera*, I. i. 151.
[316] *HW*, ii. 566. For the possibility that he died in 1190, rather than 1191 (as stated in *BT*, *Pen20Tr*, 74; *BT*, *RBH*, 172–3) see no. 487 and note.
[317] *HW*, ii. 583–4 and n. 46.
[318] Nos 499, 501, 503–6, 508–9.
[319] *HW*, ii. 634, 638 and n. 131, 648, 683; *BT*, *Pen20Tr*, 85, 91, 104; *BT*, *RBH*, 190–1, 206–7, 232–3.
[320] This section is indebted to Smith, 'Dynastic succession', 227–8.
[321] No. 511.
[322] *BT*, *Pen20Tr*, 105; *BT*, *RBH*, 234–5; no. 513 (the document names the brothers in the order Gruffudd, Maredudd, Hywel and Madog Fychan, quite possibly indicating their relative seniority).
[323] No. 323 and note.

in September 1257, after the failure of Henry III's invasion of north Wales the previous month, that Gruffudd submitted to Llywelyn.[324] (Hywel ap Madog, the most prominent of Gruffudd's younger brothers, remained in the king's service in November 1257, but appears with Gruffudd among Llywelyn's supporters in September 1267.[325] At his death, which occurred before December 1269, he held the manor of Eyton in Maelor Gymraeg and half the commote of Cynllaith apart from Llanarmon.)[326] Gruffudd remained loyal to Llywelyn until his death in December 1269; his brother Madog Fychan died in the same month, and both men were buried at Valle Crucis.[327]

Gruffudd ap Madog married Emma, daughter of Henry Audley, before March 1258, and later granted her Maelor Saesneg and Eyton in Maelor Gymraeg for the rest of her life.[328] Her possession of these lands was confirmed in December 1270, with Llywelyn ap Gruffudd's approval, by her four sons with Gruffudd, namely Madog, Llywelyn, Owain and Gruffudd, although her title to Eyton was challenged by her daughter-in-law Margaret, widow of Madog Fychan ap Gruffudd.[329] These sons divided the rest of northern Powys between them, although it is possible that the partition took the form of a *parage* by which the eldest of these, Madog ap Gruffudd, granted Dinas Brân as well as Maelor Gymraeg, was intended to enjoy superiority over his brothers. (Gruffudd Fychan received Iâl and Edeirnion, while Cynllaith was divided between Llywelyn and Owain.)[330] If so, however, these arrangements were overtaken by the conquest of Powys Fadog by Edward I's forces in spring 1277, when Madog agreed to divide northern Powys with Llywelyn ap Madog alone following the latter's submission to the king the previous December.[331] Most of Powys Fadog fell under the overlordship of the king, though it was agreed in the Treaty of Aberconwy that, whereas Gruffudd Fychan ap Gruffudd should do homage to Edward for Iâl, Llywelyn should receive his homage for Edeirnion, one of the few territories whose lords remained the prince's vassals after 1277.[332] (Gruffudd Fychan's title to Edeirnion was disputed by his sister-in-law Margaret, widow of Madog Fychan ap Madog.)[333] Madog ap Gruffudd died shortly after the treaty, by 10 December 1277.[334] The following year his mother Emma Audley was compelled to quitclaim her lands in Maelor Saesneg, with its castle of Overton, to Edward I in return for rents in England of 100s. a year.[335] The three remaining sons of Gruffudd ap Madog sided with Llywelyn ap Gruffudd in 1282, and their lands were confiscated by the crown. Llywelyn ap Gruffudd ap Madog, already in conflict with the men of Shropshire before war broke out, was killed at Cilmeri on 11 December 1282 alongside his namesake, the prince of Wales;[336] his half of Cynllaith was granted to

---

[324] Smith, *Llywelyn*, 93–4, 111; *CPR 1232–47*, 430; cf. ibid., 268.
[325] *CLR 1251–60*, 409; no. 363, c. xi. Gruffudd and Hywel received gifts from the king in the 1240s and in 1255: *CLR 1240–5*, 270, 274; *CLR 1245–51*, 47; *CLR 1251–60*, 254.
[326] No. 516; *WAR*, 248; *HW*, ii. 747, n. 162.
[327] *BT, Pen20Tr*, 115; *BT, RBH*, 258–9.
[328] Nos 515–16.
[329] Nos 517, 526; see also no. 520. Margaret was a sister of Llywelyn ap Gruffudd of Gwynedd: cf. Smith, *Llywelyn*, 38 and n. 7.
[330] *HW*, ii. 747–8; Lloyd, *Owen Glendower*, 9; Smith, 'Dynastic succession', 228–9.
[331] No. 527.
[332] No. 363, c. xiv.
[333] No. 530.
[334] *CWR*, 161.
[335] No. 519 and note.
[336] Nos 533–8; Smith, *Llywelyn*, 565.

Roger Mortimer's new lordship of Chirk, while the other half, held by his brother Owain, was granted to Queen Eleanor. Gruffudd Fychan (d. 1289) quitclaimed Iâl to John de Warenne, earl of Surrey, in 1283, but was allowed to hold Glyndyfrdwy from the king as a tenant at will. His descendant, Owain Glyndŵr (d. *c*.1415), was proclaimed prince of Wales over a century later on 16 September 1400.[337]

Southern Powys: the lineage of Owain Cyfeiliog (d. 1197)

Owain Cyfeiliog was the eldest son of Madog ap Maredudd's elder brother Gruffudd ap Maredudd ap Bleddyn (d. 1128) and thus could have hoped eventually to succeed to the kingdom of Powys. Madog appears to have recognized the potential threat represented by his nephew, for in 1149 he granted Owain and his brother Meurig the cantref of Cyfeiliog, and by Madog ap Maredudd's death in 1160 Owain had extended his power-base eastwards, as by then he also possessed a court at Welshpool.[338] Although he joined the Welsh alliance under Owain Gwynedd in resisting Henry II's invasion in 1165, from the 1170s Owain Cyfeiliog formed close ties with the king, whose support helped him to establish a broad hegemony in southern Powys at the expense of Madog ap Maredudd's sons, notably Owain Fychan, killed in 1187 by Owain Cyfeiliog's sons Gwenwynwyn and Cadwallon.[339] (The division of Mochnant along the river Rhaeadr between Owain Cyfeiliog and Owain Fychan when they combined to expel their uncle Iorwerth Goch from the cantref in 1166 was of enduring significance, as it came to mark the boundary between northern and southern Powys.)[340] Owain founded the Cistercian abbey of Strata Marcella, a daughter house of Whitland, *c*.1170, where he was buried after his death in 1197, and had probably retired there in 1195, when his son Gwenwynwyn assumed the effective leadership of southern Powys.[341]

Most of Gwenwynwyn's surviving acts are in favour of Strata Marcella, situated near his principal court of Welshpool, and reflect the continuing patronage of the monastery by his lineage. The earliest of these shows that he held Cyfeiliog, with its castle at Tafolwern, by 1185 or 1187, presumably as an *apanage* under his father, just as Owain Cyfeiliog had held it under Madog ap Maredudd.[342] After his father's retirement to Strata Marcella in 1195 Gwenwynwyn launched attacks on the Marchers along the Anglo-Welsh border, recovered Welshpool castle after its capture by royal forces in 1196 and annexed Arwystli the following year. In the wake of the deaths of his father and the Lord Rhys of Deheubarth in 1197, he sought to assume the leadership of native Wales: as well as intervening in the succession disputes in Deheubarth on behalf of Maelgwn ap Rhys, in 1198 Gwenwynwyn 'gathered a mighty host to seek to win for the Welsh their original rights and to restore their bounds to their rightful owners'. These ambitions were curbed, however, by the failure of the ensuing siege of Painscastle in Elfael, which ended in a major Welsh defeat (13 August 1198).[343]

---

[337] Lloyd, *Owen Glendower*, 9–11; nos 531–2.
[338] *BT, Pen20Tr*, 57; *BT, RBH*, 128–9; Smith, 'Dynastic succession', 211; 'Gwaith Owain Cyfeiliog', ed. Williams, 193–8 and no. 14.
[339] *BT, Pen20Tr*, 63, 73; *BT, RBH*, 144–5, 170–1; *Gir. Camb. Op.*, vi. 142–5 (*IK* II. 12); Charles-Edwards and Jones, '*Breintiau Gwy'r Powys*', 196–7, 199–204.
[340] *HW*, ii. 520.
[341] No. 539; *HW*, ii. 583; *BT, Pen20Tr*, 79; *BT, RBH*, 180–1.
[342] Nos 541–2; the former charter, dated 9 May 1185, is of doubtful authenticity.
[343] *HW*, ii. 583–7; *BT, Pen20Tr*, 76, 79–80 (quotation at 79); *BT, RBH*, 176–83.

By December 1199 Gwenwynwyn had resumed his father's policy of détente with the crown, which regarded him as a useful ally against an ascendant Llywelyn ap Iorwerth in Gwynedd, and on 11 April 1200 he was granted the royal manor of Ashford in Derbyshire. It was probably at about this time that he married Margaret Corbet, daughter of Thomas Corbet of Caus.[344] However, after Llywelyn ap Iorwerth abandoned his proposed invasion of southern Powys in 1202 Gwenwynwyn resumed his attacks on the Marchers and lost the favour of King John, who temporarily confiscated Ashford in 1204 and then, far more seriously, seized and imprisoned Gwenwynwyn at Shrewsbury in October 1208, in response to the latter's expulsion of Geoffrey fitz Peter from Blaenllyfni in the lordship of Brecon. The ruler of southern Powys was compelled to promise twenty hostages in return for his release, and his lands were to be taken into royal custody. This gave Llywelyn ap Iorwerth the opportunity to fulfil his ambition of 1202, and the prince of Gwynedd immediately occupied Gwenwynwyn's lands, holding them until he was driven out by John's forces on c.30 November 1210.[345]

Although he owed his restoration to the king, Gwenwynwyn resented the royal custody of his castles of Tafolwern and Mathrafal and joined Llywelyn in the Welsh rising of 1212.[346] Yet Llywelyn's dominance by 1215 seems to have made Gwenwynwyn susceptible to John's attempts to detach him from the prince: the king granted him Montgomery by 28 January 1216 and restored the manor of Ashford to him the following April.[347] According to *Brut y Tywysogyon*, the ruler of Powys 'made a solemn pact with John' in 1216, renouncing his homage to Llywelyn; when diplomatic efforts failed to recall him to the prince's allegiance, Llywelyn expelled him from his lands by military force. Gwenwynwyn died in exile later in 1216, after 27 June.[348]

Southern Powys remained in the hands of Llywelyn or his sons for the rest of the prince's life, but Gwenwynwyn's son and heir, Gruffudd ap Gwenwynwyn, was restored to his father's lands by Henry III in August 1241 in return for his homage and hostages and a fine of 300 marks (£200).[349] Gruffudd had probably spent part of his exile since 1216 in the lordship of Caus with the family of his mother Margaret Corbet (d. c.1251), as well as in the manor of Ashford in Derbyshire. (Though it has been argued that Margaret is last mentioned in the sources in 1245,[350] an inquisition into tithes at Ashford and other manors in Derbyshire in 1251 implies that she was still alive then, as it refers to *dominicis terris Griffini filii Wenunwen militis et matris eius*.)[351] The manor appears to have been resumed by the crown after Gwenwynwyn's death, as one third of it was assigned to his widow Margaret, in February 1223, followed by a grant of (the remaining?) two-thirds in August 1226. In February 1242 Gruffudd ap Gwenwynwyn was given royal assent to assign the manor as dower to his wife Hawise Lestrange, sister of John Lestrange of Knockin

[344] Morgan, 'Trewern', 131; cf. no. 579.
[345] *HW*, ii. 619–21, 633; Stephenson, 'Politics of Powys Wenwynwyn', 50–1; *BT, Pen20Tr*, 83, 84; *BT, RBH*, 188–9; no. 576.
[346] *BT, Pen20Tr*, 86; *BT, RBH*, 194–5; Stephenson, 'Politics of Powys Wenwynwyn', 52.
[347] *HW*, ii. 649; no. 578.
[348] *BT, Pen20Tr*, 92 (quotation); *BT, RBH*, 206–9; *AC*, 72 (B); *HW*, ii. 649–50 and n. 194 (citing *Rot. Pat.*, 189a, a letter from John to Gwenwynwyn dated at Corfe, 27 June 1216).
[349] *BT, Pen20Tr*, 106; *BT, RBH*, 236–7; *Rot. Fin.*, i. 350–1.
[350] Lloyd, 'Border notes', 52; Morgan, 'Territorial divisions [I]', 40.
[351] Cox, 'Ancient documents', 143.

(Shropshire), though he continued to grant land there after that date. The manor was permanently confiscated following Gruffudd's agreement with Llywelyn ap Gruffudd of Gwynedd in December 1263.[352]

Even before his restoration in August 1241 Gruffudd seems to have been drawn into violent territorial disputes with his uncle Thomas Corbet of Caus, disputes which continued periodically until Corbet's death in 1274.[353] Gruffudd also recovered the land along his southern border between the Rhiw and the Helygi after the death in 1244 of Maredudd ap Rhobert of Cedewain, who had been allowed to keep it for his lifetime.[354] However, in January 1257 Llywelyn ap Gruffudd, determined to extend his authority in Wales further after his recent victories in Perfeddwlad, Meirionnydd and Ceredigion, invaded southern Powys and burned Welshpool; Gruffudd held on to Montgomery and some other lands, but was driven into exile when Llywelyn returned to complete the conquest in the autumn after Henry III's withdrawal from Degannwy on 8 September.[355] Though he probably paid visits to the manor of Ashford in Derbyshire, Gruffudd remained active in the Marches during the following years, continuing his attacks on the lands of Thomas Corbet in alliance with his brother-in-law John Lestrange.[356] Gruffudd occupied Gorddwr in the summer of 1263 and in September was ordered by the crown, no longer tolerant of his attacks in the March, to restore this territory, together with the land between the Camlad and the Severn, to Corbet. In addition, some of his Marcher allies, notably another brother-in-law, Hamo Lestrange, ceased their support for the baronial party and resumed their allegiance to Henry III. In order to retain his territorial gains in the March and also to prevent further attacks by Llywelyn ap Gruffudd, Gruffudd felt compelled to renounce his fealty to the king and come to terms with the prince of Gwynedd. The resulting agreement, concluded with Llywelyn at Ystumanner on 12 December 1263, provided for Gruffudd's restoration to the lands taken from him in 1257 in return for his homage and fealty. In addition, co-operation was envisaged in further campaigns in the March, with Gruffudd keeping all conquests north of the Camlad, the prince all those to the south.[357]

The *rapprochement* with Llywelyn lasted for a decade. However, by the end of 1274 Gruffudd had fled Welshpool for Shrewsbury and Llywelyn's forces had annexed Powys once more. At the root of this dramatic change was the discovery of the abortive plot by Dafydd ap Gruffudd, Llywelyn's brother, and Owain ap Gruffudd ap Gwenwynwyn to assassinate Llywelyn on 2 February 1274 and proclaim Dafydd as prince in his place. On 17 April 1274 both Owain and his father, Gruffudd, were tried at Llywelyn's new castle of Dolforwyn in Cedewain – whose construction was probably an important contributory factor in ensuring Powysian involvement in the plot – and confessed that they had offended against their fealty to the prince. Gruffudd was re-granted his lands apart from Arwystli and the territory on the northern borders of Cedewain between the Rhiw and the Helygi, which were confiscated by Llywelyn, to whom Owain surrendered as a hostage.[358] In the

---

[352] See note to no. 583.
[353] See note to no. 593.
[354] No. 591.
[355] *BT, Pen20Tr*, 110–11; *BT, RBH*, 248–51; *AC*, 91–2 (B); *HW*, ii. 719, 722.
[356] No. 599; Stephenson, 'Politics of Powys Wenwynwyn', 56.
[357] No. 358 and note.
[358] Nos 603–4.

autumn, however, Owain confessed the full extent of the plot, prompting Llywelyn to send five nobles to Welshpool about the beginning of December to confront Gruffudd with the details. After wining and dining the emissaries, Gruffudd had them imprisoned and fled to Shrewsbury that night. Llywelyn subsequently captured and burned Welshpool castle and occupied Gruffudd's territory.[359]

Gruffudd remained loyal to the crown for the rest of his life. He re-established his authority over southern Powys, including Arwystli, after the fall of Dolforwyn to royal forces on 8 April 1277.[360] The following month he made territorial provisions for his wife Hawise that also safeguarded the interests of his eldest son Owain and later, probably early in 1278, provided for a division of his lands among his sons which likewise attempted to secure Owain's dominance as chief lord of southern Powys after his death.[361] He also sought to recover the territory between the Rhiw and the Helygi, seized by Llywelyn in 1274, and received royal support both against Llywelyn's legal claim to Arwystli and in his own claim to the homage of the lords of Mechain.[362] His loyalty to the crown ensured that Gruffudd, uniquely among major Welsh rulers, retained his lands, now accorded the status of a barony, after the conquest of 1282–3. After his death in the spring or summer of 1286 he was succeeded by Owain, in accordance with the terms of the territorial settlement made in 1278. Owain died in 1293, leaving a two-year-old heir, Gruffudd, who died in June 1309. By 26 August Gruffudd ab Owain's sister Hawise the younger had been given in marriage to John Charlton, who did homage for the barony to Edward II two years later. Gruffudd ap Gwenwynwyn's widow Hawise Lestrange died in November 1310, and her lands passed to her daughter and son-in-law.[363]

Mechain: the lineage of Owain Fychan (d. 1187)

With the support of either the prince of Gwynedd or the English crown the descendants of Owain Fychan ap Madog maintained a lordship over the cantref of Mechain that was largely independent of the rulers of southern Powys until 1281.[364] In 1167–70 Owain Fychan briefly enjoyed a wide hegemony in Powys in alliance with Owain Gwynedd, but the death of the latter deprived him of a vital supporter and he failed to prevent the ascendancy of his first cousin Owain Cyfeiliog, who may have been behind the treacherous attack by night at Carreghofa in 1187 in which Owain Fychan was killed by Owain Cyfeiliog's sons Gwenwynwyn and Cadwallon.[365] His elegy by Cynddelw claims that Owain Fychan was lord of Mechain, Cynllaith and Mochnant Is Rhaeadr, and in a legal case in 1278 his grandson Maredudd ap Llywelyn ab Owain produced a charter by Henry II confirming Owain in possession of Mechain together with five Marcher townships and the land of Carreghofa. The jury in that case stated that Maredudd's ancestors had been adherents of Llywelyn, 'prince of Wales' (clearly a reference to Llywelyn ap Iorwerth), when they were

---

[359] *BT, Pen20Tr*, 116–17; *BT, RBH*, 260–3; *LW*, liii–lv; Stephenson, 'Politics of Powys Wenwynwyn', 46–9; Smith, *Llywelyn*, 369–77.
[360] Ibid., 415–18.
[361] Nos 606–7.
[362] Nos 605, 608; Smith, *Llywelyn*, 469–89; *CWR*, 211.
[363] For the history of southern Powys after the conquest see Morgan, 'Barony of Powys'.
[364] For Mechain see further ibid., 38–42.
[365] *BT, Pen20Tr*, 73; *BT, RBH*, 170–1; *Gir. Camb. Op.*, vi. 142–3 (*IK* II. 12); Charles-Edwards and Jones, '*Breintiau Gwŷr Powys*', 198–204.

conquered by Gruffudd ap Gwenwynwyn's ancestors.[366] This could imply that Gwenwynwyn had occupied Mechain in 1187 and that Owain Fychan's sons Llywelyn and Owain Fychan (II) gained seisin of the cantref only after Llywelyn ap Iorwerth's expulsion of Gwenwynwyn from Powys in 1208 or 1216.[367] In any case, both sons held Mechain under Llywelyn ap Iorwerth's overlordship.[368] In addition, they almost certainly held land in the adjacent cantref of Mochnant by 1222.[369]

After Llywelyn's death in April 1240 Llywelyn and Owain sided with Henry III against Dafydd ap Llywelyn. Llywelyn ab Owain was dead by July 1240, being succeeded in his share of Mechain by his eldest son Llywelyn Fychan, who, with Owain Fychan, paid a fine of £60 to the king for seisin of the commote of Mochnant Uwch Rhaeadr on 9 May 1241.[370] This is the last occurrence of Owain in the sources; he had died by the end of 1244.[371] By March 1258 Llywelyn Fychan, together with his younger brothers Owain and Maredudd, had abandoned their allegiance to the crown and submitted to Llywelyn ap Gruffudd, probably following the latter's expulsion of Gruffudd ap Gwenwynwyn from southern Powys the previous year.[372] Llywelyn Fychan probably died by December 1276, and left two sons, Gruffudd and Maredudd.[373] Mechain fell to forces loyal to Edward I in February or March 1277. Gruffudd ap Gwenwynwyn asserted his claim to the lands of Owain and Maredudd and was eventually granted the homage of Maredudd and his co-heirs by the king on 8 November 1281.[374] By November 1277 Maredudd and Owain claimed only half of Mechain Iscoed, and also acknowledged that their nephews, the sons of Llywelyn Fychan ap Llywelyn, enjoyed the same rights as they did in the land.[375] It is possible that the nephews also held most of Mechain Uwchcoed. However, the other half of Mechain Iscoed appears to have been annexed either by Gruffudd ap Madog (d. 1269) of northern Powys, who had laid claim to the whole cantref against Gruffudd ap Gwenwynwyn, perhaps in 1245, or by his sons, two of whom, Gruffudd Fychan and Llywelyn Fychan, held part of Mechain by 1278. Llywelyn Fychan's lands in Mechain were granted to Gruffudd ap Gwenwynwyn in 1282.[376]

SENGHENNYDD

Senghennydd, a cantref lying between the Taff and the Rhymni, was the most easterly of the Welsh lordships in Blaenau Morgannwg, the uplands of the Marcher lordship of

---

[366] *HW*, ii. 553 and n. 85; *GCBM I*, no. 13, lines 12, 21, 31; *WAR*, 237.

[367] Morgan, 'Barony of Powys', 38.

[368] Cf. *Rot. Pat.*, 45a (1204); *Rot. Claus.*, i. 362b (1218); *CR 1237–42*, 124.

[369] No. 611.

[370] The Llywelyn ap Llywelyn who gave homage to Henry III at Windsor at Midsummer 1240 was presumably Llywelyn ab Owain's son, and on 14 July 1240 the king complained that Dafydd ap Llywelyn prevented Owain Fychan and his nephews from obtaining seisin of the lands adjudged to them by the royal court: *CLR 1226–40*, 477; *CR 1237–42*, 359–60. Fine in 1241: *Rot. Fin.*, i. 342.

[371] Llywelyn ap Llywelyn 'of Mechain' and 'the two sons of Owain Fychan' were among the barons of north Wales addressed as supporters of Dafydd ap Llywelyn on 6 January 1245: *CR 1242–7*, 348.

[372] No. 328; Morgan, 'Barony of Powys', 39.

[373] No. 612 names only Owain and Maredudd; *HW*, ii. 709, n. 93.

[374] Nos 612–16; *CWR*, 211.

[375] *WAR*, 244.

[376] Morgan, 'Barony of Powys', 39–41.

Glamorgan. The origins of its dynasty are obscure. According to a late fifteenth-century genealogy, Ifor ap Meurig (Ifor Bach) was the grandson of a certain nobleman (*uchelwr*) of Senghennydd.[377] In 1158 the men of Ifor Bach, as he was already known in his lifetime, killed Morgan ab Owain of Gwynllŵg, the neighbouring Welsh lordship to the east of Senghennydd, and in the same year Ifor kidnapped Earl William of Gloucester, his wife Hawise and their infant son from Cardiff castle and released them only after the earl had restored lands seized from him.[378] In common with the rulers of Glamorgan and Gwynllŵg, Ifor was allied to the dynasty of Deheubarth, for he married Nest, a daughter of Gruffudd ap Rhys. The date of Ifor's death is unknown, but seems to have occurred by *c*.1174, as the grant by his son Gruffudd ab Ifor to found a hermitage or abbey in Senghennydd at Pendar was probably made in or very shortly after 1174, and in the following year Gruffudd was present at the council of Gloucester with his maternal uncle, the Lord Rhys.[379] A later charter by which Gruffudd granted land at Leckwith, together with the bodies of himself and his mother for burial, to Margam Abbey shows that Nest died no earlier than December 1193.[380] This grant is striking, as it suggests that Gruffudd claimed land south-west of Cardiff, although the clause providing for an equivalent land to be given in Senghennydd if he was unable to warrant the grant suggests that his tenure of Leckwith was insecure at best. Gruffudd died in 1211 at the Cistercian abbey of Llantarnam near Caerleon; it is unknown whether the bequest of his body to Margam was honoured.[381]

Gruffudd had two brothers, Cadwallon and Maredudd, both of whom led troops for Henry II in France in 1188; Cadwallon ab Ifor also served John in Normandy in 1203.[382] The extent to which these brothers shared land and authority with Gruffudd in Senghennydd is hard to assess. That Cadwallon, at least, enjoyed some prominence there is suggested by the reference in 1197 to the fortification by Hywel ap Iorwerth of Caerleon of *castrum de Cadwalan*, quite possibly signifying the motte at Twyn Castell, Gelli-gaer (cmt. Senghennydd Uwch Caeach), and by Walter Map's account of a *Cadolanus* at Gelli-gaer.[383] In 1211, probably after Gruffudd's death, Cadwallon raided English territories in Glamorgan, an action which no doubt explains the confiscation of certain lands in Cornwall that were restored to him by King John in September 1212.[384] However, it appears that Gruffudd exercised supremacy over his brothers in Senghennydd: both of his charters were issued in his name alone, without reference to their consent, and it was his son Rhys ap Gruffudd who succeeded him.[385] Rhys died in 1256 and was succeeded in turn by his son

---

[377] *EWGT*, 105. For the origins of the cantref and its dynasty see further *HW*, i. 277 and n. 273; Smith, 'Kingdom of Morgannwg', 24–5; Crouch, 'Slow death', 31.

[378] *Gir. Camb. Op.*, vi. 63–4 (*IK* I. 6); 'Chronicle of the thirteenth century', 274; *AM*, i. 15.

[379] No. 616; *BT, Pen20Tr*, 71; *BT, RBH*, 164–5.

[380] No. 617.

[381] *BT, Pen20Tr*, 86; *CW*, 34.

[382] *Pipe Roll 34 Henry II*, 106–7; *Gir. Camb. Op.*, iii. 303; *HW*, ii. 637 and n. 124.

[383] *Pipe Roll 9 Richard I*, 194; Walter Map, *De Nugis Curialium*, 198–201; Smith, 'Kingdom of Morgannwg', 35; RCAHMW, *Glamorgan III. 1a*, 70–1.

[384] *AC*, 68; *Rot. Claus.*, i. 123b; Smith, 'Kingdom of Morgannwg', 42.

[385] Nos 616–17 (admittedly the first of these is known only from Earl William's confirmation). Gruffudd's supremacy may also be reflected in his being named before Cadwallon in a list of pledges in 1199: *Llandaff Episcopal Acta*, no. 44. Rhys is attested as lord of Senghennydd from 1230 onwards and was an ally of Dafydd ap Llywelyn of Gwynedd in 1245: *PR 1225–32*, 412; *HW*, ii. 674 and n. 109, 700, n. 40, 703; Smith, 'Kingdom of Morgannwg', 35; Altschul, 'Lordship of Glamorgan', 47–50.

Gruffudd ap Rhys, who allied himself with Llywelyn ap Gruffudd.[386] In January 1267 Gilbert de Clare captured Gruffudd ap Rhys, annexed the lordship of Senghennydd and began building a castle at Caerphilly. Llywelyn ap Gruffudd claimed authority over Senghennydd, destroying Caerphilly castle in October 1270.[387] Although Gruffudd ap Rhys was not restored, it seems that his family was not completely dispossessed, as Llywelyn ap Gruffudd, better known as Llywelyn Bren, who held lands in Senghennydd and led a revolt in Glamorgan in 1315–16, was probably his son.[388]

II. DIPLOMATIC ANALYSIS OF THE ACTS

Over fifty years ago J. Conway Davies wrote that 'one of the most clamant needs in Welsh medieval historical research is detailed work on diplomatic forms used in Wales.'[389] Subsequent scholarship has advanced understanding of these forms in several important respects: the work of Wendy Davies on the pre-Norman charters extant in edited form in the Book of Llandaff and that of David Crouch and Julia Barrow on the episcopal acts respectively of Llandaff and St Davids are notable cases in point.[390] As far as the acts issued by twelfth- and thirteenth-century Welsh rulers are concerned, several scholars have followed J. Conway Davies's example and discussed the diplomatic of individual documents or collections of documents in studies extending from Keith Williams-Jones's article editing Llywelyn ap Iorwerth's charter for Cymer Abbey to Graham Thomas's volume of Strata Marcella charters.[391] However, the first overview of the diplomatic of charters issued by Welsh rulers of this period only appeared in 2000, in a paper by Charles Insley that drew on his work for the present edition.[392] Building on these earlier studies, the following analysis begins by examining the nature of the corpus of acts in this edition before turning to consider the diplomatic of those acts extant as texts. The discussion of diplomatic is subdivided by territory. It opens with the acts of the rulers of Gwynedd as these account for almost half the texts published in the present work; they can therefore be analysed in greater detail than those of any of the other Welsh dynasties and provide a framework for discussing the corpus of texts as a whole. The final part of the discussion attempts to draw some conclusions about the agencies responsible for the production of acts.

---

[386] *HW*, ii. 713; 'Chronicle of the thirteenth century', 280.
[387] Ibid., 282; nos 366, 375; Altschul, 'Lordship of Glamorgan', 52, 54–6.
[388] Smith, 'Rebellion of Llywelyn Bren', 74–5.
[389] Davies, 'Records of the abbey of Ystrad Marchell', 6. Cf. Jack, *Medieval Wales*, 52.
[390] Davies, *Llandaff Charters* (and cf. *eadem*, 'Latin charter-tradition'); *Llandaff Episcopal Acta*, xxxii–xliv; *St Davids Episcopal Acta*, 14–27. See also Griffiths, 'Authors of urban records'.
[391] Davies, 'Grant by David'; *idem*, 'Grant by Llewelyn'; Williams-Jones, 'Llywelyn's charter to Cymer', 49–54; Smith, 'Dower', 349–53; Smith, 'Land endowments', 153–4; Crouch, 'Earliest original charter'; Pryce, 'Church of Trefeglwys', 25–32; *Ystrad Marchell Charters*, 104–11. For an important recent palaeographical study see Patterson, *Scriptorium of Margam*.
[392] Insley, 'From *rex Wallie*'.

TYPES OF DOCUMENTS AND THEIR TRANSMISSION

Of the 618 documents contained in this edition, 444 (71.8 per cent) survive as texts, while the remaining 174 (28.2 per cent) are known only from mentions in other sources.[393] Six of the 441 texts are spurious charters, and the authenticity of a further four charters and two letters is dubious.[394] The remaining 432 authentic texts comprise 198 charters, 67 letters patent,[395] 106 letters,[396] 35 agreements,[397] 9 petitions, 6 sets of *gravamina* and 2 related texts (all sent to Archbishop Pecham), 7 records of dispute settlements and 2 memoranda. Of these 432 texts, 177 (about 41 per cent) are extant as originals. The distribution of the corpus by type is further illustrated in Tables 1–3.[398]

These figures conceal considerable variations between the different Welsh kingdoms and lordships with respect to both numbers and types of documents. Tables 4–6 illustrate some of these variations with reference to the territories by which documents are grouped in the present work. Admittedly, such a territorial division is to some extent arbitrary and open to emendation. In particular, the appearance of Powys as a single unit is arguably misleading in that no ruler after Madog ap Maredudd (d. 1160) exercised authority over the whole of the kingdom, which fragmented into several smaller territories. Nor do the figures differentiate between individual rulers within each territory, combining, for example, documents for powerful princes of Gwynedd such as Llywelyn ap Iorwerth and Llywelyn ap Gruffudd with members of the dynasty whose authority was restricted to certain areas within Gwynedd. Nevertheless, crude though it is, the territorial distribution set out here serves to highlight some important characteristics of the corpus of documents.

The pattern that emerges from these tables is in part a reflection of the differing size and political importance of the various territories. Thus, it is hardly surprising that almost half the documents derive from Gwynedd, the dominant power in native Wales for much of the twelfth and thirteenth centuries, or, conversely, that minor polities such as Cedewain and Senghennydd are each represented by only small numbers of acts. A more important deter-

---

[393] Admittedly the number of lost documents known from mentions could be slightly greater than the figures given here suggest: cf. nos 36–7, 577 and p. 25, n. 204 above. If so, however, this would not substantially affect the present analysis.

[394] Spurious: nos 179, 218–19, 497–8, 510. Dubious: nos 82, 192, 220, 256, 541, 555.

[395] Although letters patent are neither uniform in their diplomatic nor always easy to distinguish from charters, they contain sufficient distinctive features in common to merit classification as a distinct category: see below, pp. 59, 65.

[396] Namely letters with a special address sent to one or more named individuals.

[397] Agreements extant in ratifications issued by Welsh rulers (e.g. nos 300–1, 361, 402) are classified as letters patent. The category of agreement comprises documents, often described by the term *conventio* or using parts of the verb *convenire*, drawn up between a ruler and another party in which the parties are referred to in the third person (e.g. nos 81, 252, 284, 291, 358, 375, 551), records of arbitration between a ruler and another party issued by ecclesiastics (e.g. nos 43, 52, 339, 363) and also agreements with English kings or others extant only in letters patent issued by the other party (e.g. nos 221, 266, 328, 576).

[398] Although the category of 'original' is not strictly applicable to petitions or to the two memoranda (nos 398–9) – documents lacking formal diplomatic structure or evidence of validation through sealing – included under 'Other' in the following tables, they have been classified as such here on the assumption that the surviving copies were those sent by the ruler concerned. The other originals under 'Other' consist of records of judgements, two of them issued jointly with ecclesiastics (nos 16, 17, 181, 230).

Table 1 Types of documents

	Charters	Letters patent	Letters	Agreements	Petitions	Other	*Total*
Originals	87	6	67	3	8	6	177
Copies	110	62	39	32	1	11	255
Spuria	6	–	–	–	–	–	6
Dubia	4	–	2	–	–	–	6
Deperdita	104	12	41	6	11	–	174
Total	311	80	149	41	20	17	**618**

Table 2 Percentage of each type of document in the corpus of 618 acts

Charters	Letters patent	Letters	Agreements	Petitions	Other
50.5%	12.8%	24.1%	6.6%	3.2%	2.8%

Table 3 Percentage of each type of document in the corpus of 432 acts extant as authentic texts

Charters	Letters patent	Letters	Agreements	Petitions	Other
45.9%	15.5%	24.5%	8.1%	2.1%	3.9%

Table 4 Total numbers of acts, including spuria, dubia and mentions

	Charters	Letters patent	Letters	Agreements	Petitions	Other	*Total*
Arwystli	13	–	–	–	–	–	13
Cedewain	3	3	–	–	–	2	8
Deheubarth	46	17	6	6	3	3	81
Elfael and Maelienydd	8	7	–	–	1	–	16
Glamorgan	65	5	1	–	–	1	72
Gwynedd	65	32	131	25	10	8	271
Gwynllŵg	17	1	–	–	–	1	19
Powys	92	14	11	10	6	2	135
Senghennydd	2	1	–	–	–	–	3

Table 5 Total numbers of acts extant as authentic texts (numbers of originals in brackets)

	Charters	Letters patent	Letters	Agreements	Petitions	Other	*Total*
Arwystli	12 (5)	–	–	–	–	–	12 (5)
Cedewain	1 (1)	2	–	–	–	2 (2)	5 (3)
Deheubarth	13 (1)	13	4 (1)	6	3 (2)	3	42 (4)
Elfael and Maelienydd	2 (2)	7	–	–	–	–	9 (2)
Glamorgan	56 (47)	5 (5)	1 (1)	–	–	1 (1)	63 (54)
Gwynedd	43 (5)	30 (1)	93 (58)	23 (1)	1 (1)	8 (3)	198 (69)
Gwynllŵg	13 (2)	1	–	–	–	1	15 (2)
Powys	56 (24)	9	8 (7)	6 (2)	5 (5)	2	86 (38)
Senghennydd	1	1	–	–	–	–	2

Table 6 Percentage of corpus of acts extant from each territory

	Total of 618 documents	*Total of 432 authentic texts*
Arwystli	2.1%	2.8%
Cedewain	1.3%	1.2%
Deheubarth	13.1%	9.7%
Elfael and		
Maelienydd	2.6%	2.1%
Glamorgan	11.6%	14.6%
Gwynedd	43.7%	45.8%
Gwynllŵg	3.1%	3.5%
Powys	22.0%	19.9%
Senghennydd	0.5%	0.4%

Table 7 Acts extant in sources now in The National Archives: Public Record Office

	Number of texts	*Percentage of number of texts for each territory*
Arwystli (12)	–	0%
Cedewain (5)	2	40.4%
Deheubarth (43)	34	79.0%
Elfael and		
Maelienydd (9)	6	66.7%
Glamorgan (64)	–	0%
Gwynedd (203)	137	68.5%
Gwynllŵg (15)	8	53.8%
Powys (91)	37	40.7%
Senghennydd (2)	–	0%
Totals (444)	224	50.5% overall

Note: the total number of extant texts (including those of spurious or dubious authenticity) from each territory is given in brackets.

minant of the numbers and types of documents extant or known from each territory, however, is the nature of archival survival. Of course, to a significant extent both factors are interrelated. In particular, the attempts by rulers of Gwynedd to secure recognition of their paramount position in native Wales from the king of England brought them into extensive diplomatic relations with the crown not matched by other Welsh rulers, resulting in the preservation of both originals and copies of their letters and other communications among the royal archives. Almost 70 per cent of all extant texts issued by rulers of Gwynedd are preserved only in the royal archives now held in The National Archives: Public Record Office. Yet the importance of those archives in the transmission of Welsh rulers' acts goes well beyond both Gwynedd and letters or agreements concerning Anglo-Welsh relations. As Table 7 shows, just over half of the 444 texts published in this edition are extant only in sources deriving from the chancery, exchequer and other departments of English government. The proportion is even higher with respect to documents known only from mentions in other sources (Table 8).

The Edwardian conquest was a major factor in ensuring the preservation of Welsh acts

Table 8 Acts known only from mentions in sources (including documents published in this edition) now in The National Archives: Public Record Office

	Number of acts	Percentage of total number of references
Arwystli (1)	–	0%
Cedewain (3)	3	100%
Deheubarth (38)	28	73.7%
Elfael and Maelienydd (7)	7	100%
Glamorgan (8)	3	37.5%
Gwynedd (68)	58	85.3%
Gwynllŵg (4)	2	50%
Powys (44)	39	88.7%
Senghennydd (1)	–	0%
Totals (174)	140	80.5% overall

Note: the total number of documents known from mentions from each territory is given in brackets.

in English royal archives. Welsh documents covering the period 1217–92, mostly preserved in the exchequer in two receptacles, one containing *littere Wallie*, the other *scripta Wallie*, were copied *c*.1292 into the register known as Liber A, the earliest source for 64 of the texts published here.[399] In addition, many Welsh rulers' charters for religious houses, both texts and mentions, are known only from royal inspeximuses issued after the conquest. These are particularly important for the transmission of such charters issued by rulers of Deheubarth.[400] Most religious houses which had received grants from native rulers secured confirmations of these by the crown over the four decades from 1285 to 1324, and many obtained further inspeximuses from later kings.[401] That there was no general move by Edward I immediately after the conquest to issue confirmations, let alone new charters re-granting lands, shows that, in contrast to some of the Black Prince's officials in 1348,[402] the king accepted the validity of grants by native rulers. The contexts in which inspeximuses were obtained would repay further investigation. Some, at least, are probably explicable in terms of specific opportunities and perceived threats. For example, it is likely that the Augustinians of Ynys Lannog Priory took advantage of the presence of Edward I in May 1295 at nearby Llan-faes, his headquarters during the final phases of the campaign against the revolt of Madog ap Llywelyn, to seek royal confirmation of their charters in a period

[399] Texts of a further 15 acts extant in earlier sources are also copied in Liber A. For the compilation and sources of Liber A see *LW*, xxvii–xxxiii; Smith, *Llywelyn*, 324–5.
[400] Nos 25–9, 33–5, 41, 47, 49–50, 55, 61–3, 68, 82, 90–1.
[401] The earliest royal inspeximuses were as follows: Strata Florida (27 May 1285); Basingwerk (12 June 1285); Goldcliff (1 July 1290); Valle Crucis (24 April 1295); Ynys Lannog (4 May 1295); Dolgynwal (10 December 1316); Strata Marcella (12 March 1322); Talley (24 March 1324); Cymer (26 March 1324); Aberconwy (24 March 1332); Combermere (12 January 1331); Chertsey (Cardigan) (1 July 1349). In addition, Henry II confirmed one of the Lord Rhys's charters for Strata Florida (no. 25) and John included grants by Welsh rulers in his confirmations for Neath (6 January 1208), Cwm-hir (27 December 1214) and Whitland (27 December 1214).
[402] See Usher, 'Black Prince's *quo warranto*'.

of insecurity, while Edward II issued his inspeximus for Strata Marcella in March 1322 during the temporary royal custody of the barony of Powys following the capture and imprisonment of its lord, John Charlton I, the previous January.[403]

The importance of English archives in the preservation of Welsh rulers' acts is all the greater when, in addition to the departments of royal government, one takes into account copies of documents in sources such as ecclesiastical and lay cartularies (notably the Haughmond and Mortimer cartularies),[404] the *Chronica Majora* of Matthew Paris[405] and the register of Archbishop Pecham[406] as well as originals deriving from monastic and lay archives.[407] Very few acts derive from continental sources, though three letters of Owain Gwynedd are extant only in a late twelfth-century letter collection from Saint-Victor, Paris now held in the Vatican Library and a letter from Llywelyn ap Iorwerth to Philip Augustus remains in the Archives Nationales in Paris.[408]

Only a minority of texts of acts derive from archives which have survived in Wales. In part, this is explicable by unfavourable political circumstances. The contested and territorially fluctuating authority exercised by Welsh dynasties was probably not conducive to the establishment and maintenance of archives, while the eventual extinction of native rule caused a crucial break in the continuity of the archives that were kept.[409] Consequently, such archives – emanating mainly from Gwynedd – have been preserved only to the extent that they were of interest to Edward I's officials after the conquest.[410] An additional factor, however, is the limited number of archives surviving from religious houses in Wales. Two monastic archives are of great importance. By far the largest is that of Margam Abbey in Glamorgan, whose originals, together with copies on the abbey's rolls, are the source of all the extant texts of acts issued by the rulers of Glamorgan and Senghennydd.[411] In addition, 35 original charters survive from Strata Marcella from the century or so after the abbey's foundation *c*.1170, of which 28 were issued by Welsh rulers, especially Gwenwynwyn ab Owain Cyfeiliog (d. 1216) of southern Powys.[412] Although comparison with Edward II's

---

[403] Cf. Walker, 'Welsh war of 1294–5', xl; Morgan, 'Barony of Powys', 25–6. Charlton was restored to his lands later in 1322 and by the end of the decade sought to replace the Welsh community at Strata Marcella with English monks, and to have it transferred from its mother house of Whitland to Buildwas Abbey: *Ystrad Marchell Charters*, 31–3. Valle Crucis also obtained an inspeximus from Edward I at Llan-faes, 24 April 1295; whether this was related to the revolt of Madog is unclear. See also Williams-Jones, 'Llywelyn's charter to Cymer', 48–9, for the background to Edward II's inspeximus for Cymer in 1324 and, for the possible circumstances that led the monks of Aberconwy and Combermere to produce spurious charters for confirmation by Edward III, see notes to nos 218 and 497.

[404] Haughmond Cartulary: nos 1–2, 197–205, 207–8, 225–7, 258, 289, 480, 546. Mortimer Cartulary: nos 244, 259, 317, 424.

[405] Nos 111, 284, 300.

[406] Nos 77, 101–2, 428–31, 454–5, 538.

[407] Nos 22, 226, 471, 582–5, 597.

[408] Nos 193–4, 196, 235. Madog ap Maelgwn's charter for Cwm-hir appears to have been acquired by the Bibliothèque Nationale in Paris only *c*.1886: Tibbot, 'Abbey Cwmhir relic abroad', 67.

[409] One analogy is provided by episcopal archives, which were more likely to suffer loss and destruction than those of more stable and powerful governments during vacancies when authority was uncertain or divided: cf. Cheney, *English Bishops' Chanceries*, 99.

[410] See below, p. 58.

[411] For the Margam charters see Patterson, *Scriptorium of Margam*.

[412] Nos 8–12, 16–17, 231, 282, 482–3, 487–8, 499, 504, 508, 544–5, 548, 551, 553, 556, 563, 569, 575, 578, 581; *Ystrad Marchell Charters*, nos 25, 55, 70, 72, 83, 86.

Table 9 Acts issued by rulers of Gwynedd, 1120–1283

	Total	Charters	Letters patent	Letters	Other	Average annual output
1120–c.1200	18	13	–	5	–	0.2
Llywelyn ap Iorwerth c.1194–1240	51	18	5	25	3	1.1
Dafydd ap Llywelyn 1240–6	24	7	6	10	1	4.0
Llywelyn ap Gruffudd 1246–82	107	10	14	68	15	2.9

Note: the figures given are for the total numbers of known acts, both texts and documents known only from mentions in other sources. Acts of spurious or dubious authenticity are omitted. The figures for 1120–c.1200 exclude acts of Llywelyn ap Iorwerth whose opening dating limits have been assigned to the 1190s. Acts issued jointly by the brothers Owain ap Gruffudd and Llywelyn ap Gruffudd are omitted. Agreements are included under 'Other' only if these contain evidence of having been validated by the ruler through sealing.

inspeximus for the abbey in 1322 and other sources suggests that at least a further 31 original charters by native rulers have been lost,[413] the granting of the inspeximus was clearly not in itself inimical to the survival of the originals it confirmed. Nevertheless, losses of native rulers' charters for Welsh religious houses have been extensive: no originals are extant from either of the Cistercian houses of Gwynedd, Aberconwy and Cymer, from Whitland and Strata Florida in Deheubarth or from Llantarnam in the territory ruled by the dynasty of Gwynllŵg. The same is true of Basingwerk and Neath, originally Savigniac foundations, as well as of the Lord Rhys's Premonstratensian foundation of Talley and of the Augustinian priories of Ynys Lannog, Bardsey and Beddgelert in Gwynedd. Cwm-hir and Valle Crucis are each represented by two originals, and only one is extant for the nunnery of Llanllugan in Cedewain.[414] Nor have cartularies survived from Welsh houses patronized by native rulers, although the enrolled copies made by Margam in the thirteenth century served a similar purpose and the late fifteenth-century cartulary of Haughmond Abbey in Shropshire contains copies of Welsh rulers' charters concerning that house's churches of Trefeglwys in Arwystli and Nefyn in Llŷn.[415]

The ways in which Welsh rulers' acts have been transmitted are clearly relevant to any assessment of the extent to which the surviving corpus is representative of the numbers and types of documents originally produced. Let us begin by considering the question of output. Here attention will be focused on acts issued by rulers of Gwynedd, as these form the largest single collection of documents in this edition, accounting for over 40 per cent of the total (see Table 6). The analysis includes all known twelfth-century acts issued by

---

[413] Nos 5–7, 13, 61, 69, 484–5, 490–1, 542–3, 552, 554, 557–62, 564–8, 570–4, 580.
[414] Nos 108, 113, 496, 513, 18.
[415] For the enrolment of charters at Margam see Patterson, *Scriptorium of Margam*, 51–3. Neath, Strata Florida and Whitland kept registers of their property which are no longer extant: see no. 120; Williams, *Welsh Cistercians*, 219–20.

Table 10 Acts of Llywelyn ap Gruffudd

	Total	Charters	Letters patent	Letters	Other	Average annual output
1246–54	5	4	–	–	1	0.6
1255–67	38	2	7	24	5	2.9
1268–76	31	2	1	24	4	3.4
1277–82	33	2	6	20	5	5.5

members of the dynasty but its coverage of the thirteenth century is restricted to the three most dominant princes.

The figures in these tables necessarily give only a general impression, in part because, in Table 9, they smooth out highs and lows in production over a particular reign, but also because they refer only to documents which have happened to survive or be mentioned in other sources. Even so, it is clear that the number of known acts, though increasing over the period, is low by comparison with those of English magnates, let alone English kings. For example, there survive 400 charters issued between 1107 and 1191 by the family of Mowbray, 200 (plus a further 88 known from references) by the earls and countesses of Gloucester from the early twelfth century to 1217, and 469 by the earls of Chester c.1071–1237.[416] By Henry II's reign the annual output of extant royal letters exceeds 100 a year.[417] In Scotland, almost 600 acts are known, over 500 of them extant as texts, for William the Lion (1165–1214), making an average output of about twelve a year.[418] Even in the final years of Llywelyn ap Gruffudd's rule, average annual output totalled only 5.5. On the other hand, the number of Welsh rulers' acts compares favourably with those issued by Welsh bishops, although admittedly this is not strictly to compare like with like. As Julia Barrow has shown, thirteenth-century bishops of St Davids (1200–80) managed an output of between one and two acts a year, and the output at Llandaff was even lower, whereas by the early thirteenth century English sees (excluding Canterbury) averaged between six and fourteen acts a year, a rate of output which increased further thereafter.[419]

Yet, if the known annual average output of acts was only 5.5 in 1277–82, this was still five times the average output of Llywelyn ap Iorwerth and almost thirty times the average output for 1120–c.1200. That the number of acts increased over this period is hardly surprising: throughout western Europe the numbers of charters and letters produced and preserved in the twelfth and thirteenth centuries grew dramatically, as monasteries receiving endowments became more numerous and royal, seignorial and ecclesiastical administrations became more bureaucratic.[420] In a modest way, Wales, including Gwynedd, participated in these wider trends. Yet was the contrast between the twelfth and thirteenth centuries as stark as the figures presented here suggest? It is certainly the case that losses of twelfth-century charters and letters may have been significantly higher than those of thirteenth-century acts. This is suggested by the fact that none of the twelfth-century

[416] *Charters of the Honour of Mowbray*, ed. Greenway; *EGC*; *Chester Charters*; cf. Insley, 'From *rex Wallie*', 182.
[417] Clanchy, *From Memory*, 60, Fig. 1.
[418] *Acts of William I*, ed. Barrow.
[419] *St Davids Episcopal Acta*, 14–16.
[420] See, for example, Clanchy, *From Memory*, 57–78.

Table 11 The foundation of Cistercian houses in Wales known to have received charters from Welsh rulers

	Date of foundation	Number of charters received in the names of Welsh rulers
Aberconwy (Gwynedd Uwch Conwy)	1186	2
Basingwerk (S) (Gwynedd Is Conwy)	1131	12
Cwm-hir (Maelienydd)	1143(?) & 1176	10
Cymer (Meirionnydd)	1198 × 1199	2
Llanllugan (Cedewain)	c.1216 × 1217(?)	1
Margam (Glamorgan)	1147	61
Neath (S) (Glamorgan)	1130	4
Strata Florida (Ceredigion)	1164	14
Strata Marcella (Powys Wenwynwyn)	c.1170	58
Valle Crucis (Powys Fadog)	1200 × 1201	10
Whitland (Dyfed)	1140	5

Note: (S) denotes a house founded as a Savigniac abbey. The figures in the final column include both texts and mentions but exclude spuria and dubia.

Gwynedd acts before the reign of Llywelyn ap Iorwerth derives from English royal archives, whereas the enrolment of documents in the royal chancery, inaugurated in John's reign, helped to preserve the texts of a substantial proportion of thirteenth-century charters and letters. Nevertheless, even if twelfth-century acts stood a slimmer chance of survival than those of the thirteenth century, there are strong grounds for supposing that both ecclesiastical and political changes led to the production of a greater number and range of documents from c.1200 onwards.

To begin with ecclesiastical changes, all surviving charters issued by princes of Gwynedd in favour of religious houses recorded grants to reformed orders of continental origin, principally the Augustinians or Cistercians, whose foundations in Wales opened a new chapter in the ecclesiastical history of the country. The same is generally true of other Welsh rulers, although traditional Benedictine houses were also patronized by rulers of Deheubarth and Gwynllŵg.[421] The spread of the Cistercians in *pura Wallia* was especially significant. About 59 per cent of all the charters in this edition (that is, 185 out of 312) are in favour of Welsh Cistercian houses.[422] Moreover, most of the houses patronized by Welsh rulers were founded in the later twelfth or early thirteenth centuries (Table 11). True, Neath, originally a Savigniac foundation, received some grants from the dynasty of Iestyn ap Gwrgant in Glamorgan in the second quarter of the twelfth century.[423] On the other hand, that dynasty's patronage of Margam seems to have taken off only about four decades after the abbey's foundation in 1147, in the wake of Morgan ap Caradog's territorial expansion in the rising that followed the death of William, earl of Gloucester and lord of Glamorgan,

---

[421] Nos 22, 463–72, 474.
[422] These figures include both texts and mentions. The percentage is the same if charters of spurious or dubious authenticity – 2 for Aberconwy, 1 for Margam and 5 for Strata Marcella – are excluded from the samples, leaving 179 out of a total of 302.
[423] Nos 119–20.

in November 1183 and the grant to Morgan of the fee of Newcastle by Prince John in 1189.[424] Likewise Welsh rulers are not known to have patronized Whitland or Basingwerk before the last two decades of the twelfth century, although the former house may have begun to receive patronage from the Lord Rhys in the mid-1160s.[425]

As regards political changes, exposure to the increasingly bureaucratic modes of government in England from John's reign almost certainly contributed to a significant increase in the numbers of documents, especially letters, issued by Welsh rulers, particularly those of Gwynedd. Of course, the danger of arguing from silence is even greater when it comes to written communications between Welsh rulers and English kings than it is with regard to charters issued for churches. Whereas the vast majority of letters from thirteenth-century princes of Gwynedd to the king have been preserved either as originals or copies in the royal archives, the six surviving twelfth-century letters have been transmitted to us in literary and historical texts: the earliest, sent in 1120 from Gruffudd ap Cynan to Archbishop Ralph of Canterbury, in Eadmer's *Historia Novorum*, four of Owain Gwynedd's in letter collections, the fifth (admittedly of dubious authenticity) in Gerald of Wales's *De Invectionibus*.[426] Since Gruffudd ap Cynan and his son Owain Gwynedd wrote to the archbishop of Canterbury, and Owain also to Louis VII of France, it is reasonable to assume that they sent letters to English kings as well.

None the less, if written communications between the rulers of Gwynedd and the English crown were probably nothing new in 1200, the character of such communications underwent significant changes in the thirteenth century. In particular, attempts were made to define the princes' relations with the English king in written agreements to a degree not seen before. The impetus for these developments came from the crown. As Rees Davies has argued with reference to John and Henry III, 'the rule of the written word was to make overlordship more precise, more vertebrate, more enduring'.[427] Of course, it is possible that texts have been lost of similar agreements made in the twelfth century. Chronicle accounts refer to Welsh rulers swearing fealty to Henry II and Richard I, as well as to doing homage, and Roger of Howden even refers to Welsh rulers entering into a peace agreement (*foedus pacis*) with Richard I at Worcester in 1189.[428] It is probably significant, however, that none of these accounts mentions, let alone preserves the text of, a written statement of the obligations incurred; by contrast, Howden preserved texts of Henry II's treaties with William the Lion of Scotland at Falaise in 1174 and with Ruadrí Ua Conchobair (Rory O'Connor) of Connacht at Windsor in 1175.[429] The earliest surviving written agreement between an English king and a Welsh ruler is the peace concluded by Llywelyn ap Iorwerth with John's representatives on 11 July 1201.[430] Further agreements followed in the thirteenth century, and, together with diplomatic correspondence, witness to the importance attached to written communications in negotiating Anglo-Welsh relations.

In addition, both Llywelyn ap Iorwerth and especially Llywelyn ap Gruffudd sought to

---

[424] See above, p. 20.
[425] Nos 29, 47, 213, 216, 492–5.
[426] Nos 191–6.
[427] Davies, *Domination and Conquest*, 94–6; quotation at 96.
[428] *Gesta*, ed. Stubbs, ii. 87–8.
[429] *Anglo-Scottish Relations*, ed. Stones, 1–5 (Roger may have been a witness); Flanagan, *Irish Society*, 312–13.
[430] No. 221.

reinforce their authority over other Welsh lords by documentary means. Thus, Gwenwynwyn ab Owain of southern Powys is reported to have given Llywelyn ap Iorwerth documents setting out the terms of his confederacy with the prince,[431] while the exchequer Liber A contains texts of twelve letters, dating between 1256 and 1278, in which the senders, Welsh lords outside Gwynedd, undertook to stand as sureties for the fealty (and in some instances also the homage) to Llywelyn ap Gruffudd of a named person or persons.[432] Although it could be argued that the crucial guarantee of political loyalty in these latter cases was suretyship, an institution deeply embedded in Welsh society whose validity depended on commitments made orally and visually, it is significant that Llywelyn sought to secure these commitments further by formalizing them in writing.

It is likely, then, that there was a real increase in the numbers of charters issued by Welsh rulers for religious houses from the later twelfth century onwards and also, especially in Gwynedd during the thirteenth century, in the numbers of letters sent to English kings and their officials. By contrast, it is doubtful whether the same is true of acts issued in favour of the laity in Wales. First, even if grants to Marcher lords and other members of a ruling dynasty (such as wives or sons) are included, charters for lay beneficiaries in Wales are few: for example, there survive only three from Llywelyn ap Iorwerth,[433] five from Llywelyn ap Gruffudd[434] and four from Gruffudd ap Gwenwynwyn.[435] Some of these grants transferred, or confirmed the transfer of, new land to the recipient, and several explicitly exempted the recipient from various services to the prince. In one case, Llywelyn ap Iorwerth's confirmation of the purchase of lands by his seneschal Ednyfed Fychan in 1230, it is stated that the prince has allowed Ednyfed and his heirs to keep the document (strictly a letter patent rather than a charter), implying that it could be used as evidence in the future.[436] We know, from post-conquest evidence, that Llywelyn made a number of grants to Ednyfed and his family of lands on privileged tenurial terms, yet the extents which refer to these grants nowhere explicitly refer to charters.[437] In any case, such grants were themselves exceptional (and far fewer by Llywelyn ap Gruffudd's time, probably because the prince could less easily afford to dispose of his land in this way), and so, even if they were normally made in writing, this would not imply large-scale charter production for laymen. Nor is there anything to suggest that free proprietors required written confirmation from the prince of their right to inherited patrimonial land.[438] In addition, although by the thirteenth century Welsh rulers fostered the development of towns, this edition contains only one charter granting privileges to an urban community, namely that issued by Gruffudd ap Gwenwynwyn for Welshpool.[439]

---

[431] No. 577.
[432] Nos 66, 72, 79–80, 86–8, 100, 106–7, 525, 612.
[433] Nos 239, 259–60.
[434] Nos 317–18, 322, 423–4.
[435] Nos 593, 602, 606–7. Other examples are nos 15, 69, 71, 78, 84, 96, 124, 126, 441, 457, 473, 477, 515–16, 526, 531, 610.
[436] No. 260.
[437] *Rec. Caern.*, 19, 33; *Survey of the Honour of Denbigh*, 127–8, 203, 228.
[438] Cf. Jenkins, 'Lawyer looks at Welsh land law'; Stephenson, *Governance*, 190–1.
[439] No. 593. Cf. Griffiths, 'Authors of urban records', esp. 159–60. It should also be noted that in the post-conquest period the burgesses of Llan-faes claimed to hold their privileges by virtue of charters granted by the native princes: ibid., 163, n. 16, citing *CAP*, 82–3 (text of petition printed in Lewis, *Mediaeval Boroughs*, 295).

Second, it is difficult to assess the extent to which business documents were produced for administrative purposes within Welsh kingdoms or for communications between Welsh rulers. True, as already mentioned, letters from Welsh lords to Llywelyn ap Gruffudd were copied in Liber A, as were several agreements between Llywelyn and other Welsh rulers.[440] However, the pattern of archival transmission may mean that documents of interest to the English crown, or presented to it for confirmation, stood a much greater chance of being preserved than those produced for internal administrative needs.[441] Take mandates from princes to officials in Wales. Only two of these survive in the names of thirteenth-century princes, one from Dafydd ap Llywelyn to the bailiffs of Brecon, the other from Llywelyn ap Gruffudd to the bailiffs of Perfeddwlad; significantly both are extant in early modern copies ultimately derived from copies made by the churches which the bailiffs were ordered to protect, namely Leominster Priory and the see of St Asaph.[442] On the whole, however, such documents – like most administrative writs in twelfth-century England – probably stood little chance of being preserved as their importance was essentially ephemeral.[443] It is therefore reasonable to assume that more were produced than now exist; indeed there are occasional references to other examples. Thus, in 1244 Dafydd ap Llywelyn 'sent messengers and letters to summon to him all the princes of Wales', while in 1267 × 1276 the bailiff of Builth acknowledged the receipt of a mandate from Llywelyn ap Gruffudd addressed to him and other bailiffs in the middle March.[444] Likewise, the writing of financial accounts is likely to have been more common, by the later years of Llywelyn ap Gruffudd at least, than is suggested by the exiguous surviving evidence for them, namely an account rendered by the castellan of the prince's new castle of Dolforwyn in 1274, preserved in the exchequer Liber A.[445]

To sum up the discussion so far, the pattern of textual transmission may well mean that the known corpus of acts provides a distorted picture of what originally existed, not only on account of inevitable losses but also because certain categories of documents may be under-represented, especially those of ephemeral importance written for internal administrative purposes. The difficulty remains, however, of assessing how far that picture is distorted. On the basis of the sample assembled here, it has been suggested that, even allowing for losses, the output of documents was low, and owed much to demands by ecclesiastics and English kings. The following diplomatic analysis will bring further evidence to bear on these issues, as the form of the extant texts reveals a great deal about the nature and extent of the uses Welsh rulers made of documentary modes.

---

[440] For the agreements see nos 316, 323, 347, 358 and cf. no. 368.
[441] Smith, *Llywelyn*, 325, comments that the sample of internal administrative documents from Llywelyn ap Gruffudd's reign is small, making it difficult to know how far the prince had developed routine bureaucratic procedures.
[442] Nos 307, 369.
[443] Cf. Clanchy, *From Memory*, 58, 151.
[444] *BT, RBH*, 238–9; no. 364. Maredudd ap Rhys's obligation in 1261 to provide military service 'at the order' (*ad mandatum*) of Llywelyn ap Gruffudd could presuppose the sending of a written mandate: no. 347, c. iv.
[445] *LW*, 23–4; cf. Stephenson, *Governance*, 22–4; Davies, *Conquest*, 264.

GWYNEDD

Internal features
Charters and letters patent

Charters are grouped together here with letters patent, extant from 1218 onwards, on account of the basic similarities in their form and, to a significant extent, their formulae. In addition, variations in the terminology used to describe acts that were sealed patent suggest that the distinction between *carte* and *littere patentes* was less well developed in Gwynedd than in the royal chancery of thirteenth-century England.[446] Thus acts that otherwise conform in their diplomatic and function to charters are occasionally termed *littere patentes*,[447] while documents classified here as letters patent are usually referred to simply by the terms *littere* and/or *scriptum* (though *instrumentum* is also used in no. 361), and two even refer to themselves by the term *carta*.[448] At the same time, a broad distinction is discernible between these two types of act. Letters patent differ from charters not only with respect to their diplomatic, especially in the formulae of their corroboration clauses and also in the absence, mostly, of witness lists, but also with respect to their purpose.[449] Whereas charters record grants of property and rights, normally in perpetuity, letters patent usually announce either the acceptance of obligations, particularly in agreements with the English crown, or grants of limited duration such as safe conducts or the appointment of diplomatic envoys. They thus bear a resemblance to letters patent issued by the English royal chancery.[450] The only exceptions are Llywelyn ap Iorwerth's grant of Norton and Knighton to Ralph Mortimer and the same prince's confirmation of the purchase of land at Rhos Fynaich by Ednyfed Fychan, which, since it was explicitly issued as a title deed for the purchaser, is arguably a charter, notwithstanding the description of it in the corroboration clause as being *scripto ac patenti*.[451]

The earliest extant letters patent from Gwynedd were three issued by Llywelyn ap Iorwerth at Worcester in March 1218 that announced various terms of the peace settlement with the regency government of Henry III, and the majority of other examples likewise declared obligations undertaken by the prince of Gwynedd with respect to the English crown. It may be that the use of letters patent in Gwynedd originated in the context of Anglo-Welsh diplomacy and that royal example in England was a crucial stimulus for the development of this class of document, whose use was subsequently extended to political relations both within Gwynedd and between it and other Welsh principalities; agreements

---

[446] Cf. Chaplais, *English Royal Documents*, 4, 19–20. The attitude towards these documents may have been more similar, rather, to that in the royal exchequer of the late 1170s reflected in the phrase *cum cartis et aliis scriptis patentibus* in *Dialogus de Scaccario*, ed. Johnson, 31. Compare also the reference to the king's issuing of a 'patent seal' in the Iorwerth Redaction's version of the laws of court: below, p. 135.

[447] Nos 286, 289.

[448] Nos 254, 456. Although the endorsement of no. 304 refers to the document as *carta*, the terms used in the text are *littere* and *scriptum*.

[449] Witness lists do occur, however, in nos 254 (termed a *carta*), 260, 304, 309 (and also no. 211); the corroboration clause of no. 361 names those who consented to the agreement.

[450] Cf. Chaplais, *English Royal Documents*, 19, and also *Vocabulaire*, ed. Ortí, 98. The terminology of the latter work is generally followed in the present discussion both for types of acts and for the constituent parts of documents' diplomatic.

[451] Nos 259–60.

in this form with rulers of Deheubarth survive from 1251 and 1258, as do statements of obligations to Llywelyn ap Gruffudd issued by rulers of Powys Fadog and Deheubarth from 1256, 1258 and 1260.[452] However, since the surviving sample of documents is probably skewed in favour of those relating to the English crown, this impression may be misleading. Moreover, as the following analysis will show, the diplomatic of most letters patent from thirteenth-century Gwynedd shows little evidence of direct borrowing from those issued by English kings, but seems to be indebted rather to ecclesiastical models.

The twelfth century

All but one of the twelve texts of charters issued in the twelfth century by members of the Gwynedd dynasty other than Llywelyn ap Iorwerth record grants in favour of Haughmond Abbey.[453] The exception is Gruffudd ap Cynan's charter for Aberconwy in 1190 × 1199.[454] Six of these open with an address (*inscriptio*). This is general in three cases: *Universis sancte matris ecclesie filiis et fidelibus*,[455] *Omnibus sancte Dei ecclesie filiis tam presentibus quam futuris*[456] and *Universis Dei fidelibus tam presentibus quam futuris*.[457] The last formula is adapted in the collective addresses in nos 200 and 202 by inserting *Francis et Anglis* after *fidelibus*, whereas no. 199 has *omnibus hominibus infra parochiam de Neuyn'*. The greeting (*salutatio*) reads *salutem in domino* in four of these charters, *salutem* alone in nos 198–9.[458] The style (*intitulatio*) employed in acts issued by rulers of Gwynedd is considered in a separate section below.

The text in all the charters is written in the first person singular apart from no. 201, issued jointly by Dafydd ab Owain and his wife Emma. The notification (*notificatio*) in seven charters uses forms of *scire* (the verb normally used in English royal charters, followed generally also by baronial charters); forms of *noscere* occur in four, and *manifesto* is used by Dafydd ab Owain in no. 199. It may be significant that six of the seven examples of *scire* occur in charters issued by Dafydd ab Owain, his wife Emma and their son Owain ap Dafydd with respect to grants in Ellesmere; three of these directly mirror English royal practice in their use of *Sciatis me* followed by the dispositive verb(s) in the perfect infinitive.[459] The perfect or perfect infinitive is used for the dispositive verbs in all cases: most charters combine *dare* and *concedere*, though no. 203 has *dedi et quietum clamavi*, both of Owain ap Dafydd's confirmations for Haughmond combine *concedere* and *confirmare* and Gruffudd ap Cynan ab Owain's charter for the same house has *concessi et dedi et hac carta mea confirmavi*.[460] Nine charters have corroboration clauses that refer to the permanence given the grant by the charter and the author's seal. Apart from nos 200 and 202, grants of Stockett to Haughmond by Dafydd ab Owain and Emma respectively whose corroboration clauses are identical, the

---

[452] Nos 66, 85, 316, 329, 525; see also no. 368.
[453] Nos 197–205, 207–8.
[454] No. 206.
[455] No. 197.
[456] No. 198.
[457] No. 205.
[458] On greeting formulae see further Ruelle, '*A tous présents*', and Lanham, '*Salutatio' Formulas*, which shows that the formulae cited here are extremely common.
[459] Nos 200–5. The formula *sciant . . . quod ego* also occurs in Gruffudd ap Cynan's charter for Haughmond in 1195 × 1199 (no. 207).
[460] Nos 204–5, 207.

formulae used vary. For example, Owain ap Dafydd uses two different clauses, one in the present tense, the other in the perfect (as is usual in these clauses), in his confirmations to Haughmond,[461] while the clause in Gruffudd ap Cynan's charter for Aberconwy differs from that of his charter for Haughmond.[462] The variety in the corroboration clauses in charters for Haughmond, which account for eight of the nine examples, suggests that that house did not try to impose uniformity, and makes it difficult to determine how far the wording in any of these cases was drafted by the beneficiary.

Four charters for Haughmond also have injunctive clauses that are clearly indebted to English royal writs, which in turn influenced English private charters and Scottish royal acts.[463] All open with *Quare volo*, followed by (*firmiter*) *precipio*: for example, *Quare volo et firmiter precipio ne quis*,[464] though no. 199 is more elaborate (*Quare volo et super foresfacturam meam vobis omnibus precipio quatinus*, followed by a prohibitive clause, *Prohibeo itaque ne quis*). All twelve charters have witness lists, but only Gruffudd ap Cynan's charter for Aberconwy contains a dating clause, a feature of other charters for Welsh Cistercian houses in this period, namely a place-date followed by the year of incarnation and month.[465]

Llywelyn ap Iorwerth

Of the fifteen texts of charters extant in the name of Llywelyn ap Iorwerth, nos 218–19 in favour of Aberconwy are clearly spurious and no. 256, for the Hospitallers of Dolgynwal, contains some suspicious features that cast doubts on its authenticity. In addition there survive texts of seven letters patent, five of which concern agreements with Henry III.[466]

All but two of Llywelyn ap Iorwerth's authentic charters contain a general address and greeting.[467] The address appears to have been standardized from the mid-1220s, but displays some variation before then. Nos 213 and 216, early charters for Basingwerk, have *omnibus sancte matris ecclesie filiis tam presentibus quam futuris*, a formula elaborated in no. 229, issued for Cymer in 1209, by the addition of *ad quorum notitiam tenor presentium literarum pervenerit*. Three of the four charters for Haughmond have *omnibus/universis* (*Dei/Cristi*) *fidelibus* (*tam presentibus quam futuris presens scriptum inspecturis*), and a similar address occurs in Llywelyn's charter of submission to John in 1211 (*Omnibus Cristi fidelibus presentem cartam inspecturis*).[468] The address in Llywelyn ap Iorwerth's three letters patent at Worcester in 1218 is different again (*Universis tam presentibus quam futuris ad quos*

---

[461] Nos 204–5.

[462] Nos 206–7.

[463] *Transcripts*, ed. Stenton, xxxiii; Stringer, 'Charters of David', 87. Compare, for example, Henry II's charter for Haughmond in 1155 × 1162 (*Quare volo et firmiter precipio quod dicti canonici habeant et teneant bene et in pace, libere et quiete et honorifice omnia predicta imperpetuum*): *Cart. Haugh.*, no. 30 (though this goes on to add a prohibitive clause, *Et prohibeo ne quis dampnum vel molestiam aliquam eis faciat*); see also ibid., nos 23, 151.

[464] No. 198; nos 197 and 203 are similar.

[465] No. 206: *Datum apud Porthaethay' anno ab incarnatione domini millesimo c . . . mense iunii*. For dating clauses in charters for Strata Florida, Aberconwy's mother house, see nos 28, 35, 50, 55, and cf. also *Ystrad Marchell Charters*, 108–9. In this respect the charters for Haughmond resemble private charters in England, which are rarely dated before the late thirteenth century: *Transcripts*, ed. Stenton, xxxii.

[466] Nos 240–2, 254, 259–60, 274.

[467] The exceptions are nos 231, 239 (as well as the spurious nos 218–19).

[468] Nos 225–7, 233.

presens scriptum pervenerit).[469] This resembles some contemporary episcopal acts rather than the general addresses of royal letters patent, which usually included the phrase *omnibus has litteras inspecturis* in the period 1216–20, though *omnibus ad quos presentes littere pervenerint* became most common thereafter.[470] Unfortunately, surviving episcopal acts from Bangor are few, but an act of Bishop Cadwgan (1215–35/6) has *omnibus Cristi fidelibus ad quos presens scriptum pervenerit*, an address also used by Bishops William II (1219–29) and Elias (1230–40) of Llandaff;[471] similar addresses are used by bishops of St Davids in the same period.[472] By contrast, Reiner, bishop of St Asaph (1186–1224) seems to have favoured *universis sancte matris ecclesie filiis tam presentibus quam futuris*,[473] though one of his acts opens with the address *Omnibus Cristi fidelibus presens scriptum visuris vel audituris*.[474] The three authentic charters and two letters patent from 1230 onwards use the address *has litteras visuris vel audituris*.[475] Since each of these documents is for a different beneficiary or recipient, it would appear that its use was controlled by the prince's clerks.

No clear pattern emerges from the greeting used. The most common is *salutem*,[476] followed by *salutem in domino*,[477] with the addition of *eternam* in nos 258–9 (one for Ynys Lannog Priory, the other for Ralph Mortimer). The latter formulae are probably indebted to episcopal or monastic diplomatic.[478] The use of *salutem in Cristo* is restricted to nos 213 and 216, both charters for Basingwerk, and may reflect beneficiary drafting, though earlier charters for the abbey from Owain Brogyntyn have only *salutem*.[479] Likewise *salutem in vero salutari* is confined to two Haughmond charters,[480] and *salutem et pacem* to no. 229 for Cymer; since the latter formula is paralleled in two charters for Cymer's mother house of Cwm-hir, it almost certainly represents diplomatic practice common to both those monasteries.[481]

Llywelyn's charters and letters patent exhibit a movement towards the use of the plural of majesty normal in English (and perhaps to a lesser extent Welsh) episcopal acts by *c.*1180

---

[469] Nos 240–2. A variation on this, namely *Omnibus ad quos presens carta pervenerit*, is used in the prince's instrument of submission to Henry III in 1223 (no. 254).

[470] See, for example, *PR 1216–25*, 3, 34, 145, 225, 235, 243; *Foedera*, I. i. 198; Chaplais, *English Royal Documents*, 19.

[471] *Cart. Haugh.*, no. 793. Cf. *Llandaff Episcopal Acta*, nos 59–60, 62–4, 69–70, 75, 81–2 (some of these open with *Universis*).

[472] *Omnibus*/*Universis sancte matris ecclesie filiis ad quos presens scriptum pervenerit* is common in the acts of Bishops Geoffrey (1203–14) and Iorwerth (1215–29) of St Davids: *St Davids Episcopal Acta*, nos 50–2, 54–5, 58–61, 71, 77, 79, 86–7. Cf. *EEA*, vii. lxxxiii–lxxxiv for similar addresses in early thirteenth-century Hereford episcopal acts.

[473] *Cart. Haugh.*, nos 667, 1111.

[474] Shrewsbury, Shropshire Records and Research Centre, MS 6001/6869, fo. 161r (cd., *Cart. Haugh.*, no. 859).

[475] Nos 258–60, 272, 274. The formula also occurs in no. 256, dated 1225, but of dubious authenticity. The future participles used in this formula are first attested in no. 250 (for Ynys Lannog, 1221): *hoc scriptum visuris vel audituris*.

[476] Nos 213, 227, 233, 241, 254, 274 (and also no. 256).

[477] Nos 240–1, 260, 272.

[478] Cf. *Cart. Haugh.*, nos 615–18, 667, 793; *Ystrad Marchell Charters*, no. 70; nn. 471–2 above.

[479] Nos 492–4.

[480] Nos 225–6; it should be noted that the formula is lacking in the charters of Dafydd ab Owain, Emma and Owain ap Dafydd in respect of Stockett (nos 200, 202, 205). For other examples of the formula see no. 522; *Cart. Haugh.*, nos 27, 1148, App. C, no. ix; Ruelle, '*A tous présents*', 1665.

[481] Nos 108, 113; below, p. 104.

and adopted by the English royal chancery from the coronation of Richard I in 1189.[482] Llywelyn's earliest charters, issued in favour of Basingwerk no later than 1202, use the first person singular.[483] However, the first person plural is used as early as 1205 × 1211 in two Haughmond charters as well as, mostly, in the 1209 charter for Cymer,[484] and in all but one of Llywelyn's letters patent from 1218 and all three authentic charters from 1221 (the same is also true of letters to individuals from 1220 at the latest).[485] Yet there are exceptions: a 1209 confirmation charter for Strata Marcella (an original), together with charters for John in 1211 and Morgan Gam in 1217 and a letter patent (termed *carta*) for Henry III in 1223 have the first person singular.[486] True, each of these instances is possibly explicable in terms of the particular circumstances in which the document was drawn up. In the first case, the usage may reflect drafting by the monks, most of whose Welsh benefactors used the first person singular;[487] the charter for Morgan Gam was quite possibly modelled on a previous document issued by the Braose lord of Gower; while the drafting of the instruments of submission in 1211 and 1223 may have been supervised by royal clerks seeking to diminish Llywelyn's status. Nevertheless, it remains notable that the prince was unable to impose a consistent use of the first person plural in his acts until after 1223.

The text of three charters for religious beneficiaries – Cymer (1209), Ynys Lannog (1221) and the problematic Dolgynwal charter dated 1225 – opens with an arenga or pious preamble, an extremely rare feature among the acts of Welsh rulers.[488] That in the Cymer charter is particularly notable as it proclaims the prince's duty to preserve peace, especially for religious, thereby enunciating an ideal of rulership, whereas the latter two examples are variations on the common theme of the need to ensure that the act will last in perpetuity.[489] The notifications in Llywelyn's charters and letters patent show a marked preference for forms of *noscere* over *scire*.[490] The use of *scire* is restricted to Llywelyn's instrument of submission to King John in 1211, the charter to Morgan Gam in 1217 and one of the three

---

[482] Chaplais, *English Royal Documents*, 13; Cheney, *English Bishops' Chanceries*, 58; *St Davids Episcopal Acta*, 26.

[483] Nos 213, 216. The same is true of the two spurious charters for Aberconwy dated 1199 (nos 218–19).

[484] Nos 225–6, 229; cf. no. 227.

[485] Charters: nos 250, 258, 272 (and also no. 256). Letters: below, p. 71.

[486] Nos 231, 233, 239, 254.

[487] The only exceptions are nos 5 and 8 issued by rulers of Arwystli.

[488] Nos 229, 250, 256. The only other example is no. 544, a charter of Gwenwynwyn for Strata Marcella (1191). The use of the arenga is likewise rare among the charters of the earls of Chester: Hudson, 'Diplomatic and legal aspects', 159. Cf. also *Llandaff Episcopal Acta*, xl; *St Davids Episcopal Acta*, 23; and, more generally, Cheney, *English Bishops' Chanceries*, 72–5; Fichtenau, *Arenga*. It is possible that the inclusion of an arenga formed part of native Welsh diplomatic originating in the pre-Norman period, as several examples occur among the charters preserved in the Book of Llandaff. However, since the preambles in the Llandaff charters are both few and different in form (often referring to the grantor) from the arengas in the present edition, it is unlikely that the latter were influenced by any such Welsh tradition. Cf. Davies, *Llandaff Charters*, 132–3, 142; Insley, 'From *rex Wallie*', 187, n. 33.

[489] The duty of the ruler to protect the Church was a common theme of arengas in Danish royal diplomas (1140–1223), the majority of which, in contrast to the charters of Welsh rulers, included an arenga: Damsholt, 'Kingship', esp. 69–70.

[490] See also below, p. 138 and n. 1065.

letters patent issued at Worcester in 1218.[491] Nearly all the remaining documents use forms of *noscere*: the formula *noverit universitas vestra nos* followed by the dispositive verb(s) in the perfect infinitive is particularly common;[492] there are also three examples of *noveritis me/nos* followed by the perfect infinitive.[493] The only exceptions are the charters for Cymer (1209) and Ynys Lannog (1221), which have *duximus confirmare* and *duximus notificare* respectively.[494]

The dispositive verbs in a majority of charters include *concedere*, combined with *dare*,[495] *confirmare*[496] or *conferre*.[497] The combination of *concedere* and *confirmare* is confined to three confirmations (one for Basingwerk, two for Haughmond), and the occurrence of *confirmare* and, later, *commendare* in no. 229 is consistent with the charter's purpose as a general confirmation of Cymer's lands and rights. However, the confirmation for Haughmond in no. 227 has *dare* alone, as does no. 231, which, though ostensibly a fresh grant, is in fact a confirmation for Strata Marcella,[498] and usage overall is inconsistent, each of the combinations occurring in charters for different beneficiaries issued at different periods of the prince's reign. The description of the lands and appurtenances granted is usually fairly succinct, although the Cymer charter includes a lengthy list of lands with detailed boundary clauses, including perambulations, in common with other charters for Welsh Cistercian houses.[499]

None of the charters has an injunctive clause, and only one authentic charter (in favour of Haughmond) contains a prohibitive clause.[500] Corroboration clauses occur in all the charters apart from no. 227, which is incomplete, and also in all letters patent. The formulae of these clauses vary, but those in the charters for Basingwerk are similar to each other and the same is true of the Haughmond charters as well as, to a lesser extent, the prince's two charters for Ynys Lannog.[501] The corroboration in Llywelyn's charter for Strata Marcella bears comparison with episcopal as well as other lay charters for that abbey, and may be ultimately indebted to the diplomatic of episcopal acts.[502] In all these cases, the corrobo-

---

[491] Nos 233, 239, 242.

[492] Nos 216, 225–6, 240, 242, 258–9, 272.

[493] Nos 227, 241, 254.

[494] Nos 229, 250.

[495] Nos 216, 227, 239 (and also the spurious nos 218–19).

[496] Nos 213, 225, 258; all three verbs are used in nos 226 and 272, both of which record fresh grants.

[497] Nos 250, 259 (and also no. 256).

[498] The dispositive clauses of Welsh rulers' charters for Strata Marcella usually combine *dare* with *concedere* and/or *confirmare*, the only other examples of the use of *dare* alone occurring in nos 13, 283, 544–5, 563.

[499] No. 229 (the same is true of the spurious no. 218 for Aberconwy); cf. below, pp. 100, 126.

[500] No. 258. Prohibitive clauses also occur in the Aberconwy charters (nos 218–19).

[501] Basingwerk: nos 213, 216. Of the three Haughmond examples, the corroboration in no. 225 (*Et ut ista concessio et confirmatio nostra perpetue firmitatis robur optineat eam presenti carta sigilli nostri appositione roboravimus*) is almost identical to that of no. 258 (and no. 546, a confirmation for Haughmond by Gwenwynwyn), and very close to that of no. 226. The final clauses of the corroborations in the two Ynys Lannog charters are particularly similar to each other: *Et ut hec donatio et concessio rata et inconcussa tam a nobis quam a nostris heredibus usque in perpetuum permaneat, eam sigilli nostri munimine fecimus roborari* (no. 250); *Ut igitur hec nostra donatio in posterum robur optineat firmitatis, eam presenti scripto et sigilli nostri munimine fecimus roborari* (no. 272).

[502] The corroboration in no. 231 for Strata Marcella (*Sed quia presens etas prona est ad malum unde si possit extorquere lucrum, tam propria sigilli mei impressione quam bonorum ac fidelium virorum*

ration probably reflects ecclesiastical influence. The corroboration clauses in the letters patent form a distinctive, though not uniform, group. Two of the letters issued at Worcester in 1218 have *in huius rei testimonium presenti scripto sigillum nostrum apponi fecimus*, whereas in 1223, 1230 and 1238 the corroboration opens with the phrase *in cuius rei testimonium*.[503] These clauses were probably influenced by ecclesiastical or, perhaps, English private acts, which in turn were indebted to royal letters patent.[504] However, none of Llywelyn's acts borrows any of the full clauses used in royal letters patent, including the standard formula by Henry III's reign, *in cuius rei testimonium has litteras nostras fieri fecimus patentes*.[505] Most corroboration clauses of charters refer to the document as *carta*, as does no. 254, Llywelyn's statement of undertakings to Henry III in 1223, in common with the document's address. The other letters patent use *scriptum* (or *scripto ac patenti* in no. 260 for Ednyfed Fychan), while no. 213, a charter for Basingwerk, reflects papal influence, at least ultimately, in its reference to *pagina*.[506] No. 229 for Cymer is unique among Llywelyn's charters in containing a warranty clause.

Apart from nos 227 and 233 all charters have witness lists, as do nos 254 and 260, a further reflection of the latter documents' affinities with charters despite their conforming in some respects with the diplomatic and substance of letters patent. Nos 259 and 272, a letter patent in favour of Ralph Mortimer and a charter for Ynys Lannog respectively, both end with the valediction *Valeat universitas vestra semper in domino*. Four authentic charters have dating clauses, as do two of the letters patent.[507] The majority of these open with the past participle *dat'* or *datum*, though one letter patent (1218) has *acta* and one charter for Ynys Lannog (1221) has *actum*.[508] All have place-dates apart from no. 229 for Cymer. Nos

---

atestatione hanc meam donationem munivi et corroboravi) bears comparison with that in no. 9, issued for the abbey by Cadwallon ap Hywel of Arwystli in 1206 (*Et quia presens etas prona est ad malum unde sibi conatur extorquere lucrum, hanc meam predictam venditionem tam sigilli mei impressione quam bonorum virorum attestatione munivi et coroboravi*). See also nos 10, 503–4, 554, 564. The earliest extant example of such a corroboration occurs in a charter of Bishop Alan of Bangor datable to 1195 × 1196 (*Sed quoniam ad malum presens etas prona est et ingeniosa et id calumpniose temptat infringere unde sibi lucrum conatur extorquere, hanc donationem et venditionem sigilli nostri impressione confirmamus*), and this may have been the model for the other corroborations referred to here: *Ystrad Marchell Charters*, no. 16.

[503] Nos 240–1, 254, 260, 274. The clause in the third Worcester document (no. 242) is essentially an elaboration of that used in nos 240–1.

[504] Cf. Cheney, *English Bishops' Chanceries*, 76; Stringer, 'Charters of David', 92. The acts of Bishop Iorwerth of St Davids include *in huius rei testimonium presenti scripto nostrum apponi fecimus sigillum*, *in cuius rei testimonium his litteris patentibus sigillum nostrum apponi fecimus* and *in cuius rei testimonium presenti scripto sigillum nostrum duximus apponendum*: *St Davids Episcopal Acta*, nos 71, 80, 86, 88. Cf. *Llandaff Episcopal Acta*, nos 75, 81–4, 88. However, the corroboration clauses in the few surviving acts of Bishop Reiner of St Asaph (1186–1224) and Bishop Cadwgan of Bangor (1215–35/6) lack the formula *in cuius/huius rei testimonium*. Thus one of Reiner's acts reads *Et ut hoc factum nostrum debite stabilitatis robur optineat presens scriptum sigilli nostri munimine roboravimus*: Shrewsbury, Shropshire Records and Research Centre, MS 6001/6869, fo. 161r, and see also ibid., fos 130v, 150r, 161v (cd. *Cart. Haugh.*, nos 859, 667, 793, 862).

[505] Cf. Chaplais, *English Royal Documents*, 19–20 (which also shows that the phrase *in huius rei testimonium* was used in corroboration clauses of letters patent under King John).

[506] Cf. Guyotjeannin, 'L'influence pontificale', 90, 91.

[507] Nos 229, 231, 242, 250, 260, 272. The same is true of the two spurious texts for Aberconwy and the charter for Dolgynwal: nos 218–19, 256.

[508] Nos 242 and 250.

229, 250, 260 and 272 include the year of incarnation or grace and the latter three acts also bear the day of the month according to the Roman calendar (as do the spurious nos 218–19 for Aberconwy). No. 242, a letter patent concerning Llywelyn's agreements with the crown at Worcester in 1218, is dated by the regnal year of Henry III together with the day of the month according to the Roman calendar.[509]

Gruffudd ap Llywelyn and Dafydd ap Llywelyn

Two texts of charters of Gruffudd ap Llywelyn are extant from his father's lifetime: both were issued in favour of Strata Marcella in 1226.[510] In common with most other Welsh rulers' charters for that abbey, including Llywelyn's charter of 1209, they lack an address and open with the notification, each of which uses forms of *noscere* (followed by the construction *quod ego* and dispositive verb(s) in the perfect tense).[511] The text in both is written in the first person singular. Unlike no. 282, no. 283 has a corroboration clause that refers to the charter as *pagina*, as well as a warranty clause, placed, unusually, after the witness list. Both are dated by the year of the incarnation, without place-dates.

Three charters of Dafydd ap Llywelyn, two for Ynys Lannog (1229 and 1238) and one for Haughmond (1238 × April 1240), date from Llywelyn's reign, but only one from after his succession as prince of Gwynedd, namely a confirmation for Basingwerk of July 1240.[512] All four charters are confirmations. The address in each of the three charters dating from his father's reign (*Universis/Omnibus* (*Cristi fidelibus*) *has litteras visuris vel audituris*) resembles that used by Llywelyn himself in the same period, and the greeting, *salutem in domino*, is common in Llywelyn's acts. The address and greeting (*in Cristo salutem*) in Dafydd's charter for Basingwerk are identical to those in Llywelyn's charters for that house, and the placing of Dafydd's name at the beginning of the address is also paralleled in one of Llywelyn's charters.[513] The three charters issued in Llywelyn's lifetime use the first person plural, thereby matching the plural of majesty used by Llywelyn himself at the same period; presumably this reflected Dafydd's status as his father's designated heir. The notifications of all Dafydd's charters open with the same formula (*Noverit universitas vestra*), followed in three cases by *nos* and the dispositive verb(s) in the perfect infinitive and in the Basingwerk charter by *quod ego* and the dispositive verbs in the present tense (a construction also found in Llywelyn's charters for Basingwerk). The function of all four charters as confirmations is reflected in their use of *confirmare* in the disposition, preceded by *concedere* in three cases. Nos 286 and 289, for Ynys Lannog and Haughmond respectively, refer to themselves in their corroboration clauses as *littere patentes*, whereas nos 288 and 292 use the term *scriptum*. In addition, no. 292, for Basingwerk, includes a warranty clause. Apart from no. 288 each charter contains a witness list. Nos 286, 288 and 292 have dating clauses with a

---

[509] The dating clause in no. 256 for Dolgynwal, a charter of dubious authenticity, is also dated by Henry's regnal year but gives the day and month according to the ecclesiastical calendar.
[510] Nos 282–3.
[511] Of the thirty-four texts of Strata Marcella charters contained in this edition, only three, all issued by rulers of Arwystli, contain an address and greeting (nos 5, 8, 581). Only two use *scire* in the notification (nos 6, 578), while two others lack a verb, with the disposition following a verbal invocation or arenga (nos 539, 544); the remaining thirty use forms of *noscere*, especially *notum sit quod ego* followed by a verb in the perfect tense.
[512] Nos 286, 288–9, 292.
[513] Cf. nos 213, 216.

place-date followed by the year of grace or incarnation and a day in the ecclesiastical calendar; no. 286 for Ynys Lannog closes with the same valediction as nos 259 and 272 issued by Llywelyn in favour of Ralph Mortimer and Ynys Lannog respectively.

In addition there survive six letters patent issued by Dafydd following his submission to Henry III at Gwerneigron in August 1241. These afford the earliest clear influence of the English royal chancery on the princely acts of Gwynedd: two contain the normal address in royal letters patent (*omnibus ad quos presentes littere pervenerint*),[514] and this is only slightly modified in the rest by the insertion of *Cristi fidelibus* after *omnibus*.[515] All have the greeting *salutem*, as was standard in royal acts, but the greeting was of course extremely widespread and had been used by Llywelyn ap Iorwerth and other members of the Venedotian dynasty. It is, however, likely that royal influence explains the use in all these letters patent of the first person singular. This seems to have been imposed on Dafydd owing to his weakness following his surrender to Henry, for the prince had used the first person plural during his father's lifetime and reverted to this usage in letters after his renewal of hostilities against the crown in 1244–5.[516] This interpretation is also supported by the demeaning style adopted by Dafydd in these letters.[517] The corroboration clauses are similar, though not identical, to those in Llywelyn's letters patent; the most common is *in cuius rei testimonium presenti scripto sigillum meum apposui*.[518] All Dafydd's letters patent apart from no. 304 have dating clauses introduced by *actum* with a place-date (*apud N.*) followed by the day of the month and the king's regnal year.

Llywelyn ap Gruffudd and his brothers

The last rulers of independent Gwynedd are represented by texts of thirteen charters and nineteen letters patent: five issued by Owain ap Gruffudd (including two letters patent jointly with Llywelyn ap Gruffudd);[519] twenty-two by Llywelyn ap Gruffudd;[520] three by Dafydd ap Gruffudd;[521] and two by Rhodri ap Gruffudd.[522]

Apart from Llywelyn's earliest surviving charter, for Ralph Mortimer (1241), and a letter patent announcing an agreement with Henry III and the Lord Edward (1262),[523] all these acts contain a general address and greeting. The address in charters usually takes the form *Universis/Omnibus Cristi fidelibus has litteras visuris vel audituris*, in common with several charters of Llywelyn ap Iorwerth and Dafydd ap Llywelyn; the use of *sancte matris ecclesie*

---

[514] Nos 301, 303.

[515] Nos 300, 302, 304–5.

[516] Nos 286, 288–9, 307–8. Admittedly, the use of the first person singular in the Basingwerk charter (no. 292) shows that the crown was not alone in denying Dafydd the plural of majesty after his accession even if, in this case, the usage stemmed essentially from adapting the model of Llywelyn's charter. That political submission could be influential in this regard is suggested, though, by Llywelyn ap Iorwerth's use of the first person singular in no. 254, a letter patent of 1223 announcing his willingness to make amends to the king and his men for damages caused in raids on Shropshire.

[517] See below, p. 78.

[518] Nos 300–1, 304–5; nos 302–3 are more elaborate, as they refer to sealing also by the bishops of Bangor and St Asaph.

[519] Nos 309–10, 313–14, 316.

[520] Nos 317–18, 320–2, 329–30, 335–6, 349, 361–2, 367–8, 397, 402–5, 407, 423–4.

[521] Nos 441, 456–7.

[522] Nos 458–9.

[523] Nos 317, 349.

filiis presentibus et futuris instead of *Cristi fidelibus* in Llywelyn ap Gruffudd's charter for Basingwerk follows the pattern of earlier Gwynedd charters for the same beneficiary.[524] Variations on these formulae, sometimes including the substitution of the future participle *inspecturis* for *visuris* (and occasionally *audituris* as well), occur in the two letters patent issued jointly by Owain and Llywelyn, in seven of those issued by Llywelyn alone, in Dafydd's letter patent of 1283 and in Rhodri's letter patent of 1280.[525] However, Owain's two letters patent announcing agreements with Henry III in 1244,[526] together with Llywelyn ap Gruffudd's ratification of the treaty of Aberconwy in 1277 and three of the four accompanying documents,[527] are modelled on the address normal in royal letters patent: most have *omnibus Cristi fidelibus ad quos presentes littere pervenerint*, though no. 309 has *presens scriptum* instead of *presentes littere* and no. 405 follows the royal address precisely (*omnibus ad quos presentes littere pervenerint*). As with Dafydd ap Llywelyn's letters patent in 1241, royal influence on the address appears in the context of submission to the English crown, suggesting that royal clerks may have had a hand in drafting the documents. The most common form of salutation is *salutem in domino*,[528] sometimes elaborated by the addition of *sempiternam*[529] or, in no. 318 (1243), *eternam*. The remaining charters and letters patent simply have *salutem*.[530]

Owain ap Gruffudd's two letters patent announcing his obligations to Henry III in 1244 are written in the first person singular, but his charter for Ynys Lannog in 1247 has the first person plural, in common with all previous charters to that house by members of the dynasty, including that issued by Llywelyn ap Gruffudd earlier that year.[531] Of the two charters issued by Llywelyn during the reign of his uncle Dafydd ap Llywelyn, no. 317, for Ralph Mortimer in 1241, is written in the first person singular, while no. 318, for Einion ap Maredudd in 1243, uses the plural of majesty, as do the rest of Llywelyn's charters (extant from 1247 onwards) apart from no. 321, a confirmation for Basingwerk in 1247 which follows the diplomatic of earlier Gwynedd charters for that house in its use of the first person singular. The same is true of all letters patent in Llywelyn's name alone (extant from 1258 onwards). The plural is also used by Dafydd ap Gruffudd in his charters of 1260 and 1283 and his letters patent of the latter year, and by Rhodri ap Gruffudd in his quitclaim to Llywelyn in 1272 (though Rhodri's letter patent of 1280 is in the singular).[532] The notifications in all the charters use forms of *noscere*, especially the formula *noverit universitas vestra*, usually followed by *nos* and the perfect infinitive.[533] The letters patent also show a marked preference for forms of *noscere*, with only two examples of *scire*; in addition, *volo devenire notitiam* occurs in no. 309, *significamus* in no. 316 and *inspeximus* in no. 402 (Llywelyn's ratification of the treaty of Aberconwy).

---

[524] Nos 318, 320–1; cf. nos 213, 216, 292. No. 458, issued by Rhodri ap Gruffudd, lacks *Cristi fidelibus*, reading *Universis presentes litteras visuris vel audituris . . . .*
[525] Nos 314, 316, 329–30, 335, 361–2, 368, 404, 456, 459.
[526] Nos 309–10.
[527] Nos 402–3, 405, 407.
[528] Nos 310, 313, 320, 330, 336, 361–2, 368, 402–3, 405, 407, 424, 456.
[529] Nos 329, 397, 423, 441, 459.
[530] Nos 309, 314, 316, 321–2, 335, 404, 458.
[531] Nos 309–10, 313.
[532] Nos 441, 456–9.
[533] The exceptions are no. 317 (*Noverint universi quod ego*) and no. 397 (*notum facimus . . . quod*), both followed by a verb in the perfect tense, and no. 320 (*Noveritis nos* followed by the perfect infinitive).

The verbs in the dispositive clauses of charters are in the perfect tense or perfect infinitive, the only exception being no. 397, Llywelyn's charter of liberties for St Asaph, which uses the present. Most charters include the verb *dare*, usually combined with *confirmare* and/or *concedere*, though Llywelyn's quitclaims to Ralph Mortimer in 1241 and Roger Mortimer in 1281 have *quietum clamare* (combined with *remittere* in the latter), and the charter for St Asaph in 1276 × 1277 has *fatemur et recogniscimus*.[534] The dispositive verbs in letters patent vary according to the subject matter of the document, and several use the present rather than the perfect tense.[535] All charters and all the letters patent apart from no. 330, a letter of credence for representatives of Llywelyn ap Gruffudd, contain a corroboration clause. As with Llywelyn ap Iorwerth, the form of the clause differs between the two types of document. In charters, a variety of formulae are used to emphasize that the document has been sealed in order to ensure its permanence. In contrast to the majority of late twelfth- and early thirteenth-century charters, only no. 318 (1243) also refers to the document itself as helping to reinforce the grant (. . . *eam presenti scripto et sigilli nostri munimine fecimus roboravi*). Most letters patent, on the other hand, include the phrase *in cuius rei testimonium*, derived ultimately from royal letters patent, in formulae previously used by Llywelyn ap Iorwerth and Dafydd ap Llywelyn in documents of that type. As in its address, no. 405, one of Llywelyn ap Gruffudd's acts concerning the treaty of Aberconwy, borrows the royal formula directly (*in cuius rei testimonium has litteras nostras fieri fecimus patentes*). In most cases, though, the corroboration clause includes the noun *sigillum* combined with a form of the verb *apponere*: for example, *In cuius rei testimonium nostrum sigillum hiis litteris patentibus fecimus apponi*,[536] or, fairly consistently from 1265 onwards, *In cuius rei testimonium presentibus sigillum nostrum fecimus apponi*.[537] Not surprisingly, both Dafydd ap Gruffudd's acts of 2 May 1283 contain almost identical corroboration clauses: *In cuius rei testimonium sigillum nostrum presenti carte fecimus apponi*.[538] Two of Llywelyn's charters have a warranty clause, one, in favour of Basingwerk (1247), 'against all men and women', the other, for St Asaph (1276 × 1277), 'against all men'.[539]

Each charter concludes with a witness list as does no. 309, announcing Owain ap Gruffudd's agreement to serve Henry III in 1244.[540] All acts, apart from no. 317, Llywelyn ap Gruffudd's earliest charter (1241), also contain a dating clause. The letters patent by which Owain ap Gruffudd, together with Llywelyn in 1248, announce agreements with Henry III are dated by the day of the month and the king's regnal year, thereby resembling Dafydd ap Llywelyn's letters patent of 1241.[541] The remaining letters patent, together with all charters containing complete dating clauses, have the year of the incarnation (usually *anno domini*, though nos 320, 424 and 459 have *anno gratie*) and, apart from no. 368, the day of the month calculated according to either the ecclesiastical or, in the case of four charters, the Roman calendar.[542] (That Llywelyn ap Gruffudd's charter for Ynys Lannog in

---

[534] Nos 317, 397, 424.
[535] Nos 335–6, 361–2, 404–5.
[536] No. 335; no. 336 is very similar.
[537] Nos 362, 402–4, 407.
[538] No. 457; no. 456 differs only in its word order.
[539] Nos 321, 397.
[540] No. 361 (Pipton, 1265) also effectively has a witness list, as the names of those present are introduced by the phrase *presentibus et consencientibus* after the corroboration clause.
[541] Nos 309–10, 314.
[542] In no. 397 the dating clause has been abbreviated to *Datum etc.*

April 1247 was drafted by a different clerk from that of Owain for the same house in September of that year is suggested by the use of *anno gratie* and the ecclesiastical calendar in the former, as distinct from *anno domini* and the Roman calendar in the latter.)[543] The addition of Edward I's regnal year in Llywelyn's quitclaim to Roger Mortimer of 9 October 1281 is probably explicable by the context of the prince's accompanying agreement with Mortimer on the same day, which opens with a similar dating clause.[544] Apart from four letters patent,[545] all acts also have place-dates. The dating clauses in all letters patent and also in seven charters are introduced by *datum*, *dat'* or *data*; of the remaining charters, two open with *datum et actum*, one with *actum* and one with *acta*.[546] Only two letters patent contain a valediction.[547]

Letters

The clerks who drafted letters for rulers of Gwynedd generally conformed to western European epistolary conventions of the period. Thus, in letters to kings, bishops and popes, the name of the addressee appears before that of the sender, whereas other Welsh lords, together with officials of the princes and those of the English crown, such as the justice of Chester, are named after the ruler of Gwynedd.[548] This sensitivity to distinctions of rank reflected the great importance attached to the greeting (*salutatio*) in the teaching of epistolary style (*ars dictandi* or *dictamen*).[549] Some of the greetings used by Llywelyn ap Iorwerth in letters to Henry III referred to the relationship established by Llywelyn's marriage to Henry's half-sister Joan: *Karissimo fratri et domino suo excellentissimo*, *Karissimo domino et fratri suo* and *Reverendo domino et fratri karissimo*.[550] Likewise, Dafydd ap Llywelyn addressed Henry as *Excellentissimo domino suo et avunculo*.[551] The greetings of Llywelyn ap Gruffudd's letters to both Henry III and Edward I almost all open with the phrase *Excellenti/Excellentissimo domino suo*.[552] All rulers of Gwynedd were careful to acknowledge the king of England as their lord and to include his full title in the address. Llywelyn ap Gruffudd further emphasized his subordination to Edward I by

---

[543] Nos 320, 313. The Roman calendar is also used in Llywelyn's charter for Einion ap Maredudd (1243) and in Dafydd's confirmation (1260) for Einion's son (nos 318, 441), as well as in Rhodri's quitclaim to Llywelyn (1272) (no. 458).

[544] Nos 424–5.

[545] Nos 314, 330, 335–6.

[546] Nos 424 (1281), 458 (1272), 321–2 (both 1247).

[547] Nos 314 (Owain and Llywelyn, 1248) and 459 (Rhodri, 1280).

[548] Nos 263, 307–8, 369, 378–9, 410, 414 (and also no. 220, whose authenticity is dubious). A partial exception to this pattern is no. 194, in which Hugh, bishop of Soissons is named after Owain Gwynedd, perhaps because the letter was sent to Hugh in his capacity as Louis VII's chancellor. His position as Henry III's justiciar presumably explains why Hubert de Burgh is named before Llywelyn ap Iorwerth in no. 243. Note also how Llywelyn is named before Eva de Braose in no. 261, but after her brother William Marshal in no. 262.

[549] Cf. Schaller, 'Dichtungslehren', 261–2; Camargo, *Ars Dictaminis*, 22–3. The same principles were followed in the diplomatic correspondence of the English royal chancery: Chaplais, 'English diplomatic documents', 46–7.

[550] Nos 244–5, 255. Joan addressed her brother as *Karissimo suo domino et fratri suo karissimo* (no. 280).

[551] Nos 298–9.

[552] For parallels in letters to Henry III from other lords see Chaplais, *Diplomatic Documents*, 160–2 (nos 240–2). A variation occurs in no. 418 (1279): *Viro magnifico ac domino suo excellenti*.

referring to himself as *suus devotus*, *(suus) devotus vasallus* and similar phrases in letters from 1275 onwards.[553]

Although most greetings include *salutem*, their form is varied, just as in diplomatic correspondence the English royal chancery elaborated its normal greeting of *salutem* to create more courteous phrases.[554] Several of Llywelyn ap Iorwerth's letters bear the greeting *salutem et se totum*, a formula continued by Dafydd ap Llywelyn.[555] The greeting *cum (debita) dilectione salutem* likewise occurs in letters sent by both of those princes.[556] In 1262–3 the greeting normally used by Llywelyn ap Gruffudd in letters to the king is *salutem et affectum ad obsequia*.[557] This appears to have been discontinued thereafter, however, and from 1274 the most common greeting, first attested in 1269, is *salutem et paratam ad beneplacita voluntatem*.[558] Greetings to popes were appropriately submissive and have parallels in the diplomatic correspondence of other rulers: for example, *salutem et tam devotam quam debitam tanto patri cum honore reverentiam* (Dafydd ap Llywelyn, 1241) or *devota pedum oscula beatorum* (Llywelyn ap Gruffudd, 1275).[559]

According to the conventions of *ars dictaminis*, the greeting (*salutatio*) of a letter was followed by an *exordium* (or *captatio benevolentiae*), which prepared the recipient for the message and/or request contained respectively in the *narratio* and *petitio*, the latter often being closely related to the final part known as the *conclusio*.[560] From 1220 at the latest the *exordium*, *narratio* and/or *petitio* of letters from Llywelyn ap Iorwerth were consistently written in the first person plural, a practice continued by Dafydd ap Llywelyn and Llywelyn ap Gruffudd. The six twelfth-century letters exhibit a varied pattern: Gruffudd ap Cynan's letter to Archbishop Ralph of Canterbury consistently uses the first person plural as does that of Owain Gwynedd to Archbishop Thomas Becket;[561] however, Owain's earlier letter to Louis VII is written in the first person singular and the later one, together with that to Louis's chancellor, Hugh de Champfleury, in a mixture of the first and second person plural.[562] The earliest authentic texts of letters sent by Llywelyn ap Iorwerth, datable to 1212, also combine the first and second person plural, though with a preference for the

[553] The earliest example was probably either no. 384 or no. 385. In any case, the formula was certainly used no later than May 1275: no. 386. It also occurs in a letter to Pope Gregory X of September 1275: no. 390. For the earlier use of the formula in letters to Llywelyn from lords of Deheubarth see below, p. 96.

[554] Cf. Chaplais, 'English diplomatic documents', 47.

[555] Nos 244–5, 248–9, 268, 298–9. Cf. nos 280 and 315: *salutem et se ipsam* (Joan); *salutem et se ipsos* (Owain and Llywelyn sons of Gruffudd). The formula occasionally occurs in letters in England from early in Henry III's reign: see, for example, Chaplais, *Diplomatic Documents*, 68 (no. 89) (from Guido de Pochoneria to Hubert de Burgh, August 1220).

[556] Nos 243, 255, 261, 307–8.

[557] Nos 351, 353, 355–7.

[558] The earliest examples are nos 370, 380, 384–6. (For continental examples of the formula see Ruelle, '*A tous présents*', 1664.) Cf. no. 327 (1257): *salutem et paratam ad obsequia voluntatem*. One exception is no. 401 (February 1277): *salutem et fidelitatem sibi debitam pro viribus observare*. This seems to be an unusually late example of an 'independent-infinitive-phrase *salutatio*', a form of greeting well established by the mid-twelfth century but rare after 1200: cf. Lanham, '*Salutatio*' *Formulas*, 10–11, 42–55, esp. 53, 55.

[559] Nos 294, 390. Cf. Lanham, '*Salutatio*' *Formulas*, 9; Chaplais, 'English diplomatic documents', 47.

[560] Camargo, *Ars Dictaminis*, 22–3.

[561] Nos 191, 195.

[562] Nos 193–4, 196.

former.[563] The first person plural is consistently used from May 1220, though the switch from the first person singular may have occurred at some point between 1215 and 1219.[564]

Until 1269 letters usually end with a petition, injunction (in mandates to officials) or other concluding statement, often followed by a final greeting or valediction, usually *Valete*, but sometimes a more elaborate phrase such as *Valeat excellencia vestra diu in domino*.[565] Occasionally, the valediction is preceded by a declaration that further information will be given orally by the bearer of the letter.[566] Corroboration clauses are rare. Although two of Llywelyn ap Iorwerth's letters refer to sealing, this is simply in order to explain the use of the privy rather than the great seal.[567] However, three of Dafydd ap Llywelyn's letters in 1241 – one to Henry III's magnates, the others to the king himself – include a corroboration clause opening with the phrase *in cuius rei testimonium*,[568] as does a letter of Llywelyn ap Gruffudd to the bishops of Bangor and St Asaph in 1274.[569] All four letters are extant only in copies. These clauses are similar to those in letters patent with general addresses; indeed, nos 299 and 383 refer to the document as *littere patentes* (the other two corroboration clauses use the term *scriptum*). This may suggest that the clause was reserved for letters sealed patent, but was considered unnecessary for those, probably the vast majority, sealed closed. As elsewhere in Europe in this period, it is likely that sealing was the normal means of authenticating letters (in common with charters), though the status of the bearer was also crucial in this respect.[570]

One important development under Llywelyn ap Gruffudd was the addition, almost always at the end of the letter, of a dating clause, normally introduced by *Dat'*. This practice first occurs in nos 369–70, both of 1269, and is normal thereafter; it was also followed in Princess Eleanor's letters, none of which is earlier than 1279, but not in those of Dafydd ap Gruffudd.[571] The dating clause consists of a place-date followed by the day of the month (calculated variously) and also, in a minority of cases, the year of incarnation (*anno domini*). As the latest letter whose text survives before 1269 belongs to 1263,[572] it may be that the decision to include a dating clause similar to those used in letters patent with

---

[563] Nos 234–5. The latter, to Philip Augustus, only uses the plural when Llywelyn speaks on behalf of both himself and the other Welsh princes.

[564] May 1220: nos 246–7. No. 237 (1215 × 1216) uses the first plural, but much of the letter is illegible. The first plural is consistently used in nos 238 and 243–5, each of which has a *terminus a quo* earlier than 1220. The only surviving letter of Joan (no. 280) (probably 1230 × 1231) is in the first person singular. The usage of Dafydd ap Gruffudd's clerks varied according to the nature of the letter.

[565] No. 249; cf. nos 246, 294, 298, 315, 327, 351, 353.

[566] For example, nos 245–6, 249.

[567] See below, pp. 86, 87.

[568] Nos 296, 298–9. Such a clause is lacking in Dafydd's letter to the pope in 1241 (no. 294) and in nos 307–8 of 1244–5.

[569] No. 383.

[570] Cf. Constable, *Letters and Letter-Collections*, 47, and no. 196, discussed in Pryce, 'Owain Gwynedd', 17–18. The importance of sealing as a mark of authentication is assumed in Gerald of Wales's allegation that, before his appointment to the see of Bangor in 1215, Cadwgan, then abbot of Whitland, delivered to the abbot of Clairvaux a letter with a false seal (*literas . . . sigillo adulterio signatas*), ostensibly from Llywelyn ap Iorwerth, offering lands for the foundation of a new abbey: *Gir. Camb. Op.*, iv. 166 (*Speculum Ecclesie*, III. 7).

[571] The only exceptions are nos 413 (an original letter to Edward I) and 428 (a letter to Archbishop Pecham, extant only in copies); the omission of a dating clause in no. 410 is not significant, as the copy of the letter is incomplete, ending *etc.*

[572] No. 357.

general addresses was an innovation introduced in the wake of Llywelyn's recognition as prince of Wales in 1267.

Agreements

The following overview of agreements involving members of the dynasty of Gwynedd excludes those announced or ratified in the form of letters patent issued by a Venedotian ruler, a category of document already discussed above. Instead, it focuses attention on fourteen other documents, including bipartite chirographs, validated by the ruler's seal[573] and also refers to nine texts of agreements known only from documents issued by the English king or other lords, on the assumption that the latter contain terms to which Venedotian rulers had agreed.[574] Moreover, in at least one of these latter cases it is clear that a similar document, now lost, was issued in the name of the prince of Gwynedd.[575]

Twelve of the texts concern truces, peaces and other agreements with the English crown.[576] Of these, six – five involving Llywelyn ap Iorwerth, one Llywelyn ap Gruffudd – survive only as ratifications in royal letters patent.[577] No. 363, the Treaty of Montgomery (1267) is extant in the form of a letter patent issued by the papal legate Cardinal Ottobuono, the mediator responsible for overseeing the negotiations, and not surprisingly exhibits elements of papal diplomatic. Of the remaining five agreements with the crown, that negotiated on behalf of Llywelyn with John's representative in 1201, described as a *forma pacis*, was a memorandum of articles of agreement authenticated by the seals of the archbishop of Canterbury and the justiciar, whereas the remaining four, three of which date from the 1240s, the fourth from 1260, may be classified as *conventiones* (as each includes either the phrase *ita convenit* or the term *conventio*), originally drawn up in the form of bipartite indentures or chirographs according to their corroboration clauses.[578]

Nine of the eleven agreements with parties other than the English crown are likewise described as chirographs; indeed, no. 252 is extant as one half of an original bipartite chirograph indented at the top. The only exceptions, both dating from 1261, are no. 345, described as a letter patent sealed by the arbitrators of the agreement, and no. 347, whose corroboration clause refers merely to sealing by Llywelyn ap Gruffudd and the bishops of Bangor and St Asaph.[579] The terms used to describe these agreements vary: *conventio* (or *ita convenit* or *sic convenitur*) occurs in six cases,[580] *compositio* in two[581] and *finalis concordia*

---

[573] Nos 252, 284, 291, 312, 323, 342, 346–7, 358, 363, 366, 375, 425, 447.

[574] Nos 221, 266–7, 269–70, 328, 331, 345.

[575] No. 328 (1258), a letter patent issued by the Comyns, is described as a chirograph in the corroboration, which states that the seals of Llywelyn ap Gruffudd and his magnates were attached to *consimili scripto*; this shows that the original chirograph also contained a similar letter patent issued by Llywelyn.

[576] In addition, seven other texts of such agreements are extant as ratifications in princely letters patent (nos 274, 300–1, 336, 349, 361–2) and no. 402, the Treaty of Aberconwy (1277), in both royal and princely letters patent.

[577] Nos 266–7, 269–71, 331.

[578] Nos 221, 284, 291, 312, 342. Cf. Rowlands, '1201 peace', 155; Chaplais, 'English diplomatic documents', 45 (which notes the use of bipartite indentures for treaties between the English crown and rulers who were not kings such as the counts of Flanders).

[579] No. 328 is a letter patent which derived from a bipartite chirograph: see n. 187 above.

[580] Nos 252, 312, 323, 328, 366, 375.

[581] Nos 346–7.

and *fedus pacis et insolubilis concordie* in one each.[582] Of particular interest are the four agreements made by Llywelyn ap Gruffudd (in one case jointly with his brother Owain) with members of other Welsh dynasties between 1250/1 and 1263.[583] These were almost certainly drawn up the prince's clerks and reflect the prince's readiness to try and formalize his political relationships within Wales by the same written means already well established in negotiating Anglo-Welsh relations. One notable feature of these agreements is their sanction clauses, in which each party submits itself to the jurisdiction of prelates and accepts that it will be excommunicated for any breach of the terms agreed and also renounce any exceptions under canon or civil law which might impede that excommunication.[584] Further evidence of ecclesiastical influence on the drafting of no. 358, the agreement between Llywelyn ap Gruffudd and Gruffudd ap Gwenwynwyn in 1263, is the opening formula of perpetuity (*ad perpetuam rei geste memoriam*), an alternative to the apostolic greeting in papal diplomatic that was used, for example, by Ottobuono four years later in his letter patent announcing the Treaty of Montgomery, though the ensuing description of the agreement as a *finalis concordia* seems indebted to English common law.[585]

The rulers' styles

The address or, where this is lacking, the notification of most acts issued by rulers exercising or claiming paramount authority over Gwynedd use a style (*intitulatio*) in referring to the author of the act. This is invariably the case with Llywelyn ap Iorwerth, Dafydd ap Llywelyn and Llywelyn ap Gruffudd (as well as Dafydd ap Gruffudd after he had succeeded his brother as prince of Wales). The few acts extant before Llywelyn ap Iorwerth's ascendancy in Gwynedd from 1199 show some variety in this respect. In his sole surviving act, a letter to the archbishop of Canterbury in 1120, Gruffudd ap Cynan is named simply as *Criphinus*, without title or patronymic.[586] However, his son Owain Gwynedd adopted the assertive titles *rex Wallie* or *Walliarum rex* in 1140 and 1163–5, replacing the latter by *Waliarum princeps* in a letter to Louis VII of France in 1165 × 1166.[587] It may be inferred from letters of Pope Alexander III and Thomas Becket that Owain also used the titles *princeps Wallie* and *Walensium princeps* by 1169.[588] The switch from *rex* to *princeps* was almost certainly regarded as articulating an elevation in status. As *rex* was used by a variety of twelfth-century Welsh rulers, some of whom exercised only very limited power, it had arguably become devalued and thus offered a less effective expression of the dominance over native Wales to which Owain aspired than *princeps*, literally 'principal ruler', with its Roman imperial connotations

---

[582] Nos 358, 425. No. 345 uses no single term to describe the agreement reached by the arbitrators.

[583] Nos 316, 323, 347, 358.

[584] See further Walters, 'Renunciation of exceptions'; Smith, *Llywelyn*, 326–7. Cf. the agreement between Henry III and Dafydd ap Llywelyn at Gloucester in 1240 (no. 291), in which the parties submit themselves to the jurisdiction of the papal legate Otto, who may use ecclesiastical censure to compel observance of the terms of the arbitration.

[585] Cf. Giry, *Manuel de diplomatique*, 695; no. 363. Smith, 'Disputes and settlements', 840–1, observes that no. 366, an agreement with Gilbert de Clare (1268), contains 'many of the ingredients and hallmarks of the *compromissio* familiar to canon lawyers'.

[586] No. 191.

[587] Nos 192–6.

[588] *CTB*, ii. 840, 972, 976 (nos 190, 223, 225).

– a term used, moreover, by powerful territorial rulers on the Continent, including the dukes of Normandy both before and after 1066.[589]

To judge by the surviving evidence, however, the title 'prince of Wales' lapsed in Gwynedd after Owain Gwynedd's death (though it was adopted by his nephew Rhys ap Gruffudd of Deheubarth).[590] Until 1230, the territorial element in the rulers' styles is *Norwallia* ('North Wales' or 'Gwynedd'), not 'Wales'. Dafydd ab Owain styled himself *rex Norwallie* in two charters for Haughmond in 1177 × 1187 and 1177 × *c*.1190, but also used *princeps Norwallie* in one charter of 1186 × 1194, a title also adopted by his nephew Gruffudd ap Cynan ab Owain in *c*.1190 × 1199.[591] In most of his charters and letters before 1230 Llywelyn ap Iorwerth is styled *Lewelinus princeps Norwallie*. A papal letter may indicate that he had adopted this style as early as the autumn of 1199.[592] However, a few documents, none later than 1212, insert a patronymic: for example, *Lewelinus Gervasii filius Norwallie princeps*.[593] As none of the documents where the patronymic appears survives in the original, it is impossible to be certain that its use is authentic, though its appearance in the agreement with King John's representatives in July 1201 may reinforce the case for regarding it as an authentic early style, even if that agreement was drafted by English chancery clerks.[594]

The same problems arise in considering the most remarkable style found in any of Llywelyn ap Iorwerth's acts, namely *Lewelinus filius Gervasii Dei gratia princeps Norwalie*. This occurs in a letter, probably datable to *c*.May × 4 August 1212, extant in four early modern copies, of which three include the phrase *Dei gratia*. Unfortunately, it is extremely difficult to establish the relationship between the different copies and in particular to determine whether those containing the phrase are likely to be more reliable than the one that does not, although there is some evidence to suggest that the omission resulted from abbreviation.[595] As the claim to rule by the grace of God is unique among all known acts issued by twelfth- and thirteenth-century Welsh rulers, and since the copies are so late, there are grounds for suspecting that the phrase is a later interpolation. However, the possibility that it is authentic cannot be ruled out. If, as is likely, the letter was sent at the height of Llywelyn's recovery of power in the summer of 1212, it could represent an experiment designed further to promote the prince's dominance over other Welsh lords in defiance of

---

[589] Pryce, 'Owain Gwynedd', 20–3; Crouch, *Image of Aristocracy*, 85–93; Werner, 'Kingdom and principality', 243–8, 276, n. 3; *Acta of William I*, 87. Closer to Gwynedd, the earl of Chester was called *princeps* in Lucian's tract 'In Praise of Chester' *c*.1194: Crouch, 'Administration', 71.

[590] Nos 26, 28.

[591] Nos 198 (*David rex filius Owini*), 199 (*David rex Norwallie*), 200 (*David filius Owini princeps Norwallie*), 206 (. . . *Kynan filius Northwallie princeps*); cf. no. 202. Gruffudd ap Cynan ab Owain is named with a patronymic but no title in no. 207 (1195 × 1199).

[592] *Reg. Innocenz' III.*, ii. 403–1 (no. 224) (24 November 1199).

[593] No. 229; cf. no. 234, cited below. No. 220, of dubious authenticity, has *Lewelinus filius Ioruert princeps Norwallie*. Though *Lewelinus Gervasii filius totius Norwallie princeps* in the spurious nos 218–19 may have been based on an authentic style of the prince, *totius* was almost certainly a later interpolation.

[594] No. 221: *Leulinus filius Ioruert*. Llywelyn is also referred to by his Christian name and patronymic in royal letters of September 1199 and May 1201; the earliest royal reference to him as *Lewelinus princeps Norwallie* occurs in a letter of 16 April 1205 granting the prince Ellesmere castle as a marriage gift with Joan: *Rot. Chart.*, 23a, 104a, 147a.

[595] No. 234 and note. A marginal note near to the style in C, the manuscript that omits *Dei gratia*, states that 'It is otherwise in ye originall': Stephenson, *Governance*, 3, n. 11.

King John, and is arguably of a piece with the authoritative tone struck throughout the letter. Interestingly, the phrase *per Dei gratiam* occurs, albeit with reference to the forming of a confederacy with other Welsh *principes* rather than as part of the prince's style, in Llywelyn's letter to Philip Augustus of France, likewise datable to the summer of 1212.[596] Yet, if the style in no. 234 is authentic, it failed to catch on: Llywelyn was content in all his other surviving acts before 1230 to style himself simply *princeps Norwallie*.

During the last decade of his rule Llywelyn used a new style: *Lewelinus princeps de Aberfrau, dominus Snaudon'* (and variant spellings thereof). As previous scholars have noted, Llywelyn drew here on Welsh political mythology, promoted by lawyers in Gwynedd, in which the court of Aberffraw on Anglesey – the principal seat of the rulers of Gwynedd according to Gerald of Wales – represented overlordship over the other Welsh rulers.[597] This doctrine is especially clear in two Latin texts of Welsh law, Redactions B and C, compiled in Gwynedd quite possibly in the second quarter of the thirteenth century and thus contemporary with Llywelyn. According to these, only the king of Aberffraw pays gold to the king of London, whereas the other kings of Wales pay gold to Aberffraw.[598] In other words, by declaring himself to be prince of Aberffraw Llywelyn was, in effect, saying that he was prince of Wales, thereby implicitly challenging a cardinal principle he had accepted at Worcester in 1218, namely the king's right to receive the homages of all the Welsh lords.[599] At the same time, the prince emphasized the link with his patrimonial territory of Gwynedd in the title 'lord of Snowdon'.[600] Thus the new style drew a new distinction between, on the one hand, Llywelyn's aspirations to Wales-wide authority as prince of Aberffraw and, on the other, his position as territorial lord of Gwynedd or Snowdon.[601] Moreover, the style enabled the prince to articulate his claims to authority over the whole of native Wales without incurring the risk of offending either the English crown or, more importantly perhaps, Welsh opinion by explicitly claiming – as his grandfather Owain Gwynedd had done – to rule over Wales rather than Gwynedd alone. His recourse to an archaic-sounding style may point to an attempt to justify a wider territorial hegemony by appealing to an invented tradition of Welsh rulers' dependence on the ruler of Aberffraw, and of his own dependence on the 'crown of London', that stood a greater chance of acceptance within Welsh political culture than the title 'prince of Wales'.[602]

When this new style was first adopted is uncertain. The earliest dated document containing it is a charter dated at Ruthin on 18 November 1225 in favour of the

---

[596] No. 235. The same is true of no. 245, a letter to Henry III of 1219 × 1221. Cf. also Crouch, 'Administration', 70–1, for the addition of *Dei gratia* to comital styles in twelfth-century England.

[597] *HW*, ii. 682; Smith, *Llywelyn*, 17–18, 188, 284; *Gir. Camb. Op.*, vi. 81, 169 (*IK*, I. 10; *DK*, I. 4).

[598] *LTWL*, 207, 277.

[599] No. 241.

[600] I follow established usage here, though the title is probably more accurately translated 'lord of Snowdonia': Smith, *Llywelyn*, 188, n. 4.

[601] The notions that Aberffraw represented supremacy over Wales and Snowdonia represented the prince's dynastic roots are arguably implicit in the praise poem composed by the court poet Llywarch ap Llywelyn to celebrate Llywelyn's victories in the March and Deheubarth in 1217, in which Aberffraw is named first in a list of eighteen courts or castles held by the prince and Llywelyn's ancestry is explicitly linked with Snowdonia: *Gwaith Llywarch ap Llywelyn*, no. 25, esp. lines 13–28, 43–9.

[602] Cf. *HW*, ii. 682; Davies, *Conquest*, 246–7; Smith, *Llywelyn*, 284.

Hospitallers of St John at Dolgynwal (Ysbyty Ifan) and extant in an inspeximus of Edward II issued in December 1316. However, since this charter is of questionable authenticity, it provides a shaky foundation for dating the change in the prince's style.[603] The next dated document of Llywelyn's bearing the new style is no. 260, a letter patent of 1 May 1230 in favour of his leading official, Ednyfed Fychan, and the style occurs in all the prince's subsequent acts. Although the royal chancery continued to refer to Llywelyn by his previous title (*princeps Norwallie*) in August 1230, it had accepted the new style by May 1231 and this was used in royal documents thereafter.[604] A time lag of a year or so between the adoption of the style and its acceptance by the royal chancery is perhaps more credible than one of over five years. Unfortunately there are no other acts of Llywelyn's dated, or definitely datable to, the period from November 1225 to May 1230, although it should be noted that the pope continued to refer to him as 'prince of North Wales' in response to petitions from Joan and from the bishops of St Davids, Bangor and St Asaph in April 1226.[605] The balance of probability, then, is that the style 'Llywelyn, prince of Aberffraw and lord of Snowdon' was a recent innovation in May 1230. Why Llywelyn made the change at this time is unknown. It did not coincide with any major increase in the prince's power, already extensive in Wales since 1216–17. The change should probably be set against the background of Llywelyn's attempts in the 1220s to secure recognition of his hegemony over the other Welsh rulers and thus of a principality of Wales, attempts that reveal his dissatisfaction with the terms of his agreements with the crown at Worcester in 1218.[606] Although this can only be speculation, it may be that the catalyst for the change was the discovery of Joan's affair with William de Braose in April 1230: the dishonour to the prince may have made it all the more imperative to promote his authority and dignity in a new style whose terms were likely to find favour with traditionalist opinion in Gwynedd.[607]

These interpretations of the significance of the new style and the chronology of its adoption are arguably supported by the apparently unprecedented style used by Llywelyn's wife Joan: *domina Wallie* ('lady of Wales'). This style was recognized by the English crown by November 1235 at the latest,[608] but when it was first adopted is uncertain. No. 280, Joan's only surviving letter, which uses the style, was probably issued in 1230 × 1231. It is, however, notable that the English chancery referred to her as 'lady of North Wales' on several occasions between March 1227 and April 1230,[609] and earlier records refer to her

---

[603] No. 256 and note.

[604] *CR 1227–31*, 368; *PR 1225–32*, 436; see also the king's letters patent announcing agreements with Llywelyn in the 1230s (nos 266–7, 269–71). The reference to Llywelyn as 'prince of Wales' in January 1229 in *CLR 1226–40*, 115 (noticed in Williams, 'Succession to Gwynedd', 394, n. 1) was probably a clerical error for 'prince of North Wales'; Llywelyn was never accorded the former title in letters from the king, nor does he appear to have adopted it in his own acts.

[605] Vatican City, Archivio Segreto, Reg. Vat. 13, fo. 122v, nos 252–3 (*CPL*, i. 109); cf. no. 279 below.

[606] Cf. Pryce, 'Negotiating Anglo-Welsh relations', 17–18.

[607] Another possibility is that the political ideology of Aberffraw's supremacy, articulated by the lawyers but probably more widely current among *literati* in Gwynedd, was itself only a recent innovation in the spring of 1230, and that the new style was simply a response to new political ideas. However, the date of the relevant legal texts makes it equally possible that the lawyers' ideology was elaborated after, perhaps even in response to, the adoption of the new style.

[608] *CPR 1232–47*, 130. The obituary notices of Joan in the Annals of Tewkesbury and Annals of Chester likewise refers to her as *domina Wallie*, as do Welsh sources composed after her death in 1237: *AM*, i. 101; *Ann. Cestr.*, 61; Jones, 'Llyfr Coch Asaph', i. 73; *BT*, *Pen20Tr*, 104.

[609] *PR 1225–32*, 112; *CR 1227–31*, 68–9, 123, 322.

simply as the king's sister and/or the wife of Llywelyn.[610] If 'lady of North Wales' was regarded as the proper title for the wife of the 'prince of North Wales', perhaps the title 'lady of Wales' was adopted in or after 1230 to assert an elevation in status commensurate with that proclaimed by Llywelyn in his new title of 'prince of Aberffraw and lord of Snowdon'.[611] If so, this would reinforce the likelihood that Llywelyn was effectively proclaiming himself prince of Wales. Of course, the style may also have reflected the special status enjoyed by Joan as the daughter and sister of kings of England; it is worth noting that Emma of Anjou, wife of Llywelyn's uncle Dafydd ab Owain, had used the title *domina*.[612] Yet, even if the style was seen essentially as something honorific, and hence acceptable, by her brother Henry III, the combination of this title with 'Wales', which brings to mind the titles of Matilda as 'lady of England' or 'the English' about a century earlier, was something new and is likely to have had a political significance.[613]

Dafydd ap Llywelyn's styles changed according to political circumstances. There is no evidence that he continued his father's title 'prince of Aberffraw, lord of Snowdon', even though in one charter issued during his father's lifetime (in 1238) he is styled *David filius domini Lewelini principis de Aberfrau, domini Snaud'*.[614] Instead, in a charter of July 1240 and three letters of March–August 1241, Dafydd reverted to his father's first consistently used title, *princeps Norwallie*.[615] Possibly the threat from his half-brother Gruffudd prompted this emphasis on Dafydd's right to rule Gwynedd. But the greatest threat to Dafydd's position came from Henry III, who was determined to prevent his nephew from maintaining the hegemony established by Llywelyn. This change in royal policy was reflected in the agreement reached at Gloucester in May 1240, just over a month after Llywelyn's death, in which Dafydd is referred to ominously as *David filium Lewelyn' quondam principis Norwallie et domini de Abberfrau*.[616] Following his surrender to Henry at Gwerneigron on 29 August 1241, Dafydd adopted an abbreviated version of this style in his own letters patent of submission: *David filius Lewelini quondam principis Norwallie*.[617] In view of his use of the title *princeps Norwallie* earlier in that year, it is very likely that this new style was imposed on the prince of Gwynedd by his royal uncle. Certainly, Dafydd no longer used this style once he had returned to the attack following the death of Gruffudd ap Llywelyn on 1 March 1244. To judge by a letter of Innocent IV, Dafydd had resumed his title of *princeps Norwallie* by June or July of that year.[618] By the beginning of 1245 he had adopted a new style, *David princeps Wallie*, thereby reviving a title last used in Gwynedd by his great-grandfather Owain Gwynedd in the 1160s.[619]

The difficulty of maintaining a consistent style from reign to reign owing to the need for each new ruler to establish his dominance is further illustrated by the acts of Llywelyn ap Gruffudd. In a letter patent announcing an agreement with Maredudd ap Rhys Gryg and

---

[610] See, for example, *Foedera*, I. i. 152, 159.

[611] It is perhaps unlikely that Joan will have adopted the style until after her release from imprisonment by Llywelyn in 1231 (cf. above, pp. 28–9).

[612] No. 202: *Domina Emma soror Henrici regis uxor David filii Owini principis Norwallie*. Cf. *BT*, *RBH*, 164–5.

[613] Cf. Chibnall, *Empress Matilda*, 102.

[614] No. 289. In two earlier charters Dafydd is styled *David filii domini L. (principis)*: nos 286, 288.

[615] Nos 292, 294, 298–9.

[616] No. 291.

[617] Nos 300–5.

[618] No. 306.

[619] Nos 307–8.

Rhys Fychan of Deheubarth in 1251, Llywelyn and his brother Owain adopted a unique style that expressed their right to rule in Gwynedd by virtue of their descent from Gruffudd ap Llywelyn: *Owenus et Lewelinus filii Griffini filii Lewelini quondam principis, heredes Norwallie*.[620] However, in acts before 1262, both charters and letters, issued in his name alone Llywelyn styles himself simply *Lewelinus filius Griffini*.[621] A partial exception is no. 328, the agreement in 1258 between the Scottish and Welsh lords, in which Llywelyn is referred to as *princeps Wallie*. However, while this provides a valuable indication of the prince's aspirations, he avoided the title in his own acts until 1262, when he adopted the style *Lewelinus filius Griffini princeps Wallie, dominus Snaudon'*.[622] This clearly echoed Llywelyn ap Iorwerth's style in the 1230s, but differed from it both in the inclusion of a patronymic and, more importantly, by the substitution of 'Wales' for 'Aberffraw', perhaps under the influence of Dafydd ap Llywelyn's late acts. The patronymic was retained in charters as late as 1281,[623] but was dropped in letters to individuals from 1269. Letters patent with a general address present a less consistent picture: the patronymic appears until at least 1265,[624] is omitted in 1269 and in the letter ratifying the treaty of Aberconwy in 1277, but is used again in other letters concerning that treaty.[625] The omission of the patronymic in letters to individuals may reflect an attempt to endow Llywelyn with greater dignity following his recognition as prince of Wales in the treaty of Montgomery in 1267. If so, however, the prince's clerks clearly failed to impose this style across the whole range of his acts.

Llywelyn's style was adapted in the four letters sent by his wife Eleanor in the period 1279–82: *Alienora principissa Wallie, domina Snaudon'*.[626] Dafydd ap Gruffudd is styled *David filius Griffini* in acts issued during Llywelyn's lifetime. Ironically, given the desperate situation he faced after his brother's death, Dafydd was the first thirteenth-century prince of Gwynedd to continue his predecessor's style, to judge by two acts issued on 2 May 1283: *David filius Griffini princeps Wallie, dominus Snawdon*.[627]

External features

Palaeography

Of the forty-six surviving texts of charters issued by rulers of Gwynedd in this period, only five are extant in the original: one in favour of Haughmond Abbey, two from the Strata Marcella archive and two for the lay beneficiaries Einion ap Maredudd and his son Madog ab Einion. The hand of no. 226, Llywelyn ap Iorwerth's charter for Haughmond (1205 × 1211), points strongly towards its being a beneficiary product, influenced by some of the devices employed by the papal and episcopal chanceries, as it is written in an early thirteenth-century formal book hand modified by the extension of ascenders and a high degree of calligraphic embellishment, especially the decorative treatment of majuscules; other notable characteristics are the use of the *titulus* as the normal suspension mark and

---

[620] No. 316.

[621] In the light of Llywelyn's other surviving acts before 1262, the inclusion of *princeps Wallie* in no. 322 is almost certainly a later interpolation.

[622] The earliest example is no. 353 or no. 354.

[623] Nos 397, 423–4.

[624] Nos 329–30, 335–6, 361–2.

[625] Nos 368, 402–5, 407.

[626] Nos 433–6.

[627] Nos 456–7; both include the prince's patronymic.

the filling out of the last line by means of stretched ligatures.[628] No. 231, Llywelyn ap Iorwerth's charter for Strata Marcella in 1209, is written in a slightly modified book hand by a scribe otherwise unrepresented among the Strata Marcella charters; the use of *uu* for *w* also occurs in no. 18, Maredudd ap Rhobert's charter for Llanllugan. No. 282, issued by Gruffudd ap Llywelyn in 1226, the only example among the Strata Marcella documents of work by another scribe, is also written in a modified book hand, but exhibits a greater degree of currency than no. 231; a conservative feature is the use of the insular abbreviation ÷ for *est*.[629] No. 318, Llywelyn ap Gruffudd's charter for Einion ap Madog in 1243, is in a fully developed cursive hand, typical for the mid-thirteenth century.[630] The confirmation issued by Dafydd ap Gruffudd in 1260 to Einion's son Madog ab Einion is written in a small, economical book hand, much less cursive than that of no. 318, and is comparable, for example, with the hands of nos 583–5, issued by Gruffudd ap Gwenwynwyn 1232 × 1250.[631]

Only one original has been found of the acts with general addresses classified here as letters patent, namely no. 304, issued by Dafydd ap Llywelyn at Westminster in October 1241. It is written in a cursive script typical of English royal scribes at that date; indeed, given the circumstances of its production, the document may well have been written by a scribe belonging to Henry III's chancery.

Of the texts of eighty-nine letters with special addresses, fifty-eight are extant in the original. The earliest, Llywelyn ap Iorwerth's letter to Philip Augustus of France (1212), resembles a charter in its appearance: it is written in a modified book hand and is sealed patent, bearing the prince's great seal attached to a parchment tag that passes through slits in the fold.[632] The remaining originals, all extant among the 'Ancient Correspondence' (SC 1) in The National Archives: Public Record Office, are mostly written in cursive hands characteristic of business records of the period. Distinguishing between these hands in order to identify the work of individual scribes is difficult and the following observations are necessarily tentative.

No. 280 (1230 × 1231), the one surviving letter of Joan, displays the fewest cursive features of the sample, its hand being closely related to the simplified letter-forms (with a minimum of curved strokes) and 'stabbing' duct made by a stylus on wax, and lacking the fluency of movement of a scribe used to writing extensively with a quill on parchment.[633] Two of Llywelyn ap Iorwerth's letters, both datable to 1220, are written in a similar, perhaps identical, neat small hand with cursive elements found as much in additions and annotations in books as in business documents at this period, and distinguished from modified book hand by the scale of the writing, width of the nib, proportions of the letter-forms and

---

[628] Cf. Hector, *Handwriting of English Documents*, 30; Chaplais, *English Royal Documents*, 50–1.

[629] For these hands, designated L and Q by Graham Thomas, see *Ystrad Marchell Charters*, 110–11 and Plates 4iii and 7i. For the distinction between current and fully developed cursive hands see Webber, 'Scribes and handwriting', 147.

[630] Davies, 'Grant by Llewelyn', 158 and Plate XIV. The hand is of a similar type to that of no. 587 (1232 × 1263), and also, for example, to Holt, 'Willoughby deeds', Plates XII (1239) and XIII (1240). Madog may be the same as the *Madoco clerico nostro* who witnessed Llywelyn ap Gruffudd's charter for Ynys Lannog in 1247 (no. 320): Stephenson, *Governance*, 226.

[631] No. 441; Davies, 'Grant by David', 32 and Plate VIII.

[632] No. 235.

[633] For 'duct', meaning 'the distinctive manner in which strokes are traced upon the writing surface', and other palaeographical terms see Parkes, *English Cursive Book Hands*, xxvi.

a more cursive duct.[634] Nos 243 (1218 × 1230), 244 (1218 × 1237), 245 (1219 × 1221) and 247 (1220) (reproduced in Plate 1) are all written in well-developed cursive hands which exhibit close similarities to each other and could therefore be the work of the same scribe. It is not impossible even that this group of letters was written by the same scribe as the previous two discussed, the differences resulting simply from the use of different grades of script.[635] Nos 249 (1221 × 1222) and 255 (1224) (reproduced in Plate 2) are written in a well-developed cursive and rapid cursive hand respectively, each by a different scribe who clearly did not write any of the previously mentioned letters. Nos 237 (1215 × 1216) and 263 (1230) are badly stained but appear to be written in similar, though probably in neither case identical, cursive hands to that of no. 249.[636] The cursive hand of no. 308 is somewhat conservative for 1245, when the letter was written on behalf of Dafydd ap Llywelyn, and could possibly be the work of the same scribe who wrote several of the letters of Llywelyn ap Iorwerth in and around 1220.[637]

The thirty-one original letters of Llywelyn ap Gruffudd, extant from 1257 to 1282, are all written in the fully developed cursive handwriting which had developed primarily for business purposes during the late twelfth and earlier thirteenth centuries, although not all of them conform in all details to the distinctive variety of this script known as anglicana used in England from the mid-thirteenth century.[638] The same is true of the four original letters of Princess Eleanor, written in the period 1279–82,[639] and the eight original letters of Dafydd ap Gruffudd, datable to between 1275 and 1282.[640] These cursive hands exhibit close similarities to each other and are therefore very difficult to distinguish. Nos 427 (reproduced in Plate 5) and 436, both dated at Nefyn, 2 February 1282, are rare exceptions, the distinctive character of the hand being supported by a common orthographic peculiarity (the spelling *Agnlie*) and method of deletion; these letters thus show the same scribe writing on behalf of both Llywelyn and Eleanor.[641] Of Dafydd ap Gruffudd's letters, nos 444, 446, 450–1 and 453 share common stylistic details, especially the use and treatment of hairline strokes (producing a somewhat spiky appearance), which suggests that they are probably written by the same scribe.[642]

---

[634] Nos 246, 248.

[635] The lower part of the *g* is strikingly similar in all five letters, though this one feature is insufficient evidence to establish a conclusive identification.

[636] Images of no. 263 are available on a website devoted to this document: *http://www.ukans.edu/carrie/ms_room/jjcrump/document.html.*

[637] Nos 243, 245–8, discussed above.

[638] For example, no. 380, reproduced in Plate 3. Cf. Parkes, *English Cursive Book Hands*, xiv–xv; Huws, *Medieval Welsh Manuscripts*, 17–18.

[639] Nos 433–6. No. 434 is reproduced in Plate 4.

[640] Nos 444–6, 448–51, 453.

[641] Some other letters may tentatively be grouped together on account of their being written in similar hands, and possibly by the same scribe, distinctive to each group: (a) nos 353, 355 and 356; (b) nos 384–6; (c) nos 393–4; and (d) nos 401 and 411. However, these identifications are by no means conclusive. Thus, in (a), the hand of no. 353 seems narrower and more upright than those of nos 355–6, suggesting a different personal duct, though this could simply result from the same scribe writing no. 353 in a more deliberate fashion. In (b), the letters *g*, *d* and *b* are somewhat different between nos 384 and 386, and in (c) no. 394 has a less distinctive *g*, different *h* and shorter descender on the *r* than no. 393. In addition, the hands of nos 370 and 376 are probably the same, while the hands of nos 377–8 are similar to each other and different from those of nos 370 and 376.

[642] The absence of this style in no. 452, whose hand is pure anglicana, arguably reinforces the likelihood that the text of that letter is a copy rather than an original.

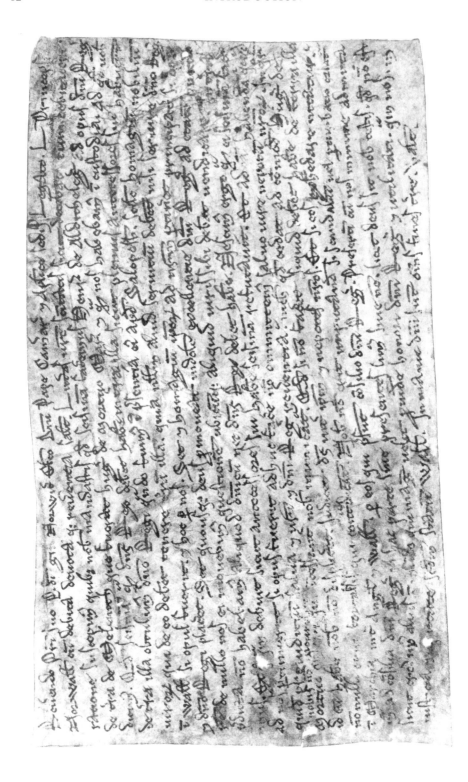

Plate 1 Letter of Llywelyn ap Iorwerth (no. 247)

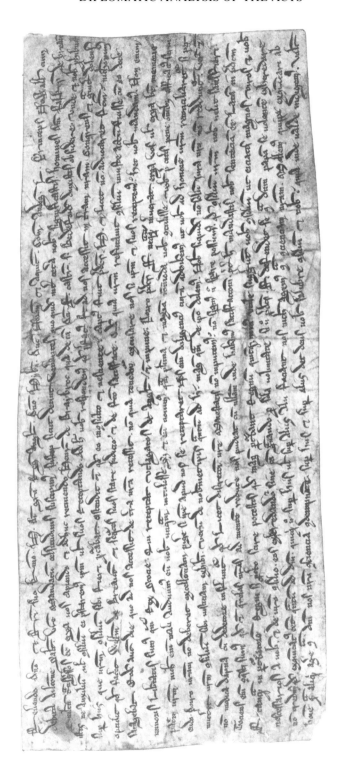

Plate 2 Letter of Llywelyn ap Iorwerth (no. 255)

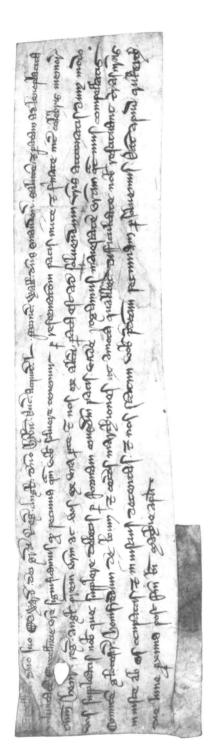

Plate 3 Letter of Llywelyn ap Gruffudd (no. 380)

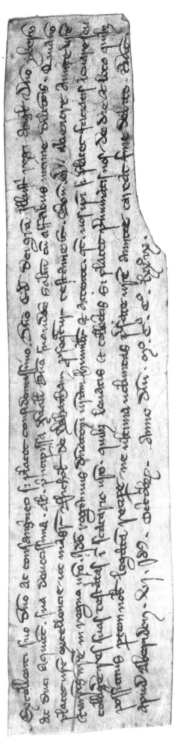

Plate 4 Letter of Eleanor, Princess of Wales (no. 434)

Plate 5 Letter of Llywelyn ap Gruffudd (no. 427)

Sealing and seals

No. 226 (for Haughmond Abbey) and nos 231 and 282 (both for Strata Marcella) were sealed on a parchment tag through horizontal slits in the fold at the foot of the charter (*sur double queue*), though in the latter two cases the seal is missing. No. 235, Llywelyn ap Iorwerth's letter to Philip Augustus, is likewise sealed *sur double queue* and includes an impression of the prince's great seal. The sealing of both Llywelyn ap Gruffudd's charter for Einion ap Madog and Dafydd ap Gruffudd's confirmation for Einion's son is unusual, as both charters were sealed on cloth tags inserted through holes in the centre of the fold at the foot of the document; neither seal survives.[643] Evidence for the sealing of Venedotian rulers' letters patent is meagre: no. 304 (1241), issued by Dafydd ap Llywelyn, is sealed *sur double queue*, while Evan Evans (d. 1788) described the original of no. 260 (1230) as having a seal attached by a tag of 'twist silk'.

Apart from no. 235, the original letters with special addresses appear to have been sealed close as they contained a tongue partially cut off the foot of the document, from right to left, which would have been tied round the letter after it had been folded; a seal would then have been applied to the loop, securing the tongue to the main parchment.[644] Several letters contain slits in the main body of the parchment through which, presumably, a tongue or tag would have passed in closing the folded document.[645] However, no traces of wax remain on any of the surviving examples and most have had their tongue completely cut away, although in a few cases the tongue remains, with the address written on its right-hand side.[646] That Llywelyn ap Iorwerth's letters, at least, were normally sealed with his great seal is suggested by two letters in which the prince felt it necessary to explain that his privy seal had been used as his great seal was not to hand, whereas the rest of his letters make no mention of sealing.[647]

Llywelyn ap Iorwerth and Dafydd ap Llywelyn are the only rulers of Gwynedd for whom seal impressions survive. How many of their twelfth-century predecessors had seals is unknown. In view of his contacts with the Anglo-Norman world it is possible that Gruffudd ap Cynan had a seal, and comparison with contemporary practice elsewhere makes it likely that Owain Gwynedd sealed the letters in his name now extant only in copies, especially as his younger brother Cadwaladr ap Gruffudd possessed a seal to judge by the corroboration clause of his one surviving charter.[648] Charters of Dafydd ab Owain, his wife Emma and their son Owain likewise show that each of these had seals, as did the brothers Gruffudd and Maredudd sons of Cynan ab Owain.[649]

For Llywelyn ap Iorwerth, the evidence of corroboration clauses is supplemented by impressions of two equestrian seals and one counterseal. The impressions, all imperfect and originally *c*.70 mm. diameter, of equestrian seals attached to documents of 1205 × 1211, 1209 and 1222 seem to be from the same matrix.[650] The first two impressions contain

---

[643] Nos 318, 441.

[644] Nos 324, 340, 343, 353–6, 370, 376–80, 384–6, 392–4, 400–1, 413, 415–22, 427. Cf. Chaplais, *English Royal Documents*, 30–1; Constable, *Letters and Letter-Collections*, 47.

[645] Nos 248, 354, 370, 378, 380, 434, 449; cf. *Letters and Charters of Cardinal Guala*, ed. Vincent, xci.

[646] Nos 354, 377, 448–9.

[647] Nos 248, 262.

[648] No. 197. Cf. Constable, *Letters and Letter-Collections*, 47.

[649] Nos 200–2, 204–8.

[650] Nos 226, 231, 252. Descriptions of last two seals in Siddons, 'Welsh equestrian seals', 305 (and

fragments of a legend: '. . . . . I PRINCIPIS : N . . . .', and 'SIGIL . . . . IPI . . . .'.[651] The legend on the last example is completely lost. An imperfect impression of a similar, yet different, equestrian seal, also originally c.70 mm. diameter, is attached to Llywelyn's letter to Philip Augustus (1212); the legend reads '+ SIGILLVM : LOELI . . . . . .'.[652] In common with most other Welsh rulers of the twelfth and thirteenth centuries as well as barons in England, Llywelyn ap Iorwerth thus used a single-sided equestrian seal as his great seal, rather than a two-sided seal, with the ruler enthroned in front and mounted on a horse on the back, used by the kings of England and Scotland from the reigns of William II and Alexander I respectively.[653]

In addition, Llywelyn possessed a privy or secret seal, an antique gem engraved with a boar lying under a tree, used as a counterseal in his agreement with Ranulf III of Chester in 1222, with the legend 'SIGILLVM . SECRETVM . LEWLINI'.[654] By 1230, to judge by Evan Evans's description of the original of no. 260, the prince had at least one other counterseal, in this case depicting a flower (Evans makes no reference to a legend on either the equestrian seal or the counterseal he described). The precise models followed by Llywelyn, indeed whether he was the first of his dynasty to use a counterseal, can only be guessed. Although the earls of Chester were precociously early among English magnates in their adoption of counterseals, the earliest example being an intaglio gem that belonged to Ranulf II in the 1140s which was also used by his successor Hugh II (1153–81), the counterseal used by Ranulf III from c.1218 was heraldic.[655] Episcopal influence cannot be ruled out: like other contemporary prelates, Bishop Cadwgan of Bangor (1215–35/6) possessed a privy seal, bearing the legend '+ S' SECRETVM . CADVCANI . EPI'.[656] However, it is equally if not more likely that familiarity with Angevin royal practice was the crucial influence, especially in view of Llywelyn's marriage to Joan. Richard I is the first king of England known to have had a privy seal, and John, as count of Mortain, used an antique intaglio gem in a finger-ring with a legend comparable to Llywelyn's ('SECRETVM IOHANNIS'); he also had a privy seal after his accession as king. Llywelyn's privy seal may likewise have been worn in a ring. Llywelyn was using a privy seal by 1220, but references in his letters suggest that this was not normally an acceptable alternative to his great equestrian seal.[657] Rather, he probably followed English royal and baronial practice and used a privy seal for private or secret correspondence and also, as in 1222 and (apparently) 1230, as a counterseal to his single-sided equestrian seal which

Plate A XIII, 2 (for no. 231); plate of seal attached to no. 252 in Harvey and McGuinness, *Guide*, 29 (Fig. 24). For a modern impression from what appears to be the same matrix see Williams, *Catalogue of Seals*, i. 34, 77 (Plate W1).

[651] It seems that more of the legend of no. 226's seal was preserved when J. B. Blakeway drew it in the nineteenth century, as he gives the reading (probably somewhat inaccurately) as '. . . . . I PRINCIPI NOWII . . . .': Oxford, Bodleian Library, MS Blakeway 17, fo. 133r.

[652] No. 235. The forelegs of the horse stretch out at less of a right-angle than those on the seals attached to nos 231 and 252. Descriptions of seal in Siddons, 'Welsh seals in Paris', 539–40 (and Plate II, no. XII); *idem*, 'Welsh equestrian seals', 304–5 (and Plate A XIII, 1).

[653] Crouch, *Image of Aristocracy*, 246; Harvey and McGuinness, *Guide*, 27, 29.

[654] No. 252, illustrated in Williams, *Welsh History through Seals*, 19; Harvey and McGuinness, *Guide*, 29 (Fig. 24).

[655] Heslop, 'Seals', 180, 183, 187–92, 194–6.

[656] Williams, 'Catalogue of Welsh ecclesiastical seals: I', 110 (and Plate XVI, no. 5).

[657] Nos 248, 262.

guaranteed that the document had been sealed with his assent. As in English aristocratic society, the possession of a counterseal was a marker of status, for it implied that the owner had a clerical office which looked after the great seal.[658]

The most intriguing evidence for seals used by the rulers of Gwynedd is an imperfect impression, originally c.(?)80–90 mm. diameter, of a two-sided seal appended to no. 304 (1241), a letter patent of Dafydd ap Llywelyn. Previous discussion of this seal has been based on an early nineteenth-century description and engraving by J. B. Blakeway. However, the recent rediscovery of the document has made it possible to compare this depiction with photographs of the seal, which appears to have been slightly less damaged when Blakeway saw it.[659] The impression shows a ruler enthroned with upright sword in his right hand in front and mounted with a shield on the back. As Blakeway noted, the impression is identical with Henry III's first great seal apart from the device on the shield, which he believed to be a lion rampant that had been cut in after the seal was originally impressed. He therefore suggested that the impression had been made from a matrix of Henry's great seal, from which the legend had been removed, and 'the lions of England scraped off to make room for the single lion of Wales'.[660]

While the close similarity to Henry III's great seal is undeniable, crucial aspects of Blakeway's interpretation concerning its character and manufacture are impossible to verify. The view that the legend had been removed from the matrix can only be speculation, as no legend survives (nor was any visible when Blakeway inspected the seal). His identification of the device on the shield as a single lion rampant, though consistent with the evidence of the engraving, remains uncertain, both because the engraving is too imprecise to permit certainty and because only about half of the shield now survives; this makes it very difficult to make out the remains of the device. Moreover, if the identification is correct, this also poses problems, as the device would correspond to neither of the heraldic shields depicted by Matthew Paris in association with Dafydd. One of these bears the arms Quarterly Or and Gules, four lions passant counter-changed, and is similar to the arms attributed to other princes of Gwynedd in thirteenth-century sources. The other, by contrast, has Or, three roundels Vert, on a chief dancetty Vert a lion passant Sable, and is attested nowhere else.[661] The existence of two different arms in Paris's manuscripts may indicate that, as in early thirteenth-century England,[662] armorials were still fluid in Wales at this period and therefore that the putative single lion rampant belonged to a context of variety and experimentation.

Be that as it may, the attraction to the prince of a two-sided seal as a visible means of augmenting his status is easy to understand. That the king tolerated, and possibly even facilitated, this calls for explanation, however. After all, from as early as their meeting at Gloucester in May 1240 Henry revealed his determination to clip his nephew's wings and

---

[658] Cf. Chaplais, *English Royal Documents*, 23–5; Crouch, *Image of Aristocracy*, 244–6; Harvey and McGuinness, *Guide*, 35–7, 58–9.

[659] Owen and Blakeway, *History of Shrewsbury*, i. 117–18. I am very grateful to David Crook for providing me with photographs and measurements of the seal, which will be fully described and discussed in a forthcoming publication by himself, David H. Williams and David Crouch.

[660] Siddons, 'Welsh equestrian seals', 305–6, supports this theory and argues that the impression was made from Henry III's first great seal.

[661] Siddons, *Development of Welsh Heraldry*, 280–2 and Plates XXI (a), (b), XXII.

[662] Cf. Heslop, 'Seals', 195.

prevent him from enjoying the same hegemony as Llywelyn ap Iorwerth.[663] Possibly, as David Crouch has suggested, the answer lies precisely in Dafydd's special relationship to the Plantagenet dynasty as a grandson of King John. Just as he was allowed by the king at Gloucester to wear a coronet known as the *garlonde*, described by the Tewkesbury annalist as the insignia of Gwynedd but which also, significantly, was comparable with the garland used in the coronation of John as duke of Normandy in 1199, so too may Dafydd have received a version of the king's great seal on that occasion as another means of demonstrating his superiority not only over other Welsh rulers but over English magnates too.[664] If the seal was a diplomatic gift from the king (in contrast to the garland, which Dafydd probably inherited from his father Llywelyn), this may suggest in turn that, at least initially, Henry was ready to concede to his nephew new trappings of power while at the same time endeavouring to diminish its substance.

It is unknown whether Dafydd ap Llywelyn's seal set a precedent for the prince's successors, as no impressions survive of the seals of Owain, Llywelyn, Dafydd and Rhodri sons of Gruffudd ap Llywelyn (or of Gruffudd himself). However, corroboration clauses in charters and letters patent not surprisingly show that these members of the dynasty possessed seals.[665] In addition, Llywelyn ap Gruffudd's privy seal was found in his breeches after his death in December 1282.[666] Together with the privy seals of Dafydd ap Gruffudd and Eleanor, this was melted down to make a chalice in 1284.[667]

ARWYSTLI

Texts of twelve charters survive in the names of rulers of Arwystli from the mid-twelfth century to 1215, four in favour of St Michael's church, Trefeglwys and/or Haughmond Abbey,[668] and eight in favour of Strata Marcella, of which five are originals.[669] The earliest charter, recording a grant by Hywel ab Ieuaf of protection and sanctuary to Trefeglwys, is extant only in early modern transcripts whose dispositive clauses are incomplete.[670]

Four charters open with a protocol consisting of the ruler's style, a general address and a greeting. In no. 1, Hywel ab Ieuaf's charter of protection for Trefeglwys, the style precedes the address (*Heuel rex Arguestli omnibus sancte ecclesie tam modernis quam futuris salutem*),[671] whereas in his sons' charters for Haughmond and Strata Marcella it follows the address. The address and greeting of no. 4, Meurig ap Hywel's confirmation to Haughmond, are the same as those in a charter for the abbey issued by Owain ap Dafydd

---

[663] No. 291.

[664] Crouch, *Image of Aristocracy*, 93–4, 203–4, 246. Interpretation is further complicated by uncertainty as to whether Dafydd's seal was the same size as Henry III's great seal or somewhat smaller.

[665] See, for example, no. 284, which refers to the seals of both Gruffudd ap Llywelyn and his wife Senana.

[666] *CAC*, 129.

[667] Taylor, 'Fragment', 256–8.

[668] Nos 1–4.

[669] Nos 5–6, 8–13.

[670] No. 1. For further discussion of the textual transmission and diplomatic of this charter see Pryce, 'Church of Trefeglwys', 18–24, 27–33.

[671] The use of *modernis* in the address is unusual among the charters in this edition, though it also occurs, in a different formula, in a charter for Cwm-hir (no. 108).

of Gwynedd at about the same period (*universis Dei fidelibus tam presentes quam futuris Meuric filius Hoel de Arwistl salutem in domino*),[672] while those in nos 5 and 8, charters of Meurig and his brother Hywel for Strata Marcella in 1198, are almost identical to each other (*universis sancte matris filiis (tam) presentibus et futuris qui presentem cartam inspexerint [N.] salutem et pacem bonam*). The remaining eight charters incorporate the style and general address in the notification. The forms of the address vary, though most include the phrase *tam presentes quam futuri* (or the equivalent in the dative), the only exception being *omnes ad quos presens scriptum pervenerit* in no. 2. There are two examples of *tam presentibus quam futuris*;[673] three of *omnibus/universis sancte matris ecclesie filii tam presentibus quam futuris* and one with the same formula in the nominative;[674] and one of *tam presentes quam futuri presentes literas inspecturi vel audituri*.[675]

Hywel ab Ieuaf is styled 'Hywel, king of Arwystli' in nos 1 and 2, but with his name and patronymic only (*Hoel filius Geuaf*) in no. 3. His sons and grandsons are all styled by name and patronymic, though a territorial name is appended to the latter in one charter of Meurig ap Hywel (*Meuric filius Hoel de Arwistl*) and in the charters issued by the sons of Owain o'r Brithdir (for example, *David filius Owyni de Bridtyr*).[676] The style in no. 10 is unusual in naming the grantor's mother as well as father, apparently because title to the lands granted derived from her (*Grifinus Coch Grifini filius de Karno ex matre Levchv filia Kadwallavn*).

The notifications in nine of the charters use forms of *noscere*, most commonly *notum sit*, followed either by *me/nos* and the perfect infinitive or by *quod ego* and the dispositive verb(s) in the perfect tense. The latter construction also occurs in the three charters, two for Haughmond and one for Strata Marcella, that use *sciant* in the notification.[677] Only two charters, both issued in favour of Strata Marcella in 1198, are written in the first person plural, the rest being in the first person singular.[678] The dispositive verbs vary: the most frequent combination is *dedi et concessi et (hac) presenti carta confirmavi* (or the equivalent in the perfect infinitive),[679] though *dedisse* is omitted in no. 4 and *dedi* is used alone in nos 2 and 13; the two charters recording sales have *vendidi*.[680] The majority of grants are said to be given in alms (*in perpetuam elemosinam, in puram/liberam et perpetuam elemosinam*), though the formula is adapted in the two sales to *in liberam (et quietam) et perpetuam possessionem*, and Dafydd ab Owain's confirmation to Strata Marcella has *iure perpetuo in possessionem*.[681] No. 1 has a sanction (*Et quicunque predicte ecclesie refugium violaverit iram Dei et omnium sanctorum incurrat*). Four charters contain corroboration clauses: one, in a charter for Haughmond, refers to sealing only, the others, all for Strata Marcella, refer to sealing and witnesses in formulae found in other charters for that abbey.[682] Dating clauses occur in seven

---

[672] Cf. no. 205.
[673] Nos 9–10.
[674] Nos 3, 11–13.
[675] No. 6.
[676] Nos 4, 11 and also 12–13.
[677] Nos 2, 3, 6.
[678] Nos 5, 8.
[679] Nos 3, 5–6, 8, 11–12.
[680] Nos 9–10. The dispositive verb is lacking in the copies of no. 1, but was probably a form of *suscipere*.
[681] Nos 9–11. No. 13 lacks any reference to alms or perpetual right.
[682] Nos 3, 6, 9–10. The clauses in the latter two charters are identical and belong to a distinctive group of corroboration clauses in the Strata Marcella charters: see above, pp. 64–5, n. 502.

charters, all for Strata Marcella.[683] These are introduced by *facta est*, the most common usage in charters for the abbey, apart from no. 10, which has *datum*, and no. 6, which is integrated into the corroboration clause. Each has a time-date (the year of the incarnation only) and five also include a place-date.[684] All charters have a witness list, usually introduced by *Hi(i)s testibus . . .*, though no. 8 is in the nominative and begins *Huius igitur donationis testes sunt*, a formula occasionally used in other charters for Strata Marcella.[685]

Eight of the charters include ecclesiastics in their witness lists, but none of these is explicitly associated with the grantor and there are no references to scribes.[686] It is difficult to determine how far the charters in favour of Trefeglwys and/or Haughmond were drawn up by the beneficiaries, though the inclusion of a sanction in no. 1 shows that it was at least heavily indebted to ecclesiastical models.[687] On account of similarities between their diplomatic and that of other charters issued for the abbey, it is likely that most if not all of the charters for Strata Marcella were written by the beneficiaries. The weakest candidates for beneficiary production are the closely related nos 5 and 8, recording a grant of Cwm Llwyd by the brothers Meurig and Hywel in 1198. These differ from all other charters issued by Welsh rulers for the abbey in their use of the first person plural and in their notification (*notum facimus universitati vestre nos* followed by the dispositive verbs in the perfect infinitive), while the inclusion of a protocol with a general address and greeting is exceptional, the only parallel being a charter issued over thirty years later by Madog ap Caswallon.[688] However, the formula *universis sancte matris filiis (tam) presentibus et futuris* in the address is common in other Strata Marcella charters, as is the use of *facta est* in the dating clause; as noted above, the form of the witness list in no. 8 is also paralleled elsewhere in the abbey's charters.[689]

The strongest candidate as a beneficiary product is no. 9, an original whose scribe also wrote three charters of Gwenwynwyn.[690] The charter is written in a modified book hand which uses the insular abbreviation ÷ for *est* and places an accent to show stress on the Welsh place-name *Llanamdéueri*.[691] Though each of the hands of the other four originals is attested only once in the Strata Marcella archive, it is probable that they, too, derived from the abbey's scriptorium.[692] These are also written in modified book hands, with the spacing of the words and the letter-forms in no. 12 creating an impression of formality particularly reminiscent of a book hand.

Each of the originals was sealed on a parchment tag inserted through the fold at the foot of the document (*sur double queue*), and two of the texts extant only in copies, one issued by Hywel ab Ieuaf, the other by Meurig ap Hywel, refer to the grantor's seal in their corrob-

---

[683] Nos 5–6, 8–11, 13.

[684] Place-dates: nos 6, 9–11, 13.

[685] Cf. nos 231, 545, 556.

[686] Nos 2–3, 5, 9–13.

[687] Pryce, 'Church of Trefeglwys', 32.

[688] No. 581.

[689] For the diplomatic of the Strata Marcella charters as a whole see *Ystrad Marchell Charters*, 104–9, and below, pp. 124–7.

[690] Nos 552, 563, 575.

[691] Thomas's Scribe E: *Ystrad Marchell Charters*, 110–11 and Plate 2ii.

[692] Nos 8, 10–12, written respectively by Thomas's Scribes D, J, N and O: *Ystrad Marchell Charters*, 110–11 and plates 2i, 4i, 5ii, 6i. The insular abbreviation ÷ for *est* occurs in the two earlier charters, nos 8 and 10, dated 1198 and 1207 respectively.

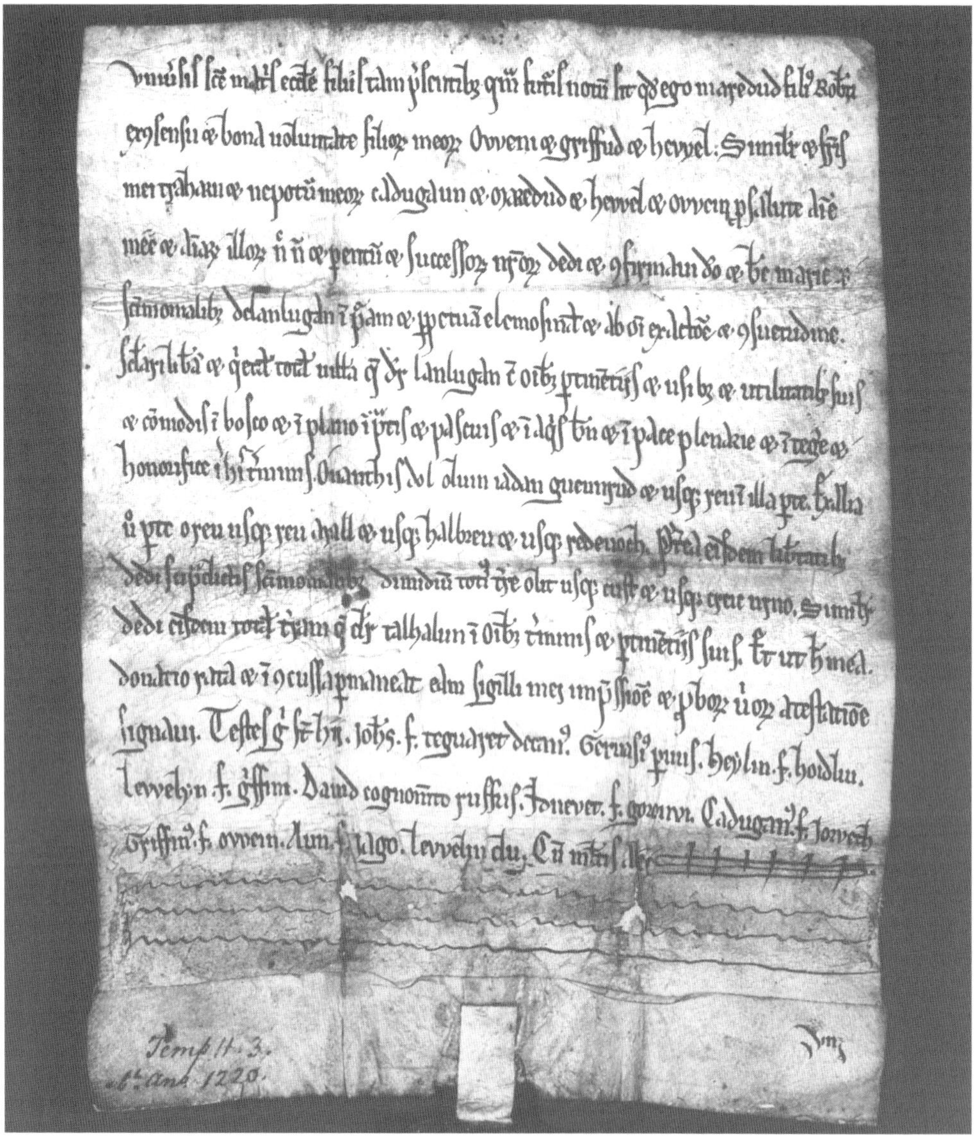

Plate 6 Charter of Maredudd ap Rhobert (no. 18)

oration clauses.[693] Three impressions of circular equestrian seals survive, each with the
horse and rider facing right.[694] Those of Hywel ap Hywel (originally *c*.60 mm. diameter)
and Dafydd ab Owain o'r Brithdir (originally *c*.50 mm. diameter) are imperfect, and most
of their legends are lost, the former reading 'SIG . . . .', the latter '+ SIG

[693] Nos 3, 6.
[694] Full descriptions in Siddons, 'Welsh equestrian seals', 307.

. . . . TIR'.[695] Though nearly complete, the seal of Madog ab Owain (originally *c*.55 mm.) is worn and bears only the remains of a legend: 'SIG . . . .'.[696]

CEDEWAIN

The five texts of acts issued by Maredudd ap Rhobert of Cedewain consist of one charter and two records of judgement in charter form, all three of which are originals,[697] together with two letters patent, extant only in copies.[698] The records of judgements, both probably datable to 1216 × *c*.1226, concern the same land dispute and were issued by Maredudd acting on behalf of his overlord Llywelyn ap Iorwerth; they are preserved among the muniments of Strata Marcella, which held part of the disputed land. No. 16 is written in a cursive hand that also wrote a charter of Gwenwynwyn for Strata Marcella in 1215, suggesting that its scribe was a monk of that abbey; the same may be true of no. 17, too, although its modified book hand is not found elsewhere among the abbey's charters.[699] No. 18 (reproduced in Plate 6), a charter datable to *c*.1216 × 1236 which records a gift to the nunnery of Llanllugan, is written in a generally upright modified book hand that endows the charter with the requisite solemnity by elongating and elaborating ascenders as well as giving descenders to *f*, *r* and long-*s*. These features are paralleled in other documents at the beginning of the proposed date range but would be conservative for its end. That its scribe was more familiar with writing manuscripts is possibly suggested by the consistent use of the ampersand rather than the tironian *nota* as an abbreviation for *et*, a usage considered old-fashioned even for book hand by this period though it remained common in liturgical manuscripts.[700]

Of the three acts in charter form, only no. 16, one of the records of judgement, opens with a protocol containing a general address (*omnibus tam presentibus quam futuris ad quos presens pervenerit scriptum*) and greeting (*salutem*). The two letters patent, both dated at Montgomery, 8 October 1223, closely resemble that issued by Llywelyn ap Iorwerth on the same occasion in most respects, including a protocol with the address *omnibus ad quos presens carta pervenerit* and greeting *salutem*.[701] General addresses, each different from either of those just cited as well as from each other, are incorporated into the notification in the other record of judgement and the charter for Llanllugan.[702] Maredudd's style in both acts recording judgements includes the title 'lord of Cedewain' as well as his name and patronymic (*Mareduth filius Roberti dominus de Kedeweinc*), whereas the charter for Llanllugan and the letters patent have his name and patronymic only.

---

[695] Nos 8, 11.

[696] No. 12.

[697] Nos 16–18.

[698] Nos 19–20.

[699] *Ystrad Marchell Charters*, 110–11 and Plates 5i and 6ii (Scribes M and P).

[700] Cf. Huws, *Medieval Welsh Manuscripts*, 176. The only other examples of originals in this edition which consistently use the ampersand are nos 22 (1146 × 1151), 108 (1179 × 1212) and 113 (1212). Perhaps surprisingly, however, it is also very common in no. 583, a charter of Gruffudd ap Gwenwynwyn written in Derbyshire 1232 × 1250. The ampersand is occasionally used in several charters for Strata Marcella, though in all these cases the clear preference is for the tironian *nota*: nos 8, 12, 231, 487, 545, 548.

[701] Nos 19–20; cf. no. 254.

[702] Nos 17–18.

The text of all the charters is written in the first person singular, that of the letters patent (only one of which is in Maredudd's name alone) in the first person plural. The notifications in the charters all use forms of *noscere* followed by *quod* and verbs in the perfect tense, whereas the letters patent have *sciatis nos* followed by the verb in the perfect infinitive. The two judgements contain lengthy narrations setting out the details of the dispute and the verdict reached; the dispositive verbs in the charter for Llanllugan are *dedi et confirmavi*, the gift is said to be in pure and perpetual alms and the boundaries of the lands are described in a mixture of Latin and Welsh found in some other charters for Cistercian beneficiaries.[703] Two charters include corroboration clauses, one, placed after the witness list, referring to the document and Maredudd's seal, the other (in the Llanllugan charter), preceding the witness list, referring to sealing and witnesses.[704] Only one letter patent has a corroboration clause, which is incomplete (*Et in huius rei testimonium etc.*).[705] None of Maredudd's acts contains a dating clause, though a time-date is referred to in the text of both letters patent. One of the records of judgement and the charter have witness lists, introduced by the phrase *Testes igitur hii sunt/sunt hii*;[706] the other record of judgement lists arbitrators in the text after the phrase *Isti igitur sunt qui affuerunt* and ends with a final greeting (*Valete*).[707] The witness lists in the letters patent are incomplete.

Each of the acts in charter form was sealed on a parchment tag inserted through the fold at the foot of the document (*sur double queue*), and the seal impression survives in each case. Those attached to nos 16 and 17 were definitely, and that attached to no. 18 almost certainly, made from the same matrix.[708] All are circular, *c*.55 mm. diameter, showing an equestrian figure riding to the right. The legend is lost on the impression attached to no. 17 and virtually lost on that of no. 16, which reads '+ . . . . C'. However, more survives of the legend on the seal of no. 18 ('. . . . EREDVD FIL . . . . . DE . . EDEV . . .'), suggesting that its original wording was something like '+ SIGILLVM MEREDVD FILII ROBERTI DE KEDEWEINC'.

DEHEUBARTH

The forty-three extant texts issued on behalf or with the consent of rulers of Deheubarth consist of fourteen charters,[709] thirteen letters patent with general addresses,[710] four letters with special addresses,[711] three petitions to the king,[712] three sets of *gravamina* sent to Archbishop Pecham in 1282[713] and six agreements. Two of the agreements are with Bishop Iorwerth of St Davids in 1222, one with the abbey of Strata Florida in 1279 and three with

---

[703] See below, p. 100.
[704] Nos 16, 18.
[705] No. 19.
[706] Nos 17–18.
[707] No. 16.
[708] Siddons, 'Welsh equestrian seals', 308.
[709] Nos 22, 26, 28, 35, 46, 50, 55, 57, 63, 71, 78, 82, 84, 97. The authenticity of no. 82 is dubious.
[710] Nos 66, 72–3, 76, 80, 85–6, 88, 93, 95–6, 99–100.
[711] Nos 70, 79, 87, 89.
[712] Nos 75, 83, 94.
[713] Nos 77, 101–2.

Payn de Chaworth, Edward I's commander in west Wales, in the spring of 1277.[714] The following comments will concentrate on the diplomatic of the charters and letters.[715]

Apart from nos 71 and 84, all the charters are in favour of ecclesiastical beneficiaries, six of them for Strata Florida. As will become evident, the diplomatic of the charters, including those for Strata Florida, exhibits considerable variety, making it difficult to assess the extent to which their drafting was controlled by beneficiaries as opposed to the ruler's clerks. However, the stark contrasts between the two surviving charters in the name of the Lord Rhys, one for Chertsey Abbey in Surrey, the other for Strata Florida, strongly suggests that at least one of these was a beneficiary product; indeed, the influence of English royal diplomatic on the Chertsey charter may well indicate that it was drawn up by the monks and presented to Rhys for authentication.[716] Otherwise, however, the example of the royal chancery had little impact on charter-writing, which, as in Gwynedd and Powys, seems primarily indebted to ecclesiastical models. On the other hand, letters patent from 1258 onwards announcing obligations to Llywelyn ap Gruffudd bear resemblances to letters patent of that prince and their drafting may have been influenced by the practices of Llywelyn's clerks, especially when they were dated at places in Gwynedd.[717]

No. 22, the earliest charter (1146 × 1151), issued by Cadell ap Gruffudd for Totnes Priory in Devon, is the only surviving original. It is written in a book hand characteristic of the mid-twelfth century, with a margin on all sides and majuscule letters at the beginning of the notification (where the opening *N* is set to the left of the rest of the text in the margin, in a manner reminiscent of initials in manuscripts) as well as of the dating clause and witness list. The ampersand is used consistently as the abbreviation for *et*. As Crouch implies, the document was probably drafted and written at Lampeter by a Welsh clerk who did not often produce charters, quite possibly the *Guffus clericus noster* of the witness list. Apart from this use of *noster*, which contrasts with the *eius* used to describe the relationship of the preceding witness to Cadell and may indicate that the scribe was more used to drafting ecclesiastical documents, the text is written in the first person singular, with the dipositive verbs *do et concedo* in the present tense. An unusual feature of the corroboration clause is its reference to Cadell's oath as well as seal. The dating clause consists of a place-date only. Though detached from the rest of the charter, the parchment tag to which the seal is attached must originally have been inserted through slits in a fold at the base, now cut away (*sur double queue*). The seal, on white wax, is incomplete, and depicts an equestrian figure riding to the right wearing a surcoat of chain mail extending to the bottom of the horse and holding a shield in the left hand and the remains of a sword in the right; the remains of a legend read '. . . . . FILII GR . . . . .'.[718]

Cadell's charter is one of only two that lack a protocol, the other being no. 71, Owain ap Maredudd's grant of dower to his wife Angharad in 1273. The remaining twelve charters have various forms of address (*inscriptio*), though all those for Strata Florida include the

---

[714] Nos 43, 52, 74, 92, 98.

[715] The distinction drawn between charters and letters patent issued by rulers of Gwynedd (above, p. 59) also applies to those of the rulers of Deheubarth, although here, too, the distinction was not rigid: cf. no. 78 (1283), referred to as a *carta* in the corroboration clause and as *littere patentes* in the additional corroboration by Llywelyn ap Gruffudd after the sealing clause.

[716] Nos 26, 28.

[717] Namely, nos 85 (Caernarfon), 88 (Abereiddon) and 100 (Dolwyddelan).

[718] See further Crouch, 'Earliest original charter', 128–30.

phrase *universis sancte* (*matris*) *ecclesie filiis* (as does Rhys Ieuanc's charter for Bishop Iorwerth of St Davids).[719] This phrase occurs in none of the letters patent, dating from 1258 onwards, most of whose addresses take the form *universis/omnibus Cristi fidelibus presentes/has litteras visuris vel audituris*, a form also used in Gruffudd ap Maredudd ab Owain's charter of 1283.[720] Three forms of greeting (*salutatio*) occur in the charters: *salutem* (not attested after 1202),[721] *salutem et pacem*[722] and *salutem in domino*;[723] each of these is used in charters for more than one beneficiary. *Salutem* is used alone in only one of the letters patent,[724] where the usual form is *salutem in domino*, with the addition of *sempiternam* in one case.[725]

The addresses and greetings in the four letters to individuals are formulated with the courtesy normal in such documents, including reference to the title of the addressee: *Illustri principi ac domino karissimo domino L. filio Griffini suus Owenus filius Maredud salutem cum honore*;[726] *Excellentissimo domino suo L. principi Wallie, domino Snaod' suus Kynan filius Maredut salutem et promtam atque paratam in omnibus ad obsequia voluntatem*;[727] *Excellenti viro et discreto domino L. filio Griffin(i) principi Wall(ie), domino Snaudon' Howel filius Resi Vrec suus semper et ubique salutem et sincere dilectionis affectum*;[728] and *A noble ber et sage sire Rob(er)t Burnel eveke de Bahdþe le ceu valet si leur pleht Howel ap Res Crik salus, reverence, servise et tous honurs*.[729] The greeting in the second example is a variation on that used by Llywelyn ap Gruffudd in his letters from 1269 onwards: *salutem et paratam ad beneplacita voluntatem*.[730]

In most charters and letters the style (*intitulatio*) of the grantor or sender consists of his name, usually followed by a patronymic but only rarely by a title. (Rulers of Deheubarth are never referred to by any title in their petitions or in agreements to which they were parties.) Both of the Lord Rhys's charters accord him a title in the protocol: *Resus filius Gruffini princeps Wallie* in the Chertsey charter (1165 × 1197), *Resus Walliarum princeps* in the Strata Florida charter (1184).[731] In addition, the latter charter uses a different style in the notification: *Resus Sudwallie proprietarius princeps*. As we have only two charters, both extant only in copies, the authenticity and significance of these styles are difficult to assess. However, the very unusualness of the phrase *proprietarius princeps* – which is unique not only among Welsh rulers' acts but also among the sources consulted in compiling the archive of the *Dictionary of Medieval Latin from British Sources* – arguably suggests that it is genuine. Moreover, its authenticity is reinforced by the likelihood that, as J. Beverley Smith has argued, *proprietarius* rendered the Welsh noun *priodor*, meaning 'proprietor' in the sense of a freeman with full rights to land established by possession for at least four generations, and

---

[719] Nos 28, 35, 50, 55, 57, 63, 82.
[720] Nos 66, 72, 76 (joint with the abbots of Whitland and Caerleon), 78, 80, 85, 88, 93, 95–6, 99–100.
[721] Nos 26, 35, 46, 50, 55.
[722] Nos 28, 57, 82, 84.
[723] Nos 63, 78, 97.
[724] No. 86.
[725] No. 85.
[726] No. 70.
[727] No. 79.
[728] No. 87.
[729] No. 89.
[730] See above, p. 71.
[731] Nos 26, 28.

thus bears comparison with the term *argluyd priodaur* (Mod. W. *arglwydd priodor*) used in the *Historia Gruffud vab Kenan*, a Welsh text of the earlier thirteenth century based on a Latin text composed in the twelfth century, which presents Gruffudd ap Cynan as the rightful owner of the patrimony (W. *tref tad*) of Gwynedd.[732] If so, the title *Sudwallie proprietarius princeps*, 'proprietary prince of Deheubarth', probably served to assert that Rhys's hereditary right to his patrimonial kingdom went back beyond the time even of his paternal grandfather Rhys ap Tewdwr (d. 1093), even though Rhys's father Tewdwr, while a descendant of Owain ap Hywel ap Cadell (d. 988), is not known to have been king of Deheubarth.[733]

If the title *Sudwallie proprietarius princeps* is authentic, this might seem to cast doubt on the authenticity of the title 'prince of Wales' in the protocol of the Strata Florida charter and therefore also in that of the Chertsey charter. That the Lord Rhys's usual title was *Sudwallie princeps* is further suggested by the reference to him as such in the style *H. filius Resi Suthwallie principis* used by his son Hywel Sais quite possibly during Rhys's lifetime and certainly by July 1198; a similar style was adopted by Rhys's grandson Maelgwn Fychan in 1198 × 1227.[734] It is also notable that Maelgwn ap Rhys adopted the style *Mailgun filius Resi princeps Swthwallie* in 1198.[735] Yet the styles in the protocols of the Chertsey and Strata Florida charters cannot be dismissed lightly. They are clearly independent of each other, as they not only occur in documents for unrelated religious houses but also, more importantly, differ in their wording and position: the Chertsey charter has *Resus filius Gruffini princeps Wallie*, placed, uniquely among the Deheubarth charters, before the address and greeting (an indication, together with the form of the notification, of the influence of English royal charters),[736] whereas that for Strata Florida (*Resus Walliarum princeps*) follows the address, omits the patronymic and has the genitive plural form of *Wallia*. As both titles were used in the later 1160s by Rhys's uncle Owain Gwynedd,[737] they were already current when Rhys's charters were issued; indeed, Owain's usage may have been directly influential here. Nor was the use of two different styles in the Strata Florida charter necessarily contradictory: *Walliarum princeps* may have referred to the wider hegemony within native Wales to which Rhys aspired, whereas *Sudwallie proprietarius princeps* referred to his authority over his ancestral kingdom of Deheubarth. If so, the charter may witness to a distinction comparable to that articulated by the title 'prince

---

[732] *Historia Gruffud vab Kenan*, 7, 10; Smith, 'Treftadaeth Deheubarth', 34, 48–9, n. 65; see also Charles-Edwards, *Early Irish and Welsh Kinship*, 280–1, 287, 294–6. The corresponding passages in *Vita Griffini Filii Conani*, ed. Russell, §§10 and 14, do not echo the Welsh legal terminology, as they simply refer to the king by the phrases *ad illum iure spectabat in illos dominari* and *dominum suum (legitimum)*. I am grateful to Paul Russell for allowing me to cite his text in advance of publication.

[733] Cf. Maund, *Ireland, Wales, and England*, 33, 37–8; Moore, 'O Rys ap Tewdwr', 54.

[734] Nos 46, 63.

[735] No. 35. Descriptions of Rhys in English chronicles vary, and cannot in any case be assumed to reflect the ruler's own style. Roger of Howden refers to Rhys by his name and patronymic and occasionally also as *rex* or *regulus* of south Wales; Ralph of Diss calls him both *australium princeps Wallensium* and *princeps Waliae*; and the obituary notices in the Annals of Tewkesbury and Annals of Winchester both have 'Rhys, king of Wales' (*rex Wallie*): *Gesta*, ed. Stubbs, i. 162, 314, 317, 355; ii. 87, 97; Diceto, i. 311, 384; *AM*, i. 55; ii. 66. Rhys's kinsman and contemporary, Gerald of Wales, referred to him as *australis Kambriae princeps* or simply as *princeps*: *Gir. Camb. Op.*, vi. 14, 112 (*IK*, I. 1, II. 2). Henry II's confirmation of Rhys's lost charter for Strata Florida refers to Rhys by name and patronymic only: *Mon. Ang.*, v. 633; no. 25. Cf. also Turvey, 'King, prince or lord?'.

[736] Cf. Chaplais, *English Royal Documents*, 13.

[737] See above, p. 74.

of Aberffraw and lord of Snowdon' used by Llywelyn ap Iorwerth in the 1230s.[738] That the title 'prince of Wales' appears not to have been adopted by any of the Lord Rhys's successors provides weak evidence, moreover, for concluding that it was never used by Rhys himself. Rather, it probably reflects the contested and limited nature of his successors' power together with the renewed dominance of Gwynedd, whose prince, Llywelyn ap Iorwerth, presided over a partition of Deheubarth in 1216.

In addition to the charters of Maelgwn ap Rhys, Hywel Sais and Maelgwn Fychan already mentioned, only two other documents use a style that consists of more than a name and patronymic. Cadell ap Gruffudd refers to his father's royal status (*Cadellus filius Grifini regis*), while in 1277 Rhys Wyndod styled himself, uniquely among the Deheubarth acts, with reference to his seat of power (*Resus Vagghan dominus de Dynevor*).[739] Rhys Wyndod is referred to as *Reso Parvo de Estrad Tywy* in the *gravamina* sent to Archbishop Pecham in October 1282.[740] In the three letters to Llywelyn ap Gruffudd loyalty to the prince is emphasized by the addition to the sender's name of the pronoun *suus*, amplified in one case by *semper et ubique*.[741]

In most charters the notification uses a form of the verb *noscere*, including four examples, all in charters for Strata Florida, of *notum facio/facimus* followed by the dispositive verbs in the perfect infinitive.[742] The notifications of the other two Strata Florida charters open with *vestre universitatis notitie innotescat quod ego* (the Lord Rhys, 1184) and *ad universitatis vestre notitiam volo pervenire* (Maelgwn Fychan, 1198 × 1227).[743] Otherwise the most common formula, attested from the late twelfth century to 1283, is *noverit universitas vestra*.[744] The letters patent likewise show a strong preference for forms of *noscere*, especially *noverit universitas vestra*.[745] Only two charters and one letter patent use forms of *scire*: the notification of the Lord Rhys's charter for Chertsey opens with *sciatis me* followed by the dispositive verbs in the perfect infinitive, a formula typical of English royal charters, as does a letter patent of Rhys Wyndod, while Maredudd ab Owain's grant of dower to his wife in 1273 has *sciant . . . quod ego*.[746] Most charters are written in the first person singular, the only exceptions being those of Maelgwn ap Rhys for Strata Florida (1198), Rhys Ieuanc for Bishop Iorwerth of St Davids (1215 × 1228) and Gruffudd ap Maredudd ab Owain for Rhys Fychan (1283).[747] Though the notification of Rhys Gryg's charter for Strata Florida in 1198 has *notum facimus* the rest of the text uses the first person singular.[748] The letters give a similarly mixed picture. A majority use the first person singular, but the plural occurs in five of the letters sent by a single ruler.[749] Neither the charters nor the letters exhibit any consistent patterns with respect to this usage, which may have depended at least as much on

---

[738] Cf. above, p. 76.
[739] Nos 22, 99. For similar usage by the rulers of Gwynllŵg see below, p. 117.
[740] No. 101.
[741] Nos 70, 79, 87.
[742] Nos 35, 50, 55, 82.
[743] Nos 28, 63.
[744] Nos 46, 57, 83, 97.
[745] Nos 66, 76, 80, 85–6, 95–6, 100; the formula is also used in two letters addressed to Llywelyn ap Gruffudd: nos 70, 79.
[746] Nos 26, 71, 99.
[747] Nos 35, 57, 78.
[748] No. 50.
[749] Nos 66, 72–3, 85, 93 (though the corroboration clause is in the singular).

the preference of the clerk drafting the document as on the wishes of the grantor or sender. The dispositive verbs usually take the form *dedisse, concessisse et* (*hac*) *presenti carta mea/nostra confirmasse* (or the equivalent in the perfect tense).[750] This is modified in the two latest charters, issued in 1283: no. 78 inserts a warranty clause (*dedisse et concessisse et contra omnes homines et feminas warantizasse*) and no. 97 is a quitclaim (*concessisse, remisisse et quietum clamasse*). No. 22, Cadell ap Gruffudd's charter for Totnes Priory, is unique among the Deheubarth charters in using the present tense (*do et concedo*).

The most remarkable of the surviving Deheubarth charters is that issued by the Lord Rhys for Strata Florida in 1184. The ruler's styles have already been discussed. The notification, itself unparalleled among the charters of Welsh rulers, is followed by a narration explaining how Rhys had built the monastery and endowed it with extensive lands and now, in 1184, confirmed all he had given in the present charter (*presentis scripti memoria stabilivi*). Three of his sons, Gruffudd, Rhys and Maredudd, had offered the same gift to the abbot of Strata Florida at the same time in the presence of Rhys and his army in the church of Llansanffraid Cwmteuddwr near Rhayader. The clause that then introduces the list of lands granted is closely modelled on a papal bull, presumably that issued by Alexander III for Strata Florida in 1165 × 1181, as the following comparison shows.[751]

Rhys's charter
... statuentes ... ut quascumque possessiones, quecumque bona idem monasterium in presentiarum possidet et custodit sive concessione pontificum, largitione principum, oblatione fidelium vel aliis iustis modis Deo propitio adepta fuerit, firma monachis illius et eorum successoribus ab omni seculari et ecclesiastica consuetudine et debito immunia et illibata permaneant. In quibus hec duximus exprimenda vocabulis propriis ...

Alexander III's bull
... statuentes ut quascumque possessiones, quecunque bona idem monasterium in presentiarum iuste et canonice possidet aut in futurum concessione pontificum, largitione regum vel principum, oblatione fidelium seu aliis iustis modis Deo propitio poterit adipisci firma vobis vestrisque[a] successoribus et illibata permaneant. In quibus hec propriis duximus exprimenda vocabulis ...

[a] nostrisque MS.

As similar borrowings occur in some episcopal acts confirming the possessions of religious houses, including those of Peter de Leia, bishop of St Davids, for Neath and Slebech,[752] it is possible that the immediate model for Rhys's charter was a confirmation by the bishop of St Davids, though neither David fitz Gerald (1148–76) nor Peter de Leia (1176–98) is known to have issued such a confirmation in favour of Strata Florida. In any event, the

---

[750] No. 35 has only *concessisse et presenti carta nostra confirmasse*, and no. 50 only *dedisse et concessisse*.
[751] See Davies, 'Papal bull of privileges'; also printed in *Liber Epistolaris*, ed. Denholm-Young, 2–3.
[752] See *St Davids Episcopal Acta*, 66, 70 (nos 43, 46), and, for some English examples, Saltman, *Theobald*, 371 (no. 148) and cf. ibid., 332, 361, 406, 530 (nos 111, 139, 183, 304); *EEA*, i. lvi; *EEA*, v. 87 (no. 114).

clause suggests that the charter was drawn up either by the beneficiary or by a cleric familiar with drafting ecclesiastical documents.

On the other hand, whereas the papal bull refers tersely to Rhys's gift of Ystrad-fflur 'with all its granges and (?)appurtenances' (*Ex dono videlicet Resi filii Griffini Stratflur cum omnibus grangis et impendiciis* (sic (?for *appendiciis*)) *suis*), the enumeration of lands in Rhys's charter takes the form of a detailed perambulation of boundaries, first, of the possessions granted by Rhys and his sons (extending in a circuit beginning and ending at Nannerth near Rhayader) and, second, of grants by 'the sons of Cadwgan'. Moreover, though mainly written in Latin, these descriptions contain a significant number of connecting words and phrases in Welsh. The first perambulation is followed by a list of 'the more distinguished places' within the bounds, while the second set of bounds is said to have been described by Rhys with his nobles and his son Gruffudd. Probably the first set of bounds were described by Rhys and his three sons, as these are named as granting all contained within them to the monks in perpetual right. It seems, therefore, that the charter records oral descriptions of the abbey's possessions made in the presence of Rhys's army in the church of Llansanffraid Cwmteuddwr.

The form of these boundary clauses is probably indebted to earlier Welsh traditions of charter writing. Both perambulation and a mixture of Latin and Welsh for the linking words occur in the boundary clauses of charters preserved in the early twelfth-century Book of Llandaff (*Liber Landavensis*), and may in some cases have formed integral parts of the texts of the charters from the mid- or late ninth century.[753] Perambulations also occur in many of the charters for Strata Marcella, which, like Strata Florida, was a daughter house of Whitland Abbey.[754] Their appearance in twelfth- and thirteenth-century rulers' charters is a conservative aspect of Welsh diplomatic by comparison with that of royal charters in England, where detailed perambulations tended to die out with the demise of the Anglo-Saxon diploma, though they continued to be used in private charters.[755] The boundary clauses of Rhys's charter are reproduced in the confirmation by his son Maelgwn ap Rhys in 1198, but later confirmations for Strata Florida simply list the places granted, possibly developing the model provided by the list of 'more distinguished places' included in Rhys's charter.[756] The detailed description of liberties that follows the enumeration of lands in Cynan ap Maredudd ab Owain's charter for Strata Florida (1280 × 1282) is suspect, and may reflect post-conquest fabrication or rewriting by the monks.[757]

Corroboration clauses occur in eight charters and all the letters, including those addressed to Llywelyn ap Gruffudd, the only exception being no. 89, a letter, in French,

---

[753] See Davies, *Llandaff Charters*, 142–4, and the examples cited there, most of which are either in Welsh or in a mixture of Welsh and Latin.

[754] *Ystrad Marchell Charters*, 106–7; below, pp. 120, 126.

[755] Cf. Clanchy, *From Memory*, 86, citing *Facsimiles*, ed. Stenton, 138–9 (no. liii: a charter granting land at Lambrigg near Kendal, Westmorland *c.*1210). In this respect Welsh practice was more similar to that in Scotland, where the inclusion of perambulations in royal charters was widespread in the thirteenth century (and later): cf. Barrow, *Kingdom of the Scots*, 72–4, 80–2; Neville, 'Charter writing', 79, 82–3. (I am grateful to Cynthia Neville for her comments on Scottish perambulations.) In both Scotland and England perambulation was used by kings and other lords as a means of settling disputed boundaries, and the same seems to have been true of Wales: *CR 1234–7*, 401; Pryce, *Native Law*, 208–10, and cf. no. 346. The recording of perambulations in charters was presumably intended to forestall any disputes over the boundaries of the lands granted.

[756] Nos 35, 50, 55 (though this includes some bounds at the end), 63, 82.

[757] No. 82 and note.

from Hywel ap Rhys Gryg to Edward I's chancellor Robert Burnell. The clauses in charters refer only to sealing, apart from no. 22, Cadell's charter for Totnes Priory, which also refers to an oath. The form of the corroboration in Rhys Ieuanc's charter for Strata Florida (1202) is unusual in declaring that the document has been sealed by the grantor's first seal and that he has not granted any charter to anyone else before this nor had any other seal than that used to confirm the present charter.[758] Presumably this was aimed against anyone who might claim to possess an earlier charter from Rhys granting all or some of the same lands. Maredudd ab Owain's grant of dower to his wife (1273) has a further corroboration clause after the dating clause stating that 'Lord Llywelyn, prince of Wales' had appended his seal to the document.[759] The formulae of these clauses vary in the charters, and only two examples in 1283 include the phrase *in cuius rei testimonium* normally used in the letters.[760] In nine of the letters the corroboration explicitly describes the document as being patent.[761] Only two charters, both from the early 1280s, contain warranty clauses.[762] One of these, Cynan ap Maredudd ab Owain's charter for Strata Florida, is unique in containing an elaborate sanction clause, invoking blessings and curses on those confirming and contravening the terms of the charter respectively. This clause almost certainly reflects beneficiary drafting and its appearance at this date is a further reason for doubting the authenticity of the charter in its present form.[763]

Dating clauses occur in half of the charters and nine of the letters patent, but never in the letters addressed to individuals.[764] A further two letters patent, concerning a debt owed by Rhys ap Maredudd to a burgess of Carmarthen, refer to a time-date in the text of the document.[765] All the dating clauses in letters patent give a place-date, the year (usually of the incarnation, though Rhys Wyndod's acknowledgement of receipt of money from Edward I in 1277 is dated by the king's regnal year)[766] and the day of the month, most commonly calculated according to the ecclesiastical calendar. Most open with *Dat'* or *Datum*, though no. 86 has *Datum et actum* and no. 93 has *Acta*. The form of the clauses in charters is more varied. Cadell's charter for Totnes Priory gives a place-date only, stating that the grant was made 'in the house of Lord Cadell above the river Teifi next to St Peter's church', while Rhys Ieuanc's charter for Strata Florida (1202) is dated by the year of the incarnation only.[767] The other five charters containing dating clauses resemble the letters patent in giving a place-date as well as the year of the incarnation and the day of the month.[768] In four charters the clause is introduced by *Dat'* or *Datum*,[769] the other three having forms of *facere*.[770]

---

[758] *Hanc autem donationem primo sigillo quod habui confirmavi et ante hanc cartam nullam aliam alicui homini dedi nec aliquod sigillum ante hoc habui quo hanc cartam confirmavi*: no. 55.

[759] No. 71.

[760] Nos 78, 97. The only letters whose corroboration clauses lack this phrase are nos 76 (issued jointly with Cistercian abbots) and 79.

[761] Nos 66, 70, 72, 76, 79–80, 85, 87, 99.

[762] Nos 78, 82. As noted above, the clause is integrated into the disposition in the former document.

[763] No. 82 and note.

[764] Charters: nos 22, 35, 50, 55, 71, 78. Letters patent: nos 66, 73, 76, 85–6, 88, 93, 99–100.

[765] Nos 95–6.

[766] No. 99.

[767] Nos 22, 55.

[768] Nos 35, 50, 71, 78, 97.

[769] Nos 35, 71, 78, 97.

[770] Nos 22, 50, 55.

All the charters contain witness lists, as does one of the letters patent, Hywel ap Rhys Gryg's declaration of homage to Llywelyn ap Gruffudd (1258).[771] Occasionally a witness is described as being the clerk or scribe of the grantor: *Guffus clericus noster*, in Cadell's charter for Totnes Priory; *A. clerico meo* in Rhys Ieuanc's charter for Strata Florida (1202), possibly identifiable with the *A. clerico nostro officiali de Kardygan* of the same grantor's charter for Bishop Iorwerth of St Davids (1215 × 1229); and *Iervasio et Iohanne notariis nostris* in Hywel ap Rhys Gryg's letter patent of 1258.[772] How far any of the persons named were involved in drawing up the document they witnessed is uncertain, and the same is true of the religious and other secular clergy who occur fairly frequently in these lists. Three of the letters end with a final greeting (*Valete*).[773]

ELFAEL AND MAELIENYDD

Surviving texts of acts issued by the rulers of Elfael and Maelienydd are very few: two charters for Cwm-hir Abbey, one in the name of Hywel ap Cadwallon (probably *c.*1210 × July 1212), the other in that of Madog ap Maelgwn (May 1212),[774] and seven letters patent. Of the latter, five, with identical texts, announce undertakings to Henry III at Shrewsbury on 14 August 1241,[775] while the other two, dated 1271 and 1276 respectively, announce obligations of suretyship incurred by lords of Elfael and others with respect to Llywelyn ap Gruffudd.[776]

Both charters for Cwm-hir are extant in the original. Each fills most of the available space on the parchment, though, unlike no. 113, no. 108 (reproduced in Plate 7) does not extend quite to the right-hand edge; the final line of text in no. 108 is filled by extending the stroke of the *t* of *presumat*, that in no. 113 by writing the final two words (*mense maio*) in majuscule letters, with those of the latter word generously spaced. Both documents are written in very similar book hands modified only by the use of a curving and elongated shaft in the *d* of no. 108 and of an elongated ascender in the *s* of no. 113. Each charter has strokes above *i* when this is doubled (for example, *filiis* and *aliis* in no. 108, *pertinentiis* in no. 113) and a dot above *y* in Welsh names. However, while the resemblances between the two charters suggest that both were produced in the same scriptorium (namely that of Cwm-hir, to judge by the dating clause of no. 113 discussed below), there are enough differences to suggest that each is the work of a different scribe. The most obvious contrast is that the hand of no. 108 slopes back to the left whereas that of no. 113 is upright. This contrast is reflected, for example, in the latter's preference for a *d* with a vertical ascender rather than one with a curved ascender; though this also occurs, it is less frequent than in the other charter. In addition, the forms of *g* differ: that in no. 113, with an open tail, is rather old-fashioned. Likewise the forms of the majuscule *G*, *N* and *S* in each charter are similar but not identical. While both are extremely conservative in their use of the ampersand, rather

[771] No. 85.
[772] Nos 22, 55, 57, 85. Note also *Gorgenew clerico domini Resi* in Rhys Gryg's agreement with Bishop Iorwerth of St Davids: no. 52.
[773] Nos 79–80, 87.
[774] Nos 108, 113.
[775] Nos 110–12, 116, 118.
[776] Nos 106–7.

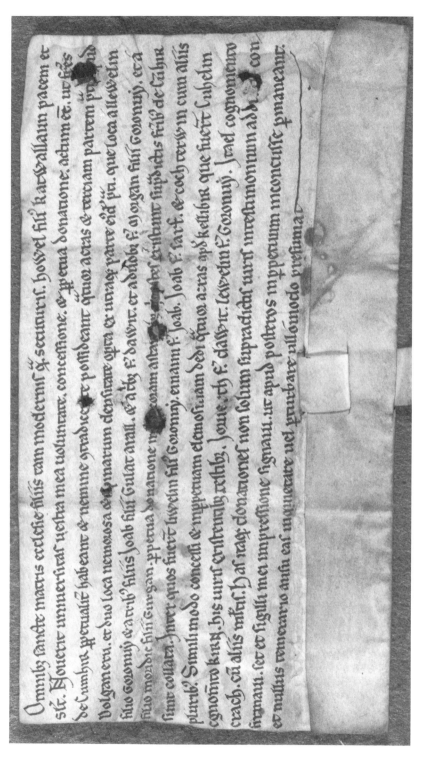

Plate 7 Charter of Hywel ap Cadwallon (no. 108)

than tironian *nota*, as the abbreviation for *et*, the central downward stroke of the ampersand in no. 113 is more vertical than that of no. 108; moreover, no. 108 uses the abbreviation more sparingly than no. 113, which never writes *et* in full. No. 108 is more conservative than no. 113 in its consistent use of a horizontal rather than wavy stroke as the common mark of abbreviation, whereas the latter uses both types of stroke. Apart from the use of the ampersand, though, the hands of both charters are compatible with production in the last quarter of the twelfth or early thirteenth century and thus not exceptionally old-fashioned for the dating proposed on historical grounds.

Each charter was sealed on a parchment tag inserted through a central slit just above the fold and slits in the fold. The seal is no longer attached to no. 108 and has not been examined. However, an earlier description states that it was a very imperfect impression on light brown wax of an equestrian seal, originally *c*.2 inches (*c*.52 mm.) diameter, with the remains of a legend 'SIGILLVM . . . .'.[777] An imperfect impression of Madog ap Maelgwn's circular equestrian seal, originally *c*.60 mm. diameter, remains attached to no. 113; the legend is lost.[778]

The diplomatic of the charters includes a number of unusual features, and neither bears close affinities with Roger Mortimer's charter for Cwm-hir in 1200.[779] Unlike Mortimer's charter, both open with a protocol in the form of a general address, style (name and patronymic in both) and greeting. The address in no. 108 reads *omnibus sancte matris ecclesie filiis tam modernis quam secuturis*, that in no. 113 *cunctis Cristi fidelibus tam presentibus quam futuris*, but the greetings differ only in their word order (*pacem et salutem*, *salutem et pacem*). The latter address also occurs in no. 229, Llywelyn ap Iorwerth's charter for Cwm-hir's daughter house of Cymer, dated 1209. The text in both charters for Cwm-hir is written in the first person singular. Each has the same notification (*noverit universitas vestra*) followed by constructions using the perfect infinitive (*mea voluntate, concessione et perpetua donatione actum esse* in no. 108, *me concessisse* in no. 113). Thereafter the diplomatic of each document is highly distinctive. No. 108 has two witness lists, one for each of the grants mentioned, which are incorporated into the preceding dispositive clauses (*multis coram astantibus qui testes existunt supradictis fratribus de Cumhir sunt collata, inter quos fuerunt . . .; his viris existentibus testibus*), and ends with a corroboration clause referring to the witnesses as well as sealing by Hywel's seal. No. 113 is more conventional in placing its witness list separately near the end, where it is followed by a dating clause, though it earlier states that the grant was made *multis coram astantibus*, a phrase also used in the formula introducing the witness list in Llywelyn's charter for Cymer. Other similarities between no. 113 and the Cymer charter are the use of the phrase *omni terra que mee ditioni subiacet* to describe the territory under the grantor's authority and the emphasis, already implicit in the greeting, on maintaining the monks' lands in peace. Thus no. 113 contains a combined corroboration and sanction clause, placed after the disposition, stating that Madog ap Maelgwn has sworn an oath with his nobles (*optimates*) that anyone infringing the terms of the grant will be disinherited and exiled from his land until restitution is made to the monks; this is followed by a further such clause declaring that Madog and his nobles have sworn never to endure the lordship of any prince (clearly meaning Llywelyn ap Iorwerth), who will be rejected by all if he presumes to make any claim on the lands granted.

---

[777] Siddons, 'Welsh equestrian seals', 306, citing Birch, *Seals*, ii. 287 (no. 5977).
[778] For a detailed description see Siddons, 'Welsh equestrian seals', 306.
[779] Cf. Charles, 'Early charter', 68–9.

The most remarkable feature of no. 113 is its dating clause: *Datum litterarum per manum domni Riredi abbatis mense maio*. This is the closest parallel among the charters in this edition with the form of dating clause that refers to a datary responsible for authorizing the issue of a document. The formula *Dat' per manum N. cancellarii* was incorporated in the dating clauses used by the papal chancery by the mid-twelfth century, and this provided at least the ultimate model for its adoption, from Richard I's accession in 1189, by the English royal chancery, whose practice in turn influenced episcopal diplomatic in England. The chancery of Philip Augustus of France (1180–1223) used the same formula in royal diplomas, and it is also attested in the early twelfth century among the acts of the archbishop of Bourges.[780] Yet, if no. 113 reflects the influence of such dating clauses, it differs from them in omitting a place-date (inserted between *Dat'* and *per manum* in papal and episcopal usage, after the *per manum* clause in acts issued by the English royal chancery) and in its inclusion of *litterarum* after *Datum*. Normally *Datum* or *Data* was taken to refer to the document, which required no further description (say, as *scriptum* or *carta*). The use of *littere* in the genitive plural here is particularly puzzling, as the noun does not agree with the neuter singular *datum*, which seems to go with the *per manum* clause: 'given/issued by the hand of Lord Rhirid the abbot in the month of May' (though *datum litterarum* could mean 'the date of the letter/document', that sense is precluded by the syntax of the rest of the dating clause).[781] The phrase *Datum litterarum* therefore seems to be ungrammatical, and the clause as a whole is perhaps best seen as an inexpert attempt to devise a *per manum* type of dating clause that would emphasize the abbot's role in executing the document. It is probably significant that the only other charter text in this edition to include the phrase *per manum* is Llywelyn's charter for Cymer, which states that the prince had confirmed the charter with his seal *per manum domini Esau tunc abbatis eiusdem monasterii* ('by the hand of Lord Esau then abbot of the same monastery').[782] Abbot Rhirid may likewise have been responsible for the sealing, and quite possibly also for the drafting if not the writing, of Madog ap Maelgwn's charter for Cwm-hir.

The five letters patent recording submissions to Henry III at Shrewsbury on 14 August 1241 essentially differ from each other only in the names of their authors (all in the style of name and patronymic).[783] Each is written in the first person singular and opens with a notification incorporating a general address (*sciant presentes et futuri*) followed by *quod* and the verb in the perfect tense. After stating the obligations undertaken the documents include a corroboration clause beginning *ad predictam autem fidelitatem observandam* (not *in cuius rei testimonium*) that refers to an oath and sealing and end with a dating clause introduced by *actum* giving the day of the month and the king's regnal year.[784]

The two letters patent concerning obligations to Llywelyn ap Gruffudd bear some resem-

[780] Cheney, *English Bishops' Chanceries*, 84–9; Chaplais, *English Royal Documents*, 13, 14; Giry, *Manuel de diplomatique*, 755.

[781] Cf. *DMLBS*, s.v. *dare* 13a–b. There is a parallel for dating by the month without the day in no. 206 for Aberconwy, though this also gives a place-date and the year of the incarnation.

[782] Note also Earl William of Gloucester's confirmation of 'the gift which Gruffudd ab Ifor made to the abbey of Margam by the hand of Brother Meilyr Awenydd' (*donationem quam Griffinus filius Ivor fecit abbatie de Margan per manum fratris Meileri Awenet*): *EGC*, 115 (no. 120), calendared as no. 616.

[783] Nos 110–12, 116, 118.

[784] The day of the month appears to have been expressed differently in different texts of the letters: see the dating clause of no. 111.

blances to the letters patent issued by that prince.[785] Both open with a similar general address and greeting: *universis presentes litteras visuris vel audituris salutem* in no. 106, with the insertion in no. 107 of *Cristi fidelibus* after *universis* and *in domino* after *salutem*. The lords of Elfael are styled not only with their names and patronymic but also with a title: *domini de Eluael* in no. 106, *domini de Eluael vch Mynyth* in no. 107. The notification in both is *noverit universitas vestra*. Each has a corroboration clause, though only that in no. 107 adheres to the standard form used in such documents (*in cuius rei testimonium sigilla nostra presenti scripto fecimus apponi*). Both letters end with a similar dating clause introduced by *datum* followed by a place-date, year of the incarnation and day of the month calculated according to the ecclesiastical calendar.

GLAMORGAN (AND SENGHENNYDD)

The sixty-four texts of acts in the names of rulers of Glamorgan all derive from the archive of Margam Abbey and comprise fifty-seven charters, five letters patent, one letter to the abbots of the Cistercian order and one judgement. Almost 85 per cent of these documents (fifty-four) are extant in the original. All but three of the charters are in favour of Margam,[786] and the letters and judgement also concern that house.[787] The two texts of acts issued by rulers of Senghennydd, one charter and one letter patent (both extant only in copies), are likewise in favour of Margam, and will be considered in this section on account of the similarities between their diplomatic and that of the Glamorgan rulers' charters for the abbey.[788]

The following analysis will concentrate on the diplomatic of the acts before concluding with a brief examination of the seal impressions attached to originals. The palaeography of originals will not be considered in detail, as the hands of the Margam documents down to *c*.1225, including all but two of those published in the present edition, have been the subject of a recent comprehensive study by Robert Patterson.[789] This has identified at least fifteen scribes, responsible for writing forty-three of the originals issued by members of the dynasty of Glamorgan, as belonging to the abbey; many of these wrote charters for more than one grantor.[790] In addition, it is likely that some of the eleven other originals, at least two of which were very probably written in the same hand, were likewise products of the Margam scriptorium, even though this cannot be established with the same confidence as is the case with the forty-three documents already mentioned.[791] The hands vary from

---

[785] Cf. above, pp. 67–70.

[786] The exceptions are nos 121 (for the abortive foundation of Pendar), 124 (for Roger Cole) and 129 (for St Leonard's church, Newcastle).

[787] Nos 123, 141, 147, 151, 181, 187, 190.

[788] Nos 617–18.

[789] Patterson, *Scriptorium of Margam*.

[790] Patterson's identifications are as follows. Scribe 1: no. 121. Scribe 12: no. 130. Scribe 16: nos 146–7, 155 (A1), 171. Scribe 17: no. 148. Scribe 18: nos 136, 153–4, 163, 164 (A1 and A2). Scribe 19: nos 141, 158, 175, 183, 185, 189–90. Scribe 20: ?no. 184. Scribe 21: no. 132. Scribe 22: no. 166. Scribe 24: nos 177, 180. Scribe 29: nos 159, 161, 165, ?167. Scribe 30: nos 133–4. Scribe 33: nos 142–3, 157. Scribe 34: nos 127–8, 144–5, 172. Scribe 38: no. 123. Scribe 42: nos 150, 170.

[791] Nos 137 and 188 are probably in the same modified book hand. Each of the other nine Margam documents published in this edition whose scribes were not identified by Patterson seems to be in a

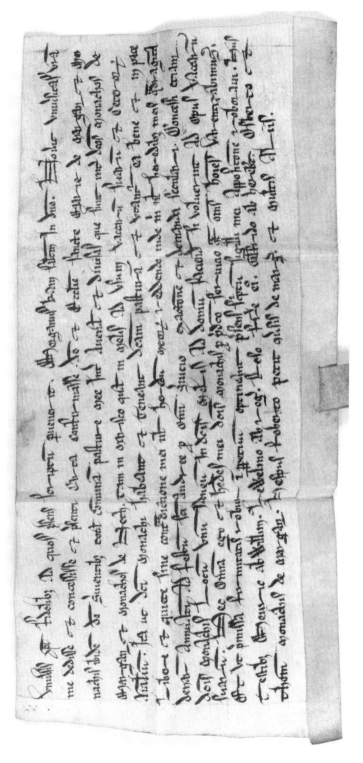

Plate 8 Charter of Morgan Gam (no. 176)

almost pure book hand to modified book hands exhibiting varying degrees of currency; all conform to types of script used at the same period in England.[792] Two originals are too late in date to fall within Patterson's remit. No. 181 (1234), the record of a judgement issued by Morgan Gam and Bishop Elias of Llandaff, is written in a current hand characteristic of that period, with many cursive features, and no. 187 (1246), a letter patent issued by Morgan ap Cadwallon in the presence of Bishop William de Burgh of Llandaff promising protection for property of Margam, is written in a modified book hand notable for its use of very elongated ascenders in the words of the first line.

Most of the charters and all the letters patent open with a protocol containing a general address, style and greeting, almost always in that order. The one exception is Morgan ap Caradog's charter for Roger Cole, the only lay beneficiary among these records, whose protocol opens with the style and also contains the only example of a collective address (*omnibus Francis, Walensibus et Anglicis ad quos presentes littere pervenerint*) and of the greeting *salutem et benevolentiam*.[793] The usual greeting is *salutem*, though *in domino* is added in two of Morgan Gam's charters (both datable to *c.*1217 × 1241) and Morgan ab Owain's letter patent announcing his final concord with Margam in 1246.[794]

In the period up to *c.*1217 two main types of general address predominate: *omnibus sancte ecclesie filiis ad quos presens scriptum pervenerit*[795] and *omnibus sancte ecclesie filiis presentibus et futuris* (with *universis* occasionally substituted for *omnibus*).[796] The choice of address probably reflects scribal preference in some cases: for example, the former formula is used in all five charters written by Patterson's Scribe 34,[797] the latter, albeit varying between *omnibus* and *universis*, in the six written by Scribe 18 (together with nearly all other charters written by this scribe).[798] The latter formula is also used consistently by Scribe 33 apart from the insertion of *matris* before *ecclesie* in no. 142.[799] Likewise the only two examples of the address *omnibus sancte ecclesie filiis* occur in charters, issued by different members of the dynasty, written by Scribe 42.[800] On the other hand, both of the principal formulae are used by Scribe 16 not only in the charters for Morgan ap Caradog and his son Lleision, but also in charters for other grantors.[801] In addition to the formulae already cited,

---

different hand: nos 124, 129, 151, 162, 168–9, 174, 176 (reproduced in Plate 8), 186. For the problems of establishing whether unidentified hands were associated with the Margam scriptorium see Patterson, *Scriptorium of Margam*, 29–30 and n. 63, 53, 56 and n. 77, 74.

[792] Ibid., 54–5.

[793] No. 124.

[794] Nos 176–7, 187.

[795] Nos 127–8, 130, 135, 144–6, 151, 161–2, 172.

[796] Nos 131–4, 136, 138–9, 143, 148, 152–5, 157, 160, 163–4, 171, 173, 617.

[797] Nos 127–8, 144–5, 172.

[798] Nos 136, 153–5, 163–4. For the use of the same address in this scribe's other charters, for both Welsh and Anglo-Norman grantors, see *Cartae*, i. 208 (no. 202); ii. 225, 270, 355, 480 (nos 220, 273, 355, 482); vi. 3216 (no. 1596). The only exception is an act of Bishop Henry of Llandaff, probably dictated by an episcopal clerk, which has a collective address and the greeting *salutem et benedictionem*: *Llandaff Episcopal Acta*, no. 55.

[799] Nos 143–4, 157; *Cartae*, i. 167 (no. 168); ii. 265 (no. 268).

[800] Nos 150, 170. The only other charter written by this scribe, for William the Harper of Bonvilston, has a more elaborate form of this address (*omnibus sancte ecclesie filiis hanc cartam visuris vel audituris*): *Cartae*, i. 210 (no. 204); cf. Patterson, *Scriptorium of Margam*, 99–100.

[801] Nos 146, 155, 171; *Cartae*, i. 161 (no. 161); ii. 245, 449, 451, 452 (nos 240, 457, 459, 460). Two other charters written by Scribe 16 are different again. William Marshal II's charter has a collective

there is one example from this period of *omnibus Cristi fidelibus ad quos presens scriptura pervenerit* and two of *omnibus sancte (matris) ecclesie filiis presentibus et futuris qui hanc cartam inspexerint*.[802] Charters after *c*.1217 are fewer than those of the preceding period and the inclusion of a protocol is less common.[803] The address in one of Morgan Gam's charters is similar to the first of the two just cited, reading *universis Cristi fidelibus ad quos presens scriptum pervenerit*.[804] His two other charters containing a protocol, together with Morgan ab Owain's letter patent announcing a final concord with Margam, have *omnibus Cristi fidelibus presens scriptum visuris vel audituris*.[805]

Charters lacking a protocol incorporate a general address in the notification. This usually refers simply to '(all) those present and future', the most common formulae being *(omnes) presentes et futuri* and *(omnes) tam presentes quam futuri*,[806] though the two examples in Morgan ap Caradog's charters are *tam presentes quam posteri* and *tam futurorum quam presencium universitas*.[807] The only other exception occurs in a charter of Lleision ap Morgan, which reads *omnes legentes et audientes hanc cartam*.[808]

In almost all cases the members of the dynasties of Glamorgan or Senghennydd are styled by their name and patronymic. Usually the element 'son of' in the patronymic is Latinized (for example, *Morganus filius Cradoci*), but two charters of Morgan ap Cadwallon, both written by the same scribe, render it in Welsh (*Morganus ab Kadwathlan*), a usage also found on the seal (but not the charters) of Morgan ab Owain ('+ S. MORGAN MAB OEIN') as well as, partially, in the charter of Rhys ap Gruffudd ab Ifor of Senghennydd (*Resus filius Griffin ab Yuor*).[809] The only exceptions to the use of a patronymic occur in the protocols of three charters of Morgan Gam and a judgement issued jointly with the bishop of Llandaff in 1234, which style him simply *Morganus Kam/Cam* (a usage followed on all three of his seals).[810] By contrast, the three charters of

---

address, and John of Bonvilston's charter inserts *presentibus et futuris* before *ad quos presens scriptum pervenerit*: ibid., i. 201 (no. 195); ii. 540 (no. 530).

[802] Nos 121 (a confirmation of *Cartae*, ii. 346–7 (no. 346), the only other example of the work of Scribe 1), 137, 188 (both written by the same, unidentified, scribe): cf. Patterson, *Scriptorium of Margam*, 81, 108, 119.

[803] The proportion of acts from this period containing a protocol is: Morgan ap Caradog (3/6); Morgan ab Owain (1/5); Morgan ap Cadwallon (0/2); Gruffudd ab Ifor of Senghennydd (0/1).

[804] No. 176.

[805] Nos 177, 180, 187.

[806] Nos 158, 165–9, 174–5, 183–6, 189–90, 618 (the last of these is a letter patent). No. 178 is slightly different: *omnes et presentes et futuri*.

[807] Nos 122, 129. The latter formula occurs, with different word order, in the notification of no. 124 (*tam presentium quam futurorum noverit universitas*), which, like no. 129, records a grant for a beneficiary other than Margam and is written by an unidentified scribe (different from that of no. 127), who may not have belonged to the abbey's scriptorium: cf. Patterson, *Scriptorium of Margam*, 29–30, n. 63, 110, 119.

[808] No. 159. The same scribe (29) uses *tam presentes quam futuri* in the notification of a charter issued on behalf of David Scurlage, as well as in the notifications of two other charters of Lleision, which have *omnibus sancte ecclesie filiis ad quos presens scriptum pervenerit* in the protocol: *Cartae*, vi. 2301 (no. 1580); nos 161, 165; cf. Patterson, *Scriptorium of Margam*, 94.

[809] Nos 189–90, 618; below, p. 114. The first two charters were written by Scribe 19: cf. Patterson, *Scriptorium of Margam*, 90. An earlier charter of Morgan ap Cadwallon styles him *Morganus filius Kaduathlan*: no. 188.

[810] Nos 176–7, 180–1; below, p. 114.

Morgan lacking a protocol style him by name and patronymic (*Morganus filius Morgani*).[811] As none of the charters is datable with any precision, it is difficult to be certain whether the styles were used simultaneously or consecutively. However, there are some grounds for supposing that *Morganus Kam/Cam* was a later development than *Morganus filius Morgani*, as two examples of the former occur in documents issued no earlier than 1230 and in 1234 respectively, while one example of the latter occurs in a charter issued no later than 2 June 1231.[812] The dropping of the patronymic in favour of a distinctive sobriquet (meaning 'the crooked' or 'the hunch-backed') may have been linked to Morgan Gam's renewed attacks in Glamorgan in the period following the death of his overlord, Earl Gilbert de Clare, in 1230 and the subsequent intervention in south Wales of Morgan's ally, Llywelyn ap Iorwerth of Gwynedd. Indeed, one of the charters that uses the style 'Morgan Gam' explicitly confirms Earl Gilbert's grants to Margam.[813]

The text in the acts is normally written in the first person singular unless it refers to a plural subject, as in charters issued in the name of more than one author or in warranty clauses that associate a grantor's kin with the obligation of warranty. The only partial exception is no. 130, a confirmation by Morgan ap Caradog of a grant by Roger Cole, which starts in the first person plural in the notification and beginning of the disposition but subsequently refers to Roger as *homo meus* and uses the first person singular in the warranty clause.

Notifications show a strong preference for forms of *scire* rather than *noscere*.[814] Charters before *c*.1217 most commonly have *sciatis me/nos* followed by the dispositive verb(s) in the perfect infinitive.[815] Ultimately derived from English royal charters, this usage was almost certainly indebted to the diplomatic of the earls of Gloucester, patrons of Margam and overlords of the native rulers of Glamorgan, as it was by far the most frequent form of notification in the charters of Earl William (1147–83) and continued to be used by Earl William's successors until Countess Isabel's sole tenure of the earldom in 1216–17, when the preferred formula became *sciant omnes tam presentes quam futuri quod*.[816] The other formulae using *scire* in the notifications of the Glamorgan rulers' charters are *sciatis quod ego*[817] and, more frequently, *sciant quod ego*,[818] followed in both cases by the dispositive verb(s) in the perfect tense. No example of the former is later, and only one of the latter earlier, than 1205. These forms also occur in the charters of the earls of Gloucester, as do the forms of *noscere* used.[819] The latter normally consist either of *noverit quod* followed by the verb(s) in the perfect tense[820] or of *noverit me* followed by the perfect infinitive.[821] There

---

[811] Nos 174–5, 178.

[812] Nos 180–1, 174.

[813] No. 180. Morgan is referred to similarly in contemporary annals: *AM*, i. 36, 37, 39 (*Morganus Cam*); ibid., 116 (*Morgan Cham*); 'Chronicle of the thirteenth century', 278 (*Morganum Gam*).

[814] The use of *noscere* is restricted to acts of Morgan ap Caradog, Owain ap Morgan, Morgan Gam, Morgan ap Cadwallon and Morgan ab Owain: nos 123–4, 129–30, 135, 137, 141, 170, 176–7, 180, 188.

[815] Nos 127–8, 131–4, 136, 139, 142–6, 148, 151, 153–4, 157, 160–4, 171–3, 617.

[816] *EGC*, 21–2.

[817] Nos 138, 150, 152, 155. Cf. *sciat quod ego* followed, unusually, by the dispositive verbs in the present tense, in no. 121.

[818] Nos 122 (1186 × 1199), 158–9, 165–9, 174–5, 178, 183–6, 189–90, 618.

[819] Cf. *EGC*, 21–2.

[820] Nos 123–4, 129, 135, 177, 180, 187.

[821] Nos 137, 141, 170, 176.

is also one example each of *notum facimus nos* and *noverint me*, both followed by the perfect infinitive.[822]

The dispositive verbs fall into two main groups. The first of these consists principally of two formulae in the perfect infinitive, neither of which occurs later than *c.*1217: *concessisse et hac carta confirmasse*,[823] largely restricted to the acts of Morgan ap Caradog and Lleision ap Morgan, and, more frequently, *concessisse et dedisse et hac/presenti carta confirmasse*.[824] Variants of the latter formula place *dedisse* before *concessisse*[825] or, in one letter patent, have only *concessisse et dedisse*.[826] The verbs in the second group are in the perfect tense. The simplest forms are either *concessi*[827] or *dedi et concessi*, the latter being restricted to two charters of Morgan ap Caradog for beneficiaries other than Margam.[828] However, most formulae in this group include *confirmavi*: *dedi et hac carta confirmavi* (in one charter of Lleision ap Morgan only),[829] *concessi et hac carta mea confirmavi* (in charters from 1213 onwards),[830] *dedi et concessi et hac presenti carta confirmavi* (in charters datable, in one case, to 1199 × 1208, the rest to within the period 1203–28)[831] and *concessi et dedi et hac carta confirmavi* (in charters datable to within the period 1193–1214).[832] Only no. 121 (1158 × 1191) places the dispositive verbs in the present tense: *concedimus et confirmamus*. The two quitclaims have *quitas/quietum clamavi*.[833]

Descriptions of lands granted are generally concise, often referring to topographical features such as rivers or streams, and lack perambulations. Corroboration clauses are relatively rare and consist mainly of statements that the grantor has sworn an oath on relics, sometimes specified as those of Margam, to observe the terms of the grant.[834] Only a minority of corroboration clauses refer to sealing.[835] One explanation for the paucity of corroboration clauses may be that these were considered less important than a warranty clause, which occurs in over 60 per cent of the Glamorgan rulers' charters, though the use of the one did not exclude the use of the other in the same charter.[836] Warranty clauses fall into two basic types. The more common is a declaration that the grantor, often with his heirs, will warrant the grant (for example, *Ego autem et heredes mei prefatam donationem predictis monachis warentizabimus contra omnes homines in perpetuum*).[837] In some charters,

---

[822] Nos 130, 188. Cf. *notum facio quod* in Morgan ap Caradog's letter to the Cistercian General Chapter: no. 147.
[823] Nos 127–8, 153, 157, 162–3, 170, 172, 188. The combination of verbs in nos 130 and 164 is the same, but these include the phrases *presenti carta nostra* and *hac mea carta* respectively.
[824] Nos 131–4, 136–7, 139, 142–3, 148, 154, 160–1, 171, 173, 617.
[825] Nos 144–6, 176.
[826] No. 141.
[827] Nos 122, 174, 177.
[828] Nos 124, 129.
[829] No. 165.
[830] Nos 166–8, 175, 178, 180.
[831] Nos 135, 155, 183–6, 189; the last charter inserts *in perpetuam elemosinam* after *dedi*.
[832] Nos 138, 152, 159.
[833] Nos 158, 169.
[834] Nos 131, 137, 142, 154, 158, 166, 168, 183–7, 189–90, 618.
[835] Nos 121, 153, 167, 176–7.
[836] Nos 121, 131, 137, 153–4, 167, 176, 180, 183–6, 189–90.
[837] No. 133. See also nos 121, 130–1, 137, 139, 143, 146, 148, 150, 154, 160–5, 167, 171–2, 176, 180, 183–6, 189–90. The clause in no. 617 is different in that it speaks only of the consequences of the failure of the donor and his heirs to warrant the grant.

though, the clause is more complex, stating that the grantor has sworn an oath that he (and his heirs) will warrant the grant (for example, *Notandum etiam me super sanctuaria ecclesie iurasse quod ego et heredes mei prefatam donationem predictis monachis warentizabimus contra omnes homines in perpetuum*).[838] The majority of clauses warrant the grant 'against all men' (*contra omnes homines*), with the addition of 'both religious and secular' (*tam religiosos quam seculares*) in two cases.[839] However, in a few charters the clause is more specific: 'against all men and especially the sons of Wrgi and their stock';[840] 'against all men and women and especially against all Welsh';[841] 'especially against all our kin';[842] and 'against all my men and all others who wish to be with me or follow in my vicinity and especially against the men of Brycheiniog and of Senghennydd and against the sons of Seisyll ap Llywarch'.[843] In three charters (one of 1213, the others, both recording the same grant, datable to 1215 × 1222), the safeguards provided by warranty and, in the latter two cases, oaths, are supplemented by the naming of pledges.[844]

None of the acts contains a dating clause apart from the judgement issued jointly by Bishop Elias of Llandaff and Morgan Gam in 1234, which was presumably drawn up by an episcopal clerk; the clause is introduced by *actum* and dates the document by the year of grace and the day of the month according to the ecclesiastical calendar.[845] In addition, the year of Morgan ab Owain's final concord with Margam (1246) is given after the notification in his letter patent announcing the agreement,[846] while the texts of several charters mention the date when rent was paid by Margam to the grantor for the lease granted.[847] Charters normally have a witness list, and Morgan ap Caradog's letter to the Cistercian abbots ends with a final greeting (*Valete in domino*).[848] None of the witnesses is described as being the scribe of the charter and none of the clergy listed is explicitly associated with the grantor.

All the original acts issued by members of the dynasty of Glamorgan contain evidence of sealing. The seal was suspended on a parchment tag inserted through slits in the fold at the bottom of the document (*sur double queue*), with the exception of the only act by a female grantor, Gwenllian ferch Morgan, which has a silk cord of twisted pink and yellow thread rather than a tag.[849] Surviving seal impressions are numerous and varied. Cadwallon ap Caradog's seal, known from only one impression, is circular, originally *c.*60 mm. diameter, with the horse galloping to the right and bearing the legend '+ SIGILL'. CADW . . . NI . FI . . . . RATOCI'.[850] His brother Morgan ap Caradog had two equestrian seals. (1) The earliest, both of whose impressions are attached to charters datable to 1158 × 1191, is circular, origi-

---

[838] No. 134. See also nos 132, 136, 138, 152–3, 155, 173, 175, 178, 188.
[839] Nos 138, 155.
[840] No. 173.
[841] No. 180.
[842] No. 186.
[843] No. 190.
[844] Nos 167, 185–6.
[845] No. 181.
[846] No. 187.
[847] Nos 133–4, 136, 142–4, 166–7.
[848] No. 147. No. 171 ends *Hiis testibus* and leaves a blank space where the names of witnesses could have been inserted, features which may indicate that it was a draft.
[849] No. 169.
[850] No. 121; Siddons, 'Welsh equestrian seals', 299.

nally *c*.50 mm. diameter, and shows the horse galloping to the right; the more complete legend reads '+ SIGILLVM : . . . . GANI : FIL[II] : CRATOCI'.[851] (2) The second seal, of which there are numerous impressions from no later than 1199 onwards, is almost circular (*c*.58 × *c*.53 mm.), shows the horse walking to the right and bears the legend '+ SIGILLVM MARGAN : FILII CARADOCI'.[852] Only one impression survives of the seal of Maredudd ap Caradog, brother to Cadwallon and Morgan. This is circular, originally *c*.50 mm. diameter, showing a spiral branch of foliage terminating in a fleur-de-lys in the centre of the design and bearing the legend '+ SIGILLVM . MOREDVC. FILII. CARADOCI'.[853]

Owain ap Morgan ap Caradog had two seals, and two impressions survive of each. (1) The first, attached to charters written no later than 1208, is circular, originally *c*.40 mm. diameter, showing the device of a dexter hand and vested arm holding a lance-flag; the more complete legend reads '+ SIGILL' : HOWENI : F . . . . NI'.[854] (2) The impressions of Owain's other seal are attached to charters issued no earlier than *c*.1208. This is circular, *c*.40 mm. diameter, and shows a knight on a horse galloping to the right, with the legend '+ SIGILL' . OWENI . FIL . MORGAN'.[855] The chronology of the extant impressions may indicate that the use of these seals was consecutive and that Owain commissioned the equestrian seal after the death of his father Morgan ap Caradog *c*.1208.

The sequence and appearance of Lleision ap Morgan's three seals are as follows. (1) A circular seal, originally *c*.55 mm. diameter, showing the device of a figure kneeling on the left before an enthroned abbot who is blessing him with his right hand and holding a book in his right hand and bearing the legend '+ SIGILLVM . LEISAN . FILII . MORGANI'.[856] In three cases the sealing tag states that the impression derives 'from the first seal' (*de primo sigillo*). The broadest dating limits for the charters having impressions of this seal are 1203–10, the narrowest 1205–*c*.1208. The design of the seal is remarkable, and appears to portray Lleision's submission to the abbot of Margam, perhaps signalling a reconciliation between the two men following disputes that Lleision is known to have had with the abbey during his father's lifetime.[857] (2) In two cases, one datable to 1203 × 1205, the other to *c*.1208 × 1210, there are duplicate charters recording the same grant from which are suspended impressions of an oval seal (*c*.42 × *c*.38 mm.), showing a knight on a horse galloping to the right and bearing the legend '+ SIGILL' LEISAN FIL' MORGANI', whose tag is inscribed 'from the second seal' (*de secundo sigillo*).[858] (3) The most numerous impressions, extant from 1205 onwards, are of another equestrian seal, circular, *c*.55 mm. diameter, showing the horse galloping to the right and bearing the legend

---

[851] NLW, Penrice and Margam Ch. 54 (*Cartae*, ii. 346–7 (no. 346)); no. 121 ('+ S . . . . ANI . FILII . . . . CI'); Siddons, 'Welsh equestrian seals', 298.
[852] No. 130. See also nos 123–4, 127–9, 132–4, 136–7, 142–6, 148, 153; NLW, Penrice and Margam Chs. 90, 92–3, 95 (*Cartae*, i. 167; ii. 400–1, 448–9, 450 (nos 168, 409, 456, 458))).
[853] No. 150.
[854] Nos 151, 170.
[855] Nos 161, 172 (legend incomplete); Siddons, 'Welsh equestrian seals', 301.
[856] Nos 154, 155 (A1), 163, 164 (A2); the legend is incomplete on the seal attached to no. 155.
[857] Williams, *Welsh History through Seals*, 22; cf. nos 151–2. It is possible that Margam was responsible for commissioning or even making the seal, though the earliest surviving abbatial seals (of *c*.1170 and 1256) show the abbot standing, not enthroned: cf. Williams, 'Catalogue of Welsh ecclesiastical seals: IV', 142 (nos 220a, 220b, 221) and Plates XIII–XIV.
[858] Nos 155 (A2), 164 (A1); Siddons, 'Welsh equestrian seals', 300.

'+ SIGILLWM . LEISAVN . FILII . MORGAN'.[859] The text of one charter to which an impression of this seal is attached explains that Lleision had previously had two seals with which he had sealed various charters for the monks, presumably a reference to the first and second seals already mentioned.[860] To judge by the dates of the charters from which the surviving impressions are suspended, all three seals were in use simultaneously at least during the last years of Morgan ap Caradog (1205–c.1208). However, it appears that (3) was the only seal used after 1210, and perhaps after c.1208, suggesting that this was Lleision's principal if not sole seal after the death of his father c.1208.

Impressions survive of three seals of Morgan Gam. (1) One, attached to a charter datable to c.1217 × 1240, is circular, c.35 mm. diameter, showing the device of a fleur-de-lys and bearing the legend '+ SIGILLVM MORGANI CA(M)'.[861] (2) A circular equestrian seal, c.40 mm. diameter, showing the horse galloping to the right and, in the better impression, bearing the legend '+ [S]IGILLV. . [M]ORGANI . GAM *'.[862] The charters to which these impressions are attached are both datable to c.1217 × 1241. (3) A pointed oval equestrian seal, c.40 × c.28 mm., which unusually shows a rider holding a sword in his left hand on a horse that stands facing left; the legend on the best impression reads '+ SIGILLVN . NODGANI . CAM'.[863] Two of the impressions are attached to documents dated 1234.[864]

None of the remaining seals to be discussed is equestrian. The only impression of Gwenllian ferch Morgan's seal is oval, c.37 × c.30 mm., but unfortunately is too worn for either the device or the legend to be recoverable.[865] The impressions, all from the same matrix, attached to Morgan ab Owain's charters and letter patent are of a pointed oval seal, c.35 × c.25 mm., showing a fleur-de-lys device and bearing the legend '+ S. MORGAN MAB OEIN'.[866] Two impressions, both from the same matrix and attached to charters written by the same scribe datable to c.1217 × 1228, survive of the circular heraldic seal of Morgan ap Cadwallon, c.33 mm. diameter, which bears the device of a lion passant facing right and the legend '+ SIGILL' : MOGANI : FILII : KADFV'.[867]

---

[859] Nos 165, 168 and, with legends incomplete, nos 157–9, 166–7; Siddons, 'Welsh equestrian seals', 300.

[860] No. 168 (1215 × 1217): . . . *sicut carta predicti Morgan' patris mei testatur et similiter sicut carta mea quam inde habent cum parvo sigillo meo testatur quod primo habui. Nam ante hoc sigillum quo presens carta sigillatur habueram duo sigilla quibus predicti monachi habent diversas cartas sigillatas quas eis confirmo.*

[861] No. 175.

[862] No. 176 (the letters are supplied from the legend of the impression attached to no. 177: '+ S . . . . . . MOR. . . . .'); Siddons, 'Welsh equestrian seals', 300.

[863] NLW, Penrice and Margam Ch. 1973 (*Cartae*, vi. 2299–2300 (no. 1578)); Siddons, 'Welsh equestrian seals', 299.

[864] No. 181; BL, Harl. Ch. 75 B 40 (*Cartae*, vi. 488–9 (no. 490)).

[865] No. 169.

[866] Nos 183, 185, 187; only the impression attached to the first of these is complete.

[867] Nos 189–90.

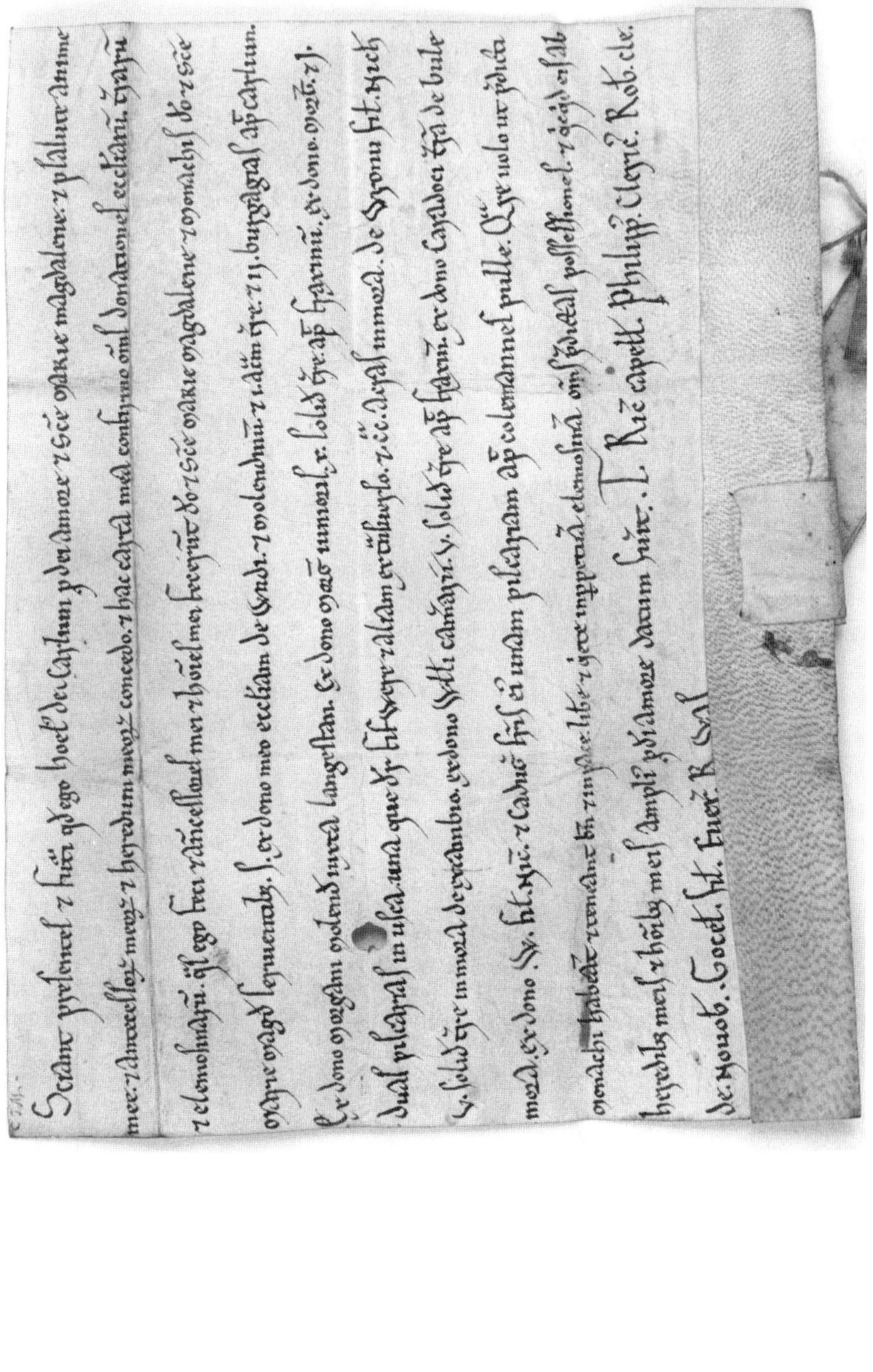

Plate 9 Charter of Hywel ap Iorwerth (no. 471)

GWYNLLŴG

The fifteen extant texts of acts issued by rulers of Gwynllŵg comprise thirteen charters, of which eight are in favour of Goldcliff Priory,[868] one letter patent[869] and one final concord made in the presence of Hywel ap Iorwerth.[870]

Two of the charters, both for Goldcliff, survive as originals. Both are datable on the basis of their contents to 1184 × 1217, with no. 471 being later than no. 469. No. 469 is written in a very fluent current hand, exemplifying a type of disciplined rapid writing that became widely used from the 1190s onwards though it is found earlier, including among English royal scribes from the 1180s. The currency of the hand is reflected, for example, in the use of a loop to form the shaft of *d* in some instances and the extension of the foot of the elongated *z*-shaped abbreviation for *-us* by a follow-through stroke that sometimes runs into the first letter of the following word. No. 471 (reproduced in Plate 9) is written in a modified book hand, with the elongation of ascenders and addition of descenders (rather clumsily in the case of some of the letters *r*), of a kind that is characteristic of the late twelfth or early thirteenth century. It therefore displays far fewer elements of currency than no. 469 (though use is made of a two-compartment *g* characteristic of cursive script),[871] and both the proportions of letters and spacing between lines are more generous than those in the other charter.[872] The seals of both charters are lost, as is the tag of no. 469. No. 471 retains a parchment tag inserted through a slit in the fold and no. 469 has one slit just above, and another in, the fold.

Five of the charters and the letter patent open with a protocol including an address and greeting (*salutem* in all cases).[873] In three of the charters the address follows the style,[874] whereas in the other three documents the address comes first.[875] Unusually among the documents in this edition four of the charters contain a collective address. In the earliest, a charter for the church of Rumney datable to 1147 × 1157, this is combined with a special address: *Domino suo Willelmo consuli Gloce' et Mabilie matri eius et omnibus amicis suis et hominibus.*[876] The formulae in the other charters all include the phrase 'all their/his men, French, English and Welsh': *omnibus hominibus suis Francis et Anglis atque Walensibus* in a charter for Goldcliff, with the addition of a general address (*et omnibus Cristi fidelibus*) in a later charter for the same house issued by Hywel ap Iorwerth (possibly modelled on Robert de Candos's foundation charter of the early twelfth century);[877] and *omnibus amicis*

---

[868] Goldcliff: nos 463–4, 469–72, 474–5. Other charters: nos 462, 465, 467, 473, 477.

[869] No. 478.

[870] No. 476.

[871] Cf. Webber, 'Scribes and handwriting', Plate VI, note. Note also the continuation of the top of the ascender of *s* into the top of the ascender of the following *t* in *Langestan*. On the other hand, a more conservative feature is the absence of a horizontal stroke through the minim stroke in the tironian *nota* (in contrast to the usual practice in no. 469).

[872] No. 471 has minim strokes of *c*.2 mm. rather than *c*.1 mm. in no. 469, and space between lines of *c*.9 mm. rather than *c*.5 mm.

[873] The final concord opens with a verbal invocation (*In nomine sancte et individue Trinitatis*): no. 476.

[874] Nos 464–5, 469.

[875] Nos 462, 474, 478.

[876] No. 462.

[877] Nos 464, 469. Cf. *Mon. Ang.*, vi: ii. 1022: *universis hominibus suis Francis, Anglis et Wallensibus et omnibus sancte ecclesie Dei fidelibus.*

et hominibus Francis, Anglis et Walensibus in the charter for St Gwynllyw's church, Newport, and Gloucester Abbey.[878] The remaining charter (1184 × 1217) and the letter patent (1233) both have general addresses.[879] The eight charters that open with a notification all incorporate a general address, usually *presentes et futuri*.[880]

The styles adopted exhibit some variation. Each of the three charters issued jointly by the brothers Morgan and Iorwerth sons of Owain has a slightly different style: *Morganus et Ierueuert filii Oni, Morganus filius Oeni et Geruerdus frater meus* (the use of the first person is explicable by the incorporation of the style in the notification rather than in a protocol) and, without patronymic, *Morganus et Ioruerdus frater eius*.[881] Morgan ap Morgan is styled by his name and patronymic in a charter for St Gwynllyw's church and Gloucester Abbey, as is Hywel ap Iorwerth in what seems to be his earliest charter, issued in favour of Glastonbury (*Hoelus filius Ioruerthi filii Oeni*).[882] However, the rest of Hywel's charters, all but one of which are for Goldcliff, reflect a desire to promote his status by omitting the patronymic and adding either 'of Caerleon' (*Hoelus de Karliun*),[883] a style also used in the final concord dated 30 March 1211,[884] or, in what was probably a subsequent development designed further to advertise his authority, 'lord of Caerleon' (*Hoelus dominus de Karliun*).[885] Likewise Hywel's son Morgan is styled by his name and patronymic in his charter of 1221 × 1230 but as 'Morgan of Caerleon' in his letter patent of 1233.[886] Hywel ap Iorwerth is the earliest Welsh ruler known to have adopted a style incorporating a toponymic referring to the seat of his power, and the change reveals his openness to aristocratic fashion in England and France as well as, perhaps, his determination to capitalize upon the legendary associations of Caerleon as the site of Arthur's court as depicted by Geoffrey of Monmouth.[887]

The text in all acts issued by a single author is written in the first person singular. The notifications of the charters show a clear preference for forms of *scire*, most commonly in the construction *sciant . . . quod ego* followed by the dispositive verbs, usually in the perfect tense, though one of Hywel ap Iorwerth's charters for Goldcliff has the present tense.[888] One charter issued by Morgan and Iorwerth in 1154 × 1158 imitates English royal and baronial usage in having *sciatis nos* followed by the verbs in the perfect infinitive.[889] Only two charters use forms of *noscere*, one for Rumney church in 1147 × 1157, the other for Glastonbury in 1179 × 1184, as does the letter patent.[890] In addition, two of Hywel ap

---

[878] No. 465.

[879] Nos 474 (*universis Cristi fidelibus ad quos presens scriptum pervenerit*); 478 (*omnibus Cristi fidelibus hoc scriptum visuris vel audituris*).

[880] Nos 463, 470–1, 472–3, 475, 477. The only exception is no. 467 (*universis ecclesie Dei fidelibus clericis et laicis presentibus et futuris*).

[881] Nos 462–4.

[882] Nos 465, 467.

[883] Nos 469–72.

[884] No. 476.

[885] Nos 473–5.

[886] Nos 477–8.

[887] Crouch, *Image of Aristocracy*, 274; cf. Holt, 'What's in a name?', esp. 184–91, 193–4.

[888] Nos 463, 470, 471 (present tense), 472–3, 475, 477.

[889] No. 464. No. 465, Morgan ap Morgan's charter for St Gwynllyw's church and Gloucester Abbey, has *sciatis quod ego*.

[890] Nos 462, 467, 478.

Iorwerth's charters for Goldcliff have *notificetur me* followed by the dispositive verbs in the perfect infinitive.[891] The most common combination of dispositive verbs is *concedere* and *confirmare* (albeit in various forms),[892] with the addition of *dare* in two cases;[893] in addition, there is one example each of *dare* and *concedere*, of *donare* and *concedere* and of both *concedere* and *dare* alone.[894] As Walker has argued, the use of the formula *in feudo et elemosina* and the placing of the *pro salute* clause towards the end of the text may suggest that the charter for Rumney church was drawn up by a local clerk with little experience of drafting such documents.[895] A *pro anima* clause also comes towards the end of one of Hywel ap Iorwerth's charters for Goldcliff.[896]

The injunctive clause in one of Hywel ap Iorwerth's charters for Goldcliff is indebted to royal example (*Quare volo et firmiter precipio ne . . .*).[897] Two charters for the same house, one issued by Morgan and Iorwerth in 1154 × 1158, the other by Hywel ap Iorwerth in 1184 × 1217, include an almost identical sanction clause, which in the earlier document reads: *Prohibemus igitur ex parte Dei et nostra ne quis huius nostre confirmationis paginam audeat infringere, quod siquis fecerit maledictione Dei omnipotentis et nostra ipse et tota eius progenies perpetuo feriatur.*[898] This is almost certainly derived from the more elaborate sanction clause in Robert de Candos's foundation charter for Goldcliff: *Prohibeo igitur ex parte Dei omnipotentis et ex parte Marie matris domini et Beate Marie Magdalene et mea nequis hanc donationem meam audeat infringere, quod siquis fecerit maledictione Dei omnipotentis et Sancte Marie et Beate Marie Magdalene et mea ipse et tota eius progenies perpetuo feriatur.*[899] Seven charters contain a corroboration clause, each of them worded differently. Of these, four refer only to sealing,[900] two to the charter and sealing and one to sealing and witnesses.[901] In addition, one charter of Morgan and Iorwerth sons of Owain for Goldcliff (1154 × 1158) incorporates a corroboration clause in the disposition that refers to the charter and, unusually, the grantors' joint seal: *. . . et presentis scripti testimonio et sigilli nostri appositione confirmavimus . . .*[902] The corroboration clause in the letter patent is incomplete but seems to have followed the standard form in such documents (*In cuius etc. huic scripto sigillum meum apposui*),[903] and that in the final concord contains a comparable formula likewise referring to sealing.[904]

None of the documents has a dating clause, though the final concord includes a time-date in the text giving the year of the incarnation and day of the month according to the Roman

---

[891] Nos 469, 474.
[892] Nos 464, 469–74.
[893] Nos 475, 477.
[894] Nos 462–3, 465, 467.
[895] No. 462; *Cart. Bristol*, no. 49, n.
[896] No. 470.
[897] No. 472. There is also an echo of royal usage in no. 471 (*Quare volo ut . . .*). Cf. above, p. 61.
[898] No. 464. The clause in no. 474 differs only in the use of the first person singular and in changing the word order to *confirmationis mee*.
[899] *Mon. Ang.*, vi: ii. 1022 (with punctuation and orthography slightly amended).
[900] Nos 469, 472, 475, 477.
[901] Nos 465, 473–4.
[902] No. 463.
[903] No. 478.
[904] No. 476: *In huius ergo concordie testimonium H. Dei gratia Landavensis episcopus . . . presenti scripto sigilla sua apposuerunt.*

calendar.[905] All the charters have witness lists apart from no. 465, whose text is incomplete (and the names in no. 462 have not been preserved). No witness is described as the scribe of the document. Although most witness lists include one or more clerics, only one is referred to explicitly as being attached to the grantor (Hywel ap Iorwerth), namely *Urbano clerico meo et canonico Landavensi* in no. 467; this Urban also occurs in Margam charters of 1140 × 1148 and 1148 × 1183.[906] The Bartholomew *clerico camerarii* of no. 473 was also associated with Hywel if, as is likely, the chamberlain referred to was in the ruler's service.

POWYS

This analysis of the diplomatic of the acts of rulers of Powys will begin with the earliest document, a charter of Madog ap Maredudd, before moving on to discuss the acts, first, of the rulers of northern Powys, and, second, those of Owain Cyfeiliog and his descendants, rulers of Powys Wenwynwyn (together with two acts issued by lords of Mechain). A separate section will follow on the styles adopted by Powysian rulers, and the final part of the discussion will examine their seals. It should be stressed at the outset that there are no explicit references in the documents to scribes responsible for their drafting and/or writing. Many include in their witness lists monastic or secular clergy who could have undertaken such work, but only two of these are associated specifically with the author of the act (Gruffudd ap Gwenwynwyn in both cases): William *de Ekun* 'then cleric of the castle' (that is, Pool) in 1271 and 'Brother Giles, a Cistercian monk, then chaplain of the lord' in 1277.[907]

Madog ap Maredudd
The earliest surviving text of the charter of Madog ap Maredudd for St Michael's church, Trefeglwys, Arwystli (1132 × 1151) is contained in the cartulary of Haughmond Abbey, which presumably acquired the original charter when the church was later granted to Haughmond.[908] The document is unique among the charters in this edition in that its diplomatic conforms with that of the 'Celtic' charter-tradition which originated in pre-Norman Wales.[909] The most distinctive characteristic of this tradition is the use of the third person, in a past tense; other defining features are 'the consistent inclusion of three constituent parts, disposition, witness list and sanction'.[910] Madog's charter adheres to this form, with a notification incorporating a general address (*Notum sit omnibus quod*) and the grantor's style followed by a disposition whose verb (*dedit*) is in the perfect tense and third person singular, a blessing and sanction (*Qui custodierit sit benedictus et qui non custodierit sit maledictus*) and a witness list. The formula *in sempiterno graphio* ('in everlasting writing') at the end of the disposition is extremely unusual in twelfth-century charters, but is paralleled in Asser's Life of Alfred and the twelfth-century Life of St Carannog. Further evidence of

---

[905] No. 476.
[906] *Llandaff Episcopal Acta*, xxii.
[907] Nos 602, 606. In addition, 'Henry cleric of the Lord Madog' appears in the witness list of Madog ap Gruffudd's spurious charter for Combermere: no. 498.
[908] Pryce, 'Church of Trefeglwys', 18.
[909] No. 480. This analysis is based on Pryce, 'Church of Trefeglwys', 24–7, which follows the criteria set out in Davies, 'Latin charter-tradition'.
[910] Ibid., 262.

local drafting is the use of *sata*, apparently derived from *satum*, a biblical measure of grain, as the unit for measuring the land granted. Both the form and the vocabulary of the charter strongly suggest, then, that the charter was drafted by a Welsh ecclesiastic – perhaps from the neighbouring *monasterium* of Llandinam in Arwystli whose abbot is one of the witnesses – familiar with an indigenous tradition of diplomatic that differed from both the diploma and the writ charter of Anglo-Norman England.

Edeirnion, Penllyn and Powys Fadog, 1176–1236

The following discussion of the acts extant from the northern regions of Powys will fall into two parts divided chronologically by the death of Madog ap Gruffudd in 1236. The authentic acts from the earlier period consist almost entirely of charters for the Cistercian houses of Basingwerk, Strata Marcella and Valle Crucis. The only charter for lay benefici- aries (whose text is corrupt) relates to the foundation of Valle Crucis; there also survives one letter patent in favour of Shrewsbury Abbey.[911] The number of authentic charters issued by each ruler is as follows: Elise ap Madog, three;[912] Owain Brogyntyn, five;[913] Madog ap Gruffudd, eight.[914] The letter patent is in the name of Hywel ap Madog.[915] The diplomatic of the three spurious charters for Combermere Abbey in Cheshire will not be considered here.[916]

Eight charters survive in the original. All were issued in favour of Strata Marcella by Maredudd ap Hywel, Elise ap Madog and Madog ap Gruffudd in the period 1176–1228 apart from Owain Brogyntyn's charter for Valle Crucis (1207), which is written in a modified book hand.[917] The charters for Strata Marcella are likewise written in modified book hands, including four, for three different grantors, by Graham Thomas's Scribe A.[918] Each of the remaining charters was written by a different scribe (C, F and S), of which the last two display a greater degree of currency than the first.[919] Scribe A also wrote four, and Scribe C one, of Gwenwynwyn's charters.[920] As with other Welsh rulers' charters for Strata Marcella, it is very likely these documents were drafted and written by the abbey's monks and the Valle Crucis charter was also probably a beneficiary product.

The case for beneficiary production is reinforced by the diplomatic of the seven charters in favour of Strata Marcella, as this resembles that of the charters of Gwenwynwyn and other Welsh rulers for the abbey. For example, each opens with a notification incorporating a general address (*omnibus sancte matris ecclesie filiis tam presentibus quam futuris* or its equivalent in the nominative, apart from no. 499, which omits *sancte matris ecclesie filiis*, and no. 508, which adds *presens scriptum inspecturis vel audituris*); and each uses a form of *noscere* in the notification, followed by *quod ego* and the dispositive verbs in the perfect tense. Perambulations are used to describe the lands granted in nos 483 and 488, both

---

[911] Nos 500, 522.
[912] Nos 483, 487–8.
[913] Nos 492–6.
[914] Nos 499–501, 503–4, 506, 508–9.
[915] No. 522.
[916] Nos 497–8, 510 and notes.
[917] No. 496; *Ystrad Marchell Charters*, 110 and Plate 3iii (Scribe I). This is the only charter identified by Graham Thomas as being in the hand of this scribe.
[918] Nos 482–3, 488, 504.
[919] Nos 487 (C), 499 (F), 508 (S). No. 508 is reproduced in Plate 10.
[920] See below, p. 124.

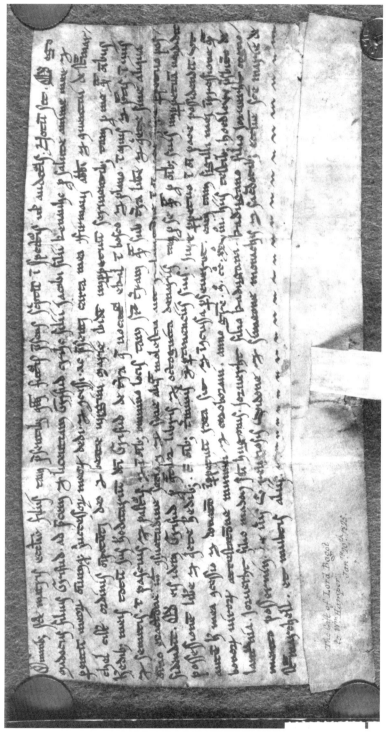

Plate 10 Charter of Madog ap Gruffudd (no. 508)

issued by Elise. All except no. 487 have a corroboration clause referring to sealing and witnesses and all except no. 499 contain a dating clause, though its form varies.[921]

Of Owain Brogyntyn's four charters for Basingwerk, all extant only in copies, nos 492–3 and 495 exhibit important resemblances to each other in their diplomatic. Nos 492–3 are very similar. Both contain a protocol with the address *omnibus sancte matris ecclesie filiis tam presentibus quam futuris* and the greeting *salutem* (a shortened form of the address is incorporated into the notification in no. 495); the notification reads *noverit universitas vestra quod ego* followed by the dispositive verb (*do*) in the present tense; and the corroboration clause is identical. The notification in no. 495 takes the form of *notum sit . . . quod ego* followed by the dispositive verb in the perfect tense, and the wording of the corroboration clause is somewhat different from that in the other two charters (though, like these, the verbs are in the present tense, and reference is made to sealing and witnesses). All three charters include a phrase in the disposition in which Owain promises to demand nothing but spiritual services from the monks (*nisi* (*tantum*) *eorum orationes et erga Deum beneficia*), and the witness lists are all in the nominative (*Hii autem sunt testes . . .*). These similarities in their diplomatic make it very likely that the charters were drafted by the beneficiaries, especially as they record new grants, rather than confirmations based on earlier charters. The fourth charter, no. 494, differs from the others in some respects, notably in its address (*universis fidelibus ad quos presens carta pervenerit*), contained in a protocol with the greeting *salutem*; in its omission of the phrase referring to spiritual benefits; in its reference to the charter and sealing in the corroboration clause; and in its placing of the witness list in the ablative (*Hiis testibus . . .*). On the other hand its notification combines elements in the other Basingwerk charters, reading *noverit universitas quod ego* followed by the dispositive verbs in the perfect tense. None of the charters has a dating clause.

The diplomatic of the four charters for Valle Crucis from this period (excluding the foundation charter granted to its mother house of Strata Marcella) exhibits considerable variety.[922] Not surprisingly, there are some similarities with the diplomatic characteristic of the Strata Marcella charters. For example, three lack a protocol and incorporate the address in the notification, of which two take the form of *notum sit . . . quod ego* followed by the dispositive verbs in the perfect tense. In addition, the corroboration clause of one of these is clearly indebted to that used in several Strata Marcella charters from 1195 × 1196 onwards.[923] Unlike many Strata Marcella charters, however, none of those for Valle Crucis contains a perambulation in its description of the lands granted. If, as is likely, the Valle Crucis charters were drafted by the monks, the admittedly small sample suggests that they eschewed standardization. Thus, no. 496, issued by Owain Brogyntyn in 1207, opens with a notification unique among the Valle Crucis and Strata Marcella charters (*Cognoscat presens etas et sciat postera quod ego . . .*, followed by the dispositive verb in the perfect tense), and the witness list is integrated with the corroboration clause (*Ceterum ne qua possit in posterum prefate donationi oriri calumpnia, quod gestum est sigilli nostri munimine*

---

[921] All include the year of the incarnation (placed in the corroboration clause in no. 508). Nos 483 and 487–8 add the day of the month (which is also referred to earlier in the text in no. 504). Place-dates are given in nos 483, 487–8, 504.

[922] Nos 496, 501, 503, 506.

[923] No. 503: *Et ut hec mea donatio rata sit et intemerata, quia moderni proni sunt ad malum unde sibi aliquid temporalis lucri extorquere potuerint, sigilli mei impressione confirmavi et corroboravi.* Cf. above, pp. 64–5, n. 502.

et testimonio litterarum roboravimus necnon et testes affuerunt quorum nomina in presenti pagina subarantur, scilicet . . .). One of Madog ap Gruffudd's charters opens with a protocol and its notification echoes English royal and baronial usage, reading *sciatis me* followed by the dispositive verbs in the perfect infinitive.[924] No. 506, a later charter of Madog, dated 1222, differs from the others for Valle Crucis in containing both a warranty clause and a sanction clause allowing the Church to impose penalties on any infringing the terms of the grant. Though each charter omits a place-date, the dating clauses vary: the year of the incarnation is incorporated in the disposition of no. 501 and in the corroboration of no. 503; in no. 496 a time-date follows, and in no. 506 precedes, the witness list (both have the year of the incarnation, but the former adds the month). No. 501 ends with a final greeting (*Valete*).

Powys Fadog, 1236–83

Texts of nine charters, four letters patent with general addresses and three letters to Edward I survive from this period. Four of the charters are in favour of ecclesiastical beneficiaries (three for Valle Crucis, one for the church of St Asaph),[925] five in favour of lay beneficiaries (three for Emma, wife of Gruffudd ap Madog, one for Edward I and one for John de Warenne, earl of Surrey and Sussex).[926]

Only one charter, issued in favour of Valle Crucis (1247), survives in the original.[927] It is written in a modified book hand, a somewhat conservative feature by the mid-thirteenth century, when such hands were becoming rare, especially among the charters of major beneficiaries. The three letters to Edward I are all written in cursive hands typical for the later thirteenth century.[928]

The diplomatic of the charters varies, even between texts for the same beneficiary. Four open with a protocol.[929] This consists of a verbal invocation (*In Dei nomine amen*) in no. 529, quite possibly reflecting beneficiary drafting by a clerk of St Asaph, and a general address, style and greeting in the rest. The address is different in each case, though the phrase *visuris vel audituris* occurs in three charters (and also two letters patent).[930] The greeting in letters patent is *salutem*, with the addition of *in domino sempiternam* in no. 532, issued by Gruffudd Fychan ap Gruffudd in 1283, a formula also used in the same ruler's charter of that year;[931] Gruffudd ap Madog's charters for Valle Crucis have *salutem eternam in domino* and *salutem in domino*.[932] The letters to Edward I contain suitably deferential greetings: *salutem et paratum in omnibus famulatum*;[933] *salutem, reverenciam et honorem*;[934] and *salutem, obedientiam, reverentiam et ad genua famulatum*.[935]

[924] No. 501. No. 500, Madog's charter for the heirs of Llanegwestl, also uses *scire* in the notification, albeit in the form *sciant . . . quod*.
[925] Nos 511, 513–14, 529.
[926] Nos 515–16, 519, 526, 531.
[927] No. 513.
[928] Nos 530, 533, 535.
[929] Nos 511, 513, 529, 531.
[930] Nos 511, 513, 524–5, 531.
[931] No. 531.
[932] Nos 511, 513.
[933] No. 530.
[934] No. 533.
[935] No. 535.

The text of all charters issued by a single ruler is written in the first person singular and the same is true of two letters patent and one letter with a special address.[936] The notifications of four charters and two letters patent use forms of the verb *noscere*, the rest forms of *scire* (*sciant* followed by *quod ego/nos* in the charters, *sciatis quod* in the letters). The corroboration clauses in nos 511 and 513, both for Valle Crucis, are very similar; that in no. 514, a later charter for the same abbey, bears some resemblances to these, including the use of *inposterum* rather than *imperpetuum*.[937] In three charters the corroboration clause includes the phrase *in cuius/huius rei testimonium* also used in all the letters patent.[938] There is only one example of a warranty clause.[939] Dating clauses occur in five of the charters and three of the letters patent, but vary in their form. Three of the former and two of the latter include place-dates. All include the year of the incarnation and also, apart from no. 511, the day of the month.

Owain Cyfeiliog and Gwenwynwyn ab Owain

The twenty-one surviving texts of charters issued by Owain Cyfeiliog and his son Gwenwynwyn ab Owain all derive from the archive of Strata Marcella apart from one charter of Gwenwynwyn in favour of Haughmond. Of Gwenwynwyn's nineteen charters for Strata Marcella, ten are extant as originals[940] together with a modern facsimile of another original and two single-sheet copies written by the same scribe of the late thirteenth or possibly even early fourteenth century.[941] The eleven originals (including the facsimile) from Gwenwynwyn's lifetime were written by six different scribes, including four by Thomas's Scribe A and three by Scribe E;[942] each of the remaining four charters was written by a different scribe (B, H, C and M).[943] Apart from H all of these scribes wrote charters for other grantors too.[944] Only the hand of Scribe M (who wrote the latest charter, dated 1215) is wholly cursive, the others being examples of modified book hands; that of Scribe B is especially close to a book hand.[945] All of this evidence strongly suggests beneficiary production. Indeed, Thomas has convincingly concluded that all the original charters in favour of Strata Marcella issued by Welsh grantors in the period up to 1215 'were probably drawn up and written in its own scriptorium'.[946]

---

[936] Nos 523, 532–3. Though no. 532 refers to the king as *dominus noster*, the rest of the letter patent is in the first person singular. The first person plural is used consistently in a letter patent of Madog Fychan (1246) and in a letter of Gruffudd Fychan (1279): nos 524, 530.

[937] The corroboration clauses of some earlier charters for Valle Crucis and Strata Marcella also have *inposterum*, though the usage is by no means consistent and *imperpetuum* also occurs: see, for example, nos 488, 496, 544, 553, 563, 575.

[938] Nos 516, 519, 523–5, 531–2.

[939] No. 516.

[940] Nos 544–5, 548, 551, 553, 556, 563, 569, 575, 578. No. 551 is included here though it records an agreement with the monks.

[941] Nos 552, 541, 555. The authenticity of the latter two charters is questionable.

[942] Scribe A: nos 548, 551, 553, 569. Scribe E: nos 552, 563, 575.

[943] Nos 544 (B), 545 (H), 556 (C), 578 (M).

[944] Nos 482–3, 488, 504 (A); *Ystrad Marchell Charters*, no. 16 (Alan, bishop of Bangor, 1195 × 1196: B); no. 487 (C); no. 9 (E); no. 16 (M).

[945] For further palaeographical analysis, including the identification of conservative features such as the use of the insular symbol ÷ as an abbreviation for *est*, see *Ystrad Marchell Charters*, 110–11. Images of original charters for Strata Marcella preserved among the Wynnstay Estate Records in the National Library of Wales may be viewed at *http://www.llgc.org.uk/drych/drych_s018.htm*.

[946] *Ystrad Marchell Charters*, 110.

In common with most other charters issued by Welsh rulers for Strata Marcella, neither that of Owain Cyfeiliog nor any of those of Gwenwynwyn contains a protocol with an address and greeting. However, nos 539, 542 and 544 open with the verbal invocation *In nomine sancte et individue Trinitatis* (followed by *amen* in no. 544). Two of these, nos 539 (*c*.1170) and 544 (1191), lack a notification, the former proceeding immediately to the dispositive clause (*Ego Oenius filius Griffini . . . concessi et dedi . . .*), the latter, uniquely among the Strata Marcella charters, containing an arenga, followed by *Forma igitur hec est. Ego Guenoingven Owini filius de Keueiliauc . . . Deo et abbatie de Estrat Marchell dedi perhenniter possidenda . . .* Both of these charters appear to be indebted in these respects to the diploma. The source of this influence is uncertain. It is unlikely to derive from native Welsh charter-writing, as, to judge by the extant examples, this differed markedly in its form from the diploma.[947] Although the diploma continued to be used in England until the mid-twelfth century despite the increasing dominance of the writ charter, it was unusual thereafter.[948] One possibility is that knowledge of the diploma derived from the abbey's mother house, Whitland (founded 1140), a daughter of Clairvaux whose original community presumably included monks from Burgundy. Although no texts of charters for Whitland are extant from the twelfth century, the earliest example being that issued by King John in 1214,[949] beneficiary drafting at Whitland, under the influence of continental models, may well explain the unusual features of no. 539, Owain Cyfeiliog's foundation charter for Strata Marcella, especially since the charter was granted to Whitland. This in turn probably influenced the redaction of nos 542 and especially 544 in the name of Gwenwynwyn. That the monks of Clairvaux were familiar with the diploma is shown by the numerous examples of such documents issued in favour of that monastery by bishops and secular rulers. For instance, several acts of Godfrey, bishop of Langres open with the same invocation as that in the Strata Marcella charters and likewise omit a notification: *In nomine sancte et individue trinitatis. Ego Godefridus . . .*[950] Moreover, these could have a witness list rather than *signa*.[951]

Apart from nos 542 and 544, Gwenwynwyn's charters for Strata Marcella open with a notification that incorporates a general address. The address is usually *universis/omnibus sancte matris ecclesie filiis tam presentibus quam futuris* (given in the nominative where *noscant* is used in the notification).[952] The same address is also found in the protocol of no.

---

[947] Cf. above, pp. 119–20.

[948] Compare, for example, the foundation charter for Quarr Abbey, a Savigniac house, in 1141 × 1145: *Charters of the Redvers Family*, ed. Bearman, 68–9 (no. 17). Cf. also ibid., 76–7, 88–90, 115–18 (nos 27, 42, 76). However, these charters differ from those for Strata Marcella considered here in that the dispositive clause following the arenga is introduced by *quapropter*, and not all open with a verbal invocation. Galbraith, 'Monastic foundation charters', 215–16, notes that the diploma 'still lingered on in documents drawn up in monastic houses' in mid-twelfth-century England, though by then it had been almost entirely displaced by the writ charter in the royal chancery and in baronial house-holds.

[949] *Mon. Ang.*, v. 591.

[950] Waquet, *Recueil*, 45–6, 51–2, 62 (nos 19, 27, 41).

[951] For example, ibid., 62 (no. 41). It should be added that, on the Continent, the diploma was still considered to be 'peculiarly appropriate for a solemn charter of foundation': Galbraith, 'Monastic foundation charters', 214.

[952] Exceptions are *omnibus tam clericis quam laicis, tam presentibus quam futuris* (no. 542), and *tam presentibus quam futuris* (also in the nominative) (nos 548, 575, 578).

546, Gwenwynwyn's charter for Haughmond, where it precedes the greeting *eternam in domino salutem*. (There are no close parallels for this address in the charters for Haughmond issued by rulers of Gwynedd and Arwystli.)

The notifications of Gwenwynwyn's charters all use forms of *noscere* apart from no. 578, the ruler's last known charter for Strata Marcella (1215), which has *sciant*. The most common form, found in twenty-three of the thirty-five charters issued by Welsh rulers for Strata Marcella, is *notum sit quod ego* followed by the dispositive verb(s) in the perfect tense, though three charters for Strata Marcella have *noscant* followed by the same construction (also found in no. 578). By contrast, no. 546, for Haughmond, has *noverit . . . nos concessisse*. All the Strata Marcella charters are written in the first person singular. The use of the first person plural in the Haughmond charter is paralleled in Llywelyn ap Iorwerth's charters for that house, though those issued by earlier rulers of Gwynedd and members of the dynasty of Arwystli use the first person singular.[953] The dispositive verbs usually consist of *dare, concedere* and *confirmare*, either all combined (for instance, *dedi, concessi et (hac presenti carta) confirmavi*)[954] or only one or two of these, while charters in which Gwenwynwyn participates in, and thus confirms, sales of land by freemen have *vendidimus* or *vendidi*.[955] In the charters for Strata Marcella the description of lands granted often takes the form of a perambulation, a characteristic of other charters issued by Welsh rulers for that house.[956] Owain Cyfeiliog's charter lacks a corroboration clause,[957] as do three of Gwenwynwyn's charters (all for Strata Marcella, including one document in the form of a *conventio*).[958] Most corroboration clauses in the Strata Marcella charters refer to sealing and witnesses, though nos 552–3 also mention the charter itself and no. 549 refers only to the charter and witnesses. The corroboration clause in no. 546 for Haughmond is almost identical to that in two of Llywelyn ap Iorwerth's charters for that house and refers only to sealing.[959] None of the charters of Owain Cyfeiliog or Gwenwynwyn contains a warranty clause.

Each charter contains a witness list, usually introduced by the formula *his testibus*, though that of Owain Cyfeiliog has the unusual *testificantibus hiis*,[960] while three of Gwenwynwyn's charters for Strata Marcella have a formula in the nominative that includes *igitur* (*testes igitur huius donationis sunt* or, in one case, *testes igitur ex parte mea sunt*).[961] Owain Cyfeiliog's charter lacks a dating clause, but such clauses occur in thirteen of Gwenwynwyn's charters, all for Strata Marcella. Nine of these have the verb *facta est*,[962] one has the phrase *data est et confirmata* and two open with *datum*.[963] The use of the phrase *actum pupplice* in no. 544 (1191) may be further evidence of continental influence on that

---

[953] See above, pp. 60, 63, 90.
[954] Nos 541–2, 555, 569, 578.
[955] Nos 552–3, 554 (*vendiderimus*), 575.
[956] Nos 539, 541–2, 544–5, 549, 552, 555, 556, 563–4, 569. Cf. *Ystrad Marchell Charters*, 106–7, and above, pp. 100, 120.
[957] No. 539.
[958] Nos 551 (*conventio*), 556, 569. No. 565 includes a clause in which Gwenwynwyn confirms the grantors' donation and sale with his seal and witnesses.
[959] Cf. nos 225–6.
[960] No. 539.
[961] Nos 544–5, 556.
[962] Nos 541–2, 552–3, 555, 564–5, 569, 575.
[963] Nos 556, 563, 578.

charter, as the formula was normal in the dating clauses of acts of Louis VI and Louis VII of France (though it fell into disuse under Philip Augustus).[964] Six of the dating clauses have place-dates. All have time-dates including the year of the incarnation, with the addition in six cases of the day of the month, calculated according to the Roman calendar.[965] Again, no. 544 is very unusual, as it also gives the regnal year of Richard I of England (*regnante rege Anglie Ricardo nomine anno iio*), echoing the recent innovation of dating English royal charters by regnal year introduced at Richard's accession in 1189.[966] Only no. 554 ends with a final greeting (*Valete*).

Powys Wenwynwyn (and Mechain), 1216–82

The texts of acts issued by members of the dynasty of Powys Wenwynwyn after the death of Gwenwynwyn in 1216 are more varied, with respect both to their type and to their beneficiaries and addressees, than those of Owain Cyfeiliog and Gwenwynwyn. In addition to thirteen charters (for ten different beneficiaries, only two of them ecclesiastical),[967] there survive two letters patent with general addresses[968] and four letters with special addresses.[969] Ten of the charters and all the letters are in the name of Gruffudd ap Gwenwynwyn. All the acts are in Latin apart from the latest document, a letter of October 1282 to Edward I's chancellor Robert Burnell, which is written in French.[970] Only two texts survive of acts issued by the lords of Mechain, namely a letter patent of 1276 and a letter to Edward I of 1277.[971]

Five charters and one *conventio* are extant as originals. Two of these documents are written in pure cursive hands typical of the mid-thirteenth century.[972] The only charter in favour of Strata Marcella, issued by Madog ap Caswallon (1231 × 1232), was written by Thomas's Scribe U in a modified book hand containing several cursive forms, notably the use of *d* with a looped ascender; this hand is not attested elsewhere among the original charters of Strata Marcella.[973] Each of the three charters datable to 1232 × 1250 recording the same grant of Gruffudd ap Gwenwynwyn to Matthew fitz Thomas is written in a different hand. No. 583 is a hybrid, containing some elements of contemporary cursive script together with some features, such as the form of *g* and the fusion of *d* and *e*, from the contemporary small book hands, and is very conservative in its use of the ampersand. No. 584 is a slightly modified small book hand whose basic duct lacks any cursive features, and no. 585 a small book hand modified to a slightly greater extent than no. 580 (for

---

[964] Giry, *Manuel de diplomatique*, 745–6, 754; see also, for example, *Recueil des actes de Louis VI*, ed. Dufour, 59 (no. 29); Luchaire, *Etudes sur les actes de Louis VII*, 18. A more distant echo of this phrase occurs in the preamble to an act of Bishop Guy of Bangor for Haughmond Abbey datable to 1177 × c.1190 (*Ne quid a nobis intuitu pietatis et honestatis puplice et solempniter gestum est . . .*): *Cart. Haugh.*, no. 1212.

[965] Nos 541–2, 544, 556, 565, 569.

[966] Cf. Chaplais, *English Royal Documents*, 14.

[967] Nos 579, 581–5, 587–8, 593, 602, 604–7, 610.

[968] Nos 586, 604.

[969] Nos 596, 600, 605, 608. As it is written entirely in the third person, no. 597, a *conventio* between Gruffudd ap Gwenwynwyn and Adam fitz Peter of Longstone, is excluded from the present discussion.

[970] No. 608.

[971] Nos 612, 614.

[972] Nos 587, 597.

[973] No. 581; *Ystrad Marchell Charters*, 110 and Plate 8ii.

example, in its form of common mark of abbreviation and the elongated descender of the
-us abbreviation). The four original letters with special addresses are written in cursive
hands typical of the period at which they were written.[974]

Only three charters are in favour of religious houses. Madog ap Caswallon's charter for
Strata Marcella (1231 × 1232) differs from earlier charters issued for that abbey by
members of the dynasty in its having a protocol, in its use in the notification of *noverit
universitas vestra* followed by the dispositive verbs in the perfect infinitive and in its
inclusion of a warranty clause.[975] The two charters for Lilleshall Abbey, one issued by
Gwenwynwyn's widow Margaret Corbet in 1223 × *c.*1251, the other by Gruffudd ap
Gwenwynwyn in 1232 × *c.*1245, bear clear resemblances to each other in their diplomatic,
including the absence of a protocol or dating clause, a notification phrased *sciant presentes
et futuri* followed by the dispositive verbs *dedi, concessi et hac presenti carta mea confirmavi*
and similar warranty and corroboration clauses.[976]

Both charters for Lilleshall recorded grants made by virtue of their grantors' tenure of
the manor of Ashford in Derbyshire, and their diplomatic also resembles that of Gruffudd
ap Gwenwynwyn's charters for lay beneficiaries in that manor, although the wording of the
corroboration clauses in these is different.[977] The same notification also occurs in nos 602
and 607, issued in 1271 and 1278 for Gruffudd's sons Llywelyn and Owain respectively,
although these, in common with all but one of Gruffudd's charters for Welsh beneficiaries,
lack a warranty clause.[978] By contrast, the charters for Welshpool and Gruffudd's wife
Hawise[979] differ from the ruler's other charters in opening with an address and greeting and
in their notifications, which use forms of *noscere* followed by the dispositive verbs in the
perfect infinitive. The addresses are different, though that in the Welshpool charter
(*omnibus fidelibus hanc presentem cartam inspecturis vel audituris*) has some affinities with
those in Gruffudd's letters patent (*universis Cristi fidelibus* (*presentes litteras visuris vel
audituris*)).[980] The greeting of the Welshpool charter, *salutem in domino*, is also used in the
two letters patent and is expanded to *eternam in domino salutem* in the charter for Hawise.
(The letter patent of the lords of Mechain has *salutem* only.)[981] The greetings in letters with
special addresses vary, though there seems to be have been some preference for including
reverentia or its French equivalent: *salutem et se ipsum semper ad pedes*;[982] *salutem et tam
debitam quam devotam in omnibus cum humilitatis subiectione reverentiam*;[983] . . . *honorem et
reverentiam/saluz et honurs et reverences*.[984] All of Gruffudd's acts are written in the first
person singular apart from two charters and three letters; four of the documents using the
first person plural date from 1277 or later.[985] The corroboration clauses of his letters patent

---

[974] Nos 596, 600, 608, 614.
[975] No. 581.
[976] Nos 579, 582.
[977] Nos 583–5, 587–8. No. 587 lacks a warranty clause.
[978] The exception is no. 593 for Welshpool.
[979] Nos 593, 606.
[980] Nos 586, 604. The extended form of this address also occurs in no. 612, the letter patent of the
lords of Mechain.
[981] No. 612.
[982] No. 596.
[983] No. 600.
[984] Nos 605, 608. In no. 614, the letter of the lords of Mechain to Edward I, the greeting is *salutem
et paratam ad obsequia cum honore voluntatem.*
[985] Nos 586, 605–8.

(and that of the lords of Mechain) contain the phrase *in cuius rei testimonium/testimonio* characteristic of such documents.[986] Only two charters and two letters patent, including one issued by the lords of Mechain, contain a dating clause (place-date, year of the incarnation and day of the month).[987]

The rulers' styles

Uniquely among the acts in this edition Madog ap Maredudd is styled with reference to the people of his kingdom, as opposed to the kingdom itself or a place within it: 'Madog, king of the Powysians' (*Madauc rex Powissensium*).[988] The styles of the northern Powysian rulers in the period before 1236 lack titles with the exception of no. 482 (1176), the sole surviving act of Maredudd ap Hywel, which reads *Mareduth filius Howel, dominus provincie que dicitur Edeyrniaun*. Elise ap Madog and Madog ap Gruffudd are consistently styled by their name and patronymic alone.[989] Owain Brogyntyn is styled in the same fashion (*Owinus Madoci filius*) in no. 496, his charter for Valle Crucis, but all his charters for Basingwerk have *Owinus de Porkinton*, thereby referring to his birthplace at Porkington near Oswestry and omitting his patronymic. Owain is also referred to by the latter style (*Oenus de Porchinton*) in the pipe rolls in the 1160s as well as in Llywelyn ap Iorwerth's charter of submission to King John in 1211.[990] An important development after the death of Madog ap Gruffudd in 1236 is the adoption in some acts issued by his sons and grandsons of styles associating them with the lordships of either Bromfield (Maelor Gymraeg) or Iâl. The earliest examples are letters patent of Hywel ap Madog (1241) and Madog Fychan ap Madog (1246), which style their authors *Hoel filius Madoc de Brumfeud* and *Mad' Vechan filius Mad' quondam domini de Bromfeld* respectively.[991] In his earliest acts Gruffudd ap Madog follows the pattern established under his father Madog ap Gruffudd, being styled by his name and patronymic only,[992] but his three latest charters, from 1254 onwards, add the title 'lord of Bromfield' (*dominus de Bromfeld*).[993] It is not clear whether this style was continued by Gruffudd's four sons in 1270, with *domini* in the nominative plural, or whether this was in the genitive singular and referred to Gruffudd: *Madocus, Lewelinus, Owenus, Griffinus filii Griffini domini de Bromfeld*.[994] In her only surviving act Emma, Gruffudd's wife, is styled 'Emma of Bromfield'.[995] In two of his acts Gruffudd's son Gruffudd Fychan uses a style that includes the title 'lord of Iâl': *Griffinus Vychan filius Griffin' ab Mad' dominus de Yal* (1278) and *Griffinus Vachan dominus de Yal* (1279).[996] By contrast, the two

---

[986] Nos 586, 604, 612.

[987] Nos 602, 604, 606 (where it is combined with the corroboration), 612.

[988] No. 480. The closest parallel is the title *Walensium princeps* possibly used by Owain Gwynedd: above, p. 74. However, neither Owain nor any other ruler of Gwynedd is known to have included the title *rex/princeps Norwalensium*, as distinct from *Norwallie*, in his style.

[989] Likewise, the legend on Madog ap Gruffudd's seal(s) seems to have read *Sigillum Madoci filii Griffini*: below, p. 131.

[990] *HW*, ii. 494 and n. 31; no. 233.

[991] Nos 523–4.

[992] Nos 511, 513.

[993] Nos 514–16.

[994] No. 526.

[995] No. 519.

[996] Nos 529–30.

acts issued after the Edwardian conquest of his lands in 1283 lack a title.[997] The same is true of two letters from Llywelyn ap Gruffudd ap Madog to Edward I in 1277 × 1282.[998]

The style used by Owain Cyfeiliog and his descendants in Powys Wenwynwyn usually consists simply of the grantor's name and, in most cases, patronymic.[999] However, in five of Gwenwynwyn's charters this is followed by 'of Cyfeiliog', the latest of which, dated 1215, also adds 'lord of Montgomery'.[1000] Likewise, the style on his second, and perhaps his third, seal is 'Gwenwynwyn of Cyfeiliog'.[1001] In addition, three other charters of Gwenwynwyn accord him the title 'prince of Powys', combined with 'lord of Arwystli' in one case: *Wennunwen Powisie princeps et dominus Arwistili* (1197 × 1208 or 1210 × 1216), *Wenunwin Owini filius princeps Powis* (1197 × 1216) and *Wenunwen' Powisie princeps* (1204).[1002] Most acts of Gruffudd ap Gwenwynwyn simply give his name and patronymic, as does at least one of his seals.[1003] However, two charters style him 'Gruffudd ap Gwenwynwyn, lord of Cyfeiliog',[1004] and a third has 'Gruffudd ap Gwenwynwyn of Cyfeiliog'.[1005] The title 'prince' (*princeps*) never appears in Gruffudd's style. The greetings in two letters to the English king stress Gruffudd's humility by referring to him respectively as *suus humilis miles* and *suus humilis et fidelis*.[1006]

In their letter patent Owain and Maredudd sons of Llywelyn ab Owain and their fellow grantors are styled by name and patronymic only, but in their letter to Edward I the style of the sons of Llywelyn ab Owain includes the title 'lords of Mechain': *sui ligii et devoti filii Lewelini ab Owein domini de Mechein*.[1007]

Sealing and seals

Neither the single surviving charter of Madog ap Maredudd (d. 1160) nor that of Owain Cyfeiliog (d. 1197) contains any reference to sealing.[1008] By contrast, corroboration clauses in charters and letters patent issued by the other members of the dynasty of Powys show that these rulers all possessed seals.[1009] All the original charters were sealed on a parchment tag inserted through a fold at the foot of the document (*sur double queue*), whereas the original letters appear to have been sealed close, as each retains the remains of a tongue cut off the foot and also, with one exception, sets of slits through which the tongue could have passed after the letter was folded.[1010] Seal impressions survive for Elise ap Madog, Owain

---

[997] Nos 531 (*Griffinus Vaughan filius Griffini de Bromfeud'*), 532 (*Griffinus Vaghan filius Griffini filii Madoci*).

[998] Nos 533 (*L. filius Grifini de Brumfyld*), 535 (*Lewelinus filius Griffini filii Madoci*). The former style is also used in Llywelyn's petitions to the king: nos 534, 536–7.

[999] The patronymic is omitted in nos 548, 565 and 578, all of which style Gwenwynwyn with a title.

[1000] Nos 541–2, 544, 555, 578 (*Wennunwen de Keueilliauc dominus de Mungumeri*).

[1001] The first seal included his patronymic as well as 'Cyfeiliog': below, pp. 131–2.

[1002] Nos 548–9, 565.

[1003] See below, p. 132.

[1004] Nos 593, 602.

[1005] No. 583.

[1006] Nos 600, 605.

[1007] Nos 612, 614.

[1008] Nos 480, 539.

[1009] Although occasionally late twelfth- and early thirteenth-century charters lack corroboration clauses mentioning sealing: nos 487, 501, 506, 556, 569.

[1010] Nos 530, 533, 535 (no slits), 596, 600, 608, 614. Cf. above, p. 86.

Brogyntyn, Madog ap Gruffudd, one of Madog's sons, Gwenwynwyn and Gruffudd ap Gwenwynwyn. All of these rulers used equestrian seals apart from Gruffudd ap Gwenwynwyn, whose seals were heraldic.

Elise ap Madog and Owain Brogyntyn are represented by one impression each, both fragmentary, perhaps originally *c*.50–55 mm. diameter, with the legend lost and showing remains of an equestrian figure facing right.[1011] Two impressions of circular equestrian seals survive for Madog ap Gruffudd, both possibly from the same matrix. One, originally *c*.72 mm. diameter, bears the legend '+ SIGILL . . . . . I GR. . . . I.'[1012] The other, attached to a charter issued over twenty years later, was also originally *c*.72 mm. diameter; it is very worn and no legend is visible. Uniquely among the Powys charters, however, this has the impression of a counterseal on the back: oval, *c*.30 × *c*.26 mm., from a late antique intaglio gem with a bust in profile, facing right, and bearing the legend '. . . . . ADOCI . FILII . GRIF . . . .'.[1013] Remains of an equestrian seal, probably circular, originally *c*.50 mm. diameter, with its legend lost, are attached to a charter issued by Gruffudd ap Madog and his brothers in 1247; since it is placed furthest left of the four seals originally attached to the document, it may have belonged to Gruffudd, the first-named grantor.[1014]

Gwenwynwyn had three circular equestrian seals, all of similar design but of different sizes.[1015] To judge by the dates of the charters to which they were attached, the sequence of seals is as follows.

A, originally *c*.50 mm. diameter: charters of 1197 × July 1202 and 4 March 1201.[1016]
B, *c*.60 mm. diameter: charters of 1197 × 1208 or 1210 × 1216, (possibly) 1199, 25 March 1201 × 24 March 1202, 1205, 1207.[1017]
C, *c*.70 mm. diameter: charters of 1197 × 1216, 1215.[1018]

The lack of precise dates for several of these charters, together with the uncertainty over the matrix used for the seal known only from a facsimile of a charter of 1199, make it difficult to determine how far use of these seals overlapped.[1019] However, it seems that B had superseded A by 1205 at the latest and possibly already by March 1201, and that C had superseded B by 1215 at the latest and possibly in or after 1207. Only one of these impressions, from B, has a complete legend: 'SIGILL : GVENVUNWIN : DE : KEVEILIAVC'.[1020] The legend on A seems to have included 'KEVEILIAVC', but added Gwenwynwyn's patronymic: 'SIGIL . . . . F[I]L : OV . . . . C';[1021] 'SIGILL : . . . . E

[1011] Nos 483, 496; Siddons, 'Welsh equestrian seals', 301–2.
[1012] No. 504 (1207).
[1013] No. 508 (1228); Siddons, 'Welsh equestrian seals', 303; Birch, *Catalogue of Seals*, ii. 285 (no. 5957).
[1014] No. 513; Siddons, 'Welsh equestrian seals', 303–4 (which estimates the seal's original diameter as *c*.60–70 mm.).
[1015] For detailed descriptions see ibid., 302–3.
[1016] Nos 545, 556.
[1017] Nos 548, 563, 569, 575. Possibly the imperfect impression shown on the facsimile of the lost original of no. 552 (1199) was also from this matrix: Siddons, 'Welsh equestrian seals', 302; *Ystrad Marchell Charters*, 163.
[1018] Nos 551, 578.
[1019] Cf. Siddons, 'Welsh equestrian seals', 295.
[1020] No. 569.
[1021] No. 556.

. . . . . . VI . . . .'.[1022] The full legend probably read 'SIGILL : GVENVUNWIN : FIL : OVINI (: ?DE) : KEVEILIAVC' (or similar spellings of the proper nouns). The legend on C clearly ended with 'KEVEILIAVC', but the impressions are too fragmentary to permit reconstruction of its full wording: 'SIGIL . . . . LIAVC'; '. . . . . . WEN . . . .'.[1023]

Gruffudd ap Gwenwynwyn had at least three circular heraldic seals. The smallest, originally c.28 mm. diameter, shows a lion rampant on a triangular shield and bears the legend 'S' GRIFINI FIL' WENVNWEN'.[1024] Another, perhaps originally c.35 mm. diameter though too imperfect for its original size to be confidently reconstructed, shows a fragment of a lion rampant on the left of a triangular shield that is larger than the shield on the previous seal; its legend is lost.[1025] The largest seal, originally c.40 mm. diameter, is extant only in an imperfect impression which shows a worn triangular shield with no device visible and bears only illegible fragments of a legend.[1026] In addition there is a late nineteenth-century description of probably one of these seals: 'Armorial shield, Heater-shaped, of green wax, bearing a lion rampant and surrounded by the following legend – + S' CRIFINI (sic) FIL' WENVNWEN'.[1027] That the lion rampant was Gruffudd's heraldic device is confirmed by a roll of arms in c.1280, in which Gruffudd appears with the arms: Or, a lion rampant Gules.[1028]

THE PRODUCTION OF ACTS

The documents assembled in this edition show that the acts issued by twelfth- and thirteenth-century Welsh rulers corresponded, by and large, to documentary forms used elsewhere in western Europe, especially in England. Thus most charters conform to the writ charter in their diplomatic structure and, where originals survive, their methods of sealing; the letters patent adopted from the early thirteenth century were indebted to episcopal and English royal example; and letters were drafted by clerks who followed the conventions of *ars dictaminis*. These resemblances with diplomatic elsewhere reflect the increasing exposure of Wales to external influences in this period as the result of Anglo-Norman and English conquest and settlement, diplomatic relations with the English crown and the establishment and patronage of religious houses of English and continental origin. It is significant that the only act which adheres entirely to native Welsh conventions of diplomatic is Madog ap Maredudd's charter for the native *monasterium* of Trefeglwys; by contrast, grants and confirmations by Welsh rulers to Trefeglwys after it had been granted

---

[1022] No. 545.

[1023] Nos 551, 578.

[1024] No. 582. Another, imperfect, impression of this seal is attached to no. 587 (illustrated in Siddons, *Development of Welsh Heraldry*, 291, fig. 94). Dimensions of shield: approximately 16 × 13 × 16 mm.

[1025] No. 585. The remaining impression of the seal is c.25 mm. diameter. Dimensions of shield: approximately 22 × 15 × 22 mm. Possibly this was from the same matrix as that used to seal no. 597, originally c.35 mm. diameter, which could not be removed for inspection from its sealing bag.

[1026] No. 583. Dimensions of shield: approximately 25 × 21 × 21 mm.

[1027] No. 588.

[1028] Siddons, *Development of Welsh Heraldry*, 2, 291.

to Haughmond Abbey, an Augustinian foundation in Shropshire, are recorded in writ charters.[1029]

Yet, within this overall trend towards conformity with wider norms, the diplomatic of charters in particular exhibits considerable variety. Probably the most important reason for this variety was the continuing importance of beneficiary production by religious houses whose individual preferences in diplomatic in turn reflected differing political and cultural contexts. To take the most obvious example, in their basic diplomatic forms the charters issued by the dynasty of Iestyn ap Gwrgant from the 1180s or 1190s onwards for Margam resemble those of Anglo-Norman benefactors who had already patronized the abbey for a generation, and differ markedly from Welsh rulers' charters for Strata Marcella, founded *c.*1170 by Owain Cyfeiliog. Though the latter charters, together with those in favour of other Cistercian houses of the Whitland filiation that were founded by Welsh rulers, are mostly in the form of the writ charter, some are more eclectic in their diplomatic than charters for Anglo-Norman foundations such as the priories of Cardigan and Goldcliff or Margam Abbey – notably in their adoption of both the native tradition of perambulations (especially where these combine both Welsh and Latin descriptors) and, quite possibly in a few Strata Marcella charters, the continental diploma. Other features which suggest that monastic drafters were experimenting in their redaction of charters are the borrowings from a papal bull in the Lord Rhys's charter for Strata Florida (1184) and the attempt, unique among the acts in this edition, to construct a dating clause naming a datary in Madog ap Maelgwn's charter for Cwm-hir (1212).[1030]

It does not follow, of course, that all charters contained in this edition were produced by beneficiaries; moreover, letters patent and, above all, letters must normally have been drafted and written by clerks either attached to a ruler's household or employed by a ruler on an ad hoc basis (say, members of a religious community). Unfortunately, the documents extant from territories other than Gwynedd never refer to individuals in terms that point to their responsibility for drawing up an act, although in a few cases – from Deheubarth, Gwynllŵg and Powys – a witness is identified as a cleric of the act's author and thus possibly as the act's redactor.[1031] It is therefore difficult to estimate the proportion of charters drafted by beneficiaries rather than by clerks employed by Welsh rulers or to determine the secretarial arrangements at those rulers' disposal. However, enough evidence survives to explore these issues with respect to Gwynedd. Since this was the most powerful native polity for most of the period covered by this work, it is likely that its princes exercised greater control over the production of acts, and possessed a more developed secretariat, than any of the other Welsh dynasties. Therefore, while necessarily tentative, the following observations have implications for understanding the production of acts on behalf of all Welsh rulers, not just those of Gwynedd.

The evidence for how acts issued by rulers of Gwynedd were produced, including the question of whether those rulers had a chancery, has received careful consideration from David Stephenson and J. Beverley Smith.[1032] The present discussion will confirm and

---

[1029] See above, pp. 60–1, 89–90, 119–20. The term 'writ charter' is used here as a term of convenience for charters in letter-form: cf. Galbraith, 'Monastic foundation charters', 205; *Acts of William I*, ed. Barrow, 69.

[1030] Nos 28, 113.

[1031] Above, pp. 102, 119.

[1032] Stephenson, *Governance*, 26–39; Smith, *Llywelyn*, 319–29. See also the valuable comments in Insley, 'From *rex Wallie*', 195–6.

amplify their conclusions by examining, first, the direct testimony for the existence of a princely secretariat and, second, the inferences that may be drawn about the drafting of acts from the form and wording of the documents themselves. The key issue here is not whether the rulers of Gwynedd had the clerical resources to compose and write documents on their behalf (they clearly did), but rather how far those rulers exercised control over the production of acts, both in terms of the proportion of documents drawn up by, or at least under the supervision of, clerks in the princes' service and in terms of the degree of uniformity imposed on the documents' diplomatic. Closely related to this issue is the question of how strictly one defines the term 'chancery'. To anticipate the conclusions of the present discussion, there is little to suggest that the rulers of Gwynedd, let alone those of other Welsh territories, had a chancery in the sense of an organization responsible for the issue of documents according to a clear set of rules intended to prevent fraud.[1033] In what follows it may therefore be more helpful to bear in mind the broader definition of a chancery proposed by several recent scholars, namely 'an organization responsible for the validation of acts, rather than, necessarily, for their production'.[1034]

No source from twelfth- and thirteenth-century Gwynedd refers explicitly to a princely chancery. Moreover, as previous scholars have noticed, there are few references in the extant acts to individuals bearing titles indicative of a secretarial role. The title of chancellor (*cancellarius*) is applied to two men: Master Instructus, the first witness to a charter of Llywelyn ap Iorwerth for Ralph Mortimer datable to 1230 × 1240, and quite possibly to 1230,[1035] and Master David, archdeacon of St Asaph, who appears in several documents issued by Dafydd ap Llywelyn in 1240–1.[1036] There are no further references to a chancellor, but Master Iorwerth (Gervase) is described by Llywelyn ap Gruffudd as his vice-chancellor (*clericum nostrum et vicecancellarium*) in a letter to Edward I in 1277.[1037] It has been plausibly suggested that the vice-chancellor was a full replacement for the chancellor, rather than his deputy, the office of chancellor having either lapsed or become purely nominal.[1038] (A possible parallel is provided by the papal chancery, where the office of chancellor was suppressed after the death of Cardinal John of S. Maria in Cosmedin in June 1213 and its functions transferred to the vice-chancellor, albeit in this case because the chancellor was thought to have become too powerful.)[1039]

As elsewhere in Europe, the origins of the office of chancellor lay in the rulers' chapel. This is made clear by a passage in the Iorwerth Redaction, a lawbook composed in early thirteenth-century Gwynedd, dealing with the *offeiriad teulu*, literally 'the priest of the military household', who acted as chaplain to the royal court.[1040] According to this

---

[1033] Cf. Clanchy, *From Memory*, 56.

[1034] *Acta of William I*, 97, following Guyotjeannin *et al.*, *Diplomatique médiévale*, 223–4.

[1035] No. 259; cf. nos 252, 280, and Stephenson, *Governance*, 30, 224–5.

[1036] Nos 292, 296, 298–9; cf. Stephenson, *Governance*, 31, 223. Even if the title was intended to confer prestige on the bearer without necessarily implying regular performance of secretarial duties, its appearance reflects at least an aspiration on the part of these rulers towards a formal secretarial organization: cf. Crouch, 'Administration', 87–8.

[1037] No. 400; cf. Stephenson, *Governance*, 224.

[1038] Stephenson, *Governance*, 37.

[1039] Cf. Giry, *Diplomatique médiévale*, 685 and n. 2; Cheney, 'Office and title of the papal chancellor', 372–3; Guyotjeannin *et al.*, *Diplomatique médiévale*, 225; *Vocabulaire*, ed. Ortí, 71–2.

[1040] For further discussion of the Welsh lawbooks' rules on the *offeiriad teulu* see Pryce, 'Household priest'.

lawbook, one of the priest's entitlements is 4*d*. 'for every patent seal which the King gives for land and earth, or for other great matters'.[1041] Likewise the queen's priest is entitled to 4*d*. 'for every patent seal which the Queen issues'.[1042] As J. Goronwy Edwards pointed out, the reference to sealing suggests that, by the early thirteenth century at least, the household priest had assumed functions typical of a chancellor.[1043] Nevertheless, the precise significance of the passage for understanding the secretarial role of the household priest remains uncertain. That the text speaks of the king giving a patent seal, rather than a charter or letter, arguably assumes a situation in which charters were presented by beneficiaries for authentication by the seal, and the payment of 4*d*. to the priest may imply that he was entrusted with its keeping. (There might also be the implication that the payment represented a fee due from the beneficiary of a charter for its authentication, a practice attested elsewhere in medieval Europe, though the other payments to which the priest was entitled came from the king and the members of his court.)[1044] Since, however, the lawbook is concerned with detailing the priest's privileges rather than his duties, it would be rash to conclude that the priest's secretarial responsibilities were limited to sealing: his part in drafting or engrossing documents may have been ignored simply because no financial perquisites were attached to it rather than because it was non-existent. Indeed, a fourteenth-century lawbook seems to have interpreted the rule on sealing as referring to the priest's making letters patent in which the king granted land.[1045]

The legal rules on the household priest, together with the references to a chancellor in the 1230s and early 1240s, suggest that a secretariat had evolved by the second quarter of the thirteenth century, headed by a member of the secular clergy.[1046] Though there are no references to a chancery or chancellor under Llywelyn ap Gruffudd, the numerous letters sent in his name imply the existence of 'a secretariat directed by a principal officer in constant attendance upon the prince'.[1047] Even if, as is possible, the role of this principal officer was mainly supervisory, the rulers of Gwynedd were able to draw on the services of clerks, at least some of whom must have been capable of drafting and writing documents.[1048] This will certainly have been true of the three individuals each described in witness lists as being a *notarius* of the act's author: Einion in Dafydd ap Llywelyn's charter for Ynys Lannog in 1229, John (or Ieuan?) (*Iohannes*) in Llywelyn ap Iorwerth's charter for the same house in 1237, and Madog *filius Magistri* in Llywelyn ap Gruffudd's charter for

---

[1041] *Ior*, §7/9 (*Ef a dely pedeyr keynnyavc o pob ynseyl agoret a rodho e brenhyn am tyr a daear neu am negesseu mavr ereyll*); trans. *LTMW*, 12.

[1042] *Ior*, §23/4 (*Ef a dele pedeyr keynnyavc o pob ynseyl agoret a rodho e urenhynes*); trans. *LTMW*, 29.

[1043] Edwards, 'Royal household', 172 (followed by Stephenson, *Governance*, 28–9).

[1044] Cf. Bishop, *Scriptores Regis*, 31; *Charters of the Honour of Mowbray*, ed. Greenway, lxx; Guyotjeannin *et al.*, *Diplomatique médiévale*, 244.

[1045] *Ancient Laws*, ed. Owen, ii. 658–9 (XIV.xxi.26: MS *H*): *ac am bob llythyr egoret am dir a daear a wnel lle rhoddo y brenhin dir cynn[?i]f pedeir ceinioc a geiff* ('and he shall have fourpence for every letter patent for land and earth in which the king gives (?)acquired land'). A triad, of uncertain date, in other Welsh lawbooks explicitly refers to the household priest reading or making a letter (in the Cyfnerth Redaction) or a charter (in Latin A) in the king's presence: Pryce, 'Household priest', 90.

[1046] Master Instructus and Master David were secular clerics, as were the clergy who held the benefice known as *offeiriad teulu* ('household priest') in post-conquest Gwynedd: Pryce, 'Household priest', 91–2.

[1047] Smith, *Llywelyn*, 321–2.

[1048] See, for example, nos 196, 252, 267, 298, 318, 320, 458; Stephenson, *Governance*, 34–9.

Heilin ap Tudur in 1281 (Madog is named after the prior of Ynys Lannog, described as Llywelyn's chaplain).[1049] In all these cases, *notarius* meant a scribe who wrote acts rather than a notary public.[1050] Given the tiny size of the sample, it is difficult to determine whether the associations of the three charters in which the term occurs with the Augustinians of Ynys Lannog are merely coincidental, or whether they indicate that the notaries named were canons of that house, thereby implying in turn that Ynys Lannog played a special role in the production of the rulers' acts.

Also relevant to a consideration of the production of acts on behalf of rulers of Gwynedd is the nature and extent of their archives. That important documents received by the princes were kept is suggested by Llywelyn ap Iorwerth's reference in his letter to Philip Augustus to preserving the king's letter in 'the aumbries of the church'.[1051] The common practice by the thirteenth century of drawing up agreements with both the crown and other lords in the form of bipartite indentures ensured that the Venedotian party could retain a copy of the agreement; thus was Llywelyn ap Iorwerth able in 1216 to despatch prelates 'and other great men of authority' to Gwenwynwyn of Powys, 'and with them the tenor of the cyrographs and the charters and the pact and the homage which he had done to him, to beseech him to return' to the prince's side.[1052] In addition, the letters patent recording obligations to Llywelyn ap Gruffudd by other Welsh lords from the 1250s were almost certainly conserved in Gwynedd, whence they eventually reached the royal exchequer and were copied in Liber A.[1053] Indeed, Llywelyn's acts occasionally mention or cite earlier letters or agreements, showing that texts of these were available to the prince's clerks. For example, one letter, datable to early 1257, refers to *littere conventionis* with the king, while another letter, dated 22 January 1277, cites *in extenso* a recent letter to the prince from Edward I.[1054] Likewise, in 1275 Llywelyn sent copies of the Treaty of Montgomery, presumably derived from a text of the letter patent issued by Cardinal Ottobuono in 1267, to both Pope Gregory X and the archbishops of Canterbury and York and their suffragans, and the prince cited clauses from the Treaty of Aberconwy in *gravamina* sent to Archbishop Pecham in 1282.[1055] It has plausibly been suggested that churches, and especially Cistercian monasteries, served as record repositories. The best evidence for this relates to Maredudd, abbot of Aberconwy.[1056] In July 1278 Maredudd, together with the dean of Arllechwedd, made an inspeximus of the record of the legal process against Gruffudd ap Gwenwynwyn and his son in 1274, while at a judicial hearing before Edward I in September 1278 the abbot produced, on behalf of Llywelyn, Rhodri ap Gruffudd's quitclaim to the prince of 1272.[1057] It is also significant that Llywelyn sent Pope Gregory X's confirmation, dated 18 August 1274, of the agreement with his brother Dafydd to the bishops of Bangor and St Asaph for

---

[1049] Nos 286, 272, 423.

[1050] Cf. Giry, *Diplomatique médiévale*, 825–6; *Vocabulaire*, ed. Ortí, 70; Prevenier, 'La chancellerie', 51, 59–60.

[1051] No. 235.

[1052] See note to no. 577.

[1053] Above, pp. 51, 58.

[1054] Nos 327, 400.

[1055] Nos 390–1, 429. To judge by their content, the citations in the *gravamina* derive, not from a registered copy of the text of the treaty ratified by Llywelyn, but, rather, from the text ratified by Edward I.

[1056] Stephenson, *Governance*, 33–4; Smith, *Llywelyn*, 322.

[1057] Nos 603, 458.

their inspection with a letter dated at Llanfair Rhyd Gastell on 20 December 1274: this not only shows that neither of the bishops had been entrusted with custody of the papal letter but may also indicate that it had been preserved by the Cistercians of Aberconwy, as Llywelyn's letter was sent from one of their granges.[1058]

Whether outgoing documents were registered is, by contrast, uncertain. It is difficult to believe that no copies were made of letters to kings of England and other potentates to which reference might be made in future negotiations, although specific references to earlier letters are lacking.[1059] Registered copies might also have provided models for the prince's clerks and could explain, for example, the fairly consistent addresses and greetings used by Llywelyn ap Gruffudd in his letters to Henry III and Edward I. In addition, the fact that the style adopted by Llywelyn ap Gruffudd from 1262 onwards ('Llywelyn (ap Gruffudd), prince of Wales and lord of Snowdon') was adapted from that used by his grandfather Llywelyn ap Iorwerth in the 1230s ('Llywelyn, prince of Aberffraw and lord of Snowdon') implies that documents containing the latter style were known to Llywelyn ap Gruffudd's clerks. Yet these diplomatic features could equally reflect familiarity with letters received from the crown and/or the use of formularies rather than with copies of earlier princely acts.

How far can a study of the diplomatic and, where originals survive, the external appearance of acts contribute to an understanding of the circumstances of their production, including the nature of the rulers' writing office and the extent of its role? Referring in particular to the charters issued by the thirteenth-century princes of Gwynedd, David Stephenson counselled caution in relying on diplomatic analysis in this connection.[1060] Certainly, as far as charters are concerned, the relatively small number of extant texts, and the transmission of most of these in copies which probably do not precisely reproduce the wording of the originals, make it difficult to draw firm conclusions about the agencies responsible for their production. Nevertheless, taken together with the other evidence already discussed in this section, a consideration of some aspects of diplomatic, both of charters and of other types of documents, may at least help to identify a range of possibilities.

Any assessment of the role of a princely secretariat in the production of charters needs to take account of other types of documents issued in the princes' name whose drafting cannot normally have been undertaken by beneficiaries. The appearance from Llywelyn ap Iorwerth's reign of letters patent with a distinctive corroboration clause testifies to the existence of a secretariat capable of devising new forms of acts of a fairly standard type.[1061] Furthermore, throughout this period rulers of Gwynedd had access to clerks who wrote letters on their behalf to individuals. Many of these letters reflect the influence of the *ars dictaminis* and familiarity with the conventions of diplomatic correspondence, and from the mid-thirteenth century some letters and also texts of agreements with other Welsh lords reflect a knowledge of Romano-canonical law in their clauses renouncing exceptions which could have been invoked to avoid the spiritual penalties accepted in the event of failure to

---

[1058] No. 383.

[1059] The dating of Llywelyn ap Gruffudd's letters from 1269 onwards could have facilitated reference, but none of the extant acts refers to a dated letter of this kind.

[1060] Stephenson, *Governance*, 27–8.

[1061] Above, pp. 59, 65. However, the drafting of some letters patent of Dafydd ap Llywelyn and Llywelyn ap Gruffudd may have been supervised, or even carried out, by clerks of the royal chancery: above, pp. 67–8.

meet obligations.[1062] From 1269 letters with special addresses were subject to greater standardization, with the omission of Llywelyn ap Gruffudd's patronymic in the style and the introduction of a dating clause.[1063] The original letters extant from *c*.1220, and especially from the mid-thirteenth century, onwards demonstrate the availability of clerks competent in the cursive handwriting normally used for business documents throughout north-western Europe at this period. Unfortunately, it is unknown how many clerks were employed by a ruler at the same time or the extent to which these were attached to the itinerant court rather than to local centres, be they princely *maerdrefi* such as Rhosyr or Cistercian granges such as Abereiddon and Rhydgastell.[1064]

The evidence provided by the documents just discussed strongly suggests that the princes possessed secretarial resources capable of producing charters. The problem, however, lies in determining how far the production of charters can be explained in these terms. In approaching this problem, it is important to emphasize that the appearance in charters of features characteristic of ecclesiastical acts is not in itself conclusive with regard to determining the agency responsible for their production. Letters patent and other documents issued on behalf of rulers of Gwynedd which cannot have been written by beneficiaries or addressees reveal a debt to the diplomatic of ecclesiastical documents such as episcopal acts: the preference for forms of *noscere* in notifications and the formulae of corroboration clauses in letters patent are cases in point.[1065] Therefore, charters produced by a ruler's secretariat may have been just as likely as those produced by a religious house to exhibit a marked ecclesiastical complexion.

Nevertheless, there can be little doubt that some charters in the names of Venedotian rulers were written by beneficiaries. This practice became increasingly less common in the major European kingdoms in the twelfth and early thirteenth centuries, though a combination of beneficiary production and chancery production continued longer in some other polities and lordships: for example, monasteries and other ecclesiastical establishments presented charters they had written to Philip Augustus's chancery in France as late as 1190, but had virtually ceased to do so by the end of the reign in 1223, while beneficiaries still drew up 30.5 per cent of comital acts in Flanders 1191–1206.[1066] As has been shown, all the princes' charters for Basingwerk share distinctive features, notably the use of the first person singular and the present tense in the disposition, which strongly suggest that these documents were drafted by the monks and then presented to the ruler for sealing. The same is true of the charters of Llywelyn ap Iorwerth and his son Gruffudd ap Llywelyn for Strata

---

[1062] See above, pp. 70–2, 74. This is not to claim that all letters were skilful compositions: no. 378 (1273) is clumsily drafted, for example.

[1063] Above, pp. 72, 79.

[1064] Probably at least four scribes wrote letters for Llywelyn ap Iorwerth, but it is uncertain how far their periods of activity overlapped, and the numbers of scribes in Llywelyn ap Gruffudd's service are even more difficult to determine: above, pp. 80–1.

[1065] Above, pp. 63–4, 65, 66, 68. A preference for *noscere* is also shown by some non-royal lay grantors in England at this period, and it has been argued that *scire* was largely abandoned there in private acts by about the mid-thirteenth century: Stringer, 'Charters of David', 85. See also Insley, 'From *rex Wallie*', 188; n. 1067 below.

[1066] Guyotjeannin *et al.*, *Diplomatique médiévale*, 106, 111–12, 229; Dufour, 'Peut-on parler?', 261; Prevenier, 'La chancellerie', 39–45. For beneficiary production in twelfth- and early thirteenth-century England and Scotland see *Charters of the Honour of Mowbray*, ed. Greenway, lxvii–lxix; Stringer, 'Charters of David', 95.

Marcella, as these contain several distinctive features (for example, the lack of an address and the form of the notification) also found in the charters of non-Venedotian rulers for that monastery. Another strong candidate as a beneficiary product is Llywelyn's charter for Cymer, a lengthy and rather clumsily constructed document with several features reminiscent of episcopal acts, as Keith Williams-Jones observed.[1067]

It would be rash to conclude, however, that charters for ecclesiastical beneficiaries were invariably written by the latter and then presented to the ruler for authentication. The problems of determining the agency responsible for drafting charters are illustrated by those in favour of Haughmond, the single largest group of Venedotian charters for the same beneficiary, extant from the mid-twelfth century to the 1230s. These exhibit considerable variation in their diplomatic, although confirmations naturally tend to adhere to the phraseology of the dispositive clause of the charter being confirmed.[1068] It does not necessarily follow, of course, that Haughmond canons had no part in the drafting of these documents; but, if they were responsible, they appear not to have imposed a consistent house style, an impression supported by variations in the diplomatic of charters issued by other benefactors preserved in the abbey's cartulary. The six charters in favour of Ynys Lannog from the period 1221–47 pose similar problems of interpretation. The earliest, no. 250, differs from the rest in its inclusion of an arenga and in the form of its notification. The others admittedly have the same type of notification (*noverit universitas vestra* followed by *nos* and the dispositive verb(s) in the perfect infinitive); but this is also the most common form of notification in charters for other beneficiaries, including Haughmond. Moreover, if the canons of Ynys Lannog drafted the charters in their favour, differences in the corroboration and dating clauses suggest at the very least that, as with their fellow Augustinians at Haughmond, they did not try to standardize their diplomatic.

Variations in the diplomatic of charters for the same religious house may, of course, indicate that the documents were drawn up, not by the beneficiary, but by clerks employed by the grantor. Unfortunately, the extent to which diplomatic analysis can identify charters as deriving from a ruler's secretariat is difficult to assess. True, some charters issued by the same ruler for different beneficiaries share common elements of diplomatic that could indicate central control over their production. The apparent emergence of a standard form of address including the phrase *has litteras visuris vel audituris* in both charters and letters patent of Llywelyn ap Iorwerth from no later than 1230 onwards is a notable case in point, as is the widespread occurrence from the early thirteenth century onwards of the notification *noverit universitas vestra* followed by the dispositive verb(s) in the perfect infinitive. Likewise, the use of the term *littere patentes* by Dafydd ap Llywelyn to describe two charters for different beneficiaries issued during his father's lifetime suggests that these were drawn up by a clerk of Dafydd.[1069] Yet, viewed overall, the diplomatic of the princes' charters is not sufficiently standardized to demonstrate conclusively that their production lay entirely in the hands of a secretariat: the occurrence of common formulae could, perhaps, reflect supervision by a ruler's clerk of drafting by a beneficiary or simply

---

[1067] Williams-Jones, 'Llywelyn's charter', 49–54. The case for beneficiary production is reinforced by the appearance of several distinctive formulae found also in two charters for Cymer's mother house of Cwm-hir: above, pp. 104–5.

[1068] Compare, for example, nos 204–5 with nos 200–2.

[1069] Above, pp. 62, 64, 66. Cf. the differences between the charters issued by Owain ap Gruffudd and his brother Llywelyn for Ynys Lannog 1247 (nos 313, 320).

widespread fashion. (The notification cited above including the formula *noverit universitas vestra* is commonplace,[1070] and in any case is not used in all of Llywelyn ap Iorwerth's acts.) Similarly the general consistency with which charters use a ruler's current style need not indicate direct involvement by the grantor's clerks in drafting the document, as a beneficiary could have ascertained the style prior to drafting in order to ensure that the charter would be acceptable when it was presented for authentication. Analysis is further complicated by the fact that, irrespective of who drafted them, charters recording confirmations or further grants to a beneficiary might draw on previous charters in its favour. This is clearly true of some of the Haughmond confirmations and of the charters for Basingwerk issued by Dafydd ap Llywelyn and Llywelyn ap Gruffudd, while the survival of originals shows that Dafydd ap Gruffudd's charter for Madog ab Einion ap Maredudd in 1260 not only drew heavily on the phraseology of Llywelyn ap Gruffudd's charter for Madog's father Einion in 1243 but also copied its method of sealing.[1071]

The difficulties of trying to draw a sharp distinction between charters drawn up by beneficiaries and those produced by the princes' own clerks suggest that such a distinction is unhelpful in the context of twelfth- and thirteenth-century Gwynedd. Instead, it may be more useful to think in terms of differing degrees of interaction between the rulers' secretariat and beneficiaries. At the very least, the secretariat – originating in the rulers' chapel and supervised by a cleric sometimes bearing the title of *cancellarius* by the second quarter of the thirteenth century – validated charters written by beneficiaries through the attachment of the ruler's seal. In addition, however, it is likely that in some cases its role extended to dictating part or all of the text as well, although how far it was responsible for the engrossment of charters is impossible to determine given the paucity of originals.[1072] Such a mixture of beneficiary and chancery production has many parallels elsewhere in western Europe in the twelfth century, but was increasingly unusual in the thirteenth.

This is consistent in turn with the evidence that the secretarial organization possessed by thirteenth-century rulers of Gwynedd lacked the institutional identity and complexity characteristic of royal, episcopal or magnate chanceries in thirteenth-century England, Scotland or France. Notwithstanding the moves towards some standardization of formulae, the surviving acts display a variety in their diplomatic which suggests that no systematic effort was made to impose uniformity and also probably that the numbers of documents issued were fairly low.[1073] In addition, there is no evidence for the inclusion in dating clauses of formulae referring to a datary such as *per manum N. cancellarii* or of dating by the ruler's regnal year, nor for the use of sealing with different coloured cords or waxes to distinguish between different types of document.[1074] These absences demonstrate

---

[1070] For examples in English private charters see *Transcripts*, ed. Stenton, 8–11, 23–5 (nos 17–19, 22, 40–5); *Charters of the Redvers Family*, ed. Bearman, nos 55, 61, 63, 65, 72, 108–9, 118.

[1071] Nos 318, 441.

[1072] The resemblances between the diplomatic of nos 231 and 282, original charters respectively of Llywelyn ap Iorwerth and Gruffudd ap Llywelyn for Strata Marcella, and other charters for that house by non-Venedotian grantors suggest that they were written by scribes of the abbey, though neither hand is attested elsewhere among the charters from the abbey's archive.

[1073] Cf. Galbraith, 'Monastic foundation charters', 214; Clanchy, *From Memory*, 85.

[1074] Cf. Cheney, *English Bishops' Chanceries*, 83–7; Chaplais, *English Royal Documents*, 15, 19; Dufour, 'Peut-on parler?', 254; *Vocabulaire*, ed. Ortí, 99, 103–5. For a *per manum* formula referring to the beneficiary, the abbot of Cwm-hir, in a charter of Madog ap Maelgwn of Maelienydd see no. 113, discussed above, pp. 104–5.

that the rulers of Gwynedd did not develop the full potential of written acts as expressions of their authority. The same is true of the rarity of collective addresses naming all a ruler's subjects[1075] as well as of changes in styles. Moreover, although the rulers' acts owed much to ecclesiastical models, ecclesiastical influence did not extend to an emphasis on the sacral aspects of rulership through the insertion of the formula *Dei gratia* into rulers' styles or the widespread inclusion of an arenga.[1076] Therefore, while the rulers of Gwynedd possessed a secretarial organization responsible for validating and also – especially in the case of letters patent and letters – producing acts in their name, even under Llywelyn ap Gruffudd that organization was limited in its scope and ambition.

Outside Gwynedd, it appears that rulers' secretarial arrangements were much more informal still, probably not extending beyond the employment of one or more household clerks, while the production of charters in favour of churches remained largely in the hands of beneficiaries. True, the surviving documents show that Welsh rulers possessed adequate means to issue acts in their name that conformed to wider contemporary European, and particularly English, diplomatic norms. Yet the continuing variations in diplomatic forms and formulae, and the limits to the control over the production of acts exercised even by the rulers of Gwynedd, suggest that the impression given by the low numbers of known documents is not grossly misleading: even allowing for losses, as clearly we must, it is unlikely that the surviving sample is merely the tip of a huge documentary iceberg. A picture of restricted output would be consistent with the case for regarding the increase in the production of acts from the late twelfth century onwards as being to a considerable degree demand-led: religious houses sought charters, diplomacy with the English crown generated correspondence and written agreements (and in turn encouraged thirteenth-century princes of Gwynedd, especially Llywelyn ap Gruffudd, to give documentary expression to their hegemonic aspirations vis-à-vis other native rulers).[1077]

This is not to imply that rulers were reluctant to issue acts or oblivious to their potential as expressions of status and authority. Nevertheless, a variety of factors may have been inimical to realizing that potential to the full. Political circumstances were frequently unfavourable: especially after the territorial fragmentation of Powys and Deheubarth, Welsh polities outside Gwynedd were small and their rulers' power correspondingly restricted; and even in Gwynedd, both dynastic conflicts and pressure from the English crown led to succession struggles that can hardly have been beneficial to the development of a secretarial organization capable of providing continuity in the form of documents from reign to reign. The lack of titles in many lesser rulers' styles and the changing styles of even the rulers of Gwynedd, who were fully aware of the importance of this aspect of diplomatic, are a further reflection of the fragmented and often disputed nature of authority in *pura Wallia*.[1078] The legal context also merits consideration. While Welsh lawyers composed lawbooks as aids to legal instruction and emblems of their learning and prestige, the law they contain allows virtually no role for documents. The readiness of Welsh rulers to challenge aspects of native law on occasion does not seem to have extended to this overwhelming reliance on non-literate modes.[1079] In particular, as disputes over land among

[1075] Insley, 'From *rex Wallie*', 187–8.
[1076] See above, pp. 63, 75–6, and cf. Flanagan, 'Context and uses', 118–23.
[1077] See above, pp. 55–7.
[1078] Cf. Davies, *Conquest*, 252, 253; above, pp. 74–9, 90, 93, 96–8, 104–5, 109–10, 117, 129–30.
[1079] Pryce, 'Context and purpose', 55–8; *idem*, 'Lawbooks and literacy'.

the laity were usually resolved by oral and visual procedures, there was little incentive for the laity to obtain charters from rulers. Therefore, in contrast to the common law of thirteenth-century England, Welsh law did not encourage the use of documents in legal cases, let alone stimulate the increasingly precise and standardized drafting of charters.[1080] The acts issued by Welsh rulers thus raise important questions about both the power of those rulers and their uses of documentary forms. It is hoped that the present edition will encourage further research on those questions as well as on other aspects of twelfth- and thirteenth-century Wales.

EDITORIAL METHOD

All documents extant as texts are published in full, while those known from mentions in other sources are normally published only in calendared form. The collection is arranged in alphabetical order by territory, and within each territory by individual rulers, grouped where appropriate by particular lineages of the ruling dynasty. Acts issued jointly by more than one Welsh ruler are assigned to the first ruler named (thus nos 309, 314–16 are grouped as acts of Owain ap Gruffudd rather than of his brother Llywelyn). As far as possible, rulers within each territory or dynastic subdivision thereof are placed in chrono-logical sequence. The acts of each ruler are likewise arranged in chronological order, albeit only approximately so, as many documents lack time-dates and can only be assigned to within broad dating limits; in these cases, the document's place in the sequence is governed by its *terminus a quo* together with the principle of increasing imprecision (thus an act datable to 1170 × 1175 would precede one datable to 1170 × 1200). Lost documents are indicated by an asterix placed before the series number, and spurious documents by a cross preceding the series number.

After the heading and calendar of each document follows the date, if given in the text, or limiting dates; the latter are separated by a multiplication sign and appear within square brackets (for example, [1240 × 1246]). If the latter limiting date is preceded by a minus sign, the document was issued before that date. For acts extant as texts there follows a list of manuscripts, designated by sigla: A for originals (A1 and A2 where two originals survive), B, C, D etc., usually in chronological order, for copies; unless stated otherwise, B is the basis for the edition of texts for which no original survives. Post-medieval copies are normally referred to only where no medieval copies survive (references to some post-medieval copies omitted here may be found in the appropriate entries in *H*). Where the original is extant, brief descriptions are given of its medieval endorsements, its dimensions (greatest width and greatest depth, together with depth of the fold-up where applicable) and sealing arrangements. In the case of copies, the approximate date of the manuscript is provided; rubrics are printed only where these illuminate the contents of the document or archival arrangements. Where applicable, details of previous editions and calendars follow the list of manuscripts. Any textual notes come immediately after the text of the document, and historical notes discussing matters such as authenticity, dating or place-names are placed at

---

[1080] Cf. Galbraith, 'Monastic foundation charters', 214; Chibnall, 'Dating the charters'.

the end. In the case of lost acts, published here in calendared form, the date or dating limits are followed by the source of the reference and, where appropriate, by historical notes.

The spelling of originals has been retained, except that *i* is used to represent both *i* and *j* and *u* is used as a vowel, *v* as a consonant. The same principles apply to copies, but these also regularize the use of *c* and *t* according to the practice of Classical Latin (for example, *compositio*, *donatio*); in addition, in the case of post-medieval copies initial *ch* has been amended to *c* (for example, *carta*, not *charta*) and the dipthong *æ* to *e*. Contractions are expanded silently except in respect of proper nouns, where the extension of abbreviated forms is indicated by brackets if the full form of the personal name or place-name is clear. Names indicated by an initial only are not extended. In Latin texts, vernacular words other than proper nouns are italicized. Capitalization follows modern practice in respect of both originals and copies. Conjectural readings are supplied within square brackets, and inter-lineations and other insertions placed within the marks ` ; dots indicate letters or words that are unrecoverable. Modern punctuation, including the expansion of the ampersand and tironian *et*, has been applied in the case of both originals and copies. In order to facil-itate reference, numbers have been assigned to the individual clauses of some of the longer texts, especially agreements. Manuscripts are collated, but where a text survives in the original the readings of any copies are normally not noted.

Where they have been identified, place-names are spelled in their modern form in the calendars of documents (in the case of lost documents which are calendared only the form given in the source is also provided in brackets); where the name has changed, the name used today follows in square brackets (for example, *Porth Hoddni [Aber-porth]*). Guidance on the location of place-names, including in many cases Ordnance Survey national grid references, is provided as appropriate in the endnotes to documents. In dating, the modern practice of starting the year on 1 January is followed. With respect to acts bearing time-dates, it is likely that, from the later twelfth century onwards (when all of these acts were written, the earliest being no. 482, dated 1176), the beginning of the year was usually calcu-lated in Wales from the Annunciation (25 March), as this was common among the Cistercians – the beneficiaries and almost certainly also the drafters of the earliest extant Welsh examples – as well as in England from the late twelfth century onwards. However, this may not have been universal practice, for the chronicles generically known as *Brut y Tywysogyon* indicate that Welsh annalists sometimes calculated the beginning of the year from Christmas Day (25 December), another date widely used in western Europe, especially up to the twelfth century but also later by Benedictine chroniclers in England, including Matthew Paris (cf. Giry, *Manuel de diplomatique*, 107–9, 124–5; *Handbook of Dates*, 9–13; *BT, Pen20Tr*, lxiv–lxv). These points are especially pertinent in respect of time-dates consisting of the year of grace only. If they are not explained in an endnote to the document, dating limits are based on the discussion of the historical background of each territory in Part I of the Introduction or, particularly with regard to reigns of kings, pontif-icates of bishops and dates of parliaments in England, on *Handbook of Dates* or *Handbook of British Chronology*.

ARWYSTLI

HYWEL AB IEUAF
(d. 1185)

1 St Michael's church, Trefeglwys

Notification [that he has received] under his protection the monasterium *founded in the township called Trefeglwys to the honour of God and St Michael [and all the land called] Bryn Bedwyn, with the consent and gift of the heirs, namely Ednyfed, Iago and Bleddrws, from the ditch of the cemetery to the Gleiniant, and in addition from his own patrimony [the land of Tregymer] from the cross as far as the Gleiniant and Maes Ysgor-fawr near Nant Carno, free of all claim and without render as a refuge for all who have fled to the aforesaid church or to places pertaining to it. May whoever violates the refuge of the aforesaid church incur the wrath of God and all the saints. Witnesses.*

[1143 × 1151]

B = Cardiff County and City Library MS 3.11, pp. 3–4 (incomplete). s. xvi².
C = Oxford, Bodleian Library, Dugdale MS 39, fo. 100v (incomplete). *c.*1583.
Pd. from B, Pryce, 'Church of Trefeglwys', 52–3 (and trans.); from a Wynnstay MS dated 1640 destroyed in 1858, Williams, 'Wynnstay MSS.', 331.
Cd., *H*, no. 2.

Heuel rex Arguestli omnibus filiis sancte ecclesie tam modernis quam futuris salutem. Notum sit vobis omnibus [quod ego] monasterium constitutum in villa que dicitur Trefeglus ad honorem Dei et Sancti Mich(ael)is [et totam terram que vocatur] Bren Betguin, ex consensu et dono heredum, scilicet Idneuet, Iaco, Bledrus, a fossa cimiterii usque ad Gelmant, et insuper de feodo meo proprio [terram de Trefgymer] a cruce usque ad Gelmant et ᵃ⁻Maes Scoruaur iuxta Nant Carno,⁻ᵃ in mea defensione [suscepi] absque omni calumpnia ᵇ⁻libere et quiete sine redditu ad refugium omnibus quicunque confugerint ad predictam ecclesiam vel ad loca pertinentia ad eam.⁻ᵇ Et quicunque predicte ecclesie refugium violaverit iram Dei et omnium sanctorum incurrat. His testibus scilicet: Catel rege Sudgualie etc.

ᵃ⁻ᵃ *omitted* C. | ᵇ⁻ᵇ etc. C.

The conjectural readings are mostly those of Pryce, 'Church of Trefeglwys', which provides a full discussion of this charter and argues (at 28–33) that the early modern copies, though abbreviated, derive from an authentic document issued on behalf of Hywel ab Ieuaf.

The dating limits are set by the presence in the witness list of Cadell ap Gruffudd, king of Deheubarth from 1143 but probably incapacitated after he was badly injured by Normans from Tenby in 1151 (*BT, Pen20Tr*, 58; *BT, RBH*, 130–3; *HW*, ii. 502–3). The Peniarth 20 version of the *Brut* says that Cadell set off on his pilgrimage 'around the calends of winter', i.e. 1 November; *Annales Cambriae* assign the pilgrimage to 1157=1156, after the death of Maredudd in 1155 (*BT, Pen20Tr*, 178; *AC*, 46). For the lands, all of which lay in the vicinity of Trefeglwys (SN 971 906), see Pryce, 'Church of Trefeglwys', 34–7 (with map). For the right of sanctuary granted see further Pryce, *Native Law*, ch. 7. See also Madog ap Maredudd's charter for Trefeglwys (no. 480 below).

2 Haughmond Abbey
Grant in perpetual alms of all the land of Bryn Bedwyn from the ditch of the cemetery to the Gleiniant, the land of Tregymer from the cross to the Gleiniant and all the land of Cilceirenydd with all the adjacent wood, namely from (?) Nantheilyn (Nantelin) to the river Cerist, to be held freely for ever for the salvation of himself and all his kin. Witnesses.

[1143 × 1151]

B = Shrewsbury, Shropshire Records and Research Centre MS 6001/6869 (Haughmond Cartulary), fos 214v–215r. s. xv ex.
Pd. from B, *Cart. Haugh.*, no. 1214.
Cd., *H*, no. 1.

Sciant omnes ad quos presens scriptum pervenerit quod ego Hoelus rex Arewestil dedi in perpetuam elemosinam ecclesie Sancti Ioh(ann)is Evangeliste de Haghmon' totam terram que vocatur Brenbedwin a fossa cimiterii usque ad Gleinant et terram de Trefkemer a cruce usque ad Gleinant et totam terram de Kilgrennith [fo. 215r] cum toto nemore adiacente, videlicet a Nantelin usque ad amnem quem vocatur Kerist, habenda et tenenda inperpetuum integre, libere et quiete pro salute anime mee et omnium parentum meorum in bosco et plano, in pratis et pascuis et in omnibus libertatibus. Hiis testibus: domino Mauricio episcopo, Reso fratre eius, Iorvert presbitero etc.

Since the grant is made to Haughmond Abbey, it is later than no. 1 above, which refers only to the *monasterium* of Trefeglwys, though no later than 1151, for the grant was confirmed by Bishop Meurig (Maurice) in a charter witnessed by Cadell ap Gruffudd (*Cart. Haugh.*, no. 1219). The charter may thus be assigned to a later point in the same date range as no. 1.

3 St Michael's church, Trefeglwys, which Bleddrws built and is subject to Haughmond Abbey
Grant in perpetual alms, for the salvation of the souls of himself, his predecessors and his heirs, with the consent of his heirs, the magnates of his land and those whose patrimony it was, of all the land called Bryn Bedwyn from the ditch of the cemetery to the Gleiniant and to the Trannon, and in addition from his own patrimony the land of Tregymer from the cross to the

Gleiniant and whatever is contained from the cross in the opposite direction to Redwastaroth *and again from the same cross to the Trannon and whatever is contained below the aforesaid cross and* Redwastaroth *and waters of the Trannon and the Gleiniant; quittance of pannage for all their pigs in the wood of Pen-prys and all the common pasturage of Tregymer and* Penvin *for their livestock and horses together with Hywel's wherever the latter have pasture, and a place in these pastures to build a vaccary wherever they wish; and all the land of Cilceirenydd with all the adjacent wood, namely from (?)Nantheilyn* (Nanthelin) *to the river Cerist and to the hollow* (pant) *of (?)Trawsbren* (Trauspren) *and to* Cattestan *and all the marsh. These are to be held freely for ever with all their appurtenances, liberties, free customs and easements in wood, plain, meadows, pastures, ways, waters, mills and all places without any claim from Hywel or from his heirs in the future. Sealing clause; witnesses.*

[1143 × 12 August 1161]

B = Shrewsbury, Shropshire Records and Research Centre MS 6001/6869 (Haughmond Cartulary), fo. 214v. s. xv ex. Rubric: De donatione diversarum terrarum ibidem sub duplici carta. Pd. from B, *Cart. Haugh.*, no. 1213.
Cd., *H*, no. 3.

Sciant universi sancte matris ecclesie filii tam presentes[a] quam futuri quod ego Hoel filius Geuaf consensu heredum meorum et magnatum terre mee et eorum quorum patrimonium erat dedi et concessi et hac presenti carta mea confirmavi in puram et perpetuam elemosinam pro salute anime mee et antecessorum meorum et heredum meorum Deo et ecclesie Sancti Mich(ael)is de Treffeglus quam Bletherus edificavit, que est in subiectione Dei et Sancti Ioh(ann)is Evangeliste de Haghmon', totam terram que vocatur Brenbedwin a fossa cimiterii usque ad Gleinant et usque ad Trennon, et insuper de feodo meo proprio terram de Trefgemer a cruce usque ad Gleinant et quicquid equaliter continetur a cruce ex opposito usque ad Redwastaroth, et iterum ab eadem cruce equaliter usque ad[b] Trennon et quicquid continetur infra predictam crucem et dictam Redwastaroth et aquas de Trennon et Gleinant, et quietantiam pannagii ad omnes porcos suos in bosco de Penpres et omnem communam pasturam de Trefgemer et de Penvin averiis suis et haraciis suis cum meis vel ubicumque mea averia et haracia mea adeunt pasturam adeo libere et eorum habeant absque ulla calumpnia ut aliqua pastura liberius et melius in elemosinam dari poterit et in hiis predictis pasturis locum ad faciendum boveriam ubicumque placuerit, et totam terram de Kilgrenuith' cum tote nemore adiacente, videlicet a Nanthelin usque ad amnem qui vocatur Kerist et usque ad pant de Trauspren et usque ad Cattestan et totam moram, habendam et tenendam libere et quiete et honorifice et inperpetuum cum omnibus pertinentiis suis, libertatibus et liberis consuetudinibus et eisiamentis in bosco et plano, in pratis et pasturis, in viis et semitis, in aquis et stagnis et molendinis et in omnibus locis sine aliqua calumpnia de me vel heredibus meis in posterum facienda. Et quoniam volo quod hec mea donatio et concessio perpetuitatis robur optineat presenti scripto sigillum meum apposui. Hiis testibus: Mauric(i)o episcopo, Reso fratre eius etc.

[a] presentis B. | [b] a B.

As the charter acknowledges the subjection of Trefeglwys to Haughmond it can be no earlier than 1143 (see note to no. 2 above). The first witness, Bishop Meurig (Maurice) of Bangor, died on 12 August 1161. The charter is probably later than no. 2 since it not only gives the boundaries of the lands in greater detail but also grants pasture rights and quittance of pannage (Pryce, 'Church of Trefeglwys', 41–2). The English place-name *Cattestan*, lit. 'Cat's stone', has not been identified (cf. Smith, *Place-Names of the West Riding IV*, 159). Bleddrws is also mentioned as the founder of Trefeglwys in no. 480 below, where he is described as a monk. The rubric in the cartulary suggests that the text was copied from a duplicate copy of the original charter (see *DMLBS*, 737, s.v. *duplex* 3).

MEURIG AP HYWEL
(*fl.* 1185–1208)

4 St Michael's church, Trefeglwys and Haughmond Abbey

Grant confirming in perpetual alms all the land they have at Trefeglwys by the gift of his father Hywel and of other faithful people, namely Bryn Bedwyn from the ditch of the cemetery to the Gleiniant, all the land of Tregymer from the cross to the Gleiniant and all the land of Cilceirenydd, with all their appurtenances in wood, plain, meadows, pastures, ways, waters, mills and easements, to be held for ever free of all secular service and exaction. Witnesses.

[Probably 1185 × *c.*1208]

B = Shrewsbury, Shropshire Records and Research Centre MS 6001/6869 (Haughmond Cartulary), fo. 215r. s. xv ex.
Pd. from B, *Cart. Haugh.*, no. 1215.
Cd., *H*, no. 4.

Universis Dei fidelibus tam presentibus quam futuris Meuric filius Hoel de Arwistl salutem in domino. Noverit universitas vestra me concessisse et presenti carta confirmasse Deo et ecclesie Sancti Mich(ael)is de Treffeglus et canonicis de Haghmon' in liberam et perpetuam elemosinam totam terram quam habent apud Trefeglus ex donatione Howeli patris mei et aliorum fidelium, scilicet Brenbedwin a fossa cimiterii usque ad Gleynant et totam terram a cruce usque ad Gleynant de Trefkem(er)e et totam terram de Kilgremit cum omnibus pertinentiis suis in bosco et plano, in pratis et pasturis, in aquis et stagnis et molendinis et omnibus locis et omnibus eysiamentis, tenenda inperpetuum libere et quiete ab omni seculari servitio[a] et exactione. Hiis testibus: Iorwerth filio Howel etc.

[a] *omitted* B.

This charter is difficult to date with any precision. It was probably issued after the death of Meurig's father Hywel ab Ieuaf in 1185. Morgan proposed a date range of 1185 × 1197 on the assumption that Meurig succeeded Hywel in Arwystli and was in turn succeeded by his brother Owain o'r Brithdir (d. 1197) ('Territorial divisions of Montgomeryshire [I]', 31–2). However, no. 6 below shows that Meurig was still alive in 1208. More persuasively, Rees suggested a date *c.*1197, shortly after Owain's death (*Cart. Haugh.*, no. 1215, n.).

5 Strata Marcella Abbey

Grant of the land called Cwm Llwyd in perpetual alms, free of all debt and exaction, both secular and ecclesiastical, with all its bounds and appurtenances and all rights of use, including fisheries, above the earth and beneath it, for the salvation of the souls of himself, his father, mother, predecessors and successors, just as previously his brother Cadwaladr gave and confirmed with his seal after receiving 15 marks from the monks. The boundaries of this gift are: from Pennant Bacho to the river Llwyd and on either side of that river with all its bounds and appurtenances. Witnesses.

1198

> B = NLW, Wynnstay Estate Records (transcript by William Jones of Dôl Hywel, Llangadfan). 18 July 1795.
> Pd. from B, *Ystrad Marchell Charters*, no. 19.

Universis sancte matris ecclesie filiis tam presentibus quam futuris qui presentem cartam inspexerint Meyrug filius Howel salutem et pacem bonam. Notum facimus universitati vestre nos dedisse et concessisse et presenti carta confirmasse Deo et Beate Marie et monachis de Stratm(ar)chell terram que vocatur Cwm Llwyd in puram et perpetuam elemosinam, liberam ab omni debito et exactione tam seculari quam ecclesiastica, in omnibus finibus suis et terminis et pertinentiis, in bosco[a] et plano, in culto et in inculto, in pratis et pasturis, in moris et pascuis, in piscariis et piscationibus, et in omnibus usibus et utilitatibus, super eandem terram et subter, pro remedio et salute anime mee et patris et matris et antecessorum et successorum meorum, sicut ante me Cadwalader frater meus dedit et sigillo suo confirmavit etiam suscepto pretio quindecim marcarum a prefatis monachis de Stratm(ar)chell. Isti autem sunt termini eiusdem donationis: a loco qui dicitur Pennan Bacho usque ad fluvium qui dicitur Llwyd et ex utraque parte amnis eiusdem in omnibus terminis suis et pertinentiis suis. Facta est vero hec donatio anno ab incarnatione domini m° c° nonagesimo.[b] His testibus: Meredyth monacho, d ...... eo ... de Strat(march)ell,[c] Madog filio Meuryg.

[a] bosto B. | [b] 1198 B*; cf. no. 8 below.* | [c] Strat . . . ell B.

For the place-names see *Ystrad Marchell Charters*, 117. Cwm Llwyd was situated in the township of Esgeiriaeth, par. Trefeglwys, Arwystli.

6 Strata Marcella Abbey

Grant, freely and in perpetual alms for the salvation of the souls of himself and his parents, of all the land called Dyffrynmerthyr, from Dengwm to Cwm Llwyd, and Cwm Llwyd with all its bounds and appurtenances on both sides of the river as the Llwyd runs to the Clywedog. Further gift with the same liberty on behalf of himself and his heirs of all the land called Perfedd Fynydd with all its bounds and appurtenances. Sealing clause; witnesses.

Strad Dewi, 1208

> B = NLW, Wynnstay Estate Records (transcript by William Jones of Dôl Hywel, Llangadfan). 18 July 1795.
> Pd. from B, *Ystrad Marchell Charters*, no. 56.

Sciant tam presentes quam futuri presentes literas inspecturi vel audituri quod ego Meyrig filius Howell dedi, concessi et presenti carta mea confirmavi Deo et Beate Marie et monachis de Stratmarchell [Deo]ᵃ ibidem in perpetuum servientibus, libere et quiete, bene et integre, in puram et perpetuam elemosinam, pro salute anime mee et parentum meorum totam terram que vocatur Dyffryn Mertyr, a Dengwn usque Cwm Llwyt, et Cwm Llwyt cum omnibus terminis suis et pertinentiis suis, tam in boscoᵇ quam in plano, tam in montibus quam in silviis,ᶜ ex utraque parte amnis et sicutᵈ ducit Llwyd usque Clawedawc. Dedi insuper et iisdem monachis in eadem libertate tam pro me quam pro heredibus meis omnem terram que dicitur Perveth Fynydd cum omnibus terminis suis et pertinentiis. Ut autem hec mea donatio rata sit in perpetuum eam tam sigilli mei impressione quam bonorum virorum attestatione munivi et corroboravi anno ab incarnatione domini millesimoᵉ ducentesimoᶠ octavo apud Strad Dewi. His testibus: Griffino Goche, Cadwalader filio Howel, Meurig filio Griffini cum multis aliis.

ᵃ *omitted* B. | ᵇ bosto B. | ᶜ sylviis B. | ᵈ B *inserts* amnis et sicut. | ᵉ milessimo B. ᶠ ducentessimo B.

All the lands granted are situated in the parish of Trefeglwys, Arwystli (*Ystrad Marchell Charters*, 124).

CADWALADR AP HYWEL
(*fl.* 1185–96)

*7 Strata Marcella Abbey

Grant in perpetual alms, for the salvation of the souls of himself and his parents, free of all custom and exaction, of all the land from the stream called Bacho to the river Dengwm, together with the sale for 15 marks of the pasture from the Dengwm to Cwm Llwyd.

[Probably 1185 × December 1196]

Mention only, in a confirmation by Alan, bishop of Bangor datable to 16 April 1195 × December 1196 (*Ystrad Marchell Charters*, no. 16). The charter was probably issued after the death of Cadwaladr's father, Hywel ab Ieuaf, in 1185 (cf. ibid., 59). The sale of Cwm Llwyd was also confirmed by Cadwaladr's brothers in 1198 (no. 5 above and no. 8 below).

HYWEL AP HYWEL
(*fl.* 1185–98)

8 Strata Marcella Abbey

Grant of the land called Cwm Llwyd in perpetual alms, free of all debt and exaction, both secular and ecclesiastical, with all its bounds and appurtenances and all rights of use, including fisheries, above the earth and beneath it, for the salvation of the souls of himself, his father, mother, predecessors and successors, just as previously his brother Cadwaladr gave and confirmed with his seal after receiving 15 marks from the monks. The boundaries of this gift are: from Pennant Bacho to the river Llwyd and on either side of that river with all its bounds and appurtenances. Witnesses.

1198

A = NLW, Wynnstay Estate Records, Ystrad Marchell Charters, no. 18. Early modern endorsements; approx. 218 × 94 + 11 mm.; two central horizontal slits, one just above the fold, one in the fold, for a tag (*c.*6 mm. wide) which exits through a slit in the base of the fold; sealed on tag. Circular seal, white wax, imperfect, originally approx. 60 mm. diameter; equestrian, facing right; legend: SIG ...
Pd. from A, *Ystrad Marchell Charters*, no. 18.
Cd., Davies, 'Strata Marcella documents', 169 (no. 8).

Universis sancte matris ecclesie filiis presentibus et futuris qui presentem cartam inspexerint Howel filius Howeli salutem et pacem bonam. Notum facimus universitati vestre nos dedisse et concessisse et presenti carta confirmasse Deo et Beate Marie et monachis de Stradmarhel terram que vocatur Cumluit in puram et perpetuam elemosinam, liberam ab omni debito et actione tam seculari quam ecclesiastica, in omnibus finibus suis et terminis et pertinentiis, in bosco et plano, in culto et in inculto, in pratis et pasturis, in moris et aquis, in piscaturis et piscationibus, et in omnibus usibus et utilitatibus, super eandem terram et subter, pro remedio et salute anime mee et patris et matris et antecessorum et successorum meorum, sicut ante me Katwaladyr frater meus dedit et sigillo suo confirmavit etiam suscepto precio quindecim marcarum a prefatis monachis de Stradmerhel. Isti autem sunt termini eiusdem donationis: a loco qui dicitur Pennan Bacho usque ad fluvium qui dicitur Luyt et ex utraque parte eiusdem fluvii in omnibus terminis suis et pertinentiis. Facta est vero ista donatio anno ab incarnatione domini m° c° nonagesimo viii°. Huius igitur donationis testes sunt: Madocus filius Grifini, Morgant filius Ris, Lowelin filius Rodri, Ioab filius Maredut, Gorony filius Keldelu, David filius Iacob, Madocus filius Owini.

The text is very similar to no. 5 above, also dated 1198 but containing a different witness list.

CADWALLON AP HYWEL
(*fl.* 1185–1206)

9 Strata Marcella Abbey
Sale for 8 pounds of silver in free and perpetual possession of the following lands: Pennant Bacho, Dyffrynmerthyr, Cwm Llwyd and Cwmbuga in all their bounds, half of Deupiw, half of Ysgor-fawr and half of the land from the Arannell to Rhydyfoch, Aberbrydwen and Rhiw Caenesied; the monks shall possess these lands and pastures in perpetual right, freely without any secular exaction or custom. Further grant for the aforesaid price of all the pastures within the bounds of Arwystli, namely from the Severn towards Powys, to be possessed freely in perpetual right. Sealing clause; witnesses.

Llandovery, 1206

A = NLW, Wynnstay Estate Records, Ystrad Marchell Charters, no. 42. Endorsed: Cadwallaun filius Howel (s. xiii[1]); early modern endorsements; approx. 190 × 132 + 14 mm.; two central slits in fold for a tag (c.9 mm. wide) which exits through a slit in the base of the fold; seal missing.
Pd. from A, *Ystrad Marchell Charters*, no. 42.
Cd., Davies, 'Strata Marcella documents', 176–7 (no. 20); *H*, no. 190.

Notum sit tam presentibus quam futuris quod ego Cadewallaunt filius Hewel vendidi monachis de Stradmarchell pro octo libris argenti in liberam et quietam et perpetuam possessionem istas terras in omnibus terminis suis et pertinentiis: scilicet Pennanbacho et Deffrenm(er)thir et Cumlluit et Cumbuga in omnibus terminis suis; similiter et dimidietatem[a] Deupiu et dimidietatem Escoruaur et dimidietatem terre tam in bosco quam in plano ab Aranell usque ad Redhouoch; insuper et Ab(er)bredwen et Reucanesseit. Volo igitur ego prefatus Cadewallaun ut prefati monachi omnes predictas terras et pasturas libere et quiete, bene et in pace et sine aliqua exactione vel consuetudine seculari iure perpetuo possideant, in bosco videlicet in plano, in aquis, in viis, in pratis, in molendinis, in pasturis et in omnibus usibus suis et utilitatibus. Dedi insuper et concessi predictis monachis pro prenominato precio omnes pasturas infra terminos Arwistili, scilicet ab Hauren versus Powis, iure perpetuo, bene et in pace, libere et quiete possidendas. Et quia presens etas prona est ad malum unde sibi conatur extorquere lucrum hanc meam predictam venditionem tam sigilli mei impressione quam bonorum virorum attestatione munivi et coroboravi. His testibus: Gurgeneu priore de Cumhir, Philippo monacho de Alba Domo, Kediuor monacho de St(ra)dflur, Seisil monacho, Kediuor Crec, Kediuor filio Griffud, Madoco filio Yeuuaf conversis de St(ra)dmarchell, Hoideleu decano, Laurentio sacerdote, Meuric filio Morgant, Meiler filio G(ri)ffud, Peredur filio Ioruerth, Kadugano filio G(ri)ffud. Facta est autem hec mea predicta venditio apud Llana(m)deueri in manu I. prioris de St(ra)dmarchell anno videlicet ab incarnatione domini m° cc° vi°.

[a] dimietatem A.

For the lands, located in the parishes of Trefeglwys, Llanidloes, Carno and Llanwnnog, see *Ystrad Marchell Charters*, 123; Pryce, 'Church of Trefeglwys', 37. Why the sale was made at Llandovery in Cantref Bychan, well to the south of Arwystli, is unclear. Had Cadwallon been exiled from Arwystli following its occupation by Gwenwynwyn of Powys in 1197? It may be significant that in 1204 the sons of Gruffudd ap Rhys had seized Llandovery castle from their uncle Maelgwn ap Rhys, who had captured it with Gwenwynwyn's help the previous year (*BT, Pen20Tr*, 82; *BT, RBH*, 186–7).

GRUFFUDD GOCH AP GRUFFUDD CARNO
(*fl.* 1207–16 × *c.*1226)

10 Strata Marcella Abbey
Sale, by Gruffudd Goch son of Gruffudd of Carno by Lleucu daughter of Cadwallon, in free and perpetual possession of the following lands: Pennant Bacho, Dyffrynmerthyr, Cwm Llwyd and Cwmbuga, half of Deupiw, half of Ysgor-fawr and half of all the land from the Arannell

to Rhydyfoch, namely Blaen Carno with all its bounds and appurtenances along a circuit, and the lands the monks have at Aberbrydwen and all the land of Rhiw Caenesied; the monks shall possess these lands and pastures in perpetual right, freely without any secular exaction or custom. Further grant of all the pastures within the bounds of Arwystli, namely from the Severn towards Powys, to be possessed freely in perpetual right. Sealing clause; witnesses.

Llanwnnog, 1207

A = NLW, Wynnstay Estate Records, Ystrad Marchell Charters, no. 54. Early modern endorsements; approx. 176 mm. wide at top, 193 mm. wide at bottom × 195 mm. deep + 20 mm.; single central horizontal slit for a tag; tag and seal missing.
Pd. from A, *Ystrad Marchell Charters*, no. 54.
Cd., Davies, 'Strata Marcella documents', 180–1 (no. 26).

Notum sit tam presentibus quam futuris quod ego Grifinus Coch Grifini filius de Karno ex matre Levchv filia Kadwallavn vendidi monachis de Stratmarchell in liberam et perpetuam possessionem istas terras in omnibus terminis suis et pertinentiis, scilicet Pennanbacho et Defrenmerthir et Cumlluit et Cum Buga, similiter et dimidietatem Deupiu et dimidietatem Scoruaur et dimidietatem totius terre que est ab Arannell usque Ridewoch, scilicet Blain Karno in omnibus terminis et pertinentiis suis per circuitum, et terras quas habent in Aberbredwen et totam terram que dicitur Riucanesseit. Volo igitur ut prefati monachi omnes predictas terras et pasturas libere et quiete, bene et in pace, et sine aliqua exactione vel consuetudine seculari iure perpetuo possideant, in bosco videlicet in plano, in aquis, in viis, in pratis, in molendinis, in pasturis et in omnibus usibus suis et utilitatibus. Dedi insuper et concessi predictis monachis omnes pasturas infra terminos Arwistili, scilicet ab Hauren versus Powis, iure perpetuo, bene et in pace, libere et quiete possidendas. Et quia presens etas prona est ad malum unde sibi conatur extorquere lucrum hanc meam predictam venditionem tam sigilli mei impressione quam bonorum virorum munivi atestatione et corroboravi. His testibus: Gervasio monacho, Aniano monacho, Kediuor Cryc et Kediuor conversis de Stratmarchell, duobus filiis Ioruert, Enniaun et Grifri, et duobus filiis Goronuy, Gurkenev et Benwin, duobus quoque filiis Grifut Hyrvein, Yewaph et D(avi)d et multis aliis. Datum aput Lan Wynnavc anno ab incarnatione domini m cc° septimo.

The description of Gruffudd Goch in the notification as *Grifini filius de Karno ex matre Levchv filia Kadwallavn* is very unusual in its naming of the grantor's mother. As the lands are the same as those granted by Cadwallon ap Hywel in no. 9 above, it was presumably this Cadwallon who was Lleucu's father and thus Gruffudd Goch's grandfather (rather than uncle, *pace Ystrad Marchell Charters*, 67). The mother seems to have been named, therefore, because it was through her that Gruffudd Goch derived his title to the lands; this may well imply in turn that Cadwallon had no son living when the grant was made. Llanwnnog (SJ 022 938) lies about 4 miles south-east of Carno in Arwystli.

DAFYDD AB OWAIN O'R BRITHDIR
(*fl.* 1197–1216 × *c.*1226)

11 Strata Marcella Abbey

Grant and confirmation, for the salvation of the souls of himself and his parents, of all the lands, gifts and liberties which all his predecessors and other heirs of Arwystli have sold or given to the monks, namely Pennant Bacho, Dyffrynmerthyr, Perfedd Fynydd, Cwm Llwyd and Cwmbuga as far as Rhyd-y-benwch in all their bounds, all the land they had at Deupiw and Ysgor-fawr and half of all the land from the Arannell to Rhydyfoch, Aberbrydwen and Rhiw Caenesied; the monks shall possess these lands and pastures in perpetual right, freely without any secular exaction or custom, so that no other monks may have any property, use or pastures in the same region from the river Severn towards Powys. He has confirmed by oath before the witnesses written below that neither he nor any of his kin will inflict, or allow to be inflicted, injury or damage on the abbey on behalf of himself, his brother, son or nephew or of any man. He will not receive the monks' goods from anyone against the monks' will but will compel, as far as he can, those receiving these to restore them and will not allow those injuring the monks into his company. Witnesses.

Llandovery, 1215

A = NLW, Wynnstay Estate Records, Ystrad Marchell Charters, no. 59. Endorsed: Carta D(avi)d filii Owei(n) de Bridtir (s. xiii med.); early modern endorsements; approx. 255 mm. wide × 130 mm. deep on left, 140 mm. deep on right + 19 mm.; two central horizontal slits, one just above, one in, the fold, for a tag (*c.*13 mm. wide) which exits through a slit in the base of the fold; sealed on tag. Circular seal, green wax, imperfect, originally approx. 50 mm. diameter; equestrian, facing right; legend: + SIG ... TIR.
Pd. from A, Jones *et al.*, 'Five Strata Marcella charters', 53; from A, *Ystrad Marchell Charters*, no. 59.
Cd., Davies, 'Strata Marcella documents', 184–5 (no. 31); *H*, no. 5.

Omnibus sancte matris ecclesie filiis tam presentibus quam futuris notum sit quod ego D(avi)d filius Owyni de Bridtyr dedi et hac presenti carta mea confirmavi Deo et Beate Marie et monachis de St(ra)tmarchell pro salute anime mee et parentum meorum totas terras cum pertinentiis suis et omnes donationes et libertates quas omnes alii heredes et antecessores mei de Arustili predictis monachis aut vendiderunt aut dederunt, scilicet Pennantbacho et Defrenmerthyr et Peruetminit et Cu(m)lluit et Cumbuga usque ad Ridpenhoch cum omnibus terminis suis; similiter et totam terram quam habuerunt de Deupiu et de Scoruaur et dimidietatem totius terre ab Arannell usque ad Ridywoch et Aberbredwen et Ryucanesseit, libere et quiete, bene et in pace et sine aliqua exactione vel consuetudine seculari iure perpetuo in possessionem. Iam dictis monachis dedi in bosco, in plano, in aquis, in viis, in pratis, in pasturis, in molendinis et in omnibus usibus suis et utilitatibus et terminis et pertinentiis suis, ita ut nulli alii monachi habeant aliquam proprietatem aut usum vel pasturas apud eandem regionem a fluvio Hawren versus Powis. Ego quoque D(avi)d filius Owini iuramento confirmavi coram subscriptis testibus ita quod nec ego neque aliquis ex his qui mihi parent memorate domui nec pro me nec pro meo fratre vel filio vel nepote vel aliquo homine malefaciam vel dampnum inferam neque inferri proposse permittam. Eorum et bona a nemine illis invitis recipiam sed recipientes proposse ad restitutionem compellam et eorum malefactores in mea societate non dimittam. Hiis testibus: D(avi)d abbate de St(ra)tm(archell), T. priore, D(avi)d priore de St(ra)tm(archell), D(avi)d parvo converso de illa domo, Vrien canonico de Tallh(au), Rírid decano de St(ra)ttywi, Teguaret filio L., Gervasio filio E., Madoco filio I. converso de St(ra)tm(archell), Mil filio I. cum duobus suis filiis G(ri)fut et Ioab, G(ri)fut Coyc, Meuric filio M., Meilir filio G(ri)fut, G(ri)fri filio Laud', Peredur cum duobus filiis, Alan et multis aliis. Facta est hec donatio apud Llanamdiuri anno ab incarnatione domini m° cc° x°v° in manu D(avi)d abbatis.

Dafydd's father Owain o'r Brithdir died in 1197. For the possible significance of the place-date compare the note to no. 9 above. In 1215 Llandovery castle was probably held by Rhys Ieuanc ap Gruffudd ap Rhys, who had captured it two years previously; it was granted to Rhys Ieuanc's uncle Maelgwn ap Rhys by Llywelyn ap Iorwerth at Aberdyfi in 1216 (*BT, Pen20Tr*, 88, 92; *BT, RBH*, 198–9, 206–7). Stephenson, 'Politics of Powys Wenwynwyn', 43, suggests that the charter is probably datable to January × March 1216. Rhyd-y-benwch identified by Stephenson (pers. comm.) at SN 857 873.

MADOG AB OWAIN O'R BRITHDIR
(*fl.* 1197–1215)

12 Strata Marcella Abbey

Grant, confirming in perpetual alms, free of all secular exaction, custom and service, all the lands and pastures possessed by the monks in the region of Arwystli through the gifts of his brothers, co-heirs and predecessors, so that no other monks may have property, use or pastures in that region from the river Severn towards Powys. The names of the lands justly possessed by the monks in perpetual possession from him and his predecessors are: Dyffrynmerthyr, Cwmbuga, Cwm Llwyd and thence to Cyfeiliog, half of Deupiw, half of Ysgor-fawr, half of Aberbrydwen, half of all the land from the Arannell to Rhydyfoch and Rhiw Caenesied with all their bounds and appurtenances. Witnesses.

1215

A = NLW, Wynnstay Estate Records, Ystrad Marchell Charters, no. 60. Endorsed: Confirmacio super Cu(m)buga Madoci filii Oweyn de Briddyr (s. xiii[1]); early modern endorsements; approx. 232 × 153 + 20 mm.; two central horizontal slits, one just above, one in, fold, for a tag (*c.*11 mm. wide) which exits through a slit in the base of the fold; sealed on tag. Circular seal, white wax, imperfect, originally approx. 55 mm. diameter; equestrian, facing right; legend: SIG . . . .
Pd. from A, *Ystrad Marchell Charters*, no. 60.
Cd., Davies, 'Strata Marcella documents', 185–6 (no. 32); *H*, no. 6.

Universis sancte matris ecclesie filiis tam presentibus quam futuris notum sit quod ego Madocus filius Owini Debriddir dedi et hac presenti karta mea confirmavi Deo et Beate Marie et monachis de St(ra)march(ell) in puram et perpetuam elemosinam et ab omni exactione et consuetudine et servitute seculari liberam et quietam totas terras et pasturas quas p[redicti] monachi de regione que vocatur Arustli possident et tenent per donationem fratrum meorum et coheredum et antecessorum meorum, ita ut nulli alii monachi habeant proprietatem aut usum vel pasturas in eadem regione a fluvio Sabrina versus Powis. Hec sunt autem nomina terrarum quas memorati monachi in propriam et perpetuam possessionem a me et a meis antecessoribus iure et iuste possident, scilicet Defren Merthyr et Cum Buga et Cum Luit et inde usque Keuelioc et dimidietatem Deupiu et dimidietatem Scoruaur et dimidietatem Aberbredewen et dimidietatem totius terre ab Aranell usque Rit Euoch et Riu Kanesseit cum omnibus terminis et pertinentiis suis in bosco et in plano, in pratis et in pasturis et molendinis et in omnibus usibus et utilitatibus suis bene et in pace, plenarie et integre et honorifice. Hec donatio facta est anno incarnati verbi mᵒ ccᵒ xvᵒ. Hiis testibus: Owino Debrogint' cum filiis duobus scilicet Kadugano et Howel, Iohanne et Aniano monachis, Gervasio filio E., Madoco filio I. conversis de St(ra)tmarch(ell).

See nos. 9–11 above and no. 13 below. The presence in the witness list of Owain Brogyntyn ap Madog ap Maredudd, himself a patron of Strata Marcella (see nos. 490–1 below), may indicate that Madog ab Owain had taken refuge with him in his lands of Dinmael and Edeirnion.

OWAIN AB OWAIN O'R BRITHDIR
(*fl.* 1197–1216 × *c.*1226)

13 Strata Marcella Abbey
Grant, confirming all the lands which all his predecessors and other heirs of Arwystli have sold or given to the monks, namely Pennant Bacho, Dyffrynmerthyr, Perfedd Fynydd, Cwm Llwyd and Cwmbuga as far as Rhyd-y-benwch, all the land they had at Deupiw and Ysgor-fawr and half of all the land from the Arannell to Rhydyfoch, Aberbrydwen and Rhiw Caenesied, so that no other monks may have any property, use or pastures in the same region from the river Severn towards Powys. He has confirmed by oath that he will protect the monastery and its possession as far as he can and observe this gift for ever. Witnesses.

Llandovery, 1215

B = NLW, MS 1641B, ii, pp. 117–18 (incomplete; lacunae supplied from no. 11). s. xviii/xix.
Pd. from B, *Ystrad Marchell Charters*, no. 61.
Cd., *H*, no. 7.

Omnibus [sancte matris ecclesie filiis tam presentibus quam futuris]ᵃ notum sit quod ego Owynus filius Owini de Britdirᵇ dedi monachis de Stratmarchell totas terras [cum pertinentiis suis et omnes donationes et libertates]ᶜ quas omnes alii heredes et antecessores mei de Arustili predictis monachis aut vendiderunt aut dederunt, scilicet Pennant Bacho et Defren Merthir et Pervetminit et Cumlluit et Cumbuga usque Ridpenhoch et totam terram quam habuerunt de Deupiu et de Scoruaur, et dimidietatem totius terre ab Aranell usque ad Ridywoch et Aberbredwen, et Riucanesseit [possideant et teneant per donationem meorum et heredum et antecessorum meorum, ita]ᵈ ut nulli alii monachi habeant aliquam proprietatem aut usum vel pasturas apud eandem regionem a fluvio Hauren versus Powis. Ego quoque predictus Owinus iuramento confirmavi domum de Stratmarchell et eius res et possessiones pro posse meo defensurum et presentem donationem perpetuo observaturum. His testibus: D(avi)d abbate, T. priore [p. 118] de Stratmarchel …ᶜ et multis aliis. Facta est hec donatio apud Llanamdiwri anno ab incarnatione domini millesimo[e] ducentisimo decimo quinto in manu Davit abbatis.

[a] B *has* x x *here to indicate omitted material.* | [b] *corrected in* B *from* Brithdir. | [c] B *has* x x x *interlined here to indicate omitted material.* | [d] B *has* x x x x *here to indicate omitted material.* [e] milessimo B.

As far as can be judged given its incomplete state of preservation, this charter was very similar to that issued at Llandovery in 1215 by Owain's brother, Dafydd (no. 11 above), and both charters may well have been issued on the same occasion.

CEDEWAIN

MAREDUDD AP RHOBERT
(d. 1244)

*14 Strata Florida Abbey
Grant in free alms of the land of Aber-miwl (Aberunhull) *in Cedewain.*

[1171 × 1244; possibly *c*.1211 × 1244]

Mention only, in a letter patent of Edward I dated at Abergavenny, 24 October 1291 (*CPR 1281–92*, 459). The letter appoints a commission of oyer and terminer on receipt of a complaint from Strata Florida that, whereas Maredudd had granted this land to the abbey by charter in free alms, Edmund Mortimer, who now held certain of Maredudd's lands, asserted that the monks were bound to find all necessary victuals for him and his household on each Friday of the year and distrained them of their oxen and beasts at their grange of Aber-miwl. The dispute with Mortimer was settled in 1293 (Williams, *Cistercian Abbey of Strata Florida*, 141–2). Although there is no other evidence explicitly corroborating this grant, its credibility is strengthened by the facts that Maredudd died at Strata Florida in 1244 having assumed the Cistercian habit and that the abbey held the grange of Aber-miwl by 1291; indeed, *Brut y Tywysogyon* appears to refer obliquely to it in 1263 (*BT, Pen20Tr*, 106, 113; *BT, RBH*, 238–9, 252–3; *Taxatio*, 289; Williams, *Cistercian Abbey of Strata Florida*, 142–3). It is quite likely that Maredudd was also the donor of the abbey's grange of Gelynnog (Celynog Hill SO 051 972), about 7 miles north-west of Aber-miwl (The Court, Aber-miwl SO 158 944), par. Tregynon (*Taxatio*, 289; Williams, *Cistercian Abbey of Strata Florida*, 136–40; Williams, *Atlas*, 57). The grant can be no earlier than the beginning of Maredudd's lordship in Cedewain, the date of which is uncertain.

*15 Juliana de Lacy, his wife
Assignation of land in dower.

[Probably *c*.1205 × *c*.1220]

Mention only, in a letter close of Henry III dated at York, 4 January 1252 (*CR 1251–3*, 185). The king's letter orders Guy de Rochford to protect Maredudd Sais and Juliana de Lacy, his wife, in the seisin and liberties pertaining to the land which Maredudd ap Rhobert,

Juliana's former husband, assigned her in dower. It is not known whether Maredudd's grant was in written form (cf. note to no. 69 below). Juliana may have been a daughter of Walter de Lacy (d. 1241), lord of Ewias Lacy and Weobley (Herefs.) and Stanton Lacy, Ludlow and Child's Ercall (Shrops.) (Morgan, 'Territorial divisions [I]', 11). For the date of the marriage see above, p. 6.

16 Judgement concerning the lands of Deupiw and (?)Hiriaeth (*Hirard*)

Notification that the dispute between, on the one side, Gwrgenau, Benwyn, Madog, Ieuaf and Dafydd sons of Gruffudd Hirfain, Caradog ap Griffri, Ithel and Iorwerth sons of Cyfnerth ap Gwyn and their other co-heirs and, on the other, the men who used to be called ffetaniaid, *over the lands called Deupiw and (?)Hiriaeth* (Hirard), *has been settled as follows. Llywelyn ap Iorwerth, lord of Arwystli, set a specified day for all the aforesaid men at Llandinam so that the case might be settled there by the arbitration of good men knowledgeable in the laws of that land. But because Llywelyn could not be present at the hearing he appointed Maredudd to preside over the case in his place. Many good men, from both Cedewain and Arwystli, gathered on the day and at the place appointed. Then the men known as* ffetaniaid *claimed hereditary right in the aforesaid lands of Deupiw and (?)Hiriaeth* (Hirard) *and at their request accepted arbitrators known in our tongue as* dadferwyr *from the better men of Arwystli, who, after diligent and prudent discussion, determined at Llandinam that the* ffetaniaid *had, and should have, no right in the aforesaid lands of Deupiw and (?)Hiriaeth* (Hirard). *After this there was discussion of this arbitration and it was adjudicated again, and thus the* ffetaniaid *were totally deprived of right in those lands for ever. All the above was done in the sight of the good men whose names are written below: John ap Cynwrig, priest of Llandinam, his son Gruffudd, Cynyr ap Cadwgan, abbot of Llandinam, Einion ap Cynfelyn, Gwrgenau Bach,* segynnab *of Llandinam, Iorwerth ap Hywel, dean of the land, the two seneschals of Llywelyn, namely Madog Tanwr and Einion ab Ednywain, Einion and Griffri sons of Iorwerth ap Gwrgenau, stewards of that land, Cadwgan ap Gruffudd, Gruffudd Goch ap Gruffudd Carno, Mil ab Ithel, Cedifor ap John, Maredudd ap Cunedda, Gruffudd ap Meilyr, Gruffudd ab Ieuaf, Madog Goch, Gwrgenau ap Glasadain, Ithel ap Caradog; good men from Cedewain: Heilin ap Hoedlyw, Dafydd Goch, Iorwerth Fychan, clerk, Cadwgan ap Iorwerth, Ednyfed ap Goronwy, Einion ap Budr ei Hosan ['Dirty-hose']. Thus on that day all the claim of the men called* ffeta-niaid *was fully removed from the aforesaid lands for all time. Sealing clause.*

[Probably 1216 × c.1226]

A = NLW, Wynnstay Estate Records, Ystrad Marchell Charters, no. 64. Early modern endorse-ments; approx. 188 × 231 + 14 mm.; two central horizontal slits in fold for a tag (c.8 mm. wide) which exits through a slit in the base of the fold; tag broken off at the base. Circular seal found loose in 1977, green wax, imperfect, originally approx. 55 mm. diameter; equestrian, facing right; legend: + ...C. Seal was attached to the charter in 1949. (See *Ystrad Marchell Charters*, 205.)
Pd. from A, *Ystrad Marchell Charters*, no. 64.
Cd., Davies, 'Strata Marcella documents', 182–3 (no. 29); *H*, no. 9.

Omnibus tam presentibus quam futuris ad quos presens pervenerit scriptum Mareduth filius Roberti dominus de Kedeweinc salutem. Noverit universitas vestra quod controversia que vertebatur inter Gurgéneu et Benuen et Madocum et Ieuaf et David filios Griffud Hyruein et Caradocum filium Grifri et Ithael et Ioruerd filios Kéfnerth filii Gwin et ceteros coheredes suos, et inter viros qui cognominabantur *fettáneit*, de terris que appellantur Déupiu et Hírard hac ratione terminata est et sopita. Lewelinus videlicet filius Ioruerd dominus Arwistili diem nominatum omnibus predictis viris apud Llandinan prefixit ut ibidem ad arbitrium bonorum virorum et iura terre illius scientium eadem causa sopiretur. Sed quia idem Lewelinus colloquio illi interesse non potuit, me in loco suo super eandem causam constituit. Convenerunt itaque ad diem et locum prefixum quam plures boni viri tam de Kedeweinc quam de Arwistili. Tunc viri qui cognominabantur *fettáneit* ius heredi- tarium in predictis terris, scilicet Deupiu et Hirard, petierent. Qui ad peticionem suam xxiiii[or] arbitros qui lingua nostra vocantur *datuérwer* de melioribus viris Arwistili acceperunt. Qui veritate eiusdem cause diligenter atque prudenter discussa arbitrabantur ibidem, scilicet apud Llandínan, quod idem viri qui cognominabantur *fettaneit* nullum habebant nec habere debent ius in terris predictis, scilicet Deupiu et Hirard. Et post hoc facta est discussio super illud arbitrium et illud idem iterum adiudicatum est et sic viri illi scilicet *fettaneit* omnino disiudicati sunt de illis terris usque in sempiternum. Facta sunt autem hec predicta in conspectu bonorum virorum quorum nomina subscripta sunt. Isti igitur sunt qui affuerunt: Ioh(ann)es filius Kenewreic sacerdos de Llandínan, Griffud filius eius, Kenir filius Cadug(aun) abbas Llandinan, Einniaun filius Kenuelin, Gurgeneu parvus *sengennab* Llandinan, Ioruerd filius Hewel decanus terre, duo senescalli Lewelini scilicet Madoc(us) Tan(ur) et Einniaun filius Edenewein, Einniaun et G(ri)fri filii Ioruerd filii Gurgeneu prepositi illius terre, Cadug(aun) filius G(ri)ffud, G(ri)ffud Cóic filius G(ri)ffud Carno, Milo filius Ithael, Kediuor filius Ioh(ann)is, Mareduth filius Knétha, G(riffu)d filius Meil(ir), G(ri)ffud filius Ieuuaf, Madoc(us) Goch, Gurgeneu filius Clasádein, Ithael filius Karadoc. Isti insuper boni viri de Kedewein interfuerunt: Héilin filius Hoideleu, David Coch, Ioruert Bochan clericus, Cadug(aun) filius Ioruerd, Ideneuet filius Goron', Einniaun filius Budrihossan. Et sic ablata est omnis calumpnia illo die virorum qui dicebantur *fettaneit* plenarie omni tempore a predictis terris. Et ut hec predicta rata et inviolabilia in perpetuum et sine omni reclamatione permaneant ego predictus Maredud ea tam presentis scripti munimine quam sigilli mei impressione coroboravi. Valete.[a]

[a] *horizontal stroke of* t *extends to fill rest of line* A.

This and the following document (no. 17) are unique examples of records of dispute settlement under native Welsh law in the twelfth and thirteenth centuries. Stephenson, *Thirteenth Century Welsh Law Courts*, 10–14, shows that both documents refer to the same case and argues that they are datable to one of the periods in which Llywelyn ap Iorwerth exercised direct authority over Arwystli, namely from 1208 to 1210 and again from 1216 until his transfer of the cantref to his son Gruffudd by 1226 (see nos 282–3 below). The witness lists are compatible with either of those date ranges. However, since Maredudd was hostile to Llywelyn in 1211–12 and is first recorded as an ally of the prince in 1215, the earlier date range is unlikely. Conversely, the description of Llywelyn as 'lord of Wales' in no. 17 could point in favour of the period after the prince had re-established, and further extended, his hegemony from 1212 onwards, a hegemony vividly illustrated by his partition of Deheubarth at Aberdyfi in 1216. This, together with the fact that the scribe of the present document also wrote a charter of Gwenwynwyn for Strata Marcella in 1215 (no. 578 below; *Ystrad Marchell Charters*, 110), led Thomas to suggest that both documents were written *c*.1216 – although he also suggested that the case itself may have taken place in 1208 × 1210, following

Stephenson's (questionable) view that the witnesses are more compatible with the earlier date (ibid., 21–2). Whether or not the documents are contemporary with the case, the balance of probability supports the later date range of 1216 × c.1226.

Both documents record the first stages of the case, heard before Maredudd at Llandinam, but no. 17 adds the outcome of an appeal to 'wise men' (*sapientes*), very probably meaning experts in native law (cf. Pryce, 'Lawbooks and literacy', 43), and concludes by noting that the *ffetaniaid* had previously been deprived of the lands they claimed in the days of Hywel ab Ieuaf (d. 1185). No. 17 also differs from the present document in referring to Llywelyn both as 'prince' and as 'lord of Wales', whereas here he is simply 'Llywelyn ap Iorwerth, lord of Arwystli', and, above all, in its clear antipathy to the plaintiffs, referred to in both documents by their nickname of *ffetaniaid*, 'sack-men, plunderers' (*Ystrad Marchell Charters*, 19, n. 3). This hostility almost certainly reflects the outlook of Strata Marcella, which had bought half of Deupiw from its heirs by August 1204 (see no. 559 below and also nos 9, 11–13 above): if successful, the *ffetaniaid's* claim would have undermined the abbey's title to that land. As already noted, the present document was written by the same scribe as wrote a charter of Gwenwynwyn in favour of Strata Marcella in 1215, and no. 17 was likewise written by a scribe from the abbey, among whose muniments both documents were preserved. The twenty-four arbitrators from Arwystli, referred to by the Welsh term *dadferwyr* (derived from the verb *dadfer*, 'to pronounce judgement, adjudge': *GPC*, s.vv.), are the same as the twenty-four *obtimates provincie de Arwistli* of no. 17. The latter document also records that the *ffetaniaid* refused the offer of *difinitio proborum virorum quod dicitur deduriht* (Mod. W. *dedfryd*). This may be a reference to the procedure mentioned in some Welsh lawbooks for settling land disputes known as *dedfryd gwlad*, 'verdict of the country', in which *henaduriaid gwlad/cantref*, 'elders of the country/cantref' hear both parties and return a verdict which forms the basis of the judges' judgement (*Welsh Medieval Law*, ed. Wade-Evans, 47; *LTWL*, 385; cf. ibid., 353, 357, 394–5, 396, and also the reference to the *seniores patrie* of Arwystli in no. 480 below).

Deupiw was probably the tenement now called Pen Clun in the township of Manledd, par. Llanidloes (SN 930 874), and *Hirard* may probably be identified as Hiriaeth (SN 959 872) (*Ystrad Marchell Charters*, 119 and Map III).

The present document highlights the importance of the native ecclesiastical foundation of Llandinam, with its priest, (?lay) abbot and steward (*segynnab*); for the last term, derived from Lat. *secundus abbas*, see Binchy, 'Some Celtic legal terms', 223, and also no. 440 below. The *abbas*, Cynyr ap Cadwgan, is also named in no. 17 as one of the *sapientes* summoned to hear the appeal; his sons were said by Llywelyn ap Gruffudd in 1281 to be official judges (*ynaid*) in Arwystli and a fifteenth-century Welsh lawbook attributes to him a lawbook which he passed on to his sons and grandsons (Pryce, *Native Law*, 34–5).

17 Judgement concerning the lands of Deupiw and (?)Hiriaeth (*Hirard*)

Notification that he has been appointed by Prince Llywelyn, lord of Wales, to settle the dispute between the heirs of (?)Hiriaeth (Hirarht) and Deupiw and the men called ffetaniaid, *who were claiming those lands against the aforesaid heirs. The claim of the* ffetaniaid *was settled lawfully and justly as follows on the peremptory day in the lawful place, namely Llandinam. First they were offered the decision of worthy men which is called* dedfryd *but they did not want that, knowing that they would gain nothing from it. Afterwards they agreed that twenty-four nobles of the province of Arwystli should decide by oath whether they had any right in the aforesaid lands. But all these nobles swore publicly that they knew nothing of their right in the lands. Then, although their claim ought to have been finished, they requested again that the case should be decided by the judgement of wise men. The wise men of Arwystli proceeded in the case, namely Cynyr ap Cadwgan and Ieuaf ap Iorwerth as well as Ednyfed ap Goronwy and Iorwerth Pastan from Cedewain and other wise and discrete men from other provinces; they decided that the* ffetaniaid, *and their offspring for ever, were not the heirs of the aforesaid lands, and the other true heirs asserted this judgement before many witnesses. When the* ffetaniaid *realized that their right was failing on all sides, they withdrew having been judged. But these* ffetaniaid *were similarly deprived lawfully and justly of these lands in the days of Hywel ab Ieuaf. Witnesses.*

[Probably 1216 × c.1226]

A = NLW, Wynnstay Estate Records, Ystrad Marchell Charters, no. 65. Early modern endorsements; approx. 177 × 82 + 17 mm.; two central horizontal slits, one just above, one in, fold, for a tag (*c*.9 mm. wide) which exits through a slit in the base of the fold; sealed on tag. Circular seal, green wax, imperfect, originally approx. 55 mm. diameter; equestrian, facing right; legend missing. Pd. from A, *Ystrad Marchell Charters*, no. 65.
Cd., Davies, 'Strata Marcella documents', 183–4 (no. 30); *H*, no. 10.

Universis fidelibus notum sit quod ego Maredud filius Rob(er)ti dominus de Kedewig constitutus a principe Lewelino Wallie domino ut dirimerem controversiam que versabatur inter heredes de Hirarht et de Deupiw et inter illos qui dicuntur *fetanieht* qui reclamabant contra predictos heredes pro illis terris. Die igitur peremtoria loco legitimo scilicet Landinan coram sapientibus et optimatibus reclamatio illorum qui dicuntur *fetanieht* et eorum calumpnia iure et iuste hoc modo terminata est et sopita. Primo igitur oblata est eis difinitio proborum virorum quod dicitur *deduriht* set noluerunt scientes ex hoc nil se posse adinvenire. Postea vero consenserunt ut[a] xxiiii[or] obtimates provincie de Arwistli de eorum calumpnia iureiurando decernerent si aliquid iuris de predictis terris haberent. Set et illi omnes obtimates publice iuraverunt nil se scire de illorum iure in predictis terris. Set eorum reclamatio tunc cum deberet finiri pecierunt iterum ut predicta causa per iudicium sapientum decisioni mandetur. Processerunt igitur in causam sapientes de Arwistli, scilicet Kenher filius Kadugan, Ioab filius Ioru(er)ht, de Ked(e)wig vero Idneuet filius Goronui, Ioru(er)ht Pastan et alii sapientes et discreti de aliis provinciis qui diiudicaverunt illos scilicet *fetanihet* non esse heredes de predictis terris cum semine eorum inperpetuum, aliis veris heredibus hoc iudicium contestantibus coram multis testibus. Illi autem qui dicuntur *fetanihet* cum cernerent ius suum ex omni parte deficere diiudicati recesserunt. Set et in diebus Howeli filii Ioab similiter illi *fatanihet* iure et iuste illis terris privati sunt. Testes igitur hii sunt: Ioru(er)ht decanus filius Howeli et Cuneda frater eius, duo filii Owin Brihtir scilicet D(avi)d et Owin, duo filii Ioru(er)ht scilicet Enniaun et G(ri)fri, Mil filius Ithael, Madauc Tanhur, tres filii G(ri)fud filii Kadugan scilicet Meilir, Seisihll, Ioru(er)ht, G(ri)fud filius Meilir, Ada(m) filius Ioru(er)ht, Gorgeneu filius Gl[a]sad(e)in, Enir vates, Kediuor filius Ioh(ann)is, P(er)edur filius Ioru(er)ht, G(ri)fud filius Ioab.

[a] consenserunt xxiiii[or] obtimates ut *with transposition marks after* consenserunt *and* ut *in* A, *indicating that* ut *should be moved to here.*

See note to no. 16 above.

18 Llanllugan Nunnery

Grant, with the consent of his sons Owain, Gruffudd and Hywel, his brother Trahaearn, and his nephews Cadwgan, Maredudd, Hywel and Owain, for the salvation of the souls of himself, the aforesaid men, his parents and successors, in perpetual alms, free of all secular exaction and custom, of the whole township of Llanllugan with all its appurtenances in these bounds: from the stream below the meadow (nanthisdol), *(?)from the grove to beneath* (oluin iadan) *(?)the red moor* (Gueunrud) *and as far as the Rhiw on one side, from the Rhiw to the other Rhiw and as far as* Halbreu *and* Rhydyfoch *on the other side. Further grant with the same liberties of half the land of* Lit *as far as* Cust *and as far as* Craig Urno. *Further grant of all the land called* Talhalun *with all its bounds and appurtenances. Sealing clause; witnesses.*

[Probably *c*.1216 × 1236]

A = Cardiff, Glamorgan Record Office, CL/DEEDS/I/3250. Foot left: Temp. H.3. ab[t.] ano. 1220 (s. xix); foot right: vii (s. xiii); endorsed: He[(?)c carta] Mared(ud) filii Rob(erti) pro Llanllugan (?s. xiii); early modern endorsement; approx. 150 × 202 + 22 mm.; central slit in fold for a tag (*c*.11 mm. wide) which originally exited through fold (now damaged); sealed on tag. Circular seal, green wax, imperfect, originally approx. 55 mm. diameter; equestrian, facing right; legend: … M]EREDVD FIL[II……]DE[K]EDEV …

Pd. from A, Jones, 'Some account of Llanllugan', 305–6 (and trans.); from A, Morgan, 'Early charter of Llanllugan nunnery', 119; from Jones, 'Pearmain', 'Vill of Llanllugan', 40–1 (and trans.). Cd., *H*, no. 11.

Universis sancte matris ecclesie filiis tam presentibus quam futuris notum sit quod ego Maredud filius Rob(er)ti ex consensu et bona voluntate filiorum meorum Ovvein et Griffud et Hevvel, similiter et fratris mei Traharn et nepotum meorum Cadugaun et Maredud et Hevvel et Ovvein, pro salute anime mee et animarum illorum necnon et parentum et successorum nostrorum dedi et confirmavi Deo et Beate Marie et sanctimonialibus de Lanlugan in puram et perpetuam elemosinam et ab omni exactione et consuetudine seculari liberam et quietam totam villam que dicitur Lanlugan cum omnibus pertinentiis et usibus et utilitatibus suis et commodis in bosco et in plano, in pratis et pascuis et in aquis, bene et in pace, plenarie et integre et honorifice in hiis terminis: *o* nanthisdol, *oluin iadan* Gueunrud et usque Reu in illa parte; ex alia vero parte *o* Reu usque Reu *arall* et usque Halbreu et usque Redeuoch. Preterea eisdem libertatibus dedi supradictis sanctimonialibus dimidium totius terre *o* Lit usque Cust et usque Creic Urno. Similiter dedi eisdem totam terram que dicitur Talhalun in omnibus terminis et pertinentiis suis. Et ut hec mea donatio rata et inconcussa permaneat eam sigilli mei impressione et proborum virorum atestatione signavi. Testes igitur sunt hii: Ioh(anne)s filius Teguaret decanus, Gervasi(us) parvus, Heylin filius Hoidliu, Levvelyn filius G(ri)ffini, David cognomento Ruffus, Idnevet filius Goronvi, Cadugan(us) filius Iorveth, Griffin(us) filius Ovvein, Aun filius Iago, Levvelin Du cum multis aliis.

In February 1278 Gruffudd ap Gwenwynwyn claimed before the king's justices that Maredudd ap Rhobert had occupied thirteen townships between the Rhiw and the Helygi (Luggy Brook) in time of war before the death of Gruffudd's father Gwenwynwyn in 1216, and eventually an agreement was made allowing Maredudd to hold these lands for the rest of his life (*WAR*, 240; no. 591 below). The occupation probably took place when Llywelyn ap Iorwerth drove Gwenwynwyn from Powys into exile in 1216 (Morgan, 'Territorial divisions [I]', 11). Since Llanllugan (SJ 058 023) lay in the region between the Rhiw and the Helygi, the grant is unlikely to be earlier than *c*.1216 (Morgan, 'Early charter of Llanllugan nunnery', 117, which favours a date *c.*1216–17). Nor can it be later than 1236, for Maredudd's son Owain, named as consenting to the grant, died in that year (*BT, Pen20Tr,* 104; *BT, RBH,* 232–3). A date earlier in this date range would be consistent with the occurrence of two of the witnesses, Gruffudd ab Owain and Awn ab Iago, in 1207 (no. 575 below), and may be supported by the presence of Heilin ap Hoedlyw, Dafydd Goch (Ruffus), Ednyfed ap Goronwy and Cadwgan ap Iorwerth, all of whom occur in, probably, 1216 × *c.*1226 (nos 16–17 above). For the place-names see Morgan, 'Early charter of Llanllugan nunnery', 118; Williams, 'Cistercian nunneries', 157–8. As the boundary clause makes clear, there are two branches of the river Rhiw, one just to the south of Llanllugan, the other almost 1 mile to the north (the former is marked on modern Ordnance Survey maps as River Rhiw, the latter as Afon Rhiw). The first set of bounds appear to describe the township of Llanllugan, although the extent to which their Welsh names represent specific place-names rather than simply topographical descriptors is unclear. *Halbreu* (or *Halbren*?) probably contains the element *hâl*, 'moor(land), down' (*GPC,* s.v. *hâl*[3]). The lands of the second and third grants have not been identified. For further discussion of the Cistercian nunnery of Llanllugan see Williams, 'Cistercian nunneries', 157–63.

19 Letter patent concerning Henry III

Notification that he has undertaken and sworn on relics at the request of Llywelyn, prince of North Wales, that if Llywelyn does not give satisfaction in accordance with the judgement of the Church to Henry and his men concerning the damages he and his men have inflicted from the day of the capture of Kinnerley castle to the day of his absolution, namely Saturday on the morrow of the octaves of Michaelmas [7 October] 1223, Maredudd will give satisfaction within a reasonable term fixed by the archbishop of Canterbury, and has bound himself and his Christianity to do this. Sealing clause; witnesses.

[Montgomery, 8 October 1223]

B = TNA: PRO, C 66/28 (Pat. R. 7 Henry III), m. 1d (contemporary enrolment).
Pd. from B, *Foedera,* I. i. 170; from B, *PR 1216–25,* 411.
Cd., *H,* no. 283.

Omnibus ad quos presens carta pervenerit Mereduc filius Rob(erti) salutem. Sciatis nos manucepisse et tactis sacrosanctis iurasse ad preces Leulini principis Norwall(ie) quod nisi satisfecerit secundum iudicium ecclesie domino H. regi Anglie et suis de dampnis eis illatis per ipsum Leulinu(m) et suos a die captionis castri de Kinardesl' usque ad diem absolutionis ipsius Leulini, scilicet usque ad diem sabbati proximam post octabas Sancti Mich(aelis) anno regni ipsius domini regis vii, ego eis inde satisfaciam ad terminos rationabiles quos mihi prefiget dominus Cantuar(iensis) archiepiscopus; ad quod faciendum me et cristianitatem meam obligavi. Et in huius rei testimonium etc.[a] Testibus predictis.

[a] B *inserts* Hiis *struck through.*

See no. 254 below, which names the witnesses.

20 Letter patent concerning Henry III

*Notification that Maredudd, Robert ap Madog and Maelgwn ap Rhys have undertaken on
behalf of Madog ap Gruffudd of Bromfield and Elise ap Madog that they will give the same
oath and obligation within the term set by the archbishop of Canterbury as they have given by
their letters patent concerning the giving of satisfaction to the king and his men for the injuries
inflicted by Llywelyn and his men from the day of the capture of Kinnerley castle to the day
of his absolution, namely Saturday on the morrow of the octaves of Michaelmas [7 October]
1223, if Llywelyn has not given satisfaction in this matter.*

[Montgomery, 8 October 1223]

B = TNA: PRO, C 66/28 (Pat. R. 7 Henry III), m. 1d (contemporary enrolment).
Pd. from B, *Foedera*, I. i. 170; from B, *PR 1216–25*, 411–12.
Cd., *H*, no. 297.

Omnibus ad [quos]ᵃ presens carta pervenerit Mereduc' filius Rob(erti), Rob(ertus) filius
Maddoc, Mailgon' filius Res' salutem. Sciatis nos manucepisse pro Maddoc' filio Griffin(i)
de Bro(m)feld' et Elysse filio Maddoc quod idem sacramentum et eandem obligationem
facient infra terminum quem dominus Cantuar(iensis) archiepiscopus eis prefiget, quam
nos fecimus per litteras nostras patentes de satisfaciendo domino H. regi Angl(ie) et suis de
dampnis eis illatis per Leulinu(m) et suos a die captionis castri de Kinardesl' usque ad diem
absolutionis ipsius L., videlicet usque ad diem sabbati proximam post octabas Sancti
Mich(ael)is anno regni ipsius H. regis viiᵒ, nisi prefatus L. eis inde satisfecerit. Testibus
predictis.

ᵃ *omitted* B.

See no. 19 above and nos 44 and 254 below. The witnesses are named in no. 254. Robert ap
Madog (d. 1224) was a tenant in Middleton (Shrops.) who had fought with Llywelyn in
1223 and whose widow nursed one of Llywelyn's daughters (*HW*, ii. 666, n. 67; Morgan,
'Territorial divisions [I]', 25–6, 29; *Ystrad Marchell Charters*, 87).

*21 Letter patent concerning Henry III

*Notification that he will act as a pledge in support of undertakings given by Senana for the
release of her husband Gruffudd ap Llywelyn.*

[Shrewsbury, 12 August 1241]

Mention only, in an agreement between Senana and the king dated at Shrewsbury, 12
August 1241 (no. 284 below). Presumably the letter patent was similar to that concerning
these matters issued on the same occasion by Hywel ap Madog of Bromfield (no. 523
below).

DEHEUBARTH

CADELL AP GRUFFUDD
(d. 1175)

22 Totnes Priory

Grant in alms, for the souls of himself, his father, mother and all his friends, of the church of St Peter of Mebwynion with all its appurtenances, including tithes, meadows and fisheries, as the monks held it in the time of King Henry. In order that they may possess their property in peace for ever he confirms this with his oath and seal. Witnesses.

Cadell's house above the river Teifi next to St Peter's church [1146 × 1151]

A = Exeter, Devon Record Office, 312M/TY18. Endorsed: de Mabonio (in hand of charter); approx. 211 × 69 mm.; original base fold trimmed away, and new slit to left of original slit, for a tag (*c*.11 mm. wide); sealed on tag. Circular seal, white wax, imperfect, originally approx. 70 mm. diameter; equestrian, facing right; legend: ... FILII GR...
Pd. from A, Crouch, 'Earliest original charter', 131 (and plate); from A, Watkin, *History of Totnes Priory*, i. 46–7 (trans. only, and plate, ibid., ii, Plate VI).
Cd., *H*, no. 17.

Notum[a] sit omnibus tam presentibus quam futuris quod ego Cadellus filius Grifini regis pro anima mea et pro anima patris mei et matris mee et pro animabus omnium amicorum meorum do et concedo in elemosinam monachis Totonie ecclesiam Sancti Petri de Mabonio cum omnibus appendiciis suis, scilicet in terris et decimis, in pratis in nemoribus, in aquis in piscaturis, sicut tenuerunt tempore Henrici regis. Et ut monachi et homines sui firmam pacem habeant et in perpetuum res suas possideant sacramento et sigillo meo hoc confirmo. Hec facta sunt in domo domini Cadelli super aquam de Teiui iuxta ecclesiam Sancti Petri. Testes: Canaan decanus avunculus Cadelli, David frater Cadelli, Coured dapifer eius, Guffus clericus noster, Cadiuor presbiter et multi alii.

[a] *majuscule* N *set to left of left-hand margin of rest of text* A.

For a full discussion of this charter see Crouch, 'Earliest original charter', which locates the church of St Peter *de Mabonio* at Lampeter, cmt. Mebwynion. Cadell captured the castle of Lampeter in 1146, but appears to have been incapacitated as ruler of Deheubarth after he was badly beaten by Norman knights near Tenby in 1151. As Crouch argues, the 'house' of

Cadell may well have been Lampeter castle. The charter reveals that Totnes Priory had already held the church at Lampeter during the reign of Henry I (1100–35), and Crouch plausibly suggests that the original grantor was Stephen, constable of Cardigan. The witness list names two kinsmen of Cadell who are otherwise unattested: an uncle, Cynan, described as dean, and a brother, Dafydd; the presence of the steward, Coured, who presumably held the office of *distain* in Cadell's court, is also notable.

RHYS AP GRUFFUDD (THE LORD RHYS)
(d. 28 April 1197)

*23 Slebech Commandery
Grant of the land of Ystradmeurig (Stratmeurich).

[1164 × 28 April 1197]

Mention only, in a confirmation of the possessions of the Hospitallers of Slebech Commandery issued by Peter, bishop of St Davids, 7 November 1176 × 16 July 1198 (*St Davids Episcopal Acta*, 72 (no. 46)). The gift is listed immediately after the grant of the church of Ystradmeurig by Roger de Clare, earl of Hertford, and is likely to post-date that grant as Rhys's grant of Llanrhystud to Slebech includes the church (no. 24; cf. no. 58 below). If so, Rhys's grant is datable to after his conquest of Ceredigion from Roger, largely accomplished in 1164 and completed in 1165 (see *BT, Pen20Tr*, 63–4; *BT, RBH*, 144–7). Ystradmeurig (SN 703 675), cmt. Mefenydd, Ceredigion was the site of a castle, garrisoned by Roger and seized by Rhys in 1164, who probably rebuilt it in stone by *c*.1190; the castle was captured by the warband of Rhys's son Maelgwn in 1193 and finally destroyed by Maelgwn in 1208 (see Turvey, 'Defences of twelfth-century Deheubarth', 115; *BT, Pen20Tr*, 75, 83; *BT, RBH*, 174–5, 188–9). Ystradmeurig originally lay at Domen (SN 718 677), on the Afon Meurig about 1 mile east of the present site, and the name appears to have been transferred to the present site with the construction of the castle in the twelfth century (Wmffre, 'Language and history', II. ii. 888, 903). The presence of the castle possibly indicates that only part of the township of Ystradmeurig was alienated to the Hospitallers; it may therefore be significant that the summary does not state that 'the whole land' was given, in contrast to nos 24 and 58 below.

*24 Slebech Commandery
Grant of the whole land of Llanrhystud (Riustud) *with the township, church, mill and all its appurtenances and liberties.*

[Probably 1164 × 28 April 1197]

Mention only, in a confirmation of the possessions of the Hospitallers of Slebech Commandery issued by Peter, bishop of St Davids, 7 November 1176 × 16 July 1198 (*St Davids Episcopal Acta*, 72 (no. 46)). The grant probably belongs to the same period as no. 23 above. A castle was built at Llanrhystud (SN 537 696), located on the border between the commotes of Mefenydd and Anhuniog, by Cadwaladr ap Gruffudd ap Cynan in 1149; it was seized by Cadell, Maredudd and Rhys in 1151 but recaptured and burned shortly afterwards by Hywel ab Owain Gwynedd; like Ystradmeurig, the castle was occupied by Roger de Clare in the summer of 1158 (*BT, Pen20Tr*, 57, 60; *BT, RBH*, 128–31, 138–9). As there are no further references to the castle after 1158, it is uncertain whether it continued in use after Rhys's conquest of Ceredigion in 1164–5. By 1229 half of Llanrhystud was held by Ednyfed Fychan, husband of the Lord Rhys's daughter Gwenllian (see note to no. 84 below), though Slebech's title to the whole of Llanrhystud was confirmed in 1231 × 1232 by Bishop Anselm of St Davids in an inspeximus for Slebech reciting an inspeximus of Bishop Iorwerth reciting Bishop Geoffrey's inspeximus of Bishop Peter's confirmation charter (*St Davids Episcopal Acta*, 123–7 (no. 108)).

*25 Strata Florida Abbey

Grant of the field between Hendref Kynuanden *and the torrent of (?)Buarth y Re* (Buarthegre) *and thence to the Teifi* (Tew), *and Hirgarth* (Hirgarth) *to the Fflur* (Flur) *and the Teifi* (Teuu), *of (?)Llangareth Hedegan* (Lanhereth' Hedegen), *of the brook called* Pistruth *from Celli Angharad* (Kelly Agaret) *to the Teifi* (Teuu), *of Llys Pennardd* (Lispennard), *of Ystrad-fflur* (Strad Flur), *of Cefncastell* (Keuencastell), *of (?)Gelliau Anaw* (Kellyeu Anau), *of Maes Glas* (Mais Glas), *of Pennal [Blaen Pennal]* (Pennal) *to the Aeron Ddu [Afon Ddu]* (Ayrondu) *and to the Camddwr* (Camduuour), *of Cefn Perfedd [Esgair]* (Kennenperuet), *of (?)Cerlliau* (Kellieu Wremdeuoy) *and Maes Bre* (Maisbre), *of Ffynnonoer [Swydd-y-ffynnon]* (Fennanoyr) *and (?)Rhyd-y-felin* (Ritheuelin) *up to Maes Bre* (Maisbre) *and of (?)Tŷ-poeth* (Derspoith) *and Rhiwarth* (Riwardh) *to the sea.*

[1165 × 3 March 1182]

Mention only, in a confirmation of Henry II, dated at Winchester, confirmed in an inspeximus of Edward I, dated at Westminster, 27 May 1285 (TNA: PRO, C 77/6, m. 2; pd., *CWR*, 300–1; *Mon. Ang.*, v. 633; trans. Williams, *Cistercian Abbey of Strata Florida*, App., xiii–xiv). As Geoffrey Plantagenet witnesses Henry's charter as chancellor, it was issued after the resignation of Geoffrey as bishop-elect of Ely and his appointment as royal chancellor on *c*.6 January 1182, and before the consecration at Angers on 3 July 1183 as bishop of Lincoln of Walter de Coutances, who witnesses as archdeacon of Oxford (assuming that *magistro Walt' de Const' Exon' archidiacono* contains a scribal error for *Oxon' archidiacono*). As the king was on the continent after 3 March 1182, the confirmation charter may be assigned to *c*.6 January × 3 March 1182, when Henry was in the vicinity of Winchester awaiting a crossing to France. The confirmation cannot, therefore, refer to the charter Rhys issued in favour of Strata Florida in 1184 (no. 28 below), which differs from Henry's confirmation in its description of the lands granted and also explicitly confirms earlier grants. (The only place-names in the present charter also contained in no. 28 are Celli Angharad, Ystrad-fflur, Maes Glas and possibly (?)Tŷ-poeth (*Derspoith*).) That Rhys issued at least one charter for Strata Florida before 1182 is also shown by an undated bull of confirmation and privileges for Strata Florida granted by Pope Alexander III (d. 30 August 1181), which confirms Rhys's gift of *Stratflur cum omnibus grangis et impendiciis* (sic) *suis* (Davies, 'Papal bull of privileges', 200; *Liber Epistolaris*, ed. Denholm-Young, 2). However, as the grant is referred to so concisely in the bull, it is uncertain whether it was the same as that confirmed by Henry II. The present charter is thus datable to between

Rhys's assumption of the patronage of Strata Florida following his conquest of Ceredigion in 1165 and Henry's confirmation. I am grateful to Nicholas Vincent for help in dating Henry's charter.

Many of the places named were located in cmt. Pennardd, Ceredigion, including Llys Pennardd, presumably the original commotal centre and apparently the same as the grange *Pennarth iuxta predictum monasterium* of the *Valor Ecclesiasticus* (*OP*, iv. 484); if the identification with this grange is correct, Llys Pennardd was probably the site to which the abbey was moved from its original location at Ystrad-fflur, also granted by Rhys, i.e. Henfynachlog (immediately south of Old Abbey Farm SN 718 646) in the valley of the river Fflur, about 2 miles south-west of the present ruins at SN 746 657 (cf. Jones Pierce, 'Strata Florida', 20). The following place-names are likewise locatable in the same commote: Cefncastell, possibly identifiable with Cefngaer (SN 723 665); Maes Glas (SN 667 621); Pennal, now Blaen Pennal (SN 625 639) and the neighbouring Aeron Ddu, now the Afon Ddu, the northernmost source of the river Aeron; Cefn Perfedd (cf. Esgair SN 665 652, or Esgair Berfedd SN 748 593); and (?)Cerllïau (*Kellieu Wremdeuoy*) (SN 701 617). Other place-names seem to refer to places in commotes to the west and north of Perfedd: Ffynnonoer (now Swydd-y-ffynnon SN 692 658), par. Lledrod-uchaf, cmt. Mefenydd; (?)Rhyd-y-felin (*Ritheuelin*) (SN 593 792), par. Llanfihangel-y-Creuddyn, about 2 miles south-east of Aberystwyth; (?)Tŷ-poeth (*Derspoith*) (SN 537 629), par. Llanbadarn Trefeglwys, cmt. Anhuniog; and Rhiwarth (*Riwardh*), possibly near Castell (SN 494 623), par. Llanbadarn Trefeglwys. For most of these identifications see Wmffre, 'Language and History', II. ii. 571, 573, 578, 598, 646–7, 757, 877, 1016; iii. 1285.

26 Chertsey Abbey

Grant in perpetual alms, for the salvation of the souls of himself and of his father and mother and for the salvation of his wife and sons, of the cell of Cardigan with all its appurtenances: namely St Mary's church, Cardigan, with the castle chapel of St Peter and the two carucates of land pertaining to it north of the road leading towards Blaen-porth, Canllefaes up to Arthur's ford, and land beyond the cemetery of St Mary's church for establishing burgages; St Peter's church, Y Ferwig, with its chapels and half a carucate adjacent pertaining to it; the church of Holy Trinity called Llandduw with one carucate adjacent which is the sanctuary of the church; and tithes of mills, fisheries and all that can be tithed within the parishes of the aforesaid churches as well as tithes of the food and drink of Cardigan castle. The monks and their men shall be free of all secular lawsuits throughout Rhys's land, answering only to the Church, and shall have the same freedom as Rhys and his men in lands, waters and mills within and outside the borough. Witnesses.

[November 1165 × 28 April 1197]

B = TNA: PRO, C 66/416 (Pat. R. 3 Henry VI, pt. 1), m. 13 (reciting an inspeximus of Henry, prince of Wales of an inspeximus of Richard II of an enrolment before Thomas de Bradeston, justiciar of Edward, prince of Wales, at Carmarthen, 17 June 1359, 22 November 1424).
C = TNA: PRO, C 66/424 (Pat. R. 7 Henry VI, pt. 1), m. 17 (reciting an inspeximus of Edward, prince of Wales, 1 July 1349, 19 November 1428).
Pd. from B, *CPR 1422–9*, 258–9; from C, ibid., 522; from B, Pritchard, *Cardigan Priory*, 144–5; from C, ibid., 147–8.
Cd., *H*, no. 18.

Resus filius Gruffini[a] princeps Wall(ie) omnibus Cristi fidelibus tam presentibus quam futuris ad quos [b-]presentes littere pervenerint salutem[-b]. Sciatis me pro salute anime mee [c-]et pro animabus patris mei et matris mee[-c] et pro salute uxoris mee et filiorum meorum dedisse et[d] concessisse et hac presenti carta mea confirmasse Deo et ecclesie Sancti Petri et abbati et monachis de Certeseya et eorum successoribus imperpetuum in liberam [c-]et puram[-c] et perpetuam elemosinam cellam[e] de Cardygan[f] cum omnibus pertinentiis suis, scilicet ecclesiam Sancte Marie de Cardygan[f] cum capella Sancti Petri de castello et cum duabus carucatis terre ad eam pertinentibus que iacent ab aquilonari parte vie que ducit versus Blaenporth'[g] et Canclauas[h] usque ad vadum Arthuri[i] et cum terra extra cimiterium ecclesie Sancte Marie de[j] burgagia facienda et cum omnibus pertinentiis, ecclesiam Sancti [k-]Petri de Berwik[-k] cum capellis suis et dimidia[l] carucata terre adiacente et ad eam pertinente et cum omnibus pertinentiis,[m] ecclesiam Sancte Trinitatis que dicitur Landov cum una carucata terre adiacente que est refugium ecclesie et cum omnibus pertinentiis suis, decimas de molendinis et piscariis et de omnibus que decimari possunt infra parochias predictatum ecclesiarum, decimas etiam de redditibus et de cibo et de potu de castello de Cardygan[f] et de omnibus que decimari possunt ut et ipsi et homines sui [n-]liberi sint[-n] et quieti ab omni actione[o] seculari per totam terram meam, ita ut nichil alicui respondeant de aliquo nisi sancte ecclesie et ut ipsi et homines sui habeant et teneant et possideant eandem libertatem in omnibus quam ego et homines mei habemus in bosco et plano, in pratis,[p] pascuis et pasturis, in aquis et molendinis infra burgum et extra in[q] omnibus rebus et in omnibus locis. Huius donationis et concessionis testes sunt: dominus Walt(er)us abbas Sancte Marie de Cameys,[r] magister Matheus clericus, Steph(an)us[s] capellanus, Trahern filius Rodin,[t] Mailgun[u] et Gruffinus[v] filii domini Resi principis, Hengeuereit[w] constabularius, Will(elmu)s Wallens(is), Ioh(ann)es prepositus, Turstanus filius eius, Lamb(er)tus de Floundres,[x] Walt(er)us palmarus,[y] Cradoc[z] presbiter, Silbrutus[aa] de Bristowe, Will(elmu)s parmentarius, Iordanus Coterell, Alfredus palmarus,[y] Ioh(ann)es et Rob(er)tus filii Milesont,[ab] Rob(er)tus filius Louredi,[ac] Ph(ilipp)us frater eius et multi alii.

[a] Griffini C. | [b-b] presens scriptum pervenerit C. | [c-c] *omitted* C. | [d] *omitted* C. | [e] ecclesiam C. [f] Cardigan C. | [g] Bleynporth' C. | [h] Cantlauas C. | [i] Arturi C. | [j] ad C. | [k-k] Sancti Petroci de Berwyke C. | [l] dicta C. | [m] C *inserts* suis. | [n-n] sint liberi C. | [o] exactione C. | [p] C *inserts* et. | [q] cum C. [r] Kemeys C. | [s] Seph(an)us B. | [t] Redyn C. | [u] Mailgon C. | [v] Griffin(us) C. | [w] Henguereth' C. [x] Flandres C. | [y] Palmarius C. | [z] Cradeo C. | [aa] Aylbrutus C. | [ab] Milcent C. | [ac] Leuredy C.

This is almost certainly a confirmation, possibly with some augmentation, of grants to Chertsey made by the Clare lords who established the town of Cardigan after their conquest of Ceredigion in 1110; the Benedictine priory at Cardigan, which never attained conventual status, thus seems to have been an Anglo-Norman foundation (Malden, 'Possession of Cardigan priory', 154–5; Griffiths, *Conquerors*, 281–2). The charter was issued after Rhys completed his reconquest of Ceredigion by capturing Cardigan *c.*1 November 1165 and before his death in 1197. A date between Rhys's succession as sole ruler of Deheubarth in 1155 and Roger de Clare's recovery of Ceredigion in the summer of 1158 is unlikely, as Rhys's hold on Ceredigion was less secure then than it was after 1165; an earlier dating would also imply an improbably long term of office for the first witness, Walter, abbot of St Dogmaels, who occurs elsewhere in 1198 and 1203 (Knowles *et al.*, *Heads of Religious Houses*, 107). *Hengeuereit* also occurs in 1198 (no. 35 below). The references to

Cardigan castle could indicate a date after this was rebuilt by Rhys in the summer of 1171 following its destruction in 1165 (*BT, Pen20Tr*, 64, 67; *BT, RBH*, 146–7, 154–5). Also potentially relevant with respect to dating is a bull of confirmation and privileges issued by Pope Alexander III (d. 30 August 1181), dated at Tusculum, 17 July, which confirms Chertsey's possession of Cardigan Priory with the churches of the Holy Trinity (Llandduw), St Peter's chapel, Cardigan and St Michael's church, Tre-main (Pritchard, *Cardigan Priory*, 149–50). The bull is probably datable to 1171, 1172 and 1180, all years in which Alexander dated documents at Tusculum in July. After his return from exile in France in the autumn of 1165 the pope was definitely elsewhere in that month in 1166, 1168–70, 1173–7, 1179 and 1181; in 1167 he was at Rome on 1 July and had reached Benevento by 2 August, while in 1178 he was at the Lateran on 29 June but had reached Tusculum by 21 September (*PL*, 200, cols 458–61, 730–2, 878–82, 1183, 1184–5, 1272–3 *et passim*). Unfortunately, however, it is difficult to tell whether the bull was issued before or after Rhys's charter. If it was earlier, why did Rhys omit St Michael's church, Tre-main (SN 235 466), about $3\frac{1}{2}$ miles north-east of Cardigan on the way to Blaenannerch; if later, why did the bull not include St Peter's church, Y Ferwig (SN 183 496), about 2 miles north of Cardigan? By contrast, the next surviving papal confirmation for Chertsey, issued by Alexander IV on 3 April 1258, does include St Peter's church, Y Ferwig, as well as the priory, churches and chapel confirmed by Alexander III (Pritchard, *Cardigan Priory*, 150–1). The church of Y Ferwig was portionary, and other evidence shows that Rhys's grant consisted of only one portion (see no. 90 and note below).

Henry Owen (*OP*, iv. 461) convincingly identified *Canclauas* as Can-llefaes (Canllefas-ganol (*sic*) SN 214 483), located about 3 miles north-east of Cardigan, near Pen-parc, rather than Tan-y-groes, about 8 miles north-east of Cardigan beyond Blaenannerch (as maintained by Pritchard, *Cardigan Priory*, 28), an identification supported by Wmffre, 'Language and History', II. i. 22. However, Owen's suggestion that 'Arthur's ford' was Rhyd Fach, on a branch of a brook joining the Teifi at Cardigan, has been questioned by Wmffre (ibid., 34), who argues that it could have been Treprïor (SN 230 488), which belonged to the priory's estates, or else a ford near Penbont (SN 236 488). For the possible identification of Llandduw (Llanddwy) as Capel (SN 188 475) see ibid., 3–4. For the significance of the description of the carucate of land attached to the church of Holy Trinity (Llandduw), cmt. Is Coed, as the church's *refugium* see Pryce, *Native Law*, 169–72 (and, for the church's location and other examples of the name 'Llandduw', Griffiths, *Conquerors*, 298, n. 19; *OP*, iii. 319–20). The use of the term 'carucate' here and elsewhere in the charter reflects the influence of Anglo-Norman settlement, although it need not follow that all the lands to which the term was applied were originally granted by Anglo-Normans. The witness list points to trading connections between Cardigan and Bristol: apart from the appearance of Silbrutus (or Aylbrutus) of Bristol, Jordan Coterell can be identified with the man of that name whose purchase, with his father Ralph Coterell of Cardigan, of land near Fromebridge (Somerset) was confirmed by Robert fitz Harding (d. 1171) and his son Maurice fitz Robert (d. 1191) (*Cart. Glouc.*, i. 173–4, 252 (nos 47, 252)). I am grateful to John Cottrell for this identification and for providing the references. The place-name Gotrel-fawr (SN 176 479) possibly derived from Jordan Coterell (Wmffre, 'Language and History', II. i. 7).

*27 Talley Abbey
Confirmation of the land of the church of St Michael, Penbryn (Penbrin)*, within these bounds: from the cemetery of the church along the highway to the cross and from the cross along the highway to the ford in the Beron* (Bern) *in the direction of Porth Hoddni* (Porthotni) *[Aber-porth], along the Beron* (Bern) *to the Saith* (Seit)*, and along the Saith* (Seyt) *to the sea; from the other side of the cemetery to the Hoffnant* (Hotnant) *and along the Hoffnant* (Hotnant) *to the sea.*

[Probably 1180 × 28 April 1197]

Mention only, in an inspeximus, presumably of the original charter, of Edward II dated at Westminster, 24 March 1324 (TNA: PRO, C 66/160, m. 21; pd., *Mon. Ang.*, iv. 163; also, with trans., Daniel-Tyssen, *Royal Charters*, 70–1; cd., *CPR 1321–4*, 402; *H* no. 20). Rhys probably founded the Premonstratensian house of Talley (Talyllychau; cmt. Caeo, Cantref Mawr) in imitation of Rannulf de Glanville, Henry II's justiciar 1180–9, who was the most important patron of the Premonstratensians in England in the 1180s and with whom Rhys had close contact during that period (Smith and O'Neil, *Talley Abbey*, 5–6; Smith, 'Treftadaeth Deheubarth', 46, n. 39). Penbryn (SN 293 522) was located in cmt. Is Coed, Ceredigion. Porth Hoddni seems to have been an earlier name for Aber-porth (SN 258 514); the *Hotnant* (Hoddnant) of the charter is now called the Hoffnant, a stream which enters the sea to the north of Penbryn (A. C. Evans *apud* Daniel-Tyssen, *Royal Charters*, 71, n. 2; *OP*, iii. 440–1; Thomas, *Enwau Afonydd*, 150–1; see further Wmffre, 'Language and History', II. i. 91, 93; iii. 1319). Rhys made other grants to Talley, including, presumably, the site of the abbey, for he is named among earlier donors in confirmations by Maredudd ab Owain and Rhys Fychan ap Rhys Mechyll (see nos 68 and 90 below). However, neither of those confirmations refers explicitly to charters issued by Rhys or makes clear which of the possessions listed were originally granted by him.

28 Strata Florida Abbey
Notification that he began to build the monastery called Ystrad-fflur and has cherished it after it was built, increasing its possessions in plains, agricultural land and mountain pasture, for the salvation of his predecessors and successors, and in 1184 has again confirmed in writing all gifts that he has bestowed on the abbey. Three of his sons, Gruffudd, Rhys and Maredudd, offered the same gift at the same time in the hand of the abbot, ordering firmly before many of the army with Rhys in St Brigit's church, Rhayader [Llansanffraid Cwmteuddwr], that the monks and their successors may keep, undiminished and immune from all secular and ecclesiastical custom and obligation, whatever possessions they now possess from popes, princes or the faithful or by other just means. The names of these possessions are: Nannerth in its bounds from Nant y Fleiddast [Nant-y-sarn] to the Wye, from the Wye to Nant y Dernol and thence to its source; then across to the source of the Ystwyth, along the Ystwyth to the Taflogau, from the bottom of the Taflogau to its source; then across to the Marchnant and thence to the Meurig; thence to the Teifi; thence to the Camddwr-fach, along the Camddwr-fach to its source; thence along Pant Gwaun to the Camddwr-fawr, then by the Camddwr across to Hirfain Cadaithin *to the Aeron towards the dyke between Trecoll and* Brinnrit*, along the dyke to its head; thence to the source of Nant y Gelli-hir, then directly to the stream 'between Buarthcaron and Dinas (?)Drygwyr'; thence as that stream leads to the grange of Castell*

Fflemish; then from the grange from the other side of the stream across the hill as Pant Gwaun leads to the stream between Maes Glas and Trebrith, *along the stream to the Teifi; thence to Maes Treflyn [Maesllyn], then directly to Llyn Maesllyn, thence to the lake; Nant Llyn directly across to (?) Penllannerch; thence directly across the mountain above Celli Angharad, that mountain being the boundary; across to the source of the Camddwr [Blaencamddwr], along the Camddwr to the Tywi, thence up on both sides to the source; then directly from the source of the Tywi to the source of the Arban, along the Arban to the Claerwen; thence to the Elan; thence along the Elan to* Groen Gwinnion; *thence up to Tal* Lluchint; *thence to the top of the ridge, along the ridge to the source of the Risca; thence across the mountain to Llam yr Unben where the boundaries of the aforesaid land of Nannerth intermix equally with the boundaries described. Rhys, his aforenamed sons and all his descendants make over to the monks of Strata Florida in perpetual right whatever is contained within the bounds traced by the circuit. These are the names of the more distinguished places in those bounds: Moel Gediau, Nant Elmer, Nant Eyrin, Nant Morauc, Brithu(n), Abercoil, Abermethen, Stratgimurn, Celli Camgoed, Prysgau Einion, Ystrad-fflur, Rhydfendigaid [Pont Rhydfendigaid], Dol-fawr, Llwyn-y-gog, Tref-y-Gwyddel, Ffynnonoer [Swydd-y-ffynnon], Celli Bryn Teifi, Esgair Berfedd, Castell Fflemish, Maes Glas. From the gift of the sons of Cadwgan and their heirs and of our lordship: Cefn-y-rhyd, Esgairsaeson, half of Bronwennau beyond Esgair to the Arth where the sons of Saesog have established their buildings, (?) Tŷ-poeth with its appendages and these are its bounds, described by Rhys with his nobles and his son Gruffudd: from the mouth of the Meilyr up along the Arth to the dyke which begins at the spring of Bleiddudd, from the spring to the hollow, along the hollow to (?) Ffosbleiddaid [fossam* Bileyneyt, *'the Dyke of the Bondmen'], along the dyke to the hollow of the Gwaun between Marchdy and Bryn Llyn Du* (Brinn Llende), *along the hollow to the dyke which is the boundary between Marchdy and the township called* Ardiscinkiwet *which Gwenllian granted to the monks in perpetual alms with the counsel of Rhys and his sons; that dyke is the boundary to the sea, thence to Aberarth, the Arth to the mouth of the Meilyr and along the shore and sea from Aberarth to Aberaeron. They grant the weirs and all fishing to the monastery for ever as well as one day and night each week from Rhys's own fishing. Witnesses.*

Llansanffraid Cwmteuddwr, 1184

B = TNA: PRO, C 77/6 (Welsh Roll, 13 Edward I), m. 2 (in an inspeximus, 27 May 1285).

C = TNA: PRO, C 66/153 (Pat. R. 14 Edward II, pt. 1), m. 5 (in an inspeximus of B, 10 November 1320).

D = TNA: PRO, C 53/123 (Ch. R. 10 Edward III), m. 6 (in an inspeximus of C, 2 October 1336).

E = TNA: PRO, C 66/308 (Pat. R. 4 Richard II, pt. 1), m. 13 (reciting an inspeximus of D by Edward the Black Prince 28 October 1369, 20 October 1380).

F = TNA: PRO, C 66/417 (Pat. R. 3 Henry VI, pt. 2), m. 5 (in an inspeximus of E, 8 July 1425).

G = TNA: PRO, C 66/605 (Pat. R. 23 Henry VII), m. 9 (in an inspeximus of F, 4 March 1508).

Pd. from B, *CWR*, 298–300; from D, *Mon. Ang.*, v. 632–3; from D, Roberts, 'Documents and charters', 196–8 (trans. only); from a transcript by Walter Davies (Gwallter Mechain, 1761–1849), Williams, *Cistercian Abbey of Strata Florida*, App., x–xiii (trans. only); from ibid., Williams, 'Further excavations', 50–3.

Cd., *CPR 1317–21*, 527 (from C); *CChR 1327–41*, 382 (from D); *CPR 1377–81*, 551 (from E); *CPR 1422–9*, 294 (from F); *CPR 1494–1509*, 567 (from G); Green, *Crosswood Deeds*, 1; *H*, no. 19.

Universis sancte matris ecclesie filiis presentibus et futuris Resus Walliar(um) princeps salutem et pacem. Vestre universitatis notitie innotescat quod ego Resus Sudwall(ie) proprietarius princeps venerabile monasterium vocabulo Stratflur edificare cepi et edificatum dilexi et fovi, res eius auxi et possessiones in quantum suffragante domino valui, ampliavi terram campestrem et agriculturam et montuosam ad animalium pasturam devota mente ad remedium anime et predecessorum et successorum meorum, quantum sibi congruebat indulgens et omnem quidem donationem quam eidem monasterio contuli anno iterum ab incarnatione domini m° c° lxxx° quarto presentis scripti memoria stabilivi. Tres etiam filii mei scilicet Griffinus, Resus et Meredud eandem donationem eodem tempore et loco in manu abbatis de Stratflur' optulerunt, statuentes firmiter coram multis de exercitu in ecclesia Sancte Brigide apud Raiadr' mecum ut quascumque possessiones quecumque bona idem monasterium in presentiarum possidet et custodit sive concessione pontificum, largitione principum, oblatione fidelium vel aliis iustis modis Deo propitio adepta fuerit, firma monachis illius et eorum successoribus ab omni seculari et ecclesiastica consuetudine et debito immunia et illibata permaneant. In quibus hec duximus exprimenda vocabulis propriis: Nanneirth in terminis suis, id est Nant hi Wleidast *hit ar* Wy, Guy *hit in* Hedirnaul deinde *hit blain*, deinde in transversum usque Blain Ystuith', Istuith *in hit* usque Taualogeu, *gwailaut* Tawlogeu *hit hi blein*, deinde per rectum transversum usque Marchnant, Marchnant usque Meuric, Meuric usque Teywy, Teiwy *hit* Camdur Wechan, Camdur Wechan *in hit*, *hit blain*, deinde sicut ducit Pant Gueun *hit hi* Camdur Waur, postea per Camdur in transversum *hi ar* Hirwein Cadaithin usque Airon sicut ducit usque fossam que est inter Tref Coll' et Brinnrit, *foss hit hi blain*, *o wlain hi* fossam recte *hi benn* Nant hi Gellyhir, deinde recte *hit ar hi nant* inter Vuarth Caraun et Dinas Dritwir, deinde sicut amnis ille ducit usque grangiam que vocatur Castell hi Flemis, de grangia postea ex alia parte amnis trans collem sicut ducit Pant Gueun *hit hi nant* inter Mais Glas et Trebrith, *in nant hit ar* Deiwy, Teywy *hit hi* Mais Tref Linn, Mais Tref Linn recte *hit in* Blinnbuden, Llinbuden *hit hi llinn*, Nant Llin recte per transversum usque Llannerch hi Guinthwa, *o* Lannerch hi Guinthwa recte per transversum montis *hi ar* Gelly Hagharat, mons ille postea terminus est recte in transversum usque *blain* Camdur, Camdur sicut ducit usque Tiwy, Tiwy deinde sursum ex utraque parte *hi hit blain*, recte postea *o wlain* Tiwy *hit hi blain* Arban, Arban *in hit* usque Calarwenn, Calarwenn usque Elan, Elan[a] exinde usque Groen Gwinnion, *hi* Groen recte sursum *hi* Tal Lluchint, *o* Tal Lluchint *hi cewyir hir esceir ar esceir ar hit* usque *blain* Riscant, *o wlain* Risca per transversum montis usque Llam hi Vnben, ubi fines prenominate terre que appellatur Nanneirth istis terminis quos duximus pariter intermiscentur. Set et quicquid continetur infra terminos prescriptos per circuitum, in campo et silva, in aquis et pratis et pascuis, in culto et inculto, ego Resus et prenominati filii mei et tota posteritas mea predictis monachis de Stratflur et eorum successoribus iure perpetuo mancipamus. Et hec [sunt] nomina locorum in eisdem terminis excellentiorum: Moil Gediau, Nann Elmer, Nann Eyrin, Nann Morauc, Brithu(n), Ab(er)coil, Abermethen, Stratgimurn, Kelly Camgoit, Priskieu Enniaun, Stratflur, Ryt Wendigait, Dol Waur, Lluingos, Tref hi Guydil, Finnaun Oyer, Kellieu Brinn Deuy, Esceir Perweith, Castell Flemis, Mays Glas. Ex donatione vero filiorum Cadugaun et eorum heredum et nostri dominii Cewyn hi Rit, Esceir Saisson, dimidia pars vero Branwennu preter Esceir *hi tu ar* Arth ubi filii Seissauc edificia sua fundaverunt, Tref Boith cum apendiciis suis et hii sunt termini eiusdem, describente Reso cum optimatibus suis et etiam Griffino filio eius: *o* Aber Meylyr sursum *ar hit* Arth usque fossam que manat de fonte Bleydud, *or fannaun hir pant*, *pant in hit* usque fossam Bileyneyt, *hi foss ar hit* usque Pant Gweun inter Marchidi et Brinn Llende, *hi pan ar hit* usque fossam que est terminus inter Marchidi et villam que vocatur

Ardiscinkiwet quam optulit Gwenliant predictis monachis in perpetuam elemosinam cum consilio nostro et filiorum nostrorum, fossa vero prefata in termino est usque ad mare, mare vero usque ad ostium Arth, Arth *hit in* Aber Meilir, et in litore et mari ab ostio Arth usque ad ostium Ayron. *Coredeu* et omnem piscaturam sepedicto monasterio offerimus imperpetuum, et etiam de propria mea piscaria unum diem et unam noctem in qualibet septimana. Huius vero universe donationis isti sunt testes: duo filii Llaudent, Grifri et Res, Iorwerth filius Edniweyn, Ediorwerth' filius Kediuor, duo filii Lewelin, Gurgeneu et Cadugaun, Maredut filius Riderch et Gugaun Stacca, Grifut filius Bledint *o* Wabudrid et Maredut filius Einnaun filii Bledint *o* Werthrinnaun.

ᵃ Elam B.

The church of St Brigit of Rhayader was Llansanffraid Cwmteuddwr (SN 968 677) (Williams, *Cistercian Abbey of Strata Florida*, 65; *OP*, iii. 456). Rhys had built a castle at Rhayader, cmt. Deuddwr, Gwerthrynion in 1177 at a time of close relations with the Welsh lord of Gwerthrynion, Einion ap Rhys, who had married a daughter of Rhys by 1175. Rhayader seems to have remained in Rhys's hands until 1194, for the Welsh chronicles report that it was burned in that year by the sons of Cadwallon ap Madog of Maelienydd after Rhys had built it for the second time, presumably recently (*BT, Pen20Tr*, 70, 72, 75; *BT, RBH*, 164–5, 168–9, 174–5; Smith, 'Middle March', 79–80; *idem*, 'Treftadaeth Deheubarth', 31–2). The significance of Rhys's presence with an army near Rhayader in 1184 is uncertain, as there is no other evidence for his presence there in that year. Nor is it known whether the charter was issued before or after his meeting with Henry II at Worcester in July 1184, followed by further talks at Gloucester in that month, meetings in which Rhys sought to make peace after having led attacks against Anglo-Norman castles in south-east Dyfed in 1183–4 (*Gesta*, ed. Stubbs, i. 314, 317; Smith, 'Treftadaeth Deheubarth', 37; Gillingham, *English in the Twelfth Century*, 62–4).

Identifications of place-names in this charter mainly follow Wmffre, 'Language and History', II. ii. 577, 578, 586, 587, 589, 593, 615, 639, 644, 710, 721, 740, 873–4, 893, 896–7, 898–9, 907, 917–18; iii. 1318, 1324, 1327; see also Williams, *Cistercian Abbey of Strata Florida*, App., xi–xiii; *OP*, iii. 456–8; and note to no. 25 above for Maes Glas, Ystrad-fflur, Ffynnonoer and Tŷ-poeth. The first perambulation follows an arc in an anti-clockwise direction beginning at Nannerth (Nannerth-fawr SN 947 716), a district north-west of Rhayader, extending into Ceredigion and finishing back at the southern boundary of Nannerth. Nant y Fleiddast (which marks the southern boundary of Nannerth) has been identified with the modern Nant-y-sarn, which descends into the Wye at SN 944 708, about 3 miles north-west of Rhayader, and Nant y Dernol joins the Wye about 2½ miles farther north-west at SN 920 746. *Blain Ystuith'* (the source of the Ystwyth) is located at Blaencwm (SN 827 754), par. Ysbyty Ystwyth, cmt. Mefenydd; the Taflogau is the present Nant Gau, a tributary of the Ystwyth (cf. Dologau SN 771 733); the Marchnant was a name for the upper reaches of the Meurig; the Camddwr-fach and Camddwr-fawr join the river Teifi north-west and south-west of Strata Florida at SN 705 661 and SN 677 623 respectively. Trecoll (SN 644 624): par. Llanbadarn Odyn, cmt. Pennardd. Dinas (?)Drygwyr (*Dritwir*) may be the same as Llwyngwinau-isaf (SN 670 634), par. Caron Is-clawdd, cmt. Perfedd. The grange of Castell Fflemish lay to the south-west of the abbey (Castell Fflemish earthwork SN 654 632). Maes Treflyn is the modern Maesllyn (SN 690 631), par. Caron Is-clawdd, cmt. Pennardd, and Llyn *Buden* the adjacent Llyn Maesllyn (SN 692 628). Llannerch y *Guinthwa* is probably Penllannerch (SN 698 627), par. Caron Uwch-clawdd (Wmffre, 'Language and History', II. ii. 615), just to the east of Llyn Maesllyn, rather than Garn Gron (SN 740 611), about 4 miles north-east of Tregaron (as suggested in *OP*, iii. 457; see also note to no. 76 below). The Camddwr whose source is at Blaencamddwr (SN 752 585), par. Caron Is-clawdd and which flows into the river Tywi is different from the Camddwr-fach and Camddwr-fawr, tributaries of the Teifi mentioned earlier in the charter's first perambulation. Llam yr Unben (lit., 'the hero's leap') has been identified with the crag of Craig Gwalch, part of the rocky ridge about 1 mile south-west of Nannerth-fawr (SN 947 716) above the lower course of Nant-y-sarn (*OP*, iii. 457–8). The places named within the bounds described in the first perambulation include the original site of the abbey at Ystrad-fflur (Henfynachlog, immediately south of Old Abbey Farm SN 718 646), Pont Rhydfendigaid (SN 730 665), Dol-fawr (SN 716 672), Llwyn-y-gog (SN 727 676) and Castell Fflemish (quite possibly Tŷ-hen, SN 662 634, rather than the earthwork about ½ mile to its south-west at SN 654 632). Tref-y-Gwyddel may be identifiable with Llwyngwyddel (SN 740 686), par. Gwnnws Uchaf, cmt. Mefenydd, though this is uncertain (Wmffre, 'Language and History', II. ii. 896–7).

The lands granted by the sons of Cadwgan include Esgairsaeson (SN 638 646), par. Blaenpennal, cmt. Pennardd, and half of Bronwennau (SN 550 624) and Tŷ-poeth (SN 537 629), both par. Llanbadarn Trefeglwys, cmt. Anhuniog. It has been argued that 'the dyke of the bondmen' (*fossam Bileyneyt*) was Ffosbleiddiaid (SN 687 670), and that the second element of the place-name has been re-analysed and *bileiniaid* (Mod. W.) replaced by *bleidd-iaid*, 'wolves' (Wmffre, 'Language and History', II. ii. 873–4). The boundaries listed include Aberarth (SN 479 637) and Aberaeron (SN 458 629). *Coredeu* has been taken as the plural form of the Welsh noun *cored*, 'weir'; it has been cited as the earliest example of the place-name Coredydd (SN 474 638), just to the south-west of Aberarth (ibid., 721).

For discussion of Rhys's styles, including the use of *Walliarum princeps* in the protocol of the present charter, see above, pp. 96–8. The introductory clause to the list of possessions in the disposition from *quascumque possessiones quecumque bona* to *exprimenda vocabulis propriis* largely consists of standard formulae in papal bulls of privilege, and is almost certainly derived from the bull issued in favour of Strata Florida by Alexander III, datable to 1165 × 30 August 1181 (see above, p. 99). No. 35 below shows that the Gwenllian who granted *Ardiscinkiwet* was Rhys's wife. The witness Gwgon *Stacca* is probably the same person as the Gwgon *Stake* who, with his sons, committed offences against the Church in Dyfed (including the seizure of 200 sheep from the cemetery of St Michael's church, Laugharne), according to Gerald of Wales in a letter complaining about the behaviour of Bishop Peter de Leia of St Davids (1176–98) (*Gir. Camb. Op.*, i. 314, 315 (*Symbolum electorum, ep.* xxxi)).

*29 Whitland Abbey

Confirmation of grants by John of Torrington, namely the land in which the abbey is situated, the land called Hendy-gwyn (Hentywin), Tresgrigh', Ysgrafell (Eskeyrevell'), Cefnfarchen (Keuenkenuargan), Ffynnonoer (Fonenonnayr), Cilgryman (Kylg(re)man'), Trefhowystell, Synod, Onnen (Omen'), Keredic', all the wood of Cardiff (Gardif'), the land of Bryn Alltudion (Brinnaltudyon), Kyldugeyn', and the land of Trefgrinn. Further confirmation of the land of Goscelin the knight, given by Hywel Sais. Grant and confirmation of other lands: the land of Ystlwyf (Oyst(er)layth'), *Llanfihangel Abercywyn* (Lanuiyhangell'), *Pen-ffos* (Penfos), *Cefnllengath* (Keuentlengath'), *Blaengwyddno* (Blanwytheno), *Llanfihangel-cilfargen* (Kylvargeyn'), *Pen-fai* (Penuey), *Rhyd-maen-gwyn* (Ridemangwyn'), *Cefn-y-drum [Cefn-llech-clawdd]* (Keuenerdrim'), *the share of the sons of Maredudd of Cilrhedyn* (Kylredin'), *namely Rhosllefrith [Pistyll-llefrith]* (Rosleuerich'), *Bronclyd* (Broncled'), *Nant Gynwrig* (Nant' Genewrich'), *Maenor Forion* (Maynoruoreon'), *Esgair-gair* (Eskerkayr'), *Maenor Grug-whyl* (Maynar' Cruchuyl'), *Rhuddlan Deifi* (Rudelan'), *Tir-newydd* (Dinenwyn'), *Crug-erydd* (Craic Cryr), Kumkeltlybroc', *Maescrugiau* (Cruggeggwallem'), *Capriscwm* (Capriscu(m)), *Darren-fawr* (Nantarran'), *(?)Fadfa* (Dadanethchorannimus), *Blaenbedw-fawr* (Bylandbedewe), *Blaensaith* (Blandseyth'), *Esgairsaith* (Eskyrseith') *and one carucate at Porth-bychan [Llanborth]* (Porthbegan').

[*c*.25 December 1189 × 1195]

Mention only, in a confirmation of King John dated at Worcester, 27 December 1214 (TNA: PRO, C 53/12, m. 3; pd., *Rot. Chart.*, 206a; *Mon. Ang.*, v. 591; Daniel-Tyssen, *Royal Charters*, 73–5 (and trans.); cd., *H*, no. 37). For the foundation and early history of the Cistercian abbey of Whitland (cmt. Amgoed, in the Anglo-Norman lordship of St Clears), whose original site appears to have been at Little Trefgarn, near Haverfordwest, see *HW* ii. 594; Cowley, *Monastic Order*, 22. It has been assumed here that the *carta sua* of Rhys in which he confirmed the grants of John of Torrington and Hywel Sais was the same as the *carta sua* in which Rhys granted and confirmed the additional lands listed; if two charters were meant, the second would probably have been referred to as *alia carta sua* (cf. *Ystrad Marchell Charters*, nos 8–10, 27–32). As Rhys's charter confirmed a grant by his son Hywel Sais, it was issued after Hywel was granted the castle, and thus lordship, of St Clears following the castle's capture by Rhys around Christmas 1189, and is unlikely to be later than Hywel's loss of the castle to William de Braose in 1195 (*AC*, 57, 60). This dating is also compatible with the attribution of several of the lands confirmed to grants by John of Torrington (d. 1203), who succeeded his brother Alan as lord of Great Torrington in Devon in 1185 and was keeper of the castles of Pembroke and Carmarthen at the beginning of John's reign; presumably John of Torrington acquired the lordship of St Clears at some point between the mid-1160s, when it was held by William fitz Hay, and the 1180s (see Sanders, *Baronies*, 48; Rowlands, 'Making of the march', 150, 224, n. 40; *Gir. Camb. Op.*, i. 28, 59). It may be significant in this connection that a William fitz Hay appears in 1166 as a tenant in Devon of John of Torrington's father William fitz Robert, lord of Great Torrington (*Red Book of the Exchequer*, ed. Hall, i. 256).

    For some of the lands named here see A. C. Evans's notes *apud* Daniel-Tyssen, *Royal Charters*, 73–5; Williams, *Atlas*, 66–8; Wmffre, 'Language and History', II. i. 125, 138, 316, 322, 324, 325, 331; iii. 1413. I am also greatly indebted to Terry James and the Carmarthenshire Antiquarian Society for supplying an extract from their place-names database. Beginning with John of Torrington's grants, Hendy-gwyn, 'the old white house', was probably situated at or near a house close to the river Taf formerly known as Whitland Farm, and thus about 1 mile to the south of the final site of the abbey (SN 208 181) which took its name (*OP*, iv. 380–1). Whether the abbey was first located at Hendy-gwyn after its move from Little Trefgarn is uncertain. Ysgrafell (SN 729 370), par. Cilycwm, cmt. Malláen. Cefnfarchen (SN 166 191), par. Llangeler, cmt. Emlyn Uwch Cuch. Ffynnonoer may be identifiable with the farm of that name (SN 238 420), par. Maenordeifi, cmt. Emlyn Is Cuch (cf. Charles, *Place-Names of Pembrokeshire*, i. 388), and thus about 1 mile south-west of Pen-fai (see below). Cilgryman (Cilgryman Fawr SN 234 252), par. Llanwinio, cmt. Peuliniog. Synod: land in the vicinity of Synod Inn (SN 404 544), about 4 miles south of New Quay (the name is also preserved in several farms, e.g. Synod Uchaf SN 399 538, Synod Isaf SN 393 545), par. Llannarth, cmt. Caerwedros. Onnen: possibly about 2 miles north-east of Synod in the vicinity of Esgaironnen Fawr (SN 418 568), par. Llannarth, or about 2½ miles north-west at Brynonnen (SN 373 572), par. Llanllwchaearn, cmt. Caerwedros. It is uncertain whether *Keredic'* is a separate place, or rather an abbreviation for Ceredigion; if the latter, the charter roll's reading *Omen' et Keredic'* is presumably an error for *Omen Keredic'* or *Omen in Keredic'*. The forest of Cardiff lay within the grange of Is Coed, which included the final site of the abbey (*OP*, iv. 369–70; Williams, *Atlas*, 66). The land of Goscelin the knight has not been identified.

The remaining lands listed appear to be fresh grants or confirmations by the Lord Rhys. Ystlwyf was a commote in Cantref Gwarthaf which included the parish of Llanfihangel Abercywyn (SN 303 133) (cf. *OP*, iv. 364). The other place-names identified were located in other commotes in Dyfed, Ystrad Tywi and Ceredigion. Pen-ffos, par. Llangeler (Pen-ffos-du SN 378 362), cmt. Emlyn Uwch Cuch. Llanfihangel-cilfargen (SN 568 244), par. Llangathen, cmt. Cetheiniog. Blaengwyddno (Upper Blaengwyddno, now The Grange, SN 149 123), par. Llanbedr Felffre (Lampeter Velfrey); Pen-fai (SN 252 425), par. Llandygwydd, cmt. Is Coed. Rhyd-maen-gwyn (SN 223 291), par. Llanfyrnach, cmt. Uwch Nyfer. Cefn-llech-clawdd (SN 363 392), par. Llangeler, cmt. Emlyn Uwch Cuch. Cilrhedyn (Cilrhedyn church SN 279 349), cmt. Emlyn Is Cuch. Pistyll-llefrith (SN 229 214), par. Llanboidy, cmt. Amgoed. Maenor Forion (SN 394 388), par. Llangeler. In par. Llanwenog, cmt. Gwynionydd: Maenor Grug-whyl (SN 486 424), Rhuddlan Deifi (SN 493 430) and Tir-newydd (SN 496 483). In par. Llandysiliogogo, cmt. Caerwedros: Crugerydd-isaf (SN 422 503), Maescrugiau (SN 368 524), Darren-fawr (SN 412 487), (?)Fadfa (SN 430 493) and Blaenbedw-fawr (SN 367 516). In par. Penbryn, cmt. Is Coed: Blaensaith (Blaensaith-uchaf at SN 279 497), the adjacent Esgairsaith and Llanborth (SN 296 521) (see also *OP*, iii. 441; note to no. 27 above).

Most of the lands apparently granted originally by Rhys, rather than by John of Torrington or Hywel Sais, lay outside the lordship of St Clears in Ceredigion, Emlyn and Ystlwyf. Since these territories had been held by Rhys since *c.*1165 it is possible that he first granted some or all of the lands to the abbey before his conquest of St Clears in 1189, and that these earlier grants were merely confirmed by the present charter (although some may of course have originally been granted by Anglo-Norman lords before *c.*1165). That Rhys's patronage of Whitland pre-dated 1189 is plausible, given that the earliest known abbots of the house, in the 1160s and early 1180s, were Welsh; that Rhys assumed the patronage of Whitland's daughter house Strata Florida in 1165; and that the Cadwaladr ap Rhys who was buried at Whitland in 1186 may have been a son of Rhys (*EGC*, 117–18 (no. 125); *HW*, ii. 596–7; *BT, Pen20Tr*, 72, 73; *BT, RBH*, 168, 170; Bartrum, 'Plant yr Arglwydd Rhys', 99).

*30 The abbot of Cîteaux
Letter, concerning the disgraceful character of William Wibert's life.

[1194 × 28 April 1197]

Mention only, in an account by Gerald of Wales of letters he sent to the abbot of Cîteaux in support of his complaints about William Wibert, abbot of the Cistercian abbey of Biddlesden (Bucks.) (*Gir. Camb. Op.*, i. 216 (*Symbolum electorum, ep.* iv). Gerald says that similar letters were also sent by the bishop of Llandaff, the abbot of Neath, the priors of Cardiff and Brecon and the dean of William de Braose. In 1193 Wibert, then a monk of Biddlesden who enjoyed the patronage of Queen Eleanor, had accompanied Gerald on three missions to Wales and allegedly spread malicious rumours about his companion which led to Gerald's loss of favour at court (ibid., 203–13 (*ep.* i)). This suggests that Gerald sent the letters no earlier than 1194, the year in which he appears to have departed from royal service – a conclusion supported by the reference to a letter from the bishop of Llandaff, as William of Saltmarsh died in 1191 and his successor Henry was not conse-crated until 12 December 1193 (cf. Richter, *Giraldus*, 84–7; Bartlett, *Gerald*, 58, n. 1; *Llandaff Episcopal Acta*, xiv–xv). However, the letters are possibly datable to *c.*1196, as in a letter sent in 1198 to Archbishop Hubert Walter of Canterbury referring to Wibert's deposition as abbot of Biddlesden in that year, Gerald states that he first met Wibert at Queen Eleanor's court during Richard I's captivity in Germany (ibid., 295 (*ep.* xxviii)), and his own letter to the abbot of Cîteaux claims that that meeting had occurred three years previously (ibid., 203 (*ep.* i)). Yet the letter of 1198 implies a date in 1194, for Gerald alleges that four years or more had elapsed since sending his letter of complaint against Wibert to the abbot of Cîteaux and that he had been temporarily reconciled with Wibert at Oxford in 1196 (ibid., 293–4 (*ep.* xxviii)). The dating limits proposed reflect this chronological uncertainty.

ANARAWD AB EINION AB ANARAWD
(*fl. c.*1163–*c.*1176)

*31 Commandery of Slebech
Grant of one carucate of land at Beggerden (Berngdona).

[Probably 1163 × 16 July 1198]

Mention only, in a confirmation of the possessions of the Hospitallers of Slebech Commandery issued by Peter, bishop of St Davids, 7 November 1176 × 16 July 1198 (*St Davids Episcopal Acta*, 71 (no. 46)). It is likely that this is the same Anarawd as that of no. 32 below, and that the grant was made after the death of his father Einion ab Anarawd in 1163 (*BT, Pen20Tr*, 62; *BT, RBH*, 142–3). Beggerden was situated in Narberth hundred, Pembs., between Minwear Brook, which runs through Conaga Dingle and joins the Eastern Cleddau at SN 029 131, and another tributary of the Eastern Cleddau less than ½ mile to its south (Charles, *Place-Names of Pembrokeshire*, ii. 527). According to a Latin schedule written *c.*1600 of grants to the Hospitallers of Slebech, Raymond fitz Martin granted one carucate, i.e. 100 acres at Beggerden (*Beuegerduna*) with all its appurtenances, in perpetual alms, with a seal (NLW, Slebech 247; cd., Charles, 'Records of Slebech', 193).

*32 Commandery of Slebech

Grant of his manor and township of Dolbrivaur *with all its appurtenances, in pure alms.*

[Probably 1163 × 16 July 1198]

Mention only, in a Latin schedule written *c.*1600 of grants to the Hospitallers of Slebech (NLW, Slebech 247; cd., Charles, 'Records of Slebech', 194; *H*, no. 39). R. Fenton added the present grant to that of no. 31 above in his version of Bishop Peter's confirmation (*St Davids Episcopal Acta*, 72; see also note to no. 64 below). *Hanarana filius Ermaun princeps et dominus* is clearly Anarawd ab Einion ab Anarawd rather than his grandfather Anarawd ap Gruffudd ap Rhys (d. 1143). *Dolbrivaur* has not been identified.

MAELGWN AP RHYS
(d. 20 November 1230 × 14 February 1231)

*33 Whitland Abbey

Grant of the land of Penllwynyrebol (Peynluin' et Evaul') *and* Kathanen.

[1190 × 27 December 1214]

Mention only, in a confirmation of King John dated at Worcester, 27 December 1214 (TNA: PRO, C 53/12, m. 3; pd., *Rot. Chart.*, 206a; *Mon. Ang.*, v. 591; Daniel-Tyssen, *Royal Charters*, 75 (and trans.); cd., *H*, no. 38). The grant is not included among the lands confirmed by the Lord Rhys (no. 29 above) and is therefore likely to be later than that confirmation. Penllwynyrebol is identifiable with Llwynyrebol (SN 132 261), par. Cilymaenllwyd, cmt. Amgoed, on the Carmarthenshire side of the Eastern Cleddau about 3 miles south-east of Maenclochog. *Kathanen* has not been identified.

*34 Cwm-hir Abbey

Grant of the land of Dyffryn Melindwr (Dyfryn Melynduuer).

[Probably summer 1197 × October 1208 or 1211 × early 1216;
possibly August 1222 × *c.*1230]

Mention only, in a letter patent of Edward II, dated at Westminster, 9 June 1318 (TNA: PRO, C 66/149, m. 5; trans. Rees, 'Account of Cwmhir abbey', 258; cd., *CPR 1317–21*, 163; *H*, no. 42). Dyffryn Melindwr (SN 656 801), cmt. Perfedd, Ceredigion is located inland from Aberystwyth, in the vicinity of Capel Bangor, and takes its name from Afon Melindwr, a tributary of the river Rheidol. Maelgwn presumably gained control of Perfedd after capturing his brother Gruffudd ap Rhys in 1197, but lost it after Llywelyn ap Iorwerth occupied the commote in 1208. Although Maelgwn recovered Aberystwyth and Perfedd in

1211, it passed to the sons of Gruffudd ap Rhys at Llywelyn's partition of Deheubarth at Aberdyfi early in 1216. Possibly Perfedd formed part of the lands of Rhys Ieuanc granted to Maelgwn by Llywelyn upon Rhys's death in August 1222.

35 Strata Florida Abbey

Confirmation, for the salvation of the souls of himself and of his father, mother, predecessors, successors and of all his friends and kin, and for prosperity in this life and for future reward, of all gifts which his father Rhys, the good prince and eminent founder of the abbey, granted it in lands, meadows, pastures, waters, fisheries and other appurtenances, in all their liberties, so that the monks may keep in perpetual alms, peacefully and honourably, undiminished and quit of all secular service and exaction, whatever possessions they now possess, or will possess in future, from princes or the faithful or by other just means. The names of these possessions are: Nannerth in its bounds, from Nant y Fleiddast to the Wye, from the Wye to Nant y Dernol and thence to its source; then across to the source of the Ystwyth, along the Ystwyth to the Taflogau, from the bottom of the Taflogau to its source; then across to the Marchnant and thence to the Meurig; thence to the Teifi; thence to the Camddwr-fach, along the Camddwr-fach to its source; thence along Pant Gwaun to the Camddwr-fawr, then by the Camddwr across to Hirfain Chadaythuy *to the Aeron towards the dyke between Trecoll and* Brynbyt, *along the dyke to its head; thence to the source of Nant y Gelli-hir, then directly to the stream 'between Buarthcaron and Dinas (?) Drygwyr; thence as that stream leads to the grange of Castell Fflemish; then from the grange from the other side of the stream across the hill as Pant Gwaun leads to the stream between Maes Glas and* Trebrith, *along the stream to the Teifi; thence to Maes Treflyn [Maesllyn], then directly to Llyn Maesllyn; thence to Nant Llyn; thence directly across to (?) Penllannerch; thence directly across the mountain to Celli Angharad, that mountain being the boundary; across to the source of the Camddwr [Blaencamddwr], along the Camddwr to the Tywi, thence up on both sides to the source; then directly from the source of the Tywi to the source of the Arban, along the Arban to the Claerwen; thence to the Elan; thence along the Elan to* Groen Guynnion; *thence up to Tal* Lluchint; *thence to the top of the ridge, along the ridge to the source of the Risca; thence across the mountain to Llam yr Unben where the boundaries of the aforesaid land of Nannerth intermix equally with the boundaries described. Maelgwn confirms and grants to the monks for ever whatever is contained within the bounds traced by the circuit. These are the names of the more distinguished places in those bounds: Moel* Gedyau, *Nant* Elmer, *Nant* Eyrin, *Nant* Morauc, Brithcum, Abercoyl, Aber Methen, Stratgenmurn, *Celli Camgoed, Prysgau Einion, Ystrad-fflur, Rhydfendigaid [Pont Rhydfendigaid], Dol-fawr, Llwyn-y-gog, Tref-y-Gwyddel, Ffynnonoer [Swydd-y-ffynnon], Celli Bryn Teifi, Esgair Berfedd, Castell Fflemish, Maes Glas. From the gift of the sons of Cadwgan and their heirs and of our lordship: Cefn-y-rhyd, Esgairsaeson, half of Bronwennau beyond Esgair to the Arth where the sons of Saesog have established their buildings, (?) Tŷ-poeth with its appendages and these are its bounds, described by his father Rhys with his nobles: from the mouth of the Meilyr up along the Arth to the dyke which begins at the spring of Bleiddudd, from the spring to the hollow, along the hollow to (?) Ffosbleiddaid [*fossam Bileynetd, *'the Dyke of the Bondmen'], along the dyke to the hollow of the Gwaun between Marchdy and Bryn Llyn Du, along the hollow to the dyke which is the boundary between Marchdy and the township called* Ardiscinkywet *which his father Rhys of pious memory granted with the consent of his wife and of Maelgwn's brothers;*

that dyke is the boundary to the sea, thence to Aberarth, the Arth to the mouth of the Meilyr and along the shore and sea from Aberarth to Aberaeron. He grants all fishing to the monastery for ever as well as one day and night each week from Maelgwn's own fishing. Confirmation of the pastures of Penweddig, as his father and brother Gruffudd gave them, so that no other monks may think that they have right there. Witnesses.

Strata Florida, 22 January 1198

B = TNA: PRO, C 66/153 (Pat. R. 14 Edward II, pt. 1), m. 5 (in an inspeximus, 10 November 1320).
C = TNA: PRO, C 53/123 (Ch. R. 10 Edward III), m. 6 (in an inspeximus of B, 2 October 1336).
D = TNA: PRO, C 66/308 (Pat. R. 4 Richard II, pt. 1), m. 13 (reciting an inspeximus of C by Edward the Black Prince 28 October 1369, 20 October 1380).
E = TNA: PRO, C 66/417 (Pat. R. 3 Henry VI, pt. 2), m. 5 (in an inspeximus of D, 8 July 1425).
F = TNA: PRO, C 66/605 (Pat. R. 23 Henry VII), m. 9 (in an inspeximus of E, 4 March 1508).
Pd. from D, Roberts, 'Documents and charters', 199–201 (trans. only); from an abbreviated text in BL, MS Harl. 6068 (s. xvi/xvii), Williams, *Cistercian Abbey of Strata Florida*, App., xiv.
Cd., *CPR 1317–21*, 527 (from B); *CChR 1327–41*, 382–3 (from C); *CPR 1377–81*, 551 (from D); *CPR 1422–9*, 294 (from E); *CPR 1494–1509*, 567 (from F); *H*, no. 22.

Universis sancte ecclesie filiis presentibus et futuris qui hanc cartam inspexerint Mailgun filius Resi princeps Swthwall(ie) salutem. Notum facimus universitati vestre nos pro salute anime nostre et patris et matris et antecessorum nostrorum et successorum et omnium amicorum et parentum, pro prosperitate vite presentis pariter et future mercedis remuner-atione concessisse et presenti carta nostra confirmasse Deo et Beate Marie et monachis de Stratflur Deo ibidem servientibus tam presentibus quam futuris imperpetuum omnes donationes quas pie memorie pater meus Resus bonus princeps eiusdem monasterii magnificus fundator predicto loco et monachis superioribus contulit in terris et pratis et pasturis, in aquis et moris, in bosco et plano, in mari et fluminibus et piscaturis et pisca-tionibus tam maris quam fluviorum, in omnibus libertatibus et consuetudinibus, bonis, possessionibus tam mobilibus quam immobilibus, prope et longe, in portubus et vicis, in viis et catellis, super terram et sub terra et in ceteris omnibus rebus quas habent in presenti et possident, vel deinceps Deo propitio sunt habituri largitione principum seu donatione quorumlibet fidelium seu quibuslibet aliis iustis modis ut habeant et possideant bene et in pace, libere et quiete, pacifice et honorifice absque omni servitio et seculari exactione, integre et absque omni diminutione, in puram et perpetuam elemosinam tam habita quam habenda, deinceps iustis modis et titulis quocumque tempore adquisita. In quibus hec propriis vocabulis indicamus: Nanneyrth cum terminis suis, id est Nant hi Bleidasti *hytt har* Gwy, Guy *hitt en* Hedernaul *hytt hi blain*, deinde in transversum usque *blain* Estuid, Estuid *eni hitt* usque Tauologeu, *gwailaut* Tauologeu *hytt hy blain*, deinde per rectum transversum usque ad Marchnant, Marchnant usque Meuric, Meuric usque Teyui, Teuy *hytt* Camdur Bechan, Camdur Bechan *en hy hytt hyt hy blain*, deinde sicut ducit Pant Guin, *en hy hytt hit en* Camdur Maur, postea per Camdur in transversum, *hytt aar* Hirwen Chadaythuy usque Ayron, Ayron sicut ducit usque fossam que est inter Tref Collh et Brynbyt, fossam *hytt hy blain*, *o hy blain hitt foss'* recte *hytt en phen* Nanet Herthelthli Hir, deinde recte *hiit aar nanit* inter Buhart' Caraun et Dinas Deretwir, deinde sicut amnis ille ducit usque ad grangiam que vocatur Castell Flemis, de grangia postea ex alia parte amnis trans collem sicut ducit Pant Gwyn *hiit he nant* inter Mahys Glaas et Trebrith, *hyd e nant eni hytt hytt aar* Theyui,

Theyui *eni hytt hytt* Mays Tref Linn, Mays Tref Lin recte *hytt in* Llinbuthen, Lynnbuthen *hytt en* Nantlin, Nanthlyn recte per transversum usque Hlannerch Chundena, *o* Lannerch Chundena per transversum montis *hytt aar* Ghelli Angaraut, mons ille postea terminus est, recte in transversum usque *blain* Camdur, Camdur sicut ducit usque Thewy, Thewy deinde sursum ex utraque parte *hytt hi blain*, recte postea *o blain* Tewy *hytt en blain* Arban, Arban *en hy hytt* usque Clarwen, Clarwen usque Helan, Helan exinde usque Groen Guynnion, *hy* Groen recte sursum *hy* Tahlluchint, *o* Talluchint *hyt cheuen ir oscher ar escheeyr aar hy hytt usque blain* Riscant, *o blain* Riscant per transversum montis usque Lhaam her Vnpenn, ubi fines prenominate terre que appellatur Nanneyrth istis terminis quos duximus pariter inter-miscentur. Set et quicquid continetur infra prescriptos terminos per circuitum, in campo et silva, in aquis et pratis et pascuis, in culto et inculto, ego Mailgun prefatis monachis confirmo et concedo habenda imperpetuum. Et hec nomina locorum in eisdem terminis excellentiorum: Moyl Gedyau, Naant Eylmer, Naant Eyrin, Naant Morauc, Brithcum, Abercoyl, Aber Methen, St(ra)tgenmurn, Kellhi Cham Choyt, Prischeu Enniaun, St(ra)tflur, Bur Wendigeyit, Dool Maur, Hluin Gog, Threef he Guidel, Fennanoir, Kelheu Brinn Deuy, Escheir Perueth, Chastell Fleymis, Mays Glaas. Ex donatione vero filiorum Cadugaun et eorum heredum et nostri dominii: Cheuen he Reet, Escheyr Sayson, dimidia vero pars Branwenneu preter Escheer *hi tu aar* Arth ubi filii Seisauc edificia sua fundaver-unt, Tref Boyth cum appendiciis suis. Et hi sunt termini eiusdem, quos descripsit Resus pater meus cum optimatibus suis: *o* Aber Meiller sursum *ar hi hitt*, Arth usque fossam que manat de fonte Bleydud, *o fennaun hir pant*, *pant eni hytt* usque fossam Bileynetd, *ef foss' ar hi hittd* usque Pant Gweun inter Marchdi et Brin Hlenlde *hlie pant ar hi hyttd'* usque fossam que est terminus inter Merchdi et villam que vocatur Ardiscinkywet quam dedit pater meus pie memorie Resus predictis monachis consilio coniugis sue et filiorum fratrum meorum. Fossa vero prefata in termino est usque ad mare, mare vero usque ad hostium Arth, Arth *hitt en* Haber Meiller, et in littore et in mari ab ostio Arth usque ad hostium Ayron. Piscaturas et omnes piscationes sepedicto monasterio offerimus imperpetuum, et etiam de propria mea piscatura et piscaria unum diem et unam noctem in qualibet septimana. Confirmo etiam sepedictis monachis de St(ra)tflur pasturas de Penwedic sicut pater meus et frater Griffinus eas illis dederunt, ut nulli alii monachi ibidem se ius habere putent. Hiis testibus: Reso filio Griffini qui etiam hanc confirmationem nostram sua donatione roboravit, et Reso filio Gervasii, Reso filio Retherch, Griffri et Griffino filiis Cadugan, Henkeuereth, Griffri[a] ab Lauden, Ioruerth filio Kediuor, Adam parvuo, Vrien filio Kediuor, Reso filio Lauden. De religiosis: Philipp(o) abbate de St(rat)marchel, David abbate de Lhalel', *tait* Seisill et *teit* Ithel, Aniano suppriore, Philipp(o) monacho, Godefrido de M(ar)gan. Dat' xi kalendas februarii in domo de St(ra)tflur anno m° c° xc^{mo} viii° ab incarnatione domini.

[a] Griffini B *(cf. no. 28 above)*.

The boundary clauses of this charter closely resemble those of Rhys ap Gruffudd's charter of 1184 for Strata Florida which it confirms (no. 28 above). The only new grant is that of the pastures of Penweddig, the cantref in northern Ceredigion comprising the commotes of Genau'r-glyn, Perfedd and Creuddyn. The first witness was Rhys Ieuanc (d. 1222), son of Maelgwn's half-brother Gruffudd ap Rhys (d. 1201). Maelgwn had captured Gruffudd following their father's death in late April 1197, resulting in Gruffudd's imprisonment by

Maelgwn's ally Gwenwynwyn of Powys, who subsequently handed him over to the English. Gruffudd was still in prison at Corfe castle when the present charter was issued, although he was released in July 1198 and proceeded to recover much of Ceredigion from Maelgwn (*BT, Pen20Tr*, 78–80; *BT, RBH*, 178–83; *HW*, ii. 584–6).

*36 Strata Florida Abbey

Grant of one or more of the following: Marchdy Mawr and Marchdy Bychan, Pencoed [-uchaf], Tynrhos (Rossan) *and Esgair* Mayntemull*, Rhiwonnen* (Riu Annum)*, Blaen-pistyll and Celli-gwenyn.*

[Probably 22 January × 14 December 1198]

Mention only, in a charter of Rhys Gryg dated at Strata Florida, 14 December 1198 (no. 50 below). These grants are different from, and probably later than, those confirmed by Maelgwn in no. 35 above. Since the confirmation of the grants in no. 50 refers to charters, in the plural, it attests to at least two missing acts of Maelgwn. At least four of the places granted were located in cmt. Mebwynion: Pencoed-uchaf (SN 580 524) and Tynrhos (SN 578 533), both par. Llangybi; Rhiwonnen (SN 570 546), par. Ystrad; Celli-gwenyn (SN 571 524), par. Silian (Wmffre, 'Language and History', II. i. 452, 478, 492, 493). For Marchdy Mawr and Marchdy Bychan compare nos 28 and 50; they are presumably the same as Dau Farchdy in no. 55.

*37 Strata Florida Abbey
See no. 36 above.

*38 Strata Florida Abbey
Grant of Ffynnon Mebwyn.

[22 January 1198 × 1202]

Mention only, in a charter of Rhys Ieuanc ap Gruffudd ap Rhys dated 1202 (no. 55 below). The place is included neither among the grants of Maelgwn referred to in Rhys Gryg's charter of 14 December 1198 nor in Maelgwn's charter of 22 January 1198 (nos 35–6 above); it is also listed in the charter for Strata Florida issued by Maelgwn's son Maelgwn Fychan (no. 63 below). Ffynnon Mebwyn (SN 544 512): cmt. Mebwynion, Ceredigion (*OP*, iv. 499; Wmffre, 'Language and History', II. i. 426).

*39 Strata Florida Abbey
Grant of Morfa-bychan.

[22 January 1198 × 1202]

Mention only, in a charter of Rhys Ieuanc ap Gruffudd ap Rhys dated 1202 (no. 55 below). See note to no. 38 above. The place is also listed in the charter for Strata Florida issued by Maelgwn's son Maelgwn Fychan (no. 63 below). The grange of Morfa-bychan was located in par. Llanllwchaearn, cmt. Caerwedros, Ceredigion (Morfa-bychan SN 565 771) (Williams, *Atlas*, 57; Wmffre, 'Language and History', II. ii. 818).

*40 Strata Florida Abbey
Grant of (?) Tre'r-bryn (Treff Bryn).

[22 January 1198 × 1202]

Mention only, in a charter of Rhys Ieuanc ap Gruffudd ap Rhys dated 1202 (no. 55 below). See note to no. 38 above.

*41 King John
Grant of the castle of Cardigan and the adjacent commote of Is Hirwern.
    [*c*.11 December 1199 × *c*.22 July 1200; probably *c*.11 December 1199 × 11 April 1200]

Mention only, in a charter of King John granting to Maelgwn the four cantrefs of Ceredigion, apart from these lands, dated at Worcester, 11 April 1200 (*Rot. Chart.*, 44a; cd., *H*, no. 40). In a charter dated at Poitiers, 11 December 1199, John stated that Maelgwn had returned and quitclaimed to him the castle of Cardigan and the adjoining commote; in return, Maelgwn was granted the four cantrefs of Ceredigion as well as Cilgerran and Emlyn (*Rot. Chart.*, 63a–b). To judge by John's charter of 11 April 1200, the transaction appears to have been completed by that date, although the Peniarth 20 version of *Brut y Tywysogyon* and the *Cronica de Wallia* state that Maelgwn sold Cardigan to John in 1200 'about the feast of Mary Magdalene' (22 July) (*BT, Pen20Tr*, 80–1; *CW*, 32); by contrast, the other Welsh chronicles place the event in 1200, with no further indication of date (*BT, RBH*, 182–3; *BS*, 196–7; *AC*, 62 and n. 4). None of these record and narrative sources explicitly states that Maelgwn's surrender was in written form. Is Hirwern was not in fact a commote but rather the half of the commote of Is Coed located west of the river Hirwern (*HW*, ii. 618 and n. 31).

*42 Cathedral chapter of St Davids
Letter from Maelgwn and Rhys ap Rhys (Rhys Gryg), urging the chapter to stand firmly with Archdeacon Gerald for the dignity of St David, or else they and all the worthy men of their land would be the chapter's chief enemies for ever.

[Shortly before 20 January 1202]

Mention only, in Gerald of Wales's *De jure et statu Menevensis ecclesie* (*c*.1218) (*Gir. Camb. Op.*, iii. 197; cd., *Episc. Acts*, i. 318 (D. 341); *H*, no. 314). Gerald refers to the support he received from Maelgwn and Rhys, through both messengers and letters, at a meeting of the chapter held on 20 January 1202 to consider his bid to secure recognition as bishop-elect of St Davids as well as of the right of St Davids to metropolitan status. A letter of support was also allegedly received from Llywelyn ap Iorwerth (no. 222 below).

43 Agreement with Iorwerth, bishop of St Davids

Thomas, Albinus and Elias, respectively dean, chancellor and treasurer of Hereford cathedral, judges delegate, announce that the dispute between Iorwerth, bishop of St Davids and Maelgwn concerning Llandovery, Cenarth Mawr and other lands in the bishop's statement of claim has been settled as follows. Maelgwn and his son and heir Maelgwn [Fychan] have acknowledged the bishop's right to all the land of Llandovery with its appurtenances and the bishop, with Maelgwn's consent, is to receive the homage of Maelgwn Fychan for that land, in return for the service of providing safe conduct for the bishop whenever he travels through that land and a procuration for the bishop in the castle of Llandovery at least once a year, the men of that tenement will serve in the bishop's army like other men of St David. Maelgwn and Maelgwn Fychan restored all of Cenarth Mawr, with its mill, fish-trap and other appurtenances to the bishop, who has granted to Maelgwn Fychan for his lifetime half of the mill and of the fish-trap, and the service of the sons of Ivon *and their men from the land of Tal-y-bryn [Dol-y-bryn], so that all these grants will be restored to the bishop after Maelgwn Fychan's death without dispute. Maelgwn and Maelgwn Fychan likewise restored all the other lands named in the bishop's statement of claim, namely Maenordeifi, (?)Llannerch Aeron* (Lanarthayron), *Gartheli,* Merthirgci'onant, *Pen-boyr, Cenarth Bychan [Cilgerran], Clydai,* Lansuluet, Lanechren *in Gwynionydd, (?)Abergwaun [Fishguard]* (Aberguemi), *Trewyddel [Moylgrove], Eglwys Wythwr [Monington] and the whole commote of* Est(r)iat *[(?)Ystlwyf] apart from the lands the bishop himself holds there. Maelgwn and Maelgwn Fychan recognized the right of the bishop and church of St Davids in all these lands according to the bounds assigned in the* graphium *of St David, and Maelgwn Fychan received the restored lands of the bishop from the bishop for his lifetime in return for an annual render of one sparrowhawk at St David's township of Cenarth Mawr on 1 August. Sealing clause; witnesses.*

1222

B = BL, Harl. MS 6280, fos 39v–40v (in an inspeximus of Bishop Anselm of St Davids dated 10 June 1239). s. xvi[1].
Pd. from B, *St Davids Episcopal Acta*, 122–3 (no. 107).
Cd., *Episc. Acts*, i. 332–4 (D. 455); *H*, no. 296.

Omnibus Cristi fidelibus ad quos presens scriptum pervenerit [fo. 40r] Thom(as) decanus, A. cancellarius, E.[a] thesaurarius Hereford' salutem in domino. Ad vestram volumus notitiam devenire quod lis mota inter Gervasiu(m) dominum Men' ex una parte et Mailg' filium Resi ex altera coram nobis a domino papa iudicibus delegatis super Lanandebery et Kenarthvaor et terris aliis per compositionem quievit, cuius forma hec est. Sciant presentes et futuri quod cum Gervasius Menev' episcopus nobilem virum dominum Mailg' filium Resi coram Th(oma) decano, A. cancellario et E. thesaurario Hereford' iudicibus a domino papa delegatis traxisset in causam nomine ecclesie sue petens ab ipso Lanamdevery cum pertinentiis suis et Kenarth Vaor cum pertinentiis suis et alias terras in editione[b] episcopi coram iudicibus proposita nominatas tandem lis inter ipsos mota tali fine conquievit, videlicet quod dictus Mailg' et Mailg' filius suus et heres eius recognoverunt ius ecclesie Menev' et episcopi in tota terra de Lanamdeveri cum pertinentiis et dictus episcopus de voluntate et consensu Mailg' maioris recepit[c] homagium predicti Mailg' iunioris de terra illa tenenda de episcopo Men' et de sua ecclesia per tale servitium, scilicet quotiens episcopus Men' per partes illas transitum fecerit dictus Mailg' si voluerit episcopus salvum conductum illi prestabit in eundo et redeundo et eidem episcopo faciet procurationem suam in castello de Lanamzeuery sicut in suo adminus semel in anno et homines de tenemento illo ad summonitionem episcopi ibunt in exercitum suum sicut alii homines Sancti David. Terram vero de Kennarth Vaor totam integre cum molendino et gurgitio et aliis pertinentiis reddiderunt prefati Mailg' maior et Mailg' iunior predicto [episcopo]ᵈ ut ad ecclesiam Men' pleno iure pertinentem et idem episcopus de voluntate Mailg' maioris concessit Mailg' iunioriᵉ ad vitam suam medietatem de molendino et de gurgitio et servitium filiorum Ivon et suorum de terra de Talebrin, ita quod post vitam ipsius redeant ille medietates molendini et gurgitii et totum servitium de Talebrin ad manus episcopi sine qualibet reclamatione et impedimento integre, quiete et solute. De terris aliis in predicta editione nominatis, scilicet Maynor Teiui, Lanarthayron, Garehely, Merthirgci'onant, Penbeyr, Kenartvech(a)n, Cledey, Lansuluet, Lanechren in Guenouit, Aberguemi, Trefgoithel, Eglois Goithir et toto [fo. 40v] commod' de Est(r)iat preter terras quas ipse episcopus tenet in Est(r)iat: in omnibus hiis terris cum earum pertinentiis secundum divisas in graphio Sancti David assignatas similiter recognoverunt sepedicti Mailg' maior et Mailg' iunior ius episcopi et ecclesie Menev' et easdem episcopi episcopo et ecclesie Menev' restitutas per manum episcopi recepit Mailg' iunior de consensu patris sui ad totam vitam suam tenendas de episcopo Menev', reddendo inde annuatim episcopo unum espervarium in villa Sancti David de Kenarth Vaor ad festum Sancti Petri ad vincula. Ut igitur compositio ista perpetuum stabilitatis robur optineat presenti scripto cyrographato sigillis partium mutuo appensis est confirmata. Actum anno gratie millesimo cc° xx° secundo. Hiis testibus: de Alba Landa et de Thalelech abbatibus, I. priore de Brechon', H. archidiacono Men', magistro W. de Capella, magistro Mathia canonico Menev', Ph(ilipp)o de Lanuays, A. filio Ithayl, magistro Thoma Briton, Rog(er)o de Burth, Walt(er)o de Brech' clerico, Aaron filio Resi, Lewlino filio Cradauc filii Eniau(n), Vossalin filio Gug', Owein filio Eniaun, Will(elm)o Coch' et multis aliis.

ᵃ Et. B. | ᵇ edificatione B. | ᶜ recepet B. | ᵈ *omitted* B. | ᵉ *corrected from* iunior B.

For a similar agreement in 1222 between Bishop Iorwerth and Maelgwn's brother Rhys Gryg see no. 52 below; fuller discussion of both documents is provided in Pryce, 'Dynasty of Deheubarth'. The identification of the commote of *Est(r)iat* is uncertain. Barrow tentatively suggests Ystlwyf (*St Davids Episcopal Acta*, 122). Although the usual form for this commote in Latin texts is *Oysterlath* or variants thereof, this identification may well be correct, as Ystlwyf lay in Cantref Gwarthaf, which formed part of Maelgwn's share in Llywelyn ap Iorwerth's partition of Deheubarth at Aberdyfi in 1216. Moreover, according to Gerald of Wales in his *De jure et statu Menevensis ecclesie* (*c.*1218), St Davids had lost Ystlwyf (*Oisterlaf*) during the pontificate of Bishop David fitz Gerald (1148–76), presumably as the result of the Lord Rhys's conquest of the commote, confirmed by Henry II in 1171 (*Gir. Camb. Op.*, iii. 155; see also note to no. 46 below). The same work also asserts that Cenarth Mawr (the original name of Cenarth) had been alienated from the church by Bishop Wilfrid (1085–1115) after the death of Rhys ap Tewdwr in 1093 (ibid., 152). Gerald had already blamed Bishop Peter de Leia (1176–98) for failing to recover these losses in a letter of complaint about the bishop to the chapter of St Davids (ibid., i. 309 (*Symbolum electorum, ep.* xxxi)).

Apart from Llandovery in Cantref Bychan and, quite possibly, Ystlwyf, the identifiable places named in the agreement were located in the cantrefs of Emlyn and Cemais in Dyfed and in Caerwedros, Mebwynion and Gwynionydd, commotes in Ceredigion Is Aeron. Dol-y-bryn was a township pertaining to Cenarth (SN 268 416), cmt. Emlyn Uwch Cuch. Maenordeifi (Maenordeifi church SN 228 432; Vaynor SN 234 429), cmt. Emlyn Is Cuch. Llannerch Aeron (Allt Llannerch Aeron in vicinity of SN 485 595) and Gartheli (SN 585 565), cmt. Mebwynion. (I am grateful to Gerald Morgan for suggesting that *Lanarthayron* probably represents Llannerch Aeron rather than Llannarth (SN 423 578), cmt. Caerwedros, as the latter is some distance from the Aeron.) Pen-boyr (SN 358 363), par. Llangeler, cmt. Emlyn Uwch Cuch. Cilgerran (SN 191 431), cmt. Emlyn Is Cuch. Clydai (SN 251 355), cmt. Emlyn Is Cuch. Moylgrove (SN 118 447) and Monington (SN 135 438), cmt. Is Nyfer, Cemais. *Aberguemi* may well be a corrupt reading of *Abergweun*, i.e. Fishguard (Abergwaun), cmt. Uwch Nyfer, Cemais, a possession of St Davids alienated during the pontificate of Bishop Bernard (1115–48) according to Gerald of Wales (*Gir. Camb. Op.*, iii. 154). For the use of the Welsh form of the place-name in another source composed at St Davids in the thirteenth century see *AC*, 67 (*Fissegard, id est, Abergweun*: C text, *s.a.* 1210).

The *graphium* of St Davids was a book recording the possessions of the church (Richter, 'New edition', 248; see also Davies, 'Charter-writing', 103–4 and no. 480 below).

*44 Letter patent concerning Henry III

[Text presumably as no. 19 above.]

[Montgomery, 8 October 1223]

Mention only, in a note on the patent roll after the text of no. 19 above, issued by Maredudd ap Rhobert of Cedewain, naming Maelgwn ap Rhys among those that *Eodem modo fecerunt cartas suas* (*PR 1216–25*, 411; cd. *H*, no. 315).

GRUFFUDD AP RHYS
(d. 25 July 1201)

*45 Strata Florida Abbey

Grant of Ystrad-ffin and y Groen Gwennon.

[Probably 1184 × 25 July 1201]

Mention only, in a charter of his son Rhys Ieuanc (no. 55 below). The charter was probably issued after the Lord Rhys's charter for Strata Florida in 1184 (no. 28 above), to which Gruffudd gave his assent, as that charter does not include Ystrad-ffin among the lands granted. Ystrad-ffin (SN 788 466) may have formed the nucleus of the abbey's Nant-bau grange in the vicinity of Llanfair-ar-y-bryn, cmt. Hirfryn, Cantref Bychan (Williams, *Atlas*, 58; see also *OP*, iv. 385–6, 499–500).

HYWEL SAIS AP RHYS
(d. 1204)

46 The church of Llanfihangel Abercywyn and its chaplain

Notification that in Hywel's presence Hywel son of Iduardus, with the consent of his heirs, has granted in perpetual alms, for the souls of himself, his parents and his sons, 24 acres of arable from the land close to the church on the east and west sides and 5 acres from the meadows close to the church on the south and west sides. Hywel ap Rhys confirms this gift with his seal at the grantor's request. Witnesses.

[7 November 1176 × 16 July 1198; possibly no later than 1195]

> B = TNA: PRO, C 66/234 (Pat. R. 25 Edward III), m. 12 (in an inspeximus of King Edward III, 5 August 1351).
> Cd., *CPR 1350–4*, 126–7; *Episc. Acts*, i. 299 (D. 272); *H*, no. 21.

Omnibus ad quos presens scriptum pervenerit H. filius Resi Suthwallie principis salutem. Noverit universitas vestra quod constitutus in presentia nostra Howelus filius Iduardi assensu et consensu heredum suorum dedit et concessit pro anima sua et pro animabus parentum et filium suorum ecclesie Sancti Michael(is) de Ab(er)cownen et capellano ibidem ministraturo viginti quatuor accras terre arabilis de terra proxima eidem ecclesie ex orientali et occidentali parte et quinque accras de pratis proximis dicte ecclesie ex australi et occidentali parte in puram et perpetuam elemosinam. Hanc vero donationem gratam et acceptam habentes nos eandem caritatis intuitu ad petitionem dicti H. filii Iduardi sigilli nostri munimine confirmamus. Hiis testibus: domino P. Men(evensi) episcopo, Richero archidiacono de K(e)m(er)d', Philippo filio Resi, Gugaun' Stuke, Iohann(e) filio Guriat, Ioh(ann)e et Thoma capellanis, Liweli(n), Martino, Gregorio clericis et multis aliis.

The first witness, Peter de Leia, bishop of St Davids, was consecrated on 7 November 1176 and died on 16 July 1198 (*St Davids Episcopal Acta*, 7–8). Llanfihangel Abercywyn (SN 303 133) lay in the commote of Ystlwyf, one of the conquests confirmed to Rhys by Henry II in September 1171; Hywel Sais was shortly afterwards released to his father by the king, who had held him as a hostage (*BT, Pen20Tr*, 66–7; *BT, RBH*, 154–7; see also note to no. 43 above). It is unknown when Hywel exercised lordship in Ystlwyf, although he was given the neighbouring lordship of St Clears after its conquest by Rhys ap Gruffudd in late December 1189. Llanfihangel Abercywyn appears among the grants which Rhys ap Gruffudd confirmed to Whitland Abbey in a lost charter datable to between about Christmas 1189 and 1195, although it is uncertain whether the church was originally granted then or at an earlier date (see no. 29 above). As the present charter makes no reference to Whitland, it may have been issued before patronage of the church was granted to the abbey and thus no later than 1195.

*47 Whitland Abbey

Grant of the land of Goscelin the knight (miles).

[*c.*25 December 1189 × 1195]

Mention only, in a lost confirmation of the Lord Rhys datable to *c.*Christmas 1189 × 1195 (no. 29 above).

RHYS GRYG AP RHYS
(d. 1233)

*48 Strata Florida Abbey
Confirmation of all gifts by his father.

[1184 × 14 December 1198]

Mention only, in a charter of Rhys Gryg for Strata Florida dated 14 December 1198 (no. 50 below). The charter is unlikely to be earlier than 1184, when Rhys was named as one of the sons of Rhys ap Gruffudd who confirmed the latter's grants to Strata Florida in that year (no. 28 above), although it is unknown whether he issued a separate charter on that occasion.

*49 Talley Abbey
Confirmation of all the lands given by Gwrgenau and Rhys sons of Maredudd (Gurgeneu et Rys filiorum Morydyk) *and by their sons Dafydd* (Dauit)*, Isrl', P(ri)srl'* (sic)*, Meurig* (Meuryt)*, Morgan and Morfran* (Morwran)*, as contained in these bounds: from the heap of stones which is the boundary between the aforesaid donors and the sons of Heilin* (Heylyn) *next to the stream of Nawmor* (Nan Mhaur) *across to the edge of Moelfre* (Moylwre)*, thence across to the ford of Caregog* (Carregauc) *in Nant Gwen* (rivulum Guen)*, thence along the Gwen* (Guen) *to its source, thence across to Cwmbyr* (Cumbyr)*, and along that to the Crwys* (Croys)*, and along that stream to its source, thence along the valley to the source of the Pib* (blayn Pyb)*, and along that stream to Rhydforynion* (Rytmorynnion)*, thence along the Marlais* (Marleys) *to another Marlais* (Marleys)*, and along the latter Marlais* (Marleys) *towards its source to the mouth of Nant-y-fedwen* (Nantywetwen)*, and along that stream to its source, and thence across to the Blodeuen* (Bloteneu)*.*

[28 April 1197 × 1233]

Mention only, in an inspeximus of Edward II, dated at Westminster, 24 March 1324 (TNA: PRO, C 66/160, m. 21; pd., *Mon. Ang.*, iv. 162–3; Daniel-Tyssen, *Royal Charters*, 65; Long Price, 'Talley Abbey', 173–4 (trans. only); Owen, 'Contribution to the history', 42–3; cd., *H*, no. 31). Since the inspeximus refers to *Resus Resi filius principis Sudwallie*, the donor must be Rhys Gryg rather than Rhys Fychan ap Rhys Mechyll as assumed in *H*, no. 31. The confirmation was probably issued after the death of Rhys Gryg's father, the Lord Rhys; Rhys Gryg was confirmed in possession of all Cantref Mawr except Malláen by Llywelyn ap Iorwerth in 1216 (*BT, Pen20Tr*, 92; *BT, RBH*, 206–7; see also Smith, '"Cronica de Wallia"', 262–5). The lands granted formed the abbey's grange of Gwyddgrug, to the north-west of Brechfa (SN 525 303), cmt. Mabudrud, Cantref Mawr (Long Price, 'Talley Abbey', 174, n. 1; see also Jones, 'Boundaries', 525, and Richards, 'Carmarthenshire possessions', 118–19, which includes a map).

50 Strata Florida Abbey

Grant in perpetual alms, for the souls of himself and his father, mother, predecessors and successors, free of all secular and ecclesiastical exaction of those lands as described more fully in the charters of his brother Maelgwn, namely Marchdy Mawr and Marchdy Bychan, Pencoed[-uchaf], Tynrhos (Rossan) *and Esgair* Mayntemull, *Rhiwonnen* (Riu Annum)*, Blaen-pistyll and Celli-gwenyn. Rhys gives these with all their liberties as Maelgwn's charters attest. Gift of his body for burial wherever he happens to die. Grant of all gifts of his father as in Rhys's other charter. Witnesses.*

Chapter-house of Strata Florida, 14 December 1198

B = TNA: PRO, C 66/153 (Pat. R.14 Edward II, pt. 1), m. 6 (in an inspeximus, 10 November 1320).
C = TNA: PRO, C 53/123 (Ch. R. 10 Edward III), m. 6 (in an inspeximus of B, 2 October 1336).
D = TNA: PRO, C 66/308 (Pat. R. 4 Richard II, pt. 1), m. 13 (reciting an inspeximus of C by Edward the Black Prince 28 October 1369, 20 October 1380).
E = TNA: PRO, C 66/417 (Pat. R. 3 Henry VI, pt. 2), m. 5 (in an inspeximus of D, 8 July 1425).
F = TNA: PRO, C 66/605 (Pat. R. 23 Henry VII), mm. 9–10 (in an inspeximus of E, 4 March 1508).
Pd. from C, *CChR 1327–41*, 383; from D, Roberts, 'Documents and charters', 201–2 (trans. only)).
Cd., *CChR 1317–21*, 527 (from B); *CPR 1377–81*, 551 (from D); *CPR 1422–9*, 294 (from E); *CPR 1494–1509*, 567 (from F); *H*, no. 23.

Universis sancte ecclesie filiis qui[a] presentem cartam inspexerint Resus filius Resi salutem. Notum facimus universitati vestre me dedisse et concessisse et presenti carta mea confirmasse pro salute anime mee et patris mei et matris et antecessorum et successorum meorum Deo et Beate Marie et monachis de St(ra)tflur in perpetuam et puram elemosinam liberam et quietam ab omni servitio et tam seculari quam ecclesiastica exactione has terras cum terminis suis et pertinentiis sicut plenius diffinite et descripte sunt in cartis Mailgonis fratris mei qui eas prius dedit, videlicet Marchdi Maur et Marchdi Bichan in terminis suis, Penncoyth, Rossan et Escheyr Mayntemull *har hi hit* et Riu Annu(m) cum finibus suis ac terminis et Blain Pistill in suis terminis et Kelly Gwenyn in suis terminis et pertinentiis. Has terras dedi ego Resus predictis monachis imperpetuum in bosco et plano, in pratis et pasturis, in aquis et moris, in piscaturis et piscationibus, in terra et subtus terra, in omnibus libertatibus et consuetudinibus per omnia et in omnibus sicut carte Mailgonis fratris mei testantur et describunt. Et insuper sancto monasterio de St(ra)tflur dedi corpus meum in fine sepeliendum ubicumque me et qualicumque morte contigerit occumbere. Et etiam omnes donationes quas pie memorie pater meus eidem monasterio dederat concessi universaliter sicut in alia carta mea plenius habetur. Hanc donationem feci monachis et monasterio de St(ra)tflur anno ab incarnatione domini m° c° nonagesimo octavo nonodecimo kalendas ianuarii in capitulo coram conventu. Testibus: Aniano suppriore, Ithayl et Elidir monachis. Et de secularibus testibus: Owino Barrath filio Howely, Elydir filio Owini, Gwyaun Seis et Maredut fratre eius, Kadugaun filio Owini Waby, Griffud filio Iorwerth Wyneu et multis aliis.

[a] in B.

For the place-names in this charter see no. 36 above.

*51 Strata Florida Abbey

Grant of Coed Mawr.

[14 December 1198 × 1202]

Mention only, in a charter of Rhys Ieuanc ap Gruffudd ap Rhys dated 1202 (no. 55 below). The grant was probably later than Rhys Gryg's charter of 14 December 1198, as this does not include Coed Mawr. The place has been identified as Coed Mawr (Coedmawr-uchaf SN 630 578) in the township of Gwynfil, cmt. Pennardd, Ceredigion (*OP*, iv. 501).

52 Agreement with Iorwerth, bishop of St Davids

*Agreement before Dean Thomas, Albinus the chancellor and T. (*recte *E[lias]), treasurer of Hereford, judges delegate, when Iorwerth claimed from Rhys in the name of his church the whole commote of Llandeilo Fawr [Maenordeilo] with its appurtenances, namely the lands between the Dulais* Luswlith *and the stream* Hylig, *the* maenor *of Llanddarog, the township of Llangynnwr and the lands of Abergwili which Gwgan Sais and Cedifor ab Ynyr and other nobles had held unjustly, namely that Rhys and his son Maredudd and heirs recognized the right of the church and bishop of St Davids in those lands with their appurtenances. Rhys has restored the lands below [i.e. west of] the Dulais to the bishop and his church up to the border of the commote of Cetheiniog except for the lands of Cerrig Gwrgenau, the land of Owain ap Cadwgan, the land of the smiths of the court of Dinefwr and the lands of the canons of Talley, which Rhys or his men have given to the church of Llandeilo Fawr or the house of Talley in perpetual alms with the consent of the bishop and chapter of St Davids. Rhys and his sons have restored to the bishop and his church all the lands of Abergwili which Cedifor ab Ynyr and Gwgan Sais and other nobles had detained unjustly. Rhys and his sons are obliged to warrant the lands of Abergwili with a mill to St Davids against Gwgan Sais and Cedifor ab Ynyr and others and against all men of the (?) Welshry. Rhys and his sons have done homage for all the other aforesaid lands to the bishop and sworn on relics that they will faithfully support him and his church, men, lands and possessions and provide an annual render of a goshawk on the feast of St John the Baptist [29 August]. Rhys and his sons are also obliged to make the men of the aforesaid tenements come to the bishop's army at his summons. Sealing clause; witnesses.*

1222

B = BL, Harl. MS 6280, fos 40v–41r. s. xvi[1].
Pd. from B, *St Davids Episcopal Acta*, 176–7 (App., no. IV).
Cd., *Episc. Acts*, i. 352–3 (D. 454); *H*, no. 295.

Sciant presentes et futuri quod cum Gervasius Men' episcopus nobilem virum Resum filium Resi coram T. decano, A. cancellario et T. thesaurario Hereford(ensi) iudicibus a domino papa delegatis traxisset in causam nomine ecclesie sue petens ab ipso totum commotum de Lanteilawmaur cum pertinentiis suis, terras etiam inter amnem Diueleis Luswlith et rivulum Hylig similiter et mainaur de Lantarauch et villam de Kelnur et terras de Ab(er)wili quas Gugan(us) Seys et Kediuor filius Enyr et alii nobiles iniuste tenebant, tandem inter ipsos lis mota talis fine conquievit, videlicet quod dictus Resus Iunior et Mareduch' filius eius et heredes recognoverunt ius ecclesie Men' et episcopi in terris nominatis cum pertinentiis suis. Terras vero de subtus Dyueleys plene et integre cum omnibus pertinentiis reddiderunt prefatus Resus et filii sui domino Men' et ecclesie sue usque ad [fo. 41r] terminos de commoto de Ketheinauch ut ad ecclesiam[a] Men' pleno iure pertinentes preter terras de Kerric Gurgeneu et terram Oweni filii Gadug' et terram fabrorum curie de Dinewr et terras canonicorum de Talelech', quas ipse vel sui dederunt ecclesie de Lanteilowmaur vel domui de Talelech' liberas et quietas in perpetuam elemosinam de voluntate episcopi et assensu capituli Men'. Preterea prefatus Resus et filii eius reddiderunt domino Men' et ecclesie sue omnes terras de Aberguili quas Kediuor filius Enyr et Gogan Seys et alii nobiles iniuste detinebant ut ad ecclesiam Men' pleno iure pertinentes. Tenentur etiam predictus Resus et filii sui domino Men' liberare, pacificare, warantizare easdem terras de Ab(er)guili cum molendino contra dictos nobiles Goganu(m) Seys et Kediuor filium Enyr et alios et contra omnes homines terre[b] Walensicor(um). De terris autem aliis prenominatis fecerunt dominus Resus et filii eius homagium domino Men', tactis sacrosanctis iurati quod manutenebunt ipsum et ecclesiam suam, homines, terras et possessiones suas ubique fideliter et sine malo ingenio, reddendo annuatim unum hastorium ad festum Sancti Ioh(ann)is Bapt(ist)e de terris nominatis. Tenentur etiam dicti Resus et filii eius facere homines de tenementis predictis venire in exercitum episcopi ad[b] eiusdem summonitionem. Ut igitur compositio ista perpetuum stabilitatis robur optineat presenti scripto cyrographato sigillis partium mutuo appensis est confirmata. Actum anno gratie millesimo cc^mo xxii^do. Hiis testibus: de Sancto Dogmael' et de Tallelech' abbatibus, Henr(ico) filio Rob(er)ti, Walt(ero) filio Bartholom(eo), Nich(olo) filio Meyler', Ioh(an)n(e) filio Assev', Will(elm)o filio Martini, Nich(olo) filio Samuel canonicis Men', de Pebydiauk et de Cantremaur decanis, G. priore de Tallelech, Ph(ilippo) canonico eiusdem domus, Gogan' officiali; de laicis Oweno filio Kadug', Grif' filio Elyder, Traharn filio Hoile, Ior filio Gogan filii Meilas, Gorgenew clerico domini Resi, magistro Ioh(anne) clerico domini Menev' et multis aliis. In cuius rei testimonium presenti scripto sigillum nostrum duximus apponendum.

[a] ecclesiarum B. | [b] tempore B. | [c] et B.

For a similar agreement dated 1222 between Iorwerth and Rhys's brother Maelgwn see no. 43 above. It has been suggested that the present document was drafted by the last two witnesses, Gwrgenau, clerk of Rhys and Master John, clerk of Bishop Iorwerth (*St Davids Episcopal Acta*, 177). The Dulais *Luswlith* is probably Afon Dulais, which joins the Tywi about $1\frac{1}{2}$ miles north-west of Llandeilo Fawr at SN 647 240; the *Hylig* may be Nant Gurrey-fach, which joins the Tywi about $1\frac{1}{4}$ miles to the south-west at SN 634 227. The following lands, described as appurtenances of cmt. Maenordeilo, lay west and south-west of Llandeilo Fawr: Llanddarog (SN 503 166), cmt. Is Cennen; Llangynnwr (SN 430 203), cmt. Cedweli; and Abergwili (bishop's palace SN 441 210), cmt. Gwidigada. Rhys Gryg had dismantled the castle of Dinefwr, near Llandeilo Fawr, in August 1220 (see no. 248 below). That 'the land of the smiths of the court of Dinefwr' was granted to, presumably, the church of Llandeilo Fawr indicates that smiths had formerly enjoyed a position in the court of Deheubarth, including tenure of land free of rent or service, similar to that set out in the Welsh lawbooks' tractate on the royal court, but that this was no longer the case by 1222 (see e.g. *LTWL*, 331, and cf. Griffiths, *Conquerors*, 262). Talley's lands lay north of the Nant Llwyd, cmt. Maenordeilo.

*53 Letter patent concerning Henry III
[Text presumably as no. 19 above.]

[Montgomery, 8 October 1223]

Mention only, in a note on the patent roll after the text of no. 19 above, issued by Maredudd ap Rhobert of Cedewain, naming Rhys Gryg among those that *Eodem modo fecerunt cartas suas* (*PR 1216–25*, 411; cd. *H*, no. 316).

*54 Letter patent concerning Henry III
[Text presumably as no. 20 above.]

[8 October 1223]

Mention only, in a note on the patent roll after the text of no. 20 above, issued by Maredudd ap Rhobert, Robert ap Madog and Maelgwn ap Rhys, stating that *Eodem modo fecit cartam suam per se Resus Crek* (TNA: PRO, C 66/28, m. 1d; pd., *PR 1216–25*, 411–12; cd., *H*, no. 317).

RHYS IEUANC AP GRUFFUDD
(d. August 1222)

55 Strata Florida Abbey
Grant in perpetual alms, for the salvation of the souls of himself and his parents, of all the gifts of his father Gruffudd of pious memory, of his grandfather Rhys and of all Rhys's sons as their charters attest. The names of the principal places are: Rhydfendigaid [Pont Rhydfendigaid], Ffynnonoer, Castell Fflemish, Rhiwonnen and Ffynnon Mebwyn, in all their bounds and appurtenances as contained in the charters of Maelgwn; Coed Mawr in the bounds defined in the charter of Rhys son of Rhys Fawr, Morfa[-mawr] and Dau Farchdy and from Marchdy to the Cledan and Ardischyn Keuet, Cefngwrthafarn[-uchaf], Gwrthwynt[-uchaf] and Bronwennau, in all the appurtenances and bounds attested in the monks' charters; Morfa-bychan in the bounds defined in Maelgwn's charter, Trefaes[-uchaf] in all its bounds, Safn-y-ci [Tanbwlch] in the bounds which Gruffudd ap Cadwgan gave the monks in perpetual alms; Y Dywarchen [Tirmynach], Llan Vessyl, Argoed y Gwenyn [(?)Argoed-fawr], Baucharn, Taflogau, Pwllpeiran and Bodcoll in all the bounds attested in the monks' charters; (?)Tre'r-bryn in the bounds defined by Maelgwn's charter, Ystrad-ffin and y Groen Gwennon in all bounds defined by the charter of his father Gruffudd; Cefn Iolo (Keuenoly), Aberdihonw, Abercoyl and Llanfadog in all their bounds and appurtenances; Nant Mora, Nannerth and Cwm Goybedauc in all their bounds. Grant also of all the pasture of Cantref Mawr and Cantref Bychan and the four cantrefs of Ceredigion and especially Penweddig in the same bounds as defined in Maelgwn's charter granting the pasture of Penweddig; of all the land between the Tywi and the Irfon, from the source of the Tywi to (?)Bwlch y Dorfa, thence from above the source of Pwll-y-wrach to the source of the Trawsnant, thence along the Trawsnant to the Tywi, thence along the Tywi to the Camddwr, thence along the Camddwr to its source. Grant also of all the land of

Elenydd and of the pasture of Cwmteuddwr, as the monks' charters concerning these attest. Rhys grants in all their liberties and good customs all the aforenamed lands and pastures and any other lands, pastures or possessions the monks have received from popes, princes and the faithful or by other just means. He has confirmed the gift with the first seal he had and has given no other charter to anyone nor had any seal before this one. Witnesses.

1202

B = TNA: PRO, C 66/153 (Pat. R.14 Edward II, pt. 1), m. 6 (in an inspeximus, 10 November 1320).
C = TNA: PRO, C 53/123 (Ch. R. 10 Edward III), m. 6 (in an inspeximus of B, 2 October 1336).
D = TNA: PRO, C 66/308 (Pat. R. 4 Richard II, pt. 1), m. 13 (reciting an inspeximus of C by Edward the Black Prince 28 October 1369, 20 October 1380).
E = TNA: PRO, C 66/417 (Pat. R. 3 Henry VI, pt. 2), m. 5 (in an inspeximus of D, 8 July 1425).
F = TNA: PRO, C 66/605 (Pat. R. 23 Henry VII), m. 10 (in an inspeximus of E, 4 March 1508).
Pd. from C, *CChR 1327–41*, 383–4; from D, Roberts, 'Documents and charters', 202–3 (trans. only)); from an abbreviated text in BL, MS Harl. 6068 (s. xvi/xvii), Williams, *Cistercian Abbey of Strata Florida*, App., xv–xvi (and trans.).
Cd., *CChR 1317–21*, 527 (from B); *CPR 1377–81*, 551 (from D); *CPR 1422–9*, 294 (from E); *CPR 1494–1509*, 567 (from F); *H*, no. 24.

Universis sancte matris ecclesie filiis qui hanc cartam inspexerint Resus filius Griffini filii Resi magni salutem. Universitati vestre notum facio me dedisse et concessisse monachis de St(ra)tflur Deo et Beate Marie ibidem servientibus pro remedio anime mee et parentum meorum in puram et perpetuam elemosinam omnes donationes quas pie memorie pater meus Griffinus et avus meus Resus et omnes filii eius dederunt sicut ipsorum carte protestantur. Principalium autem locorum nomina sunt hec: Rid Bendigeyt in omnibus finibus et pertinentiis suis, `Finnaun Oyr in omnibus finibus et pertinentiis suis, Castellh Flemys in omnibus finibus et pertinentiis suis, Ryuaunhun et Fynnaun Mebwyn in omnibus finibus et pertinentiis suis sicut in cartis Mailgonis continetur, Coyt Maur in finibus quos carta Resi iunioris, scilicet filii Resi magni difinit, Morua et Deu Marchty et de Marchty usque Caledan et Ardischyn Keuet, Keuen Guarthauarch, Torchwynt, Branwenneu, hec loca in omnibus pertinentiis et finibus quos carte quas idem monachi habent protestantur; Morua Bichan in finibus quos carta Mailgonis diffinit, Treff Mais in omnibus finibus suis, Sauan y Ky in finibus quos Griffud filius Cadugan in perpetuam elemosinam prefatis monachis dedit, Y Tywarchen, Lan Vessyl, Argoyt y Gwenneyn, Baucharn, hec loca in omnibus finibus et pertinentiis suis; Tafflogeu, Pullh Peyrant, Bothcollh in omnibus finibus quos carte predictorum monachorum de eisdem locis demonstrant, Treff Bryn in finibus quos carta Mailgonis diffinit, St(ra)tfyn, y Groen Gwennon in omnibus finibus quos carta Griffini patris mei diffinit, Keuenoly in omnibus finibus et pertinentiis suis, Aberdehonoy in omnibus finibus et pertinentiis suis, Abercoyl, Lanmadaue in omnibus finibus et pertinentiis suis, Nant Mora et Nannheyrth et Cum Goybedauc in omnibus finibus suis; insuper omnem pasturam de Cantrefmaur et de Cantrefbichan et de quatuor cantredis de Cardigan et nominatim de Pen[we]dic eo modo et eisdem terminis quos carta Mailgonis diffinit data prefatis monachis de pastura Pennwedic; totam quoque terram que est inter Tywy et Yruon, *o blain* Tywy *hyt y* Torrua, inde *yar blayn* Pullh Ydrach usque *blayn* Trosnant, inde Trosnant usque Tywy, inde sicut ducit Tywy usque Camdouyr, inde Camdouor *hyt y blayn*; totam etiam terram que dicitur Helenyt sicut carte predictorum monachorum de eadem terra protestantur; pasturam quoque de Cumhut Deudouyr sicut in cartis eorumdem monachorum predictorum continetur. Omnes terras et omnes pasturas prenominatas seu etiam quascumque alias terras aut pasturas vel possessiones quaslibet in terra et super terram in fluminibus `in mari et ubi[a] quecumque prefati monachi concessione pontificum, largitione principum, oblatione fidelium seu quibuslibet aliis iustis modis Deo propitio sunt adepti eisdem monachis dono et concedo in omnibus libertatibus et consuetudinibus bonis. Hanc autem donationem primo sigillo quod habui confirmavi et ante hanc cartam nullam aliam alicui homini dedi nec aliquod sigillum ante hoc habui quo hanc cartam confirmavi. Facta est autem hec donatio anno ab incarnatione domini m° cc° ii°. Hiis testibus: Matill' matre mea, Reso filio Riderch, Henyr Bican, Adam clerico meo, Abraham monacho, fratre Bledyn filio Ioruert, fratre Will(elm)o filio Dristan, fratre Iuor Penbras.

[a] B *inserts* ubi.

For the place-names see nos 28, 36, 38–40, 45 above and no. 63 below; *OP*, iv. 499–502; Williams, *Atlas*, 57–9. The first witness, Rhys's mother Matilda de Braose, was buried at Strata Florida beside her husband Gruffudd ap Rhys after her death at Llanbadarn Fawr on 29 December 1210 (*BT, Pen20Tr*, 84; *BT, RBH*, 190–1).

*56 King John
Quitclaim, by Rhys and his brother Owain, of all their lands in the honour of Cardigan, all the land of Cantref Bychan with the castle of Llandovery and all the land of Malláen.

[1211]

Mention only, in Bishop Walter Stapledon's calendar of exchequer records, compiled *c*.1323 (*Antient Kalendars*, ed. Palgrave, i. 113; cd., *H*, no. 25). For the context and dating of this lost charter see Smith, 'Magna Carta', 351–2. Malláen was the easternmost commote of Cantref Mawr, adjoining the commote of Hirfryn, Cantref Bychan.

57 Bishop Iorwerth of St Davids
Grant, inspired by love, in perpetual alms, of the land of Rhandir Llan-non in its ancient bounds, free of all secular exaction and custom. Witnesses.

[21 June 1215 × August 1222]

B = BL, MS Harl. 6280, fo. 72v. s. xvi[1].
Cd., *Episc. Acts*, i. 357 (D. 473); *H*, no. 26.

Universis sancte matris ecclesie filiis presentibus et futuris ad quos presens pagina pervenerit Resus filius Gruffin(i) salutem et pacem. Noverit universitas vestra quod nos pro salute anime nostre et antecessorum et successorum nostrorum dedimus et concessimus et presenti carta confirmavimus terram que dicitur Randyr Lannon in antiquis finibus et terminis suis Deo et Sancto David et Gervasio Men' episcopo et eius successoribus mero caritatis intuitu in puram et perpetuam elemosinam libere et quiete ab omni seculari exactione et consuetudine possidendam. Hiis testibus: T. abbate de Tallech, Riso, Eniaun', Blegeurit filiis Redderch, Kenan filio Rodry, A. clerico nostro tunc officiali de Kardygan, Griff(ino) filio David, Ioru(er)d filio Madauc, David Barrath, Ioh(ann)e decano de Gardyg(a)n, Iuor Penvras, David Vach ii conversis de St(ra)dflur et multis aliis.

Iorwerth was consecrated bishop of St Davids on 21 June 1215 (*St Davids Episcopal Acta*, 10). Llan-non (SN 514 668) was an episcopal township about ½ mile south of Llansanffraid, cmt. Anhuniog, Ceredigion (see *Black Book of St. David's*, 210–11). The charter was probably drafted by the *A.* described as Rhys's clerk and official of Cardigan. Ifor Penfras, lay brother of Strata Florida, also occurs in 1202 as a witness to no. 55 above.

*58 Slebech Commandery
Grant of the church of Llansanffraid (Lansanfreit) *and all the land which pertains to the township of Llansanffraid* (Lansanfreit)*.*

[21 June 1215 × August 1222]

Mention only, in an inspeximus of his predecessors' confirmations of the possessions of the Hospitallers of Slebech Commandery issued by Anselm, bishop of St Davids, 9 February 1231 × 8 February 1232 (*St Davids Episcopal Acta*, 127 (no. 108)). The grant of Llansanffraid is listed among grants explicitly said to have been made after the confirmation issued by Bishop Iorwerth, datable to 21 June 1215 × 26 January 1229 (ibid., 106–7 (no. 87)). This strongly suggests that the 'Rhys son of Gruffudd' referred to is Rhys Ieuanc ap Gruffudd ap Rhys rather than his grandfather the Lord Rhys (*pace H*, no. 33; *St Davids Episcopal Acta*, 124). As the inspeximus states that the grant was in Cardiganshire, it refers to Llansanffraid (SN 513 675), cmt. Anhuniog, about 2 miles south-west of Llanrhystud, granted to Slebech by the Lord Rhys (no. 24 above).

OWAIN AP GRUFFUDD
(d. 17 January 1235)

*59 Slebech Commandery
Grant of all the land of Moylon' *with all its appurtenances in pure and perpetual alms. Sealed.*

[Probably 25 July 1201 × 17 January 1235]

Mention only, in a Latin schedule written *c.*1600 of grants to the Hospitallers of Slebech (NLW, Slebech 247; cd., Charles, 'Records of Slebech', 194; *H*, no. 44). The grant was probably made after the death of Owain's father Gruffudd ap Rhys on 25 July 1201 (*BT, Pen20Tr*, 81; *BT, RBH*, 184–5). *Moylon'* has not been identified.

*60 Slebech Commandery
Grant of all the land of Rhosdïau (Riostoye) *with all its appurtenances. Sealed.*

[Probably 25 July 1201 × 17 January 1235]

Mention only, in a Latin schedule written *c.*1600 of grants to the Hospitallers of Slebech (NLW, Slebech 247; cd., Charles, 'Records of Slebech', 194; *H*, no. 45). See note to no. 59

above. Wmffre, 'Language and History', II. ii. 849–50 cites *Riostoye* as a form of Rhosdïau (SN 624 728), par. Llanilar, cmt. Mefenydd.

*61 Strata Marcella Abbey

Grant in perpetual alms of quittance of toll at Llanbadarn Fawr and Aberystwyth on all selling, buying and fishing and of the freedom to buy, sell and fish in those places, both on land and in the sea, without any exaction or custom.

[1222 × 17 January 1235; probably 1229 × 17 January 1235]

Mention only, in an inspeximus of Edward II dated at Tutbury, 12 March 1322 (*Ystrad Marchell Charters*, no. 77; cd., *CChR 1300–26*, 441; *H*, no. 43). The share of lands Owain inherited from his brother Rhys Ieuanc on the latter's death in 1222 probably included the cantref of Penweddig in which Llanbadarn Fawr and Aberystwyth were situated. If, as is likely, the grants in Edward II's inspeximus are listed in chronological order, the charter was issued after that of Thomas Corbet, dated 1229 (*Ystrad Marchell Charters*, 9, 29–30).

CYNAN AP HYWEL SAIS
(d. *c*.1240)

*62 Whitland Abbey

Grant and confirmation in the land of Elwyn (Elwyn) *with its appurtenances.*

[1204 × *c*.1240]

Mention only, in a letter patent of Edward II dated at Lincoln, 1 September 1315 (TNA: PRO, C 66/144, m. 23; cd., *CPR 1313–17*, 348; *H*, no. 41). The location of Elwyn may be indicated by the farm of that name (SN 232 280) about 2 miles north-west of Llanwinio, and thus probably lay in the commote of Peuliniog. Cynan's father Hywel Sais died in 1204, and Cynan seems to have died by *c*.1240 (*HW*, ii. 710, n. 99).

THE LINEAGE OF MAELGWN AP RHYS (CEREDIGION)

MAELGWN FYCHAN AP MAELGWN
(d. 1257)

63 Strata Florida Abbey

Grant in perpetual alms on behalf of himself and his heirs, for the salvation of the souls of himself, his father, mother, wife, predecessors and successors, of all grants and liberties which his father Maelgwn ap Rhys granted it in lands, meadows, pastures, waters, fisheries and other appurtenances, in all their liberties, so that the monks may keep in perpetual alms, free of all secular and ecclesiastical service for ever, whatever possessions they now possess, or will possess in future, from princes or the faithful or by other just means, as the charters of his father Maelgwn and other donors attest. The names of the principal places are: the site of the monastery at Ystrad-fflur with its bounds and appurtenances, Rhydfendigaid [Pont Rhydfendigaid], Henfynachlog, Brynhôp, Cefncastell, Llwyn-y-gog and Dol-fawr, Tref-y-Gwyddel along the Marchant to the Meurig, Dwy Taflogau with its bounds and appurtenances, Pwllpeiran with its bounds and appurtenances, Esgair Berfedd, Esgair y Prignant [Prignant-isaf], Bodcoll, 'Llywarch's heruyt *between the Rhydnant [Rhuddnant] and the Merin',* Cilmeddy, Kefryn, *Ffynnonoer [Swydd-y-ffynnon], Bryn (?) Merllyd* (Merlich) *[Penbryn], Celli-bychain, Celli Bryn Teifi, Castell Fflemish, Maes Glas, Treflyn[-fawr], Dinas (?) Drygwyr to the Aeron, Trecoll with its bounds and appurtenances, Bryn* Yrich, *Esgairsaeson, Buarth Caron, Rhiwonnen, Celli* Rumbyn, *Esgair* Maynteuylh, *Pencoed[-uchaf], Tynrhos* (Rossan), *Celli-gwenyn, Celli Angharad, Buarth* Elharth *by the boundaries in the monks' charters, Ffynnon Mebwyn with the bounds in the monks' charters, Hafod-wen, Tal Pont* Gloyued, *Hendre Forrant, Tref-y-benydd [Pontmarchog], Meuddin[-fawr], Castell* Dynauuel, *Tref y* Geudu, *Morfa-mawr, (?) Tŷ-poeth, the share-land from Nant-y-ffin to Ffynnon Bleiddudd,* Ardis Kyn Keued, *Bryn Llyn Du, Marchdy Bychan, Cefngwrthafarn[-uchaf],* Cayrtreuhyr, *Marchdy Mawr, Morfa* Menhehith, *Blaensaith, Bronwennau, Cymanfynydd, Gwrthwynt[-uchaf] with its bounds and appurtenances, Dineirth [Castell] and Tref* Ladheu *with their bounds and appurtenances, Morfa-bychan, Tre-faes[-uchaf], Safn-y-ci [Tanbwlch], Tywarchen Benweddig [Tirmynach], Pencwmbancar,* Lhanvessilh, *Argoed y Gwenyn [(?) Argoed-fawr], (?) Talbont, Castell Gwgon, Broncastellan, as contained in the monks' charters, Henllan, Nant* Eyryn, *Cwm* Gwybedauc, *Nannerth Gwy, the mouth of the Dernol to the source,* Treanil *Gwyn, all the land of Elenydd as the charters of all donors attest,* Bridcum, *Rhiw* Afwanaul, Abercoyl, y Groen Guynnion, *Llanfadog with its bounds and appurtenances, Ystrad-ffin with its bounds and appurtenances, Nant-bau,* Groen Gwynnion *and all the pasture of Ceredigion except for the portions belonging to the monks of Whitland and Cwm-hir as contained in their chirographs. Maelgwn grants and confirms, with no right of appeal for ever, all the aforenamed lands and pastures with all their bounds and appurtenances and all the aforesaid gifts, grants and liberties, as well as freedom to buy and sell and carry out all business in all his lands and lordship, with freedom from all tolls, ferry dues, bridge dues and all other customs and exactions pertaining to him on land and sea and in all places of his lordship. Sealing clause; witnesses.*

[22 January 1198 × 1227]

B = TNA: PRO, C 66/153 (Pat. R. 14 Edward II, pt. 1), mm. 6–5 (in an inspeximus, 10 November 1320).

C = TNA: PRO, C 53/123 (Ch. R. 10 Edward III), m. 6 (in an inspeximus of B, 2 October 1336).

D = TNA: PRO, C 66/308 (Pat. R. 4 Richard II, pt. 1), m. 13–12 (reciting an inspeximus of C by Edward the Black Prince 28 October 1369, 20 October 1380).

E = TNA: PRO, C 66/417 (Pat. R. 3 Henry VI, pt. 2), m. 4 (in an inspeximus of D, 8 July 1425).

F = TNA: PRO, C 66/605 (Pat. R. 23 Henry VII), m. 10 (in an inspeximus of E, 4 March 1508).

Pd. from C, *CChR 1327–41*, 384–5; from D, Roberts, 'Documents and charters', 203–4 (trans. only)); from an abbreviated text in BL, MS Harl. 6068 (s. xvi/xvii), Williams, *Cistercian Abbey of Strata Florida*, App., xvi (and trans.).

Cd., *CChR 1317–21*, 528 (from B); *CPR 1377–81*, 551 (from D); *CPR 1422–9*, 294–5 (from E); *CPR 1494–1509*, 567 (from F); *H*, no. 27.

Universis sancte ecclesie filiis tam presentibus quam futuris hanc cartam inspecturis Mailgun iunior filius Mailgonis filii Resi principis Sudwall(ie) salutem in domino. Ad universitatis vestre notitiam volo pervenire me pro salute anime mee et patris et matris et uxoris et antecessorum et successorum meorum dedisse et concessisse et presenti carta mea confirmasse Deo et Beate Marie et monachis de St(ra)tflur pro me et heredibus meis in [m. 5] puram et perpetuam elemosinam omnes donationes, concessiones et libertates quas venerabilis memorie pater meus Maelgun filius Resi eisdem monachis contulit in terris et pasturis et pratis, in aquis et moris, in bosco et plano, in mari et fluminibus, in piscaturis et piscationibus tam maris et portuum maris quam fluviorum, in omnibus libertatibus et consuetudinibus, bonis et possessionibus tam mobilibus quam immobilibus super terram et sub terra et in ceteris omnibus rebus et possessionibus quas idem monachi tenent in presenti et possident largitione principum seu donatione quorumlibet fidelium seu quibuslibet aliis iustis modis, libere ab omni servitio et exactione tam ecclesiastica quam seculari, quiete ab omni molestatione seu gravamine in perpetuum sicut carte domini Mailgonis patris mei et aliorum donatorum in amplioribus et latioribus terminis protestantur. Quorum principalia loca hec sunt: St(ra)tflur scilicet in quo loco monasterium situm est cum terminis et pertinentiis, Rit Vendikeit, Henvanchloc, Brin Hop, Keuen Castelh, Lwynychoc et Dol Maur, Tref y Gwydel sicut ducit flumen quod dicitur Marchnant usque ad aliud flumen quod dicitur Meuric, Duy Tafhologeu cum terminis et pertinentiis suis, Pulh Peyriant cum terminis et pertinentiis suis, yr Eskeyr P(er)ueth, Eskeyr y P(ri)uygnant, Bot Kolh, Heruyt Lywarch inter Ritnant et Meryn, Kylmedwyn, Kefryn, Fynnaun Oyr, Brin Merlich, Kelliheu Bykeyn, Kelheu Brin Deuy, Castelh y Flemmis, y Mais Glas, Treflyn, Dynas Drigwyr usque ad Ayron, Tref y Cholh cum terminis et pertinentiis suis, Brin Yrich, Eskeyr y Sayson, Buarth Caraun, Ryu Anhun, Kelhyeu Rumbyn, Eskeyr Maynteuylh, Pen Coyt, Rossan, Kelhy yr Guenyn, Kelhheu Eskarat, Buarth Elharth secundum terminos qui in cartis monachorum continentur, Fynhaun Mebvyn cum terminis quos monachi habent in cartis suis, yr Hauot Wen, Tal Pont Gloyued, Hen Voryon, Tref y Benny, Meudyn, Castelh Dynauuel, Tref y Geudu, y Morva, y Tref Poith, *y randyr o* Nant y Fin usque ad fontem Bleydud, Ardis Kyn Keued, Brin Lhaude, Marchty Bychan, Keuen Guardhauarth, Cayrtreuhyr, Marchty Maur, Morua Menhehith, Blay(n) Sayth, Branwenheu, Kyman Vinyd, Gurdh Wynt cum terminis et pertinentiis suis, Dyneyrd et Tref Ladheu cum terminis et pertinentiis suis, y Morua Bychan, Tref Mays, Sauyn y Ky, Tywarchen Penwedic, Ban Caru, Lhanvessilh, Argoit y Guynweyn, Tal Pont Cuculh, Castelh Gugaun, Castelham, sicut carte monachorum continent, yr Henlhan, Nant Eyryn, Cum Gwybedauc, Nanneyrd Guy, *ab*(*er*) Edernaul *hyt y blain* et Treanil Guyn et totam terram de Elenyth sicut carte omnium donatorum protestantur, y Bridcum, Ryu Afwanaul, Ab(er)coyl, y Groen Guynnion, Lhanvadauc cum terminis et pertinentiis suis, Yst(ra)t Fyn cum terminis et pertinentiis suis, Nant Bey, Groen Gwynnion et totam pasturam de Keredygyaun exceptis portionibus que ad monachos de Alba Domo et de Cumhyr pertinent sicut in eorum cirographis contineatur. Omnes igitur prenominatas terras et pasturas cum omnibus terminis et pertinentiis suis in campis et silvis, in pratis et aquis et moris et pascuis, in culto et inculto et omnes alias donationes, concessiones et libertates prenominatas, insuper libertatem emendi et vendendi et omnia negotia sua exercendi in totis terris meis et in omni dominio meo, et libertatem et quietantiam de omni theloneo et passagio et pontagio et de omnibus aliis consuetudinibus et exactionibus ad me spectantibus sive in terra sive in mari sive in portubus maris et villis et castellis sive in aliis omnibus locis dominii mei eisdem monachis dono, concedo et presenti carta confirmo, remota omni contradictione et appellatione in perpetuum. Et quia[a] volo quod hec mea donatio et confirmatio rata et inconcussa in perpetuum permaneat presens scriptum sigilli mei impressione roboravi. Hiis testibus: domino Mailgone filio Resi, Morgan filio Resi, M. archidiacono de Kardigan, David tunc priore de St(ra)tflur, Itello monacho, Dyermith converso eiusdem loci et multis aliis.

[a] qua B.

This charter is presumably later than Maelgwn ap Rhys's charter of 22 January 1198 (no. 35 above), as it contains lands lacking in the latter, and the *terminus a quo* may be somewhat later (cf. note to no. 64 below). The *M.* who witnessed as archdeacon of Cardigan must be Maelgwn Fychan's uncle Maredudd ap Rhys ap Gruffudd, who died, as archdeacon of Cardigan, in 1227 and who also occurs in 1203 × 1214 (*St Davids Episcopal Acta*, 29). Morgan ap Rhys, the second witness, was another uncle; he served his elder brother Gruffudd ap Rhys as chief of the military retinue (*penteulu*) and died at Strata Florida around the end of 1251 (*BT, Pen20Tr*, 109; *BT, RBH*, 242–3; *CW*, 41). Though the charter is presented as a confirmation of all grants made by his father 'of venerable memory', Maelgwn ap Rhys, who was the first witness, it is unclear how many of the places named here were new grants by Maelgwn ap Rhys, as the text also refers to the charters of other, unnamed grantors (these possibly included the Gruffudd ap Cadwgan who granted Safn-y-ci according to no. 55 above); it is also unclear how many of Maelgwn ap Rhys's charters were being confirmed. However, the present charter certainly includes a number of places not included in Maelgwn's charter of 1198 (no. 35 above), some of which are identified in charters of Rhys Gryg and Rhys Ieuanc ap Gruffudd ap Rhys as grants recorded in charters issued by Maelgwn (nos 50 and 55 and see nos 36–40 for texts inferred from these).

For some of the place-names see notes to nos 25, 28 and 36 above. The following identifications are indebted to Wmffre, 'Language and History', II. i. 393, 452, 463, 465, 472; ii. 584, 597, 602, 650, 693, 742, 746, 758, 876, 960; iii. 1156, 1160, 1188, 1205–6, 1326, 1358, 1412–13. Henfynachlog refers to the original site of the abbey, immediately south of Old Abbey Farm (SN 718 646), and thus Ystrad-fflur to the site of the present ruins (cf. no. 25 above). Pwllpeiran (SN 775 745): par. Gwnnws Isaf, cmt. Mefenydd, about 1 mile north-west of Cwmystwyth. Esgair y Prignant: Prignant-isaf (SN 745 755), par. Llanfihangel-y-Creuddyn Uchaf, cmt. Creuddyn; Bodcoll (SN 752 762) is in the same parish. The Rhydnant (now Rhuddnant) and Merin join at SN 769 776 to form the river Mynach, a tributary of the Rheidol, about 2 miles north-east of Devil's Bridge; *heruyt* (Mod. W. *herwydd*) in *Heruyt Lywarch*, 'Llywarch's *herwydd*' may be a variant of Mod. W. *erwydd*, 'wattling, rods'. Cilmeddy (SN 722 718): par. Gwnnws Isaf, cmt. Mefenydd. Bryn Merllyd seems to have been the original name of Penbryn (SN 689 643), par. Lledrod Uchaf, cmt. Mefenydd. Treflyn-fawr (SN 693 619): par. Caron Is-clawdd, cmt. Pennardd. Hafod-wen: Penbryn (SN 514 516), par. Dihewyd, cmt. Mebwynion. Hendre Forrant (*Hen Voryon*) (SN 491 582), par. Ciliau Aeron, cmt. Mebwynion. Tref-y-benydd (*Tref y Benny*) was an alias of Pontmarchog (SN 502 518), par. Dihewyd, cmt. Mebwynion. Meuddin-fawr (SN 487 520): par. Llannarth, cmt. Caerwedros. Blaensaith-uchaf (SN 279 497): par. Penbryn, cmt. Is Coed. Cymanfynydd (SN 566 610): par. Llanbadarn Trefeglwys, cmt. Anhuniog. Gwrthwynt-uchaf (SN 536 587): par. Trefilan, cmt. Pennardd. Dineirth has been identified as Castell (SN 494 623), par. Llanbadarn Trefeglwys, and Safn-y-ci as Tanbwlch (SN 580 793). Tywarchen Benweddig (or simply Y Dywarchen, as in no. 55 above) was the original name of the grange of Tirmynach. Pencwmbancar (SN 648 855): par. Tirmynach, cmt. Genau'r-glyn. Argoed y Gwenyn may be Argoed-fawr (SN 657 881), par. Ceulan-a-Maesmawr, cmt. Genau'r-glyn, and *Tal Pont Cuculh* may be Talbont (SN 654 891) in the same parish. Broncastellan (SN 633 840): par. Tirmynach, cmt. Genau'r-glyn. The Elenydd is the mountain tract between Ystrad-fflur and Rhayader (*HW*, ii. 513, n. 100).

This is the earliest surviving charter for Strata Florida issued by a member of the Deheubarth dynasty to include a clause quitting the monks from tolls and other payments.

*64 Slebech Commandery

Grant of half the land of Merthyr Cynlas (Merther Kynlas) *with all its appurtenances in perpetual alms. Sealed.*

[*c*.1200 × 1257]

Mention only, in a Latin schedule written *c*.1600 of grants to the Hospitallers of Slebech (NLW, Slebech 247; cd., Charles, 'Records of Slebech', 194; *H*, no. 47). The grant is also included in a version written *c*.1800 by R. Fenton of the inspeximus for Slebech issued 9 February 1231 × 8 February 1232 by Anselm, bishop of St Davids. However, the section of text including this grant is more likely to be an insertion by Fenton from NLW, Slebech 247 than a witness to a different version of Anselm's inspeximus from that preserved in Cardiff County and City Library MS 4.83 (see *St Davids Episcopal Acta*, 127–8 (no. 108)). It is unknown when Maelgwn Fychan would have first been in a position to make this grant. No. 63 above shows that he granted lands to Strata Florida during the lifetime of his father Maelgwn ap Rhys (d. 1231). As Maelgwn ap Rhys was an adult in 1188 (*Gir. Camb. Op.*, vi. 119 (*IK* II. 4)), his son could have been born in the late twelfth century; if so, the *terminus a quo* for the grant could be as early as *c*.1200. The location of Merthyr Cynlas is uncertain. It may be synonymous with or adjacent to Coed Canlas (Coed Canlas Farm SN 009 088), which had a free chapelry of St Mary (SN 014 083) in the later Middle Ages, located about 4 miles south-west of Slebech (cf. Charles, *Place-Names of Pembrokeshire*, ii. 484; *St Davids Episcopal Acta*, 189). Slebech held extensive lands in this vicinity, including Beggerden, granted (or, more probably, confirmed) by Anarawd ab Einion (no. 31 above). Another possible, but less likely, identification is Castle Cenlas (SM 866 303), about $1\frac{1}{2}$ half miles south-west of Mathry. However, Maelgwn Fychan is not otherwise known to have held land or authority in either of these areas.

*65 Letter patent concerning Henry III

Notification that he will act as a pledge in support of undertakings given by Senana for the release of her husband Gruffudd ap Llywelyn.

[Shrewsbury, 12 August 1241]

Mention only, in an agreement between Senana and the king dated at Shrewsbury, 12 August 1241 (no. 284 below). Presumably the letter patent was similar to that concerning these matters issued on the same occasion by Hywel ap Madog of Bromfield (no. 523 below).

RHYS FYCHAN AP RHYS AP MAELGWN FYCHAN
(d. 1302)

66 Letter patent concerning Llywelyn ap Gruffudd

Notification that he has given of his free will Rhys ap Iorwerth, Llywelyn ab Ieuaf and Hywel ap Goronwy as sureties to Llywelyn, prince of Wales, in the sum of £60 to be paid in three terms, namely £20 each on the calends of May, the calends of August and Michaelmas [29 September], for the townships held by Angharad, daughter of Llywelyn; each of the aforesaid men is surety for the payment of £20 at the aforesaid terms. Sealing clause.

Genau'r-glyn, 23 February 1260

> B = TNA: PRO, E 36/274 (Liber A), fo. 336r. s. xiii ex.
> Pd. from B, *LW*, 26 (no. 31).
> Cd., *H*, no. 299.

[U]niversis Cristi fidelibus presentes litteras visuris vel audituris Resus Iunior filius Resi ab Maelgvn salutem in domino. Noverit universitas vestra nos dedisse spontanea eorum voluntate Resum filium Ioruerth, Lewelinu(m) filium Ieuas, et Howelum filium Coro(n)w singulares fideiussores domino Lewelino principi Wall(ie), pro sexaginta libris legalis monete eidem solvendis in tribus terminis, videlicet in kalendis maii xx libras, in kalendis augusti xx libras et in festo Sancti Mich(ael)is Arcangeli xx libras ultimo solvendas, pro villis que fuerunt bone memorie Angarad filie[a] Lewel(ini); quisque vero virorum prenominatorum est fideiussor pro xx libris terminis predictis solvendis principi memorato. In cuius rei testimonium presentes litteras patentes sigillo nostro una cum sigillis predictorum fideiussorum fecimus roborari. Datum apud Geneu Yglyn anno domini m° cc° lix[ob] die lune proxima post festum Cathedre Sancti Pet(ri).

[a] filius B. | [b] B *inserts* nono.

The dating clause in the copy in Liber A gives the year as *anno domini m° cc° lix° nono*. This clearly contains an error and Edwards's emendation (*LW*, 26), omitting *nono*, has been accepted here. Assuming that the year began at the Annunciation (25 March), the letter was dated 23 February 1260 by modern reckoning. Although it has been argued that this would be too early for the application to Llywelyn of the title 'prince of Wales' (Stephenson, 'Llywelyn ap Gruffudd', 38, n. 8), the objection is by no means compelling given that the same title was used in the agreement with the Scottish lords of 18 March 1258 (no. 328 below). Similarly, while Rhys may have been too young to have joined Llywelyn and other Welsh lords in the 1258 agreement (Smith, *Llywelyn*, 112–13), he may have been old enough to enter into the present obligation to the prince almost two years later. Rhys Fychan's father had predeceased Maelgwn Fychan (d. 1257) in 1255. The Angharad referred to was almost certainly the daughter of Llywelyn ap Iorwerth who married Maelgwn Fychan; she was thus Rhys Fychan's grandmother and Llywelyn's aunt (cf. Smith, 'Dower', 351, n. 5). The location of the townships held by Angharad is not stated, but they presumably lay in Rhys's lands in Ceredigion.

*67 Gruffudd ap Maredudd ab Owain and the (other) heirs of Maredudd ab Owain
Grant of all Ceredigion with all its bounds and appurtenances to Gruffudd and the heirs of Maredudd ab Owain as fully as Gruffudd's predecessors held it, in return for Gruffudd's grant to him of the cantref of Penweddig.

[*c.*2 May 1283]

Mention only, in Gruffudd's grant, dated at Llanberis, 2 May 1283 (no. 78 below). It is not certain that Rhys's grant was recorded in a separate document of his own.

THE LINEAGE OF OWAIN AP GRUFFUDD (CEREDIGION)

MAREDUDD AB OWAIN AP GRUFFUDD
(d. 1265)

*68 Talley Abbey
Confirmation of all lands, churches and possessions which it has received in perpetual alms by the gifts of his father, grandfather, great-grandfather or uncles or of other magnates or nobles of Deheubarth (Decheubarch), *quit of all secular exaction, namely the land called Maerdrefi Gwynionydd* (Mayrdreui Guin nouit) *[Faerdre], Brynaeron* (Brin Yron), *Rhydowain* (Rit Iweyn), *Nant Cedifor* (Nant Kediuor), *Cynbyd Isallt* (Kynbit Ysalld), *as contained in their bounds: from the mouth of the Cerdin* (ab hostio Kerdyn) *[Abercerdin] in the Teifi towards its source to the mouth of the Cefail [Abercefail]* (Aberkeueil), *along the Cefail* (Keueil) *to its source, thence across to the head of Pant-y-moch* (blayn Pant ymoch), *thence along Pant-y-moch* (Pant ymoch) *to the dyke* (ad fossam), *thence along the dyke down to the Cletwr* (Kaletur), *thence to Abermenai* (Abermenei), *along the Mene* (Menei) *towards its source to (?)Gwaunrudd* (Gweun Ruch), *thence to the spring towards the highway coming from the source of Nant Cedifor* (blannant Kediuor), *and from the spring to that road and across that way to the little moor, and thence to (?)Blaidd-pwll* (Bleidbull / Bleidbunll), *and thence straight to the head of Y Pant-sych* (blan ypant sych), *and along that valley to the source of Nant Cedifor* (blan Nantkediuor), *descending along that stream to the mouth of the spring* (aberfinnaun), *and thence along the stream of that spring upwards to its source, and thence towards the way nearest to that spring, across that way towards the large stones lying in the field, from those stones across to Caer (?)Hyfaidd* (Kayrhuuyd/Kayrhuuid) *[(?)Pencoedfoel], and thence to (?)Gwarderwen* (Corderwen), *and thence to the spring, descending from that spring to the meadow in the valley, and thence towards the Teifi* (Teivi), *and as the bounds of the Teifi* (Teivi) *are sufficiently well known to the mouth of the Cerdin* (aber Kerdin) *[Abercerdin], where the first boundary was defined. The land of Moelhedog* (Molehehedauc) *as contained in these bounds: from Islwyn and the Cletwr* (Hescluyn Arcaletur) *to Cribin* (Cribyn), *thence to the cairn* (ircarn), *and thence along the dyke to the knoll* (cruc), *and thence to the cairn* (carn) *above the mountain, and thence to the other cairn* (carnarall) *next to Moelhedog* (Moylehaedauc), *thence to the white stone standing in the valley, thence to the source of the Cathl* (blayn Cathil)

[Blaencathl], *thence along the valley to the cairn* (carn), *and thence to the source of the Camnant* (blain Camnant), *along the Camnant to the Cletwr* (Caletur), *and thence to Islwyn* (Heslunen). *The land of Porth Hoddni* (Potthoni) *[Aber-porth] as contained in these bounds: from the sea along the Howni* (Hodyn) *towards its source to* Nant Perthwynunit, *thence along the latter stream to its source, thence along the dyke and afterwards across to the farther water dyke next to the land of the sons of Maeog* (Mayauc), *along that dyke to the dyke of Nant Helig, and thence along the Nant Helig* (Nanthelic) *to the sea. The lands of the granges of Gwyddgrug* (Gudgruc) *and Brechfa* (Brechua) *in all their bounds.*

[1235 × 1265]

Mention only, in an inspeximus, presumably of the original charter, of Edward II, dated at Westminster, 24 March 1324 (TNA: PRO, C 66/160, m. 21; pd., *Mon. Ang.*, iv. 163; Daniel-Tyssen, *Royal Charters*, 65–7; Long Price, 'Talley Abbey', 174–5 (trans. only); Owen, 'Contribution to the history', 43–4; cd., *H*, no. 29). Maredudd's father Gruffudd ab Owain died in 1235. For the place-names see A. C. Evans *apud* Daniel-Tyssen, *Royal Charters*, 65–7; Long Price, 'Talley Abbey', 174–5; Wmffre, 'Language and History', II. i. 215, 230, 242, 246, 261, 262; iii. 1295, 1301, 1320, 1325. Apart from the granges of Gwyddgrug, cmt. Mabudrud, and Brechfa, cmt. Cetheiniog, both in Cantref Mawr, the lands confirmed were all situated in Ceredigion. The lands described in the first two sets of bounds were located in the commote of Gwynionydd (see note to no. 90 below). Maerdrefi Gwynionydd refers to the district including Faerdre-fawr (SN 427 421) and Faerdre-fach (SN 421 423), and presumably also the adjacent earthwork of Castell Gwynionydd (SN 424 420). Abercerdin (SN 420 415) lay just to the south-west in the direction of Llandysul. Nant Cefail joins Afon Cerdin at SN 409 441. Pantmoch-mawr (SN 434 468) lay north of Rhydowain, and the spring referred to in *Aberfinnaun* lay just south-west of Blaencwmcedifor near Ffynnonoffeiriad (SN 430 429). Caer (?)Hyfaidd is possibly identifiable as Pencoedfoel (SN 424 427). Moelhedog (SN 446 461) was likewise situated in Gwynionydd, with Blaencathl (SN 457 467) almost 1 mile to its north-east. For Aber-porth, cmt. Is Coed, see no. 27 above.

*69 Elen, his wife

Grant in dower of Gwynionydd with its appurtenances.

[Probably shortly before 27 August 1246]

Mention only, in a ratification of the grant by Henry III dated at Woodstock, 27 August 1246 (TNA: PRO, C 66/57, m. 2; cd., *CPR 1232–47*, 487; *H*, no. 46). The grant corresponded to the nominated dower (*dos nominata*) of English common law, as the ratification states that the grant was made to Elen at the church door when Maredudd married her; the grant may not, therefore, have been in written form (Smith, 'Dower', 349–50; *Glanvill*, 58–69, esp. 64–5). Possibly the royal ratification was intended to provide a written record in addition to the memory of witnesses.

OWAIN AP MAREDUDD AB OWAIN
(d. 18 July 1275)

70 Llywelyn ap Gruffudd

Letter, declaring that Owain binds himself by the present letter patent on behalf of Hywel Fychan to the sum of £12 for having the prince's benevolence, to be paid at terms prescribed by the prince. Though Hywel is his man, Owain gives him permission to do homage and swear fealty to the prince. He sends this letter patent in witness of this.

[March 1265 × 18 July 1275]

B = TNA: PRO, E 36/274 (Liber A), fo. 335v. s. xiii ex.
Pd. from B, *LW*, 24 (no. 26).
Cd., *H* no. 288.

[I]llustri principi ac domino karissimo domino L. filio Griffini suus Owenus filius Maredud salutem cum honore. Noverit vestra preclara dominatio me cavisse vobis et obligatum esse per presentes meas patentes litteras pro Howelo Vychan in estimatione duodecim librarum pro benivolentia vestra capienda, solvendarum in terminis secundum quod vestre cederit misericordie prefigendis. Do etiam licentiam eidem H., licet homo fuerit meus, homagium faciendi vobis et fidelitatem iurandi. In cuius rei testimonium serenitati vestre presentes litteras transmitto patentes.

Owain's father Maredudd died in March 1265. The identification of the sender with Owain ap Maredudd of Ceredigion, rather than the lords of that name of Cedewain (d. 1261) or Elfael (d. *c*.1260–7), though not absolutely certain, is very likely (*LW*, 24; Smith, *Llywelyn*, 318 and n. 165).

71 Angharad ferch Owain, his wife

Grant in free marriage of the whole commote of Anhuniog with all its appurtenances and liberties, both patronage of churches and other rights, throughout the bounds of the commote, in mountains, woods, meadows, pastures, rivers, roads, arable and non-arable land, to be possessed freely by her and her heirs to be procreated by Owain, in the same liberty in which Owain previously held the commote, giving Angharad and her heirs the special power of appointing and dismissing bailiffs and all other officials in that commote without the permission of anyone. If there is a grant or exchange of lands between Owain and his brothers or other of his co-heirs which deprives Angharad of full possession of the commote, Owain has promised to provide her and her heirs with land of equal value. If Angharad is separated from Owain by the Church or any other cause, the commote will nevertheless be possessed by her and her heirs, with three exceptions: if she dies without an heir by Owain, if she enters religion or if she is taken as wife by another man; in these cases, the commote will be possessed by her heirs, if there are any, or otherwise it will revert to Owain. He has granted this charter under his seal to Angharad to ensure the permanence of the grant. Witnesses.

Llanbadarn Trefeglwys, 24 January 1273; ratified by Llywelyn, prince of Wales, 1273

B = TNA: PRO, C 146/9502. s. xiii².
Pd. from B, Smith, 'Dower', 354–5.
Cd., *H*, no. 15.

Sciant presentes et futuri has litteras visuri vel audituri quod ego Owen(us) filius Maredut filii Oweni dedi et concessi et hac presenti carta mea confirmavi totum comotum Annvnuauc integrum cum omnibus suis pertinentiis et libertatibus, tam in iure patronatus ecclesiarum quam in aliis, in terra et in mari ac aliis liberis consuetudinibus Agarat filie[a] Oweni uxori mee in liberum maritagium in omnibus terminis predicti comoti et finibus debitis suis tam in montibus quam nemoribus, in pratis, pascuis et pasturis, aquis, rivulis, viis et semitis, in terra arabili et non arabili, in humido et scicco, sibi et heredibus suis de me procreandis libere et quiete, pacifice et sine ulla contradictione tenendum et habendum et ʿetiam possidendum, scilicet memoratum comotum Annunuac in Kardigant a dicta Agarad et suis heredibus de me et heredibus meis in eadem libertate in qua antea tenui comotum sepedictum, dans eidem Agarad et heredibus suis de me et concedens specialem potestatem ponendi et deponendi ballivos[b] et omnes alios ministros in illo comoto sine consilio et licentia alicuius. Et si contingat quod alienatio inter me et fratres meos vel aliquos alios coheredes meos fuerit vel terrarum transmutatio ita quod ipsa Agarat prefati comoti dominio et possessione plenaria gaudere non poterit, ego Owen(us) tantam terram et equivalentem predicte Agarad et heredibus suis de me fideliter et mera voluntate lucrari promisi. Si autem similiter per ecclesiam vel aliquo alio casu predictam Agarat a me separari contingat nichilominus comotus ille superius nominatus a predicta Agarad et heredibus suis procreatis de me erit possidendus, istis tamen tribus casibus dumtaxat exceptis,[c] videlicet si sine herede de me procreato decesserit vel si ad religionem migraverit vel ab aliquo viro ducta fuerit in uxorem, in quibus casibus sepedictus comotus ab heredibus suis de me si sint erit possidendus, sin autem sicut prius fuit antedictus comotus ad me revertetur. Et ut hec mea donatio vel confirmatio stabilis, rata et inconcussa[d] in posterum perseveret presentem cartam sigilli mei munimine roboratam predicte Agarad dedi et concessi. Hiis testibus: Lewelino cappellano rectore de Killev, G(ri)ffino rectore de Henvenev, Lewelino cappellano vicario de Lanpadarn Tref Eglues, G(ri)fino [et][e] Oweno filiis Adaf Vaur, G(ri)ffino parvo de Killev, G(ri)ffino filio Ioruerth de Kefn Ycaerev et multis aliis. Datum apud Lanpadarn Tref Eglues die martis proxima ante conversionem Beati Pauli anno domini mᵒ ccᵒ lxxᵒ tertio. Ad hec ut predicta donatio et confirmatio super donatione predicti comoti predicte nepoti sue et heredibus suis de prenominato Oweno procreandis inposterum stabilis, rata et inconcussa permaneat dominus L. princeps Wallie presenti pagine sigillum suum fecit apponi. Datum anno domini mᵒ ccᵒ lxxᵒ tertio.

[a] filia B. | [b] ballivvos B. | [c] exeptis B. | [d] inconssia, *with dot for expunction under second* i B. [e] *omitted* B.

For a full discussion of this document see Smith, 'Dower', which argues that the form of dower corresponds essentially to the specified dower or *dos nominata* of English common law, although the reference to the grant being 'in free marriage' is unusual, as this term was normally used in assigning marriage portions. The confirmation by Llywelyn ap Gruffudd provides evidence that he had assumed the authority, previously exercised by the king (see no. 69 above), of ratifying the grants of Welsh lords by virtue of his overlordship over them recognized in the Treaty of Montgomery of 1267. Angharad was a daughter of Owain (II) ap Maredudd (d. 1261) of Cedewain; Llywelyn may have referred to her as his niece because her mother Margaret was the daughter of Maelgwn Fychan and Angharad daughter of Llywelyn ap Iorwerth (Smith, 'Dower', 350, n. 1, 351, n. 5). *Killev* in the witness list was presumably Ciliau Aeron (SN 592 501), cmt. Mabwynion; Henfynyw (SN 447 612) and Llanbadarn Trefeglwys (SN 543 631) were both in cmt. Anhuniog; Cefnycaerau may well be the farm of Cefn-y-gaer (SN 536 618), formerly in the parish of Llanbadarn Trefeglwys (ibid., 351, n. 4).

GRUFFUDD AP MAREDUDD AB OWAIN
(d. shortly before 24 March 1319)

72 Letter patent concerning Llywelyn ap Gruffudd
Notification that he is a surety or pledge to Llywelyn, prince of Wales in the sum of 20 marks for the release of Meurig ap Gruffudd, to be paid if Meurig acts unfaithfully against Llywelyn. Sealing clause.

[*c.*7 December 1271]

B = TNA: PRO, E 36/274 (Liber A), fo. 339r. s. xiii ex.
Pd. from B, *LW*, 35–6 (no. 52).
Cd., *H*, no. 286.

[O]mnibus Cristi fidelibus presentes litteras visuris vel audituris Griffud filius Maredud salutem in domino. Noveritis nos domino L. filio Griffini principi Wallie fideiussorem sive plegium esse in xx marcis sterlingorum pro Mewric filii Griffud liberatione, solvendis si idem Mewric dicto domino L. infideliter contraibit. In cuius rei testimonium predicto domino L. litteras nostras concessimus patentes sigilli nostri munimine roboratas.

See note to no. 86 below.

73 Letter patent concerning the church of Llandysul
Notification that, since there was a dispute over the patronage of the church of Llandysul in the court of Canterbury between him and the chapter of St Davids, he has given up the dispute and submitted himself to the judgement of Bishop Richard with respect to the church and the right he claims in it, promising by a corporal oath to observe whatever is ordained by the bishop in the aforesaid matter. He has also renounced all appeals, exceptions, objections and legal remedy with respect to the above. Sealing clause.

Tre-fin, 30 October 1274

B = BL, Harl. MS 6280, fos 46v–47r. s. xvi[1].
Cd., *H*, no. 287.

Universis Cristi fidelibus ad quos presentes littere pervenerint Gruff' filius Mereduci filii Oweni salutem in domino. Ad universitatis vestre notitiam volumus pervenire quod cum esset lis mota super ecclesia de Landessul in curia Cant(uariensi) inter capitulum Men' asserens dictam ecclesiam quoad ius et proprietatem ad ipsos pertinere ex parte una et nos vendicantes nobis ius patronatus in eadem ex altera, nos spontanea voluntate pro nobis et heredibus nostris, pacto modo conditione et aliis omnibus que spiritualia abhorrent reiectis, liti supradicte penitus renuntiantes, subiecimus nos ordinationi venerabilis patris domini R. Men' episcopi super ecclesia prenominata et iure quod vendicamus nobis in eadem, promittentes nos sacramento corporaliter prestito fideliter observaturos quicquid per prefatum patrem venerabilem in premissis fuerit ordinatum. Renuntiavimus etiam quoad premissa, impetratis et impetrandis appellationibus, exceptionibus, cavillationibus et omni iuris remedio. In cuius rei testimonium ac memoriam perpetuam sigillum nostrum presentibus [fo. 47r] litteris apponi fecimus. Datum apud Trefeyn tertio kalendas novembris anno domini millesimo cc^{mo} lxx quarto.

This document is closely modelled on the longer letter, setting out the details of the settlement, issued by Richard de Carew, bishop of St Davids, and likewise dated at Tre-fin, located in Pebidiog (SM 840 325), 30 October 1274 (*St Davids Episcopal Acta*, no. 144). The bishop's letter announces that Gruffudd and his heirs may retain the right of presentation to Llandysul (SN 409 417), cmt. Gwynionydd, and Hywel, the clerk presented by him, will be admitted to the church as rector; that Hywel and his successors will pay twenty marks each year to the chapter; and that the rector will present a vicar, to be continuously resident, whose vicarage will consist of one third of the church's revenues once the money due to the chapter has been paid.

74 Agreement with Payn de Chaworth, captain of the king's army in West Wales

Gruffudd and Cynan sons of Maredudd ab Owain, and their nephew Llywelyn ab Owain ap Maredudd have come to Payn de Chaworth, captain of the king's army in West Wales, willingly submitted their bodies and all their lands to the king's will and committed themselves to the custody of Payn until he considers it expedient to provide them with safe conduct to the king. Gruffudd, Cynan and Llywelyn have returned to the king two commotes, namely Mefenydd and Anhuniog, and quitclaimed their right and inheritance for ever. Those present were Nicholas fitz Martin, Geoffrey de Camville, Oliver de Dinan, Alan de Plugenet, Roger de Molis and William fitz Warin. Payn, Gruffudd, Cynan and Llywelyn have placed their seals alternately on this chirograph between them.

Carmarthen, 2 May 1277

> B = TNA: PRO, E 36/274 (Liber A), fo. 341r–v. s. xiii ex.
> Pd. from B, *LW*, 41 (no. 60).
> Cd., *H*, no. 289.

[A]nno regni regis^a Edwardi quinto in vigilia Inventionis Sancte Crucis venerunt Griffin(us) et Canan(us) filii Mareduci ap Ouwaynco [et]^b Lewelin(us) nepos eorum ad dominum Paganum de Cadurciis capitaneum munitionis domini regis in West Wall(ia) et eorum corpora et omnes terras suas voluntati [fo. 341v] domini Edwardi Dei gratia regis Angl(ie) totaliter supposuerunt, et se ipsos custodie dicti domini Pagani commiserunt quousque dictus Paganus cum viderit sibi expedire ipsis ad dominum regem salvum prestet conductum. Et idem Griffin(us) et Cananus et Leulin(us) eorum nepos domino regi duos comothos, videlicet Meuvenneth et Hannuniauk, reddiderunt et tanquam ius et hereditatem suam inperpetuum quietos clamaverunt. Huic facto presentes fuerunt domini Nichol(as) filius Martini, Galfr(idus) de Camuill', Olyuerus de Dynan, Alanus de Plokenet, Rogerus de Molis et Willelmus filius Warini. Et in cuius rei testimonium dictus Paganus et

Griffin(us) et Cananus et Leulinus huic presenti scripto cyrographato inter eos alternatim sigilla sua apposuerunt. Datum apud Kerm(er)din die et anno prenotatis.

ª B *inserts* regis *(sic)*. | ᵇ *omitted* B.

Gruffudd was negotiating with Chaworth by mid-March 1277; he was received into the king's peace pending a formal agreement by 21 March, but finally submitted only after Chaworth led a large force into Ceredigion in the following weeks. By Whitsun (16 May) Chaworth informed the king that the greatest of Deheubarth, including Gruffudd and Cynan, were on their way to him and they did homage to Edward at Worcester on 1 July (Smith, *Llywelyn*, 421–2). On account of his age, Llywelyn ab Owain was made a royal ward after the submission in May 1277 but on 15 February 1279 he did homage to the king and his lands in Ceredigion were restored to him (*BT, Pen20Tr*, 118; *BT, RBH*, 266–7; *CWR*, 180). That Mefenydd belonged to Gruffudd's share of his father's patrimony is clear from no. 75 below, suggesting that Anhuniog may have belonged to Cynan.

75 Petition to the king

Says that on the first day when he came to the king's peace, placing himself and his land at the will and grace of the king, he was deprived of half of all the land he was then holding, namely the commote of Mefenydd, which is of equal value to the other two commotes. As he cannot live from the other half, he prays the king to provide some other relief by which he might be sustained, so that he may not seem to be completely needy and destitute of all goods; he made the greatest effort in Cardigan, at his own expense, to help the royal expedition, as he has dared to tell the king's bailiffs, as he was the person of greatest power there when war broke out.

[1278]

B = *Rotuli Parliamentorum*, i. 5, no. 20 (from the Parliament Roll 6 Edward I, now lost: ibid., 1, n. *). Response: De hoc quod petit, quod rex subveniat, ei respondeatur quod rex fecit ei curialitatem de denariis apud Turrim.ª
Pd. in B.
Cd., *H*, no. 290.

Dicit Griffinus filius Mareend quod cum ipse venit ad pacem domini regis, supponens se et terram suam voluntati et gratie domini regis, primo die privatus est de medietate totius terre quam tunc tenebat, videlicet de comoto de Maywenet, qui alios duos commotos valet, ut creditur. Et cum idem Griffinus de alia medietate terre sue nullo modo vivere possit, supplicat regie magestati quatenus respiciatur de aliquo solatio unde sustentari possit, ne ad plenum videatur egere, maxime cum omnibus facta sit gratia, et ipse quasi destitutus sit omni bono, qui maiorem in partibus de Kardigan in expeditione regia sumptibus propriis subiit laborem prout ausus est dicere coram ballivis domini regis, et quia maioris fuit potestatis tempore guerre mote.

ª Trim B.

It is not clear from the printed text (B) at which of the three parliaments of 1278 (1 May, Westminster; 8 July, Gloucester; or 29 September, Westminster) the petition was presented.

According to *Brut y Tywysogyon*, Payn de Chaworth subjugated three commotes of Uwch Aeron in Ceredigion, namely Anhuniog, Mefenydd and Perfedd, after Gruffudd and his brother Cynan surrendered to him in 1277; Gruffudd was allowed home after doing homage to the king on 1 July (*BT, Pen20Tr*, 118; *BT, RBH*, 264–7). This could suggest that Anhuniog and Perfedd were the 'two other commotes' he was allowed to keep according to the petition. However, this is by no means certain. To judge by his disputes with and (if authentic) his charter for Strata Florida in 1279–80 (nos 76–7, 82 below), Cynan ap Maredudd, who was also allowed to return to Ceredigion later in 1277, held at least the commote of Pennardd, where the abbey was situated, and no. 74 above may indicate that he had also held Anhuniog before his surrender to Payn de Chaworth on 2 May 1277; Llywelyn ab Owain's share of the patrimony of Maredudd ab Owain consisted of Is Coed and half of Gwynionydd (see no. 83 below). Moreover, in July 1282 both Gruffudd and Cynan were said to hold the commotes of Mebwynion and Gwynionydd, which the king granted to Rhys ap Maredudd apart from the lands in them held by Llywelyn ab Owain at the beginning of the war (*LW*, 165–6). The identity of the 'two other commotes' thus remains uncertain. (For the lands in Ceredigion held or claimed by members of the Deheubarth dynasty in this period see also Griffiths, *PW*, 4–5.) Gruffudd eventually recovered Mefenydd by force, following his attack on Aberystwyth on 24 or 25 March 1282 (*CAC*, 44–5; *BT, Pen20Tr*, 120; *BT, RBH*, 270–1). The response to the petition ordered that a gift of money be made to Gruffudd at the Tower of London (as assumed in Bridgeman, *History*, 159; presumably *Trim* in B, printed in record type, has erroneously omitted a contraction mark).

76 Letter patent concerning a judgement by Gruffudd and the abbots of Whitland and Caerleon

Notification that, since there was a dispute for a long time over the boundaries between the abbot and convent of Strata Florida on one side and Cynan ap Maredudd ab Owain and his men of Caron on the other, finally the said parties have agreed by letters patent under a penalty of 100 marks to accept their arbitration. Having heard the cases of both sides the arbitrators have determined the boundaries as follows: from (?) Penllannerch along the monks' dyke to the stream called Chwyl, *along the* Chwyl *up to the Sychnant, up the Sychnant to its source at Bryn-mawr, from the head to the Sychnant to Y Garn Fechan [Bryngwyn Bach] next to Rhos y gwarwyfa, thence up to (?) Y Crugllainllyn [(?)Llyn Crugnant], thence through the mountain pasture to Y Garn Fawr [Garn Gron] on the mountain called Crynfynydd, from that mountain through the mountain pasture to the other* carn *by going more towards the right-hand side, from that place to the common way next to Blaenywern where the brook called Blaen Croes Fechan [Groes Fechan] has its source, and along that way to the ford in Nant Moelau Fryd [Nant y Moelau], and from that ford through the ford in Nant Llyn along the way to the ford in Nant yr Esgair Berfedd and from that ford down to the source of the Camddwr, the Camddwr is then the boundary up to the Tywi. Sealing clause.*

7 January 1280

B = TNA: PRO, JUST 1/1147, m. 26d (recited in a record of a hearing before Walter de Hopton and other royal justices at Builth, 29 July 1280).
Pd. from B, *WAR*, 301.
Cd., *H*, no. 292.

Universis Cristi fidelibus has litteras visuris vel audituris fratres L. et A. de Alba Domo et de Karlyon' dicti abbates et Griffin(us) filius M(er)eduth filii Oweni salutem in domino. Noverit universitas vestra quod cum lis et altercatio diu mote fuissent super limitibus et finibus terrarum inter abbatem et conventum de Strata Florida ex una parte et nobilem virum Cananu(m) filium M(er)eduth filii Owen(i) et homines suos de Caraun ex altera, tandem dicte partes communi consilio et assensu, scilicet dominus abbas de St(ra)ta Florid(a) pro se et conventu suo et dominus Canan(us) pro se et hominibus suis, per litteras suas patentas sub pena centum marcarum compromiserunt stare arbitrio et iudicio nostro de ambiguitate terrarum predictarum terminanda et diffinienda. Nos igitur auditis et intellectis altercatione et defensione utriusque partis prout melius potuimus et intelleximus omnem ambiguitatem dictarum terrarum per certos limites et metas in hiis terminis declaravimus et terminavimus, videlicet *o* Llanerchegeudua sicut ducit fossa monachorum usque ad rivulum qui vocatur Chwyl, et Chwyl sursum usque ad Sechnant, et Sechnant sursum recte usque ad ortum suum de Brynmaur, et de capite Sechnant recte usque ad *egarn vechan* iuxta Ros Egwaroeva, et ab illo loco directe sursum usque Ecrucllaentllyn, de Crucllaentllyn autem recte *drowe ewevn* usque *egarn vaur* in monte qui vocatur Crynvenyht, et de illo monte *drowe eweun* usque ad *egarnvrall* magis eundo versus dextram partem, et de illo loco recte usque ad viam communem iuxta Blaenewenn ubi oritur et descendit fluviolus qui dicitur Blaen Croes Vechan, et illa via sicut ducit ad vadum in Nant Moeleualvryd, et ab illo vado transeundo per vadum in Nanthlyn sicut via tendit ad vadum in Nant Ereskeyrberveth, et ab illo vado inferius usque Blaencandewr, Caendewr postea est terminus usque ad Tewy. Et ut dictum arbitrium nostrum super dictis limitibus terrarum et finibus perpetue firmitatis robur optineat, huic scripto patenti sigilla nostra apponi fecimus. Dat' anno domini m° cc° lxx nono in crastino Epiphanie domini.

See note to no. 81 below. As suggested by the reference to Cynan ap Maredudd's men of Caron, the dispute turned on land south of Strata Florida Abbey in the the later civil parish of Caron-is-clawdd. The boundaries seem to have followed a roughly south-eastern direction from *Llanerchegeudua* (probably Penllannerch SN 698 627), about 2 miles northeast of Tregaron to Blaencamddwr (SN 752 585), about 5 miles east-south-east of Tregaron, and then along the Camddwr until it flows into the river Tywi. They therefore correspond, at least broadly, to the boundary from *Llannerch hi Guinthwa* to the confluence of the Camddwr and Tywi described in less detail in the Lord Rhys's charter for Strata Florida in 1184 (no. 28 above). The monks' land lay to the north-east of the boundary, that of Cynan ap Maredudd and his men of Caron to the south-west. Bryn-mawr is possibly identifiable with Y Bryn (SN 728 616); the Sychnant with the stream whose source lies just to the north-west of Y Bryn and which flows north into Nant Gorffen at SN 716 635; *Egarn vechan* (Mod. W. Y Garn Fechan) with Bryngwyn Bach (SN 730 626); *Ecrucllaentllyn* with Llyn Crugnant (southern tip at SN 754 612); Y Garn Fawr, lit. 'the great rock or mountain' with Garn Gron (SN 740 611), the highest summit in the area; *Egarnvrall* (Mod. W. Y Garn Arall), lit. 'the other rock, mountain' with Y Garn (SN 732 607). Blaen Croes Fechan, the source of the Groes Fechan, is marked on the 6 in. Ordnance Survey map at SN 737 603. *Nant Moeleualvryd* refers to Nant y Moelau, which flows into the Groes Fawr at SN 740 594, and *Nant Ereskeyrberveth* was presumably a stream near Esgair Berfedd (SN 748 593).

77 Archbishop Pecham (grievances)

The grievances and injuries inflicted by the English on the sons of Maredudd ab Owain.

(1) After the king granted to the aforesaid nobles their own inheritances after the peace treaty, namely Genau'r-glyn and Creuddyn, the king disinherited them of those lands in contravention of his grant and peace treaty, denying them all the laws and customs of Wales and England and of the county court of Carmarthen.

(2) The king, through his justices in his county court of Cardigan, compelled them to pass judgement on the non-nobles of the country and the latter to pass judgement on them, where their predecessors never endured such things from the English.

(3) The king's justices have removed the court of the complainants' noblemen by compelling them to make satisfaction before the justices, though by right these noblemen ought to give satisfaction before the sons of Maredudd.

(4) When there was a shipwreck in the lands of the complainants, they took the goods of the wreck as their predecessors did without any prohibition by representatives of the king; but the king, contrary to their custom and law, fined them 80 marks sterling on account of that wreck and carried away all the goods contained in it.

(5) None of the complainants' men in the county [(?)recte commote] of (?)Is Coed (Vffeg') of Cardigan would have dared to come among the English for fear of prison, and had it not been because of the danger to the nobles themselves they would have done nothing against the honour of the king.

All Christians have laws and customs in their own territories and indeed the Jews living among the English have their laws, and the complainants and their predecessors had immutable laws and customs in their lands until the English took their laws from them after the last war.

[21 × 31 October 1282]

B = London, Lambeth Palace Library, Register of Archbishop Pecham, fo. 245r–v. s. xiii[2]. Some of the right-hand edge of fo. 245r is missing.
C = Oxford, All Souls College MS 182, fo. 106v. *c.* 1413.
Pd. from B and C, *Reg. Peckh.*, ii. 453–4; from (?)C, Wynne, *History of Wales*, 378–9; from (?)Wynne, Warrington, *History of Wales*, 615.
Cd., *H*, no. 293.

Ista sunt gravamina, dampna seu molestie per Anglicos illata filiis Maredud filii Oweyn.

[i] Primum est, postquam[a] dominus rex concessit predictis nobilibus suas proprias hereditates post pacis formam, videlicet Gene[u]glyn[b] et Kreudyn, prefatus vero rex contra suam donationem et pacis formam terris supradictis antedictos nobil[es] dehereditavit, denegando eisdem omnes leges et consuetudines Wallie et Anglie atque comitatus Kaer[m(er)dyn].

[ii] Secundum est, quod prefatus rex in suo comitatu de Cardigan per suos iusticiarios antedictos nobiles compell[it], ut ipsi traderent iudicium super ignobiles ac subditos patrie, et quod tales homines e contrario[c] iudicium super ips[os] apponerent, ubi nunquam antecessores eorum ab Anglicis talia sustinuerunt.

[iii] Tertium est, quod iusticiarii domini regis curiam eorum nobilium abstulerunt, compellendo homines suos [fo. 245v] proprios coram eis satisfacere, quia de iure coram predictis nobilibus deberent satisfacere.

[iv] Quartum est, quod quoddam naufragium in terris antedictorum nobilium fuit. Qui quidem nobiles bona naufragii receperunt, sicut antecessores eorum fecerunt, et hoc non[d]

fuit eis prohibitum per aliquos ex parte regis. Antedictus vero rex contra eorum consuetudinem et legem, occasione illius naufragii eosdem dampnavit in octoginta marcis
sterlingorum, atque bona que in naufragio continebantur omnino asportaverunt.[e]

[v] Quintum est, quod nullus nostrum in comitatu[c] Vffeg' de Cardigan ausus esset venire
inter Anglicos propter timorem carceris, et nisi fuisset propter periculum nobilibus metipsis
nihil contra honorem domini regis moverent.

Significant vero quod omnes cristiani habent leges et consuetudines in eorum propriis
terris, Iudei vero inter Anglicos habent leges, ipsi vero in terris suis et eorum antecessores
habuerunt leges immutabiles et consuetudines donec Anglici post ultimam gwerram[f] ab eis
leges suas abstulerunt.

[a] quamquam C. | [b] *letters in square brackets here and elsewhere in text supplied from* C. | [c] converso
C. | [d] B *inserts* fecerunt *dotted underneath for expunction.* | [e] *sic in* BC. | [f] guerram C.

For the dating see no. 428 below. Gruffudd, Cynan and their nephew Llywelyn ab Owain
brought a claim against the king to Genau'r-glyn and Creuddyn at Montgomery on 29
April 1280, and a day was given them *coram rege* a month from Easter (21 May) (*WAR*,
278–80); however, to judge by this petition, their claim failed. The phrase *in comitatu Vffeg'
de Cardigan* in the fifth petition is problematic. Here, *Vffeg'* has tentatively been taken to be
a corrupt reading of an abbreviated form of Is Coed, the commote adjacent to Cardigan
(cf. Griffiths, *PW*, 49; Rhys, *Ministers' Accounts*, 300 and n. 4); if this is correct, *comitatu*
may be a scribal error for *commoto*.

78 Rhys Fychan ap Rhys ap Maelgwn

*Grant, warranted against all men and women, of the whole of Cantref Penweddig with its
appurtenances, to be possessed freely for ever without any harassment or dispute from him and
his heirs. In exchange for this Rhys and his heirs have granted Ceredigion with all its appurtenances as fully and freely as Gruffudd's predecessors possessed it to Gruffudd and to all the
heirs of Maredudd ab Owain, while Rhys is ready to come with all his forces to Lord Dafydd,
the prince, by the feast of John the Baptist [24 June]. Sealing clause. In order that this
agreement shall be confirmed by both parties Rhys has made letters patent for Gruffudd in
these terms. Witnesses.*

Llanberis, 2 May 1283

B = TNA: PRO, E 36/274 (Liber A), fo. 383v. s. xiii ex.
Pd. from B, *LW*, 133 (no. 235).
Cd., *H*, no. 16.

Omnibus Cristi fidelibus has litteras visuris vel audituris Grufut filius Maredut filii Owein
salutem in domino. Noveritis nos pro nobis et heredibus nostris dedisse et concessisse et
contra omnes homines et feminas warantizasse Reso Iuniori[a] filio Resy filii Maelgun totam
terram de Cantref Penwedic in terminis et finibus suis, in bosco, in plano, cultis et incultis,
libere et pacifice inperpetuum possidendam sine aliqua vexatione, contradictione seu cavillatione ex parte nostra seu heredum nostrorum. Pro hac autem donatione et concessione
predictus Resus et heredes sui dedit nobis et concessit et heredibus Mareduc filii Oweyn
omnino Keredigiawn similiter in finibus et terminis suis et in omnibus aliis ad dictam

terram pertinentibus prout antecessores nostri plenius et liberius possiderunt, dum ipse R. cum toto posse suo sit paratus ad dominum David principem venire infra festum Beati Ioh(ann)is Bapt(ist)e. In cuius rei testimonium presenti carte sigillum nostrum fecimus apponi. Datum apud Llanperis anno domini M° CC° octogesimo tertio die dominica in crastino Ph(ilipp)i et Iacobi. Et ut ista conventio sit stabilis et rata et inconcussa ex utraque parte predictus Resus faciat nobis litteras suas patentes sub hac forma. Hiis testibus: Houel filio Res, Res Vichan, Goronw filio Heylyn tunc senescallo domini, Morgannt filio Mareduc, Llewelyn filio Res et multis aliis.

^a idiniori B.

Dafydd ap Gruffudd also granted Penweddig to Rhys in a charter of the same date (no. 457 below).

CYNAN AP MAREDUDD AB OWAIN
(d. shortly before 18 June 1328)

79 Llywelyn ap Gruffudd
Letter, informing the prince that he has bound himself as a surety to him for Cadwgan, Cynan's foster-son, with respect to the latter's paying £27 sterling in the prince's mercy at suitable terms fixed by the prince; Cynan is also surety for Cadwgan's constancy and fealty to the prince. He therefore prays the prince to end all anger which he has against Cadwgan. He sends this letter to ratify the above, and attests that he is a surety to all who see or read it.
[March 1265 × April 1277]

B = TNA: PRO, E 36/274 (Liber A), fo. 338v. s. xiii ex.
Pd. from B, *LW*, 34 (no. 48).
Cd., *H*, no. 284.

[E]xcellentissimo domino suo L. principi Wallie, domino Snaod'^a suus Kynan filius Maredut salutem et promtam atque paratam in omnibus ad obsequia voluntatem. Noverit vestra excellentia quod ego Kynan obligavi me fideiussorem vobis pro Kaducano alumpno meo ad solvendum xx^{ti}vii libras sterlingorum in vestra misericordia terminis competentibus a vobis sibi prefixis, similiter de ipsius constantia et fidelitate vobis debita^b sum fideiussor. Unde vestram excellentiam humiliter supplico^c quod pro Deo et amore nostro omnem rancorem quam versus ipsum habetis eidem penitus remittatis. Et ut istud ratum sit et firmum permaneat has litteras meas patentes vobis transmitto, et omnibus has litteras visuris vel audituris me fideiussorum taliter esse protestor. Valete semper in domino.

^a *sic in* B. | ^b debiter B. | ^c suplico B.

As Llywelyn ap Gruffudd used the title 'prince of Wales and lord of Snowdon' from 1262, the letter is datable to the period between the death of Cynan's father Maredudd in March 1265 and Cynan's submission to Edward I on 2 May 1277 (*BT, Pen20Tr*, 114, 118; *BT, RBH*, 256–7, 264–5; no. 74 above).

80 Letter patent concerning Llywelyn ap Gruffudd

Notification that he is a surety to Lord Llywelyn, prince of Wales, for Meurig ap Gruffudd of Elfael that the latter will be faithful and if he goes against this, Cynan will pay 10 marks sterling to the prince. He has had this letter patent made in witness of this.

[*c.*7 December 1271]

B = TNA: PRO, E 36/274 (Liber A), fo. 335v. s. xiii ex.
Pd. from B, *LW*, 24–5 (no. 28).
Cd., *H*, no. 285.

[O]mnibus Cristi fidelibus presentes litteras visuris vel audituris Kynan filius Maredut salutem in domino. Noverit universitas vestra quod ego sum fideiussor domino L. principi Wall(ie) pro Meurac Griff' de Elviel quod[a] fidelis existet et si contra hoc venire presumpserit decem marcas sterlingorum dicto domino principi Wall(ie) integraliter persolvam. In cuius rei testimonium has litteras nostras eidem principi feci patentes. Valete.

[a] B *inserts* si.

See note to no. 87 below.

81 Agreement with the abbot and convent of Strata Florida

Both parties declare that, since there have long been disputes between them concerning the limits of lands and boundaries, finally, by common consent, without any coercion, Cynan on behalf of himself and his men and the abbot on behalf of himself and his convent have submitted to the arbitration of the abbots of Whitland and Caerleon and of Gruffudd ap Maredudd, under a penalty of 100 marks, swearing that they will adhere to their arbitration and accept whatever the three arbitrators shall determine concerning all the aforesaid limits of lands. If any of them shall contravene the judgement of the arbitrators, he shall pay the other party the aforesaid 100 marks without any contradiction, on condition that the king may have twenty of the 100 marks and may distrain and compel the rebellious party fully to observe the aforesaid arbitration and to pay the remaining 80 marks to the party observing the arbitration. If the party observing the arbitration incurs any expenses in seeking justice, the disobedient party shall pay them fully to the obedient party. Sealing clause.

London, 2 November 1279

B = TNA: PRO, JUST 1/1147, m. 26d (recited in a record of a hearing before Walter de Hopton and other royal justices at Builth, 29 July 1280).
Pd. from B, *WAR*, 300-1.
Cd., *H*, no. 291.

Universis Cristi fidelibus presentes litteras visuris vel audituris Canan(us) filius M(er)educi filii Oweni et abbas et conventus de Strata Florida salutem in domino. Noverit universitas vestra quod cum diu litigium et controversia inter nos et homines nostros ex parte una et abbatem et conventum dicti monasterii ex altera hucusque fuerint exorta super limitibus terrarum et finibus, tandem ex communi nostro consensu et assensu, nulla coactione facta, ego Canan(us) pro me et hominibus meis et abbas pro se et conventu suo compromisimus sub pena centum marcarum legitime monete in tres bonos viros probos et discretos, videlicet in abbates de Alba Domo et de Karlyon et nobilem virum Griffinu(m) filium eiusdem M(er)eduth, sub iure iurando quod arbitrio dictorum trium arbitrorum in omnibus stabimus ratum et gratum habituri quicquid ipsi tres de omnibus predictis terrarum limitibus in periculo animarum suarum decreverint faciendum et statuendum. Et si aliqua pars nostrum, quod absit, contra iudicium et ordinationem supradictorum arbitrorum in aliquo venire vel contraire presumpserit, predictas centum marcas in arbitrio vallatas alteri parti arbitrio eorum obedienti sine aliqua contradictione persolvet sub hac condictione, videlicet quod dominus rex habeat viginti marcas de predictis centum marcis et ipse distringat et compellat partem rebellem ad observandum plenarie dictum arbitrium et ad solvendum plenarie reliquas octoginta marcas parti predictum arbitrium observanti. Et si alique expense fuerint facte ex parte partis obedientis arbitrio ad inquirendum iustitiam suam pars inobediens parti obedienti penitus persolvet. Et ut omnia predicta inviolabiliter observentur ego Canan(us) et ego abbas St(ra)te Floride huic scripto patenti sigilla nostra apposuimus. Dat' Lond' die veneris proxima post festum omnium sanctorum anno domini m° cc° septuagesimo nono.

The document was enrolled before Walter de Hopton and his fellow justices in acknowledgement of the agreement reached by the parties (*WAR*, 300). The terms of the arbitration award, dated 7 January 1280, were enrolled on the same occasion, immediately after the present document (no. 76 above). The agreement to accept arbitration may have been a compromise following the king's assignation on 27 July 1279 of Roger de Molis, bailiff of Llanbadarn Fawr, and Hywel ap Meurig to hear the trespasses Cynan and his men had allegedly committed against Strata Florida; if they were unable to proceed, the parties were required to appear before the king in the next parliament (*CWR*, 179; *WAR*, 197–8). Since the document is dated at London, 2 November 1279, and since a parliament opened at Westminster less than a fortnight earlier, on 20 October, it is quite possible that the parties had, indeed, appeared at the next parliament as required.

(?)†82 Strata Florida Abbey

Grant in perpetual alms, for the salvation of the souls of himself, his parents and successors of all lands, gifts, legacies, sales, pastures and liberties which his predecessor Lord Rhys the Great, prince of South Wales, and all the latter's sons and nephews, and Cynan's father the Lord Maredudd ab Owain and all his other predecessors and also Cynan's brothers Owain and Gruffudd and other faithful have given and granted in land, above and below the earth, pastures, meadows, waters, moors, cultivated and uncultivated land, fisheries in the sea, ports and rivers, in all liberties and good customs and possessions, moveable and immoveable, free of all service and ecclesiastical and secular exaction and suit of court. The names of the lands and their bounds are: the site of the monastery at Ystrad-fflur with its bounds and appurtenances, Rhydfendigaid, Henfynachlog with its appurtenances, Brynhôp, Cefncastell, Llwyn-y-gog, Dol-fawr, Tref-y-Gwyddel, Cilmeddy, Trefvnwe, Ystradmeurig apart from the acres of the lepers concerning which they have special charters, Dwy Taflogau, Pwllpeiran, Bodcoll with all its bounds and appurtenances, Trefaes[-uchaf], Y Clafdy, Ffynnonoer [Swydd-y-ffynnon] in all its bounds, Cellïau [(?)Cerllïau], Esgair Berfedd, Ynysforgan, Castell Fflemish, Maes Glas, Dinas (?)Drygwyr to the Aeron, Treflyn[-fawr], Trecoll, Tref-y-Gwyddel, Blaenaeron, Esgairsaeson in all its bounds and appurtenances, Rhiwonnen, Celli

Arwnviwe, *Bryn Perfedd [(?)Brynmadog]*, *Esgair* Vayn Temyll, *Pencoed[-uchaf]*, *Tynrhos*, *Celli-gwenyn*, *Celli Angharad*, *Buarth* Elath *apart from the part of the nuns*, *Ffynnon Mebwyn*, *Hafod-wen*, *Castell* Dynauel, Trefywedu, *Tref-y-benydd*, *Hendre Forrant*, *Meuddin[-fawr]* with all its appurtenances, *Morfa-mawr*, *Dau Farchdy* and thence to the *Cledan*, Ardiskyn Kyveth, *Cefngwrthafarn[-uchaf]*, *Blaensaith*, *Bryn Llyn Du* with all its *bounds and appurtenances, half of Bronwennau, Cymanfynydd, Gwrthwynt[-uchaf]* with its *appurtenances, Dineirth [Castell]* and *Tref* Latheu *with all their bounds and appurtenances, Morfa-bychan in all its bounds, Alltwen in its bounds, Gweirgloddallt*, Dro Ecapell *with its appurtenances, Pant Cynddelw with all its bounds and appurtenances, Trefaes[-uchaf]*, *Safn-y-ci [Tanbwlch] in all the bounds which Gruffudd ap Cadwgan gave to the monks, Tywarchen Benweddig [Tirmynach]*, *Pencwmbancar* (Ban Carv), Llanvessill, *Argoed y Gwenyn [(?)Argoed-fawr]*, *(?)Talbont*, Castell Gwgon, *Broncastellan with all its bounds and appur-tenances as contained in the monks' charters (4 acres and a meadow at Aberclarach, 8 acres and a meadow in the land of Llechwedd* lloyden, *with all the other acres which the monks have at Cefn y Fanfrech), Dyffryn Elan with all its bounds, Nant* Moraut, *Nant* Elmer, *Nant* Eyryn, *Cwm* Goybedauc, *Dyffryn y Dernol*, Treanill' Gwyn, Goletyr Maen, *Nannerth Gwy with all its bounds and appurtenances*, Abercoill, Brithen, *Rhiw* Avanaul, *Llanfadog*, Enerllyn, Talluchynt *with all its bounds and appurtenances, Aberdihonw with all its bounds and tenements, Cefn Iolo with all its bounds and appurtenances as contained more fully in the monks' charters, all the land and pasture of Elenydd in all its bounds and appurtenances, all the land of Nant-bau and* Trefflath, Pullburwe *with all its bounds and appurtenances. In order that all uncertainty is removed regarding all the said grants, especially all goods which arrive on the monks' lands through shipwreck, and above all on all the monks' coastal lands of Morfa-mawr, namely from the mouth of the Cledan to Aberarth, in all the lands of Morfa-bychan adjacent to the sea, in the lands of Alltwen, Gweirgloddallt with its bounds and appurtenances on both sides of the Ystwyth and in the acre called* Growe Ecapell *in its coastal bounds, as well as Pant Cynddelw with all its bounds and appurtenances; he has granted on behalf of himself and his heirs and successors, fully and without any challenge, all goods thrown, found or seized on these lands or shores or river-banks, and particularly he has granted and confirmed by this charter whatever is found in all the monks' lands, namely ships, skiffs, casks and other vessels, wine, honey, beer and other liquor, corn and all kinds of grain, meat, fish and all other food, gold, silver or other money, precious stones, rings and other precious objects, clothes of whatever colour, skins and animals, salt, iron and other metals and all other goods, irrespective of any secular custom, exaction or challenge of his heirs or successors. He has further granted all lands and pastures so freely that no other secular or ecclesiastical person may, at any time of the year, have any common rights in any of the monks' lands, pastures or woods nor claim or demand such rights by custom; the monks shall hold all their lands for their own use and possess them peacefully without any claim. He has granted the monks permission to construct a weir whenever they want in the river Ystwyth where they have land on both sides of that river. He has also granted freedom to buy and sell and carry out all business in all his lands and lordship, with freedom from all tolls, ferry dues, bridge dues and all other customs and exactions pertaining to him and his heirs and successors on land and sea, in ports and on shores, in townships, castles and all places of his lordship. A further confir-mation of whatever the monks receive in his lands from the offerings of the living, last wills and testaments of the dying or other just means. He is bound to maintain, on behalf of himself and his heirs and successors, all the aforesaid lands, pastures and woods with all their bounds and appurtenances, warrant them against all men and women and conserve them in peace, and has granted this for ever throughout the lands he possesses now or will possess in the future. May whosoever of his heirs and successors confirms these grants and increases them under his seal be filled with all heavenly blessing and grace and may his blessing be in all the heavenly dew above and earthly abundance below. May God weaken anyone who tries to infringe or weaken this grant and remove him soon from the face of the earth and may his name not be written in the book of life, but he shall know that he has incurred the anger and curse of almighty God, His glorious mother and all saints and elect of God as well as the anger and curse of Cynan. Sealing clause; witnesses.*

[1280 × 25 March 1282]

B = TNA: PRO, C 66/308 (Pat. R. Richard II, pt. 1), m. 12 (reciting an inspeximus of Edward the Black Prince 28 October 1369, 20 October 1380).
C = TNA: PRO, C 66/417 (Pat. R. 3 Henry VI, pt. 2), m. 4 (in an inspeximus of B, 8 July 1425).
D = TNA: PRO, C 66/605 (Pat. R. 23 Henry VII, pt. 2), mm. 10–11 (in an inspeximus of C, 4 March 1508).
Pd. from C, *CPR 1422–9*, 295–8; from an abbreviated text in BL, MS Harl. 6068, fo. 11v (s. xvi/xvii), Williams, *Cistercian Abbey of Strata Florida*, App., xvi–xvii (and trans.).
Cd., *CPR 1377–81*, 551 (from B); *CPR 1494–1509*, 567 (from D); *H*, no. 14.

Universis sancte ecclesie filiis Cananus filius Mareduth filii Oweyn salutem et pacem. Universitati vestre notum facio me dedisse et concessisse ac presenti carta mea confirmasse pro me et heredibus meis ac successoribus meis quibuscumque Deo et Beate M(ari)e et monachis de Stratta Florida, pro remedio anime mee, parentum et successorum meorum in puram, liberam ac perpetuam elemosinam omnes terras et tenementa, donationes, legationes, venditiones, concessiones, pascuas, pasturas, et libertates quas pie recordationis antecessor meus dominus Resus magnus Southwall(ie) princeps et omnes filii eius ac nepotes, et quas bone memorie dominus Maered' filius Oweyn pater meus et ceteri omnes antecessores mei, Owenus etiam et Gruffinus fratres mei ac quicumque alii fideles sive dono sive pretio seu quocumque alio iusto modo dederunt et contulerunt in terra super terram et subtus terram, in pasturis et pratis, in aquis et moris, in bosco et plano, in terra culta et inculta, in piscaturis et piscationibus tam maris et portuum maris quam fluviorum, in omnibus libertatibus et bonis consuetudinibus ac possessionibus tam mobilibus quam immobilibus hucusque habitis vel amodo habendis integre, libere et quiete ab omni servitio et exactione ecclesiastica et seculari ac qualibet secta sicut melius et plenius in amplioribus et latioribus terminis et finibus uncquam possederunt aut decetero fuerint possessuri. Quorum quedam loca et terminos propriis nominibus indicamus et nominamus: Strata Florida scilicet in quo loco situm est monasterium cum omnibus terminis et pertinentiis suis, Rydvendygheyt, Henwynatloc cum suis pertinentiis, Bryn Hop, Keuen Castell, Lloen y Goc, Dol Vaur, Tref Ygoydhell, Kylmedvywe, Trefvnwe, Strat Meur(ic) exceptis acris leprosorum de quibus habent cartas speciales, Dwe Tafflogev, Pull Peran, Bot Coll in omnibus finibus et pertinentiis suis, Trefvaes, Yclafdy, Fennaun Oyer in omnibus finibus suis, Kellyev, Esgeyr P(er)ueth', Ynys Vorgan, Castell Fle(m)mys, Mays Glas, Dynas Dricwyr usque Airo(n)n, Treflyn, Tref Ecoll, Trefigoidhel, Blain Airon, Esgeir Saisson in omnibus finibus et pertinentiis suis, Riwe Anhvn, Kelly Arwnviwe, Bryn P(er)ueth, Eskeir Vayn Teuill', Pencoet, Rossan, Kelliev Gwonyn, Kelliev Ygarad, Buarth Elath excepta parte monialium, Fennaun Vebbwyn, Hauotwen, Castell Dynauel, Tref Ywedu, Tref

Yb(er)ennyth, Hen Voron, Meudyn cum omnibus pertinentiis suis, Morva Maur, Dev Marchdi et inde usque Kaledan, Ardiskyn Kyveth, Keuen Guarth Auarth, Blayn Saith, Bryn Llauden cum omnibus terminis et pertinentiis suis, dimidia pars Browennev, Keman Vynnyd, Gurthwynt cum omnibus pertinentiis suis, Dynerth et Trefflatheu cum omnibus terminis et pertinentiis suis, Morva Bichan cum omnibus finibus suis, Allwen in terminis suis, Guerglaudhallt, Dro Ecappell' cum suis pertinentiis, Pant Kendelo cum omnibus finibus et pertinentiis suis in terra et in mari et in littore maris, Treffuaes cum omnibus perti-nentiis suis, Sauen Eky in omnibus finibus quos Gruffinus filius Cadugan eisdem monachis dedit, Tywarchen Penwedhic, Bancarv, Llanvessill, Argoit Egvenyn, Talpont Cucull', Castell Gugan, Castellan cum omnibus finibus et pertinentiis suis sicut carte monachorum continent, apud Ab(er)claragh' quatuor acras et pratum, octo etiam acras et pratum in terra illa que dicitur Llechwedlloyden', cum omnibus aliis acris quas habent ipsi monachi apud Keven Ywanvrreth, Driffryn Elan cum omnibus terminis suis, Nant Moraut, Nant Elmer, Nant Eyrin, Cumgoybedauc, Driffryn Edernawl, Treanill' Gwyn, Goletyr Maen, Nan Nerth' Goy cum omnibus finibus et pertinentiis suis, Abercoill, Brithen', By We Avanaul, Llanvadauc, En(er)llyn, Talluchynt cum omnibus finibus et pertinentiis suis, Ab(er)de Hony cum omnibus pertinentiis suis et tenementis, Keuenoly cum omnibus finibus et perti-nentiis sicut in cartis monachorum plenius continetur, totam quoque terram et pasturam de Elenyth in omnibus finibus et pertinentiis suis, totam etiam terram de Nantvey et Trefflath', Pullburwe cum omnibus finibus et pertinentiis suis. Et ut omnis scrupulositas vel ambiguitas in omni parte dictarum donationum et libertatum quas dictis religiosis dedi et concessi imposterum omnino tollatur et auferatur, specialiter omnia bona et singula que ex naufragio vel tempestate maris fractione navis aut alterius vasis cuiuscumque vel etiam ex wrek' aut alio quocumque modo aut casu ad quascumque monachorum terras devenerint aut per aliquod infortunium applicaverint et precipue in omnibus terris maritimis ipsorum monachorum de Morva Maur, videlicet de Aber Caledan usque Aber Arth', in omnibus terris de Morva Bichan que iuxta mare habentur et extenduntur, in terris etiam de Allwen, Gwyrglaudhallt in finibus et pertinentiis suis ex utraque parte Ystoyth', et in illa acra que dicitur Growe Ecappell et in finibus suis maritimis; similiter in terra monachorum que vocatur Pant Kendelo in omnibus finibus et pertinentiis suis, quecumque itaque res et omnia bona casibus superius expressis in dictis monachorum terris seu litoribus vel ripis earumdem sive in mari ex opposito terris et finibus eorumdem monachorum in proximo vel in longinquo proiecta et inventa vel capta fuerint remota omni contradictione tranquille, pacifice et integraliter prefatis monachis de Strata[a] Florida pro me et heredibus meis ac successoribus meis quibuscumque imperpetuum contuli et donavi, et nominatim quicquid proiectum fuerit vel inventum in omnibus monachorum terris et terminis tam in mari et litore maris quam extra mare, scilicet in navibus, scaphis et doliis ac aliis vasis quibus-cumque in vino, melle et cervisia et alio quocumque liquore, similiter in frumento et in omni genere bladi, in carnibus, piscibus quibuscumque et in omnibus aliis cibariis, in pecunia auri et argenti aut alia qualicumque moneta, in lapidibus preciosis, anulis, minusculis iocalibus quibuscumque, in vestubus et pannis cuiuscumque coloris, in pellibus, coriis et animalibus, in sale et ferro ac alio quocumque metallo, et insuper in omnibus aliis bonis et rebus quibus-libet ac utilitatibus non obstante dominii vel heredum aut successorum meorum quorumcumque aliqua seculari consuetudine et demanda, exactione seu contradictione prefatis religiosis integraliter contuli, donavi et concessi ac presenti carta mea confirmavi. Preterea omnes terras et pasturas dictorum religiosorum taliter liberas et quietas eisdem dedi et concessi quod nulla alia persona secularis vel ecclesiastica aliquo tempore anni habeat communitatem aliquam in aliquibus terris, pasturis et nemoribus eorundem monachorum nec aliquo tempore quasi ex consuetudine aliquis communionem aliquam seu viciniam in dictis terris et pasturis ac nemoribus in preiudicium dictorum religiosorum audeat vel presumat sibi vendicare vel exigere, set dicti religiosi omnes terras suas pasturas et nemora ad proprios usus custodient et tenebunt, ac sine aliqua calumpnia et demanda pacifice possidebunt. Dedi etiam dictis monachis liberam libertatem et licentiam faciendi et construendi gordam sive gurgitem in fluvio de Ystoyth, ubi dicti religiosi terras habent ex utraque parte fluminis quandocumque et quotienscumque placuerint eisdem et sibi viderint expedire. Similiter dedi eisdem monachis et concessi omni tempore libertatem emendi et vendendi omnia negotia sua excercendi in omnibus terris meis et in toto dominio meo et libertatem et quietantiam de omni theoloneo, passagio aut pontagio et de omnibus aliis consuetudinibus, exactionibus et demandis ad me et heredes meos ac successores meos quoscumque spectantibus vel pertinentibus sive in terra sive in mari seu in portubus et litore maris, in villis, castellis sive etiam in omnibus aliis locis dominii mei. Quicquid vero prefati monachi de Strata Florida in omnibus terris meis quas habeo vel quas habiturus sum post hoc Deo propitio de terris et pasturis vel aliis bonis et rebus quibuslibet sine comparato pretio aut oblatione viventium aut morientium testamento et ultima voluntate aut alio iusto modo poterint adipisci ratum erit eis et inconcussam pro me et heredibus meis ac successoribus meis imperpetuum. Omnes igitur terras et pasturas ac nemora predicta cum omnibus finibus et pertinentiis suis, omnes insuper donationes, concessiones et confirmationes ac libertates superius expressas et nominatas in campis et silvis, in bosco et plano, in terra arabili et non arabili, in pratis, pascuis et pasturis, in culto et inculto, in terra super terram et subtus terram, in mari et portubus ac litoribus maris, prenominatis monachis de Strata Florida pro me et omnibus heredibus meis ac successoribus meis quibuscumque custodire, integre defendere et manutenere teneor et etiam contra omnes homines et feminas warantizare et tranquillas ac pacificas in omnibus conservare et hoc in omnibus locis et terris quas in presenti habeo et possideo et quas decetero possessurus fuero et in quantumcumque Deo disponente se extenderit donatio mea, prefatas omnes donationes, concessiones, confirmationes et libertates prefatis religiosis pro me et omnibus heredibus meis ac quibuslibet successoribus dedi, contuli et concessi ac etiam imperpetuum confirmavi. Quicumque itaque de meis heredibus et successoribus has meas donationes, concessiones, confirmationes et libertates ratas habuerit et inconcussas easque sigillo suo augere et confirmare voluerit omni benedictione celesti et gratia repleatur et in omni rore celi desuper et in pinguedine terre deorsum sit benedictio eius. Qui vero infringere aut infirmare eam attemptaverit infirmet illum Deus et auferat eum cito de superficie terre et cum iustis non scribatur nomen eius in libro vite, set indignationem et maledictionem Dei omnipotentis et gloriose matris eius et omnium sanctorum et electorum Dei ac meam se noverit incursurum. Ut igitur omnes fideles has meas donationes, concessiones, libertates et confirmationes gratas, firmas et acceptas habeant et teneant imperpetuum, et ut nullus hominum uncquam possit infringere sigilli mei impressione eas roboravi. Hiis testibus: domino Aniano tunc abbate de Strata Florida, Gervasio priore, Adam suppriore, Ioh(ann)e filio Magistri, Cadug(a)no Crach' et Lli' Hagh' monachis dicte domus; de conversis fratre Madoco filio Gourgenev, Aniano Voil magistris ovium et vaccarum, fratre Gruffino et fratre Meiller filio Llewelini; de secularibus Oweyn filio Gruff' tunc archidiacono de Cardigan, Lewelino filio Kenwric tunc decano de Ult(ra) Airon', Cadugano filio Gr'

Classour et magistro Traharn' Cogh', Gruffin(o) filio M(er)ed' fratre meo, Oweyno filio Morgan filii Eynaun, Oweno filio Morgan ap Res, Hoel filio Will' Choch', Traharn' filio Ph(ilipp)i, Gwill' ap Ph', Gruffino filio Gourgenev Vychan et aliis.

ᵃ CD; Srata B.

The authenticity of this charter is open to question on account both of its textual transmission and of certain internal features. It is odd that Cynan's charter was first presented for confirmation in 1369 (to the Black Prince) rather than with the other charters issued in favour of Strata Florida by members of the Deheubarth dynasty presented to Edward II in 1320. True, this need not count decisively against the document's authenticity: after all, Edward II's inspeximus itself contained four, apparently authentic, charters not included in Edward I's inspeximus of 1285 (nos 35, 50, 55 and 63 above). Moreover, there were other charters that were never presented for confirmation (e.g. nos 36–40 above). The omissions in 1285 may reflect the circumstances of the immediate aftermath of the Edwardian Conquest: perhaps the monks thought that Edward I would be prepared to confirm the lands bestowed by the Lord Rhys, but not necessarily the grants of later Deheubarth rulers, as the earlier of Rhys's charters had been confirmed by Henry II (see nos 25 and 28 above). Yet it remains puzzling why, if they possessed Cynan's charter then, the monks passed over the opportunity in 1320 of obtaining confirmation of the uniquely comprehensive statement of their lands and liberties that it provided. One explanation could be that the present charter was written, or rewritten, in response to a challenge to the abbey's liberties, especially with respect to wreck, made at some point between 1320 and 1369, perhaps by officials of the Black Prince after he was invested as Prince of Wales in 1343. However, Strata Florida is not known to have faced such a challenge: for example, records of the *quo warranto* inquiries held in south-west Wales in 1344 by the Black Prince's officials contain no references to the abbey (cf. *Placita de Quo Warranto*, 817–21).

Most of the lands listed occur in earlier charters issued by members of the dynasty for Strata Florida and are inconclusive with regard to the present charter's authenticity. The closest parallels are with Maelgwn Fychan ap Maelgwn's charter for the abbey of 1198 × 1227, which contains many of the same lands as well as the clause on quittance of tolls and other customs (no. 63 above); some other lands, including Aberdihonw and Cefn Iolo, occur in no. 35 above. The main differences between the present charter and all earlier surviving charters for Strata Florida are the length and detail of the liberty clauses, particularly with respect to rights of wreck, and the sanction clauses. Lack of contemporary Welsh parallels makes it difficult to assess the authenticity of the liberty clauses: comparison with Llywelyn ap Iorwerth's spurious charters for Aberconwy (nos 218–19 below) could suggest that such detail was a post-conquest fabrication; yet similar clauses occur in the apparently authentic charter issued by Llywelyn for Cymer in 1209 (no. 229 below), and the liberties may have been defined so precisely in the present charter because they had been infringed by Cynan, with whom the abbey was in dispute over other matters (nos 76 and 81 above). The sanction clauses excite greater suspicion, as these are more typical of earlier medieval charter writing (cf. no. 480 below) and are unparalleled in any other authentic charters for Cistercian houses contained in this edition, the closest resemblances occurring in the spurious charters for Combermere Abbey (nos 497–8, 510 below). At the very least, the form of the sanction clauses points strongly towards beneficiary drafting.

None the less, although its authenticity is dubious, the charter cannot conclusively be shown to be spurious. The witness list is compatible with the charter's having been issued by Cynan, as Abbot Anian was Einion Sais who succeeded Philip Goch as abbot of Strata Florida in 1280 (*BT, Pen20Tr*, 120; *BT, RBH*, 268–9). If authentic, the charter was probably issued between 1280 and the outbreak of war in Ceredigion on 24 or 25 March 1282. True, Cynan's authority in Ceredigion was less extensive than the charter implies, but Cynan may have welcomed the opportunity to assert his status as a descendant of the Lord Rhys and the monks to obtain a reinforcement of their written title to lands and rights. Cynan had been allowed to return to his lands in Ceredigion after surrendering to the king in the summer of 1277. He sided with Llywelyn ap Gruffudd in the war of 1282 and submitted, together with his brother Rhys, to William de Valence in or soon after mid-January 1283; however, after a period in the king's service from March to July, Cynan sided with the Welsh cause again and was captured and imprisoned at Bridgnorth in August 1283 (*BT, Pen20Tr*, 119, 120; *BT, RBH*, 266–7, 268–71; Griffiths, *Conquerors*, 50–1; Walker, 'William de Valence', 420; Smith, *Llywelyn*, 572, n. 209). It is possible that the confirmation represented the final stage in Cynan's reconciliation with Strata Florida following the dispute over lands settled on 7 January 1280 and acknowledged before the royal justices at Builth on 8 July (see nos 76 and 81 above). If so, the charter may well have been issued in 1280, soon after the succession of Einion as abbot, at a date unknown, in that year.

The nuns whose land is excluded from the grant of Buarth *Elath* belonged to the Cistercian nunnery of Llanllŷr (SN 543 561), cmt. Mebwynion, a daughter house of Strata Florida located about 14 miles south-west of the abbey (cf. *HW*, ii. 603). The name of the witness Cadwgan ap Gruffudd Claswr (*Classour*) may indicate that his father Gruffudd was or had been a member or tenant of the native ecclesiastical community of Llanddewibrefi, refounded as a collegiate church in 1287 (Evans, 'Survival of the *clas*', 38–9).

LLYWELYN AB OWAIN AP MAREDUDD
(d. 1309, before 3 May)

83 Petition to the king and his council
Llywelyn, in the custody of the bishop of St Davids at the king's command, prays that the king and his council will make restitution to him of half of Gwynionydd and of Gwestfa (?) Gwasgarawg (Waskarou), of which Rhys ap Maredudd has disseised him by the suggestion which he made at the king's court, so that Llywelyn shall not be disinherited as he has in no wise been against the king or his peace.

[Probably 28 July 1282 × 1283]

A = TNA: PRO, SC 8/278, no. 13891. Endorsed: Fiat ei littere in cancellario quod senescallus Westwall(ie) reddat ei partem suam ipsum contingentem etc. (s. xiii ex); approx. 181 × 66 mm. Cd., *CAP*, 465–6; *H*, no. 294.

A nostre seignour le roy e a sun conseil prie Lewelin ab Oweyn, ke est en la garde le eveske de Sein David par le comandement nostre seignour le roy, ke nostre seignour le roy lui face restitucioun de la meyté del commot de Gonyonith e de Westwa Waskarou des queus Rees ab Mereduk' lui ad deseysi par suggeçtioun ke il fist a la court nostre seignour le roy, issi ke le vant[a] Lewelin ne seit deserité desi come il n'at esté en nul point encontre nostre seignour le roy ne encontre sa pees.

[a] levant *spelled as one word in* A.

Llywelyn ab Owain and his lands were placed under royal wardship following his submission, along with his uncles Gruffudd and Cynan sons of Maredudd ab Owain, on 2 May 1277. The petition can be no earlier than 15 February 1279, when Llywelyn did homage to Edward and was restored to his lands (see no. 74 and note above). However, the reference to disseisin by Rhys ap Maredudd points strongly towards a *terminus a quo* of 28 July 1282, when Rhys was granted Mebwynion and Gwynionydd by the king, and proceeded to occupy these commotes, including, contrary to the terms of the grant, the lands which Llywelyn had held in them at the beginning of the war. On 21 October 1283 Rhys was ordered to restore to Llywelyn, still a minor, the lands of which he had been seised, through his guardian, at the outbreak of war in 1282 (*LW*, 165–6, 159–60 (nos 290, 282)). However, a later date in 1283 cannot be ruled out, as it is possible that Rhys sought to challenge that order, perhaps by the *suggeçtioun* at the king's court referred to in the petition. In any event, the endorsement shows that the petition was successful: the king instructed the seneschal of West Wales to restore Llywelyn to his share of patrimony. Alone among his dynasty, Llywelyn retained his patrimony in Ceredigion until his death, when he held a commote (that is, the half-commote of Is Coed Uwch Hirwern) and half a commote (presumably Gwynionydd) together with a *gwestfa* (presumably that claimed in the present petition) from the king by the tenure of *pennaeth* or Welsh barony. If *Westwa Waskarou* represents Gwestfa Gwasgarawg, it probably consisted of enclaves of Gwynionydd in Mebwynion, namely Dihewyd (SN 486 560) and Trefigod (*CIPM* v. 42–3; Griffiths, *PW*, 5, 9; *idem, Conquerors*, 51; Wmffre, 'Language and History', II. iii. 1395) rather than the Gwestfa Gwasgarawg of either Anhuniog or Creuddyn farther north in Ceredigion (cf. ibid., 1367, 1375).

THE LINEAGE OF RHYS GRYG (YSTRAD TYWI)

RHYS MECHYLL AP RHYS GRYG
(d. 1244)

84 Gruffudd ab Ednyfed and his heirs by Rhys's kinswoman Gwenllian

Grant of Maenor Llansadwrn and (?) Tyllwyd and Kylwede *with all their appurtenances,* Taliaris, *which was the land of Lady Gwenllian, with all its appurtenances, and Cwmbleog [Cwm-liog] with all its appurtenances apart from the land of* Kymrechor, *to be held from Rhys and his heirs for ever, free of all service and exaction pertaining to Rhys and his heirs apart from army service and feeding Rhys's household on the land of Cwmbleog as it was rendered. Witnesses.*

[1236 × 1244]

B = TNA: PRO, C 66/160 (Pat. R. 17 Edward II, pt. 2), m. 24 (in an inspeximus, 24 March 1324).
C = TNA: PRO, C 66/187 (Pat. R. 10 Edward III, pt. 1), m. 40 (in an inspeximus of B, 10 March 1336).
Cd., *CPR 1321–34*, 398 (from B); *CPR 1334–8*, 227 (from C); *H*, no. 28.

Omnibus Cristi fidelibus ad quos presens scriptum pervenerit Resus iunior filius Resi Crehc salutem et pacem. Noverit universitas vestra me dedisse et concessisse et hac presenti carta mea confirmasse G(ri)f(ino) filio Ednewet et heredibus suis de Gue(n)llian consobrina mea Maenaur La(n)sadurn et Tehlwe et Kylwede' cum omnibus pertinentiis, et Taleiyares que fuit terra domine Wenlliant cum omnibus pertinentiis, et Cum Bleauhc cum omnibus perti-nentiis excepta terra Kymrechor. Concessi autem dicto G(ri)ff(ino) et dictis heredibus suis omnes predictas terras cum omnibus pertinentiis suis habendas et tenendas de me et heredibus [meis]ᵃ imperpetuum, libere et quiete ab omni servitio et exactione que ad me vel ad heredes meos pertineat,ᵇ excepto servitio exercitus de omnibus dictis terris et pastus familiarium super terram de Kombleauhc prout solutus fuit. Hiis testibus: G(ri)ff(ino) filio Rad(ulfo), magistro Lowarhc, Karwet filio Tuder, Ada filio Lowarhc et multis aliis.

ᵃ *supplied from C, where the word is interlined.* | ᵇ *sic in* B.

Gruffudd ab Ednyfed was a son of Ednyfed Fychan (d. 1246), steward of Llywelyn ap Iorwerth, and his wife Gwenllian (d. 1236), a daughter of the Lord Rhys and thus Rhys Mechyll's aunt; by October 1229 Ednyfed held Llansadwrn, together with Cellan and half of Llanrhystud in Ceredigion, which had presumably formed Gwenllian's marriage portion (*CW*, 38; *PR 1225–32*, 271; Lloyd, 'Age of the native princes', 178). It is notable that the present charter emphasizes descent from Gruffudd's mother and thus implies that the lands being granted and confirmed were inherited from Gwenllian; if so, it is no earlier than 1236. The centre of Maenor Llansadwrn was Llansadwrn (SN 695 315), cmt. Maenordeilo; *Tehlwe* may be Tyllwyd (SN 718 338), about 2 miles north-east of Llansadwrn. Taliaris (Taliaris House SN 640 280) was a township about 3 miles north-east of Llandeilo Fawr, cmt. Maenordeilo. Cwmbleog (now Cwm-liog SN 656 347) lay about $3\frac{1}{2}$ miles south-west of Caeo (see map in Richards, 'Carmarthenshire possessions', 115; no. 90 below). Gruffudd died in or shortly after 1256 and was buried in Bangor (Smith, *Llywelyn*, 45; 'Gwaith Dafydd Benfras', 497). The descendants of his brother Goronwy held the three townships of Cellan, Llechweddlwyfai in Creuddyn and Rhydonnen in Perfedd in 1344 (Griffiths, *PW*, 9).

HYWEL AP RHYS GRYG
(d. in or after 1286)

85 Letter patent concerning Llywelyn ap Gruffudd

Notification that he has done homage of his own accord to his lord Llywelyn for the lands which he has generously granted him, namely Mabelfyw and others, and has sworn his fealty and homage to Llywelyn by a corporal oath so that if he should withdraw from his fealty or good service to him and his heirs, he grants that the bishops of Bangor and St Asaph may pronounce sentence upon him without any delay and that he and his heirs shall be deprived for ever of the said lands and of all others in Wales. Hywel attaches his seal to this letter patent of obligation; he implores the said bishops to attach their seals along with his and that they will undertake what he has granted above if he should unfaithfully withdraw from his obligations. Witnesses.

Caernarfon, 11 August 1258

B = TNA: PRO, E 36/274 (Liber A), fos 342v–343r. s. xiii ex.
Pd. from B, *LW*, 45 (no. 68).
Cd., *H*, no. 298.

[U]niversis Cristi fidelibus presentes litteras visuris vel audituris Howel filius Rys salutem in domino sempiternam. Noverit universitas vestra nos nobili viro et karissimo domino nostro, domino Lewelin(o) filio Griffin(i) pro terris ac possessionibus quas nobis liberaliter contulit, videlicet Mab Elvyw et alias, nostrum homasium ultro fecisse et nostram fidelitatem et nostrum homasium prestito corporali iuramento eidem iurasse quod si ab ipsius vel suorum heredum fidelitate vel bono servitio ad nos pertinente recesserimus, concedimus et volumus nos et nostris in hoc concentientes extunc per venerabiles patres dominos episcopos Bangor et de Sancto Assaph sine dilatione aliqua promulgari et nos et nostros heredes insuper predictis terris ac omnibus aliis in Wall(ia) in perpetuum carituros et privandos. In cuius rei testimonium nostrum sigillum hiis patentibus litteris nostris obligatoriis fecimus apponi. Et predictos episcopos attentius exoramus ut sua sigilla presentibus apponant una cum nostro, eaque que supra concessimus effectu mancipaturos si nos contigerit,[a] quod absit, a premissis infideliter resilire. Datum apud Kaer yn Arvon anno domini mᵒ ccᵒ lᵒ octavo dominica proxima ante assumptionem [fo. 343r] Beate Marie. Hiis testibus: Reso filio Griffin(i), Geron' senescallo nostro, Lewelino filio Rys, Trahaearn filio Gruffin(i), Enn' Parvo, Howel filio Enn', Gruffud Grach, David et L. filiis Kenan, Iervasio et Iohanne notariis nostris et multis aliis. Valete.

[a] contingerit B.

Mabelfyw was a commote in Cantref Mawr. Presumably the document was drawn up by one or both of the notaries named at the end of the witness list.

86 Letter patent concerning Llywelyn ap Gruffudd

Notification by Hywel, Trahaearn ap Gruffudd, the two sons of Trahaearn ap Cadwgan, the two [sons of Einion ap] Gwallter, and the two sons of Arawdr ab Owain that they stand surety, individually and as a group, on behalf of Einion Sais concerning the 200 marks to be paid to their lord Llywelyn ap Gruffudd, prince of Wales and lord of Snowdon, if Einion shall fail to restore into the prince's hands his son, a hostage freed by their pledge, when the prince wishes to take him back, or if Einion shall withdraw from his homage and fealty to the prince. The senders renounce all exceptions, petitions, objections and all remedies of civil or canon law that would be valid against the present obligation. Sealing clause.

Rhyd-y-briw, 7 November 1271

B = TNA: PRO, E 36/274 (Liber A), fo. 338v. s. xiii ex.
Pd. from B, *LW*, 33–4 (no. 47).
Cd., *H*, no. 300.

[U]niversis ad quos presentes littere pervenerint Howelus filius Resi Cric, Trahayrn filius Grufud, duo filii T(ra)hayrn filii[a] Cadwgaun, duo [filii Ennii][b] filii Gualter et duo filii Arawdyr filii Owein salutem. Noverit universitas vestra nos esse fideiussores et obligatos singulos et in solidum pro Cannaun[c] Seis de ducentis marcis solvendis domino nostro Lewelino principi Wall(ie), domino Snaudon', si dictus Enniau(n) filium suum dictum obsidem et per pleviniam nostram deliberatum non restituerit in manus domini principis quando voluerit ipsum repetere, vel si dictus Enniau(n) ab homagio et fidelitate domini principis recesserit. Renuntiamus etiam omni exceptioni, impetrationi, cavilationi et omni remedio iuris civilis vel canonici contra presentem obligationem valituris. In cuius rei testimonium presentibus litteris nostris sigilla nostra apposuimus. Datum et actum apud Rith Pryw anno domini m° cc° septuagesimo primo in crastino Beati Leonardi.

[a] filio B. | [b] *supplied from* LW, *28 (no. 35).* | [c] *recte* Enniaun *[cf. LW no. 35].*

Einion Sais *de Brecon* issued his own letter, also dated at Rhyd-y-briw, 7 November 1271, announcing that he had given these sureties to Llywelyn for the release of the hostage, and placing himself under the jurisdiction of the bishop of St Davids, who could excommunicate him if he broke the stated terms (*LW*, 28–9 (no. 35)). In fact, Einion later disregarded his loyalty to Llywelyn, for he and Meurig ap Gruffudd (see no. 87 below) were among Edward I's captains when the king sought forces from Brecon in the war of 1277 (Smith, 'Llywelyn ap Gruffudd and the March', 15–16). By contrast, Madog ab Arawdr, one of the sureties, who were freemen from Ystrad Tywi, supported the prince in later conflicts (Smith, *Llywelyn*, 318). For the significance of this and other guarantees to Llywelyn of the loyalty of men in Brecon, Builth and Elfael in November and December 1271 see *LW*, xliv–xlv; Smith, *Llywelyn*, 357–8. Rhyd-y-briw (SN 919 283) was located just north-west of Defynnog, Cantref Selyf, Brycheiniog, about half way between Brecon and Llandovery; possibly the castle there was built by Llywelyn (*LW*, 29; Smith, *Llywelyn*, 416–17 and n. 99).

87 Llywelyn ap Gruffudd

Letter, declaring that he stands surety to Llywelyn for Meurig ap Gruffudd in the sum of 20 marks if Meurig is disobedient or unfaithful to the prince.

[*c*.7 December 1271]

B = TNA: PRO, E 36/374 (Liber A), fo. 337r. s. xiii ex.
Pd. from B, *LW*, 30 (no. 38).
Cd., *H*, no. 301.

[E]xcellenti viro et discreto domino L. filio Griffin(i) principi Wall(ie), domino Snaudon' Howel filius Resi Vrec suus semper et ubique salutem et sincere dilectionis affectum. Vestre dominationi et excellentie duco si placet declarandum quod ego vester sum fideiussor pro Marucio filio Griffin(i) si vobis fuerit inobediens vel infidelis `ad persolvendum vobis xx^{ti} marcas. In cuius rei testimonium litteras meas vobis mitto patentes. Valete.

As Edwards argued (*LW*, 30), the letter seems to refer to the same person as the Meurig ap Gruffudd of Elfael for whose homage and fealty to Llywelyn Einion ap Cynwrig and others acknowledged themselves to be sureties in a letter dated at Sychdyn near Mold, 7 December 1271 (*LW*, 26 (no. 32)), and thus probably belongs to about the same date. See also nos 72 and 80, and note to no. 86, above.

88 Letter patent concerning Llywelyn ap Gruffudd

Notification by Hywel and Trahaearn ap Gruffudd that they stand surety to the prince for Madog ap Cynwrig in the sum of £32, for the release of Madog on a day and at a place to be assigned to them by the prince. They renounce all benefits of canon and civil law and all petitions which could impede the said suretyship. If Hywel defaults in the payment of the share due from him of the said money, Trahaearn binds himself to pay it. Sealing clause.

Abereiddon, 26 May 1275

B = TNA: PRO, E 36/274 (Liber A), fo. 342v. s. xiii ex.
Pd. from B, *LW*, 44–5 (no. 67).
Cd., *H*, no. 302.

[O]mnibus has litteras visuris vel audituris Howel' filius Resi et T(ra)haeary filius Gruffud salutem in domino. Noveritis nos fideiussisse domino Lewelino principi Wall(ie) pro Madoco filio Kynwric ad solvendum prefato principi xxx^{ta} duas libras sterlingorum legalis monete pro deliberatione eiusdem Madoci ad certum diem et locum que nobis dictus princeps duxerit assignanda. Renuntiamus etiam omni beneficio iuris tam canonici quam civilis nec non omni impetrationi litterarum que dictam fideiussionem poterint impedire. Si autem contingat quod Howelus filius Resi defficiat in solutione portionis ipsum contingentis de dicta pecunia ego T(ra)haeary obligo me in solidum totum residuum dicte pecunie soluturum ^{a–}in forma predicta.^{–a} In cuius rei testimonium sigillum nostrum hiis litteris apposuimus. Datum apud Aberidon anno domini m° cc° lxx° quinto die dominica proxima post festum ascensionis domini.

^{a–a} in forma predictam in forma predictam B.

This Trahaearn is a witness to Hywel's oath of fealty to Llywelyn in 1258 (no. 85 above) and thus seems to have been one of Hywel's men (*H*, no. 302, n.). The Madog ap Cynwrig of the document has not been otherwise identified.

89 Robert Burnell, bishop of Bath and Wells

Letter, requesting, on account of the great trust he has in the bishop and his aid, that the bishop will do all he can to help Hywel with the king regarding peace, and that the king will have mercy on Hywel. Requests the bishop to act so that he and all his [i.e. Hywel's] friends may be bound to him always as their dear lord. Requests the bishop to inform him what the king wishes to have of Hywel so that he may be restored to his land.

[April 1277 × 7 January 1278]

A = TNA: PRO, SC 1/23, no. 140. No endorsements; approx. 210 × 27 mm.; five sets of double slits for insertion of a tag; mounted, foot cut away.
Cd., *CAC*, 123; *H*, no. 308.

A noble ber et sage sire Rob(er)t Burnel eveke de Bahdþe le ceu valet si leur pleht Howel ap Res Crik salus, reverence, servise et tous honurs. Je ws pri cher sire pur deu et pur la grant[a] fiaunce ke je ay en ws et en vohtre grant ayde, ke ws me voilez estre en aye en tote la ma ...[b] ke ws savez et poez vere mun seignor le ray de sa pes, e ke il eyt mersi de mai;[a] ke sachez sire ke cete ma fiaunse est en ws; taunt en facez sire pur deu ke je et tous mes amis ws seent `ceo dis tenu cum a lur cher singnor a remenaunt. Sal' et cher sire par deu me maundez quai[a] le roy vehdera de may[a] aver pur mai mettre en ma terre.

[a] *sic in* A. | [b] *end of word illegible* A.

Hywel left Deheubarth to join Llywelyn ap Gruffudd in Gwynedd after Rhys ap Maredudd surrendered to the crown in April 1277, and he and his men were granted the king's protection for one year on 7 January 1278 (*BT, Pen20Tr*, 118; *BT, RBH*, 264–5; *CWR*, 161; no. 92 below).

RHYS FYCHAN AP RHYS MECHYLL
(d. 1271)

*90 Talley Abbey
Grant and confirmation in perpetual alms of all the lands, possessions, churches and other things which his great-grandfather Rhys the Great (magnus), *his grandfather Rhys [Gryg], his uncles, his cousins or kin or nobles of the land gave or bequeathed to the monastery, namely Cefn-blaidd* (Keuenblich), *Llechwen-dderi* (Lewedderi), *half of Cwmbleog* (hanner Cumblehauc) *[Cwm-liog], Bryngwyn[-mawr]* (Brynwyn), *Bryn-y-llech* (Brin yllech) *in the ancient bounds, Trallwng Elgan* (Tallunelgan), *the parcel of land at Crug-y-bar* (Cruchar), *Penrhos* (Penros) *apart from the land of the sons of Bleddri Goch* (Bledri Chcok), *Ynysdywyll* (Ynistewythh), *Tre-wern* (Tremywern), *Cynwyl Gaeo [Caeo]* (Kynwyl), *Cilmaren* (Kilmaren), *the parcel of land with a meadow between the two streams below the church of Cynwyl Gaeo [Caeo]* (Kynwyl) *and above the same church between the two streams, Llanddewi['r Crwys] [Llan-crwys]* (Landewy) *as far as Rhiw-rhisgen* (Riurisken) *and Gwardderwen* (Coirderwen) *next to Prenfol Gwallwyn* (Prenual Gwallwyn), *Llwynywermwnt* (Llini Wermon), *Penfynydd* (Penuenit), *the Gorddogwy* (Gordogui) *as far as Hirfaen Gwyddog* (Hyruayngudauc), *Rhosybedw* (Rospedyr); *the grange of Gwyddgrug* (Gudgruc) *and Nawmor* (Nanmaur); *the grange of Brechfa* (Brechba), *Brynyreidion* (Bryn yredion`), *Castellgweirann, Maen-y-cynghellor* (Mayn ykyghellaur), *Cilcyngen* (Kylbyngen) *and all the land between the said grange (?) and the Cloidach* (inter dictam grangiam de Cleudach); *the*

grange of Brwnws [Maenor Frwnws] (Brunus) *in its bounds; Llwyn-yr-ynn* (Penllunyrhyt) *at Llandeilo-fawr* (Lanteilaumaur), *Ynysdeilo* (Ynisteilau), *Llodre Iago* (Llodre Iaco), *Cilcynan* (Kylkynan), *Gwyddynys* (Gudynys) *and Ynysyradar* (Ynysiradar); *the land which Gwas Teilo* (Guaistelau) *gave; the land of the church at Abercennen* (Aberkennen); *the land of the church at Talhardd* (Talharch); *Cefnmeirch* (Keuenmeirch) *and Llangeinwyry [(?)Llwyncwnhwyra]* (Lankeinwyry), *Dolhywel* (Dolhowel) *between Is Cennen* (Iscenac) *and* Henwen; *the grange of Carreg Cennen* (Karreckennen) *and Cilymaenllwyd* (Kilmanlut) *in their bounds; and half of Cilwr* (Kilwr). *In Ceredigion* (Kereidigaun): *Porth Hoddni [Aber-porth]* (Potthothni) *in the ancient bounds, Faerdre* (y Uardrem), *Rhydowain* (Ryt Yweyn), *Nant Cedifor* (Nantkedemor), *Bryn Aeron* (Brynyron), *Cynbyd* (Kynbit), *Moelhedog* (Moilehedauc), *together with the mills and common pasture of all Rhys's land. A further confirmation of all the churches possessed by the abbey for its own use just as pertained to the lord of the land: the church of St Cynwyl* (Kynwyl) *[Caeo] with the chapels of Llansadwrn* (Lansadurn), *Llanwrda* (Lanurdam), *Pistyllsawel* (Pistillsawil), *Llanpumsaint* (Lanipymseynt) *and others belonging to it; Llandeilo-fawr* (Lanteilau Vaur) *with its chapels and other appurtenances; the churches of St David, Dinefwr* (Dinewr), *of Llandyfeisant* (Lanteuassan) *and of St Michael, Aberbythych [Llanfihangel Aberbythych]* (Abirbythich); *the chapel of Carreg Cennen* (Karreckennen); *Llanegwad Fawr* (Lanogwat Vaur) *with the chapels of Llandeilo Frwnws* (Lanteilau Brunus), *Llanyhirnin* (Lanehernyn), *St Michael, Llech Feilir [Llanfihangel Llech Feilir]* (Lechmeilir) *and its other appurtenances; Llandeilo Brechfa* (Lanteilau Brechua) *in Ceredigion* (Keredigaun), *the church of St Michael, Penbryn [Llanfihangel Penbryn]* (Penbrin) *with the chapels of Baglan* (Baglan), *Brithdir* (Brithtir), *Caerllegest* (Karligheit) *[(?)Betwsifan], Porth Hoddni [Aber-porth]* (Potthothni) *and the chapel of the sons of Ithel ap Rhael* (Ydhal filii Rael); *the churches of Llangoedmor* (Lancoytmaur), *of Y Ferwig* (Berwyk) *and of St David, Dolhywel* (Dolhowel).

[1244 × 1271; possibly 1258 × 1271]

Mention only, in an inspeximus, presumably of the original charter, of Edward II dated at Westminster, 24 March 1324 (TNA: PRO, C 66/160, m. 21; pd., *Mon. Ang.*, iv. 162; Daniel-Tyssen, *Royal Charters*, 60–5; Long Price, 'Talley Abbey', 167–73 (trans. only); Owen, 'Contribution to the history', 39–46; cd., *H*, no. 30). The dating limits of the charter are set by the death of Rhys Mechyll in 1244 and Rhys Fychan's own death in 1271.

For the place-names see Long Price, 'Talley Abbey', 167–72; Richards, 'Carmarthenshire possessions'; Wmffre, 'Language and History', II. i. 51, 94–5, 109, 125, 218, 242, 254, 506–8; cf. also Jones, 'Boundaries'. Several of the lands named lay in the vicinity of the abbey itself (SN 633 327), cmt. Caeo, including Cefn-blaidd (SN 647 334), Bryngwyn-mawr (SN 647 347), Trallwng Elgan (a township north of Talley), Tre-wern (SN 652 322) and Cilwr (SN 605 238). Llangeinwyry (if now Llwyncwnhwyra SN 608 290) lay about 3 miles south-west of Talley. Cynwyl Gaeo was the original name of Caeo (SN 657 398), and Cilmaren (SN 690 388) the centre of a grange of that name in the south-east corner of Cynwyl Gaeo parish. The grange included Crug-y-bar (SN 658 379) and Cwmbleog (now Cwm-liog SN 656 347). The latter, 'apart from the land of *Kymrechor*', was granted by Rhys Mechyll to Gruffudd ab Ednyfed Fychan in 1236 × 1244 (no. 84 above). It is unknown whether *Kymrechor* was the half of Cwmbleog confirmed to Talley in the present charter, or whether Rhys Fychan had resumed half of the land granted by his father to Gruffudd, perhaps after Gruffudd's death in or shortly after 1256.

The grange of Llan-crwys (SN 644 451), originally called Llanddewi'r Crwys, cmt. Caeo, lay in the eastern part of the parish of that name and included Llwyn-y-wermwnt (Llwyn SN 643 438) and Rhosybedw (SN 631 447) as well as, in par. Cellan, cmt. Mebwynion, Prenfol Gwallwyn (now Carregbwci SN 645 479) and Hirfaen Gwyddog (SN 624 464). The grange of Gwyddgrug (Gwyddgrug SN 466 357) lay south-east of Pencader in par. Llanfihangel Iorarth, cmt. Mebwynion (see no. 49 above), and that of Brechfa to its south-east (Brechfa SN 526 303), including Brynyreidion (SN 507 300). The river Cloidach (or Clydach) flows into the Cothi at SN 542 306. The grange of Maenor Frwnws lay farther south, centring at the confluence of the rivers Cothi and Tywi, with the chapel of Llandeilo Rwnws alias Ynysdeilo (SN 494 203) on the north bank of the Tywi. Lands located around Llandeilo Fawr (SN 629 222), cmt. Maenordeilo, include Llwyn-yr-ynn (SN 594 275), Abercennen (SN 631 215), Talhardd (621 202) and the grange of Carreg Cennen and Cilymaenllwyd, which lay about 2½ miles south-east of Llandeilo Fawr (Carreg Cennen House SN 653 193; Cilymaenllwyd SN 665 198). Apart from Aber-porth (see no. 27 above) the lands named in Ceredigion appear to have been located north-east of Llandysul, cmt. Gwynionydd (see no. 68 above): Faerdre (Faerdre-fawr SN 427 422), Rhydowain (Rhydowain-fawr SN 435 452), Nant Cedifor (Blaencwmcedifor SN 434 433), Bryn Aeron, probably in the vicinity of Afon Geyron, which flows into the Afon Cletwr at SN 448 440, south of Alltyrodyn and Moelhedog (SN 446 461). Cynbyd lay in the same area.

Chapels of Cynwyl Gaeo (Caeo): Llansadwrn (SN 696 315) and Llanwrda (SN 713 316), both in cmt. Maenordeilo, Pistyllsawel (SN 618 362), cmt. Caeo, and Llanpumsaint (SN 419 291), cmt. Gwidigada. Also in cmt. Maenordeilo: the church of Llandeilo Fawr and chapels of Dinefwr (SN 611 217) and Llandyfeisant (SN 609 224). Cmt. Is Cennen: Llanfihangel Aberbythych (SN 590 197) and Carreg Cennen. Cmt. Cetheiniog: church of Llanegwad (SN 520 214) and its chapels, including Llandeilo Rwnws (Ynysdeilo) and Llanhernin (SN 507 216). Llandeilo Brechfa may be Cefn Brechfa (SN 238 500), cmt. Is Coed, Ceredigion, rather than Llandeilo Brechfa (SN 526 303), cmt. Cetheiniog (Wmffre, 'Language and History', II. i. 94–5). For Llanfihangel Penbryn, cmt. Is Coed, see no. 27 above; Brithdir (SN 338 481), Caerllegest (probably the older name of Betwsifan SN 301 477) (Wmffre, 'Language and History', II. i. 95, 113) and Llangoedmor (SN 199 458) lay in the same commote. The grant of Y Ferwig consisted of only a portion of that church, as the *Valor Ecclesiasticus* reveals that its revenues were divided equally between its vicar, the prior of Cardigan and the abbot of Talley (Cowley, *Monastic Order*, 171; no. 26 above).

*91 Talley Abbey

Grant and confirmation, in perpetual alms, of the portion of the land of Esgeirnant (Eskeirnant) *between* Nant Velyn Coyg and *the dyke* (fossata) *made from the Dulais* (Dulais) *up towards the chapels, and from that dyke up through the valley to the great heap of stones and thence to* Guenucolman*, and thence along the boundary between the grove and the field towards Blaen Penfynydd* (blain Penuenit) *to the dyke, and thence along the valley up to Crug Cledwyn* (Cruc Cletwin)*, and thence to* Carntoll*, and thence up to Rhyd Garegog* (Ryt Karreggabg) *above the next stream beyond* Karntoll*, descending along that stream to its mouth, where it flows into the Crymlyn* (Krymlyn)*. A further grant in the same charter of all the land between the stream descending from the spring of Gwenllian* (Gueliant) *and the abbey, and from that spring all the grove up to the source of Nant Cwmbyr* (blain Nant

Cu(m)byr), *and thence all the land called Esgair Cuhelyn* (Eskair Cuelyn). *A further confirmation of all lands, renders and possessions which the abbey has by the gift of Rhys the Great* (Resi magni), *great-grandfather of Rhys, or by the gift of any of his heirs or of other magnates of south Wales with all their liberties and profits.*

[1244 × 1271]

Mention only, in an inspeximus, presumably of the original charter, of Edward II dated at Westminster, 24 March 1324 (TNA: PRO, C 66/160, m. 21; pd., *Mon. Ang.*, iv. 162; Daniel-Tyssen, *Royal Charters*, 64–5; Long Price, 'Talley Abbey', 172–3 (trans. only); Owen, 'Contribution to the history', 42; cd., *H*, no. 30). For the dating see note to no. 90 above. Both grants consisted of lands in the immediate vicinity of Talley Abbey. Esgeirnant was located to the east and south-east (Pant-yr-esgair SN 646 319); the Crymlyn is a tributary of the river Cothi (Abercrymlyn SN 641 350), south of Cwm-liog (see note to no. 90 above). Ffynnon Gwenllian (the spring of Gwenllian) lay just to the south of the abbey, on the south-east corner of Mynydd Cefnros near Penrhiwgeingwen (SN 634 316); for Nant Cwmbyr cf. Cwmbyr (SN 634 321) (Long Price, 'Talley Abbey', 172–3; see also the map in Richards, 'Carmarthenshire possessions', 111).

RHYS AP MAREDUDD
(d. 2 June 1292)

92 Agreement with Payn de Chaworth, captain of the king's army in West Wales

Terms of agreement for making peace with Payn, who has full power by letter(s) patent of the king to receive the Welsh into the peace and fealty of the king, with the consent of the barons and soldiers of the army and of other soldiers and faithful men of the king in West Wales.

(1) Concerning the castle of Dinefwr and the lands of Maenordeilo, Malláen, Caeo and Mabelfyw, when the king has power in these, he will show Rhys full justice and make full restitution to him as justice demands.

(2) Rhys will do homage to the king at the latter's order and where it pleases him, and fealty to Payn on behalf of the king whom he represents in these parts.

(3) The king grants that he will never remove Rhys from his homage without Rhys's agreement, nor distrain him to do suit at any county or court unless the king holds the county in demesne.

(4) Rhys grants to the soldiers and others of the king's army free access to and exit from his castles, and permission to store victuals there in suitable places assigned by him.

(5) He will allow, and aid with all his strength, passes to be made within and outside his land through which the king's war can be advanced, and as often as necessary he will go on campaign with all his forces of horse and foot, as often as he is reasonably requested.

(6) If it happens that by Rhys's advice and agency Gruffudd ap Maredudd ab Owain comes to the king's peace, on condition that Rhys gives up the right he claims in Gwynionydd and Mebwynion, the king will make him reasonable restitution elsewhere as right demands when it has been fully declared.

Payn on behalf of the king, and Rhys on behalf of himself, his heirs and his freemen nominated for this purpose by Payn, have sworn on relics faithfully to observe all the above terms, and have attached their seals to this chirograph together with the seals of the king's barons of the said army and of other barons of West Wales, namely Ralph d'Aubigny, Roger de Molis, John Beauchamp, John de Mohun, Alan de Plugenet, Oliver de Dinan, Patrick de Chaworth, Geoffrey de Camville, Nicholas fitz Martin and William fitz Warin, who were all present at this agreement and obliged themselves with Payn on behalf of the king that the king will faithfully observe all the contents of this document and will issue a letter patent of confirmation for Rhys by the Ascension [6 May] 1277. Sealed for further security by Richard, bishop of St Davids.

Carmarthen, 11 April 1277

B = TNA: PRO, E 36/274 (Liber A), fos 339v–340r. s. xiii ex.
C = ibid., fo. 409v.
Pd. from B, *LW*, 36–7 (no. 54); from C, *Foedera*, I. ii. 542.
Cd., *H*, no. 303.

[A]nno regni regis Edwardi quinto die dominica in quindena Pasche[a] apud Kermerdin[b] per dominum Paganu(m) de Cadurciis capitaneum munitionis domini regis[c] in West Wall(ia) habentem plenariam potestatem per litteras domini regis patentes recipiendi Walenses ad pacem eiusdem domini regis et fidelitatem, assensu et consensu baronum et militum eiusdem munitionis et aliorum militum et fidelium domini regis West Wallie, talis facta est conventio super reformatione pacis Resy[d] filii Mereducis[e] videlicet:

[i] quod de castro de Dinevor[f] et de terra Maynertilau[g] et de terra de Mablaen[h] et de terra de Cayo et Mabelueu,[i] dominus Edwardus rex Angl(ie) cum in predictis castro et terris habuerit potestatem dicto Reso plenariam exibebit[j] iustitiam, et secundum quod ius suum deposcet[k] predicto Reso plenariam faciet restitutionem.

[ii] Et predictus Resus faciet homagium[l] domino regi ubi sibi placuerit ad suum mandatum, et fidelitatem loco domini regis domino Pagano qui locum eius tenet in hac parte.

[iii] Et dominus rex concedit quod dictum Resum sine spontanea eiusdem voluntate nunquam amovebit ab homagio suo, nec ipsum distringet vel distringi permittet ad sectam faciendam ad comitatum aliquem vel curiam nisi dominus rex dictum comitatum teneat et habeat in dominico.

[iv] Et dictus Resus militibus et aliis munitionis domini regis concedit in castris suis liberum receptaculum, introitum et exitum quotiens voluerint et opus fuerit, et quod possent in eisdem sua victualia reponere, et ad hoc loca competentia eisdem assignabit.

[v] Passus etiam tam in terra sua[m] quam aliena per quos guerra domini regis possit promoveri facere permittet,[n] consulet et pro suis viribus cum toto posse suo adiuvabit, et quotiens opus fuerit cum omni posse suo tam equitum quam peditum ibit in expeditionem guerre[o] quotiens super hoc rationabiliter summonitus fuerit et requisitus.

[vi] Et si contingat quod per consilium et procurationem dicti Resi[p] Griffin(us) filius Mereducis[e] ap Ovayn[q] veniat ad pacem domini regis, ea conditione quod dictus Resus eidem remittat ius suum quod habere clamat in Gunyoniuh[r] et Mebunyaun,[s] dominus rex dicto Reso alibi secundum quod ius suum deposcet cum plene fuerit declaratum rationabilem faciet restitutionem.

Hec autem omnia et singula firmiter et fideliter observanda dominus Paganus de Cadurciis pro domino rege et dictus Resus pro se et [t]heredibus suis[t] `et suis liberis hominibus quos ad hoc dictus Pagan(us) eligere voluerit et nominare, tactis sacrosanctis[u] iuraverunt, et huic scripto in modum cyrographi [v-]inter partes confecto[-v] sigilla sua alternatim una cum sigillis baronum domini regis dicte munitionis et aliorum baronum West Wallie apposuerunt, videlicet dominorum Radulphi de Aubenyee,[w] Rogeri[x] de Molis, Iohannis de Bello[y] Campo, Iohannis de Moun, Alani de Pluuenet,[z] Olyueri[aa] de Dinan,[ab] Pat(ri)cii de Cadurc(iis), Galfridi[ac] de Camuile, Nichol(ai) filii Martini et Willelmi filii Warini, qui omnes presenti conventioni interfuerunt et una cum domino Pagano pro domino rege una[fo. 340r]nimiter se obligaverunt quod dominus rex omnia in presenti scripto contenta bene et fideliter tenebit et observabit, et dominus rex infra ascensionem domini anni prenominati predicto Reso suas litteras faciet patentes confirmatorias. Datum die, anno et loco prenominatis. Et ad maiorem securitatem huius conventionis fideliter observande venerabilis pater dominus R. permissione divina Menevensis episcopus presenti scripto sigillum suum apposuit.

[a] pasce C. | [b] Kermerdyn C. | [c] C *inserts* et fidelitatem assensu et consensu baronum *struck through*. [d] Rysy C. | [e] Mereduci C. | [f] Dynevor C. | [g] Mayn(er)tylau C. | [h] Mathlaen C. | [i] Mabelveu C. [j] exhibebit C. | [k] deposset B. | [l] C *inserts* dicti *struck through*. | [m] *omitted* B. | [n] C *inserts* `et in. [o] gwerre C. | [p] Resy C. | [q] Ouayn C. | [r] Guynyonuith C. | [s] Mebunnaun C. | [t-t] suis heredibus C. [u] sacrosannctis B. | [v-v] confecto inter partes C. | [w] Aubeney C. | [x] Rog(er)o B. | [y] Bella B. [z] Plolenet C. | [aa] Olyuery C. | [ab] Dynan C. | [ac] Galfridus B.

For the background and significance of Rhys ap Maredudd's submission to the king see Smith, '"Cronica de Wallia"', 281–2; *idem, Llywelyn*, 419–21. Rhys was received into the king's peace before 21 March but, like his brother Gruffudd, did not swear fealty to Edward on that day as expected because, so Patrick de Chaworth was informed, they feared that the king's forces would not remain in the area after Easter, leaving them unprotected (*CAC*, 71–2). The submission recorded in the present agreement followed a meeting at Whitland Abbey originally arranged by Chaworth to continue military operations. Nicholas de Molis and Geoffrey de Camville were related to Rhys as their ancestors had married daughters of the Lord Rhys. It is possible that the *Cronica de Wallia* was composed at precisely this juncture by a Whitland monk, as it seems to reflect Rhys's aspirations for the restitution of the whole of Ystrad Tywi in 1277. For the subsequent submissions of Rhys Wyndod and of Rhys ap Maredudd's brother Gruffudd see no. 74 above and no. 98 below.

93 Letter patent concerning his agreement with the king

Notification that, since at his initiative he has come into the peace of the king through Payn de Chaworth, captain of the king's army in West Wales, by certain agreements with the king, Rhys obliges himself by the present letter firmly to observe all the agreements set out in the letter of peace. If he or his heirs contravene these agreements, all the lands which they hold from the king or his heirs shall be lost for ever. Rhys and his heirs place themselves under the jurisdiction of the church of Rome, Canterbury and their diocesan bishop, who by the authority of the present letter may compel them, at the king's will, to adhere to these terms by excommunication, interdict and all power which holy Church may exercise, together with the secular arm, against those rebelling against it; they also renounce all appeal, objection and remedy of all laws that could weaken the strength of the present letter. Sealing clause.

Carmarthen, 11 April 1277

B = TNA: PRO, E 36/274 (Liber A), fos 343v–344r. s. xiii ex.
Pd. from B, *LW*, 48 (no. 73).
Cd., *H*, no. 304.

[U]niversis Cristi fidelibus presentes litteras visuris vel audituris Resus filius Mereduci salutem in domino. Cum ad pacem domini Edwardi regis Anglie per dominum Paganum de Cadurciis capitaneum munitionis eiusdem domini regis in West Wallia[a] ad nostram instantiam fuerimus reformati per certas conventiones inter dominum regem per predictum dominum Paganu(m) loco eiusdem domini regis et nos initas et concessas, ad easdem conventiones omnes et singulas prout in littera reformationis pacis predicte continetur firmiter observandas tenore presentium nos obligamus, quod si nos vel heredes nostri contra conventiones predictas aliquatenus venire presumpserimus omnes terre nostre quas de domino rege tenebimus vel eius heredibus nobis et nostris heredibus ipso facto perdite sint in perpetuum et forisfacte, subicientes nos et heredes nostros iurisdictioni et coheircioni ecclesie Romane et Cantuar(iensis) et episcopi nostri diocesani qui pro tempore fuerit, qui nos auctoritate presentium absque alterius onere probationis pro voluntate predicti domini regis ad hoc compellant per sententiam excommunicationis interdicti et per omnem potestatem quam sacrosancta ecclesia in sibi rebelles una cum brachio seculari poterit excercere, renuntiantes in hac parte omni appellationi, cavillationi et omni iuris remedio per quod robur presentium aliquatenus posset infringi. In cuius rei testimonium presenti scripto sigillum meum apposui. Acta apud Kermerdin [fo. 344r] die dominica in quindena Pasche anno domini m° cc° septuagesimo septimo.

[a] Wallie B.

See note to no. 92 above.

94 Petition to the king and his council

As he had right to the castle of Dinefwr and Payn de Chaworth and his companions promised him this castle on behalf of the king if they could conquer it from Rhys Fychan [i.e. Rhys Wyndod] and his men; and seeing that the king is now seised of the castle and its appurtenances and greatly desires to hold it in the manner that he holds it, Rhys prays the king that he will grant him the value of this castle and of as much land as pertains to it elsewhere in the land where it will be of less damage to the king.

Also, as Hywel ap Gruffudd owes suit at Rhys's court of Llansadwrn, and after Hywel was made a knight he refused to do this suit, Rhys prays that he may have a writ to the king's bailiffs of Dinefwr to distrain Hywel to perform this suit at the aforesaid court as he used to do in the time of Rhys's father.

Also, as Maredudd ap Rhys, Rhys's father, was founder of Talley Abbey and its abbot is obliged to hold his lands from Rhys by performing a certain service to Rhys and to no other, Rhys prays the king to prohibit his bailiffs of Dinefwr from preventing the abbot from performing his service to Rhys as his patron, which service he is obliged to do of right.

[Probably 24 April 1277 × January 1278]

A = TNA: PRO, SC 8/63, no. 3122. No endorsement; approx. 183 × 89 mm.
Cd., *CAP*, 97–8; *H*, no. 306.

Ceo mustre a nostre seignour le rey e a son conseil Res le fiz Mareduce, ke com il en ad droit al chastel de Dyneuor e sire Payn de Chauworth' e ses compaignons premistrent a luy de par nostre seignour le rey icel chastel s'il le purreynt conquere sur Res Vaghan e les soens, e desicom nostre seignour le rey est ore seisi de cel chastel od les apurtenaunces e le desir mult tenire en la manere k'il le tient, le avantdyt Res fiz Mareduce prie nostre seignour le rey k'il luy face avere la value de cel chastel e de tant de terre com al chastel apent aliurs en la terre ou moyns serreit a grevaunce nostre seignour le rey.

Derechef com Howel ab Griffyn doyt une seute a la curt le avaundyt Res de Lensadorn', e memes celuy Howel pus k'il fu fet chevalere de cele seute fere sei ad il sustret, le avaundyt Res prie ke il eyt un bref a les bailiffs nostre seignour le rey de Dyneuor' a destreindre le avaundyt Howel a fere cele seute a l'avaundite curt com il soleit fere al tens le pere memes celuy Res.

Derechef com Mareduce ab Res pere le avaundyt Res esteyt fundur del abbeye de Taltleuhau e le abbé de cel leu deyt tenir ses terre[a] de memes celuy Res pur certeyn service fesaund[a] a luy e a nul autre, memes celuy Res prie nostre seignour le rey k'il defent a ses baillifs de Dyneuor k'il ne desturbent mye le abbé avaundyt a fere le service a memes celuy Res com a son avowé, le quel service il luy deyt fere de dreit.

[a] *sic in* A.

As it states that Dinefwr was held by the king, the petition must be later than the surrender of Rhys Wyndod, lord of Dinefwr, on 24 April 1277 (no. 98 below). Despite his earlier hopes of recovering Dinefwr for himself (no. 92 above), here Rhys merely sought compensation for its value. Hywel ap Gruffudd was a son of Gruffudd ab Ednyfed, whose possession of Llansadwrn had been confirmed by Rhys Mechyll in 1236 × 1244 (no. 84 above). The bailiff of Dinefwr, appointed by the crown after the conquest of Deheubarth in 1277, was instructed to make jurors join Hywel ap Maredudd and John de Perres when on 8 November 1279 the king ordered the latter to hold an inquisition into a claim by Hywel ap Gruffudd and his brother Rhys that Rhys ap Maredudd had unjustly occupied their land in Caeo (*CWR*, 179–80). Although the description of Rhys's father Maredudd as the founder of Talley Abbey was exaggerated, as the house was in fact founded by the Lord Rhys (see note to no. 27 above), Maredudd did issue a confirmation of the abbey's lands and his son Rhys was granted confraternity of the Premonstratensian order in 1280 (no. 68 above; Smith and O'Neil, *Talley Abbey*, 6). The assertion of his rights to homage and service from the abbot was probably a response to Talley's seizure into the king's hands, which had occurred by 6 January 1278, when the abbey was granted royal protection for two years (*CPR 1272–81*, 251). The second and third petitions were thus aimed at the tightening of royal jurisdiction, administered from Dinefwr after its fall to Edward's forces in late April 1277, and the document was probably sent no later than the end of that year or early in 1278. For further discussion see Smith, 'Origins of the revolt', 154; Griffiths, *Conquerors*, 68–9.

95 Letter patent concerning Laurence Bacin, burgess of Carmarthen

Notification that he is obliged to repay Laurence or his attorney £12 12s., in pennies or penny-rents, by the feast of the apostles Philip and James [1 May] 1278; if he fails to pay Laurence this by the said term, the latter should have white dry wool by the said feast in payment of the said money. Sealing clause.

[30 April 1277 × 1 May 1278]

B = TNA: PRO, E 36/274 (Liber A), fo. 381r. s. xiii ex.
Pd. from B, *LW*, 127 (no. 219).
Cd., *H*, no. 309.

Omnibus Cristi fidelibus has litteras ʿvisuris vel audituris Resus filius Mareduc(i) salutem in domino. Noverit universitas vestra me teneri Laur(entio) Bacyn, burgensi de K(er)merdin, in xii libris et xii solidis sterlingorum ex causa mutui eidem vel suo attornato citra proximum festum apostolorum Ph(ilipp)i et Iacobi anno domini mº ccº septuagesimoª octavo in denariis vel denariatis solvendis, et si dictam pecuniam domino Laur(entio) ad dictum terminum me solvere non contingat, volo quod habeat lanam albam et siccam ad ʿdictum festum apostolorum Ph(ilipp)i et Iacobi in dicte pecunie solutione. In cuius rei testimonium presenti scripto sigillum meum apposui.

ª septimo B.

As Edwards noted (*LW*, 127), the document was drafted in anticipation of 1 May 1278, the date of the *proximum festum* of St Philip and St James. Laurence Bacin may be identified with the wealthy Carmarthen burgess, Laurence Bacy or Pacy, who lent £150 to pay royal forces in Carmarthen and Cardigan in 1245 and 1246 and who held seven burgages, as well as the lease of a mill on the Tywi for 30*s*., in 1268 (*CPR 1232–47*, 458, 476; *CLR 1240–5*, 316; Griffiths, *Conquerors*, 180).

96 Letter patent concerning Alice, widow of Laurence Bacin, her son Peter and Peter's executors

Notification that he has granted all the wool due to him in 1278, so that they may accept every stone in place of 5s., in payment of his debt to Laurence.

[Probably shortly after 1 May 1278]

B = TNA: PRO, E 36/274 (Liber A), fo. 354r. s. xiii ex.
Pd. from B, *LW*, 69 (no. 122).
Cd., *H*, no. 32.

Omnibusª Cristi fidelibus has litteras visuris vel audituris Res(us) filius Mereduc(i) salutem in domino. Noverit universitas vestra me, fide mea prestita, Alicie relicte Laur(entii) Bacin et Petro filio suo et executor(ibus) dicti Laur(entii) totam lanam meam concessisse me in anno isto contingentem, videlicet anno domini mº ccº septuagesimo octavo, ita tamen quod quamlibet petram pro v solidis recipiant et in debito in quo teneor Laur(entio) Bacin collocari faciant. In cuius rei testimonium presens scriptum sigilli mei inpressione corroboravi.

ª o *in margin with space for majuscule* o *before* mnibus B.

As it clearly refers to the debt described in no. 95 above, payable by 1 May 1278, this document was probably written shortly after that date (*LW*, 69).

97 Edward I

Grant and quitclaim, on behalf of himself and his heirs, of the castle of Dinefwr with its demesnes and the gwestfa *of* Sclogans *pertaining to the said castle, and all right and claim in these, so that neither he nor his heirs will be able to claim or demand any right in these or any exchange for them. Sealing clause; witnesses.*

Acton Burnell, 16 October 1283

B = TNA: PRO, E 36/374 (Liber A), fo. 379r–v. s. xiii ex.
Pd. from B, *LW*, 122 (no. 212).
Cd., *H*, no. 313.

Omnibus Cristi fidelibus ad quos presentes littere pervenerint Resus filius Mereduci salutem in domino. Noverit universitas vestra me concessisse, remisisse et quietum clamasse pro me et heredibus meis domino meo Edwardo illustri regi Angl(ie), domino Hib(er)n(ie) et duci Aquit(anie) et heredibus suis castrum de Dineuor cum dominicis et cum *westua* de Sclogans ad illud castrum spectantibus et totum ius et clamium quod habui vel habere potui in predictis castro dominicis et cum *westua* de Sclogans, ita quod nec ego vel heredes mei aliquod ius vel clamium in predictis castro dominicis et *westua* de Sclogans vel escambium pro eisdem exigere vel vendicare poterimus in perpetuum. In cuius rei testimonium presentibus litteris sigillum meum apposui. Hiis testibus: Will(el)mo de Valenc(ia), Henr(ico) de Lacy comite Lync', Ioh(an)ne de War(re)nna comite Surr', Iohanne de Vescy, [fo. 379v] Ottone de Grandisono, Reginaldo de Grey, Rob(er)to de Tybetot, Steph(an)o de Penestr', magistro Rob(er)to de Schardeburgo decano Ebor(acensi), Rob(er)to filio Ioh(ann)is et aliis. Datum apud Actone Burnel sexto decimo `die octobris anno `regni predicti domini regis undecimo.

Rhys ap Maredudd was the only member of the dynasty of Deheubarth to support Edward I in 1282, and was rewarded by the king with grants of the commotes of Mebwynion and Gwynionydd in Ceredigion, granted to his father by Henry III but never implemented, as well as of Malláen and Caeo in Cantref Mawr. This document shows, however, that he failed in his long-cherished ambition of recovering Dinefwr (Smith, '"Cronica de Wallia"', 273–4). The *gwestfa* of *Sclogans* pertaining to Dinefwr castle may be identified with the *villa de Scleygon* referred to by Edward I's surveyors as part of the Dinefwr estate in 1280 and the *Trefscoleygyon* of an inquiry of 1318, and thus seems originally to have been a settlement in which the clerks (Mod. W. *ysgolheigion*) of the royal court of Dinefwr lived, or at least from which they drew an income, comparable to the lands of the court smiths and physicians of Dinefwr in the vicinity (Griffiths, *Conquerors*, 262 and references cited there). *Gwestfa* originally denoted a food render due from freemen to the king, but by the thirteenth century it is used within the commotes of Ceredigion and Ystrad Tywi as a term for the administrative unit from which the render (or its commutation) was due (Charles-Edwards, *Early Irish and Welsh Kinship*, 369–82; Rees, *South Wales and the March*, 202–5; Jones Pierce, *Medieval Welsh Society*, 318–23). It is this later, territorial sense of the term which seems to be used here.

RHYS WYNDOD AP RHYS FYCHAN
(d. 1302)

98 Agreement with Payn de Chaworth, captain of the king's army in West Wales

Rhys surrendered himself and his castles totally to Payn and submitted himself to the king's will. On behalf of the king Payn granted to Rhys that he may have the same seisin of his castles and lands as he had on the day that he came until the king's will be settled concerning himself and his lands and castles, so that the knights and others of the king's army may have free access to and exit from the castles as often as is necessary for the king's war and as Rhys or his representative shall be required by the captain of the said army. Rhys will remain with Payn until the latter may safely conduct him to the king. Those present were Nicholas fitz Martin, Geoffrey de Camville, Oliver de Dinan, Alan de Plugenet, Roger de Molis and William fitz Warin. Payn and Rhys have attached their seals alternately to this chirograph.

Dinefwr, 24 April 1277

> B = TNA: PRO, E 36/274 (Liber A), fo. 344r. s. xiii ex.
> Pd. from B, *LW*, 49 (no. 74).
> Cd., *H*, no. 305.

[A]nno regni regis Edwardi quinto in vigilia Sancti Marci Ewangel(iste) venit Resus filius Resi Vaghan ad Paganu(m) de Cadurc(iis) capitaneum munitionis domini regis in partibus West Wall(ie) et se ipsum, castra sua et totaliter commisit et supposuit voluntati domini regis gratiam ipsius si placet requirendo. Et idem Paganus ex parte domini regis eidem domino Reso concessit quod habeat et teneat eandem seysinam quam habuit die quo venit castrorum et terrarum sua[rum]ᵃ quousque de ipso et suis terris et castris fiat quod domini regis sederit voluntati, ita tamen quod milites et alii munitionis domini regis liberum habeant receptaculum, introitum et exitum in castris eiusdem quotiens in expeditionem guerre domini regis opus fuerit et idem Resus vel qui locum eius tenuerit per capitaneum munitionis predicte fuerit requisitus. Et idem Resus cum dicto Pagano commorabitur quousque per ipsum cum tempus fuerit ad dominum regem salvo conducatur. Huic facto presentes fuerunt domini Nichol(aus) filius Martini, Galfrido de Camuill', Olyuerus de Dynan, Alanus de Plokenet, Roge(rus) de Molis et Will(elmu)s filius Warini. Et in huius rei testimonium Paganus et Resus huic scripto cyrographato inter eos alternatim sigilla sua apposuerunt. Datum apud castrum de Dyneuor die et anno prenotatis.

ᵃ *ink rubbed away here* B.

See nos 92 and 94 above.

99 Letter patent concerning Edward I

Notification that he has received a loan of 20 marks from the king, through the hands of Payn de Chaworth, to be paid to either of these or to a representative bearing the present letter on the feast of Holy Trinity [23 May] 1277 without further delay. Rhys binds all his moveable and immoveable goods wherever they may be found to distraint by the king, as amends for the said money if it happens that he defaults on payment by the prescribed term. He has found

Madog ab Arawdr as his surety who has made himself the principal debtor together with Rhys.
He has had this letter patent made as evidence of the obligation.

Carmarthen, 3 May 1277

B = TNA: PRO, E 36/274 (Liber A), fo. 208r. s. xiii ex.
Pd. from B, *LW*, 201–2 (no. 352).
Cd., *H*, no. 307.

[U]niversis Cristi fidelibus presentes litteras visuris vel audituris Reus[a] Vagghan dominus de Dynevor salutem in domino. Sciatis me recepisse mutuo de denariis domini Edwardi regis Angl(ie) per manus domini Pagani de Cadurciis viginti marcas bonorum et legalium sterlingorum eisdem vel alicui certo nuntio presentes litteras deferenti solvendas in festo Sancte Trinitatis anno regni regis E. quinto sine ulteriori dilatione, et ad hoc obligo omnia bona mea mobilia et immobilia ubicumque fuerint inventa districtioni et cohercioni dicti domini regis ut me distringere possint ad solutionem prefate pecunie dampnorum etiam interesse si me in solutione predicte pecunie termino prefixo, quod absit, deficere contingat. Et ad maiorem huius rei securitatem Maddocu(m) ab Aurauder fideiussorem inveni qui se una mecum prefate pecunie principalem constituit debitorem. In cuius rei testimonium has litteras meas domino regi et dicto Pagano fieri feci patentes. Datum apud Kermerdin die Inventionis Sancte Crucis anno regni regis Edwardi prenominato.

[a] *sic in* B.

It is striking that Rhys styles himself 'lord of Dinefwr', a style not found in his other surviving acts, although he had lost Dinefwr when he surrendered to the king on 24 April (nos 94 and 98 above). Madog ab *Aurauder* is quite possibly the same person as the Madog ab Arawdr who acted as a surety for the loyalty of Einion Sais of Brecon in 1271 (no. 86 above).

100 Letter patent concerning Llywelyn ap Gruffudd

Notification by Rhys and Llywelyn ap Rhys Fychan, Gruffudd and Cynan sons of Maredudd ab Owain and Hywel ap Rhys Gryg that they have bound themselves as sureties to Llywelyn, prince of Wales for Madog ap Trahaearn ap Madog, that he will give homage and fealty to the said prince. If Madog departs from his fealty in any way, they are sureties for him to Llywelyn in the sum of £100 sterling, £20 to be paid to Llywelyn by each of them when required. Sealing clause.

Dolwyddelan, 18 May 1278

B = TNA: PRO, E 36/274 (Liber A), fo. 342r. s. xiii ex.
Pd. from B, *LW*, 43 (no. 64).
Cd., *H*, no. 310.

[U]niversis Cristi fidelibus has litteras visuris vel audituris Resus Iunior et Lewelinus filius Resi Vachan, Griffin(us) et Conanus filii Maredud ab Owein, et Owelus filius Resi Gric salutem in domino. Noverit universitas vestra quod obligavimus nos fideiussores domino Lewelino filio Griffini principi Wall(ie) pro Madoco filio Trahaearn ab Madauc ad prestandum homagium suum simul et fidelitatem principi memorato, ita quod si contra dictam fidelitatem in aliquo devenerit, fideiussores sumus pro eodem Madoco prefato Lewelino in centum libris sterlingorum bone et legalis monete eidem persolvendis quilibet vero pro xx^{ti} libris cum ab eodem fuerimus in hoc requisiti. In cuius rei testimonium presentibus litteris sigilla nostra apposuimus. Datum apud Dol Wydelan anno domni m° cc° lxx° octavo xviii° die maii.

Madog ap Trahaearn may be identified with the son of Trahaearn ap Madog of Brecon who presented a petition to the king shortly after the 1277 war, complaining that Llywelyn ap Gruffudd had seized his son after the latter had tried to join his father in going over to Edward during the war (*CAP*, 468, with revised dating and discussion in Stephenson, 'Llywelyn ap Gruffydd', 45; Smith, *Llywelyn*, 417 and n. 103).

101 Archbishop Pecham (grievances)

(1) After Rhys granted his castle of Dinefwr to the king after the last peace agreement, when Rhys was in the tent of Payn de Chaworth, six of Rhys's noble men were killed, concerning whom he has never had amends or justice.

(2) When John Giffard claimed Rhys's patrimony at Hirfryn, Rhys sought from the king the law of his country or the law of the county court of Carmarthen, in which court Rhys's predecessors were accustomed to have law when they were in unity with the English and under their lordship; because Rhys has had no law and totally lost his aforesaid land, they wished to compel him to appear in the county court of Hereford, where his predecessors have never answered.

(3) The English have committed injuries in Rhys's lands, especially in respect of churchmen: at St David's church, Llangadog they have made stables and stationed prostitutes and carried away all goods that were kept there and burned all the houses; in the same church, by the altar, they also struck the chaplain on his head with a sword and left him half-dead.

(4) In the same region they have plundered and burned the churches of Llandingad and Llanwrda, and have plundered other churches in those parts of their chalices, books and all other ornaments.

[21 × 31 October 1282]

B = London, Lambeth Palace Library, Register of Archbishop Pecham, fo. 245r. s. xiii².
C = Oxford, All Souls College MS 182, fo. 106r. *c*.1413.
Pd. from B and C, *Reg. Peckh.*, ii. 451–2; from (?)C, Wynne, *History of Wales*, 377; from (?)Wynne, Warrington, *History of Wales*, 614.
Cd., *H*, no. 311; Edwards, *Letters of a Peacemaker*, 26–7.

Ista sunt gravamina per dominum regem et suos iusticiarios illata Reso P(ar)vo de Estrad Tywy.

[i] Primum est, postquam dictus Ris dedit et concessit domino regi castrum suum apud Dynewr post ultimam pacis formam, qui dictus Resus tunc temporis erat in tentilio domini Payn de Gadurcy, eodem tempore interfecti fuerunt vi^a nobiles viri domini Ris, de quibus satisfactionem nec iustitiam unquam habuit, quod fuit eidem dampnum et gravamen.

[ii] Item, Ioh(anne)s Gyffard^b calumpniavit eum Resu(m) super hereditatem propriam apud Hirurym^c, quicquid Res(us) inquisivit a domino rege legem patrie sue aut legem comitatus Kaeruerdyn,^d in quo comitatu antecessores dicti Rys solebant habere leges

quando fierent in unitatem Anglicor(um) et sub eorum dominiis; quod idem Rys nullas leges habuit, et suam terram predictam totaliter amisit, vellent ipsum instringere[e] in comitatu Hereford', ubi nunquam antecessores eius responderunt.

[iii] Preterea, in terris prefati Resi talia gravamina fuerunt per Anglicos facta, maxime pertinent ad ecclesiasticos, videlicet in ecclesia Sancti David que vocatur Lanngadawc[f] fecerunt stabula et meretrices collocaverunt et omnia bona que in ea continebantur omnino asportaverunt atque totas domos combusserunt; et in eadem ecclesia iuxta aram percusserunt capellanum cum gladio ad capud eius et eum reliquerunt semivivum.

[iv] Item, in eadem patria ecclesiam Dyngad et ecclesiam Lannwrdaf spoliaverunt et combusserunt, ceterasque ecclesias in partibus illis omnino spoliaverunt calicibus et libris ac omnibus aliis ornamentis et rebus.

[a] sex C. | [b] Giffard C. | [c] *sic in* BC. | [d] Kaermerdyn C. | [e] *sic in* BC (*?for* distringere). [f] Lanngadawoe C.

For the dating of these *gravamina* see note to no. 428 below. The claim on Hirfryn, a commote in Cantref Bychan, formed part of a lengthy legal case between John Giffard (d. 1299) and his wife Matilda on the one hand and Rhys Wyndod on the other, which began on 14 January 1279 and had not been resolved when war broke out in March 1282 (summarized in *WAR*, 163–73 with reference to assize rolls calendared in ibid., 261–2, 268–70, 289–91, 294, 310–11, 312, 315, 316–17, 321, 327–8, 331–2, 338–40). Giffard had seized part of Hirfryn from Rhys in the 1277 war and used the legal case to try and extend his lands in Cantref Bychan (Smith, *Llywelyn*, 489–90).

LLYWELYN AP RHYS FYCHAN
(*fl.* 1271–83)

AND

HYWEL AP RHYS FYCHAN
(*fl.* 1271–82)

102 Archbishop Pecham (grievances)

After the peace between King Henry and the prince [i.e. Llywelyn ap Gruffudd] at Rhydchwima, the king granted their homage to the prince and confirmed this by his charters; accordingly they were faithful to the prince according to the terms of the grant. King Edward has disinherited them, so they have not had their lands by law or by grace.

[21 × 31 October 1282]

B = London, Lambeth Palace Library, Register of Archbishop Pecham, fo. 245r. s. xiii[2].
C = Oxford, All Souls College MS 182, fo. 106r–v. *c.*1413.
Pd. from B, *Reg. Peckh.*, ii. 452–3; from (?)C, Wynne, *History of Wales*, 378; from (?)Wynne, Warrington, *History of Wales*, 614–15.
Cd., *H*, no. 312.

Gravamina Lywelini[a] filii Ris[b] et Howel eiusdem[c] fratris[d] per dominum regem illata sunt hec. Postquam in forma[e] pacis inter dominum Henricu(m), tunc temporis regem Anglie, et dominum principem apud Rydchwima, tunc prefatus rex concessit et per cartas suas confirmavit prefato principi homagium predictorum nobilium, ex quo predicti nobiles fuerunt fideles et constantes cum prefato principe iuxta eorum donationem et cartarum suarum confirmationem. Edward(us) nunc rex Anglie predictos nobiles dehereditavit,[f] ita quod non habuerunt terras suas nec per legem nec per gratiam.

[a] Lewelini C. | [b] Rys C. | [c] *omitted* C. | [d] C *inserts* eius. | [e] formam C. | [f] C *inserts* denegando eisdem omnes leges et consuetudines Wallie.

For the dating see note to no. 428 below. The brothers refer to the Treaty of Montgomery (no. 363, c. x below).

ELFAEL

EINION CLUD AP MADOG
(d. 1177)

*103 Cwm-hir Abbey
Grant of the land of Carnaf (Karnaf) *with the wood called Coed-yr-ynys* (Cohedrenis).

[1 August 1176 × 1177]

Mention only, in a confirmation of King John dated at Worcester, 27 December 1214 (*Rot. Chart.*, 206a; cd., *H*, no. 192). The dating limits are set by the (?re-)foundation of the abbey on 1 August 1176 (*HW*, ii. 600; Remfry, *Political History of Abbey Cwmhir*, 1) and Einion's death in 1177. Carnaf grange was located near Clyro (SO 213 438), cmt. Elfael Is Mynydd (Williams, *Atlas*, 41).

EINION O'R PORTH AB EINION CLUD
(d. 1191)

*104 Cwm-hir Abbey
Grant of lands of Cabalfa (Kenbalva), Speyf *and Waun Mynachlog* (Wenn').

[Probably 1177 × 1191]

Mention only, in a confirmation of King John dated at Worcester, 27 December 1214 (*Rot. Chart.*, 206a; cd., *H*, no. 193). The grant was probably made between the death of Einion's father in 1177 and that of Einion himself in 1191. Cabalfa grange was located near Clyro and *Speyf* (*recte Speys*: cf. Smith, 'Middle March', 92 (no. 11) for *terra de Brymlegh que vocatur la Speys*) to its north-east, just across the modern Anglo-Welsh border in Brilley (SO 261 492), Herefs.; Waun Mynachlog was in Llansanffraid-yn-Elfael (SO 099 548) (Williams, *Atlas*, 41; Remfry, *Political History of Abbey Cwmhir*, 3, 6).

LLYWELYN AB ANARAWD AB EINION O'R PORTH
(*fl.* 1198–1214)

*105 Cwm-hir Abbey

Grant of Cefnhir (Kokylbir'), *Gwern-y-bwlch* (Guuernebowys), *Kylerumey and Cnwch* (Enight').

[*c.*13 August 1198 × 27 December 1214]

Mention only, in a confirmation of King John dated at Worcester, 27 December 1214 (*Rot. Chart.*, 206a). For the identification of Llywelyn ab Anarawd (*Lewlin' fil' Amaranth'*) as a grandson of Einion o'r Porth see Remfry, *Political History of Abbey Cwmhir*, 7, which also locates the lands as lying on the border between Elfael and the commote of Llythyfnwg. The charter was probably granted after Anarawd was killed at the battle of Painscastle, 13 August 1198.

MADOG AB OWAIN AP MAREDUDD
(*fl.* 1260–82)

106 Letter patent concerning Llywelyn ap Gruffudd

Notification by Madog and Gruffudd sons of Owain and Iorwerth ab Owain, lords of Elfael, Hywel ap Goronwy, bailiff of Buellt, Einion ap Madog, bailiff of Gwerthrynion and Melwyn of Buellt that they have taken Llywelyn ab Einion ap Cedifor, Iorwerth ap Llywelyn ab Adda, Philip, Madog, Einion and Dafydd sons of Ithel Chwyth, *Dafydd ab* Ydean, *Llywelyn ap Gruffudd ap Cynwrig, Dafydd ap Goronwy ap Cynwrig and Iorwerth his brother, Iorwerth* Seig, *Cedifor ap* Tanakyr *and Gruffudd his brother, Gwalchmai the reeve and Dafydd ab* Ybryth, *Maredudd his brother, Llywelyn ap Madog, Llywelyn ap Caradog Hen, Adda Fychan, Llywelyn ap Maredudd ab Adda, Iorwerth Fychan the beadle, Cadwgan ap Cadwallon, Llywelyn Gethin, Einion Foel ab y Maer (son of the steward) and Cadwgan ap Madog as sureties for £40 to be paid to the lord prince for the release of Iorwerth ap Llywelyn and for his constancy and fealty in homage and service to the prince. Iorwerth should give his son as a hostage to the lord prince for his fealty when the prince chooses. As the sureties have no seals the senders have had their seals attached to this letter. Since the prince did not wish to trouble the sureties for the payment of the said money, he has bound the six senders for the payment if Iorwerth is found to be unfaithful to the prince in any way.*

Builth, 30 November 1271

B = TNA: PRO, E 36/274 (Liber A), fo. 341r. s. xiii ex.
Pd. from B, *LW*, 40–1 (no. 59).
Cd., *H*, no. 505.

[U]niversis presentes litteras visuris vel audituris Madocus et Griffin(us) filii Oweni, Ioruerth filius Oweni domini de Eluael, Howelus filius Gyrowe ballivus de Buelld, Ennyaun filius Madauc ballivus de Gwerthrynyon et Melwyn de Bueld salutem. Noverit universitas vestra nos suscepisse Lewelinum filium Enniaun ab Kediuor, Ioruerth filium Lewelini ab Adam, Ph(ilippum), Madauc, Enniaun, David filios Ithael Chwyth, David ab Ydean, Lewelinum[a] vab Gruffut ab Kynwric, David vab Goronw vab Kywrid, Iorwerth fratrem suum, Ioruerth Seig, Kediuor ab Tanakyr, Griffinum fratrem suum, Gwaltiney prepositum, David ab Ybryth, Mared' fratrem suum, Lywelin vab Madauc, Lywelin ab Karadauc Hen, Adam Wychan, Lywelin vab Mared' filium Adam, Ioruerth Vychan bedellum, Kadwgaun vab Cadwallawn, Lywelyn Gethyn, Enniaun Voel vab y Maer, Kadwaun ab Madauc in fideiussores pro quadraginta libris bone et legalis monete domino principi solvendis pro deliberatione Ioruerth ab Lywely(n) et pro eius constantia et fidelitate in homagio et servitio domini principis. Dictus autem Ioruerth debet dare domino principi filium suum in obsidem quem dictus princeps elegerit pro dicta sua fidelitate. Quia vero prescripti fideiussores in confectione presentium sigilla non habeant ideo sigilla nostra hiis litteris fecimus apponi. Et quia predictus dominus princeps nolebat inquietare prefatos fideiussores super solutione dicte pecunie ideo voluit ipse nos sex obligare pro dictis quadraginta libris sibi solvendis si prefatus Ioruerth infidelis in aliquo inveniatur contra principem memoratum. Datum apud Llanveir in Bueld anno domini m⁰ c⁰ c⁰ septuagesimo primo in festo Beati Andree apostoli.

[a] Lewelini B.

For the context and significance of this document see Smith, 'Llywelyn ap Gruffudd', 15–16; *idem*, *Llywelyn*, 357–8. For a genealogy of the rulers of Elfael which traces the descent of Madog and his brothers from Maredudd ab Einion Clud see Remfry, *Political History of Abbey Cwmhir*, 18.

107 Letter patent concerning Llywelyn ap Gruffudd

Notification by Iorwerth ab Owain and Madog ab Owain, lords of Elfael Uwch Mynydd, Ifor ap Gruffudd, bailiff in Elfael Is Mynydd of Llywelyn ap Gruffudd, prince of Wales and lord of Snowdon, Cadwgan ab Einion, dean of Elfael, Goronwy Fychan, rector of Llansanffraid, Owain ap Meurig of Builth, Hywel ab Ifor, Madog ab Ithel, Einion ap Madog, the prince's bailiff of Gwerthrynion and Meurig ap Dafydd that they have bound themselves, of their own free will, to the prince for the release of John ap Hywel ap Meurig from the prince's prison in the sum of £60, to be paid if John presumes to leave the unity and fealty of the prince, so that each of them will pay £6 to the prince. Sealing clause.

Brynysgefyll, 7 May 1276

B = TNA: PRO, E 36/274 (Liber A), fo. 341v. s. xiii ex.
Pd. from B, *LW*, 41–2 (no. 61).
Cd., *H*, no. 506.

[U]niversis Cristi fidelibus presentes litteras visuris vel audituris Iuor filius Griffini ballivus domini Lewelin filii Griffini principis Wallie, domini Snaudone apud Elualel is Mynyth, Ioruerth filius Oweni, Madoc(us) filius Oweni domini de Eluael vch Mynyth, Caduganus filius Enniaun decanus de Eluael, Goronwe Vycan rector ecclesie de Lannsanffered, Owen(us) filius Meuric de Bueld, Howelus filius Iuor, Madocus filius Ithael, Annianus filius Madauc ballivus domini principis de Gwerthrynnyon et Meuryc filius David salutem in domino. Noverit universitas vestra quod nos non vi nec metu coacti set spontanea nostra voluntate ducti obligavimus nos predicto domino principi pro deliberatione Ioh(ann)is filii Howely ab Meuryc de carcere domini principis pro sexaginta libris sterlingorum bone et legalis monete sibi solvendis si dictus Ioh(ane)s ab unitate et fidelitate prefati domini principis presumpserit discedere quoad vixerit, ita videlicet quod quilibet nostrum persolvat memorato domino principi sex libras de dicta paccatione. In cuius rei testimonium sigilla nostra presenti scripto fecimus apponi. Datum apud Brynsceuyll in manerio predicti Iuor filii Griffini anno domini m° cc° lxx° vi^to in crastino Beati Ioh(ann)is ante Portam Latinam.

Shortly afterwards Madog ab Owain refused to be associated with the obligation, and on 13 May 1276, at the instance of Hywel ap Meurig (John's father), Abbot Cadwgan of Cwm-hir pledged all the lands and possessions he held from Llywelyn for £40 for John's release (*LW*, 32–3, 44 (nos 44, 65)). Hywel ap Meurig had been constable of the Mortimer castle of Cefnllys and also served the crown in Anglo-Welsh negotiations (Smith, 'Middle March', 86–7).

MAELIENYDD

HYWEL AP CADWALLON AP MADOG
(d. 2 × 4 August 1212)

108 Cwm-hir Abbey
Grant of 4 acres and a third part of a meadow at (?) Dolygarn (Dolganeru), together with two wooded, thorny places on either side of that meadow, which were granted as a perpetual gift to the abbey by Llywelyn ap Goronwy, the three sons of Ieuaf ap Gwlad Arall, the three sons of Dafydd, the two sons of Morgan ap Goronwy and the son of Moriddig ap Gwgan before witnesses including Llywelyn ap Goronwy, Einion ab Ieuaf, Ieuaf ap Sarf and Coch Terwin. Further grant in perpetual alms of 4 acres at (?) Caeliber (Kellibir), which belonged to Cuhelyn Kirn, *before witnesses including Iorwerth ap Dafydd, Llywelyn ap Goronwy and Ithel Crach. Sealing clause.*

[1179 × July 1212; probably *c.*1210 × July 1212]

A = BL, Add. Ch. 26727. Endorsed: Howel super Dolganherv (s. xiii¹); modern endorsement; approx. 202 × 113 + 25 mm; one central slit just above the fold and one through the fold for a tag (*c.*16 mm. wide) which exits through a slit in the base of the fold. Seal missing. There are some small holes in the parchment.
Pd. from A, Owen, *Catalogue*, iii. 750.
Cd., *H*, no. 189.

Omnibus sancte matris ecclesie filiis tam modernis quam secuturis Howel filius Katwallaun pacem et salutem. Noverit universitas vestra mea voluntate, concessione et perpetua donatione actum esse ut fratres de Cumhir perpetualiter habeant et nemine contradice[n]te

possideant quatuor acras et terciam partem prati[s ap]ud Dolganeru et duo loca nemorosa
et spinarum densitate operta ex utraque parte eiusdem prati; que loca a Llewelin filio
Goronuy et a tribus filiis Ioab filii Gulat Arall et a tribus filiis Dawit et a duobus filiis
Morgan filii Goronuy et a filio Moridic filii Gurgan perpetua donatione m[ultis] coram
astan[ti]bus [qui te]stes existunt supradictis fratribus de Cu(m)hir sunt collata, inter quos
fuerunt Liwelin filius Goronuy, Einaun filii Ioab, Ioab filii Sarf et Coch Terwin cum aliis
pluribus. Simili modo concessi et in perpetuam elemosinam dedi quatuor acras apud
Kellibir que fuerunt Cuhelin cognomento Kirn, his viris existentibus testibus: Ioruerth filio
Dawit, Lewelin filio Goronuy, Itael cognomento Crach cum aliis multis. Has itaque
donationes non solum supradictis viris in testimonium add[idi et] confirmavi set et sigilli
mei impressione signavi ut apud posteros inperpetuum inconcusse permaneant et nullus
temerario ausu eas inquietare vel perturbare ullomodo presumat.

Hywel's elder brother Maelgwn ap Cadwallon (d. 1197) succeeded their father Cadwallon
ap Madog after the latter's death on 22 September 1179; both Maelgwn and Hywel were
expelled from Maelienydd by Roger Mortimer in 1195. The charter was almost certainly
issued in the period between Hywel's restoration to Maelienydd c.1210 × 1212 and his
execution at Bridgnorth 2 × 4 August 1212 (cf. Smith, 'Middle March', 80–1; idem, 'Cymer
abbey', 102–3; Remfry, 'Cadwallon ap Madog', 20; notes to nos. 113 and 234 below).
However, a copy of the charter by George Owen of Henllys (d. 1613) states, without any
explanation, that the grant was made in 1194 (BL, Harl. MS 6068, fo. 77v, cited in Remfry,
'Native Welsh Dynasties', 156). Caeliber (Caeliber-isaf SO 213 928, Caeliber-uchaf SO 193
923) lay in Ceri, in the grange of Gwern-y-go, about $2\frac{1}{4}$ miles south-west of Montgomery,
Dolygarn (SO 086 785) on the river Eithon, almost 1 mile north-west of Llanbadarn
Fynydd in Maelienydd (Williams, Atlas, 40; Remfry, Political History of Abbey Cwmhir, 3,
5).

*109 Cwm-hir Abbey
Grant of the land of (?)Hopton (Fortun').

[1179 × 1212; probably c.1210 × July 1212]

Mention only, in a confirmation of King John dated at Worcester, 27 December 1214 (Rot.
Chart., 206a; cd., H, no. 194). For the dating limits see note to no. 108 above. Although
Lloyd ('Border notes', 49–50) took Fortun' to be Forden (SJ 227 011), cmt. Gorddwr, there
are strong grounds for identifying it as Hopton (SO 227 910; Hopton Uchaf 223 905;
Hopton Isaf SO 238 906). First, Hywel ap Cadwallon is not otherwise known to have held
lands in Gorddwr; second, Hopton – like Caeliber, almost 3 miles to its north-west, also
granted by Hywel (no. 108 above) – formed part of Cwm-hir's grange of Gwern-y-go
(Morgan, 'Territorial divisions [I]', 23 and n. 53; Remfry, Political History of Abbey
Cwmhir, 4 and n. 17; Williams, Atlas, 40; cf. no. 114 below).

CADWALLON AP HYWEL AP CADWALLON
(*fl.* 1212–41)

110 Letter patent concerning Henry III and Ralph Mortimer

Notification that he has sworn on relics that from this day and for the rest of his life he will be faithful to the king and his heirs and serve him with all his strength and power, and will faithfully observe a truce with Ralph Mortimer until Michaelmas [29 September] 1241. For the observation of this fealty and this truce he has placed himself under the jurisdiction of the bishops of Hereford and of Coventry and Lichfield, or whichever of them the king chooses, so that if he contravenes his fealty or the truce in any way they may excommunicate him and all his men and place his lands under interdict until he has made full amends for that transgression. If no peace is agreed with Ralph Mortimer before Michaelmas and Cadwallon wages war against Ralph, Cadwallon will not be bound by the aforesaid oath as long as he remains faithful to the king and his heirs. If war is waged after the aforesaid deadline, the king will nevertheless allow Cadwallon and his men to be received in his land like his other faithful men. He binds himself to observe the aforesaid fealty by the aforesaid oath and by fixing his seal to this writing.

[Shrewsbury] 14 August 1241

B = TNA: PRO, E 36/274 (Liber A), fo. 346r–v. s. xiii ex.
Pd. from B, *LW*, 54–5 (no. 80).
Cd., *H*, no. 500.

[S]ciant presentes et futuri quod ego Kadwathlan filius Hoel tactis sacrosanctis iuravi quod ab isto die in antea omnibus diebus vite mee ero ad fidelitatem domini regis Angl(ie) et heredum suorum et serviam eis fideliter et devote cum omnibus viribus meis et toto posse meo quandocumque indiguerint servitio meo, et treugam inter dominum Radulfu(m) de Mortuo Mari et me initam usque ad festum Sancti Mich(ael)is anno regni domini H. regis filii regis Ioh(ann)is vicesimo quinto ex parte mea fideliter observabo. Et tam ad fidelitatem domino regi et heredibus suis observandam in perpetuum quam ad treugas predictas observandas usque ad terminum predictum supposui me iurisdictioni domini Herefordens(is) episcopi et domini Covventrens(is) et Lichefelden(sis) episcopi vel alterius eorum quem dominus rex ad hoc elegerit, ut si in aliquo contra fidelitatem domini regis[a] vel heredum suorum vel contra observantiam predictarum treugarum venero liceat eis vel alteri eorum quem dominus rex ad hoc elegerit personam meam et omnes [fo. 346v] meos excommunicare et terram meam interdicere donec de transgressione ipsa satisfecero ad plenum. Et si forsitan infra predictum festum Sancti Michael(is) inter predictum Radulfum de Mortuo Mari et me nulla pax fuerit reformata, licet post festum illud guerram moveam predicto Radulfo non obligabit me predictum iuramentum dum tamen erga dominum regem et heredes suos fidelitatem observem continuam sicut predictum est. Et si guerra post predictum terminum inter nos moveatur, nichilominus dominus rex sustinebit quod ego et mei receptemur in terra sua sicut alii fideles sui. Ad predictam autem fidelitatem observandam tam domino regi quam heredibus suis obligo me per iuramentum predictum et per sigilli mei appositionem quod huic scripto apposui ad maiorem observationem predictorum. Actum quartodecimo die augusti anno eodem.

[a] heredis B.

For the context and significance of the submissions recorded here and in nos 111–12, 116 and 118 below see Smith, 'Middle March', 82–3, which notes that all five lords had gone to see the king at Worcester the previous February, presumably to claim Maelienydd, and emphasizes that the terms set out here did not allow for their reinstatement in their ancestral territory. It is likely that Cadwallon and his brothers Maredudd and Owain (nos 112–13 below) were sons of the Hywel ap Cadwallon ap Madog executed in 1212 rather than of the Hywel ap Cadwallon ap Maelgwn of no. 118 below (Morgan, 'Territorial divisions [I]', 27, 31, *pace* Smith, 'Middle March', 82). For the place-date see no. 118 below.

MAREDUDD AP HYWEL AP CADWALLON
(*fl.* 1212–41)

111 Letter patent concerning Henry III and Ralph Mortimer
[Text as no. 110 above.]

[Shrewsbury] 16 August 1241 (B), 14 August 1241 (C)

B = Cambridge, Corpus Christi College MS 16, fo. 172v. s. xiii med.
C = TNA: PRO, E 36/274 (Liber A), fos 346v–347r. s. xiii ex.
Pd. from B, *Matthaei Paris . . . Historia*, ed. Parker, 842; from B, Paris, *CM*, iv. 319–20; from C, *LW*, 56–7 (no. 82); from Parker, *Matthaei Paris . . . Historia*, ed. Wats, 625; from (?)Parker or Wats, Wynne, *History of Wales*, 356–7; from (?)Wynne, Warrington, *History of Wales*, 601–2.
Cd., *H*, no. 503.

Sciant presentes et futuri quod ego Merduc(us)[a] filius Howel[b] tactis sacrosanctis iuravi quod ab isto die in antea omnibus diebus vite mee ero ad fidelitatem domini regis Angl(ie)[c] et serviam ei[d] fideliter et devote cum omnibus viribus meis et toto posse meo quandocumque indiguerit servitio meo, et treugam[e] inter dominum Rad(ulfum) de Mortuo Mari et me initam usque ad festum Sancti Mich(aelis) anno regni regis[f] H.[g] xxv[oh] ex parte mea fideliter observabo. Et tam ad fidelitatem domino regi[i] in perpetuum observandam quam ad treugas[j] predictas observandas usque ad terminum predictum supposui me iurisdictioni domini H(er)efordensis episcopi et domini Coventr(ensis)[k] et Lich(efeldensis) episcopi vel alterius eorum quem dominus rex ad hoc elegerit, ut si in aliquo contra predictam[l] fidelitatem domini regis[m] vel contra observantiam predictarum treugarum venero[n] liceat eis vel [o]eorum alteri[-o] quem dominus rex ad hoc elegerit personam meam et omnes meos excommunicare et terram meam interdicere donec de transgressione ipsa[p] satisfecero[q] ad plenum. Et si forsitan infra predictum festum Sancti Mich(aelis) inter predictum Rad(ulfum) de Mor(tuo) M.[r] et me nulla pax fuerit reformata, licet post festum illud guerram moveam predicto Rad(ulfo) non obligabit me [s]predictum iuramentum[-s] dum tamen erga dominum regem[t] fidelitatem observem continuam sicut predictum est. Et si guerra post predictum terminum inter nos moveatur, nichilominus dominus rex sustinebit quod ego et mei receptemur in terra sua sicut alii fideles sui. Ad [u]predicta autem observanda[-u] domino regi et[v] heredibus suis[w] obligo me per iuramentum predictum et per sigilli mei appositionem quod huic scripto apposui ad maiorem confirmationem[x] predictorum. [y]Act' in crastino assumptionis Beate M(ari)e anno regni regis H. xxv[o].[-y]

[a] Mereduc C. | [b] Hoel C. | [c] C *inserts* et heredum suorum. | [d] eis C. | [e] trewgam C. | [f] C *inserts* domini. | [g] C *inserts* filii regis Ioh(ann)is. | [h] vicesimo quinto C. | [i] C *inserts* et heredibus suis. | [j] treugas C. | [k] Covventrens(is) C. | [l] *omitted* C. | [m] C *inserts* vel heredum suorum. [n] venerint B. | [o–o] alteri eorum C. | [p] predicta C. | [q] satisfacero B. | [r] Mari C. [s–s] iuramentum predictum C. | [t] C *inserts* et heredes suos C. | [u–u] predictam autem fidelitatem observandam tam C. | [v] quam C. | [w] C *inserts* in perpetuum. | [x] observationem C. | [y–y] Actum quartodecimo die augusti anno eodem C.

See note to no. 110 above. The verbal differences between B and C indicate that the copy in B derives from a different text of the document from that in C.

OWAIN AP HYWEL AP CADWALLON
(d. May 1251 × August 1253)

112 Letter patent concerning Henry III and Ralph Mortimer
[Text as no. 110 above.]

[Shrewsbury] 14 August 1241

B = TNA: PRO, E 36/274 (Liber A), fo. 347v. s. xiii ex.
Pd. from B, *LW*, 57–8 (no. 84).
Cd., *H*, no. 504.

[S]ciant presentes et futuri quod ego Oweyn filius Hoel tactis sacrosanctis iuravi quod ab isto die in antea omnibus diebus vite mee ero ad fidelitatem domini regis Angl(ie) et heredum suorum et serviam eis fideliter et devote cum omnibus viribus meis et toto posse meo quandocumque indiguerint servitio meo, et treugam inter dominum Rad(ulfu)m de Mortuo Mari et me initam usque ad festum Sancti Mich(ael)is anno regni regis Henr(ici) filii regis Ioh(ann)is vicesimo quinto ex parte mea fideliter observabo. Et tam ad fidelitatem domino regi et heredibus suis observandam in perpetuum quam ad treugas predictas observandas usque ad terminum predictum supposui me iurisdictioni domini Hereford(ensis) episcopi et domini Coventrens(is) et Lichefeld(ensis) episcopi vel alterius eorum quem dominus rex ad hoc elegerit, ut si in aliquo contra fidelitatem domini regis vel heredum suorum vel contra observantiam predictarum treugarum venero liceat eis vel alteri eorum quem dominus rex ad hoc elegerit personam meam et omnes meos excommunicare et terram meam interdicere donec de transgressione ipsa satisfecero ad plenum. Et si forsitan infra predictum festum Sancti Mich(aeli)s inter predictum Rad(ulfu)m de Mortuo Mari et me nulla pax fuerit reformata, licet post festum illud guerram moveam predicto Rad(ulf)o non obligabit me predictum iuramentum dum tamen erga dominum regem et heredes suos fidelitatem observem continuam sicut predictum est. Et si guerra post predictum terminum inter nos moveatur, nichilominus dominus rex sustinebit quod ego et mei receptemur in terra sua sicut alii fideles sui. Ad predictam autem fidelitatem observandam tam domino regi quam heredibus suis obligo me per iuramentum predictum et per sigilli mei appositionem quod huic scripto apposui ad maiorem observationem predictorum. Actum quartodecimo die augusti anno eodem.

See note to no. 110 above.

MADOG AP MAELGWN AP CADWALLON
(d. 2 × 4 August 1212)

113 Cwm-hir Abbey

Grant in perpetual alms with all their bounds and appurtenances of the lands of (?) Bryn-y-groes (Brin e Crois), *(?) Caer Whitton* (Cayrwetun), *and Maes* Ecrocvr. *He has granted these free for ever from all secular exaction and service and confirmed this gift, with his nobles, before many, so that anyone who presumes to contravene or in any way disturb this gift may be disinherited and banished from all the land under Madog's authority until he gives it up in peace to the monks. The nobles have sworn before many that they will never endure the dominion of any prince over them; this will be rejected by all if he (that is, the prince) presumes to make any claim over those lands unless he gives them up in peace and protects them with the monks. Witnesses.*

May [1212]

A = Paris, Bibliothèque Nationale, Nouvelles acquisitions latines 391. The parchment is mounted, and only the top and bottom of the dorse can be examined. Endorsed: Madauc super Caruetu, Brin Crois, Mo . . . (s. xiii; ink seems to have been rubbed away at the end, but no more letters visible under ultraviolet light); modern endorsements; approx. 130 × 114 + 18 mm.; three central slits, one above fold and two in fold, for a tag (*c*.17 mm. wide) which exits through the lower slit in fold; sealed on tag. Circular seal, brown wax, imperfect, originally approx. 60 mm. diameter; equestrian, facing right; legend lost. A piece of paper, containing a fragment of printed text in English (s. xvi), is attached to the back of the seal.

Pd. from A, d'Arbois de Jubainville, 'Charte originale', 86–7; from A, Tibbott, 'Abbey Cwmhir relic', 64–5 (with photograph and trans.).

Cd., *H*, no. 191.

Cunctis Cristi fidelibus tam presentibus quam futuris Madauc filius Maylgun salutem et pacem. Noverit universitas vestra me concessisse monachis de Cumhyr Deo et Beate Marie ibidem servientibus atque in perpetuam elemosinam dedisse terram que dicitur Brin e Crois in cunctis finibus et omnimodis pertinentiis suis; terram quoque que dicitur Cayrwetun similiter plenarie in cunctis finibus suis; similiter etiam terram que vocatur Mays Ecrocvr in cunctis pertinentiis et utilitatibus suis, in bosco et plano, in pratis et aquis, in silvis et campis atque omnimodis utilitatibus suis. Has itaque iam dictas terras in terminis suis et infra circumquaque in perpetuam donationem ab omni exactione et servitio seculari liberas et quietas supradictis monachis concessi et dedi et multis coram astantibus eandem donationem cum optimatibus meis sic iuramento confirmavi ut quisquis huic donationi contraire vel illam quoquo modo perturbare deinceps presumpserit ab omni terra que mee ditioni subiacet extraneus et exheredatus fiat donec illam in pace prefatis monachis dimittat. Similiter et optimates coram multis iuraverunt se nunquam passuros cuiuslibet super se principis dominium, set ab omnibus respuendum et relinquendum si aliquam calumpniam super his terris inferre presumpserit, nisi eas in pace dimiserit et cum monachis custodierit. His testibus: domino Maredud filio Rob(er)ti, T(ra)hayarn filio G(ri)fut Weleu, Grifino filio Heylin, Ioruerth filio Meyravn cum [a]multis aliis.[a] Datum litterarum per manum domni Riredi abbatis [a]mense maio.[a]

[a–a] *words written in majuscule letters* A.

This charter can be no later than May 1212, as Madog was executed at Bridgnorth in August of that year. The remarkable sentence stating that the nobles had sworn never to accept the lordship of a prince must refer to Llywelyn ap Iorwerth, who complained of Madog's attitude towards him in a letter of *c*.1210 × 4 August 1212 (no. 234 below). It is uncertain when and how Madog secured a position in Maelienydd which would have made these grants effective; that they were effective is shown by the abbey's subsequent quitclaim of two of the lands, *Karwyton'* and *Bryncroys*, to Ralph Mortimer in 1241 × 1242 (Smith, 'Middle March', 91 (no. 8); Remfry, *Political History of Abbey Cwmhir*, 8, 12–13). After Maelienydd was conquered by Roger Mortimer in 1195 the native lords sought refuge in Gwynedd; in the letter cited above Llywelyn claimed to have fostered Madog. One possibility is that Llywelyn helped to restore Madog to Maelienydd, in the wake of his recovery in 1212 following his defeat by John the previous year (cf. Smith, 'Middle March', 81). However, as Remfry has argued (*Political History of Abbey Cwmhir*, 8–12), Madog may have gained a foothold in Maelienydd through an agreement with Roger Mortimer. Madog owed King John £100 26*s*. 8*d*. for the king's *benevolentia* by Michaelmas 1210, a payment received by the sheriff of Hereford by Michaelmas 1211 (*Pipe Roll 13 John*, 233). The payment is very probably related to the account in the Wigmore chronicle that Madog and his uncle Hywel ap Cadwallon fined heavily with John in order to have their claim to hold Maelienydd as tenants of Roger Mortimer heard by a jury at Shrewsbury (cf. also Smith, 'Cymer', 115, n. 17). Although the chronicle states that they lost the claim (*Mon. Ang.*, vi: i. 350), the present grant may indicate that Mortimer granted Madog some land in Maelienydd. That an agreement had been reached between the two is possibly indicated by the association of two of the witnesses of the present charter with Mortimer: Trahaearn's father was the same person as the *Grifino Velu* who witnessed Mortimer's charter for Cwmhir in 1200, which was also witnessed by Gruffudd ap Heilin (Charles, 'Early charter', 69). The charter's implicit defiance of Llywelyn is consistent with an independent initiative by Madog to recover Maelienydd, perhaps taking advantage of the prince's discomfiture following John's devastatingly effective campaign against Gwynedd in the summer of 1211; it may be significant that the first witness, Maredudd ap Rhobert of Cedewain, was on John's side in August 1211. If so, this would suggest that the charter was issued in May 1212. *Bryn e Crois* may be identifiable with Bryn-y-groes (SO 060 580), located in Elfael about 2 miles south of Llandrindod Wells. Alternatively, Remfry has suggested that all three places lay in the south-east of Maelienydd in the vicinity of Pilleth (SO 256 682) and Whitton (SO 271 673) (*Political History of Abbey Cwmhir*, 3, 8).

MAREDUDD AP MAELGWN AP CADWALLON
(*fl.* 1197–*c*.1249)

*114 Cwm-hir Abbey

Grant of (?)Llechelwyddan (Leghwython'), *(?)Sarffryn* (Sarfbrun'), *Cefn-pawl* (Kenepawel'), *Fforchegel* (Forghekeyl), *Buddugre* (Buthygfre), *Dolvolblich', (?)Duthlas* (Butharch'), Nanrim, *(?)Dyfanner* (Dynanner), *(?)Rhiwlyfnan* (Ryulnynan'), *Crug* (Cruthas), *Delyneyn', the grange of (?)Gwanan* (Gwenweyn), *(?)Caer Ogyrfan* (Cayrogheren'), *Llaethdy* (Laythde), *half of Nant-ddu* (Nantdu), *Gwern-y-go* (Guernegof), *Biggegwenith', (?)Dolygarn* (Dolganhenru), *part of (?)Caeliber* (Kellybir), *(?)Gwenrhiw* (Gwenriw'), *(?)Pabyllwydd* (Peblewith'), *common pasture throughout Maelienydd and Ceri, the lands of Maes* Ecrogur (Maysecrogur), *(?)Caer Whitton* (Kayrwetin') *and (?)Bryn-y-groes* (Breinecrois) *sold for the castle of Cymaron* (Caminarum).

[August 1212 × 27 December 1214]

Mention only, in a confirmation of King John dated at Worcester, 27 December 1214 (*Rot. Chart.*, 205b–206a; cd., *H*, no. 196). As it includes lands granted by Maredudd's uncle Hywel ap Cadwallon and brother Madog ap Maelgwn (nos 108 and 113 above), the grant was probably a confirmation issued after the execution of those grantors early in August 1212 (by which time Madog and also, presumably, Maredudd had been restored to Maelienydd). After Madog's execution Maredudd was the principal native lord in Maelienydd, and it is significant that John's confirmation opens with these grants (see note to no. 234 below; Remfry, *Political History of Abbey Cwmhir*, 3–4). It follows that Lloyd's suggestion (*HW*, ii. 594 and nn. 106–7) that John's confirmation confused the donor with Maredudd ap Madog, ruler of Maelienydd 1140–6, should be rejected. The reference to the sale of *Maysecrogur*, (?)Caer Whitton (*Kayrwetin'*) and (?)Bryn-y-groes (*Breinecrois*) for Cymaron castle (SO 153 703) is puzzling; as Madog ap Maelgwn's charter granting these lands makes no mention of such a sale (no. 113 above), it may have been agreed with Maredudd as a condition of his confirmation (cf. *OP*, iii. 335; Remfry, *Political History of Abbey Cwmhir*, 11).

For identifications of place-names see Charles, 'Early charter', 72–3; Williams, *Atlas*, 40–1; Remfry, *Political History of Abbey Cwmhir*, 3–6, 15. Most of the lands seem to be located in Maelienydd, beginning with those in the vicinity of the abbey, which, together with lands in the parish of Llanbadarn Fynydd, formed Golon manor: Llechelwyddan (location lost); Sarffryn, possibly identifiable with Carreg Wiber, about $1\frac{1}{2}$ miles south-east of Llandrindod Wells (Carreg Wiber farm SO 081 593; see *OP*, iii. 300); Cefn-pawl (SO 067 706), about $\frac{3}{4}$ mile south-east of Cwm-hir; Buddugre (Buddugre Hill SO 089 700), about 2 miles south-east of Cwm-hir; Tŷ Faenor (Dyfaenor SO 072 711), about 1 mile east of Cwm-hir. *Cayrogheren'* may represent Caer Ogyrfan, possibly identifiable with Carreg-y-frân (SO 184 789), about 1 mile south-west of Bugeildy (RCAHMW, *Radnor*, 25). Llaethdy (SO 069 800), Nant-ddu (Blaen-nant-ddu SO 108 819, Nanty SO 101 813), (?)Gwenrhiw (possibly Gwenthriw SO 193 904) and Pabyllwydd lay in the parish of Llanbadarn Fynydd. Gwern-y-go (SO 222 919), about $2\frac{3}{4}$ miles south of Newtown, was the centre of the grange of that name in Ceri. See also notes to no. 108 above (for Dolygarn and Caeliber) and no. 113 above (for *Maysecrogur*, (?)Caer Whitton and (?)Bryn-y-groes).

*115 Cwm-hir Abbey
Grant of (?) Cilgwnfydd (Kylwylft) *and Llechryd* (Lechricht').

[August 1212 × 27 December 1214]

Mention only, in a confirmation of King John dated at Worcester, 27 December 1214 (*Rot. Chart.*, 206a; cd., *H*, no. 195). Although the donor is referred to only as Maredudd, it is likely that Maredudd ap Maelgwn was meant. Since the grants here are listed separately from those in no. 114 above, they were presumably contained in a different charter, probably issued later in the same date range as no. 114. Both lands seem to have lain in Elfael. *Kylwylft* is probably Cilgwnfydd (Cilgwnfydd Farm SO 035 543), about ½ mile north-east of Llechryd (SO 030 537), located about 2 miles north-west of Builth Wells (see Remfry, *Political History of Abbey Cwmhir*, 3, 7).

116 Letter patent concerning Henry III and Ralph Mortimer
[Text as no. 110 above.]

[Shrewsbury] 14 August 1241

B = TNA: PRO, E 36/274 (Liber A), fo. 347r–v. s. xiii ex.
Pd. from B, *LW*, 57 (no. 83).
Cd., *H*, no. 501.

[S]ciant presentes et futuri quod ego Mereduf filius Mailgun tactis sacrosanctis iuravi quod ab isto die in antea omnibus diebus vite mee ero ad fidelitatem domini regis Angl(ie) et heredum suorum et serviam eis fideliter et devote cum omnibus viribus meis et toto posse meo quandocumque indiguerit servitio meo, et treugam inter dominum Rad(ulfu)m de Mortuo Mari et me initam usque ad festum Sancti Mich(ael)is anno regni regis H. filii regis Ioh(ann)is vicesimo quinto ex parte mea fideliter observabo. Et tam ad fidelitatem domino regi et heredibus suis in perpetuum observandam quam ad treugas predictas observandas usque ad terminum predictum supposui me iurisdictioni domini Hereford(ensis) episcopi et domini Covventr(ensis) et Lichefel(densis) episcopi vel alterius eorum quem dominus rex ad hoc elegerit, ut si in aliquo contra fidelitatem domini regis vel heredum suorum vel contra observantiam predictarum treugarum venero liceat eis vel alteri eorum quem dominus rex ad hoc elegerit personam meam et omnes meos excommunicare et terram meam interdicere donec de transgressione predicta satisfecero ad plenum. Et si forsitan infra predictum festum Sancti Mich(ael)is inter predictum Rad(ulfu)m de Mortuo Mari et me nulla pax fuerit reformata, licet post festum illud guerram moveam predicto Rad(ulf)o non obligabit me iuramentum predictum dum tamen erga dominum regem et heredes suos fidelitatem observem continuam sicut predictum est. Et si guerra post predictum terminum inter nos moveatur, nichilominus dominus rex sustinebit quod ego et mei receptemur in terra sua sicut alii fideles sui. Ad [fo. 347v] predictam autem fidelitatem observandam tam domino regi quam heredibus suis in perpetuum obligo me per iuramentum predictum et per sigilli mei appositionem quod huic scripto apposui ad maiorem observationem predictorum. Actum quartodecimo die augusti anno eodem.

See note to no. 110 above.

*117 Henry III

(?) Petition by Maredudd, and Hywel ap Cadwallon, to be restored to one half of Ceri as their right.

[Shortly before 7 May 1249]

Mention only, in an order by Henry III to William de Oddingeseles, keeper of the castle of Montgomery, to hold an inquisition into the claim dated at Westminster, 7 May 1249 (*CIM*, i, no. 76; *H*, no. 507). As the king merely says that Maredudd and Hywel came to see him under safe conduct to pray for their land to be restored, there is no certainty that their petition was also presented in writing. The inquisition was held at Montgomery on 27 May 1249 and found that Maredudd and Hywel had been the rightful heirs of the land in time of peace and gave charters of fealty to John Lestrange, then bailiff of Montgomery (possibly a reference to no. 116 above and no. 118 below); however, they had subsequently broken their fealty by siding with Dafydd ap Llywelyn when he occupied the lands of Gruffudd ap Gwenwynwyn (a reference to the prince's campaigns in 1245–6). Maredudd and Hywel continued to claim half of Ceri in 1250, when an inquisition held on 11 June found that they had rebelled against the king (*CIM*, i, no. 84; see further Morgan, 'Territorial divisions [I]', 31–2).

HYWEL AP CADWALLON AP MAELGWN
(fl. 1234–50)

118 Letter patent concerning Henry III and Ralph Mortimer
[Text as no. 110 above.]

[Shrewsbury] 14 August 1241

B = TNA: PRO, E 36/274 (Liber A), fo. 346v. s. xiii ex.
Pd. from B, *LW*, 55–6 (no. 81).
Cd., *H*, no. 499.

[S]ciant presentes et futuri quod ego Hoell(us) filius Cadwatlan tactis sacrosanctis iuravi quod ab isto die in antea omnibus diebus vite mee ero ad fidelitatem domini regis Angl(ie) et heredum suorum et serviam eis fideliter[a] et devote cum omnibus viribus meis et toto posse meo quandocumque indiguerint servitio meo, et trewgam inter dominum Rad(ulfu)m de Mortuo Mari et me initam usque ad festum Sancti Mich(aelis) anno regni regis H. filii regis Ioh(ann)is vicesimo quinto ex parte mea fideliter observabo. Et tam ad fidelitatem domino regi et heredibus suis in perpetuum observandam quam ad trewgas predictas obser-vandas usque ad terminum predictum supposui me iurisdictioni domini Hereford(ensis) episcopi et domini Coventr(ensis) et Lichefeld(ensis) episcopi vel alterius eorum quem dominus rex ad hoc elegerit, ut si in aliquo contra fidelitatem domini regis vel heredum suorum vel contra observantiam predictarum trewgarum venero liceat eis vel alteri eorum quem dominus rex ad hoc elegerit personam meam et omnes meos exommunicare et terram meam interdicere donec de transgressione predicta satisfecero ad plenum. Et si forsitan infra predictum festum Sancti Mich(aelis) inter predictum Rad(ulfu)m de Mortuo Mari et me nulla pax fuerit reformata, licet post festum illud guerram[b] moveam predicto Rad(ulf)o non obligabit me iuramentum predictum dum tamen erga dominum regem et heredes suos fidelitatem observem continuam sicut predictum est. Et si guerra post predictum terminum inter nos moveatur nichilominus dominus rex sustinebit quod ego et mei receptemur in terra sua sicut alii fideles sui. Ad predictam autem fidelitatem observandam tam domino regi quam heredibus suis in perpetuum obligo me per iuramentum predictum et per sigilli mei appositionem quod huic scripto apposui ad maiorem observationem predictorum. Actum quartodecimo die augusti apud Salop' anno eodem.

[a] B inserts de *struck through.* | [b] trewgam B.

See note to no. 110 above.

GLAMORGAN

RHYS AB IESTYN
(fl. c.1130–c.1140)

*119 Neath Abbey

Grant, with the consent of his sons Iorwerth (Iouerd), Owain (Oein) and Hywel (Hoel), of the land of Llanilid (terram de Saint Ilith) with the church and all its appurtenances.

[1130 × (?)c.1140]

Mention only, in a confirmation charter of King John dated at Burbage, 6 January 1208 (TNA: PRO, C 53/8, m. 4; pd., *Mon. Ang.*, v. 259; *Rot. Chart.*, 174a; *Cartae*, ii. 316 (no. 318); cd., *H*, no. 108). Neath Abbey was founded as a Savigniac house by Richard de Granville in 1130 (Cowley, *Monastic Order*, 21). Llanilid (SS 978 813) lay in the lordship of Rhuthin, which may have been taken over by a member of the St Quintin family of Talyfan at some point after this grant, perhaps in the mid-twelfth century, but the precise chronology is uncertain (Smith, 'Kingdom of Morgannwg', 25).

*120 Neath Abbey

Grant of land between the Neath and the Tawe called Reses Lege/Risleg *in exchange for Cilybebyll.*

[c.1136 × (?)c.1140]

Mention only, in Rice Merrick's *Morganiae Archaiographia* (1578–84) drawing on the lost medieval Register of Neath Abbey (*Rice Merrick*, 39, 54, 109). The same source explains that Rhys had received the land from Richard de Granville *pro bono pacis* (almost certainly in 1136), and subsequently exchanged it with the monks for Cilybebyll (ibid., 39, 54; Crouch, 'Robert, earl of Gloucester', 230). Cilybebyll (SN 744 047) likewise lies between the Neath and the Tawe, just east of the latter about $1\frac{1}{2}$ miles north-east of Pontardawe.

MORGAN AP CARADOG
(d. *c*.1208)

121   The Cistercian Order, Brother Meilyr and the brothers of Pendar

Confirmation, by Morgan and his brothers Cadwallon and Maredudd, by their common assent, of the gift by Caradog Uerbeis *of the whole land between the three rivers of the Ffrwd, Clydach and Llysnant, with the wood of Llwynperdid, free of all secular exactions. Sealing clause. If the necessity arises they will bring their power to warrant the grant against all. Witnesses.*

[1158 × October 1191]

A = BL, Harl. Ch. 75 B 29. Endorsed: Sigill' Marga(n). Kadawl' (s. xii/xiii); approx. 193 × 128 + 20 mm.; two slits in fold on left for a tag (*c.*9 mm. wide) which exits through a slit in the base of the fold; sealed on tag. Circular seal, red wax, imperfect, originally approx. 60 mm. diameter; equestrian, facing to right; legend: + SIGILL' . CADW . . . NI . FI . . . RATOCI. Two slits in centre of fold for a tag (*c.*9 mm. wide) which exits through a slit in the base of the fold; sealed on tag. Circular seal, red wax, imperfect, originally approx. 50 mm. diameter; equestrian, facing right; legend: + S . . . ANI . FILII . . . CI. There are no slits through the right-hand side of the fold.
Pd. from (?)A (a charter 'obtained from the MS. collections of Mr. Hugh Thomas'), *Mon. Ang.*, vi: iii. 1630; from A, *Cartae*, ii. 239–40 (no. 234).
Cd., Owen, *Catalogue*, iii. 562; *H*, no. 49.

Omnibus Cristi fidelibus ad quos presens scriptura pervenerit Margan et Kadawalan et Meriedoc filii Caradoci salutem. Sciat universitas vestra quod ego Margan scilicet et fratres mei Kadawalan et Meriedoc communi assensu donationem concedimus et confirmamus quam Caradocus Uerbeis fecit Deo et Sancte Marie et ordini Cist(er)ciensi et fratri Meilero et fratribus de Pendar, scilicet totam terram que iacet inter has tres aquas, videlicet Frutsanant et Cleudach et Nantclokenig, in plano et in bosco qui boscus dicitur Hlowenrop(er)deit liberam et quietam et ab omnibus secularibus exactionibus inmunem. Hanc terram predictis fratribus a Caradoco U(er)beis in perpetuam datam elemosinam ut libera inperpetuum maneat et quieta sigilli nostri atestatione sanctimus et confirmamus. Et ad eam illis warezizandam[a] et manutenendam contra omnes et ubique si emerserit necessitas posse nostrum prestabimus. Huius confirmationis testes sunt: Kadaraut filius Eniau, Grunu filius Rewalan, Bleðin filius Breauel, Seisil filius Weueric, Will(elmus) filius Gurgwenu, Hlewarh filius Iewaf, Mariedud filius Gurga(n), Dunewal filius Iewan, I(us)tin(us) filius Reðerth.

[a] *sic in* A.

This charter is presumably later than that issued 1158 × *c*.1174 by Gruffudd ab Ifor of Senghennydd to establish Pendar (no. 616 below). One of the grantors, Cadwallon ap Caradog, had died by the time Gerald of Wales completed the first recension of his *Itinerarium Kambriae* in October 1191 (*Gir. Camb. Op.*, vi. 69 (*IK* I. 7)). The absence of Owain, another son of Caradog, suggests a date after Cadwallon's murder of Owain during the lordship in Glamorgan of William, earl of Gloucester (1147–83) and the reign of Henry II (1154–89) (ibid.). For Caradog *Uerbeis*'s charter see *Cartae*, ii. 346–7 (no. 346). It states that his grant was made with the consent of Morgan, Cadwallon and Maredudd *de quorum feudo terra illa erat* as well as Caradog's three brothers, his son and his wife. Caradog received a countergift of 20s. from Meilyr and the brothers of Pendar and confirmed the grant by his oath and by the seal of Morgan ap Caradog, as he lacked a seal of his own; the witness list is completely different from that of the present charter. *Hlowenroperdeit* is identifiable with the farm of Llwynperdid (ST 043 938), and the land in the charter formed a holding of at least 640 acres substantially coterminous with the four farms of Tir Fanheulog, Buarth y Capel, Glog and Cribyn Du, par. Llanwynno (Llanwynno ST 030 956), west and north-west of Ynys-y-bŵl in the lordship of Meisgyn (Corbett, 'Historical notes', 387; Cowley, 'Monastic Order', 36; RCAHMW, *Glamorgan III. ii*, 295–6 (which is incorrect in identifying this as the site of Pendar, as no. 616 shows that this lay, originally at least, in Senghennydd)). Gray, 'Hermitage', 122 (map), 147–9, suggested that Pendar was located at Cwm Pennar or Cefn Pennar.

122 Margam Abbey

Grant of pasture between the Afan and the Neath, from the Afan to the road leading from the chapel of Caradog to Baglan, in the sand dunes (melis) *and in the marshes, in return for 20s. annually.*

[November 1186 × January 1199]

B = NLW, Penrice and Margam Roll 2090/3. s. xiii[1]. Rubric: Carta Morgani de pastura in Melis [a]filii Caradoci[a].
C = NLW, Penrice and Margam Roll 2093/10. s. xiii[1]. Rubric: Morgan(us) de pastura in Mel(is). (Roll damaged on right-hand side.)
Pd. from B, *Cartae*, vi. 2287 (no. 1566).
Cd., Birch, *Catalogue*, iv: i. 175, 182; *H*, no. 73.

Sciant tam presentes quam posteri quod ego Morgan(us) filius Caradoci[b] concessi abbati et monachis de Marg(an) pasturam inter Auen(am)[c] et Neth, ab Auena usque ad viam que vadit a capella Caradoci [d]usque Bagalan,[-d] totam omnino [e]pasturam tam[-e] in melis quam in mariscis, et hoc pro xx[f] solidis annuatim dandis.

[a-a] *added in a hand of s. xiii med.* | [b] Cradoci C. | [c] Auene C. | [d-d] *omitted in* C. | [e-e] *lacuna in* B *because of hole in parchment.* | [f] xx[ti] C.

The grant is probably later than Pope Urban III's confirmation for Margam of 18 November 1186, which includes the grange of *Mieles*, located just to the east of the Afan, whose site was occupied by the former farms of Upper Court (SS 767 896) and Lower Court (SS 765 896) near Port Talbot railway station, but is silent on land to the west of that river, which flowed into the sea along a course a little to the south-east of the present estuary (*Cartae*, i. 186 (no. 181); RCAHMW, *Glamorgan III. ii*, 267, 269–70 and map at 273). Its pairing with *in mariscis* suggests that *melis* was used in the present charter merely as a descriptor of a sandy area (cf. the place-name Meols on the Wirral, derived from Old Norse *melr*, 'sandbank'), or ground above high-water mark, rather than specifically as a proper noun to denote the grange (cf. ibid., 269; *OP*, iii. 349–50, n. 4). However, the rubrics in the Margam rolls could imply that by the early thirteenth century *melis* was understood in the latter sense, and thus as an extension of Meles grange along the coast west of the

Afan in the direction of Baglan (SS 753 923). In any case, the land presumably lay within Margam's possessions in the marsh of Afan confirmed by Countess Isabella of Gloucester in 1189 × January 1199 (*EGC*, 126 (no. 137)).

123 Letter patent concerning Caradog ap John

Notification that in Morgan's presence Caradog has quitclaimed and abjured to the monks of Margan all the land between the two Afans [(?)i.e. the Afan and the Pelenna], which he had claimed from the monks, and has found Morgan and Meurig Broch as his sureties.

[November 1186 × c.1208]

A = NLW, Penrice and Margam Ch. 2020. Endorsed: Cradoci filii Ioh(ann)is (s. xii/xiii); modern endorsement; approx. 202 mm. wide at top, 220 mm. wide at bottom, 59 mm. deep on left, 43 mm. deep on right, including tongue (*c*.11 mm. wide) and wrapping-tie (*c*.8 mm. wide); sealed on tongue. Almost circular seal, reddish brown wax, worn impression, approx. 58 × 53 mm. diameter; equestrian, facing right; legend: SIGILLVM [M]ARGAN FILII CARADOCI.
B = NLW, Penrice and Margam Roll 288/5. s. xiii[1].
Pd. from B, *Cartae*, ii. 397 (no. 404).
Cd., Birch, *Catalogue*, i. 93; iv: i. 147; *H*, no. 321.

Omnibus sancte ecclesie filiis presentibus et futuris ad quos presens scriptum pervenerit Margan(us) filius Karadoci salutem. Noverit universitas vestra quod Karadocus filius Ioh(ann)is liberam et quitam clamavit monachis de Marg(an) et coram me abiuravit totam terram que est inter duas Auenas, quam ipse Karadoc(us) a prefatis monachis calengiza-verat, quietam clamavit de se et de omnibus suis. Et super hoc plegios invenit me et Meuric[a] Broc.

[a] *corrected from (?)*meis *in* A.

If *inter duas Auenas* refers to the river Afan and the river Pelenna which flows into it from the north-west at Pont-rhyd-y-fen (SS 793 941) (Birch, *Margam*, 384), the charter is unlikely to be earlier than November 1186. Margam had received grants from Morgan ap Caradog west of the Afan by 1189 × January 1199, but no grants in that area are included in Pope Urban III's confirmation of 18 November 1186 (*EGC*, 126 (no. 137); *Cartae*, i. 185–90 (no. 181)).

124 Roger Cole

Grant, for his service, of 20 acres from Morgan's demesne in the fee of Newcastle above the spring called Comeriswil, *to be possessed in hereditary right free of all service by a render of 1 pound of cumin annually within the octaves of Michaelmas [29 September–6 October]. Further gift of same liberty as in Morgan's demesne with respect to the land's appurtenances. Morgan's sons Lleision and Owain have given their assent. Sealing clause; witnesses.*

[29 August 1189 × c.October 1203]

A = NLW, Penrice and Margam Ch. 88. Endorsed: Donacio Morgani Rog(er)o Cole (s. xiii med.) in dominio suo de Novo Castello (s. xiv in.); approx. 162 × 92 + 14 mm.; two central slits in fold for a tag (*c*.17 mm. wide) which exits through a slit in the base of the fold; sealed on tag. Almost

circular seal, red wax, originally approx. 58 × 53 mm. diameter; equestrian, facing right; legend:
+ SIGI … MARGA … RADOCI.
Pd. from A, *Cartae*, ii. 392–3 (no. 398).
Cd., Birch, *Catalogue*, i. 30; *H*, no. 59.

Morgan(us) filius Cradoci omnibus Francis, Walensibus et Anglicis ad quos presentes littere pervenerint salutem et benevolentiam. Tam presentium quam futurorum noverit universitas quod ego Morgan(us) famulo meo Rogero Cole pro servitio suo xx acras terre de dominio meo in feudo Novi Cast' desuper fontem quemdam qui dicitur Comeriswil dedi et concessi, quam sibi et heredibus suis de me et de heredibus meis iure hereditario possidendam permisi solidam et quietam ab omni servitio reddendo annuatim unam libram cumini intra octabas Sancti Mich(aelis). Insuper ei eandem libertatem que ad dominium meum spectat et suis sequacibus in viis et in planis, in pascuis, in nemore, in foro, in mora et in omni comunione donavi. Huic donationi ut rata permaneat filii mei Leison et Oeneus assensum prebuerunt. Et eandem ego scripti serie et testium comprobatione et sigilli appositione confirmavi. Hiis testibus: domino Rog(er)o abbate de Margan, domino Urbano archidiacono, G. sacerdote, Helia clerico, Walt(er)o preposito, David Puin(el), Will(el)mo Alewi, Herb(er)to Loc, Ioruerh, Ris filio Oenei, Rogero Aiþhan et multis aliis.

Abbot Roger, the first witness, was no longer abbot in November 1203, when Innocent III issued a bull to Abbot Gilbert of Margam (*Cartae*, ii. 282 (no. 282)). Although it has been stated that Roger was abbot 1196–1203 (Birch, *Margam*, 156, n. 2; Williams, 'Fasti Cistercienses', 189), the exact length of his abbacy is uncertain. Conan was still abbot in March 1188 (*Gir. Camb. Op.*, vi. 67 (*IK*, I. 7)), but it is unknown when he was succeeded by Roger, who occurs during the pontificate of Henry, bishop of Llandaff, 12 December 1193–8 or 12 November 1218 (*Cartae*, i. 218, 224 (nos 213, 218)). Urban (III), archdeacon of Llandaff, occurs before 1179 and in 1214 × 1216 (*Llandaff Episcopal Acta*, xix). The *terminus a quo* for the charter is therefore provided by Morgan's receipt of Newcastle in 1189 from John, count of Mortain, who acquired the earldom of Gloucester after his marriage to Countess Isabella on 29 August 1189 (Smith, 'Kingdom of Morgannwg', 38–9; *EGC*, 5). For Morgan's confirmation of Roger Cole's subsequent donation of this land to Margam see no. 130 below.

*125 Einion ap Rhirid

Grant of half of Ketherec's *land in the territory of Newcastle, which belongs to Einion by hereditary right and which was granted to him by his lord Morgan.*

[29 August 1189 × 22 July 1207]

Mention only, in a charter issued by Einion granting the land to Margam Abbey (*Cartae*, ii. 367 (no. 370); cd., *H*, no. 110). Morgan's grant is not explicitly said to have been in written form. For the *terminus a quo* see note to no. 124 above. Einion's grant to Margam is included in King John's confirmation charter for the abbey of 22 July 1207 (*Cartae*, ii. 308 (no. 306)).

*126 Rhys Goch

Grant of half of Ketherec's *land in the territory of Newcastle, which belongs to Rhys by hereditary right and which was granted to him by his lord Morgan.*

[29 August 1189 × 22 July 1207]

Mention only, in a charter issued by Einion granting the land to Margam Abbey (*Cartae*,
ii. 366–7 (no. 369); cd., *H*, no. 110). Morgan's grant is not explicitly said to have been in
written form. For the dating see note to no. 125 above.

127 Margam Abbey

Confirmation of gifts in perpetual alms of 10 acres by Robert [ap] Gwion (Wian) *and 10 acres
by Roger [ap] Gwion* (Wian) *in Newcastle near* Blakeston*, to be held free of all service,
custom and exaction for ever. Witnesses.*

[29 August 1189 × c.1208; possibly 1205 × c.1208]

> A = NLW, Penrice and Margam Ch. 2023. Endorsed: Confirmatio Morg(ani) de terra Rob(er)ti
> Wia[n] et Rog(er)i Wian apud Novum Castellum (s. xii ex. × s. xiii med.); approx. 136 × 112 + 31
> mm.; two central slits in fold for a tag (*c*.12 mm. wide) which exits through a slit in the base of the
> fold; sealed on tag. Almost circular seal, red wax, edges chipped, originally approx. 58 × 53 mm.
> diameter; equestrian, facing right; legend: + SIGI . . . AN . . . OCI.
> B = NLW, Penrice and Margam Roll 292/17. s. xiii. (Omits witness list.)
> Pd. from A, *Cartae*, vi. 2285 (no. 1564).
> Cd., Birch, *Catalogue*, i. 115; iv: i. 148; *H*, no. 70.

Omnibus sancte ecclesie filiis ad quos presens scriptum pervenerit Morgan(us) filius
Cradoci salutem. Sciatis me concessisse et hac carta confirmasse monachis de Margan in
perpetuum decem acras quas dedit eis Rob(er)tus Wiein et decem acras quas dedit eis
Rog(er)us Wiein in territorio de Novo Castello iuxta Blakeston in perpetuam elemosinam
tenendas libere et quiete ab omni servicio, consuetudine et exactione sicut ulla elemosina
liberius teneri et haberi potest in perpetuum. Hiis testibus: Reso Coh, Esp(us) filio
Kistelard, David Puignel, Ric(ardo) Waleis, Hereb(er)to Palmario.

For the grants of Robert and Roger sons of Gwion (*Wian*), both undated, see *Cartae*, ii.
448–9 (nos 456–7). Neither refers to *Blakeston*. The relationship between these grants and
that of Robert in 1197, in which he granted 40 acres to Margam, 10 in alms and 30 on a
six-year lease, is unclear (ibid., 447–8 (no. 455)). The present charter can be no earlier than
1189, when Morgan received Newcastle (see note to no. 124 above), and may be later than
Robert's grant of 1197. It is possible that it was issued on the same occasion as no. 128
below, as the last four witnesses also witness the latter charter, which confirms a grant by
the first witness, Rhys Goch; if so, the present charter may be datable to 1205 × 1208.

128 Margam Abbey

Confirmation of the gifts by Rhys Goch of the half of the land which belonged to Ketherech
*in the territory of Newcastle and by Einion ap Rhirid of the other half of the same land as
attested in their charters. If they are disseised for any reason, the monks will nevertheless hold
the land in peace as Morgan's alms. Witnesses.*

[29 August 1189 × c.1208; probably May 1205 × c.1208]

A = NLW, Penrice and Margam Ch. 2021. Endorsed: Confirmatio Morg' de donatione Resi Cohed apud Novum Castellum (s. xiii in.); approx. 200 × 61 + 20 mm.; two central slits in fold for a tag (c.14 mm. wide) which exits through a slit in the base of the fold; sealed on tag. Almost circular seal, red wax, approx. 58 × 53 mm. diameter; equestrian, facing right; legend: + SIGILLVM MA . . . N FILII CARADOCI.
B = NLW, Penrice and Margam Roll 292/9. s. xiii.
Pd. from A, *Cartae*, ii. 399–400 (no. 408).
Cd., Birch, *Catalogue*, i. 114; iv: i. 147; *H*, no. 75.

Omnibus sancte ecclesie filiis ad quos presens scriptum pervenerit Morgan(us) filius Cradoci salutem. Sciatis me concessisse et hac carta confirmasse monachis de Margan donationem quam fecit eis Resus Coh in territorio Novi Castelli de medietate terre que fuit Ketherech et donationem quam fecit eis Enian filius Ririd de reliqua medietate eiusdem terre in omnibus sicut carte ipsorum testantur. Et si forte propter aliquam causam dissaisiati fuerint, nichilominus monachi tenebunt predictam terram in pace et quiete in perpetuum sicut elemosinam nostram. Testibus: Rog(ero) filio Wiain, Kenewrec fratre eius, Espus filio Kistelard, David Puignel, Hereb(er)to Palm', Ric(ardo) Waleis.

The grants by Rhys Goch and Einion ap Rhirid are not extant but are included in King John's confirmation charter for Margam of 22 July 1207 (*Cartae*, ii. 308 (no. 306)). As there is no mention of them in any previous confirmation for the abbey, including that issued by John on 15 May 1205 (*Cartae*, ii. 291–2 (no. 287)), it is likely that they were made after May 1205 and therefore that Morgan's confirmation can be no earlier than that date. As the land confirmed was in Newcastle the present charter can in any case be no earlier than 1189 (see note to no. 124 above).

129 St Leonard's church, Newcastle

Grant, for the souls of himself and of his father and mother, of 40 acres above Tythegston in perpetual alms free of all service. Further grant to the church and its custodians and men of all its rights and free customs in lands, tithes, chapels, mills and other appurtenances, so that it may possess these as perfectly as it did in the time of the earl. Witnesses.

[29 August 1189 × c.1208]

A = NLW, Penrice and Margam Ch. 2022. No medieval endorsement; approx. 183 × 99 + 12 mm.; two central slits, one just above the fold, one on the fold, for a tag (c.16 mm. wide), which exits through a slit in the base of the fold; sealed on tag. Almost circular seal, red wax, very imperfect, originally approx. 58 × 53 mm. diameter; both the device and the legend are completely unrecoverable.
Pd. from A, *Cartae*, vi. 2287–8 (no. 1567).
Cd., Birch, *Catalogue*, iv: i. 148; *H*, no. 57.

Noverit tam futurorum quam presencium universitas quod ego Morgan(us) filius Karadoci dedi et concessi ecclesie Sancti Leonardi de Novo Castello de Ruthelan xl acras terre desuper Sanctum Tuddocum per divisas constitutas in perpetuam elemosinam libere et quiete ab omni servicio tenendas pro anima mea et animabus patris et matris mee. Insuper ecclesie `et custodibus et hominibus eiusdem omnia iura sua et liberas consuetudines in terris, in decimis, in capellis, in planis, in pascuis, in viis, in semitis, in aquis, in pratis, in nemore, in comunione, in molendinis et in omni loco quiquid ad prescriptam pertinet ecclesiam concessi et carta mea confirmavi, ut habeat et possideat plene et perfecte libere et quiete sicut umquam melius et liberius plenius et perfectius in temporibus comitis tenuit. Hiis testibus: Helia capellano, Ioh(anne) capellano, Will(elm)o de Cantelo, Oen filio Wrgenu, Rob(erto) et Rog(er)o filiis Wihan, Walt(er)o preposito et aliis pluribus de hundredo.

The presence of this charter in the Margam archive is puzzling, as the church of St Leonard's, Newcastle (SS 902 800) and its chapel at Tythegston (Llandudwg) (SS 858 788) had belonged to Tewkesbury Abbey since at least the 1140s and there is no record of Margam's possessing the church during Morgan's lifetime (see *Llandaff Episcopal Acta*, nos 3, 31; *AM*, i. 99, 168). For the *terminus a quo* see note to no. 124 above.

130 Margam Abbey

Confirmation, for the salvation of the souls of himself and his ancestors, of the gift in perpetual alms by his servant Roger Cole of his free land at Newcastle, which Morgan gave him for his service, so that the monks may have that land in return for the 4 acres which lie to the east of the stream called Hellenewelle Lache *near the land of* Coitkart *by the bounds in Roger's charter, free of all service and secular exaction, disturbance and custom. Morgan warrants the grant against all men. Witnesses.*

[29 August 1189 × *c*.1208]

A = NLW, Penrice and Margam Ch. 2019. Endorsed: Confirmatio Morgani de dono R. Cole apud Novum Castrum (s. xiii in.); approx. 143 × 75 + 14 mm.; two central slits in fold for a tag (*c*.12 mm. wide) which exits through a slit in the base of the fold; sealed on tag. Almost circular seal, red wax, approx. 58 × 53 mm. diameter; equestrian, facing right; legend: + SIGILLVM MARGAN FILII CARADOCI.
B = NLW, Penrice and Margam Roll 292/20. s. xiii. (Omits witness list.)
Pd. from A, *Cartae*, vi. 2286 (no. 1565); from B, ibid., ii. 395 (no. 401).
Cd., Birch, *Catalogue*, i. 115; iv: i. 147; *H*, no. 72.

Omnibus sancte ecclesie filiis ad quos presens scriptum pervenerit Morgan(us) filius Cradoci salutem. Notum facimus universitati vestre nos pro salute anime nostre et antecessorum nostrorum concessisse et presenti carta nostra confirmasse monachis de M(ar)gan donationem quam Rog(er)us Cole homo meus et serviens fecit eisdem in puram et perpetuam et liberam elemosinam de libera terra sua apud Novum Castellum quam dedi ei pro suo servitio, ut videlicet ipsi monachi habeant ipsam terram quam dedit eis pro iiii^{or} acris que iacent ad orientem rivuli qui vocatur Hellenewelle Lache proxime terre de Coitkart per divisas que carta ipsius Rog(er)i continentur sine omni servitio et seculari exactione et molestia et consuetudine. Et ego ipsam donationem contra omnes homines warentizo. Testibus: Will(el)mo tunc cellarario de M(ar)gan, Godefrido monacho, Walt(er)o magistro de Lantgewi, Helia clerico Novi Castelli, Walt(er)o preposito, Moysete et Thom(a) de Novo Castello, Iordan(o) et Gregorio et Rog(er)o conversis de Margan, Reso^a filio Resi ab Blether', David Pugnel, Ioh(ann)e Soro et aliis multis.

^a *corrected in* A *from* Resus (-us *erased*).

This confirmation must be later than Morgan's grant to Roger (no. 124 above). The first witness, William, cellarer of Margam, occurs elsewhere in 1207 (*Cartae*, ii. 312–14 (nos 314, 316)). For the charter of Roger Cole confirmed here see *Cartae*, ii. 394 (no. 400), which states that it was sealed by Morgan as Roger lacked a seal of his own and that Roger received a countergift of one bezant. The boundary clause is more detailed than that of the present charter; no names of witnesses are preserved.

131 Margam Abbey

Grant in perpetual alms, with the consent of his heirs and friends, of all the land of Resolven with all its appurtenances between the river Gwrach and the river Clydach and between the river Neath and the great road which leads through the mountains from Torbethel to Glyn-wrach, all the produce of the river Neath between the Gwrach and the Clydach, and the common pasture of all his land in the mountains between the river Afan and river Neath, to be held free of all secular service, custom and exaction. Morgan and his heirs will warrant all this against all men for ever. He has sworn on relics, on behalf of himself and his heirs, faithfully to observe all the above. Witnesses.

[12 December 1193 × June 1199]

B = NLW, Penrice and Margam Roll 543/4. s. xiii[1].
C = NLW, Penrice and Margam Roll 2089/12. s. xiii.
D = NLW, Penrice and Margam Roll 2093/16. s. xiii[1]. Rubric: Morgan(us) de Rossaulin.
E = NLW, Penrice and Margam Ch. 212 (inspeximus of Earl Hugh Despenser, 9 October 1338).
Pd. from B, *Cartae*, i. 179 (no. 174).
Cd., Birch, *Catalogue*, ii. 6; iv: i. 175; *Episc. Acts*, ii. 698 (L. 309); *H*, no. 50.

Omnibus sancte ecclesie filiis presentibus et futuris Morgan(us) filius Caradoci[a] salutem. Sciatis me consilio et consensu heredum et amicorum meorum concessisse et dedisse et hac carta confirmasse Deo et ecclesie Sancte Marie de Marg(an) et monachis qui ibidem Deo serviunt in [b-]puram et[-b] perpetuam elemosinam totam terram de Rossaulin[c] cum omnibus pertinentiis[d] in bosco[e] et plano, in pratis et pasturis, in aquis et in omnibus aliis aisiamentis suis per has divisas, scilicet quicquid continetur inter aquam que dicitur Wrach[f] et aquam que dicitur Cleudachcu(m)kake[g] [h-]et inter aquam de Neth[i] et viam magnam que vadit per montana de Torbethel[j] usque ad Glinwrach[k] [-h] et omnes comoditates aque de Neth[i] inter[l] duas aquas prenominatas,[m] scilicet Wrach[n] et Cleudachcu(m)kake,[g] [h-]et communem pasturam totius terre mee in montanis inter Auena(m) et Neth[i],[-h] ad habendum et tenendum libere et quiete ab omni servitio et consuetudine et exactione seculari, sicut ulla elemosina liberius haberi et teneri potest. Et hoc totum warantizabimus[o] eis ego et heredes mei contra omnes homines imperpetuum.[p] Et hec omnia me fideliter et firmiter tenere super sacrosancta iuravi pro me et heredibus meis. Teste:[q] domino[m] Henr(ico) Land'[r] episcopo, Nicolao[s] Gobion,[t] Helia[u] decano de Novo Cast',[v] Ric(ardo) decano de Boneuill',[w] Henr(ico) presbitero de Brigtune,[x] Ruathlan[y] et Mauricio fratribus eius,[z] Will(elm)o filio Alewani,[aa] David Puignel.[ab]

[a]C(ra)doci C. | [b-b] *omitted* CDE. | [c] Rossaulyn C; Rossoulyn E. | [d] DE *insert* suis. | [e] boscho D.
[f] Wrac D; Wrak' E. | [g] Cleudachu(m)kake D. | [h-h] *omitted* C. | [i] Neht D.
[j] Thorbethel D. | [k] Glinwrak' E. | [l] C *inserts* illas. | [m] *omitted* C. | [n] Wrac D.
[o] warentizabimus E. | [p] C *inserts* Similiter dedi prefatis monachis in elemosinam communem

pasturam totius terre mee inter Auenam et Neth. | ^q *sic in* BD; Test' CE. | ^r Landaven' CDE.
^s Nich' CD; Nich(ola)o E. | ^t Gubion CE. | ^u Elya C; Helya D. | ^v Castello CE.
^w Boneuiliston' C; Bonevilest' D; Boneuileston' E. | ^x Briggetone C; Briggetune E.
^y Rualthan CE. | ^z eiusdem CE. | ^{aa} Alewyny C; Alewini DE. | ^{ab} Pugnel CE.

Henry was consecrated bishop of Llandaff on 12 December 1193 (*Llandaff Episcopal Acta*, xv). Resolven is included in Countess Isabella's confirmation for Margam, issued no later than the annulment of her marriage to John by Norman bishops shortly after 19 June 1199, as the confirmation charter styles her 'countess of Gloucester and Mortain' (*EGC*, 126 (no. 137); cf. Diceto, ii. 166–7). Resolven was originally granted to Margam by *Canaythen* with the assent of his lord Morgan ap Caradog, who had given him the land after *Canaythen* had been blinded while held as a hostage by William, earl of Gloucester (1147–83) (*Cartae*, ii. 347–8 (no. 347)). The grange occupied the whole of Resolven Mountain, between Nant Gwrach in the north-east and the Clydach Brook, which flows into the Neath at SN 829 031, in the south-west, and between the river Neath in the north-west and the mountain road – probably identifiable with the Cefn Ffordd – from Torbethel (Banwen Tor y Betel SS 823 998) to Glyn-wrach (Blaengwrach SN 874 041) in the south-east (RCAHMW, *Glamorgan III. ii*, 266–7).

132 Margam Abbey

Grant in alms, with the consent of his kinsmen and friends, of all the land of Pultimor *with all its easements and appurtenances, free of all secular service, custom and exaction by paying him and his heirs half a mark annually at Michaelmas for all service. Morgan and his son Lleision have sworn on the relics of the church of Margam that he and his heirs will warrant all this against all men for ever. Witnesses.*

[12 December 1193 × June 1199]

A = NLW, Penrice and Margam Ch. 89. Endorsed: Carta Morgani filii Caradoci de terra de Pultimor (by scribe of charter); approx. 191 × 109 + 35 mm; two central slits in fold for a tag (*c.*19 mm. wide) which exits through a slit in the base of the fold; sealed on tag. Almost circular seal, brown wax, of which only part of the right-hand side is visible, originally approx. 58 × 53 mm. diameter; equestrian, facing right; legend: [+ S]IGILLVM …
B = NLW, Penrice and Margam Roll 2093/1. s. xiii. (Roll damaged.)
Pd. from A, *Cartae*, ii. 398 (no. 406); from B, ibid., vi. 2288 (no. 1568).
Cd., Birch, *Catalogue*, i. 31; ibid., iv: i. 180–1; *Episc. Acts*, ii. 697–8 (L. 307); *H*, no. 51.

Omnibus sancte ecclesie filiis presentibus et futuris Morgan(us) filius Caradoci salutem. Sciatis me consilio et consensu parentum et amicorum meorum concessisse et dedisse et hac carta confirmasse Deo et ecclesie Sancte Marie de Margan et monachis ibidem Deo servientibus in elemosinam totam terram de Pultimor cum omnibus aisiamentis et pertinentiis suis ut habeant et teneant eam in perpetuum liberam et quietam ab omni servitio et consuetudine et exactione seculari reddendo mihi et heredibus meis annuatim ad festum Sancti Michael(is) dimidiam marcam pro omni servitio. Et ego et Leysan filius meus affidavimus et super sacrosancta ecclesie de Margan iuravimus quod hoc totum ego et heredes mei adquietabimus et warentizabimus predictis monachis contra omnes homines in perpetuum. His testibus: domino Henr(ico) Landav(ensi) episcopo, Helya decano de Novo Castello,

David Puignel, H(er)berto Palm(er)io, Wasmero filio Iago, Nichol(ao) Gobiun, magistro Walt(er)o de Bergeueni.

For the dating see no. 131 above. *Pultimor* was located in the vicinity of Llanfeuthin (Llanvithyn Farm ST 051 712) in the Llancarfan valley (Pierce, *Place-Names of Dinas Powys*, 97–9). The confirmation charter by Morgan's son Lleision was very probably issued on the same occasion as the present charter (no. 152 below).

133 Margam Abbey

Grant, with the consent of his sons, in alms and free of all secular service, custom and exaction of all the meadow which belonged to Alewi *between Ralph's house and* Orgares *dyke, and all Morgan's meadows between* Orgares *dyke and the chapel, and all the meadow which belonged to David* Puinel *and the meadow of Ieuan* Braut Waith, *for an annual render of 1 silver mark at Michaelmas for all service. Morgan has received five years' render in advance after Michaelmas 1199. Hereafter he will never receive more than three years' render in advance. He and his heirs will warrant the gift against all men for ever. Witnesses.*

[Shortly after 29 September 1199]

A = NLW, Penrice and Margam Ch. 51. Endorsed: Morg' de pratis de Auene (s. xiii med.) et diversis aliis terris (s. xv/xvi); Karadoci (s. xiii[1]); approx. 136 × 146 + 17 mm.; two central slits in fold for a tag (*c*.12 mm. wide) which exits through a slit in the base of the fold; sealed on tag. Almost circular seal, green wax, very imperfect, originally approx. 58 × 53 mm. diameter; equestrian, facing right; legend unrecoverable.
B = NLW, Penrice and Margam Roll, 288/2. s. xiii[1]. (Roll damaged.)
C = NLW, Penrice and Margam Roll, 2093/11. s. xiii[1].
Pd. from A, *Cartae*, ii. 247–8 (no. 243).
Cd., Birch, *Catalogue*, i. 18–19, 93; *H*, no. 53.

Omnibus sancte ecclesie filiis presentibus et futuris Margan(us) filius Karadoci salutem. Sciatis me consilio et consensu filiorum meorum concessisse et dedisse et hac karta confirmasse Deo et ecclesie Sancte Marie de Marg(an) et monachis ibidem Deo servientibus in elemosinam liberam et quietam ab omni servicio et consuetudine et exactione seculari totum pratum quod fuit Alewi inter domum Radulfi et Orgares Walle, et universa prata mea que sunt inter Orgares Walle et capellam, et totum pratum quod fuit D(avi)d Puinel et pratum Yewan Braut Waith, reddendo michi et heredibus meis annuatim ad festum Sancti Michaelis unam marcam argenti pro omni servicio. Et sciendum quod pre manibus accepi redditum v annorum anno ab incarnatione domini m° c° nonagesimo nono post festum Sancti Michaelis. Et notandum quod nunquam deinceps pre manibus accepturus sum nisi redditum trium annorum. Ego autem et heredes mei prefatam donationem predictis monachis warentizabimus contra omnes homines in perpetuum. His testibus: Helia decano, Worgano capellano de Auene, Meuric Map et Griphino fratre eius, Howelo filio Griphini, Ruatlan map Wrgi, Morgenu Cole, David Puinel, Will(elm)o filio Alewi, H(er)berto filio Palmari.

These lands were located on the coast just west of the river Afan (cf. Birch, *Margam*, 396; *Cartae*, vi. 2208 (no. 1510)). *Orgares* dyke is identifiable as the sea-wall which in the Middle Ages formed the northern bank of the Afan estuary, beginning on the west at SS 758 883 and ending at SS 763 882 (RCAHMW, *Glamorgan III. ii*, 270 and n. 11). See also nos 134–5 below.

134 Margam Abbey

Grant, with the consent of his sons, in alms and free of all secular service, custom and exaction of all the land which begins at Pultschathan *and leads by the dyke to Pwll Ifor* (Yuores Pulle) *and thence to the boundaries between Morgan and the men of Baglan and returns by the alder grove beneath the mountain to* Pultschathan, *for an annual render to him and his heirs of 5s. at Michaelmas for all service. Grant to the monks of free entry and departure to take all produce from the land and to do as they will with the land. Morgan has received £10 16d. from that farm in 1199, after Michaelmas. He has sworn on the relics of the church that he and his heirs will warrant the gift against all men for ever. Witnesses.*

[Shortly after 29 September 1199]

A = NLW, Penrice and Margam Ch. 2017. Endorsed: Carta prima Morgani de donatione eiusdem in marisco de Auene (s. xii/xiii) inter Puleschathan et Yvores pulle et divisas de Baglande (s. xvi); approx. 170 × 157 + 18 mm.; two central slits in fold for a tag (*c.*16 mm. wide) which exits through a slit in the base of the fold; sealed on tag. Almost circular seal, green wax, chipped at the edges and worn, originally approx. 58 × 53 mm. diameter; equestrian, facing right; legend unrecoverable.
B = NLW, Penrice and Margam Roll 2093/7. s. xiii[1].
Pd. from A, *Cartae*, vi. 2275–6 (no. 1554); from B, ibid., 2276–7 (no. 1555).
Cd., Birch, *Catalogue*, iv: i. 146, 181; *H*, no. 54.

Omnibus sancte ecclesie filiis presentibus et futuris Margan(us) filius Karadoci salutem. Sciatis me consilio et consensu filiorum meorum concessisse et dedisse et hac karta confirmasse Deo et ecclesie Sancte Marie de Marg(an) et monachis ibidem Deo servientibus in elemosinam liberam et quietam ab omni servicio et consuetudine et exactione seculari totam terram que incipit a Pultschathan et vadit per fossatum usque ad Yuores Pulle et inde usque ad divisas que sunt inter me et homines de Bagelan et revertitur per alnetum sub monte usque ad Pultschathan, quicquid includitur intra has metas, reddendo michi et heredibus meis annuatim ad festum Sancti Michael(is) quinque solidos pro omni servicio. Et sciendum quod concessi predictis monachis liberum ingressum et egressum et precipiendis omnes commoditates quas habere poterunt de prefata terra et ut faciant de terra ipsa quicquid voluerint. Et ego Margan(us) pre manibus accepi x libras et sexdecim denarios de predicta firma anno ab incarnatione domini m° c° nonagesimo nono post festum Sancti Michael(is) eiusdem anni. Notandum etiam me super sanctuaria ecclesie iurasse quod ego et heredes mei prefatam donationem predictis monachis warentizabimus contra omnes homines in perpetuum. His testibus: Helia decano, Worgano capellano de Auene, Meuric Map et Griphino fratre eius, Howelo filio Griphini, Ruatlan map Wrgi, Morgenu Cole, David Puinel, Will(elm)o filio Alewi, Herberto filio Palmeri.

This charter was written by the same scribe, and contains the same witness list, as no. 133 above (cf. Patterson, *Scriptorium of Margam*, 94, 109, 119). *Pultschathan* was located near the coast in the marsh of Afan, west of the river Afan (Birch, *Margam*, 397). Presumably the mountain was Mynydd Dinas (summit at SS 761 915). For another grant in the same area see no. 122 above.

135 Margam Abbey

Grant, with the consent of his heirs, of 2 acres of meadow and 1 acre of arable land in the marsh of Afan which was held by Ieuan BrautVait, from whom the monks held them when he was alive, in perpetual alms, for the soul of Ieuan. Witnesses.

[October 1199 × c.1208]

B = NLW, Penrice and Margam Roll 288/3. s. xiii[1].
Pd. from B, *Cartae*, ii. 397–8 (no. 405).
Cd., Birch, *Catalogue*, i. 93; *H*, no. 71.

Omnibus sancte ecclesie filiis ad quos presens scriptum pervenerit Morgan(us) filius Cradoci salutem. Noverit universitas vestra quod ego Morgan(us) ex communi consensu et assensu heredum meorum dedi et concessi et hac presenti carta confirmavi ecclesie Beate Marie de Marg(an) et monachis ibidem Deo servientibus duas acras prati et unam arabilem iacentes in marisco de Auene que fuerunt Iowan BrautVait, de quo vivente predicti monachi eas tenuerunt, libere et quiete et in pace, in puram et perpetuam elemosinam sicut ulla elemosina liberius ac commodius dari potest aut haberi imperpetuum, ita quod monachi decetero pro supradictis acris nemini respondebunt. Et sciendum quod has tres acras ego Morgan(us) dedi monachis de Marg(an) imperpetuum pro anima Iowan BrautVait. Hiis testibus: Wrgano sacerdote, David Puignel, H(er)berto, Iuor filio Iowan, Galfrido filio H(er)b(er)ti et multis aliis.

Morgan granted Ieuan's meadow to Margam shortly after 29 September 1199 (no. 133 above); the present charter may well be later than that grant, as it also grants an acre of arable next to the meadow and, unlike no. 133, demands no render in lieu of service.

136 Margam Abbey

Grant, with the consent of his sons Lleision and Owain and the rest, of the land which begins at Pultscathan and leads by the water dyke to the dyke of Sanan, and thence to the dyke of Caradog, and thence by another dyke to the land of Ieuan ap Tatherec, and thence to the road of Marcuth, and thence to the alder grove beneath the mountain, and thence returns by the dyke made by the monks by the alder grove to Pultscetan. All the land within these bounds he grants in perpetual alms, free of all secular service, exaction and custom, for an annual render of 5s. at Michaelmas for all service. Grant to the monks of free entry and departure to take all produce from the land and to do as they will with the land. Morgan has received £10 16d. in advance from the render in the year in which the charter was made, namely 1200, after Michaelmas. He has sworn on the relics of the church that he and his heirs will warrant the gift against all men for ever. Witnesses.

[Shortly after 29 September 1200]

A = NLW, Penrice and Margam Ch. 59. Endorsed: Carta Morgani secunda continens primam donationem eiusdem et donationem Leysan cum additamento in marisco de Auene (s. xiii in.); Karadoci de terra sub alneto v[s] (s. xiii/xiv); approx. 182 × 210 + 24 mm.; two central slits in fold for a tag (c.13 mm. wide) which exits through a slit in the base of the fold; sealed on tag. Almost circular seal, green wax, approx. 58 × 53 mm. diameter; equestrian, facing right; legend: + SIGILLVM MARGAN FILII CARADOCI.
B = NLW, Penrice and Margam Roll 2093/8. s. xiii[1].

Pd. from A, *Cartae*, ii. 255–6 (no. 255).
Cd., Birch, *Catalogue*, i. 21–2; iv: i. 181; *H*, no. 58.

Universis sancte ecclesie filiis presentibus et futuris Morgan(us) filius Cradoci salutem. Sciatis me concessisse et dedisse et hac carta confirmasse monachis de Marg(an) consilio et consensu filiorum meorum Leisan videlicet et Oeni et reliquorum terram que incipit a P(u)ltscathan et vadit per fossam aquariam usque ad fossam Sanan, et inde usque ad fossam Cradoci, et inde per aliam fossam usque ad terram Yeuan filii Tatherec, et inde ad viam Marcuth, et inde ad alnetum sub monte, et inde revertitur per fossam quam monachi fecerunt per alnetum usque P(u)ltscetan. Omnem hanc terram et quicquid includitur inter has metas concessi et dedi ego Morgan(us) predictis monachis in perpetuam elemosinam ut habeant et teneant eam liberam et quietam ab omni servitio seculari et exactione et consuetudine reddendo mihi et heredibus meis v solidos ad festum Sancti Michael(is) singulis annis pro omni servitio. Et sciendum quod concessi predictis monachis liberum ingressum et egressum ad percipiendas omnes commoditates quas habere poterunt de prefata terra et ut faciant de terra ipsa quicquid voluerint. Notandum etiam quod ego Morgan(us) pre manibus accepi x libras et sexdecim denarios ab ipsis monachis de redditu predicte terre anno illo quo hec carta facta fuit, scilicet anno ab incarnatione domini m° cc° post festum Sancti Michael(is) eiusdem anni. Set et super sanctuaria ecclesie iuravi quod ego et heredes mei prefatam donationem predictis monachis warantizabimus contra omnes homines in perpetuum. Hiis testibus: Kenewrec presbitero de Langauelac, Cuelin Archer, Yoruerd filio Hoeli, Griffino Du, Ithenard filio Griff', Morgano filio Griff', Wrunu filio Mauricii, Win filio Gesurei, Herb(er)to filio Palmari, Ythel filio Helie.

The land was situated west of the Afan close to that granted in no. 134 above. See also note to no. 137 below.

137 Margam Abbey

Grant, with the consent of his sons, of the land in his marsh which lies next to the land he first gave the monks, as attested in the charter between them, namely whatever is contained between the aforesaid land and the monks' dyke which surrounds it; that dyke leads to the road of Marchut *and extends to the broad dyke and by that dyke to the dyke of Caradog and thence turns along the dyke of* Sanan *to the arable, afterwards descending towards Pwll Ifor. All this land he granted in perpetual alms, free of all secular service, exaction and custom. The land shall be joined to the previous land and included under the same rent. His first-born son Lleision has sworn on the relics of Margam that he will hand over the land to the monks without claim or trouble for ever. They will warrant the land against all men. Witnesses.*

[October 1200 × *c*.1208]

A = NLW, Penrice and Margam Ch. 2025. Endorsed: Morg' de Mora de Auene (s. xiii[1]); modern endorsement; approx. 172 × 136 + 13 mm.; two central slits, one just above fold and one in fold, for a tag (*c*.20 mm. wide). Seal no longer attached but presumably is that now kept with charter in box, almost circular, brown wax, originally approx. 58 × 53 mm. diameter; equestrian, facing right; legend unrecoverable.
B = NLW, Penrice and Margam Roll 2093/9. s. xiii[1].

Pd. from A, *Cartae*, vi. 2282 (no. 1561).
Cd., Birch, *Catalogue*, iv: i. 148; *H*, no. 74.

Omnibus sancte ecclesie filiis presentibus et futuris qui hanc cartam inspexerint Morgan(us) filius Cradoci salutem. Noverit universitas vestra me consilio et consensu filiorum meorum concessisse et dedisse et presenti carta confirmasse Deo et Beate Marie et monachis de M(ar)ga(n) in marisco meo iuxta terram quam prius dedi eis sicut carta inter nos facta testatur terram illam que iacet ei proxima in parte occidentali, scilicet quecumque includitur inter predictam terram et fossatum eorum quod circumcingit eam. Quod videlicet fossatum incipit ad viam Marchut et extenditur in directum ad latum fossatum et per illud fossatum ad fossatum Cradoci et inde flectitur per fossatum Sanan usque ad terram arabilem, postea vero descendit usque ad Pulth Yuor, id est ad divisas terre predicte. Hanc igitur totam terram concessi et dedi prefatis monachis in puram et perpetuam elemosinam ut habeant et possideant eam liberam et quietam ab omni servitio seculari, exactione et consuetudine sicut ulla elemosina teneri possit liberius. Et hec terra priori terre adiungetur et sub eodem censu computabitur. Et sciendum quod filius meus primogenitus Lheison super sacras reliquias monasterii de M(ar)ga(n) iuravit quod dimittet terram illam prefatis monachis sine calumnia et vexatione inperpetuum. Et warantizabimus eam contra omnes homines. His testibus: Will(elmo) de Punchard' monacho, Iord' et Cnaithur et Rob(erto) Pulmor conversis de M(ar)ga(n), Mauricio presbitero, H(er)berto filio Palmarii, David Pugniel et Rob(erto) filio Palm(arii) et multis aliis.

The previous grant of land which the present charter augments is almost certainly that granted in no. 136 above; the land described here lies to the west of that in no. 136. If so, the present charter can be no earlier than October 1200.

138 Margam Abbey

Grant in alms, with the consent of his heirs and friends, of the common pasture of all his land from the east side of the Neath for as long as his land extends, free of all secular service, custom and exaction, so that he or his heirs will never allow any religious men into that pasture apart from the monks of Margam. They have sworn on relics that they will faithfully observe this and warrant it for ever against all men, both religious and secular, as their alms. Witnesses.

[1203 × 1205]

B = NLW, Penrice and Margam Roll 543/16. s. xiii[1].
C = NLW, Penrice and Margam Roll 2093/15. s. xiii[1]. (Roll damaged.)
Pd. from B, *Cartae*, i. 180 (no. 175); from C, ibid., vi. 2283 (no. 1562).
Cd., Birch, *Catalogue*, ii. 8; *H*, no. 62.

Universis sancte ecclesie filiis presentibus et futuris Morgan(us) filius Caradoci[a] salutem. Sciatis quod ego consilio et consensu heredum et amicorum meorum concessi et dedi et hac carta confirma [b]-vi Deo et Sancte Marie de Marg(an) et monachis[-b] qui ibidem Deo serviunt in elemosinam communem pasturam totius terre mee ex estparte[c] de Neth[d] quantum terra mea durat in longum et in latum, ubique et in bosco et in plano ad [b]-omnia aisiamenta sua, ad habendum et tenendum[-b] libere et quiete ab omni servitio,[e] consuetudine et exactione seculari sicut ulla elemosina liberius haberi et teneri potest, ita quod nunquam admittemus neque ego neque heredes mei aliquos [b]-viros religiosos in pasturam ipsam preter-[b] predictos monachos. Et sciendum quod super sanctuaria iuravimus quod hec omnia firmiter et fideliter observabimus et predictis monachis warantizabimus contra omnes homines tam [b]-religiosos quam seculares in perpetuum sicut-[b] elemosinam nostram. Hiis testibus:[f] Helya tunc decano, Maur' presbitero, Henr(ico) presbitero, David presbitero, Rogero filio Wian, David Puignel, Ioh(ann)e Sóor, Gruni filio Io . . . [g]

[a] Cradoci C. | [b-b] *omitted* C. | [c] hestparte C. | [d] Neht C. | [e] C *inserts* et. | [f] B *ends here.* | [g] *end of witness list lacking in* C *because of damage to roll.*

According to no. 141 below, Morgan granted part of the pasture east of the river Neath to Neath Abbey in 1205, having previously confirmed an earlier grant of it to Margam in a charter issued in the time of Abbot Gilbert (1203–13).

139 Margam Abbey
Grant in alms of all his land between the Witherel *and* Ellenepulle lake *and 50 acres at* Rofleslond *near to the monks' land at* Clacckeston *which they have from Herbert Scurlage, free of all secular service, custom and exaction. He and his heirs will warrant this for ever. He has made the grant for the souls of his mother and father and of all his ancestors and for his own salvation when he gave himself to Margam in the hands of Abbot Gilbert. Further grant that, if dies in the secular world, his body shall be buried at Margam. Witnesses (not named).*
[1203 × c.1208]

> B = NLW, Penrice and Margam Roll 292/11. s. xiii. Rubric: Carta Morg(ani) filii Cradoci de l acris et de adiectione alterius.
> Pd. from B, *Cartae*, ii. 396 (no. 403).
> Cd., Birch, *Catalogue*, i. 114; *H*, no. 60.

Omnibus sancte ecclesie filiis presentibus et futuris Morgan(us) filius Karadoci salutem. Sciatis me concessisse et dedisse et hac carta confirmasse Deo et ecclesie Sancte Marie de Marg(an) et monachis ibidem Deo servientibus in elemosinam totam terram quam habui inter Witherel et Ellenepulle lake et l acras de Rofleslond proximiores terre eorum apud Clacckeston quam habent de H(er)b(er)to Scurlag, ut habeant et teneant predictam terram liberam et quietam ab omni seculari servitio, consuetudine et omni exactione, sicut ulla elemosina liberius teneri potest. Et hoc totum warantizabimus eis ego et heredes mei in perpetuum, et hanc elemosinam feci eis pro anima patris mei et matris mee et pro animabus omnium antecessorum meorum et pro salute mea quando reddidi me domui de Marg(an) in manibus G. abbatis. Et hoc posui tunc in mea concessione, quod si in seculo obiero corpus meum apud Marg(an) sepelietur. Hiis testibus.

Gilbert was abbot of Margam by the autumn of 1203 (see note to no. 124 above). The precise meaning of the phrase *quando reddidi me domui de Margan in manibus G. abbatis*, which suggests that Morgan submitted to the abbey, is uncertain. (Latham, *Word-List*, 396 s.v. *redditio* cites the usage *reddo me* (*alicui*), 'to become the (feudal) man of', 1201.) The lands granted were all situated in the fee of Newcastle. *Clacckeston* has been identified as Candleston (Candleston Farm SS 870 780), between Tythegston and Merthyr Mawr (Birch,

Margam, 387). However, it may have lain further north, as no. 143 below shows that it was near Llangewydd (Llangewydd Court Farm SS 872 814) and Laleston (SS 875 978), respectively about 2 miles and 1 mile north of Candleston. Likewise no. 180 below refers to *Roueslonde* as being in the vicinity of Laleston. Llangewydd was granted to Margam about the middle of the twelfth century by Roger of Halberton with the consent of William Scurlage and by William son of William Scurlage, and confirmed as the grant of these and Herbert Scurlage by Pope Urban III on 18 November 1186 (*Llandaff Episcopal Acta*, nos 24–5; *Cartae*, i. 186 (no. 181); RCAHMW, *Glamorgan III. ii*, 287).

*140 Neath Abbey

Grant of land in perpetual alms between the Afan (Auene) *and the Neath* (Neth), *namely (?)the Port Way* (Portwer) *and thence to the sea, 65 acres of arable near to their houses, the whole island within the large pool, all the land outside the (?)dyke* (valdam) *and common pasture, and all his land between the Afan* (Auene) *and the Thaw* (Thawi).

[Probably 1205 × 6 January 1208]

Mention only, in a confirmation by Lleision ap Morgan mentioned in a confirmation of King John dated at Burbage, 6 January 1208 (no. 156 below). The *terminus a quo* is based on Morgan's statement in no. 141 below that the monks of Neath held nothing from him in his land east of the Neath before he granted them pasture there in 1205. *Portwer* may be the Port Way, the main route through Glamorgan (the modern A48; cf. Griffiths, 'Native society', 181 (Fig. 1); RCAHMW, *Glamorgan III. ii*, 102). *Thawi* has been taken as the river Thaw, which flowed into the Bristol Channel at the ancient port of Aberthaw, whose site is now located in the hamlet of West Aberthaw (ST 024 668), rather than the river Tawe: as the latter lies west of the Neath, it is unlikely that the grant distinguished land between it and the Afan from land within that area that lay between the Afan and the Neath.

141 Letter patent concerning Margam Abbey

Notification that he granted to Margam common pasture and easements of his land in the time of Abbot Conan almost thirty years previously. Afterwards, many years later in the time of Abbot Gilbert, he granted the same gift more expressly in a charter. As the monks of Neath had nothing at that time from Morgan's land in the mountains on the east side of the Neath, overcome by greed on account of poverty he granted in 1205 a certain part of the same pasture by charter to the monks of Neath. He has ordered this truthful testimony to be written so that the truth will be known to all and the dispute between the two houses concerning that pasture will be settled more easily and justly.

[25 March 1205 × 28 May 1208; possibly 25 March 1205 × *c*.August 1206]

A = BL, Harl. Ch. 75 B 31. Endorsed: Morg' pro domo de Marg' de communi pastura sua ex estparte de Neth (s. xiii in.); approx. 200 × 177 + 19 mm.; two slits through centre of the fold for a tag (*c*.13 mm. wide) which exits through a slit in the base of the fold; sealed on tag. Almost circular seal, red wax, imperfect, originally approx. 58 × 53 mm. diameter; equestrian, facing right; legend: + SIGILLVM MAR ...
Pd. from A, *Cartae*, ii. 391–2 (no. 397); from A, Clark, 'Lords of Avan', 20; from A, Clark, 'Contributions toward a cartulary', 41–2.
Cd., Owen, *Catalogue*, iii. 562; Birch, *Catalogue*, ii. 8; *H*, no. 68.

Omnibus ad quos presens scriptum pervenerit Morgan(us) filius Caradoci salutem. Noverit universitas vestra me concessisse et dedisse monachis de Margan' communem pasturam et aisiamenta terre mee in bosco et in plano tempore Conani abbatis fere triginta annis transactis. Postea vero tempore Gileb(er)ti abbatis pluribus iam annis transactis eandem donationem eis expressius incartavi sicut carta quam inde habent testatur. Cum monachi de Neth eo tempore nichil omnino haberent de terra mea in montanis ex estparte de Neth, anno autem ab incarnatione domini millesimo ducentesimo v° cupiditate victus propter penuriam quandam partem eiusdem pasture monachis de Neth incartavi. Hoc testimonium veritatis ideo scripto mandavi ut nota sit omnibus veritas et controversia inter duas domos de eadem pastura facilius et iustius terminetur.

The letter is unlikely to be later than 28 May 1208, when, as arbitrators appointed by the Cistercian General Chapter, the abbots of Fountains, Wardon and Boxley settled the dispute over pasture rights between Margam and Neath in the district between the rivers Neath and Afan: Neath was allowed to keep the third closer to it and Margam was allocated the remaining two-thirds (*Cartae*, ii. 330–2 (no. 329); see further Cowley, 'Neath versus Margam', 7–9). In a letter addressed to the Cistercian Order (no. 147 below), probably datable to about August 1206, Morgan insisted that he had granted the pasture to Neath for a period of two years only. The omission of this qualification from the present document may well indicate that it was written earlier than that letter. Conan was abbot of Margam *c*.1166–90 (Cowley, *Monastic Order*, 49; cf. Williams, 'Fasti Cistercienses', 189; note to no. 124 above). See also no. 140 above.

142 Margam Abbey

Grant in fee farm of all the land and meadow within these bounds: from the land the monks had from Payn de Turberville as the stream called Witherel *leads to the great road called* Grenewei, *and by that road to Scurlage's land of* Crokerhille; *the part of the moor from the stream descending from* Treikic *towards the west to the bounds of Scurlage's land and thence to the stream which descends from* Treikic *towards the east, and thence to the great stone on the east side of the stream, and thence to the thicket of* Altherelin, *and from the stream on the east side of* Redeforde *to* Torres, *and from north of* la More *to the arable land beneath* Treikic. *All this he has granted, with the consent of his sons Lleision, Owain and all the others, to be held for ever from him and his heirs for an annual render of 10s. at Michaelmas for all service, custom and exaction, of which he has received five years' render in advance in 1205. Further grant of all the easements of his land at Newcastle; also of the land which belonged to Walter* Lageles, *to be held for the same farm the monks used to pay to Earl William, namely 8s. 4d. at four terms of the year. Morgan and his sons have sworn faithfully to observe all this for ever. He and his heirs have granted all these lands in perpetual alms free of all secular service, custom and exaction apart from the stipulated farm. Witnesses.*

[Probably *c*.29 September 1205]

A = NLW, Penrice and Margam Ch. 85. Endorsed: Donatio Morg(ani) in feudo Novi Castelli (s. xiii[1]); approx. 155 × 311 + 18 mm.; two central slits in fold for a tag (*c*.12 mm. wide) which exits through a slit in the base of the fold; sealed on tag. Almost circular seal, red wax, approx. 58 × 53 mm. diameter; equestrian, facing right; legend: + SIGILL ... MAR ... DOCI'.
B = NLW, Penrice and Margam Roll 2093/3. s. xiii[1].

C = NLW, Penrice and Margam Roll 292/1. s. xiii.
Pd. from A, *Cartae*, ii. 299–300 (no. 295).
Cd., Birch, *Catalogue*, i. 29–30, 113; *H*, no. 61.

Omnibus sancte matris ecclesie filiis presentibus et futuris Morgan(us) filius Caradoci salutem. Sciatis me concessisse et dedisse et hac carta confirmasse Deo et ecclesie Beate Marie de Margan et monachis ibidem Deo servientibus in feudo firmam totam terram et pratum infra hos terminos, scilicet a terra quam monachi habent de Pagano de Turberewile sicut rivulus qui dicitur Witherel vadit ad magnam viam que dicitur Grenewei, et sicut eadem via vadit ad terram Scurlage que dicitur Crokerehille; preterea partem more a rivulo qui descendit de Treikic ultimus versus occidentem usque ad terminos terre Scurlage, et inde usque ad rivulum qui descendit de Treikic versus orientem, et inde usque ad Magnum Lapidem ex hest parte rivuli, et inde usque ad dumetum Altherelin, et a rivulo ex hest parte de Redeforde usque ad Torres, et ex *north* de la More usque ad terram arabilem subtus Treikic. Hec omnia ego Morgan(us) concedentibus filiis meis Leisan et Owein et omnibus aliis concessi predictis monachis habenda et tenenda in perpetuum de me et heredibus meis reddendo annuatim pro omni servicio, consuetudine et exactione decem solidos tantum ad festum Sancti Michaelis, ex quibus pre manibus accepi redditus quinque annorum anno ab incarnatione domini m° cc° v°. Concessi etiam eis aisiamenta terre mee apud Novum Castellum in bosco et in plano, in moris, in pasturis, in aquis, in semitis, in viis. Et preterea terram que fuit Walt(er)i Lageles tenendam de me et heredibus meis per eandem firmam quam reddere solebant Will(elm)o comiti, scilicet octavo solidos et iiii^{or} denarios ad iiii^{or} terminos anni. Et sciendum quod ego et filii mei iuravimus nos hec omnia fideliter et absque dolo servaturos inperpetuum. Hec omnia ego et heredes mei dedimus predicte domui in elemosinam perpetuam liberam et quietam ab omni seculari servicio et consuetudine et exactione preter nominatam firmam. His testibus: Wilfrid(us) sacerdos, Lucas clericus, Rob(ertus) Segin, Rob(ertus) Samson, Alaithur, Resus Coh, Roger(us) Wian, Roger(us) Aithan, David Puignel, Wrunu filius Cadugan, Meuric filius Luarch, Youuaf frater eius, Roger(us) Cam, Anaraud filius Cnaithur, Ysaac filius Rohhan, Seisil filius Loharch, Traharn filius Seisil, Walt(er)us prepositus, Ric(ardus) faber, Walt(er)us de Marcros, Cradoc frater Resi Coh, Madoc filius Wrunu, Meuric filius Cadugan et multi alii.

For Earl William of Gloucester's grant to Walter *Lageles* of the land which his father held (i.e. Laleston) for 8*s.* per annum see *EGC*, 104 (no. 105). Walter granted it to Margam by November 1186 (*Cartae*, i. 186 (no. 181)).

143 Margam Abbey

Grant of 50 acres of arable near Clakeston *near the land of Llangewydd in perpetual alms, free of all service, custom and exaction. Confirmation of the gift of Robert ap Gwion* (Wian) *by the same bounds as attested in his charter to the monks. A further grant of 80 acres in alms between* Clakeston *and Laleston to hold of him and his heirs for an annual render of 40d. at Michaelmas, of which he he has received five years' render in 1205. He and his heirs will warrant this for ever as their alms. Witnesses.*

[Probably *c*.29 September 1205]

A = NLW, Penrice and Margam Ch. 86. Endorsed: Donatio Morg(ani) de terra quam nobis dedit apud Novum Castellum (s. xiii[1]); approx. 155 × 204 + 22 mm.; two central slits in fold for a tag (*c*.13 mm. wide) which exits through a slit in the base of the fold; sealed on tag. Almost circular seal, red wax, approx. 58 × 53 mm. diameter; equestrian, facing right; legend: + SIGILLVM MARGANI [F]ILII CARADOCI.
B = NLW, Penrice and Margam Roll 2093/4. s. xiii[1].
C = NLW, Penrice and Margam Roll 292/2. s. xiii.
Pd. from A, *Cartae*, ii. 297–8 (no. 293).
Cd., Birch, *Catalogue*, i. 30, 113; *H*, no. 67.

Omnibus sancte ecclesie filiis presentibus et futuris Morgan(us) filius Caradoci salutem. Sciatis me concessisse et dedisse et hac carta confirmasse Deo et Beate Marie et ecclesie de Margan et monachis ibidem Deo servientibus in puram et perpetuam elemosinam liberam et quietam ab omni servitio, consuetudine et exactione quinquaginta acras terre arabilis iuxta Clakeston proximiores terre de Langewi. Concessi etiam eis donationem quam fecit Rob(ertus) filius Wian per easdem divisas sicut carta ipsius quam monachi inde habent testatur. Preterea concessi et dedi eis quaterviginti acras in elemosinam habendas et tenendas de me et heredibus meis in perpetuum inter Clakeston et Lagelestan reddendo annuatim pro omni servicio et consuetudine et exactione quadraginta denarios ad festum Sancti Michael(is), ex quibus pre manibus accepi redditus quinque annorum anno ab incarnatione domini m° cc° v°. Et ego et heredes warentizabimus eis inperpetuum sicut elemosinam nostram. His testibus: Wilfrid(us) sacerdos, Lucas clericus, Rob(ertus) Segin, Rob(ertus) Samson, Alaithur, Resus Coh, Rog(erus) Wian, Rog(erus) Aithan, David Puinel, Wrunu filius Cadugan, Meuric filius Luarh, Youaf frater eius, Rog(erus) Cam, Anaraud filius Cnaithur, Ysaac Rohhan, Seisil filius Luarch, Traharn filius Seisil et multi alii.

For Robert ap Gwion (*Wian*) see also no. 127 above. All the witnesses of the present charter occur, in the same order, in no. 142 above, written by the same scribe (Patterson, *Scriptorium of Margam*, 96, 110), though the latter charter contains a further six names. These similarities, together with the identical clauses on receiving advance payment of five years' render in 1205, strongly suggest that both charters were issued on the same occasion. For the place-names see note to no. 139 above.

144 Margam Abbey

Grant in perpetual alms of the meadow which belonged to Coh *in the marsh of Afan by Margam Burrows* (Bergas), *to be held of him and his heirs freely for an annual render of 15d. at Michaelmas for all service; he has received three years' render in 1205. Philip Moel has quitclaimed the same meadow before Morgan, his lord, and sworn an oath and given pledges that neither he nor his heirs will ever claim it. Witnesses.*

[Probably *c*.29 September 1205]

A = BL, Harl. Ch. 75 B 30. Endorsed: Donatio Morg' de prato Cohd (s. xiii in.); in marisco de Avan (s. xv); approx. 141 mm. wide at top, 131 mm. wide at bottom × 131 mm. deep + 28 mm.; two slits in centre of fold for a tag (*c*.18 mm. wide) which exits through a slit in the base of the fold; sealed on tag. Almost circular seal, red wax, originally approx. 58 × 53 mm. diameter; equestrian, facing right; legend: + SIGILL . MARGANI . FILII . CA ... CI.
B = NLW, Penrice and Margam Roll 288/10. s. xiii[1].

Pd. from A, *Cartae*, ii. 298 (no. 294).
Cd., Owen, *Catalogue*, iii. 562; Birch, *Catalogue*, i. 94; *H*, no. 66.

Omnibus sancte ecclesie filiis ad quos presens scriptum pervenerit Morgan(us) filius Cradoci salutem. Sciatis me dedisse et concessisse et hac carta confirmasse Deo et ecclesie Sancte Marie de Margan et monachis ibidem Deo servientibus in puram et perpetuam elemosinam pratum quod fuit Coh in marisco de Auene iuxta Bergas habendum et tenendum de me et heredibus meis libere et quiete, reddendo annuatim pro omni servitio ad festum Sancti Michael(is) xv denarios. Et ego pre manibus accepi redditum trium annorum anno ab incarnatione domini m° ducentesimo v^{to}. Et sciendum quod Philipp(us) Moel quitum clamavit predictum pratum coram Morgano domino suo et iuramentum prestitit et plegios dedit quod nunquam illud calumniabit nec ipse nec heredes eius. Hiis testibus: David Puignel, Hereb(er)to filio Palmarii, Ithenard filio Ithel, Philippo, Ric(ardo) Waleis.

It is unclear why Birch (*Margam*, 7, 157–8, followed by Gray, 'Hermitage', 149) thought that the *Coh* mentioned in this charter was a hermit. For the identification of *Bergas* as Margam Burrows, south-east of the old mouth of the Afan, see Birch, *Margam*, 385 and cf. RCAHMW, *Glamorgan III. ii*, 273.

145 Margam Abbey

Grant in perpetual alms of the land which belonged to Walter Laheles to be held freely in return for an annual render of 2s., to be paid as 6d. at four terms of the year, for all service, custom and exaction. He has granted the rest of the annual render which the earl used to receive, namely 6s. 4d., to the monks for his soul for the feeding of the poor by the monastery on Maundy Thursday, and wishes that his alms be assigned to this annual feeding for ever. Witnesses.

[October 1205 × *c*.1208]

A = NLW, Penrice and Margam Ch. 87. Endorsed: Donatio Morg(ani) de vi solidos et iiii^{or} de Lahelest' (s. xiii^1); approx. 174 × 93 + 20 mm.; two central slits in fold for a tag (*c*.18 mm. wide) which exits through a slit in the base of the fold; sealed on tag. Almost circular seal, red wax, approx. 58 × 53 mm. diameter; equestrian, facing right; legend: + SIGILLVM MARGAN FILII CARADOCI.
B = NLW, Penrice and Margam Roll 292/3. s. xiii.
Pd. from A, *Cartae*, ii. 395–6 (no. 402).
Cd., Birch, *Catalogue*, i. 30, 113; *H*, no. 76.

Omnibus sancte ecclesie filiis ad quos presens scriptum pervenerit Morgan(us) filius Cradoci salutem. Sciatis me dedisse et concessisse et hac carta confirmasse monachis de Morgan^a in perpetuam elemosinam terram que fuit Walteri Laheles tenendam et habendam libere, pacifice et quiete reddendo mihi et heredibus meis annuatim pro omni servitio, consuetudine et exactione ii^{os} solidos ad iiii^{or} terminos anni, scilicet ad unumquemque terminum vi denarios. Nam totum reliquum quod comes solebat accipere et ego post ipsum ad annuum redditum de illa terra, scilicet vi solidos et iiii^{or} denarios dedi predictis monachis pro anima mea ad mandatum pauperum faciendum per conventum in cena domini. Et volo ut hec elemosina mea in perpetuum in domo de Margan inviolabiliter ad hoc annuum mandatum faciendum assignetur. Hiis testibus: Walt(er)o Luuel, Ernulfo constabulario de Kenefeg, Stephano clerico, Griffino filio Kneithur, Reso Coh, David Puignel, Kenewrec filio Loarh, Thoma filio Ric(ardi) et multis aliis.

^a *sic in* A.

This charter was presumably issued later no. 142 above, datable to about Michaelmas 1205, which required the full render of 8*s*. 4*d*.

146 Margam Abbey

Grant, with the consent of his sons Lleision and Owain, of all the land which belonged to Walter Laheles *with all its appurtenances in perpetual alms for the souls of himself and his ancestors and successors. He and his heirs will warrant this grant as their alms against all men for ever. He and his heirs quitclaim for ever all the annual render which the earl and afterwards Morgan used to receive from that land, namely 8*s. 4*d. If any service, to the king or anyone else, is demanded from that land, he and his heirs will perform it so that the monks are free from all secular service, exaction and custom for ever. Witnesses.*

[October 1205 × *c*.1208]

> A = NLW, Penrice and Margam Ch. 91. Endorsed: Morg' de viii solidis et iiii^{or} denariis de Lahelestun' (by scribe of charter); approx. 170 × 107 + 7 mm.; two central slits, one just above fold and one in fold, for a tag (*c*.14 mm. wide) which exits through a slit in the base of the fold; sealed on tag. Almost circular seal, green wax, edges chipped, originally approx. 58 × 53 mm. diameter; equestrian, facing right; legend: + SIGILLVM [M]AR ... [F]ILII ...
> B = NLW, Penrice and Margam Roll 2093/5. s. xiii¹.
> C = NLW, Penrice and Margam Roll 292/14. s. xiii. (Omits witness list.)
> Pd. from A, *Cartae*, ii. 329 (no. 328); from C, ibid., 399 (no. 407).
> Cd., Birch, *Catalogue*, i. 31, 115; *H*, no. 77.

Omnibus sancte ecclesie filiis ad quos presens scriptum pervenerit Morg' filius Cradoci salutem. Sciatis me consilio et consensu Leisan et Owein filiorum meorum dedisse et concessisse et hac carta confirmasse Deo et ecclesie Beate Marie de Marg(an) et monachis Deo ibidem servientibus totam terram que fuit Walt(er)i Laheles cum omnibus pertinentiis suis in perpetuam elemosinam pro anima mea et pro animabus predecessorum et successorum meorum, habendam et tenendam libere et quiete sicut ulla elemosina potest liberius haberi et teneri. Et ego et heredes mei warantizabimus eis hanc donationem sicut elemosinam nostram contra omnes homines in perpetuum. Et totum annuum redditum quem comes solebat accipere et ego post ipsum de illa terra, scilicet viii solidos et iiii^{or} denarios, ego et heredes mei predictis monachis quitum clamavimus in perpetuum. Si vero aliquod servitium sive domini regis sive alicuius alterius de illa terra fuerit aliquando requisitum, ego et heredes mei illud faciemus ita quod monachi quieti erunt et liberi ab omni servitio, exactione et consuetudine seculari in perpetuum. His testibus: Will(elm)o de Lichevelt et Rob(er)to de Pultimor converso de M(ar)g(an), Wurgano presbitero, Madoco filio G(ri)f', Hoel filio Rog(er)i, David Pugneil.

As it remits the whole of the rent for Laleston, this charter may be assigned to a later date in the same date range as no. 145 above.

147 The father abbots and monks of the Cistercian order

Letter, informing them that, though a long time previously he granted and confirmed by charter to the monks of Margam the pasture of all his land on the east side of the Neath, he later granted to the monks of Neath that they could share in the pasture of a certain part of his land for two years only; these two years will have elapsed on the Michaelmas following the Michaelmas which is imminent. There are still witnesses who were present at this agreement who know how true this is. The monks of Neath never had any agreement with Morgan concerning this pasture before this two-year agreement nor had any charter from him; they never frequented this pasture in Morgan's lifetime before this agreement. The monks of Neath never had a charter from Morgan's father nor did they ever frequent this pasture in his father's lifetime. Morgan wishes to communicate this truthful testimony so that the recipients will be able to deliver a more secure judgement on the dispute concerning this pasture between Neath and Margam. All, both old and young, living in Morgan's land know that the monks of Neath never frequented this pasture before the aforesaid two-year agreement nor were ever seen there previously with their herds.

[*c*.August 1206]

A = NLW, Penrice and Margam Ch. 2024. Endorsed: Morg' de pastura sua ex estparte de Neth pro domo de Marg(an) (s. xiii in.); modern endorsement; approx. 170 × 91 + 7 mm.; two central slits, one just above fold, one in fold, for a tag (*c*.8 mm. wide); sealed on tag. Seal missing.
Pd. from A, *Cartae*, vi. 2284–5 (no. 1563).
Cd., Birch, *Catalogue*, iv: i. 148; *H*, no. 322.

Universis dominis et patribus abbatibus et monachis Cisterciensis ordinis ad quos presentes littere pervenerint Morgan(us) filius Cradoci salutem. Universitati vestre notum facio quod cum ex multo iam precedenti tempore dederim et concesserim atque carta mea confirmaverim monachis de Margan communem pasturam totius terre mee ex estparte de Neth, concessi postea monachis de Neth ut in pastura cuiusdam partis terre mee cum monachis communicarent per duos annos tantummodo, qui duo anni post imminens festum Sancti Michael(is) ad proximum eiusdem festum futurum implebuntur. Huius conventionis testes adhuc supersunt qui eidem interfuerunt qui optime sciunt quam vera est hec assertio mea. Noveritis itaque pro certo quod monachi de Neth nunquam ante hanc conventionem horum duorum annorum aliquam conventionem aliquando mecum fecerunt de pastura illa nec aliquam cartam de me unquam habuerunt, set nec pasturam ipsam frequentaverunt unquam in diebus meis ante hanc conventionem inter me et illos factam. Adhuc etiam pro certo noveritis quod monachi de Neth nullam cartam unquam habuerunt de patre meo nec in diebus patris mei pasturam illam aliquando frequentaverunt. Hoc testimonium veritatis vobis intimare volui ut cognita veritate possitis securius veram proferre sententiam super ventilatione controversie que de pastura eadem vertitur inter monachos de Neth et monachos de Marg(an). Norunt enim omnes senes cum iunioribus qui habitant in terra mea quod monachi de Neth nunquam ante predictam conventionem duorum annorum inter me et illos factam pasturam ipsam frequentaverunt nec cum armentis suis in ea aliquando antea visi fuerunt. Valete in domino.

As Morgan stated in no. 141 above that he granted some of his pasture to Neath in 1205, the two-year term mentioned in the present document was presumably due to end at Michaelmas 1207. Since the letter refers to the Michaelmas before that marking the end of the two-year as *imminens*, it was presumably written in about August 1206, and was quite possibly sent to the Cistercian General Chapter, whose annual meetings commenced on or about 14 September, in that year (cf. Cowley, *Monastic Order*, 113). Gilbert, abbot of Margam attended the General Chapter in 1206, and could therefore have taken the letter as evidence to support his case against Neath (*Statuta*, ed. Canivez, i. 326). Although the previous General Chapter had appointed the abbots of Fountains, Buildwas and Ford to settle a dispute between Margam and Neath (ibid., 317–18), it is not certain that this dispute concerned the pasture rights granted by Morgan, whose grant to Neath in 1205 may, to judge by the present document, have occurred at about Michaelmas and thus after the meeting of the General Chapter. The dispute over pasture rights was not settled until May 1208 (see note to no. 141 above).

148 Margam Abbey

Grant of 80 acres of arable on the west side of Laleston, on the north side of the road leading from Laleston towards Kenfig and on the east side of the 50 acres he previously granted, to be held in alms free of all secular service, custom and exaction for an annual render of 40d. at Michaelmas. He has received in advance all the farm for eight years, of which the first year was 1208. He and his heirs will warrant all this for ever. Witnesses.

[Probably *c.*29 September 1208]

A = NLW, Penrice and Margam Ch. 100. Endorsed: Morgani de quat' xx^{ti} acris (s. xiii^1); approx. 151 × 101 + 24 mm.; two central slits in fold for a tag (*c.*11 mm. wide) which exits through a slit in the base of the fold; sealed on tag. Almost circular seal, red wax, chipped around the edges and worn, originally approx. 58 × 53 mm. diameter; equestrian, facing right; legend: + SIG … N FILII …
B = NLW, Penrice and Margam Roll 292/12. s. xiii. (Omits witness list.)
Pd. from A, *Cartae*, ii. 328–9 (no. 327).
Cd., Birch, *Catalogue*, i. 114–15; *H*, no. 69.

Omnibus sancte ecclesie filiis presentibus et futuris Margan(us) filius Karadoci salutem. Sciatis me concessisse et dedisse et hac karta confirmasse Deo et ecclesie Sancte Marie de Margan et monachis ibidem Deo servientibus quat' xx^{ti} acras terre arabilis ex westparte de Laghelestune et ex northparte vie que vadit de Laghelestune versus Kenefeg et ex estparte illarum l acrarum quas ante dederam eis in elemosinam. Has ergo quat' xx^{ti} acras infra has metas iacentes dedi in elemosinam ad habendum et tenendum libere et quiete ab omni seculari servitio et consuetudine et exactione sicut ulla elemosina liberius teneri potest, reddendo annuatim mihi et heredibus meis solummodo quadraginta denarios ad festum Sancti Michael(is). Et sciendum quod totam firmam pre manibus accepi viii^{to} annorum quorum primus fuit annus m^{us} c^{us} c^{us} viii^{us}. Et hoc totum warentizabimus eis ego et heredes mei in perpetuum. His testibus: Helia decano, Henrico monacho, Will(elm)o de Bedinctun', Io(hann)e Sor, David Puinel, Madoc filio Meileri, Hernaldo converso, Iordano converso.

The 50 acres previously granted may have been the same as those recorded in nos 139 and 143 above, likewise located in the vicinity of Laleston in the fee of Newcastle. However, the 80 acres granted in the present charter were presumably different from the 80 acres between *Clakeston* and Laleston granted in no. 143 above, for which Morgan had received five years' farm in 1205.

CADWALLON AP CARADOG
(d. by October 1191)

*149 Margam Abbey
Grant of lands, pastures and other easements in his land.

[Probably November 1186 × October 1191]

Mention only, in a confirmation by Cadwallon's son Morgan ap Cadwallon probably datable to November 1186 × October 1191 (no. 188 below). It is likely that the present charter was issued after Pope Urban III's confirmation of Margam's lands of 18 November 1186, as neither this nor any earlier confirmation includes grants by sons of Caradog ab Iestyn (cf. *Cartae*, i. 185–90 (no. 181)). Although no. 121 above may be earlier than November 1186, that charter was in favour of the abortive foundation of Pendar, not Margam. The land granted by Cadwallon comprised or included Cefn Machen in Margam's grange of Llangeinor (see note to no. 188 below).

MAREDUDD AP CARADOG
(d. 1211)

150 Margam Abbey
Notification that, as he has been received into the full fraternity of Margam, he has taken the monastery and all its possessions, and especially its grange of Llanfeuthin, under his protection. He has also granted in perpetual alms, with the consent of his wife Nest and his heirs, for the salvation of the souls of himself, his father Caradog and his wife Nest, the right to take timber and fuel from his wood for the use of the grange of Llanfeuthin, and use of his common pasture for the cattle, horses, pigs and pasturing animals of that grange. He and his heirs will warrant all this free of all secular service, custom and exaction. The monks of Margam have given him 100s. for this gift. Witnesses.

[November 1186 × June 1199]

A = BL, Harl. Ch. 75 B 28. Endorsed: Carta Moreduch de husbote et heþbote (s. xii/xiii); approx. 240 × 97 + 19 mm.; two central slits in fold for a tag (*c.*16 mm. wide) which exits through a slit in the base of the fold; sealed on tag. Circular seal, red wax, originally approx. 50 mm. diameter; spiral branch of foliage terminating in a fleur-de-lys in the centre of the design; legend: + SIGILLVM . MOREDVC . FILII . CARADOCI.
Pd. from A, Clark, 'Some account', 28; from A, *Cartae*, ii. 229–30 (no. 224).
Cd., Owen, *Catalogue*, iii. 561; *H*, no. 56.

Omnibus sancte ecclesie filiis Moraduþ filius Karadoci salutem. Sciatis quod quoniam receptus sum in plenam fraternitatem domus de Marg(an) tunc recepi et ego domum ipsam et omnia que ad ipsam spectant et maxime grangiam illorum de Lantmeuþin cum omnibus catallis et pertinentiis suis in custodia et protectione mea sicut propria catalla mea. Et tunc concessi et dedi assensu uxoris mee Nest et heredum meorum pro salute anime mee et

Karadoci patris mei et uxoris mee Nest et omnium antecessorum meorum eidem domui in perpetuam elemosinam aisiamenta in bosco meo in usus grangie sue de Lantmeuþin quantumcumque opus habuerint ad meirimium[a] et ad focalia, et communem pasturam terre mee quantumcumque opus habuerit in usus eiusdem grangie ad boves et equos et porcos et animalia pascualia. Et hoc totum warentizabimus eis et aquietabimus ego et heredes mei ut habeant et teneant hoc totum libere et quiete ab omni seculari servitio et consuetudine et omni exactione sicut ulla elemosina liberius teneri potest. Et quoniam eis hanc donationem feci dederunt michi monachi predicte domus de Marg(an) c solidos karitatis intuitu. His testibus: Henea sacerdote, Will(elm)o sacerdote de Sancta Iulita, domina Nest uxore predicti Moraduþ, Kenewrec filio Madoc, Madoc filio Kaduga(n), Isac Sedan, Rogero filio Wiawan, Cuelin portario.[b]

[a] *nine minims after the* r *with a contraction mark over the final two minims* A. | [b] portari(us)o A.

Maredudd's grant was confirmed by Countess Isabella 1189 × June 1199 (*EGC*, 126 (no. 137)). The grange of Llanfeuthin is referred to by Hugh of Llancarfan in a notification to William, bishop of Llandaff in 1186 × 1191 (*Cartae*, i. 182 (no. 177)); however, neither the grange nor Maredudd's grant is included in Pope Urban III's confirmation to Margam in November 1186 (ibid., i. 185–90 (no. 181)). The grange lay about $\frac{1}{2}$ mile north of Llancarfan (see note to no. 132 above; RCAHMW, *Glamorgan III. ii*, 291–3).

LLEISION AP MORGAN
(d. 1214 × 1217)

151 Margam Abbey
Notification, by Lleision and Owain sons of Morgan, that they have confirmed by oath to the monks of Margam that neither they nor any of [their] men will dig or plough any of the land between the dyke of the English and Meles in the marsh of Afan. For they and their father Morgan have granted in alms to the monks all the land, both arable and non-arable and pasture, in Meles, the moor and marsh between the Afan and St Thomas's chapel for an annual render of 20s. Witnesses.

[Probably *c*.1186 × *c*.1208]

> A = BL, Harl. Ch. 75 C 36. Endorsed: Leisan et Owein de marisco de Auen' (s. xiii in.); approx. 219 × 56 + 17 mm.; single slit on right-hand side of fold, with tag and seal missing; single slit on left-hand side of fold for a tag (*c*.10 mm. wide) which exits through a slit in the base of the fold; sealed on tag. Circular seal, red wax, originally approx. 40 mm. diameter; hand holding a lance with a banner; legend: + SIGILL . HO ... NI.
> B = NLW, Penrice and Margam Roll 2090/4. s. xiii[1]. (Omits witness list.)
> Pd. from A, *Cartae*, iii. 921 (no. 809).
> Cd., Owen, *Catalogue*, iii. 569; *H*, no. 82.

Omnibus sancte ecclesie filiis ad quos presens scriptum pervenerit Leissan et Owein filii Morgani salutem. Sciatis nos pepigisse monachis de Margan et iuramento firmasse quod nec nos nec aliqui hominum aliquam fossabimus aut arabimus terram que iacet inter walda(m) Anglor(um) et Meles in marisco de Auene. Nam pasturam tocius terre tam arabilis quam non arabilis in Melis, in mora, in marisco concessimus predictis monachis et dedimus in elemosinam inter Auene et cappellam Sancti Thome tam nos quam pater noster Morgan(us) pro xx solidis annuatim nobis inde persolvendis. Hiis testibus: Worgano cappellano de Auene, Rog(er)o filio Yuor, David Puignel, Herb(er)to Palmer, Will(elm)o filio Alewi.

It is not clear whether the grant was made at the same time as the undertaking not to disturb the monks' land, and thus it could be that Morgan ap Caradog was no longer alive when the present document was issued. As the *nos* of the last sentence before the witness list clearly refers only to Lleision and Owain, the same is presumably also true of the *nobis*, implying that Morgan, though a grantor, took no share of the 20*s*. rent. On balance, however, a date during Morgan's lifetime seems likely. It is not ruled out by the wording of the document; indeed, the use of the perfect rather than pluperfect tense for the grant suggests that it was made (or perhaps renewed) when the brothers swore not to dig or plough the monks' land rather than on an earlier occasion. The witness list is likewise consistent with a date before Morgan's death: Wrgan, chaplain of Afan, occurs in 1199 and Herbert Palmer in 1199 and 1205 (nos 133–4, 144 above). Margam possessed the grange of Meles by November 1186 (note to no. 122 above). The dyke of the English or 'Gwal Saeson' was a stone wall on the southern boundary of the grange that originally crossed from the Afan to the river Ffrwdwyllt; the precise location of St Thomas's chapel is uncertain (RCAHMW, *Glamorgan III. ii*, 267–70).

152 Margam Abbey

Grant, with the consent of his kin and friends, of his father's charter concerning the land of Pultimor; he has received ten years' rent for the land from the monks in advance and will receive no more until that term is completed. He has sworn on the relics of St Mary's church at Margam to warrant that land against all men for ever. He has remitted all claims which he ever made against the monks. Witnesses.

[12 December 1193 × January 1199]

B = NLW, Penrice and Margam Roll 2093/2. s. xiii[1]. The portion of the roll containing the text of this document is in very poor condition. Unless otherwise indicated, lacunae have been supplied from G. T. Clark's text in *Cartae*, probably based on a transcript made when the roll was less damaged than it is now.
Pd. from B, *Cartae*, vi. 2289 (no. 1569).
Cd., Birch, *Catalogue*, iv: i. 181; *Episc. Acts*, ii. 701 (L. 318); *H*, no. 52.

Omnibus sancte ecclesie filiis presentibus et futuris Leisan filius Morg(ani) [salutem. Sciatis quod ego] consilio et consensu parentum et amicorum meorum concessi et dedi et hac carta confirmavi monachis de [Margan cartam Morgani patris] mei quam fecit predictis monachis de terra de Pultimor, per o[mnia sicut carta testatur]. Et sciendum quod accepi pre manibus a prefatis monachis firmam ipsius terre in x annos p … meus susceperat pre manibus firmam ipsius terre a predictis monac[his nichil omnino accep]turus donec predictus terminus compleatur. Sciendum etiam quod super sanctuaria ecclesie Beate

Ma[rie de Margan fide]liter observabo, et terram illam prefatis monachis warantizabo [contra omnes homines] in perpetuum. Et omnes calumpnias quas unquam moveram contra eos remisi eis se … [Hiis testibus: domino] Henr(ico) Land(avensi) episcopo, Helya decano de Novo Castell(o), Dau[id Puignel],[a] Hereb(er)to Palm(er)o, Wasmero filio Iago, Nichol(o) Gobion, magistro W[altero de Bergeueni].

[a] *supplied here from no. 132 above.*

This is a confirmation of Morgan's grant (no. 132 above), which stipulates an annual rent of half a mark (6*s.* 8*d.*), and was almost certainly issued on the same occasion, as the witness lists of both charters are identical.

153 Margam Abbey

Grant of all the land from the dyke of Sanan to the the water dyke and thence to Pultschatan, *granted in alms by his father as his charter attests. Lleision has sworn on the relics of the church to warrant this gift of his father against all men for ever. He has sealed this with his father's seal as he had no seal of his own. Witnesses.*

[Shortly after 29 September 1200]

A = NLW, Penrice and Margam Ch. 2026. Endorsed: Carta Leysan cum additamento donationis patris eius in Marisco de Auene (s. xiii in.); approx. 142 × 105 + 25 mm.; two central slits in fold for a tag (*c.*13 mm. wide) which exits through a slit in the base of the fold; sealed on tag. Almost circular seal, brown wax, chipped at the edges and worn, originally approx. 58 × 53 mm.; equestrian, facing right; legend: + SIGI … ADOCI.
B = NLW, Penrice and Margam Roll 288/4. s. xiii[1].
Pd. from B, *Cartae*, iii. 919 (no. 807).
Cd., Birch, *Catalogue*, i. 93; iv: i. 148–9; *H*, no. 106.

Omnibus sancte ecclesie filiis presentibus et futuris Leisan filius Morgani salutem. Sciatis me concessisse et hac carta confirmasse Deo et ecclesie Sancte Marie de Marg(an) et monachis ibidem Deo servientibus in elemosinam totam terram que extenditur in longum et latum a fossato Sanan usque ad fossam aquariam et inde iuxta eam in longum et latum usque P(u)ltschatan quam pater meus Morgan(us) dedit prefatis monachis in elemosinam per omnia sicut eius carta testatur. Et sciendum quod affidavi et super sacrosancta ecclesie iuravi quod hanc donationem patris mei prenominatis monachis warantizabo contra omnes homines in perpetuum. Et quia sigillum meum non habui sigillo patris mei hanc cartam sigillavi. Hiis testibus: Kenewrec presbitero de Langauelach, Cuelin Arther, Yeruerth filio Hoel, Griffin Du, Ythenard filio Griff', Morgano filio Griff', Wrunu filio Mauricii, Win filio Gesuredi.

This is a confirmation of no. 136 above, datable to shortly after Michaelmas 1200, and was almost certainly issued on the same occasion, as both charters are written by the same scribe (Patterson, *Scriptorium of Margam*, 89–90, 109, 119) and, more importantly, their witness lists are identical except that no. 136 includes two additional names at the end. This dating is consistent with the sealing clause, which shows that Lleision's father was present at the making of the charter.

154 Margam Abbey

Grant in perpetual alms, with the consent of his father and his friends, of all the land of Resolven with all its appurtenances between the river Gwrach and the river Clydach and between the river Neath and the great road which leads through the mountains of Torbethel to Glyn-wrach, all the produce of the river Neath between the Gwrach and the Clydach, and the common pasture of all his land in the mountains between the river Afan and river Neath, to be held free of all secular service, custom and exaction. Lleision and his heirs will warrant all this against all men for ever. He has sworn on relics, on behalf of himself and his heirs, faithfully to observe all the above. Witnesses.

[Probably *c*.1203 × 1205]

A = NLW, Penrice and Margam Ch. 112. Endorsed: Leisan de Rossaulin (s. xiii in.); modern endorsement; approx. 175 × 171 + 27 mm.; two central slits in fold for a tag (*c*.12 mm. wide) which exits through a slit in the base of the fold; sealed on tag. Circular seal, red wax, approx. 55 mm. diameter; figure kneeling on left before an abbot holding a book and blessing him; legend: + SIGILLVM . LEISAN . FILII . MORGANI. Seal tag inscribed: de primo sigillo (by scribe of the charter).
B = NLW, Penrice and Margam Roll 543/5. s. xiii[1].
C = NLW, Penrice and Margam Roll 2093/17. s. xiii[1].
D = NLW, Penrice and Margam Ch. 212 (inspeximus of Hugh Despenser, 9 October 1338).
Pd. from A, *Cartae*, iii. 928–9 (no. 816); from D, ibid., iv. 1215 (no. 968).
Cd., Birch, *Catalogue*, i. 38; ii. 6; *H*, no. 63.

Omnibus sancte ecclesie filiis presentibus et futuris Leisan filius Morgani salutem. Sciatis me consilio et consensu patris mei et amicorum meorum concessisse et dedisse et hac carta confirmasse Deo et ecclesie Sancte Marie de Marg(an) et monachis qui ibidem Deo serviunt in perpetuam elemosinam totam terram de Rossaul(in) cum omnibus pertinentiis suis in bosco et plano, in pratis et pasturis, in aquis et in omnibus aliis aisiamentis suis per has divisas, scilicet quicquid continetur inter aquam que dicitur Wrach et aquam que dicitur Cleudachcu(m)kake et inter aquam de Neth et viam magnam que vadit per montana de Torbethel usque ad Glinwrach et omnes commoditates aque de Neth inter duas aquas prenominatas, scilicet Wrac et Cleudachcu(m)kake, et communem pasturam tocius terre mee in montanis inter Auena(m) et Neth, ad habendum et tenendum libere et quiete ab omni servitio et consuetudine et exactione seculari sicut ulla elemosina liberius haberi et teneri potest. Et hoc totum warantizabimus eis ego et heredes mei contra omnes homines in perpetuum. Et hec omnia me fideliter et firmiter tenere super sacrosancta iuravi pro me et heredibus meis. Hiis testibus: Helia tunc decano de Novo Castello, Mauricio presbitero, Martino presbitero, Henr(ico) presbitero, David presbitero, Rog(er)o filio Wian, David Puignel, Ioh(ann)e Sóór, Grunu filio Ioh(ann)is et multis aliis.

This is a confirmation of Morgan ap Caradog's grant in no. 131 above, on which this charter is closely modelled. However, it is almost certainly later than Morgan's charter: although both charters have three witnesses in common, the witness list of Lleision's charter is identical to that of no. 155 below, and almost identical to that of no. 138 above, both of which are datable to *c*.1203 × 1205.

155 Margam Abbey

Grant in alms, with the consent of his father and friends, of the common pasture of all his land from the east side of the Neath as far as his land extends, free of all secular service, custom and exaction, so that he or his heirs will never allow any religious men into that pasture apart from the monks of Margam. He and his father have sworn on relics that they will faithfully observe this and warrant it for ever against all men, both religious and secular, as their alms. Witnesses.

[*c*.1203 × 1205)]

A1 = BL, Harl. Ch. 75 C 34. Endorsed: Leissan de communi pastura sua ex estparte de Neth (s. xiii in.); early modern endorsement; approx. 119 × 147 + 17 mm.; two central slits, one just above fold and one in fold, for a tag (*c*.9 mm. wide) which exits through a slit in the base of the fold; sealed on tag. Circular seal, light brown wax, imperfect, originally approx. 50 mm. diameter; figure kneeling on left before an abbot holding a book and blessing him; legend: . . . GILLVM . LEISAN . FI . . .

A2 = NLW, Penrice and Margam Ch. 109. Endorsed: Confirmatio Leisan de communi pastura (s. xiii in.); approx. 195 × 156 + 26 mm.; two central slits in fold for a tag (*c*.12 mm. wide) which exits through a slit in the base of the fold and to which is attached a circular seal, dark red wax, approx. 40 mm. diameter; equestrian, facing right; legend: + SIGILL' LEISAN FIL' MORGANI. Seal tag inscribed: de secundo sigillo (by scribe of charter).

B = NLW, Penrice and Margam Roll, 543/17. s. xiii[1]. (Omits witness list.)

C = NLW, Penrice and Margam Roll, 2093/14. s. xiii[1]. (From A2.)

Pd. from A1, *Cartae*, iii. 929–30 (no. 817).

Cd., Birch, *Catalogue*, i. 37–8; ii. 8; *H*, no. 64.

Universis sancte ecclesie filiis presentibus et futuris Leisan filius Morgani salutem. Sciatis quod ego consilio et consensu patris mei et amicorum meorum [a–]dedi et concessi[–a] et hac carta confirmavi Deo et ecclesie Sancte Marie de Margan et monachis qui ibidem Deo serviunt in elemosinam communem pasturam totius[b] terre mee ex estparte de Neth quantum terra mea durat in longum et in latum, ubique et in bosco[c] et in plano ad omnia aisiamenta sua, ad habendum et tenendum libere et quiete ab omni servitio et consuetudine et exactione seculari sicut ulla elemosina liberius haberi et teneri potest, ita quod nunquam admittemus neque ego neque heredes mei aliquos viros religiosos in pasturam ipsam preter predictos monachos. Et sciendum quod ego et pater meus super sanctuaria iuravimus quod hec omnia firmiter et fideliter observabimus et predictis monachis warantizabimus contra omnes homines tam religiosos quam seculares sicut elemosinam nostram in perpetuum. His testibus: Helia tunc decano, Maur(icio) presbitero, Martino presbitero, Henr(ico) presbitero, David presbitero, Rog(er)o filio Wian, David Pugneil,[d] Ioh(ann)e Soor,[e] Grunu filio Ioh(ann)is [f–]et aliis multis.[–f]

[a–a] concessi et dedi A2. | [b] tocius A2. | [c] boscho A2. | [d] Pugnel A2. | [e] Sóór A2. | [f–f] *omitted* A2.

This is a confirmation of Morgan ap Caradog's grant in no. 138 above, on which its text is closely modelled, and was almost certainly issued on the same occasion as both charters contain almost identical witness lists. This is a rare example among the acts in this edition of a grant extant in two originals.

*156 Neath Abbey

Grant of all the land which his father Morgan (Margo') *gave in perpetual alms between the Afan* (Auene) *and the Neath* (Neth), *namely (?) the Port Way* (Portwer) *and thence to the sea, 65 acres of arable near to their houses, the whole island within the large pool, all the land outside the (?) dyke* (valdam) *and common pasture, and all Morgan's land between the Afan* (Auene) *and the Thaw* (Thawi).

[Probably 1205 × 6 January 1208]

Mention only, in a confirmation charter for Neath Abbey of King John dated at Burbage, 6 January 1208 (TNA: PRO, C 53/8, m. 4; pd., *Rot. Chart.*, 174a; *Cartae*, ii. 316 (no. 317); cd., *CChR 1327–41*, 357; *H*, no. 111). For the dating see note to no. 140 above.

157 Margam Abbey

Grant in alms of all the gifts made to them by his father Morgan in the territory of Newcastle as attested in his charters. Witnesses.

[Probably *c.*29 September 1205]

A = NLW, Penrice and Margam Ch. 2027. Endorsed: Confirmatio Leisan de terra quam Morg' pater suus apud Novum Castellum (s. xiii¹); approx. 163 × 81 + 16 mm.; two central slits in fold for a tag (*c.*10 mm. wide) which exits through a slit in the base of the fold; sealed on tag. Circular seal, red wax, approx. 55 mm. diameter; equestrian, facing right; legend: ... SIGILLWM ... VN FILII MORGA ...
B = NLW, Penrice and Margam Roll 292/4. s. xiii.
C = NLW, Penrice and Margam Roll 2093/6. s. xiii¹. (Roll damaged.)
Pd. from B, *Cartae*, iii. 915 (no. 803).
Cd., Birch, *Catalogue*, i. 113; iv: i. 149; *H*, no. 89.

Omnibus sancte ecclesie filiis presentibus et futuris Leisan filius Morgani salutem. Sciatis me concessisse et hac carta confirmasse Deo et ecclesie Sancte Marie de Margan et monachis ibidem Deo servientibus in elemosinam omnes donationes quas eis fecit pater meus Morgan(us) in territorio de Novo Castello per omnia sicut carte ipsius testantur. His testibus: Wilfrid(us) sacerdos, Lucas clericus, Rob(ertus) Segin, Rob(ertus) Samson, Alaithur, Resus Coh, Rog(erus) Wian, Rog(erus) Aithan, David Puignel et multi alii.

This is very probably a confirmation of Morgan ap Caradog's grants in nos 142–3 above, datable to about Michaelmas 1205. As it is written by the same scribe as these (Patterson, *Scriptorium of Margam*, 96, 110, 119), and all the witnesses in Lleision's charter appear, in the same order, in both of Morgan's charters (although these add further names), it is likely that the present charter was issued at the same time as these.

158 Margam Abbey

Quitclaim of all his plaints against, and exactions from, the abbey concerning all the lands which its monks hold from him or his men in his fee. Confirmation of all grants, agreements and charters which his father Morgan ap Caradog, his brother Owain and their men made to the monks and all lands which they gave or sold them in Pultimor, *the marsh of Afan, Newcastle and all places beneath and on the mountains, so that they may hold them all freely as the charters of the aforesaid father, brother and men attest, and especially the land of Walter* Lageles *which his father gave to Margam in alms. Lleision has sworn on the relics of the monastery, namely on the body of Jesus Christ, the most precious wood of the True Cross and the relics of the holy apostles, martyrs, confessors and virgins (all of which relics are contained in one cross), placed on the high altar, that henceforth he will not disseise them of any land, plough, sow, weed, reap or remove their lands, mow or plough their meadows, or harm any of their horses or other animals in the pastures which they have in his fee on account of any anger or plaint which he has against them. If the monks offend him or fail to do for him what they ought to do by right, he will submit a claim to the bailiffs of the land and accept amends by the judgement of a court. He has sworn to observe all this for the whole of his life. Witnesses.*

[*c.*29 September 1205 × February 1207]

A = NLW, Penrice and Margam Ch. 106. Parchment slightly damaged. Endorsed: Confirmatio Leisan generalis (s. xiii in.); approx. 212 × 96 + 12 mm.; two central slits, one just above fold, one in fold, for a tag (*c.*14 mm. wide) which exits through a slit in the base of the fold; sealed on tag. Circular seal, green wax, approx. 55 mm. diameter; equestrian, facing right; legend: + SIGILLWM LEISAVN FILII MO[RG]AN.
Pd. from A, *Cartae*, iii. 916–17 (no. 805).
Cd., Birch, *Catalogue*, i. 36–7; *H*, no. 91.

Sciant omnes presentes et futuri quod ego Leisan(us) filius Morgani quitas clamavi omnes querelas et exactiones quas hactenus habui adversus domum de Margan' de omnibus terris et tenementis que monachi eiusdem domus tenent de me vel de hominibus meis in feudo meo. Insuper etiam hac presenti carta mea confirmavi eis omnes concessiones et conven-tiones et omnes cartas quas Morgan(us) filius Karadoci et Audoen(us) frater meus et homines nostri eisdem monachis fecerunt et omnia tenementa que eis dederunt aut vendiderunt tam in Pultimor et marisco de Auene quam in territorio de Novo Castello et in omnibus aliis locis sub montanis et super montana, ut habeant hec omnia et teneant libere et quiete inperpetuum sicut ulla elemosina liberius et melius potest teneri sicut carte predictorum patris et fratris et hominum nostrorum testantur, et precipue terram Walt(er)i Lageles quam pater meus dedit domui de Marg(an) in elemosinam. Et ego Leisan sciens et prudens super sanctuaria monasterii manu propria iuravi, scilicet super sacratissimum corpus domini nostri Iesu Cristi et super pretiosissimum lignum vere crucis et super reliquias sanctorum apostolorum et sanctorum martirum et sanctorum confessorum et sanctarum virginum quorum omnium reliquie in una cruce [conti]nebantur; super hec omnia [impo]sita magno altari iuravi ego sicut mihi expresse et manifeste nominabantur quod decetero de nullo tenemento suo dissaisiabo eos.... iam ... eos impediam ... faciam vel permittam terras suas arare, seminare, sarclare, metere vel colligere et asportare, neque prata sua falcare et cariare vel uoluntatem suam de omnibus rebus suis facere, neque aliquod nocumentum eis inferam vel inferri faciam aut permittam de equicio suo vel de omnibus aliis animalibus suis que habent vel habebunt in omnibus pasturis quas in feudo meo habent propter aliquam iram aut querelam quam habuerim vel forte habebo adversus eos. Set si in aliquo adversum me deliquerint vel si non faciunt mihi quod mihi de iure facere debent demonstrabo ballivis terre et per iudicium curie suscipiam inde emendationem. Et hec omnia iuravi me predictis monachis toto tempore vite mee observaturum. Hiis testibus: Walt(er)o de Sulie tunc vicecomite de Glamorg(an), Ric(ardo) Flama(n)g', Pet(ro) le

Butiller, Will(el)mo de Cantilupo, Walt(er)o Luvel, Steph(an)o clerico de Kenefeg',
Wasm(er)o, Thoma Albo de Kenef', Alaith(ur)o, Reso Coch, Griffin(o) filio Kanaith' et
multis aliis.

Morgan ap Caradog probably granted the land of Walter *Lageles* to Margam at about
Michaelmas 1205 (no. 142 above). Walter of Sully also witnesses as sheriff of Glamorgan
in two charters alongside William de Braose (d. 1211), presumably during William's
custody of Glamorgan (23 October 1202–February 1207) (*Cartae*, ii. 587–8 (nos 561–2);
Smith and Pugh, 'Lordship of Gower', 219). Falkes de Bréauté held the custody of
Glamorgan from February 1207 until January 1214 and also seems to have acted as bailiff
or sheriff there during that period (see e.g. *Cartae*, ii. 306, 312, 313, 319, 334, 338–9 (nos
302, 311–13, 319, 333, 338); *EGC*, 7). Although Walter was still sufficiently prominent in
Glamorgan in August 1213 to be the recipient, along with Richard Fleming, another
witness in the present charter, of a writ ordering an inquisition into damages incurred by
churches in the diocese of Llandaff, there is no evidence that he held the office of sheriff
during Falkes's custody of Glamorgan, and other sheriffs are attested for the period
c.1214–30 (*Rot. Claus.*, i. 164b; *Glamorgan County History*, iii. 689–90; cf. no. 159 below,
for Walter witnessing, without any title, alongside Falkes 'then sheriff of Cardiff').

159 Margam Abbey

*Grant in perpetual alms of all the land in the burrows of Afan [Aberafan Burrows] which the
monks folded in the time of his father and of himself, namely 14 acres to be held free of all
secular service, custom and exaction. The monks may put their fold wherever they wish on that
land, so that they will have all the corn from that land without giving any of it to Lleision or
his heirs, since he quitclaims all of this on behalf of himself and his heirs for ever. Witnesses.*

[*c*.1208 × 1214]

A = NLW, Penrice and Margam Ch. 2031. Endorsed: Leisan de xiiii acris in Berghes de Auene. C.
(s. xiii in.); approx. 182 × 90 + 27 mm.; two central slits in fold for a tag (*c*.15 mm. wide) which
exits through a slit in the base of the fold; sealed on tag. Circular seal, green wax, imperfect, origi-
nally approx. 55 mm. diameter; equestrian, facing right; legend: + S … M LEISAN …
MORGAN.
B = NLW, Penrice and Margam Roll 2090/5. s. xiii[1]. (Omits witness list.)
Pd. from A, *Cartae*, vi. 2290 (no. 1570).
Cd., Birch, *Catalogue*, iv: i. 150, 176; *H*, no. 80.

Sciant omnes legentes et audientes hanc cartam quod ego Leissan filius Morgani concessi
et dedi et hac carta confirmavi Deo et ecclesie Sancte Marie de Margan' et monachis ibidem
Deo servientibus in perpetuam elemosinam totam terram in Berghis de Auen' quam faldav-
erunt tempore patris mei et tempore meo, scilicet xiiii acras adminus ad habendum et
tenendum libere, quiete et pacifice absque omni servicio, consuetudine et exactione seculari,
sicut ulla elemosina liberius haberi potest inperpetuum. Et sciendum quod super terram
ipsam ponent faldam suam ubicumque voluerint, ita quod habebunt totum bladum quem
super terram ipsam lucrabuntur sine dare mihi vel heredibus meis aliquam partem, quia ego
totum quietum clamavi pro me et heredibus meis in perpetuum. Hiis testibus: Faukes tunc
vicecomite de Kardif', Walt(er)o de Sulia, magistro Rad(ulfo) Mailoc, Rog(er)o ab Yuor,
Rog(er)o ab Einiavn, Greg(orio) clerico, Herb(er)to de Auen', Will(elm)o ab Alewi,

Ioh(ann)e de Valle, Will(elm)o de Brist' monachis et Iustino converso de Marg(an) et multis aliis.

The reference to *tempore patris mei* suggests that the charter was issued after Morgan ap Caradog's death. Falkes de Bréauté, the first witness, was sheriff of Glamorgan or Cardiff (the titles appear to have been interchangeable) 1207–14 (see note to no. 158 above).

160 Margam Abbey

Grant in perpetual alms, by Lleision and his brother Owain, of all the marsh between the dyke of the English and the river Afan, and between the Afan and Margam Burrows (Berges), to be enclosed by an embankment and to be used as the monks wish, free of all secular service, custom and exaction for an annual render of half a silver mark at Michaelmas. The monks may build a bridge over the Afan between the aforesaid marsh and their land in Afan. A further grant in alms of all the pasture of the burrows of Afan [Aberafan Burrows] which the abbey held in the time of the grantors' father, for an annual render of 20s. at Michaelmas. Lleision and Owain will warrant all this for ever. When they made this gift the monks gave them 60s. in silver. They have taken Margam, with its men and moveables, under their protection against all men, and granted their bodies to the abbey for burial when they die. Witnesses (not named).

[*c.*1208 × 1217]

B = NLW, Penrice and Margam Roll 288/12. s. xiii[1]; NLW, Penrice and Margam Roll 2090/1. s. xiii[1]. (2090 is a continuation of 288.)
Pd. from B, *Cartae*, iii. 920 (no. 808).
Cd., Birch, *Catalogue*, i. 94; iv: i. 175; *H*, no. 78.

Omnibus sancte ecclesie filiis presentibus et futuris Leysan(us) filius Morg' et Owein frater suus salutem. Sciatis nos concessisse et dedisse et hac carta confirmasse Deo et ecclesie Sancte Marie de Marg(an) et monachis ibidem Deo servientibus in perpetuam elemosinam totum mariscum qui iacet inter Wallu(m) Anglor(um) et aquam de Auene et inter aquam de Auene et Berges ad claudendum fossato et faciendum inde quicquid voluerint et habendum et tenendum, libere et quiete ab omni seculari servitio, consuetudine et exactione, sicut ulla elemosina liberius teneri potest, reddendo annuatim solummodo dimidiam marcam argenti ad festum sancti Mich(aelis). Et facient pontem ultra Auene ubicumque voluerint inter predictum mariscum et terram suam de Auene. Preterea donavimus et confirmavimus[a] in elemosinam predictis monachis totam pasturam de Berges de Auene quam tenuerunt tempore patris nostri, reddendo inde annuatim xx solidos ad festum sancti Mich(aelis). Et hec omnia warantizabimus eis in perpetuum, et quando fecimus eis hanc donationem predicti monachi dederunt nobis lx solidos argenti, et nos suscepimus domum de Marg(an), homines et catalla eorum et protegendum, fovendum et manutenendam pro posse nostro contra omnes homines. Et dedimus predicte domui corpora nostra ad sepeliendum, quandocumque nos mori contigerit. Hiis testibus.

[a] *text in 288/12 ends, and text in 2090/1 begins, here.*

The reference to *tempore patris nostri* suggests that Morgan ap Caradog was no longer alive, and the association of Lleision's brother Owain may indicate that the charter was issued early in the date range. Cf. no. 151 above.

161 Margam Abbey

Grant in perpetual alms by Lleision and Owain sons of Morgan of all the meadow and land of Spinis *which the monks held in the time of their father, as it lies towards Newcastle, namely two furlongs eastwards from the muddy ford, then northwards to the land of* Seieth *and* Spinas *and whatever is beneath there, to be held free of all service, custom and exaction. They and their heirs will warrant the aforesaid land against all men as their free alms. If either of them should die, the survivor will warrant the gift. Witnesses.*

[*c.*1208 × 1217]

A = NLW, Penrice and Margam Ch. 2032. Endorsed: Leisan et Owein de terra de Spínís (s. xiii[1]); approx. 140 × 124 + 28 mm. Two slits in left-hand side of fold for a tag (*c.*11 mm. wide) which exits through a slit in the base of the fold; sealed on tag. Circular seal, red wax, approx. 40 mm. diameter; equestrian, facing right; legend: + SIGILL' OWENI FIL MORGAN. Two slits in right-hand side of fold for a tag (*c.*15 mm. wide) which exits through slit in base of fold; sealed on tag. Circular seal, red wax, imperfect, originally approx. 55 mm. diameter; equestrian, facing right; legend lost.
B = NLW, Penrice and Margam Roll 292/21. s. xiii. (Omits witness list.)
Pd. from B, *Cartae,* iii. 931 (no. 818).
Cd., Birch, *Catalogue,* i. 116; iv: i. 150; *H,* no. 86.

Omnibus sancte ecclesie filiis ad quos presens scriptum pervenerit Leissan et Owein filii Morgani salutem. Sciatis nos concessisse et dedisse et hac carta confirmasse Deo et ecclesie Sancte Marie de Marg(an) et monachis ibidem Deo servientibus in puram et perpetuam elemosinam totum pratum et terram de Spínís quam tenuerunt tempore patris nostri sicut iacet versus Novum Castellu(m), scilicet a Vado Lutoso versus orientem in longum habens duas quarentanas, inde extenditur versus *north* usque ad terram Seieth et Spinas et quicquid ibi est infra. Totam hanc terram concessimus predictis monachis habendam et tenendam in perpetuum libere, quiete et pacifice absque omni servicio, consuetudine et exactione sicut ulla elemosina liberius teneri potest. Et nos et heredes nostri warantizabimus predictis monachis prenominatam terram contra omnes homines inperpetuum sicut nostram liberam elemosinam. Siquid vero de altero nostrum humanitum contigerit qui superstes fuerit predictam donationem predictis monachis pro posse suo warantizabit. Hiis testibus: Howel filio Resi, Enea filio Rog(eri), Reso filio Rog(eri), David Puignel, Herb(er)to de Auena, Wrunu de Bagalan, Lewelino filio Meurich, Cradoco filio Meurich, Wrgano sacerdote de Auena.

This may be assigned to the same date range as no. 160 above. The precise location of *Spinis* in the fee of Newcastle is uncertain. See also no. 169 below.

162 Margam Abbey

Grant in alms of all the gifts, charters and agreements made by his father Morgan in pastures, meadows and lands in the marsh of Afan, the territory of Newcastle and Pultimor, as his charters attest. Lleision will warrant all this against all men. Witnesses.

[Probably *c*.1208 × 1217]

A = NLW, Penrice and Margam Ch. 2029. Endorsed: Confirmatio Leisan generalis (s. xiii[1]); approx. 180 × 115 + 22 mm.; two central slits in fold for a tag (*c*.17 mm. wide) which exits through a slit in the base of the fold; sealed on tag. Seal missing.
B = NLW, Penrice and Margam Roll 543/6. s. xiii[1].
C = NLW, Penrice and Margam Roll 543/18. s. xiii[1].
D = NLW, Penrice and Margam Roll 2093/18. s. xiii[1].
Pd. from B, *Cartae*, iii. 916 (no. 804).
Cd., Birch, *Catalogue*, i. 8; ii. 6–7; iv: i. 150–1; *H*, no. 84.

Omnibus sancte ecclesie filiis ad quos presens scriptum pervenerit Leissan filius Morgani salutem. Sciatis me concessisse et hac carta confirmasse monachis de Margan in elemosinam omnes donationes et cartas et conventiones quas fecit eis pater meus Morgan(us) in pasturis, in pratis, in terris in marisco de Auene, in territorio de Novo Castello, in Pultimor, in montanis, in bosco et in plano, in omnibus et per omnia sicut carte ipsius testantur. Et ego eis contra omnes homines hec omnia predicta pro posse meo warantizabo. Hiis testibus: Wurgano presbitero, Will(elm)o filio Aelwi, David Puigneil, Herb(er)to Palmario, Ric(ardo) preposito de Novo Castello, Wrunv filio Philippi.

The general nature of this confirmation and its reference to charters and *conventiones* in the plural suggest that it was issued after the death of Morgan ap Caradog.

163 Margam Abbey

Grant of all the gifts and confirmations made in alms by his father Morgan so that the monks may hold them freely as attested in his father's charters and documents. Lleision and his heirs will warrant these against all men for ever. Witnesses.

[*c*.1208 × 1217]

A = NLW, Penrice and Margam Ch. 111. Endorsed: Confirmatio Leisan de omnibus elemosinis patris sui (s. xiii in.); modern endorsements; approx. 166 mm. × 119 mm. deep on left, 129 mm. deep on right + 30 mm.; two central slits in fold for a tag (*c*.13 mm. wide) which exits through a slit in the base of the fold; sealed on tag. Circular seal, brown wax, approx. 55 mm. diameter; figure kneeling on the left before an abbot holding a book and blessing him; legend: + SIGILLVM LEISAN FILII MORGANI. Seal tag inscribed: de primo sigillo (by scribe of charter).
Pd. from A, *Cartae*, iii. 914–15 (no. 802).
Cd., Birch, *Catalogue*, i. 38; *H*, no. 88.

Omnibus sancte ecclesie filiis presentibus et futuris Leisan filius Morgani salutem. Sciatis me concessisse et hac carta confirmasse Deo et ecclesie Sancte Marie de Marg(an) et monachis ibidem Deo servientibus omnes donationes et confirmationes quas pater meus Margan(us) fecit eis in elemosinam ut habeant illas ita libere et quiete in omnibus sicut carte et scripta patris mei testantur. Et ego et heredes mei warantizabimus eas prefatis monachis contra omnes homines in perpetuum. Hiis testibus: Helia decano de Novo Castello, Maur(icio) presbitero Sancti Cadoci, Henr(ico) presbitero de Ponte, David Puignel, Andrea tunc cellarario de Marg(an), Will(elm)o del[a] Val monacho, Gnait(ur)o converso eiusdem domus.

[a] *sic in* A.

Another general confirmation of Morgan's grants but issued on a different occasion from no. 162 above, to judge by the witness list. As it seems to have been issued on the same occasion as no. 164 below it is probably later than no. 162, albeit in the same date range.

164 Margam Abbey

Grant of all the gifts and agreements, especially those in Afan and Newcastle, made by his father Morgan ap Caradog and his men so that the monks may hold them as their charters attest, free of all secular custom, service and exaction. Lleision will warrant these grants against all men for ever. He made this confirmation when he granted his body for burial at the abbey. Witnesses.

[*c*.1208 × 1217]

A1 = NLW, Penrice and Margam Ch. 110a. Endorsed: Confirmatio Leisan generalis (s. xiii in.); early modern endorsement; approx. 188 × 135 + 32 mm.; two central slits in fold for a tag (*c*.12 mm. wide) which exits through a slit in the base of the fold; sealed on tag. Circular seal, brown wax, imperfect, originally approx. 40 mm. diameter; equestrian, facing right; legend: + SIGI . . . IL' MORGANI. Seal tag inscribed: de s[ecundo sigillo] (by scribe of charter).
A2 = NLW, Penrice and Margam Ch. 110b. Endorsed: Confirmatio Leisan generalis de Auen' et de Novo Castello (s. xiii[1]); approx. 135 × 161 + 16 mm.; two central slits in fold for a tag (*c*.12 mm. wide) which exits through a slit in the base of the fold; sealed on tag. Circular seal, red wax, approx. 55 mm. diameter; figure kneeling on the left before an abbot holding a book and blessing him; legend: + SIGILLVM LEISAN FILII MORGANI. Seal tag inscribed: de primo sigillo (by scribe of charter).
B = NLW, Penrice and Margam Roll 2093/12. s. xiii[1].
Pd. from A1, *Cartae*, iii. 918 (no. 806).
Cd., Birch, *Catalogue*, i. 38; *H*, no. 83.

Omnibus sancte ecclesie filiis presentibus et futuris Leisan filius Morgani[a] filii Karadoci salutem. Sciatis me concessisse et hac mea carta confirmasse Deo et Beate Marie et monachis de Margan omnes donationes et conventiones et nominatim in territorio de Auena et de Novo Castello quas pater meus Margan(us) filius Karadoci et homines eius fecerunt predictis monachis ut habeant et teneant eas sicut eorum carte testantur liberas et quietas ab omni consuetudine seculari et servitio et exactione sicut ulla elemosina liberius haberi et teneri potest. Et ego warantizabo eas prefatis monachis contra omnes homines in perpetuum. Hanc autem confirmationem feci quando corpus meum dedi prefate domui ut ibi sepeliatur cum mortuus fuero. Hiis testibus: Helia decano de Novo Castello, Maur(icio) presbitero Sancti Cadoci, Henr(ico) presbitero de Ponte, David Puignel, Andrea tunc cellarario de Marg(an), Will(elm)o de Valle[b] monacho,[c] Gnait(ur)o converso eiusdem domus.

[a] Margani A2. | [b] Val A2. | [c] monaco A2.

Both A1 and A2 are written by the same scribe (Patterson, *Scriptorium of Margam*, 89–90, 112). The confirmation should probably be assigned to a later point in the same date range as no. 162 above, as it serves to reinforce the monks' title to land specifically in Afan and Newcastle (making no reference to *Pultimor* near Llancarfan), and includes grants by Morgan's tenants as well as those of Morgan himself. The presence of Andrew as cellarer of Margam possibly supports a date after Morgan's death, as William was cellarer in 1207 (see no. 130 above). The charter was almost certainly issued on the same occasion as no. 163 above, also written by the same scribe and whose witness list is identical. It is uncertain whether Lleision's grant of his body for burial was the same as that referred to in no. 160 above.

165 Margam Abbey

Grant in perpetual alms of 2 acres of land at Gumboldes Wille, *between* Crockerehulle *and the king's meadow, to be held free of all service, custom and exaction. Lleision and his heirs will warrant the gift against all men for ever. Witnesses.*

[*c*.1208 × 1217]

> A = NLW, Penrice and Margam Ch. 2030. Endorsed: Carta Morgani de Gumboldes Wille (s. xiii); modern endorsement; approx. 148 × 82 + 23 mm.; one slit in fold to left of centre for a tag (*c*.13 mm. wide) which exits through a slit in the base of the fold; sealed on tag. Circular seal, green wax, approx. 55 mm. diameter; equestrian, facing right; legend: + SIGILLWM LEISAVN FILII MORGAN.
> B = NLW, Penrice and Margam Roll 292/24. s. xiii. (Omits witness list.)
> Pd. from B, *Cartae*, iii. 914 (no. 801).
> Cd., Birch, *Catalogue*, i. 116; iv: i. 151; *H*, no. 100.

Sciant tam presentes quam futuri quod ego Leysan filius Morgani dedi et hac carta confirmavi Deo et ecclesie Sancte Marie de Margan et monachis ibidem Deo servientibus in puram et perpetuam elemosinam duas acras terre ad Gumboldes Wulle inter Crockherehulle et pratum regis, habendas et tenendas de me et heredibus meis in perpetuum libere, quiete et pacifice absque omni servicio, consuetudine et exactione sicut ulla elemosina liberius haberi potest et teneri in perpetuum. Et ego et heredes mei predictis monachis hanc donationem warantizabimus contra omnes homines inperpetuum. Hiis testibus: Gilib(er)to de Turb(er)uill', Will(elm)o de Cantelo, Hoel filio Resi, Rog(er)o filio Yuor, Radulfo persona, Griffino filio Knaiti(ur), Wrunu filio Philippi, Ric(ardo) Waleis, Walt(er)o Marker tunc preposito, Madoc fratre Griffini, David Lug et multis aliis.

The charter probably records a new grant by Lleision after his father's death, for it neither refers to the consent nor confirms a grant of Morgan ap Caradog. This dating is supported by the presence in the witness list of Gilbert (II) de Turberville, lord of Coity from 1207 (RCAHMW, *Glamorgan III. 1a*, 220). *Crokherehulle* (*Crokerehille* in no. 142 above) was located in Newcastle (Birch, *Margam*, 388).

166 Margam Abbey

Grant of all the gifts by his father and his men and by Lleision and his men as attested in their charters. When he gave this charter Lleision remitted all plaints and exactions at issue between himself and the monks. The monks gave him 5 pounds of silver on the octaves of the apostles Peter and Paul [6 July] 1213 for this grant and confirmation. He has also restored to them their land in Newcastle which he has unjustly ploughed and sowed, namely Argolesull, *together with its corn, so that they may hold that and all their other lands freely with all their appurtenances. He has sworn on the relics of the church of Margam that he will faithfully observe all this for ever. Witnesses.*

[On or shortly after 6 July 1213]

A = NLW, Penrice and Margam Ch. 107. Endorsed: Leisan de Argolesille (s. xiii[1]); modern endorsement; approx. 162 × 130 + 30 mm.; two central slits in fold for a tag (*c*.16 mm. wide) which exits through a slit in the base of the fold; sealed on tag. Circular seal, green wax, approx. 55 mm. diameter; equestrian, facing right; legend: + SIGIL ... M LEISAVN FILII MORGAN.
B = NLW, Penrice and Margam Roll 292/23. s. xiii. (Omits witness list.)
Pd. from A, *Cartae*, ii. 337 (no. 336).
Cd., Birch, *Catalogue*, i. 37, 116; *H*, no. 92.

Sciant omnes tam presentes quam futuri quod ego Leisan(us) filius Margani concessi et hac karta mea confirmavi Deo et Beate Marie de Marg(an) et monachis ibidem Deo servientibus omnes donationes patris mei et hominum eius et omnes donationes meas et hominum meorum sicut karte mee et karte eorum testantur. Et sciendum quod quando hanc kartam predictis monachis dedi, remisi eis omnes querelas et omnes exactiones que fuerunt inter me et predictos monachos. Et pro hac concessione et confirmatione dederunt michi predicti monachi v libras argenti in octavo apostolorum Pet(ri) et Pauli anno incarnationis dominice m° cc° xiii°. Remisi etiam eis terram eorum in territorio de Novo Castello quam iniuste aravi et seminavi, scilicet Argolesull' et bladum eiusdem terre ut habeant et teneant eam et omnes alias terras suas libere et quiete cum omnibus pertinentiis et libertatibus suis. Insuper iuravi super sacrosancta ecclesie de Marg(an) quod hec omnia predicta fideliter et firmiter observabo in perpetuum. His testibus: Mauritio presbitero, Wilfrido presbitero, Radulfo clerico, Grifino ab Kneiþur, Alaiþur, Rog(er)o ab Iuor, Radulfo Mailoc, Ada(m) filio Ailwardi, Alewi Ruht, Rob(er)to Samson, Thoma Asketil.

167 Margam Abbey

Grant in perpetual alms of all the gifts by Roger ap Gwion (Wian) *and his brothers from all their land in Lleision's fief of Newcastle, to be held free of all service, custom and exaction as attested in the charters which the monks have from the sons of* Gwion (Wian). *Grant that he will never trouble the monks concerning their place in the vill of Newcastle which Walter* Lagheles *gave them in perpetual alms. Grant of all gifts and confirmations of lands by his father Morgan, the latter's men and his own men in the fee of Newcastle, to be held in perpetual alms as attested in their charters. Lleision and his heirs will warrant all this for ever. A further grant that he will never in future trouble the monks or their property in order to receive renders in advance from the lands they hold in the fee of Newcastle nor will he receive renders from them for those lands before the term stipulated in their charters. When he gave this charter the monks gave him 40s. at Christmas 1213 and he then remitted all plaints and claims which he had against them before that day. Sealing clause; pledges; witnesses.*

[25 December 1213]

A = NLW, Penrice and Margam Ch. 108. Endorsed: Carta Leisan(i) de redditu pre manibus non exigendo (s. xiii in.); early modern endorsement; approx. 220 × 116 + 24 mm.; two central slits in fold for a tag (*c.*14 mm. wide) which exits through a slit in the base of the fold; sealed on tag. Circular seal, dark green wax, approx. 55 mm. diameter; equestrian, facing right; legend: + SIGILLWM LEIS[A]VN FILII … GAN.
Pd. from A, *Cartae*, ii. 335–6 (no. 335).
Cd., Birch, *Catalogue*, i. 37; *H*, no. 93.

Sciant tam presentes quam futuri quod ego Leissan(us) filius Morgani concessi et hac mea carta confirmavi Deo et ecclesie Beate Marie de Margan et monachis ibidem Deo servientibus in puram et perpetuam elemosinam omnes donationes quas eis fecerunt Roger(us) filius Wian et fratres eius de tota terra ipsorum filiorum Wian in meo feodo Novi Castelli, ut habeant et teneant predicti monachi predictam terram libere et quiete ab omni servicio, consuetudine et exactione sicut ulla elemosina liberius haberi potest inperpetuum per omnia sicut carte filiorum Wian quas prefati monachi inde habent testantur. Preterea concessi eisdem monachis et hac carta confirmavi quod nunquam ipsos monachos vexabo vel vexari permittam de orto suo in villa Novi Castelli quem eis Walter(us) Lagheles dedit in puram et perpetuam elemosinam. Concessi etiam sepedictis monachis et hac mea carta confirmavi omnes donationes et confirmationes terrarum quas fecit eis Morg' pater meus et homines sui et omnes donationes terrarum quas eisdem monachis fecerunt homines mei in feodo Novi Castelli, ut habeant et teneant predictas terras in perpetuam elemosinam per omnia sicut carte donatorum testantur. Et hec omnia ego et heredes mei predictis monachis warantizabimus in perpetuum. Concessi insuper eisdem monachis et hac mea carta confirmavi quod nunquam in posterum sepedictos monachos vel res ipsorum vexabo vel inquietabo pro redditu pre manibus accipiendo de terris quas tenent in feodo Novi Castelli nec redditum ab ipsis monachis accipiam de eisdem terris antequam veniat terminus in cartis ipsorum constitutus et nominatus. Et sciendum quod quando eis hanc cartam dedi tunc ipsi monachi dederunt mihi xl^a solidos anno scilicet incarnationis domini m^o cc^o tercio decimo ad natale domini et tunc eis remisi omnes querelas et calumpnias quas habui versus illos ante illum diem. Et ut hec mea concessio et confirmatio firma permaneat inperpetuum eam presenti scripto confirmavi et sigillo meo roboravi. Insuper me hec omnia servaturum salvos plegios inveni, scilicet magistrum Radulfu(m) Mailoc, Gilleb(er)tum de Turb(er)uill', Walt(eru)m Luuel tunc constabularium de Kenef'. Hiis testibus: magistro Rad(ulfo) Mailoc, Gilleb(er)to de Turb(er)uill', Henr(ico) de Vmfranvill', Walt(er)o Luuel, Alaith(ur) filio Ythenard, Griff' filio Knaith(ur), Madoc fratre eius et multis aliis.

For grants by Roger ap Gwion (*Wian*) and his brother Robert see note to no. 127 above.

168 Margam Abbey

Grant of Pulthimor *with all its appurtenances in return for an annual render of half a silver mark at Michaelmas for all service, as his father's charter attests and similarly the charter they first had from Lleision with his small seal. Before the seal by which the present charter is sealed he had two seals, by which the monks have various sealed charters which he confirms. He has sworn on the relics of the church of Margam that he will faithfully observe all this. Witnesses.*

[Probably May 1215 × 1217]

A = BL, Harl. Ch. 75 C 35. Endorsed: Ultima confirmatio Leisan de Pultimor (s. xiii in.); approx. 225 × 103 + 23 mm.; single central slit in fold for a tag (*c*.13 mm. wide) which exits through a slit in the base of the fold; sealed on tag. Circular seal, green wax, approx. 55 mm. diameter; equestrian, facing right; legend: + SIGILLWM . LEISAVN . FILII . MORGAN.
Pd. from A, *Cartae*, ii. 303–4 (no. 299).
Cd., Owen, *Catalogue*, iii. 569; *H*, no. 79.

Sciant presentes et futuri quod ego Leisan(us) filius Morgan' concessi et hac presenti carta confirmavi Deo et ecclesie Beate Marie de Marg(an) et monachis ibidem Deo servientibus terram de Pulthimor cum pertinentiis suis, reddendo mihi et heredibus meis annuatim dimidiam marcam argenti ad festum Sancti Michael(is) pro omni servitio, sicut carta predicti Morgan' patris mei testatur et similiter sicut carta mea quam inde habent cum parvo sigillo meo testatur quod primo habui. Nam ante hoc sigillum quo presens carta sigillatur habueram duo sigilla quibus predicti monachi habent diversas cartas sigillatas quas eis confirmo. Et sciendum quod ego affidavi et iuravi super sanctuaria ecclesie de Marg(an) quod hec omnia servabo eis fideliter et sine malo ingenio. Hiis testibus: Mauricio capellano de Sancto Caddoco, Rog(er)o ab Yuor et Enea et Maddoco filiis eius, Ernaldo tunc constabulario de Neth, Henr(ico) capellano de Ponte, Aluredo de Dumnoc et Philippo de Berkelay servientibus Reginaldi de Brause, Steph(an)o clerico de Kenef', Alaith' filio Ythenard', Ric(ardo) de Selebi tunc suppriore de Marg(an), Will(elm)o de Lichefeld', Walt(ero) de Kard', Helya de B(ri)stoll' monachis, Iustino et Espus conversis de Marg(an) et multis aliis.

The presence of two servants of Reginald de Braose (d. 1228) among the witnesses suggests a date no earlier than May 1215, when Reginald joined his brother Giles, bishop of Hereford in taking over the de Braose lordships in the central area of the Welsh March, and probably no earlier than Giles's death in November 1215 and Reginald's subsequent marriage to Gwladus Ddu, daughter of Llywelyn ap Iorwerth, after which Reginald received the lordship of Gower from Llywelyn. Reginald lost control of Gower to Llywelyn after giving fealty to Henry III in June 1217 and never recovered it (Smith and Pugh, 'Lordship of Gower', 221–2). For Morgan ap Caradog's charter granting *Pultimor* and Lleision's first confirmation charter, both datable to 1193 × 1199, see nos 132 and 152 above.

GWENLLIAN FERCH MORGAN
(fl. c.1200–c.1217)

169 Margam Abbey
Quitclaim of all her right and claim in the meadow and land of Spinis, *which the monks had held in the time of her father and which her brothers Lleision and Owain had afterwards given in perpetual alms, as attested in the charters the monks have concerning it, by the boundaries*

*between her remaining land and their land, namely two furlongs eastwards from the muddy
ford and northwards to the land of* Seiet. *Witnesses.*

[*c.*1208 × *c.*1217]

A = NLW, Penrice and Margam Ch. 123. Endorsed: Guenthlian de terra de Spinis (s. xiii in.);
approx. 157 × 57 + 15 mm.; two central slits in fold for silk cords, pink and yellow intertwined;
sealed on cords. Oval seal, red wax, very worn, approx. 37 × 30 mm.; neither the device nor the
legend is recoverable.
B = NLW, Penrice and Margam Roll 292/22. s. xiii. (Omits witness list.)
Pd. from B, *Cartae*, iii. 931–2 (no. 819).
Cd., Birch, *Catalogue*, i. 42, 116; *H*, no. 87.

Sciant omnes tam presentes quam futuri quod ego Wenthlian filia Morgani Deo et Sancte
Marie et monachis de Margan quietum clamavi totum ius meum et clamum quod habui in
prato et terra de Spinis quam predicti monachi tenuerant tempore patris mei, quam
Leisan(us) et Owein fratres mei postea dederant eis in puram et perpetuam elemosinam
sicut in carta illorum quam inde habent continetur per divisas factas inter terram meam
residuam et terram illorum, scilicet a Vado Lutoso de Hwitherel versus orientem per duas
quarentanas et versus *north* usque ad terram Seiet. Hiis testibus: Will(elm)o de Licheffeld',
fratre Iocelino et fratre Ric(ardo) conversis de Marg(an), Ioh(ann)e de Golcl', Wrunu filio
Philipp(i), Iago Seis, Ric(ardo) Walensi et multis aliis.

This must be later than the charter of Lleision and Owain granting *Spinis* (no. 161 above).
If, as is likely, the reference to the land of Lleision and Owain (*terram illorum*) indicates that
they were alive at the time of Gwenllian's quitclaim, the charter was probably issued no
later than 1217.

OWAIN AP MORGAN
(*fl. c.*1200–*c.*1217)

170 Margam Abbey
*Grant in alms of all the gifts and confirmations made by his father Morgan ap Caradog and
his brother Lleision of lands, meadows and pastures in the marsh of Afan, of the land of
Resolven with its appurtenances, of the pastures on the east side of the Neath as far as their
land extends and of the land of* Pultimor *with its appurtenances, to be held for ever free of all
secular service and custom and all exaction. Witnesses.*

[*c.*1203 × *c.*1208]

A = BL, Harl. Ch. 75 C 37. Endorsed: Hoen(us) filius Morg' de Pultimor. De Auen'. De Rossaulin.
De pastura sua ex estparte de Neth (s. xiii in.); early modern endorsement; 132 × 115 + 23 mm.;
two central slits in fold for a tag (*c.*13 mm. wide) which exits through a slit in the base of the fold;
sealed on tag. Circular seal, dark green wax, imperfect, originally approx. 40 mm. diameter; hand
holding a lance with a banner; legend: + SIGILL . HOWENI . F . . . NI.
B = NLW, Penrice and Margam Roll 2093/13. s. xiii[1].
Pd. from A, *Cartae*, iii. 935 (no. 823).
Cd., Owen, *Catalogue*, iii. 569; *H*, no. 65.

Omnibus sancte ecclesie filiis Hoen(us) filius Margani salutem. Noverit universitas vestra me concessisse et hac karta confirmasse in elemosinam Deo et eclesie Sancte Marie de Marg(an) et monachis ibidem Deo servientibus omnes donationes et confirmationes quas fecerunt eis Margan(us) pater meus et Leisan frater meus de terris et pratis et pasturis in marisco de Auena, et de terra de Roshowelin cum pertinentiis suis, et de pasturis ex hestparte de Neht quantum terra nostra extenditur in longum et in latum, et de terra de Pultimor cum pertinentiis suis ut habeant et teneant hec omnia in perpetuum libere et quiete ab omni seculari servitio et consuetudine et omni exactione sicut ulla elemosina liberius teneri potest. His testibus: fratre Iustino et fratre Cnaiþur conversis de Marg(an), Alaiþur filio Eþenard', Rog(er)o filio Wian, D(avi)d Puinel, Morgano filio Karadoci patre meo et Leisan fratre meo.

The witness list shows that the charter was issued during the lifetime of Owain's father, Morgan ap Caradog. The grant of pastures on the east side of the Neath by Morgan and its confirmation by Lleision are datable to *c*.1203 × 1205 (nos 138 and 155 above). For the other grants mentioned, most of which pre-date 1205 and none of which is necessarily later than that date, see nos 122, 135, 137 above (land in the marsh of Afan); nos 131 and 154 (Resolven); and nos 132 and 152 above (*Pultimor*).

171 Margam Abbey

Grant in alms of all the marsh between the dyke of the English and the river Afan and Margam Burrows (Berges), *free of all secular service, custom and exaction for an annual render of half a silver mark at Michaelmas. The monks may build a bridge over the Afan between the aforesaid marsh and their land in Afan. A further grant in alms of all the pasture of the burrows of Afan [Aberafan Burrows] which the abbey held in the time of Owain's father, for an annual render of 20s. at Michaelmas. Owain will warrant all this for ever. When he made this gift the monks gave him one mark. Witnesses (not named).*

[*c*.1208 × *c*.1217]

A = NLW, Penrice and Margam Ch. 2034. Endorsed: Owein de Marisco de Auen' (s. xiii in.); approx. 126 × 100 + 18 mm.; two central slits in fold for a tag (*c*.16 mm. wide) which exits through a slit in the base of the fold; sealed on tag. Seal missing.
B = NLW, Penrice and Margam Roll 2090/2. s. xiii[1].
Pd. from A, *Cartae*, vi. 2291 (no. 1571).
Cd., Birch, *Catalogue*, iv: i. 151, 175; *H*, no. 81.

Omnibus sancte ecclesie filiis presentibus et futuris Owein filius Morgani salutem. Sciatis me concessisse et dedisse et hac carta confirmasse Deo et ecclesie Beate Marie de M(ar)gan et monachis ibidem Deo servientibus in elemosinam totum mariscum qui iacet inter walla(m) Anglor(um) et aquam de Auene et Berches ad habendum et tenendum libere et quiete ab omni seculari servitio, consuetudine et exactione sicut ulla elemosina potest liberius teneri, reddendo inde annuatim solummodo dimidiam marcam ad festum Sancti Michael(is). Et facient pontem ultra Auenam ubicumque voluerint inter predictam mariscum et terram suam de Auene. Preterea concessi et confirmavi in elemosinam predictis monachis totam pasturam de Berches de Auene quam tenuerunt tempore patris mei, reddendo inde annuatim xx solidos ad festum Sancti Michael(is). Et hec omnia warantizabo eis in perpetuum. Et quando feci eis hanc donationem dederunt mihi marcam unam. Hiis testibus.[a]

[a] *text ends c.43 mm. before end of the line, c.16 mm. above the top of the fold.*

As it lacks both a seal and witness list, though space appears to have been left for the inclusion of the latter, this may have been a draft that was never validated by Owain. The text is very similar to that of no. 160 above, datable to *c*.1208 × 1210, granted jointly by Owain and his brother Lleision, although that charter contains details lacking here, including a promise to protect Margam Abbey and its property and the donation of the grantors' bodies for burial. The present charter may simply be another record, issued by Owain alone, of the transaction recorded in no. 160 and contemporary with the latter charter; alternatively it may be a later confirmation by Owain.

172 Margam Abbey

Grant in alms of all the gifts, charters and agreements made by his father Morgan in pastures, meadows and lands in the marsh of Afan, the territory of Newcastle and Pultimor*, as his charters attest. Owain will warrant all this against all men. Witnesses.*

[*c*.1208 × *c*.1217]

A = NLW, Penrice and Margam Ch. 2033. Endorsed: Confirmatio Oweni filii Morg' generalis (s. xiii in.); early modern endorsement; approx. 183 × 86 + 23 mm.; two central slits in fold for a tag (*c*.17 mm. wide) which exits through a slit in the base of the fold; sealed on tag. Circular seal, red wax, approx. 40 mm. diameter; equestrian, facing right; legend: + S ... OWENI FIL' M ... ANI.
B = NLW, Penrice and Margam Roll 543/7. s. xiii[1].
C = NLW, Penrice and Margam Roll 2093/7. s. xiii[1].
D = NLW, Penrice and Margam Roll 292/5. s. xiii.
Pd. from A, *Cartae*, vi. 2292 (no. 1572); from D, ibid., iii. 936 (no. 824).
Cd., Birch, *Catalogue*, i. 113–14; ii. 7; iv: i. 151; *H*, no. 85.

Omnibus sancte ecclesie filiis ad quos presens scriptum pervenerit Ohein filius Morgani salutem. Sciatis me concessisse et hac carta confirmasse monachis de Margan in elemosinam omnes donationes et cartas et conventiones quas fecit eis pater meus Morgan(us) in pasturis, in pratis, in terris in marisco de Auene, in territorio de Novo Castello, in Pultimor, in montanis, in bosco et in plano, in omnibus et per omnia sicut carte ipsius testantur. Et ego eis contra omnes homines hec omnia predicta pro posse meo warantizabo. Hiis testibus: Alaithur filio Ithelnard, Heneir fratre Alaithur, Reso filio Ruathlan, Madoc filio Rog(er)i, Anharoud filio Knaithur, Heneir fratre Anharoud, Vrien filio Weir, Ithelnard filio Madoc, Kenewrec filio Madoc, Meuric filio Keþeric, Hespus filio Meiler, Philippo fratre Hespus, Elidir fratre Philippi et multis aliis.

Apart from the difference in the grantors' names, the text of this charter down to the witness list is identical to that of no. 162 above, issued by Owain's brother Lleision *c*.1208 × *c*.1210. However, since the witness lists are completely different and the charters are in different hands, they are most unlikely to have been issued on the same occasion.

CADWALLON AP MORGAN
(fl. c.1200–c.1217)

173 Margam Abbey

Grant in perpetual alms of all the land of Resolven with all its appurtenances, namely between the river Gwrach and the river Clydach and between the river Neath and the great road leading through the mountains of Torbethel to Blaengwrach, all the produce of the river Neath between the Gwrach and the Clydach and of the woods below those boundaries, including honey and birds. A further grant of all gifts and confirmations by his father Morgan and brothers Lleision and Owain between the river Neath and river Afan as their charters attest. He has given and confirmed all this in perpetual alms free of all secular service, and sworn on the relics of the church of Margam faithfully to maintain all the above grants, to warrant them against all men and especially against the sons of Gwrgi and their stock, and not to maintain or warrant any man who does violence to the abbey unless he has first made satisfaction to it. Witnesses (not named).

[c.1203 × 1217]

B = NLW, Penrice and Margam Roll 543/19. s. xiii[1].
Pd. from B, *Cartae*, iii. 913–14 (no. 800).
Cd., Birch, *Catalogue*, ii. 8; *H*, no. 101.

Omnibus sancte ecclesie filiis presentibus et futuris Cadwalan filius Morg' salutem. Sciatis me pro salute anime mee et omnium antecessorum et successorum meorum concessisse et dedisse et hac carta mea confirmasse Deo et ecclesie Sancte Marie de Marg(an) et monachis ibidem Deo servientibus in puram et perpetuam elemosinam totam terram de Rossaulin cum omnibus pertinentiis suis in bosco et plano, in pratis et pasturis et omnibus aliis aisiamentis et libertatibus suis, per has divisas, scilicet quicquid continetur inter aquam que dicitur Wrach et aquam que dicitur Claudac'kan et `inter a` aquam de Neth et magnam viam que vadit per montana de Torrebeðel usque ad Bleinwrac et omnes commoditates aque de Neth inter duas aquas prenominatas, scilicet Wrac et Cleudacu(m)kac. Insuper etiam omnes commoditates totius nemoris infra predictos terminos existentes, tam in melle et avibus quam de omnibus aliis comodis de eodem nemore provenientibus. Preterea concessi et confirmavi predicte domui de Marg(an) omnes donationes et confirmationes quas Morg' pater meus et fratres mei Leisan(us) et Owein fecerunt eidem domui inter aquam de Neth et aquam de Auene per omnia sicut carte ipsorum testantur. Hec omnia dedi et confirmavi in perpetuam elemosinam predicte domui de Marg(an) ad habendum et tenendum libere et pacifice ab omni seculari servitio, sicut ulla elemosina liberius potest teneri. Insuper etiam iuravi super sanctuaria eiusdem `ecclesie b` de Marg(an) quod hec omnia predicte domui fideliter et firmiter tenebo et warantizabo pro posse meo contra omnes homines et precipue contra filios Wrgy et eorum progeniem et quod nullum hominem manutenebo vel warantizabo qui violentiam fecerit domui de Marg(an), nisi prius eidem domui satisfecerit. Hiis testibus.

a *interlined in B by a contemporary hand.* | b ecclesie *interlined in B above* dom' *dotted underneath for expunction.*

The charter is presumably later than those of Lleision and Owain confirming Margam's land in Resolven, datable respectively to *c*.1203 × 1205 and *c*.1203 × *c*.1208 (nos 154 and 170 above), but probably pre-dates Morgan Gam's establishment of sole authority over Afan by 1217. The implicit threat from the sons and grandsons of Gwrgi may indicate that the charter is earlier than a quitclaim of land in Resolven to Margam by three grandsons of Gwrgi, namely Ifor, Tudur and Cynwrig sons of Rhiwallon ap Gwrgi, made before Gerald, archdeacon of Brecon and the chapter of Brecon (*Cartae*, ii. 596 (no. 571)). However, this does not help to refine the dating of the present charter. As the quitclaim lacks witnesses and contains no other indicators of date, it is uncertain whether the archdeacon was Gerald of Wales or his nephew Gerald de Barri the younger, in whose favour he renounced the archdeaconry in 1203 and who held the office until at least January 1247 (see *St Davids Episcopal Acta*, 28–9).

MORGAN GAM
(d. February 1241)

174 Margam Abbey
Grant, for the salvation of his soul, of the New Marsh of Afan between the monks' new dyke and the dyke of the English, to be held so freely that no livestock of his or other men will enter the marsh or be pastured there from Easter to Michaelmas. From Michaelmas to Easter let this marsh be treated like the other. If the monks ever wish to restore this marsh to cultivation they will hold it as they first held the whole marsh by their charter. Witnesses.

[Probably *c*.1217 × 2 June 1231]

A = NLW, Penrice and Margam Ch. 115. Endorsed: Carta Morg' de novo marisco de Auene (s. xiii[1]); approx. 221 × 73 + 22 mm.; two central slits in fold for a tag (*c*.16 mm. wide) which exits through a slit in the base of the fold; sealed on tag. Seal missing.
B = NLW, Penrice and Margam Roll 2090/11. s. xiii[1]. (Omits witness list.)
Pd. from A, *Cartae*, iii. 921–2 (no. 810).
Cd., Birch, *Catalogue*, i. 40; iv: i. 177; *H*, no. 107.

Sciant omnes tam presentes quam futuri quod ego Morgan(us) filius Morgani pro salute anime mee concessi Deo et Beate Marie de Margan et monachis ibidem Deo servientibus novum mariscum de Auene quod iacet inter nova(m) walda(m) suam et walda(m) Anglorum ad tenendum de me et heredibus meis adeo libere et quiete quod nulla averia hominum meorum vel aliorum intrabunt in predictum mariscum a Pasca usque ad festum Sancti Mich(aelis) vel ibidem pascentur preter propria averia predictorum monachorum. Post festum vero Sancti Mich(aelis) usque ad Pascha fiet de illo marisco sicut de alio. Si vero predicti monachi predictum mariscum aliquando voluerint redigere in culturam tenebunt illud sicut prius totum mariscum tenuerant per cartam suam. His testibus: Gregorio tunc capellano de Auene, magistro Radulfo Mailoc, Rob(e)rto Samson, Ioh(ann)e clerico, Reso filio Rog(er)i, Washauet Gille, Will(elm)o de Licheffeld, Walt(er)o de Hau(er)ford monachis de Margan, fratre Rob(erto) Pulmor et multis aliis.

The dating limits are fixed by Morgan Gam's asssumption of sole authority in Afan and the death of the second witness, Master Ralph Maelog, on 2 June 1231 (*AM*, i. 79). The New Marsh of Afan was an approximately circular area comprising about 43 acres centring on SS 761 883 located south of the old course of the Afan at Morfa Newydd (RCAHMW, *Glamorgan III. ii*, 270 and map at 273).

175 Margam Abbey

Grant in perpetual alms of all gifts, confirmations and agreements by his father Morgan and brothers Lleision and Owain and their men concerning all lands which the monks held from them in the territory or fee of Afan, in meadows and marshes and the pasture of the sand dunes (meles), *as the charters of those grantors attest, in return for the customary farm paid to the aforesaid predecessors for all service and secular exaction, namely 20*s. *for the pasture of the sand dunes* (meles), *1 mark for the meadows in the marsh and half a mark for the New Marsh. A further grant of the land of* Pultimor *with all its appurtenances as the charters of the aforesaid father and brothers attest, in return for 40*d. *annually at Michaelmas for all service. A further grant that he will not trouble the monks or their property for any renders in advance before the end of the term set out in their charters nor commit any violence within or outside their granges. A further grant that henceforth he will not trouble or impede the monks with respect to their water of Afan nor remove their sheep from their pasture for any reason or anger he has against the monastery. He will not trouble or impede them with respect to the cultivation of their lands in the fee of Newcastle while Newcastle is out of his hands, but they will have peace from him and his men even if he wages war against others for Newcastle. He has sworn on the relics of the church of Margam that he will faithfully maintain all these commitments and warrant them against all men. Witnesses.*

[*c*.1217 × 1240]

A = NLW, Penrice and Margam Ch. 2035. Endorsed: Confirmatio Morgani filii Morg' de terris de Auene et de Pultimor (by scribe of charter); early modern endorsement; approx. 168 × 157 + 13 mm.; two central slits in fold for a tag (*c*.13 mm. wide) which exits through a slit in the base of the fold; sealed on tag. Circular seal, green wax, approx. 35 mm. diameter; a fleur-de-lys device; legend: + SIGILLVM MORGANI CA(M).

B = NLW, Penrice and Margam Roll 2090/9. s. xiii[1]. (Omits witness list.)

Pd. from A, *Cartae*, vi. 2350–1 (no. 1622).

Cd., Birch, *Catalogue*, iv: i. 151–2, 176; *H*, no. 102.

Sciant omnes presentes et futuri quod ego Morgan(us) filius Morgani concessi et hac carta mea confirmavi Deo et ecclesie Sancte Marie de Marg(an) et monachis ibidem Deo servientibus in puram et perpetuam elemosinam omnes donationes et confirmationes et conventiones quas Morgan(us) pater meus et fratres mei Leisan(us) et Owein et eorum homines eisdem monachis fecerunt de omnibus terris et tenementis que de ipsis tenuerunt in territorio vel feudo de Auene, tam in pratis et mariscis quam de pastura de meles, sicut carte ipsorum quas inde habent testantur, reddendo mihi inde annuatim solitam firmam quam predictis predecessoribus meis reddere solebant, scilicet pro pastura de meles xx solidos et pro pratis in marisco i marcam et pro novo marisco dimidiam marcam pro omni servicio et seculari exactione. Concessi etiam eisdem monachis et confirmavi terram de Pultimor cum omnibus pertinenciis suis sicut carte predictorum patris mei et fratrum meorum quas inde habent testantur, reddendo mihi inde annuatim quantum ad me pertinet, scilicet xl denarios ad festum Sancti Mich(aelis) pro omni servicio. Preterea concessi prefatis monachis et hac carta confirmavi quod eos non vexabo vel res ipsorum pro aliquibus redditibus meis pre manibus ab ipsis accipiendis antequam veniat terminus in cartis eorum constitutus et nominatus et quod nullam violenciam infra grangias eorum sive extra in pratis aut bladis aut in aliquibus eorum rebus inferam aut inferri permittam. Concessi etiam eis et confirmavi quod decetero non vexabo eos nec impediam de aqua sua de Auene aut aliquid inde contra eos faciam vel fieri permittam et quod oves eorum de pastura sua non ammovebo aut ammoveri permittam pro aliqua causa vel ira quam erga prefatam domum habuero. Preterea sciendum quod eos non vexabo nec impediam de terris suis colendis quas habent in feudo Novi Castelli quamdiu ipsum Novum Castellum fuerit extra manum meam, sed de me et de meis firmam pacem habebunt licet cum aliis pro predicto Novo Castello guerram habuero. Insuper etiam super sanctuaria eiusdem ecclesie iuravi quod ego et heredes mei hec omnia fideliter et absque dolo tenebimus et prefatis monachis contra omnes homines pro posse nostro warantizabimus. Hiis testibus: Owein(o) decano, Gregor(io) presbitero de Auene, Walt(er)o clerico, Kadwathlan filio Morgani, Alaith(ur) filio Ythen', Meurich Vap, Griffin(o) ab Kanaith(ur), Ener fratre eius, Philipp(o) tunc suppriore de Marg(an), Will(elmo) de Licheff', Iordan(o) de Hau(er)ford', Will(elm)o de Diuelin, Philipp(o) de Kenef', Ric(ardo) de Beleby monachis de Marg(an) et multis aliis.

This clearly belongs to the period after Morgan Gam had succeeded his brothers Lleision and Owain in Afan, and also shows that by the time of the charter the dynasty had lost control of Newcastle (Smith, 'Kingdom of Morgannwg', 39). The first witness, Owain, rural dean of Llandaff or Penychan, occurs elsewhere in 1193 × 1218 and in 1200 × 1218, but was no longer dean by 1240 at the very latest, for Henry of Cardiff occurs as dean in 1230 × 1240 and Master Adam in 1238 × 1240 (*Llandaff Episcopal Acta*, xxv).

176 Margam Abbey

Grant of all his common pasture between the Afan and the boundaries between the monks of Margam and the monks of Neath, in the marsh and in the sand dunes (melis)*, for the use of their cattle and other animals, to be held freely without challenge by Morgan or his heirs, in return for an annual render of 40d. on the feast of St Andrew [30 November] for all secular service, exaction and claim. Further grant of one suitable place in the said sand dunes* (melis) *to build a house for their cattle. Morgan and his heirs will warrant all this against all men. Sealing clause; witnesses.*

[*c.*1217 × February 1241]

A = BL, Harl. Ch. 75 C 21. Endorsed: Carta Morgani Gam de communa pasture in Melis et in mariscis de Auene (s. xiii med.); approx. 188 × 89 + 11 mm.; single central slit in fold for a tag (*c.*6 mm. wide) which exits through a slit in the base of the fold; sealed on tag. Circular seal, green wax, originally approx. 40 mm. diameter; equestrian, facing right; legend: + … IGILLV … ORGANI . GAM *.
B = NLW, Penrice and Margam Roll 2090/13. s. xiii[1]. (Incomplete.)
Pd. from A, *Cartae*, i. 165–6 (no. 166); from A, Clark, 'Lords of Avan', 21–2; from A, Clark, 'Contributions toward a cartulary', 183.
Cd., Owen, *Catalogue*, iii. 567; Birch, *Catalogue*, iv: i. 177; *H*, no. 90.

Universis Cristi fidelibus ad quos presens scriptum pervenerit Morganus Kam salutem in domino. Noverit universitas vestra me dedisse et concessisse et presenti carta confirmasse Deo et ecclesie Sancte Marie de Margan et monachis ibidem Deo servientibus totam communam pasture mee inter Auena(m) et divisas que sunt inter dictos monachos de Margan et monachos de Neth, tam in marisco quam in melis ad usum vaccarum suarum et ceterorum animalium, ita ut dicti monachi habeant et teneant dictam pasturam et utantur ea bene et in pace, libere et quiete sine contradictione mei vel heredum meorum, reddendo inde mihi vel heredibus meis quadraginta denarios annuatim ad festum Sancti Andree pro omni servicio, exactione et demanda seculari. Concessi etiam dictis monachis locum unum idoneum in dictis melis ad domum faciendum si voluerint ad opus vaccarum suarum. Hec omnia ego et heredes mei dictis monachis pro predicto servicio contra omnes homines warentizabimus. Et ut premissa firmitatis robur in perpetuum optineant presens scriptum sigilli mei appositione roboravi. Hiis testibus: Meuric ab Willim, Lewelino ab Rog', Reso fratre eius, Galfrido ab Hereb(er)t, Osberto et Thom(a) monachis de Margan, Hespus, Roberto, Petit conversis de Marg(an) et multis aliis.

The boundaries between Margam and Neath were probably those fixed in May 1208 in settlement of a dispute between the two houses over pasture rights (see note to no. 141 above).

177 Margam Abbey

Grant, for the salvation of the souls of himself and his predecessors and successors and on the advice of his friends, supported by an oath on the relics of the church of Margam, that he will henceforth faithfully observe all charters and confirmations of his predecessors, namely his father and brothers, as well as his own charters, confirmations and agreements. A further grant and oath that he will never henceforth disseise the monks of any land they hold from him or remove their livestock from any land they hold from him for any reason. If any dispute arises, either from his or from the monks' side, amends will be made amicably between them if possible. If not, amends will be made by the arbitration of two or three good men chosen by both parties. If he does not faithfully observe all this let the church do as it is entitled, and similarly with respect to the monks if they do not observe this. Sealing clause; witnesses.

[c.1217 × February 1241]

A = NLW, Penrice and Margam Ch. 73. Endorsed: Confirmatio Morgani Kam de omnibus cartis suis et patris sui et fratrum suorum (s. xiii med.); Quod non ponamur in placitum in curia de Auena (s. xiii/xiv); early modern endorsement; approx. 225 × 105 + 15 mm.; single central slit in fold for a tag (c.7 mm. wide) which exits through a slit in the base of the fold; sealed on tag. Circular seal, green wax, very imperfect, originally approx. 40 mm. diameter; equestrian, facing right; legend: + S ... MOR ...
B = NLW, Penrice and Margam Roll 2090/12. s. xiii[1]. (Omits witness list.)
Pd. from A, *Cartae*, iii. 925–6 (no. 813).
Cd., Birch, *Catalogue*, i. 26; iv: i. 177; *H*, no. 103.

Omnibus Cristi fidelibus presens scriptum visuris vel audituris Morgan(us) Kam salutem in domino. Noverit universitas vestra quod ego consilio amicorum meorum concessi pro salute anime mee et antecessorum et successorum meorum Deo et eclesie Beate Marie de

Margan et monachis ibidem Deo servientibus et etiam super sacrosancta eiusdem eclesie iuravi quod decetero quicquid hactenus fecerit fideliter tenebo omnes cartas et omnes confirmationes antecessorum meorum, scilicet patris mei et fratrum meorum, et similiter omnes cartas meas et confirmationes et conventiones quas dictis monachis feci. Concessi etiam eisdem et confirmavi et super sacrosancta iuravi quod nunquam decetero disseisiabo eos ab aliquo tenemento quod de me tenent nec amovebo nec faciam amoveri averia eorum ab aliquibus tenementis que de me tenent propter aliquam causam. Set si aliqua contro-versia emerserit inter nos ex parte mea vel ex parte monachorum emendabitur inter nos amicabiliter si fieri potest. Quod si non potest emendabitur per arbitrium duorum vel trium bonorum virorum ex utraque parte ad hec electorum. Et si fideliter omnia ista non obser-vavero bene faciat sancta eclesia quicquid ad se pertinet; similiter et de monachis si ex parte sua ista non servaverint. Et ut hec concessio mea rata permaneat et inconcussa presenti carta sigilli mei impressione roborata eandem confirmavi. Hiis testibus: Rad(ulfo) de Novo Castello, Gregorio capellano de Auen', Rad(ulfo) persona de Neth, Reso ab Rog', Lewelino fratre eius, Rob(er)to Scoto, Iacobo tunc suppriore, Osberno et Thoma de Cantelo monachis, Riredo et Espus conversis de Margan et multis aliis.

178 Margam Abbey

Grant in perpetual alms of all the land of Resolven with all its appurtenances, namely all that lies between the river Gwrach and the river Clydach and between the river Neath and the great road leading through the mountains of Torbethel to Blaengwrach, all the produce of the river Neath between the two aforesaid rivers and of the woods below those boundaries, including honey and birds, and the common pasture of all his land between the Afan and the Neath. He has confirmed all these as the charters of his father and brothers attest, and sworn on the relics of the church of Margam faithfully to maintain all the above grants and to warrant them against all men for ever. Witnesses (not named).

[*c.*1217 × February 1241]

B = NLW, Penrice and Margam Roll 543/20. s. xiii. Rubric: Carta Morgani Cam de Rossaulin.
Pd. from B, *Cartae*, iii. 928 (no. 815).
Cd., from B, Birch, *Catalogue*, ii. 8; *H*, no. 104.

Sciant omnes et presentes et futuri quod ego Morgan(us) filius Morgani concessi et hac carta confirmavi Deo et ecclesie Sancte Marie de Marg(an) et monachis ibidem Deo servi-entibus in perpetuam elemosinam totam terram de Rossaulin cum omnibus pertinentiis suis, scilicet quicquid continetur inter aquam que dicitur Wrach et aquam que dicitur Cleudac(um)ka(n)c et inter aquam de Neth et magnam viam que vadit per montana de Torrebethel usque ad Bleinwrac et omnes comoditates aque de Neth inter duas aquas prenominatas et omnes comoditates totius nemoris infra predictos terminos, in melle et avibus et in omnibus aliis comodis de eodem nemore provenientibus et communem pasturam totius terre mee inter Auene et Neth. Hoc totum confirmavi prefatis monachis de Marg(an), sicut carte patris mei et fratrum meorum quas inde habent testantur. Et iuravi super sanctuaria eiusdem ecclesie quod hec omnia supradicta eis fideliter tenebo, et absque dolo et contra omnes homines pro posse meo warantizabo in perpetuum. Hiis testibus.

For Morgan ap Caradog's grant of Resolven in 1193 × 1199, and confirmations by his sons Lleision and Cadwallon, see nos 131, 154 and 173 above. The present charter is presumably later than Cadwallon's charter, which refers to grants by Lleision and Owain, but not Morgan Gam.

†179 Margam Abbey

Grant by Morgan and his brothers Lleision and Owain that henceforth Morgan will not trouble or impede the monks with respect to their water of Afan nor remove their sheep from their pasture for any reason or anger he has against the monastery. He will not trouble or impede them with respect to the cultivation of their lands in the fee of Newcastle while Newcastle is out of his hands, but they will have peace from him and his men even if he wages war against others for Newcastle. He has sworn on the relics of the church of Margam that he will faithfully maintain all these commitments and warrant them against all men. Witnesses.

[*c.*1217 × February 1241]

B = NLW MS 3746D, loose paper no. V (transcript by William Floyd, ?1810–?1898). s. xix. Rubric preceding transcript: Collectanea Topographica et Genealogica Vol. 8, p. 36. V. Deeds connected with Newcastle and Swansea, Glamorganshire, in the possession of C. R. Mansel Talbot, Esq. Confirmatio Morgani Gam de terris &c. Monachis de Margan.
Pd. from B, *Cartae*, iii. 925 (no. 812); from B, Clark, 'Lords of Avan', 23; from B, Clark, 'Contributions toward a cartulary', 184.
Cd., *H*, no. 98.

Ego Morgan filius Morgani et fratres mei Leisan et Owein concessi eis et confirmavi eis (scilicet monachis) quod decetero non vexabo eos nec impediam de aqua sua de Avene aut aliquid iniurie contra eos faciam aut fieri permittam et quod oves eorum de pastura non amovebo aut amoveri permittam pro aliqua causa aut ira quam erga prefatam domum habuero. Preterea sciendum quod eos non vexabo nec impediam de terris suis colendis quas habent in feodo Novi Castelli quamdiu ipsum Novum Castellum fuerit extra manum meam, scilicet[a] de me et de meis firmam pacem habebunt licet cum aliis pro predicto Novo Castello guerram fecero. Insuper et supra sanctuaria eidem ecclesie iuravi quod ego et heredes mei hec omnia fideliter et absque dolo tenebuntur et prefatis monachis contra omnes homines pro posse nostro warrantizabimus. Huius testibus: Cuichlin filio Canan, Rederch et Ririd.

[a] *sic in* B *(the corresponding passage in no. 175 reads* sed*).*

There are compelling reasons for regarding this document as spurious. It lacks both an address and a notification and the text down to the witness list is almost identical to the final part of no. 175 above, suggesting that it has been taken from that charter. The names of Lleision and Owain have clearly been interpolated, with no attempt to amend the verbs to the second person plural, and the same is true of the gloss *scilicet monachis*. The witness list is, however, completely different from that of no. 175; its source can only be guessed. (The first witness is not attested elsewhere in the Margam charters.) The form of the document and the nature of the interpolations suggest that it was written after the medieval period, perhaps in the nineteenth century.

180 Margam Abbey

Grant in perpetual alms, with the consent of his wife Matilda and other friends, of all the gifts made to them by Gilbert de Clare, earl of Gloucester in the fee of Newcastle, namely all the moor between the moor which Morgan's father granted the monks by charter and the water of Baedan, as that water descends from the west and the stream of Cuthelindelake *descends from the east from* Treykik *to* Hollake*; also all the acres which the said earl granted by charter in the territory of Laleston, from the north side of the great road which leads towards* Walderes Crosse *in* Roueles Londe *and from the south side of that road, and similarly of Laleston. These lands are to be held free of all secular custom and service as freely as in the time of Earl Gilbert as the earl's charters attest. Morgan and his heirs will warrant these lands against all men and women and especially against all Welsh. Sealing clause; witnesses.*

[25 October 1230 × February 1241]

A = NLW, Penrice and Margam Ch. 2036. Endorsed: Carta Morgani Cham de terra de Novo Castello (s. xiii med.); approx. 196 × 130 + 16 mm.; one central slit in fold for a tag (*c*.6 mm. wide); sealed on tag. Seal missing.
B = NLW, Penrice and Margam Roll 292/28. s. xiii. (Omits witness list.)
Pd. from B, *Cartae*, iii. 927 (no. 814).
Cd., Birch, *Catalogue*, i. 116; iv: i. 152; *H*, no. 99.

Omnibus Cristi fidelibus presens scriptum visuris vel audituris Morgan(us) Cam salutem. Noverit universitas vestra quod ego consilio et consensu Matildis uxoris mee et aliorum amicorum meorum concessi et presenti carta confirmavi Deo et ecclesie Sancte Marie de Margan et monachis ibidem Deo servientibus in perpetuam elemosinam omnes donationes quas fecit eis Gilleb(er)t(us) de Clar' comes Gloucest(ri)e in feodo Novi Castelli, scilicet totam moram que iacet inter illam moram quam pater meus eis dedit et incartavit et aquam de Baythan sicut dicta aqua de Baythan ab occidente et rivulus qui dicitur Cuthelindelake ab oriente descendunt de Treykik usque in Hollake, et preterea omnes acras terre quas eis dictus comes dedit et incartavit in territorio de Lagelestun' tam ex aquilonari parte magne vie que vadit versus Walderes Crosse in Roueles Londe quam ex australi parte eiusdem vie et similiter de Lagelestun'. Has omnes terras concessi et confirmavi dictis monachis ut habeant et teneant easdem libere et quiete ab omni consuetudine seculari et servitio in perpetuam elemosinam sicut umquam eas liberius et melius tenuerunt tempore Gilleb(er)ti de Clar' comiti Gloucest(ri)e in omnibus et per omnia sicut carte eiusdem Gilleb(er)ti comiti quas inde habent testantur. Et ego et heredes mei omnes dictas terras dictis monachis warantizabimus contra omnes homines et feminas et maxime contra omnes Walenses. Et ut hec mea concessio et confirmatio firmitatis robur optineat in perpetuum presente cartam sigilli mei impressione roboravi. Hiis testibus: Reymundo de Sulia, Will(elm)o de Reygni, Roberto de Cantalupo, Ioh(ann)e de Croilli, Radulfo persona de Novo Castello, Will(elm)o de Lamays tunc decano, Rob(er)to Sampsun, Gregorio capellano de Auen', fratribus Ioh(ann)e la Ware et Will(elm)o de Mora monachis, fratribus Riredo et Espus conversis de Margan, Lewelyno filio Rog(er)i, Oweno filio Alaythur, Kenewreg Coh, Lowarh filio David et multis aliis.

Gilbert de Clare, earl of Gloucester died on 25 October 1230 (*Glamorgan County History*, iii. 685). For his confirmation of the moor in Newcastle described in the present charter see *Cartae*, ii. 429 (no. 439). Ralph (d. 1259), parson of Newcastle, occurs as a canon of

Llandaff in 1230 × 1240 and 1234 and became archdeacon of Llandaff in 1243; William of Llanmaes was rural dean of Gronydd and occurs in 1230 × 1240, 1234 and 1238 × 1240 (*Llandaff Episcopal Acta*, xxii–xxiii, xxvi). *Roueles Londe* was granted (as *Rofleslond*) to Margam by Morgan ap Caradog (no. 139 above). The significance of Morgan Gam's confirmation of the grants of his late overlord while Glamorgan was in royal custody during the minority of Gilbert's heir Richard is noticed in Altschul, 'Lordship of Glamorgan', 47, 49–50, and Cowley, *Monastic Order*, 197 and n. 14.

181 Judgement concerning Margam Abbey

Judgement by Elias, bishop of Llandaff and Morgan Gam of a dispute brought before them between Rhys Goch ap Rhys Goch and Margam Abbey over land between the river Garw and the river Ogmore which Rhys claimed to possess by hereditary right, over forest rights in that land and over the damages and injuries which each party claimed to have been inflicted upon it by the other. As it has been sufficiently shown by the charters given to Margam by William de Londres and by Rhys the elder and his brothers, as well as by oral testimony, that the said land was given irrevocably to Margam in perpetual alms by Rhys the elder and his brothers, Elias and Morgan have determined, with the assent of Anian and Llywelyn, friars preachers, and of Master Maurice of Christchurch, that Margam ought to keep the said land in perpetual alms without any claim by Rhys the elder and his brothers and their heirs. With respect to the forest rights it has been provided, with the advice of discreet men, that Rhys the younger may enjoy the forest right which his father and then he enjoyed in that land. If he can prove, by the arbitration of trustworthy men and without contradiction by the monks, his right to the pasture of three houses which he claims by reason of the said forest right, let him have it; if he cannot, let him cease from claiming it. Concerning the damages allegedly inflicted on each other, Elias and Morgan have provided that, because they could not establish the truth nor would anyone else be able to inform them more fully about these matters, the damages and injuries should be remitted by both parties for ever. Both parties, namely the abbot on behalf of his house and Rhys the younger, appearing in person before Elias and Morgan, have bound themselves by oath, the abbot in the word of God and Rhys on relics, on behalf of themselves and their successors to keep the terms of this arbitration, submitting themselves totally to the jurisdiction of the bishop if either of them should presume to go against the terms. Sealing clause; witnesses.

c.4 April 1234

A = BL, Harl. Ch. 75 A 25. Endorsed: Finalis compositio inter domum de Marg(an) et Resum Coh iuniorem de terra de Egliskeinwyr (s. xiii); per arbitrium Elye episcopi La(n)d' (s. xiv); approx. 182 × 180 + 30 mm. Single slit in left-hand side of fold for a tag (c.6 mm. wide) which exits through a slit in the base of the fold, sealed on tag. Pointed oval seal, dark green wax, approx. 70 × 50 mm.; a mitred bishop standing, his right hand raised in benediction and his left hand holding a staff; legend: ELIAS ... GRA ... ENSIS . EPIS ... S; pointed oval counterseal, approx. 38 × 28 mm.; a hand raised in benediction; legend: SECRETV(M) . ELIE . LANDAVENSIS. EPISCOPI. Single slit on right-hand side of fold for a tag (c.6 mm. wide) which exits through a slit in the base of the fold; sealed on tag. Pointed oval seal, dark green wax, very imperfect, originally approx. 40 × 28 mm. diameter; equestrian, standing and facing left; legend: ... ANI ...
B = NLW, Margam Roll 293/12. s. xiii.
Pd. from A, *Cartae*, ii. 499–500 (no. 496); from A, *Llandaff Episcopal Acta*, 70–1 (no. 77).
Cd., Birch, *Catalogue*, i. 118; *Episc. Acts*, ii. 709–10 (L. 363); *H*, no. 323.

Omnibus Cristi fidelibus presens scriptum visuris vel audituris Elias divina miseratione
Land(avensis) episcopus, Morganus Cam salutem in vero salutari. Noverit discrecio vestra
quod cum esset suborta quedam controversia inter Resu(m) Goh filium Resi Goh et
domum de Margan super terra que iacet inter aquam de Garwe et aquam de Uggemore,
quam terram dictus Resus de dicta domo petebat hereditario iure possidendam, et super
forestaria in dicta terra et etiam super dampnis et iniuriis sibi invicem prout dicebatur inter
partes irrogatis, lis inter dictas partes mota coram nobis arbitris ad hoc fideliter a partibus
electis hoc fine conquievit, videlicet quod cum sufficienter nobis constaret tam per cartam
W. de London' quam per cartam Resi senioris et fratrum suorum ad hoc dicte domui de
Margan datam, et eciam per vivam vocem, quod dicta terra predicte domui de Margan in
perpetuam elemosinam a dictis Reso seniori et fratribus suis pro ipsis et heredibus eorum
irrevocabiliter esset collata, nos dictam terram sepedicte domui absque clamio predictorum
Resi senioris et fratrum suorum et ipsorum heredum in perpetua elemosina debere
remanere perpetuo sumus arbitrati, assidentibus nobis fratribus Aniano et Lewelino predi-
catoribus et magistro Mauricio de Cristi ecclesia. Super forestaria vero discretorum
virorum consilio interveniente taliter fuit a nobis provisum quod Resus iunior iure
forestarie quo usus fuit pater eius et ipse in diebus suis prout debuit quod eodem iure libere
uteretur in dicta terra. Et si pasturam quam petit ratione dicte forestarie, scilicet trium
domorum, potuerit sufficienter probare quod illam per arbitrium virorum fidedignorum et
discretorum debeat habere, monachis non contradicentibus, illam habeat; sin autem, illam
petere omnino desistat. Super dampnis vero sibi ipsis alternatim ut dicebatur irrogatis, quia
de ipsis plene nobis non constabat nec esset qui plenius super hiis nos posset certificare,
provisum fuit a nobis quod dampna et iniurie tunc inter partes irrogate remitterentur
absque reclamatione in perpetuum. Partes vero predicte, scilicet abbas pro dicta domo ex
una parte et Resus iunior ex altera, coram nobis personaliter existentes pro se et successoribus suis ad standum super predictis articulis nostre provisioni et arbitrio, abbas scilicet
in verbo Dei, Resus vero inspectis et tactis sacrosanctis, sacramento se obligaverunt submit-
tentes se omnino iurisdictioni et cohercioni episcopi si forte aliquis illorum ausu temerario
predicte nostre provisioni presumere vellet contrahire. Ad cuius rei certitudinem presenti
scripto sigilla nostra apponere curavimus. Hiis testibus: magistro Ric(ardo) de Karlyon,
domino Will(elm)o Malet, Rad(ulfo) de Novo Castro, Ioh(ann)e capellano, Rog(er)o
Sturmy, Yoruard' ab Espus et multis aliis. Actum anno gratie m° cc° xxx° iiii° circa festum
Sancti Ambrosii.

For the charters of William de Londres, lord of Ogmore and Rhys Goch the elder referred
to here see *Cartae*, ii. 451, 364–5 (nos 366, 459). In view of the clause in William's charter
stating that his forester should have custody of the wood with the advice of the abbot of
Margam it is possible that Rhys Goch the elder held this office on behalf of the lord of
Ogmore (Griffiths, 'Native society', 191; for a different view see *Llandaff Episcopal Acta*,
71). The land in dispute lay in the forest uplands of the lordship of Ogmore, in the vicinity
of Llangeinor (SS 915 877) (see further RCAHMW, *Glamorgan III. ii*, 290–1; no. 188
below). The abbey secured a further victory in this dispute *c*.1 November 1234 when, again
in the presence of Bishop Elias and Morgan Gam, Rhys Goch the younger quitclaimed to
the monks all that he claimed in Llangeinor by virtue of forest right, including the three
houses in the pasture of Llangeinor (*Cartae*, ii. 488–9 (no. 490)). It is uncertain whether the
two Dominican friars, both of whom bore Welsh names, who gave their assent to the

present judgement came from the friary at Cardiff established by February 1242, when Henry III gave the Dominicans there 5 marks, as the date of the friary's foundation is unknown (*CLR 1240–5*, 105; cf. Easterling, 'Friars in Wales', 330).

MORGAN AB OWAIN
(*fl.* 1183–1246)

*182 Margam Abbey
Grant of Hafodhalog (Hevedhaloc).

[Probably November 1186 × January 1199]

Mention only, in a confirmation of Isabella, countess of Gloucester, datable to 1189 × January 1199 (*EGC*, 126 (no. 137)); also in King John's confirmation dated at Westminster, 15 May 1205, which describes the grant as being of Hafodhalog and all it contains between the Kenfig and the Baedan (*Rot. Chart.*, 149b; *Cartae*, ii. 291 (no. 287)). This charter must have been issued before nos 183–6 below, but was probably later than Pope Urban III's confirmation of 18 November 1186, which is silent on the grant. Hafodhalog grange included the site of Hafodhalog Farm (SS 841 846), located about 1 mile north of Kenfig Hill on the west bank of the river Kenfig, and extended almost 1 mile eastwards to the river Baedan (Aberbaidan Farm SS 855 844) (RCAHMW, *Glamorgan III. ii*, 285–6). For the spelling and etymology of Hafodhalog (often incorrectly represented as Hafodheulog) see Pierce, *Place-Names in Glamorgan*, 93–4.

183 Margam Abbey
Grant in perpetual alms, with the consent of his kin and heirs, of all his land of Hafodhalog between the river Kenfig and river Baedan and towards the mountains to the cross near the high road by the same boundaries as his father Owain held it, for an annual render of 20s. to him and his heirs on the eighth day before Christmas, in lieu of all secular service, custom and exaction. They may hold this land from him and his heirs freely with all its appurtenances, apart from the aforesaid annual render of 20s. Morgan and his heirs will warrant this land for ever against all men, both relatives and strangers. If any service is demanded from that land, he and his heirs will acquit all of it. He has sworn on relics faithfully to observe all the above for ever. Witnesses.

[12 June 1215 × 1222; probably 12 November 1218 × 27 October 1219]

A = NLW, Penrice and Margam Ch. 523. Endorsed: Carta Morgani filii Oweni de Hauodhaloch (s. xiii[1]); modern endorsements; approx. 214 × 94 + 21 mm.; two central slits in fold for a tag (*c.*15 mm. wide) which exits through a slit in the base of the fold; sealed on tag. Oval seal, green wax, approx. 35 × 25 mm.; a fleur-de-lys device; legend: + S. MORGAN MAB OEIN.
Pd. from A, *Cartae*, ii. 344–5 (no. 343).
Cd., Birch, *Catalogue*, iv: i. 161–2; *Episc. Acts*, i. 350 (D. 450); *H*, no. 95.

Sciant omnes tam presentes quam futuri quod ego Morgan(us) filius Owen(i) consilio et consensu parentum et heredum meorum dedi et concessi et hac carta mea confirmavi Deo et ecclesie Beate Marie de Marg(an) et monachis ibidem Deo servientibus in perpetuam elemosinam totam terram meam de Heuedhaloc que iacet inter duas aquas scilicet Kenef' et Baithan et vadit in montana usque ad crucem que sita est iuxta magnam viam per easdem divisas per quas unquam eam melius et plenius tenuit Owein(us) pater meus, habendam et tenendam de me et heredibus meis inperpetuum, reddendo inde mihi et heredibus meis annuatim solummodo viginti solidos octavo scilicet die ante natale domini pro omni servicio, consuetudine et seculari exactione. Hanc autem terram dedi eis cum bosco et plano, cum moris et mariscis, cum pratis et pasturis, in longum et latum, cum omnibus pertinentiis et libertatibus suis, ut habeant et teneant eam de me et heredibus meis libere et quiete et pacifice sicut ulla elemosina liberius vel quietius potest teneri, salvo mihi et heredibus meis annuo redditu viginti solidorum sicut predictum est. Et ego et heredes mei hanc donationem nostram prefatis monachis warantizabimus contra omnes homines tam propinquos quam extraneos inperpetuum. Et si aliquod servicium de prefata terra aliquando requisitum fuerit, ego et heredes mei illud omnino faciemus et adquietabimus. Et sciendum quod ego Morgan(us) affidavi et super sacrosancta ecclesie de Marg(an) iuravi quod hec omnia predicta fideliter et sine dolo servabo et tenebo predictis monachis inperpetuum. Hiis testibus: domino Gervas(io) Meneuen(si) episcopo, Martin(o) Men' archidiacono, Hoel' ab Trahar', Griffin(o) ab Meur', Ric(ardo) ab Moredu, Morg(ano) Kam, Alaith', Reimu(n)do de Sulie, Will(elmo) de Sum(er)y, Will(elmo) de Reigny, Will(elmo) de Cantel', Pet(ro) Buteller', Walt(er)o Luuel, magistro Rad(ulfo) Mailoc, Will(elmo) Luuel, Thom(a) clerico, Rob(erto) Sams', Reso koch, Griff(ino) ab Kanaith' et multis aliis.

Iorwerth (Gervase) was consecrated bishop of St Davids on 21 June 1215; Master Hugh of Clun was archdeacon of St Davids by 1222 (*St Davids Episcopal Acta*, 10, 27–8). As Margam lay in the diocese of Llandaff, the charter may well have been issued during the episcopal vacancy at Llandaff between the death of Bishop Henry on 12 November 1218 and the consecration of Bishop William of Goldcliff on 27 October 1219 (Griffiths, 'Native society', 194, n. 57). The survival of four similar charters by Owain from this period suggests that he and his kin had encroached upon Hafodhalog despite his earlier grant of the land to Margam in 1186 × 1199 (no. 182 above). Probably each of the four charters was issued on a different occasion: although the witness lists of each are similar, they are not identical, and there are other differences of substance.

184 Margam Abbey

Grant in perpetual alms, with the consent of his kin and heirs, of all his land of Hafodhalog between the river Kenfig and river Baedan and towards the mountains to the cross called Kauanescros *near the high road which leads towards the source of the Kenfig until it comes to the ford called* Rideuais *and from there the boundary of the land falls into the same ford. He has given this land with all its appurtenances freely apart from an annual render of 20s. to him and his heirs on the eighth day before Christmas, in lieu of all secular service, custom and exaction. Morgan and his heirs will warrant this land for ever against all men, both relatives and strangers. If any service is demanded from that land, he and his heirs will acquit all of it. He has sworn on relics faithfully to observe all the above for ever. Witnesses.*

[12 June 1215 × 1222; probably 12 November 1218 × 27 October 1219]

A = NLW, Penrice and Margam Ch. 2051. Right-hand side of parchment slightly damaged. Endorsed: Carta Morgani filii Owein de Hauedhaloch (s. xiii[1]); approx. 239 × 154 + 30 mm.; two central slits in fold for a tag (c.12 mm. wide) which exits through a slit in the base of the fold; sealed on tag. Seal missing.
Pd. from A, *Cartae*, vi. 2338–9 (no. 1615).
Cd., Birch, *Catalogue*, iv: i. 161–2; *Episc. Acts*, i. 350 (D. 449); *H*, no. 97.

Sciant omnes presentes et futuri quod ego Morgan(us) filius Owein consilio et consensu parentum et heredum meorum dedi et concessi et hac carta mea confirmavi Deo et ecclesie Beate Marie de Marg(an) et monachis ibidem Deo servientibus in perpetuam elemosinam totam terram meam de Heuedhaloc que iacet inter duas aquas Kenef' et Baythan et vadit ad montana usque ad crucem que vocatur Kauanescros, que sita est iuxta magnam viam que tendit versus Blein Kenef' donec veniat contra vadum qui vocatur Rideuais et exinde cadit divisa eiusdem terre in predictum vadum. Hanc prefatam terram dedi prefatis monachis in perpetuam elemosinam habendam et ten[end]am de me et heredibus meis libere et quiete cum bosco et plano, cum moris et mariscis, cum pratis et pasturis, in longum et latum, cum omnibus pertinent[iis et] libertatibus suis in omnibus locis et rebus sicut ulla elemosina liberius et quietius teneri potest, salvo mihi et heredibus meis annuo redditu viginti solidorum de predicta terra quem reddent mihi et heredibus meis pro omni servitio, consuetudine et seculari exactione singulis an[nis] octavo scilicet die ante natale domini. Et ego et heredes mei hanc donationem nostram prefatis monachis warantizabimus contra omnes homines tam propinquos quam extraneos in perpetuum. Et si aliquod servicium de prefata terra aliquando requisitum fuerit, ego et heredes mei illud omnino faciemus et acquietabimus. Et sciendum quod ego Morgan(us) affidavi et super sacrosancta ecclesie de Marg(an) iuravi quod hec omnia predicta fideliter et sine dolo servabo et tenebo prefatis m[onac]his in perpetuum. Hiis testibus: domino Gervasio Meneven(si) episcopo, Mart(ino) Meneven(si) archidiacono, Hohel ab Trahar', Griffin(o) ab Meuric', Ric(ardo) ab [M]eredu,[a] Morgan' Cam, Alaith(ur), Reimu(n)d(o) de Sullie, Will(elm)o de Sum(er)y, Will(elm)o de Reigni, Walt(ero) Luuel et multis aliis.

[a] *first letter of name missing because of hole in parchment (cf. nos 183, 185–6).*

See note to no. 183 above. The boundaries of Hafodhalog are described in greater detail here than in nos 184–5 and 187.

185 Margam Abbey
Grant in perpetual alms, with the consent of his kin and heirs, of all his land of Hafodhalog between the river Kenfig and river Baedan and towards the mountains to the cross near the high road by the same boundaries as his father Owain held it, for an annual render of 20s. to Morgan and his heirs on the eighth day before Christmas, in lieu of all secular service, custom and exaction. They may hold this land from him and his heirs freely with all its appurtenances, apart from the aforesaid annual render of 20s. Morgan and his heirs will warrant this land for ever against all men, both relatives and strangers. If any service is demanded from that land, he and his heirs will acquit all of it. He has sworn on relics faithfully to observe all the above for ever. For greater security he has found pledges: Hywel ap Trahaearn, Gruffudd ap Meurig and his brothers William and Hywel, Richard ap Maredudd, Morgan Gam, Alaithur ab

Ythenard and Rhys Goch. Witnesses, the first of whom, Bishop Iorwerth of St Davids, has attached his seal to the document.

[12 June 1215 × 1222; probably 12 November 1218 × 27 October 1219]

A = NLW, Penrice and Margam Ch. 120. Endorsed: Carta Morgani filii Oweni de Hefedhaloch (s. xiii); approx. 205 × 115 + 22 mm. Two slits in left-hand side of fold for a tag (*c*.15 mm. wide) which exits through a slit in the base of the fold; sealed on tag. Pointed oval seal, green wax, imperfect, approx. 70 × 45 mm.; a bishop holding a staff in his left hand; legend: ... GILLVM GERVASII ...; an oval counterseal, approx. 50 × 30 mm., worn away on right; a bishop standing; legend: ... NSIS . EPISCOPVS. Two slits in right-hand side of fold for a tag (*c*.13 mm. wide) which exits through a slit in the base of the fold; sealed on tag. Oval seal, green wax, very imperfect, originally approx. 35 × 25 mm.; a fleur-de-lys device; legend: ... B OEIN.
Pd. from A, *Cartae*, ii. 295–7 (no. 292).
Cd., Birch, *Catalogue*, i. 41; iv: i. 161–2; *Episc. Acts*, i. 351–2 (D. 450); *H*, no. 96.

Sciant omnes tam presentes quam futuri quod ego Morgan(us) filius Oweny consilio et consensu parentum et heredum meorum dedi et concessi et hac carta mea confirmavi Deo et ecclesie Beate Marie de Marg(an) et monachis ibidem Deo servientibus in perpetuam elemosinam totam terram meam de Hauedhalok que iacet inter duas aquas, scilicet Kenef' et Baithan, et vadit in montana usque ad crucem que sita est iuxta magnam viam per easdem divisas per quas unquam eam melius et liberius tenuit Owen(us) pater meus, habendum et tenendum de me et heredibus meis inperpetuum, reddendo inde mihi et heredibus meis annuatim viginti solidos octavo scilicet die ante natale domini pro omni servicio, consuetudine et seculari exactione. Hanc autem terram dedi eis eum bosco et plano, cum moris et mariscis, cum pratis et pasturis, in longum et latum, cum omnibus aisiamentis et libertatibus suis ut habeant et teneant eam de me et heredibus meis libere et quiete et pacifice sicut ulla elemosina liberius vel quietius potest teneri inperpetuum, salvo mihi et heredibus meis annuo redditu viginti solidorum sicut predictum est. Et ego et heredes mei hanc terram prefatis monachis warantizabimus et adquietabimus contra omnes homines tam propinquos quam extraneos inperpetuum. Et si aliquod servicium de prefata terra aliquando requisitum fuerit, ego et heredes mei illud omnino faciemus et adquietabimus. Et sciendum quod ego Morgan(us) affidavi et super sacrosancta ecclesie de Marg(an) iuravi quod hec omnia predicta fideliter et sine dolo servabo et tenebo predictis monachis inperpetuum. Et ad maiorem securitatem salvo tenore carte mee eis hos plegios inveni, scilicet Hoel' filium Traharn' et Griffin(um) filium Meur' et Will(el)m(um) et Hoel(um) fratres eius et Ric(ardum) filium Mored' et Morgan(um) Kam et Alaith' filium Ythenard' et Res(um) Choch. Hiis testibus: domino Gervasio Menev' episcopo in cuius presencia hec facta fuerunt et qui in huius rei testimonium huic scripto sigillum suum apposuit, Martin(o) Men' archidiacono, magistro Mathia de Brechen', magistro H. de Clune, magistro Will(elmo) de Cap(e)lla, H(e)nr(ico) de Vmfra(m)villa, Reimu(n)d(o) de Sulie, Will(elmo) de Sum(er)y, Will(elmo) de Reigny, Will(elmo) de Cantel', Petro Buteller', Walt(er)o Luuell', magistro Rad(ulfo) Mailoc, Thom(a) clerico, Rob(erto) Samson, Griffin(o) ab Kanaith' et multis aliis.

See note to no. 183 above. This charter resembles no. 186 below in naming pledges (though in the latter Rhys Goch is a witness, not a pledge) and in its reference to sealing by Bishop Iorwerth.

186 Margam Abbey

Grant in perpetual alms, with the consent of his friends and heirs, of all his land of Hafodhalog between the river Kenfig and river Baedan and by its boundaries towards the mountains, for an annual render of 20s. at two terms, namely 10s. at Easter and 10s. at Michaelmas, in lieu of all secular service, custom and exaction. They may hold this land from him and his heirs freely with all its appurtenances, apart from the aforesaid annual render of 20s. Morgan and his heirs will warrant this land for ever and especially against all their kin. He has sworn on relics faithfully to observe all the above for ever. For greater security he has found pledges: Hywel ap Trahaearn, Gruffudd ap Meurig and his brothers William and Hywel, Richard ap Maredudd, Morgan Gam and Alaithur ab Ythenard. Witnesses, the first of whom, Bishop Iorwerth of St Davids, has attached his seal to the document.

[12 June 1215 × 1222; probably 12 November 1218 × 27 October 1219]

A = NLW, Penrice and Margam Ch. 2052. Endorsed: Morgani ab Oweyn de xx solidos vacat (s. xiii²); approx. 150 × 124 mm. including tongue (*c.* 14 mm. wide) and remains of wrapping-tie, most of which is cut away; sealed on tongue. Seal missing.
Pd. from A, *Cartae*, vi. 2337–8 (no. 1614).
Cd., Birch, *Catalogue*, iv: i. 161–2; *Episc. Acts*, i. 351 (D. 451); *H*, no. 94.

Sciant presentes et futuri quod ego Morganus filius Oeni consilio et consensu amicorum et heredum meorum dedi et concessi et hac carta mea confirmavi Deo et ecclesie Beate Marie de Margan et monachis ibidem Deo servientibus in perpetuam elemosinam totam terram meam de Hauodhalauc que iacet inter duas aquas, scilicet Kenefeg et Baithan, et per divisas suas versus montana habendam et tenendam de me et heredibus meis in perpetuum reddendo inde mihi et heredibus meis viginti solidos ad duos terminos, scilicet ad Pascha decem solidos et ad festum Sancti Mich(aelis) decem solidos, pro omni servicio et consuetudine et exactione seculari. Hanc autem terram dedi eis ut habeant et teneant eam de me et heredibus meis libere et quiete et pacifice in bosco et plano, in moris et mariscis, in pratis et pasturis, in viis et semitis, in aquis et molendinis et in omnibus aliis rebus sicut ulla elemosina liberius et quietius teneri potest et haberi, salvo mihi et heredibus meis annuo redditu viginti solidorum sicut predictum est. Hanc autem terram ego et heredes mei warantizabimus predictis monachis in perpetuum et precipue contra omnem parentelam nostram. Et sciendum quod ego Morganus affidavi et super sacrosancta iuravi quod hec omnia predicta fideliter et sine dolo servabo predictis monachis in perpetuum. Et ad maiorem securitatem salvo tenore carte mee eis pleggios inveni, scilicet Hoelum filium Traharn et G(ri)ffinu(m) filium Meuric et Will(elmum) et Hoelu(m) fratres suos et Ric(ardum) filium Moreduth, Morgan Cam, Alaitho filium Ythenard. Hiis testibus: domino Gervasio Men' episcopo in cuius presentia hec facta fuerunt et qui etiam in testimonium huius rei huic scripto sigillum suum apposuit, Martino Men' archidiacono, magistro H. de Clune, magistro Mathia de Brekon', magistro Will(elm)o de Capella, Henr(ico) de Hunfrancuill', Reimu(n)do de Sulia, Will(elm)o de Reini, Will(elmo) de Sum(er)i, Will(elmo) de Cantelo, Petro Buteiller, Walt(ero) Luuello, Griffino filio Keneithur, Ris Coch', magistro Rad(ulfo) Maeloc, Thom(a) balistario, Ioh(ann)e clerico, Rob(er)to Samson' et multis aliis.

See note to no. 183 above. This differs from the other three charters concerning Hafodhalog issued by Morgan in this period in prescribing two terms for the payment of the annual render of 20*s.* and in the singling out of Morgan's kin in the warranty clause.

187 Margam Abbey

Notification of a final concord in the presence of William de Burgh, bishop of Llandaff between Morgan and the monks of Margam, namely that Morgan, with the consent of his heirs and other friends, has reduced for ever on behalf of himself and his heirs the accustomed annual render of 20s. for Hafodhalog to 2s., to be paid annually on the eighth day before Christmas, on account of the enormous damages he has inflicted on the horses, cattle, sheep and countless other property of the monks, damages whose value was estimated by prudent men at £153 sterling. In order that this final concord be kept faithfully in the future, Morgan wishes that if he or his heirs contravene it, the bishop of Llandaff or another ordinary shall be allowed to excommunicate him and his heirs and lay an interdict on their lands until they have given full satisfaction to the monks. As further confirmation he grants that the bailiffs of the earl, and especially the bailiffs of the castles of Neath and Llantrisant, may compel him to observe the above terms. He has also sworn on relics in the church of Margam faithfully to observe all the above and to defend all the monks' goods against all men. Bishop William, in whose presence and by whose advice this concord has been made, and Richard, earl of Gloucester, have appended their seals along with that of Morgan. Witnesses.

1246

A = NLW, Penrice and Margam Ch. 140. Endorsed: Carta Morgani filii Owen de ralaxacione redditus de Hauothaloch (by scribe of the document); approx. 229 × 133 + 16 mm. Two slits in left-hand side of fold for a tag (*c*.8 mm. wide) which exits through a slit in the base of the fold; sealed on tag. Oval seal, red wax, approx. 60 × 40 mm.; a bishop standing, his right hand raised in blessing, his left hand holding a crozier; legend: ... DEI GR ... ENSIS; oval counterseal on reverse, approx. 40 × 25 mm.; the Annunciation, the Archangel Gabriel on the right greeting the Virgin on the left, and a bishop (half-length) beneath them, under a rounded arch, in prayer; legend: ... ELENS. P' . AV ... P' . TE : LIBERE ... Two central slits in fold for a tag (*c*.9 mm. wide) which exits through a slit in the base of the fold; sealed on tag. Circular seal, green wax, approx. 70 mm. diameter; equestrian, facing right; legend: ... DI. DE G ... ; circular counterseal on reverse, imperfect, approx. 70 mm. diameter; device of a shield with three chevrons between two lions; legend: RE. COMIT ... Two slits in right-hand side of fold for a tag (*c*.7 mm. wide) which exits through a slit in the base of the fold; sealed on tag. Oval seal, green wax, approx. 35 × 25 mm.; a fleur-de-lys device; legend: + S' MORGAN . MA[B] . OEIN.
Pd. from A, *Cartae*, ii. 532–3 (no. 526).
Cd., Birch, *Catalogue*, i. 48–9; *Episc. Acts*, ii. 726–7 (L. 437); *H*, no. 324.

Omnibus Cristi fidelibus presens scriptum visuris vel audituris Morganus filius Owen salutem in domino. Noverit universitas vestra quod hec est concordia finalis facta anno domini millesimo ducentesimo quadragesimo sexto coram domino Will(elm)o de Burgo Landav'episcopo inter me et monachos de Margan, videlicet quod ego Morgan(us) consensu et consilio heredum meorum et ceterorum amicorum meorum pro maximis et enormibus dampnis que dictis monachis intuli, utpote in equitio et animalibus aliis, bobus scilicet et vaccis, rebus etiam aliis quamplurimis quas hic enumerare pretermitto, quorum dampnorum summa ad centum quinquaginta tres libras sterlingorum a viris prudentibus estimabatur, redditum viginti solidorum quem mihi annuatim reddere solebant pro Hauothaloch usque ad redditum duorum solidorum pro me et heredibus meis dictis monachos relaxavi et quitum clamavi in perpetuum, ita sane quod redditum duorum solidorum octavo die ante natale domini mihi et heredibus meis annuatim reddere fideliter non omittant. Et ut hec nostra finalis concordia a me et heredibus meis fideliter et sine dolo teneatur in posterum, volo quod si contra eam ego vel heredes mei venire presumpserimus aliquando, quod absit, ut statim liceat domino episcopo Landav' vel alii ordinario qui pro tempore fuerit in me et heredes meos et in terram nostram excommunicationis sententiam vel interdicti promulgare sine cause cognitione donec plenarie dictis monachis satisfecerimus. Ad maiorem etiam huius obligationis confirmationem concedo ut ballivi domini comitis et maxime ballivi castrorum de Neth et Landt(ri)ssen ad hec predicta inviolabiliter observanda nos compellant. Iuravi insuper tactis sacrosanctis ecclesie de Margan omnia predicta me fideliter observaturum et omnia bona predictorum monachorum contra omnes homines pro posse meo defensurum. Super hiis etiam omnibus ut hec nostra finalis concordia in perpetuum firmitatis robur obtineat dominus Will(elmu)s de Burgo Landav' episcopus in cuius presentia, consilio etiam et auxilio facta est et dominus Ric(ardus) comes Glou(er)nie una cum sigillo meo sigilla sua huic scripto apposuerunt. Hiis testibus: domino Will(elm)o Landav' episcopo, magistro Pet(ro) officiali, Radul(fo) de Novo Castello, Nichol(o) tunc decano de Gronnyth, Steph(an)o Bauzain tunc vicecomite de Gla(m)morgan, Walt(er)o de Sulya, Gilleb(er)to de Vmfra(m)uill', Ioh(ann)e de Regny, Will(elm)o le Fla(m)meng, Leysano filio Morg(ani) Cha(m), Owen ab Alayth', Yoruerd' ab Espus et multis aliis.

For earlier undertakings by Morgan with respect to Hafodhalog see nos 183–6 above.

MORGAN AP CADWALLON
(*fl.* 1191–1228)

188 Margam Abbey
Grant of all the gift which his father Cadwallon made of lands, pastures and other easements in his land as his charter attests. Morgan has granted this gift by the advice and consent of his friends so the monks may hold it in perpetual alms, free of all secular service and exaction. A further grant of all pastures throughout all of his land, which he ought to inherit through his father, in all places apart from cultivated lands and meadows. He has sworn on relics to warrant this gift against all men for ever and to protect the monks and their chattels in all places. Witnesses.

[Probably November 1186 × 1228]

A = NLW, Penrice and Margam Ch. 45. Endorsed: Morgani filii Kadwatlan debet esse cum Keuemab(er)hay (s. xiii[1]); approx. 185 × 112 + 11 mm.; two slits to right of centre in fold for a tag (*c.*15 mm. wide) which exits through a slit in the base of the fold; sealed on tag. Seal missing.
B = NLW, Penrice and Margam Roll 288/9. s. xiii[1].
C = NLW, Penrice and Margam Roll 293/8. s. xiii. (Omits witness list.)
Pd. from B, *Cartae*, ii. 486 (no. 488).
Cd., Birch, *Catalogue*, i. 17, 93–4, 118; *H*, no. 55.

Omnibus sancte matris ecclesie filiis presentibus et futuris qui hanc cartam inspexerint Morgan(us) filius Kaduathlan salutem. Noverit universitas vestra me concessisse et hac carta mea confirmasse omnem donationem quam fecit Kaduathlan pater meus domui de Margan et monachis ibidem Deo servientibus de donatione terrarum quam fecit eisdem monachis et de pasturis et aliis aisiamentis in terra sua habendis per omnia sicut karta ipsius testatur. Hanc donationem ego concessi predictis monachis plenius consilio et consensu amicorum meorum ut ipsi eam habeant et possideant in puram et perpetuam elemosinam, liberam et quietam ab omni seculari servitio et exactione. Et sciendum quod[a] ego concessi predictis monachis plenius omnia pascua per totam terram meam quam pro patre meo hereditare debeo in bosco et plano et in omnibus locis exceptis terris cultis et pratis. Et hanc ipsam donationem ego iuravi super sanctas reliquias quod warantizabo eis contra omnes homines inperpetuum et quod ego protegam eos et catalla eorum et custodiam pro posse meo in omnibus locis. His testibus: Odone de Novo Burgo, Meuric filio Rogeri, Vren filio Weir, Iuor Keloit et multis aliis.

[a] *written over an erasure* A.

The grant by Morgan's father Cadwallon ap Caradog is probably datable to November 1186 × October 1191 (no. 149 above). The phrase *per totam terram meam quam pro patre meo hereditare debeo* suggests that the present charter was issued before Cadwallon's death, and thus within the same date range. If so, Morgan was both confirming Cadwallon's grant and making an additional grant of pastures in the lands he was entitled to inherit from his father. The proposed date range is compatible with the presence of the first witness, Odo of Newport, who occurs elsewhere 10 August 1186 × 1191 (*Cartae*, ii. 388; vi. 2275 (nos 394, 1553)). The endorsement refers to Cefn Machen (Cefnmachen-uchaf SS 914 866) in the abbey's grange of Llangeinor, situated at the southern end of the mountains between the Garw and Ogmore valleys in the lordship of Ogmore: cf. *Kevenmahhaj inter aquam de Vgkemor et aquam de Garwe* in a charter of Cedifor ap Ralph (*Cartae*, ii. 363 (no. 364)). For other grants in Cefn Machen and Llangeinor (alias Eglwysgeinor) by Welsh freeholders and by William de Londres (d. *c.*1200) see ibid., 363–5, 370–1, 451 (nos 365–6, 374, 459) and also no. 181 above. Of all the grants of land in this area to Margam, only that of William was confirmed by Countess Isabella of Gloucester in 1189 × 1199 and by King John on 22 July 1207, a reflection of William's superior position as lord of Ogmore (*EGC*, 126–7 (no. 137); *Cartae*, ii. 308–9 (no. 306); cf. Davies, 'Lordship of Ogmore', 287–8, 290). Morgan ap Cadwallon promised to protect the grange of Llangeinor in no. 190 below.

189 Margam Abbey

Grant in perpetual alms of the common pasture throughout his land for their stud and other livestock, apart from corn and meadow, namely eastwards along the boundaries between his land and that of Hywel ap Maredudd, westwards along the boundaries with the land of Morgan Gam, southwards along the boundaries with the land of Gilbert de Turberville and northwards as far as Morgan's land extends towards those parts, for an annual render of 1 silver mark, one half payable at Easter, the other half at Michaelmas, for all service and secular exaction. Morgan and his heirs will warrant this pasture against all men for ever. If he is unable to warrant the pasture because of war or any other reason, or if the monks are unable to reach it because of war or any other impediment, they will cease to pay the mark until they can freely frequent it. He will not permit any of his men to deny them any pasture by appropriating it, apart from corn and meadow. He has sworn on the relics of the church of Margam faithfully to observe all the above. Witnesses.

[*c.*1217 × 1228]

A = NLW, Penrice and Margam Ch. 1957. Endorsed: Carta Morg' ab Cadwathl' de communa pasture sue (s. xiii in.); early modern endorsement; approx. 212 × 95 + 19 mm.; two central slits in fold for a tag (c.15 mm. wide) which exits through a slit in the base of the fold; sealed on tag. Circular seal, green wax, approx. 33 mm. diameter; device of a lion passant facing right; legend: + SIGILL' : MOGANI : FILII : KADFV.
B = NLW, Penrice and Margam Roll 293/9. s. xiii. (Omits witness list.)
Pd. from B, *Cartae*, ii. 487 (no. 489).
Cd., Birch, *Catalogue*, i. 118; iv: i. 126; *H*, no. 105.

Sciant omnes tam presentes quam futuri quod ego Morgan(us) ab Kadwathl(an) concessi et dedi in perpetuam elemosinam et hac carta mea confirmavi Deo et ecclesie Beate Marie de Marg(an) et monachis ibidem Deo servientibus communam pasture tocius terre mee in longum et latum tam ad equitium suum quam ad cetera averia sua excepto blado et prato, scilicet versus orientem sicut divise vadunt inter terram meam et terram Hoeli filii Moreduh et versus occidentem sicut divise vadunt inter terram meam et terram Morgani Kam et versus austrum per divisas que sunt inter me et Gileb(er)tum de Turb(er)uill' et versus aquilonem quantum terra mea se extendit erga partes illas, reddendo inde mihi et heredibus meis annuatim unam marcam argenti ad duos terminos, scilicet dimidiam marcam ad Pascha et dimidiam marcam ad festum Sancti Mich(aelis) pro omni servicio et seculari exactione. Et ego et heredes mei warantizabimus eis predictam pasturam contra omnes homines inperpetuum. Quod si forte propter guerram vel aliquem alium casum non poterimus eis prefatam pasturam warantizare, vel si ipsi ad eam propter guerram vel aliquod aliud impedimentum non poterunt venire, cessabunt interim prefatam marcam reddere donec possint libere eandem pasturam frequentare. Et sciendum quod non permittam aliquem hominum meorum prohibere eis aliquam pasturam apropriando eam sibi excepto blado et prato. Et ego Morgan(us) iuravi super sanctuaria ecclesie de Marg(an) quod hec omnia predicta servabo et tenebo prefatis monachis fideliter et sine malo ingenio. Hiis testibus: Will(elm)o de Licheffeld', Rad(ulfo) portario, fratre Iustin(o), Walt(er)o Luuel, Steph(an)o clerico, Alaith', Reso Choch, Griffin(o) ab Kanaith', Eneraud fratre eius, Rog(er)o Kam et multis aliis.

The land of Morgan Gam was Afan, over which he exercised sole control from *c.*1217; the charter makes no mention of Morgan Gam's elder brothers Lleision and Owain. In 1228 Hywel ap Maredudd, lord of Meisgyn, captured, blinded and castrated his cousin Morgan ap Cadwallon and annexed Morgan's lordship of Glynrhondda (*AM*, i. 36; Altschul, 'Lordship of Glamorgan, 47). Gilbert (II) de Turberville succeeded to the lordship of Coity in 1207; the date of his death is unknown (see note to no. 165 above).

190 Margam Abbey

Notification that he has taken under his protection the grange of Llangeinor and all the livestock of the monks which are in or near his land and warrants them against all his men and associates, and especially against the men of Brycheiniog and Senghennydd and the sons of Seisyll ap Llywarch. If any of the aforesaid men seize the monks' livestock he will send his faithful retinue to free them or, failing that, he will make amends for the damage from his own property. He will not permit any of his men or associates to claim land from the monks except

in that court where they ought to give and receive justice. He has sworn on the relics of the
church of Margam faithfully to observe all the above. Witnesses.

[*c*.1217 × 1228]

A = BL, Harl. Ch. 75 C 19. Endorsed: Protectio Morg' ab Cadwal' (s. xiii[1]); approx. 205 × 78 +
17 mm.; two central slits through fold for a tag (*c*.13 mm. wide) which exits through a slit in the
base of the fold; sealed on tag. Circular seal, red wax, approx. 33 mm. diameter; device of a lion
passant facing right; legend: + SIGILL' : MOGANI : FILII : KADFV.
B = NLW, Margam Roll 293/10. s. xiii.
Pd. from A, *Cartae*, ii. 301–2 (no. 297).
Cd., Birch, *Catalogue*, i. 118; *H*, no. 320.

Sciant omnes tam presentes quam futuri quod ego Morgan(us) ab Kadwathl' recepi in
custodiam meam grangiam de Egliskeinwer et omnia averia monachorum de Marg(an) que
sunt in terra mea vel prope terram meam ad warantizandum contra omnes homines meos
et omnes alios qui voluerint mecum esse vel circa me frequentare, et maxime contra
homines de Brechineoch et de Seingeheny et contra filios Seisil ab Lowar'. Et si aliquis
predictorum hominum ceperit averia eorum ego ponam fidele posse meum ad ea liberanda;
quod si non fecero ego pepigi cum eis quod reddam eis damnum suum de meo proprio.
Preterea sciendum quod non permittam aliquem hominum meorum vel aliquem alium qui
mecum esse voluerit vel circa me frequentare terram ab eis calumniare nisi in curia illa ubi
debent rectum facere et accipere. Et ego Morgan(us) iuravi super sanctuaria ecclesie de
Marg(an) quod hec omnia predicta servabo et tenebo prefatis monachis fideliter et sine
malo ingenio. Hiis testibus: Will(elm)o de Licheffeld, Rad(ulfo) portario de Marg(an),
fratre Iustin(o), Walt(er)o Luuel, Steph(an)o clerico, Alaith', Reso Coch, Griffin(o) ab
Kanaith', Eneroud fratre eius, Rog(er)o Kam et multis aliis.

This declaration was probably issued on the same occasion as no. 189 above as it has an
identical witness list and was written by the same scribe (Patterson, *Scriptorium of Margam*,
90, 116, 128). The Seisyll ap Llywarch whose sons are referred to in the warranty clause is
quite possibly identifiable with the witness of that name in two charters of Morgan ap
Caradog in 1205; if the Trahaearn ap Seisyll who witnesses after him in those charters was
his son, he may have been one of those perceived as threatening Llangeinor in the present
document (see nos 142 and 170 above). Morgan ap Cadwallon had earlier confirmed his
father's grant of land in Llangeinor to Margam (no. 188 above; cf. also no. 181 above).

GWYNEDD

GRUFFUDD AP CYNAN
(d. 1137)

191 Ralph, archbishop of Canterbury

Letter, from Gruffudd and all the clergy and people of Wales, requesting the consecration of their bishop-elect as soon as possible, since they have lacked a pastor for many years, during which they have been without chrism or any spiritual jurisdiction. It is the archbishop's duty to aid their church, as it is a daughter of his church. However, if they fail to obtain a bishop from Ralph, they will seek one from Ireland or some other barbarous region.

[Shortly before 4 April 1120]

B = Cambridge, Corpus Christi College MS 452, p. 309. s. xii[1].
Pd. from B, Eadmer, *Historia Novorum*, ed. Rule, 259–60.

Radulfo Cantuariensis ecclesie archiepiscopo, reverendo patri, Deo hominibusque dilecto Criphin(us) et universus clerus totius Gvalis et populus, orationes, devotiones, servitium et salutem. Supplices et humi pedibus vestris prostrati paternitatem vestram deprecamur, ut electum nostrum consecretis citissime in episcopum, pro Dei amore et salute anime vestre; quia cum magna calamitate per multos annos caremus pastore, in quibus nec crisma habuimus nec aliquid cristianitatis vere. Vestrum est igitur succurrere nostre ecclesie, quia filia est vestre matris ecclesie. Et si nunc, quod absit, episcopum non habebimus ex vestra parte, queremus aliquem de Hib(er)nia insula vel de alia aliqua barbara regione. In Deo crescat dignitas vestra.

The bishop-elect was David, identified by William of Malmesbury with David the Scot, the Irish master of the cathedral school of Würzburg who accompanied Henry V of Germany on his expedition to Rome in 1111 (William of Malmesbury, *Gesta Regum*, ed. Mynors *et al.*, i. 764–5; ii. 385). A *terminus ad quem* for the letter is provided by David's consecration as bishop of Bangor on 4 April 1120 (Eadmer, *Historia Novorum*, ed. Rule, 260; his profession of obedience to Ralph is printed in *Canterbury Professions*, ed. Richter, no. 67). The see had been vacant following the flight from Gwynedd, probably in the late 1090s, of the previous bishop, Hervé, a Norman appointee consecrated in 1092 who was translated to the newly created see of Ely in 1109 (Lewis, 'Gruffudd ap Cynan', 74). There seems no reason to doubt the letter's authenticity, and Conway Davies was probably correct to regard it as 'a home-made document, and not one dictated at Canterbury' (*Episc. Acts*, ii. 552); no Canterbury writer is likely to have drafted the penultimate sentence threatening consecration in Ireland. That such petitions for consecration were preserved in Canterbury is also shown by Eadmer's citation of several from Ireland and Scotland (*Historia Novorum*, ed. Rule, 76–7, 279–80, 297–8); none of these bear close verbal resemblances to the present letter. The significance of David's appointment as bishop is assessed in Lewis, 'Gruffudd ap Cynan', 75–6.

OWAIN GWYNEDD
(d. 23(?) November 1170)

(?)†192 Bernard, bishop of St Davids

Letter, from Owain, king of Wales, and Cadwaladr, announcing their obedience from now on, although hitherto he had not enjoyed their friendship. A certain Bishop Maurice had entered the church of St Daniel like a thief, without any invitation from them, concerning whose unjust status they have decided to submit to the bishop's counsel. With the aid of God and the bishop they do not wish to have such a pastor at all, but desire to supplant him totally as is just. Although up to now they have, through pride, denied the old right of the church of St David, namely the archbishopric, they recognize it now and are ready to do penance; therefore they will not delay making satisfaction to him concerning all these matters. They beseech him to come with Anarawd ap Gruffudd to meet them on the feast of All Saints [1 November] at Aberdyfi, so that they may discuss the above-mentioned matters and strive to restore the ancient right of his church.

[February × October 1140]

B = Vatican City, Biblioteca Apostolica Vaticana, MS Reg. lat. 470, fo. 16v. s. xiii.
C = ibid., fos 17v–18r.
Pd. from B, Davies, 'Materials', 300–1; from B, 'Giraldus Cambrensis: *De Invectionibus*', ed. Davies, 142–3; from C, ibid., 146–7.
Cd., *Gir. Camb. Op.*, iii. 59 (*De Invectionibus*, II. 9); Haddan and Stubbs, i. 345; *Episc. Acts*, i. 259–60 (D. 122); *H*, no. 325.

B.[a] Dei gratia Meneven(si) episcopo Oene(us) rex Wallie[b] et Kadwaladerus[c] salutem et omne bonum. Notum sit vestre potestati, licet ante non profuerit nostra vobis amicitia, nos amodo nostram vobis propalare obedientiam. Non lateat etiam vestram clementiam quendam hominem Mauritiu(m)[d] episcopum nomine Sancti Daniel'[e] ecclesiam non per hostium sed aliunde, ut fur vel latro, nobis omnibus invitis intrasse, de cuius statu iniusto decretum est nobis vestrum inconcussum subire consilium. Talem enim pastorem nostre ecclesie animeque nostre tutorem esse Deo et vobis auxiliantibus nullatenus volumus, sed cum iustum sit, eum omnino supplantare desideramus. Hactenus autem ecclesie Sancti D(avi)d vetus ius, scilicet archiepiscopatum, superbie radice subtraximus, quod demum recognoscimus atque penitere non denegamus; ideoque satisfactionem vobis facere de omnibus hiis non protelamus. Quamobrem vestram `obtestamur dignitatem quatinus pro Dei amore nostraque petitione cum Anaraud filio G(ri)ffini in festo omnium sanctorum ad hostium Deui erga nos omni excusatione remota veniatis, ut deliberationem de supradictis agamus et vestre ecclesie antiquum ius restituere nitamur.

[a] Sernardo (*sic for* Bernardo) C. | [b] Wall' B. | [c] Kadwalladerus C. | [d] Mauricium C. | [e] Daniel C.

As the present letter is preserved only in Gerald of Wales's *De Invectionibus* (completed 1216), it is possible that Gerald forged it in order to demonstrate that the metropolitan claims of St Davids (renewed by him between 1198 and 1203) had been supported by Gwynedd rulers in the past. However, the balance of probability is against its being an outright fabrication. It is implausible that Gerald would have gone to the lengths of presenting such support in the context of a campaign by the secular power to remove a canonically consecrated bishop of Bangor. Moreover, while supportive of Bishop Bernard's campaign to secure metropolitan status for St Davids, the letter primarily reflects the objectives of Owain and Cadwaladr in Gwynedd and is therefore unlikely to have been composed at St Davids in the time of Bernard. Yet, though probably not concocted *ex nihilo*, the letter may have been doctored by Gerald to emphasize the senders' submission to St Davids, and the extent to which it represents an authentic document sent by Owain and Cadwaladr is therefore uncertain.

It is quite conceivable that the brothers sought an alliance with Bishop Bernard of St Davids in a bid to reassert control over the church of Bangor. Meurig (Maurice) gave fealty to King Stephen as bishop-elect of Bangor at Worcester on or around 3 December 1139, despite having been ordered not to do so by the archdeacon – probably Simeon of Clynnog – of his predecessor Bishop David, and was consecrated by Archbishop Theobald on or shortly after 31 January 1140 (*Chronicle of John of Worcester*, iii, ed. McGurk, 278–9, 284–5; Richter, *Giraldus*, 31). The letter appears to have been written in response to these events, and thus, inasmuch as it is authentic, after Meurig's consecration early in 1140 but before the date of the proposed meeting at Aberdyfi on 1 November, presumably in the same year. There is no evidence to show whether the meeting took place or whether Owain and Cadwaladr made any other contact with Bernard. However, despite the brothers' objections, Meurig established himself as bishop at Bangor (though when precisely is uncertain), for he later fled from his diocese to Canterbury, probably *c*.1154 × 1157, after falling out with Owain and many of his clergy on account of his attempts to promote ecclesiastical reform; it is unknown whether he returned to Bangor before his death on 12 August 1161. See *HW*, ii. 483–4; Richter, *Giraldus*, 31–2; *Letters of John of Salisbury*, i, no. 87; Pryce, 'Esgobaeth Bangor', 44–5. Bernard, bishop of St Davids 1115–48, probably began his unsuccessful campaign to secure recognition of St Davids as a metropolitan see with authority over the other Welsh bishoprics in the late 1130s (Richter, *Giraldus*, 38–52; *St Davids Episcopal Acta*, 4). Anarawd ap Gruffudd was the eldest son and successor of Gruffudd ap Rhys (d. 1137), ruler of Deheubarth. He found favour with the clergy of St Davids for killing the Flemish leader Letard Litelking, described in the Annals of St Davids as 'an enemy of God and St David', in 1137 and negotiated a truce with Owain and Cadwaladr in 1138. By 1143 he was betrothed to a daughter of Owain, and this alliance may explain why he was murdered by Cadwaladr's warband in that year (*AC*, 40–2; *BT, Pen20Tr*, 53; *BT, RBH*, 118–19).

193 Louis VII, king of France

Letter, informing the king that, since he has heard of his virtue, dignity and nobility from rumour and the truthful report of many, Owain has long desired to come to the king's notice and have his friendship. Though he has hitherto been hindered by the rarity of travellers and the distance of places between them, from now on he shall endeavour to obtain this friendship by both writing and messenger. Placing himself and his possessions at the king's command, Owain prays that, though largely unknown to him up to now, the king may deign to consider him amongst his faithful and devoted friends, and asks him to reply to this petition without delay through the bearer of the present letter.

[*c.*October 1163 × July 1165]

> B = Vatican City, Biblioteca Apostolica Vaticana, MS Reg. lat. 179, fo. 234v. s. xii ex.
> Printed from B, *HFS*, iv. 733 (no. 472); from B, Pryce, 'Owain Gwynedd', 26 (and trans., ibid., 4); from *HFS*, *RHF*, xvi. 116 (no. 357).
> Cd., Teske, *Briefsammlungen*, 398 (no. 474); *H*, no. 327.

L. gloriosissimo Francor(um) regi Owin(us) rex Walie salutem et devotissimum obsequium. Ex quo vestre virtutis magnificentiam et amplissimam vestre dignitatis ac nobilitatis excellentiam fama nuntiante et veridica multorum relatione accepi, in vestre celsitudinis notitiam venire, et dulcissimam vestram amicitiam habere, summo desiderio a multis temporibus desideravi. Sed quod hactenus, commeantium raritate impediente et locorum distantia, obtinere non potui, decetero ut obtineam tam scripto quam nuntio diligenter laborabo. Me igitur et mea, si qua vobis placent, vestre voluntati ad nutum exponens, summa precum instantia deposco quatinus me, hucusque multimode[a] discretioni vestre incognitum, inter vestros fideles et devotos amicos amodo habere dignemini. Quid autem carissime vestre dilectioni super petitione proposita placuerit, per presentium latorem michi significare non differatis. Valeant qui vos feliciter et diu regnare desiderant. Valete.

[a] multirude B.

The dating and significance of this and the other two letters from Owain to the Capetian court are discussed in Pryce, 'Owain Gwynedd'. The present letter appears to be Owain's first approach to Louis VII (1137–80) and thus pre-dates no. 196, written no earlier than September 1165. Although, in contrast to the latter, the present letter makes no mention of hostility from the king of England, the decision to seek Louis's support was probably part of a broader strategy by Owain to defy Henry II. If so, the letter is unlikely to have been written earlier than the autumn of 1163: Owain did homage to Henry II on 1 July of that year, but had apparently greatly angered the king by October through his assumption of the title 'prince'. However, Owain's defiance of the king only turned into open rebellion in the late autumn of 1164, and the initial approach may therefore have taken place between that date and Henry II's ill-fated Welsh campaign of July–August 1165 (Pryce, 'Owain Gwynedd', 4–5).

194 Hugh de Champfleury, bishop of Soissons and chancellor of the king of France

Letter, thanking God and the bishop for what the latter had written to Owain through his messenger Moses, namely that if Owain should send his messenger to the king of France again, he should make him come through the bishop, so that with his help the messenger's purpose might be accomplished more effectively. Owain is therefore sending this Moses as his messenger to consult with the bishop concerning his business, and entreats him to support Moses with respect to the king and to assist Owain's side.

[*c*. November 1163 × July 1165]

B = Vatican City, Biblioteca Apostolica Vaticana, MS Reg. lat. 179, fos 230v–231r. s. xii ex.
Pd. from B, *HFS*, iv. 729 (no. 460); from B, Pryce, 'Owain Gwynedd', 26–7 (and trans., ibid., 6); from *HFS*, *RHF*, xvi. 205 (no. 29).
Cd., Teske, *Briefsammlungen*, 397 (no. 462); *H*, no. 328.

Ow' rex Walie, suus amicus devotissimus H. Suessionensi episcopo et regis Francie cancellario, suo patri in Cristo et amico dilectissimo, debitam ac voluntariam cum salute amicitiam.[a] Deo patri, mi venerande, et vestre discretioni gratias refero, de hoc quod mihi per nuntium meum Moysen litteris vestris mandastis, ut scilicet si meum nuntium iterum mitterem domino regi Francie, per vos divertere facerem, ut vestro suffragio efficacius suum propositum effectui mancipare valeret. Unde et nunc istum M'. nuntium meum vobis mittimus consulendum de suo negotio, vos obnixe deprecando quatinus eum versus regem foveatis, et partem nostram pro Dei amore et nostro iuvetis. Valete.

[a] amiticiam B.

As it refers to an earlier embassy, this letter is clearly later than no. 193 above; indeed, Hugh's response, as reported here, may well have been to that initial approach to Louis. Like no. 193 the present letter styles Owain 'king of Wales' (*rex Walie*) and seems to be earlier than no. 196 below, which styles him 'prince' and refers to Henry II's 1165 campaign. It therefore falls somewhat later within the same date range as that suggested for no. 193 (Pryce, 'Owain Gwynedd', 6). Hugh de Champfleury, bishop of Soissons (1159–75), served as chancellor to Louis VII from 1150 to 1172, and was responsible for the transfer to Saint-Victor in Paris of letters from the royal chancery, including Owain's letters to France (Teske, *Briefsammlungen*, 34–45, 118, 179–80; cf. *CTB*, i. cix). Other petitioners likewise sought Hugh's mediation on their behalf with the king (Teske, *Briefsammlungen*, 121–2).

195 Thomas Becket, archbishop of Canterbury

Letter, stating that the archbishop will have heard how much harm has come to the right of Owain's church after the death of Bishop Maurice, and therefore expressing his great fear that, since it is his duty to care for this church, God will ascribe this harm to his negligence. The archbishop knows how much .he king of England unjustly hates Owain, so that he dishonours him as far as possible in both ecclesiastical and secular matters, regarding which Owain experiences the injurious absence of the archbishop's exile. But since in such a situation the archbishop knows how far he can have regard for his need in this matter, Owain beseeches that permission be given for his bishop to be ordained elsewhere, on condition that he gives obedience to the church of Canterbury and the archbishop as if he had been consecrated by the latter. The archbishop should agree to this petition, as Owain's subjection to him is not by any right but by free will, which will remain unchanged unless the archbishop has determined that it should not continue. If the archbishop doubts his obedience Owain will provide any security he wishes. Just as his archdeacon David is following all the archbishop's commands, so will Owain. But the archbishop should know that Owain cannot remain in this situation any longer. Owain requests the archbishop's written instructions on this matter.

[November 1164 × November 1165; probably September × October 1165]

B = BL, MS Cotton Claudius B.ii, fo. 192v. s. xii ex. Rubric: Thome Cant(uariensi) archiepiscopo Oenus rex Guallie.

C = Vatican City, Biblioteca Apostolica Vaticana, MS Vat. lat. 1220, fo. 161r–v. s. xiv ex. Rubric: Thome Canth(uaren)si archiepiscopo Denus rex Gwallie.

D = Cambridge, Corpus Christi College MS 295, fo. 103v. s. xiii in. Rubric: Th(om)e Cant(uariensi) archiepiscopo Oen(us) rex Gualie.

E = Oxford, Bodleian Library MS 937, Part (i), fos 132v–133r. s. xii/xiii. Rubric: Tho(me) Cant(uariensi) archiepiscopo Oen(us) rex Guallie.

Pd. from B, C and E, *Mat. Becket*, v. 229 (no. 121); from B, with variants from C, D and E, *CTB*, i. 234–7 (no. 57; and trans.); from Biblioteca Apostolica Vaticana, MS Vat. lat. 6027, copy (s. xvii) of C, *Epistolae*, ed. Lupus, ii. 439–40 (no. 79); from E and Lupus, *Gilberti . . . epistolae*, ed. Giles, ii. 302–3 (no. 500) (repr. in *PL*, cxc. 1055); from Giles, Haddan and Stubbs, i. 364–5.

Cd., *H*, no. 326.

[a–]Religiosissimo Dei gratia sancte Cant(uariensis) ecclesie archiepiscopo T., suo patri spirituali O. Walliar(um) rex, suus spiritualis in domino filius, debitam ac voluntariam in Cristo obedientiam.[–a] Vestre, pater mi venerande, discretionis auribus insonuit, quanta sui iuris detrimenta post mortem episcopi nostri Mauricii nostra passa fuerit ecclesia, unde et magno timore perculsi trepidamus, ne,[b] quia nobis incumbit necessitas curam et sollicitudinem huius ecclesie gerendi, Deus nostre negligentie ista imputet. Nostis quoque quantum nos inmeritos oderit rex Anglie, ita ut nostro honori[c] in ecclesiasticis et[d] secularibus negotiis pro posse deroget, in quo vestri exilii dampnosam sentimus absentiam. Sed quoniam in tali statu nostis[e] quo nostre[f] super hac re[g] indigentie consulere valeatis, vestram deprecamur obnixe clementiam quatinus, cum sic amodo esse nequeamus, nostrum alibi episcopum ordinandi licentiam tribuatis, tali tamen interveniente conditione, quod sancte Ca(n)t(uariensi) ecclesie et vobis exhibeat obedientiam, ac si vestre manus impositione consecratus fuisset. Et bene nostre[h] petitioni debetis satisfacere, quia non ius aliquod nos cogit vobis subici, sed voluntas, que semper durabit inmobilis, nisi in vobis remanserit quo minus perseveret. Quod si nos de obedientia, si hoc contigerit, suspectos habueritis, securitatem faciemus quam velitis. Et sicut archidiaconus[i] noster D(avi)d[j] vestra in omnibus precepta sequitur, sic et nos omnes faciemus. At unum tandem[k] sciatis, quod amplius sic esse non valemus.[l] Voluntatem itaque vestram super his michi litteris vestris renuntietis.

[a–a] *omitted* BCE. | [b] nec C. | [c] D *inserts* et. | [d] D *inserts* in. | [e] non estis D. | [f] *omitted* CD. | [g] C *inserts* nostre. | [h] nostri C. | [i] archiediaconus E. | [j] Davit E. | [k] tamen DE. | [l] valeamus D.

For the authority of B, and its relationship to the other recensions of Alan of Tewkesbury's collection of Becket's letters, see *CTB*, i. lxxx–xcviii, cxi. The letter was written after Becket's exile from England in November 1164 but before the archbishop's hostile reply (*MTB*, v. 230 (no. 122); *CTB*, i. 238–9 (no. 59)), written no later than November 1165, rejecting Owain's demand, a reply which in turn preceded Pope Alexander III's letter to the clergy of Bangor supporting the archbishop's stand, dated 10 December 1165 (*MTB*, v. 225–6 (no. 117)). The reference to Henry II's hatred of Owain suggests that the present letter was written after the king's campaign against the Welsh in the summer of 1165; if so, it is probably datable to September or October of that year (*CTB*, i. 234–5 (no. 57); Pryce, 'Owain Gwynedd', 9–10). Bishop Meurig (Maurice) died on 12 August 1161; the ensuing vacancy ended with the consecration of Gwion (Guy) as bishop of Bangor on 22 May 1177. The controversy caused by Owain's attempts to secure the consecration of his candidate, quite possibly Arthur of Bardsey, as bishop in succession to Meurig is illuminated by a series of letters preserved in the Becket letter collections (*MTB*, v. 225–39 (nos 117–30); *CTB*, i. 234–43, 552–5; ii. 840–1, 972–9 (nos 57–61, 114, 190, 223–5)) and is discussed in *Episc. Acts*, ii. 417–34. Archdeacon David was appointed before Meurig's death, probably on the death of Archdeacon Simeon in 1151 (ibid., 423).

196 Louis VII, king of France

Letter, informing Louis that, though the report of all proclaims him to be one in whom all can have complete trust, Owain's own experience of his clemency and kindness towards subjects and those having complete trust in him makes him choose Louis as his sole adviser to whom in difficulties he may complain of his necessity. For as often as he has sent letters informing Louis about his cares, Louis has received both the letters and their bearers benevolently and treated them kindly; and through the latter he has counselled Owain as a pious king should counsel someone having complete trust in him. Therefore, since he is surrounded by difficulties at present, Owain does not wish his kind adviser to be ignorant of the situation. Preceded by no evil deeds of his, in the past summer the king of England waged against him the war which, as Louis knows, he planned for many days with his tyranny. But when in the conflict the five armies of Owain's side came together, more of the king's men fell than his. As a result the king mutilated Owain's hostages, although he had not presented them previously for the keeping of peace. But, as all things are disposed of by the will of God rather than the wishes of man, he moved the army towards England, not through Owain's merits, but through prayers to the saints, and by their intercession with God; however, he left Owain uncertain of the outcome to the end, because he arranged neither a peace nor a truce. Angry because the result had not turned out as he had hoped, on his departure he ordered the foreigners and all whom he had gathered together to come with him against Owain again after next Easter. Therefore Owain prays Louis to inform him via the bearer of this letter whether he is resolved to wage war against the king, so that in that war Owain may both serve him by harming the king according to Louis's advice and take vengeance for the war waged against him. But if Louis does not propose this, he should inform Owain by this bearer what advice and help he wishes to give. Owain has no way of evading the king's snares without Louis's advice and help. He also commends to Louis his familiar clerk and kinsman Guiardus, so that Louis may provide him with necessities. Owain sent him before to Louis with his letters, which Louis did not believe were his, so Owain was told. But they were his, and through them he commended Guiardus to Louis. Owain also prays that, just as Louis has begun to render peaceful towards him the pope and the archbishop of Canterbury, so he will continue to do so.

[September 1165 × -24 April 1166; probably November 1165 × early March 1166]

B = Vatican City, Biblioteca Apostolica Vaticana, MS Reg. lat. 179, fo. 233r–v. s. xii ex.

Pd. from B, *HFS*, iv. 731–2 (no. 467); from B, Pryce, 'Owain Gwynedd', 27–8 (and trans., ibid., 7–8); from *HFS*, *RHF*, xvi. 117 (no. 358).

Cd., Teske, *Briefsammlungen*, 398 (no. 469); *H*, no. 329.

Excellentissimo Dei gratia L. Francor(um) regi Owin(us) Waliarum princeps, suus homo et amicus fidelis, devotissimum cum salute servitium. Cum universorum relatio, serenissime rex, te conspicuum predicet, in quo omnes possunt et debent confidere, clementia tamen mihi experimento nota et mansuetudo erga subiectos et in te confidentes, fecit me eligere te solum consultorem, ad quem in angustiis meam conquerar necessitatem. Quamtotiens enim de meo esse et mea sollicitudine litterarum inscriptione vobis nuntiavi, non tam litteras quam earum latores benevole recepisti et eos clementer tractasti. Mihi etiam per illos, Deo gratias et vobis, consuluisti prout pius rex confidenti in eo debuit. Cum itaque angustie ad presens mihi undique sint, nolo te clementem consultorem latere. Werra quam rex Anglie per multos dies, ut vobis notum est, severitate sue tyrannidis mihi excogitavit, in preterita estate, nullis malis meis precedentibus, contra me surrexit. Sed cum in conflictu quinque partis nostri exercitus convenirent, Deo gratias et vobis, ex suis plures ceciderunt quam ex meis. Quo viso, meos obsides nequiter et iniuriose demembravit, non eos mihi ante offerendo pro pace tenenda. Sed, quia non hominis proposito sed nutu Dei omnia disponuntur, movit exercitum versus Anglia(m), non nostris fortasse meritis sed humilium oratione ad sanctos et sanctorum intercessione ad Deum, usque adeo tamen me dubium relinquens, quod nec pacem nec indutias nobiscum composuit. Iratus itaque pro eventu non prospero, alienigenis et omnibus quos ad nostrum detrimentum congregaverat, in discessu mandavit ut post futuram Pascha contra nos iterum cum eo venirent. Proinde vestram clementiam obnixe deprecor quatinus per presentium latorem mihi nuntietis si animum werrandi contra eum habetis, ut in illa werra et vobis serviam nocendo ei secundum consilium vestrum et illata mihi ab eo vindicem. Quod si hoc non proponis, quid consulas, quod adiutorium mihi largiri vis, per hunc latorem mihi nuntietis. Nullam enim viam evadendi eius insidias habeo, nisi te largiente mihi consilium et adiutorium. Privatum etiam et familiarem clericum meum Guiardum et consanguineum vobis commendo, quatinus pro Dei amore et nostro ei necessaria provideatis. Misi enim eum ante in vestram presentiam cum litteris meis, quibus non credidistis, ut nobis dictum est, quod essent mee. Sed sunt he, Deum testem induco, qui per illas eum intimo corde vobis commendavi. De hoc etiam vestram clementiam obnixe deprecor, ut sicut incepistis prelatos ecclesie, videlicet apostolicum et archiepiscopum Cantuariensem, michi pacificos reddere, sic et adhuc reddatis. Valete.

For the dating of this letter see Pryce, 'Owain Gwynedd', 8–11. The reference to Henry II's war against Owain 'the previous summer' must be to the king's campaign of July–August 1165 (on which, see Latimer, 'Henry II's campaign'). If so, the letter was sent no earlier than September 1165 but before 24 April 1166, the date of the 'following Easter' mentioned as having been set for the mustering of a new royal campaign. Two considerations may allow this date range to be narrowed. First, since it makes no mention of Henry II's presence in France, the letter may have been written before the king crossed to Normandy in the second half of March 1166. True, Owain could have envisaged Louis's attacking Henry precisely because the latter was on the Continent. However, it is more likely that the letter sought to prevent the planned Easter campaign in 1166 by persuading Louis to intensify hostilities against Henry's French lands and therefore compel Henry to leave England. Second, the reference at the end of the letter to Louis's mediation with Becket and the pope (namely Alexander III) shows that it was written after both churchmen had come into conflict with Owain over the issue of consecrating a new bishop of Bangor. As Becket rejected Owain's request for a bishop to be consecrated by another metropolitan probably in October or November 1165 and had secured Alexander's support by 10 December 1165 (note to no. 195 above), Louis's mediation is unlikely to have begun before November of that year. If so, the present letter was probably sent no earlier than November 1165. The employment of the title 'prince of Wales' (*Waliarum princeps*), in contrast to the 'king of Wales' (*rex Walie*, *Walliarum rex*) used in earlier letters to the Capetian court and in Owain's letter to Becket, is consistent with such a dating. The identity of the clerk Guiardus is unknown. Despite his French name, he must have been Welsh, for he is described as Owain's kinsman.

CADWALADR AP GRUFFUDD
(d. 29 February(?) 1172)

197 Haughmond Abbey

Grant, for the salvation of the souls of himself and all his predecessors and heirs, in perpetual alms, of the church of Nefyn with all its appurtenances, all the land where the church is situated between the two small brooks and all the land of Cerniog with all its appurtenances and easements. The canons shall possess this gift free of all injury and evil custom. Sealing clause; witnesses.

[1140 × 1152 or 1157 × -12 August 1161]

B = Shrewsbury, Shropshire Records and Research Centre MS 6001/6869 (Haughmond Cartulary), fos 148v–149r. s. xv ex.
Pd. from B, *Cart. Haugh.*, no. 784 (omits sealing clause); from BL, MS Harleian 6068, fo. 10r (s. xvi/xvii; incomplete), Owen, *Catalogue*, i. 451, n. 2; from ibid., Anon, 'Trefeglwys charter', 241; from Cardiff County and City Library MS 4.101, fo. 165r (s.xvi/xvii; incomplete), *Hist. Gwydir*, 2; from a lost Wynnstay MS dated 1640 destroyed in 1858, Williams, 'Wynnstay MSS.', 4, 5 (incomplete).
Cd., Owen, *Catalogue*, i. 451; *H*, no. 113.

Universis sancte matris ecclesie filiis et fidelibus Cadwaladrus frater Owini magni salutem in domino. Notum sit universitati vestre quod ego Cadwaladrus pro salute anime mee et omnium antecessorum et heredum meorum dedi et concessi Deo et ecclesie Sancti Ioh(ann)is Evangeliste de Haghmon' et canonicis ibidem Deo servientibus in puram et perpetuam elemosinam ecclesiam de Neuyn cum omnibus pertinentiis suis et totam terram que [fo. 149r] est inter duos rivulos inter quos predicta ecclesia sita est et totam terram de Cheemhoc cum omnibus pertinentiis et aisiamentis suis in pratis et in pascuis et in omnibus aliis rebus et locis. Quare volo et precipio firmiter quatinus predicti canonici hanc meam donationem libere et quiete et absque ullo gravamine et mala consuetudine teneant et inperpetuum in pace possideant. Et ut ista mea donatio rata et firma inperpetuum maneat eam presenti scripto et sigilli mei testimonio confirmo. Hiis testibus: Mauric(i)o episcopo, David et Reso et Moyse fratribus eius, Aliz de Clara uxore mea etc.

The outer dating limits of this charter are set by the pontificate of the first witness, Meurig (Maurice), bishop of Bangor, who was consecrated on or shortly after 31 January 1140 and died 12 August 1161 (see note to no. 192 above). As Cadwaladr was expelled from Anglesey, his last remaining lands in Gwynedd, in 1152 and restored in 1157 as a result of Henry II's campaign against Owain Gwynedd, the charter is datable to either 1140 × 1152 or 1157 × 12 August 1161. One argument in favour of the latter date range is that in 1156–7, during his exile from Gwynedd, Cadwaladr held land from the king in the Shropshire manor of Ness, situated only about 10 miles from Haughmond Abbey (cf. *HW*, ii. 613, n. 5; Johns, 'Postscript', 129–30). Nevertheless, the earlier date range cannot be ruled out, for the grant could reflect the influence of Angevin patronage of Haughmond, which was considerable and with which Cadwaladr was probably familiar from the early 1140s: he fought with Ranulf II, earl of Chester (1129–53) on the Angevin side at the battle of Lincoln in 1141, and his association with the earl is also attested later in the 1140s (Pryce, 'Church of Trefeglwys', 45–6; cf. *Cart. Haugh.*, no. 784 n., which favours a date of 1141 × 1143 'when Cadwaladr was involved in English affairs').

The last witness provides further evidence of Cadwaladr's close relations with Ranulf. Lloyd, following Eyton, identified Cadwaladr's wife as an otherwise unknown daughter of Richard fitz Gilbert de Clare, the lord of Ceredigion killed by the Welsh in 1136, and thus a niece of Ranulf; Lloyd also pointed out that she could not be identified as Gilbert fitz Richard's daughter Alice, who married Aubrey II de Vere of Hedingham, Essex, as she entered a nunnery on her husband's death in 1141 (*HW*, ii. 491; Eyton, *Shopshire*, x. 257; cf. Sanders, *Baronies*, 52, n. 5). Another possibility, however, is that *Aliz* is a corrupt reading for *Adeliza* rather than *Alicia*, and that the lady was Richard's widow, and Ranulf's sister, Adeliza. This receives some support from Welsh genealogical collections, extant in manuscripts of the late fifteenth century onwards, which name *Adles ferch iarll Klaer* ('Adles daughter of the earl of Chester') as the mother of four of Cadwaladr's sons, two of whom, significantly, were named Rhicerd (i.e. Richard) and Randwlff (i.e. Ranulf), the others bearing the Venedotian dynastic names of Cunedda and Gruffudd (*EWGT*, 98). The form *Adles* is more likely to derive from *Adeliza* than from *Alicia*. It seems that Adeliza took refuge with her brother Ranulf after her husband's death in 1136 (*Chester Charters*, no. 39), and given his association with Ranulf by 1141, it is conceivable that Cadwaladr married her, thereby reinforcing his alliance with the earl while also strengthening his title to rule in Ceredigion through marriage to Richard fitz Gilbert's widow. Cadwaladr retained authority in northern Ceredigion – conquered as a result of the campaigns led by Owain Gwynedd and himself following Gilbert's death in 1136 – until 1149, when he transferred his land there to his son Cadfan, who lost it to Cadwaladr's nephew Hywel ab Owain the following year (*BT, Pen20Tr*, 57; *BT, RBH*, 128–9).

When and how long Cadwaladr held land at Nefyn is unknown. (Cerniog lay in the same vicinity, to the east of Mynydd Nefyn (Johns, 'Postscript', 130).) The Welsh chronicles refer only to his tenure of northern Ceredigion, Meirionnydd and Anglesey; but the present charter shows that he possessed land in Llŷn as well at some point. In addition, it appears that his son Richard ap Cadwaladr was *rhaglaw* of the commote of Dinllaen, where Nefyn is situated, in the early thirteenth century, indicating that Cadwaladr's lineage continued to hold land in the area after his death in 1172 (note to no. 258 below). It has been suggested that provision was made for Cadwaladr in Llŷn after he lost Meirionnydd in 1147 to his nephews Hywel and Cynan sons of Owain Gwynedd (Smith, 'Dynastic succession', 217); if so, this would further narrow the first of the two proposed date ranges. It should be added that a confirmation of Haughmond's Welsh possessions issued in 1195 × 1196 by Alan, bishop of Bangor, states that the grant at Nefyn was made by Cadwaladr and his sons Maredudd, Einion and Cadwallon (*Cart. Haugh.*, no. 794). According to the genealogical collections already mentioned, the mother of these sons was Dyddgu daughter of Maredudd ap Bleddyn (d. 1132) of Powys, whom the genealogists seem to have regarded as an earlier partner of Cadwaladr than 'Adles daughter of the earl of Chester' (*EWGT*, 98). Whether the sons issued a separate charter confirming their father's grant, or whether their participation in that grant was assumed by the bishop on the strength of their presence in the (now truncated) witness list of the present charter, can only be guessed. Also uncertain is whether the Moses named as one of Bishop Meurig's brothers was the same as the messenger of that name sent on at least two occasions by Owain Gwynedd to the Capetian court *c*.1164–5 (no. 194 above).

DAFYDD AB OWAIN GWYNEDD
(d. -27 May 1203)

198 Haughmond Abbey

Grant, in perpetual alms for the salvation of his soul, of the land which Troit de Brumm' *had of the land of (?) Boduan (*Bodanen*) in the township of Nefyn, free of all earthly customs and exactions. None of Dafydd's men shall trouble the canons concerning this in the future. Grant likewise of the tithes of his mill of Nefyn and their confirmation in perpetual alms by the present writing. Witnesses.*

[May 1177 × September 1187]

B = Shrewsbury, Shropshire Records and Research Centre MS 6001/6869 (Haughmond Cartulary), fo. 149r. s. xv ex.
Pd. from B, *Cart. Haugh.*, no. 786; from Cardiff County and City Library MS 4.101, fo. 165r (s. xvi/xvii; incomplete), *Hist. Gwydir*, 4; from a Wynnstay MS dated 1640 destroyed in 1858, Williams, 'Wynnstay MSS.', 332.
Cd., Owen, *Catalogue*, i. 451; *H*, no. 114.

Omnibus sancte Dei ecclesie filiis tam presentibus quam futuris David rex filius Owini salutem. Notum sit vobis me concessisse et in perpetuam elemosinam dedisse abbati et canonicis de Haghmon' pro salute anime mee illam terram quam Troit de Brum(m) habuit de terra Bodanen in villa de Neuyn' liberam et quietam ab omnibus terrenis consuetu-dinibus et exactionibus. Quare volo et firmiter precipio ne quis meorum in posterum predictis canonicis super hoc inquietare presumat vel in aliquo disturbet. Concedo itaque similiter predictis canonicis decimationem molendini mei de Neuin et in perpetuam elemosinam presenti scripto confirmo. Testibus: Rog(er)o Powiswlt, Gervasio fratre episcopi etc.

As Rees argued (*Cart. Haugh.*, no. 786 n.), the charter was issued after the consecration of Gwion, presumably the bishop whose brother is the second witness, to the see of Bangor in May 1177 but before Michaelmas 1187, by which date the first witness, Roger of Powys, had been succeeded by his son Maredudd (*Pipe Roll 33 Henry II*, 63; for Roger see further Eyton, *Shropshire*, xi. 31–2; Suppe, 'Roger of Powys'). Bishop Gwion confirmed this grant in a charter issued May 1177 × *c*.1190, also witnessed by 'the brother of the bishop', here unnamed (*Cart. Haugh.*, no. 791). The grant appears to have been of a piece of land in the township of Nefyn that belonged to the land of *Bodenan*. Bishop Gwion's confirmation refers to the latter land as *Bothenav* and the previous owner as *Troitbrummete*; the name of the land is given as *Bodenan* and that of its owner as *Troithbremeth* in a confirmation by Bishop Alan of Bangor in 1195 × 1196 (ibid., no. 794); and the land is called *Bothwian* in no. 207 below, issued by Gruffudd ap Cynan ab Owain in 1195 × 1199. *Bodanen/Bothenav/Bothwian* was probably the bond township of Boduan, in the vicinity of Plas Boduan (SH 327381), south-east of Nefyn, and, like it, located in the commote of Dinllaen in Llŷn (cf. Jones Pierce, *Medieval Welsh Society*, 82). Rees (*Cart. Haugh.*, no. 786 n.), implicitly identified *Bodanen* with *Bodenean*, identified by Jones Pierce as a bond township near the *maenor* of Nefyn ('Two early Caernarvonshire accounts', 150 and n. 7); elsewhere, Jones Pierce identified *Bodenean* or *Bodnean* as Boduan ('Lleyn ministers' accounts', 261). Dafydd thus appears to have granted Haughmond a detached portion of the township of Boduan in the township of Nefyn.

Early modern, highly abbreviated, copies of the charter, including those whose published texts are noted above, derive from a common archetype that was independent of B, as they contain a different witness list (e.g. *Hist. Gwydir*, 4: *Johanne de Burchelton, Rad'o de lega, Einion Seys &c.*; a full list of transcripts is given in *H*, no. 114). These witnesses also appear (with others) in no. 203 below, and they may have been transposed from that or another charter into the early modern texts of the present charter. This seems more likely than that Dafydd's original charter named them after the two witnesses in B, whose witness list is truncated, as neither of those two witnesses was included in the early modern copies.

199 The parishioners of Nefyn

Notification that he has granted his tithes in perpetual alms for the salvation of his soul to the abbot and canons of Haughmond. Dafydd orders the parishioners to pay the tithes of all fishing and all fruits of the earth to the abbot and convent as the bishop of Bangor confirms and orders in his charter; and prohibits any of his men between the two small brooks around the church from exercising lordship over the land of the canons or inflicting any injury on their men. Witnesses.

[May 1177 × c.1190]

B = Shropshire Records and Research Centre MS 6001/6869 (Haughmond Cartulary), fo. 149r. s. xv ex.
Pd. from B, *Cart. Haugh.*, no. 785.
Cd., *H*, no. 115.

David rex Norwallie omnibus hominibus infra parochiam de Neuyn' existentibus salutem. Universitati vestre presentibus litteris manifesto me concessisse et in perpetuam elemosinam pro salute anime mee abbati et canonicis de Haghmon' decimas nostras dedisse. Quare volo et super foresfacturam meam vobis omnibus precipio quatinus prenominatis abbati et conventui tam de omni piscatura maris quam de frugibus terre decimas sicut episcopus Bangorensis carta sua confirmat et precipit plenarie persolvatis. Prohibeo itaque ne quis meorum infra duos rivulos circa ecclesiam super terram predictorum canonicorum dominium exerceat nec eorum hominibus aliquam molestiam vel gravamen inferat. Hiis testibus: Wian episcopo, Madoc fratre eius etc.

The charter is datable to Gwion's pontificate, May 1177–*c.*1190 (*Cart. Haugh.*, no. 785 n.). For the bishop's charter, issued during the same date range, ordering the parishioners to pay their tithes to the canons, see ibid., no. 792; as Dafydd's letter refers to this charter and is witnessed by Gwion, both documents may have been issued on the same occasion. The Welsh form of the bishop's name, *Wian*, bears comparison with the Latinized form *Guianus* given by Gerald of Wales (*Gir. Camb. Op.*, vi. 125 (*IK* II. 6)), and contrasts with the forms *Guido* or *Wido* used by the bishop in his acts and by the English chronicler Ralph of Diss (*Cart. Haugh.*, nos 791–2, 1212, 1220; Diceto, i. 420; cf. Pryce, 'Esgobaeth Bangor', 46–7).

200 Haughmond Abbey

Grant, with the consent of his wife Emma and his heir Owain in free and perpetual alms for the salvation of the soul of himself, his wife and all his predecessors and successors of the whole of Stockett with all its appurtenances, to be held in perpetual right from him and his heirs free of all the secular service which is due to them. Sealing clause; witnesses.

[August 1186 × 25 April 1194]

B = Shrewsbury, Shropshire Records and Research Centre MS 6001/6869 (Haughmond Cartulary), fo. 209v. s. xv ex. Marginal heading: Stockett. Rubric: Donatio de Stokete.
C = Shrewsbury, Shropshire Records and Research Centre 2922/15/1, fos 1v–2r. s. xvi/xvii. Rubric: Carta David filii Owini de Stochyeta.
Pd. from B, *Cart. Haugh.*, no. 1169.
Cd., *H*, no. 116.

David filius Owini princeps Norwallie universis Dei[a] fidelibus Francis et Anglis presentibus et futuris salutem in domino. Sciatis me assensu Emme uxoris mee et Owini heredis mei dedisse et concessisse Deo et ecclesie Sancti Ioh(ann)is Evangeliste de Haghmon'[b] et canonicis ibidem Deo servientibus in liberam et perpetuam elemosinam pro salute anime mee et uxoris mee et omnium antecessorum et successorum meorum totam Stocgete[c] cum omnibus pertinentiis suis[d] in bosco, in plano, in pratis, in pasturis, in aquis, in viis, in[e] semitis et in omnibus aliis locis et cum omnibus rebus et libertatibus ad eandem terram pertinentibus, habendam et tenendam iure perpetuo de me et heredibus meis pacifice, libere et quiete pro omni seculari servitio quod ad nos pertinet. Ut itaque hec mea donatio rata et inconcussa[f] perpetuo permaneat eam presenti carta mea et sigilli[g] appositione roboravi et confirmavi. Hiis testibus: Reinero episcopo [h]de Sancto Assaph',[-h] [i-]Kenwreco filio Cadwgoen capellano, Radulpho de Lega, Will(elm)o de Culem(er)e.[-i]

[a] Cristi C. | [b] Haghem' C. | [c] Stogete C. | [d] *omitted* C. | [e] et C. | [f] C; incussa B. | [g] C *inserts* mei. [h-h] *omitted* C. | [i-i] etc. B.

As Rees argued (*Cart. Haugh.*, no. 1169 n.), the charter was issued after Reiner's conse-cration as bishop of St Asaph in August 1186 and before the confirmation of Emma's grant of Stockett to Haughmond by Richard I on 25 April 1194 (pd. in Eyton, *Shropshire*, vii. 293–4). Stockett is located in Ellesmere, which was granted to Dafydd by Henry II at Oxford in May 1177 (*Gesta*, ed. Stubbs, i. 162; *Chronica*, ed. Stubbs, ii. 134).

201 Haughmond Abbey

Grant, jointly with his wife Emma, at the request and with the consent of their son and heir Owain, for the salvation of their souls in free and perpetual alms, of all the land of Crickett with all its appurtenances, to be held as freely for ever as any other land granted in alms, and also of annual quittance of pannage for 100 pigs. Sealing clause; witnesses.

[25 April 1194 × 1197 or 9 February 1198 × May 1203]

B = Shrewsbury, Shropshire Records and Research Centre MS 6001/6869 (Haughmond Cartulary), fos 51v–52r. s. xv ex. Marginal heading: Crikcote. Rubric: Ut patet in indenturis.
Pd. from B, *Cart. Haugh.*, no. 268.
Cd., *H*, no. 119.

Sciant omnes tam presentes quam futuri quod ego David filius Owini et Emma uxor mea ad petitionem et consensum Owini filii et heredis nostri dedimus et concessimus et presenti carta nostra confirmavimus Deo et ecclesie Sancti Ioh(ann)is Evangeliste de Haghmon' et canonicis ibidem Deo servientibus pro salute animarum nostrarum in liberam, puram et perpetuam elemosinam totam terram de Crickcote cum omnibus pertinentiis suis et cum omnibus libertatibus et liberis consuetudinibus et cum omnibus communitatibus et eisia-mentis in bosco et plano, in pratis [fo. 52r] et pascuis, in aquis et moris, in viis et semitis et in omnibus rebus et locis ita libere, integre et quiete habendam et imperpetuum possi-dendam sicut unquam aliqua fuit terra liberius, plenius et quietius in elemosinam data vel dari potuit. Concessimus etiam eisdem canonicis quietantiam pannagii annuatim ad centum porcos. Unde ne aliquis heredum vel successorum nostrorum prefatos canonicos super ista donatione et concessione nostra in posterum aliquatenus inquietare presumat set rata, firma et inconcussa permaneat et imperpetuum perseveret, eam presenti carta cum sigillorum nostrorum appositione roboravimus. Hiis testibus: Ioh(ann)e de Burcheltun', Einion de Hordeleg', Rein(er)o persona de Ellesmere etc.

This charter was very probably issued after 25 April 1194, for Crickett is not included with Stockett in Richard I's confirmation of that date (see note to no. 200 above). That Dafydd appears without any title as ruler of North Wales, in contrast to nos 198–200 above, may indicate that it was issued after he lost power in Gwynedd following his defeat by Llywelyn ap Iorwerth and his allies at Aberconwy in 1194, after which Dafydd was left with only three castles, probably on the English border. It could even suggest a date subsequent to his capture by Llywelyn in 1197 and release on or shortly after 9 February 1198 (*Feet of Fines*, 79, shows that Hubert Walter went to Wales to release Dafydd on the octaves of the Purification 1198), for thereafter Dafydd remained in his lands in England until his death, having lost his last vestiges of regality in Gwynedd (cf. *HW*, ii. 588–90). *Pace* Rees (*Cart. Haugh.*, no. 268 n.), there is no compelling reason to assign Dafydd's imprisonment in 1197 as a *terminus ad quem*; while it is most unlikely to date from his captivity, the charter could have been issued during the period between his release in February 1198 and his death, which occurred no later than 27 May 1203.

EMMA OF ANJOU, WIFE OF DAFYDD AB OWAIN
(*fl.* 1151–1212)

202 Haughmond Abbey

Grant, with the assent of her husband Dafydd and her heir Owain in free and perpetual alms for the salvation of the souls of herself, her husband and all her successors and predecessors of the whole of Stockett with all its appurtenances, to be held in perpetual right from her and her heirs free of all the secular service which is due to them. Sealing clause; witnesses..

[August 1186 × 25 April 1194]

> B = Shrewsbury, Shropshire Records and Research Centre MS 6001/6869 (Haughmond Cartulary), fo. 209v. s. xv ex.
> C = Shrewsbury, Shropshire Records and Research Centre 2922/15/1, fo. 2r. s. xvi/xvii.
> Pd. from B and C, *Cart. Haugh.*, no. 1170 (witness lists only).
> Cd., *H*, no. 117.

Domina Emma soror Henrici regis, uxor David filii Owini principis Norwallie universis Dei fidelibus Francis et Anglis presentibus et futuris salutem in domino. Sciatis me assensu David mariti mei et Owini heredis mei dedisse et concessisse Deo et ecclesie Sancti Ioh(ann)is Evangeliste de Haghmon'[a] et canonicis Deo servientibus in liberam et perpetuam elemosinam pro salute anime mee et mariti mei et omnium successorum et antecessorum meorum totam Stocgete cum omnibus pertinentiis in bosco, in plano, in pratis et[b] pasturis, in aquiis, in viis, in semitis et in omnibus aliis locis et cum omnibus [c-]rebus et[-c] libertatibus ad eandem terram pertinentibus, habendam et tenendam iure perpetuo de me et heredibus meis pacifice, libere et quiete pro omni seculari servitio quod ad nos pertinet. Ut itaque hec me donatio rata[d] et inconcussa perpetuo permaneat eam presenti carta mea et sigilli mei appositione roboravi et confirmavi. Hiis testibus: Rein(er)io episcopo de Sancto Asaph, [e-]Cadwgan filio Peil(er), Cenewrick filio Cadwgan', Arthur capellano, Alano camerario domini David, Will(elm)o de Hortuna, Eigmon' filio Cadwgan, Ivone de Aelega, Widone capellano, Will(elm)o de Culem(er)e.[-e]

[a] Haghem' C. | [b] in C. | [c-c] *omitted* C. | [d] *inserted above line in* B. | [e-e] etc. B.

This charter was issued within the same date range as Dafydd's charter granting Stockett (no. 200 above), with which it bears a close verbal resemblance, apart from necessary adaptations. Three of the witnesses are common to both charters, but the present charter contains a further seven witnesses not found in no. 200, while the latter contains one, Ralph of Lee, lacking here. This could suggest that the charters were issued on different occasions, both in the presence of Bishop Reiner. Whenever it was issued, the charter demonstrates the importance Haughmond attached to obtaining Emma's consent to a grant of land in her marriage portion of Ellesmere.

203 Haughmond Abbey

Grant and quitclaim, for the salvation of the souls of herself and all her predecessors and heirs, of all the pannage of Stockett, to be held freely for ever. The canons shall be quit thereof, and no one shall presume to trouble them on that account. Witnesses.

[1194 × May 1203; possibly 1197 × *c*.9 February 1198]

B = Shrewsbury, Shropshire Records and Research Centre MS 6001/6869 (Haughmond Cartulary), fo. 210r. s. xv ex.

C = Shrewsbury, Shropshire Records and Research Centre 2922/15/1, fo. 2r–v. s. xvi/xvii.

Pd. from B and C, *Cart. Haugh.*, no. 1173 (witness lists only).

Cd., *H*, no. 121.

Sciant omnes tam[a] presentes quam futuri quod ego Emma sponsa David filii Owini dedi et quietum clamavi Deo et ecclesie Sancti Ioh(ann)is Evangeliste de Haghmon'[b] et canonicis ibidem Deo servientibus pro salute anime mee et pro animabus omnium antecessorum et heredum meorum totum pannagium de Stokeita[c] libere et quiete, integre et plenarie habendum et inperpetuum possidendum. Quare volo et firmiter precipio quod predicti canonici amodo sint inde quieti nec aliquis eos inde aliquatenus vexare presumat.[d] Hiis testibus: Viviano de Bentuna,[d] Ioh(ann)e de Burghletuna, Rei[d]n(er)io persona de Ellesm(er)e,[d] [e] Eigmon Says, Rog(er)o camer(ar)io, Radulf(o) de Lega.[e]

[a] laici C. | [b] Haghemon' C. | [c] Storkeita C. | [d–d] *omitted in C, which is damaged here.* | [e–e] etc. B.

This appears to be an additional grant to that in no. 202 above and thus later than it. Rees suggested that it was made during Dafydd's imprisonment in 1197–8 (*Cart. Haugh.*, no. 269 n.), presumably on the assumption that otherwise Emma would not have acted alone. This is possible: the grant of Crickett, including quittance from pannage, was made jointly by Dafydd and Emma (no. 201 above); and though no. 202 shows that it was possible for Emma to issue a charter independently at a time when her husband is not known to have been imprisoned, Haughmond also obtained a similar charter from Dafydd (no. 200 above). The lack of any title for Dafydd probably indicates a *terminus a quo* of 1194; that Emma refers to herself as his wife, rather than widow, provides a *terminus ad quem* of May 1203 (see note to no. 201).

OWAIN AP DAFYDD AB OWAIN
(fl. c.1180–1212)

204 Haughmond Abbey

Grant, for the salvation of the souls of himself and his father and mother, confirming his parents' gift of all the land of Crickett in free and perpetual alms with all its appurtenances and easements, to be held for ever with quittance of pannage for 100 pigs in Northwood. Sealing clause; witnesses.

[1194 × 1203]

B = Shrewsbury, Shropshire Records and Research Centre MS 6001/6869 (Haughmond Cartulary), fo. 52r. s. xv ex.

Pd. from B, *Cart. Haugh.*, no. 269 (witness list only).

Cd., *H*, no. 120.

Sciant omnes tam presentes quam futuri quod ego Owin(us) filius David concessi et presenti carta mea confirmavi Deo et ecclesie Sancti Ioh(ann)is Evangeliste de Haghmon' et canonicis ibidem Deo servientibus pro salute anime mee et patris et matris mee donationem quam David filius Owini pater meus et Emma mater mea fecerunt eisdem canonicis de tota terra de Criccote in liberam et perpetuam elemosinam cum omnibus libertatibus et pertinentiis suis et cum omnibus communitatibus et eisiamentis in bosco et plano, in pratis et pasturis, in aquis et moris, in viis et semitis et in omnibus rebus et locis libere et quiete, habenda et imperpetuum possidenda cum quietantia pannagii ad centum porcos in Nordwode. Et quia volo quod predicti canonici memoratam terram cum prefatis libertatibus et liberis consuetudinibus libere et quiete in perpetuam elemosinam possideant eam presenti scripto cum sigilli mei testimonio confirmo atque corroboro. Hiis testibus: Ioh(ann)e de Burhelt', Reynero clerico, Rog(er)o clerico, Einion'ᵃ de Hordileg', Rein(er)o de Franketon', Will(el)mo de Hothton', Rad(ulpho) de Laga, Simone de Iagedun' etc.

ᵃ *second* i *interlined in* B.

This charter confirms no. 201 above and may be assigned to the same date range. It was probably issued later within that period than no. 201, as it differs from the latter in identifying the location of the pannage as Northwood.

205 Haughmond Abbey

Grant, in free and perpetual alms, of the whole land of Stockett with its all appurtenances, to be held for ever from him and his heirs free of all the secular service that is due to him or his heirs. Sealing clause; witnesses.

[1194 × October 1204]

B = Shrewsbury, Shropshire Records and Research Centre MS 6001/6869 (Haughmond Cartulary), fo. 209v. s. xv ex.
C = Shrewsbury, Shropshire Records and Research Centre 2922/15/1, fo. 1r. s. xvi/xvii.
Pd. from B and C, *Cart. Haugh.*, no. 1171 (witness lists only).
Cd., *H*, no. 125.

Universis Dei fidelibus tam presentibus quam futuris Owin(us) filius David salutem in domino. Sciatis me concessisse et presenti carta confirmasse Deo et ecclesie Sancti Ioh(ann)is Evangeliste de Haghmon'ᵃ et canonicis ibidem Deoᵇ servientibus in liberam et perpetuam elemosinam totam terram de Stocgheteᶜ cum omnibus pertinentiis suis in bosco et plano, in pratis et pascuis, in aquis, in viis et semitis et in omnibus aliis locis et cum omnibus rebus et libertatibus ad eandem terram pertinentibus, habendam et iure perpetuo tenendam de me et heredibusᵈ meis pacifice, libere et quiete de omni seculari servitio quod ad me vel heredes meos pertinet. Ut igitur hec concessio et confirmatio mea inperpetuum rata perseveret eam sigilli mei appositione communivi. Hiis testibus: Will(el)mo filio Alani, ᵉ⁻Ioh(ann)e Ext(ra)neo, Hug(one) Pant', Hamone Ext(ra)neo, Vivien de Rossal', Stephano de Stantu(n), Odo de Hodenet, Rein(er)o clerico, Rad(ulf)o clerico, Martino capellano de Ellesm(er)e, Rob(er)to capellano, Eynianne Seis et Dooc servientibus David patris mei.⁻ᵉ

ᵃ Haghemon C. | ᵇ *omitted* C. | ᶜ Stocgeta C. | ᵈ C *inserts* suis *(sic)*. | ᵉ⁻ᵉ etc. B.

Though Rees suggested that this charter was datable to the period after Dafydd ab Owain's death in 1203 and before King John's grant of Ellesmere to Llywelyn ap Iorwerth in March 1205 (*Cart. Haugh.*, no. 1171 n.), the description of the witnesses Einion Sais and Dwywg as servants of Dafydd probably implies that he was alive at the time of the grant. In any case, the charter is most unlikely to be later than 14 October 1204, when the sheriff of Warwickshire was ordered to assign Owain land in the manor of Elmdon in exchange for his land in Ellesmere which had been kept in the king's hand on 14 October 1204 (*Rot. Claus.*, i. 12a). Indeed, John had expressed his determination to take the manor into his own hands in late May 1203, and urged that other provision be found for Owain on 2 August of that year (*Rot. Lib.*, 36, 56; cf. *HW*, ii. 616, n. 26). On the other hand, the charter is presumably later than Owain's parents' grants of Stockett, datable to 1186 × 1194 (nos 200 and 202 above), and the reference to Dafydd without any title suggests a date no earlier than 1194 (note to no. 201 above). It is unclear why the charter does not explicitly confirm the grants of Owain's parents, to which he had assented, in the same way as no. 204 above.

THE LINEAGE OF CYNAN AB OWAIN

GRUFFUDD AP CYNAN AB OWAIN
(d. 1200)

206 Aberconwy Abbey
Grant, for the salvation of the souls of himself and his predecessors, in perpetual alms, of Gelliniog with all its appurtenances, Rhuddgaer with all its bounds, Stawenan with all its bounds and appurtenances and the mill of Tal-y-bont. The monks shall possess all the aforesaid lands in perpetual alms freely, peacefully and honourably, with all customary liberties and free of all earthly service and secular exaction. Sealing clause; witnesses.

Porthaethwy, June [*c.*1190 × 1199; probably 1194 × 1199]

B = BL, MS Harley 3725 (Register of Aberconwy Abbey), fos 43v–44r. s. xiv.
Pd. from B, *Reg. Aberconway*, pp. 7–8; from B, Owen, *Catalogue*, i. 405 (witness list only).
Cd., *H*, no. 197.

[N]otum sit omnibus sancte matris ecclesie filiis tam presentibus quam futuris quod ego . . .[a] Kynan filius Northwallie princeps intuitu divine pietatis, pro salute anime mee et antecessorum meorum, dedi et concessi in puram et perpetuam elemosinam Deo, Beate Marie et monachis de Aberconwey sub ordine Cistercien(si) Deo famulantibus Kellinioc cum omnibus pertinentiis suis, Rudgaer cum omnibus finibus suis, Stawenan cum finibus et omnibus pertinentiis suis et molendinum de Talepont. Et volo ut idem monachi, tam presentes quam futuri, omnes prenominatas terras cum [fo. 44r] omnibus ad eas pertinentibus in perpetuam elemosinam possideant, bene et quiete et libere, in pace, plenarie, integre et honorifice, in bosco et plano, in pratis et pasturis, in aquis et molendinis cum omnibus libertatibus solitis et liberis ab omni terreno servitio et exactione seculari. Ut autem hec mea donatio et concessio imperpetuum firma permaneat eam presentis carte[b] munimine et sigilli mei impressione roboravi. Hiis testibus: Owen ap Ednywan, Teg' ap Robert, Cadwen Ieweryth filio, Howelo Ydrys filio et multis aliis. Datum apud Porthaethay' anno ab incarnatione domini millesimo c . . .[a] mense iunii.

[a] *lacuna in* B. | [b] cartis B.

Although the Christian name of the donor is missing from the copy in B, the original charter must have contained the name of Gruffudd, the only son of Cynan ab Owain who held authority in Anglesey, and who could claim to be 'prince of North Wales', after the Cistercians were established at Aberconwy by 1192, having moved there from their original site at Rhedynog Felen near Caernarfon given them at their foundation in 1186 (*HW*, ii. 601, n. 143; Hays, *History*, 5–6, 185). Assuming that it is authentic, the title *Northwallie princeps* suggests that the charter was issued during the period when Gruffudd ruled Gwynedd Uwch Conwy after the defeat in 1194 of Dafydd ab Owain, apparently followed by the final expulsion of Rhodri ab Owain (d. 1195) from Anglesey, a rule that ended with the conquest of Gruffudd's lands by Llywelyn ap Iorwerth during 1199 (*HW*, ii. 588–9). Gruffudd died at Aberconwy, having assumed the monastic habit, in 1200 (*BT, Pen20Tr*, 80; *BT, RBH*, 182–3; Carr, 'Prydydd y Moch', 165–6, suggests that he may have been forced to enter Aberconwy by the victorious Llywelyn). However, the title could be a later interpolation, or (more plausibly, perhaps) an expression of Gruffudd's aspirations before the defeat of Dafydd. If so, an earlier *terminus a quo* of *c.*1190 cannot be ruled out: Gruffudd seems first to have driven Rhodri from Anglesey at that date and to have maintained his hold on the island thereafter, apart from a temporary recovery by Rhodri in 1193 and possibly again in 1194 (*HW*, ii. 588; cf. Hays, *History*, 6, which dates the charter to 1188 × 1199 on the grounds that Gruffudd held Anglesey no earlier than 1188). The grange of Gelliniog, which included Rhuddgaer (SH 445 643), was in the commote of Menai, and Tal-y-bont (SH 454 666) lay nearby; the location of *Stawenan* has not been identified (Hays, *History*, 17–18). For some verbal parallels between this charter and those allegedly issued by Llywelyn ap Iorwerth in favour of Aberconwy see note to no. 218 below.

207 Haughmond Abbey and its canons at Nefyn church

Grant, for the salvation of the souls of himself and his predecessors, of Gwion the cook and his land (namely 3 acres in Nefyn), of Abraham son of Alured the cobbler, and Wasdewi and John sons of Serenna, in perpetual alms so that they shall remain for ever with St Mary's church, Nefyn and the canons of Haughmond. Also a confirmation of the gift by his brother Maredudd of Cadwgan ap John Sturry with all his land, possessions and children, and of all his predecessors' gifts of lands and tithes of mills pertaining to Edern and Boduan and tithes of fisheries, and of pastures and all easements and liberties as set forth in those predecessors' charters. Sealing clause; witness.

[April 1195 × 1199]

B = Shrewsbury, Shropshire Records and Research Centre MS 6001/6869 (Haughmond Cartulary), fo. 149r–v. s. xv ex.
Pd. from B, *Cart. Haugh.*, no. 788; from Cardiff County and City Library MS 4.101 (s. xvi/xvii; incomplete), *Hist. Gwydir*, 1; from BL, MS Harley 6068 (s. xvi/xvii; incomplete), Owen, *Catalogue*,

i. 451, n. 2; from ibid., Anon, 'Trefeglwys charter', 240; from a Wynnstay MS dated 1640 destroyed in 1858, Williams, 'Wynnstay MSS.', 332 (incomplete).
Cd., *H*, no. 199.

Sciant tam presentes quam futuri quod ego Griffin(us) filius Canaan concessi et dedi et hac carta mea confirmavi pro salute anime mee et antecessorum meorum Deo et ecclesie Sancti Ioh(ann)is Evangeliste de Haghmon' et canonicis ibidem Deo servientibus ad ecclesiam eorum de Neuyn' Wyon cocum et terram suam scilicet tres acras in Neuin et Abraham filium Aluredi sutoris et duos filios Serenne scilicet Wasdewi et Ioh(ann)em fratrem eius in perpetuam elemosinam ut libere et quiete ad ecclesiam Sancte Marie de Neuin et predictos canonicos de Haghmon' iure perpetuo permaneant. Preterea donationem Mereduth fratris mei quam fecit eisdem canonicis de Kadugan filio Ioh(ann)is Sturry cum tota terra sua et omni substantia sua et liberis suis, et omnes donationes antecessorum meorum in terris et decimis molendinorum de Ederne et de Bothwian et piscariarum et in pasturis et omnibus eisiamentis et libertatibus sicut carte antecessorum eorumdem testantur sepedictis canonicis de Haghmon' [fo. 149v] confirmavi. Ut itaque mea donatio hec et confirmatio imperpetuum stabilis et rata permaneat presenti carta et sigilli appositione eam roboravi et communivi. Hiis testibus: Reuewenard filio Edenwen etc.

The charter is almost certainly no earlier than April 1195, for neither its grants nor that of Maredudd ap Cynan (no. 208 below) which it confirms are included in Bishop Alan of Bangor's confirmation of Haughmond's possessions in his diocese, including grants by Cadwaladr ap Gruffudd and Dafydd ab Owain at Nefyn, issued April 1195 × December 1196 (*Cart. Haugh.*, no. 794). It was probably issued no later than 1199, when Gruffudd lost power in Gwynedd Uwch Conwy to his cousin Llywelyn ap Iorwerth (see note to no. 206 above).

MAREDUDD AP CYNAN AB OWAIN
(d. 1212)

208 St Mary's church, Nefyn and the canons of Haughmond
Grant, for the salvation of the souls of himself and his predecessors and heirs in pure and perpetual alms of Cadwgan ap John, with his wife and children and all his land with all its appurtenances, free of all service owed to Maredudd. Sealing clause; witnesses.

[April 1195 × 1199]

B = Shrewsbury, Shropshire Records and Research Centre MS 6001/6869 (Haughmond Cartulary), fo. 149r. s. xv ex. Rubric: De terra Ioh(ann)is Scurri.
Pd. from B, *Cart. Haugh.*, no. 787.
Cd., *H*, no. 198.

Notum sit tam presentibus quam futuris quod ego Maredud filius Canan dedi et concessi Deo et ecclesie Beate Marie de Neuin et canonicis de Haghmon' pro salute anime mee et omnium antecessorum et heredum meorum in puram et perpetuam elemosinam Caducan filium Ioh(ann)is cum uxore sua et liberis et totam terram suam cum omnibus pertinentiis suis liberam et quietam ab omni servitio quod ad me pertinet. Et ut ista donatio mea rata,[a] firma et inconcussa inperpetuum permaneat eam presens carta mea cum sigilli mei appositione confirmavi. Hiis testibus: Candelau archidiacono, Ioh(ann)e fratre eius, Griffino et Candelau canonicis de Bardeshey, Rob(er)to et Steph(an)o burgensibus de Neuin.

[a] r *in* rata *inserted as correction after* et B.

The charter is earlier than no. 207 above, which confirms the grant, but falls within the same date range as the latter. Llywelyn ap Iorwerth's confirmation (no. 258 below) says that Cadwgan's land was at Morfa Dinllaen. Bishop Alan's confirmation of April 1195 × December 1196 describes Cynddelw as archdeacon of Llŷn; by the early thirteenth century, however, the ecclesiastical status of Llŷn had been demoted to that of a rural deanery (*Cart. Haugh.*, no. 794; Pearson, 'Creation', 174–5). The description of Gruffudd and Cynddelw as canons of Bardsey may indicate that they, like the recipients of the grant, were Augustinians and therefore that Bardsey had been transferred to the Augustinian order by this date (Johns, 'Postscript', 130–1; Jones Pierce, *Medieval Welsh Society*, 392, n. 3). The last two witnesses are the earliest known burgesses of Nefyn; significantly, they were English or French to judge by their names.

*209 Cymer Abbey
Grant of lands in Neigwl (Neugol) *in free alms, free of any service or secular rent.*

[1198 × 1201]

Mention only, in Roger Mortimer's report of the findings of an inquisition into the exaction of 39*s.* per annum from Cymer Abbey, cited in a pardon to the abbey dated 12 February 1316 (*CPR 1313–17*, 395). Although the reference does not explicitly mention a charter, the description of the grant strongly suggests that it was in written form. Maredudd was expelled from Llŷn by Llywelyn ap Iorwerth in 1201 (*BT, Pen20Tr*, 81; *BT, RBH*, 182–3). Although it has been assumed that Maredudd only held Llŷn after the death of his brother Gruffudd in 1200, and that the present charter is thus datable to 1200 × 1201 (Williams-Jones, 'Llywelyn's charter', 47 and n. 19), no. 208 above shows that Maredudd held land in at least one part of Llŷn, that is, Nefyn, before Gruffudd's death, raising the possibility of an earlier *terminus a quo*. The charter may have been issued, therefore, at any time between the foundation of Cymer in 1198 or early 1199 and Maredudd's expulsion from Llŷn in 1201, apart from the period (of uncertain length) of his imprisonment following his capture after the Welsh defeat at Painscastle on 13 August 1198 (*BT, Pen20Tr*, 80; *BT, RBH*, 180–2; *HW*, ii. 586).

LLYWELYN FAWR AP MAREDUDD AP CYNAN
(d. (?)1251)

*210 Strata Marcella Abbey
Testimony concerning the sale of all the land of Pennantigi (Pennantigi) to the monks by [and in MS] all the heirs of that land.
          [Probably September 1241 × August 1251; possibly 1255 × early December 1256]

Summary only, in an inspeximus of Edward II dated at Tutbury, 12 March 1322 (TNA: PRO, C 53/108, m. 6; pd., Jones, 'Abbey of Ystrad Marchell', 315; *Ystrad Marchell Charters*, no. 84; cd., *CChR 1300–26*, 441; *H*, no. 200). Pennantigi was a vaccary – in the parish of Mallwyd (cmt. Mawddwy), and thus in Powys – which was sold to Strata Marcella by Gwenwynwyn ab Owain between March 1201 and August 1204 (no. 557 below). The description of the sale attested to by Llywelyn ap Maredudd as being *dictis monachis et omnibus propriis heredibus eiusdem terre* is probably a scribal error for . . . *ab omnibus propriis heredibus* . . ., as assumed by Jones and suggested in *CChR 1300–26*, 441. If, as is very probable, the sale by the heirs, i.e. free proprietors, of the land was part of the same transaction as Gwenwynwyn's sale, the attestation was presumably by Llywelyn ap Maredudd ap Cynan, rather than his grandson Llywelyn ap Maredudd ap Llywelyn. If so, the use of the title *princeps de Meironut* indicates that the document was issued no earlier than September 1241, when Llywelyn gained Meirionnydd, which his father Maredudd ap Cynan had lost in 1202, and no later than August 1251, when Llywelyn was succeeded by his son Maredudd (note to no. 211 below; *CR 1247–51*, 555; Stephenson, *Governance*, 143–4). If, on the other hand, the sale by the heirs took place later than Gwenwynwyn's sale, it is just possible that the document was issued by Llywelyn ap Maredudd ap Llywelyn between his succession to Meirionnydd in 1255 and expulsion by Llywelyn ap Gruffudd early in December 1256 (see note to no. 212 below).

211 Letter patent concerning Henry III
Notification that Llywelyn has promised to serve King Henry faithfully, to harm all those who are unfaithful to him and to give no support to his enemies. If he should be convicted of having acted against the king in any way, he concedes on behalf of himself and his heirs that all his land shall fall to the king and his heirs as demesne to be retained for the king's own use or to be given to whoever he wishes; Llywelyn and his heirs will retain nothing except by the king's grace, in which case they will be the king's tenants according to the customs of Welsh barons just like other Welsh barons. Witnesses; sealing clause.
                                                                                [1246, probably August]

   B = TNA: PRO, E 36/274 (Liber A), fo. 332r. s. xiii ex.
   Pd. from B, *LW*, 14–15 (no. 8).
   Cd., *H*, no. 512.

[O]mnibus ad quorum notitiam presens scriptum pervenerit Lewelin(us) senior filius Mored' filii[a] Kanani de M(er)ennoyth salutem. Noverit universitas vestra me promisisse domino H. regi Angl(ie) fideliter pro posse meo servire et omnes qui contra fidem eius sunt gravare, nullum assensum neque consensum inimicis suis adhibere. Et si forte contigerit quod in aliquo, quod absit, contra dominum regem rationabiliter fuero convictus, concedo pro me et heredibus meis domino regi et heredibus suis totam terram meam quod cedat ei et heredibus suis in dominicum, rettinendi[b] ad opus suum proprium vel dandi cuicumque voluerit sine aliquo retenemento mihi vel heredibus meis nisi fuerit de mera gratia sua vel heredum suorum, ita tamen quod dominus rex me et heredes meos teneat secundum usus et consuetudines Walens(ium) baronum prout alios barones Walens(es) tenuerit. Hiis testibus: domino N. de Mol', Rob(er)to Walerond, Griffino filio Wennonwen, Gilberto de Uall', Guidone de Briona, Mored' filio[a] Res, Mored' filio[a] Oweyn et aliis fidelibus domini regis. In cuius rei testimonium presenti scripto sigillum meum apposui.

[a] filius B. | [b] *sic in* B.

Llywelyn Fawr and his younger brother Llywelyn Fychan, sons of Maredudd ap Cynan, were restored to Meirionnydd by Dafydd ap Llywelyn following the latter's submission to Henry III in late August 1241 (*BT, Pen20Tr*, 106; *BT, RBH*, 236; *HW*, ii. 698, n. 28). For this restoration they bound themselves to pay Henry a fine of £80, the first half of which was due on 27 January 1242 (*Rot. Fin.*, i. 371). Edwards suggested that the letter may well have been Llywelyn's promise of fealty to the king on being restored, and was thus possibly datable to the autumn of 1241 (*LW*, 14–15). However, as Walker pointed out ('Anglo-Welsh Wars', 563–4 and n. 314), the combination of witnesses, including Nicholas de Molis and Robert Walerand as well as the two Pembrokeshire tenants Gilbert de Valle and Guy de Brian, strongly suggests that it was written during the passage of the royal army through Meirionnydd in 1246, probably in August (a date accepted by Smith, *Llywelyn*, 55).

LLYWELYN AP MAREDUDD AP LLYWELYN
(d. 1263)

212 Henry III
Letter, reminding the king that, because he preferred fidelity to infidelity, he has recently been expelled from his land of Meirionnydd through the force of Llywelyn ap Gruffudd and has now spent all the movable goods he had when he left. As the king has been his refuge since that time, he prays the king to look mercifully on him in his predicament and to make some temporary provision for himself and his family. He hopes to recover his land soon through the favour of God and the king.

[December 1256 × December 1259; probably December 1256 × 1257]

A = TNA: PRO, SC 1/4, no. 27. No endorsements; approx. 179 × 34 mm.; mounted, foot cut away.
Pd. from A, *RL*, ii. 123–4.
Cd., *CAC*, 28; *H*, no. 513.

Excellentissimo domino suo H. Dei gratia illustri regi Angl(ie), domino Hybern(ie), duci Norm(annie), Aquit' et comiti And' suus humilis et fidelis in omnibus Lewelin(us) filius Maredud de Meyronnid salutem et se totum. Venerande excellentie vestre karissime domino bene constat qualiter a terra mea de Meyro(n)nid, eo quo fidelitatem meam infidelitati preposui, per vim et prepotentiam Lewel(ini) filii Griffin(i) dudum fui eiectus et mobilia que habui in recessu meo de terra illa iam expendi. Et quoniam ex quo vestra regalis potentia mee tribulationis reffugium est et protectio, excellentiam vestram duxi humiliter exorandam quatinus pro Deo et pro servicio vobis semper duraturo me in angustia mea clementer et[a] misericorditer respicere dignemini, de quadam sustentatione mihi et familie mee ad tempus, si placet, facientes[b] provideri; me etenim spes est per Dei et vestri favorem terre nostre in brevi me habere recuperationem. Valeat regalis potentia vestra per tempora longiora. Valete.

[a] A *inserts* ele *which is struck through.* | [b] *corrected in* A *from* faciatis.

As Edwards argued (*CAC*, 29), the letter was presumably written not very long after Llywelyn was expelled from Meirionnydd by Llywelyn ap Gruffudd in early December 1256, and can be no later than 1259, since 'duke of Normandy' is included among the king's titles; Henry III relinquished this title in the Treaty of Paris with Louis IX of France on 4 December 1259. The description of the expulsion as having occurred *dudum* suggests a date within the early part of this date range. Llywelyn succeeded his father Maredudd ap Llywelyn ap Maredudd in 1255 and died in 1263 (Stephenson, *Governance*, 143; Smith, *Llywelyn*, 55, n. 74, 91, 155–6).

THE LINEAGE OF LLYWELYN AP IORWERTH

LLYWELYN AP IORWERTH
(d. 11 April 1240)

213 Basingwerk Abbey
Grant and confirmation of all the gifts of his predecessors, free of all earthly service and secular exaction, namely the site of the abbey with the mill before the gate; the land before the gates given by Ranulf and his brother Eneas; the land which Maredudd Wawer *had in Holywell and in the field of that township; Fulbrook with all its appurtenances and common pasture in the mountains; and* Hauotdeleweth *and* Creicgraft *with all their appurtenances. Sealing clause; witnesses.*

[1194 × c.October 1202]

B = TNA: PRO, C 53/73 (Ch. R. 13 Edward I), mm. 26–25 (in an inspeximus of King Edward I, 12 June 1285).
C = TNA: PRO, C 53/116 (Ch. R. 3 Edward III), m. 26 (in an inspeximus of B, 17 February 1329).
D = TNA: PRO, C 53/164 (Ch. R. 15–17 Richard II), m. 16 (in an inspeximus of C, 2 December 1393).
Pd. from D, *Mon. Ang.*, v. 263; from *Mon. Ang.*, H. L. J. J. W., 'Basingwerk abbey', 106 (trans. only). Cd., *CChR 1257–1300*, 291 (from B); *CChR 1327–41*, 100 (from C); *CChR 1341–1417*, 342 (from D); Stephenson, *Governance*, 201; *H*, no. 124.

Lewelinus princeps Northwall(ie) omnibus sancte matris ecclesie filiis tam presentibus quam futuris in Cristo salutem. Noverit presens viventium etas et universa futurorum posteritas quod ego Lewelinus concedo et confirmo Deo et Sancte Marie et monasterio de Basingwerk' monachisque ibidem Deo servientibus omnes donationes quas antecessores mei prefato monasterio pro suis animabus contulerunt, liberas et quietas ab omni servitio terreno et exactione seculari, scilicet locum illum in quo abbatia illorum fundata est cum molendino quod ante portam habent; terram [m. 25] que ante fores eorum iacet quam Ranulphus et frater eius Eneas predictis monachis dederunt; terram etiam quam Meredith Wawer in Haliwelle et in campo eiusdem ville habuit, et Fulebrock' cum omnibus pertinentiis suis et communitatem pasture montium cum ceteris, et Hauotdeleweth et Creicgraft cum omnibus pertinentiis suis in terris et aquis et pasturis et omnibus ceteris aisiamentis. Ne igitur aliquis contra hanc nostram paginam temere venire audeat sigilli mei impressione et testibus eam communio. Hii autem sunt testes: Ric(ardu)s filius Kadwalad', Horin filius Ulf, Meyiller filius Kadugan, Hitel filius Kenred, Griffinus filius Wskeneu, Kenwreich filius Meredit, Will(elmu)s filius Ierwerth.

The charter can be no earlier than 1194, when Llywelyn gained control of Perfeddwlad following his defeat of Dafydd ab Owain (*HW*, ii. 588–9). As Stephenson noted, the witness list contains none of Llywelyn's servants who appear fairly regularly from *c*.1215, suggesting that the charter 'may be very early' (*Governance*, 201). The strongest evidence of an early date is the absence of the church of Holywell among the possessions confirmed, indicating that this charter probably pre-dates Llywelyn's charter granting that church to Basingwerk (no. 216 below), issued no later than October 1202. Richard ap Cadwaladr, the first witness, was quite possibly the same as the Rhicert or Richard who was a son of Cadwaladr ap Gruffudd ap Cynan (d. 1172) (cf. Stephenson, *Governance*, 149–50, and nos 216, 258). The manor of Fulbrook was granted to Basingwerk *c*.1135 by Ranulf II, earl of Chester (1129–53), and Holywell by Robert Pierrepont, with Ranulf II's consent (*Chester Charters*, no. 36; *CChR 1257–1300*, 290), and included in a confirmation issued by Henry II datable to 1155 × May 1162 (*Mon. Ang.*, v. 262–3).

*214 Basingwerk Abbey
Confirmation of all his land of Mostyn, and a grant of osiers for making houses and hedges.
[1194 × August 1211, or July 1212 × 11 April 1240]

Mention only, in an inspeximus of Edward III dated at Westminster, 17 February 1329 (*CChR 1327–41*, 100; cd., *H*, no. 161). For the *terminus a quo* of this charter see no. 213 above. Llywelyn temporarily lost control of the Four Cantrefs, including the cantref of Tegeingl in which Mostyn was situated, following his submission to King John in August 1211 (no. 233 below).

*215 Basingwerk Abbey
Grant of the land and pasture of Gelli with all its appurtenances.
[1194 × August 1211, or July 1212 × 11 April 1240]

Mention only, in a confirmation by Llywelyn's son Dafydd ap Llywelyn, dated at Coleshill, 25 July 1240 (no. 292 below). For the dating limits of this charter see no. 213 above. Gelli (SJ 127 783) lay in Tegeingl to the west of the abbey in the parish of Whitford and formed the basis of the monks' township of Tre'rabad (SJ 110 785) (Williams, 'Basingwerk abbey', 106–8, with a map).

216 Basingwerk Abbey

Grant in pure and perpetual alms, for the relief of the poverty of the monks and for the souls of himself and of his father, mother and ancestors, of the church of Holywell with all its appurtenances, saving the rights which the clerks Absolom, Ivo and Adam have therein as long as they live, so that once vacant each prebend shall revert fully to the monks. Sealing clause; witnesses.

[*c*.June 1196 × October 1199; or *c*.February 1200 × *c*.February 1201;
or December 1201 × *c*.October 1202]

B = TNA: PRO, CHES 30/2 (Flint Plea Rolls), m. 5 (contemporary enrolment of letter reciting the charter presented on behalf of Edward, prince of Wales in legal proceedings at Flint, 12 April 1305).
C = TNA: PRO, CHES 30/7 (Flint Plea Rolls), m. 30 (contemporary enrolment of ?B in legal proceedings at Flint, 29 July 1336).
Pd. from B, J. E. Messham *apud* Leach, 'Excavations at Hen Blas', 42–3 (and trans., ibid., 46).
Cd., *H*, no. 118.

Omnibus sancte matris ecclesie [filiis] tam presentibus quam futuris ego[a] princeps[b] Norwall(ie) salutem.[c] Noverit universitas vestra quod caritatis intuitu ac pietatis ad sublevandum inopiam monacorum de Basingwerk[d] ego Lewel(inus) pro anima mea et anima patris mei et matris mee et antecessorum meorum predictis monachis de Basingwerk[d] do et concedo in puram et perpetuam elemosinam ecclesiam de Halywell'[e] cum omnibus pertinentiis suis ut eam habeant in proprios usus inperpetuum possidendam, salvo iure et Absolonis, Ivone[f] et Ade clericorum quod in eadem habent ecclesia[g] quamdiu vixerint, ita tunc quod singule prebende cum vacaverint unica[h] et plena integritate in predictorum usus cedant monachorum. Et ut ista donatio firma sit et stabilis sigilli mei impressione et testibus eam communio atque confirmo. Hii autem sunt testes: dominus scilicet Rawatlan(us)[i] electus de Bangor, Abrah(a)m abbas de Aberconewey, Wen[j] ap Ednewen, Ric(ard)us filius Cadwalladre[k] et multi alii.

[a] *sic in* BC; Lewelinus *omitted?* | [b] princes B. | [c] C *inserts* in Cristo. | [d] Basyngwerk C. | [e] Haliwell' C. | [f] Ivonis C. | [g] ecclesiam B. | [h] *omitted in* C, *which has a lacuna at this point.* | [i] Rawathan(us) C. [j] Wyon C. | [k] Cadewaladr' C.

Though the copies of this charter in the Flint plea rolls are evidently corrupt in their rendering of the protocol, they appear to derive from an authentic act of Llywelyn. C appears to be a copy of B, though the insertion of *in Cristo* in the greeting in C could indicate that its text derived from the exemplar presented on behalf of the prince of Wales in 1305 rather than from the enrolment containing B.

The charter is probably no earlier than about June 1196, when its first witness, Rotoland, was elected bishop of Bangor for the second time following the death of Bishop Alan of

Bangor in England on 19 May 1196. Rotoland was first elected bishop of Bangor following the death of Bishop Gwion in 1190, but his candidature seems effectively to have lapsed following the consecration of Bishop Alan on 16 April 1195. Rotoland's second election was equally unsuccessful, for Robert of Shrewsbury was consecrated bishop of Bangor by Archbishop Hubert Walter on 16 March 1197. Appeals to the papacy to confirm his election took Rotoland away from Gwynedd from about October 1199 to January 1200 and from about February to December 1201 (Hays, 'Rotoland'). Although it has been assumed that Rotoland would not have been elected without Llywelyn's approval (ibid., 12), this is questionable, since it is unlikely that Llywelyn was in control of Arfon, including Bangor, in 1196; rather, Gruffudd ap Cynan ab Owain seems to have been the dominant power in Gwynedd Uwch Conwy at that time, only succumbing to Llywelyn in 1199 (Smith, 'Cymer', 103–4). The present charter implies that Llywelyn at least tolerated Rotoland's status as bishop-elect. If so, it was probably issued before Rotoland's departure for Rome in about February 1201, for by July 1201 the prince clearly accepted Robert as bishop, swearing fealty in his presence to King John (no. 221 below). However, a later date is not impossible, for Gerald of Wales claims that he reconciled Llywelyn and Rotoland on the latter's return to Gwynedd in December 1201, and that in August or early September 1202 Rotoland handed over to him, on the prince's orders, £20 held at Aberconwy that had been collected to support Gerald's metropolitan campaign. This suggests that the prince was on friendly terms with Rotoland, even perhaps recognizing him as bishop-elect, between December 1201 and the late summer of 1202. However, it is very unlikely that Llywelyn will have continued this support once news reached Gwynedd of Rotoland's condemnation by the Cistercian General Chapter in September 1202. Rotoland left Gwynedd in about October, and after reaching France was accompanied by Gerald to Cîteaux and subsequently to Rome, which they reached on 4 January 1203 (cf. Hays, 'Rotoland', 13–15). Llywelyn is next found acting together with Bishop Robert early in 1204 (ibid., 17 and 19, n. 29). The inclusion of Rotoland in the witness list to the charter therefore points to a very early date in Llywelyn's reign, certainly before Rotoland was condemned by the Cistercians, and probably before March 1201. An early date is also indicated by the inclusion of Gwyn ab Ednywain, who witnessed several acts between the late twelfth century and 1209 (nos 206, 229, 231; cf. Stephenson, *Governance*, 215). For Richard ap Cadwaladr see note to no. 213 above.

*217 Beddgelert Priory

Grant of all the land of Cynddelw Llwyd of Pennant (cartam Lewelini magni de tota terra Kindeluluyt de Pennant).

[*c.*1199 × 11 April 1240]

Mention only, in a letter patent of Edward I dated at Canterbury, 10 May 1286, referring to a letter patent of Anian, bishop of Bangor that listed charters granted to Beddgelert by Welsh princes (TNA: PRO, C 53/74, m. 1; pd., *Mon. Ang.*, vi: i. 200; *Rec. Caern.*, 166 (Edward's letter only); cd., Gresham, *Eifionydd*, 64; Stephenson, *Governance*, 204; *H*, no. 168). The grant could have been made at any point after Llywelyn secured his domination of Gwynedd Uwch Conwy. Beddgelert Priory lay on the north-eastern edge of the township of Pennant, cmt. Eifionydd (Gresham, *Eifionydd*, 4–6).

†218 Aberconwy Abbey

Grant and confirmation in pure and perpetual alms, for the salvation of the souls of himself and all his ancestors, heirs and successors, of (1) the site in which the monastery was founded, by the following boundaries: ascending from the river Conwy to Aber-y-gyffyn, thence along the river Gyffin to a bank by Gwrydrhos, hence turning right along that bank marked by stones to the stream of Perau, hence ascending by that stream to a bank by Coed Mawr, hence by that bank to a rock nearby, hence along the top of the rocky hills to the head of the Cristionydd, hence descending to the sea and thence along the river Conwy to Aber-y-gyffin.

(2) A further grant and confirmation of lands in Creuddyn by the following boundaries: ascending from the Conwy to the little spring in the farthest part of the monks' arable land at Hennron, *hence along the upper part of the cultivated land to the large stones in Erw Morfran; thence to the public way, hence along the way to the bank above* Erwedus, *hence to the top of Carreg Wiber, hence by the upper part of Rhyforyn and the monks' arable land to the furthest part of Gwern-y-gof, hence along the hollow below Gwern-y-gof to the land of Crogfryn, hence by the boundary stones to the stream by Eglwys Rhos, hence along the said stream to the hollow in the furthest part of the monks' meadow below Crogfryn, hence along the hollow to the small brook between Bodysgallen and Bron Goch which descends into that hollow, hence to a spring, hence to a rock with a pit, hence to Carreg* Ereu, *hence to a second rock beyond Carreg Walch, hence along the upper part of the monks' cultivated land to the bank between Trefwarth and Callawr Werth, and thus along that bank to the pool below, hence along the furthest part of the monks' arable land to the grove of Iarddur ap Cynddelw, hence by the bank to the top of that bank, thence along the water-side between the arable land and the pool to Argae Felin, hence along the water to the Conwy.*

(3) A further grant of all the river Conwy and the crossing of that river, and the fishery from Aber-y-gyffin to Aberconwy.

(4) A further grant and confirmation of Ffriwlwyd by the following boundaries: ascending from the sea along the middle of a boundary bank to the river Carrog, hence along the middle of the Carrog to the small brook of Chwilogen, hence along the middle of the Chwilogen to its source, hence ascending through the marsh to Pwllberwr, hence by the channel of the marsh to Gwern-y-bleiddiau, hence along the middle of Gwern-y-bleiddiau to Waun Bant descending by a stream flowing through a glen to the river Dwyfach and then by the whole of the Dwyfach and the mill and the fishery to the river Dwyfor, thence by the middle of the Dwyfor with half of the fishery to the sea and thence along the shore to the aforesaid bank.

(5) A further grant and confirmation of Cwm by these boundaries: ascending from Hensarngwm near Pentyrch along a hollow to the river Ceiliog, hence along the middle of the Ceiliog to the brook flowing from Sychnant, hence by that brook to Clawdd Seri, hence descending by the water flowing from Clawdd Seri to the head of the Efelog brook, hence along the middle of the Efelog to Rhyd Efelog, hence ascending by a hollow to Rytnerthvoessen, *hence by the farthest hollow beyond Bryn Brych and Ynys Las to the river Carrog, and thence ascending by a hollow to Hensarngwm.*

(6) A further grant and confirmation of Rhedynog Felen by these boundaries: from the place where the river Carrog flows near a spring near Llanwnda to a hollow between Gyfynys Fechan and Ynys Ceubren to Gerthig, hence turning right along a hollow beyond Ynys Ceubren to Wern Ddofn, hence along the middle of Wern Ddofn descending to the river Gwyleyt, *hence along the middle of the* Gwyleit *to Aber Carrog near Morfa Dinlle, and thus ascending by the middle of the Carrog towards Llanwnda to the said place near the aforesaid spring.*

(7) A further grant and confirmation of Nancall by these boundaries: ascending from Aber Call by the river Call to Braich Ddu, hence to the heights of Llwyd Mawr, hence to the summit of the mountain of Llwyd Mawr to the head of Gweunydd Gwynion, hence to the head of the Maig, hence descending along the middle of the Maig to the Dwyfach, and from there by the Dwyfach to Aber Call.

(8) A further grant and confirmation of Gelliniog by these boundaries: ascending from the Menai by the river Braint to the mouth of Pwll Dwyran, hence along the middle of Pwll Dwyran to Sarn-y-gerdd, hence by a stone-marked boundary to a pool near Trefarthen, hence by the middle of that pool to the shore, hence to the Menai to the mouth of the Braint.

(9) A further grant and confirmation of the mill of Tal-y-bont with its appurtenances, the river and bank of Sarn-y-felin to Carreg Elgar and the public way at all times from Gelliniog to the aforesaid mill without hindrance from anyone.

(10) A further grant and confirmation of Bodgedwydd by these boundaries: ascending from a small island in Llyn Coron by the middle of Clawdd Iago to Carnedd Iorwerth, hence turning towards Aberffraw by a stone-marked boundary to Waun Wen, hence by a stone-marked boundary to Murddunen Cyfnerth, hence directly towards Henllys to Cors Henllys, hence turning to the right by the middle of the stream to Rhytty, hence by the middle of that stream to the mouth of Gofer Garanen as it descends into Korscallellyn, *hence ascending by the Gofer Garanen near to a stone-marked boundary to Waun Las, hence by the middle of Waun Las to Waun Fawr, hence ascending by the stream to Ffynnon-y-meirch, hence by a stone-marked boundary to the side of Bod-wrdin, hence following the stones to Cerrig Poethion, hence by a boundary turning towards Trefdraeth to the side of Trefdraeth, hence by the middle of water channel in the vicinity of Trefdraeth by the middle of Cors y Gigfran to Pyllau Halog and thence by the water channel to the aforesaid island.*

(11) A further grant and confirmation of the area of Llan-faes by its boundaries with all its appurtenances.

(12) A further grant and confirmation of Foelas, Ceirniog and Llanfair Rhyd Gastell by these boundaries: ascending from the mouth of the Gwrysgawg by the river Gwrysgawg to the wide ford at the head of the Gwrysgawg, hence by the water channel to Maen-y-siarter, hence to Cerrig Llwynogod, hence to Carnedd Rhun, hence to the spring below Moel Seissawg, hence to the head of Gwaun Eneas, hence descending by the water channel to Hen Ryd Beli, hence by the river Caledwyn below Cors Garanen, hence straight across to Esgynfaen Gwgon, hence to Llyn Alwen, hence by the middle of Llyn Alwen and the middle of the river Alwen to Rhyd Gwyn, hence by Nant Heilin Sais to the glen turning right and ascending by that glen to the head of a deep water channel below Brondengynllwyn, *hence leaving* Brondengynllwyn *on the right between the monks' boundaries by the valley to the head of the Llaethog, hence by the middle of the Llaethog to the river Nug, hence by the middle of the Nug to the river Conwy, and by the middle of the Conwy to the mouth of the Gwrysgawg.*

(13) A further grant and confirmation of Llyn Cymer by these boundaries: ascending by Llyn Cymer by the river Alwen to the mouth of Drywes, hence by the middle of the Drywes to Bon-yr-helyg-bras, hence to Nant Rhingylliaid, hence to the river Brenig and by the middle of the Brenig to Llyn Cymer.

(14) A further grant and confirmation of Llechwedd Cryn Llwyn by these boundaries: from the pool nearer to the top of Dinas Din Dunod opposite the Alwen to the place where the stream descends into the Alwen from Bwlch Dinewyd, thence across from the same stream to Bwlch Dinewyd, thence by the descent of the stream from the other part of the mountain

towards *Cerrigydrudion* to *Ynys-yr-haidd, hence from the upper part of that Ynys by the pool to the farther stream flowing from a spring, thence along a glen to the top of the great marsh towards the east, hence along that marsh to the stream running from the farther spring towards the east from the region of the Alwen, and from that spring to the lower boundary below the road, thence along that boundary to* Heliclwyneu *at the head of the stream which descends towards the Alwen, thence to Cerrig Llwydion towards the north on the height of a hill, hence to the head of the valley which descends towards Dinas Din Dunod, hence along the same valley to the aforesaid pool next to the top of that Dinas.*

(15) A further grant and confirmation of these lands at Nanhwynan, namely Gwastad Onnos, Bryngwynein, *Hafod Tandrec, Llyn Du, Cwm-y-gored, Ysgubor Din Emrys, (?)Hendref Hwynan* (Hendrefwynein), *Gwernos Deg, Pennant Morgenau, Pennant Crwn, Cwm Llain on both sides of the Llain, Cwm Erch on both sides of the Erch, Cwm Dylif on both sides of the Dylif,* Kemen Terneint *and Gwryd Cai on both sides of the* Degymni, *by these boundaries: ascending from the mouth of the Colwyn as it descends into the Fferlas [Glaslyn] along the middle of the Colwyn to the head of the Colwyn as it descends from Bwlch Cwm Llain, hence by the ridge of the rocks to the top of Wyddfa Fawr [Snowdon], hence to the top of Crib Goch, hence to the top of Wregysog, hence along the height of the rocks to the seat of Peris [(?)Gorffwysfa Peris], hence to the top of Moel Berfedd, hence directly to the place where the river Mymbyr begins to descend precipitately like a torrent, hence along the middle of the Mymbyr to Yr Afon Goch, hence ascending by that water to Llygad-yr-ych, hence to the height of Cerrig-yr-ych, hence to Llech* Edear, *hence to Bancarw, hence by the summit of the rocks of Bancarw to the head of the Teirw, hence by the river Teirw to the rock which descends into the Teirw near to the upper ford of the Teirw, hence by the small rocky hills from the side of the Gerrynt to Llechwedd Gwylfau, hence indirectly to the small mountain which looks like a castle on the right-hand side of Llechwedd Gwylfau, hence by the heights to the top of Carreg-yr-eryr, hence by the summit of the rocks to the peak of Moel Dinewyd, hence to Bylchau Terfyn, hence by the ridge of the rocks to Gorsedd* Ressygynt *as it hangs over the valley, hence turning towards Llyn Dinas along a rocky arm above the valley to the top of Clawdd Main, hence by the middle of that Clawdd to the river Fferlas, and thence by the middle of the Fferlas to the mouth of the Colwyn as it descends into Llyn Cymer.*

(16) A further grant and confirmation of Ardda and Darlas by these boundaries: ascending from the mouth of Pwll-y-ddarlas by the middle of the water to the marsh of Cowlyd, hence by the middle of that marsh to the pool above the top of the marsh and by that pool directly to Y Fign Fforchog, hence by the height of the rocks to the top of Llithrig-y-wrach, hence by the heights of that mountain towards the west to Bwlch Eryl Farchog, hence descending by that valley and its small stream, called Ffrwd Ddu, which is directly below Carreg Gwenoliaid and descends into the river Eigiau, and by the Eigiau to the marsh of the Eigiau and by that marsh and the river descending from the marsh to the river Conwy and by the middle of the Conwy to the mouth of Pwll-y-ddarlas.

(17) A further grant that the monks shall be free in perpetuity from all feeding and puture of men, horses, dogs and birds and shall not be forced to feed Llywelyn or his servants or any other secular persons under the cover of custom and that neither he nor his servants or other secular persons shall interfere with elections, depositions or resignations of abbots, but everything shall be ordained in the monastery by the religious according to the Rule.

(18) A further grant that the monks may benefit from shipwreck in their lands in the same way as Llywelyn does in his, namely that any goods which come to their lands from the sea as

a result of sinking or wreck or other misfortune shall belong entirely to the monks; similarly if ships or vessels or goods of the monks are wrecked within the prince's land those vessels and goods belong to the monks.

(19) A further grant that the monks and their servants with all their goods shall be quit of all tolls, ferry dues, road dues and bridge dues in all Llywelyn's lands and that they and their servants are free to buy and sell animals, food and drink and other goods. Similarly they and their servants and all their goods may have free passage across the Menai, Conwy, mouth of the Mawddach and the Dyfi and in all ferry-crossings throughout Llywelyn's power notwithstanding any law or custom.

(20) A further grant that if the monks' animals or other goods are stolen or temporarily lost, as soon as the monks have proved that those goods are theirs they will be handed over to them without delay. Similarly Llywelyn forbids any secular or religious person from his land apart from the monks to use the iron brand which they use to mark their animals, and if anyone's animals are found with that mark [they will be returned to] the monks.

(21) A further grant in perpetuity that the monks shall not be judged for any causes in Llywelyn's courts or any lay court, but shall be corrected in their chapter according to their order.

(22) A further grant that no one may extort from them common rights or a part of their pastures, woods or mills, but the monks may keep against all the boundaries contained in this charter and within those boundaries ploughing, buildings, mills, cultivation and other labour services.

(23) A further grant that no one may bring an action against them concerning the reception of any persons to their habit, of whatever condition, after these have made their professions, but actions may be brought against such persons during the year of probation.

(24) A further grant that if any of those who have taken monastic vows has received money or other goods incautiously from creditors or involved themselves in secular suretyships without the abbot's permission, the monastery shall not make satisfaction for those borrowings and sureties.

(25) A further grant that the monks may build mills on waters running between their lands and those of the prince or his men and may even divert those waters from their beds to their lands.

(26) A further grant that the monks may receive into their habit and service the prince's free men, spadarii *and advowry men and all having the first tonsure of whatever condition.*

And since it is a pious thing to give protection to all who leave secular vanities and worldly riches and voluntarily turn from the service of princes to the service of the king of kings, Llywelyn wishes that the monks, both present and future, shall possess all the aforesaid lands by the aforenamed boundaries, including fisheries, mills, minerals, birds, shores, harbours, shipwrecks and treasures freely in pure and perpetual alms in perpetuity, free of all earthly service and secular exaction. He also wishes that the monks shall enjoy all the aforesaid liberties throughout all his lands and throughout his principality in perpetuity. And he prohibits, on pain of his displeasure, any one from injuring the monks in contravention of this charter, since he has taken them and all their possessions under his protection. Sealing clause; witnesses.

Aberconwy, 7 January 1199

B = TNA: PRO, C 53/119 (Ch. R. 6 Edward III), m. 21 (in an inspeximus, 24 March 1332).
C = BL, Harl. MS 3725 (Register of Aberconwy Abbey), fos 63v–65v. s. xiv². (Incomplete; comparison with D shows that this recites an inspeximus of B by Edward the Black Prince 16 October 1347 before a *quo warranto* inquiry at Caernarfon, 1348.)
D = BL, Harl. MS 696 (Record of Caernarfon), fo. 90r–v. 1494. (Incomplete; reciting an inspeximus of B by Edward the Black Prince 16 October 1347 before a *quo warranto* inquiry at Caernarfon, 1348.)
Pd. from B, *Mon. Ang.*, v. 672–4; from C, *Reg. Aberconway*, 22–3; from D, *Rec. Caern.*, 146–8; from *Mon. Ang.*, Bezant Lowe, *Heart of Northern Wales*, 444–8 (trans. only).
Cd., *CChR 1327–41*, 267 (from B); Stephenson, *Governance*, 199–200; *H*, no. 122.

Notum sit omnibus sancte matris ecclesie filiis tam presentibus quam futuris quod ego Lewelin(us) Gervasii filius totius Norwall(ie) princeps intuitu divine pietatis pro salute anime mee et animarum omnium antecessorum et heredum ac successorum meorum dedi et concessi atque presenti carta mea confirmavi pro me et heredibus ac successoribus meis in puram et perpetuam elemosinam imperpetuum Deo et Sancte Marie et monachis de Ab(er)conewey sub regulari habitu Deo servituris [i] locum ipsum in quo idem monasterium fundatum est per hos scilicet terminos: ᵃ⁻ascendendo de flumine Conwy usque ad Aberegeffyn deinde totum fluvium Geffeyn usque ad quoddam *claud* iuxta Gweridros, hinc divertendo ad dexteram per illud *claud* lapidibus signatum usque ad rivulum Perhey, hinc ascendendo per illum rivulum usque ad quoddam *claud* iuxta Coetmaur, hinc per illud *claud* usque ad quandam rupem prope hinc per altitudinem collium petrosarum usque ad os Cristiani, hinc descendendo usque ad mare, et deinde per flumen Conwy usque ad Aberegeffyn.

[ii] Dedi etiam et concessi atque confirmavi eisdem monachis has terras apud Creudyn per hos videlicet terminos: ascendendo de Conwy usque ad quendam fonticulum existentem in extrema parte terre arabilis monachorum apud Hennron, hinc per superiorem partem terre ab eisdem culte usque ad lapides grandes existentes in Erw Voruran, inde usque ad communem viam, hinc per ductum vie usque ad *claud* supra Erwedus, hinc usque ad capud Carrec Wyber, hinc per superiorem partem Ryuoryn, et terre arabilis monachorum usque ad extremum partem Gwernegof, hinc per alveum desubtus Gwernegof usque ad terram Crocuryn, hinc per lapides in termino constitutos usque ad rivulum iuxta Eglwys Ros, hinc per dictum rivuli usque ad alveum, qui est in extrema parte prati monachorum subtus Crocuryn, hinc per ductum alvei usque ad descensum rivuli, qui est inter Bodesgallen et Brongoch, et descendit in dictum alveum, hinc usque ad fontem quendam, hinc per rupem proximam desuper predentem usque ad lapidem quem vocant quadratum, hinc usque ad rupem in qua est fovea, hinc usque ad Carrec Ereu, hinc usque ad secundam rupem ultra Carrecwalch, hinc per superiorem partem terre culte monachorum usque ad *claud* inter Trefwarth, et Callaurwerth, et sic per dictum illius *claud* usque ad paludem subtus, hinc per extremam partem terre arabilis monachorum usque ad nemus Eardur filii Kendelu, hinc per *claud* usque ad capud illius *claud*, inde per ripam paludis inter terram arabilem et paludem usque ad Argae Velin, hinc per ductum aque usque ad Conwy.

[iii] Concessi etiam eisdem monachis totam aquam Conwy, et eiusdem aque transitum, atque piscarium de Aber Egeffyn usque Aber Conwy.

[iv] Concessi insuper et confirmavi eisdem monachis Friwlwyt, per hos scilicet terminos: ascendendo de mari per medium cuiusdam fosse in terminum facte usque ad fluvium Karroc, hinc per medium Karroc usque ad rivulum Chwilogen, hinc per medium

Chwilogen usque *blaen* Chwilogen hinc ascendendo per paludem usque Pwllberwr, hinc per alveum paludis usque Gwernebleideu, hinc per medium Gwernebleideu usque Wennbant, hinc per medium Wennbant descendendo per quendam rivulum fluentem per quandam valliculam usque ad fluvium Dwyuech et sic descendendo totam aquam Dwyuech et molendinum atque piscariam totaliter et integre usque ad fluvium Dwyuaur, deinde per medium aque Dwyuaur cum medietate piscarie usque ad mare et abhinc per litus usque ad fossam supradictam.

[v] Concessi etiam et confirmavi eisdem monachis Kwm per hos videlicet terminos: ascendendo de Hensarngwm iuxta Pentyrch per quendam alveum usque ad fluvium Keiloc, hinc per medium Keiloc usque ad quendam rivum fluentem de Sichnant, hinc per illum rivum usque ad Claud Seri hinc descendendo per aquam fluentem de Claud Seri usque *blaen* rivi Efelauc, hinc per medium rivi Efelauc usque Rytefelauc, hinc ascendendo per quendam alveum usque Rytnerthvoessen, hinc per extremum alveum ultra Brynbrych et Enys Las usque ad fluvium Carroc, et ab hinc ascendendo per quendam alveum usque Hensarngwm.

[vi] Dedi etiam et confirmavi eisdem Redenocuelen, per hos videlicet terminos: ab illo loco quo fluvius Karroc fluit iuxta quendam fontem existentem prope Llanwnda, usque ad quendam alveum qui est inter Gefenys Vechan, et Enys Keubren usque Gerthic, hinc divertendo ad dexteram per quendam alveum ultra Enys Keubren' usque Werndofyn, hinc per medium Werndofyn descendendo usque ad fluvium Gwyleyt, hinc per medium Gwyleit usque Aberkarroc iuxta Morua Dinlleu, et sic ascendendo per medium aque Karroc versus Llanwnda usque ad dictum locum iuxta predictum fontem.

[vii] Concessi etiam et confirmavi eisdem Nankall per hos scilicet terminos: ascendendo de Aberkall per fluvium Kall usque Breichdu, hinc usque ad altitudinem Llwytmaur, hinc cacumen montis Llwytmaur usque Blangwennyd Gwyn(n)eon, hinc usque *blaen* Meyc, hinc descendendo per medium Meyc usque Dwyuech, et ab hinc per aquam Dwyuech usque Aberkall.

[viii] Concessi insuper eisdem et confirmavi Kellhineoc per hos scilicet terminos: ascendendo de Meney per fluvium Breint usque *aber* Pwllewyrran, hinc per medium aque Pwllewyrran usque Sarnygerd, hinc per quoddam *claud* lapidibus signatum usque ad quoddam stagnum iuxta Trefarthen, hinc per medium illius stagni usque Clauderadwy, hinc per illud *claud* usque ad litus, hinc directe usque ad alveum Meney, et sic per medium aque Meney usque *aber* Breint.

[ix] Concessi etiam et confirmavi eisdem molendinum de Talebont cum pertinentiis, aquam quoque et fossam de Sarn y Velyn usque Carrec Elgar, atque viam communem omni tempore de Kellhineoc usque ad molendinum predictum sine impedimento cuiuscumque.

[x] Dedi etiam et confirmavi eisdem Bodgedwyd per hos videlicet terminos: ascendendo de quadam parva insula existente in Llyn(n) Coron per medium Claud Yago usque Carned Yorwerth, hinc divertendo versus Aberfraw per quoddam *claud* lapidibus signatum usque Weun Wenn, hinc per *claud* quoddam lapidibus signatum usque Murdynen Kefnerth, hinc directe versus Henllys usque Korsenllys hinc divertendo ad dexteram per medium alvei usque Rytdu, hinc per medium illius alvei usque *aber* Gouer Garanen prout descendit in Korscallellyn, hinc ascendendo per Gouergaranen iuxta quoddam *claud* lapidibus signatum usque Weun Las, hinc per medium Weun Las usque Weun Vaur, hinc ascendendo per alveum usque Fynnony Meyirch, hinc per quoddam *claud* lapidibus signatum usque ad latus Bodwrdyn, hinc per ductum lapidum usque Cerric Poetheon, hinc per quoddam *claud*

divertens versus Trefdraeth, usque ad latus Trefdraeth, hinc per medium alvei existentis in confinio Trefdraeth per medium Kors y Gicvran usque Pylleu Haloc, et ab hinc per alveum usque ad predictam insulam.

[xi] Dedi etiam et confirmavi eisdem plateam de Lanmaes per terminos suos cum omnibus pertinentiis suis.

[xii] Concessi insuper et confirmavi eisdem monachis Voelas, Keirnauc et Llanveir Ryt Castell per hos videlicet terminos: ascendendo de Aber Gwrysgauc per fluvium Gwrysgauc usque ad quoddam latum vadum in *blaen* Gwrysgauc, hinc per alveum usque Maenesartyr, hinc usque Cerric Llwynogod, hinc usque Carned Run, hinc usque ad fontem subtus Moel Seissauc, hinc usque ad summitatem Moelseissauc, hinc usque *blaen* Gweun Eneas, hinc descendendo per alveum usque Henrytbeli, hinc per fluvium Kaletwyn usque *blaen* Kaletwyn subtus Korsgaranen, hinc directe ducta linea usque Esgynvaen Gwgann, hinc usque Llynalwen, hinc per medium Llynalwen et medium fluvii Alwen usque Rytgwynn, hinc per Nant Heilyn Seis usque ad quandam valliculam divertentem ad sinistram, et per illam valliculam ascendendo usque ad capud cuiusdam alvei profundi subtus Brondengynllwyn, hinc relinquendo Brondengynllwyn ad dexteram intra terminos monachorum per vallem usque *blaen* Llaethauc, hinc per medium Llaethauc usque ad fluvium Nuc, hinc per medium Nuc usque ad flumen Conwy, et `per medium aque Conwy usque ad Aber Gwriscauc.

[xiii] Concessi etiam et confirmavi eisdem Llyn Kemer `per hos scilicet terminos: ascendendo per Llynkemer per fluvium Alwen usque Aber Drywes, hinc per medium aque Drywes usque Bonerelic Bras, hinc usque Nant Ringhylleyt, hinc ad fluvium Brenic, et per medium Brenic usque Llynekemer.

[xiv] Concessi etiam et confirmavi eisdem Llechwedkrynllwyn per hos scilicet terminos: a *pwlle* propinquiori *tal* Dinas Dindunaut contra Alwen usque ad locum ubi rivulus descendit in Alwen de Bwlchdinewyt, inde contra eundem rivulum usque Bwlchdinewyt, inde per descensum rivuli ex alia parte montis versus Kerricedrudeon usque ad Enyserheid, hinc a superiori parte eiusdem Enys per paludem usque ad rivulum ulteriorem fluentem de quodam fonte, inde per longitudinem cuiusdam vallicule usque ad capud magne paludis versus orientem, hinc per longitudinem illius paludis, usque ad rivulum decurrentem de fonte ulteriori versus orientem e regione Alwen, et ab eodem fonte usque ad *claud* inferius subtus viam, inde per longitudinem illius *claud* ad Heliclwyneu apud *blaen nant* quod descendit versus Alwen, inde usque ad Kerricllwydeon versus aquilonem in supercilio cuiusdam collis, hinc usque super *blaen* vallis qui descendit versus Dinas Dundunaut, hinc per eiusdem vallis longitudinem usque ad supradictum *pwlle* iuxta *tal* ipsius Dinas.

[xv] Concessi insuper et confirmavi eisdem monachis has terras apud Nanhoenin, scilicet Gwastat Onnos, Bryngwynein, Hafat Tandrec, Llyndu, Chwmygoret, Scubordynemreis, Hendrefwynein, Wernosdec, Pen(n)ant Morgeneu, Pen(n)ant Crwnn, Cu(m) Llein ex utraque parte Llein, Chwmerch ex utraque parte Erch, Chwmdelif ex utraque parte Delif, Kemen Terneint et Gwryt Kei ex utraque parte Degymni, per videlicet terminos subscriptos: ascendendo de Ab(er) Colwyn prout descendit in Ferlas per medium Colwyn usque *blaen* Colwyn prout descendit de Bwlch Chwmllein, hinc per crepidinem rupium usque ad capud Wedua Vaur, hinc usque ad capud Grybgoch, hinc usque ad capud Wregyssauc, hinc per altitudinem rupium usque ad sedem Peris, hinc usque ad capud Moel Berued, hinc directe usque ad illum locum in quo fluvius Member incipit sicut torrens precipitanter descendere, hinc per medium aque Member usque Erauongoch, hinc ascen-

dendo per illam aquam usque Llegat Erych, hinc usque ad altitudinem Cerric Eryyrch[b], hinc usque Llech Edear, hinc usque Bankarw, hinc per cacumen rupium Bancaru usque *blaen* Teyrw, hinc per fluvium Teyru usque ad petram que descendit in Teyru iuxta Ryt Teyru superiorem, hinc per parvos colles petrosos a latere Gerrynt usque Llechwed Gwelvau, hinc ducta linea indirecte usque ad monticulum qui in similitudinem castelli apparet a dextera parte Llechewed Gwelvau, hinc per altitudinem usque ad capud Carrecereryr, hinc per summitatem rupium usque ad verticem Moeldinewyt, hinc usque Bylcheu T(er)uyn, hinc per cacumen rupium usque ad Gorssed Ressygynt prout pendet desuper vallem, hinc divertendo versus Llyndinas per longitudinem cuiusdam brachii petrosi desuper vallem apparentis usque ad capud Claud Mein, hinc per medium illius *claud* usque fluvium Ferlas, et deinde per medium Ferlas usque ad Ab(er)colwyn prout descendit in Llynekemer.

[xvi] Dedi etiam et confirmavi eisdem monachis Ardeu et Darlas per hos scilicet terminos: ascendendo de Ab(er)pwlledarlas per medium aque usque ad stagnum Cawlwyd, hinc per medium illius stagni usque ad paludem que est supra capud stagni, et per illam directe paludem usque ad Vygynforchauc, hinc per altitudinem rupium usque ad capud Llithrecewrach, hinc per altitudinem illius montis versus occidentem usque Bwlcheryl Varthauc, hinc descendendo per illam vallem et per illum rivulum descendentem per illam vallem[c] qui dicitur Frwt Du qui est directe subtus Carrec Gwennolyod et descendit in fluvium Eygyeu, et per fluvium Eigyu usque ad stagnum Eigyu, et per illud stagnum et per fluvium descendentem de stagno usque ad flumen Conwy et per medium Conwy usque ad Aberpwlledarlas.[-a]

[xvii] Concessi insuper eisdem monachis quod liberi sint imperpetuum et quieti ab omnibus pastibus et poturis hominum, equorum, canum et avium et non compellantur ad pascendum me aut ministros aut alios quoscumque seculares sub obtentu consuetudinis et quod circa electiones, depositiones seu resignationes abbatum tempore vacationis aut alio tempore ego nullatenus intromittam, seu ministri mei aut alii seculares minime intromittant, sed omnia in dicto monasterio facienda per religiosos ordinentur regulariter et tractentur.

[xviii] Concessi etiam eisdem ut uti et gaudere possint naufragio in omnibus terris suis et litoribus meliori modo quo in terris meis ego utor, videlicet quecumque bona seu res per submersionem aut fractionem seu per aliud infortunium ad terras suas seu ad litora terris suis convicta de mari evenerint, ipsa bona totaliter et integre sint ipsorum monachorum, similiter si naves aut scaphe aut bona ipsorum monachorum infra dominium meum per procellam maris aut naufragium aut per aliud infortunium fracta aut submersa fuerint ipsa vasa et bona sint ipsorum monachorum.

[xix] Concessi etiam eisdem monachis quod ipsi et omnes servientes sui cum omnibus bonis suis quieti sint ab omni theolonio, passagio, paasio[d] et pontagio in omnibus terris meis et quod ipsi et omnes servientes sui in terris suis libere possint emere et vendere animalia, cibum et potum atque alia quecumque bona. Et similiter ipsi et servientes sui ac omnia bona sua libere et sine quocumque pretio paratum transitum habeant per Meney, Conwey, Abermaw et Dyui, et in omnibus passagiis per omnem potestatem meam non obstante quacumque lege aut consuetudine.

[xx] [e-]Concessi etiam eisdem quod si animalia sua aut alia quecumque bona furata, rapta seu ablata vel ad tempus perdita fuerint tamcito iidem monachi illa bona probaverint esse sua, ipsis sine dilectione pacifice liberentur, similiter prohibeo ne aliqua persona secularis

aut religiosa de dominio meo preter dictos monachos utatur illo signo ferreo quo ipsi signare solent animalia sua et iumenta, et si animalia quorumcumque inventa fuerint signo ipso signata ipsis monachis libenter.

[xxi] Concessi etiam eisdem monachis imperpetuum quod pro quacumque causa dicto aut facto aut forisfacto in curiis meis aut in quacumque curia laicali nullatenus iudicentur, amercientur seu punientur, sed in capitulis suis secundum ordinem suum corrigantur.⁻ᵉ

[xxii] Concessi etiam eisdem monachis ut nullus hominum extorqueat ab eis vicinitatem aut partem de pasturis, silvis aut molendinis suis, sed ipsi monachi contra omnes custodeant et possideant fines et terminos suos in hac carta contentos et intra eosdem terminos aratras, edificia, molendina, culturas et alios quoscumqueᶠ labores pro libito suo faciant sine contradictione cuiuscumque.

[xxiii] Concessi etiam eisdem monachis quod nullus hominum possit super ipsos calumpniam seu actionem facere propter receptionem aliquarum personarum ad habitum suum cuiuscumque conditionis sint postquam ipsi recepti in dicto monasterio profiteantur, sed si qui tales personas ad religionem de seculo fugientes super aliquibus calumpniaverint, durante anno probationis et non post professionem factam, actionem suam ostendant.

[xxiv] Concessi etiam eisdem monachis ut si qui professorum dicti monasterii sine licentia et consensu abbatis sui peccuniamᵍ aut alia bona a creditoribus incaute mutuo acceperint aut secularibus fideiussionibus se inmiscuerint, monasterium predictum pro talibus mutuis et fideiussoribus minime satisfaciat.

[xxv] Concessi insuper eisdem quod licite possint super aquas currentes inter terras meas seu hominum meorum ex una parte et terras ipsorum ex altera levare et edificare molendina et etiam easdem aquas de canalibus suis ad terras suas vertere et declinare sine impedimento cuiuscumque.

[xxvi] Concessi etiam eisdem quod licite possint recipere ad habitum suum et ad famulatum suum et servitia liberos meos, spadarios et homines de advocatione mea atque omnes primam tonsuram habentes cuiuscumque conditionis extiterint sine molestia et calumpnia cuiuscumque.

Et quia pium est ut omnibus qui seculi vanitates et mundanas divitias derelinquerint et ad regis regum obsequia voluntarie convertuntur principum assuit presidium et tutela, volo pro me et heredibus ac successoribus meis quod iidem monachi tam presentes quam futuri habeant et possideant omnes terras predictas per limites et fines ac terminos prenominatos in silvis et campis, cultis et incultis, pratis, pascuis, pasturis, piscariis, stagnis, vivariis, aquis, molendinis, viis, semitis, moris, glebariis, lapidibus metallis, avibus omniumque avium nidis, litoribus, portubus, naufragiis, thesauris omnibusque rebus tam super terras suas quam sub terris suis inventis, bene et in pace, libere, quiete, integre, plenarie, honorifice, firmiter et inconcusse in liberam, puram et perpetuam elemosinam imperpetuum solutas et liberas ab omni terreno servitio et exactione seculari. Volo etiam ut iidem monachi tam presentes quam futuri omnibus predictis libertatibus, quietantiis et aliis liberis consuetudinibus per omnes terras meas et per totum principatum meum imperpetuum gaudeant et utantur. Et prohibeo sub periculo indignationis mee ut nullus hominum eisdem monachis aut servientibus suis contra hanc cartam meam preiudicium faciat aut gravamen, quoniam ipsos et omnes res ac possessiones suas sub protectione mea suscepi. Et ut hec mea donatioᶜ atque confirmatio imperpetuum firma et inconcussa permaneat, ne aliqua contentionis aut perturbationis occasio contra predictos monachos possit inposterum suboriri, eam presentis carte munimine et sigilli mei impressione roboravi. Testibus hiis: Yorwerth Gam,

Gwynn filio Ednewein, Ydon capellano meo et Madoco filio Eardur. Datum apud Aberconwy anno ab incarnatione domini m° c° xcviii° septimo idus ianuarii et principatus mei anno decimo.

ᵃ⁻ᵃ etc. CD. | ᵇ yr *written over an erasure in* B. | ᶜ B *inserts an erasure.* | ᵈ *sic in* B; pavagio C; paagio D. | ᵉ⁻ᵉ *omitted* C. | ᶠ C *inserts* faciant *and ends here.* | ᵍ *sic in* B.

Containing *c.*2,600 words, this is by far the longest charter in favour of a religious house extant in the name of a twelfth- or thirteenth-century Welsh ruler. The principal reasons for rejecting it, together with no. 219 below, as an authentic act issued by Llywelyn are set out by Insley, 'Fact and fiction', with references to earlier studies. The reasons relate both to the lands and to the liberties conceded to the monks of Aberconwy. Before considering these points, however, it should be stressed that the charter's textual history is inconclusive with respect to authenticity. The earliest surviving text is preserved in an inspeximus of Edward III dated 24 March 1332. As the majority of charters issued by the princes of Gwynedd survive only in later copies, including chancery enrolments, this is in itself unremarkable and provides very weak grounds for rejecting the text as a copy of an authentic charter issued by Llywelyn. Arguably more significant is the lack of any explicit confirmation of the charter by Edward I, even though the king issued a charter of his own to the abbey on 23 October 1284 granting new lands in exchange for those in and around its site at Conwy together with the grange of Creuddyn on the occasion of the abbey's removal about 7 miles south down the Conwy Valley to Maenan (*Mon. Ang.*, v. 674–5; cf. Hays, *History of the Abbey of Aberconway*, 70–3). Edward's charter includes a general confirmation of all grants of lands, churches, men and alms to the abbey but makes no mention of Llywelyn or any other prince of Gwynedd, and is silent on earlier charters: *Concessimus . . . et confirmavimus omnes rationabiles donationes terrarum, ecclesiarum, hominum et elemosinarum eis a quibuscumque jam collatas et imposterum conferendas vel adquirendas* (*Mon. Ang.*, v. 674). This might seem all the more striking in view of the king's readiness to confirm charters of the princes of Gwynedd in favour of Basingwerk (no. 213 above) and, especially, Ynys Lannog (e.g. nos 250, 272 below), as well as the Lord Rhys's charter for Strata Florida (no. 28 above). Edward thus clearly had no objection in principle to accepting the legitimacy of native rulers' charters for religious houses. Equally, however, such confirmations were not issued by the king so consistently as to make the lack of one for Aberconwy significant: for example, the earliest royal confirmations of princely charters for the Welsh Cistercian abbeys of Cymer and Strata Marcella date from the reign of Edward II (no. 229 below; *Ystrad Marchell Charters*, 8–9). Rather, the procuring of royal confirmations depended on the initiative of the individual monastery or priory, reflecting its particular circumstances. The circumstances at Aberconwy in 1284 were such, it could be argued, as to render any attempt to obtain a confirmation of Llywelyn's charter from Edward I at the very least impolitic, if not impractical. The main purpose of Edward's charter was to record new grants in the context of the move to Maenan; indeed, the king presented himself as refounding the abbey at Maenan (*monasterium . . . de novo apud Maynan . . . fundavimus*: *Mon. Ang.*, v. 674). In this situation he may not have wished to emphasize the abbey's connections with the defeated dynasty of Gwynedd and, more particularly, to confirm a charter whose list of lands granted by Llywelyn opened with the very lands ceded by the monks to the king, namely the site and vicinity of the abbey at Conwy and the grange of

Creuddyn. By providing a general confirmation of earlier grants Edward helped to secure the monks' title to their lands without committing himself to guaranteeing any specific grant. The king's charter need not imply, then, that the monks lacked an authentic original (or for that matter copy) of Llywelyn's charter in 1284. The same is true of King John's confirmation, dated 1 April 1202, of a lost charter of Henry II granting protection to the abbey (*Reg. Aberconway*, 10; Henry II's charter and John's confirmation were also twice confirmed by Henry III (*CChR 1226–57*, 171; *CPR 1232–47*, 504)). The silence of John's charter regarding any grant to the abbey by Llywelyn is not surprising, for the king was confirming, not earlier grants of lands to the abbey, but rather his father's grant of protection and freedom from tolls and similar dues. This may be compared with John's two charters for Whitland Abbey, both issued on 27 December 1214, one a grant of protection, the other a confirmation of grants by John of Torrington, Rhys ap Gruffudd and others (*Rot. Pat.*, 125b; *Mon. Ang.*, v. 591).

The lands granted in the charter weaken the case for its authenticity on two main counts. (The lands have been identified and discussed in Gresham, 'Aberconwy charter', and *idem*, 'Aberconwy charter: further consideration'.) First, although the wording used suggests that all the lands listed were fresh grants by Llywelyn, several, at least, must in fact have been confirmations of earlier grants by different donors (Insley, 'Fact and fiction', 241–2). This is certainly true both of Rhedynog Felen, the original site given to the community near Caernarfon in 1186, almost certainly by Llywelyn's uncle Rhodri ab Owain, and of the site of Aberconwy, granted by 1192, quite possibly together with the arable lands of Creuddyn on the other side of the Conwy (Gresham, 'Aberconwy charter: further consideration', 315–16); and it may well also be true of Gelliniog on Anglesey, granted to the monks by Llywelyn's cousin Gruffudd ap Cynan ab Owain no later than 1199 (no. 206 above). Second, and more important, the date given in the charter, 7 January 1198 (new style, 1199), is extremely suspect, as Llywelyn almost certainly lacked sufficiently widespread authority in Gwynedd to have been able to grant all the lands listed at that date; the authenticity of the dating clause is further undermined by its inclusion, unique among Welsh princely acts, of the prince's regnal year.

The liberty clauses are likewise most unlikely to have been originally written as early as 1199, for comparison with other Welsh charters for religious houses suggests that the clauses are both too generous and too precisely formulated to derive from that date; it is particularly significant that the liberties granted by Llywelyn to Cymer Abbey in 1209 (no. 229 below) are fewer and less detailed than those contained here (Insley, 'Fact and fiction', 243–6; Smith, 'Cymer', 112–13). Take, for example, the clauses relating to wreck (c. xviii): whereas the Cymer charter simply allows the monks freely to recover their own shipwrecked goods, the present charter extends this to all wrecks on their lands, thereby allowing them the same rights in this respect as the prince (cf. Smith, '*Gravamina*', 168–9; Pryce, *Native Law*, 245 and n. 41; for further comment on the liberties granted, see note to no. 219 below). The suspicions aroused by the substance of some of the liberty clauses are reinforced by the presence in at least one of them of vocabulary that appears to be anachronistic for the date given in the charter (I am grateful to David Howlett for providing me with copies of relevant slips from the archive of the *Dictionary of Medieval Latin from British Sources*). *Signum* is not otherwise attested in British sources with the meaning of a brand for livestock before 1274 nor the verb *signare* 'to mark or brand (animals)' before 1264 (c. xx). Another possibly anachronistic usage is *probatio* 'monastic profession' (c. xxiii), otherwise first attested on the Continent in a charter of 1223 and in Caesarius of Heisterbach at about the same date (Du Cange, vi. 513) and in Britain in Matthew Paris's account of the rule of St Francis *s.a.* 1227 in the *Chronica Majora* (Paris, *CM*, iii. 137). The term *via communis*, 'public way' (cc. ii, ix), is otherwise attested in British sources only from *c.*1250 (Latham, *Revised Medieval Latin Word-List*, 510, s.v. *via*). The use of *vicinitas* '(right of) common' (c. xxii) is, by contrast, not necessarily open to the charge of anachronism: though an unusual term in British sources, otherwise occurring only from 1366 onwards, it is attested in continental sources from 1168 (Du Cange, viii. 321; Niermeyer, *Mediae Latinitatis Lexicon*, 1096).

As Insley has argued ('Fact and fiction', 247–8), the most likely context for the charter's redaction was the crisis faced by Aberconwy in the wake of Edward I's conquest of Gwynedd in 1282–3. According to this interpretation, the document was drawn up by the monks as a bargaining counter in negotiations with the king prior to the move to Maenan in 1284, with the twofold purpose of defending its title to extensive lands (amounting to 38,000 acres) and asserting its right to a wide variety of liberties vis-à-vis secular authority. It is unknown whether it was presented to the king or his officials, and hence influenced Edward I's charter for the abbey, dated 23 October 1284. As already noted, that charter lacks any reference to the present document, and most of the rights granted by the king do not match those set forth in the liberty clauses of Llywelyn's charter. The closest parallels – substantive rather than verbal – occur in the clause in Edward's charter freeing the monks from tolls and related dues and allowing their ships free passage throughout the king's dominions (*Mon. Ang.*, v. 674). The overall lack of correspondence between the substance and wording of the two charters likewise makes it difficult to tell whether the present charter was drawn up in response to that issued by Edward. In either case, the redactor of the one charter could have deliberately avoided echoing the other. More specifically, some of the liberties listed in the present charter may have been included in order to try and prevent fiscal and other demands on the abbey made by Llywelyn ap Gruffudd from becoming a precedent for the new ruler of Gwynedd. It is striking that these liberties open with a grant of freedom from feeding and puture, as precisely these services had been rendered annually before the conquest from Aberconwy's grange of Ffriwlwyd to support 'certain serjeants' of Llywelyn's; this puture was extended at 8*s.* 8*d.* by Edward I, who on 10 June 1285 ordered that the monks' land should be granted quittance of this payment (*CWR*, 301, 304). The following clause (almost certainly derived from a papal bull, as argued below) on immunity from secular interference in abbatial elections, depositions and resignations probably owes its prominent position, not to any such interference by Llywelyn ap Gruffudd, but rather to the community's sense of insecurity at the time of Edward's conquest.

Analysis of its diplomatic suggests that the charter was not concocted *ex nihilo c.*1283, but drew on a number of documents held by the abbey. This is not surprising, as Aberconwy must originally have possessed more charters than those known today, issued by Henry II (with confirmations by John and Henry III), Gruffudd ap Cynan ab Owain (no. 206 above) and Llywelyn ap Gruffudd (no. 319 below). In particular, it is very likely that the abbey received one or more authentic charters from Llywelyn ap Iorwerth, who appears to have been an important benefactor as he died and was buried at Aberconwy after taking the monastic habit there in 1240 (*BT, Pen20Tr*, 105; *BT, RBH*, 236–7). As suggested below, the present charter may well represent an elaboration of precisely such a charter. However, it appears that the monks considered any such authentic charters of Llywelyn's insufficiently comprehensive and detailed to serve as an effective title deed in the troubled circumstances of the conquest of Gwynedd. Given their possession of such charters, together with their probable role in the production and conservation of princely documents (above, pp. 136–7), the monks will presumably have been well equipped to produce what could pass for authentic originals issued by the prince.

One striking feature of the present charter is the close resemblance between some of its formulae and those of Gruffudd ap Cynan ab Owain's charter for Aberconwy, datable to *c*.1190 × 1199 and probably to 1194 × 1199 (no. 206 above). This is especially true of the notification (identical words are printed in bold face).

Gruffudd's charter:

[N]otum sit omnibus sancte matris ecclesie filiis tam presentibus quam futuris quod ego [name erased] Kynan filius Northwallie princeps intuitu divine pietatis, pro salute anime mee et antecessorum meorum, dedi et concessi in puram et perpetuam elemosinam Deo, Beate Marie et monachis de Aberconwey sub ordine Cistercien(si) Deo famulantibus . . .

Llywelyn's charter:

Notum sit omnibus sancte matris ecclesie filiis tam presentibus quam futuris quod ego Lewelin(us) Gervasii filius totius Norwall(ie) princeps intuitu divine pietatis, pro salute anime mee et animarum omnium antecessorum et heredum ac successorum meorum, dedi et concessi atque presenti carta mea confirmavi pro me et heredibus ac successoribus meis in puram et perpetuam elemosinam imperpetuum Deo et Sancte Marie et monachis de Ab(er)conewey sub regulari habitu Deo servituris . . .

There are further parallels in the corroboration and dating clauses.

Gruffudd's charter:

Ut autem hec mea donatio et concessio imperpetuum firma permaneat eam presentis carte munimine et sigilli mei impressione roboravi. Hiis testibus . . . Datum apud Porthaethay' anno ab incarnatione domini millesimo c [lacuna] mense iunii.

Llywelyn's charter:

Et ut hec mea donatio atque confirmatio imperpetuum firma et inconcussa permaneat, ne aliqua contentionis aut perturbationis occasio contra predictos monachos possit inposterum suboriri eam presentis carte munimine et sigilli mei impressione roboravi. Testibus hiis . . . . Datum apud Aberconwy anno ab incarnatione domini m° c° xcviii° septimo idus ianuarii et principatus mei anno decimo.

Since no other texts of princely charters for Aberconwy survive (apart from no. 219 below, which is clearly derived from the text under discussion here), it is difficult to be certain whether the similarities between Gruffudd's charter and that attributed to Llywelyn reflect direct borrowing from the former by the latter, or whether the present charter draws upon another early charter (perhaps issued by Llywelyn himself) that incorporated elements of a house style at Aberconwy exhibited also in Gruffudd's charter. Aspects of the present charter's diplomatic certainly conform with what one might expect to find in an authentic charter of Llywelyn's issued in January 1199. In particular, the notification, whose formulae are arguably more distinctive than those of the sealing and dating clauses, is compatible with an early date in Llywelyn's reign. Forms of the verb *noscere* are used in the notifications of all but one of the prince's surviving charters (the exception being no. 250 below of 1221), and as such is perhaps not especially significant. More significant is the use of the first person singular, which occurs also in the prince's charters for Basingwerk, issued no later than 1202 (nos 213, 216 above), and Strata Marcella (1209) (no. 231 below). The notification of no. 231 most closely resembles that of the present charter: *Universis sancte matris ecclesie filiis tam presentibus quam futuris, notum sit quod ego L. Noruuallie princeps, intuitu pietatis et spe eterne retributionis pro anime mee ac parentum meorum salute dedi* ... The first person plural is used fairly consistently by Llywelyn only from 1218 onwards (above, p. 63). Admittedly the Basingwerk and Strata Marcella examples omit Llywelyn's patronymic, but this is found in other early acts, including the address of the prince's charter for Cymer Abbey in 1209 (no. 229 below: *Lewelinus Gervasii filius Norwallie princeps*; cf. also nos 220–1 below, and Stephenson, *Governance*, 199). The only unique, and thus suspect, element in the notification is its description of Llywelyn as *totius Norwallie princeps*: this could be seen either as an assertive statement of power at the time of the prince's occupation of Gwynedd Uwch Conwy (thus Stephenson, ibid.) or as a retrospective elaboration designed to reinforce the abbey's title to the lands and liberties granted by emphasizing the geographical extent of Llywelyn's authority (cf. *HW*, ii. 601, n. 144). The presence of Gwyn ab Ednywain in the witness list is likewise consistent with a late twelfth- or early thirteenth-century date (see note to no. 216 above); for Madog ab Iarddur see Stephenson, *Governance*, 99–100.

The extent to which the dispositive clauses of Llywelyn's charter were drawn or adapted from earlier texts can only be guessed in most cases. The detailed boundary clauses are inconclusive: though these might be considered archaic by the later thirteenth century, and thus to have derived from one or more earlier texts, it is notable that the lands granted to the abbey at Maenan are described in comparable detail in Edward I's charter of 1284 (*Mon. Ang.*, v. 674). The clause (c. xix) exempting the abbey from tolls and other dues may have been influenced by that in Henry II's charter of 1186 × 1189 or one of its confirmations by John or Henry III: compare *quieti sint ab omni theolonio, passagio, paasio et pontagio* with *quieti sint de tholonio, et passio, et paagio, et pontagio* in John's confirmation of 1202 (*Reg. Aberconway*, 10).

One source almost certainly used by the charter's redactor, however, was a papal bull of privileges. Although none is extant for Aberconwy, a papal bull is a plausible source for parts of the charter in view of the borrowings from such a privilege in Rhys ap Gruffudd's charter for Strata Florida Abbey, the mother house of Aberconwy, in 1184 (no. 28 above), as well as the explicit references to papal privileges in Llywelyn ap Iorwerth's charter for Cymer Abbey in 1209 (no. 229 below). A comparison of Llywelyn's charter for Aberconwy with the privileges issued by Alexander III for Strata Florida in 1165 × 1181 (Davies, 'Papal bull of privileges', 200–1; *Liber Epistolaris*, ed. Denholm-Young, 2–3) and, especially, by Urban III for Margam Abbey in 1186 (*Cartae*, i. 185–90) reveals some suggestive similarities of substance and vocabulary. This is particularly true of two clauses in Llywelyn's charter with respect, first, to interference in the internal governance of the abbey and, second, to debts incurred or suretyships undertaken by those under monastic vows.

(a) Llywelyn's charter:

. . . et quod circa electiones, depositiones seu resignationes abbatum tempore vacationis aut alio tempore ego nullatenus intromittam, seu ministri mei aut alii seculares minime intromittant, sed omnia in dicto monasterio facienda per religiosos ordinentur regulariter et tractentur. (c. xvii)

Alexander III's bull:

. . . sanctimus ut episcopus in cuius episcopatu monasterium vestrum consistit nec regularem electionem abbatis vestri unquam impendiat nec de removendo ac deponendo eo qui pro tempore fuerit contra statuta Cisterciensis ordinis et auctoritatem privilegiorum suorum se ullatenus intromittat.

Urban III's bull:

. . . Illud adicientes ut nullus regularem electionem abbatis vestrie (sic) *impediat aut de instituendo vel deponendo seu removendo eo qui pro tempore fuerit contra statuta Cisterciensis ordinis et auctoritate privilegiorum vestrorum se ullatenus intromittat.* (*Cartae*, i. 188)

(b) Llywelyn's charter:

. . . Concessi etiam eisdem monachis ut si qui professorum dicti monasterii sine licentia et consensu abbatis sui peccuniam aut alia bona a creditoribus incaute mutuo acceperint aut secularibus fideiussionibus se inmiscuerint, monasterium predictum pro talibus mutuis et fideiussoribus minime satisfaciat. (c. xxiv)

Urban III's bull:

. . . Ad hec etiam prohibemus ne aliquis monachus vel conversus sub professione domus vestre astrictus sine consensu et licentia abbatis et majoris partis capituli vestri pro aliquo fidejubeat vel ab aliquo pecuniam mutuo recipiat ultra pretium capituli vestri providentia constitutum nisi propter manifestam domus vestre utilitatem. Quod si facere presumpserit non teneatur conventus pro his aliquatenus respondere. (*Cartae*, i. 187)

Alexander III's bull for Strata Florida makes no mention of sureties or loans. This clause in Llywelyn's charter was consistent with native secular law in thirteenth-century Gwynedd, which included monks amongst those forbidden to be or give sureties (*Ior*, §66/7; trans. *LTMW*, 75–6).

Three other clauses in Llywelyn's charter may likewise be interpreted as responses to liberties granted in a papal privilege. The first is the immunity granted to the monks from the jurisdiction of lay courts, including Llywelyn's: instead, the monks should be corrected in their chapter (c. xxi). This bears comparison with Urban III's privilege for Margam that no bishop or other person should compel them to appear before synods or *conventus* outside the monastery or subject them to secular jurisdiction (*Cartae*, i. 188). Two other clauses of Llywelyn's charter refer to the receipt of those seeking to make a monastic profession. The relevant clauses in the bulls of Alexander III for Strata Florida and Urban III for Margam are as follows.

Alexander III's bull:

Si qua vero libera et absoluta persona pro redempcione anime sue nostro monasterio se conferire voluerit suscipiendi eam facultatem liberam habeatis, adicientes etiam auctoritate apostolica interdicimus ne quis fratris nostros clericos sive laicos post factam in nostro monasterio professionem absque vestra licencia suscipere audeat vel retinere.

Urban III's bull:

Liceat quoque vobis clericos vel laicos e seculo fugientes liberos et absolutos ad conversionem recipere et eos absque contradictione aliqua retinere. (*Cartae*, i. 187)

The clause in Llywelyn's charter (c. xxvi) allowing the monks to receive the prince's free men, *spadarii* and advowry men and all having the first tonsure is consistent with the privileges granted in both bulls. However, another clause (c. xxiii) suggests that Llywelyn's charter was influenced by a bull closer in this respect to that of Alexander III rather than that of Urban III, for it seems to elaborate the former's implicit distinction between novices and fully professed monks in limiting the immunity granted to the abbey from claims in respect of those who had entered the community to monks who have made their professions, explicitly adding that such claims could still be made with regard to novices during their year of probation.

A papal bull may also have influenced the dating clause, as the charter's combination of the year of incarnation and regnal year parallels papal practice. Other dated Welsh Cistercian charters contain only the year of incarnation or grace, apart from one charter of Gwenwynwyn for Strata Marcella in 1191, which also includes Richard I's regnal year (no. 544 below); while from Richard I's accession the time-date in English royal charters consists solely of the day of the month and the king's regnal year (cf. above, pp. 105, 127).

All of the borrowings and parallels noted so far are, of course, consistent with redaction in 1199 or later in Llywelyn ap Iorwerth's principate, and offer no firm evidence of redaction *c.*1283. It is possible that the charter is based upon an authentic confirmation issued by Llywelyn, which in turn was indebted to the diplomatic of Gruffudd ap Cynan's charter and a papal bull. After all, Llywelyn issued something similar for Cymer in 1209 (no. 229 below). Nevertheless, there is a compelling case for concluding that the present charter is not what it purports to be. To sum up: in contrast to the Cymer charter, it does not take the form of a confirmation and is silent on previous donors, even though Aberconwy had received at least Rhedynog Felen and the site of the abbey (probably together with Creuddyn) before 1199; the extent of Llywelyn's power in Gwynedd Uwch Conwy in early January 1199 is highly uncertain; while the liberties listed are more generous and detailed than those granted to Cymer, and contain vocabulary suggestive of redaction in the middle or later decades of the thirteenth century. While it would be rash to rule out the possibility that the lands named in the charter were confirmed, and in many cases first granted, by Llywelyn, or that the prince bestowed some of the liberties listed therein, the document cannot be accepted as an authentic act issued by the prince on 7 January 1199.

†219 Aberconwy Abbey

Grant and confirmation, for the salvation of the souls of himself and all his ancestors, heirs and successors, that the monks and all their successors shall enjoy all the following liberties throughout all his lands and throughout his principality in perpetuity.

(1) The monks shall be free in perpetuity from all feeding and puture of men, horses, dogs and birds and shall not be forced to feed Llywelyn or his servants or any other secular persons

under the cover of custom, and neither he nor his servants or other secular persons shall interfere with elections, depositions or resignations of abbots, but everything shall be ordained in the monastery by the religious according to the Rule.

(2) The monks may benefit from shipwreck in their lands in the same way as Llywelyn does in his, so that any goods which come to their lands from the sea as a result of sinking or wreck or other misfortune shall belong entirely to the monks; similarly if ships or vessels or goods of the monks are wrecked within the prince's land those vessels and goods belong to the monks.

(3) The monks and their servants with all their goods shall be quit of all tolls, ferry dues, road dues and bridge dues in all Llywelyn's lands, and they and their servants are free to buy and sell animals, food and drink and other goods. Similarly they and their servants and all their goods may have free passage across the Menai, Conwy, the mouth of the Mawddach and the Dyfi and in all ferry-crossings throughout Llywelyn's power notwithstanding any law or custom.

(4) If the monks' animals or other goods are stolen or temporarily lost, as soon as the monks have proved that those goods are theirs they will be handed over to them without delay. Similarly Llywelyn forbids any secular or religious person from his land apart from the monks to use the iron brand which they use to mark their animals, and if anyone's animals are found with that brand [they will be returned to] the monks.

(5) The monks shall not be judged for any causes in Llywelyn's courts or any lay court, but shall be corrected in their chapter according to their order.

(6) No one may extort from them common rights or a part of their pastures, woods or mills, but the monks may keep against all the boundaries contained in the great charter and within those boundaries ploughing, buildings, mills, cultivation and other labour services.

(7) No one may bring an action against them concerning the reception of any persons to their habit, of whatever condition, after these have made their professions, but actions may be brought against such persons during the year of probation.

(8) The monks may receive into their habit and service the prince's free men or advowry men or spadarii *or* hospitalarii *and all having the first tonsure of whatever condition.*

(9) If any of those who have taken monastic vows has received money or other goods incautiously from creditors or involved themselves in secular suretyships without the abbot's permission, the monastery shall not make satisfaction for those borrowings and sureties.

(10) The monks may build mills on waters running between their lands and those of the prince or his men and may even divert those waters from their channels to their lands if necessary.

(11) None of Llywelyn's servants shall enter the monks' lands for any reason to carry out any duties, nor shall anyone take the goods of the monks or their servants from their lands unless by Llywelyn's special mandate and also with the permission of the abbot.

(12) Whenever ships or vessels come to the lands of Llywelyn or the monks with wine, grain or any other merchandise, the monks may freely buy those goods and the sellers may freely sell their merchandise to the monks and their servants without the permission of anyone.

(13) If thieves, robbers or malefactors are seized or found in the granges, houses or lands of the monks by Llywelyn's officials or servants or any others, the monks and their servants may not be troubled on account of this, for it pertains to Llywelyn's officials and servants who have been assigned to keep the peace to investigate, pursue and arrest robbers, thieves and malefactors, and to the monks and their servants honourably to provide visitors and guests with provisions and hospitality.

Llywelyn wishes that the monks and their servants shall enjoy all the aforenamed liberties and other free customs which it is tedious to narrate throughout all his lands and throughout his principality without any diminution in perpetuity. And he prohibits, on the pain of his displeasure, any one from injuring the monks in contravention of this charter, since he has taken them and all their possessions under his protection. Sealing clause; witnesses.

Aberconwy, 7 January 1199

B = TNA: PRO, C 53/119 (Ch. R. 6 Edward III), mm. 21–20 (in an inspeximus, 24 March 1332). Rubric: Inspeximus etiam aliam cartam eiusdem Lewelini in hec verba.
C = BL, MS Harl. 696 (Record of Caernarfon), fos 90v–91r. 1494. (Incomplete; reciting an inspeximus of B by Edward the Black Prince 16 October 1347 before a *quo warranto* inquiry at Caernarfon, 1348.)
Pd. from C, *Rec. Caern.*, 148.
Cd., *CChR 1327–41*, 267–9 (from B); Stephenson, *Governance*, 199–200; *H*, no. 123.

Notum sit omnibus [a]sancte matris ecclesie filiis tam presentibus quam futuris quod ego Lewelin(us) Gervasii filius totius Norwallie princeps intuitu divine pietatis pro salute anime mee et animarum omnium antecessorum et heredum ac successorum meorum dedi et concessi atque presenti carta mea confirmavi pro me et heredibus ac successoribus meis in puram et perpetuam elemosinam imperpetuum Deo et Sancte Marie et monachis de Ab(er)conwy sub regulari habitu Deo servituris quod ipsi et omnes [m. 20] successores sui infrascriptis libertatibus et quietantiis per omnes terras meas et per totum principatum meum imperpetuum gaudeant et utantur:

[i] videlicet quod ipsi monachi liberi sint et quieti imperpetuum de omnibus pastibus et poturis hominum, equorum, canum et avium, et non compellantur ad pascendum me aut ministros meos aut alios quoscumque seculares sub obtentu consuetudinis, et quod circa electiones, depositiones seu resignationes abbatum tempore vacationis, aut alio tempore in dicto monasterio faciendas ego nullatenus intromittam, seu ministri mei aut alii seculares minime intromittant, sed omnia in dicto monasterio facienda per religiosos ordinentur regulariter et tractentur.

[ii] Concessi etiam eisdem monachis ut uti et gaudere possint naufragio in omnibus terris suis et litoribus meliori modo quo in terris meis ego utor, videlicet quecumque bona aut res per submersionem vel fractionem seu per aliud infortunium ad terras suas seu ad litora terris suis coniuncta de mari evenerint ipsa bona totaliter et integre sint ipsorum monachorum. Similiter si naves aut scaphe aut bona ipsorum monachorum infra dominium meum per procellam aut tempestatem maris aut naufragium, seu per aliud infortunium fracta aut subversa fuerint, ipsa vasa et bona sint ipsorum monachorum.

[iii] Concessi etiam eisdem quod ipsi et omnes servientes ac familiares sui cum omnibus bonis suis quieti sint ab omni theolonio, passagio, paagio et pontagio in omnibus terris meis, ipsique monachi et servientes atque familiares sui libere possint in terris suis emere et vendere animalia, cibum et potum atque alia quecumque bona. Et similiter ipsi et servientes ac familiares sui atque omnia bona sua liberum et paratum transitum habeant per Menei, Co(n)wy, Ab(er)mau et Dyui, et in omnibus passagiis per omnem potestatem meam, non obstante quacumque lege aut consuetudine.

[iv] Concessi etiam eisdem monachis quod si animalia aut alia quecumque bona sua rapta, furata, ablata vel ad tempus perdita fuerint, tamcito ipsi monachi illa bona probaverint esse sua ipsis sine dilatione liberentur. Similiter prohibeo ne aliqua persona

secularis aut religiosa de dominio meo preter ipsos monachos utatur illo signo ferreo quo signare solent animalia sua et iumenta, et si animalia quorumcumque inventa fuerint signo ipso signata ipsis monachis liberentur.

[v] Concessi insuper eisdem monachis imperpetuum quod pro quacumque causa, dicto vel facto seu forisfacto in curiis meis, aut in quacumque curia laicali nullatenus iudicentur, amercientur seu punientur, sed in capitulis suis secundum ordinem suum corrigantur.

[vi] Concessi etiam eisdem monachis ut nullus hominum extorqueat ab eis vicinitatem aut partem de pasturis, silvis aut molendinis suis, sed ipsi monachi contra omnes custodiant et possideant fines et terminos in magna carta sua eisdem a me concessa contentos et intra eosdem terminos araturas, edificia, molendina, culturas et alios quoscumque labores pro libito suo faciant sine contradictione cuiuscumque.

[vii] Concessi etiam eisdem monachis ut nullus hominum possit super ipsos calumpniam seu actionem facere propter receptionem aliquarum personarum ad habitum suum cuius-cumque conditionis sint postquam ipsi recepti in dicto monasterio sint professi, sed si qui tales personas ad religionem de seculo fugientes super aliquibus calumpniaverint, durante anno probationis et non post professionem factam, actionem suam ostendant.

[viii] Predicti vero monachi licite possint recipere ad habitum suum et servitia ac famulatum liberos meos et homines de advocatione mea atque spadarios seu hospitalarios omnesque primam tonsuram habentes cuiuscumque conditionis extiterint sine molestia et calumpnia cuiuscumque.

[ix] Concessi etiam eisdem monachis ut si qui professorum dicti monasterii sine licentia et consensu abbatis sui a creditoribus pecuniam aut alia bona mutuo acceperint, aut secularibus fideiussionibus incaute se immiscuerint, monasterium predictum pro talibus fideiussionibus et mutuis minime satisfacere compellatur.

[x] Concessi insuper eisdem monachis ut super aquas currentes inter terras meas seu hominum meorum ex una parte, et terras ipsorum monachorum ex altera, levare possint et edificare molendina, et etiam easdem aquas de canalibus suis ad terras suas si necesse fuerit vertere et declinare.‑a

[xi] Concessi etiam eisdem monachis ut nullus ministrorum meorum pro quacumque causa ingrediatur terras ipsorum ad aliqua officia in eisdem facienda. Et similiter ut nullus hominum bona ipsorum monachorum aut servientium seu familiarium suorum de terris suis capiat aut auferat nisi per mandatum meum speciale et etiam per licentiam abbatis monasterii predicti.

[xii] Concessi insuper eisdem ut quandocumque naves aut scaphe musto, vino aut annona aut aliis quibuscumque mercimoniis ad terras meas vel ad terras ipsorum monachorum applicuerint, ipsi monachi licite, libere et sine contradictione emere possunt illa mercimonia, et similiter venditores talium mercimoniorum licite possint vendere merci-monia sua eisdem monachis et servientibus ac familiaribus suis sine licentia cuiuscumque.

[xiii] Concessi etiam eisdem quod si fures aut latrones aut malefactores in grangiis aut domibus aut terris ipsorum monachorum per satellites aut ministros meos aut alios quoscumque capti fuerint aut inventi, ipsi monachi et servientes ac familiares sui propter hoc minime molestentur, nam ad satellites et ministros meos qui ad custodiendam pacem sunt assignati pertinet latrones, fures et malefactores investigare, prosequi et capere, ipsis vero monachis et servientibus atque familiaribus suis convenit supervenientibus et hospitibus victum et hospitium pro posse suo honorifice ministrare.

Et volo pro me et heredibus ac successoribus meis ut iidem monachi et servientes atque familiares sui tam presentes quam futuri hiis prenominatis libertatibus et quietantiis atque aliis variis liberis consuetudinibus quas longum est enarrare per omnes terras meas et per totum principatum meum sine diminutione aliqua imperpetuum gaudeant et utantur. Et prohibeo sub pena indignationis mee [b-]ut nullus hominum eisdem monachis et servientibus ac familiaribus suis contra hanc cartam meam preiudicium faciat aut gravamen, nam ipsos et omnes res atque possessiones suas sub protectione mea suscepi. Et ut hec mea donatio ac concessio atque confirmatio imperpetuum firma et inconcussa permaneat eam presentis carte munimine et sigilli mei impressione roboravi. Testibus hiis: Yorwerth Gam, Gwyn filio Ednewein, Ydon capellano meo et Madoco filio Eardur. Datum apud Ab(er)conwy anno ab incarnatione domini m° c° xcviii° septimo idus ianuarii et principatus mei anno decimo.[-b]

[a-a] et cetera ut supra et addit sic C. | [b-b] et cetera omnia ut supra in prima carta usque ad finem C.

This charter was written after no. 218 above, upon which it draws extensively and to which it refers as *magna carta sua eisdem a me concessa*. The first part (cc. i–x) repeats all the liberty clauses contained in no. 218, though the latter's clause referring to *spadarii* and advowry men has been moved back two clauses and its wording modified, especially by the addition of *hospitalarii* to those whom the monks were allowed to receive. (For *homines de advocatione*, 'advowry men' see Rees, *South Wales and the March*, 179, 221–2; Carr, *Medieval Anglesey*, 162–3. The *spadarii* of the clause bear comparison with the similarly termed *spadones* found elsewhere in post-conquest Wales and defined by Rees as 'servants or tenants of unfree status (classified with advowry and customary tenants)' (*South Wales and the March*, 293–4); while *hospitalarii* here should perhaps be taken as a variant of *hospites* in the sense of 'customary tenants' (*DMLBS*, 1176, s.v. *hospes* 5).) There follow a further three liberty clauses lacking in no. 218. Two of these deal with intrusion by the prince's officials on the abbey's lands (cc. xi, xiii), the third upholds the monks' right to purchase goods from merchant vessels (c. xii). The final clause of the disposition (*Et volo pro me . . . utantur*), followed by the sanction and corroboration clauses, are closely modelled on those of no. 218. However, the clauses in the present charter contain some significant additions, namely a further emphasis on the permanence and integrity of the grants (*pro me et heredibus ac successoribus meis, sine diminutione aliqua*) and the inclusion of references to the monks' servants and *familiares* as beneficiaries of the liberties. The witness and dating clauses are identical to those of no. 218.

If the arguments that no. 218 was drawn up *c*.1283 are accepted, the present charter, which is based upon it, must also be spurious. Insley suggests that the monks may have been prompted to reissue and amplify their privileges by the infringements of the abbey's liberties by the sheriff of Caernarfon and other royal officials in the reign of Edward II, especially in 1313 ('Fact and fiction', 248; cf. Hays, *History of the Abbey of Aberconway*, 88–92). This is possible, in view of the amercements imposed on the abbey for a variety of reasons; in particular, the first two of the new clauses, forbidding the prince's servants from intruding upon, or seizing goods from, the abbey's lands could be seen as responses to the imposition of amercements. On the other hand, if amercements were the principal stimulus for the production of the charter, it is notable that no clause explicitly prohibited their imposition; it was to the authority of Edward I's 1284 charter, rather than either of those allegedly issued by Llywelyn, that the monks appealed to Edward II in claiming that they should be quit of all amercements (*CAP*, 40). Furthermore, neither trade nor thieves, the subjects of the other two new clauses, are otherwise known to have been bones of contention between Aberconwy and the secular authorities in the early fourteenth century. The assertion of the monks' freedom to buy merchandise brought by ships appears to reinforce the earlier clause, found also in no. 218, allowing the monks and their servants freely to buy and sell livestock, food, drink and other goods. Perhaps this reinforcement was aimed at the customs officials appointed by Edward I in the Principality of Wales to supervise the staple and wine trade (Lewis, 'Contribution to the commercial history', 92), though there is no evidence that these officials sought to restrict the monk's rights in this respect.

The *satellites* and *ministri* of c. xiii have been identified with the peacekeeping officials known as *cais*. These appear to have been established by the native princes and to have been abolished after the Edwardian conquest, owing to the unpopularity of the puture to which they were entitled. However, there is some evidence to suggest that an (apparently unsuccessful) attempt was subsequently made to revive the office, perhaps in the late thirteenth century (Waters, *Edwardian Settlement*, 138; Stephenson, *Governance*, 46–50). If so, the clause may have been inserted in the charter with the aim of pre-empting any action against the monks as a result of the discovery of thieves on their lands.

Whether any of the three new clauses in the present document derive from authentic princely charters, particularly those of Llywelyn, is unknown. However, while it is conceivable that the monks discovered one or more such charters only after they had written no. 218, and that this prompted, or at least contributed to, the decision to draw up a fuller account of the abbey's liberties than that set forth in the latter document, the balance of probability is that the present charter resulted from a desire to reassert and reinforce the rights contained in no. 218 and that the additional clauses were first written at the time this supplementary charter was produced. (It should be added that, in contrast to some of the clauses already present in no. 218, none of the new clauses is paralleled in extant papal bulls for Welsh Cistercian houses.) While it is possible that the present document was composed in response to specific pressures in the second decade of the fourteenth century, the new clauses could equally reflect more general concerns among the monks about administrative and legal developments after 1284 and the potential threat posed by over-zealous officials of the Principality of North Wales. If so, the charter's redaction may be assigned to a date range of 1284 × 1332.

(?)†220 Pope Innocent III

Letter, from Llywelyn together with Gwenwynwyn and Madog, princes of Powys, and Gruffudd, Maelgwn, Rhys and Maredudd sons of Rhys, princes of South Wales, informing the pope of the dangers to souls the Welsh Church has endured after it was subjected to the power of England and Canterbury by royal violence, not by reason or by the authority of the Apostolic See. The archbishops of Canterbury have customarily preferred English bishops in Wales who are ignorant of the customs and language of the Welsh, and who are unable to preach or hear confessions without an interpreter. The archbishops have appointed these bishops not by canonical election but by intrusion and violence; or if they allow an election, they make it a pretence by summoning Welsh clergy to England and forcing them to elect a pastor there in the chambers of kings. The bishops preferred from England do not love Wales or the Welsh but persecute their bodies rather than seeking the profit of souls. Desiring to rule over the Welsh rather than being of profit to them, the bishops do not exercise the pastoral office but seize whatever they can from Wales and take it to England; there they consume everything, in abbeys and lands granted them by the kings of England, where like the Parthians they may excommunicate the Welsh as often as they are ordered. They sell and alienate to both clergy and laity the lands granted formerly by the senders' predecessors to the cathedral churches throughout Wales. On account of this the senders seize the lands from the churches, for they see that all have been given to plunder. Hence the cathedral churches of Wales have been reduced to great poverty, whereas if they had good and suitable pastors they would be noble and among the best. Moreover, whenever the English attack the princes and their land the archbishops of Canterbury immediately impose an interdict on the land and excommunicate the princes – who merely fight for their country and their liberty – by name as well as their people in general; and they order the bishops of Wales, who willingly obey them, to do the same. Hence whenever any of the Welsh fall fighting to defend their country, they fall excommunicated. Therefore they seek remedy from the pope for these and many other troubles, which the canons of St Davids with their bishop-elect, Gerald the archdeacon, will explain more fully by word of mouth, praying that he will free from servitude his sons, who have been afflicted by the English Church in the time of [the last] three bishops of St Davids. For before the times of those three, St Davids was the primatial see of all Wales, and also metropolitan from ancient times, subject only to the Roman Church. Whatever service the pope shall order the senders and their lands to do for him and the church of St Peter, they shall undertake promptly and devoutly.

[July 1199 × January 1201]

B = BL, Cotton MS Domit. V, fos 103r–104r. s. xiii.
Pd. from B, *Gir. Camb. Op.*, iii. 244–6; from ibid., Haddan and Stubbs, i. 431–2; Davies, 'Giraldus Cambrensis and Powis', 191–2 (inaccurate trans. only).
Cd., *Episc. Acts*, i. 324–5 (D. 363); *H*, no. 331.

Reverentissimo patri et domino Inn(ocentio) Dei gratia summo pontifici Lewelin(us) filius Ioruert princeps Norwallie, Wenunwen et Madoc(us) principes Powisie, Grifin(us) et Mailgo, Resus ac Mareduci(us) filii Resi principes Sutwallie salutem et debitam per omnia subiectionem. Paternitati vestre notificamus, quanta incommoda et animarum pericula ecclesia Walensica sustinuit, postquam Anglice potestati et Cantuar(iensi) per regiam violentiam, et non de ratione vel apostolice sedis auctoritate, subiecta fuit. In primis itaque Cantuar(ienses) archiepiscopi ex consuetudine nobis et genti nostre episcopos preficiunt Anglicos, morum patrie et lingue nostre prorsus ignaros, qui nec verbum Dei populo predicare sciunt nec confessiones nisi per interpretem suscipere. Illos etiam non per electionem canonicam set per intrusionem potius et violentiam in ecclesiasticis constituunt; vel si electionem quandoque sustineant, umbratilem illam et non veram faciunt, clericos nostros in Angliam vocando, et ibi in cameris regum quemcumque et quantumlibet vilem in partibus suis abiectum sibi eligere pastorem compellendo. Preterea episcopi nostri sic nobis de Anglia prefecti, quia nec terram nostram neque nos diligunt, set sicut innato quodam odio corpora prosecuntur, ita nec etiam animarum lucra querunt. Preesse quidem nobis et non prodesse cupientes, pastorale officium minime apud nos exercent, set quecumque a terra nostra, et si non recte, quocumque modo rapiunt, in Anglia(m) asportant; ibique in abatiis et terris, eis a regibus Anglie ad hoc concessis, ut quasi Parthicis a tergo et a longe [fo. 103v] sagittis secure nos quotiens iubentur excommunicare possint, cuncta consumunt. Terras etiam ob hoc olim ecclesiis cathedralibus per Wallia(m) a nostris predecessoribus devota largitione collatas, quia patriam non diligunt, tam clericis quam laicis vendunt, donant et alienant. Et nos ob hec, ex parte nostra, terras ecclesiarum, quoniam omnia quasi in direptionem data videmus, ecclesiis auferimus et occupamus. Unde ad summam miseriam et paupertatem ecclesie cathedrales in Wallia redacte sunt, que si bonis et idoneis gauderent prelatis, nobiles essent et optime. Ad hec etiam, quotiens Anglici in terram nostram et nos insurgunt, statim archiepiscopi Cantuar(ienses) totam terram nostram sub interdicto concludunt, et nos, qui pro patria nostra solum et libertate tuenda pugnamus, nominatim et gentem nostram in genere, sententia excommunicationis involvunt; et id ipsum episcopis nostris, quos ipsi ad libitum suum nobis, ut diximus, creant, et qui eis in hoc libenter obediunt, faciendum iniungunt. Unde accidit, ut quotiens in bellicis conflictibus pro patria tuenda cum gente inimica congredimur, quicunque ex parte nostra ceciderint, excommunicati cadunt. Contra hec igitur incommoda et alia multa, que canonici Meneven(ses) cum electo suo, G. archidiacono, viro venerabili et discreto, vobis viva voce plenius ostendent, a vestra sanctitate, ad quam ecclesie totius regimen spectat, cum lacrimis et singultibus remedia querimus; rogantes et communiter suplicantes, quatinus filios vestros, tantum trium episcoporum Meneven(sium) tempore ab Anglicana ecclesia miserabiliter afflictos, ab indebita servitute paterna pietate relevare ve[fo. 104r]litis. Quoniam ante illorum trium, qui nunc ultimo fuerunt, tempora ecclesia Meneven(sis) primatie Wallie totius sedes fuerat, sicut et antiquitus metropolitana, sancte Romane scilicet ecclesie solum obnoxia. Unde si oculo misericordie vestre nos super hiis respicere dignum duxeritis, quodcumque servitium, quod ferre possimus, nobis et terris nostris vobis et ecclesie Beate Pet(ri) faciendum iniunxeritis, prompta et devota voluntate suscipiemus. Valeat in domino cara nobis paternitas vestra.

The text of this letter is extant only in Gerald of Wales's *De iure et statu Menevensis ecclesiae* (*c*.1218) and, as several commentators have observed, was almost certainly drafted by Gerald himself (*Gir. Camb. Op.*, iii. 245, n. 1; *Episc. Acts*, i. 224–5; Richter, *Giraldus Cambrensis*, 122; Stephenson, *Governance*, 163). It does not necessarily follow, however, that the letter was forged. The inclusion of Llywelyn's patronymic bears comparison with the description of the prince as *Leulinus filius Ioruert* in his agreement with the representatives of King John on 11 July 1201 (no. 221 below) and as *Lewelinus Gervasii filius* in the charter for Cymer of 1209 (no. 229 below) as well as in the charters for Aberconwy, which, though not authentic in their present form, may derive from one or more authentic charters of Llywelyn for that abbey (nos 218–19 above and notes). Likewise the reference to the rulers of Powys and Deheubarth as *principes* may be compared with the description in the Cymer charter of Gruffudd ap Cynan and his brother Maredudd as Llywelyn's *conprincipes* (no. 229 below; cf. Stephenson, *Governance*, 163). It is possible, therefore, that Llywelyn and the other senders would have been happy to append their seals to this letter in their name, as Gerald claims they did (*Gir. Camb. Op.*, iii. 244).

The authenticity of the letter is, nevertheless, open to more serious challenge on account of the date implied by Gerald for its despatch. According to Gerald, the letter was taken by him on his third journey to Rome, which he reached on 4 January 1203, and was presented during the first great consistory after the Epiphany (6 January) (*Gir. Camb. Op.*, iii. 241–4); it is likewise placed in the third visit to Rome in the headings to chapters, no longer extant, of Gerald's *De rebus a se gestis* (ibid., i. 15 (c. clxix)). However, as Lloyd noted (*HW*, ii. 627 and n. 73), the letter must in fact have been written before the death of Maredudd ap Rhys, one of its senders, on 2 July 1201. Lloyd went further by also suggesting that it was probably taken by Gerald on his first journey to Rome, which he reached at the end of November 1199, a journey begun no later than October, and perhaps in August, 1199 (*Episc. Acts*, i, 211–19), on the grounds that it was quite possibly the same as the letter from Llywelyn and other princes to which Innocent III replied in a letter of 5 May 1200 ('Giraldus Cambrensis, *De Invectionibus*', ed. Davies, 149 (III. 4); the letter is absent from the pope's register). If so, the letter is datable to between Gerald's election as bishop of St Davids on 29 June 1199 and his departure for Rome by October 1199. On the other hand, Innocent III's letter of 5 May 1200 does not refer specifically to the issues raised by Llywelyn and the other princes in the letter printed here: it simply acknowledges receipt of the princes' letter commending Gerald to the pope and urges the princes to assist the church of St Davids. It may, therefore, have been written in reply to another letter from the princes, no longer extant, in which case the date range of the present letter should be extended to Gerald's second visit to Rome. Since Gerald reached Rome on that visit by 4 March, not returning to Wales until December 1201 (*Gir. Camb. Op.*, iii. 188, 196; cf. *Episc. Acts*, i. 219), and since both Maredudd ap Rhys and his brother Gruffudd died in July of that year, the letter cannot be later than February 1201 (*pace* Richter, *Giraldus Cambrensis*, 122, n. 1, which assigns it to 1202, rejecting Lloyd's arguments for an earlier date).

If Gerald's account of his third visit to Rome is taken at face value, then, there is a strong case for doubting the letter's authenticity on the grounds of anachronism: two of the purported senders of the letter had been dead for well over a year when Gerald set off for Rome with it at the end of 1202. As Richter has pointed out (ibid., 122), the letter was the only major evidence produced by Gerald according to his account of this visit. Either it was forged in 1202, perhaps drawing on a copy of an earlier, authentic, letter to Innocent III from Llywelyn and the other princes (the pope and his curia were unlikely to be aware that it contained an anachronism), or else Gerald subsequently added it to his retrospective account of his struggle to secure papal confirmation of his election as bishop of St Davids and of the metropolitan status of that see. If the latter were the case, the letter could still have been forged by Gerald, albeit without the necessity of producing what could pass as an original. Alternatively, however, he may simply have inserted into his narrative the text of a letter originally composed no later than February 1201 in order to add weight to his account of the third visit: if so, the letter could be authentic, even if the circumstances of its composition alleged by Gerald are misleading. In short, while its authenticity is doubtful, the letter cannot conclusively be shown to be spurious.

The three bishops of St Davids referred to at the end of the letter were Bernard (1115–48), David fitz Gerald (1148–76) and Peter de Leia (1176–98).

221 Agreement with the representatives of King John

(1) In the presence of Robert, bishop of Bangor, Reiner, bishop of St Asaph, Geoffrey fitz Peter, the king's justiciar and many barons and others Llywelyn has sworn, and the great men of his land have sworn after him, to observe fealty to King John for ever in respect of his life, limbs and earthly honour.

(2) Llywelyn has received from the justiciar seisin of all the lands of which he was then in possession, to hold until the king's return to England.

(3) After the king's return Llywelyn shall come at his order to do homage to him as his liege lord for the aforesaid lands.

(4) Having done homage Llywelyn shall return to his own land in peace and shall not be impleaded by anyone until he has received due summons in his own country. The king will pardon all offences committed before the day of peace.

(5) If afterwards anyone should make a claim to any of the aforesaid lands, Llywelyn will choose whether that claim will be heard according to the law of England or the law of Wales, and will only respond with regard to ownership, entirely excluding the question of possession.

(6) If he chooses the law of England, the king will convene his court in a suitable place in England and justice shall be judged there according to that law.

(7) If he chooses Welsh law, it will first be decided whether Llywelyn is entitled to have his own court or not; if he is, the case will be heard in his court.

(8) If not, the king shall send discreet men to the land of Llywelyn which is in dispute and justice will be done in their presence by Welshmen chosen for this purpose who are suspect to neither party, and the decision observed by the parties. The same shall be done regarding all other accusations against Llywelyn brought before the king or his justices.

(9) If Llywelyn or his men commit offences against the king or his men after the aforesaid peace, the king shall receive amends by the counsel of the archbishop of Canterbury and Geoffrey fitz Peter, or one of them, and of other faithful men. The archbishop of Canterbury, Geoffrey fitz Peter and the bishops, earls and barons present at the making of this peace will support Llywelyn's cause according to justice.

(10) If those who cause damage in the king's land come to Llywelyn's land, and the victims of the damage or others pursue them with cries and horns up to Llywelyn's land, Llywelyn shall restore the plunder and do justice to the malefactors.

(11) If malefactors from the king's land pass secretly through Llywelyn's land or hide there, Llywelyn has promised on oath to do all in his power to remedy this, just as if the damage had been done to him or his land.

Sealed by the archbishop and the justiciar who have undertaken that the king will confirm this peace with his seal.

11 July 1201

B = TNA: PRO, C 66/1 (Pat. R. 3 John), m. 3 (enrolled April 1202).
Pd. from B, *Foedera*, I. i. 84; from B, *Rot. Pat.*, 8b–9a; from B, Rowlands, '1201 peace', 165–6.
Cd., *H*, no. 330.

Hec est forma pacis qua Leulinus filius Ioruert venit ad servitium domini regis.

[i] Primo coram Rob(er)to Bargorensi^a et R. de Sancto Asaph' episcopis et domino G. filio Pet(ri) comite Essex' iusticiario domini regis et baronibus multis et pluribus aliis iuravit idem Leulin(us), et maiores terre sue post eum iuraverunt, fidelitatem ^b–domini regis–^b I. contra omnes homines se inperpetuum observaturos de sua vita et membris suis et de suo terreno honore.

[ii] Et idem Leulin(us) recepit de manu domini iusticiarii saisinam omnium tenementorum suorum que tunc possidebat et ea in pace tenebit usque adventum domini regis in Anglia(m).

[iii] Et cum dominus rex in Anglia(m) venerit idem Leulin(us) ad mandatum eius veniet ad eum et homagium ei faciet sicut domino suo ligio de predictis tenementis.

[iv] Et homagio facto in pace redibit ad propria nec ab aliquo implacitabitur donec in patria sua competentem receperit summonitionem, et dominus rex omnia retro forisfacta ante diem pacis si qua sunt ei condonabit.

[v] Si vero postmodum aliquis querelam moverit super aliquo tenementorum suorum predictorum, in eius electione erit utrum causa illa tractetur secundum legem Anglie vel secundum legem Wallie, et non respondebit alicui nisi de proprietate, `tamen exclusa penitus questione possessionis.

[vi] Et si secundum legem Anglie causam illam tractari elegerit, dominus rex ponet curiam suam in Anglia in loco competenti et ibi quod iustum fuerit secundum legem illam iudicabitur.

[vii] Si autem legem Walle(n)se(m) elegerit, quicumque eum super predictis in causam traxerit, primo discernetur utrum ipse Leulin(us) curiam suam habere debeat vel non; quam si habuerit, causam illam in curia sua tractabit.

[viii] Si vero curiam suam non habuerit, dominus rex mittet de fidelibus suis viros discretos in terram Leulini de qua questio fuerit coram quibus a Wallensib(us) ad hoc electis et partibus non suspectis quod iustum fuerit statuetur et a partibus firmiter observabitur. Similiter fiet de omnibus aliis de quibus decetero querele venient ad dominum regem vel iusticiarium eius de ipso Leulino.

[ix] Porro `si idem Leulin(us) aut sui domino regi vel suis forisfecerint post pacem predictam, dominus rex fideli consilio domini Cant(uariensis) archiepiscopi et domini G. filii Pet(ri) iusticiarii vel alterius illorum si ambo interesse non poterint et aliorum fidelium suorum emendationem recipiet, nichilominus predicta pace observata. Dominus etiam Cant(uariensis) et dominus G. filius Pet(ri) iusticiarius, episcopi, comites, barones qui huic paci componende interfuerunt ad honorem Dei et domini regis causam Leulini secundum iustitiam fovebint.

[x] Preterea si qui dampna in terra domini regis fecerint et in terram Leulini venerint, et dampna passi vel alii eos cum clamore et cornu usque ad terram predicti Leulini insecuti^c fuerint, idem Leulin(us) dampna restituet et de malefactoribus iustitiam faciet.

[xi] Si vero malefactores terre domini regis per terram ipsius Leulini furtive transierint vel ibi se occultaverint, super sacramentum suum promisit quod omnem diligentiam adhibebit ad hoc emendandum sicut faceret si dampna sibi vel terre sue^d illata essent. Facta fuit pax ista iii^{tio} anno regni regis Ioh(ann)is v^{to} idus iulii. Et ad maiorem huius rei securitatem dominus Cant(uariensis) et dominus G. filius Pet(ri) iusticiarius sigilla sua huic scripto apposuerunt et pepigerunt quod dominus rex pacem istam sigillo suo confirmabit.

^a *sic in* B. | ^{b-b} *sic in* B. | ^c *corrected in* B *from* insecui. | ^d suo B.

The context and significance of this, 'the earliest surviving written agreement between an English monarch and a Welsh ruler' (Davies, *Conquest*, 294), are assessed in Rowlands, '1201 peace', esp. 155–65. For briefer discussions see *HW*, ii. 614–15; Richter, 'Political and institutional background', 51–2; and Davies, 'Law and national identity', 58. The document was clearly drawn up by the royal chancery. By 13 January 1201 John had decided to extend a truce he had concluded with Llywelyn, and on 3 April the prince was granted a safe conduct to meet the king to discuss peace (*Rot. Chart.*, 100b, 103a). However, John left for Normandy in May, so the agreement was concluded with the justiciar Geoffrey fitz Peter, and the archbishop of Canterbury, Hubert Walter. John returned to England in December 1203, and it is likely that Llywelyn fulfilled his undertaking to do homage to him at a meeting in Worcester *c*.1 September 1204, and certainly must have done so before his betrothal to Joan, agreed by 15 October 1204 (*HW*, ii. 616 and n. 23, citing *Rot. Pat.*, 44a;

Rot. Claus., i. 12a; for a more cautious interpretation see Rowlands, '1201 peace', 164). Whether John subsequently confirmed the peace with his own seal, as anticipated in the final clause, is unknown. If, as is probable, a copy was also made for Llywelyn, no record of this has survived.

*222 Letter patent concerning St Davids Cathedral Chapter

Notification that, if any of the canons or clerks of the church of St Davids should lose anything on account of their supporting Archdeacon Gerald, Llywelyn would provide twofold restitution; he would also receive honourably and generously in his own land any that were driven into exile for that reason.

[Shortly before 20 January 1202]

Mention only, by Gerald of Wales in his *De iure et statu Menevensis ecclesiae* (*c.*1218), where he relates that Llywelyn sent his messenger Prior Laurence of Bardsey with the letter to the chapter of St Davids meeting on 20 January 1202 (*Gir. Camb. Op.*, iii. 196–7; cd., *Episc. Acts*, i. 318 (D. 342); *H*, no. 463).

*223 Gerald of Wales
Letter.

[Summer 1202]

Mention only, in a chapter heading to Book III, c. 138 of Gerald of Wales's *De rebus a se gestis* (1208 × 1216); the heading reads *Literae Lewelini Giraldo directae* (*Gir. Camb. Op.*, i. 13). However, since the text of Book III ends at c. 19, the chapter itself is lost and the contents of the letter are therefore unknown. To judge by its place in the list of chapter headings, the letter was sent to Gerald during his journey to Gwynedd in the summer of 1202 (cf. *Gir. Camb. Op.*, iii. 226).

*224 Basingwerk Abbey
Grant of lands and pastures in Penllyn.

[August 1202 × 11 April 1240]

Mention only, in a confirmation by Llywelyn's son Dafydd ap Llywelyn dated at Coleshill, 25 July 1240 (no. 292 below). A *terminus a quo* for the grant is provided by Llywelyn's seizure of Penllyn from Elise ap Madog in August 1202.

225 Haughmond Abbey
Confirmation in free and perpetual alms, for the salvation of the souls of himself, his father and his uncle Dafydd ab Owain of the gift of the land of Stockett by his uncle Dafydd with all its liberties and appurtenances, free for ever from all secular exaction and service as set forth in Dafydd's charter. Sealing clause; witnesses.

[16 April 1205 × August 1211]

B = Shrewsbury, Shropshire Records and Research Centre MS 6001/6869 (Haughmond Cartulary), fos 209v–210r. s. xv ex.
C = Shrewsbury, Shropshire Records and Research Centre MS 2922/15/1, fo. 1r. s. xvi/xvii. (Incomplete.)
Pd. from B and C, *Cart. Haugh.*, no. 1172 (witness list only); from Cardiff County and City Library MS 4.101 (s. xvi/xvii), *Hist. Gwydir*, 8 (incomplete).
Cd., Eyton, *Shropshire*, x. 250; *H*, no. 126.

Lewelin(us) princeps Norwallie omnibus fidelibus tam presentibus quam futuris presens scriptum inspecturis salutem in vero salutari. Noverit universitas vestra nos concessisse et presenti carta nostra confirmasse Deo et ecclesie Sancti Ioh(ann)is evangeliste de Haghmon' et canonicis ibidem Deo servientibus in liberam et perpetuam elemosinam pro salute anime nostre et animarum patris nostri et David filii Owini avunculi nostri donationem [fo. 210r] quam prefatus David filius Owini avunculus noster eisdem canonicis fecit et carta sua confirmavit de tota terra de Stokeseta cum omnibus libertatibus et perti-nentiis, in bosco et plano, in pratis et pasturis,[a] in aquis et vivariis, in[b] stagnis et piscariis, in moris,[c] viis et semitis et in omnibus aliis rebus et locis integre, libere et quiete in perpetuum ab omni exactione et servitio seculari sicut carta predicti David filii Owini testatur. Et ut ista concessio et confirmatio nostra perpetue firmitatis robur optineat eam presenti carta sigilli nostri appositione roboravimus. Hiis testibus: domino Rein(er)o episcopo de Sancto Asaph',[d] Adaph archidiacono, Ellise, Wen filio Edenweni, Wion filio Ione, Rein(er)o clerico de Ellesm(er)e, Ric(ardo) et Hug(one) filiis[e] eius, Will(elm)o de Horhtun', Rad(ulf)o de Lega.

[a] C *begins here.* | [b] et C. | [c] maioris B. | [d] B *ends here with* etc. | [e] *omitted* C.

Stockett lay in the manor of Ellesmere, granted to Llywelyn on 16 April 1205 as part of his marriage portion on his marriage to Joan; the manor had previously been held by the prince's uncle Dafydd ab Owain (d. 1203). Indeed, Thomas de Erdington, keeper of Ellesmere castle, had already been ordered to hand over the castle to Llywelyn on 23 March 1205 (*Rot. Chart.*, 147a; *Rot. Pat.*, 51b; see further *HW*, ii. 553, 616 and n. 26). Llywelyn still held Ellesmere at Michaelmas 1209 (*Pipe Roll 11 John*, 146), but had been deprived of it by June 1212, when the manor was held by Robert Lupus (*HW*, ii. 638, n. 129, citing *Testa de Nevill*, 56; there are no references to Ellesmere in the pipe rolls for 12 and 13 John). Llywelyn recovered the manor by Michaelmas 1220, when he was assigned arrears of £30 for the previous three years (*Pipe Roll 4 Henry III*, 176). Since the king presented a successor to the witness Reiner as parson of Ellesmere on 30 August 1214 (*Rot. Pat.*, 121a; cf. *HW*, ii. 631–2), the charter must have been issued between April 1205 and John's confis-cation of the manor after Michaelmas 1209 – presumably following the king's breach with the prince in the summer of 1210, and surely no later than the royal campaign against Gwynedd in the summer of 1211 (see no. 233 below). As it is a confirmation of Dafydd's grant of Stockett (no. 200 above; cf. no. 202 above), the charter may well have been issued early in this date range, shortly after Llywelyn's acquisition of Ellesmere.

226 Haughmond Abbey

Grant, for the salvation of the souls of himself, his father and his uncle Dafydd ab Owain in free and perpetual alms of the whole half of Kenwick with all its liberties and appurtenances, free of all secular exaction and service, so that the canons shall have easements there as fully as Llywelyn's men who hold the other half of the same township. Llywelyn has also granted quittance of pannage for sixty pigs wherever his men have mast within the hundred of Ellesmere. Sealing clause; witnesses.

[16 April 1205 × 1211]

A = original charter, in the care of the National Trust at Belton House, Grantham. Endorsed: (1) Carta Lewelini de Kenewek *(written over* Stochyet *struck through)* et de pannagio (s. xiii); (2) Ca[r]ta de Kenewyk' [c]um pannagio (s. xiii); approx. 223 × 133 + 23 mm.; single central slit in fold for a tag (*c*.13 mm. wide) which exits through a slit in the base of the fold; sealed on tag. Circular seal, green wax, imperfect, originally approx. 70 mm. diameter; equestrian, facing right; legend: . . . . I PRINCIPIS: N. . . . .

B = Shrewsbury, Shropshire Records and Research Centre MS 6001/6869 (Haughmond Cartulary), fo. 128v. s. xv ex. Marginal heading: Kenewike. Rubric: De donatione medietatis ville ibidem per dupplicem cartam.

Pd. from B, *Cart. Haugh.*, no. 657.

Cd., Eyton, *Shropshire*, x. 251; 'Report by Sir Frederick Kenyon', 79 (from A); *H*, no. 127.

Lewelinus princeps Norwallie universis Dei fidelibus tam presentibus quam futuris presens scriptum inspecturis salutem in vero salutari. Noverit universitas vestra nos concessisse et dedisse et presenti carta nostra confirmasse Deo et ecclesie Sancti Ioh(ann)is evangeliste de Haghemo(n)' et canonicis ibidem Deo servientibus pro salute anime nostre et animarum patris nostri et David filii Owini avunculi nostri in liberam et perpetuam elemosinam totam medietatem de Kenewich cum omnibus libertatibus et [pertinen]ciis[a] suis, in bosco et plano, in pratis et pascuis, in aquis et viis et semitis et in omnibus rebus et locis cum omnibus esiamentis liberam et quietam ab omni ex[ac]tione et servitio seculari, ita quidem quod idem canonici omnia et eadem esiamenta ita integre, libere et plenarie habeant in bosco et in omnibus aliis locis sicut homines nostri qui aliam medietatem eiusdem ville tenent plenius habere solent vel habere debent. Preterea concessimus eisdem canonicis quietantiam pannagii ad sexaginta porcos ubicumque porci nostri pesonam habuerint infra hundredum de Ellesmere. Et ut ista donatio et concessio nostra perpetue firmitatis robur optineat eam presenti carta cum sigilli nostri appositione roboravimus. His testibus: domino Reinero episcopo de Sancto Asaph, Will(elm)o filio Alani, Adaph archidiacono, Elisse filio Owini, Wen filio Edenwein, Grifino filio Iaruuortd Goeth, Wion filio Ione, Reinero clerico de Ellesmere, Ricardo et Hugone filiis eius, Will(elm)o de Hohtu(n) et [b]multis aliis.[b]

[a] *hole in parchment in* A; *missing letters supplied from* B. | [b-b] *words extended to fill rest of line by stretching* lt *ligature in* multis *and top of* s *in* aliis A.

The charter may be assigned to the same date range as no. 225 above, and lists the same witnesses, with the addition of William fitz Alan (II), lord of Oswestry (d. 1212/13) and Gruffudd ap Iorwerth Goch. It is written in a modified book hand typical of the early thirteenth century. Unlike no. 225, this was a new grant by Llywelyn, whose charter opens the section on Kenwick in the Haughmond Cartulary. The rubric to B may indicate that Llywelyn issued two originals of the charter, which could explain some of the differences between the readings of the present charter and those in B and in three early modern copies (cf. *Cart. Haugh.*, no. 657, n.). I am greatly indebted to David Crook for drawing this original charter to my attention and for providing photographs of it.

227 Haughmond Abbey

Grant, in pure and perpetual alms, with the consent of Geoffrey de Vere and Robert fitz Aer, of the whole of Newton with its moors, wastelands and appurtenances and Whitemere, free for ever from all service, tallage, scutage, aid, labour service on his manor, military service and all secular exaction.

[16 April 1205 × August 1211, or 1220 × 1230]

B = Shrewsbury, Shropshire Records and Research Centre MS 6001/6869 (Haughmond Cartulary), fo. 152r. s. xv ex. Rubric: Confirmatio predictorum.
Pd. from B, *Cart. Haugh.*, no. 806.
Cd., Eyton, *Shropshire*, x. 250; Stephenson, *Governance*, 201; *H*, no. 128.

Lewelinus princeps Norwallie omnibus Cristi fidelibus salutem. Noveritis nos concessisse et dedisse in liberam, puram et perpetuam elemosinam Deo et Sancto Ioh(ann)i evangeliste et canonicis de Haghmon' cum voluntate et assensu Gaufridi de Ver et Rob(er)ti filii Aheri totam Newtonia(m) cum moris et vastis et omnibus pertinentiis suis et Witemere libere inperpetuum ab omni servitio, taillagio, scutagio, auxilio, opere manerii nostri et excercitu atque ab omnimoda exactione seculari etc.

The rubric in B is a reference to the previous two charters in the Haughmond Cartulary in which Geoffrey de Vere (d. 1170) granted two virgates in Newton (1165–70) and Robert fitz Aer (II) (d. 1195) granted all his land in Newton to the abbey (*c.*1190–5) (*Cart. Haugh.*, nos 804–5). The Geoffrey de Vere and Robert fitz Aer referred to in Llywelyn's charter were probably the sons of the original donors; Robert fitz Aer (III) reached his majority in 1211 and died 1221 × 1231 (Eyton, *Shropshire*, ix. 312, 318; x. 250). The absence of a witness list makes it difficult to date the charter with any precision. Llywelyn's style indicates a date no later than early 1230. Otherwise, diplomatic analysis is inconclusive. Both the address and the notification are different from those in nos 225–6 above, though the address is comparable with that in the prince's charter of submission to John in 1211 (*Omnibus Cristi fidelibus presentem cartam inspecturis*), and lacks the future participles *visuris vel audituris* used in all of Llywelyn's other extant charters from 1221 (above, p. 62 and n. 475). On the other hand, the only other examples of *noveritis* in notifications in Llywelyn's acts occur in 1218 and 1223 (nos 241, 254 below). The charter may be assigned either to the same period as nos 225–6 above (1205–11) or to that following his recovery of Ellesmere by Michaelmas 1220 (cf. note to no. 256 below).

*228 King John

Letter, making undertakings to the king in respect of injuries inflicted on Gwenwynwyn while the latter was in the king's custody.

[Shortly before 24 December 1208]

Mention only, in a letter patent of King John dated at Bristol, 25 December 1208 (*Foedera*, I. i. 102; *Rot. Pat.*, 88a). John explains that he has remitted all ill will towards Llywelyn on account of his occupation of Gwenwynwyn's castles and lands and of other injuries inflicted on Gwenwynwyn while he was in the king's custody, once Llywelyn has done what he informed the king he would do in the letter delivered on 24 December at Bristol by his clerk Ystrwyth; henceforth the king will treat Llywelyn like a son and maintain and protect all his possessions. Llywelyn had occupied southern Powys following the imprisonment of Gwenwynwyn after the latter sought peace from the king at Shrewsbury on 8 October 1208, even though Gwenwynwyn's lands had been taken into the custody of the crown, and the present letter, together with John's reply, reveals the determination of both prince and king to prevent this from leading to a breakdown of the relations between them (*HW*, ii. 621–2). The undertakings made by Llywelyn are unknown, but they appear to have been fulfilled, for he remained on good terms with John throughout 1209 and joined the royal expedition against William the Lion of Scotland in the summer of that year (ibid., 622–3).

229 Cymer Abbey

Since he is bound to keep the peace, especially for those in religious orders, Llywelyn ought to ensure that they are not molested by a lack of peace. Therefore, hearing the just petitions of the abbot and monks of Cymer living under the Rule of St Benedict, his patron, he has confirmed by his seal whatever he has learned has been bestowed on them by himself or by others or by his fellow princes, so that what has been justly bestowed shall not be removed by unjust presumption in the future. Therefore he has committed clearly to this writing the names of the lands bestowed on the monks by himself and other brother princes with all their bound-aries and appurtenances, as contained in the charters and gifts of the two princes Maredudd and Gruffudd sons of Cynan, and of Hywel ap Gruffudd and others, and as fully as the said princes have given the lands and liberties.

Cymer, in which the monastery is situated with all its boundaries and appurtenances; Abereiddon and Esgaireiddon in these boundaries: the stream called Midhul *[Afon Melau]*, *which arises in the mountain called Rhobell Fawr, is the boundary and runs directly between Yr Hafod Wen and the land of Nannau to the river Mawedd [Wnion], and by the edge of that mountain directly to the hill Yr Eryl [Cefn yr Eryr], then directly to the summit of the mountain called Y Dduallt, and thence to the source of the stream called Mynach, and the Mynach as it runs to the Mawedd, and afterwards to the stream* Kreon *[Afon y Dolau] which is the boundary between Meirionnydd and Penllyn. On the other side of the river Mawedd, Cwmdadi and* Ydymant *to the boundary of Penllyn, Esgair-gawr, Cwm-y-cawr [(?)Cwm-ochr] between the Cawr [Afon Cwm-ochr] and Harnog, Brynbedwyn, Y Ddolwen with all its boundaries and appurtenances, Cefncreuan, Yr Hafod Celynnog, Nant y Ceiliogau, Brithgwm, Marchnad with its boundaries and appurtenances, Llwydiarth,* Kellileth, Kelliuorloyw, *Moel Llwydiarth [(?)Mynydd Llwydiarth], (?)Ffridd Rhos, Cwm y Gerwyn,* Bulycifreic, Ykychul, *Cwm Gelli,* Riullathhidwyn, *Esgair-neiriau,* Ycumkorsawc, *Cwm Gwernach, Rhyd-y-garnedd, part of the land of* Keuenykellynllhwyn, *all the land of Cyfnerth ap Seisyll at Tanfod, the 2 acres of Llywelyn ap Seisyll at Tanfod, the whole share of the said Cyfnerth's inheritance whether in Tanfod or in other places, Pwll-y-march, Broneunydd, the acre of Llywelyn the* rhingyll, Halneychey, Ryhuygwerython, *the share of Madog and Llywarch sons of Moriddig with the meadow of Bodowyn, the share of the three sons of Collwyn of Bodowyn and Hirdir Llanegryn, namely Cedifor, Einion and Adda, Bredyn, part of the township of Tre-faes,* Gweunyfalt, *the 2 acres of Llywelyn ap Seisyll, the acre of Cynidr, Gellisarog, Goleuwern and Cyfannedd with all their boundaries and appurtenances.*

In the province of Ardudwy: Llanelltud, Cwm-gwnin, Moel Ispri, Cesailgwm, Cwm Mynach; by a similar gift he has granted all the lands between the rivers Cain and Mawddach with all their boundaries and appurtenances: Gwynfynydd, Gwernybudeyew, *Nant y Graean, Dolgain, Nant Hir, (?)Bedd Porius* (Bethyresgyb), *Y Feidiog, Nant-y-moch and the Cain to the summit of the mountain Moel yr Wden, where the Cain has its source, and then by way of Moel yr Wden to the river Lliw and then across to the edge of the ridge of that mountain above the Lliw and by that ridge directly above the Lliw by way of Helyg-y-moch and above Eryl-y-fedwen to the stream which flows through the marshy pool called (?)Mign Lyn to Eryl-y-fedwen and then to the Lliw, which is the boundary between Ardudwy and Penllyn; and the Mawddach, which rises from the said pool and immediately becomes a stream, fixes the boundary as far as Abercain, Llwynyrhydd, Y Cerrig Llwydion,* Heskyndhu, *Hafod Dafolog,* Ybwlellwych, *Dolcenawon, as the greater part of the river Mawddach which runs near the land of Nannau marks the boundary, because the Mawddach is divided there in three streams and then they meet together as one, Yr Allt Lwyd, Cwmhesgin, Dinas Teleri, Cwm Cedryn, Rhiw Gyferthwch,* Pennarthwonawc, *Nant Las Tegwared, Nant yr Hendy, Bedd Coediwr, Y Wenallt.*

In the province of Llŷn: Neigwl with all its boundaries and appurtenances and places as follows, namely Y Gwastadfaes, Y Penrhynau, Ykurrachdyr, Rossychulyc, the land of Einion Penfras, Bryn-y-lan, Treuuoydyc, *Y Rhos [(?)Rhos-Neigwl], part of* Ydauaty, *Tref* Wykwarhet, *Ynys Gelliwig, Pant-y-llefrith, Graeanog,* Brynycrochwyt, *Trewen, Dôl Caradog, half of the township of Ceidio with a portion of land called Maen Bleiddud.*

Llywelyn will warrant and maintain all the above-named lands in the three aforesaid provinces, and any others which have been or will be bestowed on Cymer, on behalf of himself and his heirs as a perpetual gift, in fields, woods, meadows, waters, mills, pastures, fisheries, net fishing, rivers and marshes, harbours, shores and sea, liberties of ships and boats, in recovering the monks' own cargoes if these are wrecked, in taking timber and stones, birds, forest beasts and wild animals of whatever kind, in digging up metals and treasures, in mountains and groves, in all moveables and immoveables, in possessing and using all material and non-material things above or below those lands, in all benefits, free of all secular exaction or claim, without any trouble or dispute, without the custom of secular laws or any tribute, without any agreement with anyone regarding pastures or other benefits in the aforesaid lands, either in dwelling together or in partnership. Llywelyn has further granted that if any free proprietor in all the land subject to his authority makes a temporary grant of a field or pool the monks shall have the liberty to receive and take away its profit. Obeying the pope's precepts, Llywelyn has granted that papal privileges, strengthened by the authority of St Peter and St Paul, which have been or will be given to the monks shall maintain their force and remain inviolate. He shall fully exercise secular justice and willingly sustain ecclesiastical censure against those who manifestly contravene the apostolic letters, be it by burning any of the houses of the monks or shedding blood within the precinct of the said monastery or its granges and places, by detaining a man for theft or robbery, by striking a man or any irreverence, by despoiling a man or doing anything contrary to apostolic writings and indults. Llywelyn has granted this gift for the salvation of the souls of himself and his parents as a perpetual gift in pure alms, and taken the aforesaid brothers and their possessions under his protection for ever, so that none of his successors or others succeeding by hereditary right can infringe or in any way disturb or contravene it. He has confirmed the charter by his seal, by the hand of Esau, abbot of Cymer, in the presence of many from whom he has summoned suitable witnesses; witness list.

1209

B = TNA: PRO, C 66/160 (Pat. R. 17 Edward II, pt. 2), m. 23 (in an inspeximus, 26 March 1324).
C = TNA: PRO, C 66/179 (Pat. R. 6 Edward III, pt. 2), m. 9 (in an inspeximus of B, 11 August 1332).
D = TNA: PRO, C 66/426 (Pat. R. 8 Henry VI, pt. 1), m. 6 (reciting an inspeximus of an inspeximus of B by Richard II 12 May 1389 by Henry, prince of Wales 31 December 1400, 16 November 1429).
E = BL, MS Harl. 696 (Record of Caernarfon), fos 119v–120v (reciting a version of C, described as an inspeximus dated 11 August 6 Edward II of an inspeximus dated 26 March 17 Edward I, presented to a *quo warranto* inquiry on behalf of Edward, prince of Wales in 1348). 1494.
Pd. from B, Williams-Jones, 'Llywelyn's charter to Cymer', 54–7 (and trans., ibid., 57–9); from D, *Mon. Ang.*, v. 458–9 (as Cwm-hir); from E, *Rec. Caern.*, 199–201; from *Mon. Ang.* and *Rec. Caern.*, Jones, 'Cymmer Abbey', 451–4 (incomplete trans. only).
Cd., *CPR 1321–24*, 400 (from B); *CPR 1330–4*, 334 (from C); *CPR 1429–36*, 38 (from D); Stephenson, *Governance*, 201; *H*, no. 130.

Omnibus sancte matris ecclesie filiis tam presentibus quam futuris ad quorum notitiam tenor presentium literarum pervenerit Lewelinus[a] Gervasii filius Norwall(ie)[b] princeps salutem et `pacem . Cum cuntis[c] quantum in nobis est pacis beneficium conservare tenemur, hiis maxime quos commendat[d] ordo religionis, debemus solicite providere ne pacis defectu molestentur iniuste. Quo circa dilectorum fratrum nostrorum abbatis et monachorum Cisterciensis ordinis Bangor(ensis) diocesis apud Kemmer Deo et gloriose Virgini Marie devote servientium atque sub regula Sancti Bened(ic)ti nostri patroni regulariter viventium iustas petitiones exaudientes, et eorum precibus inclinantes utilitatibus eorundem diligenter providere volentes quicquid vel a nobis vel ab aliis seu a conprincipibus nostris eisdem collatum accepimus nostro sigillo duximus confirmare ne quod iuste collatum fuerit iniusta possit infuturum permutari presumptione. Eapropter terrarum eisdem monachis collatarum nomina que a nobis et `ab aliis illis fratribus principibus date sunt huic scripto liquide duximus commendare[e] cum integris terminis et pertinentiis suis, prout melius et certius et manifestius continentur in kartis[f] et donationibus duorum principum Mareduc[g] scilicet et Griffud[h] filiorum Kenan[i] et Howeli filii Griffini[j] et aliorum, et prout plenius et expressius omnes terras dictis monachis ac libertates dicti principes contulerunt et donaverunt.

Kenmer[k] videlicet in quo loco monasterium eorum fratrum situm est cum omnibus terminis et pertinentiis suis, Ab(er)ydon' et Eskeryndon',[l] in hiis terminis: rivulus qui nominatur Midhul,[m] qui de monte qui vocatur Irobell'[n] oritur, est terminus et currit directe inter locum qui dicitur Yrhauotwen[o] et terram Manhew[p] usque ad flumen Mawuheth,[q] et iterum per crepidinem dicti montis directe usque ad collem Yrerhill',[r] et item per directum usque ad cacumen montis qui dicitur Ydhuallt, ac deinde usque ad ortum rivuli qui vocatur Menach, et Menach prout certius currit usque Mauueth',[s] ac postea usque `ad rivulum Kreon[t] qui est terminus inter Meyrionyth[u] et Pennllin.[v] Ex alia parte fluminis Mauuehet,[s] Cumdadhu[w] et Ydymant[x] usque ad terminum Penllin,[v] Esgerkaur,[y] Cu(m)ykawr[z] inter Kaur[aa] et Hayrnawe,[ab] Brynbetwyn, Ydollwen,[ac] cum omnibus terminis et finibus et pertinentiis suis, Keuenkrewuan,[ad] Yrauotkelynnawc,[ae] Nantykeyliocheu,[af] Brithgum,[ag]

Marcnant[ah] cum integris terminis[ai] et pertinentiis suis, Llwydiarath,[aj] Kellileth',[ak] Kelliuorloyw, Moallhwydiath,[al] Rospeleydr,[am] Kumygerhwyn,[an] Bulycifreic,[ao] Ykychul,[ap] Cumkelly,[aq] Riullathhidwyn,[ar] Esgeyraneryn,[as] Ycumkorsawc[at] cum omnibus terminis et pertinentiis integris, Cumgwernach [au]-in cuntis terminis et pertinentiis suis,-[au] Ritcarneth,[av] partem terre Keuenykellynllhwyn,[aw] totam terram Keunerth[ax] filii Seysyll[ay] apud Tanuoth,[az] duas acras Lewelyn filii Seysill[ay] in Tanuhot,[az] totam partem dicti Keunerth[ax] de hereditate sua ubicumque fuerit sive in Tanuoth[az] sive in aliis locis esse constiterit, Pwllymarch, Broneynwth,[ba] acram Lewelyn[bb] preconis, Halneychey,[bc] Ryhuygwerython,[bd] in omnibus finibus et pertinentiis suis, partem Madawc[be] et Llewarch[bf] filiorum Morydhic[bg] cum prato de Bodyghwyn,[bh] partem trium filiorum Gollwyn de Bodywyn[bh] et de Hyrdyrllanegrin, Kedyuor,[bi] Eynyawn,[bj] Adam, Baredyn,[bk] partem terre de villa T(re)uuais,[bl] Gweunyfalt,[bm] accras duas Lewelyn filii Seysyll,[ay] accram Kenedyr,[bn] Kellywassarauc,[bo] cum omnibus terminis et pertinentiis suis,[bp] Golewern,[bq] Keunahet,[br] in omnibus terminis et pertinentiiis suis. In provincia Ardudwy: Llanhuldut,[bs] Cumgwenyn,[bt] Moylysbryn,[bu] Kesseylguin,[bv] Cummeneych,[bw] in omnibus finibus et terminis et integris pertinentiis suis; omnes terras que sunt constitute inter duo flumina Keyn et Maudhu[bx] simili donatione predictis fratribus donavimus et concessimus cum cunctis terminis et finibus et pertinentiis suis et locis quorum nomina expresse exarata[by] sunt hec: Gwynuenyht,[bz] Gwernybudeyew,[ca] Nantygaranew,[cb] Dolgeyn, Nanthyr, Bethyresgyb,[cc] Yueydyawc,[cd] Nantymoch, et Keyn postea usque ad cacumen montis Ryuhuden[ce] de quo rivulus ille Keyn ortum accipit ac postea via Ryuhuden[ce] ducente usque ad fluvium Llyw,[cf] et postea per transversum usque ad crepidinem iugi montis qui est supra Llyu[cf] et per crepidinem iugi montis illius qui directe extenditur supra Llyu[cg] per Helycymoch et supra Erhylyuedwen[ch] usque ad rivulum qui de stagno paludis que vocatur Mycyneleyn et per illam paludem defluit plane usque Erylyuedwen[ci] et deinde currit usque Lyu[cf] qui rivulus est terminus inter Arduduy[cj] et Penllyn;[v] et Maudhu[ck] qui de dicto stagno et de dicta palude surgit et statim in amnem derivatur dictas `terras terminat usque ad Ab(er)keyn, Llwynyrhit,[cl] Ykerryclluydyon,[cm] Heskyndhu,[cn] Yrhauottauolawc,[co] Ybwlellwych,[cp] Dolycanaon,[cq] per totum prout melius maior pars fluvii Maudhu[ck] que vicinior currit iuxta terram Nanheu terminat, quia[cr] Maudhu[ck] ibi in tribus rivulis dividitur[cs] et iterum in unum conveniunt, Irallthlwhyt,[ct] Cumhesgyn, Dynasteleri, Cu(m)kedryn,[cu] Ryhukeuerthuc,[cv] Pennarthwonawc,[cw] Nantylastegwaret,[cx] Nantyrhendy, Bethycoydhur,[cy] Ywenallt.

In provincia Llheyn:[cz] Neugwl[da] cum integris terminis suis et pertinentiis[db] et locis quorum nomina scribere volumus in presenti karta,[dc] videlicet Yguasdaduays,[dd] Ypennrhynew, Ykurrachdyr,[de] Rossychulyc,[df] terram Eynyawn[dg] Penuras,[dh] Brynylan, Treuuoydyc,[di] Yros, partem Ydauaty, Treu Wykwarhet, Ynyskellywyc, Pantylleuryth,[dj] Grayanawc, Brynycrochwyt,[dk] Treuywen,[dl] Dolkaradawc,[dm] dimidietatem ville Keydyau[dn] cum particula terre que vocatur Meynbleythud.[do]

Omnes igitur supranominatas in tribus prefatis provinciis terras et quascumque alias seu a nobis seu ab aliis sunt adepti vel imposterum adepturi et etiam domui de Kemm(er) et monachis eiusdem loci collatas, warantizabo et manutenebo pro me et heredibus meis a me in perpetuam donationem vel ab aliis illis datas, in campis et silvis, in pratis, aquis, molendinis, in pasturis et piscationibus, in retium stationibus, in fluminibus et stagnis, in portubus atque littoribus et mari, in navium et scapharum libertatibus, in earum onera de propriis rebus monachorum tantum si malo eventu contingat ut a procella maris fuerint confracte aut submerse habenda et tollenda sine contradictione et tallio, in omnibus lignis suscipiendis et lapidibus cuiuslibet generis, in avibus et feris silvestribus et animalibus agrestibus cuiuscumque generis vel specei[dp] fuerint habendis, in mettallis[dq] et thesauris effodiendis et deducendis, in montibus et nemoribus, in omnibus mobilibus et immobilibus, in omnibus que super dictas terras aut subtus eas continentur de rebus materialibus vel non materialibus possidendis et in proprios usus habendis, in omnibus utilitatibus et commoditatibus libere et quiete ab omni seculari exactione sive gravamine, `sine alicuius molestia aut calumpnia vel controversia, sine[dr] consuetudine legum secularium aut tributo aliquo uncquam,[ds] sine aliqua conventione cum aliquo in pasturis seu in aliis utilitatibus in prefatis terris, vel in cohabitatione aut consortio. Preterea ipsis monachis dedimus et concessimus ut si quis de heredibus in omni terra que mee ditioni subiacet agrum vel stagnum ad tempus concesserit libertatem habeant suscipiendi eorumque[dt] fructus tollendi. In omnibus quoque et ante omnia domini pape preceptis obedientes, prefatis fratribus donavimus ut[du] summi pontificis privilegia, beatorum apostolorum Petri at Pauli auctoritate roborata, ipsisque monachis sive data sive danda in omnibus vim suam obtineant[dv] et inconcussa atque inviolata permaneant. In eos vero qui apostolice magestatis apices manifeste fregerint et contra eas egerint, aut quamlibet de domibus ipsorum monachorum incendendo aut sanguinem intra septa monasterii fundendo vel etiam grangiarum aut locorum, aut hominem tenendo aut furtum aut rapinam seu hominem verberando sive aliquam irreverentiam exercendo, hominem[dw] spoliando vel aliud quid contra apostolica scripta et indulta faciendo, quantumlibet nobis caros et vicinos secularem iustitiam plenarie exercebimus[dx] et ecclesiasticam censuram in eos latam patienter et libenter sustinebimus. Hanc autem presentem nostram donationem dilectis fratribus monachis de Kemm(er)[k] sic dedimus et concessimus pro salute et remedio anime nostre et parentum nostrorum in perpetuam donationem et puram elemosinam possidendam, atque predictos fratres et eorum res et possessiones sub nostra protectione et defensione in evum[dy] protegendos suscepimus, ut nullus de posteris nostris vel aliis quisquam hereditario iure nobis succedens eam possit effringere vel aliquo modo inquietare aut ausu temerario audeat contraire. Et ut ea firma et stabilis, rata et inconcussa et inviolata ab omnibus nobis in futurum succedentibus perpetuo prenominatis fratribus perseveret, ut beneficiorum ipsorum et orationum caritatis divine intuitu ordinisque reverentia, presentem kartam[dz] nostre donationis sigilli nostri munimine et impressione confirmavimus et corroboravimus per manum domini Esau tunc abbatis eiusdem monasterii, multis coram astantibus ex quibus idoneos testes adhibuimus quorum nomina sunt hec: de religiosis, Gervasius[ea] monachus et frater Madocus conversus de Llwydyarth,[eb] religiosi de Kemm(er);[k] de secularibus vero, Gwyn filius Edneweyn[ec] senescallus noster, Eynyawn[ed] filius Rodri, magister Strwyth, Ywen[ee] et multis aliis ydoneis et fidelibus. Dat' anno ab incarnatione domini millesimo ducentesimo nono.

[a] Lywelinus E. | [b] Northwall(ie) E. | [c] cunctis E. | [d] comendat E. | [e] comendare E. | [f] cartis E. | [g] M(er)ed' E. | [h] Gruff' E. | [i] Kynan E. | [j] Gruff' E. | [k] Kymmer E. | [l] Esgeyrdon' E. | [m] Midhwl E. | [n] Yrobell' E. | [o] Hirhauotwen E. | [p] Nanheu E. | [q] Mauhach E. | [r] Yrerhyl E. | [s] Mawhech' E. | [t] Creon' E. | [u] M(er)yonnyth' E. | [v] Pennllyn E. | [w] Camudadu E. | [x] Onnant E. | [y] Esgeyrgawr et E. | [z] Cwmykawr E. | [aa] Kawr E. | [ab] Haeharnawt E. | [ac] Ydolwenn E. | [ad] Keuyneran E. | [ae] Hyrhauotgelynnawk E. | [af] Nantkeylyoukeu E. | [ag] Brithgwyn E. | [ah] Marchnant E. | [ai] et finibus ... cum integris terminis *repeated here in* E. | [aj] Llwytyarth' E. | [ak] Kellylach E. | [al] Moellwytyarth E. | [am] Rosbeleydyr E. | [an] Cwmygerwyn E. | [ao] Bwlchyfreyt E. | [ap] Ykychwl E. | [aq] Cwmkelly E. | [ar] Rywlathydwyn E. | [as] Esgeyranneired E. | [at] Ycwmkrorsgwoc E. | [au-au] Cwmkadyen', Cwmkeseil cum omnibus terminis et pertinentiis integris E. | [av] Ritgarned' E.

[aw] Keuynkelynllewyn' E. | [ax] Kefn(er)th E. | [ay] Seissill E. | [az] Tanuot E. | [ba] Wronevnyth' E.
[bb] Lewelini E. | [bc] Helvycgoy E. | [bd] Rywgerydon' E. | [be] Madoc E. | [bf] Llywarch E. | [bg] Moridic E.
| [bh] Botywyn E. | [bi] Kediuor E. | [bj] Enyo' E. | [bk] Waredyn' E. | [bl] Trevaes E. | [bm] Gwevnyfalt E.
[bn] Kendyr E. | [bo] Kellywassarawc E. | [bp] E *inserts* Govolyan cum omnibus terminis et pertinentiis
integris. | [bq] Golevwern E. | [br] Kyvannod E. | [bs] Llannvlldut E. | [bt] Cwmgwynyn E.
[bu] Moelysbryn E. | [bv] Kesseigwyn' E. | [bw] Cwmmeneych' E. | [bx] Mawdv E. | [by] extrata E.
[bz] Gwynvynyd E. | [ca] Gwernybudeyv E. | [cb] Nantygaranev E. | [cc] Bedyresgyb E. | [cd] Verydyawc E.
[ce] Rywhwden E. | [cf] Lliw E. | [cg] Llyw E. | [ch] Erylyvetwyn E. | [ci] Erylyvetwen E. | [cj] Ardudwy E.
[ck] Mawddv E. | [cl] Llwynyrhyd E. | [cm] Ykerricllwydyon' E. | [cn] Hesgyndv E. | [co] Yrhavotavolawc E.
[cp] Ybwlellwyth' E. | [cq] Dolykanavon E. | [cr] qua E. | [cs] dividuntur E. | [ct] Yralltlwt E.
[cu] Cwmkedyrn' E. | [cv] Rywgyverthwch E. | [cw] Pennyarthwonawc E. | [cx] Nantyllastegwaret E.
[cy] Bedyketwr E. | [cz] Lleyn E. | [da] Newgwl E. | [db] E *inserts* suis. | [dc] carta E. | [dd] Ygwascatvaes E.
[de] Ycwarrachdir E. | [df] Rosichulyc E. | [dg] Enyon' E. | [dh] Penvras E. | [di] Treuuorydic E.
[dj] Pantyllefvryth E. | [dk] Brynykrocwyd E. | [dl] Trefyweyn' E. | [dm] Dolgaradawc E. | [dn] Keydyaw E.
[do] Maenbleyddud E. | [dp] speciei E. | [dq] metallis E. | [dr] sui E. | [ds] unquam E. | [dt] eorum et E. | [du] et
E. | [dv] optineant E. | [dw] homines E. | [dx] excerbimus E. | [dy] omni E. | [dz] cartam E. | [ea] Iervasius E.
[eb] Llywytyarth E. | [ec] Ednyweyn' E. | [ed] Eyno(n) E. | [ee] Ywon E.

The variant readings of E are given since, as Williams-Jones pointed out ('Llywelyn's charter to Cymer', 45–6), E's text seems to derive from the original letter patent issued by Edward II in 1324 rather than from its enrolment, for it includes three place-names lacking in the latter, namely Cwm Cadian, Cwm Cesail and *Govolyan* (textual notes *au, bp*). As the inspeximus was presented to *quo warranto* commissioners in Meirionnydd, this hypothesis is credible, as is the suggestion that it was falsely attributed to Edward I in order to lend it greater authority (Williams-Jones, 'Llywelyn's charter to Cymer', 46, n. 8).

The Cistercian abbey of Cymer in Meirionnydd was founded by Llywelyn's first cousins, Maredudd and Gruffudd sons of Cynan ab Owain Gwynedd, in 1198 or early 1199 as a daughter house of Cwm-hir in Maelienydd. The present charter is the only one now extant in favour of the house and appears to have superseded previous charters; Llywelyn refers to the charters and gifts of Maredudd and Gruffudd and of Gruffudd's son Hywel. In contrast to Llywelyn's two charters for Aberconwy (nos 218–19 above), there are no grounds for doubting the authenticity of the Cymer charter: for example, it explicitly refers to previous grants by other donors rather than, as in the longer Aberconwy charter (no. 218), giving the impression that all the lands named were new grants by Llywelyn, and the dating clause appears authentic. Of the secular witnesses named, Gwyn ab Ednywain and Master Ystrwyth acted as receivers of expenses paid to Llywelyn by the king in 1209, while the presence of Einion ap Rhodri is also consistent with the charter's date in that year, if, as has been suggested, he was a son of Rhodri ab Owain Gwynedd (d. 1195) (Stephenson, *Governance*, 116, 215, 225). None of the rights and liberties listed in the final part of the charter seem to be anachronistic, and the clauses confirming papal privileges bear comparison with the tenor of papal privileges granted to other Cistercian abbeys both in and outside Wales (cf. p. 99 and note to no. 218 above). That the charter was issued at the request of the monks is also credible: probably the monks sought the prince's confirmation of their lands and liberties in response to the political upheaval created by Llywelyn's expansion into southern Powys and northern Ceredigion following Gwenwynwyn's imprisonment by King John in October 1208. See further Williams-Jones, 'Llywelyn's charter to Cymer', and Gresham, 'Cymer Abbey charter' (whose identification of the lands granted is followed in the summary of the charter given above), together with Smith, 'Cymer', Smith and Butler, 'Cistercian order', 297–309, and Pryce, 'Medieval church', 275–9 (which focus primarily on the circumstances of the abbey's foundation and the issue of Llywelyn's charter).

230 Arbitration between the abbeys of Dore and Strata Florida

All disputes between the abbot and house of Dore and the house of Strata Florida have been settled by this agreement at the entreaties of the arbitrators whom they have promised to abide by the agreement, namely the abbots of Neath, Tintern, Margam, Whitland and Aberconwy and other good men, especially Llywelyn. The abbot of Dore has remitted to Strata Florida all suits and all damages inflicted on his house, so that henceforth the abbot and convent of Strata Florida will cause Dore no trouble nor seize its property in all the lands, pastures and woods it has in Cantref Selyf as set out in the charters of Dore. Any monk or conversus of Dore or Strata Florida who infringes this peace shall be banished from his house, and will return only by permission of the General Chapter. Sealed by the arbitrators and by the abbots of both houses.

1209

A = TNA: PRO, E 326/727 (Ancient Deeds, Series B). Endorsed: Conventio inter abbatem de Dora et abbatem de Stratflur (s. xiii[1]); Cantselif (s. xv); approx. 143 × 85 + 9 mm., indented along top edge; seven tags, each *c*.8 mm. wide and each passing through two slits in the fold and exiting through a slit in the base of the fold; all seals are missing.
Pd. from A, Sayers, 'English Cistercian cases', 96–7.
Cd., *Cat. Ancient Deeds*, i. 282; *H*, no. 332.

C I R O G R A P H U M [a]

Sciant presentes et futuri quod omnes lites et querele que habebantur inter abbatem et domum de Dora et abbatem et domum de St(ra)tflur sub hac forma pacis quieverunt ad preces arbitrorum in quos compromiserunt, scilicet abbatum de Neht, de Tint(er)', de Marg(an), de Alba Domo et de Ab(er)conu et aliorum bonorum virorum, precipue Lewelini: scilicet quod abbas de Dora remisit omnes querelas et omnia dampna domui sue illata abbati et conventui de St(ra)tflur, ita ut de cetero idem abbas et conventus de St(ra)tflur nullam vexationem vel alienationem vel per se vel per aliquem[b] suorum facient abbati et domui de Dora in omnibus terris et pasturis et silvis quas habent in Cant(re) Selif iuxta tenorem cartarum de Dora. Quicumque aut monacus vel conversus de Dora vel St(ra)tflur hanc pacem infregerit, a domo sua eliminetur nec reversurus nisi per generale capitulum. Facta est 'hec pacis confirmatio anno ab incarnatione domini m° cc° ix° et munita sigillis arbitrorum et abbatum utriusque domus.

[a] *word cut through by indent* A. | [b] aiquem A.

The Cistercian abbey of Dore in Ewias (Herefs.) was founded in 1147 and received lands in Cantref Selyf in the lordship of Brecon from Walter I Clifford *c*.1170 (*Mon. Ang.*, v. 555; Williams, *White Monks in Gwent*, 37). The role of Llywelyn in the arbitration reflected the dominance he had achieved in the autumn of 1208 as a result of his annexation of southern

Powys, followed by his occupation of northern Ceredigion as far as the river Ystwyth; the prince had also handed over the district between the Ystwyth and the river Aeron, in which Strata Florida lay, to Rhys and Owain sons of Gruffudd ap Rhys (*HW*, ii. 621). The protection granted to Dore – specifically with respect to its property in Cantref Selyf, according to the document's endorsement – by a Bishop 'G.' of St Davids may have been issued by Bishop Geoffrey (1203–14) at about the same time as the present arbitration (*St Davids Episcopal Acta*, no. 53). For brief comments on the arbitration see Sayers, 'Judicial activities', 173–4; Williams, *White Monks in Gwent*, 38.

231 Strata Marcella Abbey

Grant, in the hope of eternal reward for the souls of himself and his parents of (?) Banhadlogllwydion in pure and perpetual possession, free of all secular exaction and custom so that the monks may possess that land with all its boundaries and appurtenances peacefully in perpetual right, and that no lay or ecclesiastical person may have any right or use in it except for the monks of Strata Marcella. Sealing clause; witnesses.

Dinorben, 25 November [1209]

A = NLW, Wynnstay Estate Records, Ystrad Marchell Charters, no. 58. Endorsed: Lewelin(us) super Banadellaeludion (s. xiii[1], probably by scribe of charter); early modern endorsements; approx. 120 × 140 + 20 mm.; two central horizontal slits for a tag (*c.*15 mm. wide) which exits through a slit in the base of the fold; sealed on tag. Circular seal, green wax, imperfect, originally approx. 70 mm. diameter; equestrian, facing right; legend: SIGIL . . . . . . IPI . . . . . .

Pd. from A, Jones, 'Abbey of Ystrad Marchell', 306–7; from A, Jones *et al.*, 'Five Strata Marcella charters', 52; from A, *Ystrad Marchell Charters*, no. 58.

Cd., Davies, 'Strata Marcella documents', 182 (no. 28); Stephenson, *Governance*, 200–1; *H*, no. 129.

Universis sancte matris ecclesie filiis tam presentibus quam futuris notum sit quod ego Lewelin(us) Noruuallie princeps, intuitu pietatis et spe eterne retributionis pro anime mee ac parentum meorum salute, dedi Deo et Beate Marie et monachis de St(ra)tmarchel illam terram que appellatur Banadellaucluidion in puram et perpetuam possessionem, liberam et quietam et ab omni seculari exactione et consuetudine et inquietudine extraneam, ita ut predicti monachi predictam terram cum omnibus terminis suis et pertinentiis, in omnibus utilitatibus eius usibus, sine ulla reclamatione firmiter, bene et pacifice perpetuo iure possideant, ita quod nullus sive secularis sit sive ecclesiasticus nullum in ea habeat ius aut proprietatem, usum vel usiarium, exceptis venerabilibus et mihi karissimis monachis de Stradm(ar)chel quibus affectuosa caritate et plenaria donatione prefatam terre particulam, scilicet Banelauc luidion, in omnibus terminis suis voluntarie concessi et firmissime dedi. Sed quia presens etas prona est ad malum unde si possit extorquere lucrum, tam propria sigilli mei impressione quam bonorum ac fidelium virorum atestatione hanc meam donationem munivi et corroboravi. Huius igitur donationis testes sunt: G. prior de St(ra)tm(ar)chel et I. conversus eiusdem loci; de laicis,[a] Malgun filius Ririt, Guen filius Ehtnewein, Goronui mab Trehrud Owen. Datum litterarum vii° kalendas decembris, luna xx[a] iiii[a], apud Dinnorben in manu G. prioris de St(ra)tm(ar)chel.

[a] lacis A.

As Thomas noted, the combination of the date 25 November and the reference to the twenty-fourth day of the moon means that this charter is datable to 1209, as the new moon fell on 2 November in 1209 (*Ystrad Marchell Charters*, 197, citing Giry, *Manuel de diplomatique*, 157). Llywelyn had overrun southern Powys, in which Strata Marcella was situated, in the autumn of 1208 (*HW*, ii. 621). The location of (?)Banhadlogllwydion (*Banadellaucluidion/Banelauc luidion*) is uncertain. Thomas suggested that it lay either in the township of Gwyddelwern in Edeirnion or in that of Llanelidan in the adjacent commote of Llannerch, Dyffryn Clwyd (*Ystrad Marchell Charters*, 124). The case for Llanelidan is arguably stronger. (?)Banhadlogllwydion was included among grants made to Strata Marcella by Madog ap Gruffudd of northern Powys in a charter of 1207 (no. 504 below), which states that the monks had bought the land from the sons of Iorwerth ap Cadwgan of Llanelidan. Moreover, it is striking that Llywelyn's charter records a gift rather than a confirmation, and makes no mention of the other lands granted by Madog in 1207, all located in Edeirnion. If, as is possible, Llywelyn thereby implicitly rejected Madog's lordship of (?)Banhadlogllwydion, this could strengthen the case for locating the land in Llanelidan, as Dyffryn Clwyd formed part of the Four Cantrefs held by Llywelyn since 1194. By contrast, though he had occupied Edeirnion, in August 1211 Llywelyn nevertheless recognized that Owain Brogyntyn, of the Powysian dynasty, had rights there too (no. 233 below). The charter was issued at Dinorben (SH 969 748), the prince's court for the commote of Rhos Is Dulas, and perhaps for the whole cantref of Rhos (*Survey of the Honour of Denbigh*, 222–3, 230–3; cf. Jones, 'Tribal system', 120, 122).

*232 Strata Marcella Abbey

Confirmation in free and perpetual alms of all lands as set forth more fully in the charters of the lands' donors or sellers.

[probably 25 November 1209 × November 1210; possibly 1216 × 11 April 1240]

Mention only, in an inspeximus of Edward II dated at Tutbury, 12 March 1322 (Jones, 'Abbey of Ystrad Marchell', 313; cd., *CChR 1300–26*, 440; *H*, no. 162). In the inspeximus the summary of this charter follows that of Llywelyn's grant of (?)Banhadlogllwydion (no. 231 above), datable to 25 November 1209; this could suggest that the present confirmation was issued either at the same time as, or later than, no. 231. If so, it may well have been issued during Llywelyn's occupation of southern Powys following the capture of Gwenwynwyn on 8 October 1208, an occupation ended by John's restoration of Gwenwynwyn to his principality towards the end of November 1210 (*HW*, ii. 633). It is not impossible, however, that the charter is datable to the period of Llywelyn's second occupation of southern Powys after his expulsion of Gwenwynwyn early in 1216.

233 King John

In order to receive the king's grace and good will, Llywelyn has quitclaimed to King John for ever the castle of Degannwy with Rhos, Rhufoniog with Denbigh and Ystrad, and Dyffryn Clwyd with Ruthin. He shall not intervene concerning Edeirnion and its appurtenances, save to intercede for his uncle Owain Brogyntyn, since he has never held that land from Llywelyn or any of his ancestors but rather from the king. He has granted that Hywel ap Gruffudd shall have seisin of his land until inquiry is made in Llywelyn's court. If Hywel refuses to go to that court or have inquiry made there, the king shall distrain him to do so. Llywelyn has granted that the king may do his will regarding Rhuddlan and Mold with Englefield [Tegeingl] saving Llywelyn's right and . . . to prove his right; what he has proved he shall remit to the king for as long as it pleases him. If the men of the lands remitted to the king wish to hold their lands from the king, let them give security that they will serve him faithfully and ensure that their services are received by the king alone. Llywelyn will grant the king the allegiances of whichever of his men the king chooses, and deliver to the king his son Gruffudd; if he does not have an heir by the king's daughter, Llywelyn grants to the king as his heir all his lands, both those retained and those remitted, apart from those which it pleases the king to give to the same son and to Llywelyn's men. Llywelyn will give the king for his expenses 10,000 cows, forty destriers and sixty hunters, so that the men of the lands he has remitted, both those who become the king's tenants and those who remain with Llywelyn, shall reasonably give Llywelyn an aid for the aforesaid payment. Llywelyn will deliver to the king as many hostages as he wishes from his land for his faithful service, and in order to ensure the agreement is kept Llywelyn has sworn on relics and had this charter made for the king. The bishop of Norwich, the earls William of Salisbury, William Marshal and William de Warenne and Peter fitz Herbert have undertaken that the king by this agreement has remitted all ill will and anger against Llywelyn. Sealed, at Llywelyn's request, by the aforesaid bishop, earls and Peter, and by Llywelyn himself.

12 August 1211

B = TNA: PRO, E 163/4/47, m. 6. s. xiv[1].
Pd. from B, Smith, 'Magna Carta', 361–2.
Cd., *H*, no. 131.

Omnibus Cristi fidelibus presentem cartam inspecturis Lewelinus princeps Norwall(ie) salutem. Sciatis quod pro habenda gratiam et benevolenctiam domini [mei regis Anglie] Iohannis dimisi `ei et imperpetuum quieta clamavi castrum de Gannoch' cum Ros et omnibus pertinentiis suis et Roui(n)a cum Dunbeig' et Estrede et omnibus perti[nentiis suis] et Defreneclud' cum Ruthin et omnibus pertinentiis suis. De Derenia(n) autem cum pertinentiis suis nichil me intromitto nisi supplicando pro Oeno de Porkinton [avunculo] meo quia numquam tenuit terram illam de me vel aliquo antecessorum meorum set de domino rege. Et concessi quod Hoelus filius Griffini seisinam [habeat de] terra sua ita quod postea stet recto in curia mea. Et si in curiam meam venire vel in ea recto stare noluerit, dominus rex ad hoc ipsum dist[ringere] faciet. Et concessi quod dominus rex faciat voluntatem suam de Roelan' et Monte Alto cum Englefeld' et omnibus pertinentiis suis salvo iure meo et [. . . vel . . .] petere dirationare per ius quod in eis clamo; quod disrationavero dimittam in manum domini regis quamdiu ei placuerit. Homines autem terrarum quas domino [regi di]misi si voluerint ad dominum regem venire et terras suas de eo tenere, faciant ei bonam securitatem quod fideliter ei servient et servitia sua bene ei reddent nec aliquo modo perquirent quod ab alio quam a domino rege receptentur. Faciam etiam habere domino meo regi ligantias omnium hominum meorum de quibus voluerit, et liberabo ei filium meum Griffinu(m) tenendum semper et ad faciendum inde voluntatem suam, ita quod si de filia[a] domini regis uxore mea heredem non habuero, concedo ipsi domino meo regi tanquam heredi meo omnes terras meas tam illas quas retinui quam illas quas et dimisi preter terras quas ei placuerit dare eidem filio meo et meis. Preterea dabo eidem domino meo regi pro expensis suis decem milia vaccarum et quadraginta dextrarios et sexaginta chascuros, ita quod homines terrarum quas domino regi dimisi tam illi qui ad dominum regem ibunt ut de eo terras suas teneant quam illi qui mecum remanebunt auxilium michi facient rationabiliter ad solvendam predictam pecuniam. Liberabo etiam ei obsides de terra mea quos et quot et de quibus habere voluerit pro fideli servitio meo, et pro conventione predicta tenenda et hec in bona fide et sine malo ingenio tenenda tactis sacrosanctis iuravi et hanc cartam meam eidem domino meo regi inde fieri feci. Dominus vero Norwic(ensis) episcopus, Will(elmu)s [comes Sarresberiensis], comes Will(elmu)s Mar(escallus), comes W. Warronn' et Petrus filius Hereb(er)ti manuceperunt quod dominus rex omnem malivolentiam et ind[ignationem] michi per predictam conventionem remisit quam erga me habuit usque ad diem Veneris proximam post festum Sancti Laurencii [Martiris anno regni] domini regis xiii. Et ad maiorem huius rei securitatem dominus I. Norwic(ensis) episcopus, W. comes Sarr(esberiensis), comes W. Mar(escallus), comes W. W[arronn'] et Petrus filius Hereb(er)ti ad petitionem meam sigilla sua cum sigillo meo huic carte apposuerunt.

ᵃ fidelia B.

The readings supplied within square brackets where the parchment is now illegible follow, in almost all cases, those suggested by Smith, who used an infra-red photograph.

This important charter was issued following John's successful campaign against Gwynedd in July and early August 1211 (*HW*, ii. 634–6; Davies, *Conquest*, 295–6). According to *Brut y Tywysogyon*, 'Llywelyn, being unable to suffer the king's rage, sent his wife, the king's daughter, to him by the counsel of his leading men to make peace with the king on whatever terms he could', and the prince subsequently met the king himself (*BT, Pen20Tr*, 85; also *BT, RBH*, 190–3). The present agreement contains the results of their negotiations. For a full discussion of its textual history and significance see Smith, 'Magna Carta', which emphasizes the extent of John's determination to resolve the problem posed by Wales revealed by the document, including the escheat of Gwynedd to the crown should Llywelyn die without an heir by Joan.

234 Madog ap Maelgwn and his brothers; Hywel ap Cadwallon; Maredudd ap Rhobert; Iorwerth Goch, his son Meurig and his other sons; Iorwerth and Maredudd sons of Einion Clud; Iorwerth ap Meirion; and all others in Wales

Letter, declaring that places consecrated to God, and especially to religion, should be cherished and protected from loss, and all in sacred orders, especially religious, should be venerated and not disturbed by any trouble, so that they can intercede for the salvation of Llywelyn and of all. Therefore Llywelyn prays, and orders those whom he can order, as they love his honour and wish to have free access to him and his counsel and aid, that they love the canon Walter Corbet and assist him in his business for the love of God and Llywelyn; they should also protect from theft, plunder and all damage the land of Ratlinghope and Coates which Walter has acquired for the increase of religion, land which, so Llywelyn has heard, is near to the land of Ceri, together with the men, servants, animals and other things of that place that will be necessary for the use of the brothers and poor of Christ. Walter is a kinsman and close friend of Llywelyn, much loved on account of his religion, and his brother William Corbet is Llywelyn's uncle. Therefore Llywelyn asks the recipients to have faith and peace with the aforesaid place and the brothers who will serve there and their men and possessions. If any one should inflict

*damage or any injury after this request, he shall lose Llywelyn's friendship and love. In
particular, Madog ap Maelgwn, whom Llywelyn has fostered and elevated, should not repay
good with evil but exert himself on behalf of Llywelyn's honour just as Llywelyn previously
assisted Madog.*

[Probably *c*.May × 4 August 1212]

B = Cardiff County and City Library MS 4.101 (formerly MS 83), fo. 230r. s. xvi/xvii; here 1605.
C = NLW, Peniarth MS 225B, p. 128. s. xvi/xvii.
D = *Mon. Ang.* (1st edn.), ii. 336–7. 1661. Rubric: Ex ipso autogr. penes Owenum Wyn de Gwedir,
Baronettum.
E = NLW MS 9070 (formerly Panton Papers 20), no. 2 (CI 61). s. xvii[l].
Pd., D; from D, *Mon. Ang.*, vi: i. 496–7.
Cd., *H*, no. 333.

Lewelinus filius Gervasii [a]-Dei gratia-[a] princeps Norwalie[b] dilectis sibi et cognatis et amicis
Madoco filio[c] Mailgun[d] et fratribus eius, et Hoelo[e] filio Cadewathl'[f] et M[e]redith[g] filio
Roberti et Gervasio Goch[h] et Meurik[i] filio eius et aliis filiis ipsius, et Gervasio et Meredith[g]
filiis[j] Heinoun[k] Clut[l] et Gervasio `filio Meirioun,[m] et omnibus aliis per[n] Walliam constitutis
tam notis sibi quam extraneis, salutem et in omnibus necessitatibus suis et iustis
petitionibus suis pro posse suo non minus auxilii quam consilii solatium. Quia tam vobis
quam nobis expedit omnia loca Deo consecrata, et maxime ea que sancte religioni sunt
`de putata, pie[o] caritatis affectu fovere et eorum indemnitati providere, et omnes in sacris
ordinibus constitutos et maxime viros[p] religiosos, pia devotione colere et venerari et nulla
molestia infestare[q] vel insequi, ut pacifice[r] et quiete pro nostra omniumque salute,
dominum cuius servitio se penitus manciparunt[s] iugiter possint interpellare,[t] precor vos
obnixius[u] et expostulo, et illis omnibus de vobis quibus possim[u] precipere, firmiter precipio
quatenus sicut me diligitis et honorem meum, et sicut ad me liberum accessum vultis habere
et reditum, et pro loco et tempore consilium meum et subsidium, fratrem Walteru(m)
Corbet canonicum diligatis et in negotiis suis pro Dei amore et meo promoveatis et terram
quam ipse ad honorem Dei et obsequium et sancte religionis incrementum adquisivit,[v]
scilicet Rotlincope[w] et Cotes, que terra, sicut mihi relatum est, proxima et vicina est terre de
Keri, manuteneatis et protegatis et defendatis et tam homines et servientes prefati loci quam
animalia et cetera omnia que illic sunt et futura sunt ad usum[x] fratrum et pauperum Cristi[y]
necessaria, a furto et rapina[z] et a[n] depredatione et ab omnibus aliis molestiis et
gravaminibus et damnis. Noverit enim universitas vestra quod ipse Walterus cognatus
noster[aa] est et familiarissimus, et pro religione sua et honestate mihi multum dilectus, et
frater Will(el)mi Corbet avunculi mei. Quapropter iteratis precibus rogo vos [ab]-omnes
accuratius[ac] quatinus erga iam sepedictum locum et fratres ibidem-[ab] Deo servituros et
homines illorum et omnes res[ad] suas fidem et pacem habeatis et teneatis. Si quis enim[ae] post
hanc petitionem meam ipsis[af] damnum aliquod vel iniuriam intulerit, pro certo sciat se
deinceps familiaritatem meam amissurum et amicitiam. Et precipue hoc vobis dico Madoce
fili Milgun[ag] quem nutrivi[ah] et exaltavi,[ai] [aj]-ut non reddas-[aj] mihi malum pro bono sed inten-
datis honori meo ut ego vobis amodo[ak] sicut prius consulam et succurram[al] ex animo.
Valete.

[a-a] *omitted* C. | [b] Northwallie C; Norwallie DE. | [c] filii C. | [d] Mailgwn D. | [e] Howelo D.
[f] Kadewathl' C; Cadewathlon D; Kadewathlader E. | [g] Mereduth CE; Meredith D. | [h] Goh CE.
[i] Meuric CD; Meureik E. | [j] filis B. | [k] Heinonii E. | [l] Chit E. | [m] Meirionii E. | [n] *omitted* C.

^o pio D. | ^p vivos C. | ^q *corrected from* pasifice *in* B. | ^r manciparent D. | ^s interpellere C. ^t obnoxius D. | ^u possum C. | ^v adquisiverim E. | ^w Ratlincope D; Rotelincope E. | ^x alii E. | ^y ei E. ^z rapine B. | ^{aa} meus C. | ^{ab–ab} quod C. | ^{ac} attentius E. | ^{ad} terras D. | ^{ae} CD *insert* ex vobis; autem ex vobis E. | ^{af} ipsi C. | ^{ag} Meilgun C; Mailgwn D. | ^{ah} nutriverim E. | ^{ai} exaltaverim E. | ^{aj–aj} ne reddatis E. | ^{ak} animo E. | ^{al} suurram B.

Of the four early modern copies of this letter, at least three are associated with the Wynns of Gwydir, who claimed descent from Gruffudd ap Cynan and the dynasty of Gwynedd (*Hist. Gwydir*, 1). B occurs in a manuscript containing an autograph copy of *The History of Gwydir* by Sir John Wynn (1553–1627), though the transcript of Llywelyn's letter is not in Sir John's hand (*RMWL*, ii. 783–9; *Calendar of the Wynn (of Gwydir) Papers*, 116–18 (no. 732)); C was copied by 'Sir' Thomas Wiliems of Trefriw, a kinsman of the Wynns patronized by Sir John; while D is said by Dugdale to have been transcribed from the autograph of the letter held by Owen Wynn (1592–1660), a son of Sir John Wynn, who succeeded to the baronetcy and estate of Gwydir on the death of his brother Richard Wynn in 1649 (*DWB*, 1018–19, 1097–8). The provenance of E is uncertain. It consists of a separate sheet mounted in a volume of miscellaneous correspondence and papers of the families of Jones and Panton of Plas Gwyn, Anglesey, Price of Derwen, John Jones, dean of Bangor and Evans of St Asaph, dating from the seventeenth and eighteenth centuries (*Handlist of Manuscripts in the National Library of Wales*, iii. 107–8). E is evidently the least accurate of the extant texts, and is therefore listed after the somewhat later copy in D. Establishing the relationship between the four copies is difficult. None is obviously derived directly from any of the others. If the Wynns possessed the original of the letter, as Dugdale stated, it is possible that not only D but also B and perhaps C and/or E were transcribed from it. Unfortunately, neither D nor any of the other sources provides any physical description of the text being copied which would help to corroborate Dugdale's statement. However, it should not be dismissed out of hand: since the Wynns sought out texts of twelfth- and early thirteenth-century charters issued in favour of Haughmond Abbey by rulers of Gwynedd, they may likewise have acquired either the original or a copy of Llywelyn's letter which had once been held by Ratlinghope Priory. In any event, an ultimate provenance in the priory seems more likely than one in Gwynedd, as, even if acts issued by Llywelyn were normally registered by the prince's clerks (which is far from certain), no such registered documents appear to have survived (cf. above, p. 137). However, all the texts have undergone some modernization. C omits *Dei gratia* from Llywelyn's title (on which see further above, pp. 75–6) as well as a phrase in the clause opening *Quapropter iteratis precibus* . . . (textual note *ab*). This may indicate that Wiliems (or his exemplar) abbreviated the text, and B, of similar date, has been chosen as the principal source of the text printed here.

This letter can be no later than 1212 when its first two addressees, Madog ap Maelgwn and his uncle Hywel ap Cadwallon (together with Meurig Barach) were hanged in England (*BT, Pen20Tr*, 87; *BT, RBH*, 194–5). If the testimony given by Tudur ap Madog at Montgomery to Edward I's commission of inquiry into Welsh law in 1281 may be relied upon, the executions took place at Bridgnorth early in August 1212: according to Tudur, the three men were hanged as a result of an appeal against them for the murder of a certain William de Mora before John and his justices at Bridgnorth (TNA: PRO, C 77/2, m. 2; cd., *CWR*, 206; cf. *CIM*, i. 26 (no. 84)). Since the Welsh chronicles date the executions to 1212, and since John was present at Bridgnorth only on 2, 3 and 4 August in that year (itinerary in *Rot. Pat.*), the men presumably died on one of those days. Though Tudur was referring to events almost seventy years previously, his account is credible in view of its consistency with that in the Welsh chronicles (he names the same three individuals) and also with John's itinerary. It follows that Madog and the others were not among the hostages handed over to John as one of the terms of Llywelyn's submission in August 1211 and executed at Northampton on 14 August 1212, as assumed by Eyton, *Shropshire*, vi. 161; xi. 173.

The reference to Llywelyn's having fostered Madog ap Maelgwn suggests that Madog's father Maelgwn ap Cadwallon (d. 1197) had fled to Gwynedd with his brother Hywel ap Cadwallon after their explusion from Maelienydd by Roger II Mortimer in 1195 (Smith, 'Middle March', 81; *idem*, 'Cymer', 103–4). However, by the time the letter was written, Madog was clearly no longer in Gwynedd and seems to have established himself in the middle March: the commote of Ceri, named in the letter, lies between Madog's ancestral lordship of Maelienydd and the lordship of Cedewain, which was probably held by another of the letter's recipients, Maredudd ap Rhobert, by 1211. Indeed, Madog appears to have recovered at least part of Maelienydd, presumably with Roger Mortimer's agreement, perhaps by Michaelmas 1210 (note to no. 113 above). The implication that Madog's loyalty to Llywelyn was in doubt could relate to attempts by Madog to secure John's support in order to recover all or part of Maelienydd, independent of Llywelyn's overlordship; that the ruler of Maelienydd sought to maintain his independence is shown by his charter for Cwmhir, issued no later than May 1212, with its defiant sanction clause directed against 'the lordship of any prince', clearly meaning Llywelyn (no. 113 above). It is also worth noting that Llywelyn could not rely on Maredudd ap Rhobert's support by the summer of 1212, for in a letter of 1 September 1212 King John states that he has agreed to make payments to Madog ap Gruffudd of northern Powys, Maredudd ap Rhobert and other Welsh in his service (*Rot. Claus.*, i. 123b); in the light of this evidence Lloyd concluded that *Brut y Tywysogyon* was incorrect in naming Maredudd and Madog among Llywelyn's supporters against the king in the summer of 1212 (*HW*, ii. 638, n. 131). The dating limits of the present letter are thus Madog's return to Maelienydd, very probably no later than 1210, and his death, together with that of Hywel ap Cadwallon, in early August 1212. However, its magisterial tone, including the phrase *omnibus aliis per Walliam constitutis tam notis sibi quam extraneis* in the address, may well reflect the dominant position recovered by the prince in the summer of 1212 (cf. no. 235 below; Smith, 'Cymer', 115, n. 17, suggests that the letter was probably written in 1212).

It is uncertain when the Augustinian priory or cell of Ratlinghope (Shrops.), located on the western slopes of the Long Mynd about 10 miles from the border with Ceri and dependent on Wigmore Abbey, was founded. The land had presumably been given to Walter Corbet before 1209, for the abbot of Wigmore had made assarts and purprestures at Ratlinghope and Coates by March 1209 (Eyton, *Shropshire*, vi. 159, citing a forest assize before the justices at Shrewsbury; Eyton assigned the foundation to 1199 × 1209, and this is acccepted in *VCH, Shropshire*, ii. 80). The present letter was written after the land was donated but before a community had been established there (note the phrase *fratres ibidem Deo servituros*); the date of the community's arrival is unknown. The references to Walter Corbet as Llywelyn's *cognatus* and to his brother William Corbet as Llywelyn's uncle may indicate that the prince's mother Marared married a Corbet after the death of Llywelyn's father Iorwerth Drwyndwn (*HW*, ii. 587, n. 62; cf. Pryce, *Native Law*, 85).

235 Philip Augustus, king of France

Letter, thanking Philip, king of the French, prince of the kings of the earth, for sending to Llywelyn, Philip's faithful man, his letter sealed with his gold seal in testimony of the treaty between the kingdom of the French and the principality of North Wales, which Llywelyn will have kept in the aumbreys of the church as if it were a sacred relic, so that it may be a perpetual memorial and an inviolable testimony that he and his heirs, adhering inseparably to Philip and his heirs, will be friends to Philip's friends and enemies of his enemies; Llywelyn asks that the same will be observed by Philip towards Llywelyn and his friends. In order that this be kept inviolably, having summoned the council of his leading men and with the consent of all the princes of Wales, all of whom he has bound together in the friendship of this treaty, Llywelyn promises by the testimony of his seal to be faithful to Philip for ever, and just as he faithfully promises so he will more faithfully fulfil his promise. From the time he has received Philip's letter Llywelyn has not made truce, peace or even parley with the English, but by the grace of God he and all the princes of Wales in unanimous confederation have manfully resisted their – and Philip's – enemies, and with the Lord's help have recovered from the yoke of their tyranny a great part of the land and the strongest castles which they have occupied by deceit, and hold mightily in God that which has been recovered. Therefore all the princes of Wales request that Philip make neither truce nor peace with the English without them, knowing that the princes will not bind themselves by any agreement or price to the English in any peace or treaty, unless they have advanced knowledge of his approval.

[July × -14 August 1212]

A = Paris, Archives Nationales de France, J 655, no. 14. Permission was not granted to examine this document on account of its poor state of preservation. The text is transcribed from the 1:1 photographic facsimile in Matthews, *Welsh Records*. The description of the document and its sealing arrangements is based both on that facsimile and on information about the letter's endorsements and dimensions, together with a photocopy of the dorse, kindly supplied by the Centre d'accueil et de recherche des Archives Nationales (CARAN). Endorsed: Confederacio Loelini principis Norwallie cum domino rege Francorum sine data (s. xiv[1]); v (s. xiv), clii (struck through) (s. xiv), vii (s. xiv); pulchra (s. xiv); Scrinio lxix (s. xiv); modern endorsements; approx. 210 × 117 + 13 mm.; two central slits in fold for a tag (*c.*11 mm. wide) which exits through a slit in the base of the fold; sealed on tag. Circular seal, black wax, imperfect, originally *c.*70 mm. diameter; equestrian, facing right; legend: + SIGILLVM : LOELI . . .

Pd. from A, Teulet, *Layettes*, i. 386–7 (no. 1032); from A, *RHF*, xviii. 168, n. (a); from A, *Welsh Records*, ed. Matthews, 3–4 (and trans., ibid., 58–9); from A, Treharne, 'Franco-Welsh treaty', 74–5; from Treharne, *EHD*, iii. 306–7 (trans. only).

Cd., *H*, no. 334.

Excellentissimo domino suo Ph(ilippo) Dei gracia illustri Francorum regi Loelin(us) princeps Norwallie fidelis suus salutem et tam devotum quam debitum fidelitatis et reverentie famulatum. Quid retribuam excellentie nobilitatis vestre pro singulari honore et dono inpreciabili quo vos rex Francor(um), imo princeps regum terre, me fidelem vestrum non tam munifice quam magnifice prevenientes, litteras vestras sigillo aureo impressas in testimonium federis regni Francor(um) et Norwallie principatus michi militi vestro delegastis, quas ego in armariis ecclesiasticis tanquam sacrosanctas relliquias[a] conservari facio, ut sint memoriale perpetuum et testimonium inviolabile quod ego et heredes mei, vobis vestrisque heredibus inseparabiliter adherentes, vestris amicis amici erimus et inimici inimicis, idipsum a vestra regia dignitate erga me et meos amicos regaliter observari modis omnibus expecto postulans et expeto? Quod ut inviolabiliter observetur, congregato procerum meorum concilio et communi cunctorum Wallie principum assensu, quos omnes vobiscum in huius federis amicicia colligavi, sigilli mei testimonio me vobis fidelem inperpetuum promitto, et sicut fideliter promitto fidelius promissum adimplebo. Preterea, ex quo vestre sullimitatis litteras suscepi, nec treugas nec pacem nec etiam colloquium aliquod cum Anglicis feci, set per Dei gratiam ego et omnes Wallie principes unanimiter confederati, inimicis nostris imo vestris viriliter restitimus, et a iugo tyrannidis ipsorum magnam partem terre et castra munitissima, que ipsi per fraudes et dolos occupaverant, per auxilium domini in manu forti recuperavimus, recuperata in domino Deo potenter possidemus. Unde postulantes expetimus universi Wallie principes quod sine nobis nec treugas nec pacem cum Anglicis faciatis, scituri quod nos nullo pacto vel precio, nisi precognita voluntatis vestre benivolencia, eis aliquo pacis seu federis vinculo copulabimur.

[a] *sic in* A.

A full discussion of this letter is provided by Treharne, 'Franco-Welsh treaty', which convincingly argues that it was written after the Welsh offensives to recover the Four Cantrefs that began in July 1212 were under way, but before John's hanging of Welsh hostages on 14 August 1212, on the grounds that its silence concerning the latter event is almost certainly significant. The initiative for the alliance, already confirmed by Philip Augustus in the letter mentioned here by Llywelyn, seems to have come from the French king, as part of his diplomatic response to John's plans for a campaign to recover Normandy and other French lands lost in 1204, though he may also have been prompted by Pope Innocent III, who absolved Llywelyn and other Welsh princes of their oaths of fealty to John, and lifted the interdict on their lands, in 1212. Presumably the treaty was concluded in May or June 1212, before the despatch of Philip's letter to Llywelyn (Rowlands, 'King John and Wales', 283–4); Giles de Braose, bishop of Hereford, who had fled to France in 1208 and whose family was allied to Llywelyn, may have played a part in the negotiations (*EEA*, vii. xlvi). For the significance of the reference to Philip's golden seal, see Brunel, 'Les actes des rois', esp. 116–17. In the event, the alliance proved short-lived: after John's submission to Innocent III on 15 May 1213 Llywelyn concluded a truce with the king of England on 3 June to run until 1215, and gave no support to Philip during John's campaigns against him in 1214.

*236 Agreement with King John
Chirograph between Llywelyn and the king.
[June 1213 × May 1215; possibly June 1213 or August 1214]

Mention only, in a letter of Llywelyn to John datable to 13 June 1215 × -19 October 1216 (no. 237 below). Presumably the document was drawn up during the truce that lasted from June 1213 until May 1215 (cf. *HW*, ii. 641–3). Indeed, it may well have recorded the terms of that truce or its renewal in August 1214, as the latter was said by John to have been recorded by both parties in writing (*secundum formam ex utraque parte concessam et scripto redactam*) (*Rot. Pat.*, 120b, cited by Smith, 'Magna Carta', 356, n. 6).

237 King John

Letter, concerning pledges, English attacks, Reginald de Braose, Maelgwn and Rhys sons of Rhys and the terms of a chirograph between Llywelyn and the king.

[13 June 1215 × -19 October 1216]

> A = TNA: PRO, SC 1/1, no. 15. No endorsements; approx. 174 mm. wide × 64 mm. deep at left, 51 mm. deep at right; mounted, foot cut away. The document is badly stained and mostly illegible.

Excellentissimo . . .[a] regi Angl(ie) . . .[b] comiti And' . . .[c] / . . .[d] (?)nullo (?)modo . . .[e] ad vos venire . . .[f] / . . .[g] pro . . .[h] die nos (?)illos h. . . ille (?)licentiam et . . .[i] / . . .[j] pro (?)novem septimanis vos (?)vero . . .[k] (?)vestrem nobis (?)Brusie . . .[l] / . . .[m] nemo nobis consulit quod liberemus . . . (?)brevius plegios nobis iusticiabiles . . .[n] / . . .[o] Mailgun et Resu(m) filios Resi et alios securos. Adhuc noveritis quod (?)pro ix . . .[p] / . . .[q] die (?)homines nostros spoliaverunt, `domos fregerunt , percusserunt et vulnaverunt . . .[r] / . . .[s] salva reverentia nostra. Preterea homines vestri prosternunt . . .[t] / . . .[u] si non haberetis silvam sufficientem et vos opus haberetis (?)non (?)haberet egre . . .[v] / . . .[w] (?)Reg' de Bruisi ut secundum tenorem cirographi inter nos et vos . . .[x] / . . .[y] ab eis tempore werre. Valeat exellencia vestra diu in domino.

[a] *lacuna of c.35 mm.* | [b] *lacuna of c.50 mm.* | [c] *lacuna of c.27 mm.* | [d] *lacuna of c.58 mm.* | [e] *lacuna of c.52 mm.* | [f] *lacuna of c.32 mm.* | [g] *lacuna of c.56 mm.* | [h] *lacuna of c.7 mm.* | [i] *lacuna of c.57 mm.* [j] *lacuna of c.40 mm.* | [k] *lacuna of c.20 mm.* | [l] *lacuna of c.45 mm.* | [m] *lacuna of c.47 mm.* | [n] *lacuna of c.28 mm.* | [o] *lacuna of c.6 mm.* | [p] *lacuna of c.50 mm.* | [q] *lacuna of c.30 mm.* | [r] *lacuna of c.52 mm.* [s] *lacuna of c.43 mm.* | [t] *lacuna of c.56 mm.* | [u] *lacuna of c.25 mm.* | [v] *lacuna of c.55 mm.* | [w] *lacuna of c.28 mm.* | [x] *lacuna of c.50 mm.* | [y] *lacuna of c.40 mm.*

The summary and suggested date range are partly based on the description of the letter in the TNA: PRO typescript list. The letter appears to have been written after Llywelyn's renewal of hostilities against the crown and the Marchers in May 1215. The dating limits are the release of Rhys (Gryg) ap Rhys from royal custody on 13 June 1215, after which he began attacking Marcher castles in south Wales (*HW*, ii. 643–5 and n. 167), and John's death. In December 1215 Llywelyn led a force including both Rhys and Maelgwn which won major victories in Deheubarth, including the capture of Carmarthen. Reginald de Braose was Llywelyn's ally and son-in-law (*HW*, ii. 644–5, 648). For the chirograph between the prince and the king see no. 236 above.

238 The bailiffs of Maelienydd

Letter, notifying the bailiffs of Maelienydd that he has taken under his protection Leominster Priory, with its men and possessions, and commanding that they support and protect the monks and their possessions and defend them from injury and trouble, neither inflicting harm or trouble upon them nor allowing others to do so. If any injuries or troubles are inflicted upon the monks within their bailiwicks they should ensure that amends are made for them without delay.

[Probably 1215 × 1230; possibly 1218 × 1230]

> B = BL, Cott. MS Domit. A. iii (Leominster Priory Cartulary), fo. 74v. s. xiii med.
> Pd. from B, *Mon. Ang.*, iv. 56.
> Cd., *H*, no. 352.

Lwelin(us) princeps Norwallie baillivis de Melenith salutem. Sciatis nos sub protectione nostra suscepisse domum monachorum de Leom', homines, res et possessiones eorum, unde vobis mandamus firmiter precipientes quatinus dictos monachos, res et possessiones ipsorum manuteneatis, protegatis et defendatis ab iniuriis, molestiis et gravaminibus, non inferentes eis molestiam vel gravamen nec ab aliis eis inferri permittentes. Et si quid iniurie vel gravaminis ipsis fuerit in bailliis vestris illatum illud eis sine dilatione faciatis[a] emendari. Valete.

[a] fatiatis B.

Lloyd (*HW*, ii. 676, n. 117) suggested that this letter probably belonged to the autumn of 1231, citing a report in the Annals of Tewkesbury that Llywelyn, at about Michaelmas (29 September) 1231, burned the border areas near Painscastle, so that the prior of Leominster was compelled to make peace with him 'for a great quantity of money' (*AM*, i. 80). If so, the letter could be interpreted as marking an attempt by Llywelyn to ensure that this peace was maintained. However, Llywelyn's title in the address ('prince of North Wales') makes it very likely that the letter was written before May 1230, after which the prince seems consistently to have employed the title 'prince of Aberffraw and lord of Snowdon'. On the other hand, it is unlikely to be earlier than 1215, when Llywelyn appears to have restored the grandsons of Cadwallon ap Madog (d. 1179) after they joined him in his campaign in south Wales (Cadwallon's sons, native lords of Maelienydd, had been expelled by Roger II Mortimer in 1195), and the prince subsequently refused to recognize the claims of Hugh III Mortimer (d. 1227) or his son-in-law Ralph II Mortimer (d. 1246) to Maelienydd (see no. 234 above and nos 247, 259 below). In other words, the letter probably derives from a period in which Llywelyn is likely to have had sufficient influence in Maelienydd to intervene there on behalf of Leominster Priory. In addition, the use of the plural of majesty may suggest that the letter was sent no earlier than 1218, when this use became normal, though it is occasionally attested in the prince's acts from at least 1209 (p. 63 above). As it is unknown whether the priory had lands in Maelienydd, it is uncertain whether the mandate was designed to protect the monks' possessions there or rather to prevent attacks across the border on the priory and its lands in Herefordshire. A further indication that such attacks, and hence the need for protection, were not restricted to 1231 is provided by a series of mandates in the late twelfth and earlier thirteenth centuries issued by bishops of Hereford from William de Vere (1186–96) onwards, as well as by Bishops Geoffrey (1203–14) and Iorwerth (1215–29) of St Davids, ordering their diocesan clergy to excommunicate anyone accused by the monks of harming them or the priory's possessions, although all these documents are couched in general terms and make no specific reference to Maelienydd (*EEA*, vii, nos 212, 269, 349; *St Davids Episcopal Acta*, nos 65, 81).

239 Morgan Gam

Grant to Morgan Gam and his heirs of all the land of Landimôr with its appurtenances to be held free of all service save for that of one knight. A further grant of all the land on the east side of the river Tawe as that river falls into the sea. Sealing clause; witnesses.

[Probably summer 1217]

B = TNA: PRO, C 49/81 (formerly C49/Roll 9), m. 1 (recited before an inquisition at Carmarthen, 4 July 1355). s. xiv med.

Pd. from B, *Cartae*, iii. 1083 (no. 900) (witness list only).

Cd., ibid.; Stephenson, *Governance*, 201–2; *H*, no. 132.

Sciant presentes et futuri quod ego L. princeps Norwall(ie) dedi et concessi Morgano Cam et heredibus suis totam terram de Landymor cum omnibus [pertinentiis][a] suis, in bosco et in plano, in aquis et mariscis, in moris et in pratis, in viis et in semitis et in molendinis tenendam de me et heredibus meis, libere et quiete ab omni servitio et consuetudine et exactione preter servitium unius militis. Preterea vero dedi ei et concessi totam terram ad orientalem plagam de Tauwey sicut ipsa aqua cadit in mare. Et ut hec omnia inconcussa ei et illibata permaneant presenti carta et sigilli mei impressione corroboravi. Hiis testibus: Madoco filio G(ru)ffit Maylor, Moreduth filio Rodb(er)t, Etheuenet Vagh(a)n, Eynan filio Walhmy, Madoc filio Rired, Mailgu(n) filio Resi Crek,[b] Reso filio G(ru)ffit et multis aliis.

[a] *omitted* B. | [b] *sic in* B *?for* Mailgun filio Resi, Reso Crek.

For the inquisition at which the charter was recited see Evans, 'Some notes', 89–90, 92, n. 2. Evans erroneously dated the charter to 1231; if the last witness is Rhys ap Gruffudd ap Rhys it can be no later than 1222, and in any case the style shows that it can be no later than 1230. Stephenson argued (*Governance*, 201–2) that the witnesses point to Llywelyn's expedition to south Wales in the winter of 1215–16, culminating in the division of the lands of Deheubarth among the descendants of the Lord Rhys at Aberdyfi early in 1216 (*BT, Pen20Tr*, 91–2; *BT, RBH*, 204–6). (Stephenson also pointed out that *Mailgun filio Resi Crek* in the witness list is probably an error for Maelgwn ap Rhys (d. 1231) and Rhys Gryg.) However, the grant almost certainly took place in the summer of 1217, when Llywelyn conquered Gower from Reginald de Braose and handed it over to Rhys Gryg (Smith and Pugh, 'Lordship of Gower', 223; *BT, Pen20Tr*, 95; *BT, RBH*, 214–15), for the manor of Landimôr lay within the lordship of Gower. The 'land on the east side of the Tawe' was the manor of Kilvey, which lay between the lordship of Glamorgan, within which Morgan Gam (d. 1241) held his lordship of Afan, and that of Gower (see *Glamorgan County History*, iii, Map 3). Morgan Gam seems to have been the sole lord of Afan by 1217 (Altschul, 'Lordship of Glamorgan', 46). He appears subsequently to have granted Landimôr as a marriage portion with his daughter Matilda to Gilbert de Turberville of Coity (*Cartae*, iii. 1165 (no. 945); cf. Smith and Pugh, 'Lordship of Gower', 247; Evans, 'Lords of Afan', 28). The charter provides a unique reference to Llywelyn's demanding knight-service from another Welsh lord, albeit with respect to a manor within what had until recently been Anglo-Norman lordships (cf. Davies, *Conquest*, 245).

240 Letter patent concerning the inheritance of Gwenwynwyn

Notification that Llywelyn has received in custody from the legate Guala and King Henry, in the presence of the bishops Peter of Winchester, Reiner of St Asaph, William of Coventry, Sylvester of Worcester, Hugh of Hereford and Ranulf of Chichester and William Marshal, earl of Pembroke, Ranulf, earl of Chester and Lincoln, Saer, earl of Winchester, Walter de Lacy, Hugh Mortimer, William de Cantilupe, the chamberlain Geoffrey de Neville, Falkes de

Bréauté, Brian de Lisle, Philip of Oldcoates and other magnates and faithful men of the king, all the land which belonged to Gwenwynwyn in Wales and Montgomery, of which he had been disseised by Llywelyn and his adherents on account of the war between the late King John and his barons; the land shall be held by Llywelyn until Gwenwynwyn's heirs come of age. After they have done homage to the king the heirs shall receive the homages of the men of Gwenwynwyn's land who wish and ought to give them homage. Llywelyn will find reasonable maintenance for the aforesaid heirs, be they fostered in Wales or in England, from the revenues of the said land by the counsel of the legate and their kin, save for the reasonable dower of Margaret, former wife of Gwenwynwyn, and for the right of anyone. Llywelyn's right in the lands shall neither increase nor diminish on account of this custody. Llywelyn has sworn on relics before the magnates to observe these terms and sealed the present document.

[12 × 16 March 1218]

B = TNA: PRO, C 54/19 (Close R. 2 Hen. III), m. 9d (contemporary enrolment).
Pd. from B, *Foedera*, I. i. 150–1; from *Foedera*, Anon, 'Documents', 122–3; from *Foedera*, Bridgeman, 'Princes of Upper Powys', 109–10.
Cd., *H*, no. 335.

Universis tam presentibus quam futuris ad quos presens scriptum pervenerit Lewelinus princeps Norwall(ie) salutem in domino. Noverit universitas vestra nos recepisse a domino G. titulo Sancti Martini presbitero cardinali et apostolice sedis legato et a domino H. illustri regi Angl(ie) coram dominis P. Winton(iensi), R. de Sancto Asapf', W. Coventr(ensi), S. Wigorn(iensi), H. Hereford(ensi) et R. Cicestr(ensi) episcopis et W. Mar' comite Penbroc, R. comite Cestr(ie) et Linc(olnie), S. comite Winton(iensis), Walt(er)o de Lasy, H. de Mortuo Mari, W. de Cantelupo, G. de Nevill' camerario, Falkesio de Breaut', Brian' de Insula, Philipp(o) de Ulecot' et aliis magnatibus et fidelibus domini H. illustris regis Anglie in custodia et defensione totam terram que fuit Wenhunwen' in Wallia et in Mungum(er)i unde per nos et inprisos nostros causa guerre inter bone memorie I. quondam regem Angl(ie) et barones suos orte, disseisitus fuit, tenendam usque ad etatem heredum predicti W., ita quod heredes ipsius W., postquam homagia sua domino regi fecerint recipient homagia de hominibus terre predicti W. qui eis homagia facere voluerint et debuerint. Inveniemus autem predictis heredibus dicti W., sive custodiantur et nutriantur in Wallia sive in Angl(ia), de exitibus dicte terre rationabilem sustentationem suam per consilium domini legati et parentum eorum, salva M. quondam uxori ipsius W. rationabili dote sua et salvo iure cuiuslibet. Et causa huius custodie in dictis terris nichil nobis iuris accrescet nec in eisdem ius nostrum in aliquo minuetur. Ut autem hec omnia fideliter et firmiter observentur tactis sacrosanctis coram magnatibus iuravimus. Et in huius rei testimonium presenti scripto sigillum nostrum apponi fecimus.

This is the first of three letters patent enrolled on the close roll that were issued by Llywelyn ratifying agreements made with Henry III at Worcester. The third of these (no. 242 below) is dated 16 March 1218; the present document and the second one (no. 241 below) are undated. A royal letter dated 12 February 1218 had instructed Llywelyn to appear with his adherents to do homage to Henry at Worcester on 11 March (*Foedera*, I. i. 150), and the regent, the Earl Marshal, was present there 12–17 March inclusive, having travelled via Gloucester (10 March) and Tewkesbury (11 March) (*Rot. Claus.*, i. 354a–356a). Assuming that the present document and no. 241 were issued no later than no. 242, the first two letters patent were issued 12 × 16 March; if, as is likely, the present letter was issued at the same time as no. 241, it was probably written no later than 15 March (see note to no. 241). For contrasting assessments of the agreement reached at Worcester see *HW*, ii. 653–4; Davies, *Conquest*, 242–3; Carpenter, *Minority*, 74–8; and Smith, *Llywelyn*, 21–2.

241 Letter patent concerning the agreement at Worcester

Notification that Llywelyn has sworn on relics at Worcester before the legate Guala, in the presence of the bishops Peter of Winchester, Reiner of St Asaph, William of Coventry, Sylvester of Worcester, Hugh of Hereford and Ranulf of Chichester and William Marshal, earl of Pembroke, Ranulf, earl of Chester and Lincoln, Saer, earl of Winchester, Walter de Lacy, Hugh Mortimer, William de Cantilupe, the chamberlain Geoffrey de Neville, Falkes de Bréauté, Brian de Lisle, Philip of Oldcoates and other magnates and faithful men of the king, that he will endeavour with all his power to ensure that the castles of Carmarthen and Cardigan, with their lands and appurtenances, are handed over to the legate for the king's use and that all lands and castles occupied in defiance of the barons and adherents of the king in south Wales, be they standing or demolished, shall be handed over to the legate, saving any one's right. Llywelyn has also promised the king to strive to ensure that all the magnates of all Wales will come on a fixed day and at a fixed time to do homage and fealty to the king as their liege lord, just as they or they predecessors did to the father of the king and his predecessors. Llywelyn promises that no enemy of the king shall be received in Wales; indeed, he will pursue the king's enemy as if he were his own and do all in his power to punish or obtain amends for all injuries to the king and his men as if they had been committed against Llywelyn or his men. Sealing clause.

[12 × 16 March 1218]

B = TNA: PRO, C 54/19 (Close R. 2 Hen. III), m. 9d (contemporary enrolment).
Pd. from B, *Foedera*, I. i. 150.
Cd., *H*, no. 336.

Universis tam presentibus quam futuris ad quos presens scriptum pervenerit Lewelin(us) princeps Norwall(ie) salutem in domino. Noveritis nos coram domino G. Dei gratia titulo Sancti Martini presbitero cardinali et apostolice sedis legato, et coram dominis P. Winton(iensi), R. de Sancto Asaph', W. Couentr(ensi), S. Wigorn(iensi), H. Hereford(ensi) et R. Cicestr(ensi) episcopis et W. Mar' comite Penbr', R. comite Cestr(ie) et Linc(olnie), S. comite Winton(iensis), Walt(er)o de Lasy, H. de Mortuo Mari, W. de Cantilupe, G. de Neuill' camerario, Falkesio de Breaut', Briano de Insula, Ph(ilippo) de Ulecote et aliis magnatibus et fidelibus domini H. illustris regis Angl(ie), tactis sacrosanctis apud Wigornie iurasse quod totum posse nostrum in bona fide et sine malo ingenio apponemus ut castra de Kaermerdin et Kaerdigan, cum terris et omnibus aliis pertinentiis suis domino legato predicto, ad opus domini regi predicti reddantur et ut omnes terras et castra occupata super barones vel inprisios domini regis in Sudwall(ia), sicut sunt, vel stantia vel prostrata, reddantur eidem domino legato salvo quorumlibet iure. Ad hec sciant omnes nos bona fide predicto domino H. regi promisisse per sacramentum quod ea fecimus quod fideliter et potenter laborabimus ut omnes magnates totius Wall(ie) ad dominum regem veniant ad certum diem et locum et faciant eidem domino regi sicut domino suo ligio homagia et fidelitates sicut ipsi vel antecessores sui plenius facere solebant patri predicti domini regi et antecessoribus suis. Preterea nullum inimicum domini regis receptabimus in Wall(ia) aut receptari promittemus. Immo ipsius inimicum tamquam nostrum modis omnibus perse-quemur et omnes iniurias eidem domino regi et suis illatas pro posse nostro vindicabimus vel emendari faciemus tamquam nobis vel nostris illatis. Et in huius rei testimonium presenti scripto sigillum nostrum apponi fecimus.

See note to no. 240 above. The document names precisely the same people as being present at Llywelyn's undertakings as no. 240 and thus may well have been issued at the same time. Moreover, it was probably written no later than 15 March, when a safe conduct was issued to Welsh magnates to do homage and fealty to the king at Worcester on 22 April (*Foedera*, I. i. 151), as this safe conduct is unlikely to have pre-dated Llywelyn's undertaking in the present document to try and ensure that the Welsh magnates did homage and fealty to Henry.

242 Letter patent concerning Carmarthen and Cardigan castles

Notification that he has received in custody from the legate Guala for the use of King Henry, in the presence of the bishops Peter of Winchester, Reiner of St Asaph, William of Coventry, Sylvester of Worcester, Hugh of Hereford and Ranulf of Chichester and William Marshal, earl of Pembroke, regent of England, Ranulf of Chester and Lincoln, Saer, earl of Winchester, Walter de Lacy, William Brewer, William de Cantilupe, Hugh Mortimer, the chamberlain Geoffrey de Neville, Falkes de Bréauté, Philip of Oldcoates and other magnates and faithful men of the king, the castles of Carmarthen and Cardigan with their lands and appurtenances. The castles will be kept from the revenues of the custody, so that the king will contribute nothing nor receive anything from the custody until he is of age. Llywelyn or his heirs will return the castles to the king or his heirs just as they were received from the legate, and the guardians and bailiffs he has placed there will swear that if Llywelyn dies before the king comes of age, they will deliver the castles to the king or his heirs. If any of the custodians or bailiffs dies or is otherwise removed before the king comes of age, his successor will swear the same. As the king's bailiff Llywelyn will hold the king's court in the aforesaid castles and lands according to English law for the English, according to Welsh law for the Welsh. He will do all in his power to ensure that the king's peace, right and dignity are preserved in the custody. As a greater security for observing the aforesaid terms, Llywelyn will find the following pledges: Maelgwn ap Rhys, Rhys ap Gruffudd, Madog ap Gruffudd and Maredudd ap Rhobert. If Llywelyn does not comply with the terms, they shall distrain him or his heirs or those to whom the castles have been committed, unless they have done all in their power to comply, so that all the aforesaid terms are upheld. The pledges will swear to observe the terms. Llywelyn has also granted that his men Ednyfed Fychan, Einion ap Gwalchmai, Einion ap Rhirid and Heilin ap Rhirid may be absolved from homage and fealty to him and may aid the king and his heirs to ensure that full amends are made for breaches of the terms by Llywelyn; nor may they return to Llywelyn's homage and fealty without first making satisfaction to the king or his heirs concerning the aforesaid breaches. They have sworn to do this. Llywelyn has sworn on relics in the presence of the legate and other aforenamed men to observe these terms and appended his seal to the present document.

Worcester, 16 March 1218

B = TNA: PRO, C 54/19 (Close R. 2 Hen. III), m. 9d (contemporary enrolment).
Pd. from B, *Rot. Claus.*, i. 378b–379a.
Cd., *H*, no. 337.

Universis tam presentibus quam futuris ad quos presens scriptum pervenerit Lewelin(us) princeps Norwall(ie) salutem. Sciatis nos recepisse in custodia a domino G. titulo Sancti Martini etc. auctoritate sancte Romane ecclesie ad opus domini H. illustris regis Angl(ie) coram dominis P. Winton(iensi), R. de Sancto Asafo, W. Coventr(ensi), S. Wigorn(iensi), H. Hereford(ensi) et R. Cicestr(ensi) episcopis et W. Mar' comite Penbr' domini H. regis Angl(ie) rectore,[a] R. Cestr(ie) et Linc(olnie) et S. comite Winton(iensis) comitibus et Walt(er)o de Lascy, W. Briwer', Will(elmo) de Cantilupo, H. de Mortuo Mari, G. de Neuill' camerario, Falk' de Breaut', Phil(ippo) de Vllecot' et aliis magnatibus et fidelibus dicti domini regis castra de Kaermerdin et de Kaerdigan cum terris et omnibus aliis pertinentiis suis, que castra cum pertinentiis suis custodienda de exitibus predicte custodie, ita quod dominus rex ad hec custodienda nichil de suo ponet nec aliquid inde recipiet usque ad etatem dicti domini regis etc. Nos vel heredes nostri predicta castra cum pertinentiis suis libere reddemus dicto domino regi vel heredibus suis sicut ea recepimus a domino legato; ita quod faciemus custodes et baillivos ipsorum castrorum et terrarum cum pertinentiis quos ibi posuerimus iurare quod si nos infra etatem dicti domini regis decessimus, predicta castra cum terris et pertinentiis eidem domino regi vel heredibus suis quieta liberabunt. Et si forte quis de predictis custodibus vel baillivis infra etatem dicti domini regis decessit vel aliquo alio modo amotus fuerit, ille quem loco illius posuerimus hoc idem iurabit. Tenebimus autem ut baillivus domini regis curiam domini regis in predictis castris et terris de Angl(icis) secundum legem Anglicana(m), de Walensibus secundum legem Walense(m), salva quorumlibet iure. Faciemus autem pro posse nostro servari pacem domini regis et ius et dignitatem eiusdem in predicta custodia. Et ad maiorem securitatem super predictis firmis observandis inveniemus pro nobis plegios, scilicet Malgon' filium Resi, Resu(m) filium Griffin(i), Madoc' filium Griffini et Mareuduc' filium Rob(erti), qui, si forte dicta castra non observaverimus, nos vel heredes nostros vel illos quibus predicta castra cum terris et pertinentiis commisimus, nisi ipsi similiter predicta observaverint modis omnibus quibus potuerint, distringent ut omnia predicta domino regi vel heredibus suis fideliter observarentur et teneantur. Dicti autem plegii iurabunt quod fideliter et integre hec observ-abunt domino regi et tenebunt. Ad hec concessimus quod Etneueth' Bachan, Eygno(n) filius Walcm', Eygno(n) filius Ririt, Heylin(us) filius Reirit homines nostri recedant et omnino sint absoluti ab homagio et fidelitate nostra et domino regi et heredibus suis adhereant et eis pro posse suo sint in auxilium, ut ea que a nobis observata non fuerint plenarie emendentur. Nec alio modo ad homagium et fidelitatem nostram redeant nisi domino rege vel heredibus suis de predictis prius fuerit satisfactionem. Et hec fideliter observanda iuraverunt. Ut autem hec omnia firmiter et fideliter observemus pro posse nostro, in presentia domini legati et aliorum prenominatorum tactis sacrosanctis iuravimus et in testimonium presenti scripto sigillum nostrum apponi fecimus. Acta sunt hec apud Wigorn' xvii kalendas[b] aprilis anno regni domini H. regis Angl(ie) secundo.

[a] rector B. | [b] *interlined over* die *struck through* B.

The list of persons named as present at Llywelyn's undertakings is slightly different from that in nos 240–1 above: William Brewer appears instead of Brian de Lisle. In addition,

William Marshal is explicitly termed regent in the present document. These differences suggest that the letter patent was not issued on the same occasion as nos 240–1. Moreover, this letter appears to be later than no. 241, as it contains a compromise over the status of Carmarthen and Cardigan castles. See further the note to no. 240. The pledges named by Llywelyn (Maelgwn ap Rhys, Rhys ap Gruffudd, Madog ap Gruffudd and Maredudd ap Rhobert) were all leading supporters of Llywelyn; all appear, for example, as witnesses to Llywelyn's charter for Morgan Gam (no. 239), as do Ednyfed Fychan and Einion ap Gwalchmai, prominent councillors of the prince.

243 Hubert de Burgh

Letter, concerning the judgement given Llywelyn in the presence of the legate, the king and Hubert that . . . have a defence against a certain burgess of Worcester who impleads them regarding a certain debt . . . of war. Because Llywelyn's men are unjustly troubled contrary to this, Llywelyn asks Hubert to order the sheriff of Worcester to . . . should not trouble Llywelyn's aforesaid men, or for love of Llywelyn order that the plea be held before Hubert so that Llywelyn's men . . . acting in this matter so that they [(?)Llywelyn's men] feel that Llywelyn's entreaties have profited them and Llywelyn will thank Hubert.

[16 March 1218 × 1230]

> A = TNA: PRO, SC 1/1, no. 118. No endorsements; approx. 186 × 31 mm.; one slit on left-hand side (for insertion of a tongue or tag?); mounted, foot cut away. Approx. 43 mm. along the right-hand side of the parchment are badly stained and largely illegible.
> Cd., *CAC*, 3; *H*, no. 339.

Karissimo amico suo H. de Burg' iusticiario Angl(ie) L. princeps Norwall(ie) cum dilectione salutem. No[(?)veritis] vero quod (?)conster . . . (?)vobis in presentia domini legati, domini regis et vestra redditum fuit nobis pro iuditio quod . . . habere defensionem suam contra burgensem quendam Wigorn' quia eos inplacitat de quodam debit[o] . . . guerre. Et quoniam homines nostri contra hoc iniuste gravantur, rogamus vos quatinus precipiatis vicecomitem Wigorn' quod ipse . . . [(?)placit]um illud non gravet predictos homines nostros, vel pro amore nostro precipiatis quod placitum illud sit coram vobis ut homines nostri . . . tur et contra, si placet, inde faciatis quod ipsi sentiant preces nostras sibi profuisse et nos ad grates vobis (?)teneamur.

Edwards pointed out that Llywelyn's style means that the letter can be no later than 1230, and also that it is unlikely to have been written before Llywelyn made peace with Henry III in March 1218 (*CAC*, 3). The legate referred to will have been either Guala (1216–18) or Pandulf (1218–July 1221); unfortunately it is not clear whether the legate was still in office when the letter was written. The judgement mentioned cannot have taken place during Llywelyn's negotiations at Worcester in March 1218, as Hubert de Burgh was not present at these. One possible occasion for the judgement was Llywelyn's meeting with Pandulf and Hubert, together with Henry III and Archbishop Stephen Langton, at Shrewsbury in May 1220 (no. 245 below and note), although the judgement could, of course, have occurred during another meeting, otherwise unattested.

244 Henry III

Letter, complaining, not about the king, of whose brotherly affection Llywelyn is certain, but about his council, concerning the king's order that Llywelyn should give full seisin of the custody of his manors of Knighton and Norton to Hugh Mortimer, whereas the justiciar Hubert de Burgh and the bishop of Winchester, who are witnesses to the king's letter, were present when it was adjudged before Guala, formerly legate, that Hugh Mortimer injures Llywelyn regarding the aforesaid land and should deliver it to him. The king and his justiciar had ordered the said Hugh to comply with that judgement and hand over Llywelyn's land; but he has still not done so. Now the king alleges the custom of England against Llywelyn, though it is not against him, as the land was given to him in free marriage and he owes no service from it. Nor did Thomas of Erdington hold those manors from Llywelyn, as falsely suggested to the king, nor was he in seisin of them, since that ought to have been an exchange and he could not make an exchange without the king's permission, as was adjudged by the said legate and the great men of the king's council. Nor is that [English] custom against Llywelyn, since the son of the said Thomas holds nothing from Llywelyn in chief. May God give the king counsel to the profit and honour of both him and Llywelyn. Llywelyn should not be blamed if scandal arises as a result of the injuries and damages inflicted upon him.

[October 1218 × November 1227]

A = TNA: PRO, SC 1/4, no. 16. No endorsements; approx. 195 × 61 mm.; mounted, foot cut away.
Pd. from A, *RL*, i. 59–60.
Cd., *CAC*, 23; *H*, no. 338.

Karissimo fratri et domino suo excellentissimo H. Dei gratia regi Angl(ie), domino Hib(er)n(ie), duci Norm(annie) et Aquit' et comiti Andeg' L. princeps Norwall(ie) salutem et se totum. De vobis, domine karissime, nec volumus nec debemus conqueri, quia certi sumus quod fraternum affectum erga nos geritis. Verum de consilio vestro non modicum conquerimur super mandato quo nobis mandastis, quod plenam seisinam habere faciamus H. de Mortuo Mari de custodia maneriorum nostrorum de Knihteton' et Norton'; desicut dominus H. de Burg' iusticiarius et dominus Wint(oniensis), qui testes sunt in litteris vestris, presentes fuerunt coram domino Gaul' quondam legato ubi iudicatus fuit Hug(onem) de Mortuo Mari iniuriare nobis de predicta terra et debere deliberare nobis terram nostram. Vos etiam, domine, si recolitis, et iusticiarius vester scripsistis dicto Hug(oni) mandantes ei iudicium illud et monentes eum quod ipse deliberaret terram nostram; quod nondum facere curavit. Nunc autem allegatis consuetudinem Angl(ie) contra nos, cum tamen non sit contra nos, eo quod terra illa data fuit nobis in liberum maritagium, nec debemus alicui aliquid servitium ex ea; nec Thom(as) de Erdinton' de nobis tenuit maneria illa, sicut falso suggestum fuit vobis, nec fuit in seisina maneriorum eorundem, cum escambium[a] illud fieri deberet, nec poterat escambium facere sine licentia vestra, sicut iudicaverunt dictus legatus et prefati viri et maiores de consilio vestro. Nec est consuetudo illa contra nos, cum nichil teneat filius dicti Thom(e) de nobis in capite. Deus det vobis consilium super hiis quod et vobis et nobis cedat ad commodum et honorem. Hoc solum volumus vos scire, quod nobis non debet imputari si scandalum proveniat de iniuriis et dampnis nobis illatis. Valete.

[a] esvambium A.

As Edwards noted (*CAC*, 23), the letter must be later than the end of Guala's term as legate on 12 September 1218. Hugh (III) Mortimer of Wigmore died in November 1227 (*AM*, i. 69). Thomas of Erdington (d. 20 March 1218) was granted the manors of Knighton and Norton in Shropshire by King John on 13 March 1207 (*CChR 1226–57*, 229; see also *Rot. Claus.*, i. 85b). However, it seems that shortly before his death Erdington exchanged the manors with Hugh Mortimer for ten librates of land in Kingsworthy (Hants.) (BL, Harl. MS 1240, fo. 68v; the charter can be no earlier than 3 July 1216 when its first witness, Sylvester, bishop of Worcester, was consecrated). The exchange was confirmed by Henry III on 24 April 1218 (*PR 1216–25*, 149), but Mortimer failed to recover the manors. The charter recording the exchange contradicts one of Llywelyn's claims in the present letter, for it includes a clause whereby Erdington promised to indemnify Hugh Mortimer for any losses incurred as a result of Thomas's homage to Llywelyn (see further Eyton, *Shropshire*, xi. 347, and Crump, 'Mortimer family', 122–3, which favours a date shortly after Henry III's confirmation in 1218). However, when Llywelyn eventually quitclaimed Knighton and Norton to his son-in-law Ralph (II) Mortimer, Hugh Mortimer's brother and successor, probably in 1230, he no longer sought to deny that Erdington had held the manors for him, since he referred to the service which Erdington had previously performed to him for them (no. 259 below). As he asserts that the manors were granted to him in free marriage, Llywelyn appears to have claimed them by virtue of a royal grant on the occasion of his marriage to Joan, but independent confirmation of this claim is lacking. For Giles, Thomas of Erdington's heir, see further no. 252 below and note.

245 Henry III

Letter, asking the king to write to his council to provide Llywelyn with the safe conduct he has requested for coming to their meeting at Shrewsbury, namely the archbishop of Canterbury, the justiciar, the earl of Gloucester and Falkes de Bréauté, and Llywelyn will come there by God's grace as instructed. The bearer of the letter will inform him of other matters orally.
[late June × early July 1219, or early May 1220, or June 1221]

A = TNA: PRO, SC 1/4, no. 17. No endorsements; approx. 162 × 44 mm.; mounted, foot cut away.
Pd. from A, *RL*, i. 113–14.
Cd., *CAC*, 23; *H*, no. 343.

Karissimo domino et fratri suo H. Dei gratia regi Angl(ie), domino Hib(er)n(ie), duci Norm(annie) et Aquit' et comiti Andeg' L. princeps Norwall(ie) salutem et se ipsum. Supplicamus vobis attencius rogantes quatenus scribatis consilio vestro quod ipsi faciant nos habere conductum quem petivimus veniendo Salopesb' die nobis ibidem constituto, scilicet dominum Cant(uariensem) et dominum iusticiarium et dominum comitem Gloucestr(ie) et dominum Falk' de Breaut', et nos per Dei gratiam illuc veniemus sicut nobis iniunctum est. Cetera vobis lator presentium viva voce plenius significabit. Valete.

The letter was presumably written shortly before one of the three meetings between Llywelyn and Henry III or his representatives in the period before the fall of Falkes de Bréauté in 1224 (on which see note to no. 255 below). Edwards linked it with the second of those meetings, held on 5 May 1220, suggesting that it was sent after 1 May, when Henry wrote to the prince requesting him to appear at Shrewsbury on 4 May and authorizing

Falkes to act as safe conduct while declaring his willingness to add the archbishop of Canterbury and 'other sufficient persons' if Llywelyn wished (*CAC*, 23; *Foedera*, I. i. 159; see also note to no. 246 below). If the present letter was sent in response to the safe conduct issued on 1 May, this implies a very swift exchange of letters, for Llywelyn was at Shrewsbury by 5 May. In addition, the king's letter of 1 May makes no reference to a request for the four individuals named in the present letter to act as safe conducts, though that letter refers to an earlier request. This could mean that the earlier request, whether written or oral, reached the king after the despatch of the letter on 1 May, and the present letter was sent in response to the king's letter, reiterating the original request; if so, the present letter will have been written very shortly before 5 May. However, it is equally, if not more, likely that Llywelyn wrote in advance of his meeting at Shrewsbury either with Pandulf in July 1219 (note to no. 246) or with Henry and his great council, 27 June–3 July 1221; the king ordered the issue of letters of safe conduct for Llywelyn to attend the latter, without naming any individuals to provide safe conduct, on 23 June 1221 (*PR 1216–25*, 294; Carpenter, *Minority*, 253).

246 Pandulf, bishop-elect of Norwich and papal legate

Letter, repeating his complaints about the excesses, losses and injuries dishonourably committed against Llywelyn by the men of Pembrokeshire. If he has ever experienced a more serious war, he has never endured such dishonour as from these. There is only one reason for this, as God knows, because he has kept peace with those who hated peace lest Llywelyn be seen to disturb the kingdom and disobey Pandulf's orders. The more gently Llywelyn behaved towards them, all the more savagely did they attack him, frequently even during the truce established by Pandulf. After Llywelyn had returned home from Pandulf's presence at Shrewsbury he asked them to confirm the truce agreed by him. But they disdained to do so, replying to Llywelyn's men that they might trust in them [the men of Pembrokeshire] if they wished, or otherwise do what they ordered. Even if they had sworn to keep the truce, Llywelyn could have had little faith in them, let alone when they thus reply obscurely regarding peace. They have summoned whatever aid they could from Ireland, and their combined forces attack Llywelyn daily. Just as Llywelyn had abided by Pandulf's counsels previously, he has ordered his kinsmen and other men of his bailiwick to withdraw from their lands with their cattle to safer places. What is worse than to leave one's land in this way without taking vengeance on the aggressors, even when the means is at last near at hand? Let Pandulf see how long Llywelyn can endure such things, when they [the men of Pembrokeshire] disregard all Llywelyn's warnings and refuse to make amends for excesses committed during the truce or cease inflicting injuries. If Pandulf sends word to them that unless they behave differently he will not concern himself with them, Llywelyn believes that they will take different counsel. If not, Llywelyn asks Pandulf to inform him of his will, and hopes that God may give him counsel to the honour of the king and Llywelyn. The bearer of the letter will inform Pandulf of other matters orally.

[6 May × late August 1220]

A = TNA: PRO, SC 1/2, no. 8. No endorsements; approx. 180 × 53 mm.; mounted, foot cut away.
Pd. from A, *RL*, i. 141–3.
Cd., Anon, 'South-west Wales', 30; *CAC*, 9; *H*, no. 341.

Reverendo patri suo et domino P. Dei gratia Norwicen(si) electo, domini pape camerario et apostolice sedis legato L. princeps Norwall(ie) cum debita subiectione salutem. Quod vobis multotiens significavimus adhuc compellimur iterare non sine nimia cordis anxietate ᵃ⁻de scilicet⁻ᵃ excessibus, dampnis et inuriis quibus incessanter cum dedecore ab hominibus de Penbrocsir', qui nos vexant, infestamur. Nam et si aliquando graviorem senserimus werram, nunquam tamen, sicut credimus, tantum dedecoris perpessi sumus quantum ab ipsis sustinuimus. Cuius rei causa una sola fuit, sicut novit Deus, scilicet quod pacifici fuimus cum hiis qui oderunt pacem, ne vel regnum perturbare videremur vel vestris inobedientes consiliis et mandatis. Verum quanto mitiores vel benigniores vestris commonitionibus erga ipsos nos gerebamus, tanto atrocius et acerbius in nos ipsi insurgebant, etiam tempore treugarum frequentius, quas inter nos et ipsos statuebatis, quibus et ipsi in nullo deferebant. Necnon, cum ad propria remeassemus a presencia vestra de Salopsbr', petivimus ab eis ut treugas a nobis prolocutas confirmarent. Quod facere contempserunt; imo nostris respon-derunt quod in ipsis confiderent si vellent, sin autem facerent quod disponerent. Verum et si iurassent treugas, minimum imo nichil possemus in illis habere fiducie, ne dum cum ita sub obscure pacis enigmate nobis respondeant. Sed et quotquot potuerunt de Ybernia in auxilium sibi contra nos vocaverunt et adduxerunt, qui collato robore cum eis nos singulis diebus infestare non desistunt. Nos vero, sicut antea consueveramus ut vestris obseder-amusᵇ consiliis, cum aliud nobis consilium non restaret, precipimus nepotibus nostris et aliis hominibus de balliva nostra ut, relictis finibus suis, cum averiis suis recederent ad loca tutiora. Que werra gravior, que molestior amaritudo, quam terram sic relinquere et iniuran-tibus nullam reddere talionem, etiam cum subsit aliquando facultas. Vos, sancte pater, vos ipsi videatis quamdiu talia poterimus sustinere, cum nostris in nullo commonitionibus adquiescant, nec excessus aliquos ab eis infra treugas perpetratos velint emendare vel ab iniuriis ferendis cessare. Si ipsis mandaretis quod nisi aliter se haberent de ipsis non intro-mitteretis, credimus quod aliud caperent consilium. Sin autem, vos beneplacitum vestrum nobis significabitis, et Deus det vobis sanum consilium ad honorem domini regis et nostrum. Cetera vobis lator presencium viva voce significabit. Valeat paternitas vestra in domino. Valete.

ᵃ⁻ᵃ *sic in* A. | ᵇ obsederaremus A.

The letter was clearly written before Llywelyn launched a major campaign in south Wales, including an invasion of Pembrokeshire, at the end of August 1220. The campaign was aimed particularly at the lands of William Marshal the younger, who had succeeded to the earldom of Pembroke following the death of his father William Marshal on 14 May 1219 (*BT, Pen20Tr*, 97; *BT, RBH*, 220–1; *HW*, ii. 658–60; Walker, 'Hubert de Burgh', 472). A *terminus a quo* is provided by the reference to the truce made with the legate Pandulf at Shrewsbury. Lloyd argued that this was a reference to the meeting between Llywelyn and the legate on 10 July 1219, rather than that of 5 May 1220, on the grounds that it was 'of the nature of an appeal from one who had no design of immediate vengeance', and Edwards was inclined to agree (*HW*, ii. 659, n. 21; *CAC*, 9). By contrast, Shirley (*RL*, i. 141) assigned the letter to July × September 1220, and Walker ('Hubert de Burgh', 472, n. 1) likewise favoured 1220 rather than 1219. The case for 1220 is stronger than that for 1219. All that is known of the meeting in July 1219 derives from a letter from Pandulf to Hubert de Burgh relating that Llywelyn had come to Shrewsbury together with other Welsh

Marchers and Reginald de Braose; there is no explicit reference to a truce (*RL*, i. 136; for the date, see *HW*, ii. 656 and n. 2). In May 1220, on the other hand, an agreement was made at Shrewsbury that included a truce between Llywelyn and the Marshal and other Marchers to last until Michaelmas and the fixing of a meeting at Oxford on 2 August to hear disputes between the two parties. When Llywelyn failed to appear on 2 August, another meeting was arranged for 30 September at London; but this plan was overtaken by the prince's invasion of Pembrokeshire at the end of August (see *Foedera*, I. i. 164; *RL*, i. 143–5; and, for discussion, Carpenter, *Minority*, 191–2). It is therefore likely that Llywelyn was complaining of breaches of a truce with William Marshal agreed in May 1220 which the earl's men of Pembrokeshire had refused to confirm. As Llywelyn had no nephews, the *nepotes* referred to in the letter were presumably members of the dynasty of Deheubarth, Llywelyn's kinsmen through their common descent from Gruffudd ap Cynan (d. 1137), whose daughter Gwenllian (d. 1136) was the mother of the Lord Rhys.

247 Pandulf, bishop-elect of Norwich and papal legate

Letter, informing Pandulf that he has received his letter ordering him to give seisin to Henry of Audley for the king's use of Maelienydd, which belonged to Hugh Mortimer and which Llywelyn has had in custody. Llywelyn had offered the king the seisin to which he was entitled in that land when he was in the king's presence at Shrewsbury, namely the homage of the noble men who ought to hold that land from him, for no other service is due [from them] than to serve the king in Wales, if necessary, and this through Llywelyn. But the homage of these men belongs to Llywelyn's principality, if it please God and the king. However, until the king comes of age, Llywelyn will not institute an inquiry wherever he should claim a right for himself. In the aforesaid land Llywelyn did not use to have any demesne, nor should the king have any. Therefore Llywelyn does not know why he should give seisin to the king, after he has refused the seisin to which he was entitled like his predecessors. Llywelyn will do all he can to have that seisin, saving the right of his kinsmen, to whose prejudice, saving Pandulf's and the king's reverence, [he will do] nothing that benefits Hugh Mortimer . . . who is constantly hostile to Llywelyn. If he [(?)the king] does not do so [(?)i.e. demand seisin], Llywelyn will be pleased for him to have anything to which he is entitled from that land. Let God judge between Hugh and Llywelyn's nephews, and if he seeks to disinherit them, there will perhaps be some to oppose him. Llywelyn should not be blamed if a scandal or disturbance arises in the March between England and Wales through those who are high in the king's council, especially since Llywelyn is not admitted to the king's council with regard to this matter, whether he is present or not. Let God be a witness that there is no one in the world who wishes more than Llywelyn to see to the honour and benefit of the king in justice and equity according to the status of Wales. All the bounds of the earth are in the hand of the Lord.

[Shortly after 10 May 1220]

A = TNA: PRO, SC 1/2, no. 7. No endorsements; approx. 165 mm. wide × 101 mm. deep at left, 90 mm. deep at right; mounted, foot cut away.
Pd. from A, *RL*, i. 122–3.
Cd., *CAC*, 8–9; *H*, no. 342.

Reverendo patri suo P. Dei gratia Norwic(ensi) electo, domini pape camerario et apostolice sedis legato L. princeps Norwall(ie) cum debita devotaque reverentia salutem. Litteras vestre sanctitatis, sicut decebat, cum debita veneratione suscepimus, quibus nobis mandastis quod seisinam faceremus Henr(ico) de Alditheleg' ad opus domini regis de terra de Melenith, que fuerat Hug(onis) de Mortuo Mari et quam nos habebamus in custodia. Ad quod vobis dicimus quod seisinam quam dominus rex deberet habere in terra illa, sicut plenius antecessores sui habuerunt de terra illa, obtulimus domino regi quando fuimus in presencia eius apud Salopesb', scilicet homagium nobilium virorum qui de eo deberet tenere terram illam, quia nullum aliud servitium deberet nisi servire domino regi in Wall(ia), si opus fuerit, et hoc per nos. Sed et homagium ipsorum ad nostrum pertinet principatum, si Deo et domino regi placeret. Set quousque Deus promoveat indolem excellentie domini regis ad etatem provectiorem, de nullo nos ei movebimus questionem ubicumque aliquid iuris sibi deberet vendicare. In terra predicta non habebamus aliquod dominicum, nec dominus rex debet habere. Nescimus ergo quam ei seisinam faceremus, ex [quo][a] quam debuit sicut antecessores sui habere seisinam refutavit. Et ad eam habendam, quicquid ad nos pertinuerit, si opus fuerit, adhuc facere non ommittemus, salvo iure nepotum nostrorum, in quorum quidem preiudicium, salva et vestra et domini regis reverentia, nichil quod cedat ad commodum Hug(onis) de Mortuo Mari, `nobis non incur . . . qui incessanter nobis inimicatur. Quod si non faceret, siquid deberet habere de terra illa, id eum habere nobis non displiceret. Iudicet Deus inter ipsum et nepotes nostros, et si eos exheredare nitatur, nonnulli erunt fortassis qui contradicant. Nobis non erit imputandum, si scandalum vel perturbatio oriatur in Marchia inter Angl' et Wall' per eos qui presunt consilio domini regis, presertim cum nos minime admittamur ad consilia domini regis in hac parte, sive presentes simus sive non; licet Deus sit nobis testis quod non est, sicut credimus, alius in mundo qui magis velit providere honori domini regis et utilitati quam nos in iustitia et equitate secundum statum Wall(ie). In manu domini sunt omnes fines terre. Valete.

[a] *hole in parchment* A.

As Edwards argued (*CAC*, 9), this letter is evidently a reply to that from Henry III to Llywelyn of 10 May 1220, ordering the prince to hand over Maelienydd, in accordance with the agreement at Shrewsbury, to the custody of Henry of Audley (*Rot. Claus.*, i. 418a). The point of Llywelyn's reference to Hugh (III) Mortimer may be seen from the king's letter of 19 May ordering Henry of Audley, once he had received Maelienydd from Llywelyn, to hand it over to Mortimer (ibid.). Mortimer in fact failed to recover Maelienydd by his death in 1227. The *nepotes* referred to were Cadwallon and Maredudd sons of Maelgwn ap Cadwallon; their brother Madog (d. 1212) had been brought up by Llywelyn (Smith, 'Middle March', 81–2; no. 234 above), and this fostering may explain Llywelyn's use of kinship language here. For the term *status Wallie* see Smith, *Llywelyn*, 292 and n. 67. The final sentence seems to echo Psalm 94[95]:4 in the Roman Psalter (*quia in manu eius sunt omnes fines terrae . . .*) or the liturgical text derived from it (*In manu tua Domine omnes fines terrae*): for the latter see, for example, *Antiphonale Sarisburiense*, ed. Frere, ii. 116; iii. 171. I am indebted to Sally Harper for help with this point.

248 Henry III

Letter, informing the king that he came to the land of Rhys Gryg on the Friday before the Feast of the Decollation of St John the Baptist [28 August 1220]. When Rhys heard of Llywelyn's coming he dismantled his castle of Dinefwr, once famous and now in ruins, to which the privileges of all South Wales once belonged as if to the head of South Wales. On the same day there was a fight on the bridge of Carmarthen where many of Rhys's men were wounded and some killed, while Llywelyn's were unharmed as God willed; on the following Sunday [30 August] Rhys made peace with Llywelyn and gave him the lands of Cedweli, Carnwyllion, Gwidigada and Gower, as well as hostages that he would serve the king faithfully and do him homage by coming to the king's court accompanied by Llywelyn or by [the earl of] Chester or [the earl of] Gloucester on a day and at a place Llywelyn has assigned to him by the king's council. Afterwards Llywelyn marched to Pembrokeshire to receive amends for injuries inflicted by the men there on his lands and demesnes, if they are willing; if they are unwilling, he will attack them and never have peace with them, since they do not know how to keep a truce or peace, nor do they fear God or man or respect the Church more than a (?)kiln, having burned thirty-five churches during the war. Now they have dragged men from a church as if from a grange, concerning which let God judge between them and Llywelyn. After Llywelyn came to their parts they did not cease to inflict losses on him and seize booty, though he had still not inflicted any evil on them. Since he does not have his great seal he has sealed this letter with his privy seal.

[*c*.1 September 1220]

A = TNA: PRO, SC 1/4, no. 18. Endorsed: Domino regi (s. xiii[1]); approx. 165 × 76 mm.; sixteen sets of slits, some double, for insertion of a tongue or tag; mounted, foot cut away.

Pd. from A, *RL*, i. 176–7.

Cd., Anon, 'South-west Wales', 30; *CAC*, 24; *H*, no. 344.

Karissimo domino suo H. Dei gratia regi Angl(ie), domino Hib(er)n(ie), duci Norm(annie) et Aquit', comiti And' L. princeps Norwall(ie) salutem et se ipsum. Sciatis quod nos die veneris ante decollationem Sancti Ioh(ann)is Baptiste venimus ad terram Resi Crec. Ipse vero audito adventu nostro statim subvertit castrum suum de Dinewor, olim famosum nunc autem[a] ruinosum, ad quod tamquam ad capud Suthwall(ie) olim pertinebant dignitates totius Suthwall(ie). Et eodem die fuit conflictus super pontem de Kaermarthin ubi plures de suis vulnerati fuerunt et quidam interfecti, nostris vero illesis sicut Deus voluit, sequenti die dominica pacificatus fuit dictus Resus nobiscum et reddidit nobis terras de Ketweli et Kirnowall' et G[w]idigada et Gohir. Dedit etiam nobis obsides quod vobis fideliter serviet . . .[b] et faciet vobis homagium veniendo ad curiam vestram in comitatu nostro vel comitatu Cestr(ie) vel comitatu Glocestr(ie) ad diem et locum competentes quos ei rationabiliter de consilio vestro assignavimus. Postmodum autem iter nostrum arripuimus versus Penbrocsir' recepturi emendationes et rectituri de iniuriis nobis ab eis illatis et terras et demania nostra, si hoc facere voluerint; que si facere noluerint nos manum apponemus,[c] si Deus dederit potestatem, nec umquam cum eis pacem habebimus quia nec sciunt nec volunt treugas vel pacem servare, nec timent Deum nec verentur hominem nec defferunt ecclesie magis quam torredule qui triginta quinque ecclesias combusserunt tempore werre. Nunc vero extrahunt homines de ecclesia tanquam grangia unde iudicet Deus inter nos et ipsos. Postquam etiam venimus ad partes eorum non cessarunt nobis dampna inferre et predas capere, cum adhuc nos eis nihil mali intulissemus. Et quia sigillum magnum non habemus sigillo privato sigillavimus has litteras. Valete.

^a nunc autem *then repeated in* A. | ^b *parchment stained and illegible.* | ^c A *inserts* tamquam *struck through.*

As Edwards pointed out (*CAC*, 24), the references to the feast of the Decollation of St John the Baptist (29 August) and to an expedition in Pembrokeshire correspond with the accounts in *Brut y Tywysogyon* of Llywelyn's campaign in Pembrokeshire in 1220 (*BT, Pen20Tr*, 97–8; *BT, RBH*, 220–1). The letter was thus written shortly after the surrender of Rhys Gryg on 30 August 1220, to which it refers, but before the beginning of Llywelyn's attacks on Rhos and Daugleddau in Pembrokeshire described in the *Brut*. (For the background to these attacks see no. 246 above.) Since it is used in the context of taking Rhys Gryg to the king's court, the most likely meaning of *comitatus* in the phrase *in comitatu nostro vel comitatu Cestrie vel comitatu Glocestrie* is 'company, retinue': Rhys had agreed to go to the king in the company of Llywelyn, the earl of Chester or the earl of Gloucester. Ranulf, earl of Chester had returned to England from crusade in July 1220 and reached Chester on 16 August, when he met Llywelyn to renew their understanding of 1218 (Carpenter, *Minority*, 212).

Llywelyn's reference to the special dignity of Dinefwr (SN 614 225), near Llandeilo Fawr (cmt. Maenordeilo) shows familiarity with the idea, first attested in the writings of Gerald of Wales in the late twelfth century, that Dinefwr was the 'principal court' or 'principal seat' of South Wales (meaning the native kingdom of Deheubarth); according to Gerald, it was one of three such courts, the others being Aberffraw in Anglesey for Gwynedd and Pengwern (later Shrewsbury) for Powys (*Gir. Camb. Op.*, vi. 80–1, 169, 172 (*IK*, I. 10; *DK*, I. 4, 5)). The status of Dinefwr as the 'principal seat' of Deheubarth, just as Aberffraw was that of Gwynedd, is also proclaimed in several of the Welsh lawbooks, including Latin Redaction B, compiled in Gwynedd during Llywelyn's reign (e.g. *LTWL*, 110, 194, 207, 317, 349). See further Smith, 'Treftadaeth Deheubarth', 18–21 and references given there.

249 Henry III

Letter, requesting the king to protect Llywelyn's men of Suckley from the unjust molestation which they are suffering most unjustly on account of the debt of Roger of Clifford. Since [Llywelyn has] no advocate or patron in England other than the king, he asks the king [to order] his justices to protect Llywelyn and his men. If the king wishes to hold any investigation regarding the aforesaid manor or other manors given to Llywelyn in free marriage by the king's father of blessed memory, the bearer of this letter will reply on Llywelyn's behalf. Llywelyn has heard that the king has ordered all manors held by his father to be seized into the king's hand, but is confident that no one can make a claim regarding any of the tenements which the king's father gave in free marriage. The bearer of the letter will inform the king of other matters orally. Llywelyn asks the king to inform him of his will regarding these and other matters.

[October 1221 × February 1222]

A = TNA: PRO, SC 1/4, no. 20. No endorsement; approx. 130 mm. wide × 82 mm. deep at left, 67 mm. deep at right; mounted, foot cut away. The parchment is stained.
Cd., *CAC*, 25; *H*, no. 345.

Reverendo domino suo H. Dei gratia illustrissimo regi Angl(ie), domino Hibernie, duci
Norm(annie) et Aquit', comiti And', fratri suo karissimo L. princeps Norwall(ie) salutem
et se totum. Rogamus vos, domine, quatinus homines nostros de Sukele deffendere velitis
ab iniusta vexatione et molestia qua molestantur occasione debiti[a] (?). . .[b] Rog(er)i de
Cliforth iniustissime. Et quia nullum advocatum vel patronum . . . in Angl(ia) nisi vos, si
placet per iusticiarios vestros iuxta rationem nos `et nostros homines deffensare e . . . s.
Adhuc si vultis nos in aliquo convenire super predicto manerio vel aliis maneriis que nobis
data sunt in liberum maritagium a beate memorie patre vestro, lator presencium vobis
respondebit iuxta rationem [et] nostrum beneplacitum. Secundum hoc quod accepimus vos
precepisse seisiari omnia maneria que fuerunt patris vestri in manum vestram, securi quippe
sumus quod nemo potest nos callumpniari[c] super aliquid tenementorum que nobis pater
vester dedit in liberum maritagium. Cetera vobis lator presencium viva voce significabit.
Valeat excellencia vestra diu in domino. Beneplacitum vestrum nobis super hiis et super aliis
nobis significetis, ad quod promptum et paratum secundum posse nostrum nos invenietis.

[a] debite A. | [b] *because of a stain in the parchment it is unclear whether a word is missing here in* A.
[c] *sic in* A.

Llywelyn was granted the manor of Suckley (Worcs.), along with that of Bidford
(Warwicks.), by John on or by 19 August 1215 (*HW*, ii. 647, citing *Rot. Claus.*, i. 226b,
namely mandates to the sheriffs of the counties in which the manors lay to hand them over
to the prince's proctors *ad opus ipsius Lewelini*). However, on 30 October 1217 the king
ordered the sheriff of Worcestershire to restore seisin of Suckley to Roger of Clifford and
the manor was probably held by him until the agreement at Worcester with Llywelyn in
March 1218 (*Rot. Claus.*, i. 337b; *CAC*, 25). The prince was restored to Bidford in October
1218 (below); perhaps he recovered Suckley at about the same time. In any case, Suckley
was certainly held by Llywelyn at Michaelmas 1220 (*Pipe Roll 4 Henry III*, 189), and was
granted by the prince to John of Scotland, nephew and heir of the earl of Chester, as part
of the marriage agreement with the latter in 1222 (no. 252 below). The reference to Henry
III's order that all manors held by his father John should be seized into his hands shows
that the letter was written after 30 September 1221, when writs were issued to all sheriffs,
together with between two and four coadjutors in each county, to take into the king's hands
all demesnes of which John had been seised at the beginning of the war with his barons
(*Pipe Roll 5 Henry III*, xxxiv–xxxvi; Carpenter, *Minority*, 269–70). This attempt at the
resumption of royal lands turned out to be largely ineffective, and orders were given on 4
February 1222 for Llywelyn to be restored to full seisin of Suckley (and Bidford) (*Rot.
Claus.*, i. 487a). Though the mandates of 19 August 1215 say nothing about the nature of
the grants, a mandate of 10 October 1218, ordering Llywelyn's restoration to Bidford, states
that that manor had been given to Llywelyn in free marriage with Joan (*Foedera*, I. i. 152),
and the same is likely to have been true of Suckley, as the prince claimed in the present
letter.

250 Ynys Lannog Priory

Grant to his beloved brothers the canons of Ynys Lannog, for the souls of himself and his parents, in pure and perpetual alms, of the whole township of Bancenyn, free of all services, with all its appurtenances. Sealing clause; witnesses.

Caernarfon, 15 October 1221

B = TNA: PRO, C 53/81 (Ch. R. 23 Edward I), m. 2 (in an inspeximus, 4 May 1295).
Pd. from B, *Mon. Ang.*, iv. 581–2; from B, *CChR 1257–1300*, 459; from *Mon. Ang.*, Jones, 'Mona mediaeva', 48–9 (trans. only).
Cd., Stephenson, *Governance*, 202; *H*, no. 133.

Universis Cristi fidelibus hoc scriptum visuris vel audituris L. princeps Northwall(ie) salutem in domino. Quod pietatis confertur intuitu condigna debet firmitate stabiliri, ne perversorum malitia vel per temporis processum lapsu memorie possit permutari, quatinus firma radice stare possit imperpetuum. Hinc est quod vestre duximus notificare universitati nos pietatis intuitu et pro anime nostre et animarum parentum nostrorum salute concessisse et in puram et perpetuam elemosinam contulisse totam villam de Bageni(n)g, libere et quiete, sine omni servitio et exactione cum omnibus pertinentiis suis in bosco in plano, in pratis in pascuis, in aquis in rivis, in molendinis cum omnibus asiamentis ad eandem villam pertinentibus, infra et extra, dilectis fratribus nostris canonicis de Insula Glannauch. Et ut hec donatio et concessio rata et inconcussa tam a nobis quam a nostris heredibus usque in perpetuum permaneat eam sigilli nostri munimine fecimus roborari. Hiis testibus: patre Abraham de Aberthon', magistro Ada de Sancta Trinitate, magistro Instructo, magistro Ric(ard)o, Widone canonico de Enli, Ada clerico filio Oweyn, Ennio filio Walchmei, Ennio Bichan, Grono filio Kenor' et multis aliis. Actum apud Kaerinaruon anno gratie m° cc° xx° primo idus octobris.

Ynys Lannog, also known as Ynys Seiriol, Priestholm or Puffin Island, lies off the north-eastern coast of Anglesey close to the native ecclesiastical foundation of Penmon. According to Gerald of Wales, in the late twelfth century Ynys Lannog, meaning 'the ecclesiastical island, on account of the great number of saints whose bodies lie there', was home to a community of hermits who lived off the labour of their own hands and prohibited women from entering the island (*Gir. Camb. Op.*, vi. 131 (*IK*, II. 7)). The present charter is the earliest evidence that this native eremitical community had been transformed into one of canons, who, to judge by sources from the early fourteenth century onwards, belonged to the Augustinian order (Johns, 'Celtic monasteries', 21, 24–5). By 1237 the priory had received the landed endowments of Penmon church on the mainland (no. 272 below; for confirmations see nos 286, 288, 313, 320 below). A similar process occurred, almost certainly also at Llywelyn's initiative, with respect to the native eremitical community on Ynys Enlli (Bardsey Island) (note to no. 440 below); it is significant that a canon of Enlli was a witness to the present charter, possibly suggesting that Enlli had already become an Augustinian priory by 1221. See further Johns, 'Celtic monasteries', 21–30, 40–1, and Carr, 'Priory of Penmon'. The township of Bagenig (alternatively known as Bancenyn or Bodgeini) was presumably adjacent to, rather than an old name for and thus the same as, the township of Llan-faes (*pace* Johns, 'Celtic monasteries', 25 and n. 53; cf. Richards, *Welsh Administrative and Territorial Units*, 9, 116), as Llan-faes was a princely *maerdref* which developed into a town in the thirteenth century, and the site of a Franciscan friary founded by Llywelyn in 1237 (note to no. 272 below).

*251 Gwenllian de Lacy

Grant of four manors: Aberchwiler (Aberwhyler), *Penbedw* (Penpedow), Estradmelened' *and* Trewowr *with their appurtenances.*

[*c*.1222 × -28 July 1224]

Mention only, in a record of a case *coram rege* at Westminster, 5 May 1241 brought by Gwenllian, widow of William de Lacy against Dafydd ap Llywelyn for recovery of the manors (*CRR*, xvi, no. 1596; for the date see ibid., xxxix). Gwenllian was a daughter of Llywelyn ap Iorwerth by Tangwystl, and thus a sister of Gruffudd ap Llywelyn and half-sister of Dafydd ap Llywelyn; she had married William de Lacy (d. 1233), son of Hugh de Lacy (d. 1186) and Rose O'Connor of Connacht, by 28 July 1224, when she was captured by William Marshal's forces on the O'Reillys' crannog in Cavan, Ireland (Lloyd, 'Who was Gwenllian?', 293–4). The marriage probably took place *c*.1222–3, when Llywelyn was allied with William's half-brother Hugh de Lacy (d. 1243) against the English crown: Hugh, bearing his forfeited title of earl of Ulster, witnessed the marriage agreement between Llywelyn's daughter Helen and John of Scotland in 1222 and also supported Llywelyn in the war against royal and Marcher forces in 1223 (ibid.; Frame, *Ireland and Britain*, 158–60; no. 252 below). The manors were presumably granted to Gwenllian at her marriage, just as lands were granted in free marriage to Helen on her marriage to John of Scotland (Lloyd, 'Who was Gwenllian?', 294; no. 252 below). Aberchwiler (Gwaen Aberwheeler SJ 095 693) and Penbedw (SJ 165 682) lay in the commote of Dogfeiling, Dyffryn Clwyd, and *Estradmelened'* probably just south of Denbigh in the vicinity of the river Ystrad (Ystrad Hall SJ 062 647), cmt. Ceinmeirch, Rhufoniog, as suggested by Lloyd, 'Who was Gwenllian?', 298. *Trewowr* has not been identified. In 1282 Dafydd ap Gruffudd asserted that Gwenllian had held lands in both Dyffryn Clwyd and Rhufoniog (no. 454, c. i below).

252 Agreement with Ranulf (III), earl of Chester

Agreement in the form of a chirograph with Ranulf, earl of Chester, that the earl's nephew John of Scotland shall marry Llywelyn's daughter Helen, and that Llywelyn will give John in free marriage the manors of Bidford in Warwickshire and Suckley in Worcestershire, just as King John gave them to Llywelyn in free marriage, and the manor of Wellington in Shropshire, to be held by John and his heirs by Helen, as fully as Llywelyn held them. Llywelyn will also give John 1,000 marks of silver, and on the wedding day, on the octaves of the Assumption of the Virgin Mary [22 August], will give John full seisin of the said manors with all their appurtenances and all the muniments Llywelyn has concerning the manors from the king or others. On the same day he will ensure that John has his charter and the charter of Lady Joan, his wife, and pay John 500 marks of silver and pay the other 500 marks on the following Michaelmas [29 September]. If it should happen that Llywelyn is unable to warrant the manor of Wellington to John, Helen and their heirs because of the claim of Thomas of Erdington's heir or another reason, Llywelyn will give them a reasonable exchange in Shropshire, unless Earl Ranulf is able, by entreaty or payment, to settle that claim, in which case Llywelyn will pay him whatever the earl requests for settling the claim. On the wedding day John will assign to Helen 100 librates of land in dower, and if the earl and Llywelyn are unable to be present at the wedding, the wedding shall take place on another day fixed by their common consent. John and Helen have pledged their faith in the hand of Reiner, bishop of St Asaph, to keep this agreement, and the earl and Llywelyn have confirmed it with their oaths and seals together with many of their faithful men. Witnesses.

[4 February × -22 August 1222]

A = BL, Cotton Ch. 24/17. No medieval endorsements; approx. 182 mm. wide × 198 mm. deep at left, 210 mm. deep at right + 13 mm.; bipartite chirograph, indented at top (indentations approx. 34 mm. deep); two central slits through fold for a tag (14 mm. wide); sealed on tag. Circular seal, brown wax, imperfect, originally approx. 70 mm. diameter; equestrian, facing right; legend lost; oval counterseal on reverse, approx. 32 × 25 mm.; device of a boar passant under a tree; legend: SIGILLVM . SECRETVM . LEWLINI.

Pd. from A, *Chester Charters*, no. 411; from A, Owen, *Catalogue*, ii. 526 (witness list only); (?)from an abbreviated early modern transcript, Ormerod, *History*, i. 43 (incomplete; Ormerod states that 'the original deed whereof remained in the possession of Somerford Oldfield, Esquire, at Somerford in Cheshire, anno Domini 1653'). Abbreviated texts are contained in Oxford, Bodleian Library, Dugdale MS 15, fo. 147r (s. xvii[1]); BL, Harl. MS 2044, fo. 30r (s. xvii); BL, Harl. MS 2079, fo. 32r (s. xvii).

Cd., Owen, *Catalogue*, i. 357; *H*, no. 346.

C I R O G R A P H U M [a]

Hec est convencio facta inter dominum Rannulphum comitem Cestr(ie) et Lincoln(ie) et dominum Lewelinu(m) principem Norwallie, videlicet quod Ioh(ann)es de Scocia nepos predicti comitis de sorore sua primogenita ducet in uxorem Helenam filiam ipsius Lewelini, ita quod dictus Lewelin(us) dabit dicto Ioh(ann)i in liberum maritagium totum manerium de Budiford in Warewikisir' et manerium de Succhele in comitatu Wigornie cum omnibus pertinenciis suis, sicut dominus rex Ioh(ann)es ea illi dedit in liberum maritagium, et totum manerium de Welinton' in comitatu Salopesbir' cum omnibus pertinenciis suis infra villam et extra, habenda et tenenda dicto Ioh(ann)i et heredibus suis ex dicta Helena provenientibus, sicut idem Lewelin(us) ea aliquo tempore melius et integrius tenuit. Et preterea dabit eidem Ioh(ann)i mille marcas argenti, ita quod die desponsacionis, scilicet in octabis assumpcionis Beate Marie, faciet dominus Lewelin(us) memorato Ioh(ann)i plenaram seisinam dictorum maneriorum cum omnibus ad ea pertinentibus et cum omnibus munimentis que dominus Lewelin(us) habet de dictis maneriis tam de domino rege quam de aliis. Et nichilominus eodem die cartam suam et cartam domine Ioh(ann)e uxoris sue eidem Ioh(ann)i habere faciet, et eodem die ei solvet quingentas marcas argenti et alias quingentas marcas solvet ei in festo Sancti Michael(is) proximo sequenti. Et si forte contigerit quod [domi]nus Lewelin(us) propter calumpniam heredis[b] Thome de Erdint' vel alio casu manerium de Welint' predictis Ioh(ann)i et Helene [filie] sue et illorum heredibus guarantizare nequiverit, dominus Lewelin(us) faciet eis racionabile et competens escambium in co[mitatu S]alopesbr', nisi forte dictus [R. c]omes Cestr(ie) et Lincoln(ie) prece vel pecunia possit illam calumpniam pacificare, et tunc quicquid [(?)ad pacificand]am dictam calumpniam idem comes erogaverit, dictus Lewel(inus) solvet illud plenarie. Dictus vero Ioh(ann)es dicto desponsacionis [die] assignabit dicte Helene nomine dotis centum libratas terre, et si forte aliquis casus contigerit quod dicti comes et Lewel(inus) ad predictum diem [d]esponsacionis faciende interesse nequiverint, nichilominus alio die per eorumdem comune consilium statuendo fiat deponsacio. Et hanc convencionem firmiter et bona fide tenendam Ioh(ann)es de Scotia et Helena in manu domini Reineri episcopi de Sancto Asaph affidarunt, et dominus comes supradictus et Lewel(inus) eam iuramentis suis et sigillis suis una cum multis de eorumdem fidelibus confirmarunt. Testibus: domino Rein(ero) episcopo de Sancto Asaph, domino H. abbate Cestr(ie), domino H. de Lasci comite Ulton', P. de Orreb' iusticiario Cestr(ie), H. de Aldidel', Gualt(er)o de Daiuill', Ric(ardo) Phiton, Edeneuet Vaghan, Ennio' filio Righerit, Goronou filio Edeneuet, Heilin' filio Kenrec, Heilin filio Idhic, magistro Estruit, magistro Ada, David clerico Lewel(ini), magistro H. et Sim(one) clericis domini comitis et multis aliis.

^a *upside down* A. | ^b heredim A.

The marriage between Llywelyn's daughter Helen and John of Scotland, heir of Earl David of Huntingdon (d. 1219) and nephew and eventual heir of Ranulf (III) earl of Chester, occurred in 1222, and was negotiated 'for the purpose of effecting a lasting peace' between the prince and the earl (*Ann. Cestr.*, 50–3). John, aged almost fifteen, had passed with his English lands from the wardship of his cousin Alexander II of Scotland to that of Ranulf in March 1221 (Stringer, *Earl David*, 182–3). The marriage agreement was presumably made after the manors of Bidford and Suckley were restored to Llywelyn on or shortly after 4 February 1222 (*Rot. Claus.*, i. 487a), but before 22 August 1222, the date anticipated for the marriage. For Llywelyn's receipt of these manors from John see note to no. 249 above. The reference to a claim to the manor of Wellington (Shrops.) by the heir of Thomas of Erdington (d. 20 March 1218) was to the action of mort d'ancestor brought against Helen by Thomas's son and heir Giles in 1221 (TNA: PRO, JUST 1/733A, m. 3d, cited in Eyton, *Shropshire*, ix. 43). Thomas had been granted Wellington by John on 3 November 1212, and was already holding it by June of that year (*Rot. Chart.*, 189a; *Testa de Nevill*, 56). However, according to the record of the case in 1221, Helen alleged that she had been given Wellington by a certain *Wyandus*, that is, Gwion ap Jonas, to whom Henry III and his council had committed it. This Gwion may be identified with the man of that name who held land worth £14 in Wellington from 1194 to May 1210 (Eyton, *Shropshire*, ix. 41–3), and who witnessed two of Llywelyn's charters granting Shropshire lands to Haughmond abbey 1205 × 1211 (nos 225–6 above; see further note to no. 497 below). The case continued until at least Easter 1226, when it was deferred until the arrival of the justices in eyre, who were to settle it then irrespective of whether Helen appeared or not (*CRR*, x. 280; xi. 227 (no. 1113), 428 (no. 2134); xii. 19 (no. 113), 85–6 (no. 444), 203 (no. 1008), 445 (no. 2202)). Giles of Erdington had gained possession of the manor by 1229 (Eyton, *Shropshire*, ix. 43).

According to Matthew Paris, Helen had her husband poisoned in 1237, and the Annals of Dunstable report that she angered her father by marrying Robert de Quincy, the younger son of the earl of Winchester, as her second husband (Roderick, 'Marriage', 18, citing Paris, *CM*, iii. 394, and *AM*, iii. 146).

*253 Pope Honorius III

Petition, stating that since a detestable custom had developed in his land, whereby the son of the handmaiden was equally heir with the son of the free woman and illegitimate sons obtained an inheritance as if they were legitimate, Llywelyn has abolished this custom, that was contrary to divine and human law, with the consent of Henry, king of England, as well as the authority of Stephen, archbishop of Canterbury, and Pandulf, bishop-elect of Norwich and legate, and has ordained that henceforth the canonical sanctions should be inviolably followed in the aforesaid cases, issuing a statute whereby Dafydd, his son by his legitimate wife Joan, daughter of the late king of England, should succeed him by hereditary right in all his posses- sions. Llywelyn seeks confirmation of the statute by apostolic authority.

[*c.*April × -26 May 1222]

Mention only, in a letter from Honorius III to Llywelyn dated at Alatri, 26 May 1222, in which the pope granted the requested confirmation of the statute (Vatican City, Archivio Segreto Vaticano, Reg. Vat. 11, fo. 244r–v, no. 407; cd., *Reg. Hon. III*, ii. 73 (no. 3996); *CPL*, i. 87; *H*, no. 466). The papal letter is printed here in full as it probably preserves much of the wording of Llywelyn's letter (as assumed by Lloyd, *HW*, ii. 686, n. 185). Parts of standard formulae omitted in the registered copy are supplied within square brackets. (For the formulae see Sayers, *Papal Government*, 98–100, 104–9; some examples from original papal letters are printed in ibid., 213, 227, 243, 251–2 (nos 2, 18, 36, 46).)

[Honorius episcopus servus servorum Dei dilecto filio] nobili viro Lowelino domino Norwallie [salutem et apostolicam benedictionem]. Cum a nobis petitur[a] [quod iustum est et honestum tam vigor equitatis quam ordo exigit rationis ut id per sollicitudinem officii nostri ad debitum perducatur] effectum. Sane tua petitio nobis exhibita continebat quod cum quedam detestabilis consuetudo vel potius corruptela inolevisset in terra tue ditioni subiecta, ut videlicet filius ancille esset heres cum filio libere et illegitimi filii hereditatem sicut legitimi obtinerent, tu karissimi in Cristo filii nostri Henr(ici) regis Anglor(um) illustris domini tui accedente consensu ac etiam interveniente auctoritate venerabilis fratris nostri Stephani Cantuarien(sis) archiepiscopi sancte Roman(e) ecclesie cardinalis [fo. 244v] ac dilecti filii Pandulfi Norwicen(sis) electi tunc in partibus illis legationis officium exercentis consuetudinem seu corruptelam huiusmodi iuri divino et humano contrariam abolere ac extirpare curasti, statuendo ut in predictis casibus id decetero in prefata terra inviolabiliter conservetur quod cautum est per canonicas et legitimas sanctiones, secundum statutum huiusmodi ordinando ut David filius tuus quem ex Iohanna filia clare memorie regis Anglie uxore tua legitima suscepisti hereditario iure te succedat in omnibus bonis tuis; quare nobis humiliter supplicasti ut predictum statutum apostolico roborare munimine dignaremur. Nos igitur iustis precibus tuis benignum impertientes assensum, statutum ipsum sicut provide factum est auctoritate apostolica confirmamus[a] [et presentis scripti patrocinio] communimus. Nulli ergo[b] [omnino hominum liceat hanc paginam nostre protectionis et] confirmationis infringere [vel ei ausu temerario contraire]. Si quis autem[c] [hoc attemptare presumpserit indignationem omnipotentis Dei et Beatorum Petri et Pauli apostolorum eius se noverit incursurum]. Dat' Alatri vii. kalendas iunii anno sexto.

[a] MS *inserts* etc. usque. | [b] MS *inserts* etc. nostre. | [c] MS *inserts* etc.

As Smith has pointed out ('Dynastic succession', 218, n. 3), there is a close verbal resem- blance between the phrase in the statute regarding the son of the handmaiden being an heir with the son of a free woman and Galatians 4: 30 (which in the Vulgate reads *non enim heres erit filius ancillae cum filio liberae*). Llywelyn had obtained approval from the king, archbishop and legate at Shrewsbury on 5 May 1220 for the succession of Dafydd, his son by Joan, to the exclusion of his older but illegitimate son Gruffudd (*Foedera*, I. i. 159; *HW*, ii. 656; Carpenter, *Minority*, 191–2), and the statute was probably issued on that occasion (Powicke, *Henry III*, ii. 630 and n. 1). For further discussion of the statute's significance see Stephenson, *Governance*, 153–4; Smith, 'Dynastic succession', 218–19; and *idem*, *Llywelyn*, 12–14.

254 Letter patent concerning Henry III

Notification that he has sworn on relics to indemnify the king and his men, within a reasonable term fixed by the archbishop of Canterbury and in a suitable place, for the losses inflicted by Llywelyn and his men from the day of the capture of Kinnerley castle to the day of his absolution, namely Saturday on the morrow of the octaves of Michaelmas [7 October] 1223. Sealing clause; witnesses.

[8 October 1223]

B = TNA: PRO, C 66/28 (Pat. R. 7 Henry III), m. 1d (contemporary enrolment).
Pd. from B, *Foedera*, I. i. 170; from B, *PR 1216–25*, 411.
Cd., *H*, no. 347.

Omnibus ad quos presens carta pervenerit Leulin(us) princeps Norwall(ie) salutem. Noveritis me tactis sacrosanctis iurasse quod satisfaciam domino meo H. illustri regi Angl(ie) et suis infra terminos rationabiles quos mihi prefiget dominus Cantuar(iensis) archiepiscopus et in loco competenti, de dampnis eidem regi et suis illatis per me et meos a die captionis castri de Kinardesl' usque ad diem absolutionis mee, diem videlicet sabbati in crastino octavarum Sancti Mich(ael)is anno regni ipsius regis vii. In cuius rei testimonium huic carte sigillum meum apposui. Hiis testibus: domino S. Cantuar(iensi) archiepiscopo, domino P. Winton(iensi), domino H. Heref(ordensi), domino R. de Sancto Asaph' episcopis, H. de B(ur)go iusticiario Angl(ie), R. comite Cestr(ie) et Lincoln(ie), W. comite Sarr', W. comite Warenn(ie), W. comite de Ferrar(iis), Rob(erto) filio Walt(er)i, Petro filio Hereb(erti), Will(elm)o de Albin(iaco), Ioh(ann)e de Monem', Hugo(n)e de Mortuo Mari, Walt(er)o de Clifford, Ioh(ann)e filio Alani, Rog(er)o de Clifford', Will(elm)o de Stuteuill, Ph(ilipp)o de Albin(iaco), Ric(ard)o de Riuer(iis), Rad(ulfo) de Trubleuill' et aliis.

Though described as a *carta*, this document conforms in its substance and in the form of its corroboration to a letter patent (see p. 59 above). Llywelyn had captured the castle of Kinnerley near Knockin (Shrops.) early in 1223, and soon also took the castle of Whittington (Shrops.). On his submission at Montgomery Llywelyn agreed that Henry III should keep Montgomery and its district, and William Marshal should keep the lands he had occupied apart from those held 'in fee' (*ut de feudo*) by Llywelyn at the beginning of the war; in addition, the prince would repair and restore to Fulk fitz Warin the castles he had destroyed (*AM*, iii. 82–3; *PR 1216–25*, 481; for discussion, see *HW*, ii. 661–3; Walker, 'Hubert de Burgh', 473–5; Carpenter, *Minority*, 298, 313–14). Llywelyn's allies, including Rhys Gryg, Maelgwn ap Rhys, Maredudd ap Rhobert and Madog ap Gruffudd, proffered charters of submission at the same time (nos 19–20, 44, 53–4 above and nos 489, 507 below). According to a royal letter of 4 November 1223, the prince submitted at Montgomery on 8 October (*PR 1216–25*, 481), and thus a day after he received absolution on 7 October; the document is therefore almost certainly datable to 8 October.

255 Henry III

Letter, informing the king that he has received his message informing Llywelyn that Falkes de Bréauté has trespassed greatly against the king by seizing and detaining Henry of Braybrooke, whence the king had had Falkes's castle of Bedford besieged. Therefore the king had ordered Llywelyn not to give Falkes aid or counsel or receive his men. Llywelyn replies that Falkes has come to his land complaining about the actions procured against him by the king's council. He declared that the said Henry had been captured without his knowledge, and though he did not support the action, he offered to make William de Bréauté and his followers stand judgement and make amends for it. Since he was having his hands full in telling that the king's council denied that it had treated him unjustly, he left Llywelyn's land on the same day as he arrived. Llywelyn is not informing the king of this because he is obliged to excuse himself for receiving Falkes and his men. Llywelyn has as much liberty as the king of Scotland, who receives outlaws from England with impunity. Llywelyn has not heard that Falkes has ever done harm to the king or his late father; rather, he has brought many benefits to the king, serving the king more effectively than almost anyone else. The king should not feel angry that Falkes went to Llywelyn. Llywelyn would make greater efforts towards ensuring a reconciliation between Falkes and the king if the king's council allowed justice to be done to Falkes. Indeed, Llywelyn has more to complain of in this regard than Falkes. Not only are Llywelyn's rights not given him, but great losses are dishonourably inflicted on him. Though he does not impute anything to the king himself, Llywelyn has no hope that the king's council wishes to make satisfaction to him. Llywelyn has complained so often that he is ashamed to recall his grievances, since he has had no satisfaction for them. The king has also informed Llywelyn that a sentence [of excommunication] has been proclaimed against Falkes as a disturber of the realm, but the king should know that greater disturbance is caused to the realm by those who advise him to eject from his council great and necessary men by disinheriting and harming them without reason. If Falkes were defending himself against the pope who is wishing to disinherit him, Llywelyn does not believe that he would have been excommunicated as far as God is concerned. Whatever others may do regarding these or other matters, Llywelyn will do nothing against his conscience. He would rather be excommunicated by man than, condemned by his conscience, do anything against God. May God give the king and Llywelyn salutary counsel, which is much needed, concerning these and other matters.

[Probably July 1224]

A = TNA: PRO, SC 1/4, no. 19. No endorsements; approx. 219 × 96 mm.; mounted, foot cut away.
Pd. from A, *RL* i. 368.
Cd., *CAC*, 24–5; *H*, no. 348.

Reverendo domino et fratri suo karissimo H. Dei gratia regi Angl(ie), domino Hyb(er)n(ie), duci Norm(annie) et Aquit', comiti Andeg' L. princeps Norwall(ie) cum debita dilectione salutem. Vestre mandatum celsitudinis suscepimus[a] sicut debuit venerantes quo quidem inter cetera nobis significastis homines domini Falkes' de Breau' in multum transgressos esse erga vos, capiendo et adhuc retinendo Henr(icum) de Braybroc, qua de causa dicti F.

castrum, scilicet Bedeford', duxistis obsidere. Unde et nobis prohibuistis ne auxilium vel consilium ei prestaremus ipsum vel suos receptando. Ad hoc vobis respondemus quod prefatus F. ad nos accessit in terram nostram conquerens et graviter dolens super hiis que vestrum consilium sibi fieri procurabat. Ostendit etiam quod eo inconsulto et nesciente captus fuit predictus H., et licet non advocaret factum, nichilominus optulit quod faceret Will(elmu)m de Breaut' et sequaces suos stare iudicio et de facto satisfacere. Quod quia vestrum refutavit consilium iniuste actum fuisse cum eo docere satagebat, eodem autem die quo ad nos accessit de terra nostra recessit. Non quia teneamur excusare nos, si ipsum et suos receptemus, hec vobis mandamus. Non enim minoris libertatis sumus quam rex Scocie qui receptat utlagatos de Angl(ia), etiam impune. Porro predictus F. nequaquam meruerat erga vos vel erga beate memorie patrem vestrum nichil enim mali audivimus eum vobis unquam intulisse. Set et eum novimus quamplurima et maxima commoda vobis contulisse, vobis pre ceteris pene omnibus efficacius serviendo. Porro vestram non deberet excellentiam pigere, si ipse apud nos se receptaret. Nos enim diligentius curam adhiberemus ut vobis ad honorem reconciliaretur, si permitteret vestrum consilium sibi iusticiam exhiberi. Verum de nobismet ipsis quantum ad hoc magis quam de ipso dolemus. Nobis siquidem non solum iura nostra non redduntur, verum etiam non modica dampna cum dedecore inferuntur. Quod licet discretioni vestre maiestatis non imputemus, non speramus nec sperare possumus quod consilium vestrum nobis velit satisfieri. Tociens enim conquesti sumus quod etiam querelas nostras ad mentem reducere nos pudeat, cum nullam inde haberemus satisfactionem. Preter hec mandastis nobis sentenciam esse latam in predictum F. tanquam in perturbatorem regni, sed pro certo scire potestis quod magis perturbant regnum quicumque minus utile suggerunt vobis consilium ut eiciatis magnos viros et vobis neces-sarios a vobis et de vestro consilio, eos exheredando `et sine causa gravando, pro sola voluntate. Si vero predictus F. defendet se contra dominum papam se volentem exheredare, non credimus quod excommunicatus esset quantum ad Deum. Quicquid vero super hiis vel super aliis alii faciant nos nichil agemus contra conscientiam[b] nostram. Mallemus quippe excommunicari ab homine quam aliquid agere contra Deum, nos nostra conscientia condemnante. Super hiis et super aliis det Deus vobis salubre consilium et nobis, quia inde valde indigemus. Valete.

[a] A *inserts* suscep *struck through.* | [b] concientiam A.

William de Bréauté, brother of Falkes, seized the justice Henry of Braybrooke, a personal enemy, on 17 June 1224 and imprisoned him in Bedford castle. Though Falkes denied having instigated his brother's action, he condoned it and revolted. On 20 June Archbishop Langton and his fellow bishops excommunicated the castle garrison at Bedford, which was put under siege, as well as Falkes himself, who by then had fled. The present letter was probably written in July: as Edwards argued (*CAC*, 25), it is clearly earlier than a letter to Henry from Ranulf, earl of Chester, sent after the receipt at Chester on 4 August of a letter from Henry but before news had arrived of the surrender of Bedford on 14 August (*Chester Charters*, no. 415; cd., *CAC*, 14). It may also be somewhat later than a letter, probably also written in July, from Alexander, bishop of Coventry, in which he informed the king that he had heard that Falkes was about 3 miles beyond Chester and suggested that Henry write a friendly letter to Llywelyn asking him not receive Falkes into his lands (*CAC*, 33). Falkes was absolved on, or shortly before, 25 August, when he resigned all his possessions to the

Crown, and he publicly abjured the realm in October. For the rebellion of Falkes and its aftermath see Carpenter, *Minority*, 360–70 (and, for earlier proceedings against Falkes in 1224, ibid., 351–60).

Although Falkes's brief visit to Wales was a minor episode in his rebellion, Llywelyn seized upon the opportunity to claim disingenuously that he had as much right as the king of Scotland to receive outlaws from England, even though the prince had explicitly promised not to receive the king's enemies in the agreement with Henry at Worcester in March 1218 (no. 241 above). I am grateful to Paul Russell for his comments on the fourth sentence from the end (*Si vero predictus F. . . .*), whose sense has been rendered literally in the summary, on the assumption that Llywelyn was emphasizing the unfairness of Falkes's excommunication by saying that such a sentence would be unjustified even if it was the pope, rather than merely the king's counsellors, who wished to disinherit Falkes. For brief comment on the episode and the constitutional implications of Llywelyn's claim see *LW*, l–li, n. 2; Powicke, *Henry III*, ii. 620; Lewis, 'Treaty of Woodstock', 40–1; Walker, 'Hubert de Burgh', 477; Carr, 'Anglo-Welsh relations', 129–30; Smith, *Llywelyn*, 274–5.

(?)†256 Hospitallers of Dolgynwal

Grant, inspired by piety and for the salvation of his soul, to the house of the Hospital of Jerusalem at Dolgynwal and the brothers there serving God and St John, of the entire church of Ellesmere with its appurtenances for the use of the poor of Christ, in pure and perpetual alms, by right of patronage; so that, whenever a portion of the church becomes vacant, it will come into the possession of the said brothers without dispute. Sealing clause; witnesses.

Ruthin, 18 November 1225

B = TNA: PRO, C 66/146 (Pat. R. 10 Edward II, pt. 1), m. 2 (in an inspeximus, 10 December 1316).
C = TNA: PRO, C 66/184 (Pat. R. 8 Edward III, pt. 2), m. 19 (in an inspeximus of B, 21 October 1334).
Pd. from B, Eyton, *Shropshire*, x. 247 (incomplete).
Cd., *CPR 1313–17*, 576 (from B); *CPR 1334–8*, 34–5 (from C); Stephenson, *Governance*, 202; *H*, no. 134.

Omnibus sancte matris ecclesie filiis has litteras visuris vel audituris L. princeps de Aber(frau), dominus Snaud' salutem. Quod perpetua debet gaudere stabilitate et fidedignorum testimonio virorum debet confirmari et scriptis competentibus roborari. Vestra noscat universitas nos pietatis intuitu et pro salute anime nostre concessisse et contulisse domui Hospitalis Ierosal(em) de Dolgenwal' et fratribus Deo et Sancto Ioh(ann)i ibidem servientibus totam ecclesiam de Ellemers cum omnibus pertinentiis suis ad opus pauperum Cristi, in puram et perpetuam elemosinam, prout melius ad nos pertinet de iure patronatus donatio sive presentatio; ita scilicet quod quandocumque portio de ecclesia illa vacaverit aliqua in possessionem predictorum fratrum cedat sine aliqua contradictione. Unde ad maiorem cautelam duximus huic scripto nostrum apponere sigillum. Hiis testibus: magistro Ada de Sancta Trinitate, magistro Instructo archipresbitero de Karkeby, Edneued parvo senescallo, Ennyo parvo, Owen camerario nostro, Tegwared filio Eygyani, Grono filio Seyssill', Helin filio Ydic et multis aliis. Datum apud Ruthi(n) in octabis Sancti Martini anno regni Henr(ici) iunioris regis Angl(ie) x^{mo}.

The authenticity of this charter is questionable on the grounds that its style and dating clause seem incompatible (cf. Stephenson, *Governance*, 202). The style 'Llywelyn, prince of Aberffraw, lord of Snowdon' is not otherwise attested in the prince's acts before May 1230. Admittedly, this in itself is not conclusive, as no other acts of Llywelyn may definitely be assigned to the period from November 1225 to May 1230. However, the papal chancery still referred to Llywelyn as 'prince of North Wales' in April 1226, as did the English royal chancery as late as August 1230; the chancery's earliest known use of the title 'prince of Aberffraw and lord of Snowdon' occurs in May 1231 (above, pp. 76–7). It is unlikely that the prince would have adopted the new style in charters for ecclesiastical beneficiaries while retaining the old style for communications with the crown: both in the period up to 1225 and from 1230 onwards Llywelyn's acts are generally consistent in their use of styles irrespective of the document's beneficiary or addressee (above, pp. 75–6).

The dating clause dates the document by the king's regnal year and also seems to allude to his minority by describing Henry as *iunior*, an extremely unusual usage which could derive from a later interpolation; on the other hand, its very unusualness is arguably evidence of its authenticity, as a forger would presumably have avoided such a departure from convention. Although rare in Llywelyn's acts (and those of Welsh rulers generally), the use of the king's regnal year is not itself necessarily suspect. One of the letters patent by which Llywelyn made undertakings to the king at Worcester in March 1218 was dated by Henry's regnal year, albeit without any qualification of the king as *iunior* (no. 242 above; cf. no. 254 above). Moreover, the dating clauses of Llywelyn's charters vary according to the beneficiary, suggesting that beneficiaries influenced their drafting: those for Basingwerk and Haughmond (and also the layman, Morgan Gam) lack time-dates of any kind, while the charters for Cymer, Strata Marcella and Ynys Lannog each have different kinds of time-dates, all but one, like that of the present charter, introduced by *datum* (cf. above, pp. 65–6). Thus, while none of the other authentic charters of the prince includes the king's regnal year in its dating clause, its use in the present charter, the only extant example issued by a Welsh ruler in favour of the Hospitallers, could reflect the preference of the beneficiaries at Dolgynwal or of a local clerk at Ruthin.

Other aspects of the charter's diplomatic are inconclusive with respect to its authenticity. Although the only parallels among Llywelyn's acts for the charter's address occur in documents of 1230 or later (nos 259 (which reads *universis* rather than *omnibus*), 260, 272 below and cf. no. 258 below), it could have been used as early as November 1225 since, as already noted, no acts survive thereafter until May 1230. Moreover, the use in the address of the future participles *visuris vel audituris* is attested in a charter of 1221 for Ynys Lannog (no. 250 above). The same charter also contains an arenga, the combination of *concessisse* and *contulisse* as the dispositive verbs and three of the witnesses in the present document, including the *magistri* Adam and Instructus. Though the use of *noscat* in the notification and the form of the corroboration clause are unique, neither is sufficient to render the charter suspect, as notifications in the prince's acts employ a variety of formulae, usually including other forms of *noscere* such as *noverit*, and corroboration clauses in his charters likewise vary. The description of the grant's recipients (*domui Hospitalis Ierosalem de Dolgenwal' et fratribus Deo et Sancto Iohanni ibidem servientibus*) differs from contemporary formulae in charters issued for the Hospitallers in Essex (e.g., *Deo et Sancte Marie et Sancto Iohanni Baptiste et beatis pauperibus sancte domus Hospitalis Ierusalem*, c.1230 (*Cartulary of the Knights of St. John*, ed. Gervers, no. 170; cf. ibid., xxxiv)), but even if phrases such as the latter were preferred by the Hospitallers, the formula in the present charter could reflect idiosyncratic drafting by Llywelyn's clerk. As Stephenson noted, the witness list is 'compatible with a date of 1225 (but also with one after 1230)' (*Governance*, 202).

Independent corroboration is lacking both of Llywelyn's possession of Ellesmere church and of the existence of a Hospitaller hospice at Dolgynwal by 1225. The prince had received the castle and manor of Ellesmere from John upon his marriage with Joan in 1205 and, although he was deprived of them by 1211, they were restored to him by 1220 (Eyton, *Shropshire*, x. 236–7; *HW*, ii. 646–7). Yet in November 1221 the jurors of Pimhill hundred declared at the assizes at Shrewsbury that, though Llywelyn held the manor of Ellesmere by the king's authority, the church ought to be in the king's gift (Eyton, *Shropshire*, x. 237–8). If correct, this implies that Llywelyn either had been granted it between November 1221 and November 1225 or, more probably, had usurped the advowson in the wake of his conquests in Shropshire in 1223 (ibid., 247; Rees, *History*, 63, n. *). Ellesmere church appears to have been attached to the preceptory of Halston in Shropshire by 1294, and Ysbyty Ifan and all the Hospitaller lands in north Wales had been merged into the bailiwick of Halston by 1338, when it is referred to as the bailiwick of Halston and Dolgynwal (ibid., 68–9). That Llywelyn established or at least confirmed the presence of the Hospitallers at Dolgynwal, now known as Ysbyty Ifan ('The Hospital of John'), on the eastern bank of the river Conwy at SH 843 489, is plausible in view of the prince's almost uninterrupted tenure of the locality after the defeat of Dafydd ab Owain in 1194 together with his support for other reformed religious orders (*HW*, ii. 604; Rees, *History*, 63–4). More specifically, Llywelyn may have been motivated to support the Hospitallers by the Fifth Crusade (1217–21) or by the example of his son-in-law John de Braose, who made donations to the Hospitallers in the 1220s (a suggestion I owe to Helen Nicholson; cf. Nicholson, 'Margaret de Lacy', 634, 635). Given the prince's possession of Ellesmere from 1205, it is also possible that he granted its church to Dolgynwal.

In short, while the charter cannot conclusively be shown to be spurious on either diplomatic or historical grounds, the probable incompatibility of the prince's style with the dating clause renders the document's authenticity suspect. If so, at least either the protocol or the dating clause has been tampered with at some stage in the text's transmission. (I am grateful to Paul Brand, Nicholas Vincent and especially Helen Nicholson for their helpful comments on this charter.)

*257 Henry III

Letter (?), apologizing for the assault by some of Llywelyn's men on merchants taking provisions to the king. Llywelyn would have sent envoys if the king's councillors had been with him.

[Shortly before 8 September 1228]

Mention only, in a letter from Henry III to Llywelyn dated at Montgomery, 8 September 1228 (*CR 1227–31*, 116). Although Henry does not explicitly refer to the receipt of a letter from the prince, simply using the phrase *prout nobis significastis*, it is very likely that Llywelyn's communication was in writing (as assumed by Stephenson, *Governance*, 7). The king thanked Llywelyn for the apology and wished that subsequent actions would have been consistent with it. He would have exercised his rights of jurisdiction regarding the assault but for his respect for the prince's honour and the truce agreed at the petition of his sister, Llywelyn's wife (Joan). He did not wish the peace and love with Llywelyn to cease unless on account of injuries committed by Llywelyn. Henry warned the prince of the injuries that could threaten him if he was separated from the king's love, and denied the charge that he had been without sufficient councillors. Llywelyn ought not to have any concerns about sending his envoys to the king during the truce, which the king had ensured was observed on his side; Llywelyn should ensure that it was observed on his.

The truce referred to was probably arranged when Joan met the king at Hereford in mid-August, after receiving a safe conduct on 13 August; Llywelyn was due to meet the king at Shrewsbury on 10 September (*HW*, ii. 667–8, n. 74; Walker, 'Hubert de Burgh', 478). However, Henry and the justiciar Hubert de Burgh had begun preparations for a campaign against Llywelyn on their arrival at Montgomery on 3 September, following a Welsh attack on the garrison there at the end of August, and the king's reply to Llywelyn made it clear that he blamed the prince for the breakdown of the truce and 'implied that it was now too late to negotiate' (ibid., 478–80). For the brief and disastrous royal campaign in Ceri that commenced on 25 September see *HW*, ii. 667–9; Walker, 'Hubert de Burgh', 480–2; Davies, *Conquest*, 298.

258 Haughmond Abbey

Grant and confirmation for the salvation of the souls of himself, his ancestors and heirs of the church of Nefyn with all its appurtenances, namely all the land between the two streams between which the said church is situated; from the house of Gruffudd (?) Brydydd (Predit) with the meadow to the house of Waspatlillan; *the 3 acres which Gwion the cook gave to the canons; the two small portions of land which the bald leper once held near* Penodrayt; *the land which* Troytbrimmet *once held from the land of Boduan; and Cadwgan ap John Sturry with his wife, children and possessions and all his land at Morfa Dinllaen. A further grant of common pasture with the cattle of Llywelyn's men of Nefyn, Morfa and Botacho. Llywelyn prohibits his bailiffs or heirs from exercising lordship over the aforesaid land of the canons. A further grant and confirmation of whatever Cadwaladr brother of Owain the Great and Gruffudd ap Cynan and his brother Maredudd and Dafydd ab Owain gave to the canons. A further grant that the men of the canons shall be free as regards Llywelyn and his heirs from all earthly customs, aids, labour services, tallages, military service and other exactions. Sealing clause; witnesses.*

[1230 × 1240; possibly 1230 × 1232]

B = Shrewsbury, Shropshire Records and Research Centre MS 6001/6869 (Haughmond Cartulary), fo. 149v. s. xv ex.
Pd. from B, *Cart. Haugh.*, no. 789.
Cd., *H*, no. 138.

Lewelin(us) princeps de Aberfrau,[a] dominus Snawdini omnibus has litteras visuris vel audituris salutem eternam in domino. Noverit universitas vestra nos concessisse et presenti carta nostra confirmasse Deo et ecclesie Sancti Ioh(ann)is Evangeliste de Haghmon' et canonicis ibidem Deo servientibus pro salute anime nostre et antecessorum et heredum nostrorum ecclesiam de Neuyn' cum omnibus pertinentiis suis tam infra villam quam extra tam in terris quam in aliis rebus, videlicet totam terram inter duos rivulos inter quos predicta ecclesia sita est, et a domo Griffri Predit cum prato usque ad domum Waspatlillan, et tres acras terre quas Wyon cocus eisdem canonicis dedit, et duas portiunculas terre quas leprosus calvus aliquando tenuit iuxta Penodrayt, et illam terram quam Troytbri(m)met aliquando tenuit de terra Bodanewe et Cadug' filium[b] Ioh(ann)is Sturry cum uxore sua et liberis suis et omni substantia sua et cum tota terra sua apud Moruadinllain. Concedimus etiam predictis canonicis et eorum hominibus communem pasturam liberam et quietam cum averiis hominum nostrorum de Neuyn' et de Morua et de Botache. Inhibemus etiam ne quis ballivorum vel heredum nostrorum super terram predictorum canonicorum dominium exerceat. Preterea concedimus eis et confirmamus quicquid Cadwaladrus frater Owini magni et Griffin(us) filius Canaan et Meredut frater eius et David filius Owini predictis canonicis dederunt. Concedimus etiam quod homines predictorum canonicorum liberi sint quantum ad nos et heredes nostros ab omnibus terrenis consuetudinibus, auxiliis, operationibus, taillagiis, exercitibus et aliis exactionibus. Et ut ista concessio et confirmatio nostra perpetue firmitatis robur optineat eam presenti carta cum sigilli nostri appositione roboravimus. Hiis testibus: Griffino filio Roderi, Ric(ard)o filio Cadwaladri, Edeneuet parvo etc.

[a] Aberfiau B. | [b] filius B.

The style 'Llywelyn, prince of Aberffraw and lord of Snowdon' indicates that the charter was probably issued no earlier than 1230. If, as is likely, the Richard ap Cadwaladr of the witness list was the son of Cadwaladr ap Gruffudd ap Cynan who was *rhaglaw* of Dinllaen in Llŷn the charter is probably no later than 1232, for Philip ap Gilbert had succeeded Cadwaladr in this office by that date (Stephenson, *Governance*, 202 and 149, n. 59, citing *CIM*, ii. 166). Gruffudd ap Rhodri occurs 1226–40, Ednyfed Fychan 1215–46 (Stephenson, *Governance*, 207–9, 215). The church of Nefyn had first been granted to Haughmond by Cadwaladr ap Gruffudd (no. 197 above), the land of *Troit de Brumm* or *Troytbrimmet* in Boduan by Dafydd ab Owain (no. 198 above; see also no. 199 above), and Cadwgan ap John (Sturry) and his family and land by Maredudd ap Cynan (no. 208 above). The present charter thus confirmed these grants, defining the lands more precisely than the original charters with respect to the appurtenances of the church of Nefyn and the lands of Cadwgan (here adding that the latter's land was at Morfa Dinllaen), and explicitly exempting them from princely rights of lordship. For the township of Botacho in the commote of Dinllaen see *Rec. Caern.*, 34, and Jones Pierce, 'Lleyn ministers' accounts', 259; its name is preserved in two farms, Botacho Ddu and Botacho Wyn (Jones (Myrddin Fardd), *Enwau Lleoedd*, 120–1). The identification of Morfa Dinllaen is uncertain, as is whether it was the same as the place named Morfa: possibly one or both names referred to Morfa Nefyn (SH 286 403), that is, Morfa in the commote of Dinllaen.

259 Letter patent concerning Ralph Mortimer

Notification that Llywelyn has granted to his beloved son[-in-law] Ralph Mortimer the lands of Norton and Knighton with all their appurtenances for the due service of those lands which Thomas of Erdington gave Llywelyn, saving agreements between Llywelyn and his son Dafydd on one side and Ralph on the other. Sealing clause; witnesses.

[1230, (?)mid-June × 11 April 1240; possibly 1230]

B = BL, Harl. MS 1240 (Mortimer Cartulary), fo. 68v. s. xiv/xv.
Pd. from B, Eyton, *Shropshire*, xi. 348.
Cd., Stephenson, *Governance*, 203; *H*, no. 139.

[U]niversis sancte matris ecclesie filiis has litteras visuris vel audituris L. princeps de Aberfrau, dominus Snaudon' salutem eternam in domino. Noverit universitas vestra nos contulisse et concessisse dilecto filio nostro domino R. de Mortuo Mari terras de Nortun et de Kenithtun cum omnibus pertinentiis et libertatibus suis pro debito servitio cum libertate earumdem terrarum quod nobis faciebat Thomas de Erdintun, salvis tamen conventionibus factis inter nos et David nostrum filium ex una parte et ipsum R. ex alia parte. In cuius rei testimonium has litteras sigilli nostri munimine duximus roborandas. Hiis testibus: magistro Instructo cancellario nostro, Idneuet Vechan senescallo nostro et Griffr' filio Rodei[a] et Ennio parvo et multis aliis. Valeat universitas vestra semper in domino.

[a] *sic in B ?for* Rodri.

As Llywelyn refers to Ralph Mortimer as his son the charter must have been issued after Ralph's marriage in 1230 to the prince's daughter Gwladus Ddu, widow of Reginald de Braose (*AM*, iv. 421). The grant may have been made shortly after the marriage, as a means of further cementing the prince's new alliance with his erstwhile enemies, the Mortimers (cf. Crump, 'Mortimer family', 124; Remfry, 'Native Welsh Dynasties', 172). Crump, 'Repercussions', 205, n. 32, suggests that the marriage took place during the meeting of the regents Stephen Segrave and Ralph Neville with Llywelyn or his representatives at Shrewsbury, 11–14 June 1230; however, if, as is likely, the prince was present at the wedding, this is uncertain, as he may not have attended the Shrewsbury meeting in person (cf. ibid., 206, n. 38). According to the Wigmore chronicle, Llywelyn granted the whole of Ceri and Cedewain as a marriage portion (*Mon. Ang.*, vi: i. 350), but the present document refers only to the granting of Knighton and Norton, two manors in Shropshire that had been in dispute between Llywelyn and Hugh III Mortimer (d. 1227), Ralph's brother and predecessor as lord of Wigmore; the prince had refused to grant seisin of the manors to Hugh and, in contrast to the present document, denied that they were held of him by Thomas of Erdington (d. 1218) (no. 244 above). Yet in the undated charter recording Erdington's exchange with Hugh Mortimer of Norton and Knighton for land in Kingsworthy (Hants.), ratified by Henry III on 24 April 1218, Erdington promised to compensate Hugh for any loss incurred on account of his homage to Llywelyn, apparently for the two Shropshire manors (see note to no. 244). The witness list contains the only explicit designation in the sources of the clerk Instructus as Llywelyn's chancellor.

260 Letter patent concerning Ednyfed Fychan

Notification that Ednyfed Fychan, his seneschal, has bought with Llywelyn's consent the land of Rhosfynaich with all its appurtenances from the heirs of Dineirth, from the lineage of Marchudd and from the descendants of Dwywg in the presence of Llywelyn and the said parties. Ednyfed shall hold the land free of secular service, and none of the aforesaid heirs of Dineirth, lineage of Marchudd and descendants of Dwywg will be able to claim any right in it for ever. Ednyfed and his heirs shall pay 2s. annually to God and the church of Dineirth for

Easter lights. The boundaries of the said land are Taletaclaud *towards the west and* Aberdowyth *[the mouth of the* Dowyth*] towards the west, [i.e.] the channel nearer to the land of Dineirth which divides the same land [i.e. Rhosfynaich?] from that of Dineirth on one side and from the sea on the other. Ednyfed and his heirs shall possess for ever the said channel with all the water which descends through it to* Aberdowith *with all its appurtenances, liberties, buildings, mills and fisheries, so that no one else may fish or otherwise work in that water. Llywelyn has sealed the document at the request of the parties and granted it to Ednyfed and his heirs. Witnesses.*

Ystrad, 1 May 1230

B = NLW MS 2020B (formerly Panton MS 52; transcript by Evan Evans 1731–88), ii, fos 145r–146v. s. xviii. Rubric: Copia charte de Ros Veneych. After the transcript Evan Evans wrote (fo. 146v): 'The Prince Lewelyn ap Erwerth his seal is of green wax with the print of a man in armour of the one side, and a floure of the other side and the Tagg is of twist silk. Copia concordat cum originale. This copy from the original deed by the hand seems to be near two hundred years old. The original is wrote on vellom in an old fair court hand, and is in the custody of Edward Philip Pugh Esq. of Coetmor in Caernarvonshire, a descendant from the said Ednyvet Fychan. The hand in the original is thus'. There follows (fo. 147r) an attempt to reproduce the protocol (*Omnibus . . . salutem in domino*) in the script of the original, including contractions.
C = TNA: PRO, E 163/28/11, pp. 34–5. s. xvi[l]. Rubric: Carta de Ros Venych'.
Pd. from B, *RMWL*, ii. 859; from *RMWL*, Anon, 'Rhos Fynach charter', 129–30; from (?)*RMWL*, Bezant Lowe, *Heart of Northern Wales*, 370–1 (trans. only).
Cd., Stephenson, *Governance*, 202; *H*, no. 137.

Omnibus sancte matris ecclesie filiis has litteras visuris vel audituris L.[a] princeps[b] [c]Ab(er)frau, dominus Snaudon[c] salutem [d]in domino.[d] Noverit universitas vestra quod[e] Idnev[f] Vachan[g] senescallus[h] noster emit ex[i] assensu nostro ab heredibus de Dineyrth[j] et [k]eorum heredibus,[k] [d]a llwyth Marchudd et eorum heredibus[d] et a[i] nepotibus Dueog[l] et eorum heredibus coram nobis presentibus partibus supradictis terram de Ros Veneych[m] cum omnibus[n] pertinentiis et libertatibus suis[o] in bosco, in plano, pascuis, pasturis, pratis, semitis et aquis et in omnibus esiamentis[p] suis in mari et in terra sibi et heredibus suis habendam[q] et iure[r] hereditario in perpetuum possidendam[i] libere et quiete et absque servitio seculari, ita quod nullus predictorum heredum [fo. 145v] de Dineyrth,[j] de [s]llwyth Marchudd,[s] de nepotibus Duog[t] aliquid ius in[i] predicta terra aut in suis[i] pertinentiis in posterum poterint clamare, preterquam idem Idneved[f] et sui[i] heredes. Predictus vero Idnevd[f] et sui heredes persolvent annuatim[u] Deo[i] et ecclesie de Dineyrth[j] [d]duos solidos[d] ad luminaria erga Pasca.[v] Termini vero dicte terre sunt Taletaclaud'[w] versus occidentem et Aberdowyth[x] versus occidentem,[o] alveus propinquior terre de Dineyrth[j] qui dividit terram eandem[y] et terram de Dineyrth[j] ex una parte et mare ex altera parte. Dictum[z] vero alveum[aa] cum omni[ab] aqua que[i] descendit[ac] per ipsum alveum usque ad Aberdowith[ad] cum omnibus pertinentiis et libertatibus suis, edificiis,[ae] molendinis et piscariis dictus Idnevet[f] et sui[af] heredes[ag] [fo. 146r] absque omni calumpnia[ah] in perpetuum possidebunt, ita quod nullus alius in eadem aqua vel in aliqua parte ipsius aque possit piscari [d]vel aliter operari[d] preterquam[ai] Idnevet[f] et sui[aj] heredes.[ag] In cuius rei testimonium huic[i] presenti[ak] scripto[al] ac patenti ex consensu[am] partium sigillum nostrum poni[an] fecimus.[ao] Et idem [d]scriptum eidem[d] Idnevet[f] et suis[ap] heredibus[aq] concessimus[i] habendum. His[ar] testibus: David[as] herede nostro, Gruffud[at] filio[au] Roderici,[i] Gruffud[at] filio[av] Oweni parvo,[aw] magistro Ada,[ax] David filius[av] Electi,[ay] Philippo et[i] Bleydud[az] personis de Dineyrth,[ba] L., M., B. [bb]filiis Madauc,

Einio filio[bc] Maredud, Tuder filio Aron,[bc] Madoco filio Bondes et[bb] multis aliis. Datum apud [fo. 146v] Estrad [d]-kalendis maii[d] anno gratie [bd]-millesimo ducentesimo tricesimo.[bd]

[a] sic *on fo. 147r;* Leolinus *on fo. 145r* B. | [b] principis C. | [c–c] sic *on fo. 147r;* Aberfraw, dominus Snawdon *on fo. 145r* B; Aberffrau, dominus Snaudon C. | [d–d] *omitted* C. | [e] quo B. | [f] Edn' C. | [g] Vychan C. | [h] senesscalus C. | [i] *omitted* C. | [j] Dinerth C. | [k–k] heredibus eorum C. | [l] Duoc C. | [m] Venych C. | [n] C *inserts* suis. | [o] C *inserts* et. | [p] asiamentis C. | [q] habenda C. | [r] C *inserts* de. | [s–s] Lloithmarchud et C. | [t] Dowc C. | [u] antedict' C. | [v] Pascam C. | [w] Talart y Clawdd [in originale Taletaclaud'] B; Talykatlawd C. | [x] Aberodwydd C. | [y] eadem C. | [z] Dictus C. | [aa] alveus C. | [ab] omne C. | [ac] decendit C. | [ad] Aberodwyth C. | [ae] edificatibus C. | [af] suus. | [ag] her' C. | [ah] calumnia C. | [ai] preter ipsum C. | [aj] suum C. | [ak] presentem C. | [al] script' C. | [am] conssessu C. | [an] aponi C. | [ao] fessimus C. | [ap] s' C. | [aq] hered' C. | [ar] Hiis C. | [as] Davit C. | [at] Gruff' C. | [au] filedon' C. | [av] fillium C. | [aw] parro [in orig parvo magro] B; Enne parvo C. | [ax] Adda C. | [ay] domino(?) C. | [az] Bleuddudd C. | [ba] Dinerth C. | [bb–bb] et Karon M. Beudic ac C. | [bc] B *inserts* [in orig. fil.]. | [bd–bd] m° cc° xxx° C.

The text printed here is based on that copied by Evan Evans (Ieuan Fardd) in B as this is more complete and correct than that of the earlier copy in C. (I thank W. Rhys Robinson for drawing attention to, and providing a photocopy of, the text in C, a sixteenth-century compilation discussed in Smith, 'Land endowments', 150–3, which notices the text of the present charter at 153, n. 2, as well as Tony Carr for help with the transcription.) To judge by the note appended to his transcript, Evans saw two texts of the charter. The text in B was taken from a copy which he thought had been written almost two hundred years earlier, i.e. in the sixteenth century. However, he had also seen the original charter, describing what was presumably Llywelyn's equestrian seal and commenting that the text of the copy he had used corresponded to that of the original, whose greeting clause he also copied. As the textual notes show, the copy used by Evans had modernized the orthography of the place-names Aberffraw and Snowdon and also provided an early modern Latin form of Llywelyn's name. It is likely that the remainder of the text contains similar modernizations. Evans noted that the original charter was held by a descendant of Ednyfed Fychan, Edward Philip Pugh of Coetmor. A very similar description of the document and its ownership by Pugh, almost certainly derived from that of Evans, occurs in BL, Additional MS 14949, fo. 45v, a notebook written by Lewis Morris in the 1750s, though this cites only the opening of the protocol (*Omnibus santae matris ecclesiae filiis etc.*) followed by a summary of the witness list ('attested by his son David his heir, Gruffudd filis (*sic*) Roderici Gruffud filis (*sic*) Oweni etc.').

Edward Philip Pugh belonged to what had formerly been a prominent recusant family with its seat at Penrhyn Creuddyn who acquired the Coetmor estate in the parish of Llanllechid, Caernarfonshire, through marriage to its heiress in the third quarter of the eighteenth century. Their only son, James Pugh, sheriff of Caernarfonshire in 1776, died childless in 1800, having abandoned Coetmor House a few years earlier after its roof had been blown away by a great storm, leaving the house to fall into ruin. See *Tours in Wales by Thomas Pennant*, ed. Rhys, iii. 103; *Tours in Wales (1804–1813)*, ed. Fisher, 238, 311; Hughes, *Hynafiaethau Llandegai*, 149–51 (to be used with caution as it contains several inaccuracies, including the identification of Pugh with the house of Bodysgallen in Creuddyn); Dodd, *History of Caernarvonshire*, 59, 85, 170 and esp. 185. It is unknown what happened to the original charter after Edward Philip Pugh's day and the abandonment of

Coetmor House; the Coetmor archives are now lost (*ex inf.* Tomos Roberts, to whom I am grateful for helpful discussion of these points).

Llywelyn issued this document in confirmation of his approval of the purchase by his seneschal Ednyfed Fychan of the land of Rhosfynaich (in the cantref of Rhos) from three kin groups. To judge by its name, Rhosfynaich (lit. 'moor of the monks') had formerly belonged to an ecclesiastical community, almost certainly the church of Dineirth (alternatively known as Llandrillo-yn-Rhos) to which Ednyfed and his heirs agreed to pay 2*s.* each year (SH 832 806). Dineirth was a native foundation of some importance, and was included among the 'principal churches' in Wales to whom Gruffudd ap Cynan bequeathed 10*s.* before his death in 1137 (*Historia Gruffud vab Kenan*, ed. Evans, 31–2; *HW*, i. 240; Thomas, *History of the Diocese of St Asaph*, iii. 210–11). By 1230, however, it appears that Rhosfynaich was held by lay kin groups, suggesting that the land had become secularized in a comparable way to the endowments of some other native churches of early medieval origin in twelfth- and thirteenth-century Wales (for which see e.g. *Gir. Camb. Op.*, vi. 122 (*IK*, II. 4); Evans, 'Survival of the *clas*'). The precise location of the land is uncertain as the boundaries named in the document, *Taletaclaud* and *Aberdowyth*, cannot be identified, though Bezant Lowe implied that the *Dowyth* of the latter was the same as the brook or river, choked by the early twentieth century, known as Afon Ganol (*Heart of Northern Wales*, 373). However, the place-name is preserved in that of Rhos Fynach (*sic*) House (now Rhos Fynach Tavern) and Rhos Fynach weir, just south-east of the chapel of St Trillo on Rhos Point (SH 841 811), and the land therefore is likely to have lain in that vicinity, that is, between Dineirth (to its east) and the sea (see Bezant Lowe, *Heart of Northern Wales*, 370, 372, 374–5 and Fig. 192, reproducing a plan of 1867 showing the location of Rhos Fynach).

The 'heirs' (*heredes*) of Dineirth will have been the free proprietors of that hamlet, which belonged to the township of Llwytgoed in the commote of Rhos Uwch Dulas. 'Llwyth Marchudd' ('the lineage of Marchudd') has been described as 'the most powerful non-royal kindred in Gwynedd' (Jones, 'Pattern of medieval settlement', 47–9; for the pedigrees of 'Llwyth Marchudd', see *EWGT*, 116). Although apparently originally settled around Abergele, the settlement pattern revealed by the Survey of the Honour of Denbigh (1334) suggests that the lineage of Marchudd's son Edrud ap Marchudd established a secondary settlement at Llwytgoed and its hamlets of Gwlyptref and Dineirth, from where it subsequently expanded further into many other areas of Rhos as well as into Rhufoniog. The third kin group named, the *nepotes*, i.e. descendants or lineage (for comparable Hiberno-Latin usage see Charles-Edwards, *Early Irish and Welsh Kinship*, 156–7, 574) of Dwywg likewise held land in both Abergele and Llwytgoed and its associated hamlets in 1334. See *Survey of the Honour of Denbigh*, 245–50, 299, 301 and Table II; Owen, 'Tenurial and economic developments', 123–5, 140. Interestingly, Ednyfed Fychan himself belonged to the lineage of Edrud ap Marchudd, which continued to hold land in Dineirth in 1334 (Roberts, *Aspects of Welsh History*, 182).

Whether Llywelyn's involvement in Ednyfed's acquisition of Rhosfynaich indicates that princely assent was necessary for any such purchase of free patrimonial land, or merely that it was necessary or at least prudent in this particular instance, is difficult to tell (cf. Stephenson, *Governance*, 80, n. 76). The Welsh law texts assume that patrimony could not normally be alienated from the kindred without the consent of the donor's heirs, and a witness to Edward I's inquiry into Welsh law in 1281 declared that under that law 'no one can sell or quitclaim his patrimony' (*Ior*, §87 (trans. *LTMW*, 110); *Col*, §607; *CWR*, 195;

Smith, 'Gage and the land market', 539–40). The prince's assent to the purchase, in the presence of the parties and also, the witness list reveals, the parsons of Dineirth, will have served to dispel any doubts about the legality of the transaction and the terms by which Ednyfed and his heirs were entitled to hold the land. Most important, the issue of a *scriptum* or letter patent confirming the transaction provided the purchaser with written title to the land: the text explicitly states that Llywelyn has granted the document to Ednyfed and his heirs, who, as already noted, retained it until at least the later eighteenth century.

The dating clause of the document also merits notice. Ystrad was a manor just south of the river Ystrad, south of Denbigh, cmt. Ceinmeirch (*Survey of the Honour of Denbigh*, 2–3 and map facing 1). It lay about 17 miles from the manor of Crogen near Bala where William de Braose was executed the following day (note to no. 261 below). It is therefore possible that it was at Ystrad on 1 May that Llywelyn's magnates passed the sentence of execution on William for his alleged affair with the prince's wife Joan (Crump, 'Repercussions', 200, n. 14, citing a suggestion by A. D. Carr). Not only were the prince and his seneschal Ednyfed Fychan present at Ystrad but also, according to the witness list of the present document, Dafydd ap Llywelyn, Gruffudd ap Rhodri (one of the prince's first cousins) and a leading clerical servant, Master Adam.

261 Eva de Braose

Letter, asking Eva to inform him whether she wishes the alliance between his son Dafydd and her daughter Isabel to stand, for it will never rest with Llywelyn that it should not stand. If she does wish this, she will wish to inform him of her will regarding the alliance and the right of her daughter so that nothing worse can result from the misfortune. Llywelyn explains that he could not have prevented the magnates of his land from making the judgement they made, knowing the punishment for the dishonour and insult to him, and asks her to inform him what she proposes to do in this regard.

[Shortly after 2 May 1230]

> B = TNA: PRO, SC 1/11, no. 56a. s. xiii[i]. A copy of no. 262 follows in the same hand on the same sheet of parchment.
> C = ibid., no. 57a. s. xiii[1].
> Pd. from C, *RL*, i. 368.
> Cd., *CAC*, 51; *H*, no. 349.

L. princeps de Aberfrau,[a] dominus Snauduon'[b] dilecte amice sue domine[c] E. de Braus' cum dilectione salutem. Rogamus vos quatinus nos de voluntate vestra certificetis utrum volueritis stare confederationem factum inter David filium nostrum et I. filiam vestram, quia nunquam in nobis remanebit quin[d] confederatio illa stabit. Et si hoc volueritis, ne de malo peius possit evenire, voluntatem vestram de illa confederatione et de iure filie vestre nobis in brevi significare[e] volueritis. Et sciatis quod nullo modo possemus defendere quod magnates terre nostre non facerent iudicium quod fecerunt, vindictam de oprobrio et iniuria nostra sapientes, et quicquid inde feceritis nobis significare curetis.

[a] Auberfrau C. | [b] Snaued' C. | [c] *omitted* C. | [d] quorum B (*C's reading has been preferred as making more sense than B's, though the clause in C is grammatically incorrect, as* quin *takes the subjunctive*).
[e] singnificare C.

The judgement referred to was the sentencing to death by Llywelyn's council of Eva's husband William de Braose, lord of Brecon, Builth and Abergavenny, for his alleged adultery with Joan; according to Nicholas, abbot of Vaudy, writing to the chancellor Ralph Neville soon after 18 May 1230, William was hanged from a tree at Crogen (a princely manor near Bala) on 2 May 1230 in the presence of over 800 persons (*CAC*, 37; cf. Carr, 'Barons of Edeyrnion', 190). William was imprisoned in Gwynedd following his capture in the Ceri campaign in September–October 1228, and among the terms of his release early in 1229 was an agreement whereby his daughter Isabel would marry Llywelyn's son and designated successor Dafydd, who would receive the lordship of Builth as his marriage portion (*AM*, iii. 117). The affair with Joan seems to have started during William's imprisonment, but only came to light when the lord of Brecon visited Llywelyn's court at Easter 1230 (Easter Sunday fell on 7 April that year) and was discovered with Joan in her chamber, resulting in the imprisonment of both parties and William's execution on 2 May. Joan was released in 1231 and by May 1232 represented her husband at Shrewsbury in negotiations with Henry III (*HW*, ii. 685–6, citing *Ann. Cestr.*, 56, and *PR 1225–32*, 476). Like the letter to William Marshal (no. 262 below), the present letter shows the importance Llywelyn attached to maintaining the proposed marriage alliance between his son and Isabel, and seeks to play down his own role in William's execution by claiming that the sentence had been a decision of his magnates. The marriage did go ahead, probably receiving official sanction from the English crown when Llywelyn met the chancellor Ralph Neville, one of the regents during Henry III's campaigns in Brittany and Poitou, at Shrewsbury, 11–14 June 1230 (Walker, 'Hubert de Burgh', 483–4). For a recent discussion of these events and their significance see Crump, 'Repercussions'; see also nos 262–3 below.

262 William Marshal, earl of Pembroke

Letter, informing the earl that the magnates of Llywelyn's land would not bear not having passed the sentence on William de Braose which they passed, for William plotted to deceive Llywelyn, bringing him dishonour beyond measure by deceitfully entering his chamber. Llywelyn asks the earl to inform him whether he wishes the friendship between the earl's niece and Llywelyn's son Dafydd to stand; if he wishes this, the alliance will stand firm as far as Llywelyn is concerned. Asks the earl to inform him of his will concerning this and other matters, and assures him that he does not wish their friendship ever to be broken because of this or of anything else in the world. The earl should not be disturbed that Llywelyn has had this letter sealed by his secret seal, since he did not have his great seal with him.

[Shortly after 2 May 1230]

B = TNA: PRO, SC 1/11, no. 56b. s. xiii[1]. The copy follows the text of no. 261, on the same sheet of parchment and in the same hand.
C = ibid., no. 57b. s. xiii[1].
Pd. from C, *RL*, i. 369.
Cd., *CAC*, 51; *H*, no. 350.

Amico suo et fratri karissimo domino W. Marescall' comiti Penbroc' L. princeps etc. Vestra noverit dilectio quod magnates terre nostre nullo modo sustinerent quod non facerent[a] de Will(elm)o de Braus' iudicium quod fecerunt, qui dolum nostrum machinatus est, cameram nostram dolose intrando nobis ultra modum inferens oprobrium. Quare vestram obnixe rogamus dilectionem, de qua maximam gerimus fiduciam, quatinus voluntatem vestram nobis significare velitis utrum volueritis [stare][b] amicitiam factam inter neptem[c] vestram et filium nostrum David; quod si volueritis, ex parte nostra firmiter et perseveranter confederatio illa stabit. Valete. Beneplacitum vestrum super hiis et aliis nobis significare curetis, et pro certo sciatis quod nunquam in nobis fiet quin amicitia inter nos et vos facta firmiter et inviolabiliter inperpetuum observetur, nec propter hoc nec propter aliud in mundo. Iterum valete. Non moveat vos quod has litteras meas secreto sigillo nostro[d] sigillari fecimus, quia magnum[e] sigillum nostrum penes nos non habuimus.[f]

[a] faceren C. | [b] *omitted* BC. | [c] nepotem C. | [d] nostra C. | [e] mangum C. | [f] C *inserts* Valete.

William Marshal, earl of Pembroke, was Eva de Braose's brother. The assertion that William de Braose had entered Llywelyn's chamber corresponds to the account in *BT, Pen20Tr*, 102, which states that William was 'caught in Llywelyn's chamber with the king of England's daughter, Llywelyn's wife'; *BT, RBH*, 228–9, is similar. As in his letter to Eva (no. 261 above), Llywelyn insisted that his magnates had no choice but to sentence William to death, though here he explained the dishonour he had suffered explicitly in terms of a conspiracy by William to deceive him. Both letters claimed, therefore, that the magnates' judgement on William was justified by the magnitude of his offence against the prince. Llywelyn did not go so far as to say explicitly, however, that the judgement was in accord with Welsh law or custom.

How Welsh law, as set forth in the compilations extant in the early thirteenth century, could have been cited in support of the sentence passed on William is uncertain. In a sense the question is irrelevant, in that Llywelyn and his council are most unlikely to have consulted the law texts in this case. Yet the texts merit consideration insofar as they articulate norms that may have enjoyed currency in Welsh society beyond the restricted circles of native lawyers for and by whom they were composed. One archaic-looking passage in the opening tractate on the royal court includes 'abuse' or 'misuse' of the king's wife as one of the three causes of insult (*iniuria*, W. *sarhaed*) to the king, attracting a fine of 100 cattle from each cantref of the kingdom and other payments (for examples from two northern Welsh texts see *Ior*, §3, trans. *LTMW*, 5–6; *LTWL*, 193–4); but it is unclear whether this referred to adultery with the wife, as assumed by one fifteenth-century lawbook from south Wales, or simply to harming or obstructing her in some way (cf. *LTMW*, 221, 5.28–9n.). Note also the rule attributed to Goronwy ap Moriddig, possibly datable to the second quarter of the thirteenth century, ordaining that a woman whose adultery became known should pay *sarhaed* ('insult-price') to her husband or else be repudiated by him (Pryce, *Native Law*, 93–4). Probably more pertinent are rules that punish treason (W. *brad*) against the king or lord with death (examples in thirteenth-century vernacular lawbooks from Gwynedd in *Ior*, §115, trans. *LTMW*, 166; *Col*, §397; *Damweiniau Colan*, ed. Jenkins, §§199, 286). Usually the Latin texts of Welsh law render 'treason' and 'traitor' in these contexts as *proditio* and *proditor* (e.g. *LTWL*, 128, 231, 259), but it is worth noting that in one such passage Latin Redaction A, of the mid-thirteenth century, uses the phrase *dolum regis* (*LTWL*, 134). (For further discussion of some of these rules see Pryce, *Native Law*, 66–9, 201.) The phrase in Latin Redaction A raises the possibility that the use of *dolum* and *dolose* in the present letter reflected a conviction at the court of Gwynedd that, though Llywelyn was not his lord, William de Braose had acted in a way that was not just deceitful or guileful, but amounted to treachery, a capital offence in Welsh law.

However, irrespective of any relationship to legal norms set forth in the law texts, the letter, in common with that to Eva de Braose, is striking above all for its confident assumption that Llywelyn and his magnates were entitled to jurisdiction over William, despite his being a subject of the English king from whom he held his Marcher lordships.

263 Stephen Segrave

Letter, enclosing transcripts of letters to be directed to the king from Llywelyn by Ralph Mortimer, and also sending letters to Llywelyn's seneschal Ednyfed from W. fitz (?)Adam, seneschal of the earl of Pembroke concerning the detention of the son of Einion Fychan, who has not been committed to Llywelyn's custody in accordance with Stephen's promise to Llywelyn as conveyed by Master Instructus; the earl's bailiffs act in opposition to the king's council. Llywelyn replies that he will not release a single groom or spare any prisoner on account of Einion's son, for he had been given as if he were a foster son to Eva de Braose. Llywelyn will hold those he has in his prison, acting according to the advice of his council. Eva's chaplain excommunicates Llywelyn by name on successive Sundays . . . those seeking a pretext for waging war rashly provoke Llywelyn's anger. The said bailiffs [of the earl of Pembroke] have asked about Madog Fychan and his adherents who take themselves and their belongings from Brecon to Builth. Llywelyn replies that he would make them come to a safe and suitable place to make amends for the matters of which they were accused and would expel them from his land if they refused. If they agreed to make peace with the aforesaid bailiffs, taking with them discreet persons from Llywelyn's side . . . in their land as is customary in Wales . . . Llywelyn informs Stephen of this lest the said bailiffs tell him otherwise. Llywelyn further asks Stephen to persuade the chancellor and [Earl] Warenne to write on Llywelyn's behalf to the king regarding the prince's case. Llywelyn requests that transcripts of these letters are sent to Llywelyn by the bearer of the present letter, and the letters themselves sent as quickly as possibly in order to reach Ralph Mortimer, Llywelyn's envoy, before he crosses the sea.

[*c*.mid-June × late August 1230]

A = TNA: PRO, SC 1/11, no. 58. No endorsements; approx. 154 × 124 mm.; one slit in middle of left-hand side; mounted, foot cut away. The parchment is very badly stained and the text only partially legible.
Pd. from A, Crump, 'Repercussions', 211–12.

L. princeps de Ab(er)frau, (?)dominus (?)de (?)Snaud' . . . (?)amico (?)suo (?)domino Steph(ano) de Segraf (?)cum (?)debita dilectione salutem. Mittimus ad vos transcripta literrarum dirigendarum ad dominum regem ex part nostra per dominum R. de Mortuo Mari. Preterea quia nec volumus nec debemus 'quod omnia . . . . nobis nec significentur nec (?)super eis . . . . Mittimus igitur vobis literas directas Idneued senescallo nostro de W. filio Ade senescallo domini comitis Penbr' per quas perpend . . . eis . . . presumptose atemptent retinere filium Ennii Vachan et quod nostre non committatur custodie secundum quod promisistis nobis et mandastis per magistrum Inst(ru)ct(um), quem quidem promissionem adimplere tenemini et sicut aliud esset in causa nisi quod ballivi dicti domini comitis videantur atemptare presumentes refragari 'et contradicere iusto consilio domini regis. Nos vero respondimus quod non liberaremus unum garciferum pro dicto filio Ennii nec alicui incarcerato parceremus propter ipsum 'nec debemus quia tanquam alumpnus traditus fuit domine Eve de Brausa. Nos vero visis causis tenemus eos quos habemus in carcere (?)nostro, vero agenda nostra secundum dominum[a] `Deum et fidele consilium nostro Deo dante disponimus. Preterea dicta domina Eva habet capilanum suum qui singulis dominicis diebus excomunicat nos nominatim et . . . (?)multis nos provocant ad iram qui querentes occasionem movendi guerram quam vix sustiner(?)ent (?)pro. . . super quam curam debent habere. Ad hec questi sunt dicti ballivi de Mad' Vachan et complicibus suis qui transtulit se et sua mobilia de Brekeniauc usque ad Buelt: nos respondimus eis quod illos faceremus venire ad locum securum et competentem ad (?)emendas faciendas de hiis que eis obiciantur, quod si nollent de terra nostra expellemus eos. Si vero velint hoc facere (?)ductis cum ipsis viris discretis ex parte nostra ad faciendum pacem cum predictis ballivis ita quod eis iura sua reddentur pro . . . serviciis (?)itaque fuerint (?)dum (?)secure (?)presint (?)morari in terra sua sicut moris est in Wall', (?)fieri (?)de . . .(?)lius (?)libere (?)ad. . . . Hec (?)domino vobis significamus[b] `ne dicti ballivi presint vobis contraria significare. Valete. (?)Preterea rogamus vobis quatinus (?)introduc' (?)eis dominum cancel-larium et dominum de Warant si presens fuerit ut scribant pro nobis et (?)filio (?)nostro domino regi ut agenda nostra iniustis petentibus (?)et (?)litera promoveantur. Et literarum eorum et vestrarum (?)transcripta nobis per latorem presentium remitere non obmittatis, ipsas vero literas per (?)eundem mittatis quam citius pot(?)eritis ut consequi (?)prefatum dominum R. de Mortuo Mari et nuncium nostrum ante quam mare transierit. Iterum valete. Beneplacitum vestrum et consilium nobis significare velitis.

[a] *underlined in* A *(?for deletion)*. | [b] A *inserts* ut.

The text printed here follows that published in Crump, 'Repercussions', apart from some minor modifications, mostly made to ensure conformity with the conventions of the present edition, based on a collation with photographs of the document at *http://www.ukans.edu/ carrie/ms_room/jjcrump/frimages.html*. I am very grateful to Jon Crump for allowing me to use his edition and for having drawn attention to the document and making available a copy of his article, to whose analysis the note below is greatly indebted, in advance of publication.

The letter is addressed to Stephen Segrave, who, with the chancellor Ralph Neville, bishop of Chichester, and William de Warenne, earl of Surrey, was regent during Henry III's campaign in France in the summer of 1230 (*AM*, i. 74). The excommunication of Llywelyn by Eva de Braose's chaplain was almost certainly in response to Llywelyn's execution of William de Braose on 2 May 1230. After the execution, custody of William's lands was given to William Marshal II, earl of Pembroke, and thus fell under the control of the latter's seneschal, William of Christchurch, also known as William fitz Adam (cf. no. 265 below and note). As it seems to refer to a letter concerning the son of Einion Fychan from William fitz Adam to Llywelyn's seneschal Ednyfed Fychan that was written at some point following an agreement with Stephen Segrave concerning Madog Fychan, probably made at Llywelyn's meeting with Stephen at Shrewsbury on or about 12 June 1230, the present letter was almost certainly sent after that date, but before Ralph Mortimer, named as Llywelyn's envoy, crossed to join Henry III in Brittany towards the end of August, reaching Nantes by 1 September 1230 (*CCR 1227–31*, 433). (Crump, 'Repercussions', 207, n. 44, suggests a somewhat narrower date range, between mid-July and the end of August.) Einion Fychan was one of Llywelyn's principal officials, and the refusal of William

Marshal's bailiffs to release his son, originally handed over in fosterage to Eva de Braose, clearly rankled with the prince. The 'groom' (*garcifer*) referred to was one of the hostages from William de Braose's military retinue whom Llywelyn kept in captivity after releasing William in 1229. (The summary assumes that *dominum de Warant'* refers to William de Warenne, a possibility raised in Crump, 'Repercussions', 212, n. 67; for the form, cf. *comitem Warantie* in no. 398 below.)

*264 Ralph, bishop of Chichester and chancellor

Letter(?), informing Ralph that William of Christchurch has granted a truce between Llywelyn and the men of William's lord, and requesting the bishop to send a discreet man to the Marches to view the transgressions committed between the two lands.

[*c.*August × September 1230]

Mention only, in an undated letter from Master William of Christchurch to Ralph Neville, bishop of Chichester and chancellor (*RL*, ii. 5–6; cd., *CAC*, 35–6). Though William does not explicitly say that Llywelyn sent a letter to the chancellor, this is strongly implied by the use of the phrase *dedit in mandatis*. For the matters referred to see note to no. 265 below.

*265 William of Christchurch

Letter, in reply to William's letter asking whether he wished to keep the peace agreed at Shrewsbury concerning Madog Fychan and his accomplices as well as others, stating that he did not wish harm to be caused to the land of William's lord any more than to his own land. Llywelyn also informs William that he has sent a message to Ralph, bishop of Chichester and chancellor, saying that William has granted a truce between Llywelyn and the men of William's lord, and requested the bishop to send a discreet man to the Marches to view the transgressions committed between the two lands.

[*c.*August × September 1230]

Mention only, in an undated letter from Master William of Christchurch to Ralph Neville, bishop of Chichester and chancellor (*RL*, ii. 5–6; cd., *CAC*, 35–6). As William wrote to the chancellor the letter was clearly sent while Henry III was away from England in Brittany and Poitou between the beginning of May and 28 October 1230, leaving Ralph and Stephen Segrave as regents (cf. Powicke, *Henry III*, i. 181–3). As Lloyd argued (*HW*, ii. 671, n. 92), William's letter is one of several concerning the difficulties between Llywelyn as lord of Builth, on behalf of his son Dafydd, and William, who was seneschal of William Marshal II at the time the latter had the custody of the lordship of Brecon following Llywelyn's execution of its lord, William de Braose, on 2 May 1230 (*CR 1227–31*, 353; *PR 1225–32*, 377, 398; see also Walker, 'Hubert de Burgh', 483–4, and, for a summary of William of Christchurch's career, *Llandaff Episcopal Acta*, xvi–xvii). The 'two lands' referred to by Llywelyn were therefore Brecon and Builth. The probable date range for William's letter can be narrowed down to about September 1230 as it referred to and enclosed a letter concerning Madog Fychan from Gwyn ap Goronwy, Llywelyn's seneschal at Builth, which was clearly that sent by Gwyn to William fitz Adam datable to late summer or early autumn 1230 (*CAC*, 36, 53). (This implies that William of Christchurch was also known as William fitz Adam, a conclusion supported by no. 263 above, which refers to *W. filio Ade* as seneschal of the earl of Pembroke. See also Crump, 'Repercussions', 207, n. 43.) In addition, the conciliatory tone of Llywelyn's letter (as reported by William) with respect to Madog Fychan is consistent with that of no. 263, written no later than late August 1230. It is likely, then, that Llywelyn wrote to both the chancellor (no. 264 above) and William of Christchurch in August or early September 1230. The peace at Shrewsbury referred to in the present letter was probably agreed at the meeting there between Llywelyn and Ralph Neville on about 12 June (*HW*, ii. 671 and n. 92). In a letter to the chancellor probably written somewhat later in the autumn of 1230 William of Christchurch expressed his willingness for the bishop of Hereford, Peter fitz Herbert and the prior of Wenlock to inquire into breaches of the truce in the lordship of Brecon, suggesting that the chancellor responded to Llywelyn's request to investigate transgressions between it and the lordship of Builth (*CAC*, 35). For Madog Fychan see also no. 307 below.

266 Agreement with Henry III

Notification by the king that he has extended to the feast of St Andrew [30 November] 1232 the truce between him and his adherents from both Wales and England on the one side and Llywelyn and his adherents on the other which was negotiated by Walter de Lacy, John of Monmouth, Gilbert Basset, Walter Clifford, William fitz Warin, William de Stuteville, Amaury de Saint-Amand and Hugh of Kilpeck to last until the feast of St Andrew 1231. The terms will be the same as those of the original truce, to which Llywelyn, Owain ap Gruffudd, Rhys Gryg, Ednyfed Fychan and Gruffudd ap Rhodri appended their signa, *namely that for as long as the truce lasts all men on either side will return to their own lands and have all their holdings, both moveables and immoveables, in peace, nor will the king receive the adherents or men of Llywelyn, nor Llywelyn the adherents or men of the king, during the said truce. The men of each side shall meanwhile remain within their own borders. The king has had Master Alexander de Swereford, archdeacon of Shropshire and William de Lacy swear to observe the truce on his behalf. Sealed; witnessed by the king.*

Westminster, 30 November 1231

B = TNA: PRO, C 66/42 (Pat. R. 16 Henry III), m. 10 (contemporary enrolment).
Pd. from B, *Foedera*, I. i. 201; from B, *PR 1225–32*, 453.
Cd., *H*, no. 351.

Rex omnibus ad quos etc. salutem. Sciatis quod treugam per dilectos et fideles nostros W. de Lascy, Ioh(annem) de Monem', Gileb(ertum) Basset, Walt(erum) de Clifford, Will(elmu)m filium Warin(i), Will(elmum) de Stuteuill', Amaur' de Sancto Amando et Hug(onem) de Kilpec captam inter nos et inprisios nostros tam de Wall(ia) quam de Angl(ia) ex una parte, et L. principem de Abbefrau[a] et dominum de Snaudon' et inprisios suos ex alia parte, duraturam usque ad festum Sancti Andr(ee) anno etc. xvi° prorogavimus usque ad festum Sancti Andr(ee) anno etc. xvii°, in forma qua per predictos fideles nostros capta fuit, cui appendent signa ipsius L., Oeni filii Griffin(i), Resi Crec, Edeneuet Vacha(n), Griffin(i) filii Retheric(i), videlicet quod quamdiu dicta treuga duraverit, omnes homines tam ex parte nostra quam ex parte ipsius L. redibunt ad propria et habebunt omnia tenementa sua mobilia et immobilia in pace, nec nos infra predictam treugam recipiemus inprisios vel homines ipsius L. vel suorum, nec idem L. recipiet inprisios vel homines nostros vel nostrorum. Homines vero utriusque partis interim remanebunt infra fines suos proprios conversantes. Fecimus etiam dilectos et fideles nostros magistrum A. de Swereford', archidiaconum Salop(ie), et Will(elmum) de Lascy iurare in animam nostram quod predictam treugam fideliter et firmiter tenebimus. In cuius etc. huic scripto sigillum nostrum apponi fecimus. Teste me ipso apud Westm' xxx die novembris.

ᵃ *sic in* B.

The date of the earlier truce, due to expire on 30 November 1231, whose extension was ratified by the king in this letter, is uncertain. Llywelyn had launched an attack on south Wales at the beginning of June 1231 that resulted in his excommunication and the preparation of Henry III's third campaign against him the following month, a campaign which consisted mainly of building a new stone castle at Painscastle, where the royal army remained from 30 July to 20 September (*HW*, ii. 673–6; Walker, 'Hubert de Burgh', 485–90). By 24 November the prince had agreed to negotiate, for a safe conduct was issued on that date for his envoys, Master Instructus and Master Philip, to appear in London (*PR 1225–32*, 452). As a result of the ensuing negotiations the king extended the truce to 30 November 1232. The previous truce had presumably been agreed after 30 September, when the king was still contemplating further military action against the Welsh (*CR 1227–31*, 600), and may well have been concluded at the royal council in London *c*.23–26 October 1231 (Vincent, *Peter des Roches*, 278). There appear to have been hopes of turning the subsequent truce of 30 November 1231 into a peace, for in late January 1232 a safe conduct, valid until the first Monday in Lent (1 March), was issued to the envoys Instructus and Philip for the purpose of negotiating a truce or peace between the king and Llywelyn (*PR 1225–32*, 460). However, if such negotiations took place, they were inconclusive. For further evidence of Master Alexander de Swereford's service to the king, see *CR 1227–31*, 57, 141, 467, 513, and cf. *PR 1225–32*, 457–8.

267 Agreement with Henry III

Notification by the king that Llywelyn has promised him to stand by the provisions of his chancellor Ralph, bishop of Chichester and Alexander, bishop of Coventry and Lichfield, Richard Marshal, earl of Pembroke, John de Lacy, earl of Lincoln and constable of Chester, Stephen Segrave, justiciar of England and Ralph fitz Nicholas, the king's seneschal, together with Ednyfed, Llywelyn's seneschal and his brother Goronwy, Einion Fychan and David the clerk, regarding amends due for all excesses by Llywelyn and his men against the king and his men and the restitution to the king and his men of all lands occupied by Llywelyn and the Welsh during the war; similarly regarding the receipt of amends from the king and his men for all the lands of Llywelyn and his men occupied by the king and his men; similarly regarding the assignation to Dafydd ap Llywelyn and his wife Isabella, eldest daughter and heiress of William de Braose, of her share of her father's lands; and regarding the refusal of money to the king as amends for the said excesses and the assignation of the said portion. Sufficient security has been given regarding their faithful service to the king and the keeping of peace with him and his kingdom of England, so that no loss or danger can arise therefrom to him and the kingdom. If, during the said provision, something new arises requiring amends, Llywelyn grants that it shall be amended by the said provisors. The king accepts their provision on behalf of himself and his men, just as Llywelyn has done on behalf of himself and his men. The king has had this letter patent made as evidence of this matter. Witnessed by the king.

Shrewsbury, 7 December 1232

B = TNA: PRO, C 66/43 (Pat. R. 17 Henry III), m. 9 (contemporary enrolment).
Pd. from B, *Foedera*, I. i. 208.
Cd., *CPR 1232–47*, 3–4; *H*, no. 353.

Rex omnibus etc. Sciatis quod cum L. princeps de Aberfr(au) et dominus Snauwdon' nobis concesserit et firmiter promiserit quod stabit provisioni venerabilum patrum R. Cicestr' episcopi et cancellarii nostri et A. Coventr' et Lychefeld' episcopi, et dilectorum et fidelium nostrorum R. Marsc' comitis Penbr', I. de Lacy comitis Linc' et constabularii Cestr(ie), S. de Seg(ra)ue iusticiarii nostri Angl(ie) et R. filii Nichol(ai) senescalli nostri, una cum Ideneuet senescallo ipsius L. et W(er)renoc fratre eius, Iniano Vachan' et David clerico quam ipsi facturi sunt super congruis emendis nobis faciendis de omnibus excessibus nobis et nostris ab eo et suis factis et de restitutione nobis et hominibus nostris facienda de omnibus terris et possessionibus nostris et nostrorum, per ipsum L. et Walenses occupatis, occasione werre inter nos et ipsum mote; similiter etiam de recipienda restitutione a nobis et nostris de omnibus terris ipsius L. et hominum suorum per nos et nostros occupatis occasione werre predicte; et de assignanda David filio ipsius L. et Ysab(e)lle uxori eius primogenite filie et heredi Will(elmi) de Breus' rationabili[a] portione ipsam Isab(e)llam contingenti[b] de terris que fuerunt predicti Will(elm)i patris sui; et de refusione pecunie nobis facienda pro predictis excessibus congrue[c] emendandis et portione predicta assignanda; provisa tamen super hoc ab eisdem sufficiente securitate de fideli servitio nobis prestando et de tranquillitate nobis et regno nostro Angl(ie) observanda, ita quod dampnum vel periculum nec nobis nec regno nostro inde possit evenire. Et si, pendente provisione predicta, aliquid de novo emerserit emendandum, idem L. voluerit et concesserit quod per predictos provisores emendetur. Nos provisionem eorundem, quam facturi `sunt super omnibus premissis, gratam habemus et acceptam pro nobis et nostris, sicut prefatus L. pro se et suis. Et in huius rei testimonium has litteras patentes nostras inde fieri fecimus. Teste me ipso apud Salop' vii die decembris anno regni nostri xvii°.

[a] rationabile B. | [b] contingente B. | [c] cogrue B.

For Llywelyn's negotiations with the king in 1232 see *HW*, ii. 676–7; Vincent, *Peter des Roches*, 328, 372. According to the Annals of Tewkesbury, a three-year truce was agreed on *c*.4 December between the king and prince (*AM*, i. 88). The present document presumably records Llywelyn's agreement to abide by the decisions of the arbitrators appointed under the terms of that truce, negotiated to replace the previous truce (no. 266 above) which expired on 30 November 1232.

268 Henry III

Letter, informing the king that, since his messengers could not reach him at present because of floods and dangers on the roads, he has sent this letter by a certain courier to say that Llywelyn has kept and will keep the peace with the king and all his men, and has ordered his bailiffs and adherents to keep peace with their fellow Marchers. Llywelyn therefore asks the king to order his bailiffs in the March to keep peace with Llywelyn's men, and to inform Llywelyn of his will.

[Shortly before 21 September 1233]

B = TNA: PRO, C 54/44 (Close R. 17 Hen. III), m. 3d (contemporary enrolment). Before the text is written: Litteras Lewelin' subscriptas recepit 'dominus rex xx° die septembris scilicet 'die Sancti Math(e)i apud Kedeministr'.
Pd. from B, *Foedera*, I. i. 210; from B, *CR 1231–4*, 323–4.
Cd., *H*, no. 354.

H. regi Angl(ie) etc. L. princeps de Abber', dominus Snaudon' salutem et se totum. Quoniam propter inundationes aquarum et viarum discrimina nuntii nostri in presentiarum ad vos accedere non possent per cursorem quendam presentes litteras vobis duximus destinare per quas maiestati vestre significamus quod nos pro nobis et nostris vobiscum et cum omnibus vestris pacem tenuimus et tenebimus in futurum, et hoc dedimus ballivis nostris et inprisiis in mandatis ut pacem cum suis commarchionibus firmiter teneant et observent. Quare vestram rogamus serenitatem quatinus ballivis vestris in Marchia commorantibus detis si placet in mandatis quod cum nostris pacem teneant inviolatam. Beneplacitum vestrum si placet nobis significetis. Valeat excellentia vestra.

The letter is datable from the rubric in the close roll which states that Henry received it at Kidderminster on the feast of St Matthew (21 September). The king also referred to the receipt of what is clearly the same letter when he wrote to the constable of Whitchurch (Shrops.) from Oddington (Gloucs.) on 25 September 1233 (*CR 1231–4*, 324–5). Lloyd cited the letter as evidence of Llywelyn's continuing willingness to negotiate with Henry in 1233 (*HW*, ii. 679 and n. 132). The wider context of the crown's efforts to prevent Llywelyn allying with the rebellious Richard Marshal is examined in Vincent, *Peter des Roches*, 400–2.

269 Agreement with Henry III

Notification by the king that he has confirmed the truce agreed at Brocton on Monday [6 March] by Bishops Alexander of Coventry and Henry of Rochester sent to Llywelyn and the Earl Marshal by Edmund, then elect, now archbishop, of Canterbury and his fellow bishops, between the king and his men on one side and Llywelyn and the Earl Marshal on the other, to run until the feast of St James [25 July] the same year. The king confirms that all shall possess during the truce as at the time it was agreed, and meanwhile those on either side may go and cultivate the lands and live on them. The lands shall be common for selling, buying and other contracts, and those wishing to engage in such transactions shall be free to enter and leave the lands, so that neither side may enter the other's lands with weapons or armed force. No new castles or fortresses may be built or repaired during the truce. Neither side may abandon or infringe the truce on account of an offence caused by anyone, but trespasses committed by either side during the truce shall be amended by those persons chosen before the archbishop at Shrewsbury on Tuesday [2 May] in the same year at the meeting to be held to make peace between the said prince and Marshal, so that up to the said date the truce between the king's side and Wales shall be firm. If a dispute arises regarding the possession of lands or men between the two sides, it shall be settled by the arbitration of the persons chosen before the archbishop in the aforesaid meeting.

[9 April 1234]

B = TNA: PRO, C 66/44 (Pat. R. 18 Henry III), m. 15 (contemporary enrolment).
Pd. from B, *RL*, i. 433–5.
Cd., *CPR 1232–47*, 43; *H*, no. 355.

Rex omnibus etc. salutem. Sciatis quod treugas captas apud Broc(er)ton' die lune ante cineres anno regni nostro xviii° per venerabiles patres A. Coventr' et H. Roff' episcopos, missos per venerabilem patrem E., tunc Cantuar' electum, nunc vero Cant' archiepiscopum, et coepiscopos suos ad L. principem de Abberfr(au) et comitem Marsc', duraturas usque ad festum Sancti Iacob(i) anno eodem, inter nos et nostros ex una parte et ipsos principem et comitem et inprisios et homines suos ex altera, concessimus gratas et ratas eas habentes: quas quidem ex parte nostra firmiter faciemus observari, ita quod quilibet possideat durantibus treugis sicut possedit in earum captione; et interim liceat ex utraque parte ire, agere, terras arare, seminare et alia necessaria ad culturam terrarum et habitationem facere. Et sint terre hinc inde communes ad venditionem et emptionem et alios contractus faciendos, et liber pateat ingressus et egressus et regressus huiusmodi emptiones, venditiones vel alios contractus facere volentibus, ita tamen quod neutri parti liceat partes aut terras alterius cum armis aut vi armata ingredi, set sine armis quilibet, et liber abeat, eat et redeat. Nec liceat hinc inde castra aut fortelesca de novo construere, vel dirruta reficere vel fulcire. Non liceat etiam alteri parti a treugis recedere vel treugas infringere propter offensam ab aliquo forte illatam, videlicet ut quandocumque contingit de quibusdam indomitis personis et incorrigibilibus, set emendentur excessus ex utraque parte perpetrati tempore treuge per illas personas que eligentur coram domino archiepiscopo, die martis proxima post clausum Pascha anno eodem apud Salopesbir', in tractatu quem ibi habiturus est cum dictis principe et Mariscallo de pace inter nos et ipsos formanda; ut sic usque ad prefatum terminum firme sint treuge inter potestates nostras et nostrorum et Wallia(m). Quilibet etiam, ut predictum est, ex utraque parte teneat et possideat quod habuit et tenuit tempore captionis treugarum istarum, ita tamen quod si contentio oriatur de possessionibus terrarum vel hominum inter nos et nostros ex una parte et dictos principem et comitem et homines et inprisios eorum, contentio illa terminetur secundum arbitrium predictarum personarum que eligentur coram dicto archiepiscopo in predicto tractatu, sicut predictum est.

Richard Marshal, earl of Pembroke (1231–4), began attacking lands in royal custody in the March of south Wales in the summer of 1233, leading a baronial campaign directed against the influence at Henry III's court of Peter des Roches, bishop of Winchester, and his nephew Peter des Riveaux (for these and subsequent events, see *HW*, ii. 678–80; Powicke, *Henry III*, i. 125–36; and esp. Vincent, *Peter des Roches*, 399–445). Llywelyn joined in the Marshal's campaign from mid-October of that year and the conflict continued in south Wales and along the Anglo-Welsh border into early February 1234, when Earl Richard left Wales to defend his Irish lands against royalist forces. Soon Henry succumbed to the pressure from his bishops, led by Edmund Rich (elected archbishop of Canterbury on 20 September 1233), to make peace as part of a wider programme of reform, and the Marshal and Llywelyn agreed to the truce set out in the present document at Brocton, probably near Bishop's Castle (Shrops.), or possibly near Worthen (Shrops.), on 6 March. The truce was provisionally ratified by the king after 11 March, when a safe conduct was issued to Llywelyn's envoys (*CPR 1232–47*, 41), but no later than 28 March, when the king informed his captains at Monmouth that a truce had been agreed to run until 30 April, and that he would make a further decision with his council at London on Sunday 9 April (*CR 1231–4*, 555). The present ratification presumably derives from that council, and is thus datable to 9 April (as implied in Vincent, *Peter des Roches*, 435; by contrast, Lawrence, *St Edmund*, 132, states that the truce received royal ratification on 12 April, but this seems to be based on the position of the text on the patent roll, where it is enrolled between documents dated 12 and 15 April, and the enrolment could have been made several days after the letter was issued). The document's reference to Edmund Rich as archbishop of Canterbury is consistent with a date of 9 April, for Edmund was consecrated the previous Sunday, 2 April. A final settlement was delayed, however, by the death of the Marshal in Ireland on 16 April from wounds received after he had been treacherously attacked on 1 April at a parley with his opponents on the Curragh of Kildare (Orpen, *Ireland under the Normans*, iii. 64–6). Despite the Marshal's death, however, the meeting scheduled for 2 May at Shrewsbury for the appointment of arbitrators to supervise the truce appears to have taken place (*pace* Lawrence, *St Edmund*, 137), as Archbishop Edmund was present at Shrewsbury on 2 May and on 20 May the king wrote to the three arbitrators from Herefordshire chosen by Llywelyn (Vincent, *Peter des Roches*, 442 and n. 56; *CR 1231–4*, 562). Further negotiations followed (ibid., 564–5), resulting in a new agreement on 21 June (no. 270 below).

270 Agreement with Henry III

Notification by the king that he has confirmed the truce made at Myddle by Edmund, archbishop of Canterbury, Henry, bishop of Rochester and Alexander, bishop of Coventry between the king and his men on one side and Llywelyn and his men and adherents, both Welsh and others he had at the beginning of the war of Richard Marshal, earl of Pembroke, on the other, on Wednesday after the feast of Holy Trinity [21 June 1234], to run for two years from the feast of St James [25 July]. Each side shall have the same tenements, lands, men and homages as at the beginning of the said war in any pleading over those tenements during the truce. If in the mean time any wrong is committed, amends shall be made by supervisors chosen from both sides, with the power of making amends according to the law and custom of the March, in a suitable place in the March, regarding the same seizures and trespasses within a term which the supervisors may think fit, the truce nevertheless remaining intact. No new castle shall be fortified or demolished castle restored in the March during the truce, and lands shall be common in accordance with the terms of the previous truce made by the aforesaid bishops of Rochester and Coventry at Brocton. Master John Blund, Henry of Audley, John Lestrange and Harvey Bagot have sworn on the king's behalf to observe the truce. Witnessed by the king.

Kempton, 7 July 1234

B = TNA: PRO, C 66/44 (Pat. Roll 18 Henry III), m. 9 (contemporary enrolment).
Cd., *CPR 1232–47*, 59.

Rex omnibus Cristi fidelibus presentes litteras inspecturis salutem. Sciatis quod concessimus et ratas habemus et gratas treugas captas apud Mudel inter nos et omnes homines nostros ex una parte per venerabiles patres E. Cant' archiepiscopum, totius Angl(ie) primatem, et H. Roffens' et A. Coventr' episcopos et L. principem de Aberfrau et dominum de Snaudon' et omnes homines suos et inprisios Walenses et alios si quos habuit in principio guerre que dicebatur guerra Ric(ardi) Mar', comitis Penbr' ex alia die mercurii proxima post festum Sancte Trinitatis anno regni nostri decimo octavo, duraturas a festo Sancti Iacobi apostoli anno eodem usque in duos annos completos a predicta die Sancti Iacobi apostoli, ita scilicet quod tam nos et nostri quam predictus L. et sui sint in eisdem tenementis, terris, hominibus et homagiis in quibus fuerunt in principio dicte guerre in aliqua inplacatione super eisdem tenementis durantibus treugis predictis. Et si quid interim fuerit forisfactum, emende fiant per correctores ad hoc ex utraque parte electos qui hanc potestatem faciendi emendas secundum legem et consuetudinem March(ie) in loco competenti in Marchia de eisdem forisfactis vel transgressionibus infra terminum quem dicti correctores viderint expedire, treugis nichilominus manentibus in sua firmitate per tempus predictum. Et nullum castrum novum firmetur vel dirrutum reficiatur in Marchia durantibus treugis et terre sint communes secundum formam treugarum alias captarum per predictos Roffen' et Coventr' episcopos apud Brocton. Iuraverunt autem hanc treugam ex parte nostra in animam nostram bona fide et sine malo ingenio fideliter observandam usque ad predictum terminum dilecti et fideles nostri magister I. Blundus, Henr(icus) de Aldithel', Ioh(ann)es Extraneus et Hervious[a] Bagod. Teste me ipso apud Keninton' vii° die iulii.

[a] *sic in* B.

The agreement made at Myddle (SJ 468 236) in Shropshire, mid-way between Llywelyn's manor of Ellesmere and Shrewsbury, extended the truce made earlier in the year at Brocton (no. 269 above). For the context and significance of the agreement see *HW*, ii. 681; Lawrence, *St Edmund*, 137–8; Stephenson, *Governance*, xxii; Carr, 'Anglo-Welsh relations', 130. Henry also cited most of the text of the agreement in a letter to Richard, earl of Cornwall and Poitou, dated at Westminster, 30 June 1234 (*CR 1231–4*, 568–9).

271 Agreement with Henry III

Notification by the king that he has confirmed the truce agreed at Tewkesbury on Friday the feast of St Benedict [11 July] 1236 by Edmund, archbishop of Canterbury, between the king and his adherents on one side and Llywelyn and his adherents on the other, to run for one year from the feast of St James [25 July]. Each side shall retain those lands, men and homages which they had when the truce was made, except that Earl Gilbert Marshal shall restore to Morgan of Caerleon the lands and goods which the earl occupied during the other truce between the king and Llywelyn. If lands, castles or other goods are seized in the mean time, and this seizure is manifest, the lands and castles shall be returned immediately without waiting for any correction by the supervisors of the truce. But amends shall be made by those supervisors for moveables thus seized, the truce nevertheless remaining intact; no pledges shall be taken for any breach of the truce regarding moveables nor for any dispute preceding the agreement of the truce, but rather amends made by the supervisors as stated above. No one shall receive into his power the adherents of the other side during the truce. No new castle shall be fortified or demolished castle restored in the March during the truce, and lands shall be common in accordance with the terms of the previous truce between the king and Llywelyn.

Henry of Audley, John Lestrange and Henry of Stafford have sworn on the king's behalf to observe the truce. Witnessed by the king.

Tewkesbury, 11 July 1236

B = TNA: PRO, C 66/46 (Pat. R. 20 Henry III), m. 5 (contemporary enrolment).
Pd. from B, Brady, *Complete History*, App., 182 (no. 158); from B, *Foedera*, I. i. 229–30.
Cd., *CPR 1232–47*, 153; *H*, no. 356.

Rex omnibus ad quos presentes littere pervenerint. Sciatis quod concessimus bona fide et sine malo ingenio et ratas habemus et gratas treugas captas apud Theokesbir(iam) die veneris in festo Sancti Bened(ic)ti anno regni nostro xx° per venerabilem patrem E. Cant' archiepiscopum inter nos et ʽomnes homines et inprisios nostros apertos ex una parte, et L. principem de Abbef(ra)u[a] et dominum de Snaudon' et omnes homines et inprisios suos apertos tam Walenses quam alios ex alia parte, duraturas a festo Sancti Iacob(i) anno eodem usque in unum annum completum; ita scilicet quod tam nos et nostri quam predictus L. et sui simus in eisdem terris et tenementis, hominibus et homagiis, in quibus fuimus predicto die captionis treugarum istarum, salva Morgano de Carleon' restitutione sua tam de terris quam de bonis et mobilibus suis, que comes G. Mar' occupaverat super eum infra treugas alias inter nos et ipsum L. ultimo captas. Si quid autem interim fuerit forisfactum, per captionem terrarum vel castrorum vel bonorum mobilium, et manifestum sit de captione terrarum vel castrorum illorum, terre et castra statim reddantur, non expectata aliqua correctione emendatorum treuge. Set de bonis mobilibus ita captis, per ipsos correctores fiant emende, treugis nihilominus durantibus in sua firmitate, in forma predicta, ita quod hinc inde nulla namia capiantur pro aliqua interceptione facta infra treugas istas de bonis mobilibus, nec pro aliqua contentione ante captionem huius treuge orta; set per ipsos correctores fiant ʽinde emende sicut predictum est. ʽNullus etiam receptet in potestate sua inprisios alterius durantibus treugis. Nullum etiam castrum novum firmetur in Marchia vel dirrutum reficiatur durantibus treugis; et terre sint communes secundum formam treugarum que ultimo capte fuerunt inter nos et ipsum L. Iuraverunt autem in animam nostram ex parte nostra hanc treugam bona fide et sine malo ingenio fideliter observandam, usque ad predictum terminum, dilecti et fideles nostri Henr(icus) de Aldithel', Ioh(ann)es Lest(ra)ng' et Hernic(us)[b] de Stafford'. In cuius etc. Teste me ipso apud Theok' xi die iulii anno regni nostri xx°.

[a] *sic in* B. | [b] *sic for* Henricus B.

This agreement extended for one year the truce agreed at Myddle on 21 June 1234 (no. 270 above). In addition it stipulated that Gilbert Marshal, earl of Pembroke (1234–41), should restore to Morgan ap Hywel of Caerleon what he had seized from him during the previous truce, possibly a reference to Gilbert's capture of Morgan's castle of Machen in 1236, which Gilbert then returned to Morgan for fear of Llywelyn (*BT, Pen 20Tr*, 104; *BT, RBH*, 234–5). For the background of the struggle between Morgan and the Marshals, who had occupied Caerleon since 1217, see *HW*, ii. 653, 674, n. 108, 701, n. 43 and nos 477–8 below.

272 Ynys Lannog Priory

Grant, for the salvation of the souls of himself and his ancestors, to the prior and canons of Ynys Lannog of all the abadaeth *of Penmon, with all its appurtenances as far as the township of Trecastell, free for ever from all secular service to Llywelyn and his heirs. Sealing clause; witnesses.*

Rhosyr, 10 April 1237

> B = TNA: PRO, C 53/81 (Ch. R. 23 Edward I), m. 2 (in an inspeximus, 4 May 1295).
> Pd. from B, *Mon. Ang.*, iv. 582; from *Mon. Ang.*, Jones, 'Mona mediaeva', 49 (trans. only).
> Cd., *CChR 1257–1300*, 459–60; Stephenson, *Governance*, 203; *H*, no. 140.

Omnibus sancte matris ecclesie filiis has litteras visuris vel audituris Lewelin(us) princeps `de Aberfrau, dominus Snaudon' salutem in domino. Noverit universitas vestra nos pro salute anime nostre et antecessorum nostrorum dedisse et concessisse et hac presenti carta nostra confirmasse priori et canonicis de Insula Glannauc, Deo et Beate Marie ibidem servientibus, totam *abbadaeth* de Penmo(n)n cum omnibus pertinentiis suis, in bosco, in plano, in pascuis, in pasturis, in viis, in semitis et in omnibus aliis asiamentis suis et cum omnibus terminis et finibus suis usque ad villam que vocatur Trefekastell', a nobis et heredibus nostris eisdem priori et canonicis et eorum sucessoribus libere et quiete ab omni servitio seculari perpetuo possidendam. Ut igitur hec nostra donatio in posterum robur optineat firmitatis, eam presenti scripto et sigilli nostri munimine fecimus roborari. Hiis testibus: Anniano et Ada fratribus de ordine predicatorum, Ennio parvo, Mareduth filio Iorueth, Heylin filio Kewrid', Madoco filio Purwyn, Mareduth filio David, David Machan, Howel filio Heylin, Ph(ilippo) filio Iuor, Iohanne notario nostro et multis aliis. Datum apud Rosuer quarto id' aprilis anno gratie millesimo ducentesimo xxx septimo. Valeat universitas vestra semper in domino.

For Llywelyn's grant to Ynys Lannog in 1221 see no. 250 above. The present grant marked the final phase in the endowment of the Augustinian priory, in which it received the lands, termed the *abadaeth*, formerly held by the church of Penmon, a major pre-Norman foundation on the mainland opposite Ynys Lannog (see *HW*, ii. 689, n. 206; Johns, 'Celtic monasteries', 24–5; and, for the term *abadaeth*, Pryce, *Native Law*, 186, 244). It is worth noting that the grant coincided with another act of religious patronage by Llywelyn nearby at Llan-faes, where the prince founded a Franciscan friary as a memorial to his wife Joan, who had recently died, probably in February 1237 (*BT, Pen20Tr*, 104; *BT, RBH*, 234–5; *HW*, ii. 686 and n. 183). The prince's connections with the mendicant orders are also revealed by the first two witnesses of the present charter, the Dominican friars Anian and Adam. Whether Anian was the same as the friar of that name who preached the crusade in west Wales in 1236 is uncertain (*AC*, 82; cf. Easterling, 'Friars in Wales', 330), and the same is true of both friars' institutional affiliation, for the Dominican friary at Bangor is not attested until 1251 and that of Rhuddlan until 1258 (Roberts, *Aspects of Welsh History*, 217–18). Rhosyr (SH 420 655) was a princely court in the commote of Menai, Anglesey, whose thirteenth-century layout has been uncovered by recent excavations (Johnstone, 'Investigation into the location', 59 (Fig. 5.3), 65–7; *idem*, 'Cae Llys, Rhosyr').

*273 Henry III

Letter, prolonging the truce with the king for one year from the feast of St James [25 July] 1237 to the feast of St James 1238.

[Shortly before 16 June 1237]

Mention only, in a memorandum following the enrolment of a letter from Henry III to Llywelyn dated at Westminster, 16 June 1237; the memorandum states that Llywelyn's letter was delivered to Brother Geoffrey on Tuesday 16 June (*CR 1234–7*, 536–7; cd., *H*, no. 469). The truce being renewed is clearly no. 271 above and in his letter to Llywelyn the king confirms the extension of it that had been negotiated by Thierry, prior of the Hospital of St John of Jerusalem in England; William de Ferrers, Amaury de Saint-Amand, Richard de Grey, Hugh de Vivonne and Hubert Hose had sworn to keep its terms on behalf of the king, certain *fideles* of Llywelyn on behalf of the prince. Henry says that he is sending Simon, the clerk whom Llywelyn had sent to the king, with a letter patent on the matter to Llywelyn (see below). Henry also thanks Llywelyn for having agreed to send his son Dafydd, along with certain *fideles*, to meet him at Worcester on 29 June, and explains that he has had to postpone the meeting until 1 August, saying that he will provide safe conducts at Shrewsbury on 25 July to accompany Dafydd and the others to the meeting. The royal letter patent referred to here must be that ratifying the extension of the truce, and naming those who had sworn to uphold it on the king's behalf, dated at Westminster, 14 June 1237 (TNA: PRO, C 66/47, m. 7; pd., *Foedera*, I. i. 232; cd., *CPR 1232–47*, 186).

274 Letter patent concerning the truce with Henry III

Confirmation of the extension of the truce agreed in the twentieth year of the king's reign between the king and his adherents on one side and Llywelyn and his adherents, both Welsh and others, on the other, from the feast of St James [25 July] 1238 for one year, in accordance with the terms of the previous truce, saving all agreements and articles contained in those terms. Ednyfed Fychan, Einion Fychan, Master David archdeacon of St Asaph and Philip ab Ifor have sworn on relics on Llywelyn's behalf faithfully to observe the extension of the truce, so that amends shall be made for trespasses and breaches of the truce as provided for in the previous truce. Sealing clause.

[c.8 July 1238]

B = TNA: PRO, C 66/48 (Pat. R. 22 Henry III), m. 4d (contemporary enrolment).
Pd. from B, *Foedera*, I. i. 236.
Cd., *CPR 1232–47*, 237; *H*, no. 357.

Omnibus Cristi fidelibus has litteras visuris vel audituris[a] Leulin(us) princeps de Aberfrau et dominus de Snaudon' salutem. Noverit universitas vestra nos prorogationem treugarum inter dominum H. illustrem regem Angl(ie), dominum Hyb(er)n(ie), ducem Norm(annie) et Aq(ui)t' et comitem And' et inprisios apertos et homines suos ex una parte, et nos et inprisios apertos et homines nostros tam Walle(n)ses quam alios ex altera parte, captarum anno regni ipsius xx duraturam a festo Sancti Iacobi apostoli anno regni ipsius xxii usque in unum annum completum, ratam et gratam habere, secundum formam predictarum treugarum ultimo captarum, salvis omnibus conventionibus et articulis in illa forma contentis. Ad cuius prorogationis treugarum confirmationem, tactis sacrosanctis, fecimus dilectos et fideles nostros Ydeneuet Vacha(n), Eyna(n) Vacha(n), magistrum David archidiaconum de Sancto Asaph et Ph(ilippu)m filium Yuor iurare in animam nostram, quod eandem treugarum prorogationem, cum omnibus conventionibus et articulis predictis, fideliter et sine malo ingenio pro nobis et nostris fidelibus et imprisiis observari faciemus a predicto festo Sancti Iacobi usque in unum annum completum, ita tamen quod propter illarum treugarum prorogationem, nichilominus super transgressionibus et interceptionibus infra[b] dictas treugas hinc inde perpetratis, vel de cetero perpetrandis, fiant emende secundum alias in predictis treugis provisam. In cuius rei testimonium[c] huic scripto sigillum nostrum duximus apponendum.

[a] B *inserts* salutem *erased.* | [b] *one minim too many at the beginning of the word* B. | [c] B *inserts* huc *struck through.*

This is a further extension of the truce agreed in 1236, already renewed in June 1237 (nos 271, 273 above). The royal letter patent ratifying this extension of the truce, and Henry's letter to Llywelyn rehearsing this ratification and urging the prince to observe its terms, are dated at Reading, 8 July 1238 (*Foedera*, I. i. 235–6; cd., *CPR 1232–47*, 225). For the wider context of relations between Llywelyn and Henry in 1238–40, see Williams, 'Succession to Gwynedd', 395–6. In the face of prohibitions by the crown in early March, Llywelyn had backed off from his plan to have the other Welsh princes do homage and fealty to his son Dafydd, and relations had improved sufficiently by 26 May for the king to issue a safe conduct for envoys sent by the prince to make peace (*CR 1237–42*, 123–5; *CPR 1232–47*, 221). However, as on previous occasions, no firm peace agreement was forthcoming, and instead the present extension of the existing truce was made. On 19 October 1238 the other Welsh princes swore only fealty to Dafydd at Strata Florida Abbey (*BT, Pen20Tr*, 104; *BT, RBH*, 234–5). In view of the loss of both the patent rolls for October 1238–October 1240 and the close rolls for October 1238–October 1239 (noticed by Williams, 'Succession to Gwynedd', 402 and n. 1), as well as the evidence for continuing good relations between Llywelyn and the king, it is likely that the truce was extended again in the summer of 1239.

'THE QUEEN OF NORTH WALES'
(*fl.* 1202)

*275 Gerald of Wales
Letter.

[Summer 1202]

Mention only, in a chapter heading (*Literae reginae Norwalliae Giraldo directae*) to Book III, c. 140 of Gerald of Wales's *De rebus a se gestis* (1208 × 1216) (*Gir. Camb. Op.*, i. 13). Since the text of Book III ends at c. 19, the chapter itself is lost and the contents of the letter are therefore unknown. To judge by its place in the list of chapter headings, the letter was sent to Gerald during his journey to Gwynedd in the summer of 1202 (cf. *Gir. Camb. Op.*, iii. 226). If this dating is correct, then the sender cannot have been Joan, whom Llywelyn married in probably the spring of 1205. The identification of 'the queen of North

Wales' with Tangwystl, mother of Llywelyn's son Gruffudd, is also unlikely, as she appears never to have been married to the prince (*HW*, ii. 686; see also the reference in *Survey of the Honour of Denbigh*, 128, to *cuidam amice sue nomine Tanguestel Goch*, and note to no. 253 above). One possible candidate is a sister of Ranulf III, earl of Chester, whom, to judge by a letter of Pope Innocent III of 17 February 1205, Llywelyn married about the end of 1192 after the king of Man and the Isles delayed in sending his daughter to be the prince's wife; unfortunately there is no other evidence for this marriage and the sister has not been identified (*Reg. Innocenz' III.*, vii. 385 (no. 220); Alexander, *Ranulf of Chester*, 3, 118, n. 14; Pryce, *Native Law*, 84–5). (The date of 1192 can be deduced from the chronology given in the papal letter for the subsequent betrothal and marriage to the Manx king's daughter by Llywelyn's uncle Rhodri ab Owain, who died in 1195.)

JOAN, LADY OF WALES
(d. February 1237)

*276 King John
Letter, warning him that, if he continued with his campaign against the Welsh, he would either be killed by his magnates or handed over to be destroyed by his enemies.

[Shortly before 14 August 1212]

Mention only, in the *Flores Historiarum* of Roger Wendover (d. 1236), followed by Matthew Paris (d. 1259) in his *Chronica Majora* and *Historia Anglorum* (Wendover, ii. 61–2; Paris, *CM*, ii. 534; *idem*, *HA*, ii. 128; cd., *H*, no. 464). According to Wendover, the king, on his arrival at Nottingham (14 August 1212), ordered the hanging of twenty-eight Welsh boys who had been given as hostages the previous year following Llywelyn's submission, in revenge for the Welsh uprising that had recently broken out. Then, just as John had sat down to dinner, two letters arrived, the first from the king of Scots (William the Lion), the second from Joan, both of which warned him that, if he continued with his campaign against the Welsh, he would either be killed by his magnates or handed over to his enemies. As a result of these warnings John abandoned his campaign and returned to London, where he demanded hostages from the magnates whose loyalty was suspect. (Of Matthew Paris's two accounts, that in the *Historia Anglorum* is closer in substance to Wendover's, as the *Chronica Majora* interpolates a clause asserting, inaccurately, that John initially disregarded the letters and proceeded to Chester, and only abandoned the campaign on receiving further warnings there.) That the king called off his Welsh campaign on account of a baronial conspiracy against him is well attested in both chronicle and record sources: although originally he had ordered his forces to gather at Chester on 19 August, news of the conspiracy led him to countermand these orders at Nottingham on 16 August, and he may already have taken the decision on 14 August (*Rot. Pat.*, 94a; cf. *Rot. Claus.*, i. 121a; see further Warren, *King John*, 199–200). The reliability of Wendover's story about Joan's letter is uncertain, as this detail is not corroborated by independent accounts of John's stay at Nottingham in August 1212. However, if the story is true, John received the letter at Nottingham on 14 August.

*277 King John

Petition, requesting the king to release Llywelyn's hostages Cynwrig, (?)Bleddyn (Bleum'), Tegwared and Merwydd.

[Shortly before 18 December 1214]

Mention only, in a letter patent of King John to Engelard de Cigogné, sheriff of Gloucester, dated at Monmouth, 18 December 1214 (*Rot. Pat.*, i. 125a; *Foedera*, I. i. 126; cd., *H*, no. 465). The king ordered de Cigogné to release the hostages to Llywelyn's envoy. In a letter close of the same date the king ordered the sheriff of Gloucester that, if he had demanded a customary payment from the Welsh hostages whom Joan had requested, he should take it; however, if they were living on alms they were to be quit of it (*Rot. Claus.*, i. 181b). Though neither letter explicitly states that Joan had written to the king, her petition was almost certainly presented in a letter. The role of the sheriff of Gloucestershire in the custody of the hostages may well indicate that they were held at Gloucester; the king ordered de Cigogné to release a prisoner captured at Carrickfergus (presumably during the Irish campaign of 1210) from Gloucester on 21 December 1214 (*Rot. Pat.*, 125b). It is likely that the hostages were among those delivered to John in fulfilment of the terms of Llywelyn's submission to the king in August 1211 (no. 233 above).

*278 King John

Petition(?), requesting the king to release Llywelyn's hostage Gwyn ap Iorwerth (Wyn filium Jorves).

[Shortly before 7 January 1215]

Mention only, in a letter patent of King John to William de Cantilupe dated at London, 7 January 1215 (*Rot. Pat.*, 126a). The king states that he is releasing Gwyn to 'our beloved daughter Joan, wife of Llywelyn' and orders de Cantilupe to hand Gwyn over to Llywelyn's clerk Osturcius, bearer of the letter. De Cantilupe was a steward of the royal household (Church, *Household Knights*, 9). Though there is no explicit reference to a petition, written or oral, the king's reference to Joan strongly suggests that she had requested the hostage's release, and it is very likely that she did so in a letter delivered by Osturcius. See also note to no. 277 above.

*279 Pope Honorius III

Petition, seeking dispensation from her illegitimate birth.

[*c*.March × -29 April 1226]

Mention only, in the pope's letter legitimizing Joan, dated at the Lateran, 29 April 1226 (Vatican City, Archivio Segreto, Reg. Vat. 13, fo. 122v, no. 252; cd., *Reg. Hon. III*, ii. 417–18 (no. 5906); *CPL*, i. 109). The pope explains that he is granting the petition so that Joan's defect of birth should not detract from the honour of her husband Llywelyn and her son (i.e. Dafydd), and that he is all the more willing to do so on account of Llywelyn's faith and devotion towards the Roman Church, but without any prejudice being caused thereby to the king of England. The legitimization of Joan served further to reinforce the legitimacy of her son Dafydd, whose position as Llywelyn's designated heir had been confirmed by Honorius III in response to a petition from Llywelyn four years earlier (no. 253 above).

280 Henry III

Letter, expressing her great sadness that her enemies, and indeed the king's too, sow discord between the king and Llywelyn. Assures the king of Llywelyn's affection for him, and warns him of the danger to her of losing true friends. Requests the king on bended knee to be reconciled with those who are bound to him by an inseparable bond of love, urging him to love his friends and harm his enemies. Assures him that it is most unjust of those encouraging him to be suspicious of Instructus, clerk of the king and Llywelyn, for she believes he has no more faithful clerk in England than him; he is no less faithful to the king if he faithfully carries out Llywelyn's business, for he acts just the same on the king's behalf before Llywelyn; neither the king nor anyone else could trust Instructus if was negligent in his lord's business.

[Probably 1230 × 1231]

A = TNA: PRO, SC 1/3, no. 188. No endorsements; approx. 163 × 55 mm.; mounted, foot cut away. The top left-hand corner of the parchment is missing.
Pd. from A, *RL*, i. 487–8; from *RL*, *Letters of Medieval Women*, ed. Crawford, 54 (trans. only).
Cd., *CAC*, 20; *H*, no. 340.

[Karis]simo suo domino et fratri suo karissimo H. Dei gratia regi Angl(ie), domino Hib(er)n(ie), duci Norm(annie) et Aquit' et comiti And' I. domina Wall(ie) salutem et se ipsam. Sciatis, domine, quod tanta anxietate contristor quod nequaquam possem exprimere, eo quod inimici nostri immo et vestri prevaluerunt seminare discordias inter vos et dominum meum. Super quo non minus doleo propter vos quam propter dominum meum, presertim cum sciam quam sincerum affectum habebat et adhuc habet dominus meus erga vos, et quam inutile sit nobis et periculosum, salva reverentia vestra, veros amicos amittere et inimicos pro amicis habere. Hinc est quod, tanquam flexis genibus et fusis lacrymis, vestram rogo maiestatem quatinus in melius mutare consilia velitis et eos qui inseparabili dilectionis vinculo coniunguntur vobis reconsiliare non omittatis, quo facilius possitis et discatis et amicos diligere et inimicos gravare. Ad hec sciatis, domine, quod iniustissime suggerunt vobis nonnulli suspicionem habere de Inst(ru)cto et vestro et domini mei clerico, quo non credo vos posse habere in Angl(ia) vobis fideliorem clericum, sic me Deus adiuvet; nec ideo minus fidelis est vobis, si fideliter agit negocia domini sui, quia eodem modo[a] se habet in agendis vestris coram domino suo; nec vos nec aliquis in ipso posset confidere, si domini sui tepide vel negligenter negocia tractaret. Si itaque in aliquo mihi credere velitis, in hoc mihi fidem adhibere velitis. Valete.

[a] A *inserts* facit *struck through.*

Edwards argued that this letter is difficult to date because it is written in such general terms, and therefore assigned it to the period between the agreement at Worcester in March 1218 and Joan's death in 1237 (*CAC*, 20). Stephenson noted, however, that Master Instructus is no longer attested in Llywelyn's service after 1231, and seems to have been replaced thereafter by Master David, archdeacon of St Asaph (*Governance*, 225). Another important clue to dating is provided by the style, 'Joan, Lady of Wales'. The royal chancery addressed Joan as 'Lady of North Wales' in April 1230, but recognized her title of 'Lady of Wales' by 8 November 1235 (no. 281 below). Although it is unknown when Joan first used the latter title, its adoption may well have been related to Llywelyn's change of title from 'Prince of North Wales' to 'Prince of Aberffraw and Lord of Snowdon', a change which probably occurred in 1230 (see above, pp. 76–8). If so, this could indicate a *terminus a quo* for the letter of 1231, when Joan was released from the imprisonment imposed by her husband following the discovery of her affair with William de Braose at Easter 1230 (cf. no. 261 above; *HW*, ii. 685). It is in any case unlikely to be earlier than 1230. Taken together with the evidence relating to Instructus, the letter may well be datable, then, to 1230 × 1231, perhaps to 1231.

*281 Henry III
Petition, requesting the king to grant a pardon to Robert son of Reginald for the death of William son of Ralph of (?) Credenhill (Credenshull).

[Shortly before 8 November 1235]

Mention only, in a letter patent of Henry III granting the request dated at Daventry, 8 November 1235 (cd., *CPR 1232–47*, 130; *H*, no. 468). The letter names the petitioner as the 'Lady of Wales'. The use of this title reinforces the likelihood that the petition had been received in written form, even though no document is explicitly referred to. *Credenshull* may probably be identified as Credenhill in Herefordshire (compare the forms *Credenhull* 1291, *Cradenhulle* 1301 and *Credenhulle* 1303 cited in Bannister, *Place-Names of Herefordshire*, 53).

GRUFFUDD AP LLYWELYN
(d. 1 March 1244)

282 Strata Marcella Abbey
Grant, for the salvation of his soul in perpetual alms, without any claim, demand or secular custom, of the whole land of Hafod Owain, namely from the black dyke to the Yfyrnwy, thence to Nant Eryr, from that brook to its source, thence to Bôn y Maen Melin [Twmpath Melyn], thence to Rhydyfoch, thence via the summit of the mountain to Nanhanog [Nant Glanhanog], thence from its source to its mouth, namely Pwll Llydan; from the other side towards the river Iaen from the aforesaid black dyke in a circuit to the brook called Hwrdd [Nant y Capel], and thence to the Iaen. A further grant of common pasture throughout the land between Hafod Owain and Rhiw Maen Gwyn in breadth, and up to Derwen in length. A further grant of the land called Pennant Iaen and Cwm y Calch as set out in the charter of Gwenwynwyn, and the land below the brook called Nant Ddu to its source, thence via the summit of the mountain to Carnedd-wen. A further grant of Rhos y Garreg and Pennant Cynlling, from the source of Nant yr Ysgoliau [Nant Taren-Fedw Ddu] to the Dulas, thence to the mouth of the Dengi and thence to the source of the Dengi; similarly of the land between Dulas and Nant yr Ysgoliau as set out in the charter between the monks and the heirs of that land. A further grant of Cefn

Coch; likewise all the land between the Corf [Nant Coro] and the Einion, so that no other monks shall have any use, right of common or possession there except those of Strata Marcella. Gruffudd has granted all the aforesaid bounds and gifts pertaining to Cyfeiliog as set out in the charters of Gwenwynwyn to be possessed fully, honourably and peacefully. A further grant of Y Dugoed with all its bounds and appurtenances towards Cyfeiliog as the monks held them in the time of Gwenwynwyn, freely and quietly in perpetual possession. Dating clause; witnesses.

1226

A = NLW, Wynnstay Estate Records, Ystrad Marchell Charters, no. 68. Early modern endorsements; approx. 199 × 216 + 17 mm.; two central horizontal slits, one just above the fold, the other in the fold, for a tag (*c.*16 mm. wide) which exits through a slit in the base of the fold; sealed on tag. Seal missing.

Pd. from A, Jones *et al.*, 'Five Strata Marcella charters', 53–4; from A, *Ystrad Marchell Charters*, no. 68; from A, Jones, 'Abbey of Ystrad Marchell', 316–17 (trans. only).

Cd., Davies, 'Strata Marcella documents', 187 (no. 34); Stephenson, *Governance*, 202; *H*, no. 135.

Universis Cristi fidelibus ad quos presens pervenerit scriptum notum sit quod ego Grifinus filius Lewelini principis Norwallie concessi, dedi et confirmavi Deo et Beate Marie et monachis de St(ra)tmarchell pro salute anime mee in puram et perpetuam elemosinam, libere et quiete, sine omni reclamatione et exactione vel consuetudine seculari totam terram que vocatur Hawoth Owen cum omnibus terminis suis et pertinenciis, scilicet a fossa nigra in directum usque ad Evernow, inde usque ad Nant Ereyre, ille vero rivulus usque ad eius ortum, inde usque ad Bon Emaynmelin, inde directe usque ad Rithewohc, inde per summitatem montis usque ad Nanhanuac, inde ab eius ortu ubi oritur de subter salicibus usque ad eius exitum scilicet Puhlledan; ex altera vero parte versus fluvium qui vocatur Yhaen a predicta fossa nigra per circuitum usque ad rivulum qui vocatur Hurht, et Hurht usque ad Yhaen. Dedi insuper illis communionem pasturarum per totam terram illam que est inter Hawoht Oweyn et Riw Mayn Guin in latum, in longum vero usque ad Derwen. Dedi etiam illis terram que vocatur Pennant Yeweinc et Cu(m) Kalaht sicut melius testantur carte domini Wenunwin, terram illam etiam que est infra rivulum qui vocatur Nantu usque ad eius ortum, inde per summitatem montis usque ad Carnehtwen. Dedi similiter et terras illas, scilicet Ros Ekarrec, cum omnibus terminis suis et pertinenciis, et Pennant Kenhlling in his terminis, scilicet ab ortu rivuli qui vocatur Nant Eskoleyv prout ducit usque ad Dulas, Dulas usque ad *aber* Dengi, Dengi vero susum usque ad eius ortum; similiter terram illam que est inter Dulas et Nant Eskolev sicut melius testatur carta illa quam habent dicti monachi inter se et heredes predicte terre. Dedi etiam illis Keuenchoch cum terminis suis et pertinenciis. Eodem modo dedi predictis monachis totam terram que est inter Corfh et Enniaun, ita quod nulli alii monachi habeant in ea aliquem usum vel communionem aliquam vel proprietatem exceptis illis monachis de Stratmarchell. Omnes vero terminos predictos et donationes que pertinent ad Keveyliavc dedi illis sicut melius inde testantur carte domini Wenunwin plene et honorifice in omni pace possidendas. Dedi quoque illis Edugoeht cum omnibus terminis suis et pertinenciis versus Keueyliauc prout melius et liberius tenuerunt tempore domini Wenunwin, libere et quiete in perpetuam possessionem. Facta est autem hec mea donatio anno ab incarnatione domini m° cc° xx° vi°. His testibus: T. videlicet et I. monachis de St(ra)tmarchell, D., K. et M. conversis eiusdem domus; de secularibus vero, Grifino filio Rodri, Blehtint filio Meuric, Meylir Du, T. et M. filiis

Moruran, G. filio Daniel', G. filio Maredut, Goronvvy filio David, Huhcdreth Crutheur et multis aliis.

The grant of the land between the Corf and the Einion to the monks of Strata Marcella alone contradicted the terms of Gwenwynwyn's earlier grant (no. 563 below), which reserved the pastures of this land to Cwm-hir. The statutes of the Cistercian General Chapter show that Cwm-hir was in dispute with Strata Marcella in 1225, and the chapter appointed arbitrators in 1226 who settled this dispute, which also involved Cwmbuga, at Radnor on 15 July 1227: that part of the land between the Corf and the Einion lying in Ceredigion was adjudged to Cwm-hir, that in Cyfeiliog to Strata Marcella (*Ystrad Marchell Charters*, 23–4 and no. 70). It appears, then, that Strata Marcella obtained Gruffudd's confirmation of these lands in order to support its case in this dispute (Banks, 'Notes', 208). For the original grants by Gwenwynwyn of the lands confirmed by Gruffudd see *Ystrad Marchell Charters*, 125, referring to nos 541, 560, 562–3 and (probably) 565 below. The first two lay witnesses, Gruffudd ap Rhodri and Bleddyn ap Meurig, were associated with members of the Gwynedd dynasty on other occasions (*Ystrad Marchell Charters*, 59, 69; Stephenson, 'Politics of Powys Wenwynwyn', 46). For the identification of the Corf as Nant Coro or Corog, which flows north from Carn Bwlch-coro past Llechwedd-einion to join the Llyfnant at Glasbwll, see Morgan, 'Territorial Divisions [II]', 24.

283 Strata Marcella Abbey

Grant of all the land of Rhoswydol with all its bounds and appurtenances as set out in the charter of Gwenwynwyn. A similar grant of all the right of Dafydd Gohwe Fychan concerning that land, after he had granted all his right in Rhoswydol in the hand of Terence, monk of Strata Marcella, for two pounds which he accepted for his right by the arbitration of six trust-worthy men of Cyfeiliog; and since they had no seal Dafydd's gift has been confirmed with Gruffudd's seal. A further grant of all the donations . . . throughout Cyfeiliog as granted by his predecessor Gwenwynwyn, peacefully, without any claim, demand or secular custom. Sealing clause; witnesses. If another person should contravene the charter, Gruffudd warrants all the lands and liberties contained in it against all mortals

1246 [*recte* 1225 × -15 July 1227; probably 1226]

B = NLW MS 1641B, ii, pp. 92, 94 (s. xviii/xix).
Pd. from B, *Ystrad Marchell Charters*, no. 69.
Cd., *H*, no. 146.

Noverint tam presentes quam futuri quod ego Griffinus filius Liwelini principis[a] Norwallie dedi monachis de Stradmarchell . . .[b] totam terram que vocatur Roswidaul cum omnibus terminis et pertinentiis suis sicut melius testatur carta Wennunwen super eandem terram. Eodem modo dedi predictis monachis et concessi totum ius David cognominati Gohwe Bichan de predicta terra, ipso prius dante et concedente totum ius quod habebat de Roswidaul in manu Terentii monachi de Stradmarchell pro duabus libris quas per arbitrium sex virorum fide dignorum de Keveliauc pro iure suo accepit . . .[b] Et quia[c] sigillum non habebant predicti David donationem meo sigillo confirmavi et roboravi. Dedi insuper predictis monachis omnes donationes . . .[b] per totam terram de Keveiliauc sicut melius donavit antecessor meus Wenunnwen, bene et pacifice, sine aliqua reclamatione et exactione et consuetudine seculari. Et ut ista mea donatio et pacis forma inter me et dilectos monachos de Stradmarchell et viros de Keveliauc maneat inviolabiliter inconcussa hanc paginam mee donationis tam meo sigillo quam bonorum virorum testimonio munivi et roboravi. Anno ab incarnatione domini [d]-millesimo ducentesimo quadragesimo-[d] sexto. His testibus: H. de Alba Domo, P. de Stradfflur, M. de Valle[d] Crucis abbatibus, I. priore de Abercon(wy), T. et I. monachis de Stradmarchel, D. et K. conversis de Pola . . .[b] Eodem modo si persona altera ab ista carta recesserit omnes etiam terminos et donationes et libertates in hac carta contentas ego dominus Grifinus dictus contra omnes mortales teneor warantizare.

[a] princeps B. | [b] *passages omitted* B. | [c] qui B. | [d-d] milessimo ducentessimo quadragessimo B. [e] Valla B.

Although the charter is dated 1246, this must be a copyist's error (probably already found in the exemplar used by B's scribe, Walter Davies), as Gruffudd died on 1 March 1244. Thomas suggests that the charter was dated 1226 and was issued in the same year as no. 282 above (*Ystrad Marchell Charters*, 26–7). This is very likely, as 'MCCXXVI' could have been mistranscribed as 'MCCXLVI' at some stage before Walter Davies copied B. In any case, the witness list indicates a date range of 1225 × 1227. The 'P.' named as abbot of Strata Florida presumably succeeded Cedifor, the abbot of that house who died in 1225 (*BT, Pen20Tr*, 100; *BT, RBH*, 226–7); as (presumably the same) 'P.' was abbot of Strata Florida in July 1227, he cannot have been Cedifor's predecessor (*Ystrad Marchell Charters*, no. 70). The presence of 'M.' as abbot of Valle Crucis shows that the charter was issued before 15 July 1227, when the abbot of Valle Crucis was called 'T.' (ibid.). As 'T.' remained abbot of Valle Crucis until at least 1234 (no. 509 below), this rules out a date between 15 July 1227 and Gruffudd's imprisonment by Llywelyn in 1228 (*BT, Pen20Tr*, 103; *BT, RBH*, 232–3). It is worth adding that the monks 'I.' and 'T.' and the *conversi* 'D.' and 'K.' also appear as witnesses to Gruffudd's charter of 1226 (no. 282 above). Though not unequivocally ruled out by any of the witnesses, the period between Gruffudd's release in 1234 and the seizure of Cyfeiliog and his other lands in Powys by Dafydd ap Llywelyn after 19 October 1238 (*BT, Pen20Tr*, 104; *BT, RBH*, 234–5) is extremely unlikely, since Gruffudd refers to his father by the title *princeps Norwallie* rather than 'prince of Aberffraw and lord of Snowdon', the title Llywelyn had adopted by then; the new title is referred to in a confirmation charter of Dafydd ap Llywelyn in 1238 × 1240 (no. 289 below). If the dating proposed here is correct, then, the charter reinforces the testimony of no. 282 above that Gruffudd held lands in Cyfeiliog in the period between his loss through confiscation of Meirionnydd and Ardudwy in 1221 and his imprisonment in 1228 (*Ystrad Marchell Charters*, 26). For Gwenwynwyn's grants of Rhoswydol see nos 552–4 below. As well as confirming these past grants, the present charter confirms what appears to have been a contemporary grant by Dafydd *Gohwe* Fychan of his right in Rhoswydol, for which he received 2 pounds from the monks as agreed through the arbitration of six men of Cyfeiliog.

SENANA, WIFE OF GRUFFUDD AP LLYWELYN
(d. after 11 July 1252)

284 Agreement with Henry III

Agreement between the king on one side and Senana, wife of Gruffudd ap Llywelyn – whom his brother Dafydd holds in prison – together with her son Owain, on the other: Senana undertakes on behalf of Gruffudd to give the king 600 marks to free Gruffudd and his son Owain, so that it shall be judged in the king's court whether he should be imprisoned, and that thereafter the king's court shall make a judgement for him and his heirs according to Welsh law concerning their portion of the patrimony of Llywelyn, Gruffudd's father, which Dafydd has withheld from Gruffudd. If Gruffudd and his heirs recover by the judgement of the king's court the portion that they say is theirs of the aforesaid patrimony, Senana undertakes on behalf of Gruffudd and his heirs that they shall pay 300 marks per annum for it to the king and his heirs, namely one third in coin, one third in oxen and cattle, and one third in horses, according to the valuation of lawful men, to be handed over at Shrewsbury to the sheriff of Shropshire, and by him to the royal exchequer, namely one half at Michaelmas and the other at Easter. Senana also undertakes on behalf of Gruffudd and his heirs that they will maintain a firm peace with Dafydd concerning the portion remaining to Dafydd of the said patrimony; and that if any Welsh rebel against the king or his heirs, Gruffudd and his heirs will compel them to make satisfaction. To ensure that all the above terms are observed, Senana will give the king her sons Dafydd and Rhodri as hostages, on condition that, if Gruffudd and Owain should die before they are released, one of the aforesaid sons of Senana shall be restored to her. Senana has sworn on the Gospels on behalf of herself and Gruffudd and his heirs that they will observe all these terms, and has undertaken that Gruffudd will swear the same when he has been released. She has submitted herself in Gruffudd's name concerning the above to the jurisdiction of the bishops of Hereford and Coventry, so that the bishops, at the king's request, shall force them to observe all the terms through excommunication and interdict. Senana has undertaken to ensure that all the terms are implemented and that, after his release, Gruffudd and his heirs will confirm them and give their written instrument to the king in the aforesaid terms. This document has been drawn up as further security, so that Senana has affixed her husband's seal on the part remaining with the king and the king's seal has been affixed on the part remaining with her. Senana has given the following pledges in Gruffudd's name: Ralph Mortimer, Walter Clifford, Roger of Mold, seneschal of Chester, Maelgwn ap Maelgwn, Maredudd ap Rhobert, Gruffudd ap Madog of Bromfield and his brothers Hywel and Maredudd and Gruffudd ap Gwenwynwyn; these have undertaken all the above terms on Senana's behalf and given their charters to the king concerning them.

Shrewsbury, 12 August 1241

B = TNA: PRO, C 53/34 (Ch. R. 25 Henry III), m. 3d (contemporary enrolment).
C = Cambridge, Corpus Christi College MS 16, fo. 172r–v. s. xiii med.
D = TNA: PRO, E 36/274 (Liber A), fo. 345r–v. s. xiii ex.
Pd. from B, Brady, *Complete History*, App., 194–5 (no. 167); from B (?or Brady), Wynne, *History of Wales*, 355–7; from C, *Matthaei Paris . . . Historia*, ed. Parker, 840–1; from C, Paris, *CM*, iv. 316–18; from D, *LW*, 52–3 (no. 78); from Parker, *Matthaei Paris . . . Historia*, ed. Wats, 624–5; from (?)Brady or Wynne, Warrington, *History of Wales*, App., 600–1.
Cd., *CChR 1226–57*, 262–3 (from B); *H*, no. 362.

[a]-Sciant presentes et futuri quod ita-[a] convenit inter dominum H.[b] regem Angl(ie) illustrem ex una parte et Senanam[c] uxorem Griffini filii L.[d] quondam principis Norwall(ie) quem D(avi)d frater eius tenet carceri mancipatum cum Oweyn[e] filio suo nomine eiusdem Griffini[f] ex altera, scilicet quod predicta Senana[g] manucepit pro predicto Griffino[h] viro suo quod dabit domino regi dc[i] marcas ut[j] rex eum et predictum Oweyn[k] filium suum liberari faciat a carcere predicto, ita quod stabit iudicio curie sue si de iure debeat carcere detineri, et ut[j] rex postea iudicium[l] curie sue secundum legem Walens(em)[m] ei et heredibus suis habere faciat[n] super portione que eum contingit de hereditate que fuit predicti L. patris sui, et quam predictus D(avi)d [o]-ipsi Griffino deforciat,-[o] ita quod si idem Griffinus[h] et[p] heredes sui per considerationem curie domini regis recuperent portionem quam se dicunt contingere de hereditate predicta, eadem Senana manucepit pro predicto Griffino[q] et heredibus suis quod ipse et heredes sui imperpetuum inde reddent domino regi [a]-et heredibus suis-[a] ccc[r] marcas annuas, scilicet tertiam partem in denariis et tertiam partem in bobus et vaccis et tertiam partem in equis per estimationem legalium hominum liberandas[s] vicecomiti [t]-Salop' apud Salop'-[t] et per manum ipsius vicecomitis ad scaccarium[u] regis deferendas[v] et ibidem liberandas,[s] scilicet unam medietatem ad festum Sancti Mich(aelis) et [w]-aliam medietatem-[w] ad Pascham.[x] Eadem etiam Senana[g] manucepit[y] pro predicto Griffino[h] viro suo et heredibus suis[z] quod firmam pacem tenebunt cum prefato David[aa] super portione que eidem David remanebit de hereditate predicta. Manucepit etiam eadem Senana[ab] pro prefato[ac] Griffino[q] et heredibus suis[ad] quod si aliquis Walens(is) aliquo tempore[ae] regi vel heredibus suis rebellis extiterit[af] prefatus Griffinus[h] et heredes sui ad custum suum proprium ipsum conpellent ad satisfaciendum domino regi et heredibus suis. Et de hiis omnibus supradictis firmiter observandis dicta Senana[ab] dabit domino regi David et Rothery[ag] filios suos obsides, ita tamen quod si de prefato Griffino[q] et Oweyno[k] filio suo qui cum eo est in carcere[ah] humanitus contingat antequam inde deliberentur,[ai] alter predictorum filiorum eidem Senane[ab] reddetur reliquo obside remanente. Iuravit insuper eadem Senana[ab] tactis sacrosanctis ewangeliis pro se et[aj] prefato Griffino[q] et heredibus suis quod hec omnia firmiter observabunt, et manucepit quod prefatus[ak] Griffinus[al] idem[am] iurabit cum a carcere liberatus fuerit. Et super premissis se submisit nomine dicti Griffini[an] iurisdictioni[ao] Hereford' et Coventr'[ap] episcoporum, ita quod prefati episcopi vel [aq]-alter eorum-[aq] quem dominus rex elegerit ad requisitionem ipsius[v] regis per sentientias excommunicationis in personas et interdicti in terras eos[ar] coherceant[as] ad predicta omnia et singula observanda. Hec omnia manucepit predicta Senana[ab] et bona fide promisit se facturam et curaturam quod omnia impleantur et quod prefatus Griffinus[al] cum liberatus fuerit et heredes sui hec omnia grata habebunt et conplebunt et instrumentum suum inde dabunt domino regi in forma predicta. Ad maiorem siquidem huius rei securitatem factum est hoc scriptum inter ipsum dominum regem et prefatam[at] Senanam[ab] nomine prefati Griffini[h] viri sui ita quod parti remanenti penes ipsum dominum regem appositum est sigillum prefati Griffini[h] per manum prefate[au] Senane[ab] uxoris sue una cum sigillo ipsius[av] Senane,[ab] et parti remanenti penes ipsam Senanam[ab] nomine prefati Griffini[an] appositum est sigillum ipsius[aw] domini regis. De supradictis etiam omnibus conplendis et firmiter observandis dedit predicta Senana[ab] nomine prefati Griffini[an] domino regi plegios subscriptos,[ax] videlicet Rad(ulfu)m de Mortuo Mari, Walt(erum) de[ay] Clifford', Rog(erum) de Mo(n)te Alto senescallum Cestr(ie), Mailgu(n) filium Maylgu(n),[az] Mereduc[ba] filium Rob(erti), Griffin(um) filium Maddok[bb] de Brumfeld, Howel et Mereduk[bc] fratres eius, Griffin(um) filium Wennu(n)wen,[bd] qui hec omnia pro prefata Senana[ab] manuceperunt, et cartas suas ipsi

domino regi inde fecerunt. Actum^{be} apud Salop'^{bf} die lune proxima ante assumptionem Beate Mar(ie) anno regni^{bg bh}–ipsius^v regis^{–bh} xxv.^{bi}

^{a–a} *omitted* C. | ^b H(enricu)m C. | ^c Senenam C. | ^d Leolini C. | ^e Owenio C; Oweno D. | ^f Griffrini C. | ^g Senena C. | ^h G. C. | ⁱ secentas C; sexcentas D. | ^j CD *insert* dominus. | ^k O. C. | ^l iudicio B. ^m Wal(e)nsiu(m) C. | ⁿ facit C. | ^{o–o} deforciat ipsi Griffino C. | ^p vel C. | ^q G. viro suo C; Griffino viro suo D. | ^r trecentas C; trescentas D. | ^s liberandum C. | ^{t–t} Salopesb' C. | ^u CD *insert* domini. ^v deferendum C. | ^{w–w} alteram C. | ^x Pascha C. | ^y *omitted* C. | ^z C *inserts* manucepit. | ^{aa} CD *insert* fratre suo. | ^{ab} S. C. | ^{ac} dicto C. | ^{ad} B *inserts* quod *struck through.* | ^{ae} CD *insert* domino. | ^{af} fuerit C. | ^{ag} Rothury C; Rather' D. | ^{ah} B *inserts* hamanitus *struck through.* | ^{ai} liberentur CD. | ^{aj} C *inserts* pro. | ^{ak} dictus C. | ^{al} CD *insert* vir suus. | ^{am} eidem D. | ^{an} G. viri sui C; Griffini viri sui D. | ^{ao} CD *insert* venerabilium patrum. | ^{ap} Lichefeld' C. | ^{aq–aq} eorum alter CD. | ^{ar} eorum B. | ^{as} choerceant C. | ^{at} dictam C; predictam D. | ^{au} dicte C. | ^{av} predicte C. | ^{aw} *omitted* C. | ^{ax} superscriptos C. ^{ay} *omitted* D. | ^{az} Mailgun CD. | ^{ba} Mereduk D. | ^{bb} Maddoc C. | ^{bc} Mereduc C. | ^{bd} Wenu(n)wen' D. | ^{be} Acta C. | ^{bf} Saleposb' C. | ^{bg} *omitted* B; *supplied from* CD. | ^{bh–bh} regis ipsius C. | ^{bi} vicesimo quinto D.

Senana had tried to persuade Henry III to secure her husband's release early in May 1241 (*CRR*, xvi, no. 1595: *a die Pasce in quincque septimanas*). The present agreement was reached while the king was mustering his forces at Shrewsbury to attack Dafydd ap Llywelyn. Its significance, especially the threat posed through its envisaging a division of Gwynedd between Gruffudd and Dafydd, is assessed in Williams, 'Succession to Gwynedd', 399–400, and Smith, *Llywelyn*, 32–3, 37–9. For the charters issued by Ralph Mortimer, Roger of Mold, Walter Clifford and Hywel ap Madog see *LW*, 19–20, 35 (nos 17, 18, 51) and no. 523 below; the charters of the other pledges named are not extant (others are calendared as nos 21 and 65 above and nos 512, 521, 593 below). After Henry had defeated Dafydd in August 1241 Gruffudd was taken from captivity in Cricieth castle to the Tower of London, where he died from a fall while attempting to escape on 1 March 1244 (Smith, *Llywelyn*, 35 and n. 122, 39–40, 47–8). His youngest sons Rhodri and Dafydd were held as hostages at Chester, 1242–5 (ibid., 73, n. 145). Senana is last attested on 11 July 1252, when she witnessed a judgement in Llŷn between the ecclesiastical communities of Bardsey and Aberdaron made before her son Dafydd (no. 440 below).

DAFYDD AP LLYWELYN
(d. 25 February 1246)

*285 Gwenllian de Lacy
Confirmation of Llywelyn ap Iorwerth's grant of four manors: Aberchwiler (Aberwhyler)*, Penbedw* (Penpedow)*, Estradmelened' and Trewowr with their appurtenances.*

[*c.*1225 × -5 May 1241]

Mention only, in a record of a case *coram rege* at Westminster, 5 May 1241, brought by Gwenllian, widow of William de Lacy, against Dafydd ap Llywelyn for recovery of the manors (*CRR*, xvi, no. 1596; for the date see ibid., xxxix). Llywelyn's grant is datable to *c*.1222 × -28 July 1224; Gwenllian was Dafydd's half-sister: see no. 236 above. As the court record merely states that *eadem Wentyliana confirmacionem ejusdem David habet*, the date of the confirmation is unknown, although as Dafydd was born after August 1211 it was probably issued at a later date than his father's charter.

286 Ynys Lannog Priory

Confirmation, inspired by piety, of the gift by his father Llywelyn of all the township of Bancenyn with all its appurtenances, as freely as Llywelyn has granted it. Sealing clause; witnesses; valediction.

Ynys Lannog, 22 February 1229

B = TNA: PRO, C 53/81 (Ch. R. 23 Edward I), m. 2 (in an inspeximus, 4 May 1295).
Pd. from B, *Mon. Ang.*, iv. 582; from *Mon. Ang.*, Jones, 'Mona Mediaeva', 49 (trans. only).
Cd., *CChR 1257–1300*, 459; Stephenson, *Governance*, 202; *H*, no. 136.

Universis Cristi fidelibus has litteras visuris vel audituris David filius domini L. principis salutem in domino. Noverit universitas vestra nos divine pietatis intuitu donationem domini L. patris nostri super tota villa de Bagenig' cum omnibus pertinentiis suis dilectis nostris priori et canonicis de Insula Glannauc concessisse et presenti carta nostra confirmasse, prout melius et liberius dominus L. pater noster eisdem contulit et concessit. In huius rei testimonium has litteras nostras patentes sigilli nostri munimine fecimus roborari. Hiis testibus: Mared filio Rikardi, Ririd filio Kadugaun, L. filio Griffud, Karuet filio Tuder, Leuelino filio Rikardi, Lewelino filio Mared', David[a] filio Eniaun, Ennio notario nostro et multis aliis. Actum apud Insulam Glanauc anno gratie m° cc° vicesimo nono in die Cathedre Sancti Petri. Valeat universitas vestra semper in domino.

[a] Daud B.

This is a confirmation of no. 250 above. The first witness, Maredudd ap Rhicert (Richard) was possibly a son of Rhicert ap Cadwaladr ap Gruffudd (Stephenson, *Governance*, 148–51; see also notes to nos 197 and 258 above).

*287 Strata Marcella Abbey

Grant and confirmation of all the lands and pastures that they had from the kin of Bleddrws around the grange of Llyn-y-gadair (Lhinnegadeir) and around the vaccary of Cwmhesgin (Cumhesgin) with all their appurtenances.

[1230 × 11 April 1240]

Summary only, in an inspeximus of Edward II dated at Tutbury, 12 March 1322 (Jones, 'Abbey of Ystrad Marchell', 313–14; *Ystrad Marchell Charters*, no. 75; cd., *CChR 1300–26*, 440; *H*, no. 164). As the inspeximus styles Dafydd *filius Lewelini principis de Abberfrau*, the charter is unlikely to have been issued before 1230 or after Dafydd's accession following his father's death on 11 April 1240 (cf. no. 289 below). Thomas suggested a date range of 1229 × 1235 on the strength of the summary's place in the inspeximus (*Ystrad Marchell Charters*, 29). The lands granted were located in Penllyn (ibid., 126; Williams, *Atlas*, 60).

288 Ynys Lannog Priory

Confirmation of the gift of Penmon by his father Llywelyn, in accordance with the terms of Llywelyn's charter concerning that land. Sealing clause.

Cemais, 21 February 1238

> B = TNA: PRO, C 53/81 (Ch. R. 23 Edward I), m. 2 (in an inspeximus, 4 May 1295).
> Pd. from B, *Mon. Ang.*, iv. 582.
> Cd., *CChR 1257–1300*, 460; Stephenson, *Governance*, 203; *H*, no. 141.

Omnibus has litteras visuris vel audituris David filius ʻdomini Lewelini salutem in domino. Noverit universitas vestra nos hac presenti carta nostra confirmasse canonicis de Insula Glannauc donationem domini L. patris nostri super terra de Penmon, secundum tenorem carte quam dominus L. fieri fecit eisdem super terra predicta. In cuius rei testimonium sigillum nostrum huic scripto duximus apponendum. Datum apud Kemeys die dominica prima in quadragesima anno incarnationis dominice millesimo ccᵒ tricesimo octavo.

This is a confirmation of no. 272 above.

289 St Michael's church, Trefeglwys and the canons of Haughmond Abbey

Grant and confirmation of all the lands which Hywel ab Ieuaf and Madog ap Maredudd granted in perpetual alms with all their appurtenances and easements as set out in the charters of Hywel and Madog. Witnesses.

[19 October 1238 × 11 April 1240]

> B = Shrewsbury, Shropshire Records and Research Centre MS 6001/6869 (Haughmond Cartulary), fo. 215r. s. xv ex.
> Pd. from B, *Cart. Haugh.*, no. 1217.
> Cd., *H*, no. 142.

Omnibus Cristi fidelibus has litteras visuris vel audituris David filius domini Lewelini principis de Aberfrau,[a] domini Snaud' salutem in domino. Noverit universitas vestra nos concessisse et confirmasse Deo et ecclesie Beati Mich(ael)is de Treueglus et omnibus canonicis de Haghmon' ibidem Deo servientibus omnes terras quas Howel filius Ieuaf et Maduc filius Maredith eis in perpetuam elemosinam contulerunt cum omnibus pertinentiis suis et eisiamentis in bosco et plano et in omnibus aliis locis prout melius et liberius in cartis dictorum Howel et Maduc continetur. In huius rei testimonium has litteras nostras patentes eis dedimus. Hiis testibus: domino Ririt Bangoren(si) episcopo etc.

[a] Aberfiau B.

Dafydd's style strongly suggests that the document was issued before his father's death on 11 April 1240, as Dafydd adopted the title *princeps Norwallie* after his accession and seems no longer to have referred to his father as 'prince of Aberffraw and lord of Snowdon' (*pace Cart. Haugh.*, no. 1217 n., which dates the charter to between Dafydd's accession and Gruffudd ap Gwenwynwyn's recovery of Powys in August 1241). The witnessing by Richard, bishop of Bangor (here referred to, uniquely, by a Welsh name, Rhirid) provides a *terminus a quo* of 1237, the year of his consecration, and Stephenson was surely correct in suggesting that the charter was issued after Gruffudd ap Llywelyn was driven from southern Powys by Dafydd following the latter's receipt of fealty from the Welsh lords at Strata Florida on 19 October 1238 (Stephenson, *Governance*, 203; *BT, Pen20Tr*, 104; *BT, RBH*, 234–5). For the grants of Hywel and Madog see nos 1–3 above and no. 480 below.

*290 Tudur ap Madog
Grant of land in Pennant Gwernogon.
            [11 April 1240 × 25 February 1246; possibly April 1244 × 25 February 1246]

Mention only, in an inquisition before William Grandison and Robert Staundon at Caernarfon, 13 June 1289 (cd., *CIM*, i, no. 1468; *H*, no. 163). The inquisition found that Gruffudd ap Tudur and his brother had greater right in certain lands in Pennant *Gwernogon*, by hereditary right after the death of their father Tudur ap Madog, and by seisin, than Philip, prior of Beddgelert, on account of a grant of Dafydd ap Llywelyn, then prince of Wales. If Dafydd was styled 'prince of Wales' in the charter, this would narrow the date range to the last two years of his reign when he assumed this title (see nos 307–8 below, and cf. Stephenson, *Governance*, 221, which dates the grant to 1245 × 1246). Tudur has been identified as an important servant of both Dafydd ap Llywelyn and Llywelyn ap Gruffudd who received grants of hereditary tenurial privileges on Anglesey (ibid., 98–100, 132, 221). Although it is not clear whether Pennant *Gwernogon* was part of, or synonymous with, the township of Pennant immediately west of Beddgelert, it presumably lay near the priory (ibid., 132, n. 164; cf. Gresham, *Eifionydd*, 3–5).

291 Agreement with Henry III
Agreement between the king and Dafydd concerning the homage that Dafydd was offering to the king for his right in North Wales and concerning the lands which the king's barons, namely Gruffudd ap Gwenwynwyn and others, were seeking from Dafydd as their rights, except for the land of Mold, which, in accordance with the document recently made at Gruffudd's Cross [(?)Gresford] (apud crucem Griffini) *by the king's seneschals, for the present is excepted from the arbitration, and saving any right the seneschal of Chester may have in that land. The king has taken Dafydd's homage for his right of North Wales; both the king on behalf and with the consent of the aforesaid barons and Dafydd on behalf of himself, his men and his heirs have submitted themselves concerning all the aforesaid lands to the arbitration of the papal legate Otto, the bishops of Worcester and Norwich, Richard, earl of Cornwall and John of Monmouth on the king's side and the bishop of St Asaph, Ednyfed Fychan and Einion Fychan on Dafydd's side, so that each side will accept and observe for ever the arbitration of all or the majority of these. William de Cantilupe has sworn on behalf of the king, and Dafydd has sworn his own corporal oath, to observe these terms faithfully and they have also submitted themselves to the jurisdiction of the aforesaid legate as long as he holds his legatine office in England, so that he may coerce a party contravening the aforesaid terms by ecclesiastical censure either to observe the aforesaid arbitration or to make amends for its breach; however, Dafydd or his men may be legitimately convicted if they contravene the aforesaid terms before they have come before the legate or others whom he deputizes in a place in the Marches that is safe for Dafydd and his men, if they have been summoned, and if they have been summoned*

legitimately and fail to come, they will be considered contumacious unless they have a reasonable or sufficient impediment. After the legate's term of office has ended the parties have likewise submitted themselves to the jurisdiction of the archbishop of Canterbury and his successors. All the homages of the barons of Wales are quit to the king and his heirs by this peace, and all arsons, homicides and other evils committed by both English or Welsh are remitted, so that each side may be fully reconciled, saving any right that Dafydd may have in other lands. If any of the aforesaid arbitrators dies before this arbitration is completed, or is unable to be present at the arbitration owing to a reasonable impediment, a substitute shall be found who is not suspect to either party. The bishop of St Asaph, Ednyfed, Einion and Gruffudd ap Rhodri swear to observe the aforesaid terms and to ensure as far as they are able that they are observed by Dafydd and his men. As a further security this document has been drawn up in the form of a chirograph, so that the seals of Dafydd, the bishop of St Asaph, Ednyfed, Einion and Gruffudd are affixed to the part remaining with the king, and the king's seal is affixed to the part remaining with Dafydd. Witnesses.

Gloucester, 15 May 1240

B = TNA: PRO, C 54/50 (Close R. 24 Henry III), m. 4d in schedule (enrolled 1240).

C = TNA: PRO, E 36/274 (Liber A), fos 328v–329r. s. xiii ex.

Pd. from B, Brady, *Complete History*, App., 190–2 (no. 163); from B, *CR 1237–42*, 240–1; from C, *Foedera*, I. i. 239–40; from C, *LW*, 5–6 (no. 2); from (?)Brady, Wynne, *History of Wales*, 350–2; from an early edition of *Foedera*, Warrington, *History of Wales*, 596–7; from *Foedera*, Bridgeman, 'Princes of upper Powys', 112–13.

Cd., *H*, no. 358.

Sciant presentes et futuri quod ita convenit inter dominum H.ᵃ⁻regem Angl(ie) illustrem⁻ᵃ ex una parte et David'ᵇ filium Lewelyn' quondam principis Norwall(ie) et domini de Abberfrauᶜ altera apud Glouc' die martis proxima ante festum Sancti Dunstani anno regni ipsius regis vicesimo quarto de homagio ipsius David' quod ipse offerebat eidem domino regi pro iure suo Norwall(ie) et de terris quas barones ipsius domini regis, scilicet Griffin(us) filius Wenunwanᵈ et alii baronesᵉ domini regis, petebant versus ipsum David ut iura sua, excepta terra de Monte Alto secundum quod continetur in scripto nuper confecto apud Cruce(m) Griffin(i) per senescallos domini regis que ad presens excipitur ab arbitrio, salvo tamen in posterum iure senescalli Cestr(ie) in terra illa si quod habet, scilicet quod predictus dominus rex cepit homagium prefati David' de predicto iure suo Norwall(ie) et quod tam idem dominus rex pro prefatis baronibus suis de consensu eorundem quam prefatus David pro se et suis et heredibus eorum super omnibus terris predictis se submiserunt arbitrio venerabilium patrum O.ᶠ Sancti Nich(olai) in carcere Tull(iano) diaconi cardinalis etᵍ apostolice sedis legati, Wigorn(ensis) et Norwic(ensis) episcoporum, et nobilis viri R. comitis Pyctav(ie)ʰ et Cornub(ie) fratris ipsius domini regis, et Ioh(ann)is de Monem' ex parte ipsius domini regis et venerabilis patris episcopi de Sanctiⁱ Asaph, Idineuetʲ Vaghan,ᵏ et Eyngnan Vaghan ex parte prefati David, ita quod quomodocumque ab ipsis omnibus vel a maiori parte eorundem super premissis fuerit arbitratum utraque pars ipsorum stabit arbitrio et illud in perpetuo firmiter observabit. Et ad hec fideliter et sine fraude servandaˡ Will(elmus) de Cantelupoᵐ de preceptoⁿ regis iuravit in animam ipsiusⁿ regis, et idem David in propria persona sua corporale prestitit sacramentum, et insuper se submiserunt iurisdictioni et ordinationiᵒ prefati domini legati quamdiu in Angl(ia) legationis fungatur officio, ut partem contra premissa venientem per censuram ecclesiasticam modis omnibus quibus melius viderit expedire tam ad predictum arbitrium observandum quam ad transgressionem contra illud perpetratam emendandam valeat cohercere, ordine iuris observato, dum tamen idem David vel sui si forsitan contra predicta venire presumpserint prius coram dicto domino legato vel aliquibus aliis ad hoc ab ipso deputandis et partibus merito non suspectis in confinio March'p loco eidem David' et suis tuto legitime convincantur si ad hoc vocati venerint, vel si legitime vocati non venerint pro contumacibus habeantur nisi rationabile et sufficiens habeant impedimentum. Finitoq vero predicte legationis officio sub forma prescripta cohercioni et iurisdictioni domini Cant(uariensis) archiepiscopi et successorum suorum et ecclesie Cant(uariensis) se partes predicte submiserunt. Et sciendum quod per hanc pacem remanent domino regi et heredibus suis omnia homagia baronum Wall(ie) quieta, et remittuntur omnia incendia, homicidia et alia mala tam ex parte Anglicor(um) quam Walens(ium) perpetrata, ita quod ad invicem plene reconcilientur, salvo prefato David' iure suo si quod habet in aliis terris. Et si forte aliquis predictorum arbitrorum ante hoc arbitrium completum in fata decesserit,r vel per impedimentum rationabile predicto arbitrio faciendo non possit interesse, alius loco suo substituetur qui neutri partium merito suspectus habeatur. Ad hec prefati episcopus de Sancto Assaph,s Ideneuet et Igna(n) et Griffin(us) filius Rotherich' prestiterunt sacramentum quod quantum in eis est predicta fideliter observabunt et ab ipso David et suis modis omnibus quibus poterunt facient observari. Ad maiorem autem huius rei securitatem factum est hoc scriptum inter ipsos regem et David in modum cyrographi, ita quod parti remanenti penes ipsum dominum regem appositum est sigillum ipsius David' una cum sigillis predictorum episcopi de Sancto Assaph',s Ideneuet, Ignan et Griff(ini), et parti penes ipsum David' remanenti appositum est sigillum domini regis. Hiis testibus: venerabilibus patribus O. Sancti Nich(olai) in carcere Tull(iano) diacono cardinalik apostolice sedis legato, W. Ebor(acensi) archiepiscopo, W. Karl(eolensi), W. Wigorn(ensi) et W. Norwic(ensi) episcopis, R. comite Pict(avie) et Cornub(ie) fratre domini regis, venerabili patre episcopo de Sancto Assapho,s W. de Cantelupo,e Amaur't de Sancto Amando senescallis nostris, Ioh(ann)e Ex(tra)neo, Edenewetu Vachan, v-Ignan Vachan,-v Griff(ino) filio Retherich', David archidiacono de Sancto Assaph's et aliis.

a-a illustrem regem Anglie C. | b Dauit C. | c Aberfrau C. | d Wenunweny C. | e C *inserts* ipsius C.
f C *inserts* Dei gratia. | g *omitted* C. | h Pictavie C. | i Sancto B. | j Ideneuet C. | k C *inserts* et.
l observanda C. | m Cantilupo C. | n C *inserts* domini. | o cohercioni C. | p Marcarum C. | q finite
B. | r concesserit C. | s Asaph C. | t umaurico C. | u Edeneuet C. | v-v *omitted* B.

According to the Annals of Tewkesbury, Dafydd attended the royal council at Gloucester in May 1240 wearing the coronet 'which is called the *garlonde*, the insignia of the principality of North Wales' and submitted to the king, who both knighted him and invested him with 'all the land which his father held by right' (*AM*, i. 115). That Dafydd was so ready to settle for royal recognition of his title to Gwynedd, and thus apparently to relinquish the wider hegemony in Wales established by Llywelyn ap Iorwerth, reflected the challenge to his succession mounted within Gwynedd by his half-brother Gruffudd, who, according to Matthew Paris, waged war against Dafydd from Llywelyn's death until his capture and imprisonment in Cricieth castle at about the end of September 1240 (see Williams, 'Succession to Gwynedd', 397, 401–8, 411; Smith, *Llywelyn*, 29–32). For the term 'Welsh barons', used to stress the equality of all Welsh lords under the crown, see Carr, 'Aristocracy in decline', 104–5. Otto, cardinal deacon of St Nicholas in carcere Tulliano, held the office of legate *a latere* in England, Wales and Ireland from 12 February 1237 until January 1241, and had arrived in England in mid-July 1237 (*Councils and Synods*, II. i. 237). It is uncertain whether the bishop of St Asaph was Hugh/Hywel I (1235–40) or Hugh/Hywel II (1240–7) (cf. Stephenson, *Governance*, 169). For the identification of *crux Griffini* as Gresford see note to no. 371 below.

292 Basingwerk Abbey

Grant and confirmation, for the love of God and the salvation of the souls of himself and his father Llywelyn and his mother Joan and all his heirs, in pure and perpetual alms, of all the gifts and liberties which his father Llywelyn and his other predecessors granted to the monastery to be held for ever, free of all earthly service and secular exaction, as freely as any other alms, with all their appurtenances as set out in the present document: namely, the site of the abbey with the mills before the gate; the land before the gates given by Ranulf and his brother Eneas; the land which Maredudd Wawor *had in and outside the township of Holywell and the land which his brother, (?) Uchdryd* (Huttredus) *exchanged in the same township for his share of land in Whitford; the grange of Fulbrook with all its appurtenances and easements and the common pasture of the mountains; the church of Holywell with the chapel of Coleshill and all its other appurtenances, so that the monks may have them for their own use for ever; the land and pasture of Gelli given by his father with all its appurtenances and easements as set out more fully in the charter concerning these. A quitclaim for ever of toll throughout his land and sea on all the monks' sales and purchases. A further grant of two thirds of the tithes of fish caught in the fisheries of Rhuddlan together with the tithe of his share of the fish; the whole of Gwernhefin with all the men of that township and its appurtenances, granted by Owain Brogyntyn; Elise's confirmation of that gift; the lands and pastures in Penllyn given by his father Llywelyn, as set out in the latter's charter. Dafydd and his heirs will warrant all the aforesaid tenements to the monks against all men for ever. Sealing clause; witnesses.*

Coleshill, 25 July 1240

> B = TNA: PRO, C 53/73 (Ch. R. 13 Edward I), m. 25 (in an inspeximus, 12 June 1285).
> C = TNA: PRO, C 53/116 (Ch. R. 3 Edward III), m. 26 (in an inspeximus of B, 17 February 1329).
> D = TNA: PRO, C 53/164 (Ch. R. 15–17 Richard II), m. 16 (in an inspeximus of C, 2 December 1393).
> Pd. from D, *Mon. Ang.*, v. 263; from *Mon. Ang.*, H. L. J. J. W., 'Basingwerk abbey', 107–8 (trans. only).
> Cd., *CChR 1257–1300*, 291 (from B); *CChR 1327–41*, 100 (from C); *CChR 1341–1417*, 342 (from D); Stephenson, *Governance*, 203; *H*, no. 143.

David filius Lewelini princeps Northwall(ie) omnibus sancte matris ecclesie filiis tam presentibus quam futuris in Cristo salutem. Noverit universitas vestra quod ego David filius Leuelini, pro amore Dei et pro salute anime mee et pro animabus patris mei domini Leuel(ini) et matris mei domine Io(ann)e et pro animabus omnium heredum meorum, concedo et presenti carta confirmo Deo et Sancte Marie et monasterio de Basingwerc monachisque ibidem Deo servientibus, in puram et perpetuam elemosinam, omnes donationes et libertates quas pater meus dominus Leuelinus et alii antecessores mei prefato monasterio pro suis animabus contulerunt, tenendas imperpetuum et habendas, liberas et quietas ab omni terreno servitio et exactione seculari, sicut aliqua elemosina liberius et plenius possideri potest, cum omnibus pertinentiis suis de quibus in presenti scripto quedam placet exprimere et nominare: scilicet locum illum in quo abbatia illorum fundata est cum molendinis que iuxta portam abbatie habent; terram que ante fores eorum iacet quam Ranulphus et Enias frater eius predictis monachis dederunt; terram etiam quam Meredit Wawor in villa de Haliwelle et extra villam habuit, et terram quam Huttredus frater eius secum escambiavit in ipsa villa pro sua parte terre in Quitfordia; et grangiam illorum que apellatur Fulebrock' cum omnibus pertinentiis et aisiamentis suis et communitatem pasture montium cum ceteris; ecclesiam quoque de Haliwelle cum capella de Colsul et cum omnibus aliis pertinentiis suis, ut eas habeant in proprios usus imperpetuum integre possidendas; terram etiam et pasturam de Gethli quam habent ex donatione patris mei cum omnibus pertinentiis et aisiamentis suis per metas et divisas que in carta quam inde habent plenius continetur. Insuper quietum clamavi eis imperpetuum tolnetum totius terre mee possesse et possidende marisque possessi et possidendi in omnibus rebus vendendis et emendis ad opus ibidem Deo servientium. Preterea concessi eis et confirmavi duas partes decime piscium qui in piscariis de Rothelan capiuntur cum illa decima piscium mee partis quos homines capiunt in aqua; item ex dono Howen de Porkinton' totum Wenhewin cum omnibus hominibus eiusdem ville et cum pertinentiis; confirmationem quoque Helyse super eadem donatione; ex donatione vero domini Leuelini patris mei terras et pasturas in Penthlin per metas et divisas que nominantur in carta patris mei quam inde habent. Et ego David et heredes mei hec omnia prefata tenementa ipsis monachis contra omnes homines imperpetuum warantizabimus. Unde ut° hec mea concessio et confirmatio stabiles et inconcusse permaneant presens scriptum sigilli mei appositione roboravi. Hiis testibus: Hugone episcopo de Sancto Assaf, Edeneweth Vakan, magistro David tunc cancellario, Ennio Vakan, Gronou filio Kenewreik, Heylin' filio Kenrith', Ph(ilipp)o filio Ywor, Madoco filio Purewenn', Wronou filio Seisel et multis aliis. Dat' apud Colshull anno domini m° cc° quadragesimo in die Sancti Iacobi apostoli.

Two of the grants by Llywelyn ap Iorwerth in Tegeingl survive independently (nos 213, 216 above), as does Owain Brogyntyn's grant of Gwernhefin in Penllyn (no. 492 below). The confirmation of Owain's grant by Elise ap Madog (no. 486 below) is not extant, and the same is true of Llywelyn's grants of Gelli and of lands and pastures in Penllyn (nos 215, 224 above). The present confirmation differs from no. 213 through its inclusion of land held by (?)Uchdryd (*Huttredus*), and from no. 216 by naming the chapel of Coleshill among the appurtenances of the church of Holywell; the chapel may have been attached to the court of the lords of Tegeingl at Coleshill (Lloyd, 'Edward I and the county of Flint', 20). The charter also includes two new grants by Dafydd: quittance of toll throughout his land, and tithes of fish at Rhuddlan. Whether Hugh, bishop of St Asaph, was the first or second bishop of that name is uncertain (see note to no. 291 above).

*293 Henry III

Letter(?), informing the king that the arbitration between Dafydd and Roger of Mold has been postponed as the legate has sent no one to represent him.

[Shortly before 5 October 1240]

Mention only, in a letter from Henry to Dafydd dated at Westminster, 5 October 1240 (*CR 1237–42*, 243). Although Henry's letter makes no explicit reference to receiving a letter from Dafydd, stating only that the prince had informed the king of the matter in question (*Quia significastis nobis quod* . . .), it is very likely that this message was conveyed in writing. In his letter the king replied that the legate (Otto) would send either the prior of Wenlock or the abbot of Combermere to represent him at Kinnerton on 19 October and, since he wished the arbitration to go ahead as agreed, the king was sending the justice of Chester in his place and Henry of Audeley in that of Earl Richard of Cornwall. The arbitration had been agreed to by Dafydd at Gloucester in May 1240 (no. 291 above); however, from the autumn of 1240, with his rival Gruffudd ap Llywelyn imprisoned in Cricieth castle, the prince seems to have welcomed any opportunity to delay proceedings (see Williams, 'Succession to Gwynedd', 399).

294 Pope Gregory IX

Letter, expressing his confidence that the kingdom of England is bound to the pope by special affection, whereby the pope is obliged to provide both for the exaltation of the English Church and for the utility of the king and kingdom when the opportunity arises. Therefore Dafydd prays that, since Boniface, procurator of the church of Belley, uncle of the king, has been unanimously elected to the church of Canterbury and the king and whole kingdom of England need his counsel greatly, the pope will consider the danger that could threaten the orphan son and heir of the king should the king die and confirm the election of Boniface, so that the status of the king and English kingdom should be preserved more securely and on account of this Dafydd may be rendered more devoted to the pope and the Roman Church.

[February × August 1241]

B = TNA: PRO, E 36/274 (Liber A), fo. 334v. s. xiii ex.
Pd. from B, *LW*, 20–1 (no. 20).
Cd., *H*, no. 361.

Sanctissimo in Cristo patri G. Dei gratia summo pontifici David princeps Norwall(ie) nepos domini regis Angl(ie) salutem et tam devotam quam debitam tanto patri cum honore reverentiam. De paternitatis vestre dilectione optinemus fiduciam specialem quod inter cetera mundi regna dilectionis affectione specialis vobis regnum Angl(ie) astringatur, quapropter tam exaltationi ecclesie Anglicane quam utilitati regis et regni diligenter providere tenemini tempore opportuno. Hinc est quod cum vir venerabilis Bonofacius procurator Boliacon(ensis) ecclesie avunculus domini nostri regis Angl(ie) ad regimen Cantuar(iensis) ecclesie unanimiter et concorditer vocatus fuerit divina gratia disponente et dominus noster rex et totum regnum Angl(ie) ipsius consilio non modicum indigeant, paternitati vestre supplicandum duximus cum affectum quatinus diligenter considerantes si placet quod si humanitus de domino rege contingeret, quod Deus avertat, periculum quod de filio suo pupillo et herede posset facilius iminere, electionem factam de predicto Bonofacio in ecclesia memorata vestra dignetur clementia confirmare, ut status prefati domini nostri regis Angl(ie) et regni Anglicani melius et securius conservetur, et nos vobis ob hoc et ecclesie Romane devotiores merito reddere debeatis. Valeat in domino semper vestra sancta paternitas.

Boniface of Savoy, procurator of Belley, about 40 miles east of Lyon, and an uncle of Henry III's queen Eleanor of Provence, was elected archbishop of Canterbury on 1 February 1241 following the death of Archbishop Edmund Rich on 16 November 1240. As Edwards argued (*LW*, 21), the present letter was probably sent soon after Boniface's election, and in any case no later than news had reached Britain of Gregory IX's death on 21 August 1241. Matthew Paris alleged that Henry III went to considerable lengths in order to try and secure papal recognition of Boniface's election, reporting that the king compelled the bishops and abbots of England to append their seals to a letter praising 'beyond measure' the personal attributes of the archbishop-elect (Paris, *CM*, iv. 104–5). Dafydd's letter may bear witness to similar pressure. Boniface, one of the queen's numerous Savoyard uncles who enjoyed considerable influence at Henry's court in the period 1236–41, was eventually confirmed as archbishop by Innocent IV in September 1243 and consecrated by him at Lyons on 15 January 1245; however, he was not enthroned at Canterbury until 1 November 1249 (Powicke, *Henry III*, i. 361; Stacey, *Politics, Policy, and Finance*, 181–2).

*295 Henry III

Letter, informing the king that he has sent three of his men in his place to Worcester with respect to the arbitration.

[Shortly before 10 × 14 February 1241]

Mention only, in a letter from Henry to Dafydd dated at Woodstock, 19 February 1241 (*CR 1237–42*, 350). In his letter Henry recalled that he had requested Dafydd to provide arbitrators in place of those originally chosen who had gone overseas, in accordance with the terms of their agreement, and to proceed with the arbitration concerning the portion of Dafydd's inheritance pertaining to his wife and the claims of Roger of Mold and others. Of the three envoys announced by Dafydd only one had appeared at Worcester, without power to negotiate on the prince's behalf; the king therefore commanded Dafydd to appear at Shrewsbury on the Sunday before Palm Sunday (17 March 1241) or else to send proctors with full power to act on his behalf. As Henry was present at Worcester by 10 February and was still there on 14 February, presumably the envoy arrived during that period and Dafydd's letter was written shortly before then; the king was at Hereford on 8 February and at Evesham on 15 February and reached Woodstock by 16 February (*CR 1237–42*, 272–4; *CPR 1232–47*, 244–5). See further note to no. 293 above.

296 The magnates of Henry III

Letter, explaining that, since he has been prevented by various matters from appearing before them at Shrewsbury on the Sunday before Palm Sunday to reply to the king's barons who accuse him according to the royal mandate sent to him, he has sent his faithful men Master David his chancellor, Goronwy ap Cynwrig and Einion Fychan, bearers of the present letter, as his proctors with respect to all that pertains to him, in accordance with the peace agreement between the king and himself, in order to satisfy all according to the justice and reason in the aforesaid agreement and to receive amends for him and the portion of his inheritance pertaining to his wife. He will ratify whatever these proctors do justly with respect to the aforesaid business. Sealing clause.

[19 February × 17 March 1241]

B = TNA: PRO, E 36/274 (Liber A), fo. 334r–v. s. xiii ex. Rubric: De pace facienda inter Anglicos et Wallenses.
Pd. from B, *LW*, 20 (no. 19).
Cd., *H*, no. 359.

[V]iris venerabilibus et dilectis amicis suis magnatibus domini regis has litteras inspecturis David princeps Norwall(ie) cum dilectione salutem. Quoniam variis prepediti negotiis hac instanti die dominica ante Ramos Palmarum coram vobis apud Salop' personaliter interesse non possimus ad respondendum baronibus domini regis qui nos impetunt secundum formam mandati domini regis nobis ad hoc directi, ideo dilectos et fideles nostros magistrum David cancellarium nostrum, Goronuy filium Kenwric, Annianu(m) Parvum latores presentium duximus ad vos destinare, constituentes eosdem procuratores nostros in omnibus que ad nos pertineant, secundum formam pacis inter dominum regem et nos alias [fo. 334v] reformate, ad satisfaciendum omnibus secundum iustitiam et rationem in forma pacis predicte, et ad recipiendum nobis emendas et portionem de hered-itate sua uxorem nostram contingentem, ratum etiam et gratum erimus habituri quicquid predicti fideles nostri super prefato negotio dictis die et loco duxerint faciendum, iustitia mediante. In cuius rei testimonium sigillum nostrum huic scripto fecimus apponi. Valete.

As Edwards argued (*LW*, 20), the letter is datable to between 19 February 1241, when the summons to appear at Shrewsbury was issued, and 17 March 1241, i.e. the Sunday after Palm Sunday in that year. See also no. 295 above.

*297 Henry III
Letter, complaining about the proceedings of the king's vassals at Shrewsbury.
[17 March × 28 April 1241]

Mention only, in a letter from Dafydd to the king datable to 17 March × 28 April 1241 (no. 298 below). The present letter must be later than no. 296 above, sent in advance of the Shrewsbury meeting on 17 March, and thus was written after that meeting but before no. 298 below, sent in anticipation of a subsequent meeting on 28 April.

298 Henry III
Letter, thanking the king for remembering that he had complained to him both by letter and through his clerk Master Philip concerning the proceedings of the king's vassals whom the king has sent to Salisbury; these magnates, as Dafydd has previously told him, spurned the agreement reached at Gloucester through the legate and many other good and great men, with Dafydd's proctors contradicting them and proclaiming the protection of the pope and king, and admitted and listened to the witnesses of Dafydd's enemies, although they were not arbitrators chosen for this by the parties as provided for in the aforesaid peace agreement, nor did they have special jurisdiction over this matter. On account of this Dafydd had sent the aforesaid clerk with his complaint. In order that light be shed on the aforementioned proceedings for the benefit of the king and his common council Dafydd is sending his faithful men Tudur his seneschal, Einion Fychan, Master David his chancellor and his clerk Philip ab Ifor, his proctors

at the aforesaid meeting at Salisbury, and ratifies whatever these messengers shall do in accordance with the aforesaid agreement concerning the aforesaid matter and others that may affect him. Sealing clause.

[*c*.24 March × 28 April 1241]

B = TNA: PRO, E 36/274 (Liber A), fo. 333v. s. xiii ex.
Pd. from B, *LW*, 18–19 (no. 15).
Cd., *H*, no. 360.

[E]xcellentissimo domino suo et avunculo domino H. Dei gratia regi Angl(ie), domino Hib(er)n(ie), duci Norman(nie), Aquit(anie) et comiti And(egavie) D. princeps Norwall(ie) suus fidelis nepos et devotus salutem et se totum. Maiestati vestre grates referimus copiosas eo quod bene reduxistis ad memoriam quod vobis conquesti fuimus tam per litteras quam per magistrum Phil(i)ppu(m) clericum nostrum ad vos ex parte nostra ad hoc principaliter destinatum de processu magnatum vestrorum quos ad partes Solosbur' destinastis, qui quidem magnates vestri, sicut alias vobis significavimus, spreta que forma pacis inter vos et nos apud Glouern(iam) reformata per dominum legatum et multos alios bonos et magnos viros tam clericos quam seculares, contradicentibus procuratoribus nostris et protectionem domini pape et vestram proclamantibus, testes adversariorum nostrorum non veriti sunt admittere et exaudire, cum ad hoc non essent arbitri electi a partibus sicut provisum fuit in forma pacis predicte, nec etiam specialem super hoc haberent iurisdictionem, propter quod ut prediximus excellentie vestre querimoniam nostram per predictum magistrum clericum nostrum duximus referendam. Et ut vobis et consilio vestro communi[a] luce clarius appareat de processu memorato dilectos et fideles nostros Tuderiu(m) senescallum nostrum, Ennium Parvum, magistrum David cancellarium nostrum et Philipum filium Yuor clericum nostrum, qui fuerunt alias procuratores nostri apud Solosbur' in predicto negotio, ad vestram presentiam duximus destinandos, ratum et gratum habituri quicquid predicti nuntii nostri super prefato negotio et aliis que nos tangant secundum formam sepedictam duxerint faciendum. In cuius rei testimonium huic scripto sigillum nostrum fecimus apponi. Valeat excellentia vestra semper in domino.

[a] comuni B.

As Edwards argued (*LW*, 19), the letter was sent after the meeting at Shrewsbury on 17 March 1241 and in anticipation of another meeting there on 28 April 1241, which was attended by the four proctors named here (*CR 1237–42*, 357). As the letter reveals that Dafydd had already complained about the proceedings at the meeting on 17 March, and had apparently received a reply (no longer extant) to this from the king, the present letter is unlikely to have been written until at least about a week after the meeting.

299 Henry III

Letter, announcing that he is sending Richard, bishop of Bangor, Master David, the prince's chancellor and Philip ab Ifor to negotiate peace between the king and himself, and ratifying whatever the said envoys do concerning the said matter.

[*c*.8 × 29 August 1241]

B = TNA: PRO, E 36/274 (Liber A), fo. 405r. s. xiii ex.
Pd. from B, *LW*, 153–4 (no. 271).
Cd., *H*, no. 363.

Excellentissimo domino suo et avunculo H. Dei gratia regi Anglie, domino Hib(er)n(ie), duci Normannie, Aquit(anie), comiti Andegavie David princeps Nor(wallie) suus fidelis nepos et devotus salutem et se totum. Mittimus ad vos dilectos et speciales nostros venerabilem patrem dominum R. Bangorn(ensem) episcopum, magistrum David cancellarium nostrum, Philippum filium Yuor ad tractandum de pace inter vos et nos reformanda et confirmanda, ratum et gratum habituri quicquid dicti nuntii nostri super dicto negotio duxerint faciendum coram vobis. In cuius rei testimonium has litteras patentes sigilli nostri apositione duxerimus roborandas. Valeat excellentia vestra semper in domino.

As the letter refers to peace negotiations, it was presumably written no earlier than 8 August 1241, when Henry began gathering forces for his campaign against Dafydd, and before peace was made at Gwerneigron on 29 August. The date range can probably be narrowed, as Edwards suggested (*LW*, 154), to the second half of August, i.e. to the period after the king had made his agreement with Gruffudd ap Llywelyn's wife Senana on 12 August and proclaimed, the next day, that he would receive all the Welsh of North Wales who had made peace with him and done fealty to Gruffudd (*CPR 1232–47*, 256); and possibly even to the days following the commencement of the royal campaign on 24 August (cf. no. 284 above; Williams, 'Succession to Gwynedd', 404–5). The inclusion of Bishop Richard of Bangor among the negotiators is significant on two counts. First, it indicates that by this time he had returned to Gwynedd from exile in England, whither he had fled following Dafydd's capture of Gruffudd ap Llywelyn, apparently while under the bishop's safe conduct, around Michaelmas 1240 (see ibid., 403–4). Second, the choice of a prelate associated with Gruffudd's cause would have commended itself to the king and reflects the seriousness of Dafydd's intentions in seeking peace.

300 Letter patent concerning Henry III

Notification that he has granted to the king that:

(1) he will hand over his brother Gruffudd, together with the latter's eldest son and others whom he has imprisoned, to the king and afterwards accept the judgement of the king's court regarding whether Gruffudd should be held captive and whether any portion of the land held by his father Llywelyn ought to pertain to Gruffudd according to the custom of the Welsh, so that peace may be upheld between Dafydd and Gruffudd;

(2) security for the maintenance of that peace will be given according to the decision of the king's court;

(3) both Dafydd and Gruffudd will hold the portions pertaining to them of the aforesaid lands in chief from the king;

(4) he will restore to Roger of Mold, seneschal of Chester, his land of Mold with its appurtenances and to him and other barons of the king the seisin of lands occupied since the war between King John and Llywelyn, saving any right of property contained in an agreement, with this right to be subject to the jurisdiction of the king's court;

(5) he will restore to the king all expenses incurred through his campaign;

(6) he will make satisfaction for damage and injuries inflicted by him and his men, according to the decision of the aforesaid court, or hand over the malefactors to the king;

(7) he will restore to the king all homages which his father John had and which the king ought to have by right, especially those of all Welsh nobles;

(8) the king will not abandon any of his adherents and their seisins may remain with the king and his men;

(9) the land of Ellesmere with its appurtenances will remain with the king and his heirs for ever and the land of Englefield [Tegeingl] will be kept at his will for himself and his heirs for ever;

(10) henceforth Dafydd will not receive in his land, nor allow to be received, persons outlawed or banished by the king or his barons of the March;

(11) he will give security concerning the observance of all the aforesaid articles through hostages, pledges and other means specified by the king.

(12) In these and all other matters Dafydd will be at the wish and command of the king and obey the law in all things in his court.

Sealing clause; dating clause.

(13) Those who are detained with Gruffudd will be similarly handed over to the king until his court has decided whether and in what manner they ought to be released.

(14) In order to uphold all the aforesaid terms Dafydd has sworn on the holy cross that he has carried around with him. Hugh, bishop of St Asaph, at Dafydd's request, has promised on his order to do all the aforesaid things and will ensure that they are observed as far as he is able. Ednyfed Fychan has sworn likewise on the aforesaid cross on Dafydd's orders.

(15) Dafydd has further granted that if he or his heirs attempt to contravene the king's peace or the aforesaid articles, their entire inheritance will be forfeit to the king and his heirs.

(16) With respect to all these matters Dafydd has placed himself and his heirs under the jurisdiction of the archbishop of Canterbury and the bishops of London, Hereford and Coventry, so that all or any of them may excommunicate him and place an interdict on his land if he should attempt to contravene the aforesaid peace. He has arranged that the bishops of Bangor and St Asaph have given charters to the king in which they agree to carry out all sentences of excommunication or interdict by the aforesaid archbishop and bishops at their command.

Gwerneigron, 29 August 1241

B = TNA: PRO, C 66/49 (Pat. R. 25 Henry III), m. 2d (enrolled (?)October 1241). This version of the treaty is copied on the patent roll above that in no. 301 below. It is crossed through for cancellation, but a rubric to the text states: Non debent cancellari eo quod tam ista forma quam subsequens acceptate erant. As m. 2 of the patent roll contains documents dated in October 1241, and clearly continues from m. 3, containing documents dated earlier in October, it is likely that the present text, along with nos 301 and 303 below, were enrolled after these.

C = Cambridge, Corpus Christi College MS 16, fos 172v–173r. s. xiii med.

Pd. from B and C, Brady, *Complete History*, App. 196–7 (no. 170); from C, *Matthaei Paris . . . Historia*, ed. Parker, 842–3; from C, Paris, *CM*, iv. 321–3; from Parker, *Matthaei Paris . . . Historia*, ed. Wats, 625–6; from (?)Parker or Wats, Wynne, *History of Wales*, 359–61.

Cd., *CPR 1232–47*, 264 (from B).

Omnibus Cristi fidelibus ad quos presentes littere pervenerint[a] David filius L.[b][c]quondam principis Norwall(ie)[-c] salutem. Sciatis quod concessi domino meo H. regi Angl(ie) illustri filio domini I. regis:

[i] quod[d] Griffinu(m) fratrem meum quem teneo incarceratum una cum filio suo primo-

genito et aliis qui occasione predicti Griffini sunt in potestate mea incarcerati `tradam ^{e} et ipsos eidem domino meo regi tradam, et postea stabo iuri in curia ipsius domini regis tam super eo, utrum idem Griffinus debeat teneri captus, quam super portione terre que fuit predicti Lewel(ini)^f patris mei, si qua ipsum Griffinu(m) contingere debet secundum consuetudinum Walensiu(m), ita quod pax servetur inter me et predictum Griffinu(m)^g fratrem meum;

[ii] et^e quod caveatur de ipsa tenenda secundum considerationem curie ipsius domini regis;

[iii] et quod tam ego quam predictus Griff(inus)^g portiones nostras que nos contingent de predictis terris tenebimus in capite de predicto domino rege;

[iv] et quod reddam Rog(er)o de Mo(n)te Alto, senescallo Cestr(ie), terram suam de Muhaut cum pertinentiis, et sibi et aliis baronibus et fidelibus domini regis seisinas terrarum suarum occupatarum a tempore guerre orte inter ipsum dominum I. regem et predictum L. patrem meum, salvo iure^h proprietatis cuiuslibet pacti et instrumenti, super quo stabitur iuri hinc inde in curia ipsius domini regis;

[v] et quod reddam ipsi domino regi omnes expensas quas ipse et sui fecerunt occasione exercitus istius;

[vi] et quod satisfaciam de dampnis et iniuriis illatis sibi et suis, secundum considerationem curie predicte, vel malefactores ipsos ipsi domino regi reddam;

[vii] et quod similiter domino regi reddam omnia homagia que dominus I. rex pater suus habuit et que dominus rex de iure habere debet, et specialiter omnium nobilium Walens(ium);

[viii] et quod idem dominus rex non dimittet aliquem de suis imprisiis et quod ipsi domino regi et suis remaneant seisine sue;

[ix] et quod terra de Ellesmere^i cum pertinentiis suis in perpetuum remanebit domino regi et heredibus suis, et in voluntate sua sit retinendi terram de Englefeud^j in perpetuum sibi et heredibus suis;

[x] et quod decetero non receptabo utlagos vel foris bannitos ipsius domini regis vel baronum suorum de Marchia in terra mea nec permittam receptari.

[xi] Et de omnibus articulis supradictis et singulis firmiter et imperpetuum observandis domino regi et heredibus suis pro me et heredibus meis cavebo per obsides et pignora et aliis modis quibus dominus rex dicere voluerit et dictare.

[xii] Et in his et in omnibus aliis stabo voluntati et mandatis ipsius domini regis et iuri parebo omnibus in curia sua.

In cuius rei testimonium presenti scripto sigillum meum apposui. Actum apud Alnetu(m) iuxta fluvium Eluey de Sancto Assaph'^{k} in festo decollationis Sancti Ioh(ann)is Bapt(iste) anno predicti domini H. regis xxv.

[xiii] Et sciendum quod illi qui capti detinentur cum predicto Griff(ino)^g eodem modo tradentur domino regi donec per curiam suam consideratum fuerit utrum et quomodo debeant deliberari.

[xiv] Et ad omnia predicta firmiter tenenda ego David iuravi super crucem sanctam quam coram me deportari facio.^{e} Venerabilis etiam pater H. episcopus de Sancto Assaph'^{k} ad petitionem meam firmiter promisit in ordine suo quod hec omnia predicta faciet et procurabit modis quibus poterit observari, Edeneuth'^{l} siquidem Waghan^m per preceptum meum illud idem iuravit super crucem predictam. Actum ut supra.

[xv] ^{n}–Preterea concessi pro me et heredibus meis quod si ego vel heredes mei [C, fo. 173r]

contra pacem domini regis vel heredum suorum vel contra articulos predictos aliquid attemptaverimus, tota hereditas nostra domino regi et heredibus suis incurratur.

[xvi] De quibus omnibus et singulis supposui me et heredes meos iurisdictioni archiepiscopi Cant(uariensis) et episcoporum Lond', Hereford' et Coventr' qui pro tempore preerunt, quod omnes vel unus eorum quem dominus rex ad hec elegerit possit nos excommunicare[o] et terram nostram interdicere si aliquid contra predictam attemptaverimus. Et procuravi quod episcopi de Bangor et de Sancto Asaph cartas suas domino regi fecerunt per quas concesserunt quod omnes sententias tam excommunicationis quam interdicti a predictis archiepiscopo, episcopis vel aliquo eorum ferendas ad mandatum eorum exequentur.[-n]

[a] B *inserts* salutem *struck through.* | [b] Lewelini C. | [c-c] *omitted* C. | [d] B *inserts* deliberabo *struck through*; C *inserts* deliberabo. | [e] *omitted* C. | [f] Lowelini C. | [g] G. C. | [h] B *inserts* cuiuslibet *struck through.* | [i] Engle(s)m(er)e C. | [j] Engl' C. | [k] Asaph' C. | [l] Edeneuet C. | [m] Wangan C. | [n-n] *omitted* B. | [o] escommunicare C.

This is the first of two versions of the peace agreement made at Gwerneigron copied on the patent roll. Although struck through, the rubric states that it should not have been cancelled as both it and the following version were accepted. The most likely explanation for the existence of two versions is that the text printed here was drawn up by the parties at Gwerneigron on 29 August, and that no. 301 below was a revised text ratified by the king on 30 August, a sequence strongly suggested by the addition to the latter's dating clause stating that the agreement reached on 29 August at Gwerneigron was renewed in the king's tent at Rhuddlan the following day (a formulation also found in no. 302 below).

The text preserved in C, the autograph manuscript of Matthew Paris's *Chronica Majora*, is very closely related to that on the patent roll (B), except that Matthew copied two further clauses (cc. xv–xvi) omitted in B. Matthew's source for the text was probably Bishop Richard of Bangor, named in c. xvi, who resided at the chronicler's monastery of St Albans for much of the decade 1247–57; as Matthew composed the annals in the *Chronica Majora* for the period 1236–50 between 1245 and early 1251, he could easily have drawn on information supplied by the bishop for his account of events in 1241 (see *HW*, ii. 744; Vaughan, *Matthew Paris*, 12, 15, 35, 49–61; Williams, 'Succession to Gwynedd', 403–8; and Smith, *Llywelyn*, 35, n. 118, which observes that Matthew's inclusion of this and other texts relating to Gruffudd ap Llywelyn in 1241 'may well reflect Bishop Richard of Bangor's connection with St Albans'). It is possible that the text copied by Matthew was an earlier redaction than that preserved in the patent roll. This would explain why cc. xv–xvi occur only in C, although their omission in B could, perhaps, be the result of editing by the chancery scribe, undertaken in the knowledge that these clauses had been superseded by nos 302–3 below. The different forms of Dafydd's style in B and C may provide further evidence that each copy drew on a different exemplar. B includes the phrase *quondam principis Norwallie*, whereas C omits it, styling the prince *David filius Lewelini* without any title. The former style occurs in royal letters to the prince from at least October 1240 (*CR 1237–42*, 243, 344), the latter from at least February 1241 (ibid., 350), and neither corresponds to the style used by Dafydd in his own acts before 29 August 1241, namely *David princeps Norwallie* (although he was referred to as *David filium Lewelyn' quondam principis Norwallie* in no. 291 above, his agreement with Henry III at Gloucester on 15 May 1240).

If the precise relationship between the texts in B and C remains uncertain, the differences between the present agreement and that in no. 301 below are clear. The difference between their dating clauses has already been noticed. In addition, no. 301 lacks not only cc. xv–xvi but also c. xiii (in the last instance probably because the clause's substance was considered to be adequately covered in c. i of no. 301); moreover, there are sufficient verbal discrepancies between the remaining clauses whose substance is common to both agreements to indicate that no. 301 represents a revised version of the present document. Note, for example, how c. i of the present document has been re-drafted to distinguish more clearly between the issues of Gruffudd's incarceration and his entitlement to a share of Gwynedd in cc. i–ii of no. 301, or how c. v of the latter document is elaborated at the end by comparison with the equivalent c. iv here. More generally, whereas in the present document cc. i–x take the form of subordinate clauses dependent on *concessi* in the second sentence, cc. ii–xi in no. 301 are independent sentences, many introduced by the verb *promitto*. A comparison of the two documents thus reveals an attempt to introduce greater precision and clarity into the obligations agreed by Dafydd in the period between the initial agreement at Gwerneigron on 29 August and its ratification in the king's tent at Rhuddlan the following day. Moreover, this process continued on 31 August, as nos 302–3 below show: these letters patent amplified and gave additional solemnity to the undertakings first made in cc. xv–xvi of the present agreement, and the decision to put them in separate documents no doubt explains why they were omitted in no. 301 (and possibly also accounts for their absence from B's version of the present document).

For the campaign that led to Dafydd's surrender at Gwerneigron, on the banks of the river Elwy just north of St Asaph and about 2 miles south of Rhuddlan (cf. Gwernigron Farm, SJ 025 752), and the significance of the terms agreed, see *HW*, ii. 697–8; Powicke, *Henry III*, ii. 632–3; Williams, 'Succession to Gwynedd', 404–5; Davies, *Conquest*, 301–2; Smith, *Llywelyn*, 32–5. The charters issued by the bishops of Bangor and St Asaph referred to in c. xvi are not extant.

301 Letter patent concerning Henry III

Notification that he has granted to the king that:

(1) he will hand over his brother Gruffudd, together with the latter's eldest son and others whom he has imprisoned, to the king so that it may be investigated whether and in what manner they ought to be released.

(2) He will accept the judgement of the king's court regarding whether any portion of the land of his father Llywelyn, which is now held by Dafydd, ought to pertain to Gruffudd according to the custom of Wales or according to right as chosen by the king.

(3) If the king makes peace between Dafydd and Gruffudd, Dafydd will observe it and will give security concerning its maintenance according to the decision of the king's court.

(4) [as c. 3 in no. 300 above].

(5) Dafydd promises to hand over to the king the land of Mold with its appurtenances belonging to Roger of Mold, seneschal of Chester, together with the seisin of lands belonging to him and other barons of the king occupied since the war between King John and Llywelyn, and restore them to the king or whoever he has commanded so that the king may dispose of them according to his will, saving any right of property contained in an agreement, with this right to be subject to the jurisdiction of the king's court.

(6)–(13) [as cc. 5–10, 12, 11 in no. 300 above].
Sealing clause; dating clause.
(14) [as c. 14 in no. 300 above].

Gwerneigron, 29 August 1241; renewed at Rhuddlan, 30 August 1241

B = TNA: PRO, C 66/49 (Pat. R. 25 Henry III), m. 2d (enrolled (?)October 1241).
C = TNA: PRO, E 36/274 (Liber A), fo. 330r–v. s. xiii ex.
Pd. from C, *Foedera*, I. i. 242; from C, *LW*, 9–10 (no. 4).
Cd., *CPR 1232–47*, 264 (from B); *H*, no. 364.

Omnibus[a] ad quos presentes littere pervenerint[b] David filius Lewel(ini) quondam principis Norwall(ie)[c] salutem. Sciatis quod concessi domino meo H. regi Angl(ie) illustri filio domini[d] I. regis:

[i] quod Griffinu(m) fratrem meum quem teneo incarceratum una cum filio suo primogenito et aliis qui occasione predicti Griffini in potestate mea incarcerati sunt tradam eidem domino meo regi tali modo quod de omnibus cognoscatur utrum et qualiter debeant deliberari.

[ii] Stabo etiam iuri in curia predicti domini mei regis super portione terre que fuit predicti L.[e] patris mei cuius seisinam nunc habeo et teneo, si qua ipsum Griffinu(m) contingere debet secundum consuetudinem Wall(ie) vel secundum ius prout dominus rex elegerit.

[iii] Et si idem dominus rex pacem fecerit inter me et predictum Griff(inum) fratrem meum ipsam tenebo et servabo, et de ipsa tenenda cavebo secundum considerationem[f] curie ipsius domini regis.

[iv] Volo etiam et concedo quod tam ego quam predictus Griffinus portiones que nos contingent de predictis terris teneamus in capite de predicto domino rege.

[v] Promitto etiam quod terram de Muhaud[g] totam cum pertinentiis suis et seisinas terrarum[h] Rog(er)i de Muhaud[g] senescalli Cestr(ie) et omnium aliorum baronum et fidelium ipsius domini regis occupatarum a tempore guerre[i] orte inter dominum Ioh(ann)em regem et predictum Lewel(inum) patrem meum in manibus ipsius domini regis tradam et eidem reddam vel cui mandaverit ut de ipsis disponat ad voluntatem suam, salvo iure proprietatis cuiuslibet pacti et instrumenti super quo stabitur iuri hinc inde in curia ipsius domini regis.

[vi] Item promitto quod reddam prefato domino regi omnes expensas quas ipse et sui fecerunt occasione excercitus istius.

[vii] Item promitto quod satisfaciam domino regi de dampnis et iniuriis illatis sibi et suis secundum considerationem curie predicte, vel malefactores ipsos ipsi domino regi reddam.

[viii] Promitto similiter eidem domino regi quod reddam ei omnia homagia que dominus I. rex pater suus habuit et que dominus rex de iure habere debet, et specialiter dimitto ei homagia omnium nobilium Walensiu(m).

[ix] Porro volo et concedo quod idem dominus rex non dimittat aliquem de suis inprisiis, et quod ipsi domino regi et suis remaneant seisine sue;

[x] et quod terra de Aylesmere[j] cum pertinentiis suis imperpetuum[k] remaneat domino regi et heredibus suis, et in voluntate sua sit retinendi terram de Englefeld[l] imperpetuum[k] sibi et heredibus suis.

[xi] Insuper promitto quod decetero non receptabo in terra mea nec receptari permittam utlagatos vel forisbannitos[m] ipsius domini regis vel baronum suorum de Marchia.

[xii] Et in hiis et in omnibus aliis stabo voluntati et mandatis ipsius domini regis et iuri parebo omnibus in curia sua.

[xiii] De omnibus autem articulis supradictis et singulis firmiter imperpetuum[k] observandis domino regi et heredibus suis pro me et heredibus meis cavebo per obsides et pignora et aliis modis quibus dominus rex dicere voluerit vel dictare.[n]

In cuius rei testimonium presenti scripto sigillum meum apposui. Actum apud Alnetum iuxta ʼfluvium Elwey de Sancto Assaphʼ[o] in festo decollationis Sancti Ioh(ann)is Bapt(iste) et crastina die renovatum apud Rothelan in tentorio domini regis anno regni predicti domini [p–]H. regis[–p] xxv.[q]

[xiv] Et ad omnia predicta firmiter tenenda ego David iuravi super crucem sanctam quam coram me deportari facio. Venerabilis etiam pater Hugo episcopus de Sancto Assaphʼ[o] ad petitionem meam firmiter promisit in ordine suo quod hec omnia predicta faciet et procurabit modis quibus poterit observari. Edeneueth siquidem Vaghan per preceptum meum illud idem iuravit super crucem predictam. Actum apud Alnetu(m) ut supra.

[a] C *inserts* Cristi fidelibus. | [b] perve, *followed by* salutem *struck through* B. | [c] Nortwall(ie) C. [d] *omitted* C. | [e] Lewelini C. | [f] C *inserts* curie. | [g] Muhaut C. | [h] B *inserts* suarum *struck through.* [i] gurre B. | [j] Aillesm(er)e C. | [k] inperpetuum C. | [l] Englefeld C. | [m] forisbanitos C. | [n] dicare C. [o] Asaphʼ C. | [p–p] regis H. C. | [q] vicesimo quinto C.

See note to no. 300 above.

302 Letter patent concerning Henry III

Notification that, since he has made certain promises and agreements with the king in the recent peace agreement between them, as set out in the letter concerning those agreements made at Gwerneigron on 29 August 1241 and renewed the following day at Rhuddlan in the king's tent, he is (of his own free will and with the will and consent of the bishops of St Asaph and Bangor and his counsellors) placing himself, and all who will support him in contravening the said agreements or being against the king, together with all his land, under the jurisdiction of the archbishop of Canterbury and the bishops of London, Ely, Hereford and Coventry and Lichfield, all together and whoever jointly the king has chosen, in order that the said agreements be observed fully for ever by him and his heirs with respect to the king and his heirs. Submissive to the jurisdiction of the aforesaid prelates over himself and his supporters, he gives the aforesaid prelates full power to compel his supporters to observe the aforesaid agreement and make full satisfaction according to the king's will, if he or his men should in any way contravene the aforesaid terms. He promises that he and his heirs will observe all these terms in good faith for ever with respect to the king and his heirs. The bishops of St Asaph and Bangor have, at Dafydd's request, promised the king and his heirs on behalf of themselves and their successors that they will publish, observe and make their subjects observe the sentences issued for the aforesaid reason. Sealing clause.

Rhuddlan, 31 August 1241

B = TNA: PRO, E 36/274 (Liber A), fos 331v–332r. s. xiii ex.
Pd. from B, *Foedera*, I. i. 242–3; from B, *LW*, 12–13 (no. 6).
Cd., *H*, no. 365.

[O]mnibus Cristi fidelibus ad quos presentes littere pervenerint David filius Lewelini quondam principis Norwall(ie) salutem. Sciatis quod cum quasdam promissiones et pacta inierim[a] cum domino meo H. rege Anglie filio domini I. regis in reformatione pacis inter ipsum et me nuper facte, sicut continetur in litteris super eisdem pactis et conventionibus factis apud Alnetu(m) iuxta fluvium de Elwey de Sancto Asaph' in festo decollationis Sancti Ioh(ann)is Baptiste et crastina die renovatis apud Rothelan in tentorio domini regis anno regni predicti domini regis vicesimo quinto et sigillo meo sigillatis, ut dicte conventiones et pacta plene et efficaciter per me et heredes meos domino regi predicto et heredibus suis in perpetuum observentur, voluntate spontanea ad plenam securitatem ipsius domini mei regis et heredum suorum de consensu et voluntate de Sancto Asaph' et Bangorens(is) episcoporum et consiliariorum meorum me et omnes illos qui in hoc, quod contra pacta et conventiones predictas venirem vel contra dominum regem essem, mihi favebunt vel consilium vel auxilium prebebunt, et totam terram meam suppono iurisdictioni Cantuariens(is) archiepiscopi, Londoniens(is), Elyens(is), Herefordens(is), Coventrens(is) et Lichefeldens(is) episcoporum, omnium similiter et cuiuslibet in solidum quem dominus rex elegerit, iurisdictioni ipsorum vel ipsius in solidum quem dominus rex elegerit in me et dictos mihi faventes vel consulentes vel auxiliantes et terram prorogare intendens, predictis prelatis simul et cuilibet in solidum quem dominus rex elegerit prout predictum est dans et concedens plenam et liberam potestatem ut ad requisitionem ipsius domini regis nulla alia monitione facta per excommunicationis in me et dictos mihi faventes consiliantes aut auxiliantes et interdicti in terram sententias ad observationem ipsius forme et conventionum que in dictis litteris continentur distringant et ad plenam satisfactionem iuxta voluntatem domini regis compellant, si forte, quod Deus avertat, in aliquo contra predicta per me vel meos venirem. Et omnia hec bona fide et in perpetuum servanda domino regi et heredibus suis per me et heredes meos promitto. Venerabiles insuper patres de Sancto Asaph' et Bangorens(is) episcopi supradicti ad petitionem meam prefato domino regi et heredibus suis [fo. 332r] [b-]pro se et successoribus suis[-b] in suo ordine promiserunt quod sententias occasione predicta latas vel ferendas sicut eis mandabitur publicabunt et plenius observabunt et a subditis districte et inviolabiliter facient observari. In cuius rei testimonium tam ego quam dicti venerabiles patres de Sancto Asaph' et Bangorens(is) episcopi sigilla nostra presentibus fecimus apponi. Actum apud Rothelan in tentorio ipsius domini regis tricesimo primo die augusti anno eodem.

[a] iniero B. | [b-b] per se et successores suos B.

See note to no. 300 above.

303 Letter patent concerning Henry III

Notification that of his own free will he has undertaken to the king that he and his heirs will serve the king and his heirs faithfully all the days of their life nor will they be against him in any respect. If it should happen that they depart from their faithful service to the king or his heirs, let all their land be forfeit to the king and his heirs and pass to their use for ever. Sealed by Dafydd and, at his request, by the bishops of Bangor and St Asaph.

Rhuddlan, 31 August 1241

B = TNA: PRO, C 66/49 (Pat. R. 25 Henry III), m. 2d (enrolled (?)October 1241). (For the date of the enrolment see no. 300 above.)
C = TNA: PRO, E 36/274 (Liber A), fo. 335r. s. xiii ex.
Pd. from (?)B, Warrington, *History of Wales*, App., 603–4; from Warrington, Haddan and Stubbs, i. 469 (incomplete); from C, *LW*, 22 (no. 22).
Cd., *CPR 1232–47*, 264 (from B); *H*, no. 366.

Omnibus ᵃ⁻ad quos presentes littere pervenerint⁻ᵃ David filius L.ᵇ quondam principis Nortwall(ie)ᶜ salutem. Noverit universitas vestra me spontanea voluntate mea pepigisse domino meo H.ᵈ⁻Dei gratia⁻ᵈ regi Angl(ie) illustri quod ego et heredes mei eidem domino regi et heredibus suis omnibus diebus vite nostre constanter et fideliter serviemus nec aliquo tempore contra eos erimus, quod si forte evenerit quod a fideli servitio suo vel heredum suorum, quod absit, recesserimus, tota terra nostra erga ipsum dominum regem et heredes suos incurratur et in usus eorum perpetuis cedat temporibus. Hanc autem pactionem et concessionem sigilli mei appositione roboravi, et ad maiorem huius rei declarationem venerabiles patres Bangorens(is) et de Sancto Assaph' episcopi ad petitionem meam presenti scripto sigilla sua apposuerunt. Actum apud Rothelan xxxiᵉ die augusti anno ᶠ⁻regni predicti domini H. regis vicesimo quinto.⁻ᶠ

ᵃ⁻ᵃ etc. B. | ᵇ Lewelini C. | ᶜ Norwall(ie) C. | ᵈ⁻ᵈ *omitted* C. | ᵉ tricesimo primo C. | ᶠ⁻ᶠ *omitted* B.

See note to no. 300 above.

304 Letter patent concerning Henry III

Notification that he has granted to the king that:
(1)–(3) [as cc. 2–4 in no. 301 above].
(4) He has returned the land of Mold to the king as promised earlier, so that if he grants it to another this shall be saving Dafydd's proprietary right contained in any agreement, concerning which judgement will be made in the king's court; if the king wishes to keep it in his own hand, he may do so without any claim from Dafydd and his heirs.
(5) He will hand over to the king the lands of all the king's barons occupied since the war between King John and Llywelyn and return them to the king or whoever he commands, so that he may dispose of them as he wishes, saving Dafydd's proprietary right contained in any agreement, concerning which judgement will be made in the king's court.
(6)–(9) [as cc. 7–10 in no. 301 above].
(10) The castle and lands of Degannwy will remain for ever with the king and his heirs for the expenses of the royal expedition to Rhuddlan.
(11) [as c. 11 in no. 301 above].
(12) Henceforth he will willingly receive all the king's commands and carry them out as far as possible.
(13) Throughout their lives he and his heirs will serve the king and his heirs faithfully nor be against them at any time; if they depart from faithful service to him, all their land may be forfeit to the king and his heirs and pass to their use for ever.
(14)–(15) [as cc. 13, 12 in no. 301 above].
(16) In order to uphold all these promises, concessions and agreements Dafydd has sworn,

of his own free will as full security to the king and his heirs, on the holy cross that he has carried around with him, and with the will and consent of the bishops of St Asaph and Bangor and his counsellors he places himself, and all who will support or counsel him in contravening the said agreements or being against the king, together with all his land, under the jurisdiction of the archbishop of Canterbury and the bishops of London, Ely, Hereford, and Coventry and Lichfield, all together and whoever jointly the king has chosen. Submissive to the jurisdiction of the aforesaid prelates over himself and his supporters, he gives the aforesaid prelates full power to enforce, at the king's request, through sentences of excommunication and interdict upon him and his supporters, the observance of the promises, concessions and agreements contained in this and certain other documents made for the king and to compel them to make full satisfaction according to the king's will, if he or his men should in any way contravene the aforesaid terms.

Sealing clause; witnesses.

[Westminster, *c.* 24 October 1241]

A = original document, in the care of the National Trust at Belton House, Grantham. Endorsed: Carta David filii Leuelini quondam principis Wall(ie) facta H. regi Angl(ie) filio Ioh(ann)is regis de stando iuri in curia dicti domini H. regis et heredum suorum super portione terre que fuit dicti Leulini patris sui in Wall(ia) sine data (s. xiii); approx. 231 × 210 + 29 mm.; central slit in fold for a tag (*c.* 18 mm. wide) which exits through a slit in the base of the fold; sealed on tag. Circular two-sided seal, brown wax, imperfect, originally approx. (?)80–90 mm. diameter; ruler enthroned with sword in right hand in front, equestrian, facing right, on back; no legend survives on either side.
B = TNA: PRO, E 36/274 (Liber A), fos 330v–331v. s. xiii ex.
Pd. from B, *Foedera*, I. i. 243; from B, *LW*, 10–12 (no. 5).
Cd., 'Report of Sir Frederick Kenyon', 79 (from A); *H*, no. 367.

Omnibus Cristi fidelibus ad quos presentes littere pervenerint David filius Lewellin(i) quondam principis Norwall(ie) salutem. Sciatis quod concessi domino meo H. regi Angl(ie) illustri filio domini I. regis quod:

[i] stabo iuri in curia sua super porcione terre que fuit predicti Lewellin(i) patris mei cuius saisinam nunc habeo et teneo si qua Griffinu(m) fratrem meum contingere debet secundum consuetudinem Wall(ie) vel secundum ius prout dominus rex elegerit.

[ii] Et si idem dominus rex pacem fecerit inter me et predictum Griffinu(m) fratrem meum ipsam tenebo et servabo et de ipsa tenenda cavebo secundum considerationem curie ipsius domini regis.

[iii] Concessi etiam quod tam ego quam predictus Griffin(us) portiones que nos contingent de predictis terris teneamus in capite de predicto domino rege.

[iv] Terram etiam de Muhaut eidem domino meo regi reddidi sicut ei prius promiseram, ita quod si eam alii reddiderit salvum sit mihi ius proprietatis cuiuslibet pacti et instrumenti super quo stabitur iuri hinc inde in curia ipsius domini regis: et si eam voluerit retinere in manu sua, pro voluntate sua eam retineat sine omni clamio mei et heredum meorum.

[v] Concessi etiam quod omnium baronum et fidelium ipsius domini regis terras occupatas a tempore guerre orte inter dominum I. regem et predictum Lewell' patrem meum in manibus ipsius domini regis tradam et eidem reddam vel cui mandaverit, ut de ipsis disponat ad voluntatem suam, salvo mihi iure proprietatis cuiuslibet pacti et instrumenti super quo stabitur iuri hinc inde in curia ipsius domini regis.

[vi] Concessi etiam quod satisfaciam ipsi domino regi de dampnis et iniuriis illatis sibi et

suis secundum consideracionem curie predicte, vel malefactores ipsos ipsi domino regi reddam.

[vii] Reddidi autem eidem domino regi omnia homagia que dominus I. rex pater suus habuit et que dominus rex de iure habere debet, et specialiter dimisi ei homagia omnium nobilium Walensiu(m).

[viii] Concessi etiam quod idem dominus rex non dimittat aliquem de suis imprisiis et quod ipsi domino regi et suis remaneant saisine sue sicut predictum est;

[ix] et quod terra de Aillesm(er)e cum pertinentiis suis et terra de Engelfeld' cum pertinentiis suis in perpetuum remaneant domino regi et heredibus suis;

[x] et quod castrum et tenementa de Gannoc cum pertinentiis suis inperpetuum remaneant domino regi et heredibus suis pro expensis quas idem dominus rex et magnates sui fecerunt in expeditione sua apud Rothelan.

[xi] Insuper promisi quod decetero non receptabo in terra mea nec receptari permittam uthlagatos vel forisbannitos ipsius domini regis vel baronum suorum de Marchia;

[xii] et quod decetero omnia mandata ipsius domini regis libenter admittam et ea pro viribus meis adimplebo.

[xiii] Concessi etiam quod ego et heredes mei eidem domino regi et heredibus suis omnibus diebus vite nostre constanter et fideliter serviemus, nec in aliquo tempore contra eos erimus; quod si forte evenerit quod a fideli servitio suo quod absit recesserimus, tota terra nostra erga ipsum dominum regem et heredes suos incurratur et in usus eorum perpetuis cedat temporibus.

[xiv] De omnibus autem articulis supradictis et singulis firmiter in perpetuum observandis domino regi et heredibus suis pro me et heredibus meis cavi et cavebo per obsides et pignora et aliis modis quibus dominus rex dicere voluerit vel dictare;

[xv] et in hiis et omnibus aliis stabo voluntati et mandatis ipsius domini regis et iuri parebo in omnibus in curia sua.

[xvi] Ad has quidem promissiones, concessiones et pacta firmiter observanda et tenenda voluntate spontanea ad plenam securitatem ipsius domini regis et heredum suorum ego David iuravi super crucem sanctam quam coram me deportari facio, et de consensu et voluntate de Sancto Asaph' et Bangoren' episcoporum et consiliariorum meorum me et omnes illos qui in hoc, quod contra pacta et conventiones predictas venirem vel contra dominum regem essem, mihi favebunt vel consilium et auxilium prebebunt, et totam terram meam suppono iurisdictioni Cantuar' archiepiscopi, London', Elyen', Hereford', Coventr' et Lichef' episcoporum, omnium simul et cuiuslibet in solidum quem dominus rex elegerit, iurisdictioni ipsorum vel ipsius in solidum quem dominus rex elegerit in me et dictos mihi faventes vel consulentes vel auxiliantes et terram prorogare intendens, predictis prelatis simul et cuilibet in solidum quem dominus rex elegerit prout predictum est dans et concedens plenam et liberam potestatem ut ad requisitionem ipsius domini regis, nulla alia monitione facta, per excommunicationis in me et dictos mihi faventes, consulentes aut auxiliantes et interdicti in terram sententias ad observationem promissionum, concessionum et pactorum que in presenti scripto et in quibusdam aliis eidem domino regi inde factis continentur distringant et ad plenam satisfactionem iuxta voluntatem ipsius domini regis compellant, si forte, quod Deus avertat, in aliquo contra predicta per me vel meos venirem.

In cuius rei testimonium presenti scripto sigillum meum apposui. Hiis testibus: venerabilibus patribus W. archiepiscopo Ebor' Angl(ie) primate, R. Linc' et P. Heref' episcopis, W.

de Ferr' comite Dereb', R. Le Bigot comite Norf', H. de Albin' comite Arundell', Pet(ro) de Sabaud', Ioh(ann)e de Monem', Ioh(anne) filio Galfr(idi), Will(elm)o de Cantilupo, Herb(er)to filio Math(e)i, Bert(ra)mo de Crioil, Galfr(ido) Dispens(ario), Drogone de Barentin et aliis.

As Lloyd and Edwards argued (*HW*, ii. 698; *LW*, 12, 23), this document must be the renewal of the Rhuddlan peace at London mentioned by Richard, bishop of Bangor in 1246 (*LW*, 21–2). This is supported by the Welsh chronicles and Matthew Paris, who state that Dafydd was summoned to a council at London after his defeat by the king (*BT, Pen20Tr*, 105–6; *BT, RBH*, 236–7; *AC*, 83–4; Paris, *CM*, iv. 150), and especially by no. 305 below, dated at Westminster, 24 October 1241, which was presumably issued at or about the same time as the present document. While largely similar to the Gwerneigron agreement renewed at Rhuddlan (no. 301 above), the present agreement was more severe, adding two new concessions, including the surrender of Degannwy (cc. x and xii); c. xiii reaffirmed the terms of no. 303 above, and was further reinforced by no. 305 below, a point which could indicate that no. 305 was issued subsequently to the present document. I am very grateful to David Crook for alerting me to the existence of the original document and for providing photographs of it.

305 Letter patent concerning Henry III

Notification that, should he die without a legitimate heir, he grants, of his own free will, all the land of the principality of North Wales to the king and his heirs, so that they may succeed him in all that land for ever, and orders all his men and subjects to obey the king and his heirs as their true lords if that should happen. Sealing clause.

Westminster, 24 October 1241

B = TNA: PRO, E 36/274 (Liber A), fo. 335r. s. xiii ex.
Pd. from B, *LW*, 22–3 (no. 23).
Cd., *H*, no. 368.

[O]mnibus Cristi fidelibus ad quos presentes littere pervenerint David filius Lewelini quondam principis Norwall(ie) salutem. Sciatis quod ego totam terram principatus Norwallie ad me quoquomodo pertinentem[a] domino meo H. illustri regi Anglie filio regis Ioh(ann)is et heredibus suis, ex mera liberalitate mea et spontanea voluntate, donatione inter vivos dono et concedo si forte sine herede de corpore meo exeunte de uxore mea mihi legitime desponsata, quod Deus avertat, me decedere contingat, ita quod ipse et heredes sui in perpetuum in tota dicta terra principatus mihi succedant, precipiens omnibus hominibus et subditis meis quod si ita contingat predicto domino meo regi et heredibus suis ut veris dominis suis adhereant obediant et intendant. In cuius rei testimonium presenti scripto sigillum meum apposui. Actum apud Westm(onasterium) vicesimo quarto die octobris anno regni eiusdem domini regis vicesimo quinto.

[a] pertinente B.

See note to no. 304 above. The principle that Gwynedd should escheat to the crown after the prince's death in the absence of a legitimate heir marked a revival of a demand imposed by John on Llywelyn ap Iorwerth thirty years earlier (no. 233 above).

*306 Pope Innocent IV

Letter (?), informing the pope that war had continued for a long time between Dafydd, whose parents had given him as a (?)foster son/(?)ward (alumpnus) *to the Roman Church, and the king of England. Eventually, after both parties agreed by oath that an arbitration should be made about all disputes before the bishop of St Asaph and his colleagues, the king, ignoring the fact that he was not allowed to take any action during this arbitration, unexpectedly attacked the prince, and compelled him by violence and fear to comply with his wishes over the matters under arbitration.*

[*c*.June × -26 July 1244]

Mention only, in a mandate from Innocent IV to the abbots of Aberconwy and Cymer dated at Genoa, 26 July 1244, recited in an undated letter from those abbots to Henry III preserved in Matthew Paris, *Chronica Majora* (Paris, *CM*, iv. 398–9; Haddan and Stubbs, i. 470–1). The papal mandate is not in the pope's register (Richter, 'David ap Llywelyn', 209, n. 21). Innocent stated that he had received his information *ex parte dilecti filii nostri, nobilis viri David, principis Northwallie*, thereby probably echoing the style used by Dafydd in his letter to him. After summarizing the prince's letter the pope ordered the abbots to conduct an inquiry, since any concessions extracted by force and fear were invalid; if they found that such was the case here, they should absolve the prince from his oath to keep the terms he had sworn to observe and lift any ecclesiastical sentence imposed on his person or lands for breach of those terms. The abbots concluded their letter by summoning the king to appear before them on 20 January 1245 at Caerwys (cmt. Rhuddlan) to answer the matters raised in the mandate. Paris adds that the king and his magnates were angered by this and renewed their attacks on Dafydd (Paris, *CM*, iv. 399–400). After diplomatic overtures by Henry, the pope annulled all the actions of the abbots in a letter to the bishops of Ely and Carlisle dated at Lyons, 8 April 1245, declaring that Dafydd's predecessors had been vassals of the English kings from time immemorial and that the prince's claim to have been given as an *alumpnus* of the Roman Church was false (*Foedera*, I. i. 255; Haddan and Stubbs, i. 471–2). Thus ended Dafydd's attempt to hold Gwynedd as a vassal of the papacy (see Richter, 'David ap Llywelyn'). That the prince's claim to have been given as an *alumpnus* to the Roman Church had some foundation, though he may well have sought to make more of the relationship than had originally been intended, is shown by a letter of 29 April 1226 from Pope Honorius III to the bishops of St Davids, Bangor and St Asaph, informing them that he had taken Dafydd, whom his parents had offered *in alumpnum quasi ecclesie Romane*, under the special protection of the apostolic see (cited in Crump, 'Repercussions', 204 and n. 29).

307 Rhys ap Hywel, Gwilym Fychan, Llywelyn ap Gruffudd and Madog Fychan, bailiffs of Brecon

Letter, informing them that he has recently heard the complaint of Abbey Dore, namely that certain malefactors, on some fictitious grounds, have inflicted serious injuries on their property and persons and threaten worse. Since these malefactors have sought refuge in the bailiffs' land, he orders them to protect the possessions of the said house from the injury and violence of these and others and not to give refuge to such malefactors, especially since the monks are ready to respond to those making claims against them and to make just satisfaction if necessary. The bailiffs should act in this matter so that Dafydd's said friends [of Abbey Dore] do not suffer damage on account of the bailiffs' lack of diligence.

[July 1244 × 25 February 1246]

B = BL, Add. MS 4558, fo. 256r. s. xvii/xviii.
Cd., Owen, *Catalogue*, ii. 909; *H*, no. 371.

D. princeps Wallie karissimis et fidelibus suis Reso filio Howel, Willelmo Vachan, Lewelino filio Grufut, Madoco Vachan ballivis de Breccon salutem cum dilectione. Querela amicorum nostrorum abbatii et conventus de Dora nuper ad nos devenit, quod quidam calumpniatiores sui et malefactores, quibusdam fictis occasionibus propositis, tam rebus quam personis suis graves iniurias et molestias iam intulerunt et maiores adhuc minantur. Cum igitur dicti malefactores in partibus vestris refugium habeant, vobis precipiendo mandamus quatinus ab eorum et aliorum iniuriis et violentiis dicte domus res et possessiones pro fideli posse vestro tueri curetis nec huiusmodi malefactores suos ad refugium recipiatis – eo maxime, quod dicti boni viri parati sunt eo modo quo viros decet religiosos calumpniatoribus suis respondere et cum iustitia si necesse fuerit satisfacere – tantum super hiis facientes, ne dicti amici nostri pro defectu diligentie vestre dampnum incurrant, set ut vos merito inde commendare teneamur. Valete.

Richter argued that any act of Dafydd containing the title 'prince of Wales' was probably issued between July 1244, when Dafydd was referred to as 'prince of North Wales' by Pope Innocent IV and 8 April 1245, when the pope reversed his earlier support for the prince, who, according to Matthew Paris, had sought to make Gwynedd a papal fief (Richter, 'David ap Llywelyn', esp. 209–10; no. 306 above). As the papal mandate of 26 July 1244 called him 'Dafydd, prince of North Wales', this style had probably been used by Dafydd in his letter to Innocent; if so, a *terminus a quo* of July 1244 is, indeed, likely, reflecting the prince's greater confidence in the wake of sympathetic treatment by the pope. However, since only one other act of Dafydd survives from 1244 onwards (no. 308 below, datable to January 1245, which also contains the title 'prince of Wales'), the wider date range for the style suggested here cannot be ruled out. A date during the period of Dafydd's military successes in Wales is consistent with the letter's substance: the monks of Dore clearly believed that the prince had influence in the lordship of Brecon; and it is significant that he addressed the bailiffs of Brecon, presumably drawn from leading Welsh families in the district, as his *fideles* (though not as *his* bailiffs). The letter very probably refers to attacks on Dore's lands in Cantref Selyf in the lordship of Brecon, as these lands were the subject of several disputes and attacks in the 1240s and 1250s, including attacks by Gruffudd Fychan and other Welsh of the cantref in 1240 (Williams, *White Monks in Gwent*, 38; cf. also no. 230 above). It is unknown whether Gruffudd Fychan, described as bailiff of Walter

Clifford (III) in 1240 (*Episc. Acts*, i. 369–70 (D. 520)), was related to either Gwilym Fychan or Madog Fychan (or both) addressed in the present letter. It is possible that Madog Fychan was the same as the man of that name who fled Brecon for the lordship of Builth in the summer of 1230 (see nos 263, 265 above; *CAC*, 35–6).

308 Walerand le Tyeis and John Lestrange

Letter, recalling well that his response concerning those matters in their previous letter was sufficient. So that no anger or . . . could be found from his side . . . he has made, namely . . . he rejects [(?)the truce] which they were able . . . with difficulty from the king . . . until the feast of Peter and Paul [29 June]. He is ready to accept a truce . . . to Michaelmas [29 September] or All Saints [1 November] or longer if the king wishes. Therefore he asks them, as his special friends, that, if they have the power to confirm [the truce] on behalf of the king, to inform him without delay. He is ready . . . to act humbly towards the king, his lord and uncle . . . and restore peace with him . . . as much as is in his power . . . the king wishes to maintain him and his allies . . . Seeks a reply by letter.

[Probably January 1245]

> A = TNA: PRO, SC 1/11, no. 54. No endorsements; approx. 137 × 62 mm.; mounted, foot cut away. The parchment is badly stained, making it illegible in parts.
> Cd., *CAC*, 49–50; *H*, no. 372.

D(avi)d princeps Wallie nobilibus viris et amicis suis predelictis dominis W. le Tyeis et I. Ext(ra)neo cum dilectione salutem. Satis recolimus quod sufficientem vobis ex parte nostra fuit responsum super hiis que in litteris vestris prioribus continebantur. Ne ex parte nostra indignatio vel . . . posset inveniri . . . fecimus, videlicet . . . quas cum difficultate domino rege potuistis . . . usque ad festum Pet(ri) et Pauli refutamus. Treugas . . . ad festum Beati Michaelis vel festum omnium sanctorum vel diutius si regie cederit voluntati parati sumus accipere et confirmare ex parte [(?)nostra].ª Itaque (?) vos rogamus ut dilectos amicos nostros et speciales quod [(?)or quatinus], si potestatem habetis eum . . . confirmare ex parte domini regis nobis sine mora significare velitis. Preterea sciatis quod parati sumus omnem . . . et humilitatem gerere erga dominum regem dominum nostrum et avunculum . . . et pacem cum eo reformare pro . . . posse nostro . . . dominus rex velit nos et imprisos nostros manutenere . . . Excusationibus ideo . . . nobis litteratorie . . . significetis. Valete.

ª *word illegible* A.

On 8 January 1245 Henry III empowered Walerand Teutonicus and John Lestrange, the addressees of the present letter, together with Henry of Audeley and Hubert Hose, to make a truce with Dafydd, and on 16 January he ordered that any truce made should not become operative until he had been informed of its terms and confirmed it (*CPR 1232–47*, 447, 448). As Edwards suggested (*CAC*, 50), it is very likely that the present letter was sent during the negotiations inaugurated by the appointment of the negotiators on 8 January. The document provides important evidence for Dafydd's assumption of the title 'prince of Wales' (see note to no. 307 above).

OWAIN AP GRUFFUDD
(d. *c*.1282)

309 Letter patent concerning Henry III
Notification that he has faithfully promised the king that he and his heirs will faithfully serve the king and his heirs for ever and will never be against them. If he or his heirs should leave their fealty and service, both the two cantrefs which the king has granted him and all the other lands in Wales which pertain to him by hereditary right shall be forfeit to the king and his heirs for ever, so that neither Owain nor his heirs shall ever have any right or claim in those lands. Sealing clause; witnesses.

Westminster, 16 November 1244

B = TNA: PRO, C 66/56 (Pat. R. 29 Henry III), m. 10d (contemporary enrolment).
C = TNA: PRO, E 36/274 (Liber A), fos 332v–333r. s. xiii ex.
Pd. from C, *LW*, 16 (no. 12).
Cd., *CPR 1232–47*, 462 (from B); *H*, no. 369.

Omnibus ᵃ⁻ad quos presens scriptum pervenerit⁻ᵃ Oweyn filius Griffini salutem. Ad omnium volo devenire notitiam me firmiter ac fideliter promisisse domino meoᵇ Henr(ico) regi Angl(ie)ᶜ illustri filio scilicet regis Ioh(ann)is quod ego et heredes mei eidem domino regi et heredibus suis imperpetuumᵈ fideliter et sine omni fraude serviemus nec aliquo tempore contra eos erimus, et si, quod absit, aliquo tempore a fidelitate et servitio eorum ego vel heredes mei discesserimusᵉ tam illa duo cantreda terre que prefatus dominus rex michi commisit quam tota alia terra in Wall(ia) que me hereditarie contingere poterit domino regi et heredibus suis imperpetuumᵈ incurratur, ita quod nec ego vel heredes mei aliquod ius vel clamium in terris illis umquam habere poterimus . In cuius ᵃ⁻rei testimonium huic scripto sigillum meum apposui.⁻ᵃ Hiis testibus: Rad(ul)fo filio Nich(ola)i,ᶠ Galfr(ido) Dispens(ario), Hug(one) de Vivonia, Rob(ert)o de Muceg(ro)s,ᵍ Herb(er)to filio Math(e)i, Pet(ro) de Geneue, Ioh(ann)e de Lexinton', Nich(ol)oʰ de Boleuill', Walt(er)o de Luton',ⁱ Anketill Maloreʲ et aliis. Actum apud Westm(onasterium) xviᵏ die novembris anno eiusdem regis regni xxix.ˡ

ᵃ⁻ᵃ C; etc. B. | ᵇ me B. | ᶜ Anglor(um) C. | ᵈ inperpetuum C. | ᵉ dissesserimus C. | ᶠ Nicol(ai) C. | ᵍ Muscegros C. | ʰ Nicol(o) C. | ⁱ Luyton C. | ʲ Mallore C. | ᵏ sextodecimo C. | ˡ vicesimo nono C.

Owain was released from custody in the Tower of London, where he had been kept with his father Gruffudd (d. 1 March 1244) since September 1241, and handed over to the care of John Lestrange, justice of Chester in mid-July 1244 (*CLR 1240–5*, 252). The present and the following document show that he had been summoned to Westminster by 16 November 1244. Owain remained in England under royal protection, receiving houses from the king in Shotwick, Cheshire, on 1 November 1245, until news arrived of the death of his uncle Dafydd ap Llywelyn on 25 February 1246 (*CPR 1232–47*, 465; Smith, *Llywelyn*, 49).

310 Letter patent concerning Henry III

Notification that, of his own free will and without fear of imprisonment or any other
punishment, he has undertaken to the king and his heirs that he and his heirs will serve them
faithfully for ever and never be against them and has sworn a corporal oath regarding this. If
he should ever leave their service he places himself and his heirs under the jurisdiction of the
archbishop of Canterbury and the bishops of Worcester and Hereford, or just two of them, so
that as soon as they learn that they have not been faithful to their aforesaid lords, they may
excommunicate him and his heirs without further warning and without any appeal or remedy
of a superior court, which he has renounced on behalf of himself and his heirs, until they have
made sufficient satisfaction. Sealing clause.

Westminster, 17 November 1244

> B = TNA: PRO, C 66/56 (Pat. R. 29 Henry III), m. 10d (contemporary enrolment).
> C = TNA: PRO, E 36/274 (Liber A), fo. 332v. s. xiii ex.
> Pd. from C, *LW*, 15–16 (no. 11).
> Cd., *CPR 1232–47*, 462 (from B); *H*, no. 370.

Omnibus [a]–Cristi fidelibus ad quos presentes littere pervenerint[–a] Oweyn filius Griffini
salutem in domino. Sciatis ʽme libero arbitrio et spontanea voluntate mea et nullius metus
causa vel carceris vel alterius cruciatus pepigisse domino meo Henr(ico) regi Angl(ie)[b]
illustri filio scilicet regis Ioh(ann)is et heredibus suis quod ego et heredes mei eis imperpetuum[c] fideliter et sine fraude serviemus nec aliquo tempore alicuius favore vel odio vel
etiam federe contra eos erimus et super hoc prestiti sacramentum corporale, et si, quod
absit, ab eorum servitio[d] discesserimus aliquo tempore suppono me et heredes meos iurisdictioni et potestati[e] Cantuar(iensis) archiepiscopi, Wigorn(ensis)[f] et Heref(ordensis)
episcoporum qui pro tempore erunt, vel duorum illorum si forte omnes superstites non
fuerint, quod statim cum ad eorum notitiam[g] pervenerit quod ad fidem et servitium predictorum dominorum nostrorum non fuerimus, liceat eis sine ulteriori cognitione me vel
heredes meos excommunicare et eadem sententia ligatos tenere sine omni appellatione et
superioris fori remedio quibus pro me et heredibus meis renuntiavi donec ad sufficientem
venerimus satisfactionem. In cuius [a]–rei testimonium presentibus litteris sigillum meum
apposui[–a]. Actum [h]–apud Westm(onasterium) septimo decimo die novembris anno regni
ipsius domini regis vicesimo nono.[–h]

[a–a] C; etc. B. | [b] Anglor(um) C. | [c] inperpetuum C. | [d] B *inserts* disserimus *struck through.*
[e] C *inserts* venerabilium patrum. | [f] Wygorn(ensis) C. | [g] notiam B. | [h–h] C; ut supra B.

See note to no. 309 above. On 17 November the king wrote to all his faithful men in Wales
and the Marches encouraging them to aid Owain, whom he had released from prison, and
also made a gift to Owain of 20 marks (*CPR 1232–47*, 446; *CLR 1240–5*, 277).

*311 Beddgelert Priory

Grant of all the township of Tre'r-beirdd in the commote of Menai (super totam villam que
vocatur Tref Ybeyrd apud Kynind Meney).

[March 1246 × mid-June 1255]

Mention only, in a letter patent of Anian, bishop of Bangor, dated at Maes-y-llan, 1 April 1286 (*Foedera*, I. ii. 664; *Mon. Ang.*, vi: i. 200; Haddan and Stubbs, i. 584–5; trans. Jones, 'Arvona mediaeva', 159; cd., Stephenson, *Governance*, 204; *H*, no. 166). The reference is to a *cartam domini Oweni*, most probably identifiable as Owain ap Gruffudd rather than Owain Gwynedd (Stephenson, *Governance*, 156). The charter was presumably issued in the period between Owain's return to Gwynedd following the death of Dafydd ap Llywelyn on 25 February 1246 and Llywelyn ap Gruffudd's victory at the battle of Bryn Derwin in mid-June 1255 which resulted in Owain's imprisonment (cf. Smith, *Llywelyn*, 73).

312 Agreement with Henry III (Treaty of Woodstock)

Agreement between the king and Owain and Llywelyn sons of Gruffudd:

(1) the king has remitted to them all the war and evils that they had waged against him up to 28 April and received them in his full grace with their homages, and the heirs of Owain and Llywelyn will likewise give their homages to the king and his heirs.

(2) Owain and Llywelyn grant and quitclaim for ever to the king the Four Cantrefs, known in Welsh as Perfeddwlad, namely Rhos, Rhufoniog, Dyffryn Clwyd and Tegeingl with their appurtenances and all the river Conwy, from which cantrefs the king will profit as he deems fit, and likewise grant all the land of Mold with its appurtenances, so that neither Owain nor Llywelyn, nor their heirs, will have any right or claim in those cantrefs or in Mold.

(3) The king grants to Owain and Llywelyn and their heirs the rest of the whole of North Wales, to be held from the king and his heirs for ever; for which Owain and Llywelyn shall provide the king, at his command, with the service of 1,000 footsoldiers and twenty-four well-armed knights, together with either Owain or Llywelyn or their heirs, at their own expense, for as long as the king, his heirs or any of his side are on campaign in Wales or the March; and 500 footsoldiers and ten knights, together with Owain or Llywelyn or their heirs, for as long as the king, his heirs or representatives require their service in England.

(4) Owain and Llywelyn grant that if anyone on the king's side wishes to bring an action against them or their heirs concerning the lands of North Wales or any part of them or others, they will come at the king's command on a day, and to a place, designated in the March or Wales to respond to the claim and receive justice according to the laws and customs of Wales; a similar procedure will be followed if Owain or Llywelyn bring an action against Welsh of the king concerning lands in Wales or elsewhere.

(5) All the Welsh both of the king and of Owain and Llywelyn will recover all the lands which they had, or to which they were entitled, both in the aforesaid cantrefs and in North Wales, and will hold them as freely as they ever held them, giving the due and customary services to the lords of the fees.

(6) The homages and services of all the barons and nobles of Wales will remain with the king and his heirs for ever.

(7) If Owain and Llywelyn or their heirs contravene the above terms and wage war against the king or receive any enemy of the king or his heirs or his men, they will lose the right to all their lands, so that neither they nor their heirs will have any right or claim in those lands, which will be forfeit for ever to the king and his heirs.

In order that all the terms will be observed faithfully the seals of Owain and Llywelyn have been affixed to the part of this chirograph which will be kept by the king, and the king has fixed his seal to that which will be kept by Owain and Llywelyn.

Woodstock, 30 April 1247

B = TNA: PRO, E 36/274 (Liber A), fos 329r–330r. s. xiii ex.
C = ibid., fo. 407r–v.
Pd. from from B, *LW*, 7–8 (no. 3); from C, *Foedera*, I. i. 267.
Cd., *H*, no. 373.

[A]d roborandam concordiam et pacem perpetuam inter dominum Henricu(m) filium regis Ioh(ann)is illustrem regem Angl(ie) et Oweynum et Lewelinu(m) filios Griffini et heredes eorum facta est conventio ista inter eosdem dominum regem et Oweynum[a] et Lewelinu(m), videlicet quod

[i] idem dominus rex motus pietatis affectu remisit ex toto eisdem Oweyno[b] et Lewelino totam guerram et omnia mala que adversus eum insipienter moverant usque ad dominicam proximam ante festum [fo. 329v] inventionis sancte crucis, et eos in plenam gratiam suam et homagia eorum recepit, et similiter facient heredes ipsorum Oweyni[c] et Lewelini homagia eidem domino regi et heredibus suis.

[ii] Et iidem Oweynus et Lewelinus pro se et heredibus suis concesserunt et quietum clamaverunt in perpetuum eidem domino regi et heredibus suis Quatuor Cantredos,[d] scilicet Ros, Rowennyok, Defrenclut et Anglefeld cum omnibus pertinentiis eorum et tota rivera de Cuneway sine ullo retenemento, qui quidem cantredi vocantur lingua Wallensica Peruethelad, de quibus etiam cantredis idem dominus rex et heredes sui proficium suum facient secundum quod sibi viderint expedire; et totam terram de Monte Alto cum pertinentiis suis sine ullo retenemento, ita quod nec ipsi Oweynus[e] et Lewelin(us) nec eorum heredes aliquod ius vel clamium habebunt vel habere poterunt in ipsis cantredis aut terra de Monte Alto vel eorum pertinentiis.

[iii] Prefatus autem dominus rex pro se et heredibus suis concessit dictis Oweyno[b] et Lewelino et eorum heredibus residuum totius Northwall(ie)[f] sicut se extendit, habendum et tenendum eisdem Oweyno[b] et Lewelino et eorum heredibus de eodem domino rege et heredibus suis in perpetuum, faciendi iidem Oweynus,[e] Lewelin(us) et eorum heredes eidem domino regi et heredibus suis ad mandatum suum servitium mille peditum strenuorum et viginti quatuor equitum bene armatorum cum altero eorundem Oweyni[c] et Lewelini vel heredibus eorum qui pro tempore fuerint, propriis sumptibus eorum, in Wallia vel in Marchia Wallie quamdiu idem dominus rex vel heredes sui aut aliquis ex parte ipsorum fuerit in Wallia vel in Marchia Wallie in expeditione, et quingentorum peditum strenuorum et decenter armatorum in Angl(ia) ad custum ipsius domini regis vel heredum suorum cum altero eorundem Oweyni[c] et Lewelini vel eorum heredibus qui pro tempore fuerint sicut predictum est, quamdiu idem dominus rex vel heredes sui aut ille qui fuerit ex parte ipsorum servitio eorum opus habuerit.

[iv] Preterea concesserunt et obligaverunt se predicti Oweyn(us)[e] Lewelin(us) pro se et heredibus suis in perpetuum quod si aliquis Wallensis vel alius qui fuerit ex parte predicti domini regis vel heredum suorum eosdem Oweynu(m)[g] et Lewelinu(m) vel eorum heredes super terris Northwall(ie)[f] aut aliqua parte ipsarum vel super aliis inplacitare voluerint, venient ad mandatum ipsius domini regis et heredum suorum aut ballivi sui qui pro tempore fuerit certis die et loco quos assignare voluerint[h] in Marchia vel in Wall(ia) responsuri super hiis et iuri parituri ac secundum leges et consuetudines Wallie iustitiam recepturi: simili etiam modo fiet de predictis Oweyno[b] et Lewelino vel eorum heredibus si contra Wallenses ipsius domini regis vel heredum suorum super aliquibus terris Wallie aut super aliis moverint questionem.

[v] Omnes vero et singuli Wallenses tam prefati domini regis quam dictorum Oweyni^c et Lewelini recuperabunt omnes terras quas habuerunt vel de iure habere debuerunt tam in predictis cantredis quam in Northwall(ia), et tenebunt eas adeo libere sicut ipsas unquam tenuerunt faciendi [fo. 330r] inde dominis feodorum servitia debita et consueta.

[vi] Per hanc autem conventionem homagia et servitia omnium baronum et nobilium Wallie prefato domino regi et heredibus suis in perpetuum remanebunt.

[vii] Si vero sepedicti Oweynus^e et Lewelinus aut eorum heredes venerint contra premissa vel eidem domino regi aut heredibus suis sive etiam alicui ex suis guerram moverint vel aliquem contra ipsum dominum regem vel heredes suos aut homines ad dampnum eorum receptaverint, cadent ipsi Oweynus^e et Lewelinus et eorum heredes a iure omnium terrarum suarum ubicumque fuerint, ita quod nec ipsi nec eorum heredes neque aliquis pro eis aliquod ius vel clamium habebunt aut vendicare poterunt in ipsis terris, set predictis domino regi et heredibus suis absque omni calumpnia remaneant in perpetuum et eis incurrantur.

Ut autem omnia premissa fideliter et irrefragabiliter in posterum observentur parti huius scripti in modum cyrographi confecti que penes prefatum dominum regem residet sigilla predictorum Oweyni^c et Lewelini sunt appensa, et alteri parti que penes ipsos Oweynu(m)^g et Lewelinu(m) remanet idem dominus rex sigillum suum fecit apponi. Actum apud Wudestok'ⁱ pridie kalendas maii anno gratie millesimo ducentesimo quadragesimo septimo et regni predicti domini regis tricesimo primo.

^a Owinu(m) C. | ^b Owyno C. | ^c Owyni C. | ^d candredos C. | ^e Owynus C. | ^f Nortwallie C. ^g Owynum C. | ^h voluerit C. | ⁱ Wodestoke C.

For assessments of the significance of the Treaty of Woodstock see Lewis, 'Treaty of Woodstock', esp. 45–65, and Smith, *Llywelyn*, 58–62. Owain and Llywelyn were compelled to submit to the king after royal forces led by Nicholas de Molis reached Degannwy in spring 1247. On 5 March 1247 a truce agreed with John de Grey, justice of Chester was confirmed and extended by the king to last for five weeks from Easter (31 March), and a safe conduct was issued to Owain and Llywelyn, covering the same period, for their visit to the king at Oxford on Thursday 18 April (*CPR 1232–47*, 498). The present document records the terms of the agreement reached as a result of that visit. Although the king did not invoke undertakings made by Dafydd ap Llywelyn in 1241 whereby the whole of Gwynedd would escheat to the Crown on his death without a legitimate heir or if he or his heirs ceased to give faithful service to the king (nos 300, c. xv; 303; 304, c. xiii; 305 above), the Treaty of Woodstock nevertheless marked a significant reduction in the status of the principality of Gwynedd by comparison with the supremacy achieved by Llywelyn ap Iorwerth and even by comparison with the reign of Dafydd ap Llywelyn. In particular, it revealed the king's determination to perpetuate the division of Gwynedd Uwch Conwy between Owain and Llywelyn as well as to underline its dependence on the crown through the novel imposition of military service as a condition of the princes' tenure.

313 Ynys Lannog Priory

Confirmation of the gift and confirmation of Prince Llywelyn, Dafydd and Llywelyn, Owain's brother, with respect to all the abadaeth *of Penmon, Bancenyn and Crymlyn with all their*

*appurtenances, just as these were granted by Llywelyn, Dafydd and Llywelyn Sealing clause;
witnesses.*

Bancenyn, 17 September 1247

B = TNA: PRO, C 53/81 (Ch. R. 23 Edward I), m. 2 (in an inspeximus, 4 May 1295).
Pd. from B, *Mon. Ang.*, iv. 582; from *Mon. Ang.*, Jones, 'Mona mediaeva', 50 (trans. only).
Cd., *CChR 1257–1300*, 460; Stephenson, *Governance*, 203; *H*, no. 150.

Universis Cristi fidelibus has litteras visuris vel audituris Owenus filius Griffini salutem in
domino. Noverit universitas vestra nos divine pietatis intuitu donationem et confirmationem dominorum[a] L. principis et David et L. fratris nostri antecessorum nostrorum super
totam *habadaed* de Penmon, Baginyc et Cremlyn cum omnibus pertinentiis suis priori et
canonicis de Insula Glanwc dedisse et presenti carta nostra confirmasse, prout melius et
liberius domini L., David et L. frater noster concesserunt et contulerunt. Et ut hec nostra
donatio rata et inconcussa permaneat in posterum hanc cartam sigilli nostri munimine
fecimus roborari. Hiis testibus: Lewelino filio Ennii, Lewelino filio Griffud, Tuder filio
Madoc', Eynnawu(n) Wechan, Maredud filio Iorwerd, Guen filio Griffud, Lewelino filio
Iorwerd, David filio Ennii et multis aliis. Datum apud Bagynic xv kalendis octobris anno
domini m° cc^mo xlvii.

[a] domino B.

A similar confirmation was issued on 6 January 1247 by Owain's brother Llywelyn,
although this contains no reference to Bancenyn (no. 320 below). Llywelyn ap Iorwerth
granted Bancenyn to Ynys Lannog in 1221 and the *abadaeth* of Penmon in 1237, grants
confirmed by Dafydd ap Llywelyn in 1229 and 1238 (nos 250, 273, 286, 288 above). That
the canons sought this confirmation from Owain suggests that he held power in Anglesey
by September 1247 (Stephenson, *Governance*, 158–9).

314 Letter patent concerning Henry III
*Notification that Owain and Llywelyn sons of Gruffudd have pledged their lands on behalf of
their younger brother Rhodri, who had been delivered to the king as a hostage for the release
of their father Gruffudd, and undertaken that he will stand faithfully with the king and his heirs
and never recede from the king's fealty. Sealing clause.*

15 March 1248

B = TNA: PRO, E 36/274 (Liber A), fos 333v–334r. s. xiii ex.
Pd. from B, *LW*, 19 (no. 16).
Cd., *H*, no. 374.

[O]mnibus presens scriptum inspecturis Oweyn(us) et Lewelin(us) filii Griffini filii Lewelini
salutem. Noveritis nos super terris et tenementis nostris ad plegiationem nostram
Roderychu(m) fratrem nostrum iuniorem, qui fuerat illustri domino H. regi Anglie
liberatus in obsidem pro deliberatione predicti G. patris nostri, suscepisse et manucepisse
pro eodem quod fideliter stabit cum predicto [fo. 334r] rege et heredibus suis nec resiliet a
fidelitate ipsius predicti regis in perpetuum. In cuius rei testimonium huic scripto sigilla
nostra fecimus apponi. Actum anno sepedicti regis tricesimo secundo idus[a] martii. Valete.

[a] *sic in* B.

Rhodri was released from the king's prison on 5 May 1248 (*CR 1247–51*, 45). However, he was again in royal custody 1250–4, as a hostage in Cheshire, suggesting that he was subsequently returned to the king, probably by Llywelyn ap Gruffudd (Stephenson, *Governance*, 160).

315 Henry III

Letter, from Owain and Llywelyn sons of Gruffudd, recalling that in their peace agreement with the king it is written that certain of his Welsh should recover land which had fallen under their power, and likewise their men ought to have their lands in the king's power in Perfeddwlad . . . his and their men stood in peace, finally in the previous year John de Grey, the king's justice . . . totally disseised their men at the said place of their lands and corn nor could they have their corn . . . they would have had the king's letters to the said justice concerning the restoration to their men . . . but the said justice made frivolous objections, saying that he would do nothing unless Maredudd ap Richard of Llŷn should have certain lands which the mother of Owain and Llywelyn had in dower for a long time, and other lands not mentioned in the aforesaid peace agreement. They therefore pray the king that he will restore the said peace with respect to them and their men, as their men have been despoiled of all use of their lands for almost a year. Though many urge them to disseise Welshmen of the king holding lands in their power, especially Maredudd ap Richard who does not answer to them for the great lands which he holds of them, they wish to give all honour to the king as their lord, hoping that, having heard their complaint, he will ensure that full justice is done to them and their men. If the said Maredudd or any other complains about them to the king, they are ready to give satisfaction according to the law of Wales, as set out in the aforesaid agreement, in a suitable place in the March; this Maredudd refused to accept from them on another occasion, when he sought to bring an action against them before the abbot of Chester of good memory and Henry Turbock, constable of Chester . . . Nor should someone whom the king has appointed on their behalf in the action brought against them act as an advocate, but rather hear and settle the complaints peacefully.

[October 1249 × -2 July 1250]

A = TNA: PRO, SC 1/4, no. 129. No endorsements; approx. 226 mm. wide × 105 mm. deep at left, 94 mm. deep at right; mounted, foot cut away. Parts of the parchment are missing.
Pd. from A, *RL*, ii. 64–5.
Cd., *CAC*, 32–3; *H*, no. 375.

Excellentissimo domino suo H. Deo gratia regi Angl(ie), domino Hib(er)nie, duci Norm(annie), comiti And(egavie) et Aquitann(ie) Owenus et Lewelinus filii Griffini, sui fideles et devoti salutem et se ipsos. Maiestati vestre satis notum esse credimus quod, cum nos ad pacem vestram vestri gratia suscepistis, in forma pacis inter vos et nos scripta continetur quod quidam Walenses vestri deberent terras quas habuerant in potestate nostra recuperare, et similiter homines nostri in potestate vestra apud Beruedlat terras suas habere deberent quod quidem . . .[a] pio bene actum fuit et utriumque homines tam vestri quam nostri in bona pace steterunt, tandem anno preterito dominus Ioh(ann)es de Grey, iusticiarius vester, nescivimus . . .[b] e nostros apud dictum locum terris et blado penitus dissegiavit nec poterunt habere bladium suum . . .[c] imponendo cum ipse et de terris suis sunt usque . . .[d] rimus, litteras vestras habuissemus dicto iusticiario directas de restitutione hominibus nostris super predictis facienda. Nullam tamen poterunt homines . . .ᵉ sed potius dictus iusticiarius. Frivole contra nos excipiebat, dicens quod nichil faceret, nisi Maredud filius Ricardi de Leyn haberet quasdam terras [qu]as mater nostra habuerat pro dote longo tempore, et alias de quibus non fuerat in forma pacis predicta mentio facta. Quare vobis ea qua possumus devotione supplicamus quatinus, si placet, pro amore et servitio nostro dictam formam erga nos et nostros reintegrari faciatis, quia fere per annum homines nostri omni commodo et utilitate terrarum suarum sunt spoliati. Et licet multi nobis suaderent Walenses vestros in potestate nostra terras habentes maxime Mared' filium Ricardi qui de magnis terris quas tenet de nobis non respondet nobis in aliquo dissegiare, volumus tamen, sicut debemus, vobis tamquam domino nostro totum honorem defferre, sperantes quod audita querela nostra tam sepe per vos ipsos n[obis] et nostris facietis plenam iusticiam exhiberi. Si vero dictus Mared' vel aliquis alius coram vobis querelam deponat de nobis, parati sumus eidem secundum legem Wall(ie), sicut contin[etur] in predicta forma, in loco competenti in Marchia vestra et nostra satisfacere humiliter et devote, quod quidem sepedictus Maredud, cum nos etiam conisset in causam coram bone m[emor]ie abbate Cestr(ie) et domino H. Turbock' constabulario castri Cestr(ie), recipere a nobis alias refutavit. Tantum igitur super hoc, si placet, facere dignemini quod ex dev[otis] . . .ᶠ s reddamur devotiores et ad obsequia promptiores. Nec debet, ut credimus, aliquis quem vos statueritis pro nobis in causa mota contra nos advocati officium exercere [vel] allegare, sed potius pacifice audire querelas et diffinare. Diu valeat et vigeat excellentia vestra in domino.

ᵃ *lacuna of c.9 mm.* | ᵇ *lacuna of c.35 mm.* | ᶜ *lacuna of c.4 mm.* | ᵈ *lacuna of c.33 mm.* | ᵉ *lacuna of c.25 mm.* | ᶠ *lacuna of c.10 mm.*

As Edwards showed (*CAC*, 33), the letter was sent after the death of Roger Frend, abbot of Chester, referred to here as *bone memorie*, shortly before 28 September 1249 and before the end of John de Grey's term of office as justice of Chester on 2 July 1250. Maredudd ap Richard (or Rhicert) of Llŷn was probably a grandson of Cadwaladr ap Gruffudd ap Cynan (d. 1172). His refusal to give any service to Owain and Llywelyn for his lands suggests that he claimed princely status, and he seems to have taken advantage of the weakness of Owain and Llywelyn after spring 1247 to try and restore the fortunes of his line; he is no longer attested after 1257 (Stephenson, *Governance*, 148–51; Smith, *Llywelyn*, 57–8, 61).

316 Letter patent concerning an agreement with Maredudd ap Rhys Gryg and Rhys Fychan ap Rhys

Notification by Owain and Llywelyn sons of Gruffudd, heirs of North Wales, of an agreement with their beloved kinsmen Maredudd ap Rhys Gryg and Rhys Fychan ap Rhys the Younger [Rhys Fychan ap Rhys Mechyll], sealed by an oath on relics, of such friendship amongst themselves that each will without delay help the other and defend him against everyone in upholding his rights and recovering what has been unjustly taken as if they were uterine brothers. To reinforce this obligation each party has agreed, renouncing all right of appeal and the benefit of both canon and civil law, that the prelates of the Church shall have the power to excommunicate any party breaking its terms. If any dispute shall arise between the parties, it shall be settled by suitable men chosen by both parties. The agreement has been written in the form of a chirograph, with the seals of Maredudd and Rhys attached to the part held by Owain and Llywelyn, those of Owain and Llywelyn to that held by Maredudd and Rhys.

Caernarfon, 1 October 1251

B = TNA: PRO, E 36/274 (Liber A), fo. 410v. s. xiii ex.
Pd. from B, *LW*, 160–1 (no. 284).
Cd., *H*, no. 378.

Universis Cristi fidelibus has litteras visuris vel audituris Owen(us) et Lewelinus filii[a] Griffini filii Lewelini quondam principis, heredes Norwall(ie), salutem. Universitati vestre significamus nos et confederatos nostros pro nobis et heredibus nostris ex una parte et dilectos et speciales consanguineos nostros dominos Maredud filium Resi Gryc et Resu(m) P(ar)vu(m) filium Resi Iunioris et omnis sibi coniunctos pro se et heredibus suis ex altera, prestito corporali iuramento tactis sacrosanctis, talem amicitiam inter `nos confirmasse, videlicet quod unusquisque nostrum pro fideli posse suo sine ulla fictione et dilatione cum opus fuerit in conservando ius suum et acquirendo quod iniuste ablatum est pro loco et tempore iuvabit alium et manutenebit contra omnes viventes ac si essemus fratres couterini. Et ad huius obligationis maiorem certitudinem Cristianitatem nostram sancte matri ecclesie obligavimus in hunc modum, scilicet quod prelati ecclesie maiores et minores sub alternatione manentes in terra partis in sua fidelitate perseverantis remoto omni appellationis obstaculo et etiam renuntiando beneficio utriusque iuris canonici videlicet et civilis, habeant potestatem excommunicandi partem ab hac forma resilientem canonica commonitione premissa. Et quia fieri non potest inter mortales instigante illo qui viam pacis non cognovit quin aliquando inter quoscumque dilectos vel coniunctos aliqua succrescat contentionis vel discordie sintillula, volumus et statuimus quod si quid contentionis vertatur inter aliquos de nobis statim per viros ydoneos ex consensu utriusque partis eligendos sub districtione predicte pene sopiatur, predicta tamen forma concordie in sua firmitate nichilominus perseverante. Et si certior sit in posterum confederatio premissa scriptum istud in modum cyrographi est divisum, ita quod parti remanenti apud heredes Norwallie predictos O. et L. sigilla predictorum nobilium Mared(ud) et Resi sint appensa et econverso parti remanenti apud predictos nobiles M. et R. sigilla predictorum O. et L. sint apposita. Actum apud Caerynaruon' anno domini m° cc° l primo die dominica proxima post festum Beati Mich(ael)is Arcangeli.

[a] filius B.

It is likely that the initiative for this agreement came from Llywelyn, who may have already made a similar agreement with Madog ap Gruffudd of northern Powys in 1250 (though the correct date may be 1257: see no. 323 below), and who held the commote of Arfon Is Gwyrfai in which Caernarfon was situated (Smith, *Llywelyn*, 68; for the situation in Ystrad Tywi see also Smith, '"Cronica de Wallia"', 269; Smith, 'Origins of the revolt', 153). This is the only extant document in which Owain and Llywelyn style themselves *heredes Norwallie* (cf. Stephenson, *Governance*, 159). The agreement provides an early Welsh example of familiarity with the renunciation of exceptions (*exceptiones*), that is, defences allowed to a defendant under Romano-canonical law (Walters, 'Renunciation of exceptions', esp. 127–8).

LLYWELYN AP GRUFFUDD
(d. 11 December 1282)

317 Ralph Mortimer

Quitclaim on behalf of Llywelyn and his heirs of all his rights in the lands of Maelienydd and Gwerthrynion to Ralph and his wife Gwladus and their heirs, so that Ralph and Gwladus may hold the said lands in peace without any claim by Llywelyn or his heirs. Llywelyn has sworn on relics that he and his heirs will defend Ralph and Gwladus and their heirs in their seisin of the lands and will give them aid and counsel against all men (B only: *saving faith with the king of England*).*

[Probably August 1241]

B = BL, Harl. MS 1240 (Mortimer Cartulary), fo. 57r. s. xiv/xv.
C = ibid., fo. 58r.
Pd. from B, Smith, 'Middle March', 88–9; from C, ibid., 92.
Cd., Stephenson, *Governance*, 203; *H*, no. 144.

[N]overint universi quod ego Leulinus filius Griffini filii Leulini quondam principis Norwallie omnino quietum clamavi pro me et heredibus meis Rad(ulf)o de Mortuo Mari et Gladuse uxori sue et heredibus eorum imperpetuum totum ius et clamium si quod habui vel habere potui in terris suis de Melenid et[a] Warthren' cum pertinentiis vel in aliqua ipsarum, ita quod dicti Rad(ulf)us et Gladusa et heredes eorum dictas terras de Melenid et de Warthren' bene et pacifice teneant et possideant[b] absque omni reclamatione mei vel heredum meorum. Ego vero Leulinus tactis sacrosanctis iuravi quod ego et heredes mei dictos Rad(ulf)um et Gladusam et heredes eorum in[c] seisina dictarum terrarum pro posse nostro manutenebimus et quod erimus eis auxiliantes et consulentes in omnibus agendis eorum contra omnes homines [d-]salva fide domini regis Angl(ie).[-d] Ad maiorem autem securitatem fidelitatis nostre observande presenti carte sigillum meum apposui. Hiis testibus: Ioh(ann)e Ext(ra)neo, Walt(er)o de Clifford, Thoma Corbet, Briennio de Brompton', Henr(ico) de Mortuo Mari, Ph(ilipp)o de Mortuo Mari, Rad(ulf)o de Arace, Godredo filio regis Mannie, Tudero filio Madoc, Kynewrek Seys, Eygnone filio Cradoc et multis aliis.

[a] C *inserts* de. | [b] posseant C. | [c] C *inserts* plena. | [d-d] *omitted* C.

The quitclaim is closely related to six charters in which various Welshmen, including descendants of the native lords of Gwerthrynion, quitclaimed their rights in Gwerthrynion to Mortimer; these charters in turn bear close affinities with five letters patent dated 14 August 1241 by which members of the dynasty of Maelienydd agreed a truce with Mortimer (*LW*, 54–8 (nos 80–4); nos 110–12, 116, 118 above; Stephenson, *Governance*, 230–2; Smith, *Llywelyn*, 41–3).

318 Einion ap Maredudd of Dyffryn Clwyd

Grant, in regard for his liberty (?braint), to Einion ap Maredudd of Dyffryn Clwyd and his heirs of all his land to be possessed in perpetuity free and quit of all secular services, except in the army, to Llywelyn and his heirs. Sealing clause; witnesses.

Llannerch, 27 September 1243

A = NLW, Bachymbyd 984. No endorsement; approx. 226 × 48 + 11 mm.; two cloth tags, each through two holes in the centre of the fold; sealed on tags. Seal missing.
Pd. from A, Davies, 'Grant by Llewelyn', 158.
Cd., Stephenson, *Governance*, 203; *H*, no. 145.

Omnibus Cristi fidelibus has litteras visuris vel audituris Lewelin(us) filius Griffini salutem eternam in domino. Noverit universitas vestra nos considerantes eius libertatem dedisse et concessisse Ennio filio Maredud de Deffrencluyt et heredibus suis totam terram suam cum omnibus pertinentiis suis a nobis et heredibus nostris libere, pacifice et quiete ab omni exa[ctio]ne[a] seculari preter exercitum in perpetuum possidendam. Et ut hec nostra donatio rata et inconcussa inposterum permaneat eam presenti scripto et sigilli nostri munimine fecimus roboravi. Datum aput Llanherch anno domini m° c°c° xl tercio quinto kalendas octobr(is). His testibus: domino R. Bangor(ensi) episcopo, Ph(ilippo) filio episcopi, Tuder filio Madauc, Kenwric Seys, Ioruerd filio Grugunan, Griffino Grec, David filio Heylin, Madoco Coch clerico nostro et multis aliis.

[a] *letters supplied where the document is damaged.*

For discussion of the charter and its context see Davies, 'Grant by Llewelyn'; Stephenson, *Governance*, 229–32; Barrell and Davies, 'Land, lineage, and revolt', 33–5; Smith, *Llywelyn*, 46 and n. 33. The phrase *considerantes eius libertatem* seems to mean that Llywelyn accepted that Einion held his land on privileged terms, which would explain the exemption from all services except serving in the army. It is possible that *libertas* was used as a Latin equivalent of the Welsh term *braint*, meaning '(privileged) status', though *dignitas* was the normal translation of *braint* in the Latin texts of Welsh law (cf. Pryce, *Native Law*, 238). Dafydd ap Gruffudd confirmed the grant in a charter for Einion's son Maredudd in 1260 (no. 441 below).

*319 Aberconwy Abbey

Grant of first voidance of Llywelyn's chapels, namely St Patrick of Cemais [Llanbadrig] and St Peplicius of Caernarfon [Llanbeblig], to be held as freely as any rector held them in the time of Llywelyn his ancestor.

[1246 × 1267]

Mention only, in an inspeximus of Edward III dated at Westminster, 24 March 1332 (*CChR 1327–41*, 269; *H*, no. 165). In contrast to the preceding confirmations of charters of Edward I (23 October 1284) and of Llywelyn ap Iorwerth (nos 218–19 above) the confirmation of Llywelyn ap Gruffudd's grant lacks any explicit reference to a written document. Llywelyn's grant can be no later than 1267, as it is followed in the inspeximus by a confirmation of the collation to Aberconwy of two parts of the chapel of Cemais by R., bishop of Bangor; this must be Richard, bishop 1237–67. Both Llanbadrig, the church of the *maerdref* of Cemais (cmt. Talybolion, Anglesey), and Llanbeblig, near Caernarfon (cmt. Arfon Is Gwyrfai), appear to have been held by Llywelyn following the division of Gwynedd with his brother Owain in 1246 (Smith, *Llywelyn*, 66–7). Cf. Hays, *History of the Abbey of Aberconway*, 116–17, which errs in placing the end of Bishop Richard's pontificate in 1265, and Carr, *Medieval Anglesey*, 271.

320 Ynys Lannog Priory

Confirmation of the gift and confirmation of Prince Llywelyn and Dafydd with respect to all the abadaeth *of Penmon with all its appurtenances and the whole township of Crymlyn, just as these were granted by Llywelyn and Dafydd. Sealing clause; witnesses.*

Llan-faes, 6 January 1247

B = TNA: PRO, C53/81 (Ch. R. 23 Edward I), m. 2 (in an inspeximus, 5 May 1295).
Pd. from B, *Mon. Ang.*, iv. 582; from *Mon. Ang.*, Jones, 'Mona mediaeva', 50 (trans. only).
Cd., *CChR 1257–1300*, 460; Stephenson, *Governance*, 203; *H*, no. 147.

Universis Cristi fidelibus has litteras visuris vel audituris Lewelin(us) filius Griffini salutem in domino. Noverit universitas vestra nos divine pietatis intuitu donationem et confirmationem dominorum L. principis et David antecessorum nostrorum super totam *habadaet* de Penmon cum `omnibus` pertinentiis suis et tota villa de Cremlin, similiter prout melius et liberius domini L. et David concesserunt et contulerunt priori et canonicis de Insula Glanauc, dedisse et presenti carta confirmasse. Et ut hec nostra donatio rata et inconcussa inposterum permaneat hanc cartam sigilli nostri munimine fecimus roborari. Hiis testibus: David filio Griffini, Tuder filio Madauc, Ioru(er)t filio Grugunan senescallis nostris, Gruffudo filio Gugaun, fratre Adda Lippa, Madauc filio Bledin, Madoco clerico nostro, David Coch, assistentibus fratribus minoribus Gervasio, Mared' et David. Datum apud Lammaes anno gratie millesimo cc° xlvii die Epiphanie.

For Llywelyn's grant and Dafydd's confirmation see nos 272 and 288 above. Owain ap Gruffudd made a similar confirmation on 17 September 1247 (no. 313 above).

321 Basingwerk Abbey

Confirmation in pure and perpetual alms of all gifts and liberties and all lands granted by Llywelyn's grandfather Llywelyn, prince of Wales, Dafydd ap Llywelyn and Owain Brogyntyn and his brother Elise; namely, Boch-y-rhaeadr with all its appurtenances from the place where the Derfel descends from the mountain called (?) Arenig Fawr (Eninc), and thence following that river until it falls into the Tryweryn, and thence to the boundaries of Amnodd, and whatever is contained between (?) Arenig Fawr (Eninc) and the said rivers up to Amnodd, and half the rivers as they form a boundary between that place and other lands, and all the pasture within the following bounds: the Derfel and Buarthmeini and Pont Dâr Emrys and Helicboteweis and Rioweden and expressly the pasture by Amnodd and Blaen-lliw on both sides and Dinas Teleri up to the river called Nant Cedryn; also the whole of Gwernhefin with the men of that township and all its appurtenances, so freely that Llywelyn shall demand nothing from the monks except for their prayers and services before God, and the men of that township shall render their services henceforth to the abbot and monks, absolved from their homage to Llywelyn, with the lands held in perpetuity, free and quit of all secular service to Llywelyn and his heirs, as fully and freely as they were held in the time of his predecessors; and also common pasture throughout Penllyn, for the use of their livestock of whatever kind, and freedom to take from the woods whatever they need for houses, buildings, fire-making and other necessities. Llywelyn and his heirs warrant all these grants against all men and women.

Bangor, 8 April 1247

B = TNA: PRO, C 53/73 (Ch. R. 13 Edward I), m. 26 (in an inspeximus, 12 June 1285).
C = TNA: PRO, C 53/116 (Ch. R. 3 Edward III), m. 26 (in an inspeximus of B, 17 February 1329).
D = TNA: PRO, C 53/164 (Ch. R. 15–17 Richard II), m. 16 (in an inspeximus of C, 2 December 1393).
Cd., *CChR 1257–1300*, 291 (from B); *CChR 1327–41*, 100 (from C); *CChR 1341–1417*, 342 (from D); Stephenson, *Governance*, 203; *H*, no. 148.

Omnibus sancte matris ecclesie filiis presentibus et futuris has litteras inspecturis vel audituris Lewelinus filius Griffini salutem. Noverit universitas vestra quod ego predictus L. pro salute anime mee et parentum meorum dedi et concessi et hac presenti carta mea confirmavi Deo et Beate Marie et monasterio de Basingwerk' monachisque ibidem Deo servientibus, in puram et perpetuam elemosinam omnes donationes et libertates et omnes terras quas Lewelinus princeps Wall(ie) avus noster et David filius eius et Owinus de Porcuntona et Elysse frater eius prefato monasterio pro suis animabus contulerunt, has videlicet Bocraeder cum omnibus pertinentiis suis ab eo scilicet loco ubi Deruael descendit de monte qui dicitur Eninc, et inde semper sicut eadem aqua circuit quousque cadat in Tarwerin, et inde iterum sursum iuxta Tarwerin, donec ad fines Amnaut perveniatur, et quicquid inter Eninc et aquas prefatas continetur usque Amnaut, et preter hec medietatem aquarum sicut dividunt inter locum illum et alias terras, et totam pascuam infra terminos susbcriptos contentam, videlicet infra Deruael et Buarthmeynin et Bondaremris et Helicboteweis et Riowode(n) et pasturam nominatim per Amnaut et Blaenkyu ex utraque parte et Dinasteleri usque ad aquas que vocantur Nantkedrin; et totam Wenenin cum hominibus eiusdem ville et cum omnibus pertinentiis et aisiamentis que ad predictam villam pertinent tam libere et quiete, quod nichil ab eis exigam nisi eorum orationes et beneficia apud Deum, et quicquid pro terra sua servitii faciunt abbati et monachis prefati homines ab homagio meo absoluti deinceps facient et michi nichil vel meis, habendas imperpetuum et tenendas libere et quiete a me et heredibus meis sibi et successoribus suis absque omni seculari servitio et exactione mei et heredum meorum in proprios usus, sicut plenius et liberius tenuerunt temporibus predecessorum meorum; et communem pasturam per totam Pennantlin, ut habeant eam ad averia sua cuiuslibet generis sint, et ut ibi habeant de averiis quantum voluerint, et in quibus locis eius libuerit, cum ceteris aisiamentis, in boscis et planis, in pratis et pascuis et in omnibus aliis locis, et ut de silvis sumant quelibet voluerint ad usus suos necessaria sufficienter, sive sint viride sive sicce, scilicet ad domos, ad edificia, ad ignium fomenta et ad cetera quelibet necessaria. Et ego L. et heredes mei has omnes donationes, libertates, terras et concessiones sepedictis abbati et monachis contra omnes homines et feminas imperpetuum warantizabimus. Et ut hec mea concessio et confirmatio stabiles et inconcusse permaneant presens scriptum sigilli mei munimine roboravi. Hiis testibus: Grufut filio Edneuet, Tuder filio Madoci, David filio Will(elm)i, Bledin filio

Grufut, Yoruert filio Grugunan et multis aliis. Actum anno domini m° cc° quadragesimo septimo die lune post octabas Pasche apud Bangor.

For the charters of Llywelyn ap Iorwerth, Dafydd ap Llywelyn, Owain Brogyntyn and Elise ap Madog, together with many of the place-names, see nos 213–14, 216, 292 above and nos 486, 492–5 below. The lands confirmed lay in the vicinity of the river Tryweryn and Llyn Tegid (Bala Lake). Boch-y-rhaeadr is situated on the south-western edge of Llyn Celyn (Boch y Rhaeadr farm SH 847 397); the Derfel is probably Nant Aberderfel, which flows into Llyn Celyn at SH 850 395.

322 Iorwerth ap Gwrgunan

Grant to Iorwerth ap Gwrgunan and his heirs of one half of the township of Cwmllannerch in Nanconwy, to be possessed for ever with all its appurtenances and liberties, without any exaction or secular service. Sealing clause; witnesses.

Penmachno, 26 July 1247

B = TNA: PRO, E 163/28/11, p. 12. s. xvi[1].
Pd. from B, Smith, 'Land endowments', 163.
Cd., *H*, no. 149.

Universis Cristi fidelibus has litteras visuris vel audituris Lewelinus[a] princeps Wallie filius Gruff(ini) salutem. Noverit universitas vestra nos dedisse, concessisse[b] et hac presenti carta nostra confirmavi[c] a nobis et heredibus nostris Ier' filii Grugvgan et heredibus suis medietatem totaliter ville que vocatur Cwmlanerch apud Nan', cum omnibus suis perti-nentiis [et][d] libertatibus, similibus cum omnibus suis aysiamentis in plano[e] et in bosco, in aquis, pratis, pascuis et pasturis, sine aliqua exactione et absque aliquo servitio seculari imperpetuum possidendam. Et ut hec[f] nostra donatio robur firmitatis[g] imperpetuum optineat eam sigilli nostri[h] caractere[i] fecimus consignari. Hiis testibus: Grifino filio Edn' Vych(a)n, Tud' filio M(er)ed'uth,[j] Blethyn filio[k] Griffini, Eny' filio Kreadoc, D(aui)d Goch, Grifino[l] filio Gogon', Ithell' capellano, D(aui)d filio Ier' cum multis [aliis].[d] Acta apud Pennan anno domini m° cc° xl° vii° in crastino Sancti Iacobi apostoli.

[a] Lewellinus B. | [b] concesse B. | [c] *sic in* B *(?for* confirmasse*)* | [d] *omitted* B. | [e] pleno B. | [f] hoc B. | [g] firmittatis B. | [h] B *inserts* carast *struck through.* | [i] caracoe *with line over* oe B. | [j] *recte* Madoc. | [k] fillio B. | [l] Grifno B.

For a full discussion of this charter see Smith, 'Land endowments'. The title *princeps Wallie* is almost certainly a later interpolation, as Llywelyn is not otherwise known to have used this style before 1258 (cf. ibid., 153). The words *hac presenti carta nostra confirmavi* may be a dependent clause (as suggested in ibid., 163, n. 3), but the use of the first person singular in the verb is at variance with the use of the first person plural throughout the rest of the document and thus strengthens the case for an original reading of *confirmasse*. Iorwerth had been a close adherent of Llywelyn since at least 1243, when he witnessed the charter for Einion ap Maredudd; he also witnessed the prince's charters for Ynys Lannog and Basingwerk in 1247 (nos 318, 320–1 above). The charter shows that Llywelyn was in possession of the commote of Nanconwy in the cantref of Arllechwedd by July 1247.

323 Agreement with Gruffudd ap Madog of Bromfield

Agreement, in the form of a chirograph, between Llywelyn and Madog ap Gruffudd of Bromfield that both for as long they live will be of one confederacy and the same union against all men, great or small, whereby if one is troubled or deprived of his right by a third party of whatever nation the other will aid him with all his power without any delay or compulsion. Whenever one summons the other to him, for whatever reason or necessity, the other will bring aid to him without delay. In case either Llywelyn or Gruffudd should later act against this confederacy and union, both have placed themselves under the jurisdiction of the pope, who, at the request of either of them, may demand a sentence of excommunication and interdict against the one who breaks the said confederacy and union until he shall observe it in full. Both renounce any right of appeal or remedy in either the civil or ecclesiastical courts which would counteract such a sentence of excommunication and interdict.

20 November 1250 [*?recte* 20 November 1257]

B = TNA: PRO, E 36/274 (Liber A), fo. 403v. s. xiii ex.
Pd. from B, *LW*, 148 (no. 261).
Cd., *H*, no. 376.

Anno domini m° cc° quinquagesimo xx° die novembris facta fuit hec conventio inter dominum Lewelinum filium Griffini ex una parte et dominum Griffinum filium Madauc dominum de Bromfeld ex altera, videlicet quod ambo erunt quoad vixerint unius confeder-ationis et eiusdem unionis contra omnes homines sive maiores fuerint sive minores, ita quod si aliquis vel aliqui cuiuscumque nationis insurgant contra alterutrum ipsorum vel inqui-etent aut molestent ipsum vel presumant auferre aut detinere aliquid de iure alterutrius ipsorum, alter sine dilatione, difficultate vel compulsione cum omni posse quod habuerit et quod perquirere poterit prestabit alteri fideliter auxilium, tutamen et succursum. Item quandocumque et in quacumque occasione vel necessitate unus eorum voluerit alterum requirere vel vocare, alter indilate cum toto posse quod habuerit et quod aliunde habere poterit alteri veniet in auxilium et succursum. Ne autem alter dictorum vel Lewell(inus) vel Griff(inus) possit in posterum contra dictam confederationem et unionem venire, ambo supposuerunt se iurisdictioni domini pape quod ipse ad conquestionem alterutrius ipsorum possit demandare sententiam excommunicationis in personam et interdicti in terras et possessiones illius qui dictam confederationem et unitatem infringere presumat donec ad ipsam rediens eandem fideliter et totaliter observet. Ambo etiam renuntiaverunt pro parte sua appellationi, impetrationi, cavillationi et omni iuris remedio tam fori civilis quam eccle-siastici valituri contra dictam sententiam excommunicationis et interdicti si contra partem alterutram fuerit quod absit promulganda. Et ad plenam securitatem huius confederationis et unitatis tam dictus Lewell(inus) quam dictus Griffin(us) huic cyrografpho sigilla sua fecerunt alternatim apponi.

The date given in the document as transmitted in B is problematic. Lloyd held that 20 November 1250 was 'far too early' and favoured 1257 (cited in Smith, *Llywelyn*, 68, n. 123). In an unpublished paper delivered at Bangor in October 2002 David Stephenson supported this suggestion on the grounds, first, that an agreement with the lords of Ystrad Tywi dated 1 October 1251 was made by both Owain and Llywelyn (no. 316 above), whereas the naming of Llywelyn alone in the present agreement pointed to a date after his establishment of sole rule in Gwynedd Uwch Conwy as a result of his defeat of Owain in 1255; and, second, that Gruffudd ap Madog maintained his allegiance to Henry III after November 1250, and only defected to Llywelyn by the autumn of 1257, following the failure of the royal campaign that summer (cf. Smith, *Llywelyn*, 93–4, 111). If the date given in the document is in fact correct (as argued in ibid., 68 and n. 123), the agreement may have been aimed against any challenge from rival members of the two parties' dynasties, supported by the crown (Smith, 'Dynastic succession', 228).

*324 Beddgelert Priory

*Grant of all the land of the men of Trefan at Cenin fynydd and Llecheiddior (*super totam terram hominum de Trehan apud Kenynbeind et Lecheitaur*).*

[mid-June 1255 × 11 December 1282]

Mention only, in a confirmation of Bishop Anian of Bangor dated at Maes-y-llan, 1 April 1286 (*Foedera*, I. ii. 664; *Mon. Ang.*, vi: i. 200; Haddan and Stubbs, i. 584–5; cd., *H*, no. 171). Llywelyn's establishment of authority in the area after defeating his brother Owain ap Gruffudd at Bryn Derwin in mid-June 1255 provides a *terminus a quo* for the grant. Trefan (Trefan Hall at SH 481 393) and Llecheiddior (Plas Llecheiddior at SH 477 437) were free townships located to the south-west of Beddgelert (cmt. Eifionydd); Cenin fynydd (summit of Mynydd Cennin at SH 458 450) was a hamlet in Llecheiddior, of which the bond lands of Pant ddreiniog and Bwlch Gwyn belonged to the priory according to early modern records (Gresham, *Eifionydd*, 201).

*325 Beddgelert Priory

*Grant of all that land [of Tre'r-beirdd?] and the site of Beddgelert (*super totam terram illam et locum de Beckellers*).*

[mid-June 1255 × 11 December 1282; possibly 11 March 1269 × 11 December 1282]

Mention only, in a confirmation of Bishop Anian of Bangor dated at Maes-y-llan, 1 April 1286 (*Foedera*, I. ii. 664; *Mon. Ang.*, vi: i. 200; Haddan and Stubbs, i. 584–5; cd., *H*, no. 172). The *terra illa* of the reference probably refers back to the grant by Owain ap Gruffudd of Tre'r-beirdd (cmt. Menai, Anglesey) which immediately precedes it in the list (no. 311 above). The present grant is unlikely to be earlier than Llywelyn's capture of Owain at the battle of Bryn Derwin in mid-June 1255. However, if, as Gresham suggested (*Eifionydd*, 64), the site of Beddgelert was implicitly included in the lands in Nant Colwyn granted in no. 367 below, the charter was issued after 11 March 1269.

*326 Henry III

Letter, requesting that a way be opened by which Llywelyn could be reconciled with the king and receive his grace.

[*c.*December 1256]

Mention only, in a letter from Henry III to Llywelyn, dated at Merton, 2 January 1257 (*CR 1256–9*, 115; cd., *H*, no. 470). The king reveals that Llywelyn's letter had been taken by the abbot of Basingwerk, and replies that he would be pleased to see Llywelyn or his messengers, and is willing to provide a safe conduct.

327 Richard, earl of Cornwall and king of the Romans

Letter, thanking him for his efforts in re-establishing peace between the king and the Lord Edward, his nephew, and Llywelyn, as he has been informed by Richard's messengers, who have told Llywelyn that he should restore to the king and the Lord Edward all the land which he has recently occupied. However, Llywelyn neither will nor ought to do this because of the injuries inflicted by the bailiffs of the king upon him and his men against the terms of the peace, which he has requested to be redressed by the king without result. The king has granted the said land to the Lord Edward, making no mention of Llywelyn's complaints, and Edward, led by the counsel of Llywelyn's enemies did not cease to labour for the destruction of Llywelyn and his people. As a result, placing his hope in the goodness of God and fearing his and his people's destruction, Llywelyn by the common counsel of all the magnates of Wales has invaded the land which belongs by right to him and his predecessors. Although he has frequently offered a large sum of money to the king, queen and Edward, together with the four cantrefs of Perfeddwlad, so that the king might maintain him in the rest of the whole of North Wales, as contained in the agreeement between him and the king, they refused to accept his offer. Nor did the envoys sent most recently to the royal court seeking a reply to his offer receive anything, but waited for a long time in vain, so that he was utterly desperate. If he restored the said land to Edward on Richard's advice, Llywelyn believes that great discord would break out between him and the king on account of the injuries inflicted by Edward and his men, as happened before. Llywelyn is still ready to offer a sum of money to the king, Edward and the queen, together with the commote of Creuddyn containing the castle of Degannwy and the commote of Prestatyn containing the castle of Diserth, in return for a lasting peace. But if Richard cannot induce the king and Edward to have a lasting peace, Llywelyn is willing to offer 1,500 marks for a seven-year truce. Having regard for God and for the rights of himself and his predecessors, Llywelyn humbly begs Richard to intervene diligently and amicably on his behalf with the king and Edward so that they may receive him into their favour and peace. And Llywelyn shall not fail to show them faithful service and custom for his right in Wales. He requests Richard to inform him by letter what he will be willing to do in this matter.

[Probably 10 February × March 1257]

A = TNA: PRO, SC 1/11, no. 55. No endorsements; approx. 229 × 97 mm.; mounted, foot cut away.
Pd. from A, *RL*, ii. 312–14.
Cd., *CAC*, 50–1; *H*, no. 379.

Excellentissimo viro domino Ric(ardo) comiti Cornub(ie), regi Romanor(um) et per Dei gratiam imperatori L. filius Griffini salutem et paratam ad obsequia voluntatem. Excellentie vestre grates referimus copiosas de diligenti cura vestra circa reformationem pacis inter dominum regem et dominum Edwardu(m) nepotem vestrum ex una parte et nos ex altera, sicut per fratres predictos nuntios vestros ad nos destinatos intelleximus, qui nobis ex parte vestra consulendo dixerunt quod totam terram quam nuper occupavimus domino regi et domino E. filio suo restituere deberemus. Quod minime sustinere volumus, nec de iure debemus, propter gravamina infinita ostendenda vobis pro loco et tempore que a ballivis domini regis nobis et nostris contra formam pacis iniuste fuerunt illata; que a domino rege pluries quesivimus emendari, quorum emendam non fuimus subsecuti. Predictus autem dominus rex dedit et concessit predictam terram domino Edwardo, de querelis nostris penitus non faciens mentionem; qui ad destructionem nostram et gentis nostre, ut a probis viris et fide dignis indubitanter audivimus, consilio inimicorum nostrorum ductus die ac nocte laborare non cessabat. Propter que in bonitate Dei sperantes, et destructionem nostram et gentis nostre timentes consilio omnium magnatum Wallie communicato, qui nobiscum eiusdem pacis sunt et debent esse, predictam terram ad nos et antecessores nostros de iure pertinentem invasimus. Et licet magna summa pecunie domino regi et domine regine et domino Edwardo a nobis pluries fuisset oblata, cum quatuor cantredis de Perwetglaut, ita quod dominus rex nos manuteneret in residuo tocius Norwallie, sicut in litteris conventionis inter dominum regem et nos continetur, nostram tamen oblacionem recipere noluerunt. Nec nuntii nostri ad curiam domini regis ultimo destinati super oblacione nostra responsionem petentes, aliquam habere potuerunt, licet ibidem diu exspectarent. Propter quod omnino fuimus desperati. Et sciatis quod si iuxta consilium vestrum, ut credimus, domino Edwardo predicta terra a nobis restitueretur, perturbacionem et contencionem et magnam discordiam inter dominum regem et nos, quod absit, in brevi suboriri credebamus. Et hoc propter iniurias et gravamina a domino E. et suis nobis et nostris inferenda, sicut prius fecerunt. Adhuc parati sumus et erimus secundum fidele posse nostrum ad offerendum domino regi et domino E. et domine regine et vobis summam pecunie prout videritis expedire, cum uno comotho in quo est castrum de Gannuot, qui vocatur Creuthin, et alio comotho in quo est castrum de Disserd, qui vocatur Prestactune, pro perpetua pace habenda nobis et nostris et omnibus qui sunt nobiscum eiusdem pacis et belli. Si autem per nobilitatem vestram excellentiam dominum regem et dominum E. ad perpetuam pacem habendam inducere non poteritis, pro treugis usque ad septem annos habendis pro nobis et nostris, sicut predictum est, mille marcas cum dimidio domino regi et domino E. in terminis statuendis solvendis offere velitis. Unde nobilitati vestre, de qua maximam gerimus fiduciam, humiliter supplicamus et devote quatinus Deum habentes pre oculis et iura nostra et antecessorum nostrorum in Wallia considerantes, partes vestras versus dominum regem et E. filium suum si placet pro nobis diligenter et amicabiliter interponatis, ut ipsi ad eorum gratiam et pacem nos recipiant. Et nos eis fidele servicium et consuetum pro iure nostro in Wallia exhibere non omittemus. Et quicquid si placet super hoc facere volueritis nobis per litteras vestras significare velitis. Valeat excellentia vestra diu in domino.

Llywelyn entered Perfeddwlad at the beginning of November 1256 (Smith, *Llywelyn*, 84–5 and n. 186). This letter was almost certainly written in response to Richard's request in January 1257 for Llywelyn to desist from his attacks there, and after Henry III's grant on 10 February 1257 of safe conduct to Llywelyn's envoys to the earl, to last until 8 April of that year (Paris, *CM*, v. 613; *CPR 1247–58*, 541; discussion in *HW*,, ii. 720, n. 21, followed by *CAC*, 51, and Smith, *Llywelyn*, 97, n. 26).

328 Agreement between Walter Comyn, earl of Menteith and other Scottish lords and Llywelyn ap Gruffudd, prince of Wales and other Welsh lords

Walter Comyn, earl of Menteith, Alexander Comyn, earl of Buchan and justiciar of Scotland, William, earl of Mar, William, earl of Ross, John Comyn, justiciar of Galloway, Aymer de Maxwell, chamberlain of Scotland, Freskin de Moray, Hugh de Abernethy, William de Mowat, William Comyn and Richard Comyn brothers of John Comyn, Hugh and Walter de Berkeley, Bernard de Mowat, Reginald Cheyne, David de Lochore, John de Dunmore, William de Airth, Hector de Carrick, with their kin and liege men, greeting. Notification that on 18 March 1258 they have made an agreement of mutual alliance and friendship with Llywelyn ap Gruffudd, prince of Wales, Dafydd ap Gruffudd his brother, Gruffudd ap Madog, lord of Bromfield, Maredudd ap Rhys [Gryg], Maredudd ab Owain [of Ceredigion], Rhys Fychan, Owain ap Maredudd [ap Rhobert of Cedewain], Madog ap Gwenwynwyn, Maredudd Sais, Llywelyn Fychan, Owain and Maredudd sons of Llywelyn lord of Mechain, Owain ap Gruffudd, Madog Fychan, Owain ap Bleddyn, Hywel ap Maredudd, Elise ap Iorwerth and Gruffudd ap Iorwerth [of Edeirnon], Goronwy ab Ednyfed, Iorwerth ap Gwrgunan, Einion Fychan, Tudur ap Madog, Einion ap Caradog, Iorwerth ap Maredudd, Dafydd ab Einion, Ieuaf Goch, Rhys ab Ednyfed, with their kin and liege men. None of the parties will make any agreement with the king or magnates of England and Scotland unless the latter are bound with them in all of the present confederacy. They will not allow any forces to leave Scotland, nor help the king of England in any way, against the aforementioned prince and magnates, but rather will provide the latter with aid and counsel. If they are compelled by order of the king of Scots to make a peace or truce with the king of England or any other enemy of the prince and magnates, they will endeavour as far as possible to do so with regard to the interests of the prince and magnates, and indeed to persuade their king to uphold the present agreement. They offer safe conduct to merchants travelling from Wales to Scotland, and will induce Scottish merchants to come to Wales with their business. Each pledges his faith to Gwion of Bangor, the prince's messenger, to observe the agreement in the faith of the king of Scotland and swears an oath on the Gospels. A record of the agreement has been made in the form of a chirograph, each party keeping the half bearing the seals of the other. The prince and magnates likewise pledge their faith to the Scottish messenger Alan de Irvine and swear an oath.

18 March 1258

B = TNA: PRO, E 36/274 (Liber A), fo. 185v. s. xiii ex.
Pd. from B, *Foedera*, I. i. 370; from B, *LW*, 184–6 (no. 317).
Cd., *Calendar of Documents relating to Scotland*, ed. Bain, i. 421–2 (no. 2155); *H*, no. 380.

Omnibus sancte matris ecclesie filiis hoc scriptum visuris vel audituris Walt(er)us Cumin comes de Menetht', Alex(ander) Cumyn comes de Buchan iusticiarius Scot(ie), Will(elmu)s comes de Mar, Will(elmu)s comes de Ros, Ioh(anne)s Cumyn iusticiarius Galwedie, Aimerus de Makiswel camerarius Scotie, Fresekinus de Morauia, Hug(o) de Abirinchun, Will(elmu)s de Mohaut, Will(elmu)s Cumyn et Ric(ardu)s Cumyn fratres domini Ioh(ann)is Cumyn, Hug(o) et Walt(erus) de Berkeleya fratres, Bernardus de Mohaue, Reginaldus Cheyn, David Lochor, Ioh(anne)s Dundemor, Will(elmu)s de Erth, Ector de Karric', eorum amici, parentes et alligati universi salutem. Noverint nos anno gratie m°cc° quinquagesimo octavo, decimo octavo die mensis martii, de communi nostrum assensu et consensu cum domino Lewelin(o) filio Griffin(i) principe Wall(ie) et David filio Gruffud fratre suo uterino, Gruffud filio Maduc domino de Bromfeld, Maredud filio Ris, Maredud filio Ouener, Reso Iuniori, Oweyn filio Maredud, Madauc filio Wenwywin, Maredud Seis, Lewelin Vechan, Owein, Maredud filiis Leweliner[a] domini de Mechein, Owein filio Gruffud, Madauc Parvo, Owein filio Bledyn, Howel filio Maredud, Elisse et Grufud filiis Ioru(er)th, Gorone filio Edneuet, Ioru(er)th Gruginan, Enniay Vechan, Tudir filio Mad', Enniaun filio Karaduc, Ioru(er)th filio Maredud, David filio Enniayn, Ieuav Choch,[b] Roys filio Ednevet et eorum amicis et alligatis hanc fecisse conventionem mutue confederationis et amicitie, videlicet quod sine communi consensu et assensu prefatorum principis et magnatum decetero nullam pacem aut formam pacis, treugam aut formam treuge faciemus cum domino rege Angl(ie) aut aliquo magnate regni Angl(ie) aut regni Scotie qui tempore confectionis presentis scripti prefati principi et magnatibus et terris suis et nobis contrarii extiterint et rebelles, nisi illi ad omnem hanc eandem confederationem pariter nobiscum teneantur. Nos etiam contra prefatos principem et magnates nullam potentiam utpote excercitum, equitum aut peditum exire permittemus de Scotia nec in aliquo contra ipsos prefato regi Angl(ie) succursum prestabimus aut favorem, immo eisdem principi et magnatibus et terre sue fideliter auxiliantes erimus et consulentes. Et si contingat quod cum domino rege Angl(ie) aut quocumque viro prefatis principi et magnatibus aut nobis iam adversante per domini nostri regis Scotie preceptum pacem aut treugam inire compellamur, nos in bona fide quantum poterimus et sciemus ad prefatorum principis et magnatum suorum et terre sue commodum et honorem hoc fieri procurabimus cum effectu, nequaquam de voluntate nostra nisi per prefati domini nostri districtam compulsionem hoc fuerit et preceptum in aliquo contra presentem confederationem faciemus, immo dominum nostrum pro hac eadem confederatione nobiscum inienda et observanda quantum poterimus inducemus. Mercatoribus Wallie cum ad partes Scot(ie) cum suis negotiationibus venire valeant licentiam veniendi et prout melius poterunt negotiationes suas vendendi pacem etiam et protectionem nostram salvo et secure morandi et sine quacumque vexatione cum eis placuerit recedendi concedimus ex affectu. Mercatoribus etiam Scotie ad partes Wallie de licentia nostra cum suis venire negotiationibus persuadebimus ex corde. Ad predicta omnia et singula in fide predicti domini regis Scotie fideliter, integre et illese et sine fraude et dolo et in bona fide observanda unusquisque nostrum in manu Gwyd' de[c] Bangr' nuntii prefatorum principis et magnatum fidem suam prestitit et tactis sacrosanctis ewangeliis corporale sacramentum. In cuius rei testimonium huic scripto per modum cyrographi confecto et penes prefatos principem et magnates remanenti quilibet nostrum sigillum suum fecit apponi, predicti vero princeps et magnates in manu Alani de Yrewyn nuntii nostri similiter prestitis fide sua et tactis sacrosanctis ewangeliis iuramento consimili scripto huius confederationis et amicitie penes nos remanenti in testimonium singula sigilla sua apposuerunt.

[a] *sic in* B. | [b] Chch B. | [c] et B.

For the context and significance of this agreement, the earliest surviving document in which Llywelyn is given the title 'prince of Wales', see Barrow, 'Wales and Scotland', 311–12; Young, *Robert the Bruce's Rivals*, 57–8; Smith, *Llywelyn*, 110–14. The alliance was made when the Comyns were beginning to lose support in Scotland and the text makes clear that they felt unable to control the young king, Alexander III; by contrast, Llywelyn's supremacy over most of the other Welsh lords is clear. Smith argues that it was the Welsh who first sought the alliance, and suggests that its terms may have been drawn up at the assembly of the magnates of Wales in 1258 mentioned in *Brut y Tywysogyon* (ibid., 111, following *HW*, ii. 723, n. 42). Young likewise attributes the initiative to the Welsh, whereas Barrow suggests that it may equally well have come from the Scots.

329 Letter patent concerning Maredudd ap Rhys

Notification that Llywelyn has promised Maredudd ap Rhys and his heirs, in return for his homage, to protect him together with his heirs, men, lands and castles from the attacks and damage inflicted by his enemies, when requested to do so by Maredudd or his heirs. He has also promised and sworn that he will never capture Maredudd or have him captured, nor imprison his son or accept him as a hostage, nor take Maredudd's castles into his possession or custody. Further, he grants this letter of safe conduct in perpetuity, allowing no injury to be inflicted upon him or his men whenever they should visit Llywelyn. If Llywelyn should break the terms of this letter, he wishes that he and everyone consenting to it shall be excommunicated and denounced throughout all the churches of Wales, renouncing all benefit of both ecclesiastical and civil law. The present letter patent has been sealed with the seals of (specified) bishops, abbots and priors and of Llywelyn and drawn up in the form of a chirograph.

Ekaedu Vannebedeyr, 26 April 1258

B = TNA: PRO, E 36/274 (Liber A), fo. 413r–v. s. xiii ex.
Pd. from B, *LW*, 168–9 (no. 294).
Cd., *H*, no. 381.

Universis sancte matris ecclesie filiis presentes[a] litteras visuris vel audituris L. filius Griffini salutem in domino sempiternam. Noverit universitas vestra nos pro nobis et heredibus nostris karissimo ac fideli nostro domino Maredud filio Resi et suis heredibus promisisse fideliter sine fraude vel dolo pro fideli homagio suo, posse toto et servitio fidelibus exibitis nobis et heredibus nostris ipsum et suos heredes et homines suas terras et sua castella ab inimicorum suorum molestationibus et iniuriis magnis videlicet et notoriis in quantum poterimus defendere ac etiam custodire, cum ab ipso vel a suis heredibus [fo. 413v] suis super hoc fuerimus[b] requisiti. Promittimus etiam eidem ac iuramus corporali prestito iuramento quod ipsum amodo nunquam capiemus vel capi faciemus, et quod filium suum non incarceremus vel pro obside recipiemus et quod sua castra[c] in nostram possessionem specialem vel sub nostra speciali custodia nullatenus acquiremus vel acquiri procuremus. Insuper has litteras nostras concessimus eidem perpetuo conductorias et inter nos et ipsum obligatorias, ita quod amodo non oporteat ipsum vel suos heredes a nobis petere alias litteras conductorias vel aliquem conductum personalem preter istas cum ad nos cum suo posse vel sine fuerit accessurus, nullam iniuriam sibi vel suis contra predictum tenorem in veniendo ad nos nobiscum morando et ad sua propria redeundo illaturos vel ab aliis secundum posse nostrum inferre permissuros. Quod si a predictis vel ab aliquo predictorum infideliter voluerimus resilire, concedimus, clamamus ac volumus tam nos quam `omnes nobis in hoc consentientes ipso facto ex tunc esse sentenctia maioris excommunicationis innodatos et a communione fidelium in perpetuum separatos, volumus etiam nos ex tunc tales esse per singulas ecclesias Wallie publice denuntiari et sententiam in nos excommuni-cationis in earum qualibet promulgari donec ad nostram obligationem et fidelitatem predicto domino factam et firmatam reversi fuerimus, satisfaciendo eidem plenarie de transgressis. Renuntiamus etiam ex tunc si in predictorum aliquo deliquerimus omni beneficio cuilibet iuris tam ecclesiastici quam civilis, et omnibus constitutionibus, institutis vel instituendis ne valeant nobis ad aliquam appellationem seu defensionem vel commodum aliquod in hac parte. Et ad maiorem securitatem de omnibus supradictis integre et inviolabiliter observandis sigilla proborum virorum dominorum videlicet Bangorn(ensis) et de Sancto Assapph episcoporum, abbatum de Abercon' et de Ennlli, priorum de Bekelert et de Onyslannauc, una cum sigillo nostro hiis litteris nostris patentibus et per modum cyrographi confectis fecimus apponi. Datum anno domini m° cc° l octavo in crastino Marci Ewangeliste apud Ekaedu Vannebedeyr.

ª presentas B. | ᵇ fuimus B. | ᶜ castram B.

This document 'is the earliest surviving example of a formal agreement between Llywelyn and a prince who acknowledged his supremacy by doing homage' (Smith, *Llywelyn*, 107). However, the submission of Maredudd ap Rhys, lord of Ystrad Tywi, was short-lived, and by the summer of 1258 he had resumed his loyalty to the crown (ibid., 108; no. 333 below).

330 Letter patent concerning the abbot of Aberconwy and Master Madog

Notification that since Llywelyn cannot be present at the forthcoming parliament at Oxford, he has appointed the abbot of Aberconwy and Master Madog ap Philip as his representatives to negotiate a peace or truce, and to offer money for a peace or truce according to Llywelyn's means. Llywelyn promises to pay the sum they promise in a reasonable time, and authorizes all that they agree on his behalf regarding the above or any other matter at the said parliament.

31 May 1258

> B = TNA: PRO, E 36/274 (Liber A), fo. 337r. s. xiii ex.
> Pd. from B, *LW*, 29 (no. 37).
> Cd., *H*, no. 382.

[U]niversis Cristi fidelibus presentes litteras visuris vel audituris L. filius Griffini salutem in domino. Quoniam ad instans parleamentum Oxon(ie) personaliter accedere non possumus dilectos nostros dominum abbatem de Ab(er)con' et magistrum Madoc filium Ph(ilippi) in dicto parleamento loco nostri instituimus ad pacem nobis recipiendam et formandam vel ad treugas recipiendas et formandas et ad pecuniam pro pace vel treugis secundum posse nostrum offerendam quam secundum quod promiserint promittimus nos temporibus competentibus soluturos, ratum et gratum habituros quicquid iidem abbas et magister dicto parleamento in omnibus supradictis vel in ipsorum aliquo vel aliquibus duxerint faciendum. Datum anno domini m° cc° l° octavo die veneris proxima post octavas Sancte Trinitatis. Valete.

The context of these negotiations is discussed in Smith, *Llywelyn*, 118–20. A parliament had been called at Oxford by 19 May, and met on 10 or 11 June (*CR 1256–9*, 222; Treharne, *Baronial Plan of Reform*, 72). A safe conduct for Llywelyn's messengers was issued on 2 June (*CPR 1247–58*, 632), and a truce – not a peace – concluded on 17 June. For the notification of its terms by Llywelyn's envoys see *LW*, 27–8 (no. 33), which shows that the abbot of Aberconwy was called Anian. For the text of the resulting agreement, issued by the royal chancery, see no. 331 below.

331 Truce with Henry III and the Lord Edward

Notification by the king that he has given a truce, on behalf of himself, his son Edward and their men, both English and Welsh, to Llywelyn ap Gruffudd, through the agency of Anian, abbot of Aberconwy and Master Madog ap Philip, having full power to negotiate on Llywelyn's behalf. The truce will run from the Tuesday before the Nativity of St John the Baptist [18 June] 1258, to the feast of St Peter in Chains [1 August] 1259.

(1) Each side will retain seisin of the lands, men, castles and other things which it held at the making of the present truce.

(2) In the mean time no one from either side may enter the land of the other or trade there, without special licence.

(3) Roads and passes shall not be obstructed with woods or other means.

(4) The king and his men will be allowed access to his castles of Diserth and Degannwy and supply them as necessary; if such supplies cannot easily be transported because of a storm or other impediments at sea, Llywelyn shall, at the summons of the justice of Chester, conduct the supplies safely by land together with their guards.

(5) If any of the garrison or servants of the said castles become ill, the king may send others in their place without any hindrance from Llywelyn.

(6) If either side breaks the truce in any way, amends shall be made by trustworthy men chosen by both sides.

Imbert Pugeys has sworn in the king's name, and the abbot and Madog in Llywelyn's, to observe the above.

Oxford, 17 June 1258

B = TNA: PRO, C 66/72 (Pat. R. 42 Henry III), m. 7 (contemporary enrolment).
Pd. from B, *Foedera*, I. i. 372.
Cd., *CPR 1247–58*, 636; *H*, no. 383.

Rex omnibus etc. salutem. Sciatis quod nos pro nobis et Edwardo filio nostro primogenito et omnibus hominibus nostris Anglicis et Walensibus et aliis Leulino filio Griffini, per Anianu(m) abbatem de Aberconnewey et magistrum Madoch' filium Ph(ilipp)i plenam habentes potestatem cum litteris predicti Lewelini ad treugam nomine suo recipiendam et affirmandam, treugam damus a die martis proxima ante festum nativitatis Beati Ioh(ann)is Bapt(iste) anno domini mᵒ ccᵒ lᵒ octavo usque ad festum Sancti Pet(ri) ad vincula anno domini mᵒ ccᵒ lᵒ nono, utraque die plenarie computata:

[i] ita quod quilibet et singuli de parte utraque habeant seisinam terrarum et hominum et castrorum ac aliarum rerum secundum quod tempore confectionis presentium habuerunt.

[ii] Et quod nullus interim ex parte alterutra ingrediatur terram alterius, nec in ipsa aliquam querat vel faciat mercandisam, nisi specialiter super hoc licentiatus.

[iii] Preterea vada vel passus non obstruantur, silvas complicando vel modo alio aliter quam sit modo.

[iv] Insuper licebit nobis et hominibus nostris castra nostra de Dissard' et de Gannok' visitare, et per dictum tempus victualibus et aliis que ad dicta castra utilia vel necessaria fuerint munire cum duobus batellis utroque cum xii remis vel paucoribus, secundum quod opus fuerit; ita tamen quod, si propter tempestatem vel alia impedimenta maris dicta victualia vel res absque periculo vel alias commode cariari vel deferri non possint, dictus Lewelin(us) victualia predicta cum rebus et hominibus ad dicta castra tam in eundo quam redeundo ad summonitionem iusticiarii Cestr(ie) salvo et secure per terram duci faciet et conduci una cum custodibus eorumdem.

[v] Et si contigerit aliquem de custodibus aut servientibus dictorum castrorum infirmari, licebit nobis et nostris alium vel alios loco ipsius vel ipsorum substituere vel ponere, sine impedimento vel molestia eis inferendo per dictum Lewelin(um) aut suos in accedendo vel redeundo.

[vi] Et si aliquid ex parte utraque transgressum fuerit vel occupatum iniuste infra tempus predictorum vel in treugis precedentibus, illud per viros fidedignos ex parte utraque eligendos, diebus et locis assignandis, emendetur.

Ad predicta autem firmiter observanda, dilectus et fidelis noster Imb(er)tus Pugeys nomine nostro iuravit, et predicti abbas et Madoch(us) nomine ipsius Lewelini similiter iuraverunt. In cuius etc. Teste rege apud Oxon' xvii die iunii.

See note to no. 330 above.

*332 Letter patent(?) concerning a monk of Aberconwy
Letter of accreditation for a monk of Aberconwy, Llywelyn's envoy.
[Shortly before 27 July 1258]

Mention only, in a letter from Henry III to Llywelyn, dated at Westminster, 27 July 1258 (*CR 1256–9*, 320; cd., *H*, no. 472). The king states that the envoy claimed on Llywelyn's behalf that the truce had been broken by the king's side. For the truce see nos 330–1 above.

*333 Henry III
Letter, informing the king that Patrick de Chaworth and the constable of Carmarthen and their men, in breach of the truce agreed at Oxford, have removed Maredudd ap Rhys from Llywelyn's fealty; subsequently Maredudd, with the aid of the said Patrick and his forces, invaded Llywelyn's land of Dyfed in breach of the truce.
[Shortly before 4 August 1258]

Mention only, in a letter from Henry III to Llywelyn, dated at Westminster 4 August 1258 (*CR 1256–9*, 323–4; cd., *H*, no. 471). Henry replied that Maredudd had already entered the king's fealty by the Oxford truce. For the terms of the truce see no. 331 above. Though Maredudd had submitted to Llywelyn in April 1258 (no. 329 above), his loyalty to the king was evident by the summer, resulting in his dispossession of Ystrad Tywi by the prince's forces (see Smith, *Llywelyn*, 108, 121).

*334 Henry III
Letter, concerning amends due to Llywelyn for breaches of the truce and also concerning the making of peace with the king.
[Shortly before 13 May 1259]

Mention only, in a letter from Henry III to Llywelyn, dated at Westminster, 13 May 1259 (*CR 1256–9*, 476; cd., *H*, no. 473). The king replied that he would send certain magnates of his council together with some of his faithful men from the March of Wales to meet

Llywelyn at the ford of Montgomery on the quinzaine of Holy Trinity next (22 June 1259) to make and receive amends and to discuss peace; these emissaries would then report back to the king. The truce agreed at Oxford on 17 June 1258 was due to expire on 1 August 1259 (no. 331 above), and the present letter suggests that Llywelyn sought to replace it by a firm peace treaty with the king. In the event, only a further truce was agreed, on 25 June (no. 336 below).

335 Letter patent concerning Henry III's representatives

Notification that Llywelyn will provide safe conduct for those attending on the king's behalf the next parley to be held at the ford of Montgomery up to the Thursday next after the feast of the Nativity of St John the Baptist [26 June].

22 June 1259

B = TNA: PRO, E 36/274 (Liber A), fo. 332r–v. s. xiii ex.
Pd. from B, *LW*, 15 (no. 9).
Cd., *H*, no. 384.

[U]niversis presentes litteras inspecturis L. filius Gruffini salutem. Noveritis quod nos damus pro nobis et nostris omnibus ex parte domini regis ad instans parleamentum ad vadum aque de [fo. 332v] Mungem(er)i venientibus plenam securitatem accedendi ad dictum locum et morandi ad negotia domini regis et sua si habuerint expedienda usque ad diem iovis proximam post nativitatem Beati Ioh(ann)is Bapt(ist)e et ad propria cum suis omnibus redeundi. In cuius rei testimonium nostrum sigillum hiis litteris patentibus fecimus apponi. Datum anno domini m° cc° l nono dominica precedente proximo nativitatem Beati Ioh(ann)is Bapt(ist)e.

For the truce agreed at Montgomery on 25 June 1259 see no. 336 below.

336 Letter patent concerning a truce with Henry III

Ratification of the truce between the king of England and his men on one side and Llywelyn and his men on the other. The truce was sworn on Llywelyn's behalf by Dafydd (his brother), Rhys Fychan, Gruffudd ap Madog, Goronwy ab Ednyfed (Llywelyn's seneschal), Dafydd ab Einion, Hywel ap Cadwallon, Llywelyn ap Maredudd and others at the ford of Montgomery on the Wednesday before the feast of St Peter and St Paul [25 June] 1259, to extend from the feast of St Peter in Chains [1 August] of that year to the same feast [1 August] 1260.

29 June 1259

B = TNA: PRO, E 36/274 (Liber A), fos 336v–337r. s. xiii ex.
Pd. from B, *LW*, 28 (no. 34).
Cd., *H*, no. 385.

[U]niversis Cristi fidelibus Lewelinus filius Griffini salutem in domino. Noveritis quod nos habemus ratas et gratas treugas quas iuraverunt dilecti ac fideles nostri domini David frater noster, Rys Iunior, Griffin(us) filius Madoc(i), Goron' filius Edn' senescallus noster, David filius Enn', Howel filius Kadwallaun, Lewelin(us) filius Mared' et alii in anima nostra ad vadum aque de Mungem(er)y die mercurii proxima ante festum apostolorum Pet(ri) et

Pauli anno domini m° cc° l° nono a festo Sancti Petri ad vincula eiusdem anni usque ad idem festum anno[a] domini millesimi cc[i] sexagesimi inter dominum regem Angl(ie) et suos tam Anglicos quam Wallenses ex una parte et nos et nostros ex altera secundum quod idem nostri fideles pro nobis iuraverunt easdem treugas die et loco supradictis et ut in litteris confectis melius et plenius continetur. In cuius rei testimonium hiis litteris nostris patentibus nostrum sigillum fecimus apponi. Datum anno domini [fo. 337r] m° cc° l nono in festo apostolorum Pet(ri) et Pauli.

[a] anni B.

The truce was simply a prolongation of the truce of June 1258 that was due to expire in August 1259 (cf. no. 331 above; Smith, *Llywelyn*, 122).

*337 Henry III
Letter, informing the king of the injuries inflicted on Llywelyn and his men by Nicholas fitz Martin, constable of Carmarthen, in breach of the truce recently made between the king and Llywelyn.

[Shortly before 10 August 1259]

Mention only, in a letter from Henry III to Llywelyn, dated at Windsor, 10 August 1259 (*CR 1256–9*, 422–3; cd., *H*, no. 474). In reply the king said that he had ordered the supervisors of the truce to settle amends, as he wished the truce to be observed in full. The letter clearly refers to the truce agreed on 25 June 1259 at Montgomery, ratified by Llywelyn four days later (no. 336 above).

*338 Henry III
Letter, in which Llywelyn, in order to obtain peace with the king and to hold the lands and homages of Wales as his grandfather Llywelyn [ap Iorwerth] had held them, offers to do homage to the king for them and willingly marry a certain niece of the king. Or he would pay the king 11,000 marks, his queen 2,000 marks, and his son Edward 3,000 marks, to be paid over eighty years at £200 per annum, and would give the king two commotes, namely Prestatyn and Creuddyn, within which the castles of Degannwy and Diserth were built, and would restore to the Marchers lands in Wales occupied by him and his men. Or he would pay £700 for a seven-year truce, namely £100 per annum.

[October 1259]

Mention only, in a letter from Henry III to Llywelyn, dated at Westminster, 1 November 1259 (*CR 1259–61*, 4–5; cd., *H*, no. 475). Henry reveals that Llywelyn's letter had been brought to him by the bishop of Bangor (that is, Bishop Richard, 1237–67), and explains that he cannot reply at present because some of his council were abroad, and he was about to go to France (he departed in mid-November). The letter, as reported by Henry, provides a valuable insight into the way that Llywelyn made the hegemony enjoyed by Llywelyn ap Iorwerth the touchstone of his political ambitions. The identity of the king's niece is uncertain and no more is heard of the marriage proposal. (Although Eleanor de Montfort, whom Llywelyn eventually married, was Henry III's niece, she was only born *c*.1258 and is therefore most unlikely to be the niece referred to here.) See further Smith, *Llywelyn*, 122–5, 165; Maddicott, *Simon de Montfort*, 44, 187–8.

*339 Agreement with Richard, bishop of Bangor

Agreement by the arbitration of the arbitrators in no. 345 below, who ordained that fines for sacrilege in churches should be paid to the bishop. Both parties are bound to observe the terms subject to the same penalty.

Llandrillo [1259 (possibly November) × -29 April 1261]

Mention only, in an agreement between Llywelyn and Richard, bishop of Bangor dated at Rhydyrarw, 29 April 1261 (no. 345 below). It is very likely that the agreement was drawn up after Bishop Richard's return to his diocese in 1259, possibly after his receipt of a safe conduct from the king at Westminster on 31 October (Stephenson, *Governance*, 171; *CPR 1258–66*, 57). The agreement was presumably made either at Llandrillo-yn-Rhos or Llandrillo-yn-Edeirnion, both in the diocese of St Asaph. The reference to *litteris inter ipsas confectis* suggests that letters patent were exchanged by the prince and the bishop recording the terms of the arbitration, quite possibly in the form of a bipartite indenture similar to that recording the later composition between them on 18 August 1261 (no. 346 below). It is unclear whether the Llandrillo agreement dealt with the specific cases of sacrilege mentioned in no. 345 and also whether it covered any other matters of dispute between the prince and the bishop.

340 Henry III

Letter, (?)concerning negotiations with the king.

[1260 × November 1272]

A = TNA: PRO, SC 1/62, no. 14. No endorsements; approx. 206 mm. wide at top, 191 mm. wide at bottom, 122 mm. deep on left, 112 mm. deep on right; mounted, foot cut away. The document is very badly stained and largely illegible.

Excellentisimo (?)domino suo domino H. Dei gratia regi Agn'[a] . . .[b] duci Aquit' / . . .[c] se divine misericordie . . .[d] / . . .[e] vobis ad plenum non possumus respondere (?)aliud quod nos . . .[f] / ratas tractare volueritis sicut (?)vestri antecessores . . .[g] predecessor(?es) melius . . .[h] / . . .[e] fideliter faciamus. Et . . . super (?)ius . . .[i] / excellencia vestra semper in domino.

[a] *sic in* A. | [b] *no more than two words (probably* domino Hibernie et *or variant spellings thereof) illegible in* A. | [c] *following lines (c.90 mm. down), and beginning of next line (c.62 mm.), illegible in* A. | [d] *end of line (c.95 mm.) illegible in* A. | [e] *beginning of line (c.25 mm.) illegible in* A. | [f] *end of line (c.92 mm.) illegible in* A. | [g] *one word (c.5 mm.) illegible in* A. | [h] *end of line (c.80 mm.) illegible in* A. | [i] *end of line (c.103 mm.) illegible in* A.

The TNA: PRO list identifies this as a letter from Llywelyn to Henry III, within a date range of possibly 1256 × 1259. However, Henry appears to be addressed by the new style he adopted as a result of the Treaty of Paris in December 1259, namely *Henricus Dei gratia*

rex Anglie, dominus Hibernie et dux Aquitannie, as there is insufficient space after *regi Agn'*
for *domino Hibernie, duci Normannie*, which would have been required had the king's
previous style been followed (*Henricus Dei gratia rex Anglie, dominus Hibernie, dux
Normannie, Aquitanie et comes Andegavie*; cf. Chaplais, *Essays in Medieval Diplomacy*, I.
248–51). Since most of the text is illegible, including Llywelyn's own style, further indications of date are lacking, and the letter is therefore datable to between 1260 and the king's
death on 16 November 1272. If so, it could be identical with one of the letters within that
date range known from references in letters from Henry to Llywelyn (nos 341, 344, 348,
350, 352, 359–60, 365, 371–3 below).

*341 Henry III
Letter, possibly alleging breaches of the truce.

[Shortly before 15 August 1260]

Mention only, in a letter from Henry III to the bishop of Coventry and Lichfield, the prior
of Wenlock, Humphrey de Bohun, Roger Mortimer, James Audley and Simon Passelowe,
dated at Guildford, 18 August 1260 (*CR 1259–61*, 198; cd., *H*, no. 476). Henry informed the
recipients that he had received Llywelyn's letter, which he enclosed, at Windsor (where he
had been as recently as 15 August 1260: *CR 1259–61*, 197), and said that he could not
discuss the contents of the letter because his council was not present; however, he instructed
the recipients to arrange for amends to be paid to the king by the supervisors (*dictatores*)
of the truce, at their discretion. For the context see Smith, *Llywelyn*, 129–30.

342 Truce with Henry III and the Lord Edward
*The prior of Wenlock, Simon Passelowe and Fulk of Orby, justice of Chester, representatives
of Henry III and Lord Edward, have agreed at Montgomery to make a truce with Llywelyn
ap Gruffudd, represented by Richard, bishop of Bangor and the abbot of Aberconwy. The truce
agreed at Oxford [17 June 1258] is to be extended from the Octaves of the Assumption of St
Mary [22 August 1260] to the feast of the Nativity of St John the Baptist [24 June] 1262 as
follows.*
    *(1) Each side will retain seisin of the lands, men, castles and other things which it held at
the making of the truce at Oxford.*
    *(2) In the mean time roads and passes shall not be obstructed, nor woods folded back, other
than they were at the time of the Oxford truce.*
    *(3) The king and his men will be allowed access to his castles of Diserth and Degannwy and
supply them as necessary; if such supplies cannot easily be transported because of a storm or
other impediments at sea, Llywelyn shall, at the summons of the justice of Chester, conduct
the supplies safely by land together with their guards.*
    *(4) The garrison at Diserth shall be allowed three men, that at Degannwy two men, to come
and go in fetching supplies, and those castles shall have the same bounds as at the time of the
Oxford truce.*
    *(5) If any of the garrison of the said castles should die or leave because of illness, the king
and his son may send others in their place without any hindrance from Llywelyn.*
    (6) The lands are open to both peoples for trade during the truce.

(7) If there is any breach of the Oxford truce, or any preceding truces, the injured party may not punish the injury. Instead, the dispute will be settled by twelve trustworthy men, chosen by both parties: the twelve will hear the complaints, inquire into the truth, and what can easily be amended according to the custom of the March shall be amended. Where there is a difficulty, if the breach was by the king or Edward, the twelve will inform them, or their representatives, and the king and Edward will make amends within forty days; if the breach was by the men of the king or of Edward, the latter will compel them to make amends within forty days unless they have already made amends within that period. The same applies to Llywelyn and his men.

(8) Since homicides, pillage and thefts have frequently been committed by thieves, outlaws and others up to the present, both sides agree that any who have received, or will receive, such malefactors, or who will have allowed them passage through their lands, will be held liable for amends according to the judgement of the twelve.

(9) If any of either side shall seek amends for injuries, he shall not be allowed justice, and none the less those who have suffered damages as a result seek the judgement of the twelve, they are entitled to amends, to be enforced by their principal lord within forty days; and notwithstanding that the costs imposed by the twelve are held to have been paid, and they have been otherwise severely punished by their lord, so that the punishment of one may be the fear of many. The principal parties, i.e. the king and Edward, and Llywelyn, are bound by oath to observe all this.

(10) If the twelve need to cross the lands of either side to conduct their business, each side will provide safe conduct.

(11) If any of the twelve shall maliciously absent themselves, the king or Llywelyn shall compel their men to attend; if any do not attend, those present may choose other trustworthy men in their place, acceptable to both sides.

(12) All those chosen as arbitrators will swear on the Gospels to act in good faith and without deceit in the case.

(13) The king and Edward, and Llywelyn and his brother Dafydd, bind themselves by oath to observe the truce and to make amends.

(14) The king and Edward also promise, under the same oath, to make all their bailiffs in the March, and all barons named by Llywelyn, swear to observe the same terms, as does Llywelyn with regard to his bailiffs throughout Wales and his magnates.

(15) Llywelyn also promises by his oath that, if any of his men refuse to make amends according to the judgement of the twelve, he shall deprive the said malefactors of their possessions and lands until they make full satisfaction; the king promises the same with regard to his men.

(16) Further, it is agreed by both sides that those who suffer injury should first complain to the lord of the place where the injury was committed, or his bailiff. If amends are not made quickly, they should take their complaint to the twelve; if they cannot do this, the lord or bailiff should make the twelve convene and give justice to the plaintiff according to the custom of the March, providing a safe conduct for the time of the hearing.

Since neither the king or Edward, nor Llywelyn or Dafydd, were present, the bishop of Worcester, Fulk, justice of Chester, the prior of Wenlock and Simon Passelowe attached their own seals and those of the king and Edward to the part of the document to be kept by Llywelyn, and the bishop of Bangor and abbot of Aberconwy attached theirs and those of Llywelyn and Dafydd to the part to be kept by the king.

Montgomery, 22 August 1260

B = C 66/76 (Pat. R. 45 Henry III), m. 14 in schedule (in an inspeximus of King Henry III, 12 March 1261).
Pd. from B, *Foedera*, I. i. 404.
Cd., *CPR 1258–66*, 147; *H*, no. 386.

Anno domini m° cc° lx°, die dominica, scilicet in octabis assumptionis Beate Marie Virginis, ordinatum est apud Mumgom(er)i et provisum inter priorem de Wenloke et dominum S. Passelawe clericum et Fulconem de Orby, iusticiarium Cestr(ie), habentes potestatem ex parte domini regis Angl(ie) et domini Edwardi filii regis primogeniti treugas [capiendi]ᵃ et firmandi inter predictos dominum regem et filium suum ex una parte et dominum Lewelin(um) filium Griffini et suos ex altera, et dominum R. Bangor(ensem) episcopum et abbatem de Aberconwey habentes consimilem potestatem ex parte dicti domini Lewelin(i), scilicet quod treuga capta apud Oxon' prorogetur a die octabarum assumptionis Beate Marie usque ad festum nativitatis Sancti Ioh(ann)is Bapt(iste) m° cc l° xii in forma subscripta:

[i] scilicet quod quilibet et singuli ex utraque parte, habeant seisinam terrarum et hominum, castrorum et aliarum rerum omnium, quas habuerunt tempore treugarum, inter predictas terras initarum apud Oxon';

[ii] et quod interim vada vel passus non obstruantur, silve non complicentur aliter quam erant tempore quo predicte `treuge apud Oxon' erant date.

[iii] Insuper licebit domino regi et filio suo et hominibus suis castra de Disserht et de Cannok' visitare, et per predictum tempus treugarum victualibus et aliis que ad dicta castra necessaria sustinenda fuerint invenire cum duobus batellis utroque cum xii remis vel paucoribus, secundum quod opus fuerit; ita tamen quod si per tempestatem vel alia imped-imenta maris vel propter alia pericula dicta victualia sive res commode cariari non possint vel differri, predictus dominus Lewelin(us) victualia predicta, res et homines ad prefata castra in eundo et redeundo ad summonitionem iusticiarii Cestr(ie) salvo et secure per terram duci faciet et conducet una cum custodibus eorundem.

[iv] Convenit etiam quod hii qui sunt in munitione castri de Disserht habeant iugiter tres homines, et ipsi de munitione castri de Cannowe habeant duos homines, continue exeuntes et ingredientes dicta castra ad victualia et alia hiis qui in dictis castris commorabuntur necessaria perquirenda; et quod dicta castra habeant omnes terras per eosdem fines, metas et bundos quos habuerint tempore treugarum apud Oxon' initarum.

[v] Item, si contingat aliquem de munitione dictorum castrorum infirmarum mori vel amoveri, licebit domino regi et filio suo et suis alium vel alios loco ipsius vel aliorum substituere et ponere, sine alicuius contradictione et omni impedimento et molestia infer-endis per dominum Lewelinu(m) et suos in accedendo vel redeundo, militem scilicet pro milite, servientem pro serviente, et sic de aliis in dictis castris existentibus.

[vi] Convenit etiam quod terre sint utrique genti communes ad comercia exercenda; et quod liceat cuilibet utriusque gentis prosequi et assequi rem suam in partibus terre utriusque treugis durantibus supradictis.

[vii] Item si aliquid ex parte alterutra transgressum fuerit, captum vel occupatum a tempore treugarum apud Oxon' initarum vel in aliis treugis precedentibus usque ad finem treugarum prorogatarum de novo, non licebit de cetero illi qui iniuriam passus fuerit per se vel per aliquos de parte sua sibi de illata iniuria vindicare; set illud per xiiᶜⁱᵐ viros fidedignos per utramque partem eligendos, diebus et locis per eosdem duodecim assignandis,

reformabitur et emendabitur in hunc modum: scilicet quod dicti duodecim querimonias audiant, et super hiis veritatem de plano et sine dilatione inquirant et quod de facili emendari potuerunt incontinenter, secundum consuetudinum March(ie) emendent. Et ubi[b] difficultas fuerit, si ex parte domini regis vel domini E. filii sui transgressum fuerit, per dictos xii[cim] vel per eorum maiorem partem domino regi vel E. filio suo nuntietur vel aliquibus quos dominus rex in suis feodis et possessionibus et dominus E. in suis ad emendam faciendam deputaverunt, si dominum regem et E. filium suum in partibus contigerit esse remotis. Et si rex vel predictus E. filius suus dictas transgressiones fecerit, per considerationem dictorum xii electorum infra xl[a] dies emendentur. Et si per homines dictorum domini regis vel E. filii sui transgressiones facte fuerint, ad emendam faciendam infra predictum tempus xl[a] dierum, prout illi xii[cim] demandaverunt, per eorum dominos, ad quod faciendum per suum iuramentum astringuntur, compellantur, nisi gratam emendam dicti malefactores prestiterint infra brevius tempus sibi a predictis xii assignandum. Quod quidem de domino Lewelin(o) et suis observetur, si ex parte ipsius transgressum existat.

[viii] Et quoniam per latrones, utlegatos et latrunculos, predones et alios homicidia,[c] rapine et furta usque ad ista tempora sunt sepius perpetrata, ordinatum est de consensu utriusque partis quod omnes illi qui tales malefactores hucusque receptaverunt vel de cetero receptabunt, et qui per suas terras ipsos cum preda vel rapina transire permiserint, illis qui dampna huiusmodi sustinerint vel decetero sustinebunt de suo proprio, secundum considerationem xii prefatorum, reddere teneantur.

[ix] Et ad hoc faciendum per dominum regem et E. filium suum, si ex parte Anglicor(um) hoc fuit inpertratum, et per dominum Lewelinu(m), si ex parte Walens(ium) factum fuerit, compellantur precise; quod, si forte aliquis alterius partis iniurias sibi factas[d] per se vel per alios vindicare presumpserit,[e] de dampnis sibi a principio illatis nulla sibi fiat iustitia, et nichilominus, ad considerationem predictorum xii illis de quibus se vindicaverint, de dampnis que occasione vindicte sustinerunt et de expensis quas occasione iniurie sibi illate prosequende fecerint, per dominum principalem ex cuius parte fuerint infra xl[a] dies satisfacere compellantur. Et nichilominus sumptus quos dicti xii circa prosecutionem dicti negotii fecerint solvere teneantur, et per dominum suum cuius pacem vel treugam infregerint alias graviter puniantur, ita quod pena unius sit metus multorum. Et ad hec omnia[f] observanda principales domini, scilicet dominus rex et E. filius suus et dominus Lewel(inus) per eorum iuramenta teneantur.

[x] Item, si dicti xii necesse habeant per terras domini regis vel Lewel(ini) ad loca per eos assignanda pro dicto negotio transire, tam dominus rex et ballivi sui per terras suas quam dictus Lewel(inus) per terras suas, ad mandatum dictorum xii in eundo et redeundo, salvum conductum prebebit eisdem.

[xi] Si vero aliqui vel aliquis de predictis xii se malitiose subtraxerint, tam dominus rex suos quam Lewel(inus) suos ad veniendum ad dictum negotium in forma predicta prosequendum, per iuramenta ipsorum compellere teneantur; quod si aliquis vel aliqui dictorum xii electorum ad locum et diem per ipsos assignandos non venerint, licebit aliis qui presentes fuerint alios fidedingnos vel alium, neutri parti suspectos[g] vel suspectum, eligere ad dictum negotium perficiendum; ita scilicet quod, cum tales absentes vacare poterint, ad illud negotium perficiendum iterum assignentur vel assumantur.

[xii] Omnes autem predicti electi super ewangelia iurabunt quod bona fide et sine fraude procedent in negotio memorato, nec dimittent pro lucro, dampno, timore, odio vel amore quin negotium sibi iniunctum, ut dictum est, quam citius ut poterint prosequentur.

[xiii] Ad dictas autem treugas observandas et emenda facienda et ad omnia et singula que predicta sunt fideliter observanda et implenda, dominus rex et predictus E. filius suus et Lewel(inus) et D(avi)d frater eius se iuramento prestito astrinxerunt.

[xiv] Promiserunt etiam dominus rex et predictus E. filius suus,[h] sub iuramento eodem, quod omnes ballivos suos qui pro tempore fuerint in March(ia) et omnes barones quos dominus Lewel(inus) duxerit nominandos, et similiter dominus Lewel(inus) suos ballivos per totam Walliam et etiam magnates partis sue quos dominus rex et E. filius suus vel sui duxerint nominandos, iurare facient quod omnia predicta, quantum ad ipsos attinet, fideliter observabunt.

[xv] Promisit etiam dictus Lewel(inus) in virtute iuramenti sui quod, si malefactores aliqui ex parte sua emendas facere contempserint, quas dicti xii decreverint faciendas, et infra predictum terminum quem duxerint assignandum, dictos malefactores suis posses- sionibus et terris privabit, donec plenarie satisfecerint de transgressionibus, prout per predictos duodecim est ordinatum, quod quidem rex ex parte sua similiter observabit.

[xvi] Insuper, de consensu partis utriusque, extiterit `ordinatum´ quod hii, quibus iniuria vel dampnum fuerit illatum, primo dominum loci de cuius partibus dampnum est illatum vel ipsius ballivum debent adire suam exposituri querimoniam; quod si infra breve tempus non faciat fieri emendam, ad quod faciendum per suum iuramentum teneatur, tunc duodecim electos adeant et ibi suam querimoniam prosequantur; quod si non possint, faciat dominus vel ballivus illos xii convenire et conquerenti iustitiam secundum consue- tudinum March(ie) exhibere, et salvum sibi faciat habere conductum, quamdiu querimoniam suam prosequitur coram ipsis.

Et ut hec omnia robur optineant firmitatis dominus rex et dominus E. scripto penes dominum Lewel(inum) remanenti, et dominus Lewel(inus) et D(avi)d frater suus scripto penes dominum regem remanenti, sua apposuerunt sigilla. Et quia predicti domini in confirmatione presentium non fuerunt presentes, dominus Wygorn(iensis) episcopus et dominus F. iusticiarius Cestr(ie) et prior de Wenlak' et S. Passelewe ex parte domini regis et domini E., et predictus dominus Bangor(ensis) episcopus et dominus abbas de Aberconw' ex parte domini Lewel(ini), dictis scriptis apposuerunt sigilla sua et talia principalium apponantur.

[a] *omitted* B. | [b] B *inserts* diffil *struck through.* | [c] homicidie B. | [d] factis B. | [e] presumpseverit B. [f] B *inserts* os *struck through.* | [g] subspectos B. | [h] B *inserts* subir *struck through.*

For the truce agreed at Oxford on 17 June 1258 see no. 331 above. The background of the present truce is discussed in Smith, *Llywelyn*, 129–30.

343 Henry III

While the writer has been observing the said truce and waiting for the king to fix a day for a parley, and allowing merchants of the king and the Lord Edward free access to his lands, by both land and sea, the aforesaid justice of Chester, in breach of the truce, has presumed to prohibit free passage and trade between the two lands.

[Probably 22 August 1260 × 24 June 1264]

A = TNA: PRO, SC 1/5, no. 79. No endorsements; 203 × 19 mm.; mounted.
Cd., *CAC*, 34; *H*, no. 477.

Preter hec regum benignissime nobis observantibus dictas treugas et expectantibus a vobis prefixionem diei et loci ad parliamentum necnon et concedentibus tam mercatoribus quam aliis hominibus vestris et hominibus domini Edward(i) primogeniti vestri salvum et securum accessum ad partes nostras tam per mare quam per terram, predictus iusticiarius Cestr(ie) contra formam treugarum commeatus et commercia excerceri[a] inter utrasque terras prohibere presumit.

[a] *sic in* A.

As Edwards noted (*CAC*, 34), the letter is a fragment, lacking the names of both sender and addressee. However, the references to the Lord Edward and to the contravention of a truce by the justice of Chester show that it was sent to Henry III by Llywelyn ap Gruffudd. In view of its form, the document was presumably sent as an addendum with another letter addressed to the king (cf. no. 419 below). The truce referred to may well have been that of 22 August 1260 (no. 342 above), which initially extended to 24 June 1262 and was subsequently renewed for a further two years, to 24 June 1264 (no. 349 below). Unlike the truce of 17 June 1258 (no. 331 above), which forbade trade except under special licence, that of 1260 stated that trade should be free during the truce. The document may therefore be assigned to the period of the latter truce and its renewal, namely between 22 August 1260 and 24 June 1264 (not 1263, as stated in *CAC*, 34). One possibility, suggested by the reference to waiting for the king to fix the time and place for a parley, is that the document was sent with the prince's letter of December 1261 or early January 1262 asking the king to appoint a day for the prince's envoys to complete the peace negotiations (no. 348 below).

*344 Henry III

Letter, concerning the making of peace.

[May × June 1261]

Mention only, in an undated letter from Henry III to Llywelyn (*CR 1259–61*, 482; cd., *H*, no. 478). The king's letter is enrolled (on m. 10d) between letters dated 8 July (m. 11d) and 20 July (last letter on m. 10d). Llywelyn's letter was sent no later than June since Henry apologizes for having kept the bearer of his reply, Llywelyn's envoy Alan, until the feast of St Peter and St Paul (29 June), and also explains that he had not replied to Llywelyn's letter immediately because of the pressures of affairs of the realm, and thus had sent its bearer, Llywelyn's envoy Master Matthew, back without a reply. Matthew had also conveyed offers from Llywelyn concerning peace, apparently in addition to the contents of the latter's letter. As he was now restored to authority, Henry could deal with the matters raised by Llywelyn, who was asked to send representatives to discuss peace with the king. See further Smith, *Llywelyn*, 134. The king resumed his authority after the arrival in London on 25 May 1261 of a papal bull absolving him from his oath to observe the Provisions of Oxford, and shut himself in the Tower of London 22 June–30 July (Powicke, *Henry III*, ii. 420–1; Maddicott, *Simon de Montfort*, 209).

345 Agreement with Richard, bishop of Bangor

Anian, bishop of St Asaph, Gwyn, prior of the Dominicans of Bangor, brother Ieuaf, priest of the same convent, Philip, (?)warden of the friars [(?)minor] of Llan-faes, brother John Rufus of the same convent, Goronwy and Tudur sons of Ednyfed, Einion Fychan and Einion ap Caradog, chosen by each side as arbitrators to settle pleas between Richard, bishop of Bangor and his chapter on one side and the lord Llywelyn ap Gruffudd and his magnates on the other, after hearing the pleas of each party, have unanimously determined on the Thursday after Easter [29 April] 1261 as follows:

(1) When a cleric has done wrong anywhere, let both his person and his offence be delivered to ecclesiastical jurisdiction. But if he has raped a woman, whereby he has offended both the secular and the ecclesiastical authority, let him make amends there [i.e. in the ecclesiastical court] according to both laws. If he is charged with having found treasure, let him make amends to the lay power in the same place if he is convicted. However, concerning a lay tenement or similar offence let him make amends in the secular court. Concerning Ednyfed ap Hywel, who was accused of having found treasure, and the seal of the chapter of Clynnog attached to letters attesting to the manumission of a certain serf, such a case should be heard in the bishop's court. If anything was taken from Ednyfed on account of that treasure, let it be restored to him; and if it is proved that he found that treasure, let him make amends in the court of Llywelyn according to the law of the country. Concerning the seal, if on account of the aforesaid use of it he took anything from the canons, he ought to make restitution to them and the case should be heard and decided in the bishop's court and amends made to the injured party. However, if Llywelyn is conscious that on the aforesaid occasions he took something from Ednyfed and the canons, let him make restitution at a time fixed by the bishop of St Asaph.

(2) As regards Llywelyn ap Gruffudd's detaining the goods of shipwrecks while their possessors survive and immediatedly request the goods, the arbitrators recall that Llywelyn [ap Iorwerth] formerly prince of Wales acted thus, whether justly or unjustly; however, he surrendered such goods, not through the compulsion of any prelate but through fear of God, an example they commend to Llywelyn [ap Gruffudd] in good faith. As regards Llywelyn ap Gruffudd's similarly seizing goods cast onto, and treasures found on, the land of the Church, they do not recall that any received such goods apart from Prince Llywelyn [ap Iorwerth] and his successors.

(3) If a lay man of the bishop is charged with having found treasure, let him answer in the secular court, and if proof is lacking against him, in no way let lawful compurgation be denied him.

(4) As regards men of the bishop unfit for war, neither military service nor its commutation should be exacted from those younger than the lawful age of fourteen years; but let older men perform military service or pay the commutation.

(5) If servants of Llywelyn or his bailiffs or those of others seize the draught animals of the bishop's men for their own business without the men's assent, and if, after the men's complaint has been made to Llywelyn's bailiff, satisfaction is not made by severely punishing the robbers as a deterrent to others, Llywelyn should fine his bailiff at least 20s.

(6) Concerning the man allegedly seized in the refuge of the church on the day of its dedication, let trustworthy men from both Llywelyn's side and the bishop's be sent to see the place where he was seized, and if it can be proved in their presence that it is a place of refuge, let [Llywelyn] make full amends; otherwise, let Llywelyn enjoy possession of his prisoner. The

names of those assigned to this are: Archdeacon David of Bangor, the dean of Bangor and the archdeacon of Anglesey on behalf of the bishop, and G[oronwy] ab Ednyfed, Einion Fychan and Iorwerth on behalf of Llywelyn; and brother Ieuaf Foel was accepted as a counsellor on the feast of St Trillo [15 June] at Bangor. If one or more of these are absent, let another or others be substituted with the consent of those present.

(7) Concerning those excommunicated by name, if anyone has been excommunicated after receiving canonical warning, the lord is obliged to follow the bishop's mandate and seize him without delay when requested.

(8) Concerning those who have violated the church of Bangor and those fighting in the church of Rhosyr and at the church of Talybolion, the arbitrators reply as set out in the letters of Llandrillo, namely that the fines for these as for all acts of sacrilege belong to the bishop; therefore if they have not made amends to the bishop, let them do so fully.

(9) Concerning the married cleric who knowingly received a publicly banished person, and against whom it may be possible to bring proof, the cleric is obliged to answer in the ecclesiastical court. If he is resident in the prince's land and happens to be fined, all his fine will be given to the prince. If he is resident in the bishop's land, let the fine be divided between the bishop and the prince. If the wife of any man knowingly or willingly receives such a banished person in her husband's absence, let the woman answer in the ecclesiastical court and let the cleric not be punished on account of her deed nor be forced to answer for her unless he wishes.

(10) Concerning theft in the houses of certain clerics and men of the bishop, the goods of no one ought to be confiscated other than for theft discovered in the houses where they have their habitation, namely keywannedd, *for such a house is called merely a* halaucty *['polluted house']. The arbitrators have heard this from the elders.*

(11) If the bailiffs of Llywelyn or the bishop fine any persons in their courts, the fine ought to be halved between the bishop and the prince. The prince's bailiff should have with him someone from the bishop's side in whose presence he imposes and halves the fine, and the bishop's bailiff should do similarly in his court.

The aforesaid parties are obliged to observe these terms inviolably, under the same penalty under which they were obliged in the letters drawn up between them at Llandrillo.

The arbitrators attach their seals to these letters patent.

Rhydyrarw, 29 April 1261

B = NLW, Peniarth MS 231B, pp. 35–9. s. xvii[1]. Rubric: Forma compromissi inter dominum Bangor' et dominum principem.
Pd. from B, Haddan and Stubbs, i. 489–91.

Noverint tam presentes quam futuri quod nos Anian(us) episcopus de Sancto Assaph', frater Wyn[a] prior predicatorum Bangor', frater Iewaf eiusdem loci conventus, Ph' (?)gardianus[b] (?)fratrum[c] [(?)minorum][d] de Llanvaes,[e] frater Ioh(ann)es Rufus eiusdem loci conventus, Goron' et Tudur filii Itneuet, Enn' parvus, Enn'[f] filius Keirad', ad diffiniendas querelas motas inter dominum Ric(ardum) Bangorens(em) episcopum et suum capitulum ex una parte,[g] et dominum L. filium Griff' et suos magnates ex altera, electi ex utriusque partis consensu arbitrii, anno domini m. cc. lxi° apud Rydyrarw, die iovis proxima post festum Pasche, et utriusque partis querelas audientes, eas unanimiter diffinivimus in hunc modum.

[i] In primis, cum clericus forefecerit ubicunque, quatenus[h] personam suam tanquam offensa in foro [p. 36] ecclesiastico rendatur. Sed si mulierem rapuerit, quo regimen et sacer-

dotium offendit, ibidem satisfaciet secundum utramque legem. Si autem ei imponatur thesaurum invenisse, ibidem dominio laicali satisfaciat si fuerit convictus. De tenemento autem laicali `et finium transgressione satisfaciat in foro seculari. De Edn' filio Howel, cui imponebatur invenisse thesaurum, et de sigillo capituli de Kellynn' apposito litteris testimonialibus manumissionis cuiusdam servi, nobis videtur quod talis causa in curia episcopi debet ventilari. Et si quid occasione illius thesauri predicto Edn' fuerit ablatum, eidem restituatur; et si probetur ipsum thesaurum invenisse, in curia episcopi domino Lewel(ino) satisfaciat secundum legem patrie. De sigillo autem nobis videtur quod si occasione predicte appositionis canonicis aliquid abstulit, eisdem restitui debet et causa in curia episcopi ventilari et determinari et cui iniuriatum est satisfieri. Si autem conscientiam habeat dominus L. quod predictis occasionibus predictis Edn' et canonicis aliquid abstulit, restituatur tempore a domino Assavens(i) assignato.

[ii] Quod res de naufragio detinet possessoribus existentibus sanis et res suas instanter petentibus, recolimus dominum L. bone memorie quondam princeps Wall(ie) sic fecisse, sive iuste sive iniuste, tandem nullo prelato compellente sed ductus timore divino talia dimisisse, quod et domino L. bona fide laudamus. Quod res proiectas in [p. 37] terram ecclesie occupat similiter et thesauros inventos in terra ecclesie etc., non recolimus alium talia recepisse preter solum principem L. et suos successores.

[iii] Si imponitur homini episcopi laico invenisse thesaurum, in curia seculari respondeat, et si desit contra eum probatio, nullo modo ei denegetur legittima purgatio.

[iv] Quod homines episcopi inhabiles ad arma etc., nobis videtur quod a prius[i] pretaxatis ante legittimam[j] etatem,[k] scilicet xiiii annorum, non debet exigi expeditio neque expeditionis redemptio; seniores vero vel in expeditionem eant vel componant.

[v] Si qui servientes domini L. vel suorum ballivorum vel aliorum iumenta hominum episcopi sine ipsorum assensu ad sua negotia facienda rapiunt, nobis videtur, si eorum querimonia ad ballivum domini L. venerit et eis non satisfecerit raptores rigide puniendo ut alii terreantur, quod dominus L. debet mulctare ballivum suum in xx solidos ad minus.

[vi] De capto in die dedicationis in refugio ecclesie, ut dicitur, nobis videtur quod mittantur fide digni [l]ex parte[-l] tam[m] domini Lewelini quam episcopi qui videant locum in quo captus fuit, et si possit probari in ipsorum presentia locum refugii esse, per omnia satisfaciat; sin autem, dominus L. suo incarcerato gaudeat. Nomina autem ad hoc assignatorum sunt hec: dominus D(avi)d archidiaconus Bangor' et eiusdem loci decanus et archidiaconus Monie ex parte episcopi, et dominus G. filius Edn' et Enn' parvus et Ioru(e)rth ex parte Lewelini, et assumpto [p. 38] in conciliarium[n] fratre Iewaf Voel in festo Sancti Terillo apud Bangor'. Et `si contigerit aliquem vel aliquos abesse, loco absentis vel absentium alius vel alii cum assensu presentium substituantur.

[vii] De nominatim excommunicatis nobis videtur quod si premissa monitione canonica aliquis fuerit sententia excommunicationis innodatus, quod ad mandatum episcopi tenetur dominus ipsum capere sine dilatione cum ad hec fuerit requisitus.

[viii] De hiis qui fregerunt ecclesiam Bangor'[o] et pugnantibus in ecclesia de Rosvyr et apud ecclesiam de Taleboleon respondemus ut continetur in litteris de Llan(n)terillo quod talium sicut omnium sacrilegorum tantum emenda pertinet ad episcopum, unde si predicti episcopo non satisfecerunt, plenarie satisfaciant.

[ix] De clerico uxorato receptante puplice forbanizatum[p] scienter et possit contra ipsum probari nobis videtur quod tenetur respondere in foro ecclesiastico. Si vero faciat residentiam in terra principis et contingat ipsum multari, tota multa sua principi dabitur. Si

vero residentiam in terra episcopi faciat, mulcta dividatur inter episcopum et principem. Si vero uxor alicuius talem scienter vel volenter in eius absentia receptaverit, mulier in foro ecclesiastico respondeat et clericus ratione sui facti non puniatur nec pro ea nisi velit respondere cogatur.

[x] De furto in aliquorum clericorum domibus vel hominum episcopi nobis videtur quod nullius bona debent auferri nisi pro furto invento in domibus ubi fuerit eorum habitatio, id est [p. 39] *keywannedd*, quia talis domus dicitur tantum *halaucty*. Hoc audivimus a senioribus.

[xi] Si ballivi domini L. seu episcopi in suis curiis aliquos mul`c tent, ibi debet mul`c ta dimidiari inter episcopum et principem. Nobis videtur quod baillivus principis debet secum habere aliquem ex parte episcopi in cuius presentia mulctam faciat et factam dimidiat, et ballivus episcopi in sua curia similiter faciat.

Partes vero supradicte ad ista inviolabiliter servanda teneantur, et ad ea servanda[q] obligate sub eadem pena sunt qua in litteris inter ipsas confectis[r] apud Llan(n)derillo fuerunt obligate.

In cuius rei testimonium nostra sigilla hiis patentibus litteris fecimus apponi. Datum Rydyrarw anno domini m cc lxi° die veneris proxima post Pascham.

[a] *word added in margin with transposition signs showing that it should be inserted where dots indicate lacuna after* frater B. | [b] *(?)*naid *dotted underneath* B. | [c] fru' *underlined and dotted underneath, above which is inserted (?)*suum B. | [d] *dots indicating lacuna in* B. | [e] Llan *dotted underneath* B. | [f] *B inserts* ap *struck through.* | [g] *B inserts* d *struck through.* | [h] *B inserts* offe *struck through.* | [i] *three minims between* pri *and* s B. | [j] *(?)*legittimationem B. | [k] eta B. | [l-l] *words added in margin with transposition signs showing that they should be inserted where dots indicate lacuna after* digni B. | [m] *B inserts* ex. [n] *word dotted underneath in* B, *and second* c *possibly corrected from an* s; ociliarium *written in margin to left.* | [o] *B inserts (?)transposition sign (two parallel oblique strokes) followed by* estius *between* Ban *and* gor'. | [p] forbanizarum, *with dot beneath the* z *and an* r *written above* B. | [q] *B inserts* sub. [r] confectas B.

Robert Vaughan's transcript in B is corrupt in places, and Vaughan clearly had difficulty in reading some words in his fourteenth-century exemplar, the now lost Llyfr Coch Asaph (cf. Evans, 'Llyfr Coch Asaph', 177–81; Jones, 'Llyfr Coch Asaph', i. xi–xiii, xxxix–xliv).

For brief assessments of the agreement see Stephenson, *Governance*, 171–2, Pryce, *Native Law*, 135, and Smith, *Llywelyn*, 208–9. Parallels between its provisions and rules in Welsh law-texts regarding treasure-trove, wreck, military service, sacrilege, sanctuary and theft are noted in Pryce, *Native Law*, 191, 198, 220–1, 229–30 (including the use, confined to lawbooks compiled in thirteenth-century Gwynedd, of *halaucty*, 'polluted house' as a term for a house in which stolen goods were discovered, a term also used in no. 397, c. viii below). See also Smith, '*Gravamina*', 162, 168. The age of majority in c. iv is consistent with the statement in the lawbooks of Gwynedd that a son should be commended to a lord at the age of fourteen (*Ior*, §98/5; trans., *LTMW*, 131); the same texts envisage the use of banishment (c. ix) as a punishment for theft in certain circumstances (Pryce, *Native Law*, 202, 226, 227).

The names of the arbitrators are mostly the same as those given in no. 346 below. The most important difference is that the present text names the prior of the Bangor Dominicans as Gwyn (*Wyn*), whereas in no. 346 he is Adam. One possibility is that Adam had succeeded Gwyn by August 1261. Alternatively, the transcription in the present text may be erroneous (Vaughan seems initially to have been unable to read the name, as *Wyn* is a marginal addition) or Gwyn was Adam's original Welsh name: in either case, both names could refer to the same individual. For the feast of St Trillo (c. vi) see Baring-Gould and Fisher, *Lives*, iv. 264; by the fourteenth century one of the two annual fairs of the bishop of Bangor was held on four days focused on the feast of St Trillo (*Rec. Caern.*, 133). The churches mentioned in c. viii were both on Anglesey. Rhosyr probably referred to the church of St Peter, Newborough, adjacent to the site of the princely court at Rhosyr (SH 419 654) that formed the administrative centre of the commote of Menai. It is unknown which church was meant in the reference to Talybolion, the north-western commote of the island. The location of Rhydyrarw, also the place-date of no. 346 below, has not been identified.

346 Agreement with Richard, bishop of Bangor

Agreement made at Rhydyrarw between Richard, bishop of Bangor, and his chapter on one side and Llywelyn ap Gruffudd on the other, concerning the fixing of boundaries at Tal-y-llyn and between Llanwnda and Botellog, by the arbitration of Anian, bishop of St Asaph, Adam, prior and Ieuaf, lector of the Dominican convent of Bangor, Iorwerth and Trahaearn, friars minor of Llan-faes, and the lords Goronwy and Tudur sons of Ednyfed, Einion Fychan and Einion ap Caradog. The settlement of the boundary at Tal-y-llyn made by Llywelyn in the bishop's presence is confirmed, and the fine for moving the boundary shall be in Llywelyn's mercy. Concerning the boundary between Llanwnda and Botellog, it is agreed that this should be fixed on the quinzaine from the feast of St Michael [13 October] by Dafydd Goch ap Cyfnerth and fourteen other named men, meeting on the land where the boundary is disputed, under oath and pain of excommunication, who shall adjudicate the boundary between the said townships as they believe it was in the time of Llywelyn [ap Iorwerth] of good memory and the bishop of Bangor and his predecessors. If the said men say that the boundary has been moved to the place alleged, for which the bishop's men were summoned, Llywelyn shall receive a fine both for the moving of the boundary and the contumacy; if they assign the boundary beyond that place but on [the land held by] the bishop, Llywelyn shall receive payment only for the moving of the boundary; if they approve the bishop's boundary, Llywelyn's men shall be fined for their false accusation. If any of the aforesaid fifteen cannot be present for a necessary reason on the said day at the said place, Goronwy ab Ednyfed, Einion Fychan and Einion ap Caradog may arrange for other honest men to be chosen instead of those absent.

Rhydyrarw, 18 August 1261

B = TNA: PRO, E 36/274 (Liber A), fo. 364r–v. s. xiii ex.
Pd. from B, Anon, 'Merionethshire', 228–9; from B, *LW*, 97–8 (no. 192).
Cd., *H*, no. 387.

Hec est forma compositionis facte apud Rydyraru anno domini mᵒ ccᵒ lxᵒ primo die iovis proxima post festum assumptionis Beate Marie inter dominum R. Bang(orensem) episcopum et capitulum ex una parte et dominum Lewelinu(m) filium Griffini ex altera super terminis assignandis apud Tallyllynn et inter Lanwndaf et Botelauc per provisionem domini A. Asseven(sis) episcopi, fratris Ade prioris et fratris I. lectoris predicti Bang', Iervas(ii) et T(ra)haern fratrum minorum de Lamaes et dominorum Goron' et Tudry filiorum Edn', Enn' Parvi, Enn' filii Kerradauc, pacis reformatorum inter dictas partes,

videlicet quod dominus Bang(orensis) ex provisione dictorum virorum ratam habet assig-
nationem termini apud Talyllynn factam a domino L. episcopo et eius presentibus; item
quod findicta[a] de dicto termino amoto sit misericordia domini L. et voluntate. De termino
autem assignando inter Lamvndaf et Botelauc sic fuit provisum: quod in quindena a festo
Sancti Mich(ael)is proximo futuri debent convenire Dauid Goch filius Kywnerth, Goron'
filius Gviann, Elidyr filius Edn', Lewelin, Heylyn, Adaf filii Ynyr, Kadugaun Iunior, Mad',
Lywarch filii Kaduga(n), Kywn(er)th, Ioru(er)th Wydel, Ioru(er)th Coch filii Heylyn,
Madauc Bychan, Mared' filius Lewelyn, Kynwric Vydel, super terram ubi est contentio de
termino, et tunc ipsi iurati et sub excommunicatione in eorum veredicto assignabunt
terminum inter dictas villas secundum quod ipsi viderunt terminum usitatum tempore
Lewelini bone memorie et domini Bangor(ensis) et suorum antecessorum[b] et credunt esse
verum. Si autem dicti viri dixerint terminum usque ad locum ubi dicitur terminus amotus
et ad quem homines episcopi fuerunt citati, vindicta tam de termino amoto quam de contu-
macia erit domino Lewelino; si autem dicti viri assignaverint terminum ultra predictum
locum super episcopum, vindicta solum de termino amoto erit domino L.; si dicti viri assignaverint super partem domini L. et approbaverint terminum episcopi, capiat vindictam ab
hominibus suis qui ei falsum suggesserunt. Si autem aliqui de predictis quindecim viris
dictis die et loco [fo. 364v] non poterint interesse ex[c] necessaria causa, tunc per provisionem
Goron' filii Edn' et Enn' Parvi et Enn' filii Karad' loco absentium in periculum animarum
suarum eligantur `alii´ viri honesti. In cuius rei testimonium parti huius scripti penes
dominum L. remanenti sigillum domini episcopi et capituli Bangor(ensis) sunt appensa;
parti autem remanenti apud dominum episcopum et suum capitulum sigillum domini L. est
appensum. Datum anno die et loco supradictis.

[a] *sic in* B. | [b] accessorum B. | [c] et B.

This is one of at least three agreements, including a fuller one at Rhydyrarw on 29 April
1261, preceded by one at Llandrillo, between Richard, bishop of Bangor, and Llywelyn
following the bishop's return to Gwynedd from exile by 1259. See nos 339 and 345 above.
Tal-y-llyn may refer to the episcopal township of that name about 3 miles north-east of
Aberffraw (cmt. Malltraeth, Anglesey; Tal-y-llyn farm SH 366 734) (cf. Carr, *Medieval
Anglesey*, 39). Llanwnda (SH 475 583) is located about 3 miles south of Caernarfon.

347 Agreement with Maredudd ap Rhys

Agreement whereby Llywelyn receives Maredudd into his peace.

*(1) Llywelyn restores Maredudd to all his lands held at the time he left Llywelyn's unity,
namely Catheiniog, Mabudrud, Mabelfyw and Gwidigada.*

*(2) Maredudd shall ask Maredudd ab Owain whether he wishes to ally with him in recov-
ering their patrimony in Dyfed; if so, the lands recovered shall be divided between them apart
from the commote of Ystlwyf, which shall be held entirely by Maredudd ap Rhys. If Maredudd
ab Owain declines to co-operate thus, Maredudd ap Rhys and his heirs may possess for ever all
the lands he can recover free of any other claim.*

*(3) Maredudd ap Rhys is bound to serve Llywelyn with all his power by attacking
Llywelyn's enemies in South Wales at every opportunity.*

(4) Maredudd is bound, at Llywelyn's order, to go with all his forces on expedition with the

lords of Wales or else with some of them, except Rhys Fychan, with whom Maredudd is not obliged to go personally on expedition unless sent help by Llywelyn from North Wales. However, Maredudd is bound, at Llywelyn's order, to send all his forces with the said Rhys.

(5) If Maredudd is accused before Llywelyn, he is bound to go to Llywelyn without an escort or relics to show his innocence, if he can be innocent. If he confesses or is convicted of a charge, and makes satisfaction from his goods or lands according to the provision of worthy men of Llywelyn's court and council, he shall not be arrested, imprisoned or have hands laid on him.

(6) When requested by Llywelyn, Maredudd shall give him from his land twenty-four sons of nobles as hostages, chosen by Llywelyn.

(7) If Maredudd breaches this agreement in any way and refuses to give justice as set out, he quitclaims for himself and his heirs to Llywelyn and his heirs all his rights in his inheritance in South Wales. Moreover, he places himself under the jurisdiction of the bishops of Bangor and St Asaph, who may excommunicate him, his family and supporters, and demand that the sentence be issued also in the diocese of St Davids. Maredudd renounces all remedies of canon and civil law which could undermine the above terms.

The agreement is sealed by Llywelyn and the said bishops.

Coleshill, 6 December 1261

B = TNA: PRO, E 36/274 (Liber A), fos 366v–367r. s. xiii ex.
Pd. from B, *LW*, 104–5 (no. 199).
Cd., *H*, no. 388.

Anno domini millesimo cc° lx primo in festo Sancti Nicholai episcopi apud Conssyl facta est hec compositio inter dominum Lewelinu(m) filium Griffini ex una parte et dominum M(er)educu(m) filium Resi ex altera, videlicet quod dictus dominus L. dictum M. recepit ad pacem et benivolentiam suam sub hac forma, scilicet quod

[i] dominus L. restituit eidem M. omnes terras in quarum possessione erat tempore quo ultimo recessit ab eius unitate, videlicet Ketheinneauc, Mabudryd, Mabelvyv et Wydigada.

[ii] Dictus etiam M. debet inquirere a domino M. filio Oweni utrum velit esse unius were, consilii et auxilii cum ipso ad conquirendum ius et hereditatem suam in terra de Dyvet, et si esse voluerit quicquid poterunt communi consilio et auxilio conquirere inter ipsos dividetur preter commotum de Ystlvyf qui dicto M. filio Rys remanere debet indivisus. Si autem dictus Mareduc(us) filius Oweni requisitus hoc facere denegaverit, quicquid dictus Mareduc(us) filius Resi poterit conquirere de dicta terra remaneat sibi et heredibus [fo. 337r] suis sine clamio alicuius alterius in perpetuum.

[iii] Item dictus M(er)educ(us) filius Rys tenetur cum toto posse suo fideliter sine fictione, cavillatione, excusatione et contradictione facere per se ipsum servitium et commodum dicti domini L. infestando et opprimendo adversarios ipsius L. in partibus Sudwall(ie) quotienscumque et ubicumque viderit locum et tempus.

[iv] Item tenetur M(er)educ(us) ad mandatum domini L. ire personaliter cum toto posse suo in expeditionem cum dominis Wallie sive cum aliquo ipsorum preterquam cum domino Reso Iuniori, cum quo non tenetur ire personaliter in expeditionem nisi quando dominus L. transmiserit ad partes illas succursum de Norwall(ia). Quamvis autem non teneatur personaliter ire in expeditionem cum dicto domino Reso Iuniori nisi modo predicto, tamen ad mandatum domini L. tenetur totum posse suum mittere cum Reso prefato.

[v] Item si memoratus M. fuerit accusatus[a] super aliquo vel aliquibus coram prefato

domino L., ipse tenetur adire presentiam domini L. sine conductu vel reliquiis ostensurus suam innocentiam si poterit esse innocens. Si autem super obiecto vel obiectis eidem confessus fuerit vel convictus, si poterit facere iustitiam de bonis vel de terris suis secundum qualitatem et quantitatem sui delicti ad provisionem proborum virorum de curia et consilio domini Lewelini, ipse erit sine captione et incarceratione et manuum iniectione in personam ipsius.

[vi] Item cum dictus M. fuerit requisitus a sepedicto domino L., ipse debet dare de terra sua xxiiii[or] obsides de filiis optimatum quos elegerit Lewelin(us) memoratus.

[vii] Item si predictus M. contra presentem compositionem presumpserit in aliquo vel in aliquibus articulis venire et denegaverit facere iustitiam modo predicto, ipse quietum clamat pro se et suis heredibus domino L. filio Griffini et suis heredibus totum ius suum et clamium quod habet vel habere deberet in hereditate sua apud Sudwalliam. Preterea si prefatus M. contra supradicta vel eorum aliquod venire presumpserit ipse supponit se iurisdictioni dominorum episcoporum Bangor(ensis) et de Sancto Assaph qui pro tempore fuerint quod possint promulgare sententiam excommunicationis in personam illius, familiam et fautores eiusdem, et quod possint dictam sententiam exequendam prelatis ecclesiarum in episcopatu Menevensi ubi dictus M(er)educ(us) moram facere contigerit demandare. Renuntiat etiam prefatus M. pro se et heredibus suis omni appellationi, impetrationi, cavillationi et cuilibet remedio iuris canonici et civilis contra predicta valituris.

Ad maiorem autem huius compositionis securitatem dictus Lewelin(us) apposuit huic scripto una cum sigillis dictorum episcoporum sigillum suum.

[a] accussatus B.

Llywelyn's earlier undertakings to Maredudd on 26 April 1258 (no. 329 above) had been overtaken by subsequent events, notably the occupation of the latter's lands by Llywelyn in the summer of 1258 following the discovery of Maredudd's continuing loyalty to Henry III and the conviction of Maredudd for infidelity to Llywelyn on 28 May 1259 which resulted in his detention in Llywelyn's prison until Christmas 1259 (Smith, '"Cronica de Wallia"', 269–72). The implication (c. v) that relics gave protection comparable to that provided by an escort is consistent with principles in thirteenth-century law-texts from Gwynedd (cf. Pryce, *Native Law*, 193, 199, 201–2).

*348 Henry III

Letter, requesting the king to fix a day by which Llywelyn's envoys could be sent to complete the peace negotiations between the king and Llywelyn.

[Shortly before 8 January 1262]

Mention only, in a letter from Henry III to Llywelyn, dated at Westminster, 8 January 1262 (*CR 1261–4*, 100–1; cd., *H*, no. 479). Henry wrote that he could not reply until his son Edward returned from Gascony, whence he was expected any day. Edward arrived in England on 25 February 1262 (Powicke, *Henry III*, ii. 430–1), and an agreement was reached with Llywelyn on 4 May to prolong the truce of 1260 for a further two years (no. 349 below).

349 Letter patent concerning an agreement with Henry III and the Lord Edward

Notification that an agreement has been made on 4 May 1262 at Westminster between Henry III and the Lord Edward on one side and Llywelyn ap Gruffudd and his men on the other, namely that the truce made at Montgomery in 1260 shall be continued from 24 June 1262 to the end of two years following and all its articles remain in force; Llywelyn confirms whatever has been done in his name by the abbot of Aberconwy at the king's court.

[4 May × 24 June 1262, probably early]

B = TNA: PRO, E 36/274 (Liber A), fo. 333r. s. xiii ex.
Pd. from B, *LW*, 17–18 (no. 13).
Cd., *H*, no. 390.

Anno domini millesimo ducentesimo sexagesimo secundo in crastino Inventionis Sancte Crucis apud Westm(onasterium) provisum, ordinatum et concessum est inter dominum H. Dei gratia regem Angl(ie) illustrem pro se et domino Edwardo filio suo primogenito ex una parte et Lewelinu(m) filium Griffini et suos ex altera, videlicet quod treuge capte et firmate apud Mongom(er)i inter partes predictas anno domini m° cc° sexagesimo prorogentur a festo nativitatis Sancti Ioh(ann)is Bapt(ist)e anno predicto, videlicet millesimo ducentesimo sexagesimo secundo, usque ad finem duorum annorum proximo sequentiam integre completorum, et interim omnia in dictis treugis contenta in singulis articulis fideliter observentur et remaneant in robore suo, ratificantes et acceptantes quicquid per dominum abbatem de Ab(er)con' nomine nostro in curia domini regis factum est. In cuius rei testimonium sigillum nostrum presenti scripto apposuimus.

The letter was probably written shortly after the agreement had been made at Westminster on 4 May 1262, where the abbot of Aberconwy acted on Llywelyn's behalf, and before the renewal of the truce on 24 June. For the text of the truce agreed at Montgomery on 15 August 1260, see no. 342 above.

*350 Henry III

Letter (?), requesting that breaches of the truce by Roger Mortimer and John Lestrange in the lands of Gruffudd of Bromfield be amended.

[Shortly before 8 June 1262]

Mention only, in a letter from Henry III to Llywelyn dated at Westminster, 8 June 1262 (*CR 1261–4*, 128; cd., *H*, no. 480). Henry's letter does not explicitly state that Llywelyn's request was in written form. The king replied that he had ordered the arbitrators of the truce to convene at the ford of Montgomery for one month from the feast of St John the Baptist (meaning from 24 June, the feast of the Nativity of St John the Baptist, as shown by no. 352 below), in order to fix amends for any attacks.

351 Henry III

Letter, stating that Llywelyn has received the king's letter alleging that while the king was outside his kingdom Llywelyn had broken the truce by occupying certain castles of his men and killing and pillaging. Informs Henry that he has not committed breaches of the truce against the king or those of his men who had observed it regarding Llywelyn and his men; this is true of the barons of (?) Cheshire (Cateric'), *Staffordshire and Shropshire, who were innocent as regards Llywelyn, who was uninjured. Since certain barons of the March, who boasted that they were not included in the truce, presumed to violate it by disturbing Llywelyn's possession of certain lands, so that the men of those lands came of their own will to Llywelyn, Llywelyn inflicted retaliation on those barons and their supporters according to their faults. It is not contrary to the truce if Llywelyn receives men formerly in his seisin who come to him of their own will, as another example shows. The king will remember that the earl of Gloucester received magnates of Glamorgan who were in Llywelyn's seisin at the time of the re-estab-lishment of the said truce, but since they gave themselves to the earl of their own will Llywelyn did not complain that this was a breach of the truce. Likewise the king's bailiffs and barons of South Wales received men and lands of Dyfed which had been in Llywelyn's seisin, to which Llywelyn had not objected since they had left his unity of their own will. Hence Llywelyn had followed the example of the king and his barons in this regard. None the less, if any barons of the March or elsewhere wished to prosecute a plea against him for breaking the truce, Llywelyn is ready to make amends for any offences by his side, the arbitrators of the truce having met, provided that amends be made for his pleas. Asks the king not to move against him on account of a plea of the Marchers until he is more certain of the case: the king will certainly find very few of them to be readier than Llywelyn to show him service and honour, were he received into the king's peace. Llywelyn further complains about the attacks against him by the king's bailiff of Montgomery, together with the barons; he would have destroyed his bailiwick up to the walls of the castle were it not for his respect for the king and the truce. Asks the king to punish the bailiff since it is not fitting for Llywelyn to take vengeance on him.*

[Probably July × December 1262]

B = *Foedera*, I. i. 340–1. 1816. The source of the text printed in *Foedera* is described as 'Bundela Litterarum temp. Hen. III', the usual description used in that edition for the letters now classed as SC 1 in the TNA: PRO. The two texts preceding this letter in *Foedera*, which are ascribed to the same source, are now extant as TNA: PRO, SC 1/4, nos 23, 24 (see nos 354–5 below); however, the original of the present letter has not been traced.

Pd., B.

Cd., *H*, no. 389.

Excellenti domino H. Dei gratia illustri regi Anglie, domino Hibernie et duci Aquitannie L. filius Griffini salutem et affectum ad obsequia. Excellentie vestre literas ea qua decuit reverentia et honore suscepimus continentes vobis fuisse intimatum quod agentibus vobis extra regnum vestrum nos quedam castra hominum vestrorum occupando, homines occidendo et depredationes faciendo contra treugas, que vobis et nobis sunt communes, venire presumpsimus. Unde nobilitati vestre pro certo significamus quod nos dictas treugas hucusque non intercepimus versus vos vel vestros qui easdem versus nos et nostros obser-vaverunt illesas. Quod quidem audacter possimus ponere super barones de Cateric',[a] Staffordscir' et Sallopp', qui quidem nobis fuerunt innocui et nos eisdem fuimus indempnes. Verum quoniam quidam barones de Marchia, qui iactabant se non esse contentos sub dictis treugis, ipsas violari presumpserunt, perturbando possessionem nostram in quibusdam terris quarum seisinam adepti fuimus, hominibus terrarum volumptarie venientibus ad nos et se nobis tradentibus sine coactione et violentia, nos dictis baronibus et eorum fautoribus secundum eorum demerita persolvimus tallionem. Nec est contra dictarum treugarum formam, si homines qui prius fuerunt in nostra seisina volumptarie venientes ad nos recipiamus, quia consimile nobis aliunde datum fuit exemplum. Bene enim memini quod comes Gloucestrie recepit ad se magnates de Morgannuc qui erant in nostra seisina tempore reformationis dictarum treugarum, sed quia voluntarie se reddiderunt dicto comiti non sumus conquesti ipsum super hoc predictas treugas intercepisse. Simili modo ballivi vestri et barones de Sudwallia homines et terras de Dyuet[b] que erant in nostra seisina receperunt, nec nos oblocuti sumus vel impedivimus, quia volumptarie a nostra unitate recesserunt. Unde non omnino est nobis imputandum, set nos exemplo vestro et vestrorum baronum usi fuerimus in hac parte. Nichilominus, si aliqui barones de Marchia [c]vel aliunde[c] velint prosequi [p. 341] contra nos querelam de interceptione treugarum, nos parati erimus transgressiones, si que ex parte nostra facte sunt, emendare, convenientibus adinvicem dictatoribus treugarum loco congruo et tempore competenti, dum tamen fiant nobis emende de nostris querelis. Rogamus igitur nobilitatem et discretionem vestram quatinus non moveamini contra nos ob querelam Marchionum donec super nostro facto et causa facti reddidi fueritis certiores: pro certo enim habeatis quod paucissimos de ipsis inveniretis promptiores quam nos ad vestrum servitium et honorem, dum tamen bono modo et salvo iure nostro recepti fuissemus ad vestram concordiam. Preter hec conquerimur de ballivo vestro de Mungum' qui se et totum posse suum interponit cum baronibus nos infestantibus ac inquietantibus, cuius ballivam facere possemus destrui usque ad muros castri nisi parceremus ob reverentiam vestri et predictarum treugarum observationem. Placeat igitur vestre excellentie talem medelam apponere ad castigationem dicti ballivi quod non oporteat nos ad eius transgressiones manum apponere vindicatricem. Valete per tempora longiora.

[a] *sic in* B. | [b] Dynet B. | [c-c] Lalumde B.

Smith, *Llywelyn*, 342 and n. 15, notes that the date of 1256 assigned to this letter in *Foedera* is too early and argues that it belongs to the period of truce in 1261–2, probably *c*.1261. In fact, there are strong grounds for dating it to the period July–December 1262. Llywelyn states that the earl of Gloucester had received magnates of Glamorgan at the time of the re-establishment (*tempore reformationis*) of the truce, a reference to a renewal of the truce agreed on 17 June 1258 (no. 331 above). This lasted until 1 August 1259, and a further truce was agreed in June 1259 to last until 1 August 1260 (no. 336 above). However, the latter truce was not explicitly described as an extension of the 1258 truce, in contrast to the truce agreed on 15 August 1260 (no. 342 above). It is likely, then, that the letter's reference to re-establishing the truce refers either to the renewal of August 1260 or to its further extension agreed on 4 May 1262 (no. 349 above). A *terminus ad quem* is provided by Llywelyn's attacks on the March from December 1262 (*HW*, ii. 730; cf. Smith, *Llywelyn*, 135–6, 139–41). Further dating evidence is provided by the reference to the king's being abroad (*agentibus vobis extra regnum vestrum*) when he received complaints against Llywelyn. Henry III was in France between November 1259 and 23 April 1260, and again between July and December 1262 (Powicke, *Henry III*, ii. 820). If the renewal of the truce referred to was either that of August 1260 or that of May 1262, the letter from Henry to which Llywelyn replies here was sent during the second of the visits to France. This would be consistent with other evidence of allegations by both Llywelyn and the Marchers of breaches of the truce in the second half of 1262 (no. 350 above and nos 352–5 below). If the renewal of the truce referred to the truce of June 1259, however, this would push the beginning of the date range back to November 1259.

*352 Henry III

Letter, complaining to the king that John fitz Alan and other barons of the March have committed serious breaches of the truce against Llywelyn and his men, and seeking amends and that John and the others be prevented from committing such breaches.

[Shortly before 24 August 1262]

Mention only, in a letter from Henry III to John fitz Alan dated at Banbury, 24 August 1262 (*CR 1261–4*, 133–4). The king informs John that he has ordered the arbitrators of the truce to convene at the ford of Montgomery on the Morrow of Michaelmas (30 September). Henry's letters of the same date to Hywel ap Madog and Humphrey de Bohun, earl of Hereford (ibid., 136–8) seem to refer to the same letter, as does Henry's letter to Llywelyn of 25 August 1262 (ibid., 135–6). The last letter also explains that amends were not made for one month from the feast of St John the Baptist (24 June) because of the illness of Bohun, and that, while he would prefer to set an earlier day for the arbitrators than the Morrow of Michaelmas, his *fideles* are unable to attend before then because of other business. This suggests that Llywelyn's letter may also have referred to the failure to convene the arbitrators from 24 June (cf. no. 350 above).

353 Henry III

Letter, complaining that after the visit of Philip le Bret to Llywelyn to fix a day and place for the making of amends for breaches of the truce by both sides, the justice of Chester, the barons of that area and the sons of John Lestrange have made many attacks on the lands of Llywelyn's faithful man Gruffudd of Bromfield, burning townships, taking plunder and killing and capturing men. Last Monday, after the feast of St Matthias (?recte St Matthew), on the day fixed for a parley between Llywelyn and the justice while Llywelyn's men, and those of Gruffudd, were gathered for the parley, the justice and his men made off with great plunder from another part of Gruffudd's land. Since he cannot long endure such transgressions, Llywelyn asks the king to intervene to ensure their redress, or for lack of justice he will take his revenge.

[Possibly *c.*26 September 1262; probably *c.*28 February 1262 or *c.*27 February 1263]

A = TNA: PRO, SC 1/4, no. 22. No endorsements; approx. 200 × 75 mm.; mounted, foot cut away.
Pd. from A, *Foedera*, I. i. 339; from A, *RL*, ii. 218–19.
Cd., *CAC*, 26; *H*, no. 391.

Excellenti domino H. Dei gratia illustri regi Angl(ie), domino Hyb(er)n(ie) et duci Aquitann(ie) L. filius Griffini princeps Wall(ie), dominus Snaudon' salutem et affectum ad obsequia. Nobilitati vestre conquerando significamus quod postquam Ph(ilippus) le Brett ex parte vestra ad nos accessit, ut constitueretur dies et locus ad faciendum et recipiendum emendas secundum formam treugarum de interceptionibus earundem ex utraque parte factis, iusticiarius Cestr(ie), barones partium illarum et filii domini Ioh(ann)is Ext(ra)nei plures interruptiones et insultus fecerunt in terras dilecti et fidelis nostri domini Griffini de B(ro)mfeud', villas comburendo, predas diripiendo, homines quosdam occidendo, quosdam capiendo. Et nunc ultimo die lune proxima post festum Beati Mathie apostoli, cum dies ille esset constitutus ad habendum parliamentum inter nos ex una parte et dictum iusticiarium ex altera, hominibus nostris et hominibus dicti Griffini congregatis ad dictum parliamentum, dictus iusticiarius cum sua sequela magnam predam in alia parte terre dicti Griffini cepit et abegit. Unde, quia diu non possumus pati tales transgressiones multas pertransire, excellentiam vestram rogamus quatinus ad emendationem dictarum transgressionum sanum et maturum velitis consilium apponere, ne pro defectu iustitie necesse habeamus, quod absit, querere vindictam. Valeat nobilitas vestra.

Edwards, *CAC*, 26, argued that the letter was written shortly after Monday 25 September 1262 on the assumption that it referred to the feast of St Matthew (21 September) and because there was other evidence for attacks on the lands of Gruffudd of Bromfield in 1262 (see *CR 1261–4*, 135–6; *CPR 1258–66*, 227; no. 350 above). However, unless *Mathie* is a clerical error for *Mathei*, the feast was that of St Matthias (24 February). As a context in 1263 is arguably as plausible as one in 1262 (cf. *CPR 1258–66*, 239; nos 356–7 below), it is uncertain whether this is the earliest surviving document issued by Llywelyn in which he uses the title 'prince of Wales and lord of Snowdon' (cf. Smith, *Llywelyn*, 145–6).

354 Henry III

Letter, acknowledging receipt of the king's letter informing Llywelyn of Roger Mortimer's complaint that Llywelyn's men have invaded and destroyed the lands and castles of Roger and certain of his friends, affirming his belief that he has not broken the truce as regards the king. None the less, if he or his men are accused of breaking the truce, he is ready to make amends as laid down by the arbitrators of the truce, provided that the same is done with regard to the king and his men.

[Probably early December 1262]

A = SC 1/4, no. 23. Bottom right of tongue: domino regi (in hand of letter); no endorsements; approx. 197 × 56 mm., including tongue (approx. 12 mm. wide); four sets of double slits for insertion of a tongue or tag; mounted.
Pd. from A, *Foedera*, I. i. 340; from A, *RL*, ii. 233.
Cd., *CAC*, 26–7; *H*, no. 392.

Excellenti domino H. Dei gratia illustri regi Anglie, domino Ibernie, et duci Aquitan(ie) L. filius Griffini princeps Wallie, dominus Snaudon' salutem. Excellentie vestre literas recepimus continentes dominum Rog(er)um de Mortuo Mari vobis detulisse querimoniam, videlicet quod homines nostri terras et castra sua et quorumdam amicorum suorum invaserunt, depredaverunt et destruxerunt, unde nobilitati vestre significamus quod non credimus nos treugas nostras versus [v]os adhu[c] in aliquo intercepisse. Nichilominus, si treugarum nobis vel nostris interceptio imponatur, convenientibus dictatoribus treugarum ad invicem parati erimus de transgressionibus nobis et nostris impositis et imponendis congruas facere emendas, dum tamen similiter vobis fiat de consimilibus transgressionibus. Valete.

The letter clearly refers to the attacks on Roger Mortimer's lands which began on 29 November 1262, but pre-dates Llywelyn's own attacks in December (*CAC*, 27; cf. Smith, *Llywelyn*, 147).

355 Henry III

Letter, complaining that Roger Mortimer, Humphrey de Bohun the younger and other barons and royal bailiffs of the March have seized with a great force of men-at-arms and footsoldiers a certain castle in Llywelyn's seisin and begun to provision and strengthen it. Having been warned by Llywelyn according to the terms of the truce, they refused to leave the castle until, besieged and deprived of provisions, Llywelyn allowed them to retreat, although he could easily have forced them to surrender in a short time because of the shortage of provisions and the difficulty of escape. He is willing to make amends for any breach of the truce, following a meeting of the arbitrators of the truce, provided that these barons do likewise. He therefore asks the king not to be moved greatly against him because of the unreasonable complaints of the Marchers until the king has discussed the truth about what Llywelyn has done. Many complaints about Llywelyn are brought before the king by those who love his honour less than Llywelyn. Asks the king to send a reply by the bearer of the present letter.

[*c.*22 December 1262]

A = TNA: PRO, SC 1/4, no. 24. No endorsements; approx. 191 × 90 mm.; mounted, foot cut away.
Pd. from A, *Foedera*, I. i. 340; from A, *RL*, ii. 232–3.
Cd., *CAC*, 27; *H*, no. 393.

Excellenti domino H. Dei gratia illustri regi Angl(ie), domino Hybern(ie), duci Aquitann(ie) L. filius Griffini princeps Wall(ie) et dominus Snaudon' salutem et affectum ad obsequia. Excellentie vestre conquerando significamus, quod dominus Rog(er)us de Mortuo Mar(i), dominus Humfred(us) de Boum Iunior et quidam alii barones et ballivi vestri de Marchia cum maxima multitudine virorum armatorum et peditum intraverunt violenter quoddam castrum quod erat in nostra saisina, et illud ceperunt munire et affortiare. Et a nobis amoniti, secundum formam teugarum, de dicto castro noluerunt discedere donec obsidione posita et denegatis eis victualibus, optinuerint a nobis licentiam recedendi, quamvis possemus eos pauco tempore compellere ad deditionem propter paucitatem suorum victualium et difficultatem eis evadendi nobis invitis. Unde quia nos parati sumus, si aliqua poterunt contra nos et nostros opponi de interceptione treugarum, convenientibus ex utraque parte dictatoribus treugarum, loco congruo et tempore competenti eadem emendare; dum tamen dicti barones super hiis que versus nos transgressi sunt similes faciant emendas. Rogamus igitur nobilitatem et discretionem vestram quatinus non multum moveamini contra nos propter minus rationabiles querelas Marchionum de nobis, donec de nostro facto et de causa `facti discutiatis veritatem. Quamplures autem coram maiestatis vestre presencia de nobis defferunt querelas, qui minus diligunt proficium vestrum et honorem quam nos fecimus, si eorum posse equipararetur voluntati. Placeat igitur excellentie vestre et benignitati voluntatem vestram super premissis nobis rescribere per latorem presentium. Valete.

As argued by Edwards (*CAC*, 27), the letter refers to the recovery by Llywelyn of Cefnllys castle in Maelienydd, apparently just before his capture of Knucklas castle on 20 December 1262 (*AC*, 100), a chronology consistent with the fact that Henry seems to have been ignorant of Llywelyn's success at Cefnllys when he replied on 24 December to a letter from Mortimer, received at Dover on 20 December, which reported that Llywelyn was besieging the castle (*CR 1261–4*, 270). Edwards's suggested date of *c.*22 December 1262 is therefore probably correct.

356 Henry III

Letter, stating that Llywelyn has received the king's messengers with the letter asking him to appear in person in a month and a day from the day of the Purification of St Mary [2 March] at the ford of Montgomery, to make amends for breaches allegedly committed by him and his men. He is ready to do this as far as he can, but since, because of the shortage of time, it is difficult for him to gather together those whose presence is necessary at the meeting, he asks for it to be postponed until after Easter, and to move it to Oswestry. He also asks the king to forbid the Marchers to molest Llywelyn and his possessions, and he will likewise prohibit his men to molest the Marchers. Asks for a reply.

[February 1263]

A = TNA: PRO, SC 1/4, no. 21. No endorsements; approx. 190 × 82mm.; mounted, foot cut away.
Pd. from A, *Foedera*, I. i. 336.
Cd., *CAC*, 25–6; *H*, no. 394.

Excellenti domino H. Dei gratia illustri regi Angl(ie), domino Hybern(ie), duci Aquitann(ie) L. filius Griffini princeps Wall(ie) et dominus Snaudon' salutem et affectum ad obsequia. Nobilitatis vestre nuncios ea que decuit reverentia suscepimus et honore cum litteris vestris monentibus nos ut in mensem a die purificationis Beate Marie comperaremus personaliter apud vadum de Mungumr' ad faciendum emendas, secundum formam treugarum, de interceptionibus earundem factis per nos et nostros, ut dicitur. Ad quod faciendum parati sumus secundum quod melius poterimus. Set quia, propter brevitatem temporis, difficile est nobis coadunare illos, quos necesse habemus ut intersint dicto negocio perficiendo, maiestatem vestram rogamus quatenus prolongare velitis diem dictum usque ad terminum certum, quem volueritis post instans Pascha, cum mutacione loci usque ad Album Monasterium. Et si predicta vobis placuerint, faciatis prohibere Marchiones ne nos et nostras possessiones interim inquietent vel molestent. Et nos pro parte nostra faciemus prohibere homines nostros subiectos ut versus Marchiones pacifici sint et quieti. Quid autem super premissis placuerit vestre discretioni, ea que vobis placet celeritate nobis faciatis significare. Valete per tempora longiora.

As Smith argues (*Llywelyn*, 153, n. 50), Henry III's letter to Llywelyn of 1 March 1263 (*CR 1261–4*, 293–4) is clearly a reply to the present letter, which is therefore datable to February of that year.

357 Henry III

Letter, stating that the king's messenger Philip le Bret has told him that Roger Mortimer prevented his messenger from bringing the king's letter to Llywelyn and detained him for eight days in Radnor castle, meanwhile devasting Llywelyn's lands contrary to the contents of the letter. Afterwards Roger released the messenger, who was robbed, but did not restore the king's letter until summoned to Hereford before John de Grey and other barons of the March and compelled to restore it against his will. As a result Llywelyn had not received the king's letter until the Tuesday before the Annunciation of the Virgin [20 March]. Yet despite the shortage of time, Llywelyn will attend the parley fixed on the morrow of the close of Easter [9 April] at Oswestry. He has meanwhile ordered all his subjects to behave peacefully towards the Marchers.

[20 × 30 March 1263]

B = TNA: PRO, C 54/80 (Close R. 47 Hen. III), m. 9 in schedule (enrolled 1263).
Pd. from B, *CR 1261–4*, 297.
Cd., *H*, no. 395.

Excellenti domino H. Dei gratia illustri regi Angl(ie), domino Hib(er)n(ie) et duci Aquit'
L. filius Griffini princeps Wall(ie), dominus Snaudon' salutem et affectum ad obsequia.
Excellentie vestre significamus dominum Ph(ilippu)m le Bret nuntium vestrum nobis
intimasse quod dominus Rogerus de Mortuo Mari nuntium suum venientem ad nos cum
vestris litteris impedivit et detinuit in castro de Radenor' per octo dies, et medio tempore
dampna super terras nostras fecit et depredationes contra formam in dictis litteris
contentam. Postmodum dictum nuntium dimisit spoliatum, sed litteras vestras non restituit
donec vocatus apud Hereford' coram domino Ioh(ann)e de Grey et aliis baronibus de
Marchia eas reddidit compulsus et invitus. Propter quod litteras vestras non recepimus
usque in diem martis proximum ante annunciationem Beate Mar(ie). Nichilominus
quamvis difficile nobis sit propter temporis brevitatem nos tenebimus diem et locum parliamenti sicut nobis constituistis, scilicet in crastino clausi Pasche apud Albu(m)
Monasterium. Precipimus insuper omnibus subditis nostris ut interim pacifice et quiete se
habeant versus omnes Marchiones. Valete.

The letter was written no later than 30 March 1263, when it was forwarded by Henry to the
Lord Edward (*CR 1261–4*, 297), and no earlier than Llywelyn's receipt of Henry's letter on
20 March.

358 Agreement with Gruffudd ap Gwenwynwyn

*(1) Gruffudd of his free will did homage and swore fealty on relics on behalf of himself and
his heirs to Llywelyn and his heirs before Richard, bishop of Bangor, the abbots of Aberconwy
and Strata Marcella, Brother Ieuaf of the Order of Preachers, Master David, archdeacon of
Bangor, Addaf, dean of Ardudwy, David son of William, official of Dyffryn Clwyd, Goronwy,
Tudur and Cynwrig sons of Ednyfed, Iorwerth ap Gwrgunan, Einion ap Caradog, Dafydd ab
Einion, Cyfnerth ap Heilin, prior of Strata Marcella, Adda ap Meurig, Master Ivo, Gruffudd
ap Gwen, Einion ab Ednyfed and many others.*

*(2) In return for this homage and fealty Llywelyn granted and restored to Gruffudd all his
lands and possessions, namely Cyfeiliog, Mawddwy, Arwystli, Caereinion, Mochnant Uwch
Rhaeadr, Y Tair Swydd with their appurtenances, all the land between the Rhiw and the Helygi
with the township of Llanwyddelan.*

*(3) Gruffudd and his heirs will hold these lands in hereditary right for ever from Llywelyn
and his heirs.*

*(4) If Gruffudd should lose any part of these lands through war, and Llywelyn possesses his
lands in their entirety, Llywelyn will restore Gruffudd's losses of lands according to the
provison of the bishops of Bangor and St Asaph, the abbots of Aberconwy and Strata
Marcella, the prior of the Friars Preacher of Bangor, Brother Ieuaf of the same order,
Brothers Ieuaf Goch and Iorwerth ap Cadwgan of the Friars Minor of Llan-faes, Goronwy,
Tudur and Cynwrig sons of Ednyfed, Iorwerth ap Gwrgunan, Einion ap Caradog, David son
of William and Cyfnerth ap Heilin; if any of these men are lacking or absent the provision
shall be made by those who are present and remaining.*

(5) If Llywelyn should lose any part of his lands through war, the losses shall be restored

by Gruffudd by the provision of the said men, with compensation for the damages of both parties.

(6) If Gruffudd is able to conquer any lands beyond his bounds from the Camlad down towards Shrewsbury, Gruffudd and his heirs may keep their conquests; conquests above the Camlad shall remain with Llywelyn and his heirs.

(7) If a war or army invades Gruffudd's land without harming Llywelyn at the same time, Llywelyn will assist Gruffudd before all his other allies if he has the greater necessity.

(8) If Gruffudd loses his castle of Welshpool through war, Llywelyn will assign him another castle by the provision of the aforesaid men where he may protect his possessions and household until he has recovered his castle.

(9) All who have been enfeoffed by Prince Llywelyn [ap Iorwerth] or his son Dafydd or by Gruffudd may possess their lands unless they offend subsequently so that they ought to be deprived of the said lands.

(10) Concerning all lands and possessions granted by Llywelyn to anyone in Gruffudd's lordship, Gruffudd may decide whether to seize those lands or grant them to their possessors.

(11) Madog ap Gwenwynwyn will hold for life the commote of Mawddwy in chief from Gruffudd and his heirs.

(12) If Gruffudd should be accused before Llywelyn concerning anything, Llywelyn will not make much of the accusation unless it can be proved clearly: if it is proved, let Gruffudd give due amends according to the arbitration of the aforesaid men, saving his lands and possessions and without imprisonment and being a hostage, until he has given satisfaction; if the accusation cannot be proved fully, let Llywelyn punish the accuser according to the amount of the injury to either lord.

(13) Neither Llywelyn nor Gruffudd will receive or defend anyone offending against the other.

(14) Gruffudd will come with all his power to the aid of the lands and possessions of Llywelyn, both near and remote from Llywelyn, as necessary, if his own land is not being invaded; the men of the said lands are obliged likewise to come to the aid of Gruffudd's lands.

(15) Gruffudd is obliged to come to the army with Llywelyn as often as he is required unless an enemy invasion clearly threatens his own land.

(16) Both Llywelyn and Gruffudd will bind themselves to each other so that they are of one peace and one war, and one will not form an alliance with any others without the other.

(17) Gruffudd totally pardons the men of Powys of all offences they committed against him while they were in Llywelyn's lordship.

(18) To reinforce the above terms Llywelyn and Gruffudd have placed themselves and their heirs under the jurisdiction of the bishops of Bangor and St Asaph and the abbots of Aberconwy and Strata Marcella, so that these may jointly or separately excommunicate the persons of Llywelyn and Gruffudd and their heirs and place an interdict on their lands if they contravene any of the said articles. Llywelyn and Gruffudd renounce on behalf of themselves and their heirs all requests, appeals, delays and remedies of canon or civil law valid against the said sentences of excommunication and interdict. The said bishops and abbots at the request of the parties are bound jointly and separately to promote the said sentences against the party contravening the said agreements.

Gruffudd has attached his seal, along with the seals of the said bishops and abbots, to the part of the document remaining with Llywelyn; Llywelyn has likewise sealed the part remaining with Gruffudd.

Ystummanner, 12 December 1264 [recte 1263]

B = TNA: PRO, E 36/274 (Liber A), fos 356r–357r. s. xiii ex.
Pd. from B, Thomas, 'Montgomeryshire document', 306–11 (and trans.); from B, *LW*, 77–80 (no. 147).
Cd., *H*, no. 535.

Ad perpetuam rei memoriam geste facta est finalis concordia anno domini m° cc° lxiii°ᵃ in vigilia Beate Lucie virginis apud Ystumanneyr inter dominum Lewelinu(m) filium G. principem Wallie ex una parte et dominum Griffinu(m) filium Gwenvinwyn ex altera, videlicet quod [i] dictus dominus Gryffinus spontanea voluntate sua fecit homagium pro se et heredibus suis et tactis sacrosanctis iuravit fidelitatem dicto domino Lewelino et heredibus suis coramᵇ nobili patre domino Ricardo episcopo [fo. 357v] Bangorensi, dominis abbatibus de Aberconewey et de Pola, fratre Ieuaf de ordine predicatorum, magistro David archidiacono Bangor', Adaf decano de Arduwy, David filio Willelmi officiali Diffinclevid, Goronou, Tudur, Kynewrech filiis Ydeneweth, Ioruerth filio Gruginan, Aniani filio Karaudauc, David filio Aniany, Kyfnerth filio Heylin priore de Pola, Adaf filio Meurich, magistro Yvone, Griffino filio Gwen, Annaun filio Ydnyued et multis aliis.

[ii] Pro dicto autem homagio et fidelitate dicti G. dictus L. concessit et restituit eidem G. omnes terras et possessiones suas, videlicet Keuelauc et Maudwy in terminis suis, Arwystly in terminis suis et Keriniaun et Mochnant Uschraadir in terminis suis et Toyrsoyd cum pertinentiis suis et terminis, totam terram inter Ryu et Helegi cum villa de Lanuydelan.

[iii] Dictus vero G. et heredes sui dictas terras per metas et divisas suas de dicto domino L. et heredibus suis iure hereditario tenebunt in perpetuo [et] possidebunt.

[iv] Si vero contigerit, quod absit, dictum G. amittere aliquam partem de terris suis supradictis per gwerram, dicto L. terras suas in integrum possidente idem L. dicto G. restaurabit deperdita in terris ad provisionem subscriptorum virorum, videlicet venerabilium patrum de Bangor' et de Sancto Assaph' episcoporum, de Aberconway et de Pola abbatum, prioris fratrum predicatorum de Bangor', fratris Ieuaf eiusdem ordinis, fratrum Iouaf Goch et Ioruerth filii Cadugun de ordine fratrum minorum de Lanmaes, Goronou, Tudur, Kynweuch filiorum Ydeneueth, Ioruerth filii Grugunan, Aniany filii Keyradauc, David filii Will(elm)i et Kyfnerth filio Heylin; si vero contigerit aliquem vel aliquos prenominatorum virorum deesse vel abesse fiat dicta provisio per eos qui superstites fuerint vel presentes.

[v] Si vero contigerit dominum L. aliquam partem terrarum suarum amittere per gwerram, quod absit, sit in provisione dictorum virorum, conpensato utriusque partis dampno, deperdita dicto G. prout melius poterunt restaurare.

[vi] Si vero adiutore Deo sepedictus G. poterit aliquas terras conquirere ultra metas suas a Kiminaut inferius versus Salop', idem G. et heredes sui optineant et gaudeant conquisitis; a Kyminaut vero superius domino L. et heredibus suis remaneant conquisita.

[vii] Si vero gwerra vel exercitus dicti G. terram invadat, gwerra vel exercitu dictum L. eodem tempore non molestante, prenominatus L. succurret dicto G. pre omnibus aliis suis imprisiis si maiorem habuerit necessitatem.

[viii] Et si ita contigerit, quod absit, quod dictus G. castrum suum de Pola per gwerram amiserit ad provisionem suprascriptorum virorum dictus L. eidem assingnabit G. aliud castrum ubi possit res et familiam custodire secure donec castrum suum recuperaverit.

[ix] Omnes vero enim infeodati per bone memorie principem Lewelinu(m) vel per David filium suum aut per ipsum G. habeant terras suas et quiete possideant nisi in posterum deliquerint contra dictum Griffinum ut merito debeant dictis terris privari.

[x] De omnibus vero terris et possessionibus a domino L. quibuscumque collatis in dominio dicti G. sit in voluntate ipsius vel ipsas terras auferre vel concedere possidentibus.

[xi] Dominus vero Madocus filius Gwenuynwyn commotum de Mauduy quoad vixerit in capite tenebit de dicto G. et heredibus suis.

[xii] Si vero contigerit dictum G. accusari penes dominum L. super aliquo dictus L. non magnificabit dictam accusationem nisi manifeste possit probari; si vero probata fuerit faciat condignam emendam ad arbitrium predictorum virorum, salvis sibi terris et possessionibus suis, sine corporis sui incarceratione et ostasio, dummodo satisfacere poterit[c] et voluerit; si vero accusatio contra dictum G. ad plenum probari non poterit dictus L. animadvertit in accusatorem secundum quantitatem delicti et iniurie utrique domino satisfaciendo.

[xiii] Neuter vero dominorum L. [et] G. receptabit vel defendet contra reliquum delinquentem.

[xiv] Dictus vero G. cum toto [d-]posse suo defensabit[-d] et succurret terris et possessionibus dicti L. sibi vicinis et a dicto L. remotis quotiens necesse habuerint, terra sua sine hostili incursu existente; homines vero dictarum terrarum vice versa [d-]tenentur terris[-d] domini G. simili modo succurrere.

[xv] Dictus vero G. tenetur venire in exercitum cum domino L. quotiens ab eo fuerit requisitus nisi hostilis incursus sue terre tunc immineat manifeste.

[xvi] Uterque vero dictorum dominorum L. et G. fideliter adinvicem se tenebunt ita quod sint unius gwerre et unius pacis et nullis se confederabunt alter sine altero.

[xvii] Quicquid vero homines de [fo. 357r] Powys quamdiu fuerunt in dominio dicti L. deliquerunt contra dominum G. idem G. totaliter eis condonavit et remisit.

[xviii] Ad plenam vero prescriptorum fidem et securitatem sepedicti L. et G. supposuerunt se et heredes suos iurisdictioni venerabilium de Bangor' et de Sancto Assaph' episcoporum necnon et de Aberconewey et de Pola abbatum qui pro tempore fuerint, ipsis in se dictam iurisdictionem assumentibus, quod possint coniunctim et divisim promulgare sententiam excommunicationis in personas dictorum L. et G. ac heredum suorum et interdicti in terras eorundem si contra aliquem de dictis articulis venire presumpserint. Renuntiant etiam L. et G. pro se et heredibus suis omni appellationi, impetrationi, cavillationi et omni remedio iuris canonici vel civilis contra dictas sententias excommunicationis vel interdicti valituris; dicti vero episcopi et abbates ad petitionem partis dictas conventiones observantis tenentur coniunctim et divisim dictas sententias promulgare et easdem executioni demandare contra partem a dictis conventionibus resilientem.

In cuius rei testimonium huic parti scripture remanenti penes dominum G. dominus L. sigillum suum fecit apponi una cum sigillis dictorum episcoporum et abbatum; parti vero remanenti penes dominum L. sigillum domini G. cum ceteris predictis sigillis est appensum.

[a] lxiiii B. | [b] vel B. | [c] poterint C. | [d-d] *lacuna in* C; *supplied from no. 601 below.*

The sealing clause shows that two copies were made of the agreement, whose original presumably took the form of a bipartite chirograph, and that the present text derives from the part of the document sealed by Llywelyn and given to Gruffudd. Comparison with the version sealed by Gruffudd (no. 601 below) and other evidence shows that the date of 1264 is an error for 1263 (*LW*, 80). For the agreement's background and significance see Powicke, *Henry III*, ii. 619–20; Stephenson, 'Politics of Powys Wenwynwyn', 56–7; Smith, *Llywelyn*, 157–60, 287–91, 299–300. Llywelyn had occupied most of Gruffudd's lands in Powys in

1257 (see note to no. 596 below). In the summer of 1263 Gruffudd seized the commote of Gorddwr from Thomas Corbet of Caus together with the latter's land between the Camlad and the Severn, and in September Gruffudd was ordered to restore Corbet's lands by the crown (*CR 1261–4*, 265). The return of erstwhile allies such as his brother-in-law Hamo Lestrange to the allegiance of Henry III after their support for the baronial opposition against the king, and the ending of Henry's toleration of his attacks along the border, gave Gruffudd little choice but to relinquish his alliance with the king in favour of one with Llywelyn in order both to retain his conquests and to prevent attacks upon him by the prince of Gwynedd. As Smith has argued (*Llywelyn*, 289), the agreement articulated the important principle that Gruffudd's lands in Powys Wenwynwyn were to be held henceforth by virtue of a grant by Llywelyn as prince of Wales.

*359 Henry III

Letter, informing the king that the accomplices of Hamo Lestrange, whom Hamo had discharged in the castle of Montgomery after his withdrawal, had assaulted Llywelyn's men and killed three of them. Although he could have taken vengeance for this, he had refrained because of his reverence for the king.

[Shortly before 9 February 1265]

Mention only, in a letter from Henry III to Llywelyn dated at Westminster, 9 February 1265 (*CR 1264–8*, 94–5; cd., *H*, no. 482). Henry promised to send magnates shortly who would make suitable amends.

*360 Henry III

Letter, complaining that, although Llywelyn has frequently offered the bishop of Bangor a sufficient bond to obey the mandates of the Church if he has offended against him to the prejudice of ecclesiastical liberty, the bishop has so far refused to accept such a bond and has placed an interdict on Llywelyn's chapel on account of causes such as lay fees that pertain to lay, not ecclesiastical, jurisdiction.

[Shortly before 15 May 1265]

Mention only, in a letter from Henry III to the bishop of Bangor dated at Gloucester, 15 May 1265 (*CR 1264–8*, 117–18; cd., *H*, no. 483). Since pleas concerning lay fees in his realm pertained to the crown, Henry ordered the bishop (Richard, 1237–67) to lift the interdict or at least to suspend it until after the next parliament at Westminster, which the bishop would be attending and where the matter could be discussed. The next parliament was held at Winchester, in September 1265, though the Annals of Waverley state that, because of Llywelyn's attacks on Cheshire, it was continued at Westminster on 13 October (*AM*, ii. 102, 366; *CPR 1266–72*, 265).

361 Letter patent concerning an agreement with Henry III

Notification that, in order to have the good grace of the king towards himself and his magnates and other allies concerning all the king's grievances against them on account of the prince's attacks in the past, as well as certain castles, lordships, liberties and other rights to be held from the king as contained more fully in the letter concerning this, Llywelyn promises to pay the king 30,000 marks at Whittington or another place appointed by the king, provided that he is given one month's notice, to be paid as follows: 3,000 marks on the next Michaelmas [29 September], and then 3,000 marks annually at the same time in the same place until the total of 30,000 marks has been paid. By the present letter Llywelyn binds himself and his principality to this by the counsel and assent of his magnates, and has sworn on the Gospels that he and his magnates will pay the sum in full as stated above. He has acknowledged that he holds the principality of Wales and all he may have and hold from the king, and has promised to serve and obey him as his lord and to render all services for the principality and all he holds to the king and his heirs as his predecessors the princes of Wales were accustomed or ought to have done to previous kings of England. He has also sworn that he and his magnates will adhere to the ordinance recently issued at London by the magnates of England, and sealed by the king and many prelates, concerning the release of the Lord Edward, who had been given of his own will as a hostage for the assuring of this peace, and will aid the magnates with all his power against all who infringe the ordinance or try to oppress those magnates. He has granted his good grace to, and fully remitted all grievances against, all inhabitants of the castles and townships conceded to him by the king. He wishes that these may remain peacefully under him with all their goods, rendering to him the services owed to their lords, or if they prefer they may freely leave with all their goods and move to wherever they wish, and has promised to maintain them in all their rights like the rest of his men for as long they wish to remain under him. If he breaks the above terms, he grants that if he has not made amends within three months of being asked to do so by the king, the king will henceforth no longer be bound by the above agreements and concessions. Llywelyn's promise of obedience and payment to the king is conditional on the king's adhering to the aforesaid ordinance; if he breaks it, and Llywelyn is informed of this by the king's council established by that ordinance, Llywelyn shall be obliged neither to obey nor to pay until the king has made amends and been reconciled with his magnates.

Pipton, 19 June 1265

A = TNA: PRO, C 47/27/1, no. 17. No endorsement; approx. 240 × 170 + 22 mm.; double slit in fold for insertion of a tag. Tag and seal missing.

Pd. from A, *RL*, ii. 284–6; from A, Chaplais, *Diplomatic Documents*, 273–4 (no. 400).

Cd., *H*, no. 396.

Universis presentes litteras inspecturis vel audituris Lewelin(us) filius Griffin(i) princeps Wall(ie) et dominus de Snoudon' salutem in domino. Noverit universitas vestra quod nos pro bona gracia domini nostri H. Dei gratia illustris regis Angl(ie) pro nobis et magnatibus terre nostre ac ceteris coadiutoribus nostris habenda de omnibus rancoribus et offensis quas idem dominus noster rex concepit contra nos occasione aliquorum per nos principem predictum contra ipsum et suos attemptatorum temporibus iam preteritis et pro quibusdam castris, possessionibus,[a] dominiis, libertatibus et aliis iuribus nostris ab eodem domino nostro rege nobis concessis prout in litteris super hoc confectis plenius continetur, tenemur et bona fide promittimus dare et solvere eidem domino nostro regi triginta milia marcarum sterlingorum apud Wyttinton'[b] vel alio loco nobis ad solvendum eque ydoneo quem dictus dominus noster rex nobis duxerit prefigendum, dum tamen super hoc per unum mensem fuerimus premuniti, solvendas[c] terminis infrascriptas, videlicet in festo Beati Michael(is) proximo sequente tria milia marcarum, et sit deinceps singulis annis eisdem die et loco tria milia marcarum donec prefata summa triginta milia marcarum fuerit plenarie persoluta. Et ad hoc de consilio et assensu magnatum terre nostre nos et principatum nostrum tenore presencium obligamus. Iuravimus insuper ad sancta Dei ewangelia nos et magnates nostri predicti quod predictam pecunie summam per particulas memoratas sine aliqua diminucione[d] vel fraude integre et plenarie persolvemus diebus et loco suprascriptis, sicut predictum est. Recongnoscimus etiam quod principatum nostrum Wall(ie) et omnia que habemus et tenemus, tenemus de domino nostro rege predicto, et eidem [e-]tamquam domino[-e] servire et obedire promittimus et omnia servicia pro dictis principatu et aliis omnibus que de ipso tenemus sibi et heredibus suis facere que principes Wall(ie) predecessores nostri sibi et antecessoribus suis regibus Angl(ie) facere consueverunt aut debuerunt. Iuravimus quoque nos et magnates nostri predicti tactis sacrosanctis ewangeliis quod magnatibus regni Angl(ie) ordinacionem super liberacione domini Edwardi qui de sua voluntate pro pace regni obses datus fuerat pro pace ipsa assecuranda nuper London' provisam et domini regis ac plurimorum prelatorum regni sigillis consignatam, servare volentibus adherebimus et ad ordinacionem ipsam manutenendam[f] magnates ipsos cum toto posse nostro iuvabimus contra omnes illos qui ordinacionem ipsam infringere seu magnates ipsos gravare attemptaverint quoquo modo. Concessimus etiam bonam graciam nostram et plene ac pure remittimus omnem rancorem et omnem offensam quam nos vel nostri habuimus contra homines castra vel villas per dominum regem nobis concessas inhabitantes. Et volumus ac concedimus pro nobis ac nostris quod ipsi in domibus et terris suis cum bonis suis omnibus sub nobis pacifice commorari possint et quiete, faciendo nobis debita servitia que dominis suis facere consueverunt, aut si maluerint cum bonis suis omnibus libere recedere et quo voluerint se transferre. Et promittimus ipsos manutenere et defendere in suis iuribus, libertatibus et consuetudinibus sicut ceteros homines nostros quamdiu sub nobis voluerint commorari. Et si contra predicta venire presumpsimus, volumus et concedimus quod nisi infra tres menses postquam ex parte ipsius domini regis fuerimus requisiti hoc competenter emendaverimus, quod idem dominus [noste]r rex extunc per prescriptas convenciones et concessiones in nullo nobis teneatur. Quod autem domino nostro regi tamquam domino obedire et servire et predictam solucionem facere promisimus intelligendum est quamdiu idem dominus rex ordinacionem predictam servare voluerit, alioquin si contravenire presumpserit, et hoc per consilium suum quod secundum formam ordinacionis eiusdem habuerit nobis denunciatum exstiterit, in neutro sibi teneamur donec se super hoc emendaverit et concordaverit se magnatibus suis supradictis, post quod sibi obediemus tamquam domino et satisfaciemus ut prius. Data in castris iuxta Pyp(er)ton' die Sanctorum Gervasii et Prothasii anno domini millesimo cc° sexagesimo quinto. In cuius rei testimonium huic instrumento sigillum[g] nostrum apponi fecimus, presentibus et consencientibus Griffin(o) filio Wenn', Griffin(o) filio Madoci, Howel(o) et Madok(o) fratribus suis, Res Vychan', Howello filio Maredut, Howel(o) filio Resi, Goron' filio Etdenavet, Howen(o) filio Blethyin et multis aliis.

[a] p *corrected from* d A. | [b] *beginning of word written over an erasure in* A. | [c] *sic in* A *for* solvendas *or* solvendarum. | [d] dimunicione A. | [e-e] *written over an erasure in* A. | [f] manutendam A. | [g] sigllum A.

For a full discussion of this agreement, announced in this letter patent of Llywelyn issued at Pipton (Brec.) in the lordship of Cantref Selyf and sometimes misleadingly referred to as the 'treaty of Pipton', see Smith, *Llywelyn*, 167–70. The agreement was the result of negotiations, presumably at Hereford, between Llywelyn's representatives and Simon de Montfort, acting in Henry III's name; the king's grants are listed in a letter patent issued at Hereford, 22 June 1265 (*Foedera*, I. i. 457). The 'ordinance concerning the freeing of the Lord Edward' refers to arrangements made in London in March 1265 (Maddicott, *Simon de Montfort*, 338).

362 Letter patent concerning an agreement with Henry III

Notification that, since he has promised to pay the king 30,000 marks for his good grace and certain possessions, castles and other rights, as contained in his letter patent on this matter, Llywelyn promises to pay the balance of this payment to the king's heir or successor, or otherwise as the magnates of the realm decide, should the king die or act against the terms of the ordinance issued at London before full payment has been made, provided that the terms of the agreement are observed.

Pipton, 19 June 1265

A = TNA: PRO, C 47/27/1, no. 18. No endorsement; approx. 160 × 58 + 12 mm.; double slit in fold for insertion of a tag. Tag and seal missing. The document is slightly damaged, especially by a hole approx. 22 × 18 mm. on the upper left-hand side.
Pd. from A, *RL*, ii. 287; from A, Chaplais, *Diplomatic Documents*, 274 (no. 401).
Cd., *H*, no. 397.

Omnibus presentes litteras inspecturis vel audituris L. filius Griffin(i) princeps Wall(ie) et dominus Snoudon' salutem in domino. Cum domino nostro regi Angl(ie) illustri pro bona gracia ipsius habend[a et pro] quibusdam possessionibus, castris, dominiis, libertatibus et aliis iuribus nostris ab eodem nobis concessis triginta milia marcarum certis term[inis. . . d]are promiserimus, sicut in litteris nostris patentibus super hoc confectis plenius continetur, universitatem vestram scire vol[umus quod, si . . . dom]inum regem ante perfectam solucionem in fata decedere aut forte ordinacioni London' provise de qua in litteris nostris predictis pleni[us contin]etur contraire contigerit, nos heredi vel successori eiusdem dictam ordinacionem[a] observare volenti vel aliter ad disposicionem mag[natum] regni dictam ordinacionem observare volencium de residuo pecunie supradicte respondere et satisfacere promittimus et ad hoc tenore presencium nos obligamus, dum tamen ipsi ea pro quibus dictam pecuniam dare convenimus seu promisimus nobis faciant et teneant sicut conventum est. In cuius rei testimonium presentibus sigillum nostrum fecimus apponi. Dat' apud Pip(er)ton' die veneris proxima ante [festu]m nativitatis Sancti Ioh(ann)is Baptiste, anno domini m° cc lx° quinto.

[a] *An* e *erased at the end of this word* A.

See note to no. 361 above.

363 The Treaty of Montgomery

Ottobuono, cardinal deacon of St Adrian and papal legate, announces that God, seeing that the English and Welsh had long been divided and afflicted by conflicts and wars, has apparently now wished to end the evil by bringing them back to agreement. For Henry, king of

England and the noble man Llywelyn ap Gruffudd have reached the following peace and agreement on behalf of themselves, their successors and their men.

(1) Since it is easy to settle other discords where there is agreement of wills, all grudges, offences, injuries, trespasses and damages inflicted by Llywelyn's side on the king's, and by the king's on Llywelyn's, are fully remitted and pardoned.

(2) Since what is based on justice will be firm and lasting, with the rigour of justice tempered by grace, Llywelyn will restore to the king all possessions, lands and rights occupied in the recent war, except for Brecon and Gwerthrynion. However, concerning these and other lands which Llywelyn shall restore or retain, justice shall be observed according to the customs of the March.

(3) Llywelyn shall keep possession of Builth.

(4) In Maelienydd Roger Mortimer shall be allowed to build a castle at his will. The castle and land will be restored to Llywelyn if he can prove his right to Maelienydd.

(5) The king concedes Cedewain and Ceri to Llywelyn, who shall receive justice according to the aforesaid customs [of the March] if he claims other adjacent townships or lands, and likewise with regard to all claiming rights in the lands held by Llywelyn.

(6) Concerning the castle of Whittington, Llywelyn shall receive the same service as his predecessors, with custody being kept by him to whom the king has granted it.

(7) Llywelyn shall immediately release Robert of Mold with all his land of Hawarden; Robert shall not be allowed to build a castle there for sixty years.

(8) By this ordinance Gruffudd ap Gwenwynwyn shall not restore land held while he was with the king, before entering Llywelyn's fealty, but justice shall be done to those claiming right in it according to the aforesaid customs.

(9) The king, wishing to magnify the person of Llywelyn and honour his successors, grants by his pure liberality and grace, with the consent of the Lord Edward, to Llywelyn and his heirs the principality of Wales, so that Llywelyn and his heirs shall be called and shall be princes of Wales.

(10) He also grants the fealty and homages of all the Welsh barons of Wales, so that the barons shall hold their lands in chief from the said prince and his heirs, except for the homage of Maredudd ap Rhys, whose homage and lordship the king shall keep together with all the land which the prince is bound to restore to him, with those claiming right in that land receiving justice as has been customary amongst their peers. Whenever it pleases the king to concede the homage of Maredudd to the prince, the prince shall pay the king and his heirs 5,000 marks.

(11) Concerning Dafydd, brother of Llywelyn, it is specially ordained that Llywelyn shall restore to him all the land he held before he went over to the king. If Dafydd is not content with this, his provision shall be augmented as laid down by Gruffudd ap Gwenwynwyn, Gruffudd ap Madog, Hywel ap Madog, Owain ap Bleddyn and Tudur ab Ednyfed. If Dafydd is not content with these [(?)individuals], let him claim what he wishes and justice shall be done to him according to the laws and customs of Wales, in the presence of one or two men sent by the king to see what kind of justice will be done. All this should be done for Dafydd by next Christmas.

(12) The king gives to Llywelyn and his heirs the Four Cantrefs of Perfeddwlad to be possessed as fully as the king and his predecessors had them.

(13) For the principality, lands, homages and grants the prince and his successors will be bound to give the fealty, homage and service to the king and his heirs which he or his predecessors have been accustomed and obliged to give to the kings of England.

(14) The prince and his men and successors shall not receive in their lands, or aid, any

enemy of the king and his heirs who has been banished or fled; nor will the king and his heirs maintain or help an enemy of the prince or his heirs.

(15) All agreements and pacts between the aforesaid king and Llywelyn, or letters and documents concerning these, which contain anything contrary to the present peace and agreement or ordinance shall be considered null and void.

(16) For all the above concessions and grants, and in return for the grace and good will of the king and his sons, the prince is bound to give the king and his heirs 25,000 marks, of which 1,000 marks shall be paid within a month and 4,000 marks by next Christmas, with sufficient security for payment, and thence 3,000 marks each year at the same term at Chester Abbey, until the whole sum has been paid. Letters of quittance will be issued for the payments by the king or his representative. If the 3,000 marks are not paid each Christmas, and if Llywelyn has not paid by the following feast of the Purification of the Virgin [2 February], he shall pay a penalty of 100 marks and then 50 marks for each month in which he has failed to make the payment, and all expenses incurred by the king in this regard.

The above was discussed, ordained and accepted by the king and his eldest son as well as by Einion ap Caradog and Dafydd ab Einion, having the power and special command from Llywelyn to negotiate a peace and settlement with the king and his heirs and men and of swearing on behalf of Llywelyn and his counsellors and of doing all that is opportune regarding the peace. To reinforce the settlement oaths have been sworn on the Gospels by Robert Walerand and John de la Lynde on behalf of the king at his express command, by the same Robert on behalf of the Lord Edward, having a special command from him to do so, and by the aforesaid Einion and Dafydd on behalf of Llywelyn and his counsellors, that the king and his eldest son and Llywelyn and his counsellors will never break this peace but will observe it for ever in all its articles.

Ottobuono has sealed the document with his seal and the seals of the king and his eldest son and of Einion and Dafydd. It is dated at Shrewsbury on 25 September 1267 in the third year of the pontificate of Clement IV. And on the following Thursday, Michaelmas [29 September] Llywelyn, in the presence of Ottobuono and the king's sons, counsellors and barons, accepted and ratified the settlement and peace in all its articles, having first given homage and fealty to the king, and Llywelyn, on behalf of himself and his heirs and successors, together with Hywel ap Madog, Goronwy [ab Ednyfed], the prince's steward, Tudur ab Ednyfed and the aforesaid Einion and Dafydd, have sworn on the Gospels that they will not break this peace and settlement but observe it in all the aforesaid articles for ever. Ottobuono has confirmed the present document with his seal and the seals of the king, the Lord Edward, Llywelyn, Einion and Dafydd.

Shrewsbury, 25 September 1267 (B)/Montgomery, 29 September 1267 (C)

B = TNA: PRO, C 53/56 (Ch. R. 51 Hen. III), m. 2 (contemporary enrolment).
C = TNA: PRO, E 36/274 (Liber A), fos 327r–328v. s. xiii ex.
Pd. from C, *Foedera*, I. i. 474; from C, *LW*, 1–4 (no. 1).
Cd., *CChR 1257–1300*, 81 (from B); *H*, no. 398.

Ottobonus miseratione divina Sancti Adriani diaconus cardinalis apostolice sedis legatus ad perpetuam memoriam rei geste. Creator omnium Deus qui in tanta mundi varietate tantaque repugnantia rerum orbem in tanta concordia stabilivit ut omnia suos terminos teneant et certa lege subsistant, humanum genus quod mundi representat imaginem[a] suo secreto iuditio guerrarum dissidiis affligi permittat aliquando, et ipsum suo nutu pacis recreat unitate, ipse quippe Anglor(um) et Wallensium populos a longis retro temporibus in penam forsitan utrorumque adinvicem dissidentes multis discordiis multisque bellis afflictos oculo misericordie sue respiciens, hiis diebus volens[b] ut videtur finem malis imponere ad concordiam sua pietate reduxit. Ecce etenim dominus H. rex Angl(ie) illustris pro se, heredibus ac hominibus suis ex una parte et nobilis vir Lewelinus filius Griffini pro se, successoribus et hominibus suis ex altera super omnibus contentionibus et discordiis olim inter se habitis, ac transgressionibus et dampnis que hinc inde facta dicuntur, ad huiusmodi pacem et concordiam devenerunt.

[i] In primis siquidem quia de ceteris discordiis facile concordatur ubi concordia intervenit animorum, omnes rancores, offense, iniurie, transgressiones et dampna per Lewelinu(m) et suos illata domino regi et tenentibus partem suam et illata Lewelino et suis ab hominibus regis et tenentibus partem eius plenarie adinvicem remittuntur ac etiam condonantur.

[ii] Verum quoniam solidum et stabile permanet quod locatur super[c] iustitie fundamentum, primo que iustitie deinde que sunt liberalitatis et gratie in ista concordia et mixtim nichilominus utrimque[d] alicubi declarentur, cum plerumque concordiam parere soleat quando per gratiam sic rigor iustitie temperatur ut in hiis que petuntur a partibus iusta exhibeatur gratia et fiat iustitia gratiosa. Restituent igitur Lewelinus et sui domino regi et suis et tenentibus partem suam omnes possessiones, terras et iura per ipsum occupata et suos occasione guerre et discordie ultimo habite inter Anglicos et Wallenses, exceptis terris de Brechonia[e] et Werthrennon quarum Lewelino et suis seisina et possessio remanebit: de ipsis tamen et aliis quas idem Lewelinus restituet vel que remanebunt eidem fiet hinc inde iustitia secundum consuetudines hactenus in Marchia observatas.

[iii] Seisina etiam et possessio terre de Buyel remaneat Lewelino, cui rex concedit et dat ius quod habet in ea: de ipsa tamen fiet iustitia quibuscumque ius in ea petentibus in proprietate vel possessione secundum consuetudines prelibatas.

[iv] In terra vero de Maelenith liceat nobili viro Rogero de Mortuo Mari castrum erigere vel edificare pro suo libito voluntatis, cuius castri simul cum ipsa terra eidem Lewelino restitutio fiet si dictam terram de Maelenith prefato Lewelino ius in ea petenti adiudicari contingat.

[v] Dominus etiam rex dimittit et concedit terras de Kedewyen[f] et de Kery cum pertinentiis suis Lewelino predicto, qui si in aliis villis vel terris adiacentibus ius voluerit reclamare secundum predictas consuetudines iustitia sibi fiet, et similiter secundum easdem consuetudines fiet iustitia omnibus ius reclamantibus in terris que remanebunt prefato Lewelino[g] et suis.

[vi] De castro vero et terra de Whitinton'[h] idem Lewelinus habebit et recipiet servitium quod predecessores sui de ipsis hactenus habuerunt: guardia eiusdem militi remanente cui rex concessit eandem.

[vii] Idem nichilominus Lewelinus nobilem virum Rob(er)tum de Monte Alto cum tota terra sua de Hawordyn statim sine dilatione aliqua liberum restituet et dimittet, cui Rob(er)to usque ad triginta annos in ea castrum edificare vel erigere non licebit.

[viii] Per hanc autem ordinationem Griffinus filius Wennewen[i] si quam terram tenuit dum esset cum rege, antequam ad fidelitatem et partem iverit Lewelini, restituere minime teneatur: ius tamen in ea volentibus reclamare in proprietate seu possessione fiet iustitia secundum consuetudines supradictas.

[ix] Ceterum dominus rex Angl(ie) volens prefati Lewelini magnificare personam et in eo

ceteros honorare qui sibi hereditario iure succedent, ex mera ^j–liberalitate sua^j et gratia ^k–de assensu etiam et voluntate^-k domini Edwardi primogeniti sui dat et concedit prefato Lewelino et heredibus suis Wallie principatum, ut idem Lewelinus et heredes sui principes Wallie vocentur et sint;

[x] insuper fidelitatem et homagia omnium baronum Wallie Wallensiu(m), ut dicti barones a prefatis principe et heredibus in capite teneant terras suas, excepto homagio nobilis viri Mareduci[l] filii Resi, cuius homagium et dominium rex sibi et heredibus suis retinet cum tota terra eiusdem quam idem princeps sibi restituere et a suis statim restitui facere teneatur, de qua ius in ea reclamantibus postmodum fiet iustitia sicut inter pares suos fieri consuevit; quandocumque vero domino regi placuerit prefato principi concedere homagium Maraduci predicti, prefatus princeps eidem regi vel heredibus suis quinque milia marcarum[m] dare et solvere teneatur.

[xi] De David[n] autem fratre Lewelini predicti est specialiter ordinatum quod dictus Lewelinus sibi restituat totam terram quam idem David[n] habuit antequam ab ipso recederet et in parte domini regis esset. Qua si David[n] non fuerit forte[o] contentus, fiet sibi provisionis augmentum prout Griffinus filius Weneonwen[i] et Griffinus filius Madoc,[p] Hoellus[q] filius Madoc[p] et Owenus filius Bledhyn, et Tuderus filius Idneuaz[r] bona fide dicent, ordinabunt vel etiam providebunt. Quibus si David noluerit[s] esse contentus, quod voluerit petet, de quo secundum leges et c[on]suetudines Wallie iustitia sibi fiat,[t] uno vel duobus presentibus quos domino regi transmittere placuerit ad videndum que et qualis iustitia sibi fiet. Que omnia dicto David exhiberi debent et fieri infra festum nativitatis dominice proximo futurum, obstaculo cuiuslibet alterius dilationis seu difficultatis amoto.

[xii] Dat etiam et concedit dicto principi et heredibus suis dominus rex Quatuor Cantredos de Porthwlad adeo plene a prefatis Lewelino et heredibus habendos et possidendos sicut ipse et predecessores sui ipsos unquam[u] plenius habuerunt.

[xiii] Pro quibus principatu, terris, homagiis et concessionibus idem princeps et successores sui fidelitatem et homagium ac servitium consuetum ac[v] debitum domino regi et heredibus suis prestare et facere tenebuntur quod ipse vel antecessores sui regibus Angl(ie) consueverunt et tenebantur facere et prestare.

[xiv] Prefatus autem princeps et sui ac successores eorum non recipient in terris suis aliquem adversarium seu inimicum bannitum vel fugitivum prefati regis et heredum suorum, nec eis contra regem et heredes suos prestabunt consilium, auxilium vel favorem: dominus etiam rex et heredes sui inimicum vel adversarium principis vel heredum suorum non manutenebunt contra principem vel iuvabunt.

[xv] Omnes autem conventiones et pacta habita inter prefatum regem Angl(ie) et Lewelinum predictu(m), necnon littere et scripture super eis confecte si que forsan existant vel poterunt inveniri huic paci et concordie seu ordinationi in aliquo repugnantes, pro nullis, cassis, irritis et vacuis penitus habeantur, pace ista et concordia in sue firmitatis robore permanente.

[xvi] Ad hec pro omnibus concessionibus et largitionibus supradictis, et ut princeps ipse domini regis et filiorum suorum gratiam plenius habeat et bonam optineat voluntatem, viginti quinque milia marcarum domino re[gi] et heredibus suis pro se et suis successoribus dare tenetur, de quibus ipse princeps mille marcas infra mensem et quatuor milia marcarum usque ad proximum festum nativitatis dominice, pro quibus solvendis idem Lewelinus cavebit idonee,[w] et de[inde in] eodem termino tria milia marcarum quolibet anno apud Cestriam[x] in monasterio Cestr(ie) dicto regi vel nuntio suo ipsius regis litteras deferenti

persolvet, donec de tota summa fuerit plenarie satisfactum; de qualibet vero solutione littera de quietantia fiet per regem vel nuntium supradictum ad hoc ab ipso rege mandatum et potestatem habentem. Quod si in prefato festo nativitatis dominice summa trium milium marcarum quolibet anno non fuerit persoluta, si usque ad festum purificationis Beate Virginis proximo sequens idem Lewelinus supradictam summam non solverit, centum marcas nomine pene solvet et deinde pro quolibet mense in quo in solutione dicte^y summe defecerit quinquaginta marcas nomine pene; et nichilominus omnes expensas quas rex propter hoc fecerit et etiam interesse prestabit.

Premissa tractata, ordinata et acceptata sunt a prefatis rege et primogenito suo necnon Eynyaun^z filio Keyradauc^{aa} et David filio Eynyaun^z habentibus potestatem et speciale mandatum a prefato Lewelino firmandi pacem et compositionem cum rege predicto, heredibus et hominibus suis, et iurandi in animam predicti Lewelini et consiliariorum suorum necnon faciendi et complendi omnia que circa pacem predictam sunt oportuna. Et ad maiorem compositionis ipsius firmitatem et robur nobiles viri Robertus^{ab} Walerand et Ioh(ann)es de la Lind'^{ac} in animam ipsius regis de speciali et expresso mandato eiusdem, et prefatus Rob(er)tus in animam prefati domini Edwardi habens ab ipso super hoc speciale mandatum, et prenominati Eynyaun et David in animam predicti Lewelini et consiliariorum suorum tactis sacrosanctis ewangeliis presentialiter iuraverunt quod prefati rex et primogenitus suus et Lewelinus et consiliarii sui contra predictam pacem nullo tempore venient, set eam in omnibus et singulis suis articulis firmiter et imperpetuum^{ad} observabunt.$^{ae-}$In cuius rei testimonium presens scriptum sigilli nostri munimine una cum sigillis dictorum regis et primogeniti sui et predictorum Eynyaun et David fecimus roboravi.$^{-ae}$ Datum^{af} Sallop' anno domini m° $^{ag-}$cc° lx° sexagesimo septimo vii kalendas octobris^{-ag} pontificatus domini C.^{ah} pape iiii^{ti} anno tertio.

Et die iovis in festo Beati Mich(ael)is sequenti prefatus Lewelinus^{ai} in presentia nostra et domini regis filiorum et consiliariorum et baronum suorum suprascriptam compositionem et pacem acceptans et expresse ratificans in omnibus et $^{aj-}$singillis suis articulis,$^{-aj}$ facto primo homagio regi et prestito sacramento fidelitatis secundum formam superius anotatam,^{ak} `idem Lewelinus pro se,$^{al-}$heredibus et successoribus^{-al} suis et Hoelus filius Madok, Gronun,^{am} Goronun^{an} senescallus ipsius principis et Tuderus filius Nauet^{ao} et supradicti Eynhaun^{ap} et David ^{aq} iuraverunt tactis sacrosanctis ewangeliis se contra predictam pacem et compositionem in aliquo non venturos set eam in omnibus supradictis articulis se perpetuo servatur[os]. Et ad maiorem^{ar} roboris firmitatem nos sigilli nostri et supradicti^{as} domini regis, domini Edwardi primogeniti sui, Lewelini,^{at} Eynlaun^{au} et David sigillorum munimine presens scriptum fecimus roborari.$^{av-}$Actum apud Sallop' die dominica proxima ante festum Sancte Michaelis anno domini m° cc° lx sexagesimo septimo^{-av} pontificatus domini Clementis pape iiii anno tertio.

^{a} ymaginem C. | ^{b} voletis C. | ^{c} supra C. | ^{d} utrinque C. | ^{e} r *interlined in* B. | ^{f} Kedewien C. | ^{g} Lewino C. | ^{h} Whitenton' C. | ^{i} Wenonwen' C. | $^{j-j}$ sua liberalitate C. | $^{k\,k}$ de voluntate etiam et assensu C. | ^{l} Maraduci C. | ^{m} markarum C. | ^{n} Davit C. | ^{o} *omitted* C. | ^{p} Madoch C. | ^{q} Hoellius C. | ^{r} Idneueth C. | ^{s} voluerit C. | ^{t} fiat B. | ^{u} nunquam C. | ^{v} et C. | ^{w} ydonee C. | ^{x} Castriam C. | ^{y} predicte C. | ^{z} Eynyanti C. | ^{aa} Keyradau B. | ^{ab} C *inserts* et. | ^{ac} Lynde C. | ^{ad} inperpetuum C. | $^{ae-ae}$ *omitted* C. | ^{af} Actum C. | $^{ag-ag}$ ducentesimo sexagesimo septimo die dominica proxima ante festum Sancti Mich(ael)is C. | ^{ah} Clementis C. | ^{ai} princeps C. | $^{aj-aj}$ singulis articulis suis C. | ^{ak} annotatam C. | $^{al-al}$ successoribus et heredibus C. | ^{am} Grocion C. | ^{an} Goronu' C. | ^{ao} Eadneuet C. | ^{ap} Eynan C. | ^{aq} C *inserts* consiliarii dicti principis. | ^{ar} maioris C. | ^{as} supradictorum C. | ^{at} C *inserts* principis. | ᵃᵘ *sic for* Eyniaun B; Eynan C. | ᵃᵛ⁻ᵃᵛ Datum apud Monte(m) Gomeri anno domini milesimo ducentesimo sexagesimo septimo iii kalendas octobris C.

For the making and significance of the Treaty of Montgomery see Smith, *Llywelyn*, 177–86 and references given there. Two textual problems merit notice. First and foremost, the two surviving copies end with different dating clauses. Both texts date the agreement concluded with Llywelyn's representatives at Shrewsbury on 25 September. However, the version in the charter roll (B), while stating that Llywelyn ratified the agreement on 29 September, ends with a clause giving a date at Shrewsbury on 25 September, whereas the final clause in the Liber A version (C) gives a date at Montgomery on 29 September. One explanation for this could be that the royal chancery sought to emphasize that the substantive agreement had been made at Shrewsbury on 25 September, deliberately using the verb *Actum* rather than *Datum* in order to refer back to the agreement as distinct from Llywelyn's ratification. On the other hand, the version in C, which may well derive from the prince's archives (cf. above, p. 136), emphasized that the agreement was only fully concluded after Llywelyn had ratified it in person at Montgomery on 29 September. Note also how C further emphasizes Llywelyn's title of prince (textual notes *ai* and *at*). Which text is closer to the original document(s) issued by Ottobuono is difficult to tell, though there are strong grounds for supposing that Llywelyn did in fact ratify the treaty at Montgomery, almost certainly at the ford of Rhyd Chwima, on 29 September (Smith, *Llywelyn*, 179, n. 152). The second textual problem is the inclusion in B of two men called Goronwy, and in C of *Grocion* and Goronwy (textual notes *am* and *an*), amongst those swearing together with Llywelyn on 29 September. It is very likely that this resulted from a scribal error in the common exemplar underlying versions B and C, and that only one Goronwy – namely Goronwy ab Ednyfed, Llywelyn's seneschal – was meant (cf. Smith, *Llywelyn*, 179, n. 154). Ottobuono's letter to the pope announcing his success in establishing peace (*concordia* and *compositio*) between Llywelyn and the king is partially preserved in an early fifteenth-century formulary (Graham, 'Letters of Cardinal Ottoboni', 118–19).

*364 Rhys ap Gruffudd, Llywelyn's bailiff of Builth and Llywelyn's bailiffs of Brecon, Elfael and Gwerthrynion

Mandate, instructing the recipients not to go beyond the limits of their bailiwicks to harm the English Marchers (ad nocendum Anglicis marchianis).
[Probably 25 September 1267 × 1276; possibly *c*.June 1276]

Mention only, in a letter to Llywelyn from Rhys ap Gruffudd acknowledging receipt of the mandate and certifying that it had been observed (*RL*, ii. 156–7; cd., *CAC*, 53–4). Rhys adds that, since receiving the mandate, he has made a truce with Roger Mortimer to last until the feast of St Peter ad Vincula (1 August). However, after this truce was made Roger's bailiffs despoiled Llywelyn's merchants from Builth, Elfael, Gwerthrynion and Cardigan who had gone to the market at Leominster and imprisoned some of them; Rhys therefore seeks Llywelyn's instructions regarding what he and the prince's other bailiffs should do. As Edwards argued (*CAC*, 54), the letter can be no later than the outbreak of Edward I's first Welsh war early in 1277 and is probably no earlier than the confirmation of Llywelyn's hold of Builth, Brecon and Gwerthrynion in the Treaty of Montgomery in September 1267 (no.

363, cc. ii–iii above), although the prince had established authority over all these areas by March 1263 (cf. Smith, *Llywelyn*, 125–7, 141, 150). Llywelyn's men were detained at the markets and fairs of Leominster and Montgomery on 1 July 1276, despite a truce between Llywelyn's bailiffs and Roger Mortimer (no. 394 below); although it is uncertain whether these events were the same as those referred to by Rhys ap Gruffudd regarding Leominster only, the similarities between the two accounts could indicate that the prince's mandate was sent shortly before July 1276 (cf. Smith, *Llywelyn*, 404, n. 57). Rhys ap Gruffudd was among those killed with Llywelyn on 11 December 1282 (ibid., 565, n. 188).

*365 Henry III

Letter, complaining that Gilbert de Clare, earl of Gloucester and Hertford, has refused to restore the lands of certain barons of Wales belonging to Llywelyn's principality, contrary to the terms of the peace, though frequently requested to make restoration, and that he has occupied the land of Elfael Is Mynydd, the patrimony of Llywelyn's barons Owain [ap] Maredudd and Ifor ab Owain (Oweni Mareduc' et Yvorr filii Oweny). *He also petitions that the king should order Roger Mortimer to meet Llywelyn on a certain day to make and receive amends according to the peace, since Llywelyn has a right in the land of Maelienydd, which Roger possesses and where he has built a castle, and that the king should prohibit Roger from disturbing Llywelyn's possession of Dyffryn Tefeidiad (Tempsiter). (Possibly also asks the king to intervene to secure the release of Gruffudd Rhys, held by the earl, and requests the homage of Maredudd ap Rhys in return for the payment laid down in the treaty [of Montgomery].)*

[Probably December 1267]

Mention only, in a letter from Henry III to Llywelyn, dated at Guildford, 1 January 1268 (*CR 1264–8*, 496–7; cd., *H*, no. 486). Although Henry's letter refers only to Llywelyn's messengers, rather than explicitly to a letter from the prince, it is likely that at least some of the requests mentioned by the king were received by him in written form. Henry replied that he wished Llywelyn, the earl and Roger Mortimer to meet to discuss their disputes, and that he preferred to keep the homage of Maredudd ap Rhys, making him give due amends to the prince for trespasses against him. See further Smith, *Llywelyn*, 362 and nn. 83–4.

366 Agreement with Gilbert de Clare, earl of Gloucester and Hertford

Agreement between Llywelyn and Gilbert de Clare, earl of Gloucester and Hertford, concerning the disputes between them over men, lands, trespasses and other matters, recently discussed at Montgomery before the bishop of Exeter and his companions, sent by the king. The day fixed by the bishop and his companions concerning these matters, Wednesday 17 October, shall be postponed to 2 February [1269] following. Meanwhile the prince and earl have agreed that the bishop of Bangor, Goronwy ab Ednyfed, Tudur ab Ednyfed and Dafydd ab Einion on the prince's side, and John fitz John, John de Braose, Master Roger of Leicester, papal chaplain and Hervey de Borham on the earl's side, having sworn that they will faithfully hear the reasons proposed, shall settle the aforesaid matters according to justice. The prince and earl urge those chosen for this to proceed without regard for the hatred, favour, fear, reverence, dominion or love of anyone. The prince and earl will adhere to everything laid down by those chosen. If those chosen are unable to settle the matters within the time-limit, the prince and earl will provide for another means of settlement by 2 February. If a full settlement is not reached by either the first or the second means by 2 February, the matters shall go before the king as they were on 17 October. Concerning the men of Meisgyn and Senghennydd who the earl says have been removed from him by the prince, of whom the prince was in seisin on the day on which the present agreement was made, it is agreed that the men of Meisgyn should remain with their flocks and chattels until 2 February between Brecon and Glynrhondda, and those of Senghennydd similarly between Brecon and the river Caeach. The prince and earl have sworn to uphold all this, and attached their seals to this chirograph. The chosen arbitrators shall begin their office on Wednesday, 10 January [1269] at Eadbryn in Brecon.

Pontymynaich in Cantref Selyf, 27 September 1268

B = TNA: PRO, E 36/274 (Liber A), fo. 366r. s. xiii ex.
Pd. from B, *Cartae*, ii. 693–4; from B, *LW*, 101–3 (no. 197).
Cd., *H*, no. 399.

Die iovis proxima ante festum Sancti Mich(ael)is anno regni regis Henr(ici) filii regis Ioh(ann)is quinquagesimo secundo apud Ponte(m) Monachorum in Cantrefsely convenit inter dominum L. principem Wallie, dominum Snaudon' ex una parte et dominum G. de Clar(a) comitem Gloucest(ri)e et Hereford' ex altera super contentionibus et discordiis inter ipsos motis super hominibus, terris, transgressionibus et rebus aliis de quibus nuper apud Mongomer' coram venerabili patre episcopo Exon(iensi) et sociis suis per dominum regem ibidem transmissis agebatur, videlicet quod predicti princeps et comes consenserunt quod dies mercurii proxima post quindenam Sancti Mich(ael)is anno predicto quem super eisdem[a] predicti episcopus et socii sui prefixerunt coram domino rege, prorogetur usque in octabas purificationis Sancte Marie proximo futuras. Consenserunt etiam hiidem princeps et comes quod interim venerabilis pater episcopus Bangor(ensis), Gronno ab Edenaueth, Tuder ab Edenaueth et David ab Eynon ex parte predicti principis electi et domini Ioh(ann)es filius Ioh(ann)is, Ioh(ann)es de Breus(a), magister Rog(er)us de Leycestr(ia) domini pape capellanus et dominus Herveus de Borh(a)m ex parte predicti comitis electi,[b] prestito prius corporali sacramento quod fideliter et exquisite audiant rationes hinc inde propositas et proponendas super premissis, ea secundum iustitiam terminabunt et diffinient. Predicti vero princeps et comes bona fide iniungent suis ad predicta electis quod odio, favore, timore, reverentia vel dominio seu amore alicuius dimittent quin fedeliter[c] procedant in negotio supradicto. Et predicti princeps `et comes stabunt per omnia `et in omnibus iudicio dictorum et ordinationi, arbitrio seu laudo predictorum electorum in premissis. Et si contingat, quod absit, quod predicti electi unanimi consensu predicta negotia aliquo casu infra terminum supradictum non terminaverunt, predicti princeps et comes de alia via terminandi predicta infra predictas octabas providebunt. Et si evenerit quod predicta nec per primam viam nec per secundam infra predictas octabas terminentur ad plenum, sint omnia predicta negotia in predictis octabis coram domino rege in eo statu in quo esse debuerant coram eo predicta die mercurii post quindenam Sancti Mich(ael)is. De hominibus autem de Meyskyn et de Seinghenyz quos dictus comes dicit per dictum principem sibi esse substractos, de quibus idem princeps fuit in seisina die confectionis presentium, sic convenit inter eos quod illi de Meyskyn usque ad predictas octabas purificationis cum averiis suis et catallis morentur inter terram de Breconia et Glenrotheny, et illi de Seynghenyz similiter usque ad predictum tempus morentur cum averiis et catallis inter terram Brecon(ie) et aquam que dicitur Caayach, ita tamen quod occasione more predictorum hominum nichil predictis principis seu comiti accrescat `seu decrescat . Et ad hec omnia fideliter et sine dolo observanda, predicti princeps et comes corporale prestiterunt sacramentum. Et ad maiorem securitatem predicti princeps et comes huic scripto in modum cyrographi confecto sigilla sua alternatim apposuerunt. Et sciendum est quod dicti electi officium suum incipient die mercurii proxima post festum epiphanie domini proximo future apud Eadbryn in Brecon(ia) de die in diem procedendo donec predicta conpleverint. Actum anno, die et loco predictis.

ᵃ B *repeats* eisdem. | ᵇ electo B. | ᶜ *sic in* B *for* fideliter.

For the background to this agreement see no. 365 above; Lloyd, 'Llywelyn ap Gruffydd'; and Smith, *Llywelyn*, 342–4. It is discussed as an example of an arbitral award in Smith, 'Disputes and settlements', 840–1, which notes that Hervey de Borham, one of the earl's nominees, had been steward of the Clare estates. Lloyd ('Llywelyn ap Gruffydd', 59) identified Pontymynaich (*Pons Monachorum*) as a place near Gwenddwr (SO 065 432) in the Wye valley, where the Cistercians of Dore had a grange in the Clifford lordship of Cantref Selyf. The location of Eadbryn is uncertain. In the event, no compromise was reached, and on 14 March Henry III decided that the matter should be judged by the Lord Edward (*CPR 1266–72*, 205).

367 Beddgelert Priory

Exchange of land between Llywelyn and the prior and convent of Beddgelert with the consent of Anian, bishop of Bangor, namely that the prior and convent quitclaim to the prince and his heirs all the land of the church of Dolwyddelan beyond the ditch of the meadow adjacent to the said township; likewise all the land of the sons of Ithel ap Dafydd at Pennardd in Arfon except for the part of Iorwerth Hagr which the canons will retain; likewise all the land held by the canons at Amwlch [(?) Ymwlch] in Eifionydd. The prince grants and confirms for himself and his heirs all the land, cultivated and uncultivated, with meadows, woods and pastures within the following bounds: from the end of the old bridge over the Ferlas to the hill called Yr Wylfa, and thence to the summit of the mountain Moel Ehedog, and thence to Bwlch Meillionen, and thence to Bwlch llyfn, and thence to Bwlch trwsgl, and thence to Bwlch rin deyliaur, and thence along the boundaries between Arfon and Eifionydd to the river Colwyn, and following the course of that river to the river Fferlas, and following the course of that river to the front of the old bridge. The prince and his heirs warrant all this land to the prior and convent and their successors against all men and women for ever. The prince and prior attach their seals to the document along with the seals of the bishop and chapter of Bangor.

Caernarfon, 11 March 1269

B = TNA: PRO, E 36/274 (Liber A), fo. 351r. Rubric: littera conventionis. s. xiii ex.
Pd. from B, *LW*, 58–9 (no. 85); from *LW*, Gresham, *Eifionydd*, 61 (trans. only).
Cd., *H*, no. 152.

[A]nno domini mᵒ ccᵒ lxᵒ octavo facta est subscripta permutatio terrarum inter dominum Lewelinum principem Wallie, dominum Snaudon' ex una parte et priorem et conventum de Bedkelerd ex altera cum consensu venerabilis patris Anniani Bangoren(sis) episcopi, videlicet quod dictus prior et conventus quietumclamant inperpetuum pro se et successoribus suis dicto domino principi et eius heredibus totam terram ecclesie sue de Dolwydelan ultra fossatam prati iuxta dictam villam; item totam terram filiorum Ithael filii David apud Pennard in Aruon excepta parte Ioruerth' Hagyr que dictis canonicis remanebit; item totam terram quam prefati canonici habuerunt apud Amulch in Eyfionyd. Dictus vero princeps pro se et heredibus suis concedit, dat et confirmat totam terram cultam et incultam cum pratis, nemoribus, pascuis et pasturis infra terminos subscriptos, videlicet a capite veteris pontis super Serrlasse usque ad collem qui vocatur Yrvilua et per crepidinem illius collis usque ad supercilium montis Morlehedauc et per crepidinem illius montis usque ad locum qui vocatur Bulchmellonen et ab inde per crepidinem montis usque Bulchlliuin et ab illo loco per crepidinem montis usque Bulchtrusgil et a Bulchtrusgil usque Bulchrin deyliaur et ab illo loco secundum terminos inter Aruon et Eyfionyd usque ad fluvium Colwyn et secundum ductum illius fluvii usque ad fluvium Serlasse et secundum ductum illius 'fluvii Sesrlass usque ad frontem veteris pontis. Dictus vero princeps et eius heredes totam dictam terram infra prescriptos terminos tenentur prefato priori et canonicis ac eorum successoribus contra omnes homines et feminas inperpetuum warantizare sine aliqua calumpnia. Ut autem dicta permutatio firmitatis robur obtineat inposterum prescripti princeps et prior huic scripto alternatim sua sigilla apposuerunt una cum sigillis episcopi et capituli Bangoren(sis). Datum apud Caer in Aruon anno domini m° cc° sexagesimo octavo in vigilia Sancti Gregorii pape.

For the location of the lands exchanged see Gresham, *Eifionydd*, 4 (Map 4), 38, 61–3; Stephenson, *Governance*, 157. Dolwyddelan (SH 735 523) lay just over 9 miles north-east, Pennardd 6 miles north-west, of Beddgelert Priory (SH 591 480); *Amulch* is probably Ymwlch (Ymwlch Fawr at SH 508 410), in the detached portion of the township of Pennant (later a detached portion of the township of Trefan) that lay to the south-west of the priory. The lands granted by Llywelyn comprised half of the mountainous area of bond land in the north-eastern part of the township of Pennant, on the west side of Nant Colwyn, including Bwlch Trwsgl (SH 551 497), the pass at the head of Cwm Pennant. It has been assumed that the beginning of the year was placed at the Annunciation (25 March), and that the 1268 of the text refers to 1269 according to modern reckoning.

368 Letter patent concerning his brother Dafydd ap Gruffudd

Notification that Llywelyn has received his brother Dafydd ap Gruffudd into his peace, unity and concord and received his fealty, homage and service, in return for which he has restored to Dafydd all the lands which he used to have before he withdrew from Llywelyn's unity to the side of the king and the Lord Edward. Llywelyn gives Dafydd full security of life and limb without arrest or imprisonment, with the exception of those matters he set out in the peace talks, renouncing all sophistry or deceit or letters contrary to that peace agreement as well as all benefits of canon and civil law which could impede or break the agreement, subjecting himself to the jurisdiction of the bishops of Bangor and St Asaph, so that they may excommunicate him and his heirs if they break the agreement in any part. Llywelyn and Dafydd may, if they wish, seek papal confirmation of the agreement. If trespasses, injuries or grievances should arise between Llywelyn and Dafydd in future, these shall be settled by the bishops acting together with worthy men chosen with the consent of both sides. Llywelyn has had his seal and those of the aforementioned bishops attached to the present letter.

Aberreu, 1269

B = NLW, Peniarth MS 231B, pp. 67–9. s. xvii[1].
Cd., *H*, no. 402.

Omnibus has litteras visuris vel audituris L. princeps Wall(ie), dominus Snaudon' salutem in domino. Noveritis quod nos fide medietatis sacrosanctis recepimus dilectum fratrum nostrum D. filium Griffini in [p. 68] pacem, unitatem et concordiam nostram necnon fidelitatem, homagium atque servitium suum suscepimus pro quibus fidelitate, homagio ac servitio restituimus atque concessimus eidem omnes terras suas quas[a] habebat tempore quo ab unitate nostre recessit ad partem domini regis et nobilis viri domini Edwardi sui primogeniti. Damus etiam `et´ permittimus eidem D. plenam securitatem et suis quoad vitam et menbra sine captione seu incarceratione, exclusis tamen illis quos in prolocutione pacis expressimus, renuntiantes omni cavillationi et fraudi ac litteris impetratis contra formam istam necnon omni beneficio iuris tam canonici[b] quam civilis quod super hanc formam impedire possit vel infringere, subiacentes nos etiam iurisdictioni venerabilium patrum de Bangor et de Sancto Assaph' episcoporum coniunctim et divisim, ita quod possint excommunicationis sententiam in nos et heredes nostros promulgare si dictam formam in aliqua sua[c] parte infringimus. Liceat etiam nobis et dicto David, si voluerit, confirmationem predicte pacis et forme inferende a sede apostolica impetrare. Si autem transgressiones, alique offense seu rancores in posterum inter nos mutui emerserint, prefati episcopi adiectis sibi probis viris ex communi assensu nostro electis non suspectis alicui partium dictas transgressiones, offensas et rancores inter nos et dictum David corrigi facient et sopiri. Et ut forma supradicta in omnibus et singulis suis articulis inposterum firma maneat [p. 69] et penitus inconcussa, presentibus litteris nostrum sigillum una cum sigillis predictorum episcoporum fecimus apponi. Dat' apud Aberreu anno domini m cc sexagessimo nono.

[a] B *inserts (?)*habuit *deleted.* | [b] canonica B. | [c] sui B.

Although the Treaty of Montgomery (no. 363, c. xi above) had laid down that a settlement should be made with Dafydd by Christmas 1267, the present document shows that the negotiations took longer (Stephenson, *Governance*, 175; Smith, *Llywelyn*, 374–5). The bishops of Bangor and St Asaph were subsequently called upon to arbitrate in certain matters that were ambiguous in the agreement, and Llywelyn obtained papal confirmation of their 'interpretation and explanation' in the summer of 1274 (no. 382 below).

369 Llywelyn's bailiffs of Perfeddwlad
Mandate to his bailiffs of Perfeddwlad, in dealing with the bishop of St Asaph, to observe all the better customs which his predecessors have observed or made to be observed with the bishop's predecessors, with reference to lay fees. If there is any doubt concerning any custom conceded to the bishop's predecessors by Llywelyn or his predecessors, the bailiffs should discuss the matter within fifteen days by means of twelve trustworthy sworn men from the locality in which the doubt has arisen and observe faithfully what they find. Llywelyn makes a

pledge that he will not hear further the bishop's complaint on account of the bailiffs' default in carrying out this order.

Mold, 1 May 1269

B = NLW, Peniarth MS 231B, p. 70. s. xvii[i].
Pd. from B, Haddan and Stubbs, i. 497–8.
Cd., *H*, no. 400.

Lewelin(us) princeps Wall(ie), dominus Snaudon' ballivis suis de Beruetwlad salutem. Mandamus vobis precipientes quatinus observare studeatis cum fratre Aniano episcopo de Sancto Assaph' omnes consuetudines meliores quas predecessores nostri cum suis antecessoribus episcopis observaverunt seu nos fecimus observari, et hoc quoad feodum laycalem. Et si contigerit[a] super aliqua consuetudine per nos sive per predecessores nostros suis antecessoribus episcopis concessa dubitari, ex tunc infra quindenam per xii probos et fidedignos homines de patria in qua super hiis dubitatur, ac iuratos tactis sacrosanctis, diligenter discutiatis,[b] atque quod inde inveneritis fideliter observetis; cautionem super hoc facientes, quod pro deffectu vestro in exsequendo presens nostrum mandatum non audiamus amplius predicti episcopi querelam. Datum apud Monte(m) Altu(m) anno domini m° cc° lx° nono in die apostolorum Ph(ilipp)i et Iacobi.

[a] congerit B. | [b] B *inserts* atque *struck through.*

This letter is cited in a letter of Bishop Anian II of St Asaph (1268–93), and provides early evidence for tensions between Llywelyn and the bishop which subsequently seem to have been defused until 1274 (Jones Pierce, 'Einion ap Ynyr', 26–7; Stephenson, *Governance*, 174, 184).

370 Henry III

Letter, acknowledging receipt of the king's letter dated at Windsor, 28 April, postponing the parley at Montgomery on the morrow of Pentecost recently past [13 May 1269] to the octaves of Holy Trinity [27 May] at the same place. Since Llywelyn, replying to a letter from the Lord Edward dated at Chippenham, 25 April, has written to the latter that he would like the parley to be postponed to the next feast of St John [presumably the Nativity of St John, 24 June], he asks the king to inform him whether he wishes the parley to be held on the octaves of Holy Trinity or to be postponed further as Llywelyn has suggested in his letter to Edward, for Llywelyn is prepared to hold the parley on the date already ordered by the king.

Denbigh, Friday before Pentecost [10 May 1269; but probably 17 May 1269]

A = TNA: PRO, SC 1/4, no. 26. No endorsements; approx. 180 × 48 mm.; four slits for insertion of a tongue or tag; mounted, foot cut away.
Pd. from A, *RL*, ii. 329–30.
Cd., *CAC*, 28; *H*, no. 401.

Excellenti domino suo H. Dei gratia regi Angl(ie), domino Hybern(ie), duci Aquit(anniae) L. princeps Wall(ie), dominus Snaudon' salutem et paratam ad beneplacita voluntatem. Excellentie vestre literas recepimus datas apud Windesor' xxviii die aprilis, continentes prorogationem parliamenti quod debebat fieri apud Monte(m) Gom(eri) in crastino

Pentecostes nuper preteriti usque ad octabas Sancte Trinitatis, loco quo prius. Quia vero nos, respondentes quibusdam literis domini Edwardi primogeniti vestri datis apud Cipaham xxv die aprilis, rescripsimus eidem quod bene placeret nobis propter multas causas dictum parliamentum prorogari usque ad proximum festum Beati Ioh(ann)is vel paulo post, si eidem videretur expedire; ideo rogamus excellentiam vestram et requirimus diligenter quatinus placeat vobis nobis rescribere quid volueritis, vel dictum parliamentum teneri in octabis Sancte Trinitatis, vel ulterius prorogari secundum quod per literas nostras significavimus prefato domino Edward(o); quia nos parati erimus dictum parliamentum tenere secundum quod iam recipiemus a vobis in mandatis. Dat' apud Dinbych die veneris proxima ante festum Pentecostes.

That the letter was written in 1269 is strongly suggested by Henry III's authorization on 21 May 1269 of the Lord Edward to meet Llywelyn at Montgomery on the Thursday after the octaves of Holy Trinity (30 May) (*CPR 1266–72*, 344; cf. Smith, *Llywelyn*, 344–5). If so, there appears to be a clerical error in the dating clause. As Edwards noted (*CAC*, 28), this should presumably read *die veneris proxima post festum Pentecostes* (17 May), for the letter was written after the postponed parley due to have been held on the morrow of Pentecost (13 May), and thus after the Friday before Pentecost (10 May) of the dating clause.

*371 Henry III

Letter, informing the king that Llywelyn was delighted at the arrival of the Lord Edward at the ford of Montgomery and at his discussion there with Edward concerning matters of mutual interest to the prince and the king.

[Shortly before 26 July 1269]

Mention only, in a letter from Henry III to Llywelyn, presumably dated at Westminster, 26 July 1269 (*CR 1268–72*, 71; cd., *H*, no. 487). The enrolment of the king's letter bears no date, but his three previous letters in the close rolls are dated at Westminster, 26 July, as is another royal letter that refers to the recent presence of Llywelyn and Edward at the ford of Montgomery (*CPR 1266–72*, 385). Henry replied that, since Edward had been called to France to discuss plans for the crusade, he would no longer be able to meet Llywelyn at Chester on the feast of the Nativity of the Virgin (8 September) as had been agreed at Montgomery; the king therefore asked Llywelyn to join him and Edward at Westminster on the feast of the Translation of Edward the Confessor (13 October) and hold the discussions there; if Llywelyn was unable to attend, Henry would send Edward to meet him at (?)Gresford (*Crux Griffini*) on the Marches on the morrow of All Souls' day (3 November). For the location of *Crux Griffini* at Gresford (Denbs.), north of Wrexham on the Cheshire border (Gresford church SJ 346 550), see Powicke, *Henry III*, ii. 578 and n. 3, followed by Smith, *Llywelyn*, 345, 388; cf. also no. 291 above.

*372 Henry III

Letter, complaining to the king that amends have not been made according to the terms of the peace for trespasses against him and his men by the Marchers, and also complaining of recent trespasses by the king's men of Montgomery.

[Shortly before 24 July 1270]

Mention only, in a letter from Henry III to Llywelyn dated at Westminster, 24 July 1270 (*CR 1268–72*, 211–12; cd., *H*, no. 488). Henry replied that he wished the settlement of disputes with the Marchers to be postponed until the Lord Edward's return from the Holy Land, but that as regards the men of Montgomery he would send Robert Walerand and others to those parts by the next feast of the Nativity of the Virgin (8 September). However, in a subsequent letter to Llywelyn dated at Westminster, 24 August 1270, the king explained that Robert Walerand and his companions could no longer meet the prince on 8 September, as they were among the counsellors in attendance on the Lord Edward, whose departure for crusade had been delayed by unfavourable winds; the meeting would therefore have to be postponed until All Souls Day (2 November), so that suitable men could be chosen for it from the king's council at the parliament to be held on 13 October (*CR 1268–72*, 290–1).

*373　Henry III
Letter, declaring his readiness to observe the peace with the king, unless, against his will and without any fault on his part, he is provoked by others to act against this; and that Gilbert de Clare, earl of Gloucester, proposed to invade Llywelyn's land of Glamorgan with a large force.

[Probably shortly before 13 October 1270]

Mention only, in a letter from Henry III to Llywelyn dated at Westminster, 16 October 1270 (*CR 1268–72*, 234–6; cd., *H*, no. 489). It is likely that Llywelyn wrote before his attack on Gilbert de Clare's castle of Caerphilly on 13 October (cf. Smith, *Llywelyn*, 351).

†*374　Beddgelert Priory
Grant in free, pure and perpetual alms of various liberties to the prior and canons of Beddgelert.

Caernarfon, 25 July 1271

Mention only, in a record of *quo warranto* proceedings held before John de Delves, lieutenant of the justice of North Wales, in 1348 (*Rec. Caern.*, 166). The charter was declared to be a forgery since the wax of the seal was far too recent to date from 1271. Moreover, the prior had also stated that all charters issued by princes of Gwynedd in favour of Beddgelert had been burned, and that this had been confirmed by the bishop of Bangor in the presence of Edward I, who had accordingly issued a confirmation – recited in full in the record of the *quo warranto* proceedings – of the princes' grants dated at Canterbury, 9 May 1286. The prior was found guilty of forgery and imprisoned, only securing the restoration of the priory's temporalities and his own release by paying a fine of 100*s*. (ibid., 166–7; cf. Usher, 'Black Prince's *quo warranto*', 7–8).

375　Agreement with the bishops of Coventry and Lichfield and of Worcester
Agreement made in the camps near Caerphilly between Llywelyn, who has besieged Caerphilly castle built by Gilbert de Clare, earl of Gloucester and Hertford, on the one side, and the bishops of Coventry and Lichfield and of Worcester, sent by the king of England to take the castle into his hands and hold it until the dispute concerning it has been settled by the king's

magnates and counsellors at the ford of Montgomery according to the laws and customs of the March and the peace agreement recently made between the king and prince, on the other.

(1) The prince will lift the siege of the castle and allow the bishops to take it into royal custody, appointing their men as custodians until the king shall send custodians acceptable to both sides.

(2) The prince has promised that neither he nor his men shall wage war against the earl or his men while the dispute over the castle is pending nor take away or harbour anyone from the earl's side and that he shall not prevent the earl's men or tenants from trading with the prince's men.

(3) The bishops have promised in the king's name on behalf of the earl that the earl's garrison will withdraw from the castle and that the earl will not interfere in anything concerning the castle while the dispute is pending; nor will he allow any of his men to interfere concerning the maintenance of the castle, be it in extending or repairing its ditches, maintaining its walls or in any other extension or provisioning, other than according to what had been [agreed] on the day this document was drawn up; nor will those on the king's side who happen to be in the castle alter anything respecting its fortification; nor will the earl wage war against the prince or any of his men pending the dispute in any part where the earl and prince have adjacent lands nor take away or harbour any of the prince's men, nor prevent the prince's men and tenants from undertaking legitimate trade with the earl's men and tenants.

(4) The men of Senghennydd who are now with the prince will not descend any further with plunder and forces [but] will move back up to the places where they were when the present agreement was made, and likewise the men of Senghennydd with the earl will not move up with plunder and forces from the places they were inhabiting when the present agreement was made.

(5) The prelates have promised that the castle will not leave the king's hands until justice has been done regarding the dispute in the aforementioned form.

(6) They have also promised that the king will confirm the aforesaid agreement by his letter(s) patent.

(7) Whichever of the parties shall infringe this agreement in full or in part will be understood to have acted against the terms of the common peace.

(8) Even if thieves or malefactors commit thefts or other trespasses on either side, the said agreement will remain in force and amends will be made by the arbitration of worthy men from both lands according to the laws and customs of those parts.

(9) The bishops have assigned in the king's name a day for doing justice concerning the above, namely fifteen days after the next feast of St John the Baptist [(?)9 July 1272] at the ford of Montgomery, with the prince's consent.

The bishops have attached their seals on behalf of the king to the part of the present chirograph remaining with the prince, the seals of Dafydd ap Gruffudd and Gruffudd ap Gwenwynwyn have been attached on behalf of the prince to the part remaining with the bishops.

Caerphilly, 2 November 1271

B = TNA: PRO, E 163/1/28. s. xiii².
Pd. from B, *Cartae*, iii. 763–5 (no. 698).
Cd., *H*, no. 403.

Inter nobilem virum et excellentem dominum Lewelinu(m) principem Wallie, dominum quoque Snoudon' qui castrum de Caerfily per nobilem virum dominum G. de Clare comitem Glouc' et Hertford nuper erectum obsedit ex parte una et venerabiles patres dominos R. Coventr' et Lich' ac G. Wogorn' episcopos quos illustris rex Angl(ie) ad huiusmodi castrum in manum ipsius capiendum et tenendum quousque de contentione inter eosdem nobiles occasione ipsius castri exorta iustitia competens per magnates et consiliarios domini regis ad vadum Mo(n)tis Gomeri destinandos secundum leges et consuetudines March(ie) ac secundum formam pacis inter regem et principem dudum inite et firmate reddatur per suas literas transmiserat ex altera, in castris iuxta Kaerfili sic convenit quod [i] predictus princeps cum exercitu suo ab obsidione dicti castri recedat et ipsis episcopis liberam tribuat facultatem capiendi castrum in manus domini regis et aliquos de suis nomine domini regis in ipso ponendi quousque ipse rex aliquos custodes neutri parti suspectos nec alicui partium consanguinitate vel affinitate seu alia rationabili causa coniunctos ad ipsum castrum conservandum noviter duxerit destinandum.

[ii] Promisit etiam dictus princeps quod nec ipse nec aliquis de suis guerram contra dominum comitem vel aliquem de suis lite super prefato castro pendente huiusmodi contentionis occasione movebit, nec aliquem de parte comitis per se `vel per aliquem de parte comitis per se vel per alium abstrahi seu revocari procurabit aut venientem receptabit quodque homines vel tenentes comitis non impediet, nec impedire patietur per suos, quominus cum hominibus suis et tenentes libere contrahere valeant et cum ipsis mercaturam exercere.

[iii] Promiserunt similiter prefati episcopi nomine regis pro comite quod garnestura ipsius comitis per totum a supradicto castro recedet quodque ipse comes de illo castro pendente lite se non intromittet in aliquo, nec aliquem de suis permittet intromittere, circa refectionem ipsius castri vel in fossarum augmentatione sive reparatione vel murorum refectione vel in aliquo alio augmento seu munitione nisi secundum quod fuerat die confectionis presentium; nec etiam illi quos ex parte regis in ipso esse contigerit aliquid in eodem quo ad munitionem castri censeri valeat aliquatenus innovabunt, nec contra principem vel aliquem de suis guerram ratione predicta lite pendente movebit in aliqua parte ubi ipsi nobiles terras habent coniunctas atque confines, nec aliquem parti principis adherentem per se vel per alium abstrahi seu revocari procurabit aut venientem receptabit quodque ipse comes homines seu tenentes principis non impediet, nec ab aliis quantum in ipso est impedire patietur, quo minus ipsi cum hominibus vel tenentibus eiusdem comitis quodlibet commercium legitimum inire valeant et libere cum ipsis similiter mercaturam excercere.

[iv] Item homines de Seinghenyth similiter qui modo sunt cum principe non descendant inferius cum predis et familiis ascendant ad morandum et inhabitandum et locis ubi fuerunt tempore confectionis presentium, nec illi de Seyngheynth[a] similiter qui sunt cum comite cum predis et familiis ascendant ad morandum et inhabitandum superius a locis quibus habitabant tempore confectionis presentium.

[v] Dicti vero prelati promittunt quod dictum castrum non exibit de manibus regis donec de contentione dictorum nobilium iustitia competens exhibeatur in forma pretaxata.

[vi] Promittunt etiam se curaturos quod dominus rex confirmabit ordinationem predictam per literas suas patentes.

[vii] Et quecumque partium hanc ordinationem infregerit in parte vel in toto contra communis pacis formam venisse intelligatur.

[viii] Et licet aliqui latrones vel malefactores fecerint latrocinia aut alias transgressiones ex alterutra parte nichilominus dicta ordinatio in suo robore durabit et transgressiones emendantur per considerationem proborum virorum inter duas terras secundum leges et consuetudines partium illarum.

[ix] Supradicti quidem episcopi nomine regis diem ad iustitiam recipiendam et faciendam in forma predicta super premissis quindenam scilicet post festum Sancti Ioh(ann)is Bapt(iste) proximo futuram parti principis ad vadum Montis Gomeri de voluntate et consensu ipsius principis assignaverunt.

In quorum omnium testimonium parti presentis cirographi remanenti penes principem episcopi prefati pro rege sua sigilla apposuerunt, parti vero penes episcopos remanenti sigilla dominorum David filii Griffini et Griffini filii Guenn' pro principe sunt appensa. Dat' et act' in castris iuxta Kaerfili in commemoratione animarum anno gratie m° cc^mo septuagesimo primo.

ᵃ *sic in* B.

Gilbert de Clare began to rebuild Caerphilly castle in the spring of 1271, and in the autumn Llywelyn commenced the siege referred to in the agreement. Henry III empowered the bishops of Coventry and Lichfield and of Worcester to receive custody of the castle on 25 October 1271. The earl was not a party to the agreement, and soon regained possession of the castle by a ruse (*CPR 1266–72*, 583; Smith, *Llywelyn*, 352–4).

376 Edward I

Letter, acknowledging receipt of the king's letter dated at Westminster, 20 June, ordering Llywelyn not to build a castle in his land near Aber-miwl, nor to establish a town or market there to the harm of neighbouring lands and markets. Llywelyn is certain that the said letter has not had the king's consent and that, were the king present in his kingdom, such an order would not have been sent from his chancery. The king knows well that the rights of Llywelyn's principality are totally separate from the rights of his kingdom although Llywelyn holds his principality under his royal power, and he has heard and in part seen that Llywelyn and his predecessors have had the power to build castles, fortresses and markets within their borders without the favour of anyone or the announcement of new work. Llywelyn asks the king not to give heed to his enemies or to any others who have sought on account of the said occasion to turn the king against the prince.

Dinorben, 11 July [1273]

A = TNA: PRO, SC 1/19, no. 22. Modern endorsement; approx. 157 mm. wide × 76 mm. deep at left, 65 mm. deep at right; mounted; foot cut away.
Cd., *CAC*, 86; *H*, no. 405.

Excellentissimo domino suo E. Dei gratia illustri regi Angl(ie), domino Hybern(ie), duci Acquit(annie) amicus suus L. princeps Wall(ie), dominus Snaudon' salutem cum omni reverencia et honore. Litteris sub nomine vestre maiestatis scriptas et datas apud Westmonast(erium) xx die iunii recepimus mandantes et inhibentes discrete ne castrum construeremus in terra nostra propria prope Aber Miwl, nec villam constitueremus aut mercatum levaremus ibidem in nocumentum terrarum iacentium et in nocumentum mercatuum vicinorum. Certi ʻautem ᵃ sumus quod ʻdicte littere non emanarunt ex vestra consentia et si in regno vestro presentes essetis, ut optamus, tale mandatum de cancellaria vestra [non]ᵇ dirigeretur, quia bene novit excellentie vestre discretio quod iura nostre principatus omnino separata sunt a iuribus regni vestri quamvis nos sub regia vestra potestate teneamus nostrum principatum, `et audivistis etiam et in parte vidistis quod antecessores nostri et nos liberam habuerunt potestatem `infra suos terminos` edificandi construendi castra, fortelachias et mercatus . . . et (?) sine alicuius precatione aut novi operis nuntiatione. Vestram rogamus nobilitatis vestre benignitatem quatenus facilem aurem non adhibeatis malivolis nostris vel quibuscumque aliis qui ex dicta occasione moliti fuerunt animum vestrum contra nos exasperare. Dat' apud Dinorben in festo Bened(ic)ti abbatis.

^a *written over* enim *dotted underneath for expunction and also struck through; this and other interlineations are in the same hand as the rest of the document.* | ^b *parchment torn here.*

The royal letter referred to has been convincingly identified with that sent to Llywelyn dated at Westminster, 23 (not 20) June 1273 (*Foedera*, I. ii. 504); the feast of St Benedict in the dating clause of Llywelyn's letter must refer to the Translation of St Benedict on 11 July rather than the feast of St Benedict on 21 March (*CAC*, 86). The castle 'near Aber-miwl' was Dolforwyn (Lloyd, 'Dolforwyn', esp. 307). The letter has been described as 'among the most notable statements of [Llywelyn's] view of his status as prince of Wales', and was clearly aimed at Roger Mortimer (d. 1282), the author of the royal order (Smith, *Llywelyn*, 360–1).

377 Edward I

Letter, reminding the king that the peace agreement obtained from his late father and him allowed Roger Mortimer only to rebuild the castle of Cefnllys in Maelienydd, and once rebuilt justice would be done to Llywelyn concerning both the castle and the adjacent lands according to the laws and customs of the Marches. So far Llywelyn has not obtained this justice, although the said work has long been completed. But Roger has, to Llywelyn's prejudice against the terms of the aforesaid agreement, built a new work in the disputed land, not only a fence, as has been suggested to the king, but a deep and wide ditch, and stones and timber have been brought for the construction of a fortress unless it be prevented by the king or Llywelyn. The king should not be surprised if Llywelyn is irritated and seeks to prevent what he suspects could later harm him and his men and especially in a land in which he shall not desist from making a claim.

Mold, 22 July [probably 1273 or 1274]

A = TNA: PRO, SC 1/19, no. 35. On bottom right of tongue: Domino regi pro principe (in hand of scribe of letter); no endorsements; approx. 195 mm. wide on top, 185 mm. wide on bottom × 58 mm. deep, including tongue (approx. 10 mm. wide); mounted.
Cd., *CAC*, 94; *H*, no. 406.

Excellenti domino suo E. Dei gratia regi Anglie, domino Hibernie, duci Acq(u)itannie L. princeps Wall(ie), dominus Snaudon' salutem et debitam honorificenciam. Bene credimus quod memoriter tenet excellencie vestre discretio quod in forma pacis quam obtinuimus a felicis recordationis domino rege, patre vestro, et vobis continetur inter cetera quod dominus Rog(er)us de Mortuo Mari posset solummodo reficere castrum de Kefen y Llys in Maelienid, et refacto dicto castro, nobis fieret iusticia tam de dicto castro quam de terris adiacentibus secundum leges et consuetudines Marchiarum; quam quidem iusticiam adhuc optinere non potuimus, quamvis dictum opus dudum sit refarcitum, sed dictus Rog(er)us in preiudicium nostri contra predictam formam in dicta terra litig[iosa] novum opus construit, non solummodo haiam ut vobis fuit suggestum sed et fossata profunda et lata et attractum lapidum et lignorum ad constructionem forceleti, nisi per vos vel per nos impediatur. Non miretur igitur vestra nobilitas si nos moti sumus et queramus impedire ea que suspicamur posse nobis vel et nostris in posterum nocere et maxime in terra in qua clamium ponere non desistimus. Valeat excellencia vestra per tempora longa. Dat' apud Monte(m) Altu(m) in festo Beate Mar(ie) Magdal(ene).

As Edwards argued (*CAC*, 94), the letter could have been written in July of any of the four years from 1273 to 1276, although he plausibly favoured 1273 or 1274 on the grounds that thereafter the dispute over Cefnllys would probably have been overshadowed by larger issues (cf. nos 392 and 394 below for other disputes with Mortimer by May and July 1276). Smith (*Llywelyn*, 361, n. 82) interprets the letter as a further riposte, likewise aimed at Mortimer in July 1273, to the royal letter regarding Dolforwyn to which Llywelyn replied in no. 376 above, and notes that the present letter was dated at Mold, only about 17 miles to the south-east of Dinorben (SH 969 749), the place-date of no. 376. The peace agreement referred to is the Treaty of Montgomery, which allowed Roger Mortimer to build a castle in Maelienydd on condition that both it and the land would be restored to Llywelyn if he could prove his right to Maelienydd (no. 363, c. iv above). For the location of the castles referred to in this letter see Brown, 'Castle', 11–13.

378 Reginald de Grey

Letter, acknowledging receipt of the king's letter(s) bearing messages concerning the payment of 2,000 marks to Pontius de Mara assigned by the late King Henry and 3,000 marks owing to the king, and concerning the invitation of Llywelyn to the king's coronation on the octaves of next Easter. Since when he received the said letter(s) Llywelyn did not have any of his council with him apart from his brother Dafydd and the bishop of Bangor, who has come by chance to the said place (sic), *he cannot give a suitable answer immediately; however, on the next Michaelmas (29 September) he will send his reply to the king's regents at London. Llywelyn promises to supply the venison the king has requested by the date mentioned in Grey's letter.*

Rhyd Gastell, 3 September [1273]

A = TNA: PRO, SC 1/30, no. 139. Modern endorsement; approx. 151 × 68 mm.; four slits along top and four sets of double slits along bottom for insertion of a tongue or tag; mounted, foot cut away.
Pd. from A, *Foedera*, I. ii. 505.
Cd., *CAC*, 161–2; *H*, no. 407.

L. princeps Wall(ie), dominus Snaudon' speciali amico suo domino R. de Grei salutem et dilectionem sinceram. Litteras domini nostri regis suscepimus mandatorias super solutione duorum milium marcarum Pontio de Mora ex assignatione boni memorie regis Henr(ici) et trium milium marcarum quas solvere debemus domino regi necnon et de invitatione nostra ad sollempne festum sue coronationis in octabis Pasce proximo futur; sed quia in receptione dictarum litterarum non habuimus nobiscum de consilio nostro preter[a] solum David fratrem nostrum et[b] dominum episcopum Bangor', qui a casu venit ad dictum locum, ideo

competenter ad dicta negocia non potuimus tam festinanter respondere sed in proximo
festo Beati Michael(is)ᶜ transmittemus nostrum responsum apud London' ad illos qui
tenent locum domini regis. De venatione autem quam dominus rex a nobis petivi, nos
providebimus contra terminum de quo litera vestra fecit nobis mentionem. Dat' apud
Rydgastell die dominica proxima ante festum nativitatis Beate Virginis.

ᵃ preteat (?) A. | ᵇ A *inserts* D. *dotted underneath for expunction.* | ᶜ *the* h, *is interlined* A.

As Edwards argued (*CAC*, 162), the reference to the coming coronation on the octaves of
Easter means that this letter must have been written on 3 September 1273, for Edward was
crowned in 1274. It appears to be the same as the letter of Llywelyn enclosed by Reginald
de Grey with his letter to the archbishop of York, Roger Mortimer and Robert Burnell,
archdeacon of York (*CAC*, 39). Reginald de Grey was justice of Chester 1270–4, and
reappointed on 14 November 1281 (*CAC*, 79). Rhyd Gastell has been identified as Llanfair
Rhyd Gastell, a grange of Aberconwy Abbey lying between Ysbyty Ifan (SH 843 488) and
Gwytherin (SH 877 615) (Gresham, 'Aberconwy charter: further consideration', 313 (map),
323–6, followed by Smith, *Llywelyn*, 366, n. 96). The location of the 'said place' to which
the bishop of Bangor had chanced to come when the royal mandates arrived is unclear,
since no place is previously mentioned in the letter; possibly Rhyd Gastell was meant.

379 Recipient unknown

Letter, thanking him for the rumours ... And as he has not informed Llywelyn of the king's
coming ... of his coronation, Llywelyn asks that he ... concerning the king's coming ...
Llywelyn will go ... of Cedewain near the ford of Montgomery; that he will send some discreet
person with full power for the king to settle the complaints of the Marchers ...

Aber, 26 February [1274]

A = SC 1/30, no. 141. No endorsements; approx. 69 mm. wide at top, 100 mm. at bottom, 43 mm.
deep on left; the right half of the letter has been torn away.
Cd., *CAC*, 163; *H*, no. 490.

L. princeps Wall(ie), dominus Snaud' nobili viro . . . sinceram. Grates vobis refferimus de
rumoribus vestris et . . . et quia nos non certificastis de adventu domini regis . . . sue coronationis, rogamus vos quatenus super suo adventu de . . . de Kedeweinc iuxta vadum Mo(n)tis
Gom(er)i trahemus . . . vos quatenus mittatis aliquem discretum cum potestate regis
(?)plenarie . . . diffiniendas querelas Marchionum hinc inde facientes vestros . . . quorum
intersit comparere. Dat' apud Aber in crastino annunciationis . . .

The reference to the forthcoming coronation, to which Llywelyn was originally summoned
for 8 April (no. 378 above) but which eventually took place on 18 August 1274, places the
letter in 1274 (*CAC*, 163). See also note to no. 380 below for the commission appointed by
Edward I on 14 April 1274 to settle disputes between Llywelyn and the Marchers, a course
of action apparently proposed by Llywelyn in the present letter.

380 Edward I

Letter, informing the king that the money he is due to pay him in respect of the peace agreed with him and his late father King Henry is ready for payment to the king's attorneys provided that the king performs to Llywelyn what he should under the terms of that peace. Therefore he asks the king to compel the earl of Gloucester, Humphrey de Bohun and the other Marchers to restore to Llywelyn the lands which they have unjustly occupied and more unjustly detained, and Llywelyn will immediately pay the aforesaid money.

Cricieth, Monday after the feast of St Matthias [probably 26 February 1274]

A = TNA: PRO, SC 1/19, no. 32. No endorsements; approx. 174 mm. wide × 48 mm. deep on left, 38 mm. deep on right, including remains of tongue (53 × 6 mm.) on left-hand side; one set of double slits for insertion of a tongue or tag; mounted.
Cd., *CAC*, 92–3; *H*, no. 408.

Excellenti domino suo Edward(o) Dei gratia regi Angl(ie), domino Hyb(er)n(ie), duci Acquit(annie) L. princeps Wall(ie), dominus Snaudon' salutem et paratam ad beneplacita voluntatem. Excellencie vestre significamus quod pecunia quam vobis solvere tenemur per reformacionem pacis inite et firmate inter celebris memorie dominum Henr(icum), regem Angl(ie), patrem vestrum ac vos ex una parte, et nos ex altera, parata est ad solvendum vestris attornatis dum modo vos suppleatis nobis que supplere debetis per formam eiusdem pacis. Unde rogamus maiestatem vestram quatinus compellatis comitem Glocestr(ie), Homfredum de Boum et ceteros Marchiones ut amota qualibet difficultate nobis restituant terras nostras iniuste ab eis occupatas et iniustius detentas et nos statim vobis predictam pecuniam persolvemus. Dat' apud Crukeith die lune proxima post festum Beati Mathie apostoli.

As Edwards showed (*CAC*, 93), there are strong grounds for assigning this letter to 1274. On 6 February 1274 William de Plumpton was sent to Chester to receive the payment of tribute due from Llywelyn, but no payment was made (*CPR 1272–81*, 42–3); on 14 April 1274 the king ordered a commission to meet the parties to settle breaches of the peace in the Marches, and on 24 April the commission was authorized to make a truce between Llywelyn and Humphrey de Bohun to last until Michaelmas (29 September) (ibid., 47, 48; *CAC*, 55; cf. Smith, *Llywelyn*, 367–8 and n. 104). Bohun (d. 1298) succeeded his grandfather Henry de Bohun as earl of Hereford in October 1275 (ibid., 355).

*381 Pope Gregory X

*Petition, informing the pope that, because of continuous wars and dissensions in Wales, it is not safe for the prince and his servants, household members (*familiares*) and subjects to enter England, and yet they are summoned there for judgement by the see of Canterbury; and that meanwhile, on account of this, sentences of excommunication are issued and the prince's land is placed under interdict, thereby threatening them with dangers. Wherefore the prince humbly begs that the pope may provide a means by which the said servants, household members and subjects may avoid such dangers.*

[June × July 1274]

Mention only, in a letter from Gregory X to Robert, archbishop of Canterbury, dated at Lyons, 18 August 1274 (*Foedera*, I. ii. 515; Haddan and Stubbs, i. 500–1). The pope ordered the archbishop not to summon Llywelyn or his men to England, or to issue sentences of excommunication or interdict against them on account of this, provided that they were willing to appear before the archbishop's commissioners in Wales. See further Smith, *Llywelyn*, 380–1.

*382 Pope Gregory X

*Petition, informing the pope that formerly a dispute arose between Llywelyn and his brother Dafydd concerning certain lands, possessions and other matters, which were eventually the subject of an amicable agreement between the parties (*amicabilis super his inter partes compositio intervenit*), through the mediation of the bishops of Bangor and St Asaph, and corporal oaths were sworn to observe this agreement. Llywelyn submitted to the jurisdiction of the bishops concerning this, namely that the bishops could exercise ecclesiastical censure against the party contravening the agreement, and also interpret and explain obscurities in the agreement, if any should emerge. Afterwards a dispute arose between the parties concerning certain articles in the agreement which were dubious and obscure in some part, and the same bishops, in accordance with the terms of the submission, made a prudent and salutary interpretation and explanation concerning the doubt and obscurity in the said articles, as is contained more fully in the letter regarding this sealed by the same bishops. Requests the pope's confirmation of the aforesaid interpretation and explanation.*

[June × July 1274]

Mention only, in a letter from Gregory X to Llywelyn dated at Lyons, 18 August 1274 (*Foedera*, I. ii. 515; Haddan and Stubbs, i. 500–1). It appears that this petition was presented in a separate document from that containing no. 381 above, to which the pope also responded on 18 August, although both petitions were clearly taken to the pope on the same occasion. The present petition, which was granted by the pope, refers to the agreement between Llywelyn and Dafydd in 1269 (no. 368 above), one of whose clauses allowed the princes to seek papal approval of its terms. In December 1274 Llywelyn sent the papal confirmation of the agreement and of its interpretation by the bishops to be inspected by the latter (no. 383 below). No text of the letter containing the bishops' 'interpretation and explanation' has survived. See further Smith, *Llywelyn*, 374–5, 380–1.

383 The bishops of Bangor and St Asaph

Letter, acknowledging receipt of the bishops' letter(s) of warning stating amongst other things that Llywelyn should desist from inflicting disturbances and injuries upon his brother Dafydd and Gruffudd ap Gwenwynwyn and give due satisfaction for these, and that he should observe all articles of the agreement between him and the aforesaid lords. Let the bishops know that no oath concerning the observance of an agreement or even an agreement existed between Llywelyn and Gruffudd with regard to settling certain articles or grievances, but Gruffudd, after he had given homage and fealty to Llywelyn and recovered the lands held in chief from the prince, withdrew from Llywelyn's homage and fealty and abandoned his lands of his own volition, which is public and notorious to all throughout Wales. Moreover, Llywelyn has observed the agreement he made with Dafydd and the interpretation and explanation of the same made by the bishops, as contained in the letters regarding these sealed by Llywelyn, but Dafydd has had the temerity to break the agreement. Llywelyn had had the agreement and the explanation of its obscurity confirmed by the apostolic see via his clerks as can be seen from the apostolic letters themselves, which he is sending for the bishops' inspection with the bearer of the present letter. He therefore asks the bishops to warn his brother Dafydd to observe the agreement and explanation, and to compel him to do so by judicial sentence according to the terms of their execution of the agreement. Llywelyn sends this letter patent to the bishops sealed with his seal.

Llanfair Rhyd Gastell, 20 December 1274

B = TNA: PRO, E 36/274 (Liber A), fo. 415v. s. xiii ex.
Pd. from B, *LW*, 174–5 (no. 302).
Cd., *H*, no. 409.

Venerabilibus in Cristo patribus Dei gratia Bangorens(i) et Assevens(i) episcopis devotus eorum filius Lewelin(us) princeps Wall(ie) salutem, reverentiam et honorem. Litteras vestre venerabilitatis monitorias nuper recepimus inter cetera continentes ut inquietationibus ac gravaminibus et perturbationibus dominis Griffino filio Wennewyn et David fratri nostro inferendis etiam desistamus et de illatis satisfaciamus competenter, ac ut compositionem seu concordiam inter nos et prefatos dominos factam in omnibus et singulis suis articulis integre et absque diminutione aliqua servaremus. Sciatis igitur quod nullum sacramentum de compositione[a] aliqua observanda aut etiam compositio inter nos et dictum Griffinum[b] intercessit super aliquibus certis articulis aut gravaminibus sopiendis, sed idem Griffin(us) postquam suum homagium nobis fecerat et fidelitatem iuraverat ac terras suas de nobis in capite tenendas ex mera nostra liberalitate recuperaverat a nostro homagio et fidelitate recessit et terras suas dereliquit[c] motu proprio, quod omnibus per Walliam publicum extitit et notorium. Ceterum compositionem seu pacis formam inter nos ex una parte et David fratrem nostrum ex altera initam et firmitam ac eiusdem compositionis interpretationem et declarationem quam vos fecistis provide et salubriter prout in litteris inde confectis nostris sigillis munitis plenius continetur inviolabiliter versus prefatum David observavimus, quam ipse sue salutis inmemor versus nos infregit `ausu temerario; cuius rei signum apparet efficacissimum quod nos dicte pacis forme et obscuritatem eius declarationis confirmationem a sede apostolica per nostros clericos procuravimus sicut plenius vobis poterit innotescere per litteras ipsas apostolicas quas vobis sine vitio vel rasura mittimus inspiciendas[d] per presentium portitores. Rogamus igitur paternitatem vestram et hortamus hattentius[e] postulantes quatenus moneatis dictum David fratrem nostrum[f] ad dictam formam pacis et obscuritatis eiusdem declarationem[g] observandam sicut ex dicte compositionis et interpretationis tenore ac sui sacramenti virtute tenetur, ac ipsum secundum vestre executionis formam ad hoc sententialiter conpellatis. In cuius rei testimonium has nostras litteras patentes nostro sigillo signatas vobis mittimus. Dat' apud Lanuer Kygcastel[h] anno domini m° cc° lxx quarto in vigilia Beati Thome apostoli.

[a] composione B. | [b] Griffininu(m) B. | [c] dereliquid B. | [d] inspiendas B. | [e] *corrected in* B *from* hattentis.* | [f] vestrum B. | [g] *corrected in* B *from* declationem. | [h] *sic in* B.

The agreement between Llywelyn and Dafydd, in which both parties subjected themselves to the jurisdiction of the bishops of Bangor and St Asaph, was made in 1269 (no. 368 above). For Gregory X's confirmation, dated 18 August 1274, of the agreement and of its interpretation by the bishops see no. 382 above. The fullest account of the conspiracy of Gruffudd ap Gwenwynwyn and Dafydd against Llywelyn is provided in a letter from the dean and chapter of Bangor to Robert Kilwardby, archbishop of Canterbury, dated 18 April 1276 (*LW*, 136–8 (no. 245); see further nos 603–4 below). For the location of Llanfair Rhyd Gastell see no. 378 above.

384 Edward I

Letter, reminding the king that twelve worthy men chosen jointly by the king's and the prince's sides according to the peace agreement, meeting recently near Montgomery in the presence of Llywelyn's attorney, his steward beyond Berwyn, have judged £30 sterling to Llywelyn from the pledges of Robert le Crumpe and Gilbert le Palmar for the release of the latter, as agreed by both sides, or else that Robert and Gilbert should be restored to Llywelyn to be held in his prison. The king should not be surprised, therefore, that Llywelyn seeks what has been adjudged. And since many things have been suggested to the king by the Marchers which contain less truth than they ought, Llywelyn requests the king to send his attorneys to the March with the power to summon both sides before them and to hear and settle the quarrels between them according to the laws and customs of the Marches, and they will see which side makes unjust claims against the other.

Ardudwy, 24 January [probably 1275 or 1276]

A = TNA: PRO, SC 1/19, no. 31. No endorsement; approx. 164 × 71 mm., including remnant of tongue on left-hand side (approx. 20 × 6 mm.); mounted.
Cd., *CAC*, 92; *H*, no. 411.

Excellenti domino suo Edwardo Dei gratia illustri regi Angl(ie), `domino Hib(er)n(ie), duci Aquitt(anie) suus devotus Lewelinus princeps Wall(ie), dominus Snaudon' salutem et paratam ad beneplacita voluntatem. Noverit vestra excellencia quod duodecim probi viri (?)comuniter[a] ex parte vestra et nostra electi secundum formam pacis adiudicaverunt nobis nuper iuxta Monte(m) Gom(er)i in Marchia triginta libras sterlincorum[b] a plesiis[b] Rob(er)ti le Crumpe et Gilb(er)ti le Palmar' nobis solvendis pro eorum deliberatione sicut convenerat ex utraque parte, vel dictos Rob(er)tu(m) et Gilbertu(m) nobis restituere in nostra prisona retinendos, presente nostro senescallo de ultra Berrwyn nostro attornato coram dictis probis viris; quapropter mirari non debetis si placet si rem sic adiudicatam pettamus. Et quia multa vobis a Marchionibus suggeruntur que minus continent veritatis quam debet, vestre maiestati suplicamus quatenus mittatis probos viros attornatos `vestros apud Marchiam qui potestatem habeant vocandi partes utrasque coram eis et audiendi querelas utrarumque partium et eas diffiniendi secundum leges et consuetudines Marchiarum, et ipsi videbunt et cognoscent que partium ipsarum iniustam moveat questionem contra alteram. Dat' apud Ardududue[b] ix° kalendas februarii.

[a] *only seven minims after the c A.* | [b] *sic in A.*

The letter can be no later than February 1276, for Llywelyn had no 'steward beyond Berwyn' (in southern Denbs.) after his defeat by Edward I in November 1277 (Powicke, *Henry III*, ii. 673, n. 2); the agreement referred to must therefore be the Treaty of Montgomery and not the Treaty of Aberconwy (*pace CAC*, 92). Powicke suggested a date in 1275 or 1276, while Smith, *Llywelyn*, 405, n. 59, favours 1276. That the letter is no earlier than 1275 is possibly indicated by the use of the phrase *suus devotus* in the address, since the earliest examples otherwise known of this usage by Llywelyn occur in letters to the king and to ecclesiastical recipients dated or datable to 1275 (nos 386–7, 390–1 below).

385 Edward I

Letter, complaining that, although Llywelyn sent his steward to the Shropshire March to meet the sheriff of that land to make amends for trespasses and damages there by both sides, and the steward offered to give amends for all damages and trespasses by the prince's side, and indeed these had already been given for the most part, nevertheless the sheriff of Shropshire wished to amend nothing to us and our men unless specifically ordered to do so by the king, although the trespasses of his men were much greater and more atrocious than those of Llywelyn's, since they were committed in broad daylight with armed horses and banners unfurled by Gruffudd ap Gwenwynwyn and his sons together with no small multitude from the March of Shropshire; all of which is contrary to the peace agreement, which lays down that trespasses committed in the March should be amended according to the customs of the Marches. Llywelyn also complains that, although his men are allowed to come to markets in the king's lands and towns, the said sheriff has not allowed some men to enter Llywelyn's lands and towns with their merchandise, to Llywelyn's prejudice and injury. Therefore Llywelyn humbly asks the king to write to the said sheriff that he should make amends in all the above matters, especially since Llywelyn has made amends to him for the most part and is ready to make amends for the remaining trespasses, because the peace agreement ought not to be partly wanting with respect to any side.

Bala, Sunday before 22 February [1275–7, probably 17 February 1275]

A = TNA: PRO, SC 1/19, no. 20. No endorsements; approx. 168 mm. wide × 75 mm. deep on left, 58 mm. deep on right; mounted, foot cut away apart from approx. 15 × 5 mm. on left.
Cd., *CAC*, 84–5; *H*, no. 412.

Excellenti domino suo Ed(wardo) Dei gratia illustri regi Angl(ie), domino Hyb(er)nie, duci Aq(ui)tt' suus devotus et humilis L. princeps Wall(ie) salutem et paratam ad beneplacita voluntatem. Conquerimur vestre regie maiestati quod licet nos misissemus senescallum nostrum versus Marchiam Salops' in occursum vicecomitis dicte terre ad transgressiones et dampna ibidem emendanda que ad invicem mutuis incursibus facta fuerant, et dominus senescallus noster obtulerit omnia supradicta dampna et transgressiones a nostris facta versus vestros refarcire et iam etiam in maiori parte fuerant refarcita; tamen vicecomes Salops' nichil versus nos et nostros volebat emendare nisi hoc a vobis reciperet specialiter in mandatis, licet suorum transgressiones multo maiores et attrociores fuissent, utpote facte media die cum equis armatis et vexillis displicatis per G(ri)ffinu(m) filium Wen' et suos filios associatis eis non modica multitudine de Marchia Salops', que omnia contra pacis formam sunt, qua cavetur quod transgressiones in Marchiis facte passim debent emendari secundum consuetudines Marchiarum. Conquerimur etiam quod licet homines nostri passuri veniant ad mercatus in terris vestris et villis, dictus tamen vicecomes non permittit aliquos ad terras et villas nostras cum suis mercandisiis accedere in nostrum preiudicium et gravamen. Unde rogamus vestram maiestatem regiam humiliter et attente quatinus scribatis dicto vicecomiti si placet ut supradicta omnia versus nos faciat emendare, maxime cum nos in maiori parte versus eum fecimus emendari et residuum transgressionum parati sumus emendare, quia forma pacis versus aliquam partem non debet aliquatenus claudicare. Dat' apud Bala die dominica proxima ante cathedram Sancti Pet(ri).

As in no. 384 above, the peace referred to must be the Treaty of Montgomery rather than the Treaty of Aberconwy (*pace CAC*, 85), for Llywelyn had no lands exposed to attacks from Shropshire after November 1277. The letter can therefore be no later than February 1277. Nor can it be earlier than February 1275, since the attacks by Gruffudd ap Gwenwynwyn followed his defection from Llywelyn in December 1274 (J. B. Smith *apud H*, no. 412). One piece of evidence points in favour of 1275. On 3 February of that year Edward I expressed his pleasure that a day had been agreed upon by Bogo de Knovill, sheriff of Shropshire, and Llywelyn for the making of amends by Llywelyn for trespasses by him and his men against the king's men (*CR 1272–9*, 228). Presumably the meeting had been fixed for a date in February, and thus could be the same as that of which Llywelyn complained in the present letter; moreover, the sheriff's refusal to make amends to Llywelyn is consistent with the terms of Edward's letter, which speaks only of Llywelyn's making amends to the sheriff and his companions. The issue remained contentious in early May 1275 (*CAC*, 58), and in June Edward reiterated that Bogo should not make amends to Llywelyn until the prince had made amends (*CR 1272–9*, 241). It may well be, moreover, that Edward responded positively to Llywelyn's request that he should order the sheriff to make amends, for there survives an undated letter from Edward to Bogo de Knovill, enclosing a letter from Llywelyn and instructing the sheriff to appoint a day for a meeting at the ford of Montgomery where the prince should make amends for trespasses by himself and his men and Bogo should make amends for any trespasses by the king's men against Llywelyn; Bogo is urged to act circumspectly so that the prince should have no cause to complain of him to the king when he visited those parts (*CAC*, 57). Edwards suggested (ibid.) that Edward's letter enclosed a letter from Llywelyn received by 8 May (making the assumption that the prince's messengers at the Westminster parliament referred to by Edward in a letter of that date had presented a letter rather than merely oral messages from Llywelyn) (ibid., 58). However, in his letter of 8 May 1275 Edward ordered Llywelyn to send representatives to the ford of Montgomery, whereas in the undated letter to Bogo de Knovill he orders the sheriff to fix a day for Llywelyn to meet him in person. It is unlikely, therefore, that the letter to Bogo was written at about the same time as the letter to Llywelyn on 8 May; instead, the letter to Bogo may well have been sent in response to, and have enclosed a copy of, the present letter of Llywelyn written in February. This possibility is arguably reinforced by the king's concern in the letter to Bogo that Llywelyn should have no cause to complain about the sheriff.

386 Edward I

Letter, informing the king that, after the return of Llywelyn's messengers after the recent parliament in London ended, the men of Gruffudd ap Gwenwynwyn, who are maintained and harboured in the county of Shropshire and whose trespasses are publicly defended, seized six lots of booty from Llywelyn's lands of Swydd Ystrad Marchell, Swydd Llannerch Hudol, Swydd Eginlle, Cedewain and Arwystli and sold one part of it in broad daylight at Shrewsbury and Montgomery, and slaughtered and ate the other part, to the great damage and dishonour of Llywelyn and his men; another day they publicly decapitated one of his faithful men and took four horses from him to Montgomery. Since the piling of damages upon damages by such men is harmful to peace and the country, and the receiving of such men in the king's lands, though the king's men may in part be innocent, is in breach of the peace as much as if the king's men had committed such misdeeds, Llywelyn humbly asks the king to give consideration to this matter and write to the sheriff of Shropshire to arrest the said malefactors, whose names Llywelyn will supply, and compel them to make amends for their trespasses and to desist from any more in future, lest the prince's men, who suffer daily injuries from them, suffer continuing trouble without amends. Asks the king to send his reply by the bearer of the present letter.

Abereiddon, 22 May [1275]

A = TNA: PRO, SC 1/4, no. 25. Endorsed: Memorandum quod mandetur escaetori quod capiat in manum regis terram de [Osmu](n)deston' in comitatu Norf' et inquirat de exitibus a tempore mortis [(?)Be]sille (s. xiii²); approx. 170 mm. wide × 90 mm. deep on left, 75 mm. deep on right; mounted, foot cut away.

Pd. from A, *RL*, ii. 328–9; from *RL*, Anon, 'Miscellanea VII', 418–19.

Cd., *CAC*, 27–8; *H*, no. 413.

Excellenti domino suo H.ª Dei gratia illustri regi Angl(ie), domino Hybern(ie), duci Aquitann(ie) Lewelinus princeps Wall(ie), dominus Snaud' suus in omnibus devotus salutem et paratam ad beneplacita voluntatem. Significamus vestre regie maiestati quod post recessum nunciorum nostrorum a vobis nuper parliamento finito London', homines G(ri)ffini filii Wen', qui in comitatu Salops' defenduntur, manutenentur et receptantur in publico eorum transgressiones advocando, sex predas de terris nostris de Svydstratmarchell, Svydlannerchudvl, Svydeginlle, Kedewein, Aruistli ceperunt et earundem predictarum partem apud Salosb' et Mo(n)tem Gomeri vendiderunt pleno die, aliamque partem interfecerunt et consumpserunt, non sine nostro nostrorumque dampno non modico et vituperio; quendamque nostrum fidelem altera die decapitaverunt in puplico, eidemque quatuor abstulerunt caballos usque ad dictam villam de Mo(n)te Gom(er)i. Et quia dampna dampnis cumulare per tales vertitur in pacis et patrie nocumentum, et tales infra terras vestras receptando, licet vestri sint in parte a culpa immunes, non minus formam pacis infringatur quam si vestri talia perpetrassent. Ideoque vestram regiam maiestatem requirimus humiliter et attente quatenus consilium si placet super hoc apponere dignemini, scribentes adhuc si placet vicecomiti Salops' quatenus dictos maleficos, quos ei nominatim exponemus, capiat et per corporum districtionem compellat `eos ᵇ predictas transgressiones citius emendare, ac in posterum a consimilibus desistere, ne nostri, qui cotidianas ab eis paciuntur iniurias, continuum sine emenda paciantur incommodum. Quid autem super premissis facere volueritis nobis per latorem presencium, si placet, rescribatis. Dat' apud Aberidon in vigilia ascensionis domini.

ª *sic in* A. | ᵇ *interlined in same hand as rest of* A.

This letter was convincingly dated to 1275 by Lloyd (*HW*,, ii. 756, n. 203, followed by Edwards in *CAC*, 28) on the grounds that, first, Gruffudd ap Gwenwynwyn is not known to have made attacks on Llywelyn's lands before his flight to England late in 1274; second, Llywelyn was at Abereiddon on 25 May 1275 (no. 387 below); and third, the first parliament of Edward's reign was just over in May 1275 (namely the parliament held in London on 25 April 1275; it should be noted, though, that a parliament was also held at Westminster, 3–7 May 1276). Abereiddon was a grange of Cymer Abbey at or near the site of the present Hengwrt Uchaf in the parish of Llanfachreth, Merioneth (Smith, *Llywelyn*, 221, n. 155). The endorsement bears no relation to the contents of the letter, but refers to the estate of Osmundiston (Norfolk) held by Amaury de Bezill or Bisil, which had escheated to the crown after Amaury's death. This had taken place by 23 May 1273, when an inquisition post mortem of his estates was ordered to be held on 26 July; the writ notes that Amaury's heir was unknown because he had been born in another land (*CIPM*, ii, no. 21).

387 Robert, archbishop of Canterbury

Letter, acknowledging receipt of the archbishop's letter, which shows that the bishop of St Asaph has suggested certain things concerning Llywelyn and his men which such a man ought not to suggest to his prelate since they are untrue. The letter says that Llywelyn has moved against the bishop, who therefore defends the rights, liberties and customs of his church, especially those which the church has possessed from time out of mind, and of which Llywelyn, according to the archbishop's letter, has despoiled the church, namely of amends for trespasses by the church's vassals and similar matters. If the archbishop knew the truth about them, he would refuse to listen to the bishop concerning many things which he alleges against Llywelyn and his subjects. Therefore Llywelyn informs the archbishop that both he and his predecessors, in the time of the bishop's predecessors and in the long distant past up to the present, were in peaceful possession, or virtually so, of the aforesaid liberties and customs which the bishop claims. If he can show by charters of Llywelyn's predecessors granting the liberties and customs to the church of St Asaph that those liberties and customs belong to the church by right, Llywelyn will be ready to concede the liberties and customs to the church without dispute. If not, and Llywelyn and his predecessors were in possession of the liberties and customs, he nevertheless concedes that an inquest may be held in the parts where the bishop claims the liberties and rights by trustworthy men, excepting those suspect to Llywelyn, and the dispute shall be decided by the truth of the inquest. When a dispute arose another time between the same bishop and Llywelyn's bailiffs concerning the aforesaid liberties and customs, this was settled by common consent in the terms contained in the letter of the bishop bearing his seal, whose contents Llywelyn has forwarded verbatim to the archbishop, and which Llywelyn always has been and will be ready to observe if it pleases the bishop. Furthermore, since Llywelyn has understood from trustworthy persons that the same bishop has asserted in the archbishop's presence that he had obtained certain terms from the prince for the settling of the disputed liberties and customs, namely that he and Llywelyn would either accept the arbitration of Tudur ab Ednyfed, Llywelyn's steward, and Einion ap Caradog or resolve the dispute according to their consciences at the peril of their souls, Llywelyn declares that he is ready to accept any of the above terms, as the bishop may choose, provided that the bishop and chapter of St Asaph bind themselves sufficiently to observe them. In addition, and this is absurd, it may be gathered from the archbishop's letter that he has imposed at will tallages, levies and exactions on ecclesiastical persons, against the prelate's opposition, making the churches pay tax, which Llywelyn entirely denies. Indeed, he is and will be ready to protect churches and churchmen against molestors. If anyone wishes to complain about Llywelyn or his subjects that they have caused injury in these or any other matters, Llywelyn will make due amends as quickly as possible. He offers all this, as an obedient son, to the bishop in the archbishop's presence and offers it again to the bishop in his presence, and is ready to carry it out. Therefore Llywelyn asks the archbishop, having considered what he has told him above, not to permit the bishop to harass him any more, since he is ready to carry out what he offers. Nor should the archbishop believe, or be disturbed by, anything sinister which is suggested to him by the bishop regarding Llywelyn or his subjects, for the bishop seeks only to denigrate Llywelyn before the great and the good. Llywelyn asks the archbishop to inform him of his will regarding these matters.

Abereiddon, 25 May 1275

B = NLW, Peniarth MS 231B, pp. 71–4. s. xvii[1].
Pd. from B, Haddan and Stubbs, i. 503–5.
Cd., *H*, no. 414.

Venerabili in Cristo patri domino R. Dei gratia archiepiscopo Cant(uariensi), totius Anglie primati devotus suus L. princeps Wall(ie), dominus Snoud' salutem et summam in domino cum Dei honore reverentiam. Litteras vestras nuper recepimus, ex quarum tenore liquide perpendi potuit episcopum Assaven(sem) quedam de nobis et subditis nostris vobis insinuasse, que non deceret tantum virum prelato suo suggerere utpote contrarium veritati continentia. Continebatur enim in litteris supradictis, quod nos moti sumus erga predictum episcopum, pro eo quod ipse ecclesie sue iura, libertates et consuetudines vendicat, presertim illas, in quarum possessione vel quasi e tempore cuius non extat memoria fuit ecclesia memorata; quarum libertatum et consuetudinum possessione satis innuitur in litteris vestris supradictis nos predictam ecclesiam spoliasse, utpote de emendis pro transgressionibus vassallorum ipsius ecclesie et hiis similibus; super quibus si vobis de rei veritate constaret, eidem episcopo super multis que de nobis et subditis nostris vobis insinuat denegaretis audientiam. Unde paternitati vestre presentibus innotescere volumus, quod tam predecessores nostri quam nos, temporibus predecessorum suorum ac diu retroactis temporibus usque ad hec tempora, fuimus in possessione vel quasi pacifica libertatum et consuetudinum predictarum quod sibi vendicat. Et si per cartas [p. 72] predecessorum nostrorum super collatione predictarum libertatum et consuetudinum ab eisdem factas[a] ecclesie Assavens(i) docere poterit predictas libertates et consuetudines ad eandem ecclesiam pertinere de iure, parati erimus ecclesie libertates et consuetudines sine contentione prefate ecclesie concedere. Sin autem, licet[b] in possessione predictarum libertatum et consuetudinum nos et predecessores nostri fuerimus, prout superius continetur, concedimus tamen quod rei veritas inquiratur in partibus ubi vendicat libertates et consuetudines supradictas per viros fide dignos, exceptis personis nobis suspectis, et secundum veritatem inquisitionis contentio supradicta decidatur. Et cum alias inter ipsum episcopum et ballivos nostros super predictis libertatibus et consuetudinibus orta esset materia contentionis, de communi ipsius et nostro consensu conquievit illa contentio in forma, que in litteris ipsius episcopi sigillo suo signatis continetur, quarum tenorem de verbo ad verbum ad maiorem huius rei evidentiam vestre transmittimus paternitati; quam formam semper fuimus et adhuc parati sumus observare, si prefato episcopo placuerit. Preterea quia ex relatione fide dignorum intelleximus quod idem episcopus asseruit in presentia vestra se nobis obtulisse quasdam formas, per quas contentionem super predictis libertatibus et consuetudinibus concessit fore decidendam, videlicet quod ipse et nos staremus arbitrio sive dictis Tudur filii Ythneued senescalli nostri et Eynaun filii Keyradauc super decisione eiusdem contentionis, vel quod nos secundum conscientiam nostram in periculo anime nostre predictam con[p. 73]tentionem decideremus, ne videamus mensuram recusare, vestram paternitatem volumus non latere, quod nos parati sumus aliquam de formis supra-dictis, quam idem episcopus eligerit, acceptare; dummodo ad observandum eandem idem episcopus et capitulum ecclesie Assavens(is) se satis ydonee obligaverint. Ad hoc, quod absurdum est audire, ex litteris vestris premissis satis elici potuit, quod nos tallias, collectas seu exactiones personis imponimus ecclesiasticis ad libitum, ecclesie contradicente prelato; quantum ad hoc, ecclesias ipsas nobis facientes censuales que quidem omnino negamus. Immo parati sumus et erimus ecclesias et viros ecclesiasticos contra molestatores eorundem tueri et fovere. Si vero aliquis de nobis vel de subditis nostris conqueri voluerit, nos in premissis vel in aliquibus eorundem ipsos gravasse, tanquam Deo et ecclesie obedientes, faciemus debitam emendam super hoc fieri, cum omni qua poterimus celeritate. Hec omnia prefato episcopo in presentia paternitatis vestre, tanquam filius obedientie, offerimus, et adhuc eidem episcopo in presentia sua propria offerimus. Et parati erimus eadem ad effectum perducere. Paternitatem igitur vestram omni qua possumus devotione rogamus quatinus, habita consideratione ad ea que vobis superius significamus, nos per eundem episcopum de cetero fatigari, si placet, non permittatis; cum parati simus ea que offerimus ad effectum perducere. Nec vos, si placet, eidem episcopo aliqua sinistra de nobis et subditis nostris vobis suggerenti credere debetis, nec propter dicta sua turbari; cum nichil aliud querat, prout nobis videtur, nisi quod possit famam nostram apud bonos et graves denigrare. Volun[p. 74]tatem vestram super hiis et omnibus aliis nobis ad beneplacita vestra paratis, si vestre sederit voluntati, significare velitis. Valeat paternitas vestra diu in domino. Dat' apud Ab(er)ython viii kalendas iunii anno domini mcclxxv.[c]

[a] facte B. | [b] *word dotted underneath in* B. | [c] 1275 B.

The agreement settling earlier disputes between Bishop Anian II of St Asaph and Llywelyn's bailiffs, preserved in a letter sealed by the bishop, was very probably that announced in Llywelyn's letter patent of 1 May 1269 and confirmed in Anian's letter patent of the same date (no. 369 above). For the deteriorating relations between Llywelyn and the bishop, for which the present letter provides important evidence, see Stephenson, *Governance*, 175–7, and Smith, *Llywelyn*, 210–15, 377–84. The implications of the letter for the extent to which St Asaph's rights were supported by written title are considered in Pryce, *Native Law*, 198. For Abereiddon see note to no. 386 above.

*388 Edward I

Letter, justifying himself with regard to matters concerning himself and the bishop of St Asaph.

[Probably *c*.25 May 1275]

Mention only, in an undated and damaged letter from Edward I to Llywelyn (*CAC*, 61). The king replied that he would be ready to accept Llywelyn's justification if the bishop had not made assertions to the contrary. As Edwards suggested (ibid.), Llywelyn's letter 'may quite well have been sent at or about the same time as his letter of justification to the archbishop of Canterbury' (no. 387 above).

389 Thomas Cantilupe, bishop-elect of Hereford

Letter, acknowledging receipt of Thomas's letter stating that Llywelyn, so it is suggested, unjustly holds three townships pertaining to the church of Hereford's manor of Lydbury North, and requesting that they be restored. Wishing to listen to his just petitions, Llywelyn informs Thomas that, since the three townships had long belonged to the prince's lordship, he is not obliged to restore them at the suggestion of anyone. However, wishing to defer to Thomas in this matter, once the difficult negotiations with which he is presently engaged are over, Llywelyn will order an inquest into the ownership of the said townships, and according to the outcome of that inquest, having taken the advice of prudent men, he will hasten to put into effect what seems expedient according to God and justice. He asks Thomas so to provide for the protection of his church that Llywelyn's right is not harmed in any way.

Sychdyn, 27 August 1275

B = Hereford Record Office, AL 19/1 (Register of Thomas Cantilupe), fo. 4r. s. xiii[2].
Pd. from B, *Reg. Cantilupe*, 9.
Cd., *H*, no. 415.

Venerabili in Cristo patri domino Th(ome) Dei gratia Hereforden(si) electo suus si placet amicus L. princeps Wall(ie), dominus Snaudon' salutem et reverentiam cum honore. Litteras vestras recepimus continentes quod nos tres villas ad manerium ecclesie vestre et vestrum de Northledebur' pertinentes, prout vobis suggeritur, tenemus minus iuste occupatas; quare nobis per easdem litteras supplicastis dictas tres villas vobis benigne per nos restitui. Nos vero iustas petitiones vestras devote exaudire volentes, vobis tenore presentium innotescere volumus quod, cum dicte tres ville a diu retroactis temporibus sub dominio nostro extiterunt, ad alicuius suggestionem eas restituere de iure non tenemur, prout nobis videtur; set vobis in hac parte deferre[a] volentes, expeditis arduis negotiis quibus ad presens occupamur, inquiri faciemus ad quos dicte ville spectare spectare debeant, et secundum quod receperimus[b] in inquisitione supradicta, habito prudentum consilio, operari properabimus[c] quatenus secundum Deum et iustitiam expedire viderimus. Vos etiam, si placet, indempnitati ecclesie vestre ita prospicere velitis quod ius nostrum in aliquo non ledatur. Valeat paternitas vestra bene et diu in domino. Datum apud Sechton' vi kalendas septembris anno domini m° cc° lxx° quinto.

[a] defferre B. | [b] recepimus B. | [c] properavimus B.

The three townships referred to were Muleton (Mellington), Aston and Chestroke (Castle Wright), which between them comprised Teirtref Esgob, located between the lordships of Montgomery and Clun and forming part of the bishop of Hereford's estate of Bishop's Castle (Smith, *Llywelyn*, 160 and n. 78). The Sychdyn (SJ 246 662) of the place-date was located in the commote of Coleshill (Tegeingl), about $1\frac{1}{2}$ miles north-east of Mold and about 10 miles west of Chester; the 'difficult negotiations' mentioned by Llywelyn were with Edward I, who had summoned the prince to Chester by 22 August to do homage. The letter thus provides valuable evidence that Llywelyn was close to Chester and had begun negotiations with the king by 27 August: as Stephenson put it, 'An hour's ride could have altered the fate of the principality' (*Governance*, 234 and n. 14). See also Smith, *Llywelyn*, 221 and n. 160, 385 and n. 158, 388.

390 Pope Gregory X

Letter, recalling that the disputes and discords resulting in war had been settled in a treaty between the late King Henry and Llywelyn through the intervention of the papal legate Cardinal Ottobuono and confirmed by the oath of the king and the Lord Edward who succeeded him as king; the treaty had been committed to writing by the legate and bore his seal as well as those of the king, Edward and Llywelyn. Amongst other things the treaty states that Llywelyn and his successors ought to hold the principality of Wales from the king and his successors, so that all the barons of Wales shall hold their lands in chief from Llywelyn and his heirs, and give their homage and fealty to them, with the exception of one baron, in return for which Llywelyn and his successors are obliged to give homage and fealty to the king and his successors. It also states that the king and his successors shall not receive in their lands any enemy of or fugitive from Llywelyn, nor maintain or help them against him; the bearer of the present letter will be able to show the pope the contents of the treaty. Yet King Edward detains the lands of certain Welsh barons belonging to Llywelyn's lordship, which Llywelyn has peacefully held for a long time after the treaty; moreover the king has still not restored a certain baron who belongs with his lands to Llywelyn; and contrary to the aforementioned treaty receives, helps and maintains other fugitive and felonious barons of Llywelyn's land who have plotted Llywelyn's death, even though they seize booty and commit homicide and arson in his lands and still do not cease committing similar misdeeds. And although the king has received letters from the pope, whose contents the bearer of the present letter will be able to show, requesting him to observe the aforesaid treaty, his reverence for the letters has been such that up to now the king has done nothing. Even more dangerously, the king summons Llywelyn to give homage and fealty at an unsafe place amongst his principal enemies and above all the aforesaid fugitives and felons, a place to which Llywelyn cannot go without physical danger. And although legitimate excuses were offered in his presence regarding the above, he has refused to accept them or to assign a safe place for giving homage and fealty, which Llywelyn is ready to give in any safe place assigned to him, as long as the king observes the aforementioned treaty and corrects any breach of its articles and fulfils its terms if there has been any neglect with regard to those who ought to belong to Llywelyn. Since the king will not come to a place which seems safe for Llywelyn to give homage, Llywelyn requests that the king should send representatives to receive his fealty until a safe place is provided where he may give homage in person, which the king has refused. And since Llywelyn fears that the king acts thus to seek a pretext for rejecting the aforesaid treaty, he begs the pope to provide a remedy by compelling the party wishing to renege on the treaty to observe it, considering the dangers which will threaten the Welsh and English peoples if, through non-observance of the treaty, wars and discords have arisen anew. Since Llywelyn is so remote from the pope's court that he is denied access to it other than through his chief enemies who even guard the seas, he asks the pope not to listen to anyone spreading evil things about him or accusing him of breaking the treaty.

Treuddyn, 11 September 1275

B = TNA: PRO, E 36/274 (Liber A), fos 376v–377r. s. xiii ex.
Pd. from B, *Foedera*, I. ii. 528; from *Foedera*, Haddan and Stubbs, i. 506–8; from B, *LW*, 114–16 (no. 206).
Cd., *H*, no. 416.

Sanctissimo in Cristo patri domino Gregor(io) divina providentia summo pontifici humilis suus et devotus L. princeps Wall(ie), dominus Snoudon' devota pedum oscula beatorum. Non sine magna necessitate vestre sanctitati conpellimur intimare quod cum olim habite fuissent contentiones et discordie ex quibus guerra orta fuit et diu etiam habita inter excellentem virum dominum H. bone memorie regem Angl(ie) illustrem ex parte una et nos ex altera, tandem auctoritate sedis apostolice interveniente per venerabilem patrem dominum Ottobonu(m) Sancti Adriani diaconum cardinalem tunc eiusdem sedis in Angl(ia) legatum guerra, contentiones et discordie supradicte sopite fuerunt in quadam forma pacis inite inter prefatum dominum regem et successores suos ex parte una et[a] nos et successores nostros ex altera, iuramento tam ipsius domini regis et domini Edwardi primogeniti sui qui postea eidem successit in regno Angl(ie) et adhuc idem regnum optinet, quam etiam nostro vallata; que quidem forma pacis per eundem dominum legatum in scriptis est redacta, et tam sigillo ipsius quam sigillis predictorum domini regis et domini Edwardi quam etiam nostro roborata. In qua quidem forma inter alia continentur quod nos et successores nostri tenere debemus de ipso domino rege et successoribus suis Wallie principatum, ita quod omnes barones Wall(ie) Walenses a nobis et heredibus nostris terras suas in capite teneant, et homagia ac fidelitatem nobis et successoribus nostris faciant, unico barone excepto, pro quibus nos et successores nostri tenemur facere homagium et fidelitatem prefato domino regi et successoribus suis; continetur etiam ibidem quod idem dominus rex et successores sui non recipient in terris suis aliquem adversarium seu inimicum vel fugitivum nostrum seu successorum nostrorum, nec eos contra nos et successores nostros manutenebunt seu iuvabunt; que omnia in forma pacis predicta cuius tenorem lator presentium sanctitati vestre exhibere poterit plene continentur. Ecce pater sancte prefatus dominus Edwardus rex Angl(ie) ad presens illustris quorundam baronum Walensiu(m) terras ad dominum nostrum spectantes, in quarum pacifica possessione fuimus longo tempore post dictam formam pacis, sub dominio suo iam detinet; quemdam etiam baronum nostrum, qui per formam pacis supradicte cum terris suis ad nos de iure spectare deberet, adhuc nobis non restituit set in partem suam adhuc retinet; alios etiam barones de terra nostra fugitivos ac felones qui machinati fuerunt in mortem nostram in terra sua receptat, iuvat et manutenet contra formam pacis supradictam, non obstante quod predas in terris nostris ceperunt, homicidia, incendia comiserunt, et adhuc non cessant facere consimilia. Et licet litteras sanctitatis vestre supplicatorias receperit quod formam pacis supradictam observet, quarum litterarum tenorem idem lator presentium sanctitati vestre poterit exhibere, tamen ob reverentiam earundem usque ad hec tempora nichil facere curavit. Item quod nobis periculosius est, vocat nos ad locum nobis minus tutum inter capitales nostros inimicos et maxime fugitivos et felones supradictos ad faciendum sibi homagium et fidelitatem, ad quem locum nullo modo accedere possemus sine corporis nostri periculo. Et licet in presentia sua legitime proposite fuissent ex[fo. 377r]cusationes[b] super premissis, tamen easdem admittere seu locum tutum ad faciendum `sibi ᶜ homagium et fidelitatem nobis assignare recusavit, que quidem parati sumus facere in omni loco tuto per ipsum nobis assignando, dum ipse articulos in premissa forma pacis contentos observet, et quod transgressum fuerit contra articulos memoratos corrigat, et si que de illis que ad nos spectare debent defuerint adimpleat. Et quia non placuit eidem domino regi [ad locum]ᵈ accedere ad quem nobis pateret tutus accessus ut homagium sibi faceremus, supplicavimus eidem quod mitteret ad nos aliquos de suis qui fidelitatem a nobis reciperent quousque provideretur nobis de loco tuto in quo personaliter prefato domino regi facere possemus homagium, quod penitus facere denegavit. Et quia timemus quod idem dominus rex premissa facit ut occasionem querat divertendi a forma pacis supradicta in totum, non plus inteligentes expedire occurrere quam post negotium wlnerati remedium querere, ad pedes sanctitatis vestre provoluti excellentie vestre omni qua possumus devotione suplicamus quatinus remedium quod secundum Deum expedire videritis si vestre sederit voluntati predicto negotio apponi faciatis, partem a forma pacis supradicte resilire volentem `ad observationem eiusdem compellendo, attendentes si vestre sederit sanctitati quanta pericula rebus et personis populorum Walensium et Anglor(um) imminere poterunt si occasione forme pacis supradicte non observate guerra et discordie, quod Deus avertat, orte fuerunt de novo. Et quia constituti sumus in partibus a curia vestra adeo remotis quod non patet nobis accessus ad curiam vestram nisi per capitalesᵉ inimicos nostros qui etiam maritima custodiunt ne transitus per eadem nobis `pateat ad curiamᶠ supradictam, quantacumque nobis gravaminis inferatur, sanctitati vestre placeat quod nullus predicans de nobis sinistra seu contra dictam formam pacis aliquid nos egisse exaudiatur, nec aliquid contra nos exaudiatur quousque per aliquem discretum et fidelem cognitione premissa partibus ad locum tutum vocatis vobis ad plenum constiterit de negotio memorato. Conservet vos altissimus ecclesie sue per tempora longa. Dat' apud Trefthyn tertio idus septembris anno domini mᵒ ccᵒ lxxᵒ quinto.

ᵃ B *inserts* nos *struck through.* | ᵇexcusationis B. | ᶜ*word written over* nobis, *which is thereby deleted* B. | ᵈ *words omitted in* B *(cf. no. 391 below).* | ᵉ capitalos B. | ᶠ B *inserts* pateat *struck through.*

The letter provides a justification for Llywelyn's refusal to obey Edward I's summons to give homage at Chester by 22 August; Edward remained in and around Chester, only 12 miles from Treuddyn, until 11 September (*CCR 1272–9*, 241; Smith, *Llywelyn*, 385, 388). The treaty referred to is the Treaty of Montgomery (no. 363 above). Gregory X, as Tedaldo Visconti, had served Ottobuono during his period as legate in England and may even have been present at the making of the agreement in September 1267; in a letter of 18 August 1274 he had urged Edward I to observe the terms of the treaty (Smith, *Llywelyn*, 381, 389). The opening of the letter echoes, but does not cite verbatim, the arenga with which Ottobuono prefaced the text of the treaty.

391 Archbishop Robert of Canterbury, the archbishop of York and their suffragans

Letter, recalling past disputes and discords resulting in war between King Henry III and Llywelyn, settled by a treaty negotiated by the papal legate Cardinal Ottobuono between Henry and the Lord Edward and their successors on one side and Llywelyn and his successors on the other, corroborated by oaths and committed to writing by the legate, and bearing his seal and those of the parties. Amongst other things the treaty states that Llywelyn and his successors ought to hold the principality of Wales from the king and his successors, so that all the Welsh barons of Wales shall hold their lands in chief from Llywelyn and his heirs, and give their homage and fealty to them, with the exception of one baron, in return for which Llywelyn and his successors are obliged to give homage and fealty to the king and his successors. It also states that the king and his successors shall not receive in their lands any enemy of or fugitive from Llywelyn, nor maintain or help them against him; the abbots of Strata Florida and Aberconwy, the bearers of the present letter, will be able to show the prelates the contents of the treaty. Yet King Edward detains the lands of certain Welsh barons belonging to Llywelyn's lordship, which Llywelyn has peacefully held for a long time after the treaty; moreover the king has still not restored a certain baron who belongs with his lands to Llywelyn; and contrary to the aforementioned treaty receives, helps and maintains other fugitive and felonious barons of Llywelyn's land, namely Dafydd ap Gruffudd and Gruffudd ap Gwenwynwyn, who have plotted Llywelyn's death, even though they seize booty and commit homicide and arson in his lands and still do not cease committing similar misdeeds contrary to the treaty. And, although Llywelyn has frequently addressed his complaints, by messengers and letters, to Edward, both before his accession to the kingdom and after, he has done nothing about them up to now. Even more dangerously, the king summons Llywelyn to give homage and fealty at an unsafe place amongst his principal enemies and above all the aforesaid fugitives and felons and their executioners, a place to which Llywelyn cannot go without physical danger, especially since the aforesaid enemies show themselves publicly in the royal hall, both at table and in the chamber, and sometimes in council. And although legitimate excuses were offered by Llywelyn's messengers in the king's presence regarding the above, Edward has refused to accept them or to assign a safe place for giving homage and fealty, which Llywelyn is ready to give, along with others belonging to him and his men, in any safe place assigned to him, as long as the king confirms the treaty and fully corrects and fulfils anything which is wanting in or contrary to it. Since the king will not come to a place which seems safe for Llywelyn to give homage, Llywelyn requests that the king should send representatives to receive his fealty until a safe place is provided where he may give homage in person, which the king has refused. Llywelyn asks the prelates to advise and help the king to treat him according to the terms of the treaty, which Llywelyn does not wish to foresake, bearing in mind the dangers which could threaten the Welsh and English peoples if, through non-observance of the treaty, wars and discords should arise anew, as well as the recent papal prohibition at the council of Lyons against war between Christians lest the plans for a crusade are disturbed. And if the king declines the prelates' advice, they should excuse Llywelyn, who has no wish to create division or disturbance in the kingdom. Llywelyn requests the prelates to trust his messengers, whom he has sent to London by the day fixed by the king to excuse his absence, and asks them to inform him in writing of their will and counsel concerning those matters which the messengers communicate to them orally on Llywelyn's behalf.

Tal-y-bont, 6 October 1275

B = NLW MS 13211E, fos 8r–9r. s. xvi². Rubric: Litterae Lewelini principis Walliae ad clerum Angliae apud London convocatum in quibus pleraeque continentur causae contentionis et discordiarum inter eum et Edwardu(m) regem Angliae tunc ortarum etc. ex ipso autographo penes dominum Thomam Yale utriusque iuris doctorem illustrissimum remanente per Ed. Theloal transcriptae penultimo die Augusti 1574.

C = NLW MS 3075D, pp. 131–4. s. xvii ex. Rubric: as in B.

Pd. from (?), Powel, *Historie of Cambria*, 329–33 (trans. only); from (?), Wynne, *History of Wales*, 281–2 (trans. only); from (?)Wynne, Warrington, *History of Wales*, 569–71 (trans. only).
Cd., Haddan and Stubbs, i. 508; *H*, no. 417.

Venerabilibus in Cristo patribus ac dominis R. Dei gratia Cantuar(iensi) archiepiscopo totius Anglie primato ac archiepiscopo Eboracens(i) eorumque suffraganeis ad instans consilium London[a] congregatis suus devotus filius Lewelinus princeps Wallie, dominus Sna(u)don salutem et[b] tam debitam quam devotam in omnibus obedientiam cum reverentia et honore. Noverit vestra veneranda primitas[c] quod cum olim habite fuissent contentiones et discordia ex quibus guerra[d] orta fuit et diu etiam habita inter illustris memorie Henricu(m) regem Anglie, eius nominis tertium, ex parte una et nos ex altera, tandem authoritate sedis apostolice interveniente per venerabilem patrem dominum Ottobonum Sancti Adriani diaconum cardinalem tunc sedis apostolice in Anglia legatum guerra, [d] contentiones et discordie supradicte sopite fuerunt in quadam forma pacis inite inter predictum dominum Henricu(m) et dominum Edwardu(m) suum primogenitum nunc Anglie regem et suos successores ex parte una et nos et successores nostros ex altera, iuramentis eorum et nostro vallata; que quidem forma pacis per eundem dominum legatum in scriptis est redacta et tam sigillo ipsius quam domini Henrici tunc regis quam etiam domini Edwardi nunc regis sigillis nostroque etiam roborata. In qua quidam forma inter alia continentur, nec nos latet ut credimus, quod nos scilicet et successores nostri tenere debemus de ipso domino rege et successoribus suis Wallie principatum, ita quod omnes barones Wallie Wallenses a nobis et heredibus nostris terras suas in capite teneant, et homagia et fidelitatem nobis et successoribus nostris faciant, unico barone excepto, pro quibus nos et successores nostri tenemur facere homagia et fidelitatem prefato [fo. 8v] domino regi et suis successoribus; continetur etiam ibidem quod ʿidem dominus rex et sui successores non recipiant[e] in terris suis aliquem adversarium seu inimicum vel fugitivum nostrum seu successorum nostrorum, nec eos contra nos et successores nostros manutenebunt seu iuvabunt; que omnia in forma pacis predicta cuius tenorem venerabiles patres de Strata Florida et de Aberconwey abbates, latores presentium, vestre primitati[f] poterunt exhibere plenarie continentur. Ecce reverendi patres dominus Edwardus rex Anglie ad presens illustris quorundum baronum Wallensium terras, in quarum possessione pacifica fuimus longo tempore post dictam formam pacis, sub dominio suo iam detinet; quendam etiam baronum nostrum, qui per formam pacis supradicte cum suis terris ad nos de iure spectare debet, adhuc nobis non restituit sed in partem suam detinet; alios etiam barones de terra nostra fugitivos ac felones nostros, scilicet David[g] filium Griffini et Griffinu(m) filium Gwenwynwyn,[h] qui machinati fuerunt in mortem nostram in terra sua receptat, iuvat et manutenet, non obstante quod postmodum predas in terris nostris ceperunt, homicidia et incendia commiserint et adhuc non cessant consilia facere contra formam pacis predictam.[i] Et licet sepius querelas nostras per solemnes nuntios nostros et literas prefato domino Edwardo regi direximus, tam ante regni adeptionem quam post, tamen pro eis usque ad hec tempora nihil facere curavit. Item quod nobis periculosius est, vocavit nos postmodum ad locum nobis minus tutum inter capitales nostros inimicos et maxime fugitivos et felones supradictos et eorum spiculatores facturos sibi fidelitatem et homagium, ad quem locum nullo modo accedere possemus sine nostri corporis periculo, maxime cum predicti inimici et felones in aula regia et mensa et camera et aliquando in consilio se publice exhiberent. Et licet in presentia sua ac sui consilii legitime fuissent proposite excusationes a nostris nuntiis super premissis, tamen easdem admittere seu locum tutum ad faciendum sibi homagium et fidelitatem nobis assignare recusavit, que quidem parati sumus `adhuc ei facere in^j omni loco tuto quem nobis voluerit^k assignare una cum aliis nos et nostros tangentibus, per formam pacis supradictam, dummodo nobis eandem formam^l voluerit confirmare, et quod ex ea deest vel contra eam transgressum fuerit adimplere penitus et corrigere. Et quia sibi non placuit ad locum accedere ad quem tutus nobis pateret accessus ut eidem homagium faceremus, supplicavimus sibi quod mitteret ad nos aliquos de suis qui fidelitatis sacramentum a nobis reciperent quousque provideret nobis de loco tuto in quo secure possemus homagium sibi facere personaliter, quod similiter facere penitus denegavit. Vestram igitur [fo. 9r] primitatem^m rogamus affectuose suppli-cantes quatenus considerantes quanta pericula rebus et personis populorum Angloru(m) et Wallensiu(m) imminere poterunt si occasione forme pacis supradicte non observate^n guerra^d et discordie,^{o} quod Deus avertat, orte fuerint^p de novo, attendentes etiam inhibi-tionem domini pape nuper in consilio Lugdun' editam de guerra^d inter Cristianos non movenda ne terre sancte negotium perturbetur, apponatis consilium et auxilium versus dominum nostrum regem ut nos secundum formam pacis supradictam pertractet, cum ab ea discedere nullatenus voluerimus. Et si vestris consiliis, quod absit, noluerit accquiescere,^{q} excusatos nos habeatis qui^r nullo modo regni discidium aut perturbationem, quantum in nobis est, volumus procurare. Ceterum si placet fidem adhibeatis predictis nuntiis nostris, quos ad diem nobis a regia maiestate London^s prefixum mittimus ad nostram absentiam legitime excusandam, super his que vobis ore tenus ex parte nostra duxerint nuntianda voluntatem vestram^t et consilium una cum aliis nobis ad beneplacita vestra paratis que vestre^u cederunt voluntati, si placet, rescribentes. Dat' apud Tallybont^v vi^{ow} die octobris anno domini mcclxxv.^{x}

^{a} Londini C. | ^{b} *omitted* C. | ^{c} principalitas C. | ^{d} gwerra C. | ^{e} recipient C. | ^{f} principalitati C. | ^{g} Davidum C. | ^{h} Gurwynwyn C. | ^{i} supradictam C. | ^{j} *omitted* B. | ^{k} *corrected from* noluerit *in* B. | ^{l} C *inserts* nobis. | ^{m} principalitatem C. | ^{n} observata B. | ^{o} discordia C. | ^{p} *sic in* BC; *?recte* fuerunt *(cf. no. 390 above)*. | ^{q} accquiescere B. | ^{r} quia C. | ^{s} Londinum C. | ^{t} nostram B. | ^{u} nostre B. | ^{v} Talebont C. | ^{w} sexto C. | ^{x} 1275 BC.

The text in NLW MS 13215E, pp. 303–5 (s. xvi^2), while derived from the same exemplar transcribed in B and C, contains many corrupt readings and has therefore been ignored here. For Thomas Yale (*c.*1526–77) of Plas yn Iâl (Llanelidan), Denbs., and Edward Thelwall (d. 1610) of Plas y Ward, Denbs., see *DWB*, 933, 1110.

The ecclesiastical council referred to was presumably the gathering of the prelates in parliament at Westminster from 13 October 1275 (*AM*, iv. 265; Smith, *Llywelyn*, 387, n. 163). The text of the letter is closely modelled on that sent to Gregory X on 11 September 1275 (no. 390 above), but contains some significant differences, including a reference to Gregory X's decree on keeping peace issued at the Second Council of Lyons (7 May–17 July 1274). This decree formed part of the pope's preparations for a crusade at the second session of the council on 18 May: prelates were to compel Christian rulers and peoples in conflict to observe a peace or truce for six years, on pain of excommunication and interdict (*Decrees*, ed. Tanner, i. 312, c. 1c; cf. ibid., 305). Knowledge of the decree may have derived from the messengers who presented Llywelyn's petitions to the pope by 18 August 1274 (nos 381–2 above; Smith, *Llywelyn*, 380–1, 384, n. 157). The letter's place-date probably refers to the court of the commote of Tal-y-bont, Meirionnydd, located at or near the site of the farm of Tal-y-bont (SH 596 039) and the adjacent earthwork castle of Domen Ddreiniog in the township of Rhyd-cryw just over 1 mile south of the church and village of Llanegryn (Smith, 'Age of the princes', 37 and n. 188).

392 Edward I

Letter, recalling that Llywelyn has frequently complained that Roger Mortimer has arbitrarily taken possession of his land of Dyffryn Tefeidiad (Tempsiter), seized its men and booty and still detains them to Llywelyn's great prejudice and injury, notwithstanding that John fitz Alan, former lord of the land, granted the land and its men and other appurtenances to Llywelyn to be possessed in peace according to the terms of his letter(s) patent, unless by the judgement ... by our will it should happen to the same to obtain possession of the aforesaid land ... as [?will be clear from] the transcript of John's letter patent ... contrary to the false suggestion of Roger concerning the said land. Moreover, Llywelyn complains that the sheriff of Shropshire maintains in his bailiwick the men of Gruffudd ap Gwenwynwyn who day and night commit, and indeed (?)have committed, arson, plunder, the seizure of men and frequently homicide, so that Llywelyn can scarcely restrain those of his men who have suffered injury or damage from sometimes making distraint for the plunder and injuries from the said bailiwick without his knowledge. In addition, he complains that Payn de Chaworth frequently commits plunder, seizure of men and homicides in the land of Llywelyn's barons, concerning which neither Llywelyn nor his men have so far received justice ... which Llywelyn draws to the attention of the king until he shall have justice from him.

Dinas Teleri, 14 May 1276

A = TNA: PRO, SC 1/19, no. 23. No endorsements; approx. 192 mm. wide × 87 mm. deep on left, 75 mm. deep on right; mounted, foot cut away. The parchment is badly stained in places.
Cd., *CAC*, 86–7; *H*, no. 418.

Excellenti domino suo E. Dei gratia illustri regi Angl(ie), domino Hybern(ie), duci Aquittann(ie) suus si placet devotus L. princeps Wallie, dominus Snaudon' salutem et paratam ad beneplacita voluntatem. A vestre regie maiestatis memoria non credimus recessisse qualiter nos pluries de domino Rog(er)o de Mort(uo) Mari conquesti fuimus vobis et consilio vestro quod ipse nostram[a] terram de Dyfryn Teueidat saysiavit pro sue voluntatis arbitrio, homines et predas dicte terre cepit et adhuc eos detinere non veretur in nostrum preiudicium non modicum et gravamen, non obstante quod Ioh(ann)es filius Alani quondam dominus eiusdem terre predictam terram, homines et cetera ad dictam terram pertinentia nobis concessit quiete, pacifice possidenda secundum quod in litteris suis patentibus continetur, nisi alias iudicio . . . nostra voluntate predicte terre possessionem `eidem nanscisci contingeret, prout ex transcripto patentis littere predicti Ioh(ann)is vobis per . . . fiet fides contraria `tamen false suggestioni predicti Rog(er)i super terra memorata. Preterea vobis pro certo et bona fide conquerendo significamus quod vicecomes Solopsir' in ballivio suo manutenet homines G(ri)ffini filii Wenoewyn qui die noctuque incendia, predas, hominum captiones et frequenter homicidia perpetrant etenim perpetrarunt,[b] ita tamen quod vix possumus lesos nostros seu dampnificatos propter iniurias et dampna eis illata quasi continue `ex toto reprimere quin aliquando namia capiant predarum et iniuriarum suarum de dicta ballivia (?)nobis penitus inconsultis. Ad hec de domino Pagano de Cadurcis vobis similiter conquerendo monstramus quod ipse in terra baronum nostrum depredationes, hominum captiones et homicidia pluries exercuit, de quibus nos nec nostri sumus hactenus aliquam iusticiam esse … quod tamen vestre excellenti memorie relinquimus observandum quousque de premissis per vos iusticiam habeamus. Dat' apud Dinas Teleri xiiii° die maii anno domini m° c° c° lxx° sexto.

ᵃ *a line (c.18 mm. long) is drawn between* nostram *and* terram *in* A. | ᵇ *sic in* A *(?for* perpetraverunt*).*

Dyffryn Tefeidiad (Tempsiter) was the Welsh part of the lordship of Clun (Suppe, *Military Institutions*, 40–1). It was in Llywelyn's possession on the death of John fitz Alan III in 1272 (*CIPM*, i, no. 812), and had been held by the prince since at least late 1267 (no. 365 above) and possibly since 1263. It may be, then, that the letter patent referred to had been issued by John fitz Alan II (d. 1267) as part of an understanding with Llywelyn (Smith, *Llywelyn*, 155–6, 362 and n. 84). It is not known when Roger Mortimer occupied Dyffryn Tefeidiad: Llywelyn merely states that he had complained frequently to the king about the occupation (cf. ibid., 404–5). For earlier complaints about raids by Gruffudd ap Gwenwynwyn's men see nos 385–6, 391 above. Payn de Chaworth III (d. 1279) was lord of Kidwelly (see note to no. 393 below). Dinas Teleri was a grange of Cymer Abbey and has been identified as Craig y Dinas, par. Trawsfynydd (Williams-Jones, 'Llywelyn's charter to Cymer', 53 (no. 96 on map), 76; cf. Smith and Butler, 'Cistercian order', 305 and n. 35).

393 Robert, archbishop of Canterbury

Letter, in response to the archbishop's letter, brought by Llywelyn's clerks, asking that Llywelyn should keep peace with the Marchers. Llywelyn has strictly ordered his vassals and other men to commit no trespasses in the lands of the king or in any part of the Marches until they should receive orders to the contrary, as he has already informed the archbishop by letter. Recently, however, certain Marchers, hating peace and desiring to disturb the kingdom, have entered Llywelyn's lands in various parts of Wales with a great force of horse and foot, with flags and banners unfurled contrary to the peace, and have caused much damage there. For example, when Llywelyn's messengers were returning from the archbishop, men from the counties of Chester and Shropshire with the men of Dafydd, Llywelyn's brother, invaded the borders of Llywelyn's vassals in Bromfield with a great army and burned houses, killed men and seized booty there. Moreover, the men of Gruffudd ap Gwenwynwyn in their district, the men of the bishop of Hereford in theirs and the men of Roger Mortimer and of the earl of Hereford continue to molest Llywelyn's lands by night. Since Llywelyn's messengers have returned from the archbishop the sons of Payn de Chaworth have plundered the lands of Llywelyn's vassals and nephews, the sons of Rhys Fychan in South Wales, and killed and wounded men, burned houses and seized booty there, committing many other injuries contrary to the peace. Since Llywelyn strives with all his power for the restoration of peace with the king, a peace which is to be promoted and perfected by the archbishop, he asks the archbishop to refer the above matters to the king and persuade him to punish the aforesaid violators of the peace so severely that he compels them to make amends, preventing them from committing further injuries.

24 June [1276]

A = TNA: PRO, SC 1/30, no. 140. Endorsed: Dominus . . . Well(e)n' episcopo. Littera principis (s. xiii²); originally approx. 226 mm. wide × 90 mm. deep on left, 80 mm. deep on right; mounted, foot cut away. The top and bottom right-hand corners are missing; the parchment is stained and the ink faint along the right-hand edge of the document.

Pd. from A, Sommer-Seckendorff, *Studies*, 181–2.

Cd., *Sixth Report*, App. II, 101 (no. 1331); *CAC*, 162–3; *H*, no. 419.

Reverendo in Cristo patri ac domino R. Dei gratia Cant(uariensi) archiepiscopo, tocius Anglie primati devotus suus in Cristo filius L. princeps Wall(ie), dominus [Snaudon'] salutem et tanto patri ac domino cum obediencia reverenciam. Cum nuper nobis litteris vestris per clericos nostros demandastis, ut pacem a nobis et nostris penes Marchiones curaremus observare, nos vero mandatis vestris omnino volentes aquiescere, nostris vasallis ac aliis hominibus nostris sub pena mandavimus graviori districte precipientes quod ipsi aliquo modo nullas transgressiones in terris domini nostri regis Anglie vel in aliqua parte Marchiarum perpetrarent quousque a nobis aliud reciperent in mandatis, prout vobis antea litteris nostris significavimus. Nuper equidem quidam Marchiones pacis vestigia odientes et regni perturbacionem cupientes intraverunt terras nostras in diversis partibus Wallie cum magna multitudine tam equitum quam peditum, eciam cum vexillis et pentellis deplicatis contra formam pacis, qui non modica dispendia ibidem intulerunt. Ut vero exempla vobis pateant manifesta, noveritis in reditu nunciorum nostrorum a vestra paternitate homines de comitatibus Cestr(ie), Salop(ie) cum hominibus Dauyt fratris nostri, magno exercitu collecto, terminos vassalorum nostrorum apud Bromfeld invaserunt ibidemque domorum combustiones, hominum interfectiones, predarum captiones commiserunt. Homines autem Griffini filii Wenn' in partibus suis, episcopi Hereforden(sis) in suis, domini Rog(er)i de Mortuo Mari, domini comitis Hereford(ie), prerupto pacis federe de noctu per terras nostras non desinunt molestare. Filii nempe Pagani de Sadurcis[a] post adventum nunciorum nostrorum a vobis cum armata hominum multitudine terras vasallorum ac nepotum nostrorum, filiorum domini Resi Iunioris, in Sudwalie partibus depredarunt, ibidem homines occiderunt, alios vulneraverunt, domos combusserunt et preda ceperunt, multa alia dampna perpetrando contra formam pacis prelibate. Quia igitur ad pacem inter dominum vestrum regem et nos redintegrandam et per vos, sancte pater, promovendam et perficiendam omni nisi quo possumus hanelamus, paternitatem vestram diligenter rogamus quatinus premissa domino regi, si placet, refferentes eundem inducere dignemini ut predictas transgressiones prefatos pacis violatores ea severitate puniat ac compellat emendare ab ulteriori iniuria eos efficaciter inhibendo. Valeat paternitas vestra diu in domino. Dat' apud . . .[b] in festo nativitatis precursoris domini.

[a] *sic in A.* | [b] *the beginning of the place-name is illegible because of staining and the end is missing because the parchment has been torn away* A.

The letter must belong to either 1275 or 1276, for it was written between Gruffudd ap Gwenwynwyn's flight to Edward I in December 1274 and Edward's condemnation of Llywelyn for failing to do homage in November 1276. As Sommer-Seckendorff argued (*Studies*, 118–19), there are strong grounds for assigning it to 1276. Llywelyn approached Kilwardby in about mid-Lent 1276 (ibid., 118, 181) and the dean and chapter of Bangor wrote to the archbishop with an account of the conspiracy by Dafydd ap Gruffudd and Gruffudd ap Gwenwynwyn on 18 April 1276 (*LW*, 136–8); on 26 December 1276 Dafydd and Guncelin de Badlesmere, justice of Chester were ordered by the king to receive Llywelyn ap Gruffudd of Bromfield and his men into the king's peace and to pardon all trespasses by the Welsh of Bromfield (*CPR 1272–81*, 186), which would be consistent with attacks on Bromfield earlier in that year. It should also be noted that Llywelyn had complained of attacks by Payn de Chaworth in May 1276 (no. 392 above). The reference to Payn's sons is interesting, for Payn appears to have lacked legitimate sons by his death in September 1279: his heir was his brother Patrick V de Chaworth (d. 1283) (*CIPM*, ii, no. 310; cf. Sanders, *Baronies*, 125 and nn. 6–7, which assumes that Payn died childless). The sons referred to in Llywelyn's letter therefore presumably either predeceased their father or were illegitimate. The Rhys *Iunior* mentioned was Rhys Fychan ap Rhys Mechyll (d. 1271) of Ystrad Tywi, whose wife Gwladus was Llywelyn's sister and whose sons (Rhys Wyndod, Gruffudd and Llywelyn) were therefore Llywelyn's nephews. The earl of Hereford was Humphrey de Bohun (d. 1298) and the bishop of Hereford was Thomas Cantilupe (1275–82); Llywelyn had been in dispute with the latter in August 1275 (no. 389 above). The endorsement shows that the letter was sent on to Robert Burnell, bishop of Bath and Wells, Edward I's chancellor from 21 September 1274, suggesting that the archbishop sought to draw Llywelyn's complaints to the king's attention.

394 Robert, archbishop of Canterbury

Letter, declaring that Llywelyn has trusted in the archbishop's promise and the king's peace, which he was hoping would be observed differently as regards him and his men than it is now. When his men, both clerics and laymen, recently went, after the octaves of St John the Baptist [1 July], with their goods to the markets and fairs at Montgomery and Leominster, over 120 were seized with their goods, two deans were detained and one deacon was killed, even though a truce had been made between Llywelyn's bailiffs of the March and Roger Mortimer and safety promised to all attending the said fairs from Llywelyn's lands. Roger and other Marchers have therefore rendered themselves suspect to Llywelyn, giving cause for him to abandon the peace, which he is unwilling to do. Furthermore the king's barons and bailiffs of South Wales invade Llywelyn's lands day and night and plunder and kill his men in contempt of the king's peace and to Llywelyn's great prejudice and injury, for which, unless he believed it would harm the king, he could easily take compensation with further injuries. Therefore Llywelyn urges the archbishop, lest his efforts in restoring peace be in vain, on account of the rebellion of the said Marchers who disturb the peace, to persuade the king effectively to distrain the Marchers to observe the peace, as the archbishop has previously promised Llywelyn, so that they ensure that notice is taken of the said trespasses without delay. Otherwise Llywelyn's men, who suffer daily injuries, cannot neglect to make distraint by any means from the lands of the aforesaid Marchers. The said Marchers say, and confirm by their deeds, that during the peace talks begun by the archbishop they will continue to seize the property and persons of Llywelyn's men, so that they will detain the property and persons if peace is not restored. Llywelyn asks the archbishop to reply concerning these and other matters by the bearer of the present letter. (After the dating clause): while the letter was being written the enclosed complaints reached Llywelyn, which he is sending for the archbishop to inspect.

Rhyd Gastell, Wednesday before the feast of St Mary Magdalen [15 July 1276]

A = TNA: PRO, SC 1/23, no. 189. Endorsed: Domino Bath' et Wellen' episcopo (s. xiii²); approx. 187 × 105 mm.; mounted, foot cut away.
Pd. from A, Sommer-Seckendorff, *Studies*, 182–3.
Cd., *Seventh Report*, App. II, 257 (no. 1981); *CAC*, 126–7; *H*, no. 420.

Reverendo in Cristo patri ac domino R. Dei gratia Cant(uariensi) archiepiscopo ac tocius Angl(ie) primati suus devotus L. princeps Wall(ie), dominus Snaudon' salutem et omnimodam reverenciam cum honore. De vestre paternitatis promisso confisi paceque domini nostri regis, quam sperabamus versus nos et nostros aliter quam nunc tractatur observari. Nostri homines, tam clerici quam laici,[a] nuper post octabam Beati Ioh(ann)is Baptiste mercatus et nundinas apud Monte(m) Gom(er)i[b] necnon Lemynester adeuntes, cum rebus et mercandisiis suis treugis nichilominus captis et furatis inter ballivos nostros de Marchia et dominum R. de Mortuo Mari, securitateque promissa et clamata omnibus de terris nostris ad dictas nundinas venientibus, capti fuerunt ʼcum suis bonisʼ apud prefatas villas plus centum viginti, [c-]duoque decani sunt detenti et unus diaconus est occisus.[-c] ʼUnde prefatus Rog(er)us aliique sui commarchiones suspectos se reddunt nobis in hoc, et ab observacione pacis, a qua nisi inviti volumus declinare, materiam tribuunt divertendi. Preterea barones et ballivi domini regis de Suwallia[d] die noctuque terras nostras invadunt et homines nostros depredantur et occidunt in pacis regie contemptum et nostrum preiudicium non modicum et gravamen, quibus nisi regiam crederemus ledere maiestatem, de facili possemus obviare et versa vice gravamina gravaminibus compensare. Unde ne vester labor circa pacem reformandam sit inanis, quod absit, propter proterviam et rebellionem dictorum Marchionum qui pacem ipsam pro viribus intendunt penitus perturbare, rogamus paternitatem vestram humiliter suplicantes, quatenus caritatis intuitu dominum regem inducatis ut cum effectu distringat prefatos Marchiones ad prefate pacis observanciam, sicut nobis alias promisistis, ac ut dictas transgressiones infra pacem ipsam perpetratas sine more dispendio faciant observari. Alioquin dissimulare non possunt homines nostri, qui cotidiana sustinent dampna, quin namium pro premissis quoquo modo capere procuraverint de terris prefatorum Marchionum. Dicunt eciam et factis affirmant dicti Marchiones, quod durante pacis tractacione, quam vestra gracia incepistis, res et personas hominum nostrorum pro viribus capient sine intermissione, ita quod si pax non contingat reformari, ipsi iidem res et personas eorum detinebunt. Voluntatem vestram nobis super premissis ac aliis, que vestre cedant voluntati, nobis si placet, per presencium portatorem rescribatis. Valeat et vigeat vestra paternitas bene et diu. Dat' apud Rytgastell die mercurii proxime ante festum Beate Mar(ie) Magdal(ene). In confeccione presencium venerunt ad nos incluse querele quas vestre sancte paternitati mittimus inspiciendas.

[a] A *inserts* mercatus et nundinas *struck through* A. | [b] Som(er)i A. | [c-c] *written over an erasure in* A. [d] *sic in* A.

The reference to attacks in south Wales is consistent with a date in 1276, and Llywelyn had sought the archbishop's intervention on his behalf against the Marchers earlier in that year (nos 392–3 above; the dating is supported in *CAC*, 127; Sommer-Seckendorff, *Studies*, 119–20; and Smith, *Llywelyn*, 404 and n. 58). The archbishop's promise, mentioned twice in the letter (and on the second occasion said to involve a commitment to induce the king to punish the Marchers), may have been made in response to Llywelyn's previous letter of

24 June 1276 (no. 393 above). To judge by the endorsement, the present letter was forwarded to the chancellor, Robert Burnell. For Llanfair Rhyd Gastell see note to no. 378 above.

*395 Edward I

Letter, informing the king that he would go to Montgomery or Oswestry to do homage to the king, on condition that the king would provide him with a safe conduct, namely by the archbishop and archdeacon of Canterbury, the bishop of Winchester, the earls of Cornwall, Norfolk, Lincoln, Gloucester and Warenne, and Roger Mortimer, without any claim being made against him there in his presence; that the king should confirm by his letters the peace formerly made between him and his father Henry and Llywelyn, and ensure the fulfilment of what was denied to Llywelyn from the peace; and that the king would restore Llywelyn's wife with her escort. [Offers and petitions to the king also possibly included or appended.]

[Shortly before 14 October 1276]

Mention only, in an account of the process against Llywelyn which resulted in his condemnation as a rebel by the king and his council at Westminster on 12 November 1276 (*Foedera*, I. ii. 535; cd., *CCR 1272–9*, 360; *H*, no. 491). The account says that the letter was received at Westminster fifteen days before Michaelmas (14 October), following fruitless negotiations with Llywelyn conducted by the archdeacon of Canterbury on behalf of the archbishop of Canterbury and other prelates and magnates in the wake of the prince's failure to appear at Westminster to do homage three weeks after Easter 1276 (26 April). Llywelyn's request was rejected by the king and his council on the morrow of Martinmas (12 November). It is quite possible that the prince's letter was the same as that conveying petitions and offers (*peticiones et offra*) referred to in an undated letter from Edward I to Llywelyn (*Treaty Rolls*, no. 152). There the king informs Llywelyn that he has read the petitions and offers and shown them to his prelates and magnates in parliament, where it was decided after full discussion that they were insufficient and ought not to be accepted; if Llywelyn makes reasonable and due offers by the quinzaine of the feast of St Hilary (27 January 1277), the king will be prepared to receive them as is fitting. The wording of Edward's reply is identical to that of another royal letter to Llywelyn, dated at Westminster, 9 December 1276, cited in no. 400 below, except that in this letter the deadline for the receipt of new offers is fixed as the quinzaine of the Purification (16 February), and the king adds that they must be acceptable to his council as well as himself. This suggests that the undated letter from Edward was earlier than that of 9 December. However, it is likely that both royal letters refer to the same *peticiones et offra*; and the reference to rejection by the prelates and magnates in parliament could well be to the meeting on 12 November recorded in the account of the prince's condemnation, in which case the petitions and offers were the same as those presented in October (as assumed in Smith, 'Offra principis Wallie', 362–3). By contrast Smith, *Llywelyn*, 409 and n. 73, suggests that the king's undated letter and letter of 9 December referred to a later set of proposals, probably sent early in December 1276, on the grounds that by 9 December a month had elapsed since the prince's condemnation and also that, unlike the king's two letters, the account of that condemnation on the close roll makes no mention of Edward's readiness to receive revised offers. The issue cannot be resolved definitively. However, no other assembly of magnates and prelates is known to have met in 1276 after that which condemned Llywelyn on 12 November; moreover, if the undated letter was earlier than that of 9 December, the gap between it and the November condemnation would be reduced. The king's two letters may therefore simply reflect a softening of the king's stance vis-à-vis the prince's October proposals rather than a response to a new set of proposals.

*396 Pope Gregory X

Letter (?), informing the pope that when Eleanor, daughter of Simon de Montfort, whom Llywelyn had married, was being taken to him in Wales by sea, she was detained, and that she is still detained by royal order against her will, to the disparagement of her status and the manifest injury of the prince. Therefore Llywelyn humbly begs the pope's provision in this matter.

[c.December 1276 × -30 January 1277]

Mention only, in a letter from Pope John XXI to Edward I dated at Viterbo, 30 January 1277 (*Reg. Grégoire X*, 27–8; cited in part in Smith, 'Offra principis Wallie', 365, n. 6; cd., *H*, 492). The pope's letter does not explicitly state that Llywelyn's request was in written form. The request met with a sympathetic response, as in his letter the pope urged the king to release Eleanor, who had been captured with her brother Amaury de Montfort at the end of 1275. However, Edward I kept Eleanor imprisoned in Windsor Castle until her wedding with Llywelyn at Worcester in October 1278 (Smith, *Llywelyn*, 393, 396–402, 411–12, 448–50).

397 Bishop Anian and the dean and chapter of St Asaph

Notification that Llywelyn, for the love of God and the remission of his sins, as well as for the sake of the servants of Anian, bishop of St Asaph and the dean and chapter of that place, recognizes that all pleas throughout the diocese of St Asaph concerning wills, marriage, usury, tithes and sacrilege and matters associated with these belong to the jurisdiction of the church. Llywelyn wishes to obey the healthy warnings of the Apostolic See and the orders received recently concerning the restoration of the estate of the church of St Asaph in the following articles.

(1) When the bishop of St Asaph is dying, Llywelyn will not lay hands on the moveable goods of the church and prevent the fulfilment of the obligation intended by the dying one while healthy.

(2) He shall not impede wills, however made, by his vassals in the diocese for as long as they remain unchanged.

(3) He shall not occupy the goods of any vassal of the church although he has died intestate.

(4) If lay persons subject to Llywelyn demand undue procurations in the monasteries and churches of the diocese of St Asaph, against the will of those living in those places, or because of this those persons are molested physically or in their goods, Llywelyn grants the full correction of these trespasses to the church.

(5) He allows the church of St Asaph to exercise similar restraint against those of his servants who refuse to allow those condemned by his court to confess their sins to priests unless the servants are themselves present, nor does he wish to protect those offenders from the church's severe discipline.

(6) He shall not impose any tallages, levies or dues on ecclesiastical persons or vassals, unless they hold a fee in chief of Llywelyn or at any rate he has obtained the prelate's consent or spiritual permission for such an imposition.

(7) He grants jurisdiction over the vassals of the church of St Asaph to the bishop and chapter so that, when a vassal of the church is accused of theft, they may receive half of the amercement of those condemned in whatever way, so long as the penalty has been imposed on the condemned in person.

(8) He also grants to them half of the halaucty *due from the estates of the church.*

(9) If anyone subject to the same church has fled as a result of Llywelyn's power of banishment or any other reason, the bishop and chapter may take full possession of his goods, both moveable and immoveable, and dispose of them as they wish; nor shall Llywelyn's bailiffs interfere with such goods, unless by chance the prelates or their officials have been negligent or remiss in seizing them.

(10) No vassal of the church shall be arrested by Llywelyn's servants for any offence without the bishop's bailiffs having been consulted, unless there be danger in delay; on that occasion, let the offender, having been taken first to the bishop's court, not be denied to his guarantors, when the men of the church make enquiries about the prisoner.

(11) Llywelyn grants full jurisdiction to the bishop over trespasses committed in the bishop's courts, with the sole exception of homicide.

(12) If two men, namely Llywelyn's and the bishop's, wound or injure each other in Llywelyn's land, half of the fine for their man's trespass shall belong to the bishop and chapter; if in the church's land, the whole fine shall go to the bishop and chapter.

Llywelyn grants these and similar liberties, which the church of St Asaph has long enjoyed, to the aforesaid church, bishop and chapter and their successors in pure and perpetual alms, to be possessed for ever in peace, for the salvation of himself and of his predecessors as princes of Wales, and warrants the aforesaid rights, liberties and customs against all men for ever. Sealing clause; witnesses (not named).

[7 December 1276 × -10 February 1277;
probably 7 December 1276 × c.11 January 1277]

B = NLW, MS Peniarth 231B, pp. 74–7. s. xvii[1].
Pd. from B, Haddan and Stubbs, i. 519–21.
Cd., Stephenson, *Governance*, 204; *H*, no. 153.

Universis Cristi fidelibus presentes litteras visuris vel audituris L. filius Gruffud princeps Wallie, dominus Snaudon' salutem in domino sempiternam. Vobis omnibus et singulis notum facimus per presentes quod nos, divine caritatis intuitu et in nostrorum remissionem peccaminum, necnon[a] et intuitu servitiorum venerabilis patris domini A. Dei gratia episcopi Assaven(sis) et . .[b] eiusdem loci decani et capituli nobis impensorum, fatemur et recognoscimus omnes causas testamentarias, matrimoniales, usurarias, decimarum et sacrilegii necnon et hiis annexas per totam diocesim Assaven(sem) spectare ad forum ecclesie pleno iure. Volumus insuper salubribus sedis apostolice monitis parere pariter et mandatis que circa reformationem status Assaven(sis) ecclesie meminimus recepisse dudum in articulis infrascriptis.

[i] Decedente itaque episcopo qui pro tempore fuerit in ecclesia Assaven(si), ad occupationem bonorum ecclesie mobilium manus nostras nullatenus extendemus, quominus debitum sortiatur officium salubris de[c] intento decedentis.[d]

[ii] Testamenta insuper nostrorum vassallorum decedentium eiusdem diocesis, quandocumque condita, non impediemus quamdiu duraverint non mutata.

[iii] Nec occupa[p. 75]bimus bona alicuius ecclesie vassalli, quamquam ipse decesserit intestatus.

[iv] Quod si laici nobis subditi in domibus monasteriorum et ecclesiarum diocesis Assaven(sis) indebitas exigant procurationes, personis in eisdem locis degentibus contradicentibus et invitis, autem propter hoc per subditos ipsos personis eisdem in corpore vel in bonis molestias inferri contingat aut iacturas, quod fieri prohibemus, plenam correctionem pro transgressionibus his concedimus ad ecclesiam pertinere.

[v] Cohibitionem quoque consimilem ecclesie permittimus Assaven(si) in ministros nostros, qui non permiserint a nostra curia condempnatos nisi ipsis ministris presentibus et audientibus sua peccata sacerdotibus confiteri; nec ipsos transgressores manutenere volumus, quominus in tales ecclesia discipline severitatem valeat exercere.

[vi] De cetero etiam tallias, collectas seu exactiones aliquas, personis non imponens ecclesiasticis vel ecclesie[e] vassallis, nisi feodum a nobis in capite teneant, vel saltem supra tali impositione prelati consensum vel licentiam obtinuerimus spiritualem.

[vii] Ad hoc in vassallos ecclesie Assaven(sis) illam eisdem episcopo et capitulo concedimus iurisdictionem habere quod, accusato ipsius ecclesie vassallo aliquo super furto, medietatem amerciamenti recipiant qualitercumque condempnatorum, quousque dictata fuerit condempnationis summa in persona.

[viii] Ad ipsos etiam volumus et concedimus medietatem *halaucte* in ecclesie territorio pertinere.

[ix] Si quis insuper eiusdem ecclesie subditus per nostram bannitus potestatem [p. 76] aut quoquo modo noster fuerit fugitivus, plenam possessionem bonorum tam mobilium quam immobilium ingrediantur ipsius ac de hiis disponant pro sue libito voluntatis. Nec de[f] huiusmodi bonis volumus quod nostri ballivi se aliquatenus intromittant, nisi forte in talium occupatione bonorum prelati aut eorum officiales negligentes fuissent aut remissi.

[x] Preterea homo vassallus ecclesie pro forisfacto aliquo, irrequisitis episcopi ballivis, per nostros servientes in persona nullatenus[g] capiatur, nisi periculum sit in mora; et tunc forisfactor, ad curiam episcopi primo deductus, hominibus ecclesie captum requirentibus ad plegios nullatenus denegetur.

[xi] Transgressiones insuper in curiis episcopi perpetratas, nisi solum in casu homicidii, eidem episcopo facilitatem plenariam concedimus corrigendi.

[xii] Insuper si duo homines, noster videlicet et ecclesie, in territorio nostro vulnera ad invicem vel iniurias alias inferant, pro transgressione sui hominis ad episcopum et capitulum medietas spectet emende: verum si in territorio ecclesie, ipsa[h] totalis emenda in usum episcopi et capituli devolvatur.[i]

Hec et hiis similia, in quorum possessione vel quasi longe retroactis temporibus ecclesia extitit Assaven(sis), sepedictis[j] ecclesie, episcopo et capitulo suisque successoribus, pro salute anime nostre et nostrorum predecessorum principum Wall(ie), in puram ac perpetuam elemosinam concedimus possidenda in perpetuum pacifice et quiete. Et nos pro nobis, heredibus aut successoribus nostris, sibi et suc[p. 77]cessoribus[k] suis, contra omnes homines inperpetuum warentizamus[l] ipsa iura, libertates et consuetudines supradictas. Et ut hec nostra concessio et liberalis donatio robur optineat firmitatis, ipsas presenti carta nostra roborata sigilli nostri appensione confirmamus. Hiis testibus etc. Dat' etc.

^a nec *in* necnon *interlined above* q *struck through* B. | ^b *space with two dots* B. | ^c *interlined over* intento *struck through* B. | ^d decedentes B. | ^e B *inserts* l *struck through*. | ^f B *inserts* hiis *struck through* B. ^g B *inserts one letter struck through*. | ^h ipsam B. | ⁱ B *inserts* hoc *struck through*. | ^j B *inserts* episcopo *struck through*. | ^k B *repeats* nostris, sibi et successoribus. | ^l *corrected from* warantizabmus *(sic) in* B.

This grant of liberties must be later than the *gravamina* against Llywelyn published by Bishop Anian II of St Asaph and his chapter on 7 December 1276 (Haddan and Stubbs, i. 511–16), for it concedes many of the rights of temporal jurisdiction which the *gravamina* accused the prince of having usurped. On the other hand, it is likely to have been issued before Bishop Anian fled into English custody and attended the convocation at the New Temple on 10 February 1277 which excommunicated Llywelyn (*Councils and Synods*, ii. 820–2). The document may well be no later than early January 1277, however, since in an undated letter written at Leominster Bishop Thomas Cantilupe of Hereford refers to Llywelyn's recent restoration to the bishop of St Asaph of the liberties of his see; the bishop was at Leominster on 11 January 1277 (and at Bosbury on 7 January and at Hereford on 15 January) (*Reg. Cantilupe*, lxvi, 42, noticed in Smith, *Llywelyn*, 409, n. 71). For the background and context of the grant see also nos 369 and 387 above and Stephenson, *Governance*, 176–7, which points out that the letter appears to respond to a mandate from the pope – whose intervention in defence of the liberties of St Asaph is also mentioned in the text of the *gravamina* – rather than directly to the *gravamina* themselves. The Welsh term *halaucty* (literally, 'polluted house') in c. viii denoted the right to confiscate the goods of the owner of a house in which stolen goods were discovered (Pryce, *Native Law*, 229–30; see also no. 345, c. x above). I am grateful to Paul Russell for help with the translation of c. x.

398 Memorandum of offers and petitions to Edward I

Offers of the prince of Wales to the king.

(1) He offers to do homage at either Montgomery or John fitz Alan's Oswestry or thereabouts;

(2) also offers to pay 6,000 marks fifteen days after doing homage for troubling the king, for confirming and fulfilling the peace and for the restoration of Llywelyn's wife and consort Eleanor.

(3) The prince promises to do full justice to the barons of Wales who ought to hold [their lands] from him and who according to the terms of the peace are claiming right by the judgement of their peers in Wales; and likewise to the English barons in the March according to the customs of the Marchers, on condition that justice may equally be done by them to Llywelyn and his men according to the same laws and customs.

(4) The prince promises to pay 5,000 marks to the king for the homage of Rhys ap Maredudd ap Rhys, together with the full arrears of the money which he is obliged to pay under the terms of the aforesaid peace, at the terms stipulated in it.

The petition of the prince to the king.

He asks that the following lords provide safe conduct during his journey to the king to give homage, while he is with the king when he gives homage and during his journey home, with Llywelyn then being ready to do and receive justice as stated: the archbishop of Canterbury, the bishop of Durham, the earls of Cornwall, Gloucester and Warenne. And if the earl of

Cornwall or earl of Gloucester shall be absent, Llywelyn asks for the earl of Lincoln and the following hostages, namely Roger Mortimer, Gruffudd ap Gwenwynwyn and Dafydd ap Gruffudd, until he has returned home after doing homage.

The reasonable reasons why the prince asserts that he should be conducted by such men are:

first, the king received the prince's fugitives, Gruffudd ap Gwenwynwyn and later Llywelyn ap Gruffudd Madog, who fled to the king's land to wage war on the prince, and received their homage, it is said, contrary to the terms of the peace;

second, the king detains the prince's wife in prison though she has never offended in the kingdom and would not have entered it unless forced to do so after arrest at sea by royal command; and the prince fears that he too will be detained with her unless he is given the above safe conduct;

third, the prince is uncertain of his life and liberty because war has already been waged against him by the king, so that he dare not go to the king unless conducted by the aforesaid lords. Otherwise he would have gladly come at the king's first summons.

The prince submits to the king of France whether these reasons are reasonable or not, saving his right and safe conduct being granted to his messengers should they be sent to France.

Finally, if the aforesaid petitions and offers do not seem reasonable to the king, although, having respect for the authority and status of the prince, they seem sufficient to him and his council, the prince begs the king to inform him of his will concerning the matter by the present messengers of the prince and to prevent war in the March pending the negotiations.

[January × February 1277]

A = TNA: PRO, C 47/27/2, no. 9. No endorsement; approx. 171 mm. wide at top, 155 mm. wide at bottom × 193 mm. deep. The parchment is stained.
Pd. from A, Smith, 'Offra principis Wallie', 366–7.
Cd., *H*, no. 422.

Offra principis Wall(ie) domino regi.

[i] Offert in primis homagium suum domino regi facere . . .[a] de duobus locis, scilicet apud villam Mo(n)tis Gom(er)i seu apud Album Monasterium Ioh(ann)is [filii] Alani ˋvel circa .

[ii] Offert etiam domino rego sex milia marcarum sibi solvenda ad quindenam post factum homagium pro vexatione et interesse domini regis, ac pro confirmatione pacis inter eos dudum facte et eius suplecione; necnon pro restitutione domine Alienore uxoris sue et sue comitive.

[iii] Promittit etiam princeps facere plenam iusticiam baronibus Wallie de eo tenere debentibus secundum dictam formam pacis et reclamantibus secundum iudicium parium eorum in Wallia; necnon baronibus Anglicis in Marchia secundum consuetudines Marchiarum, ita tamen quod sibi et suis ab eis secundum easdem leges et consuetudines fiat iusticia pari modo.

[iv] Promittit etiam domino regi solvere quinque milia marcarum pro homagio Resi filii Maredud mab Rys, cum toto arreragio pecunie quam tenetur domino regi solvere per dictam formam pacis, ad terminos assignatos in ea.

Peticio principis versus dominum regem.

Pettit[b] infra scriptos dominos in conductu salvo veniendi ad dominum regem pro suo homagio sibi faciendo et morandi cum eo dum faciat homagium suum ac veniendi salvo ad propria, inde calumpniacionem alicuius ibidem ipso parato facere et recipere iusticiam ˋut diximus : dominum archiepiscopum Cantuar(iensem); episcopum Dulmensem;[c] comitem

Cornubie; comitem Gloucest(ri)e; comitem Warantie. Et si comes Cornubie defuerit vel comes Gloucest(ri)e, loco absentis pettit[b] comitem Lincol(nie) et obsides subscriptos, videlicet dominum Rog(er)u(m) de Mortuo Mari, G(ri)ffin' filium Wenoewyn et David filium G(ri)ffini, usque ad eius reventum ad propria post factum homagium.

Cause rationabiles quas pretendit princeps ut a tantis conducatur sunt hee.

Prima est quia dominus rex receptavit G(ri)ffinu(m) filium Wen' et postmodum Lewelin(um) filium G(ri)ffini Madoci fugitivos suos in terra sua ad gerrandum contra principem, ac eorum homagium recepit, ut dicitur, contra pacis formam.

Secunda causa est quod dominus rex detinet in carcere uxorem principis que nunquam in regno forefecit nec regnum intravit nisi victa et coacta ac in mari capta post inhibitionen regiam si que[d] fuit; et idem timet princeps ne et ipse detineatur cum ea nisi veniat in tanto conductu.

Tertia causa est quia dubitat de vita[e] et libertate sua eo quod gerra iam mota est a domino rege et suis contra ipsum; ita quod post gerram motam non est ausus accedere ad dominum regem homagium sibi facturus nisi in conductu predictorum dominorum. Aliter etiam et libenter venisset ad primam vocationem domini regis.

Ponit etiam princeps super dominum regem Francie de dictis causis si sint rationabiles vel non, salvo suo iure et conductu nunciorum suorum si contingat eos mitti in Francia(m) de causa.

Ad ultimum si prefate peticiones et offra non videntur domino regi rationabilia, cum tamen, habito respectu ad facultates et statum principis, sint visa sibi et suo consilio sufficientia, suplicat princeps domino regi quod ipse rex per presentes suos nuncios principis significet eidem certam voluntatem suam circa predictum negocium et offra, et quod inhibeat gerram in Marchia pendente tractatu.

[a] *parchment badly stained here in* A. | [b] *sic in* A. | [c] *sic in* A *for* Dunelmensem. | [d] qua A. | [e] via A.

For full discussion of this memorandum of proposals taken to Edward I by Llywelyn's messengers see Smith, 'Offra principis Wallie'. The reference to the defection of Llywelyn ap Gruffudd ap Madog of Bromfield, which occurred in late December 1276, means that the document can be no earlier than January 1277 (ibid., 363). The memorandum almost certainly accompanied either Llywelyn's letter of 22 January 1277 (no. 400 below) or his letter of 21 February 1277 (no. 401 below); the inclusion of Henry de Lacy amongst those sought to provide safe conduct possibly points to February, as the earl was appointed to a command on the Montgomery front in late January (Smith, *Llywelyn*, 410, n. 76). On the other hand, Llywelyn's concern to emphasize the reasonableness of his requests may indicate that the memorandum was sent in response to Edward's letter of 9 December 1276. For an earlier set of requests, received at Westminster on 6 October 1276, see no. 395 above. Cc. iii and iv of the present *offra* refer to c. x of the Treaty of Montgomery (no. 363 above); this may suggest that the claims of the 'barons of Wales' in c. iii related to the land of Rhys ap Maredudd, as the clause in the treaty speaks specifically of claims by Llywelyn's barons in the land of Rhys's father Maredudd ap Rhys (d. 1271). Llywelyn's offer to pay £5,000 for the homage of Maredudd ap Rhys had been accepted by Henry III in 1270, but it is uncertain whether the transaction was completed, and the present offer of £5,000 for the homage of his son may indicate that the payment had not been made (Smith, *Llywelyn*, 348–9, 364–5, 410, n. 77).

399 Memorandum to Edward I

Petitions the king to admit him into his peace and friendship, and to allow the archbishop of
Canterbury with certain other prelates, the earls of Cornwall, Lincoln and Warenne and Roger
Mortimer to conduct him to do homage and fealty to the king at a suitable place in the March,
on his outward journey, return and stay there, so that Llywelyn shall hold his principality from
the king as is fitting by giving homage, subjection and fealty in all. He offers 11,000 marks to
the king for his grace and peace, in addition to the rest of the money which he was already
obliged to pay, making a total of 25,000 marks to be paid.

[Probably January × February 1277]

A = TNA: PRO, C 47/27/1, no. 19. No endorsements; approx. 166 × 62 mm.
Pd. from A, Chaplais, *Diplomatic Documents*, 279 (no. 411).

Petimus supplicantes domino nostro regi ut nos ex sua gracia ad suam pacem et amiciciam
admittat, concedendo nobis in conductum ad faciendum homagium nostrum et fidelitatem
sibi in alico congruo loco in Marchia venerabilem patrem dominum archiepiscopum
Cantuarien(sem) cum quibusdam aliis prelatis, viros etiam nobiles comites videlicet
Cornubie, Linco(n)lie, Warre(n)nie et dominum Rog(er)um de Mortuo Mari, eundo et
redeundo et ibidem morando, ita quod principatum nostrum in suis libertatibus teneamus
ut decet de domino nostro rege, faciendo sibi homagium nostrum, subieccionem et fidelitatem in omnibus debitam. Offerrimus[a] autem domino nostro regi pro sua gracia et pace
habenda xi milia marcarum supra residuam peccuniam in qua sibi prius tenebamur, ita
quod summa totalis peccunie sibi solvende sit xx^{ti}v^{que} milia marcarum.

[a] offerrmus A.

Though the petitioner is not named, the content of the document shows that it must be
Llywelyn. As Smith points out (*Llywelyn*, 410 and n. 75), the document reflects the circumstances of late 1276 or early 1277 and is closely related to the petitions and offers in no. 398
above. In two respects the present text seems to be more conciliatory, and thus quite
possibly later, than no. 398. First, the prince offers to do homage 'in any suitable place in
the March', rather than specifying Montgomery or Oswestry. Second, he offers 11,000
marks for peace, whereas in no. 398 he offers 6,000 marks for peace and 5,000 marks for the
homage of Rhys ap Maredudd. Although the total payment offered is the same in both
documents, in the present text Llywelyn explicitly seeks only the king's 'grace and peace',
being silent on both Rhys's homage and the release of Eleanor. By February 1274, when he
began to refuse payments due under the terms of the Treaty of Montgomery on principle,
Llywelyn seems to have paid 15,000 of the 17,000 marks due for the period 1267–71; if so,
he still owed 10,000 of the total of 25,000 marks payable (Smith, *Llywelyn*, 364–6, esp. n.
91).

400 Edward I

Letter, citing Edward's letter received at Christmas: 'Edward has received Llywelyn's letter
containing petitions and offers. After reading these and discussing them fully in parliament
with his prelates and magnates, it has been considered that the petitions and offers are insuffi-
cient and ought not to be accepted. If Llywelyn makes reasonable and due offers by the

quinzaine of the Purification [16 February], the king will be prepared to receive them as is
fitting and as his council advises. Dated at Windsor, 9 December 1276.' Having read this in his
council ... Llywelyn asks the king to grant safe conduct to his messengers during negotiations
concerning the aforementioned matters. Llywelyn is therefore sending Anian, bishop of Bangor
and Master Gervase, his clerk and vice-chancellor, asking the king to believe what these
messengers inform him about the terms in the aforementioned letter of Llywelyn, and to reply
by the same messengers.

Aberalwen, 22 January 1277

A = TNA: PRO, SC 1/19, no. 24. No endorsement; approx. 196 mm. wide at top, 209 mm. wide at
bottom × 66 mm. deep; mounted, foot cut away. The parchment is stained, and the ink faint.
Cd., *CAC*, 87; *H*, no. 421.

Excellenti domino suo si placet domino E. Dei gratia illustri regi Anglie, domino
Hybern(ie), duci Aquitt' suus devotus L. princeps Wall(ie), dominus Snaudon' salutem et
paratam ad beneplacita voluntatem. Litteras vestras nuper in festo nativitatis domini
recepimus in hec verba: 'Edwardus Dei gratia rex Angl(ie), dominus Hyb(ernie) et dux
Aq(ui)tt' Lewel(ino) filio G(ri)ff(ini) principi Wall(ie) salutem. Litteras vestras nobis nuper
transmissas peticiones et offra quidam ex parte vestra nobis facta recepimus continentes, et
eas lectas et intellectas ostendimus in parliamento nostro prelatis, magnatibus et proceribus
regni nostri habitaque cum ipsis super huiusmodi petitionibus et offris vestris deliberatione
et tractatu pleniori, nobis et ipsis visum fuit illa minus sufficientia esse et idcirco omnino
exaudiri non debere. V[er]umptamen si rationabilia et debita offra nobis citra quindenam
purificationis Beate M(ari)e litteras (?)s . . . duxeritis faciendas, nos ea parati erimus
admittere sicut decet et consilium ratum nobis duxerit faciendum. Teste me ipso apud
Wydes' ix die decembris anno regni nostri v°.' Quibus lectis in nostro consilio . . .[a] excellentiam `vestram duximus rogandam ut securum conductum nunciis nostris concederitis in
veniendo ad vos ac ibidem morando ac iterum redeundo ad partes suas durante tractatu
super premissis super quod a vobis vestri gratia perpetravimus. Mittimus igitur ad
presenciam vestram dilectos nostros dominum Annianu(m) episcopum Bangorense(m) et
magistrum G(er)vasiu(m) clericum nostrum et vicecancellarium rogantes vestram regiam
maiestatem diligenter et attente quatinus fidem indubitatam adhibere dignemini hiis qui
predicti nuncii nostri vobis circa formam (?)in pretactis (?)litteris nostris . . . eorum parte
vestra duxerint intimanda, voluntatem et vestram per eosdem nobis super premissis si
placet significantes. Dat' apud Aberalwen in crastino die Agnetis virginis anno domini m°
c° c° lxx° sexto.

[a] c.*23 mm. illegible in* A.

As Edwards noted (*CAC*, 87), Edward had already issued a safe conduct on 14 January
1277 to last until mid-Lent (7 March) for any messenger Llywelyn might send (*CPR
1272–81*, 188). For the *peticiones et offra* referred to in Edward's letter see note to no. 395
above. The Master Gervase (most likely a Latinization of Iorwerth) referred to was
probably the same as a canon of Bangor of that name; his designation as vice-chancellor
may have meant that he was a full replacement for the chancellor (Stephenson, *Governance*,
36–7). Aberalwen (SJ 063 433) was a township belonging to Corwen, Edeirnion (Smith,
'Parishes and townships', 719, 724 (map 3)).

401 Edward I

Letter, stating that, as he desires to please the king and show him due humility, fealty and honour in all and thus obtain his friendship, Llywelyn sends petitions and offers through the archbishop of Canterbury to be presented by the bearer of the present letter. Llywelyn begs the king to show his royal clemency to those who are ready to submit themselves to him, rather than exercise the harshness of his power against those refusing to obey as suggested by those jealous of Llywelyn. He testifies before God that he loves the king more truly, faithfully and intimately than those who incite him against Llywelyn. Therefore, if the king grants Llywelyn's petitions, Llywelyn will be of greater value to the king than those who, by the king's war, now attempt to gain their own profit and advantage rather than the king's honour.

Tegeingl, second Sunday in Lent [21 February 1277]

A = TNA: PRO, SC 1/19, no. 30. No endorsements; approx. 170 × 85 mm.; mounted, foot cut away.
Cd., *CAC*, 91; *H*, no. 423.

Excellentissimo domino suo domino E. Dei gratia illustri regi Angl(ie), domino Hib(er)nie et duci Aquitann(ie) suus si placet devotus et fidelis Lewelinus princeps Wall(ie), dominus Snaudon' salutem et fidelitatem sibi debitam pro viribus observare. Cupientes vestre melite dominacioni teste Deo complacere et eidem nostram humilitatem, fidelitatem et honorem debitum in omnibus exibere ac per hec vestram amiciciam posse adipisci, peticiones et offra excellencie vestre mediante venerabili patre domino Cantuar(iensi) archiepiscopo presentanda per latorem presencium destinamus. Quapropter vestre supplicamus celsitudini quatinus afectantibus se vestre maiestati humiliare intuitu Dei et iusticie regiam clemenciam potius ostendere dignemini, quam potencie austeritatem ad suggestionem emulorum nostrorum contra obedire nolentes exercere. Testificamur insuper coram Deo ex quo nos et nostram fidelitatem in vestre claritatis amiciciam collegistis quod veracius, fidelius[a] et intimius vestram illustrem personam dileximus et diligimus, quam illi qui animum vestrum ad indignacionem contra nos incitarunt. Unde et si peticionibus nostris vestra annuerit maiestas, vestre dominacioni prestancius velebimus[b] quam illi qui modo per vestram guerram magis suum lucrum et commodium quam vestrum honorem adparere attemptant. Valeat excellencia vestra in domino. Datum apud Tegeygyl dominica secunda in quadragesima.

[a] *one minim too many before the final* s *in* A. | [b] *sic in* A *for* valebimus.

As Edwards noted (*CAC*, 91–2), the reference to war (*modo per vestram guerram*) indicates a date in 1277, since war had not broken out by the second Sunday in Lent 1282. The unusually deferential tone reflects the vulnerability of Llywelyn in the face both of the threat of full-scale war and of his excommunication on 10 February 1277 (cf. Smith, *Llywelyn*, 412 and n. 81). It is possible that the 'petitions and offers' mentioned were those presented in no. 398 above (as suggested in Smith, *Llywelyn*, 410, n. 76). However, there is a case for identifying them with the shorter memorandum in no. 399 above. The present letter and no. 399 are not only more deferential and conciliatory than no. 398 but they also share one correspondence of detail, for in both Llywelyn seeks the king's 'friendship' (*amicicia*), a term which is lacking in no. 398.

402 Letter patent ratifying the Treaty of Aberconwy

Llywelyn has inspected the articles concerning peace ordained by William of Southampton, provincial prior of the Order of Preachers in England, Robert Tibetot and Anthony Bek on behalf of the magnificent prince and Llywelyn's lord King Edward and by Tudur ab Ednyfed and Goronwy ap Heilin on behalf of Llywelyn:

'The king and prince have provided sufficient security to observe the articles agreed by the aforementioned representatives of both sides:

(1) Llywelyn places himself at the will and mercy of the king and will give him £50,000 for disobedience, damages and injuries by him and his men, seeking by this sum the king's grace and mercy.

(2) Llywelyn quitclaims to the king the Four Cantrefs as fully as the late King Henry or his son, the king, ever held, as well as all lands which the king has seized except for Anglesey. If Llywelyn makes a claim to lands occupied by others than the king outside the Four Cantrefs, the king will give him justice according to the laws and customs of the districts in which those lands lie.

(3) Llywelyn will come to give fealty to the king at Rhuddlan and before coming he will be absolved [from excommunication] and the interdict on his land lifted.

(4) Llywelyn will free his brother as follows: representatives of the king will come and, once Owain has been freed, give him the choice either of making peace with his brother, whose terms shall then be submitted to the king for confirmation, or of placing himself in the king's custody until he has been judged by the laws and customs of Wales in the place where he has trespassed, and if he is thus freed he may recover his patrimony if he wishes.

(5) Llywelyn will free Rhys ap Gruffudd and restore him to the position he had when he first discussed going over to the king.

(6) He will free Owain ap Gruffudd ap Gwenwynwyn unconditionally.

(7) He will free Dafydd ap Gruffudd ab Owain, Elise and Madog ab Einion unconditionally, as he will any others who can be shown to have been imprisoned on account of their loyalty to the king, and all trespasses and injuries arising therefrom will be totally remitted up to the present day.

(8) The names of those whose homages the king has granted to Llywelyn for his lifetime, and which will revert to the king and his heirs after Llywelyn's death: Dafydd ap Gruffudd ab Owain, Elise, the two sons of Owain ap Bleddyn and Rhys Fychan ap Rhys ap Maelgwn together with the land he now holds, for the land held by the king shall remain in the king's hands for ever; and all the aforesaid, except for Rhys ap Rhys ap Maelgwn, may hold the lands they have held from any lordship and fulfil their obligations to their lords.

(9) The lands of all others who have come into the king's peace and remain under the prince by the terms of the peace shall be restored to them as freely and fully as they held them when they came into the king's peace, and they may fulfil their obligations to their lords.

(10) The king by his grace grants and confirms to Llywelyn for his lifetime all the land which belongs by hereditary right to his brother Dafydd, and the the king will make due recompense to Dafydd for the same period; and the land given in recompense will revert to the king after the death of either Llywelyn or Dafydd.

(11) The king grants and confirms that Llywelyn and his legitimate heirs may have and hold Anglesey in the same way in which they first held it, paying 1,000 marks for it annually at Michaelmas.

(12) The king grants that all holding lands in the Four Cantrefs and in the other aforesaid

lands which the king retains, apart from those in which he has refused to grant this favour, may hold them as freely and fully as they held them before the war, with the same liberties and customs, so that those who held from the prince shall henceforth hold from the king by the accustomed services.

(13) Disputes between the prince and others shall be settled according to the laws of the March concerning matters in the March and according to the laws of Wales concerning those in Wales.

(14) Gruffudd Fychan shall do homage to the king for his lands in Iâl and to Llywelyn for his lands in Edeirnion.

(15) The king will confirm to Llywelyn all the lands which he now possesses free of any claim by himself or his heirs, with the exceptions of Anglesey, which he will confirm to Llywelyn for his lifetime and to heirs of his body as stated above, and of the portion there of his brother Dafydd after the death of the prince. The king will give satisfaction to Owain and Rhodri, Llywelyn's brothers, according to the terms agreed beforehand by the aforesaid counsellors of both sides, and the king will confirm the agreement between Llywelyn, Owain and Rhodri after it is made.

(16) Safe conduct will be provided for Llywelyn by the bishop of St Asaph and the aforesaid Robert and Anthony and others of the king's council up to 3 miles from Rhuddlan, and then by the bishop of Bath and the earl of Lincoln with their retinue, who will take him to the king at Rhuddlan and accompany him there and on his return home. Once the prince has arrived at Rhuddlan, the king will ordain a day for the prince to come and do homage to him at London, for which the king will provide safe conduct. For the fuller security of the above the prince will deliver to the king ten hostages from his land, whom the prince will be able to find without the compulsion of imprisonment or disinheritance, and Tudur ab Ednyfed has sworn on behalf of the prince and himself, and Goronwy ap Heilin and Dafydd ab Einion on behalf of themselves and others of the prince's council, that they will take effective steps in finding the said hostages and delivering them on a reasonable day to be fixed by the king.

(17) The prince has granted that he and those of his immediate council, together with twenty men from each cantref in his hands to be chosen annually by the king's representatives in the presence of the prince's bailiffs, will similarly swear that they will observe the above terms and ensure that they are observed by the prince, and if the prince contravenes them at all and fails to make amends within an adequate time, they will thenceforth leave the fealty, homage, lordship and service of the prince for the lordship of the king and resist Llywelyn to their greatest ability.

It has been sworn by Robert Tibetot, at the special command of the king, and the prince that the aforesaid articles shall be observed faithfully. The seals of the aforesaid Tudur and Goronwy have been attached to the part of the document remaining with the king, and the seals of the aforesaid prior, Robert and Anthony to the part remaining with the prince. Dated at Aberconwy, 9 November 1277.'

Llywelyn has ratified and approved these articles, which have been explained to him word by word, and sworn on the Gospels to observe them inviolably, and promises not to act against them by any fraud or trick. He has attached his seal to the present letter.

Aberconwy, 9 November 1277

B = TNA: PRO, C 77/1 (Welsh Rolls), m. 2 (November 1277).
C = TNA: PRO, E 36/274 (Liber A), fos 375r–376r. s. xiii ex.
Pd. from C, *Foedera*, I. ii. 545; from C, *LW*, 113–14 (no. 205) (in part).
Cd., *CWR*, 159 (from B); *H*, no. 425.

Omnibus Cristi fidelibus ad quos presentes littere pervenerint Lewelinus[a] princeps Wall(ie) salutem in domino. Inspeximus articulos provisos et ordinatos per fratrem Will(elmu)m de Suth(a)mpton'[b] priorem provincialem ordinis predicatorum Angl(ie), Rob(er)ti de Tybetot[c] et Anton' Bek' ex parte magnifici principis et domini nostri domini Edwardi Dei gratia regis Angl(ie) illustris, et per Tuderu(m) filium Etnyued et Goronow[d] filium Heylyn ex parte nostra, ad tractandum de pace inter ipsum dominum regem et nos specialiter assignatos in hec verba:

'Hii sunt articuli in quos frater Will(elmu)s de Suth(a)mpton' prior provincialis fratrum predicatorum Anglie, Rob(ertu)s de Tybetot[c] et Anton' Bek, dati et assignati ex parte magnifici principis domini Edwardi Dei gratia regis Angl(ie) illustris, et Tuder(us) filius Edeneuet,[e] et Gronow[f] filius Heylyn,[g] dati et assignati ex parte Lewelini filii Griffini principis Wall(ie), ad tractandum de pace inter predictos regem et principem concorditer consenserunt, in quos fideliter observandos tam dominus rex quam princeps supradicti securitatem prestabunt sufficientem.

[i] In primis quod predictus L.[h] supponet se voluntati et misericordie domini regis supradicti et pro inobedientia, dampnis et iniuriis sibi et suis illatis dabit pro pace sua habenda quinquaginta milia librarum sterlingorum, de qua summa gratiam et misericordiam sibi a dicto domino rege fieri petit.

[ii] Item dictus L.[h] dat et[i] concedit et confirmat et[j] quietum clamat pro se et heredibus suis domino regi Angl(ie)[k] et heredibus suis plenarie et sine aliqua retentione Quatuor Cantreda in finibus et terminis suis sicut clare memorie dominus H.[l] quondam rex Angl(ie) vel predictus[m] rex filius suus ea umquam plenius tenuerunt, simul cum omnibus terris quas idem dominus rex cepit et seisiri fecit in manum suam vel aliquo modo adquisivit, excepta terra Angles' de qua dominus rex pro suo facturus est dicto L.[n] gratiam specialem. Si vero idem Lewelinus ius vendicaverit in aliquibus terris quas alii preter dictum dominum[i] regem occupaverunt extra[o] Quatuor Cantreda predicta, plenariam iustitiam sibi exhibebit predictus[p] dominus rex secundum leges et consuetudines partium illarum in quibus terre ille consistunt.

[iii] Item idem L. veniet Rodolanu(m)[q] facturus domino regi sacramentum fidelitatis et antequam ibidem veniat ad presentiam regis absolutionis beneficium optinebit et interdictum terre sue relaxabitur.

[iv] Item dictus L.[h] Owenu(m) fratrem suum liberabit sub hac forma: quod aliqui ex parte domini regis venient et ipso liberato dabunt ei optionem aut quod conponat cum fratre suo predicto et[i] in formam ⌐certam pacis¬[r] gratis consentiet et postmodum supplicet domino regi quod illam pacem approbet et confirmet, aut quod ponat[s] se in custodia domini regis donec secundum leges et consuetudines Wall(ie) in loco ubi transgressus est de eo fuerit iudicatum, et si sic liberatus fuerit repetat hereditatem suam si sibi viderit expedire, et coram rege firmabitur via quam eligere voluerit de predictis.

[v] Item dictus Lewelinus liberabit Res(um) filium Griffini ⌐et restituet eum¬[t] ad statum quem habuit quando primo tractavit cum domino rege de veniendo ad pacem suam.

[vi] Item liberabit Owenu(m) filium Griffini filii Wenn'[u] pure et absolute.

[vii] Item liberabit David[v] filium Griffini ab Oweyn,[w] Elisse, Madocu(m) filium Enniaun pure et absolute, et si qui alii sunt de quibus constare poterit quod occasione domini regis capti fuerint et incarcerati similiter liberabuntur, et omnes transgressiones, iniurie et excessus hinc inde facti penitus remittuntur usque ad hodiernum diem.

[viii] Item hec sunt nomina illorum quorum homagia dominus rex concedit predicto L.[x]

principi ad vitam suam ita quod post decessum eiusdem[y] redeant ad dominum regem predictum et ad heredes suos et ad coronam suam et sint in medietate sub dominio dicti domini regis Angl(ie), videlicet: David[v] filius Griffini filii Owen(i), Elisse, duo filii Oweni filii Bledint,[z] Res(us) Vychan[aa] filius Res(i)[ah] filii Maelgun cum terra quam nunc tenet, quia de terra quam dictus rex vel sui seisiverunt nomine suo nichil sibi concedetur set in manu domini regis perpetuo remanebit; et concedit dominus rex quod omnes predicti, excepto Reso filio Res(i) filii Maelgun, terras quas prius de cuiuscumque dominio tenuerunt teneant eas et habeant faciendo dominis quod tenentur.

[ix] Item terre[ac] omnium aliorum[i] qui venerunt ad pacem domini regis et per formam pacis morabuntur sub principe eisdem restituantur ita libere et plenarie sicut eas tenebant eo tempore quo ad pacem domini regis venerunt, et faciant sibi et dominis quod tenentur.

[x] Item dominus rex de mera gratia sua concedit et confirmat prefato L.[ad] principi ad vitam suam totam terram que David fratri suo iure hereditario debetur, et dominus rex faciet eidem David alibi recompensationem conpetentem ad vitam predicti L.,[ae] et terra in recompensationem eidem David tradita, altero eorum, scilicet Lewel(ino) vel David,[v] decedente,[af] ad regem et heredes suos libere revertatur.

[xi] Item[i] concedit et confirmat dominus rex quod dictus L.[ad] et heredes sui de corpore suo legitime procreandi habeant et teneant Angles'[ag] eo modo quo prius eam tenuit, reddendo pro ea annis singulis ad scaccarium domini regis Sancti Mich(ael)is mille marcas sterlingorum.

[xii] Item concedit dominus rex quod omnes tenentes terras in Quatuor Cantred(is) et in aliis terris predictis quas dominus rex retinet[ah] in manu sua, exceptis illis quibus rex hanc gratiam facere recusavit, teneant eas adeo libere et plenarie sicut ante guerram tenere consueverunt, et eisdem libertatibus et consuetudinibus gaudeant quibus prius gaudere solebant, ita quod illi qui tenuerunt de principe de cetero teneant terras illas de rege et heredibus suis per servitia consueta.

[xiii] Item controversie et contentiones mote vel movende inter principem et quoscumque terminabuntur et decidentur secundum leges March(ie) de hiis que contingunt[ai] in M(a)rchia et secundum leges Wall(ie) de rebus contentiosis que in Wall(ia) orientur.

[xiv] Item Griffinu(s) Vychan faciet homagium domino regi de terris quas tenebit in dominio suo in Ial et Lewelino pro terris quas tenebit in dominio eiusdem in Edeyrniaun.[aj]

[xv] Item dominus rex confirmabit predicto L.[x] principi omnes terras quas nunc possidet absque ulla calumpnia sui vel [ak]heredum suorum,[ak] excepta Angles'[al] que eidem L.[n] confirmabitur ad vitam suam et heredibus suis de corpore suo procreandis sicut predictum est, et excepta portione David[v] fratris sui ibidem post decessum eiusdem principis; et satisfiet Oweno et Roderico fratribus eiusdem L.[ad] iuxta formam per predictos utriusque partis consiliarios superius nominatos prelocutam; et dictus dominus rex conpositionem inter eosdem L.,[am] Owenu(m) et Rod(er)icum cum facta fuerit in[i] modo debito confirmabit.

[xvi] Item prestabitur principi conductus per episcopum Assaven(sem) et predictos Rob(ertu)m et Anton' et alios de consilio domini[an] regis quos secum ducere voluerint usque ad tria miliaria de Rodolano, ubi occurrent principi episcopus Bath'[ao] et comes Linc'[ap] cum sua comitiva ad conducendum ipsum ad dominum regem usque ad Rodolanu(m),[q] morando et ad propria redeundo. Cum autem dictus princeps venerit Rodolanu(m), ibidem ordinabitur per dominum regem quod certo et conpetenti die eidem principi a domino rege prefixo veniet London' suum homagium ibidem domino regi facturus, et rex providebit sibi de venerabili et securo conductu eundo, morando et ad propria secure revertendo. Et

nichilominus idem princeps ad securitatem premissorum pleniorem liberabit domino regi decem obsides de nobilioribus terre sue quos perquirere poterit absque conpulsione carceris vel[aq] exheredationis, et Tuderus filius Etnyuet[e] predictus iuravit in animam dicti principis et in animam suam propriam, et Goronow[d] filius Heylyn[ar] et David[v] ab Ennyaun pro se et aliis de consilio eiusdem principis iuraverunt, quod operam dabunt efficacem de predictis obsidibus perquirendis et dicto domino regi liberandis ad diem rationabilem dicto principi per predictum dominum regem super hoc prefigendum.

[xvii] Et insuper concessit idem princeps quod ipse et illi qui sunt de consilio suo statim iurabunt, necnon et viginti homines de quolibet cantredo quod est in manu sua per fideles regis ibi singulis annis mittendos eligendi in presentia ballivorum eiusdem principis similiter iurabunt de anno in annum coram predictis fidelibus predicti domini regis, quod premissa quantum[as] ipsis est fideliter observabunt et per predictum principem observari procurabunt, et si idem princeps in aliquo contravenerit et hoc non emendaverit tempore conpetenti, extunc ipsi recedent et fidelitate homagio dominio et servitio dicti principis, et ad voluntatem et mandatum[at] domini regis predicti[i] transferent se ad regem et dominium suum et dicto L.[n] adversabuntur in quantum possunt.

Et sciendum quod per predictum Rob(ertu)m de Tybotot[c] habentem potestatem et speciale mandatum ad hoc a dicto[i] domino rege[au] necnon et per predictum principem est iuratum quod predicti[av] fideliter et inviolabiliter observabuntur hinc inde. In cuius rei testimonium scripto remanenti penes predictum dominum regem sigilla predictorum Tuderi et Goronow[d] et scripto remanenti penes predictum[aw] principem sigilla predictorum prioris Rob(ert)i[i] et Anton'[ax] sunt apposita. Acta et data[ay] Aberconewey[az] die martis proxima ante festum Sancti Martini anno domini m° cc° septuagesimo septimo.'

Quos[ba] quidem articulos nobis de verbo ad verbum expositos ratos habemus et gratos et eos approbamus et iuravimus ad sancta Dei evvangelia eosdem articulos inviolabiliter observare et promittimus pro nobis et heredibus nostris nos aliqua arte vel ingenio aliquo[bb] ipsem in contrarium non venire. In cuius rei testimonium presentibus sigillum nostrum fecimus apponi. Datum[bc] apud Abercunewey[az] die martis proxima ante festum Sancti Martini anno domini m° cc° septuagesimo septimo.

[a] Lewellinus C. | [b] Suthamptone C. | [c] Tibetot C. | [d] Goronw C. | [e] Etnyued C. | [f] Goronu C. | [g] Heyly C. | [h] Lewelinus C. | [i] omitted C. | [j] C; omitted B. | [k] C inserts plenarie struck through. | [l] Henr(icus) C. | [m] C inserts dominus. | [n] Lewelino C. | [o] ex C. | [p] prefatus C. | [q] Rodelanu(m) C. | [r–r] pacis certam C. | [s] ponet C. | [t–t] omitted C. | [u] (?)Wem'r C. | [v] Dauyd C. | [w] Owein C. | [x] Lewelyno C. | [y] C inserts principis. | [z] Bledynt C. | [aa] Vichan C. | [ab] Resy C. | [ac] C inserts illorum. | [ad] Lewel' C. | [ae] Lewelini C. | [af] decendente C. | [ag] Angleseiam C. | [ah] continet C. | [ai] contingent C. | [aj] Edeirniaun C. | [ak–ak] suorum heredum C. | [al] Angleseia C. | [am] Lewel' et C. | [an] dicti C. | [ao] Bathon' C. | [ap] Lincoln' C. | [aq] et C. | [ar] Heilyn C. | [as] C inserts in. | [at] C inserts dicti. | [au] C inserts predicti. | [av] C inserts articuli. | [aw] C inserts dominum. | [ax] Antonii C. | [ay] dat' apud C. | [az] Aberconwy C. | [ba] Et nos C. | [bb] C inserts tempore. | [bc] Dat' C.

The text printed here is that extant in two copies of Llywelyn's ratification of the treaty. Liber A also contains a text of the articles only, without any ratification (fos 378r–379v; pd., LW, 118–22 (no. 211)); another, incomplete, text of the articles only (fo. 384r–v (a marginal note on fo. 384v states that [for]ma scribitur in alio quaterno); pd. in part, LW, 136 (no. 244)); and a letter patent of Edward I ratifying and reciting the articles dated at Rhuddlan, 10 November 1277 (fos 407v–408v; pd. in part, LW, 157 (no. 279)). Summaries of the treaty's terms are also contained in several English annals and chronicles (Smith, *Llywelyn*, 438, n. 181; Davies, *Conquest*, 335, n. 1). The treaty and associated documents (nos 403–5 below) were the fruit of peace negotiations completed at Aberconwy Abbey in early November 1277; they formally concluded Edward I's first Welsh war and marked a huge reversal for Llywelyn (see further Smith, *Llywelyn*, 437–44 and references cited there).

403 Letter patent concerning Edward I

Notification that Llywelyn quitclaims to Edward I and his heirs for ever the Four Cantrefs as fully as they were ever held by Henry III or Edward, and all the lands seized or otherwise acquired by Edward from Llywelyn, except for Anglesey; the aforesaid lands are to be held free of all rights and claims by Llywelyn and his heirs for ever. If any documents are found by which this quitclaim could be infringed in whole or in part, Llywelyn grants that they shall be disregarded totally.

Aberconwy, 9 November 1277

B = TNA: PRO, C 77/1 (Welsh Rolls), m. 2 (November 1277).
C = TNA: PRO, E 36/274 (Liber A), fo. 377r–v. s. xiii ex.
Pd. from C, *Foedera*, I. ii. 546; from C, *LW*, 116–17 (no. 207).
Cd., *CWR*, 159 (from B); *H*, no. 426.

Omnibus Cristi fidelibus ad quos ᵃ⁻presentes littere pervenerint⁻ᵃ L. filius Griffini princeps Wall(ie) salutem in domino. Noverit universitas vestra quod nos pro nobis et heredibus nostris concedimus, remittimus et quietum clamamus magnifico principi et domino nostro domino Edwardo Dei gratia regi Angl(ie) illustri et heredibus suis in perpetuum Q(ua)tuor Cantreda cum terminis et finibus suis sicut clare memorie dominus H. quondam rex Angl(ie) vel predictus dominus Edward(us) nunc rex filius suus ea umquamᵇ plenius tenuerint,ᶜ et omnes terras et tenementa que idem dominus noster rex Edward(us) cepit et `capi et seisiri fecit in manum suam vel alio modo adquisivit super nos ubicumque in Wall(ia), excepta Angles',ᵈ et quicquid iuris, proprietatis, possessionis, actionis et clamii nobis et heredibus nostris conpetebat et conpetere poterat quacumque de causa vel ratione in cantred(a),ᵉ terris et tenementis predictis et terminis et finibus eorundem, habenda et tenenda eidem domino nostro regi et heredibus suis quieta et soluta de nobis et heredibus nostris in perpetuum. Et si que scripture vel instrumenta per que possit predicta concessio, remissio et quietaclamatio infringi in toto vel in parte invenianturᶠ volumus et concedimus pro nobis et heredibus nostris quod predicte scriptureᵍ vel instrumenta nullius penitus sint momenti. In cuius ᵃ⁻rei testimonium⁻ᵃ presentibus sigillum nostrum fecimus apponi. Datum ʰ⁻apud Aberconwe die martis proxima ante festum Sancti Martini anno domini mᵒ ccᵒ lxxᵒ septimo.⁻ʰ

ᵃ⁻ᵃ etc. B. | ᵇ uncquam C. | ᶜ tenuerit C. | ᵈ Angleseia C. | ᵉ C *inserts* in. | ᶠ C *inserts* de cetero. ᵍ *omitted* B. | ʰ⁻ʰ ut supra B.

See note to no. 402 above.

404 Letter patent concerning Edward I

Notification that Llywelyn agrees on behalf of himself and his heirs to pay 500 marks annually to Edward I and his heirs at Michaelmas at Chester for Anglesey and for the share of his brother Dafydd, until he has paid in full or has learned that he has paid the amount owed to Henry III and Edward; a royal letter of quittance shall be issued for each payment.

Aberconwy, 9 November 1277

B = TNA: PRO, C 77/1 (Welsh Rolls), m. 1 (November 1277).
C = TNA: PRO, E 36/274 (Liber A), fo. 377v. s. xiii ex.
Pd. from C, *Foedera*, I. ii. 546; from C, *LW*, 117–18 (no. 209).
Cd., *CWR*, 159 (from B); *H*, no. 427.

Omnibus presentes litteras visuris vel audituris L. filius Griffini princeps Wall(ie) salutem. Noverit universitas vestra nos pro nobis et heredibus nostris teneri solvere domino Edwardo Dei gratia regi Angl(ie) illustri et heredibus suis ad scaccarium suum in festo Sancti Mich(ael)is apud Cestr(iam) ᵃ⁻singulis annis quingentas marcas⁻ᵃ pro terra Angles'ᵇ et pro parte David fratris nostri quousque persolverimusᶜ velᵈ docuerimus nos persolvisse tantam quantitatem pecunie quantam debebamus domino H. quondam regi Angl(ie) patri suo et eidem domino Edwardo tanquam heredi suo, et fiet nobis littera domini regis de quietantia in singulis solutionibus pecunie supradicte. In cuius ᵉ⁻rei testimonium presentibus sigillum nostrum fecimus apponi.⁻ᵉ Datum apud Aberconweyᶠ die martis proxima ante festum Sancti Martini anno ᵉ⁻domini ccº lxxº septimo ut supra.⁻ᵉ

ᵃ⁻ᵃ quingentas marcas singulis annis C. | ᵇ Angleseye C. | ᶜ solverimus C. | ᵈ et C. | ᵉ⁻ᵉ ut supra B. ᶠ Aberconwe C.

See note to no. 402 above.

405 Letter patent concerning Edward I

Notification that Llywelyn hereby gives Edward I full power to decree that Llywelyn shall pay his brother Rhodri 1,000 marks, or less, for the portion of their inheritance which Rhodri should have held by right; the money which Llywelyn has paid Rhodri of that sum may be credited to the said sum, but nothing can be decreed beyond the said 1,000 marks.

Aberconwy, 9 November 1277

B = TNA: PRO, C 77/1 (Welsh Rolls), m. 1 (November 1277).
C = TNA: PRO, E 36/274 (Liber A), fo. 377v. s. xiii ex.
Pd. from C, *Foedera*, I. ii. 546; from C, *LW*, 117 (no. 208).
Cd., *CWR*, 159 (from B); *H*, no. 428.

Omnibus ad quos presentes littere pervenerint L.ᵃ filius Griff(ini) princeps Wall(ie) salutem in domino. Noverit universitas vestra quod nos damus magnifico principi et domino nostro domino Edwardo Dei gratia regi Angl(ie) illustri domino Hib(er)n(ie) et duci Aquit(anie) tenore presentium plenariam potestatem ordinandi quod Rotheric(us) frater noster habeat de denariis nostris usque ad summam mille marcarum vel citra pro portione que eidem debetur de omnibus terris et tenementis eundem, iure hereditario contingentibus ubicumque, ita quod nobis in dicta summa pecunia illa quam eidem Rotherico solvimus allocetur, ultra tamen dictas mille marcas[b] nichil in hac parte poterit ordinare, ratum habituri et gratum quicquid in [c‑]predicta forma[‑c] in premissis per dictum dominum nostrum regem fuerit ordinatum. In cuius [d‑]rei testimonium has litteras nostras fieri fecimus patentes.[‑d] Datum [e‑]apud Ab(er)conwey die martis proxima ante festum Sancti Martini anno domini m° c° lxx° septimo.[‑e]

[a] Luwel(inus) C. | [b] markas C. | [c‑c] forma predicta C. | [d‑d] etc. ut supra B. | [e‑e] ut supra B.

See note to no. 402 above.

406 Petition to the king

Petition to the king:

(1) on behalf of Hywel ap Rhys Gryg and his nephew Llywelyn, that their lands be restored to them;

(2) on behalf of various men of his who hold lands of Gruffudd ap Gwenwynwyn, namely Hywel ap Cadwgan, Einion ap Dafydd Sais, Madog ap Io[rwerth?] and Madog ap Rhirid, that their lands be restored to them according to the terms of the peace;

(3) on behalf of his men Iorwerth ab Ifor and Bleddyn ap Pyll, who [held lands?] in Perfeddwlad since the time of Dafydd ap Llywelyn, that their lands be restored according to the terms of the peace;

(4) seeking justice regarding the persons, arms and horses released by Llywelyn at the king's command, and the king promised to do justice regarding these if Llywelyn has imprisoned them for reasonable cause and not on account of the king;

(5) for the release of a man of Hywel ap Rhys Gryg imprisoned at Cardigan with letters of safe conduct from the king, whose release the king ordered again at Rhuddlan but he is still held in prison;

(6) that no support be granted to fugitive thieves from his lands at Cardigan who have committed homicides and thefts in Llywelyn's land and are received in the king's land;

(7) that, since certain men from the king's land have unjustly distrained upon the prince's men of Meirionnydd, the king may order justice to be done between them through the bailiff of Llanbadarn and so that the dispute is settled;

(8) on behalf of a certain man of his who has land in Cedewain, that the said land be restored to him according to the terms of the said peace.

[9 November 1277 × 14 January 1279]

A = TNA: PRO, SC 8/120, no. 6000. Endorsed: . . . ad Leulinu(m) nepotem etc. rex vult retinere terram suam tanquam sibi forisfactam ad (?) . . . [?satis]factionem princip' rex admittet ipsum ad pacem suam ita quod terra illa . . . imperpetuum (s. xiii²); approx. 170 × 149 mm.; the parchment is badly stained in places.

Cd., *CAP*, 202–3; *H*, no. 430.

Petit Lewelinus princeps Wall(ie) a domino suo rege

[i] pro Howelo filio Reso Cric et pro Lewelino nepote suo qui . . . sibi proditores extiterunt eo quod homagium sibi non fecerunt quod et . . . eis . . . secundum suam miseri‑cordiam[a] restitui faciat.[b]

[ii] Item petit pro quibusdam hominibus suis qui tenent terras de G(ri)ffino filio Wenn'

pro . . . dictos rex . . . duabus vicibus ut eis secundum formam pacis terre sue restitu . . . actum est pro litteris regalibus quorum nomina[c] hic sunt subscripta . . . Howelus filius Cadugaun, Enniau(n) filius David Seis, Madauc ab Io . . . Madauc filii Ririt.[d]

[iii] Item petit idem Lewel(inus) pro Iorw(er)t filio Iuor et Bledin filio Pill hominibus suis qui . . . apud y Bervetlat a tempore 'domini David filii Lewelini quidam principis . . . ut ille terre eisdem restituantur[e] secundum formam pacis predictam.

[iv] Item petit habere iusticiam de personis, equis et armis ab eo deliberatis mandato domini sui regis, et dominus rex promisit sibi fieri iusticiam 'de eisdem si rationabiliter ipsos incarceravit et non propter regem.

[v] Item petit deliberationem hominis Howeli filii Resi Cric qui incarceratus fuit apud Cardigan cum litteris domini regis de conductu, pro cuius deliberatione rex iterum mandavit de Rudlan set adhuc in carcere detinetur.[f]

[vi] Item petit dictus princeps quod non sustentantur quidam latrones profugiti apud Cardigan qui homicidia et furta perpetraverunt in terra dicti principis et receptantur in terra domini regis.[g]

[vii] Item petit dictus princeps quod quia quidem de terra domini regis[h] iniuste namiaverunt super homines dicti principis de Meirionnid, quod dominus rex precipiat fieri per ballivum suum de Llanpadern iusticiam equanimiter inter eosdem ut contentio dirimatur ubi pax regis debet haberi.[i]

[viii] Item petit pro quodam homine suo qui terram habet apud Kedeweig ut ei 'dictam terram[j] secundum dictam formam pacis restituatur.[k]

[a] *A* inserts eis *dotted underneath for expunction.* | [b] *followed by response in different hand:* Nichil fiat nisi de voluntate R[esi] filii M(er)ed[u]c quia antequam fecerit voluntatem suam . . . sicut . . . . | [c] *A inserts* ill *dotted underneath for expunction.* | [d] *followed by response in different hand:* Dicatur patri et filio quod fac' etc. alioquin rex fac' ad suam . . . . | [e] *corrected from* restituerantur *in* A. | [f] *response in different hand interlined in text of this petition:* Rex mittet ad inquirendum etc. quia ex tunc etc. P. (?) de Brogton'. | [g] *followed by response in different hand:* . . . tur quod non receptentur. | [h] *A inserts a word struck through.* | [i] *response in different hand interlined in text of this petition:* Mandetur sicut alias etc. | [j] *A inserts* tenet *struck through.* | [k] *followed by response in different hand:* Ynon ab David Seis. Rex faciat inquiri et extunc etc.

Cc. i–iii and viii show that the *terminus a quo* for this document is the Treaty of Aberconwy of 9 November 1277, which laid down that the lands of all those coming into the king's peace should be restored to them (no. 402, c. ix above). A *terminus ad quem* is probably provided by a memorandum concerning pleas held at Oswestry on 14 January 1279 which records that, at the king's order, Gruffudd ap Gwenwynwyn handed over the land of Trefolan in Deuddwr to Hywel ap Cadwgan (*WAR*, 263): if this was the same Hywel ap Cadwgan as that of c. ii above, the document pre-dates his restoration. Other evidence is consistent with this date range. Hywel ap Rhys Gryg and Llywelyn ap Rhys fled to Gwynedd in 1277 (*BT, Pen20Tr*, 118–19); Hywel sought the king's mercy probably in the same year, and was granted the king's protection on 7 January 1278 (no. 89 above; *CWR*, 161). Bleddyn ap Pyll (c. iii) was in Llywelyn's service on 7 May 1279 (*CR 1272–9*, 563–4). The assertion in c. v that Edward was still at Rhuddlan when he ordered the release of Hywel ap Rhys Gryg's man at Cardigan probably refers to the period up to 20 November 1277, when the king left Rhuddlan, though it could perhaps refer to Edward's next visit to Rhuddlan in September 1278 (cf. Smith, *Llywelyn*, 437, 448).

The responses to the petitions (textual notes *b, d, f, g, i, k*) are as follows: (1) Nothing may be done unless by the will of Rhys ap Maredudd; (2) Let the father and son be told that they (?)shall do etc. otherwise the king shall do . . . ; (5) The king will send to inquire etc. since then etc. P. (?) de Brogton'; (6) . . . that they may not be received; (7) Let it be ordered as previously etc.; (8) (?)Einion ap Dafydd Sais. The king shall make inquiry and then etc.

407 Letter patent concerning Edward I

Notification that Llywelyn grants on behalf of himself and his heirs to Edward I and his heirs all that belongs to him in Anglesey, which Llywelyn has by the king's grant, to be held after Llywelyn's death if he dies without heirs of his body; and grants that should he die without heirs of his body, all that belongs to him in Anglesey shall revert without any challenge or hindrance to the king and his heirs.

Aberconwy, 16 November 1277

B = TNA: PRO, C 77/1 (Welsh Rolls), m. 1 (November 1277).
C = TNA: PRO, E 36/274 (Liber A), fos 377v–378r. s. xiii ex.
Pd. from C, *Foedera*, I. ii. 548; from C, *LW*, 118 (no. 210).
Cd., *CWR*, 159 (from B); *H*, no. 429.

Omnibus Cristi fidelibus ad quos presentes littere pervenerint L. filius Griffini princeps Wall(ie) salutem in domino. Noverit universitas vestra nos concessise magnifico principi ac domino nostro karissimo domino Edwardo Dei gratia regi Angl(ie) illustri et heredibus suis quicquid ad nos pertinet vel pertinere poterit in Angles',[a] quam habemus ex concessione eiusdem domini regis, habendum post decessum nostrum, si contingat nos sine heredibus de corpore nostro procreandis decedere, et volumus et concedimus pro nobis et heredibus nostris aliis quod quicquid ad nos pertinent vel pertinere poterit in Angles',[a] si contigat nos sine heredibus de corpore nostro procreandis decedere, ad ipsum dominum regem et heredes suos integre, hereditarie et sine contradictione aliqua et impedimento[b] revertatur. In cuius rei testimonium presentibus sigillum nostrum fecimus apponi. Datum apud Aberconewey[c] die martis proxima post festum Sancti Martini anno domini m° cc° septuagesimo[d] septimo.

[a] Angleseya C. | [b] inpedimento C. | [c] Aberconwe C. | [d] lxx° C.

This grant confirmed the clause in the Treaty of Aberconwy whereby Llywelyn and the heirs of his body were allowed to hold Anglesey in return for an annual payment of 1,000 marks (no. 402, c. xi above) by making explicit that, if Llywelyn died without such heirs, Anglesey would escheat to the king. That this grant was issued a week after Llywelyn's ratification of the treaty and other grants relating to it may indicate that it was the result of further negotiations with Edward, who was quite possibly still at Rhuddlan on 16 November (Smith, *Llywelyn*, 437, n. 175).

*408 Edward I

Letter, complaining that, contrary to Welsh laws and customs, the king's justices of oyer and terminer in the Marches and Wales have had him summoned to appear at Oswestry to do and receive justice regarding certain lands in which he claims right. Further complaints concerning robberies by the men of Gruffudd ap Gwenwynwyn inflicted on Llywelyn after the conclusion of the peace; concerning men who, on account of the lands they hold of the king in Wales, withdraw their usual services to Llywelyn in respect of lands held of the prince; and concerning those who have fled from Llywelyn's distraint to the king's lands or power.

[Shortly before 4 June 1278]

Mention only, in a letter from Edward I to Llywelyn dated at Westminster, 4 June 1278 (*Foedera*, I. ii. 557–8; cd., *CWR*, 173–4; *H*, no. 493). The king replied that it was always usual, in his own time and that of his predecessors, and also according to Welsh customs, for pleas of lands that were, or ought to be, held in chief of the king in the Marches and Wales to be heard at certain days and places fixed by the justices appointed to hear and decide such pleas; so that Llywelyn's right should not be further delayed, the king has ordered certain of his subjects to hear Llywelyn's complaints concerning the lands mentioned in his letter, and to do justice to Llywelyn accordingly. The king also promised remedies for the other complaints raised by the prince.

*409 Edward I

Letter, complaining that the king sought to diminish Llywelyn's liberties in what he has written to Llywelyn concerning the bishop of Bangor, and maintaining that he has exacted from the abbot of Basingwerk only what he and his predecessors have been accustomed to receive. Llywelyn also refers to the article in the peace concerning the hearing and settling of pleas in the Marches and Wales, and urges the king not to believe sinister reports about him.

[Shortly before 14 July 1278]

Mention only, in a letter from Edward I to Llywelyn dated at Windsor, 14 July 1278 (*Foedera*, I. ii. 559–60; cd., *CWR*, 174–5; *H*, no. 494). The king replied that he did not seek to diminish Llywelyn's liberties with regard to the bishop of Bangor and that he was not displeased that Llywelyn exacted what was customary from the abbot of Basingwerk; in addition, since disputes in the Marches should be settled according to the laws of the Marches and those in Wales according to Welsh laws, Llywelyn should join the king's justices at the days and places appointed by them, and receive justice according to the aforesaid laws.

410 Walter de Hopton and his companions

Letter, asking, since Walter de Hopton and his companions will be at Oswestry this present Friday on the feast of St Mary Magdalene [22 July] to do justice regarding Llywelyn's demands and petitions, that they will say that his case regarding Welsh lands will be settled, which by Welsh law should be decided within the bounds of the disputed lands. Requests that they ratify in judgement his attorneys Adda ap Maredudd and Gruffudd Fychan, bearers of the present letter, or one of them, so that they can claim in the prince's name against Gruffudd ap

*Gwenwynwyn the lands of Arwystli together with lands attached to Meirionnydd, and proceed
in his petition according to Welsh laws and customs in the same way as if Llywelyn himself
were present.*

[Shortly before 22 July 1278; possibly Ardda, 21 July 1278]

B = TNA: PRO, JUST 1/1147, m. 9. s. xiii².
Pd. from B, *WAR*, 252.
Cd., *H*, no. 431.

L. princeps Wall(ie) etc. viro nobili et discreto domino W. de Hopton' et sociis suis assignatis etc. salutem. Quoniam datum est nobis intelligi quod vos eritis hac instanti die veneris
in instanti festo Beate Marie Magdal(ene) apud Albu(m) Mon(asterium) super demandis et
petitionibus nostris ibidem facturi iustitie complementum, ideo rogamus vos diligenter et
requirimus quatinus ex quo domino regi placuit ut dicitis ibidem causam nostram super
terris et tenementis Walensicis per vos tractari et terminari quod de iure tamen Walensico
infra limites terrarum litigiosarum deberet decidi. Ratificetis in iudicio personas attorna-
torum nostrorum, videlicet Ade filii M(er)educ et Griffini Vechan presentium exhibitorum
vel alterius illorum loco nostri ut possint nomine nostro petere terras de Arwystly una cum
terris appendiciis ad M(er)unnyh contra dominum Griffinu(m) filium Wenhunwyn ac in
ipsa nostra petitione procedere secundum iura et consuetudines Wall' eodem modo et
ordine ac si nos ipsi coram vobis personaliter staremus etc.

The letter was produced by Adda and Gruffudd at the hearing held at Oswestry on 22 July
1278 at the request of Gruffudd ap Gwenwynwyn, who inquired whether they were
authorized to represent Llywelyn; the hearing was then adjourned until 30 September
(*WAR*, 252). For another document probably prepared on behalf of Llywelyn for the
proceedings at Oswestry on 22 July see no. 603 below, a transcript dated at Ardda, a grange
of Aberconwy, on 21 July 1278; possibly the present letter was also drawn up on the same
occasion (the repetition of the adjective *instans* to describe both the Friday and the feast of
St Mary Magdalene is consistent with their being the day immediately after that on which
the letter was written). For the early stages of this legal case and the points of law at stake
see Lloyd, 'Edward the First's commission of enquiry', 6–8; Smith, *Llywelyn*, 470–4; Smith,
'England and Wales', esp. 200.

411 Edward I

*Letter, complaining that when Llywelyn with his huntsmen and young men were hunting in
Meirionnydd and a certain stag fled before his huntsmen and hounds across the river Dyfi into
the king's lands of Genau'r-glyn and was found there by the said huntsmen, the king's officers
and others came upon them and immediately summoned with cries and horns almost the whole
district, as they used to do in war. They seized Llywelyn's stag and mistreated his huntsmen,
something almost unheard of. Therefore Llywelyn prays the king to make full amends and
punish the said transgressors so that they shall not dare to behave like this again.*

Hafod-y-llan, 13 August [1278–81, quite possibly 1280]

A = TNA: PRO, SC 1/19, no. 27. Modern endorsement; approx. 163 × 63 mm.; mounted, foot cut
away.
Cd., *CAC*, 88–9; *H*, no. 432.

Excellenti domino suo domino E. Dei gracia regi Anglie, domino Hib(er)n(ie) et duci Aq(ui)tann(ie) devotus suus vasallus L. princeps Wall(ie), dominus Snaudon' salutem et paratam ad beneplacita voluntatem. Cum nos cum venatoribus et iuvenculis nostris alias eramus apud Meirionnyth in venando quidam cervus affugit ante venatores et brachetos nostros per amnem[a] de Dyui usque terras vestras de Genevyglynn et ibidem fuit inventus per dictos venatores nostros, ministeriales vestri de partibus illis et alii devenerunt ad eos et statim cum clamoribus et cornibus bannuerint ad se fere omnes de patria sicut `acrius faciebant in guerra. Nostrum equidem cervum abduxerunt a nostris venatoribus,[b] et eosdem male tractaverunt quod quidem inauditum[c] fuit penes. Unde regiam maiestatem vestram exoramus et requirimus cum affectu quatenus intuitu iusticie ac nostri si placet amore plenam emendam nobis fieri in premissis faciatur, et vobis vindictam si placet a dictis transgressoribus capiatur ne de cetero audeant taliter nos pertractare. Dat' apud Hauot y Llann xiii die augusti.

[a] amnum A. | [b] A *inserts* abduxerunt *struck through and also dotted underneath for expunction.* | [c] A *inserts* est *struck through and also dotted underneath for expunction.*

The reference to Genau'r-glyn as belonging to the king dates the document to after the Treaty of Aberconwy (*CAC*, 89). There is some evidence to indicate that it was written in 1280: Llywelyn complained to the king about problems in Meirionnydd in July 1280 (no. 419 below), and another letter of Llywelyn was dated at Hafod-y-llan on 28 August, probably in 1280 (*CAC*, 89; no. 421 below). Hafod-y-llan lay within Aberconwy Abbey's grange of Nanhwynan (Gresham, 'Aberconwy charter: further consideration', 332–8 and map facing 312).

*412 Letter concerning Edward I
Letter (patent?), declaring amongst other things that the prince would never maintain a man in his land against the king's will.

[Worcester, 13 October 1278]

Mention only, in *gravamina* submitted by Llywelyn to Archbishop Pecham, 21 × 31 October 1282 (no. 429, c. viii below). The prince alleged that Edward had forced him to hand over the letter on the morning of his wedding with Eleanor de Montfort, which took place at Worcester cathedral on the feast of the translation of St Edward (13 October) 1278, before mass, although no further demands should have been made on the prince beyond the articles agreed in the Treaty of Aberconwy (see further Smith, *Llywelyn*, 448–9).

413 Edward I
Letter, giving credence to Brother William, warden of Llan-faes Friary, whom he is sending to the king on secret business.

[*c*.1279 × March 1282]

A = TNA: PRO, SC 1/19, no. 38. Endorsed: . . . tur eo quod rex bene intellexit quod ita quod ille W. in . . . de . . . bus presencium . . . (s. xiii[2]; the parchment is stained and rubbed); approx. 170 × 36 mm.; mounted, foot cut away.
Cd., *CAC*, 96; *H*, no. 447.

Excellentissimo et karissimo domino suo domino E. Dei gratia regi Anglie, illustrissimo domino Hib(er)nie, duci Aquitann(ie) suus devotus L. princeps Wall(ie), dominus Snaudon' salutem et paratam ad beneplacita voluntatem. Quoniam dilectus in Cristo frater W. gardianus Lamaes nostre affectionis integritatem ad vestram excellenciam et ea que per vos feliciter cupimus expediri secretius novit, ideo eundem ad quedam vobis secreta succredimus proficua revelanda aliaque negocia expedienda. Ad vos duximus destinandum cui in hiis que dixerit indubitanter si placet credentes, voluntatem vestram per eundem significare velitis.

William de Merton, warden of the Franciscan friary of Llan-faes on Anglesey, is otherwise attested as acting as a messenger to Edward on Llywelyn's behalf in 1279, 1280 and 1281 or early 1282 (*CAC*, 62, 89–90, 99–100). The letter could belong to any of those years, or even be somewhat earlier, though it is likely to be earlier than the outbreak of war in March 1282 (*CAC*, 96).

414 Guncelin de Badlesmere, justice of Chester

Letter, stating that, since in the cause committed by the king to Guncelin and his companions regarding corn in Anglesey there is an obscure word, without whose explanation by the king Llywelyn will be unable to answer Guncelin if he comes to his land, Llywelyn requests him to postpone this business until the obscure word has been fully explained by the king. Llywelyn has sent to the king for this explanation and asks that Guncelin's companions be informed of this.

Aberffraw, Septuagesima Sunday [probably 29 January 1279]

B = TNA: PRO, SC 1/22, no. 96 (letter of Guncelin de Badlesmere to Robert Burnell, bishop of Bath and Wells). Probably spring 1279.
Cd., *CAC*, 111–12; *H*, no. 439.

L. princeps Wall(ie), dominus Snaudon' dilecto amico suo domino G. de Badelesm(er)e iusticiario Cestr(ie) salutem et omnem bonum. Quoniam in causa vobis commissa et sociis vestris a domino rege de negocio bladi in Angleseya quoddam verbum obscurum continetur sine cuius declaratione aperta per dominum regem non possemus vobis bono modo si ad partes nostras accederetis respondere, ideo vestram amicitiam quantum possimus requirimus quatinus pro amore nostro negotium istud differre velitis et diem assignatam ad hoc prolongare donec per dominum regem predictum verbum obscurum nobis plane declaretur, tantum super hoc faciendum quod vobis teneamus ad speciales gratiarum actiones quia pro prefati verbi declaratione ad dominum regem transmittimus et hoc significetur consociis vestris. Dat' apud Aberfrau dominica lxxᵃ.

On 11 June 1278 Edward ordered Bartholomew de Sully, Guncelin de Badlesmere and others to make and receive amends for corn and other goods unjustly carried away from the king's men in Anglesey (*CWR*, 167; cf. ibid., 162–3). However, the order seems to have been ineffective, for on 4 December 1278 the king ordered Guncelin, Brothers Llywelyn and Ifor of Bangor and Rhuddlan, Goronwy ap Heilin and Leonius son of Leonius to act without delay regarding the restitution of corn in Anglesey and other matters still to be done there for the king and his men, so that there should be no further delay (ibid., 177). It is likely that Llywelyn's letter was written in response to a renewed attempt by Guncelin to seek restitution of the corn prompted by the king's letter of December 1278, and can therefore be dated 29 January 1279. This likelihood is reinforced by Guncelin's letter to Robert Burnell, which cites Llywelyn's letter and seeks the bishop's advice lest he be blamed by the king for failing to carry out his business in Anglesey (*CAC*, 111–12).

415 Edward I

Letter, stating that, since the king has recently ordered Llywelyn by letter to send discreet and faithful men instructed in the matters concerning him and Gruffudd ap Gwenwynwyn to the next parliament, to be held on the quinzaine of Michaelmas next [14 October], to proceed in the king's presence according to the law called Hywel Dda, Llywelyn asks the king to do full justice to him or the attorneys he has sent according to that law without delay, recalling that the king had promised by the said letter that Llywelyn will be satisfied in this regard. Llywelyn has raised the said matter before the king and afterwards before his justices at great expense, and various messengers and attorneys sent to the king in various parts of England have laboured with regard to the same business, but so far he has received no fruit from their labour nor does he know by whose instigation he has been obstructed. Asks the king to act in such a manner that on account of a defect in the said law Llywelyn's rights are not harmed or delayed to his injury.

Abereiddon, 5 October [1279]

A = TNA: PRO, SC 1/19, no. 25. No endorsements; approx. 166 × 71 mm.; mounted, foot cut away.
Cd., *CAC*, 87–8; *H*, no. 441.

Illustrissimo viro et domino suo excellenti E. Dei gratia regi Angl(ie), domino Hybern(ie) et duci Aquitt(anie) suus devotus vasallus L. princeps Wall(ie), dominus Snaudon' salutem et paratam ad beneplacita voluntatem. Quam vobis per literas vestras nuper mandastis ut aliquos viros discretos et fideles nostros in negociis nos et dominum G(ri)ffin(um) filium Wenoen' tangentibus instructos ad proximum parliamentum vestrum quod erit in quindena Sancti Michael(is) proxima futura,[a] quem quidem terminum eidem G(ri)ffino prefixistis in premissis, mitteremus ad procedendum in presencia vestra secundum legem que dicitur Howelda, ideo rogamus vestram regiam maiestatem de qua plenam gerimus fiduciam diligenter et attente, quatenus si placet secundum legem predictam nobis seu nostris attornatis quos ad vestrum conspectum transmittimus plenam iusticiam sine more dispendio velitis exiberi, reducentes ad memoriam vos nobis per dictas litteras vestras promisisse quod nos erimus contenti per Dei gratiam in hac parte. Sciatis etiam quam ex quo nos ipsi coram vobis et post modum coram vestris iusticiariis dictum negocium promovimus non sine magnis sumptibus et tediis laboravimus diversique nostri nuncii et attornati ad vos quociens ad diversas partes Angl(ie) transmissi, super eodem negocio laborarunt, nec ex eorum labore fructum hucusque sentimus nec scimus quorum instinctu fuimus impediti. Tantum super premissis faciatis, si placet, quantum pre defectu dicte legis ius nostrum non ledatur nec differatur in nostrum dispendium et gravamen. Dat' apud Aberidon in crastino Beati Francisci.

[a] A *inserts* mitteremus *struck through.*

As Edwards noted (*CAC*, 88), the letter is datable to 1279, since it refers to a forthcoming parliament on 14 October, and Llywelyn was ordered to send representatives to parliament for 14 October 1279 (*CAC*, 62).

416 Edward I

Letter, thanking the king for transferring the case, first brought before the king's justices by Margaret of Bromfield against Gruffudd Fychan over the lands of Glyndyfrdwy in Edeirnion, to Llywelyn's court, since the said lands are clearly held of Llywelyn. Informs the king that he assigned Thursday, the vigil of Michaelmas [28 September] to Margaret to demand her right before Llywelyn and for Gruffudd to answer, and with the parties present Margaret showed certain charters by which she claimed the said lands. When Llywelyn pronounced that Margaret should prove the charters in judgement and provide Gruffudd with a copy of them, although urged to do this three times before Llywelyn's council, she utterly refused to do so, demanding that the said lands be delivered to her without legal cognizance. As Llywelyn saw that Margaret was poorly instructed, he assigned her another day and place to proceed in the said cause according to legal procedure. Therefore he beseeches the king, notwithstanding the false rumours of others, to uphold this process of Llywelyn's.

Abereiddon, 10 October [1279]

A = TNA: PRO, SC 1/19, no. 21. No endorsements; approx. 155 × 88 mm.; mounted, foot cut away.
Cd., *CAC*, 85–6; *H*, no. 444.

Excellenti domino suo E. Dei gratia illustri regi Angl(ie), domino Hybern(ie) ac duci Aquitt(anie) suus devotus vasallus L. princeps Wall(ie) salutem et paratam ad beneplacita voluntatem. Grates vestre dominationi referimus eo quod causam domine Margarete de Bromfild quam movit primo coram vestris iusticiariis super terris de Glynndyfyrdwy in Edernyavn ʿcontra Gruffud Vychan ᵃ ad nostram curiam declinastis cum dicte terre essent de nostro tenemento sicut clarum est. Unde vestre magnificencie significamus quod nos assignavimus diem iovis in vigiliis Beati Michael(is) dicte Margarete ad petendum coram nobis in iure ac prefato Grufud ad respondendum super premissis, et dictis partibus coram nobis competentibus predicta M. ostendit coram nobis quasdam cartas pretextu quarum dictas terras pettebat.ᵇ Et cum nos pronunciaremus ut prefata M. dictas cartas astrueret in iudicio et earum copiam dicto G. cum instancia hac petenti per nos faceret, licet primo et secundo ac tercio super hoc monita coram nostro consilio, tamen hec facere penitus denegavit petens sine iuris cognitione sibi dictas terras exhiberi. Hoc tamen quia vidimus dictam M. dicto die minus instructam assignavimus eidem M. alium diem et locum legittimum ad procedendum adhuc in dicta causa secundum iuris ordinem. Unde suplicamus vobis quatenus non obstante aliorum falso relatu teneatis pro certo hunc nostrum processum. Dat' apud Aberidon viᵒ idus octobris.ᶜ

ᵃ *interlined in the same hand as the rest of* A. | ᵇ *sic in* A. | ᶜ ocobris A.

As Edwards noted (*CAC*, 86), 28 September fell on a Thursday in 1273 and 1279; as the Treaty of Aberconwy stated that Gruffudd Fychan should hold Edeirnion of Llywelyn (no. 402, c. xiv above), the present letter is presumably later and thus datable to 1279 (*pace*

Powicke, *Henry III*, ii. 656, n. 2, which suggests a revised date of 1280). This is reinforced by the dating of a letter of Princess Eleanor at Abereiddon on 10 October 1279 (no. 434 below). Margaret was Llywelyn's sister and the widow of Madog ap Gruffudd of Bromfield (d. 1277). She had initiated her action by November 1277 and on 4 January 1278 Roger Mortimer and Walter de Hopton were ordered to do her justice (*WAR*, 246; *CWR*, 170–1). See also nos 418, 528, 530 below.

417 Edward I

Letter, thanking the king for granting their inheritance to Llywelyn's nephews, the sons of Madog Fychan of Bromfield, in the manner he has granted their uncles and kinsfolk [their inheritance]. However, Llywelyn has heard that the bishop of St Asaph and the justice of Chester, for some unknown reason, have given the whole lordship of their land to a certain bailiff of theirs from England, who disposes of their lands at his will to their prejudice. Llywelyn believes that this was done entirely without the king's knowledge, and therefore requests the king to order the said lords to remove the bailiff from his office, so that Llywelyn's nephews can administer their lands by their own bailiff as their predecessors have been accustomed in times past.

Penllyn, 15 October [1279]

A = TNA: PRO, SC 1/19, no. 34. Endorsed: Gentes patrie delinquerunt erga regem et noluerunt emendare pluries requisiti, (?)propter quod fuit terra capta in manu regis et cum emendaverint r(ex?) . . . amore ipsius, eo quod sunt nepotes sui, faciet eis inde curialitatem (s. xiii²); modern endorsement; approx. 174 mm. wide × 50 mm. deep on left, 76 mm. deep on right; mounted, foot cut away.
Cd., *CAC*, 93–4; *H*, no. 445.

Excellenti domino suo Edward(o) regi Anglie, domino Hib(er)nie ac duci Aquitt' suus in omnibus devotus L. princeps Wall(ie), dominus Snaudon' salutem et paratam ad beneplacita voluntatem. Excellencie vestre regraciamur de eo quod nostris nepotibus, filiis Madoci Vichan de Bromfeld', suam hereditatem concesistis in forma qua avunculis et consanguineis eorum circumquaque concesistis. Sed dominus episcopus Assaven(sis) et iusticiarius Cestr(ie), ut audivimus, nescimus quo motu, dedunt totum dominium terre dictorum filiorum regendum et tenendum cuidam eorum ballivo de Anglia, qui in preiudicium eorum ad suum libitum disponit et ordinat de suis terris in preiudicium eorumdem. Credimus tamen id factum esse penitus ʼvobis ignorantibus, unde rogamus vestram regiam maiestatem suplicantes, quatinus mandare velitis dictis dominis ut amoveant dictum ballivum a dicto officio quod exercet in terris dictorum nepotum nostrorum in eorum preiudicium et gravamen, ita si placet domine inclitissime quod dicti nepoti nostri possint per ballivum suum libere amministrare terras suas sicut antecessores eorum consueverunt[a] temporibus retroactis. Dat' apud Penlin xv° die octobris.

[a] A *inserts* ce *dotted underneath for expunction after* con *in* consueverunt.

As Edwards argued (*CAC*, 94), the letter appears to refer to the removal from office of Gruffudd ab Ifor as bailiff of Bromfield in July 1279, on account of his misbehaviour (*CWR*, 178); Gruffudd had been appointed as custodian of the lands for Madog Fychan's two sons in December 1277 (ibid., 161). This is consistent with the endorsement of the present letter, which states that the people of the district have done wrong against the king and though often requested to do so have refused to make amends, whence the land has been taken into the king's hand; when they have made amends, out of love of Llywelyn and because they are his nephews, the king will do them courtesy in the matter. See further Smith, *Llywelyn*, 457 and n. 33.

418 Edward I

Letter, relating that when formerly a lawsuit arose between Margaret, widow of Madog Fychan, lady of Bromfield and Gruffudd Fychan, lord of Iâl over lands in Glyndyfrdwy in Edeirnion, lands which fell to Llywelyn by the terms of the recent peace between him and the king and were later granted, with the king's permission, to Gruffudd Fychan by Llywelyn to be held of him in chief, and Margaret claimed the lands before Llywelyn in the presence of Gruffudd, who replied that he was ready to do justice to the said petition according to the judgement of Llywelyn's court; when Llywelyn enjoined upon Margaret by word of mouth to bring her claim against Gruffudd and that he was ready to show her justice according to the laws and customs of the disputed lands or according to the laws of charters if she had any from Llywelyn or his men, Margaret refused to act then before Llywelyn. She demanded that the lands be delivered to her, which by law and without the greatest prejudice to Gruffudd [?Llywelyn could not] do. Although he could have lawfully denied her a further hearing on this matter, Llywelyn assigned Margaret and Gruffudd another day and place to proceed before him, and the lawsuit having then begun and ... in Llywelyn's court Margaret fraudulently procured by false suggestion, to Llywelyn's prejudice [?the king's letter summoning] Gruffudd to Montgomery on the morrow of the day assigned to the parties by Llywelyn to answer concerning the said matter. Therefore Llywelyn humbly requests the king to order Walter de Hopton and his other justices not to proceed in the said cause to Llywelyn's prejudice ... of the said Margaret concerning her petition about the said lands belonging to Llywelyn's lordship ... to do justice. Llywelyn reminds the king that recently, in the parliament at London on the quinzaine of last Michaelmas [14 October], he informed the king about the process by a letter delivered by his messengers, and that no challenge was made to the process by the king or his council. Asks the king to inform Llywelyn and the justices of his will concerning the matter by the bearer of the present letter.

Ystumanner, 15 December [1279]

A = TNA: PRO, SC 1/19, no. 37. No endorsements; approx. 176 mm. wide at top, 186 mm. wide at bottom × 141 mm. deep; mounted, foot cut away. About one half of the bottom right-hand quarter of the document is badly stained and illegible.
Cd., *CAC*, 95–6; *H*, no. 442.

Viro magnifico ac domino suo excellenti Ed(wardo) Dei gratia illustri regi Angl(ie), domino Hybern(ie) ac duci Aquitt' suus devotus vasallus L. princeps Wall(ie), dominus Snaudon' salutem et paratam ad beneplacita voluntatem. Cum dudum lis orta fuerit inter Margareta(m) relictam Madoci Uychan dominam de Bromfild ex parte una et Griffinu(m) Uychan dominum de Ial ex altera super quibusdam terris et tenementis de Glynndeuerdwy in Ederniawn, que quidem terre per formam pacis inter vos et nos nuper initam in partem nostram cesserunt prout clarum est ac easdem postmodum per vestram licentiam concessimus dicto G(ri)ffino Uychan de nobis in capite tenendas; dictaque Margareta presente dicto G(ri)ffino et ad hoc vocato coram nobis `certo die et loco petiit sibi fieri iusticiam de dictis terris et tenementis, qui a nobis requisitus super hoc respondit se paratum secundum visum curie nostre dicte Margarete super memorata sua peticione in forma iuris satisfacere. Cumque nos viva voce iniunxerimus dicte M. ut in forma iuris ederet suam actionem contra dictum G. et quod parati essemus secundum leges et consuetudines ipsarum terrarum litigiosarum vel secundum iura cartarum si quas de nobis vel nostris habebat sibi iusticiam exibere, dicta M. noluit coram nobis tunc agere seu edere. Imo sine . . . cognitione petebat sibi dictas terras exiberi quod de iure et sine dicti Griffini maximo preiudicio facere . . . . Et nos nichilominus licet possimus contra dictam procedere de iure et sibi audientiam super hoc in posterum `denegare , assignavimus eidem M. et prefato G . . . . to diem et locum ceteros ad procedendum coram nobis in negotio memorato, et lite tunc inchoata ac pe . . . in nostra curia dicta M. fraudulenter et in preiudicium nostrum procuravit per falsam relationem seu suggestionem (?)vestra . . . (?)citandum dictum G. apud Monte(m) Gom(er)i in crastino diei ipsis partibus a nobis assignate super dicto responsurum. Unde rogamus magnificam vestram dominationem humiliter et attente quatinus iubeatis W. de Hopton' et ceteris vestris iusticiariis ne in nostrum preiudicium procedant in causa predicta . . . (?)fuimus dicte M. super dicta sua petitione de dictis terris nostrum merum dominium spectantibus iusticiam exhibere. Reducimus etiam vobis ad memoriam quod nuper in parliamento vestro London' celebrato in quindena Sancti Michael(is)[a] proximo preterita ipsum processum vobis per litteras nostras vobis a nunciis nostris ibidem porrectas signifi-cavimus, cui processui per vos seu vestrum consilium nusquam fuit contradictum. Voluntatem vestram nobis et dictis iusticiariis super premissis si placet per latorem presencium rescribatis. Dat' apud Estumanneir xv die decembris.

[a] Michal(is) A.

There are strong grounds for assigning this letter to 1279 (*pace* Smith, *Llywelyn*, 499 and n. 179, which suggests December 1278), since it refers to a later stage of the dispute between Margaret of Bromfield and Gruffudd Fychan than that described in no. 416 above, datable to 10 October 1279. It may even be, as Edwards suggested (*CAC*, 86), that no. 416 was the letter referred to as having been sent to the king at the Westminster parliament on the quinzaine of Michaelmas (14 October) informing him of the legal process. (It should also be noted that the reference to the parliament matches that in no. 415 above, where the 1279 parliament is meant.)

419 [Edward I]

Informs the king that the following complaint came to Llywelyn after the main letter in which this schedule is included was written. The king's men of Genau'r-glyn, namely Rhys ab Einion and his accomplices, having made no complaint to Llywelyn previously, have entered Llywelyn's land of Meirionnydd in broad daylight with an armed force and taken away much plunder, against the terms of the peace and the king's statutes; and Llywelyn's men from those parts, believing they would enjoy peace, went peacefully to the king's land to secure the peaceful recovery of their goods and to discover the reason for the raid. Then a worse error was committed than the former, for certain of Llywelyn's men were fatally wounded, others almost killed, and others seized by the aforesaid malefactors. Llywelyn therefore asks the king to order Bogo de Knovill, his seneschal in those parts, to ensure that the said goods be restored and amends made to Llywelyn and his men. But because justice requires it, if anyone from the king's lands wishes to demand anything from Llywelyn or his men, he will cause full justice to be done to them.

[5 January × -18 July 1280 (possibly 6 July 1280)]

A = TNA: PRO, SC 1/19, no. 26. Modern endorsement; approx. 163 × 56 mm.; mounted, foot cut away.
Cd., *CAC*, 88; *H*, no. 448.

Adhuc noveritis quod querela hic posita post confectionem magne litere in qua ista anima includitur ad nos devenit. Homines enim vestri de Genevglynn, videlicet Rys ab Enniaun et alii complices sui, nulla nobis querela seu occasione prius monstrata, terram nostram de Meirionnyd die lucente intraverunt cum manu armata et inde magnam predam ad terram suam deduxerunt, contra formam pacis et vestra statuta, ac homines nostri de partibus predictis credentes se bona pace gaudere ad rerum suarum repetit[ionem][a] pacificam modo pacifico terram vestram adiverunt, et ut scirent qua causa predicti invasores predicta bona rapuerant; tunc factus est error peior[b] priore, quia quidam e nostris fuerunt letaliter vulnerati, quidam fere occisi, quidam vero atachiati a malefactoribus antedictis. Quocirca petimus ut intuitu iusticie et pacis Bugon(i) de Kneuyll senescallo vestro de partibus illis mandare velitis ut predicta bona restituantur et emendam fieri faciat de tali facto nobis et nostris. `Sed quod iusticia exigit et requirit, si vero aliqui fuerint de partibus vestris qui aliquid petere voluerint a nobis vel a nostris, plenam eis iusticiam faciemus exiberi.

[a] *hole in parchment here in* A, *over which is a contraction mark.* | [b] *corrected in* A *from* prior.

The opening sentence shows that this document is not an independent letter but was enclosed as an addendum in another letter, referred to as *magna litera*. As Edwards noted (*CAC*, 88), the references to 'our land of Meirionnydd' and 'your men of Genau'r-glyn' and the description of Bogo de Knovill as 'your seneschal' leave no doubt that the sender was Llywelyn and the intended recipient Edward I. In addition, Edwards convincingly argued that a letter of Edward to Llywelyn of 18 July 1280 (*CAC*, 59–60) included a reply to the present complaint, providing a *terminus ad quem*. A *terminus a quo* is provided by Bogo de Knovill's appointment as justice of West Wales on 5 January 1280 (*CWR*, 182). It may be, indeed, that the *magna litera* which enclosed the present schedule was no. 420 below, datable to 6 July 1280, for Edward's letter of 18 July also deals with a major issue raised in that letter from Llywelyn, namely the dispute over shipwrecked goods claimed by Robert of Leicester. In other words, the fact that the king responded in the same letter both to this dispute and to the incident in Meirionnydd involving Rhys ab Einion may indicate that he had received complaints about both matters at the same time. Unfortunately, the physical evidence of the two documents is inconclusive. They are written in similar, but not identical, hands, and a comparison of the folds on the present document with those of no. 420 indicates that it could have fitted inside the latter.

420 Edward I

Letter, stating that ... the king's council in the last parliament in London declared that the king wished to keep the peace between them ... Llywelyn will have shown before the king through his attorneys his right to obtain Welsh law regarding the lands of Arwystli by sound reasons, as he believes, as well as by the attestations ... of prelates; he therefore humbly requests the king that ... the matter; he does not propose to trouble the king further as this now lies in the king's hands ... the prince and his men may not be burdened by further labours and expenses in this regard; for it seems that three years should suffice ... the terms of the peace may make clear to all, that the matter can be settled quickly unless it happen to be obstructed at the insti-gation of certain enemies ... was done regarding the parts which Llywelyn received from the wreck of Robert, merchant of Leicester, as Llywelyn informs the king by Brother William, warden of Llan-faes ... to whom the king told by word of mouth that he would not believe the merchant further in the matter of that wreck, since he obtained by false suggestion the king's letters to the justice of Chester about compelling Llywelyn to restore the goods seized from the wreck, and the king even intimated to Brother William in the last parliament at London, when the friar made ... concerning this matter, that he would tell the justice by word of mouth that no injury would be done to Llywelyn in this regard. Therefore Llywelyn is greatly surprised that recently the king ordered the said justice to distrain upon Llywelyn's men and goods wherever they be found until satisfaction be fully made to the said merchant for the said goods. As Llywelyn scarcely believes that the last order was issued with the king's knowledge, he prays the king to order the said justice of Chester to restore the goods of Llywelyn seized on that occasion and to desist from further distraint upon his men. Since no inquisition was ever made by the king's consent concerning this matter in Llywelyn's land, if the said merchant still wishes to say that his goods were not lost by wreck, he may come to Llywelyn's land or send a repre-sentative and Llywelyn will make diligent inquiry into the claim and full justice will be done to him. If the king wishes to allow none of these to be done, Llywelyn will humbly obey the king's will although it is contrary to his liberties.

Penrhos, 6 July [1280]

A = TNA: PRO, SC 1/19, no. 28. Modern endorsement; approx. 249 × 94 mm.; mounted, foot cut away. The right-hand top corner of the document is badly stained.
Cd., *CAC*, 89–90; *H*, no. 449.

Excellenti domino suo domino E. Dei gratia regi Angl(ie), domino Hib(er)n(ie) et duci Aquitann(ie) devotus vasallus suus L. princeps Wall(ie), dominus Snaudon' salutem et paratum ad beneplacita voluntatem. Quoniam nos . . . ximus consilium vestrum in parlia-mento ultimo London', declaravit vos formam pacis inter nos confirmatam et iuratam velle benedictus Deus et debere servare . . . ad . . . declaratum quam potuimus maiorem iuri nostri in optinenda lege Wallica de terris de Aruystili tam per rationes ut credimus eficaces quam per atestationes . . . prelatorum nuper per nostros atornatos coram vobis monstraverimus; ideo vestram excellenciam omni nisu quo possimus requirimus humiliter suplicantes quatinus . . . negocium; vos ulterius non proponimus fatigare ex quo etiam id nunc in manibus vestris pendet voluntatem vestram cum certo fine negocii nobis si placet . . . facie . . .[a] quod nos et nostri amplius laboribus et expensis in hac parte non gravemur, videtur enim quod tres anni debeant suficere ad (?)minus[b] articuli pacif . . . ipsa forma pacis omnibus elucidaret, quod ipsum negocium cito et prospere posset terminari nisi forte aliquorum instinctu adversancium contingeret impediri . . . facta fuit de partibus quas de wrecco recepimus de Rob(er)to mercatore de Leycestr', sicut per fratrem Will(elmu)m gardianum de Lannmaes vobis significamus . . . tistis, cui tunc fratri viva voce dixistis, quod illi mercatori fidem non adhiberetis ulterius in negocio de illo wrecco, ex quo per falsam suggestionem literas vestras ad iusticiarium Cestric procuravit super restitutione a nobis compellenda rerum de wrecco illo captarum; prefato etiam fratri Will(elm)o innuistis in ultimo parliamento vestro London' cum de hoc [(?)no]bis faceret . . .[c] quod prefato iusticiario vestro ore tenus diceretis quod nulla nobis molestia vel iniuria fieret in hac parte. Miramur igitur non modicum qualiter nuper iterato prefato iusticiario dedistis in mandatis ut super homines nostros et res in partibus quibuscumque inventis namiaret donec prefato mercatori de rebus prefatis omnino fieret satisfactum. Quocirca cum istud ultimum mandatum (?)vix credimus a vestra consciencia emanasse, vestram adhuc excellenciam humiliori affectu quo possumus exoramus quatinus sepedicto iusticiario vestro Cestr(ie) dare velitis in mandatis ut res nostras occasione prefata attachiatas nobis restituat et ab ulteriore namiatione super homines nostros desistat. Ex quo ut tactum est nulla unquam inquisitio per vestrum consensum de negocio isti in terra nostra transivit, si vero mercator prefatus adhuc velit dicere quod bona sua non fuerit amissa per wreccum, veniat ad partes nostras vel pro se mittat et causam discutiemus et inquiremus diligenter et sibi fiet iusticie complementum. Si autem nullum istorum velitis efectui mancipare, voluntati vestre quamquam fuerit contra nostras libertates humiliter parebimus. Dat' apud Pennros vi die iulii.

[a] *hole in parchment in* A. | [b] *five minims followed by contraction for* us A. | [c] *word illegible in* A.

As Edwards showed (*CAC*, 90), the letter may be assigned to 1280 because it refers to three years after the peace (that is, the Treaty of Aberconwy of 1277) and also because Llywelyn had been ordered to send his attorneys to discuss the Arwystli dispute at the parliament of May 1280 (*CAC*, 58–9). This dating is further reinforced if, as is very likely, Edward's letter of 18 July 1280, accepting that no inquest into the goods had been made by Llywelyn's order and ordering the justice of Chester to deliver the distrained goods to the prince (*CAC*, 59–60), was written in reply to the present letter. See also the note to no. 419 above and, for Robert of Leicester, no. 427 below.

421 Edward I

Letter, stating that after the king wrote to Bogo de Knovill, seneschal of South Wales, demanding that he seize full amends from Llywelyn or his men for trespasses, if any were committed, and amends would be made to Llywelyn by the king's men in the manner hitherto customary in those parts, for which Llywelyn sent his attorneys to do and receive justice, Bogo refused to settle the said matters in the said manner. He even wished to take all Llywelyn's men from those parts to appear before him wherever he might be and make satisfaction there and would not come to the accustomed places within those parts as was customary there, which Llywelyn believes to be against his liberty as well as against the customs of those parts. Therefore he humbly prays the king not to listen to anything to the contrary. For as God knows, Llywelyn was and will be ready to obey the king in all things and to make satisfaction to his men in the proposed manner, and first and foremost to make satisfaction to the king, and then let justice be done to Llywelyn. Requests the king to make his will known to Llywelyn and to the king's seneschal.

Hafod-y-llan, Tuesday after the feast of St Bartholomew [27 August 1280]

A = TNA: PRO, SC 1/19, no. 36. No endorsement; approx. 157 × 77 mm.; mounted, foot cut away. Cd., *CAC*, 95; *H*, no. 450.

Excellenti domino suo domino E. Dei gratia regi Angl(ie), domino Hib(er)n(ie) et duci Aquitann(ie) devotus suus vassallus L. princeps Wall(ie), dominus Snaudon' salutem et paratum ad beneplacita voluntatem. Noveritis quod postquam vos alias literatorie demandastis vestri gratia Bugon(i) de Qnovill', senescallo vestro Suthwall(ie), quod plenam emendam caperet a nobis vel a nostris de transgressionibus, si que fuerunt facte per nos, et nobis fieret talem emendam a vestris hominibus eo modo quo hactenus in partibus illis fuit usitatum, ad quod idem nostros attornatos transmisimus ad eundem facturam ibidem iusticiam et recepturam in primis, sed dominus Bugo nolebat dicta negocia modo predicto terminare. Volebat etiam omnes homines nostros de partibus illis abducere coram se ubicumque fieret et ibidem satisfacere nec accederet ad loca consueta in confiniis partium illarum prout ibidem fuit consuetum ac etiam usitatum, quod quidem credimus fieri contra nostram libertatem ac etiam contra consuetudines in illis partibus usitatis. Unde vestre excellencie suplicamus humiliter et devote quatinus si qua hiis contraria vestris auribus fuerint instillata, faciles aures si placet non tradatis. Nam ut Deus scit parati fuimus et erimus vobis in omnibus obedire vestrisque hominibus satisfacere modo proposito, primo etiam et principaliter vobis satisfacere et nobis post modum fieret iusticie complementum, voluntatem igitur vestram tam nobis quam vestro senescallo expresse in hac parte demandantes. Dat' apud Hauot y Llann die martis proxima post festum Beati Bartholomei.

The letter is datable to 1280 since Bogo de Knovill held office as justice of West Wales (that is, in south-west Wales), between 5 January 1280 and 8 June 1281 (*CAC*, 95, citing *CWR*, 182, and *CPR 1272–81*, 443). The feast of St Bartholomew (24 August) fell on a Saturday in 1280. Edward informed Llywelyn on 18 July 1280 that he had written to Bogo directing him to inquire into the trespass of Rhys ab Einion, in response to Llywelyn's complaint, quite possibly written on 6 July (*CAC*, 59–60; no. 419 and note above): this may have been the letter to Bogo referred to here. It should be noted, however, that Llywelyn had probably written to Edward a fortnight before the present letter, on 13 August 1280, with a further complaint against the king's men of Genau'r-glyn, within Bogo's area of jurisdiction (no. 411 above), and it is just possible that it was this complaint which prompted the king's letter to Bogo.

422 Edward I

Letter, stating that, although the king had written to Bogo de Knovill, justice of West Wales, ordering that the dispute between the king's men of Ceredigion and the prince's men of Meirionnydd [should be settled] in the manner accustomed in times past according to the nature of the pleas of both sides, nevertheless John de Knovill, the king's bailiff of Llanbadarn, contrary to the king's order and the long-established custom of those parts as well as Llywelyn's liberty, specifically ordered Llywelyn to send his men before him at Llanbadarn to do and receive justice there. Since this is precisely contrary to Llywelyn's liberty and the terms of the peace which Llywelyn always observes as much as in his power and wishes his men to observe, he humbly asks the king to order the said justice or his deputy in those parts to settle such matters within those lands in the manner which was always customary. Asks the king to inform Llywelyn of his will.

Tal-y-bont, Sunday after the feast of St Luke [20 October 1280]

A = TNA: PRO, SC 1/19, no. 33. Endorsed: Rex non debet cum homine suo habere Marchiam de hoc quod tangit regi. Sed rex mandat ballivo suo quod quodquod deberet fieri in Marchia, fiat ei apud Lampad' vel alibi in curia regis (s. xiii[2]); approx. 175 × 77 mm.; mounted, foot cut away. Cd., *CAC*, 93; *H*, no. 434.

Excellenti domino suo E. Dei gratia illustri regi Angl(ie), domino Hybern(ie) ac duci Aquitt' suus devotus in omnibus L. princeps Wallie, dominus Snaudon' salutem et paratam ad beneplacita voluntatem. Licet per litteras vestras nobis alias mandaveritis ac domino Bugoni de Knovill' iusticiario Westwallie ut contentio orta inter homines vestros de Keredig' et nostros de Meiron(n)yd, ut explicitur, in forma que consueta fuit temporibus retroactis secundum exigenciam querelarum utrobique,[a] verumptamen Ioh(ann)es de Knovill' ballivus vester de Lambadern contra vestrum mandatum ac longevam consue-tudinem partium `illarum necnon nostram libertatem mandavit nobis precise ut ad dictam contentionem sopiendam mitteremus homines nostros coram ipso apud Llanbadern iusticiam facturos et recepturos ibidem. Cum igitur hoc sit precise contra libertatem nostram ac contra pacis formam quam semper quantum in nobis est observamus et a nostris volumus observari, ideo rogamus excellenciam vestram humiliter et devote quatinus dare velitis in mandatis iusticiario vestro prefato vel eius vicem gerenti in partibus illis ut talia pacificentur in confinio terrarum illarum sicut semper fuit hactenus consuetum. Voluntatem vestram nobis super premissis si placet rescribatis. Dat' apud Talebont die dominica proxima post festum Beati Luce ewangeliste.

[a] *a verb such as* sopiatur *seems to have been omitted in this clause.*

The reference to Bogo de Knovill as justice of West Wales dates the letter to 1280 (see note to no. 421 above). Edwards's arguments regarding its date, based on a partial summary of the document (*CAC*, 93), should be disregarded. John de Knovill was Bogo's brother, and was granted the *gwestfa* of Llyswen (cmt. Anhuniog) by the king on 5 December 1280 (*WAR*, 66; Griffiths, *PW*, 12). The letter's place-date probably refers to the centre of the commote of Tal-y-bont, Meirionnydd, located near Llanegryn (see note to no. 391 above). The endorsement shows that the king rejected Llywelyn's argument, declaring that the king should not have a march with his man regarding what touches the king, and ordering his bailiff that whatever used to have to be done in the March should be done to Llywelyn at Llanbadarn or elsewhere in the king's court.

423 Heilin ap Tudur ab Ednyfed

Grant to Heilyn and his heirs of the land which Cadwgan ap Rhirid Goch held at Ystratygo and the lands which Richard ap Cadwaladr had in Nant Gwrtheyrn and Llithfaen, with all their appurtenances, just as the said Cadwgan and Richard held those lands, free of all secular obligation, in exchange for all the land which Llywelyn had given Heilin's father Tudur ab

Ednyfed at Pennant-lliw and in return for the fealty, homage and service of Heilin and his heirs to Llywelyn and his heirs. Sealing clause; witnesses.

Dolwyddelan, 7 August 1281

B = BL, MS Harley 696, fo. 126r (copy of proceedings at Caernarfon before the justice of North Wales, 1384). 1494.
Pd. from B, *Rec. Caern.*, 211.
Cd., Stephenson, *Governance*, 204; *H*, no. 155.

Universis Cristi fidelibus has litteras visuris vel audituris Lewelinus filius Griffini princeps Wall(ie), dominus Snaudon' salutem in domino sempiternam. Noverit universitas vestra nos dedisse et concessisse et hac presenti carta nostra confirmasse Heilyn filio Tud' ap Eden' et heredibus suis a nobis et heredibus nostris terram quam Cadugaun filius Ririt Gogh' habuit apud Ystratygo et terras quas Ricerd(us) filius Cadwaleder habuit apud Nant Gortheyrn' et Llythvaen in silvis in campis, in aquis in . . .ᵃ et in omnibus terminis et aisiamentis suis, prout dicti Cadugaun et Ricerd(us) dictas terras melius possiderunt pacifice, quiete et [ab]ᵃ omni exactione seculari libere pro tota terra quam dedissemus Tuder filio Edeneuet patri dicti Heilin apud Pennanlawe pro fidelitate, homagioᵇ et servitio suo ac heredum suorum nobis et nostris heredibus. Et ut hec nostra donatio robur firmitatis optineat imposterum has litteras sigilli nostri munimineᶜ fecimus roborari. Hiis testibus: Howelo filio Resi Gryc, Reso parvo filio Resi ap Maelgon', Lewelino filio Resi Vagh(a)n, priore de Insula Clannauc capellano nostro, Madoco filio magistri notario nostro et multis aliis. Datum apud Doluydelan anno domini millesimo ccº lxxxiº die iovis proxima ante festum Sancti Laur(entii).

ᵃ *lacuna in* B. | ᵇ homago B. | ᶜ minime B.

Heilin ap Tudur ab Ednyfed, a grandson of Ednyfed Fychan, continued his family's tradition of service to the princes of Gwynedd (Stephenson, *Governance*, 104 and n. 47, 131, 162 and n. 122, 219–21). Richard (Rhicert) ap Cadwaladr held the office of *rhaglaw* of Dinllaen in the first third of the thirteenth century and was probably a son of Cadwaladr ap Gruffudd ap Cynan (d. 1172) (ibid., 149–50). *Ystratygo*, Nant Gwrtheyrn and Llithfaen (about 1 mile south of Nant Gwrtheyrn at SH 356 432) were located in the commote of Dinllaen in Llŷn. Pennant-lliw was a township in the parish of Llanuwchllyn in the commote of Penllyn in which lay the site of Carndochan castle (SH 847 306), quite possibly built by Llywelyn after the acquisition of Pennant-lliw recorded in this charter (*Merioneth Lay Subsidy Roll*, ed. Williams-Jones, 7 and n. 5, 8, n. 6; *Rec. Caern.*, 211; Smith, 'Age of the princes', 30–1, 51).

424 Roger Mortimer

Quitclaim to Roger and his heirs of all Llywelyn's rights and claims in Cefnyraelwyd in Gwerthrynion, with its ancient boundaries, namely from the place where Nant Glascwm falls into the Wye up to the head of the same stream, and from the head of the Glascwm via Cefnffordd Cefnyraelwyd to the ditch where Gerwyn ap Cuhelyn was killed, and from the same ditch down to the Dulas, and from the Dulas to the Tylwch, and from the Tylwch up to Reydgorn where the Esgob falls into the Tylwch, and thus via the Esgob to the mouth of the

Gwernfron [(?)Nant y Saeson] with rights of lordship and all other appurtenances. Sealing clause.

Radnor, 9 October 1281

> B = BL, Harl. MS 1240 (Mortimer Cartulary), fo. 57r–v. s. xiv/xv.
> Pd. from B, Owen, *Catalogue*, ii. 230 (bounds only); from B, Smith, 'Middle March', 90.
> Cd., Stephenson, *Governance*, 204; *H*, no. 156.

Universis Cristi fidelibus presens scriptum visuris vel audituris Leuwelinus filius Griffini princeps Wall(ie) et dominus Swaudon' salutem in domino. Noverit universitas vestra nos remisisse et omnino quietum clamasse pro nobis et heredibus nostris dilecto consanguineo nostro domino Rog(er)o de Mortuo Mari et heredibus suis totum ius et clameum quod habemus vel habere poterimus in Keuenarayloyd in Warthreynon prout divise se habent et per fines antiquas, videlicet a loco illo ubi Nant Glascum cadit in Woyam usque ad capud eiusdem rivuli, et de Blaynglascum per Keuenforth Keuenarayloyd usque ad fossam[a] ubi occidebatur G(er)uyn ap Keuhelin, et de eadem fossa directe descendendo usque Diulas, et de Diulas usque Teleuh, et de Teleuh sursum usque Reydgorn ubi Escop' cadit in Teleuh, et sic per Escop usque Aberwenbran cum dominiis et aliis [fo. 57v] pertinentiis sine ullo retenemento. Nos autem dictam donationem, remissionem, quietam clamationem ratam et gratam imperpetuum habentes et hoc omnibus quorum interest notum esse volumus presentium tenore. In cuius rei testimonium presenti quiete clamantie sigillum nostrum duximus apponendum. Datum et actum apud Radenouere die Sancti Dionis(ii) anno gratie m° c° c° octogesimo primo regni regis Edwardi nono.

[a] fossa B.

Part of the boundary of Cefnyraelwyd (cf. Cefn yr Aelwyd, about $3\frac{1}{2}$ miles south-south-west of Llanidloes at SN 945 785) is traced in similar terms in Roger Mortimer's charter for Cwmhir Abbey in 1199 (Charles, 'Early charter', 68). The place-names in the boundary are discussed in ibid., 71, 74, n. 16. Cefnffordd Cefnyraelwyd was a ridgeway marking the frontier between Gwerthrynion and Arwystli (Smith, *Llywelyn*, 495). For the context and significance of this quitclaim, and of the agreement printed in no. 425 below, see ibid., 493–6.

425 Agreement with Roger Mortimer

A treaty of peace and indissoluble concord was made on 9 October 1281 between Llywelyn and Roger Mortimer, lord of Wigmore, each swearing on the Gospels to observe it in the following terms, namely that Llywelyn will ally with Roger against all mortals in all matters whenever asked and faithfully hold with him with all his power in time of war and of peace, saving his fealty in all to the king of England, his children and heirs; and Roger will ally similarly with Llywelyn and hold with him against all saving his fealty to the king of England, his children and heirs and Edmund, the king's brother. Both agree that whichever of them first violates the treaty shall be struck by anathema and interdict pronounced by the bishops of Hereford and St Asaph, following a single warning, so that he may not hear divine services and be held convicted of perjury and breach of faith until he shall satisfy God, the Church and the injured party. Llywelyn and Roger have had their seals attached to this chirograph.

Radnor, 9 October 1281

B = TNA: PRO, E 36/274 (Liber A), fo. 364v–365r. s. xiii ex.
Pd. from B, *LW*, 99–100 (no. 194).
Cd., *H*, no. 454.

In nomine patris amen. Anno domini mᵒ ccᵒ lxxx primo regni regis illustris Edwardi anno nono in festo Sancti Dionysii initum est fedus pacis et insolubilis concordie inter nobiles viros dominum Lewelinu(m) principem Wallie et dominum Snawdon' ex parte una, et dominum Rog(eru)m de Mortuo Mari dominum de Wygem' ex altera, sese sibi invicem et reciproce ad perpetue pacis observationem tactis et inspectis sacrosanctis ewangeliis iurando obligantes in forma sequente, videlicet quod dominus Lewelin(us) antedictus domino Rog(er)o predicto in omnibus negotiis quotiens, quando et ubi requisitus fuerit ab eodem contra omnes mortales adherebit et fideliter et constanter tenebit cum eodem cum toto posse suo tam tempore gwerre quam pacis, salva fidelitate in omnibus domino regi Angl(ie), liberis et heredibus suis debita et penitus illesa; et dominus Rog(er)us antedictus in simili forma dicto domino Lewelino adherebit et cum eo tenebit contra omnes salva et illesa fidelitate domino regi Angl(ie), liberis et heredibus suis et domino Edmu(n)do fratri domini regis Angl(ie) debita; volentes et concedentes ambo et eorum uterque quod qui prius huius pacifici [fo. 365r] federis vinculum presumpserit violare anathematis et interdicti vinculo per venerabiles patres Herefordens(em) et Assavens(em) episcopos unica monitione premissa percellatur, ita ut nec divina audire presumat et pro convicto super periurio et fidei violatore habeatur donec Deo et ecclesie et parti lese satifecerit de commissis. In cuius rei memoriam efficacem tam dictus dominus Lewelinus quam dominus Rog(er)us antedictus huic scripto in modo cyrographi confecto sigilla sua alternatim duxerunt apponenda. Datum et actum apud Rodenor' die et anno predictis.

See note to no. 424 above.

*426 Edward I
Letter, making requests, with reference to the Treaty of Aberconwy, concerning the plea between Llywelyn and Gruffudd ap Gwenwynwyn before Walter de Hopton and his fellow justices regarding the lands of Arwystli and between the Dyfi and Dulas.

[Shortly before 8 November 1281]

Mention only, in a letter from Edward I to Llywelyn, dated at Westminster, 8 November 1281 (*CWR*, 210–11; cd., *H*, no. 496). The king replied that he was willing to accede to Llywelyn's requests provided that no wrong was done to anyone else. After discussion with the justices he found that a writ was necessary for the plea to proceed further, or else Gruffudd would be wronged, and asked Llywelyn not to resent this. For the Arwystli dispute see nos 410 and 420 above.

427 Edward I
Letter, informing the king that when he recently issued orders via Llywelyn's messengers concerning a certain matter about which Llywelyn has frequently informed him, namely the honey and horses detained in Chester on account of a certain wreck which occurred in

Llywelyn's land before the war, that he ordered the justice of Chester to inform Llywelyn of the king's response, and when Llywelyn believed that he had a remedy for the matter, behold, the other day when he sent his messengers to Chester to make the necessary amends, they were vilely seized on the justice's orders and honey taken from them to the value of £4 sterling, at which Llywelyn is greatly surprised. If this was done on the sole authority of the justice it seems to Llywelyn that he acted unjustly; if with the king's assent at the instigation of certain persons, he is no less surprised since he has understood from the king's letters and responses that he would not allow Llywelyn to be burdened unjustly in this matter or in others. He therefore prays the king to order the said justice to release the goods thus detained. If he on whose account they were detained says that he was wronged in Llywelyn's land, let him come there and justice will be done to him according to the customs of Llywelyn's country. And so that the king will be more disposed to do this, Llywelyn informs him that when the king's attorneys, Bartholomew de Sully of good memory and Guncelin de Badlesmere, who came from the king to Llywelyn's land to receive hostages, he on whose account the goods were seized appeared before them and was told by them that he ought not to seek more than the customs of Llywelyn's country adjudged. Furthermore, when the matter between Llywelyn and Gruffudd ap Gwenwynwyn was begun and proceeded before the king's justices at Montgomery according to the laws of Wales on the day assigned for this, Llywelyn is greatly surprised how he was put in despair concerning the aforesaid matter by his messengers who were with the king at the last parliament in London, for when he believed that things were going better for him in that matter and in others he is oppressed more harshly day by day. Llywelyn prays the king to inform him of his will, with his hoped-for remedy in this regard, knowing for certain that he is more concerned with the disgrace to himself in this matter than with the profit he could ever have from that land.

Nefyn, 2 February [1282]

A = TNA: PRO, SC 1/19, no. 29. No endorsements; approx. 195 mm. wide × 130 mm. deep on left, 143 mm. deep on right; mounted, foot cut away.

Cd., *CAC*, 90–1; *H*, no. 455.

Excellenti domino suo domino Edwardo Dei gratia regi Agnlie,[a] domino Hibernie et duci Acquitann(ie) suus devotus Lewelinus princeps Wallie, dominus Snaudon' salutem et paratam ad beneplacita voluntatem. Cum nuper per nuncios nostros nobis dedistis in mandatis super quodam negocio pro quo quampluries vobis significavimus, videlicet de melle et de equis nostris apud Cestr(iam) detentis racione cuiusdam wrecci quondam ante gwerram in terra nostra facti, quod iusticiario Cestr(ie) mandaretis ut nobis super hoc responsum vestrum significaret, et cum inde credebamus habere remedium, ecce altera die cum nostros nuncios mitteremus apud Cestr(iam) pro necessariis emendis ibidem per mandatum prefati iusticiarii viliter atachiantur auferendo ab eis mell[a] nostrum usque ad valorem quatuor librarum sterelincorum de quo non modicum admiramur. Si enim hoc actum est sola prefati iusticiarii auctoritate nobis videtur quod minus iuste egit in hac parte, si vero per quorumque instinctum hoc per vestrum assensum processit non minus admiramur cum alias intellexerimus per vestras litteras et responsa quod nos in isto negocio nec in aliis non sustineretis iniuste agravari. Ideo vestre excellencie suplicamus, quatenus pro amore nostro predicto iusticiario mandare velitis si placet ut predicta bona taliter detenta faciat liberari. Si vero ille cuius occasione sunt detenta dicat sibi in aliquo iniuriatum fuisse in terra[b] nostra quandoque voluerit veniet ad nos et secundum consuetudines nostre patrie iusticia sibi fiet. Et ut meliorem voluntatem hoc faciendi habeatis, vobis notum sit quod quando nobiles viri vestri attornati bone memorie dominus Bartholomeus de Sulli et dominus Guncelinus de Badlesmer, qui ad nos venerant ex parte vestra pro obsidibus[c] recipiendis, ille cuius occasione bona prefata sunt detenta comparens ibidem coram prefatis attornatis ab eis habuit in reponso quod ultra non debuit petere quam consuetudines terre nostre iudicarent. Ad hec cum coram iusticiariis vestris apud Montem Gom(er)ii negocium inter nos et Gruffinu(m) filium Wenu(n)wyn secundum leges Wallie fuit inceptum et in eodem secundum easdem processum ibidem in die ad hoc[b] asignata, non sufficimus admirari qualiter per nuncios nostros qui vobiscum fuerunt in parliamento ultimo London' omnino positi fuimus in desperacione de negocio supradicto, cum enim credebamus melius nobiscum agi in prefato negocio et aliis semper durius de die in diem agravamur. Vobis igitur supplicamus ut voluntatem vestram in hac parte cum optato remedio significetis, scientes pro certo quod maius in hac parte oproprium[a] nostrum ponderamus quatenus lucrum quod unquam de terra illa habere possemus. Dat' apud Nevyn in purifficacione Beate Virgin(is). Valete.

[a] *sic in* A. | [b] *followed by a piece cut out of the parchment as a deletion in* A. | [c] obssidibus A.

As Edwards observed (*CAC*, 91), the letter belongs to either 1281 or 1282 for it refers to Bartholomew de Sully as 'of good memory', implying that he was dead; Bartholomew died by 29 June 1280 (*CIPM*, ii. 197). Edwards also noticed the similarity in content with Princess Eleanor's letter, also dated at Nefyn on 2 February, which is clearly datable to 1282 (no. 436 below). That both letters were written at the same time is almost certain: not only do they bear the same date, but they were written by the same scribe (note, for example, the spelling of *Anglia* in the address and the cutting of a piece from the parchment for deletion in both documents). The present letter is therefore datable to 1282. If so, the Westminster parliament referred to was that of October 1281, coinciding with the reopening of the Arwystli case at Montgomery on 6 October (*WAR*, 333–4); Edward's response to Llywelyn on 8 November 1281 shows a hardening of the king's attitude on the issue (*CWR*, 210–11). The visit to Gwynedd Uwch Conwy by Bartholomew de Sully and Guncelin de Badlesmere, justice of Chester to which the letter refers was made in order to obtain the surrender of ten hostages as required by the Treaty of Aberconwy (no. 402, c. xvi above); it must therefore have occurred after 9 November 1277 and before the death of Bartholomew de Sully in June 1280. For the case of Robert of Leicester's shipwrecked goods see also no. 420 above.

428 Archbishop Pecham

Letter, thanking the archbishop for the labour he has undertaken out of love for Llywelyn and his nation, especially since, so he informs Llywelyn, the archbishop came against the king's will. In response to his request that he come to the king's peace, Llywelyn is ready to do so as long as the king wishes to observe true peace towards him and his men. Furthermore, although Llywelyn was glad that the archbishop was staying in Wales, he will not be impeded from making peace by Llywelyn, who desires and hopes that peace be strengthened by the efforts of the archbishop more than of anyone else. Nor will be it be opportune to write to the pope on account of Llywelyn's obstinacy. Nor does Llywelyn spurn the archbishop's prayers and efforts but rather embraces them with all his heart. Nor is it necessary that the king raises his hand against Llywelyn, since he is ready to obey him, saving his rights and laws. And though the kingdom of England is specially subject to the Roman curia, *when the pope and* curia *hear how many wrongs have been inflicted on Llywelyn by the English, namely, that the peace first made was not observed towards him; then, the devastation and burning of churches and killing of ecclesiastical persons, that is, of male and female recluses and other religious, and of women and infants at the breast and in the womb, the burning of guest-houses and other religious buildings, homicides in cemeteries, churches and on altars and other acts of sacrilege horrible even to the ears of pagans, as set out more fully in other rolls Llywelyn is sending for the king's inspection – Llywelyn hopes that the archbishop will take pity on him, not to mention the* curia. *The kingdom of England will not be shaken by Llywelyn, while due peace is observed towards him. Who truly delights in the shedding of blood is clear from the facts: for the English have spared neither sex nor age nor feebleness and have shown no regard for any church or sacred place; the Welsh have not done such things. Moreover, since he greatly grieves if one held to ransom is killed, he does not protect the killer, who wanders in the woods like a thief. Concerning those who began the war at an unsuitable time, Llywelyn was ignorant of this until after the event; in any case those people assert that unless they had done that at that time, death and arrest threatened and they dared not remain in their homes nor go about unarmed, and they acted thus at that time on account of such fear. Concerning those things which he has truly done against God, Llywelyn will repent as a true Christian. Nor will it be on account of the Welsh that war continues, as long as the Welsh are unharmed as they should be; but it is right for them to defend themselves lest they be disinherited and killed. When injuries are considered to have arisen as a result, Llywelyn is ready to make amends for those committed by his side, so long as amends are made for injuries committed against him and others. He is likewise ready to make peace in the accustomed manner. However, when royal charters and treaties are not observed towards him, as they have so far not been observed, it is not possible to establish peace, nor when new and unheard-of exactions are imposed upon him and his men every day; he is sending in rolls the injuries inflicted upon him and agreements not observed according to the peace previously made. He has waged war because necessity compelled him. For he and all the Welsh were oppressed, despoiled and reduced to servitude by royal justices and bailiffs, contrary to the peace agreement and all justice, even more than if they were Saracens or Jews, as he has often informed the king. Nor has he had any amends, but always more ferocious and crueller justices and bailiffs were sent; and when these were sated by their unjust exactions, others were sent anew to despoil the people, to such an extent that the people preferred to die than to live. Nor is it necessary to gather a larger army or incite the spiritual power against Llywelyn while peace is kept towards him. The archbishop ought not to believe all the words of Llywelyn's enemies; just as they have oppressed and oppress him in deeds, so they defame him in words, alleging what they will. For they are always present with the archbishop, and Llywelyn is always absent; they oppress, Llywelyn is oppressed; and therefore let the archbishop not believe them in everything but rather examine the facts.*

[21 × 31 October 1282]

B = London, Lambeth Palace Library, Register of Archbishop Pecham, fo. 242r–v. s. xiii². Rubric: Responsiones Leuwelini principis ad articulos suprascriptos.

C = Winchester, Hampshire Record Office, A1/1 (Register of John of Pontoise), fo. 169r–v. s. xiii/xiv. Rubric: Litera L. Wall(ie) domino archiepiscopo Cant(uariensi) directa.

D = Oxford, All Souls College MS 182, fos 100v–101r. *c.*1413.

Pd. from B, Haddan and Stubbs, i. 543–5; from B and D, *Reg. Peckh.*, ii. 437–40; from C, *Reg. Pontissara*, ii. 638–40; from (?)D, Wynne, *History of Wales*, 365–7; from (?)Wynne, Warrington, *History of Wales*, 606–7; from *Reg. Peckh.*, Edwards, *Letters of a Peacemaker*, 25–6 (trans. only). Cd., *H*, no. 457.

Reverentissimo[a] patri in Cristo domino I. Dei gratia Cant(uariensi) archiepiscopo, totius Anglie primati suus humilis et devotus filius L. princeps Wallye,[b] dominus Snaudon'[c] salutem et filialem dilectionem[d] cum omnimoda reverentia, subiectione et honore. Sancte paternitati vestre pro labore vobis quasi intolerabile[e] quem assumpsistis ad presens pro dilectione quam erga nos et nostram nationem geritis, omni qua possumus devotione regratiantes [fo. 242v] vobis assurgimus, et eo amplius quod contra domini regis voluntatem venistis, prout nobis intimastis. Ceterum quod nos rogastis ut ad pacem domini regis veniamus, scire debet vestra sanctitas quod ad hoc prompti sumus dummodo idem dominus rex pacem debitam et veram nobis et nostris velit observare. Ad hec, licet[f] gauderemus de mora vestra facienda in Wallia, tamen per nos non eritis impediti quin pax fiat, quantum in nobis est, quam optamus per vestram industriam magis quam [g]alicuius alterius[g] roborari et speramus. Nec per Dei gratiam erit oportunum propter nostram pertinaciam aliquid scribere domino pape. Nec vestras paternas preces ac graves labores spernemus, sed[h] eas amplectimur omni cordis affectu, ut tenemur. Nec erit opus quod dominus rex aggrevet[i] contra nos manum, cum prompti simus ei[j] obedire, iuribus nostris et legibus nobis, ut premittitur, reservatis. Et licet regnum Anglie sit curie Romane specialiter subiectum et dilectum, tamen cum dominus papa necnon et curia Romana audierint quanta nobis per Anglicos mala sunt illata, videlicet quod pax prius formata non [k]fuit nobis[k] servata, nec pacta; deinde ecclesiarum[l] devastationes, combustiones et ecclesiasticarum personarum interfectiones, sacerdotum videlicet et inclusorum et inclusarum et aliarum religiosarum personarum passim, mulierum et infantium suggentium ubera et in utero[m] positarum; combustiones etiam hospitalium et aliarum domorum religiosarum; homicidiorum in cimiteriis, ecclesiis et[f] super altaria et aliorum sacrilegiorum et flagitiorum auditu etiam horribilium auditui paganorum; sicut expressius eadem in aliis rotulis conscripta vobis transmittimus inspicienda; speramus in primis quod vestra pia[f] et sancta paternitas clementer nobis compatietur necnon et curia supradicta. Nec per nos regnum Anglie vacillabit dum, ut premissum est, pax debita nobis fiat et servetur. Qui vero sanguinis effusione delectantur, manifestum est ex factis; nam Anglici hactenus nulli sexui vel etati seu langori pepercerunt,[n] nulli ecclesie vel loco sacro detulerunt; qualia vel consimilia Walen(ses)[o] non fecerunt. Super eo autem quod unus redemptus fuit interfectus, multum dolemus nec occisorem manutenemus, sed[h] in silvis uti[p] latro vagatur. De eo vero quod inceperunt guerram aliqui in tempore indebito, illud ignoravimus usque post factum; et[f] tamen ipsi asserunt quod nisi eo tempore hoc fecissent, mortes et captiones eis imminebant nec audebant in domibus residere nec nisi armati incedere; et sic pre timore tali tempore id fecerunt. De eis vero que fecimus contra Deum,[q] ut veri cristiani per Dei gratiam penitebimus. Nec erit ex parte nostra quod bellum continuetur dum[r] simus indempnes ut debemus; ne tamen exheredemur et passim occidamur, oportet[s] nos defendere ut valemus. Cum vero iniurie et dampna hinc inde considerentur et ponderentur, parati sumus emendare pro viribus, que ex parte nostra sunt commissa, dum de predictis iniuriis et dampnis nobis factis et aliis emenda nobis fiat. Et ad pacem firmandam et stabiliendam similiter[t] sumus prompti[u] debitis modis. Quoniam[v] tamen[f] regales carte et pacta inita [w-]nobis non[-w] servabantur,[x] sicut nec hucusque sunt observata, `non potest pax stabiliri; nec quando nove exactiones et inaudite contra nos et nostros omni die adinveniuntur;[y] vobis autem [z-]transmittimus in rotulis[-z] dampna illata et federa non s[ervata] [aa] secundum formam pacis prius factam.[ab] Quod vero guerravimus, quasi necessitas nos cogebat. Nam nos et omnes Walenses eramus adeo oppressi et subpeditati et[f] spoliati et in servitutem redacti per regales iusticiarios et ballivos, contra formam pacis et omnem iustitiam, amplius quam si Sarraceni essemus vel Iudei, sicut credimus et sepe denuntiavimus domino regi. Nec aliquam emendam habere potuimus, sed[h] semper mittebantur iusticiarii et ballivi ferociores et crudeliores; et quando illi erant saturati per suas iniustas exactiones, alii de novo mittebantur ad populum excoriandum, in tantum quod[f] populus mallebat mori quam vivere. Nec oportet militiam[ac] ampliorem convocare[ad] vel contra nos moveri sacerdotium,[ae] dum nobis fiat pax et servetur modis debitis, ut superius est expressum. Nec debetis, sancte pater, omnibus verbis credere nostrorum adversariorum; sicut enim nos factis oppresserunt et opprimunt, ita et verbis diffamant,[af] nobis imponentes quod[ag] volunt. Ipsi enim sepe vobis sunt presentes, et nos absentes; ipsi opprimentes,[ah] nos oppressi; et ideo propter Deum fidem eis in omnibus non exhibeatis, sed[h] facta potius examinetis. Valeat sanctitas vestra ad regimen ecclesie per tempora longa.[ai]

[a] [R]everendissimo D. | [b] Wall' C; Wallie D. | [c] Snoudon C. | [d] devotionem C. | [e] intollerabile CD. [f] *omitted* C. | [g-g] alterius alicuius C. | [h] set CD. | [i] aggravet CD. | [j] sibi C. | [k-k] nobis fuit C. [l] *omitted* D. | [m] veru CD. | [n] perceperunt C. | [o] Wallenses CD. | [p] velud C. | [q] dominum D. | [r] C *inserts* tamen. | [s] oportes B. | [t] simliter B. | [u] parati C. | [v] Quando D. | [w-w] non nobis C. [x] servantur CD. | [y] adveniunt D. | [z-z] in rotulis transmittimus nobis C. | [aa] *letters supplied from* CD. [ab] formatam C. | [ac] malitiam C. | [ad] convocari C. | [ae] sacdocium B. | [af] defamant C. | [ag] que CD. [ah] C *inserts* et. | [ai] longiora C.

This letter is clearly a response to the seventeen articles taken by John of Wales from Archbishop Pecham to Llywelyn on or shortly after 21 October 1282 (*Reg. Peckh.*, ii. 435–7; see further Douie, *Archbishop Pecham*, 238–40, 247; Smith, *Llywelyn*, 531–4). Pecham issued a safe conduct to John of Wales on 21 October, and the king issued a safe conduct to him for fifteen days on 24 October (*Reg. Peckh.*, ii. 421–2; *CWR*, 243). Llywelyn's letter and associated *gravamina* (no. 429 below) had been received by Pecham by the time of the first of his two meetings with Edward I to discuss Welsh matters, a meeting that took place at Rhuddlan no later than 31 October (Smith, *Llywelyn*, 534, n. 96, citing *Reg. Peckh.*, ii. 426, 465; Haddan and Stubbs, i. 540). The letter and *gravamina* are therefore datable to between 21 and 31 October 1282. For other *gravamina* sent to Pecham on the rolls referred to here see *Reg. Peckh.*, ii. 447–51, 454–63, and nos 77, 101–2 above and nos 454, 538 below.

429 Archbishop Pecham (grievances)

(1) Though it is said in the peace treaty that 'If Llywelyn makes a claim to lands occupied by others than the king outside the Four Cantrefs, the king will give him justice according to the laws and customs of the districts in which those lands lie' [no. 402, c. ii above], this article was not observed in respect of the lands of Arwystli and between the rivers Dyfi and Dulas. Although Llywelyn claimed the said lands before the king at Rhuddlan, and the king conceded that the cause might be examined according to the laws and customs of Wales, and advocates of the parties and the judges commonly called ynaid *were brought before the king, in order to*

judge concerning the said lands according to the Welsh laws, with the defendant appearing and responding, so that the matter should be finally settled on the day assigned by the king to the parties at Gloucester; although the said case had been examined in various places before the justices, and the lands were in pura Wallia and judgement had never been made concerning them other than by the Welsh laws, nor could or should the king have postponed the day, unless by the Welsh laws, nevertheless he postponed it of his own will contrary to those laws, and finally Llywelyn was summoned to various places to which he ought not to have been summoned, nor could he obtain justice unless by the laws of England, contrary to the said article. And this was done before the justices at Montgomery. When the parties had been established and confirmed in the judgement and the day given for hearing the sentence, the justices postponed the day contrary to the said laws. Then at London after many labours and expenses the king himself denied Llywelyn justice, unless he was willing to submit to judgement according to the laws of England in the said cause.

(2) 'And all trespasses and injuries arising therefrom will be totally remitted up to the present day' [no. 402, c. vii]. This article was not observed since Reginald de Grey, as soon as he was made justice, prosecuted innumerable claims against the men of Tegeingl and Rhos concerning trespasses done in the time of King Henry and Llywelyn when they possessed authority in those districts, whence the said men were much afraid and did not dare to remain in their homes.

(3) 'Rhys Fychan ap Rhys ap Maelgwn together with the land he now holds' etc. [no. 402, c. viii]. After the peace was made he was despoiled of the land of Genau'r-glyn which he then held with its men and livestock.

(4) 'The king grants that all holding lands in the Four Cantrefs and in the other aforesaid lands which the king retains may hold them as freely and fully as they held them before the war, with the same liberties and customs' etc. [no. 402, c. xii]. Against this article the said Reginald introduced various new customs, contrary to the aforesaid peace.

(5) 'Disputes between the prince and others shall be settled according to the laws of the March concerning matters in the March and according to the laws of Wales concerning those in Wales.' [no. 402, c. xiii] Contrary to this article the king sent justices to Anglesey, who presumed to judge Llywelyn's men there, imposing a jury upon them against the laws of Wales, although this or anything like it had never been done there in times past, imprisoning some, exiling others, even though the prince was ready to do justice concerning those men to all who were complaining about them.

(6) Although it is contained in the peace treaty that 'Gruffudd Fychan shall do homage to the king for his lands in Iâl and to Llywelyn for his lands in Edeirnion' [no. 402, c. xiv], the king's justices established the lady of Maelor throughout Edeirnion, the cognizance of whose cause belonged to Llywelyn and not to those justices, and yet the prince tolerated this for the sake of peace, since he was ready to show justice to the lady.

(7) 'Although the prince has submitted to the king's will, the king concedes that his will shall not extend beyond the said articles in any respect.' Contrary to this article gold was demanded for the queen, although gold had never been demanded thus from the Welsh in the time of King Henry or of any other king of England. Llywelyn paid this gold for the sake of peace, though nothing was mentioned of it in the peace treaty. In addition gold – namely 2,500 marks – was demanded for the queen mother, King Edward's mother, for the peace made in the time of King Henry, though nothing was said of this then. And unless the said marks were paid, the said Reginald threatened to seize any goods of Llywelyn he could find in the king's lands, and seize and ransom his men, until he had the full sum.

(8) Although the king had invited the prince to his feast at Worcester with flattering words, promising that he would then give him his kinswoman in marriage and enrich him with many honours, nevertheless on the day of the wedding, before mass, the king requested the prince to sign a letter containing amongst other things that the prince would never maintain a man in his land against the king's will, which could have led to all the prince's faithful men being taken away from him. Compelled by fear the prince handed over the letter with his seal, even though the peace treaty says that nothing ought to be demanded from him beyond what is contained in it.

(9) Although, according to the treaty, customs are confirmed to the prince which had been in use since ancient times, and the prince and his predecessors were accustomed by long-established custom to receive the goods of shipwrecks in their lands, the justice of Chester distrained upon the prince for goods he received from wrecks before the war, contrary to the peace. As distraint the justice took 15 pounds of honey and many horses belonging to the prince, and imprisoned his men. Moreover he seized skiffs from Llan-faes which came to Liverpool with merchandise and only released them when he had received as much money for them as he wished.

(10) When certain men of Genau'r-glyn had taken goods from others in Genau'r-glyn, although they were in the prince's lordship of Meirionnydd, the king's men of Llanbadarn took prey from Meirionnydd, and when the prince's men went to discover why they had seized the prey, they killed one, wounded others and imprisoned some. And though the peace says that amends for offences committed in the March should be made in the March, the said king's men refused to hear the prince's men anywhere but at the castle of Llanbadarn. Up to now they have been able to have no justice in this matter.

The king has wronged the prince and his men in these articles and in many others. And though the prince had frequently asked the king that the aforesaid peace should be observed towards him and his men, it was not observed at all, but every day the justices and bailiffs of the king in those parts heaped injuries upon injuries. Therefore no one should be surprised if the prince gave his assent to those who began to wage war, when the faith which Robert Tibetot swore to him in the king's name was not observed, and especially since the prince had been forewarned by faithful persons that he would be arrested by the king as soon as he arrived at Rhuddlan, and would have been captured if the king had gone there after Christmas as he had proposed. Asks the archbishop to give consideration to these and other, almost innumerable, grievances, and to labour fruitfully for the peace of both peoples for the salvation of the souls of the king, the prince and many others.

[21 × 31 October 1282]

B = London, Lambeth Palace Library, Register of Archbishop Pecham, fo. 234r–v. s. xiii[2].
C = Oxford, All Souls College MS 182, fos 101v–103r. *c*.1413.
Pd. from B and C, *Reg. Peckh.*, ii. 440–5; from (?)C, Wynne, *History of Wales*, 367–71; from (?)Wynne, Warrington, *History of Wales*, 607–11.
Cd., *H*, no. 458.

[i] Primus articulus est talis. Cum in forma pacis sic contineatur ut sequitur: 'Si vero L. ius vendicaverit in aliquibus terris, quas alii preter dictum dominum regem occupaverunt extra quatuor cantredos[a] predictos, plenariam iustitiam sibi exhibebit prefatus dominus rex secundum leges et consuetudines partium illarum in quibus terre ille consistunt.' Qui articulus non fuit observatus super terris Aroystly[b] et inter Deuy et Dyblas[c] fluviorum, pro

eo quod cum dictus L. dictas terras vendicasset coram domino rege apud Ruthelan,[d] et rex sibi concessisset causam examinare secundum leges et consuetudines Wallie, ac advocati partium fuissent introducti, et iudices qui vulgariter dicuntur *eneyd* fuissent introducti coram rege, ut iudicarent de dictis terris secundum leges Wallicanas, parte rea comparente et respondente, adeo quod eo die deberet finaliter terminari ex prefixione domini regis, qui apud Glou(er)niam existens diem predictum partibus assignavit, licet sepius in diversis locis coram iusticiariis fuisset dicta causa examinata, et terre ipse essent in pura Wallia nec umquam iudicatum fuit super eis nisi secundum leges Wallicanas, nec dominus rex posset vel deberet prorogare, nisi secundum leges Wallie, diem tamen ipsum motu proprio prorogavit et contra leges antedictas, et adultimo fuit vocatus ad loca varia ad que non debuit evocari, nec iustitiam obtinere potuit nisi secundum leges Anglie, contra illud quod in dicto articulo continetur. Et idem factum fuit coram iusticiariis apud Mont(em) Gom(er)y. Cum partes essent in iudicio constitute et firmate et dies datus ad sententiam audiendam, diem prorogaverunt contra leges memoratas. Demum apud Lond'[e] post multos labores et expensas varias, rex ipse iustitiam sibi denegavit, nisi vellet secundum leges Anglie subire iudicium in causa memorata.

[ii] Secundus articulus non servatus est talis: 'Et omnes transgressiones, iniurie et excessus hinc inde facte penitus remittuntur usque in diem hodiernum.' Iste articulus non fuit observatus quia dominus Reginald(us) de Grey, statim cum fuit factus iusticiarius, movit varias questiones et innumerabiles contra homines de Tegeyngl et Ros super transgressis que facte fuerunt in tempore domini [f]regis Henr(ici)[-f] et dicti domini L., dum dominium in partibus illis obtinebant, unde dicti homines multum timentes non audebant in suis domibus permanere.

[iii] Tertius articulus ubi dicitur 'Rys Uachan[g] filius Resi filii Maylgun, cum terra quam nunc tenet' etc. Post pacem initam fuit spoliatus de terra de Geneurglyn[h] quam tunc tenebat cum hominibus et averiis eorundem.

[iv] Quartus articulus. 'Item concedit dominus rex quod omnes [i-]tenentes terras[-i] in Quatuor Cantredis et in aliis terris quas dominus rex retinet in manu sua, teneant eas adeo libere et plenarie sicut ante guerram tenere consueverunt, et eisdem libertatibus et consuetudinibus gaudeant quibus prius gaudere solebant' etc. Contra istum articulum dictus Reginald(us) consuetudines varias de novo introduxit, et hoc contra pacis formam supradictam.

[v] Item quintus articulus: 'Controversie et contentiones mote vel movende inter principem et quoscumque terminabuntur et decidentur secundum leges Marchie de hiis que emergunt in Marchia, et secundum leges Wallie[j] de rebus contentiosis que in Wallia oriuntur.' Contra istum articulum venit dominus rex mittendo iusticiarios usque ad Mon, qui ibidem iudicare presumpserunt homines dicti L., vinetam ponendo super illos, contra leges Wallie, cum hoc vel aliud simile nunquam factum fuisset ibidem temporibus retroactis, quosdam incarcerando, alios in exilium mittendo, cum ipse idem princeps paratus esset de eisdem hominibus suis exhibere iustitie complementum omnibus querelantibus de eisdem.

[vi] Item sextus articulus. Item cum sit contentum in dicta pacis forma quod 'Griffin(us) Vachan[k] homagium faceret domino regi de terra de Yal et principi de terra de Edeyrnabu',[l] iusticiarii domini regis dominam de Maylaur introduxerunt in totam terram predictam de Edeyrnab',[m] cuius cognitio cause ad principem pertinebat simpliciter, et non ad illos iusticiarios, et tamen pro bono pacis princeps hoc tolerabat, cum ipse princeps paratus esset eidem domine super hoc iustitiam exhibere.

[vii] Septimus articulus, ubi dicitur: 'Et licet idem princeps se nostre, ut dictum est, supposuerit voluntati, nos tamen concedimus et volumus quod voluntas nostra huiusmodi ultra dictos articulos se in aliquo non extendat.'[n] Contra istum [fo. 243v] articulum exigebatur aurum ad opus regine, in qualibet solutione facta regi, cum huiusmodi aurum nunquam fuit exactum a Walen(sibus) nec in tempore domini Henrici vel alicuius alterius regis Anglie. Quod aurum exsolvit pro bono pacis, cum tamen nihil[o] de hoc tactum fuit in forma pacis vel excogitatum. Et nunc insuper exigitur a principe aurum ad opus regine senioris, matris videlicet domini E. nunc regis Angl(ie), pro pace facta in tempore domini H. regis Angl(ie), cum nihil de hoc tunc fuerat dictum vel quoquomodo excogitatum, videlicet duo milia marcarum et dimidiam. Et nisi dicte marce solverentur, minabatur [p]dictus Regin(aldus)[-p] quod bona eiusdem L. occuparet que invenire poterat in dominio regis, et homines suos capere[q] et venundare, quousque dictam summam haberet ad plenum.

[viii] Item, cum invitasset dominus rex dictum principem ad festum suum[r] Wygorn(ie) verbis blandissimis, promittendo ei quod `sibi tunc consanguineam suam daret in uxorem et multis ditaret honoribus, nihilominus[s] cum illuc venisset, in die desponsationis ante missam, petiit dominus rex unam literam consignari a principe, continentem inter cetera quod idem princeps nullum omnino hominem in terra sua teneret contra regis voluntatem vel manuteneret, ex quo posset contingere quod omnes fideles principis[t] eo ammoverentur. Quam quidem literam sibi sigillatam tradidit, compulsus per metum, qui cadere potest[u] in constantem virum, cum tamen in forma pacis ut premissum est contineatur quod nihil[o] ab eo deberet exigi ultra quod in dicta forma continetur.

[ix] Item, cum secundum eandem pacis formam consuetudines eidem principi confirmentur, quibus usus fuerat ab antiquo, ac idem princeps et antecessores sui ex consuetudine diutina et obtenta bona de naufragiis in terris suis provenientia consueverant recipere, et in suos usus convertere ad libitum, iusticiarius Cestr(ie) namium recepit super principem pro bonis que recepit de naufragiis ante guerram, contra dictam pacis formam, per quam omnia hinc inde erant remissa, et contra consuetudines antedictas. Dato etiam quod hoc esset forefactum, namium recepit tale, videlicet quindecim libratas mellis et plures equos, ac homines suos incarceravit, et hoc de propriis bonis principis antedicti. Preterea accepit schafas de Baneweys[v] que venerant apud Liuerepol cum mercandiis per mercatores, et eas nunquam deliberavit donec pecuniam pro eis acceperat, quantum volebat.

[x] Item, cum quidam homines de Geneuirglyn quedam bona abstulissent ab aliis vicinis suis de Geneuirglyn, dum essent in dominio principis de Meyon',[w] homines regis de Lampadarn predam fecerunt et acceperunt de terra principis de Meyron',[w] et cum homines sui venissent illuc ad querendum quare dictam predam receperant, unum de eis interfecerunt et alios vulneraverunt et quosdam incarceraverunt. Et cum in dicta pacis forma contineatur quod in Marchia deberent emendari que in Marchia committebantur, tamen dicti homines regis homines principis audire noluerunt alibi quam in castro de Lampadar(n),[x] et hoc contra pacis formam antedictam. Super quo hactenus nullam iustitiam habere potuerunt.

In istis articulis iniuriatus dominus rex principi et suis et etiam in multis aliis. Et licet princeps tam per se quam per suos petivisset sepius a domino rege, quod pacis formam supradictam erga se et suos faceret observari, in nullo tamen extitit observata, sed[y] omni die de novo iusticiarii et ballivi domini regis in partibus illis iniurias iniuriis et varia gravamina cumularunt. Propter quod mirum non debet videri alicui, si princeps prefatus assensum prestitit illis qui gwerrare[z] ceperunt, cum in hiis fides quam in anima domini regis sibi dominus Rob(ertu)s Tipetot iuraverat in nullo servabatur, et maxime et principaliter cum princeps fuisset premunitus a personis fidedignis quod princeps foret a rege capiendus in suo primo accessu apud Ruthelan,[d] et etiam fuisset captus si rex illuc accessisset post Natale, sicut proposuerat.

Hec gravamina et alia quasi innumerabilia, sancte pater, considerantes, nobis affectu pater[n]o compatiamini, et pro salute anime domini regis et nostre et etiam multorum aliorum ad pacem bonam utriusque populi laboretis fructuose.

[a] tancredos BC. | [b] Awystley C. | [c] Diblas C. | [d] Ruthlan C. | [e] London' C. | [f-f] H. regis C. [g] Nachan C. | [h] Geneuerglyn C. | [i-i] terras tenentes C. | [j] Gallie C. | [k] Vathan BC. | [l] Edeyrnahu C. [m] Ed' C. | [n] extendant C. | [o] nichil C. | [p-p] dicta regina C. | [q] coopere C. | [r] *omitted* C. [s] nichilominus C. | [t] C *inserts* ab. | [u] posset C. | [v] Banweys C. | [w] Merylon C. | [x] Lampadarn' C. [y] set C. | [z] guerrare C.

See note to no. 428 above and, for discussion of the *gravamina*, Smith, *Llywelyn*, 499–502, 533–4. The citations from the Treaty of Aberconwy in cc. i–vii appear to derive from the royal ratification and recitation kept by Llywelyn (rather than from a copy of the prince's own ratification in no. 402 above), as they bear some resemblances to the text of Edward's ratification enrolled in TNA: PRO, C 77/1, m. 2 (pd., *Rotulus Wallie*, 3–4). In particular, the latter text provides the only extant source containing the article cited in c. vii, an article which is lacking not only (of course) in Llywelyn's ratification but also in the copy of Edward's ratification in TNA: PRO, E 36/274 (Liber A), fos 378r–379v (pd. in part, *LW*, 157), an omission noticed in Smith, *Llywelyn*, 501, n. 184.

430 Archbishop Pecham

Letter, informing the archbishop that, in accordance with his advice, Llywelyn is ready to come into the king's grace, provided that the terms are secure and honourable. But because the terms in the articles sent to Llywelyn are not secure and honourable, as it seems to Llywelyn and his council, much to the surprise of all who heard them, in that they tend more to the destruction and ruin of him and his people than to their honour and security, his council by no means allows him to consent to them, if he wished to, and the other nobles and people subject to him would by no means consent to them on account of the undoubted destruction which could result from them. Therefore Llywelyn prays the archbishop to work prudently for a suitable, honourable and secure peace, for which the archbishop has worked so hard, with reference to the articles which Llywelyn is sending him in writing. For it is more honourable and more consonant with reason for Llywelyn to hold the lands to which he is entitled from the king than to disinherit him and hand them over to aliens.

Garthcelyn, 11 November [1282]

B = London, Lambeth Palace Library, Register of Archbishop Pecham, fo. 248r. s. xiii[2].
C = Oxford, All Souls College MS 182, fo. 111r–v. *c*.1413.
Pd. from B and C, *Reg. Peckh.*, ii. 468–9; from (?)C, Wynne, *History of Wales*, 391; from (?)Wynne, Warrington, *History of Wales*, 623–4; from *Reg. Peckh.*, Edwards, *Letters of a Peacemaker*, 30 (trans. only).
Cd., *H*, no. 460.

Reverentissimo[a] in Cristo patri ac domino I. Dei gratia archiepiscopo Cant(uariensi) ac totius Angl(ie) primati suus in Cristo devotus filius L. princeps Wallie, dominus Snaudon' salutem cum desideriis benivolentie filialis ac reverentiis multimodis et honoribus. Sancte pater, sicut vosmet consuluistis, ad gratiam regiam parati sumus venire, sub forma tamen nobis secura et honesta. Sed[b] quia forma contenta in articulis [c]ad nos[c] missis minime secura est et honesta, prout nobis et consilio nostro videtur, et de qua multum admirantur omnes audientes eo quod plus tendit ad destructionem et ruinam populi nostri ac nostram quam ad nostram honestatem et securitatem, nullo modo permittit consilium nostrum nos in eam consentire, si vellemus, aliique nobiles et populus nobis subiecti nullo modo consentirent in eandem ob indubitatam destructionem et dissipationem que inde eis possent evenire. Unde supplicamus vestre sancte paternitati quatinus ad reformationem pacis debite, honeste et secure, ob quam tot labores assumpsistis, provide laboretis, collationem habentes ad articulos quos vobis mittimus in scriptis. Honorabilius enim est et rationi magis consonum ut de domino rege teneamus terras in quibus ius habemus quam nos exheredare et eas tradere alienis. Datum apud Garthkelyn in festo Sancti Martini.

[a] Reverendissimo C. | [b] Set C. | [c–c] nobis C.

This letter was sent in response to further proposals from Pecham to Llywelyn taken by John of Wales after 6 November 1282 (*Reg. Peckh.*, ii. 466–8; cf. Smith, *Llywelyn*, 542–3). The proposals made to Llywelyn were in two parts, the first to be announced to him in the presence of his council, the second to be communicated to him in secret; the latter included the surrender by Llywelyn of his territory of Snowdonia (*Snaudonia*) in return for an earldom in England worth £1,000 per annum. Llywelyn's letter was accompanied by a reply by the prince's council (no. 431 below). The context and significance of both texts are discussed in Smith, *Llywelyn*, 535–6, 542–5. Garthcelyn has been identified as the site of a hall near or within Llywelyn's manor of Abergwyngregyn (ibid., 234). For the rejection of proposals sent to Dafydd ap Gruffudd at the same time see no. 455 below.

431 The reply of the Welsh to Archbishop Pecham

(1) Although the king has not wished to discuss the Four Cantrefs and the other lands given by him to his magnates, and Anglesey, the prince's council does not permit any discussion of these should peace be made, since those cantrefs belong purely to the prince, and the princes and their predecessors from the time of Camber son of Brutus have had the sole right to them because they belong to the principality whose confirmation the prince obtained from the papal legate Ottobuono with the consent of the king and his father, as their charters show, and because it is fairer that the true heirs hold the said cantrefs from the king for the accustomed money and services than for them to be given to strangers and newcomers; true, the lands were held by the king for a time, but only by force.

(2) All the tenants of all the cantrefs in Wales unanimously say that they have not dared to submit to the king's will so that he may dispose of them according to royal majesty, because (a) from the beginning the king has not observed towards the prince and his men treaties, oaths or charters; (b) royal officers have exercised the cruellest tyranny upon churches and ecclesiastical persons; (c) they are not obliged to the aforesaid things, since they are men of the prince, who is ready to obey the king concerning the said tenements through the accustomed services.

(3) As regards the demand that the prince submit to the king's will without reservation, since none of the said cantrefs have dared submit to the said will on account of the aforesaid reasons, their community does not permit him to submit to the said will.

(4) As regards the offer that the magnates of the realm will ensure that the prince is provided with an annual income of £1,000 in some part of England, he ought not to accept this provision since it has been procured by the magnates who seek to disinherit the prince so that they may have his lands in Wales.

(5) The prince is not obliged to abandon his inheritance and that of his ancestors in Wales since the time of Brutus, and confirmed to him by the papal legate, and receive land in England, where he is ignorant of the language, manners, laws and customs and where certain things could be maliciously imposed upon him by the inveterate hatred of the neighbouring English, who would be deprived of that land for ever.

(6) As the king proposes to deprive the prince of his original inheritance, it does not seem commendable that the king should allow him to have land in England, where he seems to have no right. And if the prince is not even permitted the barren and uncultivated land due to him by hereditary right from ancient times in Wales, he would not be permitted cultivated, fertile and abundant land in England.

(7) As regards the demand that the prince give the king absolute and perpetual seisin of Snowdonia, since Snowdonia belongs to the appurtenances of the principality of Wales, which he and his predecessors have held from the time of Brutus, his council does not permit him to renounce this and receive a place to which he is not entitled in England.

(8) The people of Snowdonia say that, even if the prince wished to give seisin of them to the king, they do not wish to do homage to a stranger of whose language, manners and laws they are entirely ignorant, since they could be captured and treated cruelly, just as the other cantrefs everywhere were treated more cruelly than the Saracens by the king's bailiffs and other royal officers, as is clear from the rolls which they have sent the archbishop.

[Garthcelyn, 11 November 1282]

B = London, Lambeth Palace Library, Register of Archbishop Pecham, fo. 248r–v. s. xiii[2].
C = Oxford, All Souls College MS 182, fos 108v–109r. c.1413.
Pd. from B and C, *Reg. Peckh.*, ii. 469–71; from (?)C, Wynne, *History of Wales*, 391–3; from (?)Wynne, Warrington, *History of Wales*, 624–6; from *Reg. Peckh.*, Edwards, *Letters of a Peacemaker*, 30–2 (trans. only).

[a]–Responsiones Walensiu(m).–[a]

[i] Primo, quod licet dominus rex de Q(ua)tuor Cantredis et aliis terris ab eo datis magnatibus suis ac de insula Engleseye[b] nullum voluerit habere tractatum, tamen consilium principis non permittit, si contingat aliquam pacem fieri, quin tractetur de premissis eo quod isti cantredi sunt de puro principis tenemento in quibus merum ius habuerunt principes et predecessores sui a temporibus Kambri filii Bruti; tum quia sunt de principatu, cuius confirmationem princeps obtinet per bone memorie Ottobonu(m) sedis apostolice legatum in [c]–regno Anglie–[c] consensu domini regis et sui patris ad hoc interveniente, sicut patet cartas eorum inspicienti; tum quia etiam equius est quod veri heredes teneant dictos cantredos de domino rege pro pecunia et servitiis consuetis quam eos dari extraneis et advenis, qui etsi fuerunt regis aliquando, tamen per vim et potentiam.

[ii] Dicunt etiam communiter omnes tenentes de omnibus cantredis Wallie quod non sunt ausi venire ad voluntatem regis ut de eis disponat secundum regiam maiestatem. [a]

Primo, quod dominus rex nec pacta nec iuramenta nec cartas servavit ab initio versus dominum suum principem et ipsos. [b] Secundo, quia regales in ecclesias et ecclesiasticas personas nunc crudelissimam exercent tyrannidem. [c] Tertio, quod non tenentur ad predicta cum sint homines principis, qui etiam paratus est de dictis tenementis domino regi obedire per servitia consueta.

[iii] Ad id quod dicitur quod princeps veniet simpliciter et absolute ad voluntatem domini regis, respondetur quod cum nulli de dictis cantredis ausi sint venire ad talem voluntatem[d] propter causas predictas, nec communitas eorum permittit principem venire ad dictam voluntatem modo predicto.

[iv] Item, quod proceres regni procurent ut dicto[e] principi provideatur in mille libratis in aliquo loco Anglie, dicatur quod illam provisionem non debet acceptare cum sit procurata per dictos proceres qui nituntur ad exheredationem principis ut habeant terras suas in Wallia.

[v] Item, idem princeps non tenetur dimittere hereditatem suam et progenitorum suorum in Wallia a tempore Bruti et etiam sibi confirmatam per Romane sedis legatum, ut dictum est, et terra in Anglia receptare,[f] ubi[g] linguam, mores,[h] leges ac consuetudines ignorat; ubi possent etiam sibi quedam malitiose imponi ex odio inveterato a vicinis Anglicis, quibus terra illa privaretur inperpetuum.

[vi] Item, ex quo rex proponit privare principem sua pristina hereditate, non videtur probabile quod rex permitteret ei habere terram in Anglia, ubi nullum ius videtur habere. Et si etiam non permittitur principi terra sterilis et inculta iure hereditario ab antiquo ei debita in Wallia, nullatenus permitteretur eidem in Anglia terra culta, fertilis et habundans.

[vii] Item, quod dictus princeps ponat dominum regem in seysinam Snaudon' absolute, perpetue et quiete. Dicatur quod cum Snaudon' sit de appendi`ci is principatus Wallie, quem ipse et antecessores sui tenuerunt a tempore Bruti, ut dictum est, consilium suum non permittit `eum renuntiare dicto loco et locum minus sibi[i] debitum in Anglia receptare.

[viii] Item, populus Snaudon' dicit quod, licet princeps vellet dare regi seysinam eorundem, ipsi tamen nollent homagium [fo. 248v] facere alicui extraneo, cuius linguam, mores legesque penitus ignorant. Quia sic posset contingere eos inperpetuum captivari ac crudeliter tractari, sicut alii can`tred i circumquaque per ballivos regis ac alios regales alias tractati fuerunt, crudelius quam Saraceni, prout patet in rotulis quos vobis miserunt, sancte pater.

[a-a] *underlined in* B. | [b] Angleseye C. | [c-c] Anglia C. | [d] B *inserts* domini regis *dotted underneath for expunction.* | [e] domino C. | [f] acceptare C. | [g] unde C. | [h] C *inserts* et. | [i] sibid C.

See note to no. 430 above. As many of the responses refer to the proposals put to Llywelyn in secret, the document shows the prince's determination to allow his council to join him in considering all Pecham's proposals (Smith, *Llywelyn*, 543).

ELEANOR, PRINCESS OF WALES
(d. 19 June 1282)

*432 Edward I

Letter, requesting a pardon of abjuration of the realm for Hugh de Traham and John de Barris, knights, John Becard, William le Clerk, Henry Cook, William Cook, Hugh, Philip, Adam, Stephen and Adam of the kitchen, who lately came to England with Eleanor and her brother, Amaury de Montfort.

[Shortly before 12 March 1279]

Mention only, in a pardon issued by Edward in response to this request, dated at Woodstock, 12 March 1279 (*CPR 1272–81*, 306; cd., *H*, no. 495). Though the pardon does not explicitly refer to the receipt of a letter from Eleanor, the reference to her by the style 'princess of Wales and lady of Snowdon' strongly suggests that the request was made in written form.

433 Edward I

Letter to her kinsman the king, informing him that she desires to hear good news about him. Therefore she humbly asks him to inform her how he is, and whether he wishes anything from her, although, so she has heard, contrary things have been told to him by certain people about her. She does not believe that he would believe any sinister reports about her husband and herself until he has learned from her whether these are true, seeing that he showed them such great honour when they were last at Worcester. She will always be ready to answer whatever the king wishes to ask concerning these or other things.

Llan-faes, 8 July [1279–81, probably 1279]

A = TNA: PRO, SC 1/17, no. 2. Modern endorsement; approx. 185 × 42 mm.; mounted, foot cut away.
Pd. from A, *Foedera*, I. ii. 584; from A, Wood, *Letters*, 54–5 (trans. only); from Wood, *Letters of Medieval Women*, ed. Crawford, 137 (trans. only).
Cd., *CAC*, 75–6; *H*, no. 440.

Excellenti domino suo et consanguineo predilecto domino E. Dei gratia regi Angl(ie), domino Hib(er)n(ie) et duci Aquitann(ie) sua devota consanguinea Alianora principissa Wallie, domina Snaudon' salutem cum ea que decet sincera dilectione consanguineo tanto et tam proprinquo. Noverit vestra excellencia quod de vestro statu bonos et prosperos rumores scire desideramus. Ideo vestram excellenciam humiliter rogamus et attente quatinus pro amore nostro statum vestrum, et si que penes nos volueritis que vestro cederint honori vel placuerint maiestati, nobis sicut consanguinee vobis humili et promte ad vestra beneplacita significare velitis, quamquam, ut audivimus, hiis contraria ab aliquibus vestre excellencie de nobis sint relata. Et tamen nullo modo credimus vos aliquibus de domino nostro vel nobis sinistra referentibus fidem adhibere donec a nobis sciretis si talia dicta continent veritatem, ex quo tantum honorem tantamque familiaritatem domino nostro et nobis, quando ultimo Wigorn' fuimus, vestra gratia exibuisitis. Quocirca quicquid circa hec vel alia que volueritis nobis demandare parate erimus semper pro viribus exequi et complere. Dat' apud Lannmaes viii° die iulii.

The meeting at Worcester was probably at Eleanor's wedding, which took place on 13 October 1278 (cf. Smith, *Llywelyn*, 448–9); if so, the letter was probably written in 1279, and can in any case be no later than 1281 (*CAC*, 76; cf. *WAR*, 79).

434 Edward I

Letter to her kinsman the king, asking him, since it does not please him for Nicholas de Waltham to execute the will of her mother Eleanor in his kingdom, to have the bequeathed goods collected in his treasury and to inform her of a day and place to receive the legacy, lest her mother's last will not be fulfilled.

Abereiddon, 10 October 1279

> A = TNA: PRO, SC 1/17, no. 1. No endorsements; approx. 205 mm. wide × 48 mm. deep on left, 35 mm. deep on right; five sets of double slits for insertion of a tongue or tag; mounted, foot cut away.
> Pd. from A, *Foedera*, I. ii. 576.
> Cd., *CAC*, 75; *H*, no. 443.

Excellenti suo domino ac consanguineo, si placet, confidentissimo domino Ed(wardo) Dei gratia illustri regi Angl(ie), domino Ybern(ie) ac duci Aquitt' sua devotissima Al(ienora) principissa Wall(ie), domina Snaudon' salutem cum affectibus intime dilectionis. Quia non placet vestre excellentie ut magister Nichol(as) de Whatham prosequatur testamentum bone memorie Alienore amice vestre et matris nostre in regno vestro, ideo rogamus dominationem vestram humiliter et attente quatinus vos ipsi, si placet, faciatis levare seu colligere res suas testatas in scacario vestro, quibus levatis et collectis, si placet, premuniatis nos de die et loco, quibus possimus partem nobis legatam recipere, ne ultima voluntas prefate vestre amicce[a] careat fine debito. Dat' apud Aberidon vi idus octobris anno domini m° c° c° lxx° ix .

[a] *sic in* A.

Nicholas de Waltham, a canon of Lincoln, had represented Simon de Montfort's widow at the royal court in 1275. In 1285 Nicholas was alleged to have conspired with Guy de Montfort, Amaury de Montfort and Llywelyn ap Gruffudd to spy against Edward; the king refused to allow him to execute the will because he was already suspect (Stephenson, 'Llywelyn ap Gruffydd', 44; Smith, *Llywelyn*, 395 and n. 18, 497).

435 Edward I

Letter to her kinsman the king, telling him that she longs to hear of his good health and prosperity. Since she has been informed that he proposes to discuss the case of her brother Amaury in the present parliament, she prays on bended knees that he will bear divine clemency in mind and mercifully receive her brother into his grace and peace. If, as she knows he does, the king condescends to act with clemency towards strangers, so all the more should he extend the hand of piety to his relative.

Ystumanner, 18 October [1279–81, probably 1279]

A = TNA: PRO, SC 1/17, no. 3. Endorsed: [Res]pondetur ei quod tracta[tum est] de statu in isto [parleamen]to et id quod fieri [potuit] est factum, et credi[tur per] id quod tractatum e[st del]iberacio frat[ris sui] sit 'multum appropinquior (s. xiii²; the letters in square brackets are hidden by the mount of the document and are supplied from the text in *Foedera*); approx. 192 mm. wide × 76 mm. deep on left, 51 mm. deep on right; mounted, most of foot cut away.

Pd. from A, *Foedera*, I. ii. 587; from A, Wood, *Letters*, 56–7 (trans. only); from Wood, *Letters of Medieval Women*, ed. Crawford, 138–9 (trans. only).

Cd., *CAC*, 76; *H*, no. 446.

Excellentissimo principi necnon consanguineo suo karissimo domino Ed(wardo) Dei gratia regi Anglie, domino Hib(er)nie, duci Aquitann(ie) sua devota Alienora principissa Wall(ie), domina Snaudon' salutem cum ea que decet sincera dilectione tanto domino et consanguineo tam propinquo. Exellencie vestre constare facimus per presentes nos, benedictus Deus, bona sanitate et prosperitate gaudere, quod de vobis scire non solum cupimus sed sitimus. Et quia nobis ab aliquibus est relatum quod in instanti parliamento de karissimi fratris nostri domini Amalrici status relevatione proponitis habere tractatum, ideo complosis manibus genibusque flexis ac gemitibus lacrimosis maiestati vestre supplicamus quatinus, divinam clemenciam ex vestri cordis intimo respicientes, que omnibus manum pietatis extendit, precipue hiis qui se ex toto corde requirunt, prefatum fratrem nostrum et consanguineum vestrum, benignitatem vestram, ut intelligimus, suppliciter postulantem, ad gratiam et pacem vestram misericorditer velitis recipere. Si enim exelencia vestra, prout sepius novimus, clementer extraneis condescendit, multo magis, ut credimus, nature vestre tam propinque manum debetis porigere pietatis. Valeat in domino per tempora longiora. Dat' apud Stu(m)anneir in festo Sancti Luce Evangeliste.

As Edwards noted (*CAC*, 76), since Amaury was not released until 1282, the letter could have been written in 1279, 1280 or 1281 (it was clearly written some time after her wedding on 13 October 1278). It is quite likely that it was written in 1279, for in one and the same letter to Edward, probably datable to 7 October 1279, Queen Margaret of France both asks Edward to show mercy to Amaury and raises the issue of Eleanor's mother's will, about which Eleanor wrote to the king on 10 October 1279 (no. 434 above; Smith, *Llywelyn*, 400 and n. 42). If so, the parliament referred to was that of October 1279. However, this reference is not itself decisive as regards dating, for parliaments were held at Westminster in October 1281 and possibly October 1280 (though the latter may have been postponed until early November). The place-date Ystumanner almost certainly refers to the court of that commote (in Meirionnydd), which was probably located close to the earthwork castle at Pennal (SH 697 003) (Smith, *Llywelyn*, 227 and n. 190; *idem*, 'Age of the princes', 37). The endorsement gives the reply that Amaury's case was discussed in that parliament and what could be done has been done, and it is believed that as a result of the discussion the release of Eleanor's brother was much closer.

436 Edward I

Letter to her kinsman the king, asking him, since she greatly desires to hear prosperous news of him, to inform her of how he is. She is greatly surprised that he allows her husband the prince to be troubled by certain merchants, who are (?)prosecuting him on a matter of no significance, seeing that the prince is ready to provide justice according to the customs of his land concerning those matters arising in that land. It seems strange that anybody complaining of the prince is believed before the case is openly discussed in the prince's land. Therefore she asks the king to provide an effective remedy in this matter. Furthermore, since she understands that certain of her men and one whom the king knows well, namely John Becard, who were captured along with her, have been restored to the king's peace through the prayers of certain persons, after she has often sought this without being heard (she did not believe that she was so estranged from the king that he would not more quickly receive them into his peace for her sake than for the sake of others); nevertheless, she prays that he will receive into his peace Hugh de Punfred, Hugh Cook and Philip Tailor, seeing that they are poor and originally from England, where they can earn a living more easily than elsewhere, it would be harsh to exile them from their native soil.

Nefyn, 2 February [1282]

A = TNA: PRO, SC 1/17, no. 4. No endorsements; approx. 174 mm. wide at top, 163 mm. wide on bottom × 88 mm. deep; mounted, foot cut away.
Cd., *CAC*, 76–7; *H*, no. 456.

Excellenti domino suo et karissimo consanguineo[a] domino Edwardo regi Agnlie,[b] domino Hibernie et duci Acquitann(ie) sua devota Elienora principissa Wallie, domina Snaudon' salutem cum ea que decet sincera dilectione tanto domino et consanguineo tam propinquo. Quia multum desideramus prospera scire de statu vestre quem Deus semper salvet et gubernet, ideo excellenciam vestram requirimus quatinus pro amore nostro statum vestrum et si que vestre excellencie placuerint nobis significetis. Ad hec non modicum admiramur de hoc quod dominum nostrum principem sustinere velitis vexari per quosdam mercatores, qui sibi in nullo perisicantur,[b] benedictus Deus, ex quo enim dominus princeps paratus est omnem iusticiam exhibere secundum consuetudines terre sue de hiis que in terra eadem fiunt vel contingunt. Extraneum videtur quod cuilibet querelanti de se credatur ante quam res ipsa lucqulenter[b] in terra sua discusciatur.[b] Ideo propter Deum remedium in hac parte eficax si placet apponatis. Ceterum quia intelliximus quod aliqui de hominibus nostris et unus quem bene noscis, scilicet Iohannes de Becar, qui nobiscum fuerunt capti per preces aliquorum sunt paci vestre restituti, et nos pro eisdem sepius vos requisivimus nec adhuc sumus exaudite, nec credebamus a vobis aliquo modo tantum elongari, quin citius pro nobis eos ad pacem[c] vestram reciperetis quam pro aliis; ideo nichilominus vobis suplicamus ut Hugone(m) de Pu(n)fred, Hugone(m) Coqum et Philipu(m) Cissorem ad pacem recipere velitis, si placet, ex quo enim pauperes sunt, et de A(n)glia oriundi ubi melius possunt quam alibi victitare, durum esset eis a proprio solo exulari. Valete. Dat' apud Nevyn in festo purificacionis Beate Virginis.

[a] cosanguineo A. | [b] *sic in* A. | [c] *followed by hole cut in parchment for deletion in* A.

As Edwards pointed out (*CAC*, 76–7), there is a strong case for dating this letter to 1282. John was pardoned at the instance of Luke de Tany on 15 January 1281 (*CPR 1272–81*, 423), and Hugh de Punfred, Hugh Cook and Philip Tailor were pardoned at the instance of Eleanor, princess of Wales, on 12 February 1282 (*CPR 1281–92*, 11), very probably as a result of this letter. Cf. no. 432 above for the pardoning of John Becard of abjuration of the realm in March 1279. The letter is written in the same hand as no. 427 above, likewise dated at Nefyn, 2 February. The form *perisicantur* is odd. It has been taken here as a mangled form of a third person plural present tense of *persequor*, i.e. either the indicative *perse-quuntur* or the subjunctive *persequantur*. (I am grateful to Paul Russell for his comments on this and other aspects of the letter's Latin.)

DAFYDD AP GRUFFUDD
(d. 3 October 1283)

*437 Beddgelert Priory
Grant of all the land of Adoer *in Pennant (*de tota terra Adoer apud Epenant*).*
       [*c*.1252 × 1263, or 1267 × November 1274, or November 1277 × 22 June 1283]

Mention only, in a letter patent of Edward I dated at Canterbury, 10 May 1286, referring to a letter patent of Anian, bishop of Bangor, that listed charters granted to Beddgelert by Welsh princes (TNA: PRO, C 53/74, m. 1; pd., *Mon. Ang.*, vi: i. 200; *Rec. Caern.*, 166 (Edward's letter only); cd., Gresham, *Eifionydd*, 64; Stephenson, *Governance*, 204; *H*, no. 168). Like nos 438–9 below, the reference is simply to a *cartam domini David*. Since the summaries follow those of charters issued by Llywelyn ap Gruffudd, it is likely that Dafydd ap Gruffudd is meant, rather than Dafydd ap Llywelyn (d. 1246) or Dafydd ab Owain (d. 1203), neither of whom – in contrast to Dafydd ap Gruffudd – are styled *dominus* in their extant acts (*pace* Gresham, *Eifionydd*, 6, 64, which identifies the grantor as Dafydd ap Llywelyn). It is uncertain when Dafydd ap Gruffudd would have been in a position to grant lands in the township of Pennant in Eifionydd: the only commotes in Gwynedd Uwch Conwy over which he is known to have exercised lordship were Cymydmaen and Cafflogion, both in Llŷn (see nos 440–1 below). However, Dafydd's landholding may well have been more extensive than the very limited amount of extant evidence for it might seem to suggest, and the grants could have been made at any point between his arrival in Gwynedd Uwch Conwy in 1252 and his capture in June 1283, apart, probably, from the periods he spent in England 1263–7 and 1274–7. The exact location of *Adoer* is uncertain.

*438 Beddgelert Priory
Grant of all the land of Tegwared ap Gwair *of Pennant (*de tota terra Tegwaret vayb *[sic]* Gueyr de Penant*).*
       [*c*.1252 × 1263, or 1267 × November 1274, or November 1277 × 22 June 1283]

Mention only, in a letter patent of Edward I, dated at Canterbury, 10 May 1286, referring to a letter patent of Anian, bishop of Bangor, that listed charters granted to Beddgelert by Welsh princes (TNA: PRO, C 53/74, m. 1; pd., *Mon. Ang.*, vi: i. 200; *Rec. Caern.*, 166; cd., Gresham, *Eifionydd*, 64; Stephenson, *Governance*, 204; *H*, no. 169). For the dating see note to no. 437 above.

*439 Beddgelert Priory

Grant of all the land which Iorwerth son of the priest and Steyraul *had in Pennant* (de tota terra quam habuerunt Iorverd vab yr efeyrat et Steyraul apud Epennant).

[c.1252 × 1263, or 1267 × November 1274, or November 1277 × 22 June 1283]

Mention only, in a letter patent of Edward I, dated at Canterbury, 10 May 1286, referring to a letter patent of Anian, bishop of Bangor, that listed charters granted to Beddgelert by Welsh princes, and also in a letter patent of Anian, bishop of Bangor, listing charters granted to Beddgelert by Welsh princes, dated at Maes-y-llan, 1 April 1286 (TNA: PRO, C 53/74, m. 1; pd., *Foedera*, I. ii. 664; *Mon. Ang.*, vi: i. 200; *Rec. Caern.*, 166 (Edward's letter only); cd., Gresham, *Eifionydd*, 64; Stephenson, *Governance*, 204; *H*, no. 167). The copy of Anian's letter patent describes Dafydd's grant as being *totam terram quam habuerit Ierberd Vab Yerfeynt, et Feraul apud Epennant*. For the dating see note to no. 437 above.

440 Agreement in his presence between the abbot and convent of Enlli (Bardsey) and the secular canons of Aberdaron and men of the *abadaeth*

A binding agreement concerning the disputes between the two parties before Dafydd, lord of Cymydmaen, in which they accepted the arbitration of five trustworthy men, namely G. prior of Enlli, Meilyr conversus *of that house, Goronwy son of* Ysopus, *L. the steward son of D., and Tegwared son of* K.

(1) *The five have determined concerning the tithes of the canons of Enlli that the secular canons of Aberdaron have pardoned the canons of Enlli of all tithes from all lands which they cultivate at their own cost. The canons of Enlli have given the church of Aberdaron sacerdotal vestments with a silver chalice and missal and will give it one pound of incense each year on the Nativity of St John [24 June].*

(2) *The abbot and convent may have all the procurations of the men of the* abadaeth *apart from the* clas-*townships.*

(3) *The men of the township of Ystohelyg are exempt from the township's procuration and* twnc *work, and shall pay 18*d. *with twelve heaped* gwehelyn *of barley each year.*

(4) *Those who are portioners in the church of Aberdaron shall pay only 12*d. *for* amobr *and* ebediw, *the laymen of the same township shall pay 12*s. *for* amobr *and* ebediw. *Those who are portioners in the church of Aberdaron anywhere in the abbot's lordship shall render 12*d. *for* amobr *and* ebediw.

(5) *If any money coming from the lands of the* abadaeth *is disputed, the secular canons will have one third of it.*

(6) *No one may be an* ynad *[judge] in the* abadaeth *unless he is appointed by the secular canons together with the abbot and convent.*

(7) *The abbot is entitled to investigate the truth concerning undecided cases arising from the secular canons.*

(8) *The sons of Trahaearn Foel are exempt from procuration and labour service. The same is true of Pwlldefaid.*

(9) *The* segynnab-*township is exempt apart from 12*d. *for* amobr *and 12*d. *for* ebediw.

(10) *The procurations of the* abadaeth *apart from Trefgraig: from each* rhandir *which renders* twnc, *twelve measures of grain – six of good wheat, six of good flour – and 2*s. *From Trefgraig: 15 measures of grain – one half of good wheat and the other of flour – and 27*d.

*(11) Bryncroes: 12*d. *for* amobr *and 12*d. *for* ebediw.

(12) The twnc *of Uwch Sely: from each* rhandir *twelve unheaped* gwehelyn *of barley and 25*d. *apart from Ystohelyg and Tredom. The procuration of Tredom: four measures of good flour and four of wheat and 16*d.*; its* twnc *is eight unheaped* gwehelyn *of barley and 16*d. *and one halfpenny and one-third of a halfpenny.*

(13) The twnc *of Is Sely apart from Cyllyfelin: from each* rhandir *53*d.*; from Cyllyfelin 43*d.

(14) Everyone holding land and a house from the canons of Enlli shall give labour services for three days at harvest. In summer whoever has a horse shall carry two cart-loads from the demesne to the court of Y Cil apart from Ystohelyg, the segynnabaid *and* Veyrth. *The others do no labour service apart from on the embankment of the mill of Aberdaron.*

(15) All those living in the abadaeth *are free to take the clerical tonsure.*

(16) Concerning the procurations of the lord of Cymydmaen it has been decided that once a year the cellarer and steward shall choose four trustworthy men from the abadaeth, *who shall impose on the wealthier and stronger 4*d. *and four measures of flour and two measures of oats and a hen; on those who are less rich 2*d. *and two measures of flour and one measure of oats; on the third group of men 1*d. *and one measure of flour; on the other men who cannot give as much 1*d. *or its value and one hen from each house which has hens.*

*(17) 2*s. *for a* dirwy croes *[cross-fine], as determined by Llywelyn, prince of North Wales.*

(18) The men of the abadaeth *are not to be compelled to use the mills of the abbot and convent.*

(19) If there is any land for which there is no one to answer for it, the abbot may hold the land until the arrival of a member of the kin who will answer.

Sealing clause; witnesses.

11 July 1252

B = BL, Harl. MS 696, fo. 157v. 1494.
Pd. from B, *Rec. Caern.*, 252.
Cd., *H*, no. 377.

Notum sit tam presentibus quam futuris quod hec realis compositio fuit facta inter dominum A. abbatem et conventum de Enlly ex parte una et canonicos seculares de Aberdaron' et homines de *abadayth* ex altera super contraversiis ortis inter dictos coram domino David filio Griffini domino de Kemedmaen que sic determinate sunt, videlicet quod predicte partes conpromiserunt in quinque viros fidedignos communiter electos, scilicet G. priorem de Enlly et Meilir eiusdem domus conversum et Goronu' filium Ysopo et L. yconomum filium D. et Teguared filium K.

[i] Predicti autem quinque viri primo determinavunt de decimis canonicorum de Enlly quod canonici seculares de Ab(er)daron condonaverunt canonicis de Enlly omnes decimationes omnium terrarum quas propriis sumptibus colunt. Et predicti canonici de Enlly dederunt ecclesie de Ab(er)daron vestimenta sacerdotalia cum calice argenteo et missali et dabunt ecclesie predicte unam libram thuris in nativitate Sancti Ioh(ann)is Baptiste annuatim.

[ii] Omnes autem procurationes hominum de *abadayth* preter *clastreuy* predictus abbas et conventus habeant et possideant.

[iii] De villa Stohelik' sic determinatum est quod homines dicte ville liberi sint de procu-

ratione et opere *twnk'* predicte ville, sic est quod reddant annuatim xviii denarios cum xii *gwyelyum* ordei cum cumilo.

[iv] De illis qui sunt portionarii in ecclesia de Ab(er)daron pro *amobr'* et *ebedyv* non reddent nisi xii denarios, layci autem eiusdem ville pro *amobr'* et *ebedyv* reddent xii solidos. Illi autem qui portionarii sunt in ecclesia de Ab(er)daron ubicumque in dominio abbatis fuerint pro *amobr'* et *ebedyv* reddent xii denarios.

[v] Si aliqua pecunia de terris et possessionibus de *abadayth* evenerit unde controversia mota fuerit canonici seculares tertiam partem habebunt.

[vi] De *ynad*[a] autem sic est quod nullus sit in *abadayth ynad* nisi in quem consenserint[b] canonici seculares simul cum abbate et conventu.

[vii] De causis dubiis que emerserint a predictis canonicis secularibus debet abbas inquirere veritatem.

[viii] Filii Trehayarn' Voel liberi sunt a procuratione et opere. Idem de Pulldeveyde.

[ix] Seginabdref' libera est preter xii denarios pro *amobr'* et tantum pro *ebedyv*.

[x] Procurationes de *abadayth'* preter Trefgrayk': de qualibet *rander* unde redditur *tunk'* xii cribratas, vi de frumento bono et sex de farina bona et ii solidis. De Trefgrayk' autem: xv cribratas, medietatem de frumento bono et aliam de farina et xxvii[tem] denarios.

[xi] Brinkroes vero pro *amobr'* xii denarios et tantum de *ebedyv*.

[xii] *Tunk'* supra Sely: de qualibet *rander* xii *gwyelyn* ordei sine cumilo et xxv denarios preter Stohelyk' et Trefdom'. De Trefdom' sic est pro procuratione dicte ville: quatuor cribratas bone farine et quatuor frumenti et xvi denarios; pro *tunk'* autem viii *gwyelyn* ordei sine cumilo et xvi denarios cum obolo et tertiam partem oboli.

[xiii] *Tunk'* subtus Sely preter Kellyvelyn': de qualibet *rander* liii denarios; de Kellyvelyn' vero xliii denarios.

[xiv] De opere autem sic est quicumque tenet terram et domum sub predictis canonicis de Enlly faciet opus per tres dies in autumpno; in estate autem qui habet equum debet cariari duas carratas de gleba usque ad curiam Ycil preter Stohelyk' et *segenabeyd* et Veyrth. Alii autem non faciunt opus nisi fossam molendini de Aberdaron'.

[xv] Omnes autem inhabitantes *abadayth'* ad suscipiendum signum clericale liberi sint.

[xvi] Procurationes domini de Kemediuaen' sic determinate sunt, quod semel in anno eligat celerarius simul cum yconomo quatuor viros fidedignos de *abadayth'*, et ipsi imponant ditioribus et fortioribus iiii denarios et iiii scutellatas farine et duas cribratas avenum cum gallina; item aliis hominibus qui non sunt tam divites imponant ii denarios et ii scutellatas farine et unam cribratam avenum; item tertiis hominibus i denarium et i scutellatam farine; item aliis hominibus qui non possunt dare tantum imponant i denarium aut eius valentiam et qualibet domo ubi fuerint galline unam gallinam.

[xvii] De *dyroy croes* ii solidos: sic determinavit dominus L. princeps Northwallie.

[xviii] Ad sectam molendinorum abbatis et conventus non sunt compellendi homines de *abadayth*.

[xix] Si aliqua terra fuerit pro qua nullus sit qui respondeat, teneat abbas predictam terram usque ad adventum alicuius de parentela qui respondeat.

Et ut hec forma pacis et concordia futuris temporibus stabilis et inconcussa permaneat sigilla domini R. Bang(orensis) et domini D(avi)d filii Griffini et domini A. abbatis de Enlly huic scripto sunt apposita. Hiis testibus: domina S. quondam uxore domini Griffini, T. decano de Lleyn', domino Will(el)mo priore de Nevyn', magistro Ric(ard)o capellano de Bodvran', G(er)vas(io) filio M., Meurik' filio R., Ioh(ann)e filio K., Ievaf' filio L. ballivo de Nevgwl, T. filio M., L. Calvo et multis aliis. Actum anno domini millesimo cc^{mo} l^{mo} ii° v^{to} idus iulii.

^a ymad B. | ^b consenserit B.

Dafydd presided over this arbitration award as lord of Cymydmaen, the westerly commote of Llŷn; the commote was probably granted to him by his eldest brother Owain, whom he served as *penteulu* (chief of the military retinue) by 1255 (Smith, *Llywelyn*, 68–9; *CW*, 40). It is notable that, according to the witness list, Dafydd's mother Senana was present at the agreement. The document is one of the very few records of dispute settlements extant from territories under native rule in thirteenth-century Wales (for other examples see nos 16–17, 339, 345–6 above), and illuminates the procedure of arbitration that was followed. The precise meaning of *realis compositio* is uncertain. Paul Brand, whom I thank for his comments on this and other aspects of the document, observes (pers. comm.) that the vocabulary is canonical and that 'the intention is clearly to create a permanent settlement between the parties that will be binding on their successors'; the use of *realis* here possibly derived from *res* in the sense of a point at issue in a court of law.

The pattern and conditions of land-holding revealed by the text have been analysed by Jones Pierce (*Medieval Welsh Society*, 391–407). As he showed, the agreement provides valuable evidence for the reform of a native Welsh ecclesiastical establishment by its detailing of the seignorial rights in Cymydmaen of the abbey of Enlli, very probably held by Augustinian canons by this date, and its relations with the native ecclesiastical establishment of Aberdaron. That the abbey of Enlli belonged to a reformed order of canons is suggested by references to its prior, cellarer, steward and *conversus* and by the implicit contrast drawn between its community and the 'secular canons' of Aberdaron, who were probably synonymous with the portioners of that church mentioned later in c. iv of the text. Moreover, in 1316 one of the canons of Enlli is explicitly said to be of the Augustinian order (*CPR 1313–17*, 537, cited by Johns, 'Celtic monasteries', 21). The present document indicates that the landed endowment of Aberdaron, referred to as the *abadaeth*, had been transferred to Enlli, and that disputes had arisen concerning dues and other rights claimed by Enlli from this and other lands on the mainland in Cymydmaen. In resolving these disputes, the agreement recognized the privileged status of the lands in the *abadaeth* and elsewhere held by the secular canons or portioners of Aberdaron: thus c. ii exempted the *clastrefi* (townships pertaining to the *clas* 'community' of the church, i.e. the portioners) from the procurations due to Enlli, and c. iv stipulated a low rate of 12*d.* for payments of both *amobr* (a fine for loss of virginity or marriage) and *ebediw* (a fee for succession to land, comparable to the Anglo-Saxon heriot) for portioners of Aberdaron, both in the *abadaeth* and elsewhere, in contrast to the 12*s.* demanded from lay tenants. The use of the Welsh terms *abadaeth* and *clastrefi* shows that the church of Aberdaron was a native institution, resembling the churches with abbots and a *clas* or canons referred to in the Welsh lawbooks (Pryce, *Native Law*, 186–7). The same is true of *Seginabdref* (lit., '*segynnab*-township') (c. ix) and *segenabeyd* (a pl. form of *segynnab*, i.e. *segynnabaid*, presumably referring here to the holders of *Seginabdref*) (c. xiv), as both contain the element *segynnab*, derived from Lat. *secundus abbas*, for a prior or steward of a native Welsh church (see no. 16 and note above).

Dafydd ap Gruffudd had a direct interest in the provision of the agreement as c. xvi lays down the annual procurations (*porthiant* dues) to which the lord of Cymydmaen was entitled from the *abadaeth*. The *dirwy croes* 'cross-fine' of the next clause (c. xvii) probably refers to a fine for breach of a cross placed on a field to mark a claim to it or its corn. The clause does not state to whom the fine was payable. According to lawbooks from early thirteenth-century Gwynedd, the *dirwy* (a fine of £3) numbered among the rights to which the king (i.e. prince) was entitled from 'abbot-land'. Since the clause follows that on procurations to the lord of Cymydmaen, and since it states that the amount of 2*s.* had been fixed by Llywelyn ap Iorwerth, it may be that the sum was received by the secular lord rather than by the abbot of Enlli; however, if *dirwy* denoted a fine of £3, as in the laws, the rest of the 'cross-fine' may have gone to the abbot (see Pryce, *Native Law*, 218–20).

441 Madog ab Einion ap Maredudd

Grant, in regard for his liberty and ancient dignity, of all his inheritance, freely and for ever in return for his service, without any demands except for serving with Dafydd in the army; also confirmation for ever of Madog as abbot of a quarter of the right of patronage of the townships of Llanynys and Gyffylliog, with the addition of a quarter of the township of Euarth Fechan in Llannerch and of the township of Bryncelyn in Cafflogion, all the land of Madog Crythor, of Dwywg ap Iorwerth, of Ithel Grafag, of Gwgan ap Cyngen apart from the land of Penrud, of Einion ap Griffri apart from one third and of Iorwerth ap Gwyn apart from one third. Dafydd has granted all these individual lands with their appurtenances to Madog and his heirs for ever, free of all secular service except for serving with Dafydd in the army. Sealing clause; witnesses.

Colion, 22 January 1260

> A = NLW, Bachymbyd 217. No medieval endorsements; approx. 268 × 87 + 20 mm.; two cloth tags, each through two slits in centre of fold; sealed on tags. Seal missing.
> Pd. from A, Davies, 'Grant by David', 29.
> Cd., Stephenson, *Governance*, 204; *H*, no. 151.

Universis Cristi fidelibus tam presentibus quam futuris has litteras inspecturis dominus David filius G(ri)ffini salutem in domino sempiternam. Noverit vestra universitas nos considerantes[a] libertatem et dignitatem antiquam Madoco filio Aniani filii Mareduth et suis heredibus totam hereditatem suam a nobis et nostris heredibus sine aliquo gravamine preter exercitum nobiscum pro suo servicio libere et quiete dedisse et concessisse in perpetuo possidendam et tenendam. Insuper dictum Madocu(m) videlicet abatem[b] super quartam partem iuris patronatus ville de Llanenys et de Kyffellyauc in perpetuo fecimus confirmare, hoc addito quartam partem de villa que dicitur Evarth Vechan de Llanerch et de alia villa que dicitur Brenkelyn de Gaflogon, totam terram Maodauc krethaur et totam terram Duuyuc filii Yorverth et totam terram Ythael Grafag et totam terram Gugaunc filii Kengen excepta terra Penrud et totam terram Aniani filii G(ri)fri excepta tercia parte et totam terram Yorverth filii Guen excepta tercia parte. Et singulas terras uniuscuiusque predictorum, in bosco in campo, in aqua in monte cum omnibus suis pertinenciis dicto Madoco et suis heredibus a nobis et a nostris heredibus libere et quiete et sine aliqua exactione seculari preter exercitum nobiscum dedimus et concessimus inperpetuo possidendas. Et ut hec nostra donatio in posterum non valeat infirmari presentem cartam sigilli nostri munimine fecimus roborari. Hiis testibus: Goronue filio Grufud, Grufud filio

Lewelini, Mareduth filio Lewelini, magistro Caducano, Ieruasio clerico, Ricardo filio Oweni et Caducano fratre eius cum multis aliis. Datum apud Colleyaun anno m° cc° xl°xix° xi° kalendas februarii.

[a] *sic in* A *(cf. no. 318 above, which inserts* eius *here).* | [b] *sic in* A.

The terms of this grant are similar to those of the charter Llywelyn ap Gruffudd issued in favour of Madog's father Einion ap Maredudd in 1243 (no. 318 above), except that the present charter also confirms Madog's rights in the lay abbacy of Llanynys and grants additional lands. The charter thus reveals the continuing importance of Madog's lineage and the desire of Dafydd to secure its support after he established himself as lord of Dyffryn Clwyd, a position achieved in the wake of Llywelyn ap Gruffudd's occupation of Perfeddwlad in late 1256 (Davies, 'Grant by David', 29; Barrell and Davies, 'Land, lineage, and revolt', 35; Smith, *Llywelyn*, 46, n. 33). The confirmation of Madog as abbot of a quarter of the patronage of Llanynys (cmt. Colion) and Gyffylliog (cmt. Dogfeiling) in Dyffryn Clwyd almost certainly refers to the church of Llanynys, which in 1402 was said in the past to have been divided among twenty-four perpetual portionaries known as *abad a chlaswyr* (by the fourteenth century the chief portioner was termed the dean, not abbot); the charter thus provides valuable evidence for the laicization of the office of abbot in a native Welsh church and of its division into portions, probably through partible inheritance (*CPL 1362–1404*, 349; Davies, 'Grant by David', 30–1; Jones, 'Llanynys quillets', 149–50; Jack, 'Religious life', 149–50; Evans, 'Early church in Denbighshire', 71–2). The grant of Bryncelyn, which was inherited by Madog's son Llywelyn, shows that, in addition to Cymydmaen (see no. 440 above), Dafydd also exercised lordship in the commote of Cafflogion in Llŷn by 1260 (Davies, 'Grant by David', 31). Euarth Fechan (cmt. Llannerch) was in Dyffryn Clwyd. The location of the lands of individual landholders named in the grant is not clear. It should be noted that the charter's place-date, Colion, refers to a commote in Dyffryn Clwyd, and the precise place where the document was issued is therefore uncertain.

*442 Henry III
Petition, requesting a pardon for William de Boulton for the death of Henry de Shagh.

[Shortly before 11 October 1266]

Mention only, in a letter patent of Henry III dated at Kenilworth, 11 October 1266 (*CPR 1258–66*, 646). The king's letter says that the pardon was given at the instance of Dafydd ap Gruffudd, but does not explicitly state that the request was in written form.

*443 Henry III
Petition, requesting a pardon for John son of John de Levre for the death of Roger Poydras of Manchester.

[Shortly before 7 September 1267]

Mention only, in a letter patent of Henry III dated at Shrewsbury, 7 September 1267 (*CPR 1266–72*, 104). The king's letter says that the pardon was given at the instance of Dafydd ap Gruffudd, but does not explicitly state that the request was in written form.

444 Edward I

Letter, informing the king again of his losses and grievances, concerning which Dafydd has expected to obtain help or amends by now. He therefore asks the king, in whom he places his trust before all others, to inform him by the bearer of the present letter of his advice, remedy and will regarding how he will best be able to aggrieve Llywelyn, prince of Wales, through the king's advice and help at this time, for unless he soon receives help and remedy from the king Dafydd will be unable to support himself and his people.

[1275 × January 1276]

A = TNA: PRO, SC 1/16, no. 107. No endorsements; approx. 170 × 45 mm.; mounted; foot cut away.
Cd., *CAC*, 74; *H*, no. 410.

Nobili et excellentissimo domino suo domino E. Dei gratia illustri regi Anglie, domino Hybern(ie) et duci Acquitt(anie) suus in omnibus humilis et semper fidelis David filius Griffini salutem et paratam semper ad sua obsequia et beneplacita voluntatem. Excellenci dominacioni vestre dignum duximus significandum dampnum nostrum, perditionem et gravamen, sicut vobis sepius significavimus prout vestre si placet occurrit conscientie, de quibus dampno et gravamine de pace aut de werra isto tempore remedium, succursum aut emendam putaverimus obtinere. Quare vestre venerande dominacioni et excellencie humiliter et devote supplicamus quatenus pro amore nostro et servicio sicut in vobis pre cunctis aliis et merito confidimus et adhuc si placet plenius confidentes consilium et remedium ac voluntatem ad presens si placet per latorem presencium nobis constare velitis, quam in isto tempore per vestrum consilium et auxilium L. principem Wall(ie) poterimus acgravare, intelligentes veraciter quod si infra breve tempus a vobis succursum et remedium invenire non poterimus nos et nostros sustentare minime valeamus. Valeat dominacioni vestra diu in domino.

Edwards argued (*CAC*, 74) that this letter was sent between Dafydd's flight from Wales in late November 1274 and the outbreak of war at the end of 1276 (see also *LW*, liv–lv; Powicke, *Henry III*, ii. 643, n. 2). However, since it refers to previous complaints to the king, it cannot have been written in the immediate aftermath of Dafydd's flight; while its strong implication that so far no support had been received from the king suggests that it was written before Dafydd learned of Edward's grant to him on 20 January 1276 of 100 marks, the first instalment payable on 19 April, the second on 29 September (*CCR 1272–9*, 266). It may even be that this grant was made in response to the present letter (Smith, *Llywelyn*, 383, n. 154).

445 Edward I

Letter, from William, earl of Warwick and Dafydd ... stating that since Madog of Bromfield has come to the king's peace ... [William] has seized and imprisoned some of Madog's men

... Seeing that Madog and his people were ... lord William promised amends but has done nothing ... Nevertheless, Madog has shown them that the sheriff of Shropshire wishes to seize ... of lands and deprive him of the suit of his tenants. The peace agreement which they made with him by the power given to them by the king states that he shall hold his lands and fees in peace. Wherefore they pray that the king will ensure that the peace which they have granted by his power is upheld. They request that he informs them of his will.

[Shortly after 12 April 1277]

A = TNA: PRO, SC 1/16, no. 108. No endorsements; originally approx. 173 × 71 mm.; mounted, foot cut away. About one-fifth of the document is torn away on the top right-hand corner.
Cd., *CAC*, 74–5; *H*, no. 424.

A lur tres honurable seynur par la grace deu rey de . . . de Warr' e Dauy le fiz Griffin honur e quant kil seu . . . sire ke pus ke Madok du Bromfeud esteit a vostre pes venu . . . sun poer e prist de la gent Madok e emprisona e des autres empris . . . dames k'il feist cele chose adrescer desi cume Madok e sa gent furent a . . . quilly sire Willam' un lur certain pur les amendes fere, mes ren de ceo ne fist . . . enz dist k'il vus ad la chose mustree e ke vus li avet comaundé k'il demore e ren neuf . . . en ceu pais. Atut iceo sire, Madok nus ad mustré ke vestre viscunte de Salobir' vent seisir en vo . . . de les terres e privere la seute de ses tenaunz. E la furme de la pes ke nus li avom fet par le poer ke v[us] nus avet baillé veut k'il teynue ses terres e ses fez em pes. Parunt vus priums sire s'il vus plest ke vus voillet ke la pes ke nus li avom par vestre poer graunté, e su nostre leauté plevie, le seit tenue. E vostre volunté si pleisir vus est sire nus voillet de `ceo maunder.

As Edwards argued (*CAC*, 75), Dafydd served with the earl of Warwick at Chester in April 1277, and the present letter was probably sent soon after the submission to them of Madog ap Gruffudd of Bromfield on 12 April (no. 527 below). The identity of the *sire Willam* referred to in the letter is uncertain.

446 Edward I

Letter, on behalf of his and the king's man, Gruffudd ap Iorwerth. The prince has deprived Gruffudd of his lands in Anglesey. Dafydd informs the king that after the last war Gruffudd has committed no offence against the prince, except only what he did in the king's service in time of war, and should therefore recover his land. He therefore prays that the king will grant him some remedy. Since the king recommended Gruffudd to Dafydd at Shrewsbury, he asks the king to receive Gruffudd's petition favourably.

[mid-October × 10 December 1277]

A = TNA: PRO, SC 1/16, no. 105. No endorsements; approx. 180 × 39 mm., including remains of tongue (approx. 80 × 3 mm.) on left-hand side; mounted, foot cut away on right-hand side.
Cd., *CAC*, 74; *H*, no. 435.

Domino E. Dei gratia illustri regi Anglie, domino Hibern(ie) et duci Acquitt(anie) suus in omnibus David filius Griffini salutem et paratam semper ad sua obsequia et beneplacita voluntatem pro dilecto nostro et homino vestro Grifut filio Ioruerth'. Quicquid domini principis terris suis et tenementis in A(n)glesia ipsum spoliavit. Dominationi vestre si placet dignum duximus significandum quod ipse[a] post ultimam werram nullam transgressionem contra dominum principem fecit, unde ipse terram suam deberet recipere, nisi tantum quod fecit in servicio vestro tempore gwerre. Quare vestram si placet exoramus venerandam dominacionem attencius supplicantes quatenus predicto G. aliquod remedium super hoc secundum quod vobis visum fuerit eidem si placet habere dignemini. Quoniam predictum G. nobis recomendavistis apud Salopesbur', ideo si placet peticionem suam humiliter benigne recipere dignemini. Valete diu.

^a ipsi A.

Gruffudd, a member of a prominent Anglesey lineage, joined Edward's service in the war against Llywelyn ap Gruffudd by the summer of 1277 (Smith, *Llywelyn*, 432–3), an action which presumably led to the confiscation of his lands referred to in the present letter. Since Dafydd refers to the king's having recommended Gruffudd to him at Shrewsbury, the letter must be later than 9 October 1277, when Edward is first attested in that town in 1277, apparently staying there until early November; he was present there again on 30 November and 10 December (*CPR 1272–81*, 234–5; *CCR 1272–9*, 404–7; *CWR*, 160, 161). However, it is unlikely to be later than 10 December 1277, when Edward granted Gruffudd custody of the lands of Madog ap Gruffudd of Bromfield; this was followed by a grant of the township of Maenan on 7 January 1278 (*CWR*, 161; cf. Smith, *Llywelyn*, 433, n. 164).

447 John Marshal

Agreement between Dafydd and his wife Elizabeth, formerly wife of William Marshal, on one side, and John Marshal, son and heir of the same William, on the other, whereby Dafydd and Elizabeth grant and quitclaim to John all the manor of Folesham in Norfolk with all its appurtenances, which Dafydd and Elizabeth have held as Elizabeth's dower, to be held by John and his heirs and assigns freely as true heirs of the manor for ever, giving the customary services each year to the chief lords of that fee. In return, John has granted to Dafydd and Elizabeth all his manor of Norton in Northamptonshire with all its appurtenances, to be held by them for the rest of Elizabeth's life as her dower, in exchange for the said manor of Folesham. After Elizabeth's death the manor of Norton with its appurtenances will revert to John without any hindrance from Dafydd or his heirs or assigns. It is agreed that if the valuation of Folesham exceeds that of Norton or vice versa, the party possessing the greater value will satisfy the party possessing the lesser in lands and homages, so that the lesser valuation is equal to the greater through the judgement of legal men chosen by both parties for this task. Sealed by the parties as a chirograph; witnesses.

[(?)Westminster] 2 January 1278

B = TNA: PRO, C 54/95 (Close R. 6 Edward 1), m. 14d in schedule (1278). There is some damage to the left-hand side of the parchment.
C = TNA: PRO, E 36/274 (Liber A), fo. 401r. s. xiii ex.
Pd. from C, *LW*, 139–40 (no. 246).
Cd., *CCR 1272–9*, 491 (from B); *H*, no. 154.

[Anno]^a regni regis Edwardi filii regis Henrici sexto in crastino circumcisionis domini ita convenit inter dominum David filium Griffini [quond]am principis Wallie et Elizabeth'^b uxorem eius que fuit uxor quondam domini Willelmi Mareschall'^c militis ex parte una, et

Ioh(ann)em [Mar]eschall'ᶜ filium et heredem eiusdemᵈ Willelmi ex altera, videlicet quod dicti dominus David et Elizabeth'ᵇ concesserunt et dimiserunt, quietum[clam]averunt, sursum reddiderunt et presenti scripto confirmaverunt prefato Ioh(ann)i totum manerium de Folesh(a)m in comitatu Norf'ᵉ cum [liber]o hundredo, advocationibus ecclesiarum, homagiis, servitiis, wardis, releviis, eschaetis, maritagiis, dominicis, curiarum adquisitionibus, pratis, pascuis, pasturis, molendinis et omnibus aliis rebus et pertinentiis expressis et non expressis ad dictum manerium spectantibus, sine aliquo retenemento, quod quidem manerium cum pertinentiis predictis dicti dominus David et Elizabeth'ᵇ tenuerunt ut dotem ipsius Elizabeth'ᵇ per mortem predictiᵈ Will(elm)i Mareschall'ᶜ quondam viri sui, habendum et tenendum predicto Ioh(ann)i, heredibus suisᶠ et assignatis suis totum predictum manerium cum pertinentiis suis libere, quiete, bene et in pace tamquam recti heredes dicti manerii in feodo et hereditate imperpetuum, facienda inde annuatim capitalibus dominis feodi illius servitia inde debita et consueta pro omnibus aliis servitiis et rebus cunctis. Pro hac autem concessione, dimissione et quieta clamatione et presentis scripti confirmatione predictus Ioh(ann)es Mareschall'ᶜ concessit, dimisit et presenti scripto suo confirmavit predictis domino David et Elizabeth'ᵇ totum manerium suum de Nort'ᵍ in comitatu Norh(a)mtonʰ cum homagiis, servitiis, wardis, releviis, eschaetis, maritagiis, curiarum adquisitionibus, ecclesiarum advocationibus, boscis, pratis, pascuis, pasturis, aquis, viis, semitis et omnibus aliis rebus et pertinentiis ad dictum manerium spectantibus sine aliqua adminutione,ⁱ habendum et tenendum dictis domino David et Elizabeth'ᵇ ad totam vitam ipsius Elizabeth'ᵇ in forma sue dotis tanquam in escambio dicti manerii de Folesh(a)m quod eadem Elizabeth'ᵇ tenuisse debebatʲ in dotem ad totam vitam suam. Post cuiusᵏ Elizabeth'ᵇ decessum dictum manerium de Norton' cum omnibus pertinentiis suis predictis prefato Ioh(ann)i, heredibus vel assignatis suis quiete et solute revertatur sine impedimento dicti domini David, heredum aut assignatorum suorum. Pactum est autem et fideliter compromissum inter partes predictas quod si extenta manerii de Folesh(a)m excedat extentam manerii de Norton' vel manerium de Norton' excedat extentam manerii de Folesh(a)m, tunc pars maiorem extentam possidens supplebit et satisfaciet parti minorem extentam possidenti in terris etᶠ homagiis, ita quod minor extenta maiori equivaleat per considerationem legalium virorum ex utraque parte ad hoc electorum et convocatorum. In cuius rei testimonium partes predicte presenti scripto cyrographatoˡ alternatim sigilla sua apposuerunt. Hiis testibus: domino Gilb(ert)o comite Glou(er)n(ie), domino Rog(er)o de Mortuo Mari, domino Rog(er)o Bygodᵐ comite marescallo, domino Ioh(ann)e de Vaus, domino Reginald(o) de Grey, domino Ric(ard)o de Brewys,ⁿ Ioh(ann)e clerico et aliis.

ᵃ *all letters within square brackets supplied from* C. | ᵇ Elizabet C. | ᶜ Marescall' C. | ᵈ B *inserts* domini. | ᵉ Norf(ol)c C. | ᶠ *omitted* C. | ᵍ Norton' C. | ʰ Norhampton' C. | ⁱ diminutione C. | ʲ debeat B. | ᵏ C *inserts* vero. | ˡ cyrografphato C. | ᵐ Bigot C. | ⁿ Breuese C.

Dafydd's style in this agreement is unique among the acts of Gwynedd in referring to his father Gruffudd as 'former prince of Wales'. Dafydd married Elizabeth, daughter of William de Ferrers, fifth earl of Derby, after the death (by 30 September 1265) of her first husband William Marshal, but no later than June 1268, when Dafydd and Elizabeth let the manor of Folesham (Carr, '"Last and weakest of his line"', 381–2, citing *CPR 1258–66*, 458; *LW*, 142–3). John II Marshal came of age on 26 June 1278, when he did homage to the king for his father's lands (*CCR 1296–1302*, 542; see also Cokayne, *Complete Peerage*, viii. 527). It is likely that the present agreement was made at Westminster, as it was later said (in November 1278) to have been made in the king's court (*CCR 1272–9*, 481). Edward I's letters are dated at Westminster in late December 1277 and on 2 January 1278, the date of the agreement, and at the Tower of London 3–5 January (*CPR 1272–81*, 249; *CCR 1272–9*, 434–5). Dafydd subsequently complained that John Marshal had failed to adhere to the terms of the agreement (no. 451 below). See also nos 448–9 below.

448 Robert Burnell, bishop of Bath and Wells

Letter, from Dafydd and his wife Elizabeth, stating that they have given various thanks to the bishop for the favours he has already done them, and requesting that he will grant them a writ of the king ordering Nicholas Stapleton and Ellis Beckingham, justices of the king assigned at Northampton on the Friday after the feast of Philip and James [1 May] not to hear the plea between them and Alberic of Whittlebury and William of Helmdon without the association of Ralph Hengham and John Lovetot or other justices. Request that he informs them of his will.
[Probably *c.*March 1278 × April 1281]

> A = TNA: PRO, SC 1/22, no. 189. On tongue: domino Dei `gratia Batton' et Wellen' episcopo (in hand of letter); no endorsement; approx. 156 × 39 mm., including tongue, cut along right-hand side (approx. 82 × 9 mm.); mounted.

Venerabili in Cristo patri ac domino R. Dei gratia Batton' et Wellenc' episcopo suus in omnibus devotus David filius Griffini et Elizabeht[a] uxor eius salutem in domino pariter cum omni reverencia et honore. De bonis et curialitatibus que nobis semper vestri gratia fecistis vobis non quas tenemus set quas possumus reddidimus multimodas gratiarum actiones, et adhuc si placet vestre venerande paternitati dign[um d]uximus attente supplicandum quatinus pro amore nostro sicut pro nobis vestri gratia assidue fecistis et in vobis confidimus breve domini regis nobis concedatis ut dirigat Nicholao de Stapilton' et E. de Bekingh(a)m, iusticiariis domini regis assignatis apud Norhanto(a)n die veneris proxima post festum Ph(ilipp)i et Iacobi, quod non exsequntur placitum quod vertitur inter nos et Albric' de Wyttelbur' et Will(elm)i de Helemedene sine asociatione Ran(ulfi) de Heng(a)m et Ioh(ann)is Louetot'[b] vel aliorum iusticiariorum. Valete in domino. Velle vestrum nobis vestris si placet significetis.

[a] Elizabht A. | [b] A *inserts* de *dotted underneath for expunction.*

Since it is addressed to Robert Burnell, chancellor from September 1274, and refers to a judicial hearing at Northampton fixed for Friday after the feast of St Philip and St James (1 May), the letter is likely to be no earlier than about March 1275; in view of Dafydd's attack on Hawarden on 24 March 1282, it was probably sent no later than April 1281. It cannot have been written in 1276 as the feast of Philip and James fell on a Friday in that year. The case referred to in the letter clearly arose with respect to the manor of Norton (Northants.), as the other parties named seem to have come from, and were probably resident in, Whittlebury and Helmdon and the hearing was to take place at Northampton. Elizabeth was granted Whittlebury, a hamlet in the manor of Norton and Whittlebury (Northants.), on 4 June 1266 (*CPR 1258–66*, 602), and thus may well already have held it before she and Dafydd received the (?rest of the) manor of Norton (Northants.) from John Marshal in exchange for the manor of Folesham on 2 January 1278 (see no. 447 above). It is uncertain whether she also received Helmdon, located about 7 miles to the west of Whittlebury, in 1266, and therefore whether the dispute is likely to have arisen only after Dafydd and Elizabeth were granted Norton in 1278. Nevertheless, the association of Elizabeth with her husband Dafydd probably indicates a *terminus a quo* of 1278, as Dafydd acquired rights of lordship in Norton only after the exchange with John Marshal on 2 January of that year.

Nicholas Stapleton and Ellis Beckingham frequently served on judicial commissions for the king, including a joint commission of oyer and terminer in Lincolnshire in June 1280 (*CPR 1272–81*, 410). Stapleton was senior justice of the Worcestershire eyre in 1275, and served as a justice of King's Bench in 1273–4 and again from 1278 (Crook, *Records of the General Eyre*, 29, 37–8, 134, 142–3; Sainty, *Judges of England*, 22). Beckingham (d. ?1305) served as an assize justice 1273–85, being described as keeper of the rolls and writs of the court of King's Bench in 1278, and was a justice of Common Bench 1285–1306 (Brand, *Origins*, 28; *CPR 1272–81*, 283). Ralph Hengham (d. 1311) was chief justice of King's Bench Michaelmas 1274–Easter 1289 and John Lovetot (d. 1294) occurs as a justice of Common Pleas Easter 1275–Michaelmas 1289 (Sainty, *Judges of England*, 6, 59; *Select Cases*, ed. Sayles, cxxxvi–cxxxvii). The outcome of the present request is unknown.

449 Robert Burnell, bishop of Bath and Wells

Letter, informing him that recently in parliament Dafydd had a certain parcel of land in Gloucestershire from John Marshal by virtue of an agreement between them, namely Charlton, and that the bailiff of (?) Cheltenham (Siltenam) is molesting Dafydd's men of that vill for a certain suit since the vill came into Dafydd's hands, since he is in remote parts and unable to plead. He therefore prays the bishop to let him have two letters from the king, one to the aforesaid bailiff and the other to the sheriff of Gloucester, instructing them to allow Dafydd's men of Charlton the same liberties and customs as they were allowed in the time of William Marshal, without any molestation and especially stating that they will not attend the aforesaid suit at (?) Cheltenham (Syltenam).

[July 1278 × 1281; possibly mid-May 1280 × 1281]

A = TNA: PRO, SC 1/22, no. 188. On tongue: domino episcopo Baton' et Wellen' episcopo (in hand of letter); no endorsement; approx. 192 × 48 mm., including tongue, cut along right-hand side (approx. 97 × 7 mm.); three pairs of double slits for insertion of a tongue or tag; mounted. Cd., *CAC*, 115; *H*, no. 436.

Venerabili in Cristo patri et domino, domino R. Dei gratia Baton' et Wellenc' episcopo suus in omnibus humilis David filius Griffini cum omni genere reverencie et honoris salutem. Excellenti paternitati vestre si placet dignum duximus significandum quod quamdam[a] particulam[b] terre in comitatu Glouern(ie) a Ioh(ann)e Mareschallo pro convencione facta inter nos de escambiis maneriorum nostrorum nuper in parliamento habuimus, videlicet Cherleton', ita quod ballius de Siltenam molestat homines nostros de predicta willa[c] pro aliquo suto ex quo predicta villa venit in manu nostra, eo quod nos sumus in partibus remotis et placitare nescimus. Quare vestram si placet exoramus venerandam paternitatem fiducialiter deprecantes quatinus pro amore nostro et sicut pro nobis vestrum gratia semper fecistis duo paria literarum domini regis ad instanciam vestram nobis habere dignemini, videlicet ad predictum ballivum et vicecomitem de Glouern', ut ipsi teneant homines nostros predictos de predicta willa^c de Cherleton' in eadem libertate et consuetudine sicuti tenuerunt tempore Will(elmi) Mareschalli, sine aliqua molestia aut gravamine et precipue quod non venient ad predictum sutum de Syltena(m).

^{a} quedam A. | ^{b} particula A. | ^{c} *sic in* A.

The outer dating limits of this letter are set by the appointment of Robert Burnell as Edward I's chancellor on 21 September 1274 and Dafydd's attack on Hawarden on 21 March 1282. However, the assertion that Dafydd received Charlton (i.e. Charlton Kings, Gloucs.) from John Marshal as the result of an agreement made 'recently in parliament' concerning an exchange of their manors strongly suggests that it was written no earlier than July 1278. John made an agreement with Dafydd and his wife Elizabeth for the exchange of the manors of Folesham and Norton on 2 January 1278, and reached his majority on 26 June of that year (no. 447 and note above); the most recent parliament before that of 1 May 1278 was held in November 1276, probably too early for John to have entered into such an agreement. Indeed, it is likely that John only came into possession of Charlton after doing homage to Edward I on 26 June 1278, although his mother Elizabeth had received a grant of £4 16s. 11d. per annum from the lands and rents of the vill (whose total value was given as £16 12s. 6d.), held by her husband William Marshal (d. by 30 September 1265), on 4 June 1266 (*CPR 1258–66*, 602; see also note to no. 447 above). If so, this would push the *terminus a quo* of the letter forward to the parliament held at Gloucester on 8 July 1278. It is possible that 'the exchange of our manors' referred to was in fact that agreed on 2 January 1278 (the only exchange of manors otherwise known to have taken place between the two parties), and that John granted Charlton to Dafydd as a means of helping to provide the annual payment of £16 14s. 1d. allotted to the latter on 3 November 1278 as compensation for the difference in value between Norton and Folesham. If so, the present letter is presumably no earlier than 1280, when Dafydd claimed that for two years since the agreement in January 1278 he had received none of the income allotted to him (see no. 451 below). As parliaments were held on 12 May and after 29 September in 1280 and on 11 May and after 29 September in 1281, this would further narrow the date range of the letter to between mid-May 1280 and late 1281.

The *Siltenam/Syltenam* whose bailiff allegedly demanded suit (?of court) from the tenants of Charlton has tentatively been identified as Cheltenham, which adjoined Charlton Kings, even though the spellings differ from those cited from late eleventh- to thirteenth-century sources in Smith, *Place-Names of Gloucestershire*, 96, 101. Most forms of the place-name have an initial consonant of *Ch*, and normally end in –*ham* (e.g. *Chiltenham*, *Cheltenham*), though *Schilteham* is attested *c*.1260 and *Shiltenham* in 1341.

450 Edward I

Letter, praying the king to grant him a market each Tuesday at Frodsham, as freely as he has granted Dafydd the vill itself. Since it is hard and tedious to stay at Frodsham without any solace of hunting, he prays that the king will grant him by letter(s) a licence to hunt in the common of that vill.

[28 September × 14 October 1278]

A = TNA: PRO, SC 1/16, no. 106. No endorsements; approx. 180 mm. wide × 45 mm. deep on left, 34 mm. deep on right, including remains of tongue (approx. 67 × 8 mm.) on bottom left-hand side; mounted; foot cut away on right.
Cd., *CAC*, 74; *H*, no. 433.

Domino E. Dei gratia illustri regi Anglie, domino Hyber(nie) et duci Acquitt(anie) suus in omnibus David filius Griffini humilis et fideliter salutem et se et sua cum omni parata voluntate ad obsequiorum beneplacita. Ego siquidem vobis et vestris prostratus ac cum omni subiectione et reverencia si placet plenius provolutus excellenciam vestram duxi exorandum et ea devotione qua possum implacandum quatinus forum seu mercaturam dicte ville de Frodssam ex curialitate vestra michi vestro et fideli si placet in omnibus collate per diem martie qualibet septimana[a] tam libere et benigne quam michi vestro in omnibus predictam villam contulistis occasione precum mearum si placet concedere velitis. Et quia durum michi esset necnon et tedium moram et habere apud Frodssah(a)m sine aliquo solacio venandi, vestram igitur excellentissimam reverenciam humiliter exoro et devote ut licentiam venandi in communi dicte ville de Frodssah(a)m michi vestro in subsidium solacii si placet per litteras vestras concedere dignemini. Valete diu in domino.

[a] septimiana A.

As Edwards noted (*CAC*, 74), both requests were granted by the king in letters close dated at Worcester, 14 October 1278 (*CCR 1272–9*, 478). Presumably Dafydd's letter was written shortly before these, but after the king granted the manor of Frodsham (Ches.) to Dafydd for life on 28 September 1278 (*CPR 1272–81*, 279).

451 Edward I

Letter, informing the king that an agreement was made between John Marshal and Dafydd concerning the exchange of their manors of Folesham and Norton, namely that if through a legal valuation Folesham should exceed the value of Norton, John would assign Dafydd the surplus in other lands and renders in recompense for the value of Norton, and Dafydd would act similarly if Norton exceeded the value of Folesham. This agreement was made before John de (?) Vaux and written in the king's rolls. According to a legal valuation made on the order of the sheriff of Norfolk Folesham exceeds the value of Norton by £16 14s. 1d. Dafydd therefore prays the king to make John fulfil the terms of the agreement as Dafydd has received nothing from the agreement for two years.

[1280]

A = TNA: PRO, SC 1/16, no. 103. No endorsements; approx. 183 × 43 mm., including remains of tongue on left-hand side (approx. 90 × 6 mm.); mounted, foot cut away on right-hand side.
Cd., *CAC*, 73; *H*, no. 452.

Domino E. Dei gratia illustri regi Anglie, domino Hibern(ie) et duci Acquitt' suus in omnibus humilis, fidelis et devotus David filius Griffini salutem et se totum promptum et paratum ad sua obsequia et beneplacita voluntatem. Excellenti dominacioni vestre dignum duximus si placet significandum quod conventio facta fuit inter Ioh(ann)em Mareschal' ex parte una et nos ex altera, de escambio maneriorum nostrorum de Folesh(a)m et

Nort(a)on, videlicet quod si manerium Folesh(a)m per legalem extentam inde faciendum excederet valorem manerii de Nort(a)on, quod predictus Ioh(anne)s nobis supplusagium illud in aliis terris et tenementis vel redditibus assignaret in recompensacionem valoris predicti manerii de Nort(a)on, et nos eidem similiter econverso quod si manerium de Nort(a)on plus excederet per legalem extentam manerium de Folesh(a)m in terris, tenementis vel redditibus `eidem assignaremus. Et ista convencio facta fuit coram Ioh(ann)e(m) de (?)Vix, et scribere fecimus convencionem illam in rotulis vestris. Set ita est quod manerium de Folesh(a)m per legalem extentam et per preceptum vestrum vicecomiti Norffolch' factam plus excedit manerium Nort(a)on in sexdecim libras quatuordecim solidos et unum denarium. Quare vestram venerandam dominacionem humiliter exoramus quatinus convencionem supradictam et sicuti est in rotulis vestris a predicto Ioh(anne) Mareschal' nobis habere velitis quia per duos annos de predicta convencione nichil habuimus. Valete diu.

For the agreement referred to here, made on 2 January 1278, see no. 447 above. Dafydd was allotted £16 14s. 1d. per annum by the king on 3 November 1278 to compensate for the difference in value between Norton and Folesham (*CCR 1272–9*, 481). As Dafydd complains here that he has not received any money for two years since making the exchange agreement with John Marshal, the letter was presumably written no earlier than January 1280 (cf. *CAC*, 73). Though the reading is not entirely clear, the letter seems to state that the original agreement had been made before John de Vaux (d. 1287), who is named as a witness to that agreement (no. 447 above). It is uncertain whether Dafydd meant that John had sanctioned the agreement in some official capacity as a royal servant, or whether he was singled out here because of his high status as a senior justice of eyre from August 1278 onwards (cf. Crook, *Records of the General Eyre*, 144–5; Sanders, *Baronies*, 47, n. 6). Note also Dafydd's emphasis on the enrolment of the agreement by the royal chancery.

452 [Edward I]

Letter, informing the king that William de Venables [obtained] a writ of entry concerning the lands of Hope and Estyn situated in Wales, which Dafydd has from the king, and brought the writ in the county court of Chester and impleaded him in that court. Dafydd attended the court in person out of reverence for the king, answering there publicly that he ought not to answer in that court, as the said land belongs to Welsh land, not to Cheshire, and with a loud voice placed the peace of God and the king throughout the said land, and withdrew. Yet William prosecuted the said plea in the said court and certain of the judges of the court adjudged Dafydd to be in default before it was declared whether the said land belonged to Welsh land or to Cheshire. However, Dafydd never gave an answer in that court nor did anyone answer for him, and the seneschal of the earl of Lincoln, who ought to have taken part in that judgement, totally opposed and contradicted it. Dafydd therefore asks the king to have the proceedings of the plea, with the judgement and the judges who made it, brought to his presence and have the plea in the county court suspended. Since the king is lord of various countries and various tongues, and various laws are administered in them and not changed, let the laws of Wales be unchanged like the laws of other nations.

[1281 × 24 March 1282]

(?)B = TNA: PRO, SC 1/16, no. 102. s. xiii ex.
Cd., *CAC*, 72–3; *H*, no. 438.

Vestre excellentissime regalitati ego Dauyd filius Griffini humiliter et devote significo quod dominus Will(elmu)s de Venabeles breve de introitu super terras Hoppe et Estun in Wallia sitas quas habeo ex collatione vestra venerabili et ex concessione fideli;[a] quod breve contra me in commitatu Cestr(ie) portavit et me super dicta terra in dicto commitatu inplacitavit. Ego ad mandatum vestrum sicut decuit ad dictum commitatum personaliter ob reverenciam vestram et iusticiarii vestri accessi respondens ibidem publice in pleno commitatu quod in dicto commitatu pro dicta terra minime respondere deberem, pro eo quod dicta terra est de terra Wallicona, et non de Cest(re)cir(a),[b] pacemque Dei et vestram per dictam terram alta voce posui, submisi et sic recessi. Quibus non obstantibus dictum placitum predictus Will(elm)us in eodem commitatu prosequebatur et eiusdem commitatus iudicatores prius quam declaratum fuerit utrum predicta terra fuerit de terra Wallicona seu Cest(er)cir(a),[b] me indeffectum quidam eorum iudicaverunt; tamen nuncquam responsum in dicto commitatu dedi nec aliquis pro me in responsum intravit, tamen senescallus domini comitis Linc', qui dicto iudicio intervenire debuit, eidem iudicio omnino contradixit et penitus reclamavit. Hinc est quod vestram excellenciam rogo devotissime et requiro quatenus processum dicti placiti cum dicto iudicio ac personis dictorum iudicatorum qui dictum iudicium dederint et illud approbaverunt si placet ad vestram presenciam venire et . . . velitis dictumque placitum in dicto commitatu decetero suspendi. Quoniam gratia Dei dominus estis diversarum patriarum et diversarum linguarum, et diverse leges tractantur in ipsis nec mutantur, si placet reverencie vestre, leges Wallie sicut leges ceterarum nationum sint immutabiles.

[a] *a verb such as* obtinuit *seems to be required in this clause.* | [b] *sic in (?)*B.

It is uncertain whether the text in SC 1/16, no. 102, is a copy or an original. The lack of a greeting, which is extremely unusual, together with the omission of a main verb in the first relative clause, is more likely to reflect clumsy drafting by a poorly trained clerk than defective copying. The presence of stitch marks along the left-hand side, and of a filing hole in the top left-hand corner, are likewise inconclusive. However, the case for considering the text a copy is possibly supported by the fact that, unlike no. 453 below and most other original letters printed in this edition from SC 1, the present document has not had its foot cut away as the result of making a tongue. In addition, the text is written in pure anglicana in a hand that differs from any used to write undoubted original letters of Dafydd (cf. above, p. 81 and n. 642).

This letter and no. 453 below relate to the same case and are best discussed together. Dafydd was granted Hope and Estyn in Tegeingl by Edward I on 23 August 1277 (*CPR 1272–81*, 227). The present letter appears to be earlier than no. 453 (*pace* Smith, *Llywelyn*, 461, n. 50), as it states that the judgement was made against Dafydd before it had been decided whether Hope and Estyn lay in Wales or in Cheshire, whereas no. 453 reports the results of such an inquisition.

No. 453 almost certainly refers to a reopening of the case brought by William de Venables in December 1281. In October 1282 Dafydd identified the justice of Chester who supported William de Venables as Reginald de Grey, who was reappointed to the office on 14 November 1281 (no. 454, c. ii below; *CFR*, i. 155), and judicial records show that

Venables proceeded against Dafydd in the county court, in Grey's presence, on 16 December 1281; however, Dafydd did not appear either on that occasion or at subsequent sessions of the court on 27 January and 17 March 1282 (*Calendar of County Court*, ed. Stewart-Brown, 35, 39–45, 49, 50). At the heart of Dafydd's complaint in no. 453 is the contention that the justice of Chester had allowed Venables to proceed with the case despite the findings of an inquisition, held by the justice on royal instructions, that causes relating to Hope and Estyn should be tried by Welsh law, as the land lay in Wales. The letter does not make clear whether any hearing, on 6 December or subsequently, had taken place when Dafydd wrote (and if so, whether he had attended the court), or whether he had merely received a summons to the court.

By contrast, the present letter explicitly mentions Dafydd's appearance in court, where he refused to plead. This cannot refer to the sessions of the court held on 6 December 1281 and 27 January and 17 March 1282, although it could, perhaps, refer to another session after 16 December, as the Chester county court records in this period are incomplete (Smith, *Llywelyn*, 461). However, it is equally, if not more, likely that Dafydd's appearance in court took place during an earlier phase of Venables's action, while Guncelin of Badlesmere was justice of Chester (16 October 1274–14 November 1281; see *CFR*, i. 31, 155). As Smith has noticed (*Llywelyn*, 461, citing *Reg. Peckh.*, ii. 460), the men of Tegeingl claimed in 1282 that in 'Dafydd's case' the decision of one justice of Chester was overturned by another (i.e. Reginald de Grey), which could indicate that Venables obtained his writ of entry during Badlesmere's term of office and that Badlesmere had eventually accepted Dafydd's interpretation of the appropriate legal procedure and forum for Venables's action after the present letter was written. It is possible, therefore, that the present letter was written either in 1281 before the summons to attend the county court on 16 December (it is unlikely that the action was brought against Dafydd earlier than that year) or, less probably, early in 1282, though still before no. 453, with reference to a court session other than those held on 27 January and 17 March which, in view of Dafydd's attack on Hawarden on 24 March, presumably took place before 17 March. (The letter could have been written some time later, though, so that 24 March remains the *terminus ad quem*.) No. 453 may be assigned to a narrower date range, namely to the period between Dafydd's receipt of a summons, presumably at some point between Grey's reappointment as justice of Chester on 14 November and the first hearing on 6 December, and the outbreak of war on 24 March 1282 (thus also Smith, *Llywelyn*, 461 and n. 50).

453 Edward I

Letter, stating that recently the king instructed the justice of Chester to hold an inquisition to discover whether the land of Hope and Estyn was in Wales or England, and accordingly the justice made an inquisition through the king's men of Tegeingl and Mold which revealed that Hope and Estyn is in Wales, not England, and that Welsh rather than English law should be used there. Nevertheless, at the instance of William de Venables, the justice impleaded Dafydd over Hope and Estyn in the county court of Chester. Dafydd therefore prays the king to grant him remedy so that he shall not be troubled further over Hope and Estyn in the county court, as he is ready to respond to William and any other plaintiff before the king's justice or bailiffs according to the Welsh laws.

[*c.*15 November 1281 × 24 March 1282]

A = TNA: PRO, SC 1/16, no. 104. No endorsements; approx. 184 mm. wide × 51 mm. deep on left, 40 mm. deep on right; mounted, foot cut away.

Cd., *CAC*, 73–4; *H*, no. 437.

Excellentissimo domino suo E. Dei gratia illustri regi Angl(ie), domino Hibern(ie) et duci Acquitt' suus si placet in omnibus Dauyd filius Griffini cum propinquitate serviendi salutem. Cum nuper vestri gratia iusticiario vestro Cest(rie) significastis litteratorie quod per bonos et fideles homines de partibus Hope et Estun inquireret diligenter utrum terra Hope et Estun fuerit in Wallia seu in Anglia ac ipse secundum tenorem mandati vestri per bonos et fideles homines de hominibus vestris de Tegeigel et de Monte Alto mihi non coniunctos exactam fecit inquisitionem per quam compertum fuit quod dicta terra Hope et Estun existit in Wallia et non in Anglia et quod secundum legem Vallensicam et non Anglicanam deduci debeat, ac ipse nichilominus[a] in dicto comitatu Cest(rie) ad instanciam Will(elm)i de Venabeles me super dicta terra Hope[b] et Estun inplacitat et inquietat, hinc est quod vestram regalitatem humiliter exoro quatinus remedium in hac parte si placet michi vestro facere velitis ne amplius in dicto comitatu Cest(rie) super dicta terra Hope et Estun iniuste videar vexari modo predicto, cum secundum leges Valensicas coram iusticiario vestro seu ballivis vestris dicto W. de Venabeles ac cuilibet alii conquerenti paratus sum respondere in forma iuris. Valeat vestra regalitas per tempora longiora.

[a] nichiominus A. | [b] *sic in* A.

See note to no. 452 above.

454 Archbishop Pecham (grievances)

(1) When Dafydd first gave homage to the Lord Edward, then earl of Chester, Edward gave him the cantrefs of Dyffryn Clwyd and Rhufoniog, with all their appurtenances, by letters patent, and confirmed this gift after he had become king and gave Dafydd corporal possession of those cantrefs. After the Lady Gwenllian de Lacy died, the king unjustly seized from him, contrary to the terms of his charter, three townships which she held for life in those cantrefs and which belonged to Dafydd by the aforesaid gift.

(2) Though Dafydd obtained the townships of Hope and Estyn by the king's gift, concerning which he was not obliged to answer except by the Welsh laws, the justice of Chester, at the instance of a certain Englishman, William de Venables, had him summoned to the county court of Chester to be judged concerning those townships. Though Dafydd frequently petitioned that he should not be harmfully proceeded against in the county court, as he was in no wise obliged to answer there for those townships, which were located in Wales, but rather he should be tried according to the Welsh laws, the king totally denied him this.

(3) The same justice of Chester harmed Dafydd by having his grove of Lleweni and woods of Hope cut down by the villeins of Rhuddlan and by others, though the justice had no jurisdiction in Dafydd's lands; and not content with the timber they sought there for erecting buildings at Rhuddlan and elsewhere in the country, they destroyed the grove and transported the timber to be sold in Ireland.

(4) Though Dafydd had caught and handed over for hanging certain men banished from the king's land who were hiding in the woods, the same justice accused Dafydd before the king as

if he defended and maintained the said malefactors, which was not true, as Dafydd had the thieves hanged and killed.

(5) Though it was provided in the peace agreement that the Welsh should be tried in their causes according to the Welsh laws, this was not observed with respect to Dafydd and his men.

Concerning these and other grievances Dafydd seeks amends, according to either the laws of Wales or customs – or even by special grace, which he also seeks from the king [as] he could obtain neither of those. Moreover he was forewarned by certain of the king's court that as soon as Reginald de Grey left the court, Dafydd would be captured or his sons captured as hostages, and he would be deprived of his castle of Hope and his woods there would be cut down. Although Dafydd had laboured greatly for the king in various wars in both England and Wales, and exposed himself and his men to various dangers and injuries and lost the nobler and stronger of his men and many beyond measure, nevertheless he was unable to obtain any justice, amends or grace concerning these and other grievances. On account of these grievances and dangers, fearing the death or either the perpetual or long imprisonment of himself or his sons, as if unwillingly compelled, he began to defend himself and his people as well as he could.

[21 × 31 October 1282]

B = London, Lambeth Palace Library, Register of Archbishop Pecham, fos 243v–244r. s. xiii².

C = Oxford, All Souls College MS 182, fo. 103v–104r. *c*.1413.

Pd. from B and C, *Reg. Peckham*, ii. 445–7; from (?)C, Wynne, *History of Wales*, 371–3; from (?)Wynne, Warrington, *History of Wales*, App., 610–11.

Cd., *H*, no. 459; Edwards, *Letters of a Peacemaker*, 26.

ᵃ⁻Hec sunt gravamina illata domino David filio Griffini per dominum regem.⁻ᵃ

[i] Cum dominus David primo venisset ad dominum Edwardu(m), tunc comitem Cestr(ie), ac homagium sibi fecisset, idem dominus [fo. 244r] Edward(us) eidem David duas cantredas, videlicet de Dyfryncluytᵇ et Kywonaut, cum omnibus suis pertinentiis, dedit plenarie, et litteras suas patentes super hoc fieri fecit, tandem etiam donationem eidem innovavit,ᶜ postquam creatus est in regem et etiam ipsumᵈ D(avi)d in possessionem illarum cantredarumᵉ induxit coporalem. Demum domina Wenliauntᶠ de Lacy mortua, tres villas quas in dictis cantredis tenuit quo ad vitam, que ad ipsam David spectebant ratione donationis supradicte, dominus rex sibi abstulit minus iuste contra tenorem carte sue.

[ii] Item, cum dictus D(avi)d ex donatione domini regis predicti villas de Hope et Eston' obtineret in Wallia, de quibus nulli respondere tenebatur nisi secundum leges Wallicanas; tandem iusticiarius Cestr(ie) fecit ipsum ad instantiam cuiusdam Anglici Will(elm)i de Vanabel nomine ad comitatum Cestr(ie) super dictis villulis ad iudicium evocari. Et licet dictus dominus David petivisset multotiens quod iniuriose contra eundem non procederetur in dicto comitatu, pro eo quod ibidem respondere nullatenus tenebatur super villis predictis, que site erant in Wallia, sed potius tractaretur ᵍ⁻[secundum] leges Wallicanas,⁻ᵍ hoc sibi plane denegavit.

[iii] Item, idem iusticiarius Cestr(ie) in gravamen dicti domini D(avi)d nemus suum de Leweny et silvas suas de Hope fecit succidi, tam per villanos de Ruthelanʰ quam per alios, cum idem iusticiarius in terris predicti domini D(avi)d nullam haberet omnino iurisdictionem; et non contenti quod meremium ibidem quererent ad edificia erigenda, tam apud Rodolanu(m)ⁱ quam alibi in patria, sedʲ nemus destruendo, meremium ibidem factum ad vendendum in Hyb(er)niaᵏ transtulerunt.

[iv] Item, cum idem dominus D(avi)d quosdam forbanitos de terra domini regis, qui in

nemoribus latitabant, cepisset ac suspendio tradidisset, tamen idem iusticiarius ipsum D(avi)d penes regem accusabat ac si ipse dictos malefactores defenderet et manuteneret, quod verisimile non erat, cum ipse David dictos latrones suspendi faceret et occidi.

[v] Item, cum esset cautum in forma pacis quod Walenses deberent in causis suis tractari secundum leges Wallicanas, istud tamen circa dictum David et suos homines in nullo extitit observatum.

De premissis vero gravaminibus et aliis, petiit idem David aliquam emendationem, vel secundum leges Wallie, vel secundum^{l} consuetudines, vel etiam ex gratia speciali, et hoc etiam petiit a domino rege, quorum neutrum potuit aliquatenus optinere. Et cum hoc premunitus fuit a quibusdam a curia domini regis, quod in primo regressu domini Reginaldi de Grey^{m} de curia, idem D(avi)d esset capiendus vel filii sui capiendi pro obsedibus; esset insuper spoliandus castro suo de Hope, et etiam silva sua ibidem succidenda. Ideo cum idem D(avi)d multum laborasset pro domino rege predicto in diversis gwerris^{n} tam in Anglia quam in Wallia, et exposuisset se et suos variis periculis et iniuriis, ac amisisset nobiliores de suis et fortiores ac multos nimis, nichilominus de dictis gravaminibus et aliis nullam omnino iustitiam, emendationem seu gratiam potuit obtinere. Propter que gravamina et pericula timens mortem propriam aut filiorum suorum vel incarcerationem perpetuam vel saltem diutinam, quasi coactus et invitus, incepit prout potuit se et suos defensare.

$^{a-a}$ *underlined by scribe of* B; *omitted in* C, *which has space for rubrication.* | ^{b} Diffryncluyt C. | ^{c} invocavit C. | ^{d} illum C. | ^{e} t *written above* d *with dot underneath for expunction* B. | ^{f} Wenliant C. | $^{g-g}$ *omitted* C. | ^{h} Ruthlan C. | ^{i} Rodelanum C. | ^{j} set C. | ^{k} Hiberniam C. | ^{l} *omitted* C. | ^{m} Gray' C. | ^{n} guerris C.

These grievances immediately follow those of Llywelyn ap Gruffudd in Pecham's register and, like the latter, are datable to 21 × 31 October 1282 (see nos 428–9 above). The Lord Edward granted Dafydd Dyffryn Clwyd and Rhufoniog (c. i), to be held until Dafydd had obtained all his inheritance beyond the Conwy and elsewhere in North Wales, on 8 July 1263; the grant was renewed by Edward I at Rhuddlan, during his first war against Llywelyn ap Gruffudd, on 10 October 1277 (*CPR 1272–81*, 231–2). For Gwenllian de Lacy, a daughter of Llywelyn ap Iorwerth and Tangwystl and therefore Dafydd's aunt, see no. 251 above. Her lands, with the custody of Rhos and Tegeingl, were granted to Reginald de Grey on his appointment as justice of Chester on 14 November 1281 (*CPR 1272–81*, 464; Smith, *Llywelyn*, 462, n. 53). For the case concerning Hope and Estyn (c. ii) see nos 452–3 above. The reference to the provision in the peace agreement allowing the Welsh to be tried by Welsh law (c. v) may be an allusion to the Treaty of Aberconwy (see no. 402, c. xiii above), although that merely conceded that Welsh law could be used in disputes between Llywelyn ap Gruffudd and others concerning matters in Wales. For similar claims to that advanced by Dafydd see *WAR*, 258, 266.

455 Archbishop Pecham
Statements on behalf of Dafydd, brother of the prince.
 (1) When he wishes to go to the Holy Land he will do so voluntarily, for God, not for man. He will not travel there against his will, as he knows that forced services are displeasing to God.

If he should later go to the Holy Land, he and his heirs should not be disinherited because of this, but should be rewarded.

(2) Since the prince and his supporters did not wage war out of hatred or a desire for riches by invading foreign lands, but rather by defending their own patrimony, rights and liberties, and the king and his supporters made war on the prince's lands out of inveterate hatred and avarice, Dafydd believes that they are fighting a just war and hopes that God will help them, by bringing divine vengeance upon the devastators of churches who have burned churches to the ground, robbed them of their sacraments, killed clergy and religious as well as the blind, deaf and dumb, suckling infants and the weak of both sexes and committed other enormities, as contained in the rolls sent to the archbishop. Therefore the archbishop should not pronounce any sentence against any others than those who have committed these actions. Those who have thus suffered from the king's supporters hope that the archbishop will give them remedy, and turn his attention to those who have committed sacrilege and their supporters, lest for lack of correction or vengeance the aforesaid evils provide an example to others for ever.

(3) Very many in Dafydd's land are surprised that the archbishop advises him to leave his own land for a foreign one land and live there among his enemies. Since he is unable to have peace in his own land, how much less will he be able to live peacefully in a foreign land among his enemies.

(4) Though it is hard to live in war, it is harder for a Christian people, which seeks only to defend its rights, to be utterly destroyed and reduced to nothing. Necessity compels Dafydd and the greed of enemies offends him. Reminds the archbishop that he said in Dafydd's presence that he would pronounce sentence on all who prevented peace because of hatred or avarice; yet it is clear who wages war for those reasons. Fear of death, imprisonment or perpetual disinheritance, non-observance of agreements and charters, tyrannical domination and many other similar things compel Dafydd to war; he is showing this to God and the archbishop and seeking the latter's help, as is clear from Dafydd's letters.

(5) Many others in the kingdom of England have offended the king yet he has disinherited none of these. If any of Dafydd's men have offended the king unjustly, they should give satisfaction without disinheritance; the archbishop is asked to work for this. If Dafydd is accused of having broken the peace, it has been more truly broken by those who have kept no agreements with him or given him any amends for grievances, as is shown in the rolls.

[Garthcelyn, 11 November 1282]

B = London, Lambeth Palace Library, Register of Archbishop Pecham, fo. 248v. s. xiii[2].

C = Oxford, All Souls College MS 182, fo. 112r–113r. *c*.1413.

Pd. from B and C, *Reg. Peckh.*, ii. 471–3; from (?)C, Wynne, *History of Wales*, 393–5; from (?)Wynne, Warrington, *History of Wales*, App., 625–6.

Cd., *H*, no. 461; Edwards, *Letters of a Peacemaker*, 32–3.

Ista sunt dicenda pro David fratre principis.

[i] Quod cum voluerit Terram Sanctam adire, hoc faciet voluntarie et ex voto, pro Deo, non pro homine. Unde invitus non peregrinabitur Deo dante, quia coacta servitia Deo novit displicere. Et si contingat ipsum inposterum Terram Sanctam adire, bona ductus voluntate, non propter hoc deberent ipse et heredes sui inperpetuum exheredari, immo potius premium obtinere.

[ii] Preterea, quia princeps et sui, causa odii ad aliquos concipiendi vel lucri captandi, non moverunt gwerram[a] alienas terras invadendo, sed[b] suam propriam hereditatem, iura

libertatesque necnon suorum defendendo, dominusque rex et sui odio inveterato et causa lucrandi terras nostras, gwerram[a] fecit, credimus in hoc iustam gwerram[a] nos fovere, et speramus in hac Deum nos velle iuvare, ac in ecclesiarum devastatores divinam ultionem convertere, qui ecclesias funditus destruxerunt ac combusserunt, sacra ex eis rapuerunt, sacerdotes, clericos, religiosos, claudos, surdos, mutos, infantes ubera lactentes ac debiles et miserabiles personas utriusque sexus occiderunt et alia enormia perpetrarunt, sicut in dictis rotulis vobis transmissis continetur. Unde absit a sancta paternitate vestra sententiam aliquam fulminare in alios quam in illos qui predicta perpetrarunt. Nos enim qui a regalibus predicta passi sumus, speramus a vobis super premissis paternum solacium et remedium obtinere, et in predictos sacrilegos eorumque fautores, qui nullo super hiis privilegio defenduntur, animadvertere, ne pre defectu digne correctionis seu ultionis in eos exercende, predicta mala inperpetuum per alios trahantur ad[c] exemplum.

[iii] Mirantur etiam quamplures in terra nostra, quod consuluistis nobis dimittere terram nostram propriam, et alienam adire inter hostes nostros conversando. Quia ex quo non possumus pacem habere in terra que nostra est ipso iure, multominus poterimus in aliena patria inter hostes nostros pacifice conversari.

[iv] Et licet durum sit in gwerra[d] et insidiis vitam ducere, durius tamen est funditus destrui et ad nichilum, nisi Deus avertat, deduci populum Cristianum, qui nichil aliud querit nisi sua iura defendere. Unde necessitas ad hoc nos cogit et inimicorum cupiditas nos offendit. Et vos, sancte pater, coram nobis dixistis quod vos sententiastis in omnes qui impediunt pacem causa odii vel lucri, sed[b] manifestum est qui sunt illi qui gwerrant[e] istis causis. Timor enim mortis et incarcerationis `vel` perpetue exheredationis, nulla observatio federum, pactorum vel cartarum, tyrannica dominatio et multa alia consimilia, cogunt nos esse in gwerris,[f] et hoc Deo et vobis ostendimus et petimus a vobis paternum adiutorium, ut patet in litteris nostris.

[v] Ad hec multi alii in regno Anglie offenderunt regem et tamen nullos exheredavit imperpetuum, ut dicitur. Unde si aliqui ex nostris ipsum offenderunt iniuste, dignum est ut satisfaciant, prout possunt, sine exheredatione, et sicut in vobis confidimus supplicamus quod ad hoc laboretis, sancte pater. Nam et si nobis imponatur quod fregimus pacem, tamen illi verius fregerunt, qui nullum fedus vel pactum nobis servaverunt, qui nullam emendam de querimoniis nobis fecerunt, ut patet in rotulis.

[a] guerram C. | [b] set C. | [c] in C. | [d] guerra C. | [e] guerrant C. | [f] guerris C.

These replies on behalf of Dafydd immediately follow nos 430–1 above, sent on 11 November 1282, and evidently belong to the same date as those documents. All three documents were written in response to proposals brought by John of Wales to Llywelyn's court at Garthcelyn after 6 November 1282. For the proposals conveyed from the archbishop to Dafydd which were rejected in the present letter see *Reg. Peckh.*, ii. 467–8. One notable feature of the present replies is their attempt to defend the warfare waged by the Welsh in terms consistent with ecclesiastical notions of a just war.

456 Letter patent concerning John ap Dafydd

Notification that he has appointed his faithful man John ap Dafydd, bearer of the present letter, to invite all the men of Builth, Brecon, Maelienydd, Elfael, Gwerthrynion and Ceri to *him as if Dafydd himself had been present, and Dafydd will be bound firmly with regard to all that John will do on his behalf concerning lands, services and other matters. Since John dared not take Dafydd's letters to each of them individually, let them place faith in the present charter (*sic*) in all things. Sealing clause. They will be ready to come to Dafydd whenever they have been requested by John in the period before the feast of John the Baptist [24 June].*

Llanberis, 2 May 1283

B = TNA: PRO, E 36/274 (Liber A), fo. 356r. s. xiii ex.
Pd. from B, *LW*, 77 (no. 146).
Cd., *H*, no. 462.

[O]mnibus Cristi fidelibus has litteras visuris vel audituris David filius Gryffini princeps Wall(ie) et dominus Snaudonie salutem in domino. Noverit universitas vestra quod nos pro nobis et heredibus nostris dedimus, concessimus et in omnibus constituimus dilectum nostrum fidelem Ioh(ann)em filium David latorem presentium ad invitandum omnes homines de Buellt, de P(re)conia, Maelienyd, Eluael, Gwerthrennyawn et Kery ad nos ac si nos fuissemus presentes, et quantumque fecerit ex parte nostra de terris et servitiis et de aliis rebus in omnibus firmiter tenemur. Et quoniam predictus Ioh(ann)es non fuit ausus singulariter ad unumquemque vestrum litteras nostras specialiter deducere, presenti carte fidem in omnibus adhybeatis. In cuius rei testimonium presenti carte sigillum nostrum fecimus apponi, dum vos eritis parati ad nos venire quandocumque fueritis ab ipso requisiti infra festum Beati Ioh(ann)is Bapt(ist)e. Datum apud Lanperis die dominica in crastino Ph(ilipp)i et Iacobi anno domini m° cc° octuagesimo tertio.

The place-date suggests that Dafydd was at Dolbadarn castle (Carr, 'Last days of Gwynedd', 18, n. 53). In the event, he was captured, together with his wife, two sons and seven daughters, on 22 June 1283, two days before the Nativity of John the Baptist set in the letter as the deadline for the lords' arrival to help him (Carr, '"Last and weakest of his line"', 392).

457 Rhys Fychan ap Rhys ap Maelgwn

Grant of the whole cantref of Penweddig with all its appurtenances, to be possessed freely for ever without any dues to Dafydd or anyone else. In return for this grant Rhys ought to come to Dafydd whenever he is required with all his men in the period before the feast of John the Baptist [24 June], and afterwards let him and his heirs be faithful to Dafydd and his heirs in all things. Sealing clause; witnesses.

Llanberis, 2 May 1283

B = TNA: PRO, E 36/274 (Liber A), fo. 355v. s. xiii ex.
Pd. from B, *LW*, 74–5 (no. 139).
Cd., Stephenson, *Governance*, 204; *H*, no. 157.

[O]mnibus Cristi fidelibus has litteras visuris vel audituris David filius Griffini princeps Wallie dominus Snawdon eternam in domino salutem. Noveritis nos pro nobis et heredibus nostris dedisse et concessisse dilecto et fideli nostro Reso Vichan filio Resi filii Maelgwn totum cantredum de Penuedic in terminis et finibus suis, in bosco et plano, cultis et incultis et in omnibus aliis pertinentiis et asyamentis, libere et pacifice possidendum sine aliquo onere vel exactione nobis seu alicui alii solvendo inperpetuum. Pro hac autem donatione et concessione predictus Resus debet ad nos venire quandocumque a nobis requisitus fuerit cum toto posse suo infra festum Beati Ioh(ann)is Bapt(ist)e, et postea quod sit[a] ipse et heredes sui nobis et heredibus nostris fidelis[b] in omnibus. In cuius rei testimonium sigillum nostrum presenti carte fecimus apponi. Datum apud Lanperis die dominica in crastino Ph(ilipp)i et Iacobi anno domini m° cc° octuagesimo tertio. Hiis testibus: Houelo filio Resy, Reso Vichan, Morgan filio Mareduc, Lewelin filio Rys, Goronow filio Heylin tunc senescallo domini et multis aliis.

[a] *sic in* B. | [b] fidel' B.

See note to no. 456 above. A similar grant of the cantref of Penweddig in northern Ceredigion was made on the same occasion as the present charter by Rhys's kinsman Gruffudd ap Maredudd ab Owain (no. 78 above). As Smith has pointed out (*Llywelyn*, 571–2), Rhys Fychan was in royal pay at the time of the grant, having sided with the king after William de Valence drove through Ceredigion early in 1283.

RHODRI AP GRUFFUDD
(d. *c*.1315)

458 Llywelyn, prince of Wales, his brother

Gift and quitclaim, of his own will, on behalf of himself and his heirs, of all the hereditary right and claim he has and ought to have in the lands and possessions of North Wales or elsewhere in the principality of Wales, in return for 1,000 marks sterling which the prince has paid in advance in order to acquire for Rhodri the marriage of Emonina, daughter of John le Botiller. Rhodri promises on behalf of himself and his heirs that he will not disturb the prince or his heirs contrary to this gift and quitclaim. Sealing clause; witnesses.

Caernarfon, 12 April 1272

B = TNA: PRO, C 54/95 (Close R. 6 Edward I), m. 4d (enrolled 11 September 1278).
C = TNA: PRO, C 47/10/43, no. 2. s. xiii ex.
D = TNA: PRO, E 36/274 (Liber A), fo. 360v. s. xiii ex.
Pd. from D, *LW*, 85–6 (no. 165).
Cd., *CCR 1272–9*, 506 (from B); *H*, no. 404.

Universis presentes litteras visuris vel audituris Roderic(us) filius Griffini salutem. Noverit universitas vestra nos mera et bona voluntate nostra dedisse et quietum clamasse pro nobis et heredibus nostris domino Lewelino principi Wall(ie) fratri nostro et heredibus suis de corpore suo nascentibus totum ius hereditarium[a] et clamium quod habemus et habere debemus in terris et possessionibus apud Norwall(iam) vel alibi per totum principatum Wall(ie) pro mille marcis sterlingorum quas dictus dominus princeps nobis solvit premanibus ad acquietandum nobis maritagium Emonine filie Ioh(ann)is le Botiller.[b] Promittimus etiam bona fide pro nobis et nostris heredibus quod non inquietabimus neque per aliquos alios inquietari procurabimus dictum dominum principem vel suos heredes de se progenitos contra presentem nostram donationem et $^{c-}$quietum clamium.$^{-c}$ Ad plenam autem prescriptorum fidem et securitatem presenti scripto sigillum nostrum apposuimus una cum sigillis venerabilium patrum de Bangor' et de Sancto Assaph' episcoporum necnon et abbatum de Aberconwey,^{d} Basingwerk'^{e} et Enlly,^{f} cum adiectione sigillorum virorum discretorum de Bangor' et de Sancto Assaph' archidiaconorum. Hiis testibus: Tudero filio Etnyuet^g senescallo Wall(ie), Anniano filio Kaeradauk,^{h} David^i filio Ennyaun,^{j} Reso filio Griffini,^{k} Kenewrico^l filio Goronow,^{m} magistro^n Will(elm)o et David clericis domini principis cum multis aliis. Datum et actum apud Kaerinaruon anno domini m^o cc^o septuagesimo^o secundo ii^o idus aprilis.

^{a} hereditatem D. | ^{b} Botelyr D. | $^{c-c}$ quietam clamationem D. | ^{d} Aberconwy CD. | ^{e} Basingwerc D. ^{f} Enlli D. | ^{g} Etnyued CD. | ^{h} Keradauk' C; Keyradauc D. | ^{i} Dauit D. | ^{j} Enniaun CD. | ^{k} Grifini C. ^{l} Kynwrico CD. | ^{m} Goronew C; Goronw D. | ^{n} magistris C. | ^{o} lxx^o C.

The text in B is a copy made during judicial proceedings before Edward I at Rhuddlan, 10–11 September 1278, when Rhodri claimed his share of the principality of North Wales. Llywelyn had the abbot of Aberconwy produce the document as evidence that Rhodri had quitclaimed his share (suggesting that it had been kept at that abbey, whose abbot was also one of the document's witnesses), but Rhodri, while acknowledging that he made the grant, said that he had received only fifty marks out of the 1,000 marks allegedly given by Llywelyn; on 11 September Rhodri agreed to the quitclaim on condition that Llywelyn find the remaining 950 marks (*CCR 1272–9*, 506–7). The text in C is preserved on a single sheet, and appears to be another copy, as it lacks any evidence of sealing, such as slits for tags, that would point to its being the original; possibly it, too, was made at the time of the 1278 hearing, as the same chancery file contains another document, damaged and incomplete, which seems to contain another copy of the record of these proceedings (TNA: PRO, C 47/10/43, no. 4). Llywelyn had agreed to pay the 1,000 marks after his submission to the king at Aberconwy in November 1277 (no. 405 above), but the case brought by Rhodri at Rhuddlan shows that he had failed to do so by September 1278.

Emonina (referred to in other sources as Edmunda or Emoina) was the only daughter and heiress of John le Botiller (Butler), Anglo-Irish lord of Aherlow (Co. Limerick), who died in 1260 (see Nicholls, 'Butlers of Aherlow', 124–5; I am very grateful to Seán Duffy for this identification and the reference). Her marriage to Rhodri never took place, presumably because he lacked the money required, and by 5 January 1275 Emonina had married Thomas de Multon (d. by May 1290) of Egremont in Cumberland; before that her lands had been held in custody by Otto de Grandson (*CDI 1252–84*, 189 (no. 1080)). If she was under the wardship of Otto in 1272, her proposed marriage to Rhodri had presumably been agreed with him and possibly also with Henry III. Thomas de Multon died by May 1290, Emonina by July 1290; their son Thomas gave homage to the king for his mother's lands on 12 May 1296 after reaching his majority (*CDI 1285–92*, 289, 340 (nos 591, 708); *CDI 1293–1301*, 135–6 (no. 296)). Rhodri subsequently married, by 1281, Beatrice (d. 1290), daughter of Sir David de Malpas, a Cheshire knight. (*Cart. Chester*, 223, 224 shows that Beatrice's first husband, William Patrick of Malpas, was dead by November 1281, as their daughter Isabel was claiming lands then as William's heir; see also Ormerod, *History*, ii. 598; *CIPM*, ii, no. 749.)

459 Letter patent concerning Llywelyn, prince of Wales

Acknowledgement of receipt from the abbot and convent of Aberconwy of 100 marks in silver on All Saints' Day [1 November] 1280 which Llywelyn, prince of Wales was obliged to pay him in that abbey on that day, and quitting Llywelyn of the payment. As evidence of this he has made this letter patent for Llywelyn.

Aberconwy, 1 November 1280

> B = TNA: PRO, E 36/274 (Liber A), fo. 341v. s. xiii ex.
> Pd. from B, *LW*, 42 (no. 62).
> Cd., *H*, no. 451.

[O]mnibus Cristi fidelibus has litteras visuris vel audituris Roserius filius Griffini salutem in domino sempiternam. Noveritis me recepisse per manus domini abbatis de Aberconeway et conventus eiusdem loci in dicta abbatia centum marchas argenti bone et legalis monete die omnium sanctorum anno gratie m° c°c° octogesimo in quibus dominus Lewelin(us) princeps Wallie `michi` in dicto die in dicta abbatia persolvere tenebatur, unde dictum dominum Lewelinu(m) de illo termino quietum clamo et me bene esse pacatum. In cuius rei testimonium litteras meas eidem domino Leuwellino fieri feci patentes. Valete. Datum apud Aberconeway dictis die et loco prenotatis.

As Edwards suggested (*LW*, 42), this money may have been due under the agreement made in September 1278 whereby Llywelyn was to pay Rhodri 950 marks (see note to no. 458 above).

*460 St Werburgh's Abbey, Chester

Quitclaim, by Rhodri and his wife Beatrice, of their rights in a spring in the field of Christleton near the boundaries between the said field and the field of Boughton, with all liberties and easements which the spring and its conduit require, as contained in the charter of Philip Burnell and his wife Isabel.

[*c.*1281 × 15 September 1283; probably 18 November 1281 × -6 November 1282]

Summary only, in the early fourteenth-century cartulary of St Werburgh's Abbey, Chester (*Cart. Chester*, 225 (no. 341); cd., *H*, no. 158). The outer dating limits of this quitclaim are fixed by Rhodri's marriage to Beatrice, which had taken place by November 1281, and (very probably) by Edward I's licence of 15 September 1283 allowing the abbey to carry its conduit from its well in the field of Christleton across its own lands and those of others and through the city wall of Chester (see note to no. 458 above and *Cart. Chester*, 226 (no. 343); *CPR 1281–92*, 75). However, if, as is probable, it was issued at the same time as or shortly after the grant it refers to by Sir Philip Burnell and his wife Isabel (Beatrice's daughter by her first marriage to William Patrick of Malpas), it pre-dated Philip's death in Luke de Tany's assault across the Menai Straits on 6 November 1282 (*Cart. Chester*, 225 (no. 340), and cf. ibid., 223). Furthermore, that grant is unlikely to be earlier than the recognition by Philip and Isabel, in a final concord at Westminster on 18 November 1281, of the abbey's right to hold certain manors which they had claimed as part of Isabel's inheritance (ibid., 222–4 (nos 336–7)). Philip was very probably a nephew of Robert Burnell, Edward I's chancellor (ibid., 223–4). Christleton (SJ 441 657) lay about 2 miles south-east of St Werburgh's in the parish of St Oswald's.

GWYNLLŴG

MORGAN AB OWAIN
(d. 1158)

*461 Glastonbury Abbey
Grant of fourteen acres in the moor of (?) Maen-brith (Meinbrit).

[15 April 1136 × 1158]

Mention only, in a confirmation of Hywel ap Iorwerth probably datable to 1179 × 1184 (no. 467 below). Gwynllŵg, the territory in which *Meinbrit* was located, was conquered by Morgan and his brother Iorwerth following their killing of Richard fitz Gilbert de Clare on 15 April 1136.

462 The church of St John the Baptist, Rumney
Greeting by Morgan and Iorwerth sons of Owain to their lord, William earl of Gloucester and Mabel his mother and to all their friends and men. They have granted in fee and alms, free of all exaction and service, 40 acres in the moor of Rumney out of the 300 acres which their lord, Robert, earl of Gloucester gave them in that moor for their service, for the salvation of the souls of themselves, the earl and their other predecessors. Earl Robert granted these things at Bristol as set out here. Witnesses (not named).

[November 1147 × 1157; possibly November 1147 × 1148]

B = Berkeley Castle Muniments, Select Book 1 (Cartulary of St Augustine's Abbey, Bristol; microfilm copies in Gloucestershire Record Office, MF 1071, and Oxford, Bodleian Library MS Film Dep. 912), fo. 27v. s. xiii[2].
Pd. from B, *Cart. Bristol*, no. 49; from B, Crouch, 'Slow death', 41 (trans. only).
Cd., *H*, no. 174.

Domino suo Will(elm)o consuli Gloce' et Mabilie matri eius et omnibus amicis suis et hominibus Morgan(us) et Iereuert filii Oni salutem. Notum vobis facimus nos dedisse et concessisse in feudo et elemosina quiete et libere et absque omni exactione et servitio ecclesie Sancti Ioh(ann)is Bapt(iste) de Ru(m)nia xl acras terre in maresco Ru(m)ni de illis tricentis acris quas dominus noster Rob(ertus) consul Gloec' nobis pro nostro servitio in predicto maresco dedit, pro salute anime nostre et predicti consulis et aliorum antecessorum nostrorum. Hec ita ut hic diffinitum est predictus Rob(ertus) consul apud Brist' concessit. Testibus etc.

The dating limits are fixed by the death of Robert of Gloucester on 1 November 1147 and that of his widow Countess Mabel in 1157 (*AM*, i. 14, 48). Mabel made a similar grant to St John's church, likewise after Earl Robert's death, of 60 acres from land in Rumney marsh given her by Robert (*Cart. Bristol*, no. 50). Earl William granted the advowson of St John's, Rumney, to the canons of St Augustine on Flat Holm (*Plata Holma*) and also, probably subsequently, granted Flat Holm to St Augustine's Abbey, Bristol; both charters are datable to 1148 × 1183 (ibid., nos 43, 45; cf. no. 46, and p. xxii). As the present grant is made only to St John's church, whose advowson was held by the earl of Gloucester, it presumably pre-dates the transfer to St Augustine's of the church, along with the community on Flat Holm, and therefore could be earlier than the foundation of the abbey in 1148 (cf. ibid., xiv–xxii). This would imply that the charter was issued shortly after Earl Robert's death, a possibility supported by the reference to Earl Robert's having consented to the grant. It is striking that William is addressed as *consul*, the title adopted by his father Robert, to whom it is also applied in the charter, but never used by William in his own acts though it was retained on his seal (*EGC*, 22–4). This, too, could point to a date shortly after Robert's death, before William's style of *comes Gloecestrie* had become well established. That *Plata Holma* denoted the island of Flat Holm, rather than that of Steep Holm which lies about $2\frac{1}{2}$ miles to its south (as suggested in *Cart. Bristol*, no. 43 n.), is suggested not only by its name but by its location close to the coast of Glamorgan and by evidence that it contained a pre-Norman ecclesiastical site (see RCAHMW, *Glamorgan I. iii*, 18, 44; *VSB*, 90–2 (*Vita S. Cadoci*, c. 29)). Steep Holm also had an Augustinian cell or hermitage by the thirteenth century, but this was dependent on Studley Priory in Warwickshire (Dickinson, *Origins of the Austin Canons*, 141, 238).

463 Goldcliff Priory

Grant and confirmation by Morgan and his brother Iorwerth, in perpetual alms, by their common consent, for the salvation of the souls of themselves and of all their ancestors and heirs, of all the gifts in Wales given by Robert de Candos, his wife Isabel and their heir Walter while they still held and peacefully possessed for a long time the lordship of the honour of Caerleon, namely lands, churches, tithes, renders, possessions and all other things in wood, plain, ways, waters and all other places as their charters and the confirmations of King Henry the elder and King Henry the younger attest. These were the grants of Robert, Isabel and Walter, for the love of God and their salvation: the church of St Mary Magdalene, Goldcliff with the chapel of Nash and all its other appurtenances in the moor of Goldcliff; the church of St Julius and St Aaron [St Julians] with all its appurtenances; and the church of the Holy Trinity near Caerleon [Christchurch] with all its appurtenances. Confirmation by this writing and their seal of all these churches and all other lands, renders and possessions granted by Robert and other faithful whose names are given in the charter of their lord King Henry the younger, who granted Morgan and Iorwerth the land. They wish the monks to hold them for ever freely, quit and in peace. In addition, being aware of the monks' holy religion, good way of life and charity, they have granted 200 acres in the moor of Goldcliff; Blenchesfeld within and without; the mill called (?) Milton (Bide); 3 acres next to that mill on the north side; 15

acres in the moor to the south of that mill; a fishery in the Usk called Five Fisheries; another
fishery on the other side of the Usk near St Nigarum; and a land near Caerleon bridge on the
east side near the water as the road and dyke form a boundary. Witnesses.

[19 December 1154 × 1158]

B = TNA: PRO, C 53/76 (Ch. R. 18 Edward I), m. 10 (in an inspeximus, 1 July 1290).
C = TNA: PRO, C 53/107 (Ch. R. 14 Edward II), m. 3 (in an inspeximus of B, 24 February 1320).
Cd., *CChR 1257–1300*, 358–9 (from B); Crouch and Thomas, 'Three Goldcliff charters', 156 (no. 5; from B); *CChR 1300–26*, 434 (from C); *H*, no. 175.

Sciant presentes et futuri quod ego Morgan(us) filius Oeni et Geruerd(us) frater meus de nostro communi assensu et voluntate donavimus et concessimus et presenti carta confirmavimus pro salute nostra et omnium antecessorum et heredum nostrorum Deo et ecclesie Sancte Mar(ie) Magdal(ene) Golcl(iue) et monachis Becci ibidem Deo servientibus in puram et perpetuam et liberam elemosinam omnes donationes quas Rob(ertu)s de Candos et Isabel uxor eius et Walt(erus) heres eorum eis dederunt in Wall(ia) dum adhuc dominium honoris de Karl(iun) optinuerunt et per longum tempus pacifice possiderunt terrarum scilicet ecclesiarum, decimarum, reddituum, possessionum et omnium aliarum rerum in bosco et in plano, in viis et semitis, in exitibus et in aquis et in omnibus aliis locis sicut carte eorum et confirmationes regum Henr(ici) scilicet senioris et Henr(ici) iunioris eis testantur. Hec sunt autem que Rob(er)tus de Candos et Isabel uxor eius et Walt(eru)s heres eorum predicte ecclesie Golcl(iue) et eiusdem loci monachis pro amore Dei et pro salute sua dederunt et concesserunt: ecclesiam scilicet Sancte Mar(ie) Magdal(ene) Golcliue[a] cum capella de Fraxino ad eam pertinente et cum omnibus aliis pertinentiis suis in mora Golcliue, ecclesiam Sanctorum Iulii et Aaron cum omnibus pertinentiis suis, ecclesiam Sancte Trinitatis iuxta Karliun cum omnibus pertinentiis suis. Has omnes ecclesias et omnes alias terras, redditus et possessiones quas prefatus Rob(er)tus et ceteri fideles quorum nomina in carta domini nostri Henr(ici) regis iunioris qui nobis terram dedit expressius annotantur ego prefatus Morgan(us) et Geruerdus frater meus sepedictis monachis Golcliue donavimus et concessimus et presentis scripti testimonio et sigilli[b] nostri appositione confirmavimus et volumus ut eas habeant et teneant libere, quiete et pacifice imperpetuum. Preterea sanctam religionem et bonam conversationem eorum et caritatem que in eis vigebat attentius perpendentes ut melius et devotius divinis operibus possint intendere ad eorum necessariam sustentationem, dedimus eis et confirmavimus ducentas acras terre in mora Golcliue et Blenchesfeld' interiorem et exteriorem et unum molendinum nomine Bide et tres acras terre iuxta predictum molendinum ex parte aquilonis et quindecim acras terre in mora versus austrum eiusdem molendini. Dedimus etiam eisdem monachis unam piscinam in Vsca que vocatur Quinque Piscarie et aliam piscinam in transversum Vsche iuxta Sanctum Nigarum et unam terram iuxta pontem de Karl(iun) ex parte orientis prope aquam sicut via et fossa dividit.[c] His testibus: Rad(ulf)o presbitero, Abrah(a)m presbitero, Will(elm)o presbitero, Cradoco filio Bernardi, Iuor filio Curedi, magistro Clemente, Hennion filio Luioard', Ythel ab Hely, Ruathlan albo.

[a] Golciue B. | [b] *corrected from* singilli *by dotting underneath* n *for expunction* B. | [c] *sic in* B.

The dating limits are set by the accession of Henry II, whose confirmation for Goldcliff, no longer extant, is referred to (*carta domini nostri Henrici regis iunioris*), and the death of

Morgan in 1158 (Crouch and Thomas, 'Three Goldcliff charters', 155 (no. 4); *BT, Pen20Tr*, 60; *BT, RBH*, 136–7). (A confirmation by Henry as duke of Normandy and count of Anjou dated at Bristol recited in the inspeximus of 1290 is spurious: *CChR 1257–1300*, 362–3; *RRAN*, iii. 143–4; Crouch and Thomas, 'Three Goldcliff charters', 155 (no. 3).) Goldcliff was founded as a priory of Le Bec-Hellouin on the rock outcrop overlooking the Severn estuary at Goldcliff Point by Robert de Candos in 1113, and the patronage passed to Morgan and Iorwerth after their seizure of the lordship of Caerleon *c*.1136 (Williams, 'Goldcliff priory', 37–40; Crouch and Thomas, 'Three Goldcliff charters', 154). *Blenchesfeld* lay in Nash (ST 343 837), about 1½ miles west of Goldcliff Priory; the mill of *Bide* is said in no. 469 below to be near Langstone (Langstone Court ST 371 894), about 5 miles north of Goldcliff Priory, and thus may be identifiable with the monks' mill at Milton, almost 4 miles north of the priory (Rippon, *Gwent Levels*, 82 and map at 81, Fig. 32; cf. Williams, 'Goldcliff Priory', 52). St *Nigarum*, apparently located west of the Usk, has not been identified.

464 Goldcliff Priory

Grant by Morgan and his brother Iorwerth of all liberties and free customs which they have in their land, so that the monks and their men may have freely, honourably and peacefully throughout their land, without any claim by the grantors' heirs, sake, soke, toll, team and infangthief with all liberties and other free customs and quittances in wood, plain, meadows, pastures, waters, mills, pools, within and outside the borough, within and outside the moor, in ways, paths and all other places, free of all pleas, assizes, castle and bridge works, fine for bloodshed, fine for fighting, tolls, murder and other homicide however, wherever or whenever committed and all secular services and exactions. The monks shall have a court at Goldcliff or wherever they deem convenient for all the aforesaid pleas. The grantors prohibit in God's name and theirs anyone from infringing this confirmation, on pain of God's curse and theirs on the transgressor and all his descendants for ever. Witnesses.

[19 December 1154 × 1158]

B = TNA: PRO, C 53/76 (Ch. R. 18 Edward I), m. 10 (in an inspeximus, 3 July 1290).
C = TNA: PRO, C 53/107 (Ch. R. 14 Edward II), m. 3 (in an inspeximus of B, 24 February 1320).
Cd., *CChR 1257–1300*, 359 (from B); Crouch and Thomas, 'Three Goldcliff charters', 156 (no. 6; from B); *CChR 1300–26,* 434 (from C); *H*, no. 176.

Morganus et Ioruerdus frater eius omnibus hominibus suis Franc(is) et Anglis atque Walensib(us) salutem. Sciatis nos concessisse et presenti carta confirmasse Deo et ecclesie Sancte Marie Magdalene de Golcl(iua) et prioribus quicumque pro tempore fuerint et omnibus eiusdem loci monachis omnes libertates et liberas consuetudines quas nos ipsi in terra nostra habemus, scilicet ut ipsi et homines sui libere, quiete et honorifice habeant et pacifice sine alicuius heredum nostrorum reclamatione ubicumque in terra sua sacam et socam et *tol* et *team* et in *infangenethef* cum omnibus libertatibus et aliis liberis consuetudinibus et quietantiis in bosco et plano, in pratis et pasturis, in aquis et molendinis, in stagnis et vivariis, infra burgum et extra burgum, infra moram et extra moram, in viis et semetis et in omnibus aliis locis et rebus solutas, liberas et quietas de omnibus placitis et querelis, de assisis et operationibus castellorum et pontium, de *blodwite* et *fichtwite*, de theloneo et passagio, de murdro et alio homicido quoquomodo, aliquo loco vel tempore perpetratum fuerit et de omnibus serviciis secularibus et exactionibus que umquam poterunt provenire. Et volumus ut habeant curiam suam apud Golcl' vel ubicumque sibi melius viderint expedire de omnibus placitis et querelis supradictis. Prohibemus igitur ex parte Dei et nostra ne quis huius nostre confirmationis paginam audeat infringere, quod siquis fecerit maledictione Dei omnipotentis et nostra ipse et tota eius progenies perpetuo feriatur. Hiis testibus: magistro Wid(one), magistro Clemunt, Crad(oco) dapifero, Ruallan albo, Iuor filio Curech', Rad(ulf)o et Will(elm)o capellanis de Karl(iun).

As this charter is most unlikely to be earlier than the general confirmation of Goldcliff's lands in no. 463 above, it may be assigned to the same date range. Five of the witnesses also occur in no. 463.

MORGAN AP MORGAN
(d. *c.*1186)

465 The church of St Gwynllyw's, Newport and Gloucester Abbey
Grant in perpetual alms, for the souls of his father and ancestors, for his own salvation and for the fraternity of St Peter's, Gloucester, of 40 acres from his land on the moor of Goldcliff, namely 20 acres at Sigille *Pill and 20 acres near Newport bridge and near the bank of the Usk, which his father gave to the church of St Gwynllyw. Sealing clause.*

[1158 × September 1186]

> B = TNA: PRO, C 150/1 (Cartulary of Gloucester Abbey), fo. 146r. s. xiv.
> Pd. from B, *Cart. Glouc.*, ii. 50.
> Cd., *H*, no. 177.

Morganus filius Morgani omnibus amicis suis et hominibus Francis, Anglicis et Walensibus salutem. Sciatis quod ego concessi ecclesie Sancti Gundlei et ecclesie Sancti Pet(ri) de Glouc(estrie) pro anima patris mei et antecessorum meorum et pro salute anime mee et pro fraternitate ecclesie Sancti Pet(ri) de Glouc(estrie) xl acras terre mee in mora Goldcliuie, videlicet viginti acras apud Pilla(m) Sigille et xx acras iuxta pontem Novi Burgi et iuxta ripam Usce, in perpetuam elemosinam quas pater meus ecclesie Sancti Gundlei dedit. Et ut donatio mea et patris mei rata et irrefragabilis perseveret, donationem patris mei et meam carta mea et sigillo meo impressa confirmavi etc.

Morgan's father Morgan ab Owain was killed in 1158. Thereafter the annual payment of 40*s.* assigned him by the English exchequer from lands in Gloucestershire was transferred to his son, named as Morgan in the pipe rolls from Michaelmas 1177 until Michaelmas 1185; in Michaelmas 1186 the recipient's name is altered from Morgan to *Hoelo filio Morgani*, and payments to this Hywel, presumably an otherwise unattested son of Morgan ap Morgan (rather than an error for his cousin Hywel ap Iorwerth, referred to in the pipe rolls as 'Hywel of Caerleon'), continued until at least 1220. See *Pipe Roll 23 Henry II*, 41; *Pipe Roll 32 Henry II*, 118; *Pipe Roll 4 Henry III*, 74; *HW*, ii. 507, n. 80 (which incorrectly assumes that *filio Morgani* in the pipe rolls for 1158–76 is an error for *fratri Morgani*, i.e. Hywel ap Iorwerth, said in the Welsh chronicles to have taken his brother's lands after his death in 1158; the identification with Morgan ap Morgan is accepted by Crouch, 'March and the Welsh kings', 287, n. 85). It appears, then, that Morgan ap Morgan died in the exchequer year 32 Henry II (29 September 1185 × 28 September 1186). Gloucester's title to St Gwynllyw's church was confirmed by a synod at Cardiff in 1156 (*Cart. Glouc.*, ii. 51–7; *Llandaff Episcopal Acta*, nos 11–13). It is by no means certain that the original grant by Morgan's father Morgan ab Owain was recorded in a charter: the present charter lacks the verb *confirmare* and its sealing clause seems to speak of a joint grant by father and son; certainly the Gloucester monks regarded Morgan ap Morgan's charter as valuable evidence of their title to St Gwynllyw's and included no charter by his father in their cartulary. If the present charter was the first record of the father's grant, this could suggest that it was issued shortly after Morgan ab Owain's death in 1158. *Pillam Sigille*, evidently one of the pills or tidal creeks in the Gwent Levels at Goldcliff, has not been located.

*466 Goldcliff Priory
Grant of the land at Nash of Richard Blunt, Sebrin, Roger, Geoffrey and Robert Crede.
[1158 × September 1186]

Mention only, in a confirmation by Hywel ap Iorwerth probably datable to 1184 × 1217 (no. 469 below). Morgan's gift of 10*s.* of land at Nash (ST 343 837) included in another confirmation by Hywel (no. 471 below) is probably the same grant. For the dating limits see note to no. 465 above.

HYWEL AP IORWERTH
(d. 1215 × October 1217)

467 Glastonbury Abbey
Grant, with his father's consent, for the salvation of himself and all his kin and ancestors, and in exchange for the tithes of Ynys Nant Teyrnon (Llantarnam) where he has established the white monks, to supplement the mensal lands of the monks at Basaleg, of 14 acres in the moor of (?)Maen-brith (Meinbrit) which Kinith'liu Glas formerly held, and confirmation of the 14 acres granted by his uncle the Lord Morgan. Further grant of land in the mountains in these bounds: the highway which comes from Riworus and leads to the church of Mynyddislwyn; in the upper part Srudhlanid and the church stream and in the lower part on two sides two streams falling into the aforesaid stream. Grants these to be possessed in alms for ever, free and quit of all gelds, gifts, aids, works and all customs in wood, plain, waters and in all places. Further grant that the monks may take what they need from his woods all necessities for the church and domestic buildings of Basaleg free of all claims, services, customs and pleas. Their pigs shall have free pannage in his woods, and their horses, oxen, cattle, all their animals and all their (?)sheep and goats free pasture throughout his land, in both wood and plain. They may have their court and all liberty and justice in all business and custom as fully and freely as Hywel has his. Witnesses.
[Probably 1179 × 1184]

B = Cambridge, Trinity College MS R. 5. 33 (Register of Glastonbury Abbey), fo. 107r. s. xiii–xiv (here s. xiv).

Pd. from B, *Adami de Domerham De Rebus Gestis*, ed. Hearne, ii. 607; from Hearne, *Mon. Ang.*, iv. 634.

Cd., *H*, no. 178.

Notum sit universis ecclesie Dei fidelibus clericis et laicis presentibus et futuris quod ego Hoelus filius Ioruerthi filii Oeni assensu et consensu eiusdem patris mei pro mea et omnium parentum et antecessorum meorum salute, et pro commutatione decimarum Emsant(er)uon ubi albos monachos institui,[a] dedi Deo et Sancte Marie Glastoniens(i) ecclesie ad supplementum victus monachorum degentium apud Basselech, xiiii acras in mora de Meinbrit quas Kinith'liu Glas olim tenuit, et quod confirmavi ibidem alias xiiii acras terre quas dominus Morgan(us) patruus meus eidem dedit ecclesie. Dedi insuper eidem ecclesie terram in montatis cuius hii sunt termini: publica strata que venit a Riworus et tendit ad ecclesiam de Menit Estlim, et in superiori parte Srudhlanid et rivulus ecclesie et in inferiori parte in duobus laceribus duo sunt rivuli in predictum rivulum descendentes. Dedi autem eas et confirmavi in elemosinam inperpetuum possidendas liberas et quietas ab omnibus geldis, dotiis et auxiliis, operibus et omnibus consuetudinibus in bosco, in plano, in aquis et in omnibus omnino locis. Concessi etiam monachis Glaston' degentibus apud Basselech ut accipiant[b] in nemoribus meis quod ei opus fuerit ad omnia necessaria ecclesie et officinarum de Basselech libere et quiete absque omni calumpnia et servitio et consuetudine omnique querela. Porcorum suorum pascionem in nemoribus meis absque pannagio habeant liberam et in omni terra mea tam in bosco quam in plano equitio suo et bobus suis et vaccis et omnibus animalibus suis cunctisque ovibus[c] suis et capris omnimodis liberam et quietam pasturam. Curiam suam et omnem libertatem et iustitiam in omni negotio et consuetudine plene et libere habeant sicut ego meam habeo. Hiis testibus: Urbano clerico meo et canonico Landavens(i), Iuoro filio Chaeryt, Cardoco[d] senescallo,[e] Meuryc et multis aliis.

[a] instatui B. | [b] accipeant B. | [c] omnibus B. | [d] *sic in* B. | [e] senescalla B.

According to the Welsh chronicles, the Cistercians were established at Nant Teyrnon (Llantarnam, also known as Caerleon, to which it was adjacent) in 1179 (*BT, Pen20Tr*, 72; *BT, RBH*, 168–9; cf. *HW*, ii. 600 and n. 139; Williams, *White Monks in Gwent*, 77). Hywel's father Iorwerth, whose consent is recorded, probably died no later than 1184. Basaleg Priory was founded about 2 miles south-west of Newport as a dependency of Glastonbury Abbey in 1100 × 1104 by Robert de la Haye, lord of Gwynllŵg (Coplestone-Crow, 'Foundation of the priories', 4). For the settlement before Hywel on 30 March 1211 of subsequent disputes over tithes between Basaleg and Llantarnam see no. 476 below. *Meinbrit* corresponds to *Metenbrith* in Robert's foundation charter; it may represent Mod. W. *Maen-brith* (lit. 'speckled stone') and seems to have been located on the coastal moor near Peterstone Gout (ST 278 807), about ½ mile north-east of Peterstone Wentlooge (ibid., 2 (map), 3, 5). *Riworus* and *Srudhlanid* have not been located, though the latter may be the same as the *Sunlich* of Robert's charter (ibid., 3, 5), a hilly area which seems to have corresponded to, or included, Mynydd Machen (ST 224 901), about 4 miles north-east of Basaleg. This could be consistent with the description in the boundary clause of the highway leading towards Mynyddislwyn (ST 193 939), about 6½ miles north-west of Basaleg, if the direction envisaged was from the south or east.

*468 Malpas Priory
Grant.

[*c.*1179 × October 1217; possibly *c.*1179 × 1184]

Mention only, of 'a dede of Hoell the son of Gerverd', in a report of documents, manuscripts and other writings delivered by the priors of Montacute and Malpas to commissioners of the court of Augmentations at Montacute, 27 December 1536 (*Mon. Ang.*, v. 174; cd., *H*, no. 187). If the use of the patronymic in the reference accurately reflects the style of the charter, this could indicate a date no later than 1184; in any case, a *terminus a quo* as early as *c.*1179 cannot be ruled out (cf. note to no. 467 above). Though the report does not explicitly state this, it is likely that the grant was in favour of the Cluniac priory of Malpas, located north of Newport in Gwynllŵg, rather than of Montacute, its mother house in Somerset. Like Basaleg Priory (see no. 467), also endowed by Hywel, Malpas Priory was founded by Robert de la Haye, possibly in conjunction with Henry I's physician Ranulf, 1107–*c.*1114 (Coplestone-Crow, 'Foundation of the priories', 8–9).

469 Goldcliff Priory
Grant and confirmation, for the salvation of himself and his heirs and for the souls of his father and all his ancestors, of all the gifts, liberties and free customs given by Robert de Candos, his wife Isabel and their heir Walter while they still held the honour and lordship of Caerleon, in lands, churches, tithes, renders, possessions, dignities, in wood, plain, ways, waters and all other places as the monks' charters from King Henry the elder and King Henry the younger attest, namely the church of St Mary Magdalene, Goldcliff with the chapel of Nash and all its other appurtenances; the church of St Julius and St Aaron [St Julians] with all its appurtenances; and the church of the Holy Trinity near Caerleon [Christchurch] with all its appurtenances. Further confirmation by this writing, with the consent of his sons and heirs Owain and Morgan, of all gifts and confirmations in the moor of Goldcliff and outside it by other faithful of his fee. Further confirmation of all gifts which his father Iorwerth and uncle Morgan confirmed in their charter, namely 200 acres in the moor of Goldcliff; Blenchesfeld *within and without; a mill near Langstone called (?)Milton* (Bide)*; 15 acres in the moor to the south of that mill; 3 acres next to that mill on the north side; a fishery in the Usk called Five Fisheries; another fishery on the other side of the Usk near St* Nigarum*; and a land near Caerleon bridge on the east side near the water as the road and dyke form a boundary. Further confirmation of the land at Nash of Richard Blunt, Sebrin, Roger, Geoffrey and Robert Crede given by Morgan the younger, son of Morgan, his uncle; he wishes the monks to do with it as is most convenient for them. Sealing clause; witnesses.*

[Probably 1184 × October 1217; possibly 1185 × October 1217]

A = Évreux, Archives départementales de l'Eure, H 9. Bottom left of fold: v bona in parte (s. xii/xiii, possibly by scribe of charter); endorsed: Alia confirmatio Hoeli de possessionibus et libertatibus (s. xii/xiii); iii (s. xiv); early modern and modern endorsements; approx. 150 mm. wide × 181 mm. deep on left, 194 mm. deep on right + 20 mm.; two central slits, one just above fold, one in fold; tag and seal missing.

Cd., *Inventaire sommaire*, ed. Bourbon, 4; Crouch and Thomas, 'Three Goldcliff charters', 156 (no. 10); *H*, no. 181.

Hoelus de Karln' omnibus hominibus suis Francis, Anglis atque Walensibus et omnibus Cristi fidelibus ad quos presens scriptum pervenerit salutem. Universitati vestre notificetur me concessisse et hac presenti carta confirmasse Deo et ecclesie Sancte Marie Magdal(e)n(e) et monachis ibidem Deo servientibus pro salute mea et heredum meorum et pro animabus patris mei et omnium antecessorum meorum omnes donationes et omnes libertates et liberas consuetudines quas Rob(ertus) de Candos et Ysabel uxor eius et Walt(erus) heres eorum eis dederunt dum adhuc honorem de Karln' et dominium optinerent in terris, in ecclesiis, in decimis, in redditibus, in possessionibus, in dignitatibus, in bosco et plano, in viis et semitis, in exitibus et in omnibus aliis rebus et locis sicut carte regum Henrici senioris et H. iunioris eis testantur, scilicet ecclesiam Sancte M(ari)e Magd(ale)n(e) Golc(iu)e cum capella de Fraxino que ad eam pertinet cum omnibus aliis pertinentiis suis, ecclesiam Sanctorum Iulii et Áaron cum omnibus pertinentiis suis, ecclesiam Sancte Trinitatis iuxta Karln' cum omnibus pertinentiis suis. Omnes etiam donationes et confirmationes quas ceteri fideles predictis monachis de feodo meo dederunt in mora et extra moram Golcl(iu)e ego Hoelus assensu et voluntate filiorum et heredum meorum Oeni et Morgani concedo et confirmo presentis scripti testimonio. Concedo preterea et confirmo sepedictis monachis omnes donationes quas eis dederunt Ioruerd' pater meus et Morg' avunculus meus et carta sua confirmaverunt, scilicet ducentas acras terre in mora Golcl(iu)a et Blenchesfeld' interiorem et exteriorem et unum molendinum iuxta Langest' quod vocatur Bide et quindecim acras terre in mora versus austrum eiusdem molendini et tres acras versus aquilonem et unam piscariam in Vscha que vocatur Quinque Piscarie et aliam in transversum Usche iuxta Sanctum Nigarun et unam terram iuxta pontem de Karln' ex parte orientis prope aqua sicut aqua et fossa dividit. Concessi etiam et confirmavi predictis monachis quandam terram apud Fraxinu(m) quam eis dedit Morganus iunior filius Morg(ani) avunculi mei, scilicet terram Ric(ardi) Blundi, Sebrini, Rogeri, Galfridi et Roberti Crede, et volo ut illam habeant et de illa faciant secundum beneplacitum suum sicut noverint sibi melius expedire. Ad maiorem igitur huius confirmationis firmitatem ne aliquando possit revocari in irritum sigilli mei testimonio presentis scriptum roboravi. Hiis testibus: magistro Widon(e), Cradoco senescallo, Cradoco forestario, Meuric fratre suo, Ric(ardo) presbitero de Golcli(ua), Rob(erto) Was, Ithel Bleith, Meurich filio Rog(er)i et multis aliis.

As the charter implies that Hywel's father Iorwerth ab Owain was dead, it is probably no earlier than 1184. The inclusion of a confirmation of a grant by Hywel's cousin Morgan ap Morgan may indicate that it was issued after Morgan's death, which probably occurred in 1185 × 1186 (see note to no. 465 above). Apart from that confirmation, the text is modelled on the confirmation by Iorwerth and his brother Morgan (no. 463 above), though it adds the topographical detail that the mill of *Bide* (probably Milton) was near Langstone (Langstone Court ST 371 894), about 5 miles north of Goldcliff Priory.

470 Goldcliff Priory

Grant of the church of Undy with all its appurtenances in perpetual alms, relinquishing all that used to pertain to him as advocate and lord. Further gift of one messuage at Caerleon quit and free of all custom and service. He has done these things for the souls of himself and his father, mother, his uncle Morgan and his ancestors. Witnesses.

                    [Probably 1184 × October 1217; possibly 1185 × October 1217]

B = TNA: PRO, C 53/76 (Ch. R. 18 Edward I), m. 10 (in an inspeximus, 1 July 1290).
C = TNA: PRO, C 53/107 (Ch. R. 14 Edward II), m. 3 (in an inspeximus of B, 24 February 1320).
Cd., *CChR 1257–1300*, 360 (from B); Crouch and Thomas, 'Three Goldcliff charters', 157 (no. 12; from B); *CChR 1300–26*, 435 (from C); *H*, no. 183.

Sciant presentes et futuri quod ego Hoelus de Karl(iun) concessi et presenti carta confirmavi ecclesie Sancte Mar(ie) Magd(alene) de Go[l]dcliue^a et monachis ibi Deo servientibus ecclesiam de Wundi cum omnibus que ad eam pertinent in perpetuam elemosinam, omnia illi relinquens que ad me spectabant meeque erant munificentie prout advocati et domini. Dedi etiam unam mansuram apud Karl(iun) solutam et quietam et liberam ab omni consuetudine et servitio. Hec autem ego Hoelus feci pro anima mea et pro anima patris [mei]^b et matris mee et avunculi mei Morgani et antecessorum meorum. Testibus: Ric(ardo) capellano, Durand capellano, Wig(er)an clerico, Will(elm)o clerico, Walt(er)o preposito, Meuric filio Dunewal' et aliis multis.

^a Godcliue B. | ^b *omitted* B; *inserted in* C.

This was probably issued later in the same date range as no. 469 above, since the present grants are not included in that confirmation. Undy church lies about 1 mile south-east of Magor at ST 440 869.

471 Goldcliff Priory

Grant and confirmation, for the love of God and St Mary Magdalene and for the salvation of the souls of himself and his ancestors and heirs, of all gifts of churches, lands and alms made by himself, his ancestors and his men, namely his own gift of the church of Undy and a mill, 1 acre and two burgages at Caerleon; Morgan's gift of a mill near Langstone; Morgan the younger's gift of 10s. of land at Nash; the gift by Morgan and Iorwerth of two fisheries in the Usk, one called Five Fisheries (Fifwere) *and the other across the river, and 200 acres in the moor; from Gronw ap Nicholas 5s. of land in the moor from an exchange; William the chamberlain's gift of 5s. of land at Nash; Caradog's gift of the land of Bulmore; the gift by Gronw ap Nicholas and his brother Cadwgan of a fishery at* Colemmanes pulle. *He wishes the monks to hold peacefully and freely, in perpetual alms, all the aforesaid possessions, and anything more given them by his heirs and men for the love of God. Witnesses.*

[Probably 1184 × October 1217; possibly 1185 × October 1217]

A = Eton College Records 64/1. Endorsed: Carta Hoel(i) de donationibus ecclesiarum et terrarum et aliarum rerum (s. xiii); Gooldeclyve (s. xv); approx. 161 × 128 + 18 mm.; central slit in fold for a tag (*c*.20 mm. wide), with cords for seal attached, which exits through a slit in the base of the fold; seal missing.
B = TNA: PRO, C 53/76 (Ch. R. 18 Edward I), m. 10 (in an inspeximus, 1 July 1290).
C = TNA: PRO, C 53/107 (Ch. R. 14 Edward II), m. 3 (in an inspeximus of B, 24 February 1320).
Cd., Crouch and Thomas, 'Three Goldcliff charters', 156 (from A); *CChR 1257–1300*, 359–60 (from B); *CChR 1300–26*, 435 (from C); *H*, no. 182.

Sciant presentes et futuri quod ego Hoel(us) de Carliun pro Dei amore et Sancte Marie Magdalene et pro salute anime mee et antecessorum meorum et heredum meorum concedo et hac carta mea confirmo omnes donationes ecclesiarum, terrarum et elemosinarum quas ego feci et antecessores mei et homines mei fecerunt Deo et Sancte Marie Magdalene et monachis Deo et Sancte Marie Magd(alene) servientibus, scilicet ex dono meo ecclesiam de Wndi et molendinum et i acram terre et ii burgagias apud Carliun, ex dono Morgani molendinum iuxta Langestan, ex dono Morg(ani) iunioris x solidos terre apud Fraxinu(m), ex dono Morg(ani) et I. duas piscarias in Usca, unam[a] que dicitur Fifwere et aliam ex transverso et cc[as] acras in mora, de Wronu filio Nich(olai) v solidos terre in mora de excambio, ex dono Will(elm)i camerarii v solidos terre apud Fraxinu(m), ex dono Caradoci terram de Bulemora, ex dono W. filio Nic(holai) et Cadug' fratris eius unam piscariam apud Colemannes pulle. Quare volo ut predicti monachi habeant et teneant bene et in pace, libere et quiete, in perpetuam elemosinam omnes predictas possessiones et quicquid eis ab heredibus meis et hominibus meis amplius pro Dei amore datum fuerit. Testes: Ric(ardus) capellanus, Philipp(us) clericus, Rob(ertus) clericus de Novob(urgo), Gocel(inus) filius Euer', R. Was.

[a] una A.

This confirmation is later than the previous charters of Hywel for Goldcliff as it names additional grants to those in no. 469 above, including the church of Undy granted in no. 470 above. (I am grateful to Tessa Webber for commenting that there are no compelling palaeographical objections to this conclusion, as the modified book hand of the present charter is consistent with a late twelfth- or early thirteenth-century date and could be later than the very fluent hand used in no. 469.) *Fifwere* is an Early Middle English rendering of the Latin *Quinque Piscarie* in earlier charters for Goldcliff. The Caradog who granted Bulmore (ST 358 915), about 1 mile east of Caerleon across the Usk, may have been Hywel's seneschal of that name (see nos 469 above, 472–3 below). *Colemannes pulle* has not been identified.

472 Goldcliff Priory

Grant, for his salvation and for the souls of his ancestors and heirs, of all that they need in his forest of Gwynllŵg. He orders that no one shall trouble or implead the monks or their servants or men subject anywhere in the moor to their lordship regarding way or water, wood or plain or anything; the monks shall have firm peace and all liberties and free customs in all things pertaining to his forest and his guarantee in going and returning. Sealing clause; witnesses.

[Probably 1184 × October 1217; possibly 1185 × October 1217]

B = TNA: PRO, C 53/76 (Ch. R. 18 Edward I), m. 10 (in an inspeximus, 1 July 1290).
C = TNA: PRO, C 53/107 (Ch. R. 14 Edward II), m. 3 (in an inspeximus of B, 24 February 1320).
Cd., *CChR 1257–1300*, 360 (from B); Crouch and Thomas, 'Three Goldcliff charters', 157 (no. 13; from B); *CChR 1300–26*, 435 (from C); *H*, no. 184.

Sciant presentes et futuri quod ego Hoelus de Karl(iun) dedi et concessi Deo et Sancte Marie Magd(alene) de Goldecliua et monachis ibidem Deo servientibus pro salute mea et animabus antecessorum et heredum meorum quecumque eis necessaria sunt in foresto meo de Wulench'. Quare volo et firmiter precipio ne aliquis illos vel servientes suos vel etiam homines suos ubicumque in mora Goldecliue suo dominio mancipatos quavis de causa inquietare vel implacitare, vexare vel aliquam molestiam illis inferre presumat de via vel de aqua, vel de bosco vel de plano vel etiam de aliqua re, set ut habeant bonam et firmam pacem et omnes libertates et liberas consuetudines in omnibus rebus ad forestum meum pertinentibus et warantum meum eundo et redeundo. Et ut hec omnia prenotata perpetuam optineat firmitatem presens scriptum sigilli mei impressione roboravi. Hiis testibus: Oeno filio meo, Morgano fratre[a] meo, Cradoco senescallo, Barth(olome)o clerico, Ioh(ann)e clerico, Ad(a) de Brydercumbe, Ric(ardo) capellano de Goldecl(iua), Gilb(er)to de Vsca et aliis.

[a] *sic in* B.

This probably falls later in the same date range as nos. 469–71 above, since the grant is not included in the confirmation in no. 471. The description of the second witness, Morgan, as Hywel's brother may be a scribal error for *filio meo*, as Hywel is not otherwise known to have had a brother of that name, whereas he did have a son called Morgan who outlived his elder sibling Owain (who died during their father's lifetime) to become Hywel's sole heir (see nos 474–5 below). If so, however, this would suggest clumsy drafting, as *Oeno et Morgano filiis meis* might be expected as in no. 473 below.

473 Iorwerth son of Caradog the seneschal

Grant, with the assent of his sons Owain and Morgan, his wife Gwerful and his daughter Gwenllian, of all the lands, possessions, liberties and free customs held free and quit by his father Caradog in hereditary right, in wood, plain, lands, waters, ways, paths, meadows, pastures, in and outside the moor of Goldcliff and in all other places, to be held of Hywel and his heirs, in peace with all secular exactions, namely 211 acres in the moor of Goldcliff between Nash *and* Quedforke *and* Pulenam, *from* Pulena *to* Buham, *all the land of* Buha, *and thence back in a circuit to* Quedforde; *30 acres at* Pulbletch *near the land of the church; 25 acres near* Pwll-pen *(Pulpen); all the land and woods from* Pulla Hameli *[(?)as] the stream there leads west to the highway and from the highway to the cross of* Gruninge *(or ?Bruninge); thence as the highway leads towards Holy Trinity church (Christchurch) near Caerleon and (?)by that highway as the nearer stream falls into the Usk, namely the stream that surrounds the land of Holy Trinity church and* Hendresemer *and the fisheries below the bounds of the aforesaid land, namely* Bocher *and its appurtenances and* Grenegur' *and all its appurtenances at Caerleon as the dyke near the bridge on the western side extends towards the old wall and between the old wall and the Usk to the port of Goldcliff, and thence as the lower part of the cobbled road leads to the park; from the aforesaid road near the dyke below the tombs to the land of the church and near the dyke of the land of the church and as the water flows into the Usk. [Further grant] of all the assart of* Perfulli *(or ?* Perthollig*) and all the other land with the meadow from the southern side of Caerleon near the other land in exchange for the land of* Gloc'. *Hywel has granted and confirmed all these by this writing and seal in return for Iorwerth's service and homage. Witnesses.*

[Probably 1184 × October 1217; possibly 31 March 1211 × October 1217]

B = London, Society of Antiquaries of London, MS Wakeman 790/33 (transcript by Thomas Wakeman, *c.*1788–1868), no foliation. s. xix.
Cd., *H*, no. 179.

Sciant presentes et futuri quod ego Hoelus[a] dominus de Carlyon assensu et voluntate filiorum meorum Oweni et Morgani et uxoris mee Wervelli et Wenlliane filie mee concessi et presenti carta mea confirmavi Gervardo filio Cradoci dapiferi omnes terras et posses- siones, omnes libertates et liberas[b] consuetudines quas tenuit et libere et quiete possedit Cradocus pater eius iure hereditario [new page] in bosco et in plano et in terris et in aquis, in viis, in semitis, in pratis et pasturis, in mora et extra moram de Golclivie et in omnibus aliis locis, tenendas de me et heredibus meis sibi et heredibus suis libere, quiete et pacifice cum omnibus secularibus[c] exactionibus, scilicet ducentas acras terre et undecim in mora Golcl(iv)e inter Fraxinu(m) et Quedforke et Pulenam et de Pulena usque Buham et totam terram de Buha, et item de Buha per circuitum usque ad Quedforde; item alibi apud Pulbletch triginta acras iuxta terram templi; item viginti et quinque acras iuxta Pulpen; item alibi de Pulla Hameli . . .[d] rivulus qui ibi est tendit versus occidentem omnem terram que ibi est et totum nemus quod ibi est usque ad viam regalem et de via regali usque ad crucem Gruninge[e] et de cruce . . .[d] sicut via regalis tendit versus ecclesiam Sancte Trinitatis iuxta Caerlyon et dicta via sicut propinquior[f] rivulus cadit in Uskam, scilicet rivulus qui claudit terram ecclesie Sancte Trinitatis et Hendresemer[g] et piscarie que sunt infra metas predicte terre, scilicet Bocher . . .[d] omnes eius pertinentes et Grenegur' et omnes suos pertinentes apud Caerlyon sicut fossa iuxta pontem a latere occidentali extenditur versus veterem murum et inter veterem murum et Uskam usque ad portam Golclive et de porta Golclive sicut inferior pars vie petrose tendit ad parcum; et item de predicta via iuxta fossam de subtus tumbas usque ad terram templi et iuxta fossam terre templi et sicut aqua vadit in Uska(m). Item ego . . .[d] predicto Gervardo totum assartum Perfulli[h] et totam aliam terram cum prato ab australi parte de Caerlyon iuxta aliam terram in excambio terre de Gloc'. Hec omnia p . . .[i] ego iam dictus Hoelus predicto Gervardo concessi et[j] confirmavi presentis scripti testimonio et sigilli mei impressione pro servitio et homagio suo. Hiis testibus: Vincentio [new page] priore de Golcl(iv)e, Oeno et Morgano filiis meis, Will(elm)o[k] Martell, Adriano filio suo, Will(elm)o fratre suo, Wrunnic Cadiger fil[iis] Michel . . .,[d] Barth(olome)o clerico camerarii, Reginaldo proposito Wondy et multis aliis.

[a] Hoellus B. | [b] liberes B. | [c] secularis B. | [d] *sic in* B. | [e] B *inserts* (or ? Bruninge). | [f] propinquor B. [g] *word underlined in* B *with question mark in margin.* | [h] ? Perthollig *in marginal note in same hand as text besides this word in* B. | [i] *sic in* B *for* (?)prenotata *(cf. no. 472 above) or* (?)predicta. | [j] *word placed within brackets in* B. | [k] Willo *without contraction mark in* B.

Wakeman gives no source for this charter, which he clearly had difficulty in copying, particu- larly the place-names. Though the text as transmitted is corrupt in places, there are no strong grounds for doubting its derivation from an authentic charter issued by Hywel. The style *dominus de Karliun* occurs in nos 474–5 below, and the diplomatic of the notification is comparable to that of no. 475 as well as nos 470–2 above. William Martel and *Wrinu et Cadigan filiis Nicholai* (rendered here as *Wrunnic Cadiger fil[iis] Michel*) also occur in no. 474. The charter must be later than no. 472 above, witnessed by Iorwerth's father Caradog. Caradog was seneschal to Morgan and Iorwerth sons of Owain in 1154 × 1158 and continued in this office under Hywel ap Iorwerth (nos 464, 472); Iorwerth succeeded Caradog as Hywel's seneschal and was succeeded in turn by his son Adam ap Iorwerth, who held the office under Hywel's son Morgan (nos 474–5; *CChR 1226–57*, 294; cf. Davies, *Conquest*, 263; Crouch, *Image of Aristocracy*, 162). The use of the style *Hoelus dominus de*

Carlyon may indicate a date after 30 March 1211, if this was a later, more assertive, elaboration of the style *H. de Karliun* used in no. 476 below. Pwll-pen (or Pwll-pan) (ST 355 877) lay almost 4 miles north of Goldcliff Priory (see Rippon, *Gwent Levels*, 48, Fig. 19; 81, Fig. 32; 82).

474 Goldcliff Priory

Grant, with the consent of Morgan, his son and heir, and of his wife and daughter, in perpetual and free alms of all liberties and free customs which he has in his land, so that the priors, community and their men may have freely, honourably and peacefully throughout their land, without any claim by Hywel's heirs, sake, soke, toll, team and infangthief with all liberties and other free customs and quittances in wood, plain, meadows, pastures, waters, mills, pools, within and outside the borough, within and outside the moor, in ways, paths and all other places, free of all pleas, assizes, castle and bridge works, fine for bloodshed, fine for fighting, tolls, murder and other homicide however, wherever or whenever committed and all secular services and exactions. The monks shall have a court at Goldcliff or wherever they deem convenient for all the aforesaid pleas. Further grant in perpetual and free alms of the part of his wood of Gwastadcoed (Wastadcoit) *given by Robert de Candos, founder of the church, in these bounds: as the Serfan* (Seruan) *leads east and all of (?) Gwerngaradog* (Wrencaradoc) *to Jordan's dyke and thence to the road leading to Catsash, from that road to* Fenanmeum, *thence to the chestnut-tree, thence to the Usk; from the other side of the Serfan to the well of Caradog Gam and thence to the Usk. Grant and confirmation of all lands and possessions within those bounds for the love of God and the salvation of himself and his heirs and the souls of all his ancestors. Further grant of the tithes of the pannage of Gwastadcoed* (Wastadcoit), *of the mill of Caerleon, of the mill of Liswerry, namely from Robert de Candos's fee, of Hywel's orchard at Caerleon, of his hunting and of honey in wood and plain; also grant of all the land of St* Nigarun *in wood and plain, of a boat for fishing in* Duruentrepulle, *of three boats in Five Fisheries and a boat in* Colennennespulle. *Hywel wishes that the monks shall have all that is contained in this document fully, without any difficulty, and possess them quit and honourably for ever. He prohibits in God's name and his anyone from infringing this confirmation, on pain of God's curse and his on the transgressor and all his descendants for ever. Sealing clause. Witnesses.*

[Probably 1184 × October 1217; possibly 31 March 1211 × October 1217]

B = TNA: PRO, C 53/76 (Ch. R. 18 Edward I), m. 10 (in an inspeximus, 1 July 1290).
C = TNA: PRO, C 53/107 (Ch. R. 14 Edward II), m. 3 (in an inspeximus of B, 24 February 1320).
Cd., *CChR 1257–1300*, 359–60 (from B); *CChR 1300–26*, 435 (from C); *H*, no. 180.

Universis Cristi fidelibus ad quos presens scriptum pervenerit Hoelus dominus de Karl(iun) salutem. Universitati vestre notificetur me concessisse[a] assensu et voluntate Morgani filii et heredis mei et uxoris mee et filie mee concessisse[b] et presenti carta confirmasse Deo et ecclesie Sancte Marie Magd(alene) de Golcl(iua) et monachis ibidem Deo servientibus in puram et perpetuam et liberam elemosinam omnes libertates et liberas consuetudines quas ego ipse in terra mea habeo, scilicet ut eiusdem loci priores quicumque pro tempore fuerint et totus similiter conventus et omnes homines illorum libere, quiete et honorifice habeant et pacifice sine alicuius heredum meorum reclamatione ubique in terra sua *sacom* et socam et *tol* et *team* et *infangenethef* cum omnibus aliis libertatibus et liberis consuetudinibus et quietantiis in bosco, in plano, in pratis et pasturis, in aquis et molendinis, in stagnis et vivariis, infra burgum et extra burgum, infra moram et extra moram, in viis et semitis et in omnibus aliis locis et rebus solutas, liberas et quietas de omnibus placitis et querelis de operationibus castellorum et pontium, de *blodwyte* et *fithwite*, de theloneo et passagio, de murdro et alio homicidio quoquo modo vel tempore vel loco perpetratum fuerit et omnibus serviciis secularibus et exactionibus que umquam poterunt provenire. Volo etiam ut habeant curiam suam apud Golcl(iuam) vel ubicumque sibi melius viderint expedire de omnibus placitis et querelis supradictis. Preterea concessi et confirmavi predicte ecclesie Sancte Mar(ie) Magd(alene) de Golcl(iua) et eiusdem loci monachis in puram et perpetuam et liberam elemosinam partem nemoris mei de Wastadcoit quam dedit illis Rob(ertu)s de Candos qui memoratam ecclesiam fundavit per tales divisiones, scilicet sicut Seruan tendit versus orientem et totum Wrenc(ra)doc usque ad fossam Iordan(i) et de fossa Iord(ani) usque ad viam que ducit Cathesh' et de illa via usque Fenanmeum `et de Fenanmeum usque ad castaneam et de castanea usque in Vscam, ex altera parte de Seruan' usque ad fontem Cradoci Cam et de fonte Cradoci usque in Vscam et omnes terras et possessiones que sunt infra prescriptas metas predictis monachis pro Dei amore et pro salute mea et heredum meorum et pro animabus omnium antecessorum meorum concessi et confirmavi. Preterea concessi illis decimam pannagii de Wastadcoit et decimam molendini de Karliun et decimam molendini de Liswiry, scilicet de feudo Rob(er)ti de Candos, et decimam pomerii mei de Karl(iun) et decimam venationis mee et decimam mellis in bosco et totam terram de Sancto Nigarun tam in bosco quam in plano et unum alveum ad piscandum in Dureuentrepulle et tres alveos in Quinque Piscariis et unum alveum in Colennennespulle. Hec omnia que in hac pagina continetur volo ut predicti monachi cum omni integritate sine aliqua difficultate habeant et perpetuis temporibus libere, quiete et honorifice possideant. Prohibeo igitur ex parte Dei et mea ne quis huius confirmationis mee paginam audeat infringere, quod siquis fecerit maledictione Dei omnipotentis et mea ipse et tota eius progenies perpetuo feriatur. Ut autem hec omnia maiorem optineant firmitatem presens scriptum tam sigilli mei impressione quam testium subscriptione roboravi. Testibus: Morgano filio meo, Griffino filio M(er)eduth', Will(elm)o Martel, Ric(ard)o filio Barth(olome)i, Nich(ol)o de Mora, Ieruerd' senescallo, Wrgeneu Cam, Wrinu et Cadigan filiis Nich(ola)i, Rob(er)to Pengrith', Seisil filio Turst', Seisil filio Ioh(ann)is, B(e)n(e)d(ic)to, Walt(ero) et Durand(o) capellanis de Goldcli(ua).

ᵃ *sic in* B; C *amends to* concessione. | ᵇ *sic in* B.

This is later than nos 469 and 473 above, as Hywel refers to Morgan alone as his heir, suggesting that his elder son Owain was dead. For the possibility that it was later than 30 March 1211 see note to no. 473 above. The charter is modelled in part on no. 464 above (whose sanction is in turn taken from Robert de Candos's foundation charter for Goldcliff), though the section from *partem nemoris mei de Wastadcoit* to *de fonte Cradoci usque in Vscam* seems to derive directly from Robert de Candos's charter, where the English name *Bechereswell'* appears to correspond to the Welsh name *Fenanmeum* (the element *fenan* = Mod. W. *ffynnon*, 'well') in the present charter (TNA: PRO, C 53/76, m. 10; pd., *Mon. Ang.*, vi: ii. 1022). The Serfan may be an example of a stream called after a personal name, Serfan or Serwan (Thomas, *Enwau Afonydd*, 86–7). Catsash (ST 375 905) lies about 2 miles east of Caerleon, just north of Langstone.

475 Goldcliff Priory

Grant, with the consent of his son Morgan, in free and perpetual alms of a pasture in the mountains, namely between the Rhymni and the Sirhywi, sufficient for forty cows and their calves, twenty mares with their foals and 100 sheep with their lambs, for the salvation of his soul and for the souls of his sons and all his friends and kin. Sealing clause; witnesses.

[Probably 1184 × October 1217; possibly 31 March 1211 × October 1217]

B = TNA: PRO, C 53/76 (Ch. R. 18 Edward I), m. 10 (in an inspeximus, 1 July 1290).
C = TNA: PRO, C 53/107 (Ch. R. 14 Edward II), m. 3 (in an inspeximus of B, 24 February 1320).
Cd., *CChR 1257–1300*, 361 (from B); Crouch and Thomas, 'Three Goldcliff charters', 157 (no. 14; from B); *CChR 1300–26*, 435 (from C); *H*, no. 185.

Sciant presentes et futuri quod ego Hoelus dominus de Karl' assensu et voluntate Morgani filii mei dedi et concessi et hac mea [carta]ᵃ confirmavi Deo et ecclesie Sancte Mar(ie) Magd(alene) de Golcl(iua) et monachis ibidem Deo servientibus in puram et liberam et perpetuam elemosinam unam pasturam in montanis, scilicet inter Remni et Serewi, sufficientem ad quadraginta vaccas cum exitu earundem et ad viginti equas cum earum exitu et ad centum oves cum exitu earundem pro salute anime mee et pro animabus filiorum meorum et omnium amicorum et parentum meorum. Et ut hec mea donatio firma et stabilis inposterum permaneat presens scriptum sigilli mei appositione corroboravi. Hiis testibus: B(e)n(e)d(ic)to capellano de Karl(iun), Durando capellano de Golcl(iua), Goreuerd' senescallo, Kadigan' filio Nich(ola)i, Phil(ippo) filio Rob(erti) Was, Rob(erto) Crandon', Ioh(ann)e Ruff(o) et multis aliis.

ᵃ *omitted in B; added in C.*

This belongs to the same date range as no. 474 above, as it also refers to Morgan as Hywel's sole heir and at least three of the same witnesses occur in both charters.

476 Final concord in his presence between Caerleon (Llantarnam) Abbey and Basaleg Priory

The prior and monks of Basaleg, of their own free will and with the assent of the prior and convent of Glastonbury, have remitted, and remit for ever in the future, to the abbot and convent of Caerleon all pleas and claims concerning all lands and tithes which the abbot and convent of Caerleon held and hold up to the day on which this final concord was made. If in future the abbot and convent of Caerleon shall acquire land or cultivated lands in the parishes of the monks of Basaleg, they will pay the tithes or compound for them amicably. The abbot and convent of Caerleon have remitted, and remit for ever in the future, to the prior and monks of Basaleg all pleas and claims that have arisen between them up to the day on which this final concord was made. For the good of peace the abbot and convent of Caerleon have given 10 marks and four oxen to the prior and monks of Basaleg. Henry, bishop of Llandaff, the abbot and convent of Caerleon, the prior and convent of Glastonbury, the chapter of the church of Llandaff and the Lord Hywel of Caerleon who is their patron [i.e. of the monks of Caerleon] have each attached their seals. Witnesses (not named).

30 March 1211

B = Cambridge, Trinity College MS R. 5. 33 (Register of Glastonbury Abbey), fo. 107r. s. xiii–xiv (here s. xiv).
Pd. from B, *Adami de Domerham De Rebus Gestis*, ed. Hearne, ii. 610; from Hearne, *Mon. Ang.*, v. 728.
Cd., *Episc. Acts*, ii. 692 (L. 290; from Hearne).

In nomine sancte et individue Trinitatis. Facta est finalis concordia inter abbatem et conventum de Karlyon Cist(erciensis) ordinis et priorem et monachos de Basselech coram viro venerabili H. de Karliun anno ab incarnatione domini m cc xi tertio kalendas aprilis, videlicet quod prior et monachi de Basselech mera et spontanea voluntate, auctoritate et assensu prioris et conventus de Glaston', remiserunt[a] abbati et conventui de Karlyun omnes querelas et calumpnias super omnibus terris et decimis quas tenuerunt et tenent predicti abbas et conventus de Karlyon usque ad diem in quo hec finalis concordia facta est, et remittunt in posterum inperpetuum. Quod si de cetero predictus abbas et conventus de Karliun in parrochiis eorum terram vel terras cultas adquisierint,[b] decimas solvent vel amicabiliter conponant. Abbas et conventus etiam de Karliun remiserunt priori et monachis de Basselech omnes querelas et calumpnias que inter eos exorte sunt usque ad diem in quo hec finalis concordia facta est, et remittunt in posterum in perpetuum. Dederunt predicti abbas et conventus de Karliun pro bono pacis antedictis[c] priori et monachis de Basselech x marcas et iiii boves. In huius ergo concordie testimonium H. Dei gratia Landavens(is) episcopus, abbas et conventus de Karliun, prior et conventus de Glaston', capitulum Landavens(is) ecclesie, dominus H. de Karliun qui eorum est patronus presenti scripto sigilla sua apposuerunt. Hiis testibus.

[a] se miserunt B. | [b] adquisierunt B. | [c] antedicti B.

The monks of Caerleon obtained a bull from Innocent III dated at Ferentino, 14 October 1208, confirming their exemption from paying tithes on both lands they brought into cultivation and cultivated lands worked by their hands or at their expense (Owen, *Catalogue*, iii. 710–11; cd., *Episc. Acts*, ii. 687 (L. 271); *Letters of Pope Innocent III*, ed. Cheney and Cheney, 133 (no. 805)). Earlier, probably 1179 × 1184, Hywel had granted land to Basaleg in commutation of the tithes of the monks of Caerleon (no. 467 above).

MORGAN AP HYWEL
(d. 1248)

477 William Marshal (II), earl of Pembroke and his heirs

Grant of the castle of Caerleon with its appurtenances to be held in chief of the king and his heirs as Hywel, his father, used to hold it and as Morgan used to hold it. Sealing clause; witnesses.

[February 1227 × -25 October 1230; possibly May 1227 × -3 May 1230]

B = TNA: PRO, C 53/28 (Ch. R. 19 Henry III), m. 12 (in an inspeximus, 11 April 1236). Rubric: Gib(er)to comite Mar(escallo).
Pd. from B, Bradney, *History of Monmouthshire*, iii. 189 (and trans.).
Cd., *CChR 1226–57*, 198; *H*, no. 186.

Sciant presentes et futuri quod ego Morgan(us) filius Hoelis dedi, concessi et hac presenti carta mea confirmavi Will(elm)o Maresc(a)llo comiti Pembr' et heredibus suis castrum de Karlyon cum pertinentiis suis tenendum capite de domino rege et heredibus suis sicut Hoelus pater meus dictum castrum cum pertinentiis suis de domino rege melius et liberius tenere consuevit et sicut ego predictum castrum cum pertinentiis suis de domino rege melius et liberius tenere consuevi. Ut autem hec mea donatio et concessio perpetue firmitatis `et stabilitatis robur optineat presentem cartam sigilli mei impressione roboravi. Hiis testibus: H. de Burgo comite Kant' tunc iustic(iario) Angl(ie), G. de Clara comite Glouc(estrie) et Hertf',[a] S. de Setg(ra)ue, Rad(ulf)o filio Nich(ola)i, W. de Gamages et aliis.

[a] Heref' B.

The outer dating limits are fixed by the creation of Hubert de Burgh as earl of Kent in February 1227 and the death in Brittany of Gilbert de Clare, earl of Gloucester on 25 October 1230 (*DNB*, vii. 318; cf. Powicke, *Henry III*, ii. 760–1). The beneficiary was therefore William Marshal II, earl of Pembroke 1220–31. If William was present when the charter was drawn up, the dating limits may be narrowed down to the period between May 1227, when he returned from a visit to Ireland that began in August 1226, and his arrival in Brittany on 3 May 1230 with Henry III, Hubert de Burgh, the earl of Gloucester and others (cf. Berger, 'Les préparatifs', 22; Carpenter, *Minority*, 354–5; *DNB*, xxxvi. 234).

Forces of the grantee's father, William Marshal I, had captured Caerleon from Morgan in October 1217 and the town remained in William's hands at his death on 14 May 1219 (*BT, Pen20Tr*, 96; *BT, RBH*, 216–17; *HW*, ii. 674, n. 108; see further Crouch, *William Marshal*, 127–8; Carpenter, *Minority*, 77). Although Llywelyn ap Iorwerth secured permission in 1220 from the regency government in England for Morgan to initiate a legal action against William Marshal II for the recovery of Caerleon, this action was unsuccessful (*Rot. Claus.*, i. 436b; Carpenter, *Minority*, 192; Walker, 'Supporters of Richard Marshal', 63). In November 1222 and January 1223 the royal government demanded that William surrender Caerleon castle to the king (*PR 1216–25*, 352; 363; Carpenter, *Minority*, 294, 299). However, these orders were ignored, as the castle was still held by the earl in August 1226, when an agreement was made between him and the king at Hereford. According to this, William, saving his hereditary right, would on 21 August entrust Caerleon castle to the king, who claimed seisin of it, and the king, saving his hereditary right, would return it to William five days later; at Michaelmas 1230 William would hand the castle over to the king, who would arrange for the disputed seisin to be judged within the next month by the Marshal's peers (*PR 1225–32*, 82–3). In accordance with this, on 27 August 1226 the royal keeper of Caerleon castle was ordered by the king to hand it over immediately to William, to whom it had been given in custody (ibid., 59). Caerleon castle was still held by William at his death on 6 April 1231 (*PR 1225–32*, 427).

The rubric shows that the inspeximus was issued for Gilbert Marshal, earl of Pembroke 1234–41, a younger brother of William II who succeeded to the earldom on the death of his elder brother, Richard Marshal (cf. note to no. 269 above). Gilbert no doubt sought royal confirmation of Morgan's quitclaim as a means of reinforcing his title to Caerleon castle, in the face of attempts by Morgan to recover it from Richard Marshal following his submission to Henry III in August 1233, attempts that continued with the support of Llywelyn ap Iorwerth in February and March 1236 (no. 478 below; *CRR*, xv, no. 489; *Foedera*, I. i. 223; *CR 1234–7*, 337, 342). Although Gilbert Marshal agreed to restore Caerleon castle to the king later in April 1236, and thus shortly after receiving the royal confirmation of Morgan's charter, the earl continued to hold it at his death in June 1241 (*CPR 1232–47*, 254; cf. *CR 1234–7*, 364–5, 369–70, 374, 381; no. 271 above).

478 Letter patent concerning Henry III

Notification that he will be faithful to his lord the king and serve him faithfully all his life. To guarantee this he has pledged all his lands to the king; if during his life he shall happen to be against the king, Hugh, bishop of Ely and his successor shall have jurisdiction over him to excommunicate his person and interdict all his land, without any appeal or challenge. Sealing clause.

[*c*.26 August 1233]

> B = TNA: PRO, C 54/44 (Close R. 17 Henry III), m. 6d (contemporary enrolment).
> Pd. from B, *CR 1231–4*, 321.
> Cd., *H*, no. 498.

Omnibus Cristi fidelibus hoc scriptum visuris vel audituris Morganus de Carleon' salutem. Noverit universitas vestra quod ego domino meo Henr(ico) regi Angl(ie), illustri filio I. quondam regis Angl(ie) illustris, fidelis ero et tota vita mea ei fideliter serviam. Et ad [hoc][a] faciendum omnes terras meas ubicumque sint ei obligavi. Et si forte, quod absit, contingat me contra ipsum esse aliquo tempore vite mee, concedo quod venerabilis pater H. Elyens(is) episcopus et successor suus, qui post eum erit episcopus eiusdem loci, in me iurisdictionem habeant ad sententiam excommunicationis ferendam in personam meam et ad totam terram meam interdicendam, remoto quolibet appello et contradictionis obstaculo. In cuius etc. huic scripto sigillum meum apposui.

[a] *omitted in* B, *but object required for* faciendum; *alternatively emend to* quod ad faciendum, *on the assumption that* et *derives from a misreading of the abbreviation for* quod.

Motivated by the hope of recovering Caerleon, Morgan was the only Welsh lord of south Wales to give his fealty in support of the king against the rebellious Richard Marshal, earl of Gloucester (Walker, 'Supporters of Richard Marshal', 63–4). The letter is enrolled between royal letters dated at Hereford on 25 and 28 August 1233 (*CR 1231–4*, 321–4), and can be no later than 26 August, when the king received Morgan and all he could bring with him into his service and promised not to make peace with the Marshal without including Morgan (*CPR 1232–47*, 24). See further Vincent, *Peter des Roches*, 389–90, and note to no. 477 above. The bishop of Ely referred to was Hugh of Northwold (1229–54). I am grateful to Paul Russell for help with the textual note.

MAREDUDD AP GRUFFUDD
(d. 1270)

*479 The bishop and chapter of Llandaff
Release of all his right to the advowsons of the churches of Machen, Bedwas and Mynyddislwyn.

[1248 × 1270]

Mention only, in a confirmation by Edward III for Bishop John de Eaglescliffe and the chapter of Llandaff of grants in mortmain to Llandaff, dated at Woodstock, 10 April 1330 (*CPR 1327–30*, 508; *Episc. Acts*, ii. 750 (L. 529)). In the confirmation the release follows the record of a transfer by Abbot Michael of Glastonbury to Bishop Elias (1230–40) and the chapter of Llandaff of the church of Basaleg and its chapels, including Machen, Bedwas and Mynyddislwyn (*CPR 1327–30*, 507–8). Maredudd succeeded Morgan ap Hywel in 1248. It is unclear why Conway Davies assigned the release to 1257–66, thereby implying a date during the pontificate of William of Radnor (*Episc. Acts*, ii. 750 (L. 529)).

POWYS

MADOG AP MAREDUDD
(d. *c.*9 February 1160)

480 St Michael's church, Trefeglwys

Grant, for the redemption of the souls of himself, his parents and all the faithful, of 40 sata, with the consent of Hywel ab Ieuaf with the elders of the country, at the request of the monk Bleddrws who first founded the church, namely from the township called Tregymer, in everlasting writing. A blessing on whoever keeps [this], a curse on whoever does not. Witnesses.

[1132 × 1151]

B = Shrewsbury, Shropshire Records and Research Centre MS 6001/6869 (Haughmond Cartulary), fo. 215r. s. xv ex.
C = Oxford, Bodleian Library, MS Dugdale 39, fo. 100v. *c.*1583.
D = Cardiff County and City Library MS 3.11, p. 3. s. xvi².
Pd. from B, *Cart. Haugh.*, no. 1216; from B (with variants from D), Pryce, 'Church of Trefeglwys', 51 (and trans.); from a Wynnstay MS dated 1640 destroyed in 1858, Williams, 'Wynnstay MSS.', 330–1.
Cd., *H*, no. 202.

Notum sit omnibus quod Madauc[a] rex Powissensiu(m)[b] Deo suffragante pro redemptione anime sue et parentum suorum necnon et omnium fidelium quadraginta sata consentiente Howel[c] filii Geuaf[d] cum senioribus patrie dedit ecclesie Sancti Mich(ael)is Bledrus rogatu monachi qui eam primitus constituit, scilicet de villa que vocatur Trefkem(er)e,[e] et hoc in sempiterno graphio.[f] Qui custodierit sit benedictus et qui non custodierit sit maledictus. Hii vero[g] sunt testes: Abraha(m) filius Benit[h] capellanus,[i–]Morcant filius Maredud, Iorwerth filius Gurgeneu[j] prepositus patrie Arguistly, Dolfin abbas Nandynan, Goronuy[k] filii Guin.[–i]

[a] CD; Madaut B. | [b] Powissentium CD. | [c] Hewel D. | [d] Euaf CD. | [e] Tref Cemer CD. | [f] CD; grathio B. | [g] *omitted* CD. | [h] Benir C; Bemr D. | [i–i] etc. B | [j] Gurgenau D. [k] Goronwy D.

The authenticity of the charter is defended and its dating and significance are assessed in Pryce, 'Church of Trefeglwys', esp. 24–7, 33–40, 48–9. Comparison with the charters of

Hywel ab Ieuaf of Arwystli (nos 1–3 above) shows that the church was located at Trefeglwys (SN 971 906) in Arwystli and that the charter pre-dated its transfer to Haughmond Abbey. Madog succeeded to Powys in 1132; Hywel granted additional lands and rights to St Michael's, Trefeglwys in 1143 × 1151 (nos 1–2 above). The present document is of particular interest as it is the latest known example from Wales of a charter whose form and formulae conform to 'Celtic' charter-writing conventions originating in the pre-Norman period. *Satum* was a biblical measure of grain equivalent to 1½ *modii*. The reference to Bleddrws suggests that he (together with his co-heirs Iago and Ednyfed, mentioned in no. 1 above) was the church's founder, probably in the second quarter of the twelfth century. Iorwerth ap Gwrgenau is similarly described as 'steward (*prepositus*) of that land', i.e. Arwystli, in a reference to his two sons in an early thirteenth-century document (no. 16 above). *Nandynan* is an early form of Llandinam (SO 026 885), the site of a major Welsh church almost 4 miles south-east of Trefeglwys; to judge by late medieval genealogies, Dolffyn was a descendant of Bleddyn ap Cynfyn (d. 1075), king of Powys and Gwynedd, and thus a kinsman of Madog (Pryce, 'Church of Trefeglwys', 24–5).

IORWERTH GOCH AP MAREDUDD
(*fl.* 1157–71)

*481 Haughmond Abbey
Grant of Aber Ceiriog (Abirokeyrok) *and Glyndw^r [Glyndyfrdwy]* (Glendur) *with its pasture and all other appurtenances.*

[1166 × 1177]

Mention only, in the cartulary of Haughmond Abbey (s. xv ex.), which attributes the record of the grant, made *ex dono Gervasi rufi*, to a bull issued by Pope Alexander III in 1177 whose full text has not survived (*Cart. Haugh.*, no. 2). *Abirkeyrok* (the form in the rubric) or *Abirokeyrok* has convincingly been identified as Aber Ceiriog, the confluence of the Ceiriog and the Dee (at SJ 318 395) about 2 miles north-east of Chirk (ibid., n.; cf. *Breudwyt Ronabwy*, ed. Richards, 1: *Aber Ceirawc yn Hallictwn*, i.e. Halton (SJ 302 398), a township near Chirk less than 1 mile west of the confluence). *Glendur* (Glyndŵr) is probably an abbreviated form of Glyndyfrdwy (SJ 148 426), located in the Dee valley about 9 miles north-west of Chirk (for the form of the place-name see Lloyd, *Owen Glendower*, 14, n. 2). Since Glyndyfrdwy was held by later members of the dynasty of northern Powys, most famously Owain Glyndŵr who took his cognomen from the estate, it seems that the present grant was ineffective or, perhaps, referred to only part of the lands of Glyndyfrdwy (cf. nos 528, 539, 531–2 below). Whereas Haughmond's title to Aber Ceiriog was recognized in the early thirteenth century (*Cart. Haugh.*, no. 3), there is no other evidence for the abbey's tenure of Glyndyfrdwy.

Iorwerth was expelled from Mochnant in 1166 by his nephews Owain Fychan ap Madog and Owain Cyfeiliog (*BT, Pen20Tr*, 64; *BT, RBH*, 148–9). Already in receipt of payments from the English exchequer since 1157, he was granted custody of Chirk castle by Henry II in April 1166, and was still exercising this responsibility in 1168 (*Pipe Roll 12 Henry II*, 59;

Pipe Roll 14 Henry II, 110). His exchequer payments rose to £91 per annum from Michaelmas 1168 to Michaelmas 1170 but ceased after forty-seven weeks of the year ending at Michaelmas 1171, possibly because he had died (Eyton, *Shropshire*, ii. 108–12; *HW*, ii. 520; Latimer, 'Henry II's campaign', 541). Although the absence of the grant from Alexander III's bull for Haughmond of 14 May 1172 may indicate that it was made after that, as suggested by Rees (*Cart. Haugh.*, no. 2 and n.; cf. ibid., App. A, i), it is probably prudent to push the *terminus a quo* back to 1166, both because this is when Iorwerth is first associated with Chirk in the sources and because he may have died by September 1171. He had almost certainly died by May 1177, as his son Madog ap Iorwerth Goch is named (after Owain Cyfeiliog and Gruffudd ap Madog of Bromfield) among the Welsh leaders attending the council of Oxford in that month (*Gesta*, ed. Stubbs, i. 162; I owe this point to Frederick Suppe).

PENLLYN, EDEIRNION AND DINMAEL

MAREDUDD AP HYWEL
(*fl.* 1142–76)

482 Strata Marcella Abbey
Grant, for the salvation of his soul, of all the land called Esgyngaenog with all its bounds and appurtenances in free and perpetual possession. Announces that Heilewydd, who once used to hold the same land, has sold all his right in it to the monks in free and perpetual possession for 2½ pounds of silver. Madog ap Llywarch, who was claiming the same land, has sold to the monks whatever right he had in it on behalf of himself and his heirs for 1 pound of silver, and given it to be possessed freely for ever. Maredudd wishes that the monks may possess all the aforesaid land with all its bounds and appurtenances in perpetual right. Sealing clause; witnesses.

1176

A = Caernarfon, Gwynedd Archives Service, XD2/1111. Endorsed: · xxviii · ; Maredud super Esgengain(auc) (s. xii/xiii); approx. 216 × 128 + 11 mm.; two central slits through fold for a tag (*c*.9 mm. wide), which exits through a slit at the base of the fold; sealed on tag. Circular seal, green wax, imperfect, originally approx. 58 mm. diameter; equestrian, facing right; legend: + SIGILL . . . . . . L. Readings of parts of the charter where the parchment is rubbed, making the text illegible, have been supplied within square brackets from Jones's transcript, made when the charter was in a better state of preservation, and incorporate minor orthographical emendations by Thomas in *Ystrad Marchell Charters*.
Pd. from A, Jones, 'Abbey of Ystrad Marchell', 21; from A, *Ystrad Marchell Charters*, no. 4.
Cd., Davies, 'Strata Marcella documents', 164–5 (no. 2); *H*, no. 48.

Omnibus sancte matris ecclesie filiis tam presentibus quam f[u]t[uris not]u[m] sit quod ego Mareduth filius Howel, dominus provincie que dicitur Edeyrniaun, dedi et concessi, pro salute anim[e mee, Deo et Beate] Marie et monachis de St(ra)dmarchell totam terram que vocatur Eskengaynauc in omnibus terminis suis et [perti]nenci[is in liber]am scilicet et quietam et perpetuam possessionem. Volo insuper ego prefatus Mareduth omnibus notum fieri quod Hely[ewith], qui aliquando eandem terram tenebat, vendidit totum suum ius eiusdem terre prefatis monachis in liberam et quietam et [perpe]tuam possessionem. Accepit autem idem Heylewith pro tota terra illa a predictis monachis duas libras argenti et dimidium. Madoc(us) vero filius Lewarch, qui eandem terram calumpniabatur, vendidit pro una libra argenti prefatis monachis pro se et pro heredibus suis quicquid iuris in terra supradicta habebat, et in manu Ithelli abbatis de Stradmarchell prenominatam terram perpetuo, libere et quiete possidendam prefatis monachis dedit. Volo igitur ego prefatus Mareduth ut sepedicti monachi totam prenominatam [terra]m in omnibus terminis s[ui]s et pertinentiis, iure perpetuo, possideant in terris et pasturis et in omnibus usibus suis et utilitatibus. E[t] ne hec [mea] predicta donatio sive prenominatorum virorum predicta venditio processu temporum ab aliquo possit violari tam sigilli [m]ei impress[ione qua]m bonor[um] virorum attestatione munivi et coroboravi. His testibus: magistro Riuaun, How[el filio Ithel, Ioruert Seithmarchauc, Ior]uerth filio Eynniaun, Meuric filio Kadugaun. Facta est autem hec mea predicta donatio et prefata ve[n]d[itio in manu prefati abbatis] anno scilicet ab incarnatione domini m° c° lxx° vi°.

Esgyngaenog (SJ 089 459) lay in the parish of Gwyddelwern, about 1½ miles north-east of Corwen (*Ystrad Marchell Charters*, 112 and Map II). The grant may well have been designed as a means of resolving a dispute over the land between Heilewydd and Madog ap Llywarch, both of whom received payments from the monks. If so, however, this did not prevent Madog's sons from trying to recover Esgyngaenog in 1207 (no. 504 below).

ELISE AP MADOG
(*fl.* 1160–1223)

483 Strata Marcella Abbey

Sale for 3 pounds in perpetual possession, free of all secular exaction and custom, of all the land called Llechweddfigyn with all its bounds and appurtenances, in wood, plain, waters, meadows, pastures and all rights of use. Its bounds are: from the mouth of the Cwm Main to its source, thence directly to Caerunwch, thence along the stream which descends near the ford of Dolwen, thence up along the stream of the ford of Dolwen to Gweunrudd, then along Gweunrudd to the place on the stream called Nantucheldref, thence down to Mynachddwr, thence up to the stream called Alarch, and along the Alarch to the Ceirw. Sealing clause; witnesses.

Esgyngaenog, 18 April 1183

A = NLW, Wynnstay Estate Records, Ystrad Marchell Charters, no. 5. Endorsed: Carte Elisse super Lechlleutin (s. xii/xiii); ·XXIX· (s. xii/xiii); early modern endorsements; approx. 167 × 180 + 16 mm.; two central horizontal slits in fold for a tag (*c.* 13 mm. wide) which exits through a slit in the base of the fold; sealed on tag. Circular seal, white wax, very imperfect, originally approx. 50–55 mm. diameter; equestrian, facing right, most of rider missing; no legend survives.
Pd. from A, Jones, 'Abbey of Ystrad Marchell', 23–4; from A, *Ystrad Marchell Charters*, no. 5.
Cd., *H*, no. 204.

Noscant universi sancte matris ecclesie filii tam presentes quam futuri quod ego Elisse Madoci filius vendidi et confirmavi monachis de St(ra)dmarchell pro tribus libris in propriam et perpetuam possessionem et ab omni exactione et consuetudine seculari liberam et quietam, plenarie et integre et honorifice, totam terram illam que vocatur Llecheudin cum omnibus terminis suis et pertinentiis, videlicet in bosco, in plano, in aquis, in pratis, in pasturis et in omnibus usibus suis et utilitatibus. Cuius autem terre veri termini sunt: ab Abercu(m)mein usque ad eius ortum, et a *blain* Cu(m)mehin in directum usque Kair Runhoh, et a Kairunhoh sicut ducit rivulus ille qui descendit propius iuxta vadum Dolwen, et inde rivus Ritdolwen susum usque Gweunrutd, et sicut ducit Gweunrutd usque ad ortum rivi qui dicitur Nanthucheldref, et inde Nanthucheldref deorsum usque Manachduuer, et a Manachduuer susum usque ad rivulum qui dicitur Alarch, et sic Alarch usque ad Geyro. Et quia volo ut hec mea venditio prefatis monachis imperpetuum in pace permaneat tam sigilli mei impressione quam testium attestatione munivi et coroboravi. His testibus: Grifino abbate de St(ra)dmarch(ell) et Philippo priore et Cadugano converso, magistro Riuaun et magistro Heylin, Howel filius Ythael, Yoruerd Seithmarchog et multis aliis. Facta est autem hec venditio apud Eskengainoc anno videlicet ab incarnatione domini m° c° octogesimo iii° quartodecimo autem kalendas maii.

Llechweddfigyn (SH 919 449) was located in the parish of Llanfor, Penllyn; Esgyngaenog lay about 10 miles to its east, in the parish of Gwyddelwern, Edeirnion (*Ystrad Marchell Charters*, 112, 113 and Map II). The Cwm Main is now known as Afon Aber-arw-wlaw and Mynachddwr as Afon Mynach (ibid., 113).

*484 Strata Marcella Abbey

Sale of all the land of (?) Nantfach (Nantfaith) *with all its appurtenances.*

[Probably 18 April 1183 × August 1202]

Mention only, in a confirmation charter of Edward II dated at Tutbury, 12 March 1322 (*Ystrad Marchell Charters*, no. 6; Jones, 'Abbey of Ystrad Marchell', 312 (from Henry VI's inspeximus, 1450); cd., *CChR 1300–26*, 440; *H*, no. 218). The document was probably issued on the same or a later date than no. 483 above, since the summary immediately follows that of no. 483 in the inspeximus (for the likelihood that each donor's grants are listed chronologically in the inspeximus see Davies, 'Records of the abbey of Ystrad Marchell', 11, followed by *Ystrad Marchell Charters*, 9). *Nantfaith* was probably an error for Nantfach (ibid., 113). If, like Llechweddfigyn in no. 483, the land was located in Penllyn, the charter was issued no later than August 1202, when Llywelyn ap Iorwerth seized Penllyn, which thereafter remained under the control of Gwynedd, although Llywelyn allowed Elise ap Madog to keep Crogen and seven townships in the commote.

*485 Strata Marcella Abbey

Grant and confirmation in pure and perpetual alms of all the lands it has in the province of Penllyn (Pellen), *namely part of (?) Cyman* (Kemman), *Bodwenni* (Badweneu) *and Pennantmaelgwn* (Pennanmaelgun) *with all their appurtenances, and thence from all the boundary of Rhiwaedog* (Rewedauk) *to the Mawddwy* (Mautho)*, and also of the land bought from Madog Hyddgam* (Maudauc Hethgam).

[Probably 18 April 1183 × August 1202]

Mention only, in a confirmation charter of Edward II dated at Tutbury, 12 March 1322 (*Ystrad Marchell Charters*, no. 8; Jones, 'Abbey of Ystrad Marchell', 312 (from Henry VI's inspeximus, 1450); cd., *CChR 1300–26*, 440; *H*, no. 217). A summary of Madog Hyddgam's sale, including its bounds, also appears in Edward's confirmation; the unnamed land lay in Penllyn in the vicinity of Llechweddfigyn (no. 483 above) and (?)Nantfach (no. 484 above) (*Ystrad Marchell Charters*, 113 and no. 7). For the date see note to no. 484 above and, for the place-names, *Ystrad Marchell Charters*, 113–14 and Map II. *Kemman* was possibly the land later called Cynllwyd in the parish of Llanuwchllyn.

*486 Basingwerk Abbey
Confirmation of Owain Brogyntyn's gift of Gwernhefin.

[*c*.1186 × August 1202]

Mention only, in a charter of Dafydd ap Llywelyn dated at Coleshill, 25 July 1240 (no. 292 above). The grant of Elise included in Llywelyn ap Gruffudd's confirmation for Basingwerk, dated at Bangor, 8 April 1247, almost certainly refers to the same confirmation (no. 321 above). For Owain's grant of Gwernhefin, datable to *c*.1186 × August 1202, see no. 492 below.

487 Strata Marcella Abbey
Grant, inspired by piety, in perpetual alms, of all the pastures of all the province of Penllyn, from the river Dŵr Anudon [Dee] to Edeirnion and in breadth from the river Ceirw to the Berwyn mountain, freely and fully. He has granted the pastures for the special use of the monks so that no other monks may possess them by purchase or gift. More importantly and dearly to Elise, he has granted the monks his body for burial as well as, at his death, two thirds of his moveables, both herds and other goods. Witnesses.

(?)Bala, 19 June 1191

A = NLW, Wynnstay Estate Records, Ystrad Marchell Charters, no. 15. Endorsed: Elisse super pasturas et corpus suum (s. xii/xiii); ... et monacorum de Basigw' ... Pe(n)lin (s. xiii in.); approx. 236 × 76 + 8 mm.; two central horizontal slits, one just above fold, one in fold, for a tag (*c*.12 mm. wide) which exits through a slit in the base of the fold; sealed on tag. Seal missing.
Pd. from A, *Ystrad Marchell Charters*, no. 15.
Cd., *H*, no. 209.

Universis sancte matris ecclesie filiis presentibus et futuris notum sit quod ego Helisse Madoci filius intuitu pietatis dedi et confirmavi Deo et Beate Marie[a] et conventui de St(ra)tmarcell in puram et perpetuam elemosinam omnes pasturas tocius provincie que appellatur Penllin, a fluvio qui vocatur Dwer Anudon usque ad Hedeirniaun et in latitudine a fluvio qui dicitur Geiru usque ad montem Berrwin, bene et in pace, libere et quiete, plenarie et integre et honorifice. [Predic]tas[b] itaque pasturas supradictis monachis specialiter in proprium usum dedi ut nullis aliis liceat easdem pasturas nec emtione nec donatione [possider]e.[b] Insuper et quod his maius et mihi carius erat predictis monachis dedi scilicet memet ipsum corpus, videlicet ad sepulturam, et in extremis meis preter terciam partem omnem meam substantiam tam in pecoribus quam in ceteris omnibus meis suppellectilibus. Iste autem donationes date sunt et confirmate apud Bala in manu Grifini abbatis coram Philippo priore et Teguaret converso cognomento Hescerrin et magistro Rwaun, de laicis vero Howel filio Hithael et Goronui fratre eius, anno videlicet secundo post mortem fratris mei Grifini quando prius predictam provinciam possedi. Memoratas itaque omnes donationes date sunt et confirmate et plenarie rate anno ab incarnatione domini m° c° nonagesimo primo xiii kalendas iulii.

[a] *word written in majuscule letters in* A. | [b] *lacuna in parchment* A.

For the place-names see *Ystrad Marchell Charters*, 116. The assertion after the witness list that the grant was made 'in the second year after the death of my brother Gruffudd, when I first possessed the aforesaid province' is problematic. The subsequent dating clause, which probably also refers to the ceremony at Bala rather than to a later confirmation at a place unstated, is dated 19 June 1191. According to the Welsh chronicles, however, Elise's brother Gruffudd ap Madog died in 1191 (*BT, Pen20Tr*, 74; *BT, RBH*, 172–3; *BS*, 188–9). By contrast, the charter implies that Gruffudd had died no later than 18 June 1190. Although Lloyd argued, without reference to the present charter, that the 1191 date was correct because the chronicles refer to an eclipse of the sun later in their entries for that year, and a notable eclipse is known from other sources to have occurred on 23 June 1191 (*HW*, ii. 566 and n. 155; *AM*, i. 21, 54), the contemporary evidence provided by the charter suggests that the chroniclers' date merits reconsideration. Even if that date ultimately derives from an annalistic entry composed soon after Gruffudd's death, the death may have been assigned to the wrong year at some point in the entry's transmission through the lost Latin chronicle of the late thirteenth century that is the basis of the Welsh versions now extant. This hypothesis gains support from the facts that the chronicles wrongly assign the fall of Jerusalem to Saladin (2 October 1187) to 1188 as well as the death of Archbishop Baldwin of Canterbury (19 November 1190) to 1191 (*BT, Pen20Tr*, 188). Gruffudd's date may likewise have been allocated to the year following that in which it occurred. If Gruffudd in fact died in 1190 (i.e. 25 March 1190 × 24 March 1191), the second year after his death could have begun as early as 25 March 1191.

The charter also raises questions about the nature and chronology of Elise's lordship in Penllyn. No. 483 above shows that he possessed land that he could sell in Penllyn in 1183, well before Gruffudd's death. The present charter may indicate, however, that it was only after the death of his brother that Elise enjoyed the rights of chief lord in Penllyn which enabled him to grant extensive pasture rights there; he is also attested as lord of Penllyn when he was expelled from his lands by Llywelyn ap Iorwerth in 1202. Yet Elise's brother Owain Brogyntyn also enjoyed – or at least claimed – extensive rights in Penllyn before 1202 (nos 492–5 below).

488 Strata Marcella Abbey

Sale for 8 pounds of the land of Gwyddelwern with the consent of the heirs of that township, in these bounds: from Helyglwyn Seithug to the dyke, along that dyke to the Gwaun and thence along to Moel Caseg and thence to the stream nearby and from that stream to the larger stream. Further grant of all the land of Esgyngaenog in its bounds, as granted by his predecessor Maredudd ap Hywel. Further grant of all the pastures in Edeirnion. He wishes the monks to possess all the aforesaid lands and pastures freely and fully, free of all exaction and custom in perpetual right, namely in wood, plain, waters, meadows and all rights of use. Sealing clause; witnesses.

Esgyngaenog, 15 May 1198

A = Caernarfon, Gwynedd Archives Service, XD2/1112. Endorsed: Carta Elisse super Guit[(?)el]wern (s. xii/xiii); early modern endorsement; approx. 163 × 167 + 15 mm.; two central horizontal slits in fold for a tag (*c.*12 mm. wide) which exits through a slit in the base of the fold; sealed on tag. Seal missing.
Pd. from A, Jones, 'Abbey of Ystrad Marchell', 30–1; from A, *Ystrad Marchell Charters*, no. 17.
Cd., Davies, 'Strata Marcella documents', 168 (no. 7); Owens, 'Rûg and its muniments', 87–8; *H*, no. 210.

Notum sit universis sancte matris ecclesie filiis tam presentibus quam futuris quod ego Elisse Madoci filius vendidi et confirmavi monachis de St(ra)dmarchell pro octo libris partem terre que dicitur Gwothélwern consensu et donatione heredum ville illius in his terminis, videlicet ab Helégluin Seithuc usque ad fossam et sic ducente eadem[a] fossa usque ad Gweun et inde in longitudine usque ad Moil Cassec et a Moil Cassec usque ad rivulum proximum sibi et a rivulo illo usque ad alium rivulum illo maiorem. Dedi insuper et confirmavi prefatis monachis totam terram que dicitur Eskengainoc in terminis suis, sicut dedit eis antecessor meus Mareduth filius Howel. Dedi etiam eis totas pasturas in Edeyrniaun. Volo igitur ut prenominati monachi totas prefatas terras et pasturas libere et quiete, plenarie et integre ct ab omni exactione et consuetudine liberas perpetuo iure possideant, videlicet in bosco, in plano, in aquis, in pratis, in pascuis, in omnibus usibus suis et utilitatibus. Et ne hec mea donatio seu venditio ab aliquo perditionis filio in posterum violetur tam sigilli mei impressione quam testium attestatione munire et coroborare curavi. His testibus: Grifino abbate de St(ra)dmarch(ell), Philippo priore, Cadugano converso, magistro Ruuaun, magistro Heilin, Howel filio Ythael, Yaruord Seithmarchoc et multis aliis. Datum apud Esgeng' anno ab incarnatione domini m° c° xc° viii° ii° idus maii.

[a] éadem A.

Gwyddelwern was located in Edeirnion; the places in the boundary clause describing it have not been identified (*Ystrad Marchell Charters*, 117). For Maredudd ap Hywel's grant see no. 482 above.

*489 Letter patent concerning Henry III

[Text presumably as no. 19 above.]

[Montgomery, 8 October 1223]

Mention only, in a note on the patent roll after the text of no. 19 above (issued by Maredudd ap Rhobert of Cedewain) naming Elise among those that *Eodem modo fecerunt cartas suas* (*PR 1216–25*, 411; cd., *H*, no. 529).

OWAIN BROGYNTYN AP MADOG
(d. 1215 × 1218)

*490 Strata Marcella Abbey
Sale and confirmation of the land of Blaenhyfed (Blainhiuet).

[*c*.1183 × August 1202]

Mention only, in a confirmation charter of Edward II dated at Tutbury, 12 March 1322 (*Ystrad Marchell Charters*, no. 9; Jones, 'Abbey of Ystrad Marchell', 312 (from Henry VI's inspeximus, 1450); cd., *CChR 1300–26*, 440; *H*, no. 220). Blaenhyfed has been identified as the farm now called Cwm Hyfed together with Llechwedd Du (SH 9129/SH 9130), par. Llangywer, Penllyn (*Ystrad Marchell Charters*, 113 and Map II). Its location suggests that the grant was no later than August 1202 (see note to no. 484 above). It is uncertain when Owain first held lands in Penllyn (cf. Carr and Smith, 'Edeirnion and Mawddwy', 138–9). No. 491 below suggests that he could have done so by 1183.

*491 Strata Marcella Abbey
Sale of part of (?) Cyman (Kemman).

[*c*.1183 × August 1202]

Mention only, in a confirmation charter of Edward II dated at Tutbury, 12 March 1322 (*Ystrad Marchell Charters*, no. 10; Jones, 'Abbey of Ystrad Marchell', 312 (from Henry VI's inspeximus, 1450); cd., *CChR 1300–26*, 440; *H*, no. 221). No. 485 above, probably datable 18 April 1183 × August 1202, confirms Strata Marcella's possession of *Kemman* and shows that the land was located in Penllyn.

492 Basingwerk Abbey
Grant, with the consent of his wife and heirs, of the whole of Gwernhefin with the men of that township and all its appurtenances in wood, plain, meadows, fields, moors, meadows, waters and other easements pertaining to that township, so freely that he will demand nothing from the monks apart from their prayers and services to God. At his orders the aforesaid men have been freed from Owain's homage and have done homage to the abbot and monks and henceforth will do all services due from their land to the latter rather than to Owain or his men. Further grant to both the monks and their men of common use of pasture throughout his land with the rest of his men. Further grant of these pastures and places: Buarthmeini, Blaen-lliw, half of (?) Amnodd and half of Cumbermeirh. Sealing clause; witnesses.

[*c*.1186 × August 1202]

B = TNA: PRO, C 53/73 (Ch. R. 13 Edward I), m. 26 (in an inspeximus, 12 June 1285).
C = TNA: PRO, C 53/116 (Ch. R. 3 Edward III), m. 26 (in an inspeximus of B, 17 February 1329).
D = TNA: PRO, C 53/164 (Ch. R. 15–17 Richard II), m. 16 (in an inspeximus of C, 2 December 1393).
Cd., *CChR 1257–1300*, 290 (from B); *CChR 1327–41*, 100 (from C); *CChR 1341–1417*, 342 (from D); *H*, no. 211.

Omnibus sancte matris ecclesie filiis tam presentibus quam futuris Owinus de Porkinton' salutem. Noverit universitas vestra quod ego Owinus de Porkinton' cum consilio et voluntate uxoris mee et heredum meorum do Deo et Sancte Marie et abbatie de Basingwerc et monachis ibidem Deo servientibus totum Guenheuing cum hominibus eiusdem ville et cum omnibus pertinentiis suis, in bosco et plano, in pascuis et campis, in moris et pratis et aquis et ceteris omnibus aisiamentis que ad villam prefatam pertinent, tam libere et quiete quod nichil ab eis exigam nisi eorum orationes et beneficia erga Deum. Et sciendum quod me iubente homines prefati ab homagio meo absoluti predictis abbati et monachis homagium fecerunt eisque deinceps quicquid pro terra sua servitii facient abbati et monachis facient et michi nichil vel meis. Pasture quoque tam ipsis quam suis hominibus per totam terram meam concedo cum ceteris meis hominibus in omnibus communionem. Preterea vero predictis monachis et abbatie prefate do et concedo in proprios usus has pasturas et hec loca, videlicet Buarthmeimni et Blainthliu et dimidium Amnauth et dimidium Cumb(er)meirh. Et ut ista donatio atque concessio imperpetuum firma sit et stabilis eam sigilli mei impressione et testibus confirmo. Hii autem sunt testes: Bleithnet' et Gervasius atque Griffin(us) filii Owini de Porkinton', Willemus[a] Seis, Guorennoc, Creicki, Deleu, Howel, Geillur et multi alii.

[a] *sic in* B.

The charter can be no later than August 1202 and probably belongs to a similar date range to no. 495 below. Gwernhefin is located towards the south-western end of Llyn Tegid (Bala Lake), on the west bank opposite Llangywer (SH 893 328; see Williams, *Atlas*, 39). Buarthmeini is on the Afon Lliw, which flows into the Dee just over 1 mile south-west of Llyn Tegid (SH 829 325), and Blaen-lliw is about 2 miles up-river to the north-west near the source of the Lliw (SH 802 339). The reading *Amnauth* has been adopted as this could represent Amnodd in the modern place-names Afon Amnodd-bwll (which flows into Afon Tryweryn at SH 805 384), Amnodd-wen and Amnodd-bwll, located almost 3 miles south-west of Basingwerk's lands at Boch-y-rhaeadr. *Cumbermeirh* has not been identified.

493 Basingwerk Abbey

Grant, with the consent of his wife and heirs, of Rhys Crach with all the land he holds of Owain in Penllyn, namely Kenereu *with all its appurtenances in wood, plain, moors, meadows, waters and other easements that pertain to the said township, so freely and quit of all secular and service and exaction that he will demand nothing from the monks apart from their prayers and services to God. At his orders the aforesaid man and his heirs have been freed from homage to Owain and his heirs and have done homage to the abbot and monks and henceforth will do all services due from their land to the latter. Sealing clause; witnesses.*

[*c*.1186 × August 1202]

B = TNA: PRO, C 53/73 (Ch. R. 13 Edward I), m. 26 (in an inspeximus, 12 June 1285).
C = TNA: PRO, C 53/116 (Ch. R. 3 Edward III), m. 26 (in an inspeximus of B, 17 February 1329).
D = TNA: PRO, C 53/164 (Ch. R. 15–17 Richard II), m. 16 (in an inspeximus of C, 2 December 1393).
Cd., *CChR 1257–1300*, 290 (from B); *CChR 1327–41*, 100 (from C); *CChR 1341–1417*, 342 (from D); *H*, no. 212.

Omnibus sancte matris ecclesie filiis tam presentibus quam futuris Owinus de Porkinton’ salutem. Noverit universitas vestra quod ego Owinus de Porkinton’ cum consilio et voluntate uxoris mee et heredum meorum do Deo et Sancte Marie et abbatie de Basingwerk’ et monachis Deo servientibus in eodem loco Res C(ra)ch cum tota terra sua quam tenet de me in Penandlin, scilicet Kenereu cum omnibus pertinentiis suis, in bosco et plano, in planis et moris et pratis et aquis et ceteris aisiamentis que ad prefatam villam pertinent, tam libere et quiete ab omni servitio et exactione seculari quod nichil ab eis exigam nisi orationes eorum et beneficia erga Deum. Et sciendum quod homo prefatus et heredes sui me iubente ab homagio meo et heredum meorum absoluti predictis abbati et monachis de Basingwerk homagium fecerunt eisque deinceps quicquid pro terra servitii facient abbati et monachis facient. Et ut ista donatio atque concessio imperpetuum firma sit et stabilis eam sigilli mei impressione et testibus confirmo. Hii autem sunt testes: Bleithent et Gervasius atque Griffin(us) filii Owini de Porkinton’.

This was probably issued either at the same time or at least within the same date range as no. 492 above, as its formulae are similar and both charters open with the same three witnesses. *Kenereu* has not been identified.

494 Basingwerk Abbey

Grant, for the salvation of the souls of himself and all his kin, both ancestors and successors, of all his pasture within these bounds: the Derfel, Pont Dâr Emrys, Buarthmeini, Elisbodernes, Riwoden and expressly the pasture of Hoberader, and by Annodd and Blaen-lliw on both sides and Dinas Teleri to the waters of Manadecbederiu and common pasture throughout Penllyn, to be held and possessed in perpetual alms free of all secular service and exaction. Sealing clause. He has faithfully undertaken and promised that he will admit or allow to be admitted no men whatsoever on whose account the monks may sustain any hindrance. Witnesses.

[*c*.1186 × August 1202]

B = TNA: PRO, C 53/73 (Ch. R. 13 Edward I), m. 26 (in an inspeximus, 12 June 1285).
C = TNA: PRO, C 53/116 (Ch. R. 3 Edward III), m. 26 (in an inspeximus of B, 17 February 1329).
D = TNA: PRO, C 53/164 (Ch. R. 15–17 Richard II), m. 16 (in an inspeximus of C, 2 December 1393).
Cd., *CChR 1257–1300*, 290 (from B); *CChR 1327–41*, 100 (from C); *CChR 1341–1417*, 342 (from D); *H*, no. 213.

Universis fidelibus ad quos presens carta pervenerit Owinus de Porkinton salutem. Noverit universitas vestra quod ego pro salute anime mee et pro animabus omnium parentum meorum precedentium et subsequentium dedi et concessi Deo[a] et Sancte Marie et monasterio de Basingwerc et monachis ibidem divino mancipatis officio totam pasturam meam infra terminos subscriptos contentam, videlicet infra Deruail et Pontem Daremeris et Buarthmeimi et Elisbodernes et Riwoden et pasturam nominatim de Hoberader et per Amenaud^b et Blaintliu ex utraque parte et Dinasteleri usque ad aquas que vocantur Manadecbederiu et communam pasturam per totam Penathlin libere et quiete absque omni seculari servitio et exactione tenendam et in perpetua elemosina possidendam. Et ut hec donatio et concessio rata permaneat et inconcussa eam presenti carta mea confirmo et impressione sigilli mei corroboro. Et ego firmiter et fideliter pepigi eis et fide mediante promisi eis quod in prenominatam pasturam viros omnino nullos ullatenus admittam vel admitti permittam unde predicti monachi de Basingwerk' aliquod sustineant impedimentum. Hiis testibus: Bleitheint, Gervasio, Griffino filiis Owini de Porkinton', Hoelo et Morgan filiis Tegit, Werich filio Kenewrec, Galthcim Bahhan, Madoc et Anaroud filiis Madoci, Kenecah, Gronou Bahhan, Gillemiheil, Madock' Hetgam, Ph(ilipp)o filio Rob(er)ti, Griffino sacerdote, David sacerdote, David Goh et multis aliis.

^a do B. | ^b *written as one word in* B.

The insertion before the witness list of the clause promising to protect the monks from disturbance in their pasture may indicate that the charter was a confirmation of previous grants of pasture, occasioned by challenges to Basingwerk's pasture rights in Penllyn, and thus was issued later than nos 492–3 above and no. 495 below. For some of the place-names see notes to nos 321, 492 above.

495 Basingwerk Abbey

Grant, with the consent of his heirs, friends and men, for the souls of himself, his heirs and his ancestors, in perpetual alms, of the water in Penllyn called Llyn Tegid, that is, Pemblemere, and all the pasture of Penllyn for the monks' livestock (of whatever kind and number and wherever they like) and their huts with all other easements in wood, plain, moors and waters; they may take whatever is necessary from the woods, both green or dry, for houses, buildings, hedges and firewood. They may have these free of all earthly service and secular exaction so that Owain will demand nothing from them apart from their prayers and services to God. Sealing clause; witnesses.

[10 August 1186 × August 1202]

B = TNA: PRO, C 53/73 (Ch. R. 13 Edward I), m. 26 (in an inspeximus, 12 June 1285).
C = TNA: PRO, C 53/116 (Ch. R. 3 Edward III), m. 26 (in an inspeximus of B, 17 February 1329).
D = TNA: PRO, C 53/164 (Ch. R. 15–17 Richard II), m. 16 (in an inspeximus of C, 2 December 1393).
Cd., *CChR 1257–1300*, 290 (from B); *CChR 1327–41*, 100 (from C); *CChR 1341–1417*, 342 (from D); *H*, no. 206.

Notum sit omnibus sancte matris ecclesie filiis quod ego Owinus de Porkinton' cum consilio et voluntate heredum meorum et amicorum et hominum meorum dedi Deo et Sancte Marie et abbatie de Basingwerk' et monachis ibidem Deo servientibus pro anima mea et pro animabus heredum meorum et antecessorum meorum in puram et perpetuam elemosinam aquam quandam in Penthlinn que dicitur Thlin Tegit, id est Pemblemere, et omnem pasturam predicte terre de Penthlinn' ut habeant eam ad averia sua cuiuslibet generis sint et ut ibi habeant de averiis quantum voluerint et in quibus eis libuerit locis necnon et sua mapalia cum ceteris aisiamentis omnibus in boscis, in planis, in moris et aquis et in omnibus aliis locis et ut de silvis quelibet sumant ad suos usus necessaria habundanter, sive sit viride, sive sit siccum, scilicet ad domos, ad edificia, ad sepes, ad ignium fomenta et ad cetera quelibet necessaria. Hec autem volo ut habeant tam libere et quiete ab omni servitio terreno et exactione seculari, ut michi nichil ab eis exigam, nisi tantum eorum orationes et erga Deum beneficia. Ut autem ista mea donatio firma sit et stabilis et imperpetuum inconcussa permaneat sigilli mei impressione eam commino et testes assigno. Hii autem sunt testes: scilicet episcopus Reinerius de Sancto Assaf, Ithail capellanus Owini, Howel constabularius Tegit, Kennewreik filius Cathlcuim, G(ri)fri Pengel, Madoc Hetegam et multi alii.

Reiner was consecrated bishop of St Asaph on 10 August 1186. The charter is unlikely to be later than August 1202 (see note to no. 484 above). A similar English name for Llyn Tegid (Bala Lake), namely *Pemmelsmere*, was used at about the same time as this charter was written by Gerald of Wales in *DK* I.5 (*Gir. Camb. Op.*, vi. 176). Lloyd suggested that the first element of the name derived from Penllyn (*HW*, i. 245 and n. 92). The punctuation adopted in the witness list assumes that the third witness, Hywel, was an official with responsibilities for Llyn Tegid and its vicinity, quite possibly based at Bala castle (*constabularius Tegit*; cf. *DMLBS* s.v. *constabularius* 2), although comparison with no. 494 above could suggest that *Tegit* was a personal name, representing an additional witness to *Howel constabularius*. Madog Hyddgam was a landholder in Penllyn who sold land to Strata Marcella (no. 485 above).

496 Valle Crucis Abbey

Grant for the redemption of the sins of himself and his parents in perpetual alms and free of all exaction of the certain piece of land at Moelfau between Gardd y Fign and Gweunrudd, in wood, plain and all rights of use. His heirs were present at the gift and gave their assent to it and defended it from all injuries. Sealing clause; witnesses.

June 1207

> A = NLW, Wynnstay Estate Records, Ystrad Marchell Charters, no. 101. Endorsed: Moil Vaue (s. xiii/xiv); early modern endorsements; approx. 206 × 65 + 6 mm.; a single central horizontal slit (torn) for a tag (missing). A loose seal found in the box with the Wynnstay group of charters is probably from this charter; probably circular, brown wax, imperfect, originally approx. 50–55 mm. diameter (fragment approx. 35 mm. × 45 mm.); equestrian, facing right; no legend survives.
>
> Pd. from (probably) A, Lhuyd, *Parochialia*, ii. 87; from A, *Ystrad Marchell Charters*, no. 101; from Lhuyd, Price, *Valle Crucis*, 239 (trans. only).
>
> Cd., Davies, 'Strata Marcella documents', 180 (no. 25); *H*, no. 214.

Cognoscat presens etas et sciat postera quod ego Owinus Madoci filius pro redemptione meorum peccaminum meorumque parentum concessi[a] monachis de Valle Crucis Deo et Beate Marie ibidem servientibus quandam terre particulam in puram et perpetuam elemosinam et ab omni exactione liberam et quietam que est apud Moyluav inter Garht Hevigin et Weun Ryth in bosco `et [b] in plano, in omnibus usuagiis. Huic donationi mei heredes affuerunt sub suo eam examine concedentes et ab omnibus iniuriis defendentes. Ceterum ne qua possit in posterum prefate donationi oriri calumpnia quod gestum est sigilli nostri munimine et testimonio litterarum roboravimus necnon et testes affuerunt quorum nomina in presenti pagina subarantur: scilicet Einniaun mab Einniaun mab Kathvor, Mevryg mab Kadugaun, Ioh(anne)s mab Edneveyn, Madauc map Gorgeneu, Einniaun map Ioab et multi alii. Anno ab incarnatione domini mᵒ ccᵒ viiᵒ mense iunii.

ᵃ conscessi A. | ᵇ *inserted into* A *by a different, possibly contemporary, scribe.*

Moelfau was probably Moelfre-fawr (SH 958 472) in the parish of Llangwm, cmt. Dinmael (*Ystrad Marchell Charters*, 128 and Map II).

NORTHERN POWYS (POWYS FADOG)

OWAIN AP GRUFFUDD MAELOR
(d. 1197)

†497 Combermere Abbey
Grant, for the souls of himself, his ancestors and successors, of the tithe of all the fish and fishery arising from the weirs, nets or devices of whatever kind throughout the river Dee, on either bank of the river throughout his lordship of Overton and Bromfield, and of the tithe of all the toll from his mill of Overton, with all increase in tolls or mills built on the said river. For his ancestors granted the monks these. If the animals of the monks or their men should be stolen or caught or lost by any means, they have Owain's permission to take them freely wherever they may be found on his land. Whoever of his heirs and men shall maintain his peace with the monks and benefit them, let him have the blessing of God and all the saints in heaven and on earth. Whoever is the miller of Owain or his heirs and keeper of the fishery shall give the monks his faith and oath on good relics faithfully to render tithe as God sends the fish, so that Owain shall not lose his alms and the monks have no loss. Whoever the monks place there or have in their place shall receive the tithe of fish and of all the toll of the mill and of the fisheries as the fish is caught, so that it may be sent faithfully and immediately to the monks as it pleases them. May all who shall uphold and render these alms lawfully after the days of myself and my brothers, and their relations, have the blessing of God, St Mary, all the saints and St Michael; may anyone who holds back, takes away or diminishes them have the vengeance of St Michael. Owain wishes that the monks may receive his alms so that he may receive a reward from God in heaven. Witnesses.

22 March 1195

B = TNA: PRO, C 53/117 (Ch. R. 4 Edward III), mm. 3–2 (reciting a spurious inspeximus of Edward I 13 May 1287, 12 January 1331).
Pd. from B, *Mon. Ang.*, v. 325 (witness list incomplete).
Cd., *CChR 1327–41*, 206–7; *H*, no. 222.

Owynus filius Griffini de Bromfeld' omnibus sancte matris ecclesie filiis presentibus quam futuris salutem. Sciatis me dedisse, concessisse et presenta carta mea confirmasse Deo et Beate Marie Sanctoque Mich(ael)i et monachis de Cumb(er)mare et eorum successoribus, pro salute anime mee et antecessorum et successorum meorum, decimam totius piscis et piscarie de gurgitibus quam de retibus vel ingeniis qualitercumque evenientibus sive contingentibus qui capitur per totam aquam de De, ubique prope et longe per totum dominium meum de Ouerton' et Bromfeld' ex utraque parte aque per totum, et decimam totius tholnei de molendino meo de Ou(er)ton' cum omni incremento tholneorum vel molendinorum quomodocumque vel ubicumque super aquam predictam edificari continguntur. Nam antecessores mei hec illis dederunt. Et si animalia eorum vel hominum eorum furata fuerint vel ullo modo capta vel perdita, licentiam meam habeant et plenam potestatem libere ea capiendi ubicumque super terram meam reperta fuerint. Igitur quicumque heredum meorum et hominum pacem meam illis bene tenuerint et eos beneficerit, benedictionem Dei omnipotentis habeat et omnium sanctorum in celo et in terra. Quicumque fuerit molendinarius meus vel heredum meorum et custos piscarii, dabit fidem suam et iuramentum monachis super bonas reliquias fideliter se decimaturum sicut Deus piscem miserit et sicut venerit ne ego perdam elemosinam meam et monachi aliquod dampnum habeant. Quicumque etiam monachi ibi posuerint vel habuerint in loco suo recipiet decimam de pisce et totius tholnei de molendino et de piscariis sicut captus fuerit piscis ut fideliter et statim monachis mittatur, sicut illis placuerit. Omnes vero qui hanc meam elemosinam bene et legitime post meos dies et meorum fratrum servaverint et persolverint, Dei benedictionem et Sancte Marie et omnium sanctorum et Sancti Mich(ael)is habeant et omnes eorum cognationes; qui autem retinuerit vel abstulerit vel diminuerit, vindictam Sancti Mich(ael)is veniat super eum in capitu[a] suo. Amen.[b] Volo enim ex toto corde et in animo ut in pace bona [m. 2] elemosinam meam recipiant ut a Deo retributionem in celis suscipiam. Testes huius donationis sunt isti: Sharuerd dapifer, Eiruc, Eleuauth, Madoc filius Bleionn, Seisil filius Heylin nepos Kadrouth, Matheus filius Seisil Pibin, Rob(er)tus filius Simonis, Kenewreich' filius Oweni Pren Powis, David Coc(us), Meuric filius Enionn, Sheuan Cogh et tota curia domini et alii satis qui hec viderunt anno domini m° c° xc° v°, litera dominicalis A, prima die post festum Sancti Benedicti.

[a] *sic in* B. | [b] ame *with contraction mark over* m *in* B.

As *CChR 1327–41*, 208, points out, the inspeximus ostensibly issued by Edward I confirming a charter of Gwion (*Wyon*) ap Jonas (*Mon. Ang.*, v. 324–5), followed by the present charter and nos 498 and 510 below, is spurious, as it is dated at Woodstock, 13 May 1287, whereas Edward I was in Gascony from the autumn of 1286 until the summer of 1289, accompanied by Robert Burnell, named as third witness to the inspeximus (cf. also Prestwich, *Edward I*, 305). In addition, the Combermere monks presented another spurious inspeximus of Edward I dated at Acton Burnell, 6 February 1282, as well as other charters they had embellished, to Edward III in 1331 (*CChR 1327–41*, 203, 206). Kettle has observed that the grants of tithes by the lords of Bromfield and Overton are known only from this inspeximus and also that their form is highly suspect ('Religious houses', 151, n. 37). Their transmission in a spurious inspeximus, together with the evident readiness of the Combermere monks to fabricate and tamper with other charters presented for confirmation in 1331, provide strong grounds for doubting the authenticity of both the present charter and the other charters contained in the same alleged inspeximus of Edward I.

By the early fourteenth century Combermere, a Cistercian abbey founded in 1133 as a Savigniac house on the southern edge of Cheshire near the Shropshire border at SJ 590 442, about 3 miles north-east of Whitchurch, was in severe economic difficulties, which resulted in its being taken into royal custody in 1315 and again in 1328. It was presumably in order to try and improve the abbey's fortunes that the monks presented the spurious inspeximus of 13 May 1287 and other suspect charters to Edward III in 1331 (ibid., 153). The recitation of the charters granting fishing rights in the Dee in an alleged inspeximus of Edward I is probably explicable by the fact that since 1284 the commote of Maelor Saesneg, in which Overton was situated, had formed part of the county of Flint, which in turn was attached to the earldom of Chester, held by the king's son (Williams (ed.), *History of Flintshire*, 88–91). The monks may well have claimed that those rights had received the sanction of Edward I in order to confer legitimacy on them in 1331.

The question remains, though, whether there was any genuine basis to the charters recited in Edward I's alleged inspeximus of 13 May 1287. If the crucial issue from the monks' point of view was to assert that the grants had received royal confirmation after the Edwardian conquest, it might be that they drew upon authentic charters. However, the form of the first two in particular suggests that, at the very least, any authentic texts underlying them were tampered with. The first charter recited – whose substance and wording were followed, with some adaptations, in the present charter and, to a lesser extent, in nos 498 and 510 below – is in the name of Gwion (*Wyon*) ap Jonas and is undated. Gwion may be identified with the *Wion filio Ione* who witnessed two charters of Llywelyn for Haughmond Abbey in 1205 × 1211 and who held land in Wellington (Shrops.) between 1194 and 1210 (see nos 225–6 above and note to no. 252 above). Gwion's father Jonas (d. 1174 × 1175) held Overton castle for Henry II in 1168, as had Jonas's brother Roger of Powys (d. 1186 × 1187) in 1159 (*Pipe Roll 6 Henry II*, 26; *Pipe Roll 14 Henry II*, 110; see further Suppe, 'Roger of Powys', esp. 7–8, 10). Roger's son Meurig sought confirmation of Whittington and Overton from King John in 1200, quite possibly indicating that the family had retained possession of these manors since the deaths of Jonas and Roger. This would be consistent with the royal favour enjoyed by Meurig and his cousin Gwion in Richard I's reign: both guarded a castle in 'Denbigh', perhaps located in Edeirnion, in 1196–7, and the crown granted Gwion annual revenues of £7 from Wellington from 1194 to at least 1206 (Suppe, 'Roger of Powys', 17–18). Although there is insufficient evidence to establish whether Gwion ever held Overton after the death of his father Jonas, and, if so, for how long, the connections of the family of Roger and Jonas with this castle and manor, located about 21 miles south-west of Combermere, suggest that Gwion could have granted tithes of fish and milling there to the abbey by 1195, and that these could have been confirmed and amplified by Owain ap Gruffudd, Madog ap Gruffudd and Gruffudd ap Madog after they had established their authority over Overton and Maelor Saesneg. (Note how, whereas Gwion's charter refers only to his lordship of Overton, the three charters that follow in the spurious inspeximus, including the present text, extend the grant to encompass the lordship of Overton and Bromfield.) No. 515 below shows that mills and a weir numbered among the appurtenances of the manor of Overton by the third quarter of the thirteenth century.

Analysis of the present charter is hampered by the lack of any other charters of Owain ap Gruffudd with which it might be compared. However, as with Gwion's charter, which immediately precedes it in the inspeximus and whose form and wording are very similar, the elaborate sanction clauses, as well as the reference to God sending fish, strongly suggest a degree of beneficiary redaction well beyond what was normal in Welsh rulers' charters of the late twelfth century. In addition, both the clause *Nam antecessores mei hec illis dederunt* and the blessing clause in the next sentence but one sit awkwardly in the disposition; even if the initial part of the disposition (down to *edificari continguntur*) derives from an authentic charter, these clauses, together with the sanction clauses at the end, could well be later interpolations. As regards the witness list, the heavy preponderance of Welsh names might suggest that it derives from an authentic record of 1195; moreover, *Madoc filius Bleionn* could represent the Madog ap Bleddyn ap Tudur ap Rhys Sais whom early modern sources identified as a first cousin of Roger of Powys and his brother Jonas (Bartrum, *WG*, iv, Tudur Trefor 2). On the other hand, the forms *Sharuerd* and *Sheuan*, presumably representing Iorwerth and Ieuan, excite suspicion, and the same is true of the name *Pren Powis* (literally, 'tree', '(piece of) wood' or 'timber' of Powys), irrespective of whether this is an epithet for the Owain of *Kenewreich' filius Oweni* or a separate name. On balance, both the context of its transmission and its wording make it unlikely that the charter is an authentic act issued by Owain.

MADOG AP GRUFFUDD MAELOR
(d. 1236)

†498 Combermere Abbey

Grant in perpetual alms of all the gifts given for ever by his father Gruffudd, namely the tithe of all the fish and fishery arising from the weirs, nets or devices of whatever kind throughout the river Dee, on either bank of the river throughout his lordship of Overton and Bromfield, and of the tithe of all the toll from his mill of Overton, with all increase in tolls or mills built on the said river. For his ancestors granted the monks these. Further grant of 7 acres in Overton. Whoever is the miller of Madog or his heirs and keeper of the fishery shall give the monks his faith and oath faithfully to render tithe as God sends the fish, so that Madog shall not lose his alms and the monks have no loss. He orders that wherever the monks should come to his land they should be received with great honour, so that if any persons, having seen and heard this document, should do to the contrary, let he who has dishonoured Madog be subject to his forfeiture. Declares that he has granted this from his heart and confirmed it in faith with his right hand before God. Witnesses.

Borewardston', 5 January 1197

B= TNA: PRO, C 53/117 (Ch. R. 4 Edward III), m. 2 (reciting a spurious inspeximus of Edward I 13 May 1287, 12 January 1331).
Cd., *CChR 1327–41*, 207; *H*, no. 223.

Madocus filius Griffini de Bromfeld' hominibus suis presentibus et futuris salutem. Sciatis me dedisse, concessisse et hac presenti carta mea confirmasse Deo et Beate Marie de Cumb(er)mare et monachis ibidem Deo servientibus in liberam, puram et perpetuam elemosinam omnes donationes quas pater meus Griffinus eisdem monachis et eorum successoribus imperpetuum dedit, videlicet decimam totius piscis et piscarie de gurgutibus sive de retibus quam de ingeniis[a] qualitercumque contingentibus qui capitur per totam aquam de De, ubique longe et prope per totum dominium meum de Ou(er)ton' et Bromfeld' ex utraque parte aque predicte per totum, et decimam totius tholnei de molendino meo de Ou(er)ton cum omni incremento tholneorum vel molendinorum quomodocumque vel qualitercumque et ubicumque super aquam predictam edificari contiguntur. Nam antecessores mei hec illis dederunt. Concedo etiam et confirmo eisdem monachis septem acras terre in Ouerton'. Et quicumque fuerit molendinarius meus vel heredum meorum ad predictum molendinum et custos piscarie, dabit fidem et iuramentum fideliter legitime se decimaturum sicut Deus piscem miserit et sicut venerit, ne ego predictam elemosinam meam et monachi aliquod dampnum habeant. Preterea precipio ut ubicumque sepedicti monachi super terram meam venerint cum magno honore recipiantur, ita ut quicumque hiis litteris visuris vel audituris, si contra fecerint, in meo forisfacto sit qui me dehonoravit. Et in fine huius carte illud sciatis qui[b] sic ex corde illis concessi et volo teneri et dextere mee fide coram Deo eam illis firmavi. Hiis [testibus]: Oweyon et Hener filiis Ione, Huba Grec, Griffin(us) Seis et Richeris Seis, Eleuauth, Anaun, Daniel Coc', Karadoch filio Hugo(n)is, Enun filio Edneueth', Henrico clerico domini Madoci, Dauit Yal Vauhel[b] et multis aliis qui hec viderunt et audierunt apud Borewardston' anno domini m° c° xc° vii°, E dominicali litera siclo i°.

[a] *one minim too many in* B. | [b] *sic in* B.

For the general issues that throw doubts on the authenticity of this charter see note to no. 497 above. Although it lacks the blessings and curses of no. 497, which immediately precedes it in the inspeximus, its substance is similar, including the reference to God sending fish. The main substantive differences are, first, the grant of 7 acres in Overton and, second, the order that the monks should be received 'with great honour' whenever they should come to Madog's land. If the charter was adapted from no. 497 there would be strong grounds for rejecting its authenticity, given the likelihood that no. 497 was fabricated by the monks, at least in its extant form. True, this is not the only possible explanation for the similarities with no. 497: that charter, together with the charter of Gwion ap Jonas, could have been fabricated using material from the present charter; alternatively, the similarities could represent a common core of material derived from one or more authentic charters that were subsequently rewritten by the monks of Combermere. The use of *Sciatis me* in the disposition, as also in Owain's charter (that of Gwion has *Sciatis quod ego*), is inconclusive, since, although most of Madog's other charters use forms of *noscere, Sciatis me* also occurs in a charter of 1202 for Valle Crucis (no. 501 below). The witness list could derive from an authentic charter. If, as seems probable, the first witness represents Gwion (rather than Owain) ap Jonas, he is independently attested in the late twelfth and early thirteenth centuries and, with Ynyr, numbers among Jonas's sons as recorded by late fifteenth- and sixteenth-century genealogists (note to no. 497 above; Bartrum, *WG*, iv, Tudur Trefor 8). Hwfa Gryg (*Huba Grec*) may be identifiable with Hwfa Gryg ap Hwfa ap Sandde, regarded by the genealogists as a descendant of Rhys Sais and thus a kinsman of Jonas's sons, and Einion ab Ednyfed (*Enun filius Edneueth'*) may be identifiable with Einion ab Ednyfed ap Cynwrig ap Rhiwallon, whose descendants were associated with Maelor Saesneg (ibid., Tudur Trefor 20, 39). *Eleuath* also occurs in no. 497. The location of the place-date,

Borewardston', is uncertain. It possibly represents the township of Burton (SJ 355 575), about 4 miles north-east of Wrexham in Bromfield/Maelor Gymraeg.

Nevertheless, even if we suppose that the present charter was not merely adapted from no. 497, several features excite suspicion. As with the latter charter, the clause beginning *Nam antecessores mei* could be an interpolation; indeed, it sits even more awkwardly here than in no. 497 because of the earlier reference, lacking in Owain's charter, to a previous grant by Madog's father Gruffudd. The clause on receiving the monks 'with great honour' in Madog's land may also point to tampering or outright fabrication by the monks. Although its form and formulae are less suspect than those of no. 497, the context of its transmission makes it difficult to accept that the charter is authentic.

499 Strata Marcella Abbey (for the foundation of Valle Crucis Abbey)

Grant, for the desire of the eternal homeland and inspired by love rather than the desire of transitory fame, of the township of Llanegwestl with all its bounds for the building of a monastery in honour of God and the Virgin Mary so that a community of the Cistercian order may perpetually serve God there. He has given this at the request of the following four abbots: Peter of Whitland, Deiniol of Strata Florida, Philip of Strata Marcella and Rhirid of Cwm-hir. He has given the aforesaid township to the said Cistercian community free and quit, and granted other lands he was holding by hereditary right in Powys, namely (?)Llanycyfail with all its bounds and appurtenances, (?)Rhiwdderch with all its bounds, Banhadlen with all its bounds, half of the township of Buddugre with all its bounds and appurtenances, Creigiog with all its bounds and appurtenances, Cwmbrwynog with all its bounds, Cefnlluestau with all its bounds and appurtenances, Twng with all its bounds and appurtenances, half of the township of Mwstwr with all its bounds and appurtenances, and parcels of lands at Wrexham, Bersham and Acton. He has granted the lands named free and immune from all secular exaction and service with all their bounds and appurtenances in wood, plain, waters, mills, meadows, pastures, timber and stones. Sealing clause; witnesses.

[1200 × 24 March 1201; possibly *c.*December 1200 × *c.*February 1201]

A = Ruthin, Denbighshire Record Office, Wynnstay Estate Archives DD/WY/4202. Early modern endorsement; approx. 193 × 152 + 30 mm.; central slit in fold torn. Tag and seal missing.
B = TNA: PRO, C 53/81 (Ch. R. 23 Edward I), m. 3 (in an inspeximus, 24 April 1295).
Pd. from A, *Ystrad Marchell Charters*, no. 26; from B, Jones, 'Valle Crucis', 412–13; from transcript of B in Cardiff County Library MS 4.83, p. 94 (s. xvii), *Mon. Ang.*, v. 637 (under Strata Marcella); from Jones, Price, *Valle Crucis*, 243–4 (trans. only).
Cd., *CChR 1257–1300*, 457 (from B); *H*, no. 225.

Notum sit omnibus tam presentibus quam futuris quod ego Madoc(us) G(ri)fini filius eterne patrie desiderio et caritatis intuitu non transitorie laudis apetitu dedi et concessi et hac presenti carta mea confirmavi Deo et Beate Marie et monachis de St(ra)tmarkell villam que vocatur Lly(n)hequestel cum omnibus terminis suis ad construendum ibidem monas-terium in honorem Dei et Beate genitricis semperque Virginis Marie et ut conventus Cist(er)ciensis ordinis ibi iugiter Deo militaret. Hanc inquam dedi rogatu venerabilium personarum videlicet iiii^{or} abbatum quorum ista sunt nomina: Petrus dictus abbas de Alba Domo, Deniawal de St(ra)tflur, Phillipp(us) abbas de St(ra)tmarhell, Ririd de Cu(m)hyr. Dedi etiam predictam villam iam dicto conventui Cist(erciensis) ordinis ibidem Deo servienti liberam et quietam, cui etiam alias terras dedi et concessi quas hereditario iure apud Powys possidebam quarum ista sunt nomina: Lanhekeveyl cum omnibus terminis et pertinentiis suis, Ryuderch cum omnibus terminis suis, Banhadlen cum omnibus terminis suis, medietatem ville que dicitur Buducure cum omnibus terminis et pertinentiis suis, Creychauch cum omnibus terminis et pertinentiis suis, Cu(m)bruynauch cum omnibus terminis suis, Keuenlluhesteu cum omnibus terminis et pertinentiis suis, Tong cum omnibus terminis et pertinentiis suis, medietatem ville que dicitur Mystuyr cum omnibus terminis et pertinentiis suis, et de aliis terris particulas quasdam inde de Wrechtessham et de Berertessha(m) et de Actun. Has itaque iam nominatas terras dedi Deo et Beate Marie et monachis Cist(erciensis) ordinis apud Valle(m) Crucis Deo servientibus liberas et quietas et immunes ab omni exactione et servitute seculari cum omnibus terminis et pertinentiis suis in bosco, in plano, in aquis, in silvis, in molendinis, in pratis, in pascuis, in lignis tam succidendis quam cremabilibus, in lapidibus efodendis sive collendis. Et ut hec mea donatio rata sit et apud posteros firma et stabilis imperpetuum multorum virorum atestatione et sigilli mei munimine confirmavi. His testibus: Pphill(ippo)[a] abbate de Pola, Phill(ippo) abbate de Valle Crucis, Hug(one) monacho, I. monacho, R. converso; de laicis, Keyrradauch filio Hug(onis) et M. et G. fratribus eius, Edneweyn Seys et I. fratre eius et multis aliis.

[a] *sic in* A.

The charter cannot be dated precisely. No. 501 below shows that a monastery was established at Valle Crucis by 1202. One group of manuscripts containing lists of Cistercian foundations assigns the foundation of Valle Crucis to 28 January 1201, another to 1199 (i.e. 25 March 1199 × 24 March 1200) (Janauschek, *Originum Cistercensium*, 205; Price, *Valle Crucis*, 29). The former date is probably more consistent with the Welsh chronicles, which place the building of Valle Crucis abbey at the end of their entries for 1200, which could imply a date as late as 24 March 1201, and 28 January 1201 was accepted as correct by Janauschek and Lloyd (*BT, Pen20Tr*, 81; *BT, RBH*, 182–3; Janauschek, *Originum Cistercensium*, 299; *HW*, ii. 602). Unfortunately it is unclear to which stage in the foundation process the dates in the Cistercian lists refer: to the appointment of the abbot, to the granting of the land for the abbey or to the arrival of the community at Valle Crucis? As it gave the site for the construction of the abbey to the mother house Strata Marcella, the charter was clearly issued early in the process of foundation, probably shortly after the appointment of the second witness, Philip, as abbot of the daughter community, but before that community had arrived at Valle Crucis. If a crucial stage in the abbey's foundation was reached on 28 January 1201, the charter was probably issued between about December 1200 and February 1201. However, if the foundation date of 28 January 1201 is discounted, the evidence of the Welsh chronicles indicates a date range of 1200 × 24 March 1201, similar to the date of *c.*1200 proposed in Jones, 'Valle Crucis', 407, and *Ystrad Marchell Charters*, 169. (I am grateful to Janet Burton for her comments on the problems of dating the abbey's foundation.)

For the places named in the charter see Williams, *Atlas*, 64–5; *Ystrad Marchell Charters*, 118; and, for Mwstwr (par. Corwen, Edeirnion), Pierce, 'Welsh *mystwyr*', 127–8. Later evidence shows that the half of Buddugre granted was Buddugre'r-abad and that the abbey received only half of the township of Creigiog, namely Creigiog Uchaf; like the township of Banhadlen, these lands were located in the parish of Llanarmon-yn-Iâl (no. 506 below;

Pratt, 'Fourteenth-century Bromfield and Yale', 94–5). Cefnlluestau lay in the parish of Whittington (Shrops.) and Twng in the parish of Wrexham; Bersham and Acton were likewise located near Wrexham, the site of the abbey's most substantial outlying grange (Wrexham Abbot). According to the tithe map, Cwmbrwynog was situated at SJ 065 378, about 2 miles north-east of Llandrillo-yn-Edeirnion (I am grateful to R. Geraint Gruffydd for this identification).

500 Ednyfed and Philip sons of Gwaeddnerth

As the proprietors and heirs of Llanegwestl, namely the sons of Kamron *and the sons of Ednyfed and the sons of* Guhann *and their sons, leaving the township of Llanegwestl where the abbey has now been built, had come to Bromfield by voluntary exchange, and Madog had granted them and their sons the township of Northcroft and half of the township of Stansty to be held in inheritance by them and their legitimate heirs from him and his heirs, the aforesaid heirs of Llanegwestl unanimously granted, before Madog and many others, to Ednyfed and Philip sons of Gwaeddnerth as much property to each of them in Northcroft and half the township of Stansty as each of them used to have in those places. All of them [i.e. the heirs] confirmed this on oath to them [i.e. Philip and Ednyfed] and their heirs in perpetual inheritance. (?)Acceding to the (?)just petitions of Ednyfed and Philip, Madog has granted the gift to them from the aforesaid heirs and given it to them freely, without (?)any single [(?)payment] of a legal penny, to be held for ever from him and his heirs and corroborated it with his seal in this charter. They [i.e. Ednyfed and Philip] will know and others will give assurances as is contained in their charter concerning theft, fighting and breach of Madog's prohibition after a cross has been placed as is the custom of the country. If they should pay [(?)recte shall wish] to move to another place in Madog's land let them go and return in peace. Let none of Madog's men dare to accept or hold a gage from them [i.e. Philip or Ednyfed] for any debt which Madog may owe him. Witnesses.*

[1200 × -15 January 1207]

B = BL, Add. MS 21253, fo. 187r. s. xv (here s. xvi/xvii).
C = Oxford, Bodleian Library, MS Rawlinson B.464, fos 123v–124v. *c.*1700.
D = NLW MS 1506C, pt. ii, p. 68. *c.*1700.
Pd. from D, Lhuyd, *Parochialia*, i. 100–1; from Lhuyd, Price, *Valle Crucis*, 260–1 (trans. only).
Cd., *H*, no. 224.

Sciant omnes tam presentes quam futuri quod, cum proprietarii[a] et heredes de Llanheguestel,[b] scilicet filii Kamron et filii Edene[v]ed et filii Guhann[c] et[d] filii eorum, villam illam de Llanheguestel[b] ubi nunc abbatia constructa est relinquentes[e] ad Bromefeld[f] advenissent per eorum voluntariam commutationem[g] et ego Madoc(us) filius Gri'[h] eis et filiis eorum villam de Nordcrofd[i] et medietatem ville[j] de Stanesti in hereditatem sibi et heredibus de eorum co[r]poribus legitime procreatis de me et de heredibus meis tenendam concessissem et dedissem, ipsi omnes prefati proprietarii[k] et heredes qui fuerant de Llanheguestil[l] unanimiter concedentes coram me et coram multis dederunt Idneued et Philipo[m] filiis Guaidnerd[n] tantam proprietatem unicuique eorum in prefata villa de Nordcrofd[o] et medietatem ville de Stanesti quantam omnino[p] unusquisque[q] eorum in eisdem locis haberet.[r] Et hoc iureiurando[s] confirmaverunt[t] omnes eis et heredibus eorum [u]in perpetuam[u] hereditatem.[v] Ego vero Madoc'[w] (?)iustis[x] predictorum Ideneved et

Philipi[y] petitionibus[z] (?)adquiescens[aa] donationem predictorum heredum eis taliter factam concessi et eandem ipsis et heredibus suis dedi quiete et libere sine unaquaque[ab] [(?)redditione] legalis[ac] denarii de me et heredibus meis in [ad-]perpetuum tenendam[-ad] et hac presenti carta cum impressione sigilli mei coroboravi.[ae] Ipsi vero scient[af] et alii ut in carta eorum continetur de furto, de pugna et de fractione[ag] prohibitionis mee fixo cruci signo sicut mos est patrie satisfacient. Si solverint[ah] ad alium locum in terra mea se transferre,[ai] pacifice eant et redeant. Nullus[aj] etiam meorum pro aliquo debito quo[ak] ego ei[al] tenear audeat vadem eorum accipere vel[am] detinere. Hii[an] sunt testes: dominus Philipus[ao] abas[ap] de Valle Crucis,[aq] Alixander[ar] persona de Wrixham[as] et filii eius, D(avi)d cappelanus[at] et filii eius, Moesses[au] campanarius et filii eius, filii Hugo(nis), filii Idneved,[av] filii Blethyn,[aw] filii Nenham,[ax] filii Madoc',[ay] filii Elidir, filii Caduchan,[az] filii Meilir,[ba] Ririd Senior, filii Trahacharn,[bb] filii Meridhu,[bc] filii Norne[bd], filii Idhael,[be] filii Kyndelhw,[bf] filii Edeneued et[d] plures multi.

[a] CD; proprietari B. | [b] Lan Heguestel C; Lan Egwestel D. | [c] Enhann *inserted above* Guhann *dotted underneath* C; Inhan D. | [d] C *inserts* et. | [e] C *inserts* ad Bromfeld; D *inserts* Bromfield. | [f] Bromfeld C; Bromfield D. | [g] CD; commumtationem B. | [h] Grifri CD. | [i] Nordcroft C; Vordcroft D. | [j] villam D. | [k] CD; propretarii B. | [l] Lenheguestyl C; Lan Egwestel D. | [m] Philippo CD. | [n] Guaednerd CD, *with one dot each under* a *and first* e *in* C. | [o] Nordcroffd C; Nordcroft *corrected from* Vordcroft D. | [p] CD, *with four dots under abbreviated form of word* (ono *with line over first two letters*) *in* C; avo B. | [q] CD; unusgusque B. | [r] CD; haberent B. | [s] CD; iurervrando B. | [t] confirmarunt CD. | [u-u] CD; imperpetuum B. | [v] B *inserts* Et. | [w] Madocus CD. | [x] iustitie BCD. | [y] Philipo BC; Phillippo D. | [z] potitionibus D. | [aa] adquesenem B; ad questen'en' C; ad questenden' D. | [ab] una' BC; una D; *the text is clearly corrupt here.* | [ac] D; laicalis B; lagalis C. | [ad-ad] perpet. tenend. C; porpetitensad D. | [ae] corroboravi CD. | [af] CD; scint B. | [ag] de fracione B; defracione, *with three dots under* fra *in* C *and three dots under* acio *in* D. | [ah] CD [(?)*recte* voluerint]; (?)solv(er)vet B. | [ai] transferr' B; transferd' C; transford' D. | [aj] quibus CD, *with four dots underneath in* C. | [ak] que BCD. | [al] si D. | [am] et D. | [an] Hi CD. | [ao] Philippus D. | [ap] abbas CD. | [aq] CD; Cucis B. | [ar] Alexander CD. | [as] Wrexham CD. | [at] capellanus CD. | [au] Moses CD. | [av] Edenyved C; Edneved D. | [aw] C *inserts* Bledyn, *with* h *above* d, *deleted followed by* Blethin; Blethin D. | [ax] Nonham D. | [ay] Madoc CD. | [az] Caducham, *with three dots under* m *in* C. | [ba] CD; Milir B. | [bb] Trahaiharn *corrected from* Trahayharn C; Trahayern D. | [bc] Meride'h n C; Meridehn D. | [bd] Uorne, *with three dots under the* U *in* CD. | [be] Ithael CD. | [bf] Kyndelhin C; Kyndethin D.

The version of the 'Summary of Answers' to Edward Lhuyd's 'Parochial Queries' in NLW MS 1506C is mostly if not entirely copied from that in Bodleian Library, MS Rawlinson B.464 (Lhuyd, *Parochialia*, ii. 3), and a comparison of the texts of the present charters strongly suggests that D is a copy of C, albeit one containing scribal errors and emendations. B and C are independent transcripts of the same text, which itself must have been a copy of the charter rather than the original in view of the corrupt readings common to both B and C. Though both transcripts contain errors, on balance B seems to provide a more faithful copy than C and has thus been taken as the principal source for the text printed here. The text in B is written on a flyleaf at the end of a fifteenth-century Valle Crucis manuscript (fo. 1v names *Anianus dominus abbas Valle Crucis*) containing Latin homilies for Sundays throughout the year that belonged in 1633 to John Edwards of Stansty (fo. 85r; cf. Huws, *Medieval Welsh Manuscripts*, 192 and n. 27). The present charter immediately follows no. 514 below in C and D, where no. 514 is preceded by a rubric indicating that both charters derived from copies at the beginning (and thus probably on the opening flyleaves) of a *Liber Homiliarum* owned by the antiquarian Robert Davies (1658–1710) of Llannerch near Denbigh (on whom see *DWB*, 163; Emanuel, 'Gwysaney manuscripts', 327–8). The earliest comprehensive catalogue of the Llannerch manuscripts, dated 1740, lists three Latin manuscripts that could correspond to Lhuyd's description (ibid., 329–30; Emanuel, *Catalogue of the Gwysaney Manuscripts*, 15–16, 27 (nos 13, 22)). Two of these, both of the fifteenth century, are still extant, one containing Philip Repingdon's *Sermones super evangelia dominicalia*, the other homilies by Gregory the Great and Bede, but neither contains copies of the charters copied in *Parochialia*; possibly these were contained on the paper sheets, now worn off, pasted inside the covers of the original binding of Repingdon's sermons. The present location of the volume described in 1740 as 'Homilies on all the Sundays of the year' is unknown (it clearly cannot be BL, Add. MS 21253, as this contains the text of only one of the charters, at the end of the manuscript). The charters were copied together in C and D presumably because both dealt with the freemen of Llanegwestl who had been granted lands near Wrexham in exchange for their original holdings after Llanegwestl had been given for the foundation of Valle Crucis. (I am indebted to Tony Carr for help with transcribing, and dating the hand of, the text in B.)

The text of the present charter is evidently corrupt as transmitted, especially in the section *Ego vero Madoc'* … *in perpetuum tenendam*, and the emendations made are necessarily tentative. (I am very grateful to Paul Russell for commenting on the text and suggesting improvements to my interpretation of it.) Nevertheless, the extant copies probably derive from an authentic charter issued by Madog, as the text is essentially coherent and contains no obvious anachronisms. Abbot Philip of Valle Crucis occurs in no. 499 above, as do three (named) sons of Hugh, who are probably identifiable with the *filii Hugonis* of the present witness list. Apart from their first element, the forms of the place-name Llanegwestl in B (*Llanheguestel*, *Llanheguestil*) and C (*Lan Heguestel*, *Lenheguestyl*) seem to retain early thirteenth-century orthography, being similar to *Llynhequestel* in no. 499, *Llineguest'* in no. 504 and *Linneguestel* in no. 506. The reference to Madog's prohibition being indicated by a cross is consistent with procedures in Welsh law whereby a lord placed a cross on disputed land or crops to prohibit their use until the dispute was resolved (Roberts, 'Legal practice', 311–14; Haddan and Stubbs, i. 524–5). The charter must be later than no. 499 above, as the latter was issued before the abbey had been built at Valle Crucis, and earlier than 15 January 1207, when the abbot of Valle Crucis was Dafydd (no. 504 below). Northcroft and Stansty were townships about 1 mile north-west of Wrexham (Palmer, *History of the Thirteen Country Townships*, 183, 186; Pratt, 'Fourteenth-century Bromfield and Yale', 95 and map at 106). According to no. 514 below, Madog's son Gruffudd granted Northcroft (and possibly also half of Stansty) to Valle Crucis.

501 Valle Crucis Abbey

Grant of all the pasture of all his land, namely Maelor Saesneg and the provinces of Maelor, Iâl, Nanheudwy and Cynllaith, apart from what the heirs of those provinces have occupied for their own use, so that the monks may have common pasture throughout the aforesaid provinces, in which no other religious men may have any power to have, buy or rent anything. He has granted this free of all secular exaction and custom in perpetual alms for the redemption of the souls of himself and his ancestors. Witnesses.

1202

B = TNA: PRO, C 53/81 (Ch. R. 23 Edward I), m. 3 (in an inspeximus, 24 April 1295).
Pd. from B, Jones, 'Valle Crucis', 414; from Jones, Price, *Valle Crucis*, 245 (trans. only).
Cd., *CChR 1257–1300*, 457; *H*, no. 226.

Madocus Griffini filius omnibus qui hoc scriptum visuri sunt vel audituri salutem. Sciatis me dedisse et concessisse et presenti carta mea confirmasse Deo et Beate Marie et conventui de Valle Crucis anno ab incarnatione domini m° cc° ii° omnem pasturam totius terre mee, scilicet Malaur Saisnec et provincie de Maylaur et Yayl et Nanheudu et Kenylleid, excepto hoc quod heredes earundem provinciarum ad opus suum sibi occupaverint, ita ut iam predictus conventus communitatem pasture habeat ubique in predictis provinciis in quibus nulli alii religiosi viri habeant potestatem aliquam vel facultatem habendi aliquid vel emendi vel conducendi. Hec dedi eis libere et quiete et pacifice ab omni exactione et consuetudine seculari in puram et perpetuam elemosinam in anime mee et antecessorum meorum redemptione. Hiis testibus: Ph(ilipp)o capellano filio Ioseph, Edneuein de Cau' de Kilkein, Riud Seis et multis aliis. Valete.

The term *heredes* ('heirs') here refers to ordinary free landholders (cf. Pryce, 'Church of Trefeglwys', 29).

*502 Gerald of Wales
Letter.

[Summer 1202]

Mention only, in a chapter heading to Book III, c. 139 of Gerald of Wales's *De rebus a se gestis*, which reads *Literae Madoci principis Powisiae Giraldo directae* (*Gir. Camb. Op.*, i. 13). The chapter itself is lost. For further detail and the dating see note to no. 223 above.

503 Valle Crucis Abbey
Grant, inspired by divine reward for the redemption of the souls of himself and his [(?)ancestors], with the advice of his nobles, in perpetual alms without any challenge and free of all exaction, that if any of the faithful of his land wishes to give or sell something to the monastery, or take something with him when entering religion there, this may be allowed. Sealing clause; witnesses.

1205

B = TNA: PRO, C 53/81 (Ch. R. 23 Edward I), m. 3 (in an inspeximus, 24 April 1295).
Pd. from B, Jones, 'Valle Crucis', 414–15; from B, *CChR 1257–1300*, 457–8; from Jones, Price, *Valle Crucis*, 245–6 (trans. only).
Cd., *H*, no. 227.

Notum sit tam presentibus quam futuris qui hoc scriptum visuri sunt vel audituri quod ego M. Griffini filius intuitu retributionis divine pro anime mee et meorum redemptione cum consilio optimatum meorum concessi et dedi monachis de Valle Crucis ibidem Deo et Beate Marie servientibus in puram et perpetuam elemosinam, absque aliqua contradictione et ab omni exactione liberam et quietam, ut siquis fidelium de terra sua eidem monasterio caritatis intuitu aliquantum donare voluerit vel vendere vel seipsum religioni in prefato monasterio conferendo aliquid secum afferre, licitum sit a nobis et donatum. Et ut hec mea donatio rata sit et intemerata, quia moderni proni sunt ad malum unde sibi aliquid temporalis lucri extorquere potuerint, sigilli mei impressione confirmavi et corroboravi anno ab incarnatione domini m° cc° v°. Hiis testibus: Kemaldanch, Grifri Seis filii Hoba, Siuiaun mab Idneued, Edneweyn Seis, Ievaf, Moab, Maredud, Idneued Was et multis aliis.

504 Strata Marcella Abbey

Grant, for the salvation of the souls of himself and his father in free and perpetual alms, of all the land of Esgyngaenog with all its bounds and appurtenances, which his ancestors together with the heirs of that land sold the monks to be possessed in perpetual right and the monks possessed in peace before his lordship in Edeirnion. Further grant and confirmation of the part of the township of Gwyddelwern which the monks bought from his ancestors Elise and Owain, and the heirs of that land with all its bounds and appurtenances. Further grant of the land of (?)Banhadllogllwydion which they bought from the sons of Iorwerth ap Cadwgan and their co-heirs of Llanelidan with all its bounds and appurtenances. Announces that during his lordship in Edeirnion that Iorwerth, Griffri and Gruffudd sons of Madog ap Llywarch claimed part of Esgyngaenog, which their father had previously given in perpetual possession to the monks, but later they gave all their hereditary right in Esgyngaenog, for the salvation of their souls in free and perpetual possession, to the monks, so that neither they nor their heirs may have any claim against the monks in the future. The aforesaid gift of the aforesaid men was made on 15 January 1206 [=1207] in the hand of David, abbot of Valle Crucis and I. prior of Strata Marcella at Corwen before Seisyll the priest and clergy and good men, namely Meurig and Llywarch sons of Cadwgan, Madog ap Brochwel, Einion ab Ieuaf, Cynig ab Idnerth, Madog ap Gwrgenau Saithmarchog, Iorwerth ab Einion, Iorwerth ap Hywel, Einion ap Cadfor, Iddon ap Iorwerth. Madog wishes the monks to possess the aforesaid lands with all their bounds and appurtenances in perpetual right, freely and in peace, without any secular exaction or custom, in wood, plain, waters, pastures, meadows, ways, paths and all rights of use. Sealing clause; witnesses.

The castle in Cynllaith, [15 January × 24 March] 1206 [=1207]

A = Caernarfon, Gwynedd Archives Service, XD2/1113. Endorsed: · xxxv · (s. xiii[1]); Madoc(us) filius G(ri)ffud super Eskengainauc et ceteris possessionibus nostris sub eo (s. xiii); approx. 168 × 263 + 8 mm.; two central horizontal slits for a tag (*c.*6 mm. wide) which exits through a slit in the base of the fold; sealed on tag. Circular seal, green wax, originally approx. 72 mm. diameter, detached from charter; equestrian, facing right; legend: + SIGILL … I GR … I. Parchment rubbed in places making text illegible. Most of the lacunae have been supplied from the text printed by Jones in 1871, on the assumption that the charter was in a better state of preservation when he transcribed it.
Pd. from A, Jones, 'Abbey of Ystrad Marchell', 305–6; from A, *Ystrad Marchell Charters*, no. 52. Cd., Davies, 'Strata Marcella documents', 179 (no. 24); Owens, 'Rûg and its muniments', 88; *H*, no. 228.

Omnibus sancte matris ecclesie filiis tam presentibus quam futuris notum sit quod ego Madoc(us) filius G(ri)fini dedi et concessi pro salute anime mee et pro anima patris mei monachis de St(ra)dmarchell in liberam et quietam et perpetuam elemosinam totam terram que vocatur Eskengainauc in omnibus terminis suis et pertinen[t]iis, quam terram antecessores mei bene et in pace, libere et quiete, iure perpetuo possidendam simul cum heredibus terre ipsius eis vendiderunt et ipsi monachi ante dominium meum in Edeirni[a]un ea[n]dem terram in pace possederunt. Dedi etiam et confirm[a]vi prefatis monachis partem illius ville que dicitur Gwthelwern quam emerunt ab Helisse et Owino antecessoribus meis et ab heredibus terre [illiu]s in omnibus terminis suis et pertinentiis. Dedi insuper et concessi eisdem monachis totam terram que v[oc]atur Banhadelauclludiaun quam emerunt a filiis Ioruerd filii Kadugaun et coheredibus suis de Llanhelidan in omnibus terminis suis et perti- nentiis. Volo etiam ego prefatus Madoc(us) ad omnium pervenire noticiam quod temporibus dominii mei in Edeirniaun filii Madoci filii Lewarch, scilicet Ioruerth et G(ri)fri et G(ri)ffud, calumpniati sunt partem predicte terre, scilicet Eskengainauc, quam pater eorum prenominatis monachis in perpetuam donationem et possessionem antea dederat, postea vero Deo donante in melius conversi, totum suum ius hereditarium predicte terre, scilicet Eskengainauc, pro salute anime sue in liberam et perpetuam possessionem pro se et pro heredibus suis eisdem monachis dederunt, ita u[t nec] ipsi nec heredes sui contra ipsos monachos aliquam inde unquam [in] posterum habeant calumpniam. Facta est autem hec prefata donatio predictorum virorum anno ab incarnatione domini m° cc° vi octavodecimo videlicet kalendas februarii in manu domini D(avi)d abbatis de Llineguest' et I. prioris de St(ra)dmarhell apud Coruain coram Seisil sacerdote et coram clero et coram viris bonis, scilicet Meuric et Lewarch filiis Kadúg', Madauc filio Brochwalc, Eynniaun filio Ieuaf, Kenig filio Idnerd, Madauc filio Gurgenev Seithmarchauc, Ioruerd filio Eynniaun, Ioruerd filio [Ho]wel, Eynniaun filio Catuor, Ithon filio Ioru[e]rt. Volo igitur ego prefatus Madoc(us) ut sepe[dicti] monachi prefatas terras in omnibus termin[is suis et pertinen]tiis libere et quiete, bene et in [pace], sine aliqua exactione vel consuetudine seculari [iure perpetu]o possideant in bosco [videlicet][a] in plano, in aquis, in pasturis, in pratis, [in vii]s et semitis et in omnibus usibus suis et utilitatibus. Et quia pres[en]s etas prona est ad malum unde sibi conatur ext[or]quere lucrum tam hanc meam p[redictam don]ationem quam predictorum virorum sigilli mei impressione et bonorum viror[um attestatione muni]vi. His testibus: Yeuaf filio [Mar]edud, [Ioruer]d filio Eynniaun, [Eynniaun filio …], Ririd et Kenewreic filiis Doh[o …], Ru[in filio …]. Facta est [autem hec mea predicta donatio] anno predicto in manu predicti abbatis apud castellum in Kenlleith.

[a] *Jones, followed by Thomas, reads* in declino. *The text at this point is no longer legible, but comparison with other Strata Marcella charters suggests* scilicet *or* videlicet; *the latter seems more likely in the light of Jones's reading.*

The *anno predicto* of the dating clause is 1206 (i.e. 25 March 1206 × 24 March 1207). The charter must be later than the quitclaim at Corwen on 15 January 1207 to which it refers. Esgyngaenog (SJ 089 459), near Corwen, cmt. Edeirnion, was originally granted to Strata Marcella in 1176 by Madog's kinsman Maredudd ap Hywel, whose charter records that Madog ap Llywarch had renounced his claim to the land (no. 482 above). (?)Banhadloglllwydion (*Banhadelauclludiaun*) was located in the vicinity of Llanelidan, cmt. Llannerch, or Gwyddelwern, cmt. Edeirnion (see note to no. 231 above). Seisyll the priest was presumably the same person as the Seisyll dean of Corwen in no. 506 below.

The place-date may well refer to the motte and bailey at Sycharth, best known as a residence of Madog's descendant Owain Glyndŵr (d. c.1415). Sycharth (SJ 205 258), situated near Llansilin at the entrance to the valley of the Cynllaith, is the only known site of a castle in the commote of Cynllaith. As Domesday Book records that Cynllaith was

held by Rainald de Bailleul, sheriff of Shropshire (*D.B.* i. 255a), the castle may originally
have been Norman. Although there is no written evidence for Sycharth, apart possibly from
the present charter, until Iolo Goch's famous poem describing Glyndŵr's house there at the
end of the fourteenth century, it is reasonable to suppose that it was used by the rulers of
Powys as the commotal centre of Cynllaith after the district came under their authority,
probably from the time of Madog ap Maredudd (d. 1160) (cf. *HW*, ii. 493–4). Madog's son
Gruffudd ap Madog appears in control of the area west of Oswestry in 1188 and his descendants seem to have held Cynllaith until it was lost by Owain Glyndŵr (ibid., 566). See
Richards, 'Sycharth'; Hague and Warhurst, 'Excavations at Sycharth', esp. 108–9, 113, 121;
King, *Castellarium Anglicanum*, i. 102–7, esp. 104 and map facing 102; Davies, *Revolt of
Owain Glyn Dwˆr*, 131 (which comments that Sycharth 'was almost certainly the site of the
court (W. *llys*) of the native Welsh lord of the area in earlier days', a view also expressed,
more tentatively, by Lloyd in *HW*, i. 246).

*505 Valle Crucis Abbey
Grant of the township of Halton (Hatchton).

Overton, 1218

Mention only, in a list of deeds held *c*.1880 by the trustees of Sir Richard Puleston at
Worthenbury vicarage, Flintshire (Anon, 'Historical MSS. Commission', 149). What
happened to the charter after the list was made is unknown; it is not among the documents
in the Puleston Collection deposited in the National Library of Wales. Halton (SJ 302 398)
lies about 1 mile north-east of Chirk, cmt. Nanheudwy.

506 Valle Crucis Abbey
*Grant and confirmation, with the consent of Lady I. his wife, for the salvation of the souls of
himself and all his ancestors and successors, in perpetual and peaceful alms, free of all secular
or ecclesiastical exaction and custom, of all the township of Llanegwestl, the township of
(?) Llanycyfail* (Lanegeiuel), *the township of Halton, the land of Twng, the portion of land at
Acton, the land at Wrexham and Creigiog, half the township of Buddugre, Banhadlen,
Cwmbrwynog, Cambwll, (?) Gwernfeifod* (Gimeruh Meivoch), *Cwm Ceffyl, half the township
of Mwstwr and Cefnlluestau with all their bounds and appurtenances, as their charters set out,
in wood, plain, meadows, pastures, waters, mills, moors, fields, woods, all good liberties and
customs and all rights of use above and below the ground, to be possessed quit of all disturbance for ever. He will warrant these lands against all men forever. He has consented that
ecclesiastical men may restrain with the authority of the Church whoever has presumed to
disturb the monks concerning the said lands contrary to this gift. Witnesses.*

1222

B = TNA: PRO, C 53/81 (Ch. R. 23 Edward I), m. 3 (in an inspeximus, 24 April 1295).
Pd. from B, *Mon. Ang.*, v. 637 (wrongly under Strata Marcella); from B, Jones, 'Valle Crucis',
413–14; from Jones, Price, *Valle Crucis*, 244–5 (trans. only).
Cd., *CChR 1257–1300*, 437; *H*, no. 230.

Universis sancte matris ecclesie filiis tam presentibus quam futuris notum sit omnibus quod ego Madocus filius Griffini consensu et assensu domine I. uxoris mee pro salute anime nostre et ominum antecessorum et successorum nostrorum[a] dedi, concessi et hac presenti carta mea confirmavi Deo et Beate Marie et monachis de Valle Crucis in puram et perpetuam et pacificam elemosinam, absque ulla exactione et consuetudine seculari vel ecclesiastica, totam villam que dicitur Linneguestel et villam de Lanegeiuel et villam `de Hallhtun et terram que dicitur Tonc, portiunculam quam predicti monachi habent de Hactum et terram quam habent de Wrechcessam et de Kreichauc et dimidietatem ville que vocatur Buthucbre et Bahadlen, Cum Bromauc, Camp(ro)ulh, Gimeruh, Meivoch et Cum Kefil et dimidietatem ville que dicitur Mistuir et Keuen Luesteu cum omnibus terminis et pertinentiis suis, sicut eorum carte protestantur in bosco, in plano, in pratis et pasturis, in aquis et molendinis, in moris, in campis et silvis, in omnibus libertatibus et consuetudinibus bonis `in omnibus utilitatibus et comodis super terram et subtus, quiete ab omni molestatione inperpetuum possidendas. Warantizabimus etiam easdem terras dictis monachis pro posse nostro contra omnes homines in perpetuum. Quicumque contra hanc donationem nostram predictos monachos super predictis terris molestare presumserunt, consensimus etiam ut viri ecclesiastici auctoritate sancte ecclesie eorum insolentiam compescant. Facta est hec donatio nostra anno incarnationis dominice m° cc° xxii° . Hiis testibus: Owein mab Trahaiarmh, Yeuvaf filio Maredud, David Rouffo, Iorverth mab Kachwallaun, Seisel decano de Coruain, Iohanne Ruffo; de religiosis autem I. tunc temporis abbate, I. suppriore, G. magistro conversorum et R. monacho et multis aliis.

[a] nostro B.

This is largely or wholly a confirmation of earlier grants. Many of the lands were granted in Madog's foundation charter for Valle Crucis (no. 499 above). Halton was granted in 1218 (no. 505 above). *Langeiuel* is probably the same place as *Lanhekeveyl* and *Llannekeivil* in no. 499 above and no. 511 below (*OP*, iv. 533), and *Gimeruh Meivoch* may be a corrupt reading of Gwernfeifod (SJ 094 290), a grange about 2 miles north-west of Llanrhaeadr-ym-Mochant, given as *Wernmeiuoch* in no. 511, rather than an unidentified name followed by Meifod, a township in Nanheudwy (cf. Williams, *Atlas*, 65; Lloyd, *Powys Fadog*, i. 159 and n. 11; Lloyd, 'Gwern Feifod'). The initial *I.* stood for a form of Iseult, as *Ysota* is the name given to Madog's wife in no. 526 below (and *Yseuda* in the spurious no. 510 below). It is therefore difficult to identify her with Gwladus ferch Ithel, an alleged descendant of Morgan Hir of Gwent, named by later genealogists as Madog's wife (Bartrum, *WG*, i, Bleddyn ap Cynfyn 4; iv, Morgan Hir 1).

*507 Letter patent concerning Henry III

[Text presumably as no. 19 above.]

[Montgomery, 8 October 1223]

Mention only, in a note on the patent roll after the text of no. 19 above (issued by Maredudd ap Rhobert of Cedewain) naming Madog among those that *Eodem modo fecerunt cartas suas* (*PR 1216–25*, 411; cd., *H*, no. 528).

508 Strata Marcella Abbey

Grant and confirmation, for the salvation of the souls of himself and his parents and all his successors, on behalf of himself and all his heirs, at the request and with the permission of Gruffudd Gryg ab Iago ab Cynog, of all Gruffudd's hereditary right in the land of Ekal, *in wood, plain, waters, meadows, townships, paths, pastures and in all places above and below the earth, to be possessed freely in peace and perpetual right without any secular exaction or custom or any disturbance or challenge. Gruffudd sold this to the monks for £4 6s. 8d. on behalf of himself and his heirs in perpetual possession, to be possessed freely in perpetual right and peace with all its bounds and appurtenances. Sealing clause; witnesses.*

1228

A = BL, Add. Ch. 10637. Endorsed: Madauc filius G(ri)fud super Ekal (s. xiii[1]); modern endorsement; approx. 195 × 104 + 22 mm.; two central horizontal slits in fold for a tag (*c.*13 mm. wide) which exits through lower slit; sealed on tag. Circular seal, brown wax, imperfect, originally approx. 72 mm. diameter; equestrian, facing right; no legend survives; oval counterseal, approx. 30 × 26 mm., impression of late antique oval intaglio gem with bust in profile, worn, facing right; legend: ... ADOCI . FILII . GRIF ...
Pd. from A, *Ystrad Marchell Charters*, no. 71.
Cd., Owen, *Catalogue*, iii. 704; *H*, no. 231.

Omnibus sancte matris ecclesie filiis tam presentibus quam futuris presens scriptum inspecturis vel audituris notum sit quod ego Madocus filius Grifud ad precem et licentiam Grifud Crihc filii Iacobi filii Kenauhc pro salute anime mee et parentum meorum omniumque successorum meorum dedi et concessi ac presenti carta mea confirmavi abbati et conventui de St(ra)tmarchel Cisterciensis ordinis omnipotenti Deo et Beate Virgini Marie ibidem imperpetuum servientibus tam pro me quam omnibus heredibus meis totum ius hereditarium dicti Grifud de terra que vocatur Ekal in bosco et plano, in aquis et pratis, in villis et semitis, in pascuis et pasturis et in omnibus omnino locis tam super terram quam sub terra, libere et quiete sine aliqua omnino exactione vel consuetudine seculari et sine aliqua molestia aut reclamatione in omni pace iure perpetuo possidendum, quod eis idem Grifud pro quatuor libris et octoginta denariis tam pro se quam pro omnibus suis heredibus[a] imperpetuam vendidit possessionem, libere et quiete cum omnibus terminis et pertinenciis suis, iure perpetuo in omni pace possidendum. Ut autem hec mea concessio et donatio imperpetuum rata sit et inconcussa perseveret eam tam sigilli mei impressione quam bonorum virorum attestatione munivi et coroboravi anno gratie m° cc° xx° viii°. Hiis testibus: Hoedlevv presbitero de Lant(er)nia, Ioruerht filio Madoci filii Hugonis, Ioruerht filio Kadugani, Kadugano filio Ioruerht cognomento Possernin; de viris vero religiosis Widone et Simeone monachis et sacerdotibus ecclesie Sancte Marie de St(rat)marchell et multis aliis.

[a] *word written after following* libere et quiete *in* A.

Ekal is unlocated. Thomas suggests that it probably lay in Penllyn (*Ystrad Marchell Charters*, 125). However, as Penllyn had been annexed by Llywelyn ap Iorwerth of Gwynedd since 1202, a location in Edeirnion, where Strata Marcella also held lands, is more likely.

509 Valle Crucis Abbey

Grant by the freemen of Llangollen, namely Hywel and Bleddyn sons of Cynwrig, Iorwerth, Tudur and Adda sons of Madog, Meurig ap Philip, Adda and Einion sons of Goronwy Wich, Iorwerth the clerk son of Ednywain, Iorwerth ap Cadwgan, Cynwrig ab Arthen, Cynwrig ab Idnerth, Gwion ap Cadwgan, Cynwrig ap Heilin and the other heirs of Llangollen, on behalf of themselves and their heirs, of a site for a fishery on the other side of the Dee that pertains to part of their township of Llangollen, in perpetual alms, free and quit without any challenge and disturbance. Since they were lacking a seal Madog ap Gruffudd placed his seal on this charter at their request. After some time had passed a dispute arose between the said heirs of Llangollen and the abbey about building the fishery which was settled as follows. After many disputes the heirs of Llangollen chose by common consent five monks with the abbot of Valle Crucis by whose decision they would abide, accepting whatever the monks and abbot should determine concerning the legal action initiated by the heirs about the other bank of the river Dee that pertains to the township of Llangollen. On the day fixed between both parties by the lord prince and his seneschal I. Fychan, the abbot gathered with his prior and four monks nominated by the heirs, namely H. ab Iago, Philip master of lay brothers, David the precentor and N. ab Ieuaf, who, knowing the truth about the aforesaid matters, affirmed on oath before I. seneschal of Madog, Awr and Owain sons of Ieuaf, I. priest of Llandysilio, W. ap Iorwerth, Adda Fychan of Llangollen and Awr Fychan ap Hywel that what they bought from the heirs of Llangollen was free without any challenge or disturbance for them to build and repair their fishery as they pleased on the bank of the river that pertains to Llangollen. But Madog has granted on behalf of himself and his heirs full power to the abbey to build and repair the aforesaid fishery on both banks of the Dee. Sealing clause; witnesses.

1234

> B = TNA: PRO, C 53/81 (Ch. R. 23 Edward I), m. 3 (in an inspeximus, 24 April 1295).
> Pd. from B, Jones, 'Valle Crucis', 415–16; from Jones, Price, *Valle Crucis*, 246 (trans. only).
> Cd., *CChR 1257–1300*, 458; *H*, no. 232.

Sciant presentes et futuri has litteras inspecturi quod nos liberi homines de Lancollien, videlicet Howel et Bledhunt filii Kenwric, Ioruert, Tudir et Adam filii Madauc,[a] Meuric filius Philippi, Adam et Enniaun filii Goronu Wich, Gervasius clericus filius Edneweyn, Gervasius filius Kadugaun, Kenwric filius Arthien, Kenwric filius Ydnerth, Wyaun filius Kadugaun, Kenwric filius Heylin et ceteri heredes de Lancollien dedimus et concessimus pro nobis et heredibus Deo et Beate Marie et conventui de Valle Crucis Cisterciensis ordinis Deo ibidem servientibus locum piscarie ex altera parte fluminis que vocatur Deuerdiw, que spectat ad partem ville nostre de Lancollien, in puram et perpetuam elemosinam, libere et quiete sine ulla reclamatione et molestia. Et quia sigillo carebamus ad petitionem nostram ʽdominus Madocus filius Griffini super hanc cartam sigillum suum apposuit. Elapso postea quodam temporis spatio, orta est controversia inter dictos heredes de Llancollien et dictum abbatem et conventum de Valle Crucis pro edificatione piscarie, que tandem tali modo sopita est, videlicet quod dicti heredes de Lancollien communi assensu post multas contradictiones et querelas elegerunt v monachos cum predicto abbate de Valle Crucis ut eorum starent diffinitionem, gratum et ratum habentes quicquid predicti monachi cum predicto abbate in verbo veritatis adiurati de questione ab eis mota super alteram partem ripe amnis que dicitur Deuerdue que spectat ad villam de Wancollien[b] arbitrantes terminarent. Die vero ad hoc constituto a domino principe et suo senescallo I. parvuo inter ambas partes, convenerunt predictus abbas cum suo priore et iiii[or] monachis ab ipsis nominatis, scilicet H. filio Iacobi et Philippo magistro conversorum, D(avi)d tunc temporis cantore et N. filio Ieuvaf, qui omnes predicti monachi rei veritatem scientes super premissis in verbo veritatis iurantes coram I. senescallo domini Madoci et Haur et Oweyn filiis Ieuvaf et I. sacerdote de Llan Tessiliau et W. filio Ioruerth, Adam parvuo de Lancollien et Haur parvuo filio Howel dixerunt affirmantes quod emerunt a predictis heredibus de Llancollien liberum esse sibi et quietum sine aliqua reclamatione et molestia piscariam suam edificare et restaurere prout ipsis placuerit et quotiens expedierit super ipsam partem amnis que spectat ad villam de Lancollien. Sed et ego Madocus filius Griffini dedi et concessi pro me et heredibus meis abbati et conventui de Valle Crucis plenariam potestatem construendi et restaurandi predictam piscariam ex utraque parte super fluvium que dicitur Deuerdiw. Et in huius rei evidentiam et memoriam perpetuo conservandam donationem meam necnon et predictorum heredum de Lancollien sigilli mei impressione et bonorum viro atestatione roboravi. Hiis testibus: T. tunc temporis abbate, M. priore, H. et P. et D. et N. monachis, I. sacerdote de Lantessiliau et A. et W. clericis, Haur et Oweyn filiis Ieuwaf, Haur parvo filio Howel et multis aliis, anno incarnationis domini m° cc° xxx° iiii°.

[a] Madaut B. | [b] *sic in* B.

This record of a dispute settlement between the freemen of Llangollen and Valle Crucis falls into three parts: (i) a charter by the freemen granting the abbey a place for a fishery on the bank of the Dee pertaining to their township of Llangollen, sealed by Madog; (ii) a narrative of a subsequent dispute settled before Madog's seneschal and others by the arbitration of five Valle Crucis monks; and (iii) a confirmation and amplification of that judgement by Madog, who granted Valle Crucis the right to build a fishery on both banks of the river and sealed the document. The document gives the strong impression that the freemen were compelled to yield to overwhelming pressure from the abbey and its patron Madog, not least in their having to accept a judgement based on the arbitration of five monks. On balance it is more likely that this reflects the realities of power at Llangollen in the early 1230s than later documentary fabrication by the monks. Certainly Madog's son Gruffudd included 'the monastery's fishery above the Dee on either side' in his confir-mation charter for Valle Crucis in 1236 (no. 511 below). Llandysilio was presumably Llandysilio-yn-Iâl. *T.* also occurs as abbot of Valle Crucis in 1227 (*Ystrad Marchell Charters*, no. 70). Stephenson has suggested that 'the lord prince' was Llewelyn ap Iorwerth, Madog's overlord, and *I. parvus* therefore Ednyfed Fychan, Llywelyn's seneschal (Stephenson, *Governance*, 13 and n. 9). Though possible, this is unlikely, as Llywelyn exercised no direct rights of lordship in Iâl (in contrast to Arwystli, where Maredudd ap Rhobert acted on the prince's behalf in a case noticed below) and an *I.*, admittedly not qualified as *parvus*, appears later in the text as Madog's seneschal.

The document bears some resemblances to the two charters issued, earlier in the thirteenth century, by Maredudd ap Rhobert of Cedewain recording the settlement of a dispute over lands in Arwystli in which Strata Marcella Abbey had an interest, especially in the central role played by the secular lord in giving judgement (nos 16–17 above). However, there are also important differences in form and substance. Maredudd's charters open respectively with a salutation and notification in his name and do not cite any document by either of the parties; and the procedure in Arwystli was according to native Welsh law, without involving Strata Marcella, whereas the freemen of Llangollen are said to have accepted the decision of monks from the abbey whose rights they challenged. Cf. also no. 513 below.

GRUFFUDD AP MADOG
(d. December 1269)

†510 Combermere Abbey
Grant in perpetual alms, for the salvation of the souls of himself, his father Madog and mother Iseult (Yseuda) *and all his ancestors and successors, of the tithe of all the fish and fishery arising from the weirs, nets or devices of whatever kind throughout the river Dee, on both sides of the river throughout his lordship of Bromfield and Overton, and of the tithe of all the toll from his mill of Overton, with all increase in tolls or mills built on the said river. For his uncle Owain gave [these] to the monks in his lifetime and Gruffudd's father confirmed [them]. Further confirmation and grant of 5 acres in Overton. Whoever is the miller of Gruffudd or his heirs and keeper of the fishery shall give the monks his faith and oath faithfully to render tithe as God sends the fish, so that Gruffudd shall not lose his alms and his kin and the monks have no loss. Whoever the monks place there or have in their place shall receive the tithe of the mill and of the fish as it is caught, so that it may be sent faithfully and immediately to the monks. Declares that he has granted this from his heart and confirmed it in faith with his right hand before God. Witnesses.*

[1236 × 1269]

B = TNA: PRO, C 53/117 (Ch. R. 4 Edward III), m. 2 (reciting a spurious inspeximus of Edward I 13 May 1287, 12 January 1331).
Cd., *CChR 1326–46*, 207–8; *H*, no. 234.

Griffinus filius Madoci de Bromfeld omnibus ecclesie filiis presentibus et futuris salutem. Sciatis me dedisse, concessisse et hac presenti carta mea confirmasse Deo et Beate Marie Sanctoque Mich(ael)i et monachis de Cumb(er)mare et eorum successoribus, pro salute anime mee et patris mee Madoci et matris mei Yseude et omnium antecessorum et successorum meorum, in liberam, puram et perpetuam elemosinam decimam totius piscis et piscarie de gurgitibus quam de retibus vel ingeniis qualitercumque evenientibus sive contingentibus qui capitur per totam aquam de De ubique prope et longe per totum dominium meorum de Bromf(eld) et de Ou(er)ton ex utraque parte aque per totum et decimam totius tholnei de molendino meo de Ou(er)ton cum omni incremento tholneorum vel molendinorum quomodocumque vel ubicumque super aquam predictam contigerint edificari. Nam awnculus[a] meus Owynus in vita sua [hec] eis dedit et pater meus confirmavit. Confirmo etiam eisdem monachis et concedo quinque acras terre in Ou(er)ton. Et quicumque fuerit molendinarius meus vel heredum meorum ad predictum molendinum et custos piscarie, dabit fidem et iuramentum monachis fideliter et legitime se decimaturum sicut Deus piscem miserit et sicut venerit, ne perdam elemosinam meam et parentes mei et monachi aliquod dampnum habeant. Et quecumque[b] monachi ibi posuerint vel habuerint in loco suo recipiet decimam tholnei et piscis sicut captus fuerit ut fideliter et statim monachis mittatur. Et in fine huius carte illud sciatis quod sic ex corde habeant imperpetuum omnia supradicta concessi et volo teneri, quod dextere mee fide coram Deo cum illis firmavi. Hiis testibus: Eynon filio Griffini, Gahruard' tunc disteyn, Owel' filius eius, Gahruard Wahan, Ada filio Osbern, Gahruard' filio Cadugaun, Ioh(ann)e filio Lonhardi, Simone clerico de Monte Alto et aliis.

ª *sic for* avunculus *in* B. | ᵇ *sic in* B; *(?)rectius* quicumque *(cf. no. 497 above).*

This charter confirms, and is based upon, nos 497–8 above, allegedly issued by Owain ap Gruffudd and Madog ap Gruffudd, and presents the same problems of authenticity as those (see note to no. 497). The present charter may have some authentic basis, including the witness list, where (?)Iorwerth (*Gahruard'*), referred to unusually by the Welsh term *distain*, usually rendered *senescallus* in Latin, bears comparison with the Iorwerth (*Gervasius*) *senescallo meo* of Gruffudd's confirmation for Valle Crucis in 1236 (no. 511 below). The naming of Madog's wife as *Yseuda* also suggests at least that the redactor of the charter was well informed about the grantor, as she is called *Ysota* in no. 526 below (and *I.* in no. 506 above). Nevertheless, the charter gives the impression of having been constructed by borrowing sections from both no. 497 and no. 498; the apparent revision of the clause *Nam … confirmavit* explicitly to refer to Owain and Madog is suspicious; and the syntax is faulty in places. It is therefore difficult to accept this as an authentic charter of Gruffudd in its extant form.

511 Valle Crucis Abbey

Grant and confirmation, for the redemption of the souls of himself and his parents, of all gifts, liberties and dignities – both secular moveables and ecclesiastical benefices – given to the abbey by his father Madog ap Gruffudd, with all their bounds and appurtenances, above and below the earth, in perpetual alms, namely Llanegwestl, (?)Llanycyfail, Celli (?)Fforchog (Vorkauc), (?)Rhiwdderch, Banhadlen, Buddugre, Creigiog, Wrexham, Twng, Halton, Cefnlluestau, Cwm Ceffyl, Abelauc, Mwstwr, (?)Gwernfeifod (Wernmeuioch), Hethuren and the monastery's fishery above the Dee on either side. Further confirmation of the gifts of Madog's co-heirs, namely Cwmbrwynog, Cambwll and Gweunrudd by Owain Brogyntyn and his sons and (?)Gwernfeifod (Gwarn Mevoc) by the sons of Owain Fychan. Sealing clause; witnesses.

1236

> B = TNA: PRO, C 53/81 (Ch. R. 23 Edward I), m. 3 (in an inspeximus, 24 April 1295).
> Pd. from B, Jones, 'Valle Crucis', 416; from Jones, Price, *Valle Crucis*, 247 (trans. only).
> Cd., *CChR 1257–1300*, 458–9; *H*, no. 233.

Universis sancte matris ecclesie filiis has litteras visuris vel audituris Griffinus filius Madoci salutem eternam in domino. Noverit universitas vestra me dedisse, concessisse et hac presenti carta mea confirmasse omnes donationes, libertates, dignitates, sive in mobilibus tam in secularibus quam in ecclesiasticis beneficiis, quascumque pie memorie pater meus Madocus filius Griffini donavit et contulit abbati et conventui Cisterciensis ordinis apud Vallem Crucis Deo et Beate Marie servientibus in redemptionem anime mee et parentum meorum de me et heredibus meis in omnibus terminis et pertinentiis suis, super terram et subtus terram, in puram et perpetuam elemosinam pacifice et quiete. Nomina autem predictorum sunt hec: scilicet Linneswestel,[a] Llannekeivil, Kelli Vorkauc, Rinttirht, Bannach Len, Buthucbre, Kreichauc, Wreccesham, Tunch, Halitun, Keuenlluesteu, Cumkefil, Abelauc, Mustoir, Wernmeiuoch, Hethuren, piscariam etiam monasterii supra Deuerdui ex utraque parte.[b] Donationes etiam coheredum eiusdem Madoci, videlicet Owini Porkintun et filiorum eiusdem de Cumbruinauc, Campull, Weunruth, filiorum etiam Owini parvi de Gwarn Mevoc eisdem monachis confirmavi. Et ut hec mea confirmatio rata et inconcussa permaneat inposterum eam presenti scripto et sigilli mei impressione duxi roborandam. Hiis testibus: Gervasio senescallo meo, Ytail filio Griffini, Madoco Rufo, Goronu filio Ioruerth; de religiosis, Philippo tunc temporis priore de Valle Crucis, Yuone monacho, Philippo et Ric(ard)o fratribus de ordine predicatorum et multis aliis. Facta est confirmatio anno gratie m° cc° xxxvi° .

[a] *sic for* Linnegwestel *in* B. | [b] pate B.

For the charters originally granting many of these lands see nos 496, 499, 505–6, 509 above. *Wernmeiuoch* and *Gwarn Mevoc* both probably represent Gwernfeifod, a grange north-west of Llanrhaeadr-ym-Mochnant (see note to no. 506 above), the different forms reflecting derivation from different charters, namely that of Madog ap Gruffudd (no. 506 above) and an otherwise unknown charter issued by Llywelyn and Owain Fychan sons of Owain Fychan (d. 1187) (calendared as no. 611 below; cf. *HW*, ii. 769). If correct, this suggests that Gwernfeifod had originally been granted by Llywelyn and Owain Fychan. Comparison with two of Madog's charters for Valle Crucis (nos 499, 506 above) shows that the drafters of charters did not always take the care seen here to attribute grants to the original grantors: in Madog's charters Cwmbrwynog and Cambwll appear simply as his own grants. Owain Brogyntyn (d. *c.*1218) and Owain Fychan were Madog's paternal uncles. That they and their sons are described as Madog's *coheredes* is striking: even if the impetus for this description came from the monks, it presumably had Gruffudd's approval. It is unknown to which house(s) the two Dominican witnesses, Philip and Richard, were attached, but their presence, like that of the Dominicans Adam and Anian in a charter of Llywelyn ap Iorwerth the following year (no. 272 above), provides important early evidence for Welsh rulers' association with the mendicants.

*512 Letter patent concerning Henry III

Notification that he will act as a pledge in support of undertakings given by Senana for the release of her husband Gruffudd ap Llywelyn.

[Shrewsbury, 12 August 1241]

Mention only, in an agreement between Senana and the king dated at Shrewsbury, 12 August 1241 (no. 284 above). Presumably the letter patent was similar to that concerning these matters issued on the same occasion by Hywel ap Madog of Bromfield (no. 523 below).

513 Valle Crucis Abbey (judgement and confirmation)

Notification by Gruffudd, Maredudd, Hywel and Madog sons of Madog and Einion ap Gruffudd that the dispute between the sons of Ieuaf ap Maredudd and the abbey over the bounds between Creigiog and Alltgynbyd has been settled by submitting it to their arbitration with the permission of both parties. By the common consideration of themselves and other worthy men they have adjudged Creigiog for ever to Valle Crucis in its widest bounds as given by Madog ap [Gruffudd] ... they have ordained that the monks should pay ... the sons of Ieuaf five pounds of silver or its equivalent value, so that the sons of Ieuaf (?)will renounce once and for all whatever right they used to say they had in the aforesaid bounds on a day and in a place in the presence of the arbitrators and many others. But because it is clearer than light that the aforesaid action was brought against the monks most unjustly, and so that this should not henceforth be made a precedent by others with an evil inclination, by their common consent and that of their lawful men, providing for the future peace of the monks, they have confirmed to the abbey for ever by this charter the monastery of Valle Crucis with all its possessions, renders, tenements and lands with their appurtenances and bounds in woods, pastures, waters, fisheries, mountains, moors, groves and all else pertaining to it above and below the earth, in perpetual alms, for the salvation of the souls of themselves and their ancestors and successors, as set out in Madog's charters and theirs. They acknowledge that they are bound henceforth to maintain, protect and favour with all their power the aforesaid monks in all their rights against all men, so that neither they nor any others may bring an action against the monks over the aforesaid lands and bounds or trouble them in any way in this regard. Let the monks be in their original peace, liberty and security so that they may more easily and devoutly follow their calling by serving God and praying continually for the grantors. Sealing clause; witnesses.

9 December 1247

A = NLW Peniarth MS 208. Endorsed: (?)Creygeo (last three letters are uncertain; s. xiii); approx. 355 mm. wide × 216 mm. deep on left, 234 mm. deep on right + 40 mm.; four pairs of slits through fold for parchment tags, of which three survive (one on far left *c*.9 mm. wide, one next to it on left *c*.8 mm. wide, and one on far right *c*.9 mm. wide), each passing through a slit in the base of the fold; sealed on tags. Only one seal survives, attached to tag on far left: circular, red wax, very imperfect, originally approx. (?)50 mm. diameter; equestrian, facing right; no legend survives. Charter damaged in several places.
Pd. from A, Wynne, 'Valle Crucis', 228–9; from A, Anon, 'Valle Crucis abbey – award', 100–1; from A, *RMWL*, i. 1032–3; from Anon, Price, *Valle Crucis*, 241–2 (trans. only).
Cd., *H*, no. 516.

Omnibus Cristi fidelibus presentes literas visuris vel audituris Grifinus, Maredut, Howelus, Madocus filii Madoci et Eenni(us) filius Grifini salutem in domino. Noverit universitas vestra quod controversia oborta inter filios Yvaf filii Maredut ex una parte et abbatem et c[onv]entum de Valle Crucis ex parte altera super terminis inter Creygauc et Alhd Kenbeber tali modo est sopita, ita videlicet quod permissione utriusque partis in nos comp[?romissum e]st. Nobis vero conferentibus ad invicem super hac causa provisum est quod Creygauc in terminis suis melioribus et amplioribus sicut dominus Madocus filiu[s Griffini] ... s m ... st ... donavit predictis monachis de Valle Crucis communi consideratione nostra et aliorum virorum proborum ex sententia inperpetuum adiudicavimus. N ...ᵃ partes finaliter habende et tenende providimus quod predicti monachi quinque libras argenti vel earundem valorem memoratis filiis Yvaf sicut ... ᵃ reformata est coram nobis convenit inter eos persolverent, ita dumtaxat quod sepedicti filii Yvaf pro se et pro heredibus suis quicquid iuris in predictis [terminis] se [h]abuisse dicebant ipsis die et loco nobis presentibus et multis aliis simul et semel omnino renunciabunt.[b] Sed quia perspeximus[c] et luce clarius constat [quod pre]dicta lis contra monachos nimis iniuste mota est, et ne hoc de cetero a ceteris exquisita industria et malo ingenio in consequentiam traheretur, de communi consilio nostro et legalium hominum nostrorum paci et quieti monachorum in posterum providentes monasterium de Valle Crucis cum omnibus possessionibus, redditibus et tenementis [et] omnibus etiam terris cum pertinenciis et terminis in silvis, in pascuis et pasturis, in aquis et piscariis, in montibus et moris [et] nemoribus, in omnibus aliis rebus super terram et subtus ad idem monasterium pertinentibus, in puram et perpetuam elemosinam pro salute animarum nostrarum et antecessorum necnon et successor[um n]ostrorum prout melius et efficacius in cartis domini Madoci divisim et gregatim et nominatim prout etiam in munimentis nostris eisdem monachis collatis et concessis ... ti ... abbati et conventui de Valle Crucis Deo et Beate Marie ibidem servientibus carte nostre presentis munimine perenniter confirmare decrevimus. Profitemur siqu[idem] et presencium literarum nostrarum atestatione contestamur nos teneri de cetero predictos monachos cum omni iure suo et iusticia pro viribus nostris contra omnes homines [man]utenere, protegere, favendo fovere et deffensare, ita quod nec nobis nec ullis aliis liceat contra pred[icto]s monachos litem movere vel super memoratis terris et [termi]nis ipsos in causam trahere vel aliquo modo in hac parte vexare aut perturbare. Sed sint in pristina pace, [?libert]ate et securitate ut possint facilius, devocius, fiducialius ad id ad quod [s]umpti sunt Deo desservire et pro nobis ad ipsum iugiter preces fundere. Facta est autem hec confirmatio nostra anno gratie m° cc° xl° vii° quinto idus decembris. Et ut hec donatio i[n po]sterum rata sit et inconcussa presentes literas sigillorum nostrorum inpressione duximus roborandas. Hiis testibus: de religiosis videlicet, dompno Madoco abbate tunc tempore de Valle C(ru)cis, Yuone priore, Nennio et Philippo monachis eiusdem loci, Adam filio P(er)edur, Ierusio fratribus de ordine predicatorum; de secularibus de Malaur, Lewely[no filio] Madoci, Itello et Kenuirtho[d] filiis Grifri Seys, Ioruerth et Ennio filiis Yvaf, Madoco filio Melir; de Yal, Lewelyno filio Ynir, Madoco filio Ioruert, Caducano Rufo, D ... de Kilken; de Kenleht, Madoco et Philippo filiis Ph(ilipp)i filii Alexandri; de Mohtnant,[d] Ytello filio Goronu filii Kaducani, Madoco Rufo et [mul]tis aliis.

[a] *lacuna of 53 mm. in A.* | [b] renunciarunt A. | [c] perspetximus A. | [d] *sic in A.*

Einion ap Gruffudd was probably a son of Gruffudd Iâl ap Madog (d. 1238), brother to the other grantors. That each of Madog ap Gruffudd's surviving sons, together with their nephew, were called upon to settle the dispute may indicate that they were all perceived by the monks and/or the sons of Ieuaf to be Madog's heirs, even though Gruffudd ap Madog alone had issued a confirmation for the abbey, including Creigiog, shortly after his father's death in 1236 (no. 511 above). It is unclear how far this indicates that Gruffudd, who is named first, had to struggle against his brothers to establish supremacy in Powys Fadog (cf. Smith, 'Dynastic succession', 227). *Alhd Kenbeber* was almost certainly Alltgynbyd, whose name survives at Allt Gymbyd Farm (SJ 205 549) less than $\frac{1}{2}$ mile to the south of Creigiog Uchaf (SJ 204 555) and about 1 mile south-east of Llanarmon-yn-Iâl (Williams, *Atlas*, 65).

514 Valle Crucis Abbey

Grant, with the consent of his heirs and for the salvation of the souls of himself and his ancestors, in perpetual alms, of the township of Northcroft with its bounds and appurtenances [(?)and half of the township of Stansty with all its bounds and appurtenances] which he gave in exchange to the men of Llanegwestl and their heirs, together with those men and their heirs with their service and homage, so that henceforth they shall not answer to him or his heirs for any secular service or exaction but be subject in all things to the abbot and convent of Llanegwestl [Valle Crucis]. They will be judged by the abbot and his court for all offences except for homicide and theft, nor will they will be punished concerning these until they have confessed publicly or been convicted according to the custom of the country. Further grant to the same men of rights of common in the woods, pastures and waters of his demesnes and they shall exercise all diligence and care. Let Madog's freemen grant the same to each of their men. Further grant and confirmation by the counsel of worthy and lawful men that if any of the aforesaid heirs of Llanegwestl staying at Stansty is charged with theft or homicide, (?)let them remain in their hafodydd *[summer residences]. Sealing clause; witnesses.*

Maner', 8 September 1254

B = Oxford, Bodleian Library, MS Rawlinson B.464, fos 122v–123v. *c.*1700. Rubric: Liber Homiliarum. Ante hunc librum hec occurrunt.

C = Anon, 'Valle Crucis abbey: additional particulars', 151–2 (printed transcript of a copy made (?)s. xvii[1] owned by W. W. E. Wynne of Peniarth). 1846.

D = NLW MS 1506C, pt. ii, p. 67. *c.*1700. Rubric: Liber Homiliarum. Ante hunc librum hec occurrunt.

Pd. C; from D, Lhuyd, *Parochialia*, i. 100; from Lhuyd, Price, *Valle Crucis*, 242–3 (trans. only).

Cd., *H*, no. 237.

Sciant tam presentes quam futuri hoc scriptum inspecturi[a] vel audituri quod ego Griffinus[b] filius Madoci dominus de Bromfield consilio et assensu heredum meorum dedi et concessi et hac presenti carta mea confirmavi Deo[c] et Beate Marie et monachis Cistricensis[d] ordinis apud Len Egwestel[e] Deo et Beate Marie servientibus, pro salute anime mee et animarum meorum antecessorum,[f] in puram et perpetuam eleemosynam villam que dicitur Northcroft[g] cum terminis et pertinentiis suis[h] quod[i] dedi in excambium hominibus de Len Egwestel[j] et heredibus eorum simul[k] [fo. 123r] cum ipsis hominibus et heredibus eorum et servitio eorum et homageo,[l] ita quod de cetero mihi aut heredibus meis de aliquo servitio vel exactione seculari non respondeant, sed abbati et conventui de Leneguestel[m] in omnibus sint subiecti. Et de omnibus excessibus suis stabunt iudicio supradicti abbatis[n] et curie[o] sue excepto iudicio homicidii et furti, nec etiam de[p] hiis gravabuntur[q] donec confessi[r] fuerint publice vel convicti iuxta morem[s] patrie. Preterea concessi eisdem[t] hominibus communitatem[u] nemorum et pascuorum[v] et aquarum[w] dominicis meis et omnimodam diligentiam et operam adhibebunt.[x] Hoc idem liberi homines mei unicuique[y] eorum hominum[z] concedant. Insuper etiam concedo et per consilium proborum virorum[aa] et legalium confirmo quod si alicui[ab] aut aliquibus de predictis heredibus de Leneguestel[ac] apud Stansti commorantibus[ad] furtum aut homicidium imponantur,[ae] quod Wallice[af] [(?)vocatur] *havodit* commorentur.[ag] Et ut hec mea donatio et huius carte mee[ah] confirmatio in posterum perseverent[ai] et rata et inconcussa perseverent[aj] hanc[ak] cartam sigillo meo [al]munivi et [al]roboravi.[am] Hiis testibus[an] meis[ao] scilicet: Lewelino[ap] filio Madoci, Ierusio[aq] senescallo meo, [fo. 123v] Haur[ar] et Griffri[as] filiis Gevav,[at] Gervasio[au] filio Grufud,[av] magistro[aw] Madoco filio Philipi,[ax] domino[p]

Aniano tunc abbate,[ay] domino Madoco[az] quondam[ba] abbate,[ay] Hennio,[bb] Helica,[bc] Philippo[bd] et Aniano[be] monacis[bf] et multis aliis. Dat' apud Maner'[bg] die nativitatis Beate Virginis Marie anno ab incarnatione domini millesimo[bh] ducentisimo[bi] quinquagesimo[bj] quarto.

[a] suspecturi C. | [b] Gruffinus C. | [c] dio C. | [d] Cistrensis C. | [e] Len *corrected from* Lan *in* B; Lenegwystl D. | [f] C *inserts* et successorum. | [g] Worth Croft D. | [h] B *inserts* et medietatem ville de Stanestiae cum omnibus terminis et pertinentiis suis, *with* pertinentiis *struck through after* omnibus; *all the words are placed within square brackets, with marginal note* this was interlined; D *inserts* et medietatem ville de Stanesti cum omnibus terminis et pertinentiis suis; *all the words are placed within square brackets, with marginal note* this was interlined. | [i] C; que BD. | [j] Len *corrected from* Lan *in* B; Lanegystl C; Lenegwystl D. | [k] imp' C. | [l] homagio C. | [m] Lanegwestl C; Len Egwestel D. | [n] abatis C. | [o] cu'liae [sic pro Curiae] C. | [p] *omitted* C. | [q] gravab'[tr] C; grūvict' BD. | [r] C; concessi BD. | [s] moremte [sic] C. | [t] iisdem D. | [u] *omitted* D. | [v] pascuarum C. | [w] D *inserts* communitatem. | [x] adhibebant BD (*but future makes more sense than imperfect*); adhibebo ut C. | [y] C; unius *with three dots underneath and* viam *inserted above it in* B; unius *with three dots underneath, followed by* viam *in* D. | [z] BD *insert* eis. | [aa] C; meorum BD. | [ab] B *repeats* quod si alicui. | [ac] Lanygwystl C; Len Egwestel D. | [ad] morantibus C. | [ae] imponatur D. | [af] Walice C. | [ag] *the syntax of this conditional clause is unclear, possibly because of lacunae in the text; it is uncertain whether* havodit *is the subject or the object of* commorentur *in the principal sentence.* | [ah] inde C. | [ai] proerseveraverint C. | [aj] perserverint C. | [ak] C; nunc BD. | [al-al] muniri BD. | [am] roborar' C. | [an] D *inserts a word deleted.* | [ao] meipso C. | [ap] Lewilino CD. | [aq] *vertical stroke of* I *descends below lower horizontal stroke and has three dots underneath it in* B; Iervasio C; Iernsio D. | [ar] Hanr *with three dots under the* a *and* n *in* BD; Henr' C. | [as] Gruffri C. | [at] Ier' C; Ievav D. | [au] Iervasio CD. | [av] Gruffinae C; Grufudh D. | [aw] maro D. | [ax] Phillip C; Phillipi D. | [ay] abate C. | [az] Madaco C. | [ba] quandam C. | [bb] *three dots under the* H *in* B; *omitted* C. | [bc] *three dots under the* H *with an* n *written above in* D. | [bd] Philipo C; Phillippo D. | [be] Anniano D. | [bf] monachis C. | [bg] C; Maner'um B; Manerum D. | [bh] D; millessimo B; milessimo C. | [bi] ducentissimo BCD. | [bj] quinquagessimo BCD.

As with no. 500 above, D is almost certainly a copy of B. A note prefacing the text in C, published in 1846, states that it was 'transcribed from a copy written in the character of about the reign of Charles I. This copy is in the possession of W. W. E. Wynne, Esq., who has never seen the original, and knows nothing more of the transcript he possesses than that he found it amongst a large collection of old deeds relating to his family property' (Anon, 'Valle Crucis abbey: additional particulars', 151). The rubric to B (followed by D) shows that its text cannot have been copied from the early modern transcript that later belonged to W. W. E. Wynne (d. 1880). It is uncertain whether the transcripts in the book of homilies copied in B and in the deed copied in C were made from the same text of the charter (either an earlier copy or the original). Much turns here on C's omission of the clause *et medietatem ville de Stanesti . . . et pertinentiis suis*, described as an interlineation in B, followed by D (textual note *h*). If the interlineation was simply a correction by B's source made after checking his transcript against the text of the charter, this would suggest that he used a different text from the source of the transcript copied in C. It is possible, though, that B's source copied a text similar to that in C and then interpolated the clause after copying Madog ap Gruffudd's charter (no. 500 above) – which followed the present charter in the book of homilies according to B – and noticing that Madog granted half of Stansty as well as Northcroft to the freemen of Llanegwestl. In addition, the final clause could imply that lands in Stansty were subsumed in the grant of Northcroft and the freemen of Llanegwestl and need not have been specified in the disposition (see below). It may be, then, that in its omission of the clause on granting half of Stansty C is more faithful to the text of the lost original charter than B, and the same is true of some other readings (e.g. *confessi* and *unicuique* at textual notes *r* and *y* respectively). However, in other respects the standard of transcription in B is higher than that of C, including the rendering of the place-name Llanegwestl and of some personal names in the witness list. The text published here is therefore based on B with emendations from C, and omits the clause on granting half of Stansty in view of the possibility that this is a later interpolation.

Although all are corrupt in parts, the extant texts probably derive from an authentic charter issued by Gruffudd. The notification is very similar to that of no. 515 below, and the occurrence of Madog as former abbot in the present charter is consistent with its date of 1254 as he witnessed no. 513 above as abbot of Valle Crucis in December 1247. Later medieval evidence shows that the abbey possessed Northcroft and Stansty (Palmer, *History of the Thirteen Country Townships*, 183 and n. 1, 186). The meaning of the final clause is not entirely clear, perhaps because the text as transmitted is incomplete. Earlier in the charter Gruffudd excluded theft and homicide from the jurisdiction over the men of Llanegwestl transferred to the abbot of Valle Crucis, and the final clause seems to elaborate this principle with respect to freemen of Llanegwestl temporarily resident in the township of Stansty over the summer: *havodit* (Mod. W. *hafodydd*) denoted (a) summer residences; (b) a flock or herd sent to a summer pasture (*GPC*, s.v. *hafod*). The sense may be that, in the event of their being accused of theft and homicide, the freemen could remain in their summer dwellings in Stansty pending trial. Alternatively, *havodit* may be the subject of *commorentur*, in which case the meaning would be that the summer flocks could remain (presumably at Stansty) while those accused went off to answer the charges against them. In either case, this could imply that (half of) Stansty had been granted to Valle Crucis along with Northcroft. (I am very grateful to Paul Russell for his helpful comments on the problems posed by the text.)

515 Emma Audley, his wife

Grant, with the consent of his heirs, of all the land of Maelor Saesneg for her lifetime, namely the manor of Overton with its mills, weir and all other appurtenances, the township of Hanmer with its appurtenances, the township of Llannerch-panna with its appurtenances, Knolton with its appurtenances and all the townships within the bounds of Maelor Saesneg as freely as he had that land. However, she may not give, sell, pledge or in any way alienate the said land or any part of it, but after her death it will revert to him or his heirs and may not be withdrawn from the lord of Wales. Sealing clause; witnesses.

[Probably September 1257 × September 1266; possibly
21 October 1268 × December 1269]

B = TNA: PRO, C 145/35 (39). 1277.
Pd. from B, Seebohm, *Tribal System*, App. D, 103–4.
Cd., *CIM*, i, no. 1095; *H*, no. 235.

Sciant presentes et futuri quod ego Griffinus filius Madoci dominus de Bromfeld assensu[a] et consensu heredum meorum dedi et concessi et hac presenti carta mea confirmavi domine

Emme uxori mee legitime filie domini Henr(ici) de Audidele totam patriam que vocatur Maylorseysnec quoadvixerit, videlicet manerium de Ou(er)ton cum molendinis et gurgite et omnibus aliis pertinentiis suis, villam de Hengem(er)e cum suis pertinentiis, villam de Lanerpanna cum suis pertinentiis, Cnolton' cum suis pertinentiis et omnes villas que infra limites predicte patrie de Mailorseysnec continentur prout ego melius et liberius dictam patriam habui et dare potui, ita tamen quod non possit dictam patriam vel aliquam partem eiusdem dare, vendere vel invadiare vel aliquomodo alienare, set post obitum illius predicta patria ad me vel heredos meos revertet et quod dicta terra a domino Wall(ie) non subtrahatur. Et ut hec mea donatio et concessio quoadvixerit rata et stabilis permaneat presens scriptum sigilli mei inpressione robboravi.[b] Hiis testibus: domino Aniano episcopo de Sancto Asaf, domino Yarwarth abbate de Valle Crucis, Madoco, Leulino, Oweno, Griffino filiis meis, domino David decano de Bromfeld, Nenneau filio Ener, Ririt filio Ener, Griffry filio Ener, Yeua Vawan, Gorono filio Hithel, Bledint filio Yarwarth et aliis.

[a] assenssu B. | [b] *sic in* B.

The stipulation that Maelor Saesneg should remain under the 'lord of Wales' shows that the charter can be no earlier than September 1257, when Gruffudd switched allegiance from the English crown to Llywelyn ap Gruffudd, remaining loyal to the prince thereafter (cf. Smith, *Llywelyn*, 93–4, 111). Although the jurors in the inquisition of 1277 at which the charter was produced as evidence claimed that Gruffudd had granted both Maelor Saesneg and Eyton (no. 516 below) 'when he married Emma' (*quando Emmam . . . duxit in uxorem*), the grants must have been later, as both charters are witnessed by the couple's four sons. The marriage took place before 9 March 1258, when Henry III ordered an extent to be made of land formerly held by Gruffudd as his wife's dower in the Shropshire manor of Lee Cumbray; Emma's first husband, Henry Tuschet (d. by 20 November 1242), had been lord of Lee Cumbray (*CIM*, i, no. 239; Eyton, *Shropshire*, vii. 343–5). The presence of Iorwerth as abbot of Valle Crucis is inconclusive as regards dating: he also occurs in 1270 (no. 526 below), but it is unknown when he succeeded Einion, abbot in 1254 (no. 514 above). The *terminus ad quem* depends, therefore, on whether the first witness was Anian I of St Asaph (1249–66) or Anian II (1268–93). There are two possible indications in favour of Anian I. First, Llywelyn is referred to as *dominus Wallie*, 'lord of Wales', rather than *princeps Wallie*, 'prince of Wales', the title he adopted from 1262 onwards and conferred upon him by Henry III in the Treaty of Montgomery of September 1267 (no. 363, c. ix above); if the charter was drawn up after that treaty, one might expect it to use the terms 'prince' or 'principality'. Second, although there is some overlap between the witness lists of the present charter and no. 516 below granting Eyton to Emma, there are enough differences to suggest that they were issued on different occasions. Therefore, while the Bishop Anian of no. 516 was clearly Anian II, this may not necessarily be true of the present charter. If, as seems likely, the grant of Eyton was an additional endowment following the death of Gruffudd's brother Hywel ap Madog, it may be that Hywel, who last occurs in September 1267, was still alive when the present charter was issued. On the other hand, neither argument is sufficiently compelling completely to rule out a date after Anian II's consecration in October 1268.

Llannerch-panna (SJ 411 392) is located about ½ mile south-west of Penley; Knolton referred either to the settlement of that name about $2\frac{1}{2}$ miles south-west of Penley at SJ 378 390 or Knolton Hall, about $1\frac{1}{2}$ miles south-west of Overton at SJ 352 406.

516 Emma Audley, his wife

Grant, with the consent of his heirs, of all his manor of Eyton in Maelor Gymraeg with all its appurtenances within and outside the township, in demesnes, woods, parks, fields, plains, meadows, pastures, ways, paths, waters, weirs, fisheries, mills and all liberties and easements together with a certain land which lies within the enclosure of the park of Eyton which the Lord Hywel of pious memory bought from all the heirs of Erbistock, paying them 12 gallons of ale or its value annually at Michaelmas [29 September], as well as another piece of land in the aforesaid park which the heirs of Erbistock voluntarily granted to Gruffudd. The manor is to be held from Gruffudd and his heirs throughout Emma's life as freely and fully as he ever had it, though after her death it will revert to him or his heirs, for an annual render at Michaelmas of one pair of white gloves worth one penny for all secular service and exaction. Gruffudd and his heirs will warrant and defend Emma's title to the manor with all its appurtenances against all men as long as she lives. Sealing clause; witnesses.

[21 October 1268 × December 1269]

> B = TNA: PRO, C 145/35 (39). 1277.
> Pd. from B, Seebohm, *Tribal System*, App. D, 104.
> Cd., *CIM*, i, no. 1095; *H*, no. 236.

Sciant presentes et futuri quod ego Griffinus filius Madoci dominus de Bromfeld' assensu et consensu heredum meorum dedi, concessi et hac presenti carta mea confirmavi domine Emme uxori mee legitime filie domini Henr(ici) de Aldedeleg' totum manerium meum de Eytune in Malauorkemeraec cum omnibus pertinentiis suis infra villam et extra, in dominiis, in boscis, in parcis, in campis, in planis, in pratis, in pascuis, in pasturis, in viis, in semitis, aquis, stagnis, vivariis, gurgitibus, piscariis, molendinis et in omnibus libertatibus et aisiamentis quas habui vel hab[ere] potui et in omnibus aliis pertinentiis suis predicto manerio spectantibus una cum quadam terra que iacet infra clausum parci de Eytune quam dominus Howelus pie memorie emit de omnibus heredibus de Herbystoke, reddendo eisdem annuatim xii galones cervisie vel pretium earumdem ad festum Sancti Mich(ael)is, una cum quadam particula alia terre que iacet in parco predicto quam heredes `de Erbystoke spontanea eorum voluntate tradiderunt mihi; habendum et tenendum de me et heredibus meis sibi in tota vita sua adeo libere et integre sicuti ego umquam liberius et plenius illud habui vel habere potui, `ita tamen quod post decessum predicte domine Emme revertatur predictum manerium cum omnibus pertinentiis suis mihi vel heredibus meis, reddendo inde annuatim mihi et heredibus meis ipsa unum par albarum cyrotecarum de pretio uni denarii ad festum Sancti Mich(ael)is pro omni servitio seculari, exactione et demanda. Ego vero dictus Griffinus et heredes mei predictum manerium cum omnibus pertinentiis suis sicut predictum est predicte domine Emme quamdiu vixerit contra omnes homines warantizabimus et defendemus. In cuius rei testimonium huic scripto sigillum meum apposui. Hiis testibus: fratre Aniano tunc episcopo de Sancto Assaph', fratre Gervasio tunc abbate de Valle Crucis, Madoco, Lewelino, Oweyno, Griffino filiis meis, David' tunc decano de Bromfeld', Iuua filio Ahur, Ahur filio Iuuaf, Huua filio Ioreuert,[a]

Greno filio Ioreuert, Lewelino filio Eyner, Iuua Vauehan, Nennio filio Ener, Ithenauet filio David' et aliis.

^a Lereuret B *(cf. no. 526)*.

The first witness, Anian, bishop of St Asaph, must be Anian II, consecrated 21 October 1268, rather than Anian I (d. September 1266), as the charter was written after the death of Gruffudd's brother Hywel ap Madog, which occurred after 29 September 1267 (no. 363 above). The jurors in the inquisition of 1277 at which the charter was produced declared that the manor of Eyton had escheated to Gruffudd on the death of his brother Hywel (Seebohm, *Tribal System*, App. D, 102). Erbistock (SJ 356 414) is located about 1 mile west of Overton, which lies on the other side of the Dee in neighbouring Maelor Saesneg, and about 2 miles south of Eyton.

EMMA OF BROMFIELD
(*fl.* 1258–82)

*517 Margaret, widow of Madog Fychan ap Gruffudd
Grant, in exchange for Margaret's quitclaim of Eyton, of that manor at farm, to be held from Emma for the term of Emma's life for an annual rent at Overton of 10 marks, 5 marks payable at Easter, 5 at Michaelmas [29 September]. If there is any default on the payment Emma is entitled to resume the manor without any hindrance or claim from Margaret; it will also revert to Emma if Margaret dies during her lifetime.

[28 November × December 1277]

Mention only, in a record of proceedings at Oswestry on 28 November 1277 before Anian II, bishop of St Asaph, Ralph de Farningham and Walter de Hopton, at which Emma claimed Eyton from Margaret (*WAR*, 245–6). The assize roll explicitly states that the quitclaim and grant were recorded in an indenture between the two parties. This was probably the charter referred to by Margaret in a petition of 1283 × 1284 which presents her claim to hold Eyton in the same terms as those recorded in the assize roll (no. 528 below). The agreement may have been made shortly after the initial hearing of the claim on 28 November 1277, as the reference to it appears on a schedule sewn on to m. 7 of the assize roll and states that Margaret quitclaimed Eyton after the court had decided to hold an inquisition in the case. However, the wording suggests that Margaret made her concession to Emma before an inquisition was held.

*518 Llywelyn ap Gruffudd ap Madog
Agreement that he might hold the township of Llanarmon in Cynllaith with its appurtenances, with 30s. rent in the township of Trefor in the land of Nanheudwy and with a rent called amobr *from all the lands, in return for £7 per annum at two terms until the end of Emma's life, on condition that if he should die before her, these should return to her.*

[Probably February 1278 × 11 December 1282]

Mention only, in a petition to Edward I and his council datable to 11 December 1282 ×
1283 (no. 520 below).

519 Edward I

Grant and quitclaim of all her lands and tenements with their appurtenances in Maelor
Saesneg, to be held free and quit by the king and his heirs or assigns so that neither she nor
anyone on her behalf may be able to have, claim or demand anything in the said lands and
tenements in the future. Sealing clause; witnesses.

[(?)Westminster, 10 × 15 November 1278]

> B = TNA: PRO, C 54/95 (Close R. 6 Edward I), m. 1d (in an enrolment of *c*.15 November 1278).
> Cd., *CCR 1272–9*, 513; *H*, no. 240.

Noverint universi presens scriptum visuri vel audituri quod ego Emma de Brumfeld'
concessi, remisi et imperpetuum quietumclamavi magnifico principi domino Edward(o)
regi Ang(lie) illustri omnes terras et tenementa cum pertinentiis que habui vel aliquo modo
habere potui in Maylorseiseneich', habenda et tenenda eidem domino regi [et]ᵃ heredibus
vel assignatis suis libera, quieta et soluta, ita quod nec ego nec aliquis per me vel pro me in
dictis terris et tenementis cum pertinentiis aliquid habere, clamare vel exigere possimus in
futurum. [In]ᵃ huius rei testimonium presenti scripto sigillum meum apposui. Hiis testibus:
venerabili patre Thom(a) Hereford(ensi) episcopo, Rog(er)o de Mortuo Mari, Rog(er)o de
Clifford', Rob(er)to de Tibetot, Antonio Bek', Hugone filio Otonis, Walt(er)o de Helyun,
Ioh(anne) de Louetot, Nich(ol)o de Stapelton' et aliis.

ᵃ *omitted* B.

A memorandum after the enrolment in the close roll states that the charter was delivered
for custody to Master Thomas Bek, keeper of the wardrobe, on 15 November 1278 (*CCR
1272–9*, 513). The king made a grant for life to Emma, dated 10 November at Westminster,
of 100*s.* per annum in farms from the town of Derby and the manors of Claverley (Shrops.)
and Tettenhall (Staffs.) in exchange for her quitclaim of all her lands in Maelor Saesneg
(*CPR 1272–81*, 282–3). The present quitclaim was also probably issued at Westminster, a
conclusion supported by the presence of the first witness, Bishop Thomas Cantilupe of
Hereford, at his London residence of Tottenham on 8 November 1278 (*Reg. Cantilupe*,
lxvi). Emma had declared her readiness to make an exchange before Walter de Hopton at
Oswestry in February 1278, following her restoration to Maelor Saesneg, previously in the
king's hand, and an agreement to this effect was made with the king shortly before 3
October (*WAR*, 239; *CChancW*, i. 4; see also Seebohm, *Tribal System*, App. D, 101–2;
WAR, 244–5; *CWR*, 162).

520 Petition to the king and his council

Emma shows that her husband Gruffudd ap Madog, lord of Bromfield enfeoffed her with the
township of Llanarmon in Cynllaith with its appurtenances, with 30s. rent in the township of
Trefor in the land of Nanheudwy and with a rent called amobr (ambroges) *from all the lands;*
she has a charter from her lord for the township of Llanarmon and confirmation from her son

for the rent and the amobr. *Then Emma agreed with her son Llywelyn that he should hold the aforesaid land and rent in return for £7 per annum at two terms until the end of Emma's life, on condition that if Llywelyn should die before her, these should return to her according to the terms of a document between them. Then in the war of Wales Llywelyn died, and Roger Mortimer seized all his lands and the aforesaid lands and rents. She has therefore been deprived of her right. She therefore prays the king and his council, as he is the chief lord and can do justice to all, to enable her to have seisin of the aforesaid land and rent.*

[11 December 1282 × 1283]

A = TNA: PRO, SC 8/262, no. 13080. Endorsed: Emma que fuit uxor Griffyn Maddok habet diem usque crastinum et loquendum est cum domino rege (s. xiii[2]); approx. 170 × 86 mm.; parchment badly stained, especially at bottom right-hand side.
Cd., *CAP*, 441; *H*, no. 521.

Emme ke fu femme Griffuh a[a] Madok je dis seignour de Brumfeud mustre [a] nostre seignour le reys e a soen conseil qe `issi come soen seignur avandit la feffa de la vile de Lanerman en Kenthleth ové les apertenances e de xxx s. de rente en `la vile de Trevaur en la terre de Nanheudo e de une rente ke l'en appele ambroges `de totes les terres , e de la vile de Lanarman si ad ele chartre de soen segnour[a] e de la rente e des ambroges si ad ele confermement de ses finz; puis si covint l'avandite Emme et un Lewelyn soen fuiz, ke cely Lewelyn tenit l'avandite terre e l'avandite rente rendant a l'avandite Emme vii livres par an a ii termes dekes a terme de vie de l'avandite Emme par iceu condicion, qe si l'avandit Lewelyn morsit[b] avant la dame, ke l'avandite chose retornast a l'avandite Emme solom la forme de un escrit qe est entre eus; pus en cete guerre de Gales morust l'avandit Lewelyn, e sire Rog[er] de Mortuemer si seisi totes les terres l'avandit Lewelyn e les terres e les rentes avanditz. Dunc la dame si est deforcee de soen dreit. Dunc cele Emme si prie a nostre seignor le rey e son conseil, issicome il est chef seignor e puyt fere dreytur a touz, ke il li face aver seisine ... de l'avandite terre e de l'avandite rente.

[a] *sic in* A. | [b] *sic in* A (*?for* morist).

Llywelyn ap Gruffudd ap Madog, Emma's son, died with Llywelyn ap Gruffudd, prince of Wales on 11 December 1282 (Smith, *Llywelyn*, 565). Trefor (SJ 270 425) lay about 3½ miles east of Llangollen. *Ambroges* is derived from the Welsh term, *amobr*, a payment due under Welsh law to a woman's lord in respect of a sexual relationship, both marital and extra-marital, that continued to be levied by Marcher lords after the Edwardian conquest (Davies, 'Status of women', 96–7, 103–6, 110–12). The lands had been in dispute between Emma and Llywelyn before February 1278, when he restored Llanarmon and half of Trefor to his mother for the second time after a hearing before the Hopton commission at Oswestry (*WAR*, 238; cf. *CWR*, 170–1). The document agreeing that Llywelyn could hold the lands during Emma's lifetime, calendared as no. 518 above, may have been a compromise made subsequent to that restoration.

MAREDUDD AP MADOG
(d. 1256)

*521 Letter patent concerning Henry III
Notification that he will act as a pledge in support of undertakings given by Senana for the release of her husband Gruffudd ap Llywelyn.

[Shrewsbury, 12 August 1241]

Mention only, in an agreement between Senana and the king dated at Shrewsbury, 12 August 1241 (no. 284 above). Presumably the letter patent was similar to that concerning these matters issued on the same occasion by Hywel ap Madog of Bromfield (no. 523 below).

HYWEL AP MADOG
(d. *c*.1268)

522 Letter patent concerning Shrewsbury Abbey
Notification that his dispute with the abbot and convent of Shrewsbury over a certain portion in the church of Oswestry which Seisyll once held by the authority of the bishop of St Asaph was settled as follows on the octaves of St Laurence [17 August] before Master Adam son of David and Master Richard Sais acting on behalf of the bishop of St Asaph: having heard the right of the abbot and convent in the said portion and recognized it by inspecting their muniments, Hywel has resigned any right he used to think he had in that portion into the hands of Master Adam and Master Richard; he has also withdrawn all claims concerning that portion.

Oswestry church, [17 August] 1217

    B = NLW MS 7851D (Cartulary of Shrewsbury Abbey), p. 109. s. xiii/xiv.
    Pd. from B, *Cart. Shrews.*, ii. 332–3 (no. 122b).
    Cd., *H*, no. 229.

Omnibus Cristi fidelibus ad quos presens scriptum pervenerint Howelus filius Madoc(i) filii Griffini salutem in vero salutari. Noveritis quod lis mota inter dominum abbatem et conventum Salop' ex una parte et me ex altera super portione quadam in ecclesia de Albo Monasterio quam Seysil' quondam tenuit auctoritate domini Assaph' et aliquamdiu ventilata, demum in octabis Beati Laurent(ii) coram magistris Ada filio D(avi)d et Ricardo Seys' vicem domini Asauens(is) gerentibus in hunc modum quievit; scilicet quod ego, audito iure dictorum abbatis et conventus in dicta portione et cognito ex inspectione munimentorum ipsorum, quicquid iuris credebam me habere in dicta portione resignavi in manus predictorum magistrorum A. et R. Resignavi etiam coram eisdem in iudicio omnibus impetratis et impetrandis super illa portione. Facta est autem hec resignatio anno ab incarnatione domini m° cc° xvii° in predicta ecclesia.

This document is included on the assumption that its author was the Hywel ap Madog ap Gruffudd attested elsewhere as one of the sons of Madog ap Gruffudd of Bromfield, although his name is not qualified by 'of Bromfield', in contrast to no. 523 below. If the identification is correct, Hywel was a young man when he issued the notification, as he lived for over another fifty years. The possibility that Hywel initially pursued a clerical career would be strengthened if he is also identifiable with the Hywel ap Gruffudd of Bromfield who was parson of Myddle, Shropshire, in 1232 (*PR 1225–32*, 457–8). For the widespread occurrence of portionary churches in Wales at this period see Palmer, 'Portionary churches'.

523 Letter patent concerning Henry III

Notification that has appointed himself a pledge for Senana wife of Gruffudd ap Llywelyn, and undertaken to the king on her behalf that she will firmly observe all she has agreed in the name of her husband respecting the liberation of himself and his son Owain from the prison in which his brother Dafydd detains them and respecting the portion which pertains to Gruffudd of the inheritance of his father Llywelyn, of which Dafydd deprives him. Sealing clause.

Shrewsbury, 12 August 1241

> B = TNA: PRO, E 36/274 (Liber A), fo. 332v. s. xiii ex.
> Pd. from B, *LW*, 15 (no. 10).
> Cd., *H*, no. 514.

[O]mnibus hoc scriptum visuris Hoel filius Madoc de Brumfeud salutem. Sciatis quod ego me constitui plegium Senane uxoris Griffini filii[a] L. quondam principis Norwall(ie) et manucepi pro ea erga dominum meum H. regem Angl(ie) illustrem quod omnia que conventionavit eidem domino meo nomine prefati viri sui pro liberatione sua et Oweyni[b] filii sui a carcere in quo David frater eius eos detinet et pro portione que ipsum G. contingit de hereditate que fuit predicti L. patris sui et quam prefatus D. frater eius ei deforciat, domino regi firmiter observabit. In cuius rei testimonium huic scripto sigillum meum apposui. Actum apud Salop' die lune proxima ante assumptionem Beate Marie anno regni ipsius domini regis vicesimo quinto.

[a] filius B. | [b] Oweynu(m) B.

See no. 284 above.

MADOG FYCHAN AP MADOG
(d. December 1269)

524 Letter patent concerning Henry III

Notification that he gives surety that Tudur ab Ednyfed will faithfully serve and adhere to the king and his heirs subject to a penalty of 50 marks. If Tudur should withdraw from his fealty to the king, Madog or his heirs will be bound to the king or his heirs to pay the said penalty at terms to be fixed by the king. Sealing clause.

[September 1246]

B = TNA: PRO, E 36/274 (Liber A), fo. 337v. s. xiii ex.
Pd. from B, *LW*, 30–1 (no. 40).
Cd., *H*, no. 515.

[U]niversis Cristi fidelibus has litteras visuris vel audituris Mad' Vechan filius Mad' quondam domini de Bromfeld salutem. Noverit universitas vestra quod nos fideiubemus et manucapimus pro Tuder filio Idneued quod fideliter serviet et adherebit domino regi et heredibus suis in posterum sub pena quinquaginta marcarum; si, quod absit, dictus Tud(er) a fidelitate domini regis recesserit, nos vel nostri heredes tenebimur domino regi vel suis heredibus ad solutionem dicte pene terminis a domino rege prefigendis. In cuius rei testimonium hiis litteris nostrum sigillum apponi fecimus.

As Edwards argued (*LW*, 31), this seems to refer to the terms for Tudur ab Ednyfed Fychan's release from prison; on 4 September 1246, at London, Tudur swore to serve the king faithfully and five days later, at Woodstock, he did homage to Henry for all his lands and promised to be faithful to him (*LW*, 50–2 (nos 77, 76)). Neither of the latter documents refers to the giving of sureties. The evidence for Tudur's imprisonment in 1245 and subsequent release is summarized in Stephenson, *Governance*, 219.

525 Letter patent concerning Llywelyn ap Gruffudd

Notification by Madog, together with Owain ap Bleddyn and Gruffudd ap Iorwerth, that they are sureties for Iorwerth ap Cynwrig Goch in respect of the £12 to be paid to Llywelyn ap Gruffudd at the following terms: £4 at the next feast of the Nativity of the Virgin [8 September], £4 at the following All Saints' Day [1 November] and £4 at the following feast of St Andrew the apostle [30 November]. Sealing clause.

July 1256

B = TNA: PRO, E 36/274 (Liber A), fo. 339r. s. xiii ex.
Pd. from B, *LW*, 35 (no. 50).
Cd., *H*, no. 517.

[U]niversis Cristi fidelibus presentes litteras visuris vel audituris Madoc(us) Wawan filius Madoci ab Griffin(us), Owen(us) filius Bledhyn et Griffin(us) filius Yoruerd salutem. Noverit universitas vestra nos esse fideiussores pro Yoru(er)ed filio Kenwric Goch de xii libris solvendis domino Lewelino filio Griffini terminis subscriptis, in proximo festo nativitatis Beate Virginis iiii libras, in festo omnium sanctorum sequenti iiii libras et in sequenti festo Beati Andree apostoli iiii libras. In cuius rei testimonium presentibus litteris sigilla nostra apposuimus. Datum anno domini m° cc° lvi^{to} mense iulii.

Madog's fellow sureties were his kinsmen Owain ap Bleddyn and Gruffudd ap Iorwerth, grandsons of Owain Brogyntyn, lords in Edeirnion and Dinmael. Iorwerth ap Cynwrig has not been otherwise identified.

MADOG FYCHAN AP GRUFFUDD
(d. 1277)

526 Lady Emma, their mother

Grant and confirmation by Madog, Llywelyn, Owain and Gruffudd sons of Gruffudd of all the lands and tenements which their father Gruffudd gave her in his lifetime, namely the land of Maelor Saesneg with its appurtenances, the manor of Overton with the mill, weir and all other appurtenances, the township of Hanmer with all its appurtenances, Llannerch-panna with its appurtenances, Knolton with its appurtenances and all townships within the bounds of Maelor Saesneg; the manor of Eyton in Maelor Gymraeg with the mill, park and all other appurtenances and two pieces of land in that park, one of which Hywel ap Madog bought from all the heirs of Erbistock, rendering them twelve gallons of ale or its value each year at Michaelmas [29 September], the other which the aforesaid heirs voluntarily handed over to Gruffudd, the grantors' father; and the township of Llanarmon [Llanarmon Dyffryn Ceiriog] with its appurtenances in Cynllaith together with the lands of Llwythder and Prestimand' *that their grandmother Iseult* (Ysota) *bought with the consent of their grandfather Madog and father Gruffudd from Cadwgan, Rhirid and Einion sons of Dwywg. All these lands with their appurtenances are to be held by Emma from the grantors and their heirs for her lifetime as freely as contained in the charters made for her by Gruffudd. Sealing clause; witnesses.*

Dinas Brân, 22 December 1270

B = TNA: PRO, C 145/35 (39). 1277.
Pd. from B, Seebohm, *Tribal System*, App. D, 105.
Cd., *CIM*, i, no. 1095; *H*, no. 238.

Sciant presentes et futuri quod nos Madocus, Lewelin(us), Owen(us), Griffinus filii Griffini domini de Bromfeld' concessimus et hac presenti carta nostra confirmavimus domine Emme matris nostre quoad vixerit omnes terras et omnia tenementa que dominus Griffin(us) pater noster in vita sua eidem dedit et concessit, videlicet patriam de Mailor Saisenec cum suis pertinentiis, manerium de Ou(er)ton' cum molendino et gurgite et omnibus aliis pertinentiis, villam de Hagnem(er)e cum suis pertinentiis, Lannerpanna cum suis pertinentiis, Colton' cum suis pertinentiis et omnes villas que infra limites patrie de Mailor Saisenec continentur, manerium de Eyton' in Mailor Kemerac cum molendino et parco et omnibus aliis pertinentiis et duabus particulis terre in dicto parco contentis, quarum unam emit dominus Houvelus filius Madoci de omnibus heredibus de Herbestoc, reddendo eisdem annuatim xii galones cervisie vel pretium earumdem ad festum Sancti Mich(ael)is, aliam vero particulam tradiderunt predicti heredes de Herbestoc sponte sua domino G. patri nostro, villam de Lanarmon cum suis pertinentiis in Kenlleiton' una cum terris illis quas domina Ysota avia nostra ex consensu domini Madoci avi nostri `et domini G. patris nostri emit de Cadegon et Ririt et Einon filiis Doyoc que vocantur Lloytteir et P(re)stimand', habenda et tenenda omnia predicta tenementa cum suis pertinentiis de nobis et heredibus nostris quoad vixerit prout liberius et melius continentur in cartis eidem a predicto G. patre nostro confectis. Et ut hec nostra concessio et presentis carte nostre confirmatio quoad vixerit rata permaneat presentem cartam sigillis nostris roboravimus. Hiis testibus: domino Aniano episcopo de Sancto Asaf, David decano de Bromfeld', fratre Kenewrike priore de Ruthlan,[a] domino Gervasio abbate de Valle Crucis, Nenneau filio

Ener, Baric filio Ener, Yaruorth Uoyl filio Yaruorth' Uauhan, Madoco Uauhan filio Madoci filii Oweyn, Blethint filio Yaruorth', Huua filio Yaruorth, Madoco filio Yeiuaf, Eynon filio Lewelini, Gorono filio Yaruorth, Lewelino filio Ener, Howelo filio David, Yeua filio Aur, Aur filio Yeiua, Meuric Vauhan, Ithel filio Gorono, Yaruorth filio Wyon, Yeua Vauhan et aliis. Datum [apud][b] Dynasbran in crastino Beati Thome apostoli anno domini m° cc° lxx°.

[a] Buthlan B. | [b] *omitted* B.

All the lands listed down to Llanarmon Dyffryn Ceiriog were granted to Emma by Gruffudd ap Madog in nos 515–16 above. Her son Llywelyn later seized Llanarmon, being forced to restore it twice; by his death he had made an agreement with Emma whereby he was allowed to hold it for his lifetime (nos 520–1 above). Llwythder was a township north-north-east of Llanarmon Dyffryn Ceiriog just across the river Ceiriog in the vicinity of Tower farm (Llwythder-uchaf SJ 162 333, Llwythder-isaf SJ 165 335). According to the jurors in the inquisition of 1277 at which the charter was produced as evidence, the present charter was confirmed by Llywelyn ap Gruffudd, prince of Wales, 'who confirmed all gifts' (Seebohm, *Tribal System*, App. D, 102; cf. Smith, 'Dower', 352). Lloyd suggested that the charter was probably issued shortly after Gruffudd's death and that this therefore possibly occurred in December 1270 rather than December 1269 as stated in *Brut y Tywysogyon* (*Owen Glendower*, 9 and n. 1). The place-date almost certainly refers to Gruffudd's new castle at Dinas Brân (SJ 222 431), situated on a hill north-east of Llangollen (King, 'Two castles', esp. 116, 130).

527 Agreement with William Beauchamp, earl of Warwick and Dafydd ap Gruffudd

Agreement for Madog's restoration to peace. Madog shall hold his land from the king in chief as his ancestors used to do and those tenants who sided with him may hold their lands and rights fully from him, so that he shall inflict no injury or harm on those who came to peace before him, all previous disputes between them being set aside entirely. Madog shall have as his share the land of Bromfield [Maelor Gymraeg] and its appurtenances and his brother Llywelyn shall have Nanheudwy with its appurtenances; the rest of their inheritance shall be divided equally between them. If the castle of Dinas Brân is captured by the forces of the king, the king shall be permitted either to demolish it or restore it to Madog; if the castle is restored to Madog by grant of the king or any other means, Madog shall be permitted to demolish it or keep it intact; if wishes to keep it, let him give his brother Llywelyn the value of the part of the castle pertaining to Llywelyn in land elsewhere according to the decision of Dafydd ap Gruffudd and Peter de Montfort. As Madog claims right in the land of Hope, and Dafydd makes a similar claim, it is agreed that the king shall keep that land in his hand until inquisition is made concerning their right by twelve worthy and lawful men of Cheshire and another twelve Welshmen suspect to neither party, and right shall be done according to the verdict of that inquisition. As Madog makes claims in the lands of Kinnerley, Croesfaen, Penllyn Is Meloch and Deuddwr, it is agreed by this peace that the king shall be obliged to do what is just to him in this regard. It is also agreed that the king shall remit entirely all trespasses committed by Madog and his men, and Madog shall remit all trespasses against him and his men. If Llywelyn ap Gruffudd happens to eject Madog from his land, the king shall be obliged to

provide aid for the maintenance of himself together with houses to live in until he is able to
return to his own land in peace. The duplicates of this document have been sealed reciprocally.

Chester, 21 April 1277

B = TNA: PRO, E 36/274 (Liber A), fos 345v–346r. s. xiii ex.
Pd. from B, *LW*, 53–4 (no. 79).
Cd., *H*, no. 519.

Hec est conventio facta inter Will(elmu)m de Bello Campo comitem Warr' et David filium
Griffini ex parte una et Madocu(m) de Bromfeud ex altera de pacis reformatione ipsius
Madoci, videlicet quod idem Madoc(us) teneat terram suam de domino rege in capite sicut
antecessores sui tenere solebant[a] et quod tenentes illi qui ad partem suam acciderint integre
terras et iura sua de ipso teneant, ita tamen quod ipsis qui ad [fo. 346r] pacem prius quam
ipse Madoc(us) venerunt dampnum, molestiam vel gravamen non inferat, omnibus inter
eos contentionibus hactenus habitis penitus remissis. Et quod dictus Madoc(us) habeat ad
propartem suam terram de Bromfeud cum pertinentiis, et quod Lewelin(us) frater suus
habeat Nanheudoy cum pertinentiis, et residuum hereditatis eorum inter eos equaliter
dividatur. Et si contingat quod castrum de Dynasbran per posse domini regis capiatur,
extunc liceat domino regi ipsum prosternere vel dicto Madoco restituere, et si castrum illud
extraditione domini regis vel alio quoquo modo eidem Madoco restituatur liceat eidem
Madoco ipsum prosternere vel integrum tenere; quod si ipsum tenere voluerit extunc faciat
Lewelino fratri suo extensionem partis castri ipsum Lewelinu(m) contingentem in terra alibi
per considerationem David filii Griffini et domini Pet(ri) de Monte Forti. Et quia dictus
Madoc(us) clamat ius in terra de Hope, ac dictus David clamium similiter apponit, ex hoc
ita convenit quod dominus rex terram illam in manu sua teneat quousque per xii[cim] probos
et legales homines de comitatu Cestr(ie) et alios xii[cim] Walenses utrique parti non suspectos
per ipsum dominum regem de iure eorum inquiratur, et secundum illius inquisitionis
veredictum fiat ius utrique eorum. Preterea cum dictus Madoc(us) clamium apponat in
quibusdam terris, scilicet Kynardynlle et Croesvaen et Penllinhismeloch et Dewdwer,
convenit ita per pacem istam quod dominus rex id quod iustum fuerit in hiis eidem Madoco
facere teneatur. Convenit etiam quod dominus rex omnes transgressiones sibi per predictum
Madocum et suos hactenus illatas penitus remittat, et quod idem Madoc(us) remittat
quicquid ei et suis transgressum fuerit. Et si contingat quod Lewelin(us) filius Griffini
dictum Madocu(m) a terra sua eiciat, quod dominus rex extunc eidem Madoco auxilium
sustentationi sue una cum domibus inhabitandis providere teneatur donec ad propria
pacifice redire poterit. In quorum omnium testimonium presentibus inter eos dupplicatis
sigilla sua mutuo sunt appensa. Datum et actum apud Cest(riam) xii die aprilis anno regni
regis Edwardi quinto.

[a] solent B.

Madog was compelled to make this agreement after royal forces under the earl of Warwick
and Dafydd ap Gruffudd advanced on Powys Fadog from Chester in the spring of 1277,
thereby posing the threat of disinheritance in favour of his younger brother Llywelyn, who
had submitted to the crown in late December 1276 (*CPR 1272–81*, 186; Smith, *Llywelyn*,
423–4). Resistance continued at Dinas Brân until 10 May, when the garrison set the castle
on fire in the face of an impending assault by the earl of Lincoln; the castle was then

abandoned (ibid., 424). The agreement entailed a new division of Powys Fadog, different from that made after the death of Gruffudd ap Madog both in the portions allocated to Madog and Llywelyn and in its exclusion of their brothers Owain and Gruffudd, who later sought to defend their interests by challenging the original division before the royal justices in November 1277 and February 1278 (*WAR*, 246–8). Smith has suggested that under the terms of the original division Madog held the greater part of Powys Fadog, together with Dinas Brân, symbol of the principality's unity, as the result of *parage*, and that the present agreement, which reduced his share to Llywelyn's advantage and raised the possibility of Dinas Brân's destruction, reflected the great political pressures he faced by April 1277 ('Dynastic succession', 229 and n. 3). Peter de Montfort, a prominent Warwickshire baron close to the king with strong Shropshire connections, was among those granted protection on 2 February 1277 until midsummer while in Wales on the king's service; it may be significant in the present context that he was a brother-in-law of James Audley (d. 1272) and thus also of Madog ap Gruffudd's mother Emma Audley (Cox, 'County government', 15–16, 31; Prestwich, *Edward I*, 22, 25, 38; *CPR 1272–81*, 191). Presumably the inquisition concerning Hope found in favour of Dafydd ap Gruffudd, who was granted Hope and Estyn by the king on 23 August 1277 (*CPR 1272–81*, 227; for subsequent disputes over the land between Dafydd and William Venables of Chester see nos 452–3 above). Of the other lands claimed by Madog, Kinnerley is located just south of Knockin, and Croesfaen (alternatively known as Ruyton of the Eleven Towns) lies about 8 miles south-east of Oswestry at SJ 395 222, Penllyn Is Meloch was the part of the commote of Penllyn north of the river Tryweryn, abutting at one point onto Edeirnion, and Deuddwr a commote between Ystrad Marchell and Oswestry. For problems faced by Madog shortly after this agreement see no. 445 above.

MARGARET, WIFE OF MADOG FYCHAN AP GRUFFUDD
(*fl. c.*1241–84)

528 Petition to the king
She took the manor of Eyton at farm from the wife of Gruffudd ap Madog for 10 marks per annum for the term of her life, and the earl of Warenne has disseised her of it and keeps her out wrongfully. She therefore prays the king to do her right, and [(?)likewise] regarding the township of Sontley, for which she has a good charter and from which the earl keeps her out wrongfully.

Further prays the king to do her right regarding Gruffudd Fychan, who keeps her out of two townships, namely Corwen and Cilmaen-llwyd, for which she has good charters from the same Gruffudd.

[12 February 1283 × May 1284]

A = TNA: PRO, SC 8/168, no. 8393B. Endorsed (1): Ista mulier tant[um] dereliquid versus regem quod rex non tenetur facere ei gratiam set perquirat versus comitem rex de dicta terra (s. xiii ex); (2) Griffinus dicat quod habet terras de traditione domini unde (?)sine domine . . .ᵃ [(?)provi]der' (s. xiii ex); approx. 181 × 51 mm.
Cd., *CAP*, 287; *H*, no. 520.

Margerete ke fu la femme Madauk Vechan prist a ferme le manere de Eyton' de la femme Griffin ab Madawc pur x mars par an a terme de vie, e le cunte de Waran la ad desseysi e la tent hors a tort. Dunc ele pri nostre seynur le rey ke il la face dreytur, e …[b] une vile ke ad `a nun Sonly de quele ele ad bone charte e le cunte la tent hors a tort.

Derechef ele prie nostre seynur le rey ke il le face dreyt de Griffin le Petit ke la tent hors de ii viles, çoe est asaver Corvain e Kylmainloyt, de queles ele ad bone charteres de meme celi Griffin.

[a] *one illegible word* A. | [b] *an illegible word followed by* de i *dotted underneath for expunction* A.

Since the second endorsement states that Gruffudd claimed to hold the disputed land by royal grant, the petition can be no earlier than 12 February 1283, when, at Warenne's request, Gruffudd Fychan was granted Glyndyfrdwy – in which Corwen and Cilmaenllwyd (near Carrog) were located – as a tenant at will of the king (*CWR*, 266; cf. Lloyd, *Owen Glendower*, 10). John de Warenne (d. 1304), earl of Surrey, was granted Maelor and Iâl by Edward I on 7 October 1282, thereby becoming the first Marcher lord of Bromfield and Yale (*CWR*, 240). Both Eyton and Sontley, about 2 miles north-west of it at SJ 331 468, were located in Maelor Gymraeg. Margaret refers to her agreement with Emma, widow of Madog ap Gruffudd of Bromfield, in November 1277, by which she received Eyton from her at farm for 10 marks per annum (5 marks at Easter, 5 marks at Michaelmas); this followed Margaret's quitclaim of the manor to Emma resulting from the latter's successful claim to it as her dower before the justices at Oswestry, where she alleged that Llywelyn ap Gruffudd had seized it during the war and granted it to Madog Fychan ap Gruffudd, who had in turn enfeoffed Margaret with it as dower (*WAR*, 245–6; no. 517 above; for Gruffudd ap Madog's grant to Emma of Eyton, in Maelor Gymraeg, in 1268 × 1269 see no. 516 above). Margaret claimed half of Glyndyfrdwy as her dower from Gruffudd, to whom Llywelyn ap Gruffudd had granted it, at the same sessions at Oswestry in November 1277 (*WAR*, 246). This suggests that Gruffudd had not obeyed Edward I's order from Chester on 18 July 1277 to allow Margaret to hold half of Glyndyfrdwy, which her husband Madog had assigned to her for life (*CCR 1272–9*, 399).

The present petition does not appear to be the same as Margaret's claim to these lands, against the same parties, in the chancery at Aberconwy on 27 May 1284, as on that occasion she argued that she had received the lands as dower, whereas here her claim rested on charters, without reference to dower; in addition, the claim in May 1284 referred to Cilmaenllwyd as Hafod Cilmaenllwyd (*Hawoth Kylimanllwynt*) (*CCR 1279–88*, 297). The substantive difference is significant: in May 1284 Margaret based her claim to the lands on the same grounds as those given in November 1277, even though she had eventually conceded then that Eyton rightfully belonged to Emma. The petition, by contrast, claimed the lands by virtue of charters granted by Emma and Gruffudd Fychan. Although the significance of this contrast for dating the petition is difficult to assess, the petition is probably earlier than the claim presented at Aberconwy. On 30 May 1284, presumably in response to that claim, Edward granted Margaret 5 marks per annum out of charity (*CWR*, 285; cf. *CAP*, 288, which interprets this as a sign of the king's hostility to Margaret). It is unlikely that this grant had been made when the first endorsement was written, stating that 'This woman has offended the king so greatly that he is not obliged to do her favour but let the king inquire of the earl concerning the said land'.

GRUFFUDD FYCHAN AP GRUFFUDD
(d. 1289)

529 The church of St Asaph

Grant, made voluntarily in good health, with the consent of his co-heirs and nobles, for the salvation of the souls of himself and his ancestors and successors, of all the land within these bounds: from the old boundary of the township of Llanedegla towards the southern part of that township to the stream called Geneth *in Welsh, and along this in breadth in the western part of that land, and in length towards the east to the other stream called Nant yr Erw* Fordin *in Welsh, and in the breadth of that headland across from that place on the mountain of* Darvant *which [extends] from the northern part of that land which can be ploughed easily without (?)heath to the said stream of* Geneth *– both the cultivated and uncultivated land within those bounds with their appurtenances. The bishop and his successors may turn the uncultivated land there to cultivation without any hindrance, as they see fit, and may do as they wish with all the land within the aforesaid bounds, saving that if they extend their cultivation towards the said mountain of* Barnauc *to the (?)heath beyond that now in cultivation, they may not make any enclosures round their crops there nor restrict the dykes or pastures of others beyond a breadth of one middling acre, whose breadth shall be estimated by good and lawful men if there is any doubt concerning it. He wishes that the pastures and turbaries on both sides of the aforesaid mountain shall be common as they used to be from of old for the men of the bishop as for his own men. Further grant that the bishop and his successors may have the wood within the aforesaid bounds reserved for their use, to be held with its appurtenances as freely as he and his predecessors held it in past times, so that by this gift the boundaries of other lands, commotes or parishes are not changed at all. Sealing clause; witnesses.*

'On the land itself', 9 February 1278

B = NLW, MS Peniarth 231B, pp. 87–9. s. xvii[1]. Rubric: Transcriptum donationis terre de Botidris. Pd. from NLW, SA/MB/2 (*c.*1700), fo. 18r–v, a transcript of NLW, MS 7011D (s. xvii), p. 45, which in turn was copied from B, Willis, *Survey of St Asaph*, ii. 28–30 (on the relationship between these transcripts see Evans, 'Llyfr Coch Asaph', 181–2; Jones, 'Llyfr Coch Asaph', i. xiv, xxii); from abbreviated text in NLW, SA/MB/2, fo. 40r, Anon, 'Index to "Llyfr Coch Asaph"', 329.
Cd., *H*, no. 239.

In Dei nomine amen. Sciant presentes et futuri quod anno incarnationis dominice mcclxxviii[a] feria v[a] quinto videlicet idus februarii ego Griffin(us) Vychan filius Griffin' ab Mad' dominus de Yal, in bona corporis mei sanitate ex mera et spontanea voluntate mea, de assensu benivolo et voluntate coheredum et nobilium hominum meorum et procerum, do et concedo per presentes pro salute anime mee [et][b] antecessorum et successorum meorum Deo et ecclesie cathedrali de Sancto Assaph et venerabili patri domino A. Dei gratia eiusdem loci episcopo et suis successoribus episcopis qui pro tempore fuerint in ecclesia predicta Assavens(i) totam terram sitam infra terminos subscriptos, videlicet a termino ville de Llandegla antiquo versus australem partem ipsius ville usque ad rivulum qui Wallice dicitur Geneth, et hoc in latitudine in parte occidentali ipsius terre, et extendit se versus orientem in longitudinem usque ad alium rivulum qui Wallice dicitur [p. 88] Nant yr Erw Fordin, et in latitudine illius capitis terre extendit se ab illo loco montis Darvant qui ex parte aquilonari illius terre que commode arari poterit sine brueto[c] usque ad dictum rivulum Geneth, tam terram inibi nunc cultam quam non cultam infra terminos predictos cum eius pertinentiis, ita videlicet quod dictus dominus episcopus et successores sui predicti in ecclesia Assavens(i) terram inibi non cultam redigere valeant ad culturam sine quovis impedimento, prout sibi viderint expedite, et de tota illa terra infra terminos predictos contenta commodum suum facere pro suo libito voluntatis, salvo quod si versus dictum montem Barnauc culturam suam amplicaverint usque ad bruetum[d] ultra id quod nunc consistit in terra culta nequeant aliquas circa sata sua ibidem clausuras facere vel fossata et aliorum pasturas restringere ultra latitudinem unius acre mediocris, cuius latitudo si super eam dubium oriatur per bonos viros et legitimos debet fideliter estimari. Pasturas si quidem ex utraque parte montis predicti et turbarias hominibus dicti domini episcopi et successorum suorum dictorum sicut hominibus nostris propriis volumus et concedimus esse communes prout esse consueverunt ab antiquo. Concedimus insuper dicto domino episcopo et suis successoribus predictis quod nemus infra terminos predictos situm ad libitum suum custodiri [p. 89] faciant motu suo, habendum et tenendum cum suis pertinentiis tam libere et quiete sicut nos et nostri predecessores eam liberius tenuimus temporibus retroactis, ita tamen quod per hanc nostram donationem limites aliarum terrarum, commotorum seu parochiarum nullatenus immutentur. Et ut hec nostra donatio et concessio robur optineat perpetue firmitatis eam sigilli mei impressione duximus roborandum. Hiis testibus: Mareduco filio Lewel' ballivo nostro de Yal, Goronv filio Iorverth Goch, Gruffud ap Ior' ap Run, Lewel' ap Yeuaf, fratre Iuoro[e] priore de Rudlan, Ioh(ann)e Penbed', Ednevet[f] Du filio Ior' et multis aliis. Datum super ipsam terram v idus februarii anno prescripto.

[a] 1278 B. | [b] *omitted* B. | [c] *sic in* B (*?for* bruario). | [d] *sic in* B (*?for* bruarium). | [e] B *inserts* de *struck through*. | [f] B *inserts* filio Ior' d *struck through*.

Llandegla (SJ 196 524) lay in the centre of the commote of Iâl. According to Robert Vaughan's rubric in B, the land granted was called Bodidris, a name preserved in Bodidris Hall, north-east of Llandegla at SJ 205 536. Possibly *Darvant/Barnauc* was the mountain to the east of Llandegla now known as Moel Garegog. Bishop *A.* of St Asaph was Anian II (1268–93); he subsequently made an agreement with certain tenants of Llandegla on 8 June 1278 (NLW, MS Peniarth 231B, p. 166; Jones, 'Llyfr Coch Asaph', i. 76). Dominicans had been established at Rhuddlan by 1258; the witness Brother Ifor undertook various administrative duties following the Treaty of Aberconwy (Roberts, *Aspects of Welsh History*, 217, 222–3).

530 Edward I

Letter, stating that, since Margaret widow of Madog Fychan, lady of Bromfield, harasses him excessively by bringing actions against him sometimes before the king's justices, sometimes before Llywelyn, prince of Wales, over certain lands and tenements of Glyndyfrdwy in Edeirnion which he holds in chief from the prince with the king's consent, he humbly requests the king to advise him before whom he is obliged to answer in the said matter. He knows that if he answers before the king's justices concerning the said lands that he holds in chief of Llywelyn, the prince may confiscate them for contempt of his court as he is able to do by right if wishes; but if he does not answer before the justices, he fears that they or Margaret will

somehow turn the king against him. Gruffudd therefore requests that he and the justices be
informed of the king's will in this matter.

[*c*.September × *c*.December 1279]

A = TNA: PRO, SC 1/21, no. 31. No endorsements; approx. 183 × 66 mm.; sixteen sets of double
slits for insertion of a tongue or tag; mounted, approx. 44 × 9 mm. of foot cut away on right.
Cd., *CAC*, 107; *H*, no. 525.

Viro magnifico ac excellenti domino suo E. Dei gratia illustri regi Angl(ie), domino
Hib(er)nie, duci Aquitann(ie) suus devotus Griffinus Vachan dominus de Yal salutem et
paratum in omnibus famulatum. Quoniam Margareta relicta Madoci Vachan domina de
Bromfeld nos fatigare ultra modum trahendo nos in causam quandoque coram vestris iusticiariis et quandoque coram domino Lewelino principe Wallie super quibusdam terris et
tenementis de Glynndyuyrdue in Edeirnyaun quas per vestram licenciam per concessionem
et donationem dicti principis de eodem tenemus in capite, id[eo rogam]us[a] inclitam dominationem vestram humiliter et attente quatinus nobis in hac parte consulere dignemini coram
quo teneamur in dicto negocio respondere, scientes quod si de dictis terris quas de prefato
principe tenemus in capite coram dictis vestris iusticiariis in suum preiudicium responde-
bimus, dubitamus ne dictus princeps dictas terras nobis auferat propter fori sui
contemptum sicut de iure poterit si voluerit; si autem coram iusticiariis vestris non respon-
debimus, timemus ne ipsi vel dicta Margareta procurent quoquo modo contra nos movere
vestram animam, quod absit. Voluntatem igitur vestram in premissis dictis iusticiariis ac
nobis rescribere velitis. Valeat excellencia vestra diu in domino.

[a] *letters supplied where parchment torn* A.

Edwards argued (*CAC*, 107) that the letter was sent not long before no. 416 above (10
October 1279), which shows that the king had allowed the case to go to Llywelyn's court as
the disputed lands were held from the prince, and that the hearing was held on 28
September 1279, with another day fixed for a subsequent hearing. However, no. 418 above
(15 December 1279) shows that Margaret procured a letter summoning Gruffudd to
Montgomery on the day after that fixed by Llywelyn for that second hearing, and this
provides an equally, if not more, plausible context for the present letter. Gruffudd Fychan
was allowed to hold Edeirnion from the prince in the Treaty of Aberconwy (no. 402, c. xiv
above). Margaret had claimed lands from Gruffudd in Glyndyfrdwy since November 1277
and continued to do so until at least May 1284 (no. 528 above and note).

531 John de Warenne, earl of Surrey and Sussex

Grant and quitclaim on behalf of himself and his heirs of all the land of Iâl with all renders,
services and customs of free tenants, villeins and villein services of that land and all its other
appurtenances, rights and liberties which he ever had in inheritance from his father Gruffudd,
so that neither he nor his heirs may be able to claim any right in future in the aforesaid land
and appurtenances against the earl, his heirs or any others holding the lands or appurtenances.
Sealing clause; witnesses.

[Probably January × 12 February 1283]

B = TNA: PRO, C 54/100 (Close R. 11 Edward I), m. 9d (contemporary enrolment).
Cd., *CCR 1279–88*, 229; *H*, no. 241.

Omnibus Cristi fidelibus presens scriptum visuris vel audituris Griffinus Vaughan filius Griffini de Bromfeud' salutem in domino sempiternam. Noveritis me concessisse, remisisse et imperpetuum pro me et heredibus meis quietum clamasse nobili viro Ioh(ann)i de Warenn' comiti Surr' et Sussex' et heredibus suis totam terram et tenementum de Yal cum omnibus redditibus et servitiis et consuetudinibus libere tenentium, villanis et villenagiis terre eiusdem et omnibus aliis pertinentiis suis, iuribus et libertatibus ad predictas terras et tenementa redditus et servitia, villanos et villenagia qualitercumque spectantibus que aliquando habui in proprietatem hereditatis predicti Griffinis patris mei me contingentem, ita quod nec ego nec heredes mei in dictis terra et tenemento redditibus vel servitiis, villanis vel villenagiis vel aliqua eorum parte cum pertinentiis suis versus prefatum comitem vel heredes suos vel quoscumque alios dictam terram et tenementum redditus et servitia, villanos et villenagia vel eorum partem cum pertinentiis suis tenentes, quicquam iuris vel clamis in posterum apponere vel vendicare seu quoquo modo clamare possimus. In cuius rei testimonium presenti scripto sigillum meum apposui. Hiis testibus: Galfrido de Neuill', Thoma de Chaworth', Adriano filio Alani, Guncel' de Badelosmor', Anselmo de Gyse, Will(elm)o Peyforer, Will(elm)o de Chaworth', Saero de Huntingfeud, Edmu(n)do de Deyncurt, Ioh(ann)e de Haueresham, Walt(er)o de Sancto Martino, Ioh(ann)e le Tieys militibus et multis aliis.

Although many of the documents, including the present one, enrolled on the dorse of m. 9 of the close roll are undated, one of those preceding Gruffudd's quitclaim is dated 11 January 1283 and the first of those following it which have dates are dated 15 and 20 February 1283 respectively (*CCR 1279–88*, 228–31). The documents on m. 9 are dated between 23 November 1282 and 12 January 1283, those on m. 8 between 29 January and 23 March 1283 (ibid., 197–204). The quitclaim is probably no later than 12 February 1283, when, at Warenne's request, the king granted Gruffudd Glyndyfrdwy to be held at will, presumably as compensation for the loss of Iâl, granted to Warenne by the king on 7 October 1282 (*CWR*, 240; see also no. 532 below).

532 Letter patent concerning Edward I

Notification that, since the king has granted, at the request of John de Warenne, earl of Surrey, that he may hold the land of Glyndyfrdwy from the king at his will, on condition that Gruffudd will issue a document acknowledging that he has no hereditary right in holding the said land except at the king's will, he wishes all to know that he claims nothing in the aforesaid land except at the king's will. He has made this letter patent as testimony of this.

Llanegwestl [Valle Crucis] Abbey, 4 March 1283

B = TNA: PRO, C 54/100 (Close R. 11 Edward I), m. 8d (contemporary enrolment).
Cd., *CCR 1279–88*, 231; *H*, no. 527.

Omnibus Cristi fidelibus ad quos presentes littere pervenerint Griffinus Vaghan filius Griffini filii Madoci salutem in domino sempiternam. Sciatis quod cum dominus noster Edwardus Dei gratia rex Angl(ie) illustris ad requisitionem nobilis viri domini Ioh(ann)is de Warenna comiti Surr' concesserit michi Griffino quod teneam terram de Glindou(er)do de ipso domino rege ad voluntatem suam, ita tamen quod ego Griffinus inde eidem domino regi faciam litteras meas per quas fatear me nullum ius hereditarie in tenantia predicte terre nisi ad voluntatem ipsius domini regis, scire vos omnes et singulos volo quod nichil aliud in predicta terra clamo nec clamare potero nisi ad voluntatem predicti domini nostri regis sicut predictum est. In cuius rei testimonium has litteras meas eidem domino regi fieri feci patentes. Data in abbatia de Thlanegustel' iiii^to die martii anno gratie m° cc° octogesimo secundo regni autem predicti domini nostri regi undecimo.

The king's grant of Glyndyfrdwy at will was made on 12 February 1283 (*CWR*, 266). Gruffudd remained a tenant at will for the lands until his death in 1289, notwithstanding an abortive attempt in July 1284 to secure letters patent granting his lands by barony (Lloyd, *Owen Glendower*, 10 and n. 5).

LLYWELYN AP GRUFFUDD AP MADOG
(d. 11 December 1282)

533 Edward I
Letter, praying that, as William Butler proposes to despoil Llywelyn's men of a certain piece of land between Maelor Saesneg and William's land, the king will write to his bailiffs of Shrewsbury ordering that Llywelyn's land may be as it was in the time of his father and grandfather, or else that it may remain common pasture until the king inquires into the truth. Thanks the king greatly for honouring the bearer of this letter, who is Llywelyn's kinsman, with countless pennies; the king may have certain faith in him.

[1277 × March 1282]

A = TNA: PRO, SC 1/19, no. 40. No endorsement; approx. 198 × 27 mm.; six sets of double slits for insertion of a tongue or tag; mounted, foot cut away.
Cd., *CAC*, 97; *H*, no. 522.

E. Dei gratia regi Aglie,^a domino Ibernie, domino Aq(ui)tannie L. filius G(ri)fini de Bru(m)fyld salutem, reverenciam et honorem. Super hoc, domine rex reverande, quod Wylelm(us) dy Butiler de quadam particula terre que iacet inter Maelaur Saesnec et patriam dicti Wylelmi meos homines proponit spoliare, vestram reverensiam^a dignum duco exorandam quatenus vestras literas ad vestros ballivos de Salobsburia destinare dignemini ut dicta terra sit amodo nostra ut ucusque in tempore patris mei nedum etiam avi fuit, alioquin in comunem pascuam permaneat quousque veritatem inquiratis. Insuper grates ago honori vestro multimodas eo quod latorem presencium nedum et meum consanguineum innumerabilibus denariis honorastis. Valete fidem ei adibentes indubiam.

^a *sic in* A.

The letter is datable to between Llywelyn's submission to the king at the end of December 1276 and the outbreak of war in March 1282. William Butler (d. 1283) was the eldest son of Ralph Butler (d. 1281) and Matilda Pantulf, heiress of Wem, Shropshire. Although

William had no interests in Wem, he held Loppington (SJ 471 293), about 2 miles to its west and about 3 miles south of Bettisfield in the southern tip of Maelor Saesneg; presumably the reference to William's *patria* was to Loppington, rather than to his other holding at Doddington, located about 5 miles east of Ludlow and thus considerably farther away from Maelor Saesneg (see Eyton, *Shropshire*, ix. 169–73; Sanders, *Baronies*, 94–5; *CIPM*, ii. 319–20 (no. 529)). On 2 October 1261 William was granted permission by the king to marry Angharad (*Ankeretta*), niece of James Audley (*CPR 1258–66*, 177; cf. Eyton, *Shropshire*, ix. 173, for a reference to her as *Ageharet* in assizes of 1292). As James Audley was a brother of Emma, Llywelyn's mother, and since the niece bore a Welsh name, it is possible that Angharad was a daughter of Gruffudd ap Madog and Emma; if so, William was Llywelyn's brother-in-law.

›

534 Petition to the king

Seeks remedy since, though he and his ancestors held the wood of Lledrod with its lands, tenements, meadows and other surroundings freely and in peace together with houses built on the said lands, the men of Oswestry and their neighbours, driven by greed, occupied the aforesaid wood with its lands, tenements, meadows and other surroundings without any cause, and similarly appropriate the court which belonged to him and his ancestors at Lledrod and harvested the corn growing on the said lands and carried it away. Although Llywelyn had been impleaded by the aforesaid men for the aforesaid wood, he was not impleaded at all for the aforesaid lands, tenements, meadows, houses and court.

[1277 × March 1282]

A = TNA: PRO, SC 8/192, no. 9565. No endorsement; approx. 183 × 37 mm.
Cd., *CAP*, 319–20; *H*, no. 523.

Lewelinus filius Griffini de Brumfeld petit remedium super eo quod cum ipse et antecessores sui temporibus retroactis boscum de Lederod cum terris, tenementis, pratis et aliis circumstantibus libere et in pace cum domibus super dictis terris edificatis optinuerent, ac homines de Albo Monast(er)io et eorum convicini cupiditate inducti predictum boscum cum terris, tenementis, pratis et aliis circumstantibus sine aliqua causa sibi apropriaverunt et occupaverunt, et curiam que sua fuit et antecessorum suorum apud Ledrod similiter apropriarunt[a] et blada in dictis terris crescentia messuerunt et asportaverunt. Tamen licet predictus Lewelinus per predictos homines de bosco predicto fuisset implacitatus, de terris ˋautem , tenementis, pratis, domibus et curia predictis nullatenus fuit implacitatus.

[a] *sic in* A.

The petition is datable to between Llywelyn's submission to the king at the end of December 1276 and the outbreak of war in March 1282. Lledrod was located in Cynllaith, about 1½ miles north-east of Llansilin; the name is given to two farms (SJ 215 303 and SJ 224 297) and to the hill called Mynydd Lledrod (SJ 216 309). It was therefore different from the wood of Coedgaer, located about 1 mile south-east of Lledrod, which was the subject of another dispute between Llywelyn and the men of Oswestry (see note to no. 536 below). For further complaints concerning Lledrod see nos 535, 538 below.

535 Edward I

Letter, stating that, as the king knows, a dispute has arisen between the sons of John fitz Alan of Oswestry and Llywelyn over certain woods which Llywelyn's ancestors had and which he, his father, grandfather and great grandfather possessed by hereditary right; moreover they have unjustly taken over Llywelyn's land adjoining the said woods, attacked the houses of his villeins, cut down and carried away the crops, plundered and totally destroyed his court and inflicted many other injuries on him. Llywelyn therefore prays the king to come to his assistance with justice. The king should not believe the paternal and maternal kin of those at Oswestry as they are not impartial between the latter and Llywelyn; nor should credence be given to the vassals and tenants of those at Oswestry. In addition the Welsh from whom Llywelyn withdrew during the king's war do not grieve greatly but rather rejoice at Llywelyn's trouble and molestation. Llywelyn has no other support than the king, from whom he seeks special remedy as his special protector and lord. Asks the king to state his will regarding these and other matters.

[1277 × March 1282]

A = TNA: PRO, SC 1/19, no. 41. No endorsement; approx. 176 × 59 mm.; mounted; approx. 90 × 9 mm. of foot cut away on right.
Cd., *CAC*, 98.

Illustrissimo domino suo domino E. Dei gratia regi Angl(i)e, domino Hyb(er)nie, duci Aquitan(nie) suus in omnibus fidelis Lewelinus filius Griffini filii Madoci salutem, obedientiam, reverentiam et ad genua famulatum. Quia sicut innotuit excellencie vestre inter nobiles viros filios Ioh(ann)is filii Alani heredes de Albo Mon(asterio) et me vestrem super quibusdam silvis controversia fuit orta, quas silvas habuerunt antecessores mei et iure hereditario possiderunt[a] ab antiquo ego, silicet[a] pater meus, avus et atavus, insuper terram meam predictis silvis contiguam sibi appropriaverunt et hoc iniuste et sine equitate, item domos villanorum nostrorum invaserunt, sagetes fallcaverunt et asportaverunt, curiam meam dirripuerunt et funditer everterunt et multas alias molestias mihi intulerunt, supplico vestre excellencie et reverencie quatinus in vestro fideli viro iustitia mediante subvenire velitis, scientes pro veritate quod non debetis fidem adhibere cognatis illorum de Albo Mon(asterio) ex parte patris et ex parte matris quia inter me et illos non sunt communes; item vassallis eorum et terram tenentibus de eisdem non est fides contra me adhibenda. Preterea Wallences a quibus recessi tempore werre vestre non multum dolent set gaudent de vexatione mea et gravi molestia. Ideo quia non est mihi succurssus ab alio requirendo nisi a vobis domino meo, ad vos tanquam ad tutorem et dominum meum specialem dirigo gressus paupertatis mee petens a vobis remedium speciale. Beneplacitum vestrum si placet super hiis et aliis mihi constare velitis.

[a] *sic in* A.

This refers to the same circumstances as no. 534 above and may be assigned to the same date range. John fitz Alan III of Oswestry died in 1272; his son and heir Richard I (d. 1302) came of age in 1287 (Sanders, *Baronies*, 71).

536 Petition to the king

Informs the king concerning his plea at the recent parley at Oswestry that he received there neither the law of Wales nor the ancient custom of his kin and the king's ancestors in the March of Oswestry, but only what he will narrate in this document.

First, at the suggestion of certain of his enemies an inquisition was made against him, which was never done in the time of his and the king's ancestors, by the men of Ellesmere; these are his enemies as they are men of Roger Lestrange, who acts as bailiff at Oswestry, and no trust ought rightfully to be shown them.

Second, they [i.e. the men of Ellesmere] admitted against him the men of Whittington, who are his enemies and claim other lands that are rightfully his, whom he neither proposes nor ought to trust.

Third, they similarly admitted against him men of John Lestrange of Knockin, who are his enemies, as John Lestrange was obliged to give homage to John fitz Alan and is the son of Roger Lestrange's brother and Roger is bailiff in the district of Oswestry; because of this Llywelyn would not have been obliged to trust them.

It is not surprising that he was by no means willing to endure this inquisition, held in his absence.

Further states that those justices who were there on behalf of the king in other causes, namely Hywel ap Meurig and Walter of Bedewardyn, *were advocates against him in that cause and by no means colleagues and counsellors of the king's justice Walter de Hopton.*

Concerning Walter de Hopton, though he may be a just and faithful man, it was related to Llywelyn that he was obliged to give homage to Roger Mortimer and John fitz Alan; if that was true, Llywelyn would not accept him as judge.

Prays for the sake of God, his faithful service and the king's justice that the king will let him have either the law of Wales, as the king granted him previously, or the ancient custom of his ancestors and the possessors of Oswestry in the cause between him and the hundred of Oswestry.

[14 January 1279 × November 1281; probably 14 January × c.February 1279]

A = TNA: PRO, SC 8/196, no. 9770. No endorsement; approx. 149 mm. wide at top, 137 mm. wide at bottom × 257 mm. deep.
Cd., *CAP*, 325–6; *H*, no. 518.

Significat devote domino suo regi Lewelin(us) filius Grifini de Bromfeld' ligius et fidelis suus de placito suo in parliamento nuper aput Album Monast(erium) quod ipse non habuit ibidem legem Wallie neque antiquam consuetudinem parentum suorum et vestrorum antecessorum in partibus Marchie Albi Monast(erii) nisi secundum quod vobis in sedila[a] ista narrabimus.

Primo. Ex sugestione quorumdam adversariorum nostrorum inquisicio facta fuit contra nos, quod nunquam fuit temporibus antecessorum vestrorum videlicet et nostrorum, de hominibus de Ellesm'; adversarii nostri qui homines sunt domini Rog(er)i Ext(ra)nei, qui quidem Rog(er)us est in loco ballivi aput Albu(m) Monast(erium), quibus nullam fidem de iure debetur exhiberi.

Secundo. Quod ipsi[b] receperunt contra nos homines de Witintun qui quidem sunt adversarii nostri et calumpniant nos de terris aliis de iure nostro, quibus fidem minime adhibere proponimus neque debemus.

Tercio. Quod ipsi receperunt similiter contra nos adversarios nostros, videlicet homines domini Ioh(ann)is Ext(ra)nei de Crowkyn, ita quod dictus Ioh(ann)es Ext(ra)neus homagium suum deberet reddere domino Ioh(ann)i filio Alani et quod antedictus Ioh(ann)es est filius fratris domini Rog(er)i Ext(ra)nei et nepos ipsius et dominus Rog(er)us Ext(ra)neus sicut diximus est ballivus in provincia Albi Monast(erii) et propter hoc fidem eisdem non debuissemus adhibere.

Et ᶜ ista inquisicio⁻ᶜ aliqua via noluimus sustinere quod non est mirum et in absencia nostra fuit.

Iterum si placet significamus quod illi iusticiarii qui fuerunt ibi pro vobis in aliis causis, videlicet Houwel filius Meuric et Walt(er) de Bedewardyn fuerunt advocati contra nos in illa causa et nichilominus fuerunt acsessores et conciliarii Walter' de Hoptun iusticiario vestro.

Item de Waltero vero de Hoptun, licet sit iustus homo et fidelis, tamen relatum fuit nobis quod reddere deberet homagium domino Rog(er)o de Mortuoᵈ Mari et domino Ioh(ann)i filio Alani, et si illutᵃ esset verum ipsum in iudicem non acciperemus.

Idioᵃ supplicat vobis antedictus Lewelin(us) pro Deo et pro fideli servicio suo et pro iusticia vestra quod vos faciatis sibi habere unum de duobusᵉ inter ipsum et hundredum Albi Monast(erii) aut legem Wallie, sicuti alias eidem consessistis, aut antiquam consuetudinem antecessorum suorum et possessorum predicti Albi Monast(erii).

ᵃ *sic in* A. | ᵇ ipse A. | ᶜ⁻ᶜ *sic in* A. | ᵈ Mortio A. | ᵉ duobis A.

The petition can be no later than November 1281, as Hywel ap Meurig, a prominent royal servant in Wales, was dead before the end of that month (*CCR 1279–88*, 142; *WAR*, 117–20). Legal proceedings before Walter de Hopton and other justices were held at Oswestry on 27 November 1277, 9 February, 22 July and 30 September 1278 and 14 January 1279 (*WAR*, 122–3). However, it was only on the last of these occasions that a case between Llywelyn and the men of Oswestry is known to have been heard, and no other proceedings are recorded at Oswestry until 5 June 1284. There is a strong likelihood, therefore, that the petition was written not long after 14 January 1279, when Llywelyn appeared before Hopton to deny charges that he had attacked carpenters from Oswestry who had felled timber in the wood of Coedgaer near Oswestry on 5 January 1278, following an earlier appearance before the king, almost certainly in August 1278, who had adjourned the case before Hopton and his fellow justices on 14 January 1279. Hopton and his colleagues decided that Llywelyn and his men should appear before them at Montgomery on 5 September 1279, and also that an inquiry should be made whether Llywelyn consented to the attack or not. A marginal note adds that Llywelyn was summoned at the plaint of the men of Oswestry to the king's parliament (*WAR*, 262–3; *CAC*, 154–5). Presumably this was the case referred to when the Easter parliament at Westminster in 1279 committed to Walter de Hopton a dispute between Isabella Mortimer and Llywelyn, prince of Wales 'concerning the trespass of the wood of Oswestry' (*totum negocium inter Isabellam de Mortuo Mari et Lewelinum principem Wallie de transgressione bosci Albi Monasterii*) (*Rotuli Parliamentorum Anglie*, ed. Richardson and Sayles, 7). A letter to the king from Hopton and his fellow justices, datable to shortly after the Oswestry hearing of 14 January 1279, also states that an inquisition was taken after Llywelyn's appearance before them, though on a different question from that recorded in the assize roll: according to the letter, the inquisition sought to establish whether the wood of Coedgaer was in the seisin of the king or in that of Llywelyn and his men on the day when the attack took place; the jurors replied that it was in the king's seisin (*CAC*, 155). It may well be that it was to one of these inquisitions that Llywelyn objected in the petition. That jurors were assembled from Ellesmere, Whittington and Knockin is credible, as, after Llywelyn's death, twelve jurors from each of these manors, together with Welshpool, testified before Hopton on 5 June 1284 in another inquisition at Oswestry with regard to a later attack on Oswestry by Llywelyn and others on Palm Sunday (6 April) 1281 (*WAR*, 351–3; the attack is misdated to 1282 by Davies, who linked it to the beginning of the Welsh war, in ibid., 206–8). Coedgaer probably lay in the township of Pentre-gaer, with its hillfort of Coed-y-gaer, located in woods at the top of a hill overlooking the river Cynllaith, about $3\frac{1}{2}$ miles west of Oswestry at SJ 232 289 (*VCH Shropshire*, i. 376).

Roger Lestrange had been granted Ellesmere on 24 November 1275 (*CPR 1272–81*, 125). His nephew John Lestrange (V) of Knockin (d. 1309) succeeded John Lestrange (IV) after the latter's death *c*.26 February 1276 (*CAP*, 326; cf. Eyton, *Shropshire*, x. 369–70). Inquisitions post mortem show that Walter de Hopton held nearly all his land from the fitz Alans and Mortimers; John fitz Alan III had died in 1272 (*WAR*, 105; Sanders, *Baronies*, 71). Hostility towards Ellesmere and Whittington is vividly conveyed in Llygad Gŵr's urging of attacks on these places in his praise poem to Llywelyn from this period ('Gwaith Llygad Gŵr', ed. Lynch, no. 28). The wider context of Llywelyn's disaffection from the crown in the years before 1282, which stemmed in considerable measure from the denial to him of Welsh law in legal procedures, is considered in Davies, *Conquest*, 347; Smith, *Llywelyn*, 458–9.

537 Petition to the king

Petition for the grant of a market at Llanarmon on Tuesdays; this would not be harmful to any neighbouring market as the nearest market in one direction, towards Oswestry, is 6 leagues away and in the other direction at least 12 leagues away. Further petition for an annual fair in the same township, for four consecutive days from the second day after Michaelmas [1 October], as freely as Gruffudd ap Gwenwynwyn has markets and fairs in his lands by the king's grant.

[Probably shortly before 7 November 1279]

A = TNA: PRO, SC 8/192, no. 9566. No endorsement; originally approx. 171 × 56; bottom right-hand corner torn away.
Cd., *CAP*, 320; *H*, no. 524.

Lewelinus filius Griffini de Brumfeld' petit de gratia domini regis quod idem dominus rex sibi forum apud Lanarmon die martis concedere dignetur, quod quidem forum nullo foro convicino erit nocivo quia forum propinquior ex parte una versus Albu(m) Monast(er)ium distat a prefato foro per sex leucas et ex parte alia per duodecim leucas ad minus. Petit etiam de gratia domini regis unum diem nundinarum in anno apud villam predictam, videlicet die secundo proximo `post festum Sancti Mich(ael)is et quod idem nundine durare valeant per quatuor dies continuos adeo libere, sicut Griffin(us) filius (?)Vennini[a] fora et nundinas suas habet in terris suis per concessionem domini regis.

[a] Ve *followed by eight minims, of which the fifth and the last have strokes above them* A.

The petition can be no later than 7 November 1279, when the king granted Llywelyn and his heirs a weekly market on Tuesday at Llanarmon in the cantref of Cynllaith, and an annual fair there on the vigil, feast and morrow of St Silin and St Garmon (*CChR 1257–1300*, 213). The royal grant shows that the township was Llanarmon Dyffryn Ceiriog. As 1 October was the feast day of St Silin at Llansilin, about 4 miles south-east of Llanarmon, and was also one of the feasts of St Garmon (Baring-Gould and Fisher, *Lives of the British Saints*, iii. 77, 79; iv. 206), there is no discrepancy between the date for the fair in the petition and that of the grant, although the latter was slightly less generous in allowing a fair for only three days. That the grant referred to the feast of St Silin and St Garmon, rather than Michaelmas, could, perhaps, indicate that it resulted from a later petition than the present one; but the contrast could equally be explicable in terms of an oral message communicated with the present petition.

538 Archbishop Pecham (grievances)

Complaint about the constable and men of Oswestry, who despoiled him of a third of the township of Lledrod and the court of his father without observing the law of the country or custom.

The aforesaid constable and his accomplices despoiled Llywelyn of the common pasture which he used in the past, without observing the law of the country, and fined him £70 on account of that pasture.

The king of England granted letters to a certain bastard, Gruffudd Fychan of the township of Kynaston, to litigate against Llywelyn in order to obtain all his lordship; on account of these letters Llywelyn spent £200 sterling.

The aforesaid constable forced Llywelyn to send two of his nobles to him to be hanged, though these noble men should not have been hanged. The kin of these men would have been unwilling to stop this hanging [(?) that is, redeem the nobles from hanging] for £300 sterling. Afterwards the constable twice imprisoned sixty of Llywelyn's men, giving no reason in advance except that a certain boy let out a certain cry, and they could not leave his prison until each paid 10s. for his release.

When Llywelyn's men came to market to sell their cattle, the constable would have the cattle led away to the castle and afterwards neither restored them nor paid the seller. In particular, the constable and his men took Llywelyn's herds to their own land and did with them as he wished.

The king's justices forced Llywelyn to hand over a certain township to the sons of Einion ap Gruffudd, who had not obtained that township from either Llywelyn or his predecessors, without observing the law of the country in this regard.

The aforesaid constable took away the horse of Llywelyn's bailiff without any reason: nothing was owing to the constable nor has the bailiff obtained any amends yet.

When Llywelyn was wanting to go the the township of Caehowel with the king's letters in order to appear there on the day assigned to him, the sons of Gruffudd ap Gwenwynwyn and knights of Roger Lestrange, on Roger's advice, imprisoned Llywelyn and his men to their considerable injury. Llywelyn and his men would have been unwilling to stop [(?) that is, redeem themselves from] this injury for £300 sterling nor was he able to get away from the same men until he found sufficient security.

[21 × 31 October 1282]

B = London, Lambeth Palace Library, Register of Archbishop Pecham, fo. 247r. s. xiii[2].
C = Oxford, All Souls College MS 182, fos 109v–110r. c.1413.
Pd. from B, *Reg. Peckh.*, ii. 463–5.
Cd., *H*, no. 526.

Conqueritur vobis, domine archiepiscope Cant(uariensis), totius Angl(ie) primas, Lewelin(us) filius Griffini filii Madoci de constabulario de Cruceoswaldi regis et de hominibus eiusdem ville, qui predictum Lewelinu(m) tertia parte cuiusdam ville que vocatur Ledrot et curia patris sui sine observatione iuris patrie sue vel consuetudine nequiter spoliarunt.

Preterea predictus constabularius et sui complices eundem L. communi pastura qua predictus L. usus fuit temporibus retroactis, ordine iuris patrie minime observato, spoliarunt et in lxx libris occasione predicte pasture condempnarunt.

Ceterum, dominus rex Anglie concessit quasdam literas cuidam bastardo, scilicet Griffino Vachan de villa Gynwrith, ad litigandum contra eundem Lewelinu(m) pro toto dominio suo obtinendo, quarum literarum occasione idem L. expendit cc libras sterlingorum legalis usualisve monete.

Iterum, predictus constabularius compulsit predictum L. ad mittendum duos suos nobiles ad eos suspendendos ad predictum constabularium,[a]qui quidem[a] viri nobiles suspendi minime debuissent, quam suspensionem nollent parentes predictorum hominum sustinuisse pro ccc libris sterlingorum. Postmodum predictus constabularius incarceravit bis lx homines predicti L. nulla premissa ratione nisi quod quidem garcio emisit quandam vocem, nec potuerunt evadere suum carcerem donec quilibet eorum solvit x solidos pro sua deliberatione.

Item, quando homines predicti L. venirent ad forum ad suos boves vendendos, predictus constabularius faceret boves deduci ad castrum, nec postmodum boves restitueret nec pretium solveret venditori. Presertim idem constabularius et sui ceperunt iumenta predicti Lewelini[b] ad terram suam propriam, et de eisdem iumentis fecerunt suam voluntatem.

Preterea, iusticiarii domini regis compulserunt predictum L. ad tradendum quandam villam filiis Aniani filii G(ri)ffini, qui quidem predictam villam nec a se nec a predecessoribus fuerunt consecuti, ordine iuris patrie sue in hac parte minime observato.

Item, predictus constabularius abstulit equum ballivi predicti L. sine aliqua ratione, nec sibi aliquid debebatur, nec adhuc predictus ballivus satisfactionem aliquam est consecutus.

Ceterum, quando predictus Lewelin(us) volebat adire villam que vocatur Kaerlon cum litteris domini regis ad comparendum ibidem in die sibi assignata, filii Griffini filii Gwenynnyn[c] et armigeri domini Rog(er)i St(er)mui ex consilio Rog(er)i eundem L. et suos incarcerarunt, in sui iniuriam et suorum non modicam lesionem. Quam iniuriam et lesionem nollet predictus L. et sui sustinuisse pro ccc libris[d] sterlingorum, nec ab eisdem potuit evadere donec invenit pro se sufficientem cautionem.

[a-a] quicquid BC. | [b] L. C. | [c] Gwenynny C. | [d] marcis C.

This was one of the series of complaints sent by Llywelyn ap Gruffudd, prince of Wales together with his letter to Pecham of 21 × 31 October 1282 (no. 428 above); that the present document was sent with the *gravamina* which precede it in Pecham's register is clear from the phrase *Hiis et aliis receptis in scriptis* … written immediately after it (*Reg. Peckh.*, ii. 465). For Lledrod see no. 534 above. As Edwards tentatively suggested (*CAC*, 97), the common pasture may be the same as that referred to in no. 533 above. In 1281 Gruffudd Fychan of Kynaston (SO 245 632), about 5 miles south-west of Presteigne, cmt. Llwythyfnwg, and his brothers and uncle claimed, by virtue of their descent from Iorwerth Goch, the lands of Nanheudwy, Mochnant Is Rhaeadr and half of Cynllaith from Llywelyn ap Gruffudd ap Madog in sessions before Walter de Hopton and his fellow justices (*WAR*, 319, 320, 324). Llywelyn, together with his brother Owain and mother Emma likewise faced legal claims, brought before Hopton between February 1278 and July 1281, from Gruffudd, Maredudd, Einion, Owain, Hywel and Dafydd sons of Einion ap Gruffudd to the townships of Tregeiriog, Nantyr and Llangollen Fechan in Nanheudwy, Dolwen, Llwythder and Sgwennant in Cynllaith and Hafod-wen (alias Marrington), just south-east of Chirbury, Shropshire (ibid., 238, 256–7, 318, 320; cf. ibid. 302, 305); presumably it was one of these that Llywelyn was forced to surrender to the sons of Einion. (I am grateful to Paul Russell for his help with the phrase *nolo … sustinuisse pro* in the fourth and final paragraphs, where the meaning seems to be that the sum of money demanded as redemption from the punishments was impossibly high.)

SOUTHERN POWYS (POWYS WENWYNWYN)

OWAIN AP GRUFFUDD (OWAIN CYFEILIOG)
(d. 1197)

539 Whitland Abbey (for the foundation of Strata Marcella Abbey)
Grant, for the salvation of the souls of himself, his father, mother and other ancestors, of Ystrad Marchell within these bounds: from one side of the Severn to the dyke between Rhydhesgyn and (?) Argyngroeg (Crengai) and from that dyke to the sheep pit and then around the bright grove [Goleugoed] to the gallows; thence between the meadow and the wood to the stream, thence through the middle wood to the stream in (?) Trelydan (lata villa) and along to the boundary of Argemunre, and thence by the summit of Allt Wrgy to the horse's pit [Pwll y Ceffyl] and thus back to the Severn; free of all custom and payment of tithe and other customs, in wood, plain, waters and other rights of use, for the building of an abbey for God and the ever-Virgin Mary. Witnesses.

[c.1170]

B = TNA: PRO, C 53/108 (Ch. R. 15 Edward II), m. 6 (in an inspeximus, 12 March 1322).
C = TNA: PRO, C 66/470 (Pat R. 28 Henry VI, pt. 1), m. 7 (in an inspeximus of B, 14 March 1450).
Pd. from B, *Mon. Ang.*, v. 637; from B, *Ystrad Marchell Charters*, no. 1; from C, Jones, 'Abbey of Ystrad Marchell', 16–17.
Cd., *CChR 1300–26*, 438 (from B); Davies, 'Strata Marcella documents', 164 (no. 1) (from B); *H*, no. 203.

In nomine sancte et individue Trinitatis. Ego Oenius filius Griffini, intuitu caritatis, pro salute anime mee et antecessorum meorum, patris videlicet mei et matris mee ceterorumque predecessorum meorum, concessi et dedi fratribus Cistersiensis ordinis, ecclesie scilicet Beate atque perpetue Virginis Marie de Alba Domo, Stratmarghel hiis contentam finibus: ab uno latere Hauren usque ad fossam que est inter Ridheschin et Crengai, et ab eadem fossa usque ad puteum ovium, et sic circuiens clarum nemus terminus pretenditur usque ad patibula, ab hinc vero procedit inter pratum et silvam usque ad rivulum aque, de hinc autem per medium nemus usque ad rivum qui est in lata villa, quo disterminante, progreditur usque ad terminum Argemunre, et ab eiusdem termino per supercilium clivi Worgy usque puteum caballi, et sic concluditur in Hauren; liberam et quietam ab omni consuetudine et redditu decimarum aliarumque consuetudinum respectibus, in bosco et plano et aquis ceterisque omnimodis utilitatibus, ad edificandam abbatiam Deo in honore semper Virginis Marie. Testificantibus hiis: D(avi)d filio Goluinn, Suglen filio Caradauc, Iohanne filio Gueid Woit, Beauuoir clerico; laicis: Gorgeniu filio Grifri, Celuie filio Chengret, Meurich filio Grifri, Chenvellin filio Dolfin, Ioruerd filio Wiaund, Caldellin filio Rog(er)i et fratre eius Chengret, Riaunal filio Budor, Rob(er)to filio Caradauc.

The date of the foundation of Strata Marcella is uncertain but there are strong grounds for assigning the beginning of conventual life to 1170. Most manuscripts containing lists of Cistercian foundations state that a community arrived from Whitland on 22 July 1170, and this date was accepted by Janauschek. The Register of Aberconwy Abbey also places the foundation in 1170. However, some lists date the beginning of conventual life to 1169 and several others assign the foundation to 10 July 1172 (Janauschek, *Originum Cistercensium*, 160, 296; cf. Davies, 'Records of the abbey of Ystrad Marchell', 7; *Ystrad Marchell Charters*, 11). Since the beneficiary of the present charter is Whitland, it was probably issued prior to the beginning of conventual life in, most likely, 1170. One unusual feature of the charter is the rendering of several Welsh place-names in Latin, including *clarum nemus* for Goleugoed (i.e. a wood of scattered trees that would allow in plenty of light) and *lata villa* for Trelydan (Lloyd, 'Goleugoed'). For the location of the lands, carved out of the commote of Ystrad Marchell, see *Ystrad Marchell Charters*, 112 and Map I.

*540 Strata Marcella Abbey

Grant in perpetual alms of all the land of Abraham Dafydd (Dadauut) *ap Collwyn in wood, plain and other appurtenances, i.e. half of Trefnant* (Trefnant).

[1170 × 1197]

Mention only, in a confirmation charter of Edward II dated at Tutbury, 12 March 1322 (*Ystrad Marchell Charters*, no. 2; Jones, 'Abbey of Ystrad Marchell', 308 (from Henry VI's inspeximus, 1450); cd., *CChR 1300–26*, 439; *H*, no. 215). Davies asserted, without any supporting evidence, that the charter 'can be safely dated before 1185, probably nearer 1170 than 1185' ('Records of the abbey of Ystrad Marchell', 7). However, the only secure · *terminus ad quem* is Owain's death in 1197, as assumed by Thomas (*Ystrad Marchell Charters*, no. 2). Owain's grant was a confirmation, and is followed in the inspeximus by a summary of a grant issued by Abraham himself (ibid., no. 3). Trefnant was situated to the west of the abbey, in the parish of Guilsfield, and was later known as Trefnant y Mynech (ibid., 112 and Map I).

GWENWYNWYN AB OWAIN CYFEILIOG
(d. 1216)

(?)†541 Strata Marcella Abbey

Grant, inspired by piety, for the salvation of the souls of himself, his father, mother and all his ancestors and successors, in free alms and perpetual possession, without any claim, exaction or secular custom, of all the land of Hafod Owain with all its bounds from the black dyke directly to Yfyrnwy, Yfyrnwy to Nant yr Eira, Nant yr Eira to its source, thence by the summit of the mountain to Bôn y Maen Melin, thence directly to Rhydyfoch, thence by the summit of the mountain to the source of Nanhanog, along Nanhanog to Pwll Llydan; from the other side of the aforesaid black dyke in a circuit to the stream called Hwrdd, along the Hwrdd to the Iaen, along the Iaen upwards to the ford near Talerddig, and from that ford by the hollow to Gweunrudd where the stream begins which descends to Pwll Llydan, and along that stream to Pwll Llydan. Further grant of Cwm-y-calch with all its bounds and appurtenances, on one side from the mouth of the stream which descends into the Iaen along to Bwlch y Llogail, and thence by the summit of the mountain to Rhiw y Gof, and thence again by the summit of the mountain to Blaen Bodreiswal; on the other side, Y Bryn Du from the Iaen by the summit of the mountain to the aforesaid Blaen Bodreiswal. Further grant of Pennant Cynlling in these bounds: along Nant yr Ysgoliau from its source to the Dulas, along the Dulas to the mouth of the Dengi, up the Dengi to its source. Further grant of the land between the Dulas and Nant yr Ysgoliau. The monks may possess the aforesaid lands in all their bounds in peace, without any secular exaction, claim or custom, in wood, plain, waters, pastures, all uses, rights of use and liberties, in perpetual right. Sealing clause; witnesses.

Tafolwern, 9 May 1185

B = NLW, Wynnstay Estate Records, Ystrad Marchell Charters, no. 11. s. xiii ex. Endorsed: iiii[a] (s. xiii ex); early modern endorsements; approx. 264 × 220 + 13 mm.; two off-centre horizontal slits, one just above fold, one in fold, for a tag (*c.*8 mm. wide) which exits through a slit in the base of the fold; sealed on tag. Seal missing, though linen bag which contained it remains.
Pd. from B, *Ystrad Marchell Charters*, no. 11.
Cd., Davies, 'Strata Marcella documents', 166 (no. 4); *H*, no. 205.

Noscant tam presentes quam futuri sancte matris ecclesie filii quod ego Wennunwen filius Oweni de Keveyllauc intuitu pietatis pro salute anime mee et patris mei et matris mee et omnium antecessorum meorum et successorum dedi et concessi et hac presenti carta mea confirmavi [a–][Deo et Beate Marie et monachis de Stradmarchell][–a] in liberam et quietam et puram elemosinam et perpetuam possessionem, libere et quiete, bene et in pace, sine omni reclamatione et exactione et consuetudine seculari totam terram que vocatur Hauot Oweyn cum omnibus terminis suis a fossa nigra in directum usque ad Ev(er)envy, Evernoy usque ad Nant[b] Ereyre, Na(n)t Erere usque ad eius ortum, ab ortu eius per summitatem montis usque ad Bon Emaen Melyn, inde directe usque Red Evoch, de Redevoch per summitatem montis usque ad ortum Nanhanauc, Nanhanauc per longum usque Pullydan; ex altera parte a predicta fossa nigra per circuitum usque ad rivulum qui vocatur Hvrd, Hurd in longum usque Hyaen, Hyaen in sui longitudine sursum usque ad vadum iuxta Talerdic, et a vado illo per concavitatem terre usque Wevn Rvd ubi oritur rivulus qui descendit ad Pullydan, et rivulus ille usque Pullydan ubi relinquimus. Dedi eciam Cu(m)ekalch cum omnibus terminis suis et pertinentiis ex una parte ab *aber* rivuli qui descendit in Haen in sui longitudine usque ad Bulch Ellogeyl, et ab illo loco per summitatem montis usque ad Ryv Egof, et inde iterum per summitatem montis usque Blaen Bodreyswal; ex alia parte Ebre(n)dv de Hyaen per summitatem montis usque ad dictum locum Blaen Bodreyswal. Dedi etiam Penant Kenlle(n)g in hiis terminis: ab ortu rivuli qui vocatur Nant er Esgollev in sui longitudine usque Dulas, Dulas in longum usque ad Aberdengy, Deng vero sursum usque ad eius ortum; similiter et terram illam que est inter Dulas et Nant Erescollev. Volo igitur ego prefatus Wennunwyn ut prenominati monachi predictas terras in omnibus terminis suis bene, in pace et quiete sine aliqua exactione et calumpnia vel consuetudine seculari, tam in bosco quam in plano, in aquis, in viis et semitis, in pascuis, in pasturis et in omnibus usibus et utilitatibus^c suis et in omnibus omnino libertatibus iure perpetuo possideant. Et ne aliquis successorum meorum istam meam donationem instigante diabolo infringere conetur eam tam sigilli mei impressione quam bonorum virorum atestatione munivi et corroboravi. Hiis testibus: Goronvy ab Eynavn, Morvran ab David, magistris Heylyn et Rvuavn, Daniele presbitero, Meilyr ab Nenav, Cadugavn ab Ednyuet, Kener ab Kadugavn. Facta est autem hec mea donatio in manu G(ri)ffini abbatis apud Dwalwern anno gratie m° c° lxxx° quinto vii° idus maii.

^a–a *omitted* B. | ^b Nat B. | ^c utiltatibus B.

As this charter is in a late thirteenth- or possibly even early fourteenth-century hand, a hybrid of book hand and cursive probably written by the same scribe as that of no. 555 below, it is clearly not an original issued by Gwenwynwyn (cf. *Ystrad Marchell Charters*, 110, 111). Admittedly it does not necessarily follow that the text of the charter is spurious, as it could have been copied from an authentic original. The diplomatic bears resemblances to that of authentic charters of Gwenwynwyn and all the witnesses apart from Daniel the priest and Cadwgan ab Ednyfed appear in other Strata Marcella charters (cf. ibid., 48, 52, 60, 66, 79, 80). On the other hand, resemblances to no. 555 are neither so close or unique as to point firmly to drafting by the same late thirteenth-century scribe: the notification is different in each charter, and though the corroboration is almost identical to that in no. 555, it also occurs in no. 542 (admittedly extant only in an early modern copy), likewise dated at Tafolwern, and could therefore reflect drafting at that grange rather than later scribal invention. The substance of the grant is credible as Gruffudd ap Llywelyn's confirmation for Strata Marcella, extant in an original dated 1226, includes grants of Hafod Owain, Cwm-y-calch and Pennant Cynlling and makes clear that these had been granted in Gwenwynwyn's charters (no. 282 above). Nevertheless, the wording of the perambulations is not sufficiently close in both charters to demonstrate that Gruffudd ap Llywelyn's confirmation and the present charter drew on the same charter of Gwenwynwyn. More generally, the charter's diplomatic is not conclusive proof of its text's authenticity, as a scribe with access to the Strata Marcella archive could have drawn upon formulae and witness lists in other charters to concoct a text containing what he believed to have been a genuine grant. Above all, the external appearance of the charter, got up to look like an original complete with sealing tag (and apparently also a seal), excites suspicion. If it was intended as a replacement for an authentic original, why was such a replacement considered necessary? If it is assumed that that original was in so poor a state of preservation that it could no longer provide sufficient title to the lands granted, how could it have been copied accurately? At the very least, there can be no certainty that the present charter contains a reliable copy of the charter of Gwenwynwyn that it purports to be; and it could simply be a fabrication of a charter recording a grant believed, probably correctly, to have been made by that prince for which no charter survived.

Hafod Owain (SH 927 027) formed part of the grange of Talerddig and lay 1 mile southwest of Talerddig itself. For Tafolwern see note to no. 542 below.

542 Strata Marcella Abbey

*Grant, inspired by love and holy religion, for the salvation of the souls of himself and his parents, in perpetual alms, of the land of Talerddig with all its bounds and appurtenances, on one side having Nanhanog as far as its mouth, thence extending to the Garthbrandu and along the Garthbrandu to the mountain. Further grant of Ystrad (?) Powyson (Estradpowison), Bryndu, Newydd Fynyddog with its bounds, Pennant Iaen with its bounds, Bodreiswal, Pennant Bacho with its boundary towards Arwystli to the mouth of the Dengwm and along the Dengwm to its source, as well as Mochrhaeadr, Nantmeichad, *Munam* and* Nancorreden *with their bounds and appurtenances, thence all the mountains pertaining to Cyfeiliog, namely from the side of the woods of Cyfeiliog with their bounds towards Arwystli and towards Deheubarth, namely to Nannerth Pumlumon and to Gwryd Cai, and from Gwryd Cai as the Rheidol flows thence to the mouth of Camddwr Cyfeiliog, and by Camddwr Cyfeiliog from its mouth to its source and to the top of Helygenwenddydd. Further grant of Cefn Coch and Cwmcoch up as far as Camddwr Cyfeiliog. Further grant of all the pasture between Camddwr Cyfeiliog and Camddwr Ceredigion. The monks may possess the aforesaid lands and pastures with their bounds in peace, without any disturbance or secular custom, in wood, plain, waters, pastures, all uses and rights of use, in perpetual and pure right, so that no other religious men may ever have any share or common right with them in the aforesaid lands and pastures. Sealing clause; witnesses.*

Tafolwern, 10 May 1187

B = NLW Bodewryd MS 102D, fo. 164r. s. xvii[1].
Pd. from B, *Ystrad Marchell Charters*, no. 12.
Cd., *H*, no. 207.

In nomine sancte et individue Trinitatis. Notum sit omnibus tam clericis quam laicis tam presentibus quam futuris quod ego Gwenvnwin filius Owini de Keueilliauc, caritatis intuitu et sancte religionis effectu, pro salute anime mee et parentum meorum, dedi et concessi et confirmavi Deo et Beate Marie et[a] monachis de[b] Stradmarchell in liberam et puram et perpetuam elemosinam terram que vocatur Talherthic cum omnibus terminis suis et pertinentiis, ex uno scilicet[c] latere habens Nanhanauc usque ad exitum exinde tendens Garthbrandu et pertinens Garthbrandu usque ad montem. Dedi insuper et concessi eisdem prefatis monachis eodem modo Estradpowison et Brindu et Newiduenadauc cum terminis suis et Pennanyewen(n)c cum terminis suis et Bothreiswall et Pennanbacho cum termino suo versus Arwsteli usque ad Ab(er)dengum et De(n)gu(m) exinde usque ad principium, insuper et Mochraiadre et Nanmeichat et Muna(m) et Nancorreden cum terminis suis et pertinentiis, exinde omnia montana ad Keueilliauc pertinentia, scilicet ex latere silvarum Keueilliauc cum terminis suis versus Arwsteli et versus Deheubarth, scilicet usque ad Nannerth[d] Pimpluman, et usque ad Gurhetkei, et a Gurhetkei prout inde Ridaul usque ad

Abercamduur Keueilliauc, et per Camduur Keveilliauc^c ab exitu usque ad principium, et usque ad summum Helegenwendec.^{e} Dedi etiam et concessi prenominatis monachis Keuencohc et Cumcoch susum usque ad Camduur Keueilliauc. Insuper et totam pasturam que [est]^f inter Kamdur Keuilliauc et Camduur Karedigiaun eis dedi et confirmavi. Volo igitur ego prefatus Gwenunwin ut prenominati monachi omnes prefatas terras et pasturas cum terminis suis, bene et in pace et quiete et sine omni vexatione sive consuetudine seculari, tam in bosco quam in plano, in aquis et in viis et in omnibus usibus suis et utilitatibus, perpetuo atque puro iure possideant, ita quod nulli alii viri religiosi unquam habeant cum eis partem aliquam vel communionem de prefatis terris sive pasturis. Ac ne aliquis successorum meorum istam meam donationem instigante diabolo infringere conetur^g tam sigilli mei inpressione quam bonorum virorum attestatione eam munivi et coroboravi. His testibus: magistro Heilin, magistro Riuaun, Daniel filio sacerdotis, Moruran filio D(avi)d, Goronuo filio Eynniaun, Madauc filio Kenillin, Eynniaun filio Lowarch, Goronuo filio Seisil, Kenir filio Kadugaun, Griffutd filio Edenewein, Eynniaun filio^h Goronuo, Grifri Dv, Meilir filio Nennau, Hetllell Kenig, Karadauc Parvo et multis aliis. Facta est autem hec donatio in manu G(ri)fini abbatis apud Dewalwern anno videlicet ab incarnatione domini millesimo centesimo octogesimo septimo sexto vero idus maii.

^{a} B *inserts* monacis *struck through.* | ^{b} B *inserts* Stradmarcell *struck through.* | ^{c} B *inserts word struck through.* | ^{d} B *inserts* Pimplym(m)on *deleted by underlining.* | ^{e} *corrected from* Helegenwendet *in* B. | ^{f} *omitted* B. | ^{g} conatur B. | ^{h} B *inserts* Groni *struck through.*

See note to no. 541 above and, for the lands, *Ystrad Marchell Charters*, 115–16 and Map III. Tafolwern (SH 888 026) lies adjacent to Llanbrynmair and about 2½ miles north-west of Talerddig (ibid., 114 and Map III). It possessed a castle in the 1160s and was probably the site of the court of the lord of Cyfeiliog; though it was granted to Rhys ap Gruffudd of Deheubarth in 1167, his tenure of the castle appears to have been short-lived (*BT, Pen20Tr*, 62, 64; *BT, RBH*, 142–3, 148–9). Together with no. 544 below the charter provides important evidence that Gwenwynwyn held the commote of Cyfeiliog for a decade before his father's death in 1197 (cf. Davies, 'Records of the abbey of Ystrad Marchell', 9; 'Canu Owain Cyfeiliog', ed. Williams, 197).

*543 Strata Marcella Abbey

Grant, with all his brothers, of all the land of Moedog (Moidauk) *and Bryn Onnen* (Brenhonen), *and half of the land which was in dispute between the townships of Gaer* (Kaer) *and Trefnant* (Crefnant), *namely the half which was said to belong to Gaer* (Kair).

[Probably 10 May 1187 × 1199]

Mention only, in a confirmation of Edward II dated at Tutbury, 12 March 1322 (*Ystrad Marchell Charters*, no. 13; Jones, 'Abbey of Ystrad Marchell', 309 (from Henry VI's inspeximus, 1450); cd., *CChR 1300–26*, 439; *H*, no. 219). As Davies argued ('Records of the abbey of Ystrad Marchell', 11), there are strong grounds for supposing that the summaries of Gwenwynwyn's grants in Edward II's inspeximus appear in chronological order. The present charter is preceded in the inspeximus by a copy of no. 542 above, dated 10 May 1187, and followed by no. 552 below, dated 1199 (*Ystrad Marchell Charters*, 15). For the lands, to the south-west of the abbey in the parish of Castell Caereinion, see ibid., 116.

544 Strata Marcella Abbey

As nothing is more effective than writing against oblivion and challenge and nothing should hinder the intention of holy work, he has ordered the terms of his gift and alms to be written down to perpetuate the memory of them. These are the terms. Grant, moved by divine inspiration, for the souls of himself and his parents, in perpetual possession for the use of the monks, of the Dengwm from its source to its mouth, Nantmeichad from its source to Mochrhaeadr, Newydd Fynyddog, Pennant Bacho, Bodreiswal and Pennant Iaen with all fields, mountains and woods in the mountains. Sealing clause; witnesses.

Tafolwern, 22 February 1191

> A = NLW, Wynnstay Estate Records, Ystrad Marchell Charters, no. 14. Endorsed: pennan Bahcho (s. xiii[1]); early modern endorsements; approx. 207 × 228 + 17 mm.; two central horizontal slits, one just above fold, one in fold, for a tag (*c.*14 mm. wide) which exits through a slit in the base of the fold; sealed on tag. Seal missing.
> Pd. from A, Jones *et al.*, 'Five Strata Marcella charters', 50–1; from A, *Ystrad Marchell Charters*, no. 14.
> Cd., Davies, 'Strata Marcella documents', 167 (no. 5); *H*, no. 208.

In nomine sancte et individue Trinitatis amen. Quam oblivioni et calumpnie nichil efficatius adversatur quam scriptura et operationis sancte propositum nulla debet occasio impedire, huius siquidem rationis intuitu ad perpetuendam memoriam donationis et elemosine mee formam eius scripto decrevimus annotandam. Forma igitur hec est. Ego Guenoingven Owini filius de Keueiliauc divina ammonitus inspiratione pro mea et parentum meorum animabus Deo et abbatie de Estrat Marchell dedi perhenniter possidenda et monachorum usui profutura Dengum a summa usque ad exitum, Nantmeichat similiter a principio usque Moch Raiader, Negued Uenedauc et Pennanbacho, Botreiswal, Pennan Iegueinc cum omnibus campis et montibus et silvis in montibus existentibus. Ne qua igitur possit in posterum oriri calumpnia donationem meam et elemosinam sub scriptione testium et sigilli mei munimine roboravi. Testes igitur ex parte mea sunt: Einiaun filius Bledgint, Einiaun filius Laurentii, Daniel filius sacerdotis de Keueiliauc, Griffri Niger, Meiler filius Riawal, Gorgonius filius Einiaun Kenewal, Tegwareth filius Idneueth de Goinet, Madauc filius Genillin. Ex parte autem ecclesie sunt: Grifinus abbas, Gorgonius filius Meinon monachus, frater Helfinus, magister Rogerus, Sulienus archidiaconus, magister Helias, Mabin clericus. Actum pupplice apud Dewalguern incarnati verbi anno m° c° xc° regnante rege Anglie Ricardo nomine anno ii° octavo kallendas[a] marcii.

[a] *sic in* A.

For the lands, located in Cyfeiliog and Arwystli, see *Ystrad Marchell Charters*, 115–16 and Map III. The dating clause is highly unusual among charters of Welsh rulers in including the regnal year of an English king (for another, more problematic, example see no. 256 above).

545 Strata Marcella Abbey

Grant, in honour of the undivided Trinity and glorious Virgin Mary, inspired by piety, for the salvation of the souls of himself, his parents and his heirs in perpetual alms, free of all exaction

and custom, with the full gift of the heirs, of the land called Dyffrynmerthyr from the Dengwm
to Cwm Llwyd, Cwm Llwyd on both sides of the river with all its bounds and appurtenances
in wood and plain, and the Llwyd to the Clywedog. Sealing clause; witnesses.

[1197 × 7 July 1202]

A = NLW, Wynnstay Estate Records, Ystrad Marchell Charters, no. 51. Endorsed:
Guennu(n)w(en) super Defreinmerthir (s. xiii in.); early modern endorsements; approx. 165 mm.
wide at top, 182 mm. wide at bottom × 116 mm. deep + 12 mm.; a single central horizontal slit in
fold for a tag (*c.* 13 mm. wide); sealed on tag. Circular seal, green wax, imperfect, originally approx.
50 mm. diameter; equestrian, facing right; legend: SIGILL: ... E ... VI ... .
Pd. from A, *Ystrad Marchell Charters*, no. 51; from A, Jones, 'Abbey of Ystrad Marchell', 302
(trans. only).
Cd., Davies, 'Strata Marcella documents', 178 (no. 23); *H*, no. 253.

Universis sancte matris ecclesie filiis tam presentibus quam futuris notum sit quod ego
Wennuinwin filius Ovini in honore individue Trinitatis et gloriose Virginis Marie intuitu
pietatis pro redemptione anime mee et parentum meorum nec non et heredum meorum in
perpetuam et quietam elemosinam et ab omni exactione et consuetudine liberam dedi
monachis de Stratmarchel cum plenaria donatione heredum terram illam que vocatur
Defreynmerthyr a Dencum usque Cu(m) Luit, et Cu(m) Luit ex utraque parte amnis cum
omnibus terminis suis et pertinentiis tam in bosco quam in plano, et Luit usque Clawedauc.
Et ut hec donatio firma et rata imperpetuum habeatur eandem donationem proborum
virorum atestatione et sigilli nostri inpressione confirmo atque corroboro. Testes igitur
huius donationis sunt: Goronuy filius Enniaun, Kenyr filius Kadugaun, Meilir Du,
Teguaret filius Ydneuet, Meilir filius Nennyau, Heynniaun filius Deheweint, Moruran filius
Cuhelin, Kadugaun filius Grifini, Daniel filius Kendelu sacerdotis.

The date range of 1197 × 1205 suggested by Davies ('Records of the abbey of Ystrad
Marchell', 10) is preferable to that of 1206 × 1215 proposed by Thomas (*Ystrad Marchell
Charters*, no. 51). The first witness, Goronwy ab Einion, otherwise appears in dated
charters between 1185 and 1201, but is absent from charters dated 7 July 1202, 1204 and
1205 (nos 564–5, 569 below). His prominence in the witness lists suggests that he was a
leading adherent of Gwenwynyn, a supposition supported by the fact that his son Gwên ap
Goronwy held the office of *distain* or steward in the time of Gruffudd ap Gwenwynwyn;
according to late medieval genealogists, Goronwy was married to Meddefus, daughter of
Owain Cyfeiliog (Morgan, 'Territorial divisions [II]', 26–8; *Ystrad Marchell Charters*, 66).
In view of his importance, Goronwy's absence from the witness lists of Gwenwynwyn's
charters from 1202 onwards, including the confirmation charter for Strata Marcella of July
1202 (no. 564 below), is significant and probably indicates that he was dead by the time
those charters were issued. As Dyffrynmerthyr and Cwm Llwyd were situated in Arwystli,
the charter can be no earlier than 1197, when Gwenwynwyn annexed the cantref (*Ystrad
Marchell Charters*, 123; *BT, Pen20Tr*, 79; *BT, RBH*, 180–1). Although, as Thomas pointed
out (*Ystrad Marchell Charters*, 16), Dyffrynmerthyr was confirmed to the abbey by
Cadwallon ap Hywel of Arwystli in 1206 (no. 9 above), it is unlikely that the present charter
is a confirmation of Cadwallon's grant, which was far more comprehensive in the lands it
included.

546 St Michael's church, Trefeglwys and Haughmond Abbey

Grant and confirmation of all their holdings at Trefeglwys, namely Bryn Bedwyn from the ditch of the cemetery to the Gleiniant, Tregymer and Cilceirenydd to Nansodelant *and to the Cerist, with all their appurtenances in wood, plain, meadows, pastures, waters, mills and all easements. Sealing clause; witnesses.*

[1197 × 1208; possibly 1210 × 1216]

> B = Shropshire Records and Research Centre MS 6001/6869 (Haughmond Cartulary), fo. 215r. s. xv ex.
> Pd. from B, *Cart Haugh.*, no. 1218; from a Wynnstay MS dated 1640 destroyed in 1858, Williams, 'Wynnstay MSS.', 331 (incomplete).
> Cd., *H*, no. 246.

Universis sancte matris ecclesie filiis tam presentibus quam futuris Wenniniwin filius Owini eternam in domino salutem. Noverit universitas vestra nos concessisse et presenti carta confirmasse Deo et ecclesie Sancti Mich(ael)is de Trefeglus et canonicis de Haghmon' omnia tenementa que habent apud Trefeglus, scilicet Brinbeguin a fossa cimiterii usque ad Gleinant, de Trefkemer et Kilgrenit usque Nansodelant et usque Cherist, cum omnibus pertinentiis suis in bosco et plano, in pratis et pasturis, in viis et semitis, in aquis et stagnis et molendinis et omnibus eisiamentis. Et ut hec concessio et confirmatio nostra perpetue firmitatis robur optineat eam per sigilli nostri appositionem roboravimus. Hiis testibus: Iuliano archidiacono de Pouwis etc.

The grant can be no earlier than 1197, when Gwenwynwyn conquered Arwystli; the cantref, together with Gwenwynwyn's other lands, was occupied by Llywelyn ap Iorwerth 1208–10 and again from 1216 (see notes to nos 16, 545 above). As the charter is a confirmation of Haughmond's lands in Trefeglwys and its vicinity it was probably issued shortly after Gwenwynwyn occupied Arwystli in 1197.

*547 Cwm-hir Abbey

Grant of the land of Cwmbuga (Cumbuga) *with all its appurtenances,* Kellmeigen *with its appurtenances, common pasture throughout Arwystli and Cyfeiliog,* Gwarthkerwyt, *Esgair-y-maen* (Esceir y Maen) *and (?)G ... yuedw with all its appurtenances.*

[1197 × 1208 or 1210 × 1216; probably 1197 × 24 March 1202]

Mention only, in an inspeximus of Edward II dated at Westminster, 9 June 1318 (TNA: PRO, C 66/149, m. 5; pd., Rees, 'Account of Cwmhir abbey', 258 (trans.); cd., *CPR 1317–21*, 163; *H*, no. 262). For the dating limits see note to no. 546 above. Cwmbuga was also granted to Strata Marcella by Cadwallon ap Hywel of Arwystli in 1206 (no. 9 above), and title to the land was adjudged to Cwm-hir in the arbitration of disputes between it and Strata Marcella in 1227 (*Ystrad Marchell Charters*, 23–4 and no. 70). Whether this settlement meant that the arbitrators had discovered that Gwenwynwyn's grant preceded that of Cadwallon is not known. Gwenwynwyn granted all the pastures of Cyfeiliog to Strata Marcella 25 March 1201 × 24 March 1202 (no. 563 below). Since this charter explicitly reserved the pastures between the Corf and the Einion to Cwm-hir, it was probably issued after the present charter, with the reservation representing a compromise in recognition of the earlier grant of all the pastures of Cyfeiliog to Cwm-hir. Cwmbuga and Esgair-y-maen were on the slopes of Pumlumon in Arwystli and were named as possessions of the abbey in the diocese of Bangor in the papal taxation of 1291 (*Taxatio ecclesiastica*, 293; Banks, 'Notes to the account of Cwmhir abbey', 205; Williams, 'Cistercian abbey of Cwm Hir', 403).

548 Strata Marcella Abbey

Confirmation in free and perpetual possession of (?)Garddllifain (Garddlliuein), *Cwmbyr* (Cumber) *and Hafod Gwgan, and thence all the land upwards in wood and plain to Rhydyfoch and to Rhyd ar Gwm Owen, with all their bounds and appurtenances. The monks have bought these lands from him and the true heirs of the lands for 16 pounds of silver in perpetual possession. The monks may possess all the aforenamed lands with all their bounds and appurtenances freely, without any secular exaction or custom in perpetual right, in wood, plain and all rights of use. Sealing clause; witnesses.*

[1197 × 1208 or 1210 × 1216]

A = NLW, Wynnstay Estate Records, Ystrad Marchell Charters, no. 50. Endorsed: blain Karno (s. xiii in., in red textura in a contemporary hand, possibly that of the scribe of the charter); early modern endorsements; approx. 212 × 129 + 13 mm.; two central horizontal slits in fold for a tag (*c*.7 mm. wide) which exits through a slit in the base of the fold; sealed on tag. Circular seal, green wax, approx. 60 mm. diameter; equestrian, facing right; legend: SIGILL: GVENVUNWIN: … KEVEILIAVC.
Pd. from A, *Ystrad Marchell Charters*, no. 50.
Cd., Davies, 'Strata Marcella documents', 178 (no. 22); *H*, no. 254.

Notum sit tam presentibus quam futuris quod ego Wennunwen Powisie princeps et dominus Arwistili hac presenti carta mea confirmavi monachis de Stradmarchell in liberam et quietam et perpetuam possessionem istas terras: scilicet Gardlliuein, Cumber et Hauot Gwgaun, et inde totam terram susum tam in bosco quam in plano usque ad Red Houoch et usque ad Red Arcum Howen in omnibus videlicet terminis suis et pertinentiis; quas terras prenominati monachi a me et ab ipsarum terrarum veris heredibus pro sexdecim libris argenti in perpetuam possessionem emerit. Volo ergo ego prefatus Wennu(n)wen ut predicti monachi totas prenominatas terras in omnibus terminis suis et pertinentiis libere et quiete, bene et in pace et sine aliqua exactione vel consuetudine seculari iure perpetuo possideant in bosco scilicet in plano et in omnibus usibus suis et utilitatibus. Et ne huic nostre venditioni aliquis contraire presumat tam sigilli mei impressione quam bonorum virorum attestatione munivi et coroboravi. His testibus: Suliano archidiacono, Gervasio decano de Arwistili, magistro Helia, magistro Mabin, Daniel filio sacerdotis, Philippo sacerdote, Iohanne sacerdote filio Kenewreic, Edenewein sacerdote, Aniano et Grifri filiis Gervasii, Vrgeneu et Benuen filiis Goronui, Kener filio Cadugauni, Meiler filio Nenneaun, Madoco et Rob(er)to filiis Griffud Hiruein, Karadauc filio Grifri Were, Eyniaun filio Luarch, Euelueu filio Kengen.

The witness list is compatible with either of Gwenwynwyn's periods as lord of Arwystli. It is unclear why Davies, 'Records of the abbey of Ystrad Marchell', 10, proposed a date range of 1200 × 1206, nor why Thomas assigned the charter to 1206 × 1215 (*Ystrad Marchell Charters*, no. 50). For the lands, in Arwystli, see ibid., 122, 124.

549 Strata Marcella Abbey

Notification that all the land called Coedllyn with all its bounds and appurtenances, in wood, plain, meadows, pastures, waters, paths and all rights of use and profits, has been sold by its heirs to the monks for £22 in inviolable and perpetual possession. Gwenwynwyn has given and confirmed the aforesaid land, which all the heirs sold with one will and equal consent, in perpetual alms, free of all secular exaction, custom and service. Sealing clause; witnesses. The bounds of the land are from the pool of Coedllyn to the river Yfyrnwy, thence to Aberdyfnant, thence to the mouth of Pwlldu, from Pwlldu to Cefnffordd, thence to the red ford, thence to the aforesaid pool.

[1197 × 1208 or 1210 × 1216]

> B = NLW, Wynnstay Estate Records, Inspeximus of Elizabeth I, Shrewsbury, 5 April 1584.
> Pd. from B, *Ystrad Marchell Charters*, no. 49.
> Cd., *H*, no. 255.

Universis sancte matris ecclesie filiis tam presentibus quam futuris notum sit quod tota terra que vocatur Coitllin cum omnibus terminis et pertinentiis suis in bosco et plano, in pratis et pascuis, in aquis et semitis et omnibus usibus et utilitatibus suis et comodis vendita est ab heredibus suis universis monachis de Stradmarchell pro xx duabus libris in irrefraga-bilem et perpetuam possessionem; scilicet ego Wenunwin Owini filius princeps Powis predictam terram, quam omnes heredes pro condigno pretio una voluntate et pari consensu prefatis monachis vendiderunt, dedi et confirmavi Deo et Beate Marie et monachis de Stradm(ar)chell in puram et perpetuam elemosinam, ab omni exactione et consuetudine et servitute seculari liberam et quietam. Et ut predictam terram memorati monachi incon-cusse et plenarie perpetuo possideant legitimam heredum venditionem et nostram donationem mee carte munimine et proborum virorum attestatione confirmamus atque coroboramus. His testibus: priore et monachis[a] de Stradmarchell, Teguaret converso, Adam[b] sacerdote, Mareduc filio Howel, Ioruer[th][c] Bochan filio I. Chorh, Kadugaun filio G(ri)f(ri), Gurgeneu filio Madauc, Ieuaf filio Owini, Rurit `Choch, Rurit filio Howel, G(ri)fud filio Hetnewein, Ieuaf Pengil et multis aliis. Predicte terre `veri termini sunt de stagno Coitllin usque fluvium Ewernwy, de predicto fluvio usque Aberdywnant, de Aberdywnant usque *aber* Pulldu, de predicto loco, scilicet Pulldu, usque Kewenforth, de Kewenforth usque Vadum Ruffum, de Vado Ruffo usque predictum stagnum.

[a] monaco mone B. | [b] *sic in* B. | [c] *parchment torn* B.

The title 'prince of Powys' indicates that the charter was issued after the death of Gwenwynwyn's father Owain Cyfeiliog in 1197. Coedllyn centred on Llyn Coethlyn (SJ 014 141) in the north-west of the township of Cyffin, about 2 miles north of Llangadfan, in Caereinion (Davies, 'Property and landownership', 38 and n. 20; *Ystrad Marchell Charters*, 123–4).

*550 Strata Marcella Abbey

Grant of all the land of Caledffrwd.

[1197 × 1208 or 1210 × 1216]

Mention only, in no. 581 below.

551 Agreement with Strata Marcella Abbey

Agreement between Gwenwynwyn and his heirs and the abbey concerning the fishery in Cyfeiliog above the river Dyfi that all produce of the fishery shall be divided equally between the prince and the monks. Likewise all work, labour, conservation, restoration and expenses will be shared by both parties. Gwenwynwyn has granted half of the fishery to the monks in free and perpetual alms, immune from all secular exaction, for the souls of himself and his parents and heirs. Witnesses.

[1197 × 1208 or 1210 × 1216; possibly 25 March 1201 × 1208 or 1210 × 1216]

A = NLW, Wynnstay Estate Records, Ystrad Marchell Charters, no. 35. Endorsed: Wenunnwen super m[e]diete piscarie de Deui (s. xiii med.); early modern endorsements; half of bipartite chirograph; approx. 162 × 84 + 10 mm.; at top of document two central horizontal slits in fold for a tag (*c.*7 mm. wide) which exits through a slit in the top of the fold; sealed on tag. Circular seal, green wax, imperfect, originally approx. 70 mm. diameter; equestrian, facing right; legend: SIGIL . . . . . . LIAVC.
Pd. from A, *Ystrad Marchell Charters*, no. 35.
Cd., Davies, 'Strata Marcella documents', 174 (no. 16); *H*, no. 249.

Hec conventio est inter Wennunwen filius Owini et heredes eius et monachos de Stradmarchell de piscario apud Keueillioc super fluvium Deui, ita ut omnis proventus eiusdem piscarii equaliter inter principem et monachos prefatos in duas partes dividatur. Sic etiam opus et labor et conservatio et restauratio et in omnibus expensa communiter ab utrisque habeatur. Dedit itaque prefatus princeps W. memoratis monachis dimidium predicti piscarii in liberam et perpetuam elemosinam et ab omni exactione seculari quietam et immunem pro anima sua et parentum et heredum suorum. His testibus: Daniel filio Kendelv sacerdotus, Daniel sacerdote de Pennegoys, Kening sacerdote de Machenthleith, Ruin clerico, Gorono filio Eyniavn, Meyler filio Rywallavn, Riwallaun et Madavc filiis Genillin, Owein et Eyniavn, Pobien et Maredvth filiis Philippi filii Vchtred et multis aliis.

C Y R O G R A P H U M ª

ª *top half of word (not indented)* A.

As Davies argued ('Records of the abbey of Ystrad Marchell', 10), the reference to Gwenwynwyn as 'prince' suggests that the agreement was made after the death of his father Owain Cyfeiliog in 1197; in addition, it is possible that the grant of a fishery in Cyfeiliog was no earlier than the grant of pastures in that commote of 25 March 1201 × 24 March 1202 (no. 563 below). It is quite likely that Gruffudd ap Maredudd ap Philip, one of the hostages named in Gwenwynwyn's agreement with King John on 7 October 1208 (no. 576 below), was a son of the last witness (*Charters of Ystrad Marchell*, 79).

552 Strata Marcella Abbey

Sale, by Gwenwynwyn and the men who used to possess the land of Rhoswydol in peace, in free and perpetual possession of all the land with its appurtenances within these bounds: from the mouth of the stream between Rhoswydol and Byrhedyn as that stream leads upwards to its source, then directly to the grove called Blaen Ceulan, by that grove between the grove and field to Rhiw Hithiar, the land called (?) Rhoscylchedd (Róskelchet)*, and on the other side from the mouth of the stream which is between Rhoswydol and Byrhedyn, up along the Crewi to Cwm (?) Crewi* (Eréruit) *and by the stream which runs there to its source, as well as the mountains which pertain to those lands. They have sold all the aforesaid land with all its appurtenances for 5½ pounds, to be possessed freely, without any secular exaction or custom in perpetual right. Sealing clause; witnesses.*

Ystrad Marchell, 1199

A = original charter, now lost.

B = facsimile of A, in Jones, 'Abbey of Ystrad Marchell', facing p. 35. Although the original charter was said to have been restored to Wynnstay, it is not among the Wynnstay Archives in NLW or Denbighshire Record Office, Ruthin. The facsimile shows a fold-up at the base, two central horizontal slits in fold with a tag which exits through a slit in the base of the fold; sealed on tag. Circular seal, imperfect; equestrian, facing right; legend: … GILL: GVENWNV … .

Pd. from A, Jones, 'Abbey of Ystrad Marchell', 33–4; from a photograph of A (probably B), Jones, [Untitled], 384; from B, *Ystrad Marchell Charters*, no. 20.

Cd., Davies, 'Strata Marcella documents', 169–70 (no. 9); *H*, no. 243.

Omnibus sancte matris ecclesie filiis tam presentibus quam futuris notum sit quod ego Wennunwen filius Owini et viri quorum fuit terra que nominatur Roswidaul et qui eam in pace possidebant vendidimus monachis de Stradmarchel in liberam et quietam et perpetuam possessionem totam terram cum omnibus pertinenciis suis que est infra istos terminos, scilicet ab *aber* rivuli qui est inter Roswidaul et Barrédin sicut ducit idem rivulus susum usque ad eius ortum, et inde in directum usque ad nemus quod dicitur Blain Kailan, et per idem nemus scilicet inter nemus et campum usque Riu Híthiar, et terram que nominatur Róskelchet, et item ex alia parte ab *aber* rivuli qui est inter Roswidaul et Barrédin, Créwi susum in longum usque ad Cum Eréruit et per rivulum qui ibi currit usque ad eius ortum; insuper et quantum pertinet de montibus ad terras illas. Vendidimus autem eisdem monachis pro quinque libris et dimidia totam prefatam terram cum omnibus pertinentiis suis in bosco scilicet in plano, in aquis et pascuis et in omnibus utilitatibus suis, libere et quiete, bene et in pace et sine omni exactione vel consuetudine seculari iure perpetuo possidendam. Et ne processu temporis hec nostra venditio ab laiquo possit violari ego prenominatus Wennunwen eam presentis scripti munimine et sigilli mei impressione et testium attestatione coroboravi. His testibus: Sig(e)ri(us) prior, Aaron cellerario, Tegwaret, Daniel, Goron', Elfin conversis de domo predicta; de secularibus vero, Daniele filio sacerdotis, Goron' filio Einn', Meiler filio Riawal, Maredud filio Philippi, Einniaun filio Llewarch. Facta est autem predicta venditio apud St(ra)dmarch(el) anno ab incarnatione domini m° c° nonagesimo nono.

Rhoswydol (Rhoswydol Farm SN 839 977) was located on the border between the parishes of Darowen and Penegoes in Cyfeiliog (*Ystrad Marchell Charters*, 117 and Map III).

553 Strata Marcella Abbey

Sale by Gwenwynwyn and all the heirs of the land called Rhoswydol in perpetual possession for 5¼ pounds of all the land called Rhoswydol with all its bounds and appurtenances, freely and immune from all secular exaction, custom and service. Sealing clause; witnesses.

Ystrad Marchell, 1199

A = NLW, Wynnstay Estate Records, Ystrad Marchell Charters, no. 21. Endorsed: Wenu(n)wi(n) super Roswidaul (s. xii/xiii); early modern endorsements; approx. 195 × 107 + 14 mm.; two central horizontal slits in fold for a tag (*c.*12 mm. wide) which exits through a slit in the base of the fold; sealed on tag. Seal missing.

Pd. from A, *Ystrad Marchell Charters*, no. 21.

Cd., Davies, 'Strata Marcella documents', 170 (no. 10); *H*, no. 244.

Noscant universi sancte matris ecclesie filii tam presentes quam futuri quod ego Wennunwen Owini filius et omnes hered[e]s terre que dicitur Roswidaul vendidimus monachis de Stradmarchell in propriam et perpetuam possessionem pro quinque libris et dimidia omnem terram que appellatur Roswidavl cum omnibus terminis et pertinentiis suis in bosco et in plano, in aquis et pascuis et cum omnibus usibus et utilitatibus suis, libere et quiete et ab omni exactione et consuetudine et servitute seculari immunem. Ista conventio facta est anno ab incarnatione domini m° c° nonogesimo nono apud Stradmarchell in manu S. prioris. Et ne in pos[ter]um predicta conventio improborum nequicia inquietetur vel perturbetur ego predictus Wennunw(en) eam carte mee munimine et sigilli mei impressione et testium attestatione confi[rmavi]. Hi[i]s testibus: A. cellerario, Tegwaret, Daniel, Gorronui, Elfin conversis eiusdem domus, Daniele filio s[a]cerdot[ti]s, Gorr[onui] filio Eynniavn, Meiler filio Riawal, Mareduth filio Philippi, E[y]nnia[vn] filio Llwarch et multis aliis.

See note to no. 552 above.

554 Strata Marcella Abbey

Sale, at the request and with the consent of the elders of Cyfeiliog, of the land called Rhoswydol for £3, with all its bounds and appurtenances and immune from all exaction. Sealing clause; witnesses.

[*c.*1199]

B = NLW MS 1641B, ii, p. 12. s. xviii/xix.

Pd. from B, *Ystrad Marchell Charters*, no. 22.

Universis[a] [sancte matris ecclesie filiis tam presentibus quam futuris] notum sit quod ego Wennunwen filius Owini rogatione et consensu seniorum de Kiuilhoc vendiderimus[b] terram illam que vocatur Roswidaul monachis de Stradmarcell pro tribus libris cum omnibus finibus et pertinentiis suis ab omni exactione immunem. Et quia moderna generatio suadibilis est ad malum unde sibi lucrum possit extorquere predictam terram carte mee confirmatione et sigilli nostri impressione signavimus et corroboravimus. Additis his testibus: Daniele filio sacerdotis, Goronui filio Einaun, Meileir Du, Einnaun filio Luarth, Madaoc filio Gnillin, Pobien, Maredut filiis Philippi. Valete.

[a] B *inserts* x x x *to indicate missing words.* | [b] *sic in* B.

As it is related to the sales in nos 552–3 above the charter was probably issued at about the same date as these.

(?)†555 Strata Marcella Abbey

Grant in perpetual alms, for the salvation of the souls of himself, his parents and all his heirs and successors, of all the land of Dolwen with all its appurtenances in wood, plain, waters, mills, woods, mountains, pastures and all other profits pertaining to that land, in these bounds: on one side, along the Nodwydd from the place where it descends into the Yfyrnwy to its source, thence by the middle of Cefnbrwynennau to the source of the Bolo, thence to the source of the Cannon, thence along the boundary of Caereinion and Cyfeiliog to the source of the Yfyrnwy, along the Yfyrnwy to the aforesaid source of the Nodwydd; to be possessed freely, without any secular exaction, claim or custom, in all their uses, rights of use and liberties, in perpetual right. Sealing clause; witnesses.

Tafolwern, 1200

B = NLW Wynnstay Estate Records, Ystrad Marchell Charters, no. 23. s. xiii[2]. Endorsed: ·VIII· (s. xiii[2]); early modern endorsement; approx. 273 × 100 + 10 mm. Two central horizontal slits, one just above fold, one in fold, for a tag (*c.* 11 mm. wide) which exits through a slit in the base of the fold; sealed on tag. Seal missing, though linen bag which contained it remains.
Pd. from B, *Ystrad Marchell Charters*, no. 23.
Cd., Davies, 'Strata Marcella documents', 171 (no. 11); *H*, no. 245.

Omnibus sancte matris ecclesie filiis tam presentibus quam futuris notum sit quod ego Wenunwyn filius Oweni de Keveillauc dedi et concessi et hac presenti carta mea confirmavi Deo et Beate Marie et monachis de St(ra)tmarchell Deo ibidem servientibus, in puram et perpetuam elemosinam, pro salute anime mee et parentum meorum et omnium heredum et successorum meorum, totam terram Dolwen cum omnibus pertinentiis suis in bosco, in plano, in viis, in semitis, in aquis, in molendinis, in silvis, in nemoribus, in montanis, in pascuis, in pasturis et omnibus aliis comodis ad dictam terram spectantibus in hiis terminis: ex una parte videlicet Nodwyd de loco ubi descendit in Ewernoe per longitudinem Nodwyd usque ad eius ortum, ab ortu eius per medium Kevenbrvynennau usque Blaenbolo, de *blaen* Bolo usque *blaen* Kannon; deinde sicut ducit terminus Kereinavn et Keuellyauc usque *blaen* Evernoe, Ewernoe in sui longitudine usque ad predictum locum Abernodwyd. Volo igitur ego predictus Wenunwen ut prenominati monachi omnes prefatas terras in predictis [terminis][a] bene et in pace, libere et quiete sine aliqua exactione vel calumpnia seu consuetudine seculari, in omnibus omnino usibus et utilitatibus et libertatibus suis iure perpetuo possideant. Et ne aliquis heredum meorum vel successorum istam meam donationem instigante dyabolo infringere conetur eam tam sigilli mei impressione quam bonorum virorum atestatione munivi et corroboravi. His testibus: Aniano ab Kenvelin, Sullen archidiacono, Goronwy ab Eynavn, magistro Heylin, Gruffud ab Edneweyn, Kadugavn ab Griffri, David Coch, Edneweyn Flam et multis aliis. Facta est autem hec mea donatio anno domini m° cc° apud Duwalern.

[a] *omitted* B.

The charter is written in a similar hybrid hand to that of no. 541 above, probably by the same scribe, and therefore cannot be an authentic original issued by Gwenwynwyn. For the general problems of determining whether the text is a copy of an authentic charter see note to no. 541 above. In contrast to the lands named in no. 541, Dolwen is not said by any earlier source to have been granted by Gwenwynwyn, but he may have made such a grant as the abbey held the land later in the Middle Ages (*Taxatio ecclesiastica*, 289 (*Delwen*); *Ystrad Marchell Charters*, no. 89; cf. Williams, *Atlas*, 60, 61). Dolwen (Dolwen Farm SH 975 075) lay in the parishes of Llanerfyl and Llangadfan, cmt. Caereinion (*Ystrad Marchell Charters*, 117–18 and Map III).

556 Strata Marcella Abbey
Grant in perpetual alms of all the land called Rhiw Caenesied with all its bounds and appurtenances in plain and wood, waters and pastures and other uses and profits, free and immune from all secular exaction, custom and service. The true boundary of the land is, in length, from Carno to the ford of the river Rhiw at Cwmowen and, in breadth, from the river Ffinnant to the river Brydwen. Witnesses.

Ystrad Marchell, 4 March 1200 [=1201]

> A = NLW, Wynnstay Estate Records, Ystrad Marchell Charters, no. 33. Endorsed: Wennu(n)win super Riu kanesseit ·IX· (s. xii/xiii); early modern endorsements; approx. 150 × 84 + 14 mm.; a single central horizontal slit in fold for a tag (*c.*9 mm. wide); sealed on tag. Circular seal, green wax, imperfect, originally approx. 50 mm. diameter; equestrian, facing right; legend: SIGIL . . . . . . F[I]L : OV . . . . . . C.
> Pd. from A, *Ystrad Marchell Charters*, no. 33.
> Cd., Davies, 'Strata Marcella documents', 172 (no. 14); *H*, no. 247

Universis sancte matris ecclesie filiis tam presentibus quam futuris notum sit quod ego Wenuinwin Owini filius dedi et confirmavi Deo et Beate Marie[a] et monachis de St(ra)tmarcell in puram et perpetuam elemosinam omnem terram illam que vocatur Riu Kaenessiet cum omnibus terminis et pertinentiis suis in plano et bosco, in aquis et pasturis et in ceteris usibus et utilitatibus suis et in omnibus commodis, liberam et quietam et immunem ab omni exactione et consuetudine et servitute seculari. Predictam itaque terram supradictis monachis bene et in pace, libere et quiete, plenarie et integre et honorifice dedi, cuius verus terminus est a Carno in longitudine usque ad vadum fluminis qui dicitur Riu apud Cu(m)hewen, et in latitudine a fluvio Finnant usque ad fluvium qui dicitur Bretwen. Ista autem donatio data est et confirmata ut sit rata et inconcussa apud St(ra)tmarcell in manu Philippi abbatis coram conventu quarto nonas marcii anno ab incarnatione domini m° ducentesimo. Testes igitur huius donationis sunt: Hoitliw Seis, Grifri filius Ioruert, Madocus cognomento Tanwr, Meuric filius Resi, Teguaret filius Etneuet, Ioruert filius Riwallaun, Huveluiu filius Kengen.

[a] *word written in majuscule letters* A.

Assuming that the scribe began the year at the Annunciation (25 March) the charter was issued in March 1201 by modern reckoning. Rhiw Caenesied lay to the east of Carno (SN 964 965) in the parish of Llanwnnog, Arwystli (*Ystrad Marchell Charters*, 119 and Map III).

*557 Strata Marcella Abbey
Sale of all the land of Pennantigi (Pennanttiki).

[Probably 4 March 1201 × August 1204]

Mention only, in a confirmation charter of Edward II dated at Tutbury, 12 March 1322 (*Ystrad Marchell Charters*, no. 27; Jones, 'Abbey of Ystrad Marchell', 310 (from Henry VI's inspeximus, 1450); cd., *CChR 1300–26*, 439; *H*, no. 264). This and the following five grants appear in Edward II's inspeximus between summaries of no. 556 above, dated 4 March 1200 (1201 by modern reckoning) and before no. 565 below, dated 1 September 1204. Pennantigi (Pennantigi Uchaf SH 813 161) was the location of a vaccary in the parish of Mallwyd, cmt. Mawddwy (*Ystrad Marchell Charters*, 118 and Map III).

*558 Strata Marcella Abbey
Grant in perpetual alms of all the land of Aberbrydwen (Abrebretwen) *with all its appurtenances which the monks had from the heirs of that township.*

[Probably 4 March 1201 × August 1204]

Mention only, in a confirmation charter of Edward II dated at Tutbury, 12 March 1322 (*Ystrad Marchell Charters*, no. 28; Jones, 'Abbey of Ystrad Marchell', 310 (from Henry VI's inspeximus, 1450); cd., *CChR 1300–26*, 439; *H*, no. 265). See note to no. 557 above. Aberbrydwen was situated at the confluence of Nant Brydwen with Nant Carno in Arwystli at SN 994 957 (*Ystrad Marchell Charters*, 118).

*559 Strata Marcella Abbey
Grant of the land of Deupiw (Deupiu) *which the heirs of that land sold to the monks.*

[Probably 4 March 1201 × August 1204]

Mention only, in a confirmation charter of Edward II dated at Tutbury, 12 March 1322 (*Ystrad Marchell Charters*, no. 29; Jones, 'Abbey of Ystrad Marchell', 310 (from Henry VI's inspeximus, 1450); cd., *CChR 1300–26*, 439; *H*, no. 263). See note to no. 557 above and, for Deupiw in Arwystli, note to no. 16 above.

*560 Strata Marcella Abbey
Grant of all the land below these bounds: from the stream between Hafodwen (Hauodwen) *and Pennant Iaen* (Penanhihewen) *to the river Twymyn* (Toymen) *and along that river to Nant Derwen* (Deren) *and from that stream to the mountain.*

[Probably 4 March 1201 × August 1204]

Mention only, in a confirmation charter of Edward II dated at Tutbury, 12 March 1322 (*Ystrad Marchell Charters*, no. 31; Jones, 'Abbey of Ystrad Marchell', 310 (from Henry VI's inspeximus, 1450); cd., *CChR 1300–26*, 439; *H*, no. 266). See note to no. 557 above. For the lands, including Hafodwen (SN 912 999), in the parish of Llanbrynmair, Cyfeiliog, see *Ystrad Marchell Charters*, 119 and Map III.

*561 Strata Marcella Abbey
Sale of a third of the township of Gaer (Gaer) *with all its appurtenances.*

[Probaby 4 March 1201 × August 1204]

Mention only, in a confirmation charter of Edward II dated at Tutbury, 12 March 1322 (*Ystrad Marchell Charters*, no. 30; Jones, 'Abbey of Ystrad Marchell', 310 (from Henry VI's inspeximus, 1450); cd., *CChR 1300–26*, 439; *H*, no. 267). See note to no. 557 above. Gaer was situated to the south-west of the abbey, in the parish of Castell Caereinion (*Ystrad Marchell Charters*, 116 and Map I).

*562 Strata Marcella Abbey
Sale of half of the township of Rhosgarreg (Rose Carrec) *specifically with all its appurtenances.*

[Probably 4 March 1201 × August 1204]

Mention only, in a confirmation charter of Edward II dated at Tutbury, 12 March 1322 (*Ystrad Marchell Charters*, no. 32; Jones, 'Abbey of Ystrad Marchell', 310 (from Henry VI's inspeximus, 1450); cd., *CChR 1300–26*, 439; *H*, no. 268). See note to no. 557 above. Rhosgarreg (SN 8088 955) was situated in the parish of Isygarreg, Cyfeiliog (*Ystrad Marchell Charters*, 119).

563 Strata Marcella Abbey
Grant for the salvation of his soul, in free and perpetual alms, of all the pastures of the whole province of Cyfeiliog within these bounds: from Bôn y Maen Melin to Llwyn y Groes, thence directly to the source of the Nanhanog, along the Nanhanog to its source, thence to the mouth of Nant Garth Brandu, along that stream to its source, thence directly to Carneddwen, thence to Gobleithau, and from the head of Gobleithau along Nant Teiling from its source to its mouth, then along the Bacho to the mouth of the Dengwm, then along the Dengwm to its source, then to Gelligogau, then to the Rheidol and along the Rheidol to Gwryd Cai, then again along the Rheidol to the source of Camddwr Cyfeiliog, and from the source of Camddwr Cyfeiliog to its source, thence directly to the source of the Einion, and along the Einion to its mouth, then by the Dyfi to the mouth of the Dulas, then along the Dulas to its source, then directly to (?)Cefn y Bwlch (Kenghulf), *then to the source of the Llwydo, along the Llwydo to its mouth and then along the Dyfi to the mouth of Nant Llywelyn* (Llewenith), *along Nant Llywelyn to its source, then directly to Rhyd Pebyllfa above the Clywedog, and then along the Clywedog to the Gwernach (Nant y Saeson), along the Gwernach to its source, then along the higher mountain to Rhyd Derwen, along the Derwen to the Yfyrnwy, thence along Nant yr Eira to the Lledwern, from the source of the Lledwern directly to Bon Maen Melin. All these pastures within these bounds are to be possessed in wood, plain and all places freely, without any secular exaction or custom in perpetual right, so that no other monks or nuns may have any property or common rights within these bounds, except for the the monks of Cwm-hir, to whom at the petition of the monks of Strata Marcella Gwenwynwyn has granted pastures between the Corf and the Einion, and except for the monks of Cymer, to whom, also with the consent of Strata Marcella, he has granted Llwydiarth and Cwm-celli on the other side of the river. He wishes that the monks of Strata Marcella may possess all the aforesaid pastures within the aforenamed boundaries, apart from the aforesaid parts, fully in perpetual right. Sealing clause; witnesses.*

1201

A = NLW, Wynnstay Estate Records, Ystrad Marchell Charters, no. 34. Endorsed: Wenu(n)win super omnes pasturas de Keueliac (s. xiii med.); Keueilliac (s. xiii med.); early modern endorsements; approx. 170 × 231 + 16 mm.; two central horizontal slits in fold for a tag (c.9 mm. wide) which exits through a slit in the base of the fold; tag broken off at fold; originally sealed on tag. Detached circular seal found loose in box in 1989, green wax, imperfect, originally approx. 60 mm. diameter; equestrian, facing right; no legend survives.

Pd. from A, *Ystrad Marchell Charters*, no. 34; from an unidentified transcript owned by Mr Edward Herbert of Montgomery, Meyrick, 'On a deed of gift', 448–9 (incomplete); from an unidentified transcript, Pennant, *Tour in Wales*, ii. 497–8; from Pennant, Anon, 'Documents illustrative of the history of the princes', 117; from Pennant, Jones, 'Abbey of Ystrad Marchell', 297–9 (trans. only); from a transcript in NLW, Llanstephan MS 156 (s. xvii), *RMWL*, ii. 735; from a transcript owned by Price Loveden M. P., W. B. J., 'Charter of Gwenwynwyn'.

Cd., Davies, 'Strata Marcella documents', 173 (no. 15); *H*, no. 248.

Omnibus sancte matris ecclesie filiis tam presentibus quam futuris notum sit quod ego Wenunwen filius Owini dedi Deo et gloriose Virgini Marie et monachis de Stradmarchell pro salute anime mee in liberam et quietam et perpetuam elemosinam omnes pasturas totius provincie que dicitur Keueilliauc infra istos terminos: scilicet a Bon Main Melin usque ad Lluin Ecrois, et inde in directum usque ad *blain* Nanhanauc, et inde Nanhanauc usque ad eius *aber*, et inde usque ad Abernant Karthbrandu, et per longitudinem ipsius rivuli usque ad suum *blain*, et inde directum usque ad Carnethwen, et inde usque ad Gobleitheu, et a *pen* Gobleitheu *blain* Nant Teyling usque ad suum *aber*, et inde Bacho usque ad *aber* Dengum, et inde per Dengum usque ad eius ortum, et inde usque ad Keilligogeu, et inde usque ad Reidiaul et per Reidiaul usque ad Gwrhet Kei, et inde Reidiaul iterum usque ad *aber* Camdwr Keueiliauc, et ab *aber* Camdwr Keueiliauc usque ad eius ortum, et inde in directum usque ad *blain* Eynniaun, et sic per Eynniaun usque ad eius *aber*, et inde per Deui usque ad *aber* Dwlas, et inde per Dwlas usque ad eius ortum, et inde in directum usque ad Kenghulf, et inde usque ad *blain* Lloido, et per Lloido usque ad eius *aber* et inde Deui usque ad *aber* Llewenith, et sic per Llewenith usque ad eius ortum, et inde in directum usque ad Red Pebellua super Clawedauc, et inde per Clawedauc usque ad Gwernach, et per Gwernach usque ad eius ortum, et inde sicut ducit mons superior usque ad Red Derwen, et sic per Derwen usque ad Euernoe, et inde Nant Er Heyre usque ad Lledwern, et a *blain* Lledwern in directum usque ad Bon Main Melin. Omnes itaque pasturas dedi ego predictus Wennunwen prenominatis monachis infra prefatos terminos tam in bosco quam in plano et in omnibus locis libere et quiete, bene et in pace et sine omni exactione vel consuetudine seculari perpetuo iure possidendas, ita videlicet ut nulli alii monachi nulle etiam sanctimoniales aliquam habeant in pasturis proprietatem vel communionem infra predictos terminos, exceptis monachis de Cumhyr quibus peticione monachorum de Stradmarchel concessi pasturas inter Corf et Eynniaun, et exceptis monachis de Kemm(er) quibus etiam consensu eorumdem monachorum de Stradm(archell) Lloidarth et Cumketlli ex altera parte fluvii concessi. Volo ergo ego prenominatus Wennu(n)wen ut sepedicti monachi de Stradmarchell omnes predictas pasturas infra prenominatos terminos, exceptis partibus predictis, plenarie et integre iure perpetuo possideant. Et ut hec mea donatio firma in posterum et stabilis ab omnibus teneatur eam presentis scripti munimine et testium attestatione premunivi. His testibus: Suliano archidiacono, magistro Heilin, magistro Mabin, Eynniaun filio Rod(r)i, Kadug' filio Grifri, David Goch, Edenewein Flam, Goronoy filio Eynniaun. Datum anno ab incarnatione domini anno m° cc° i° in manu P. abbatis.

For the bounds of the commote of Cyfeiliog described here, including the identification of the Corf as Nant Coro or Corog, see Morgan, 'Territorial divisions [II]', 22–4; *Ystrad Marchell Charters*, 119–21 and Map III. Gwenwynwyn also granted, very probably at an earlier date, all the pastures of Cyfeiliog to Cwm-hir (no. 547 above). Despite the present charter's explicit reservation to Cwm-hir of the pastures between the Corf and the Einion, those pastures featured among the matters in dispute between Cwm-hir and Strata Marcella settled by Cistercian arbitrators in 1227: the pastures in Ceredigion were adjudged to Cwm-hir, those in Cyfeiliog to Strata Marcella (*Ystrad Marchell Charters*, 23–4 and no. 70).

564 Strata Marcella Abbey

Grant, inspired by love, for the salvation of the souls of himself, his parents and his heirs, of all the land of Ystrad Marchell with all its bounds and appurtenances in wood, plain, waters and meadows, in perpetual alms, free from all exaction and custom. The boundary of the land is, in length, from the horse's pit [Pwll y Ceffyl] to the mouth of the Belau, along the Belau to the river which descends from (?) Trelydan (lata villa), *along that river to (?) Gwengwŷdd* (Guengwith), *then straight to the summit of the wood where the farther dyke appears, thence to Ffynnon Tysilio and thence in a straight line to the Severn. Further grant of all the land called Rhydhesgyn Isaf and Rhydhesgyn Uchaf and all the bright grove [Goleugoed] with all its bounds and appurtenances, in perpetual right. Sealing clause; witnesses.*

Ystrad Marchell, 7 July 1202

B = TNA: PRO, C 53/108 (Ch. R. 15 Edward II), m. 6 (in an inspeximus, 12 March 1322).
C = TNA: PRO, C 66/470 (Pat. R. 28 Henry VI, pt. 1), m. 7 (in an inspeximus of B, 14 March 1450).
Pd. from B, *Ystrad Marchell Charters*, no. 36; from C, Jones, 'Abbey of Ystrad Marchell', 300–1.
Cd., *CChR 1300–26*, 438 (from B); Davies, 'Strata Marcella documents', 174 (no. 17) (from B); *H*, no. 250.

Universis sancte matris ecclesie filiis tam presentibus quam futuris notum sit quod ego Wennunwen filius[a] Owini intuitu caritatis pro salute anime mee et parentum necnon et heredum meorum dedi [et][b] concessi Deo et Beate Marie et monachis apud Stradmarchell Deo servientibus totam terram que dicitur Stradmarchell cum omnibus terminis et pertinentibus suis in bosco et plano et aquis et pratis in perpetuam et quietam elemosinam et ab omni exactione et consuetudine liberam, cuius terre verus terminus est in longitudine a puteo caballi usque Abbel(er)eloure, ab Eb(er)eleu eodem flumine terminante usque ad fluvium qui descendit a lata villa et illo fluvio terminus observante usque Guengwith, et abhinc recto tramite usque ad summitatem silve, ubi ulterior fossa apparet et de hinc usque ad fontem Tessiliau et de fonte recta linea usque ad Haueren nominatim. Etiam dedi prefatis monachis ego[c] predictus Wennunwen omnem terram que dicitur Redheskyn inferius similiter et Redheskyn superius, totum etiam clarum nemus cum omnibus terminis suis et pertinentibus, ut ipsi easdem terras iure perpetuo libere et quiete possideant. Set quoniam ingeniosa ad malum presens est etas et id calumpniose temptat infringere unde sibi lucrum conatur extorquere hanc donationem proborum virorum attestatione et sigilli nostri impressione corroboravimus. Hiis testibus: Suliano archidiacono et duobus filiis eius Eyniaun et Idenevet, magistro Helin, Morauc filio Ioh(ann)is, Leulino filii Oweni, Hoidelou Seis Peruhanndir,ᵈ Hodewein Fflam, Howel filio Kenewrec, Meuric filio Kenewreic, Madoco filio Grifri, Gruffud filio Gervasii, Traharn filio Ideneuet, Eynniaumᵉ filio Kenewreyc, Eynniaumᵉ filio Dehewent, Iaruord filio Riwatlam, Edenewein Seis et multis aliis. Facta est autem hec donatio apud Stramargchell coram conventu nonas iulii anno ab incarnatione domini mᵒ ccᵒ secundo.

ᵃ B *inserts* predicti, *referring to the donor in the preceding charter cited in the inspeximus.* | ᵇ *omitted* B. | ᶜ eo B. | ᵈ *it is uncertain whether* Peruhanndir *should be taken with* Hoidelou Seis *or as a separate name.* | ᵉ *sic in* B.

This is a confirmation of Owain Cyfeiliog's foundation charter for Strata Marcella (no. 539 above).

565 Strata Marcella Abbey

Notification that Meurig Sais ap Griffri, his brother Gruffudd and their sons, nephews and co-heirs of the land called Perfeddgefn granted, for the salvation of their souls, in perpetual alms, free of all secular exaction and custom, all the land of Perfeddgefn in these bounds, namely from the mouth of the Gwernach up to Gweunrudd which is the boundary between Caereinion and Cyfeiliog, along the stream which descends from there to the river Marchno and then along the Marchno to the mouth of the Gwernach, in wood, plain and all rights of use. After the death of the aforesaid brothers Meurig and Gruffudd, their sons, nephews and co-heirs sold for 5 pounds of silver in perpetual possession, free of all exaction and secular custom, all the following land: from the mouth of the Sguthan up to its source, then directly to Llyn Coch Hwyad, thence to the source of the Gwernach, then along the Gwernach to the Marchno, then along the Marchno down to the mouth of the Sguthan, thence climbing the side of the mountain to the Gwibedyn and along the Gwibedyn to the Marchno. They sold the aforesaid land in wood, plain, waters and all rights of use so that the vendors ought to warrant it against all claiming it or injuring the monks on its account. As the aforesaid donors and vendors had no seals, Gwenwynwyn, prince of Powys, has at their request and with their consent confirmed the lands to the monks with his seal and the witnessing of the good men who were present at the gift and sale and granted, for the salvation of his soul, the same lands in free and perpetual possession. Witnesses.

Ystrad Marchell, 1 September 1204

B = NLW, Wynnstay Estate Records, Inspeximus of Elizabeth I, Shrewsbury, 5 April 1584.
Pd. from B, *Ystrad Marchell Charters*, no. 37; from B, Jones, 'Abbey of Ystrad Marchell', 303–4 (trans. only).
Cd., Davies, 'Strata Marcella documents', 175 (no. 18); *H*, no. 251.

Sciant tam presentes quam futuri quod Meuric Seis filius G(ri)fri et G(ri)ffud fratri eius, scilicet filius eiusdem G(ri)fri, et filii eorum et nepotes et coheredes terre que dicitur P(er)uerthgefn, dederunt et concesserunt pro salute anime sue monachis de Stradmarchell Deo et Beate Marie ibidem servientibus, in puram `et quietam et perpetuam elemosinam, et ab omni exactione vel consuetudine seculari liberam, totam terram que dicitur P(er)uethgefn[a] in his terminis: scilicet ab Ab(er)gwernach susum usque ad Gweunruith qui est terminus inter Kereinium[b] et Keueilliauc, et sicut ducit rivulus qui inde descendit usque ad fluvium qui dicitur Marchno, et inde Marchno iusum in longum usque ad Ab(er)gwernach, tam in bosco quam in plano et in omnibus usibus suis et utilitatibus. Post mortem vero predictorum fratrum, scilicet Meuric et G(ri)ffud, filii eorum et nepotes et coheredes sui vendiderunt predictis monachis pro quinque libris argenti in quietam et perpetuam possessionem, et ab omnni exactione vel consuetudine seculari liberam, totam terram subscriptam in terminis suis: videlicet Ab(er)scuthon susum *hid i blain*, et inde in directum usque ad Llincoh hoyat, et inde usque ad Blaingwernach, et inde Gwernach in longum usque ad Marchno, et inde Marchno iusum usque ad Ab(er)scuthon `et ab Aberscuthon per ascensum lateris montis usque ad Gwibedyn', et sicut ducit Gwibedyn usque Marchno. Hanc predictam terram vendiderunt prefati heredes prenominatis monachis in bosco, scilicet, in plano, in aquis, in omnibus usibus suis et utilitatibus, ita sane quod venditores ipsius terre debent eam warantizare predictis monachis contra omnes eam calumpniantes sive molestiam aliquam prefatis monachis pro illa facientes, et quia predictarum terrarum datores vel venditores sigillum non habuerunt, ego Wenunwen' Powisie princeps, illorum petitione et consensu, prefatas terras sigilli mei impressione et bonorum virorum attestatione qui donationi et venditioni presentes aderant prefatis monachis confirmavi et pro salute anime mee ipsas terras in liberam et quietam et perpetuam possessionem eis dedi et concessi. His testibus: magistro Heylin, Suliano archidiacono et duobus filiis eius, Eynniaun et Ideneuet, magistro Mabin, Kefnert clerico, Yeuuaf Penkil, G(ri)ffud filio Edenewein, Yeuuaf Dv et multis aliis. Facta est autem hec confirmatio anno videlicet ab incarnatione domini m° cc° quarto apud Stradmarchell kalendas vero septembris.

[a] P(er)uethgefu B. | [b] *nine minims follow the* e *in* B.

For the lands, in Caereinion, see *Ystrad Marchell Charters*, 121–2 and Map III.

*566 Strata Marcella Abbey

Grant of half the township of Ysgor-fawr (Scoruaur) *and of the land of Blaen Carno* (Blainkarno).

[September 1204 × 1206]

Mention only, in a confirmation charter of Edward II dated at Tutbury, 12 March 1322 (*Ystrad Marchell Charters*, no. 38; Jones, 'Abbey of Ystrad Marchell', 310 (from Henry VI's inspeximus, 1450); cd., *CChR 1300–26*, 439; *H*, no. 269). The grant is listed immediately after a summary of no. 565 above, dated 1 September 1204. A *terminus ad quem* is probably provided by no. 9 above, dated 1206, which appears to be a confirmation of earlier grants and includes half of Ysgor-fawr. For the lands, in the parish of Carno, Arwystli, see Pryce, 'Church of Trefeglwys', 37; *Ystrad Marchell Charters*, 122 and Map III.

*567 Strata Marcella Abbey

Confirmation of Cwm Arannell (Cum Raunel), *(?) Garddllifain* (Gardliueinn), *Y Bedwosed* (Ebedwosset) *and Hafod Gwgan* (Hauot Gugan) *with appurtenances.*

[September 1204 × 1206]

Mention only, in a confirmation charter of Edward II dated at Tutbury, 12 March 1322 (*Ystrad Marchell Charters*, no. 39; Jones, 'Abbey of Ystrad Marchell', 311 (from Henry VI's inspeximus, 1450); cd., *CChR 1300–26*, 439). This immediately follows no. 566 in Edward II's inspeximus and may be assigned to the same date range. For the lands, in Arwystli, see *Ystrad Marchell Charters*, 122 and Map III.

*568 Strata Marcella Abbey

Confirmation of all the land of Blaen Carno (Blankarno) *in wood and plain with all its appurtenances.*

[September 1204 × 1206]

Mention only, in a confirmation charter of Edward II dated at Tutbury, 12 March 1322 (*Ystrad Marchell Charters*, no. 40; Jones, 'Abbey of Ystrad Marchell', 311 (from Henry VI's inspeximus, 1450); cd., *CChR 1300–26*, 439; *H*, no. 270). This immediately follows no. 567 in Edward II's inspeximus and may be assigned to the same date range. Blaen Carno was also granted in no. 566 above.

569 Strata Marcella Abbey

Grant, for the salvation of the souls of himself and his father and mother, in perpetual alms, of all the pastures of the province of Mochnant within these bounds: in length, from Dolauwennau near Abercynllaith to Cwm Fagel; in breadth, from Cynorion to the river Yfyrnwy and Llanwddyn. The monks shall possess all these pastures without any secular exaction or custom in perpetual right in wood and plain within the aforenamed bounds and within all other bounds not named which Gwenwynwyn possesses, so that no other religious in that province shall have pastures, lands or possessions there, except for the Hospitallers who already have lands there; as for the rest, they shall not proceed to occupy lands or pastures by request, payment or any other means.

12 February 1205

A = NLW, Wynnstay Estate Records, Ystrad Marchell Charters, no. 41. Endorsed: Wennu(n)w' super pasturas Mocha(n)t (s. xiii[1]); early modern endorsement; approx. 175 × 145 + 21 mm.; two central horizontal slits in fold for a tag (*c.*7 mm. wide) which exits through a slit in the base of the fold; sealed on tag. Circular seal, green wax, approx. 60 mm. diameter; equestrian, facing right; legend: SIGILL : GVENVUNWIN : DE : KEVEILIAVC. The parchment is stained in places.
Pd. from A, *Ystrad Marchell Charters*, no. 41.
Cd., Davies, 'Strata Marcella documents', 176 (no. 19); *H*, no. 252.

Noscant universi sancte matris ecclesie filii tam presentes quam futuri quod ego Wennu(n)wen Owini filius pro salute anime mee et patris et matris mee dedi et concessi et confirmavi Deo et Beate Marie et monachis de Stradmarchell in puram et perpetuam elemosinam omnes pasturas provincie que dicitur Mochnant infra istos terminos: in longum scilicet a Dolewennev iuxta Aberkenllith usque ad Cum Uagel, in latum vero a Kenneureon usque ad fluvium qui dicitur Eu(er)noe et Llanwothin qui est terminus similiter. Volo igitur ut prefati monachi omnes predictas pasturas bene et in pace et sine aliqua exactione vel consuetudine seculari iure perpetuo tam in bosco quam in plano possideant infra prenominatos terminos et infra omnes reliquos hic non nominatos quos ego Wennunwen predictus plane possideo, ita ut nulli alii viri religiosi in eadem provincia aliquam unquam habeant pasturam aut terram sive possessionem nisi tantum fratres Hospitalarii qui terras iam adquisitas habeant; de cetero vero in terrarum sive pasturarum occupationem non processuri nec prece nec pretio neque aliquo alio modo. His testibus: magistro Heilin, magistro Mabin, Eynniavn filio Kadugavn, Eynniavn filio Madauc, G(ri)ffud filio Howel, Morithic filio Aearthur, Kellennin filio Ythael, Gurgenev filio Yago et multis aliis. Facta est autem hec donatio apud St(ra)dmarchell anno scilicet ab incarnatione domini m° cc° iiii° pridie idus februarii.

For the boundaries of the commote of Mochnant Uwch Rhaeadr described here see *Ystrad Marchell Charters*, 122–3. The reference to the lands already held by the Hospitallers in the commote must refer to their grange of Llanwddyn, located to the south and west of Lake Vyrnwy, and is valuable evidence that they had received those lands by February 1205, considerably earlier than the first reference to their possession of Llanwddyn *eo nomine* in 1338 (see Rees, *History*, 66, 128; Davies, 'Property and landownership', 52; Silvester, 'Llanwddyn hospitium', 64–5, 67 (map)).

*570 Strata Marcella Abbey

*Grant of all the land of (?)*Enatht'mant *with all its appurtenances and of* $55\frac{1}{2}$ *acres in* Ystradelfeddan (Estradeluedant)*, Tyddyn-prid (Tethinpride) and Trehelyg (T(re)pherhlic).*

[1206 × 1216]

Mention only, in a confirmation charter of Edward II dated at Tutbury, 12 March 1322 (*Ystrad Marchell Charters*, no. 44; Jones, 'Abbey of Ystrad Marchell', 311 (from Henry VI's inspeximus, 1450); cd., *CChR 1300–26*, 440; *H*, no. 271). As this follows the sale of half of Rhandir Gwion in Edward II's inspeximus, the charter was probably issued no earlier than 1206 (see no. 575 below). The lands lay to the south-west of the abbey (*Ystrad Marchell Charters*, 123 and Map I).

*571 Strata Marcella Abbey

Grant of the land of Sychdyn (Sechtin) with all its bounds and its appurtenances which the heirs of that land sold to the monks.

[1206 × 1216]

Mention only, in a confirmation charter of Edward II dated at Tutbury, 12 March 1322 (*Ystrad Marchell Charters*, no. 45; Jones, 'Abbey of Ystrad Marchell', 311 (from Henry VI's inspeximus, 1450); cd., *CChR 1300–26*, 440; *H*, no. 272). The grant immediately follows no. 570 in Edward II's inspeximus and may therefore be assigned to the same date range.

Sychdyn (SH 999 074) was located adjacent to Dolwen in the parish of Llanerfyl, Caereinion (*Ystrad Marchell Charters*, 123 and Map III; cf. no. 555 above).

*572 Strata Marcella Abbey

Grant of all the right which Heilin Coyc *had in wood and plain, waters and meadows and all rights of use in the township of Ystradelfeddan* (Strateluedam)*, of the right of the two sons of Gwgan* (Gugan) *in that township and of 10½ acres in that township.*

[1206 × 1216]

Mention only, in a confirmation charter of Edward II dated at Tutbury, 12 March 1322 (*Ystrad Marchell Charters*, no. 46; Jones, 'Abbey of Ystrad Marchell', 311 (from Henry VI's inspeximus, 1450); cd., *CChR 1300–26*, 440; *H*, no. 273). The grant immediately follows no. 571 in Edward II's inspeximus and may therefore be assigned to the same date range. Ystradelfeddan lay to the south-west of the abbey in the parish of Welshpool (*Ystrad Marchell Charters*, 123 and Map I).

*573 Strata Marcella Abbey

Sale in free and perpetual possession of all the land of Clegyrnant (Clegirnant) *with all its appurtenances.*

[1206 × 1216]

Mention only, in a confirmation charter of Edward II dated at Tutbury, 12 March 1322 (*Ystrad Marchell Charters*, no. 47; Jones, 'Abbey of Ystrad Marchell', 311 (from Henry VI's inspeximus, 1450); cd., *CChR 1300–26*, 440; *H*, no. 274). The grant immediately follows no. 572 in Edward II's inspeximus and may therefore be assigned to the same date range. Clegyrnant (SH 921 076) was situated in the parish of Llanbrynmair, Cyfeiliog (*Ystrad Marchell Charters*, 123 and Map III).

*574 Strata Marcella Abbey

Grant of the land of Esgairgelynnen (Eskeirgelennen) *with all its appurtenances.*

[1206 × 1216]

Mention only, in a confirmation charter of Edward II dated at Tutbury, 12 March 1322 (*Ystrad Marchell Charters*, no. 48; Jones, 'Abbey of Ystrad Marchell', 311 (from Henry VI's inspeximus, 1450); cd., *CChR 1300–26*, 440; *H*, no. 275). The grant immediately follows no. 573 in Edward II's inspeximus and may therefore be assigned to the same date range. Esgairgelynnen (SH 916 060) was situated in the parish of Llanbrynmair, Cyfeiliog (*Ystrad Marchell Charters*, 123 and Map III).

575 Strata Marcella Abbey

Sale in free and perpetual possession for 18 pounds of silver of all the land called Rhandir Gwion with all its bounds and appurtenances both above and below the hill, in wood, plain, meadows, pasture and all rights of use, with the advice and consent of Gwion ap Gwion and his sons, the heirs of that land, who had previously sold their half of the same to the monks for a very worthy price; likewise the other half has been sold in perpetual possession with the advice and consent of Llywelyn, Gruffudd and Goronwy sons of Owain ap Cynddelw and of Iorwerth and Awn sons of Iago. The monks may possess the aforesaid land with all its bounds and appurtenances fully, freely and honourably without any secular exaction or custom in perpetual right. Sealing clause; witnesses. Half of the land was sold in 1206, the other half the next year.

[1207]

A = NLW, Wynnstay Estate Records, Ystrad Marchell Charters, no. 53. Endorsed: Totum Randir Gwiaun (s. xiii in.); ·XX· (s. xiii in.); Wenu(n) super Bacchdreynan (s. xiii med.); early modern endorsements; approx. 223 × 115 + 10 mm.; two central horizontal slits in fold for a tag (*c.*9 mm. wide) which exits through a slit in the base of the fold; sealed on tag. Circular seal, green wax, imperfect, originally approx. 60 mm. diameter; equestrian, facing right; legend: SIG … LIAVC. Pd. from A, *Ystrad Marchell Charters*, no. 53.
Cd., Davies, 'Strata Marcella documents', 177 (no. 21); *H*, no. 256.

Notum sit tam presentibus quam futuris quod ego Wennu(n)wen filius Owini vendidi monachis de Stradmarchell in liberam et quietam et perpetuam possessionem pro xviii libris argenti totam terram que dicitur Randir Gwiaun in omnibus terminis suis et perti-nentiis tam super clivum quam subter, in bosco scilicet et in plano, in pratis et pasturis et in omnibus usibus suis et utilitatibus. Hanc autem predictam terram vendidi prenominatis monachis consilio et consensu heredum ipsius terre, scilicet Gwiaun filii Gwiaun et filiorum eius, ipsi namque dimidietatem eiusdem terre pro condigno precio eisdem monachis in perpetuam possessionem vendiderunt; similiter consilio et consensu filiorum Owini filii Kendelo, scilicet Luelini et G(ri)ffud et Goronoy, insuper et filiorum Yago, videlicet Ioruerth et Aun, alia dimidietas ipsius terre predictis monachis imperpetuam possessionem vendita est. Volo ergo ego prefatus Wennunwen ut sepedicti monachi totam predictam terram in omnibus terminis suis et pertinentiis plenarie et integre, libere et quiete, bene et in pace et honorifice et sine aliqua exactione vel consuetudine seculari iure perpetuo possideant. Et ne hec predicta venditio in posterum possit ab aliquo violari tam sigilli mei impressione quam bonorum virorum attestatione munivi. His testibus: Suliano archidi-acono, magistro Helia, Lewelino filio Owini, Kadugano filio G(ri)fri, Edenewein Flam, David Goch, Ioh(ann)e Glaswen. Facta est autem venditio dimidietatis predicte terre anno ab incarnatione domini m° cc° vi° et relique dimidietatis in anno proximo sequenti.

The date may be inferred from the text of the charter. Rhandir Gwion lay in the township of Ystradelfeddan, south-west of the abbey in the parish of Welshpool (*Ystrad Marchell Charters*, 123 and Map I).

576 Agreement with King John
Gwenwynwyn has granted and sworn on the holy Gospels that he will faithfully serve the king concerning himself and his land for ever and that he will answer in the court of the king at his summons concerning all that is declared against him. He will give the king the following twenty hostages, namely Maredudd ap Cadwgan ap Griffri, Gwyn ap Gronw ab Einion, Rhirid Goch

ap Meurig, Robert ap Dafydd Goch, Iorwerth ap Madog ap Iorwerth, Llywelyn ap Trahaearn ab Ednyfed, Einion ab Ednywain Fflam, Madog ab Einion of Hewent, the first-born son of Llywelyn ap Llywarch, Hywel ap Genillin ap Rhirid, Gruffudd ab Einion ap Cynfelyn, Einion ap Hywel Sais, Gruffudd ap Maredudd ap Philip, Cynfelyn ab Einion ap (?)Iorwerth (Yeperuerd'), Madog ap Mil ab Ithel, the first-born son of Meurig ap Cynwrig by his wife, Tudur ap Meilyr, the first-born son of Kellonin by his wife, Madog ap Cynon, Gruffudd ab Einion ap Sulien. It was agreed that within eight days from the feast of St Denis [9 October] Gwenwynwyn will give the king at least twelve of the aforesaid twenty hostages, otherwise Gwenwynwyn will remain with the king as one who has incurred forfeiture, so that the king will be able to do with his body as he wills. With respect to the remaining eight hostages Gwenwynwyn will remain in the custody of the king where it pleases the latter, or will let the king have the pledges which the king wishes to have until he lets the king have the eight hostages. In the mean time the king has taken Gwenwynwyn's land into custody so that violence will not be inflicted upon it; if this [i.e. violence] were to be done, the king would make amends for it. After Gwenwynwyn has handed over the aforesaid twenty hostages his body will be released. Witnesses.

Shrewsbury, 7 October 1208

B = TNA: PRO, C 66/8 (Pat. R. 10 John), m. 3d (contemporary enrolment).
Pd. from B, *Foedera* I. i. 101; from B, Anon, 'Documents illustrative of the history of the princes', 119–20; from B, Bridgeman, 'Princes of Upper Powys', 106–7.
Cd., *Rot. Pat.*, 91b; *H*, no. 531.

Hec est conventio facta inter dominum I. regem Angl(ie) et Wennunen filium Hoeni de Keueliac apud Salopebur' vigilia Beati Dionis(ii) anno regni eiusdem domini regis decimo, scilicet quod idem Wenn' concessit et iuravit tactis sacrosanctis ewangeliis quod fideliter serviet `eidem domino regi de se et de terra sua in perpetuum et quod stabit iure in curia[a] `ipsius regis ad summonitionem suam de omnibus que erga ipsum proponentur. Et inde dabit domino regi viginti obsides subscriptos, scilicet Mereducu(m) filium Kadugan filii Griffrin, Wen filium Wronu filii Eyneon, Rired Goh' filium Meuric, Rob(ertum) filium David Goh, Yereuerd' filium Madoc filii Yereuerd', Leuelin' filium Trahern' filii Hedeneuit, Eyneon filium Hedeweni Flam, Madocu(m) filium Eyneon de Hewent, primogenitum filium Cuelin filii Lowerh, Howelu(m) filium Genetlin filii Rired, Griffinu(m) filium Eyneon filii Keuelin, Eyneon filium Hohel Seys, Griffin(um) filium Mereduc filii Philipp(i), Konuelin filium Eynean filii Y`e p(er)uerd', Madoc filium Milon' filii Iyel, primogenitum filium Mouric filii Kenewrec de sponsa sua, Tuder filium Meiler, primogenitum filium Kellonin de uxore sua, Madoc' filium Kenon, Griffin(um) filium Eyneon filii Sulien. Convenit etiam inter eosdem quod a predicto die Sancti Dionis(ii) infra octo dies sequentes reddet idem Wenn' ipsi domino regi duodecim obsides ad minus de predictis xx obsidibus, alioquin idem Wenn' remanebit domino regi tamquam forisfactus suus, ita quod dominus rex de corpore ipsius facere potuerit voluntatem suam. Pro viii vero obsidibus qui restant liberandi preter predictos xii obsides, remanebit idem Wenn' in custodia domini regis ubi domino regi placuerit, vel tenantias quas dominus rex habere voluerit ei habere faciet tenendas donec predictos viii obsides ei habere fecerit. Dominus vero rex suscepit interim terram ipsius Wenn' in custodiam, quod fortia ei non inferetur; quod si fieret, dominus rex id faceret emendari. Postquam autem idem Wenn' predictos xx obsides domino regi ut dictum est liberaverit corpus ipsius Wenn' deliberabitur. Testibus: domino P. Wint(oniensi) episcopo, W. comite Warenn', W. comite Sarr', Rob(erto) filio Walt(er)i, Will(elmo) de Cantilup(o), Will(elmo) filio Alan(i), Rob(erto) Corbet, Hug(one) Pantolf, Ioh(ann)e Ex(tra)neo et aliis.

ᵃ B *inserts* domini *struck through.*

The agreement followed a visit by Gwenwynwyn to Shrewsbury to seek peace from the king, who had reacted strongly to Gwenwynwyn's attacks on Peter fitz Herbert in the lordship of Brecon; upon his arrival at Shrewsbury Gwenwynwyn was arrested and imprisoned and his lands placed in royal custody (*HW*, ii. 619–21). Two of the hostages, Gruffudd ab Einion and Gruffudd ap Maredudd, were released to Gwenwynwyn in spring 1215 (Smith, 'Magna Carta', 352). The significance of the agreement for the intensification of royal lordship over Welsh rulers is noticed in Davies, *Conquest*, 294.

*577 Agreement with Llywelyn ap Iorwerth
Document(s) setting out the terms of his confederacy with and homage to Llywelyn.

[1212]

Mention only, in the *Cronica de Wallia* and *Brut y Tywysogyon*, which state that in 1216 Gwenwynwyn 'renounced and scorned the oaths and pledges and charters which he had given to Llywelyn ap Iorwerth and to the princes and the leading men of Wales and England' and made a pact with King John; Llywelyn then 'sent bishops and abbots and other great men of authority to him, and with them the tenor of the cyrographs and the charters and the pact and the homage which he had done to him, to beseech him to return' (*BT, Pen20Tr*, 92; also *BT, RBH*, 206–9; *CW*, 36: *despectis iuramentis, fide, cartis scriptis, cyrographis que domino Lewelino et principibus ac magnatibus Wallie dederat*). Both the number of documents issued by Gwenwynwyn and the number and identity of the recipients apart from Llywelyn are uncertain. However, the most likely context for the document(s) is the 'solemn pact' Llywelyn made with Gwenwynwyn and other Welsh lords in 1212 (*BT, Pen20Tr*, 86; *BT, RBH*, 194–5; cf. *CW*, 34).

578 Strata Marcella Abbey
Grant, for the salvation of the souls of himself, his ancestors and successors, in free and perpetual alms, of the usufruct of all the lands adjoining his town of Montgomery which are under his lordship, so that no other religious, be they monks, canons or any other kind, may acquire or possess freely, for a price or by any other means any possession in lands, pastures or anything else pertaining to the use of the monks of Strata Marcella in all the aforesaid lands and the town of Montgomery, unless by permission of the monks of Strata Marcella, apart from lands which religious men had acquired there before his lordship. Sealing clause; witnesses.

1215

A = NLW, Wynnstay Estate Records, Ystrad Marchell Charters, no. 62. Endorsed: Wenu(n) super usuaria de Mu(n)gum(eri) (s. xiii med.); early modern endorsements; approx. 202 × 137 + 18 mm.; two central horizontal slits in fold for a tag (*c.*8 mm. wide) which exits through a slit in the base of the fold; sealed on tag. Circular seal, brown wax, imperfect, originally approx. 70 mm. diameter; equestrian, facing right; legend: … WEN … .

Pd. from A, *Ystrad Marchell Charters*, no. 62.

Cd., Davies, 'Strata Marcella documents', 186 (no. 33); *H*, no. 257.

Sciant tam presentes quam futuri quod ego Wennu(n)wen de Keueilliauc dominus de Mungum(er)i pro salute anime mee necnon et antecessorum et successorum meorum dedi et concessi et hac presenti carta mea confirmavi monachis de Stradmarchel in liberam et quietam et perpetuam elemosinam usuaria omnium terrarum ville mee de Mungum(er)i adiacentium que meo subdite sunt dominio, ita ut non liceat aliquibus religiosis, monachis scilicet vel canonicis vel etiam quibuslibet aliis aliquam possessionem in terris sive in pasturis sive etiam in quibuslibet aliis que ad utilitatem predictorum monachorum spectare poterint gratis vel precio vel etiam aliquo modo in omnibus predictis terris vel et in ipsa villa de Mungum(er)i adquirere vel possidere, nisi ex permissione et bona voluntate predictorum monachorum de St(ra)dmarchel, exceptis terris quas ante ibidem dominium meum viri religiosi sibi adquisierant. Et ne hec mea predicta donatio processu temporum ab aliquo infirmari possit eam tam sigilli mei impressione quam bonorum virorum attestatione munivi et coroboravi. His testibus: Suliano archidiacono, Enniaun et Ideneuet filiis eius, David Ruffo, Einniaun Parvo, Cadug' filio G(ri)f(ri), Meiler Pigot. Datum anno ab incarnatione domini m° cc° xv°, eodem scilicet anno quo prius eandem terram predictam possedi.

The king had granted Montgomery to Gwenwynwyn by 28 January 1216, when it was exempted from lands granted to William de Cantilupe (*Rot. Claus.*, i. 246b: *salva Wennunwen' terra de Mongumery quam dominus rex ei concessit quamdiu ei placuerit*). Stephenson suggested that the royal grant was made in January 1216 and that the charter was therefore datable to between January and 24 March, on the (probably correct) assumption that the year was reckoned to begin on the Annunciation (25 March) ('Politics of Powys Wenwynwyn', 43). However, the reference in the close roll could mean that Montgomery had already been granted to Gwenwynwyn before 28 January 1216, though, to judge by the present charter, no earlier than 25 March 1215. The place referred to was Old Montgomery, site of the castle of Hen Domen (SO 213 980), rather than the modern town of Montgomery 1 mile to its south (*Ystrad Marchell Charters*, 15).

MARGARET CORBET, WIFE OF GWENWYNWYN AB OWAIN
(d. *c*.1251)

579 Lilleshall Abbey

Grant in free and perpetual alms of one messuage with a croft above the Wye which she bought from Thomas fitz Robert of Hope, 1½ acres above (?)Priestcliffe Low (Prestelowe), 1 acre in Waledale and ½ acre in (?)Stan Low furlong (Scanlowefurlong'), to be held from her and her heirs freely and honourably as free and perpetual alms. She and her heirs will warrant the aforesaid lands to the monks against all men for ever. Sealing clause; witnesses (not named).

[February 1223 × *c*.1251]

B = BL, Add. MS 50121 (Lilleshall Cartulary), fo. 47r. s. xiii med.–s. xv (here s. xiii ex.; recited in a record of a *quo warranto* case held in London, 10 May 1271).
Pd. from B, *Cart. Lilleshall*, no. 246 (omits warranty clause).

Sciant presentes et futuri quod ego Margareta que fui quondam uxor Wenu(n)win dedi et concessi et hac presenti carta mea confirmavi Deo et ecclesie Beate Mar(ie) de Lill' et canonicis ibidem Deo servientibus in liberam, puram et perpetuam elemosinam unum mesuagium cum crofto super Weye quod emi de Thom(a) filio Rob(er)ti de Hop' et unam acram terre et dimidiam super P(re)stelowe et unam acram in Waledale et dimidiam acram in Scanlowefurlong', habendas et tenendas de me et heredibus meis libere et quiete, pacifice et honorifice sicut liberam, puram et perpetuam elemosinam. Ego vero Margareta et heredes mei predictas terras predictis canonicis contra omnes homines inperpetuum warentizabimus. Et ut hec mea donatio et concessio et confirmatio rate et stabiles inperpetuum permaneant eam presenti scripto et sigilli mei inpressione roboravi. Hiis testibus.

Margaret, a daughter of Robert Corbet of Caus, appears to have been Gwenwynwyn's second wife (Bartrum, *WG*, i, Bleddyn ap Cynfyn 29). As the grants were from Margaret's lands in Derbyshire, the charter can be no earlier than 6 February 1223, when the king assigned Margaret one third of the manor of Ashford with its appurtenances (*Rot. Claus.*, i. 532b; cf. ibid., 536b); there followed a grant of (the remaining?) two-thirds of the manor on 29 August 1226 (*Rot. Fin.*, i. 146; cf. ibid., 178; *Rot. Claus.*, ii. 178b; *Book of Fees*, i. 374). Although Margaret's son Gruffudd ap Gwenwynwyn was granted the manor of Ashford on 9 June 1232, the grant explicitly excluded the lands held by his mother in dower and she appears to have still held land in the manor in 1251 (*CR 1231–4*, 70; Cox, 'Ancient documents', 143; cf. no. 595 below).

The Wye referred to must be the river which flows east and then south-east from Buxton past Ashford in the Water (SK 195 697) and Bakewell into the Derwent at SK 260 654. Hope (SK 172 834) lies about 12 miles north of Ashford in the Water. *Prestelowe* may be identifiable with the Priestcliffe Low near Priestcliffe (SK 140 720), about 4 miles north-west of Ashford in the Water, referred to as *Prestlowe yatt* in 1640 (Cameron, *Place-Names of Derbyshire*, i. 169). For *Scanlowefurlong* cf. Stan Low in the parish of Hazlebadge in High Peak hundred (ibid., 118). Lilleshall Abbey, an Augustinian house in north-eastern Shropshire near the border with Staffordshire (*Cart. Lilleshall*, xi; Chibnall, 'Houses of Augustinian canons', 70–80), also received a grant from Gruffudd ap Gwenwynwyn, made with his mother's consent (no. 582 below).

CASWALLON AB OWAIN CYFEILIOG
(*fl.* 1197–1209 × 1229)

*580 Strata Marcella Abbey
Grant in perpetual alms of the land and township of Ystradelfeddan (Stradeluedun) *with all its appurtenances.*

[*c.*1209 × *c.*1229]

Mention only, in a confirmation charter of Edward II dated at Tutbury, 12 March 1322 (*Ystrad Marchell Charters*, no. 57; Jones, 'Abbey of Ystrad Marchell', 313 (from Henry VI's inspeximus, 1450); cd., *CChR 1300–26*, 440; *H*, no. 276). For the identification of this Caswallon with the son of that name, probably illegitimate, of Owain Cyfeiliog named in no. 581 below see *Ystrad Marchell Charters*, 24, 61. The charter is difficult to date. It may well be later than the grants by Gwenwynwyn datable to 1206 × 1216 of lands and rights in Ystradelfeddan, a township to the south-west of the abbey, since those grants are less comprehensive than that of Caswallon (nos 570, 572 above). In Edward II's inspeximus the grant comes between charters of Llywelyn ap Iorwerth (no. 231, dated 25 November 1209) and Gwenwynwyn's brother-in-law Thomas Corbet, dated 1229 (*Ystrad Marchell Charters*, no. 72).

MADOG AP CASWALLON AB OWAIN CYFEILIOG
(*fl. c.*1209–32)

581 Strata Marcella Abbey
Grant and confirmation, for the salvation of his soul, in free and perpetual alms, of all the abbey's lands, to be possessed for ever fully and without any secular exaction or custom, in lands, pastures and all bounds, appurtenances, uses and all possessions and liberties, as the charters of its donors and vendors testify, namely of Owain Cyfeiliog and his sons Gwenwynwyn, Caswallon and Maredudd, of Madog ap Gruffudd, Owain Brogyntyn and Elise [ap Madog] and of all other donors and vendors. He will warrant all these with his faithful power against all men. Further grant in honour of the dedication of the church of all the land of Caledffrwd as contained in the charter of Gwenwynwyn which they have. Sealing clause; witnesses.

Ystrad Marchell, 10 March 1231 [=1232]

A = NLW, Wynnstay Estate Records, Ystrad Marchell Charters, no. 80. Endorsed: Madoc(us) filius Kasswallaun super omnia tenementa nostra (s. xiii); early modern endorsements; approx. 178 × 116 + 14 + 15 mm. (double fold); two central horizontal slits, one just above fold, one in fold, for a tag (*c.*11 mm. wide) which exits through a slit in the base of the fold; sealed on tag. Circular seal, green wax, imperfect, originally approx. 50 mm. diameter; equestrian, facing right; legend: +S … D … CASW … AVN.
Pd. from A, *Ystrad Marchell Charters*, no. 80.

Omnibus sancte matris ecclesie filiis tam presentibus quam futuris ad quos presens pervenerit scriptum Madoc(us) filius Kaswallani salutem. Noverit universitas vestra me concessisse, dedisse et presenti carta confirmasse pro salute anime mee monachis de St(ra)dmarchell Deo et Beate Marie ibidem servientibus, in liberam et quietam et perpetuam elemosinam, omnia tenementa sua, plenarie et integre, bene et in pace et sine aliqua exactione vel consuetudine seculari imperpetuum possidenda, in terris videlicet et in pasturis et in omnibus terminis suis et pertinentiis et utilitatibus et omnibus possessionibus[a] suis et libertatibus, sicut carte donatorum suorum vel venditorum melius et plenius protestantur, scilicet Owini de Keueliauc et filiorum eius Wenunwin et Kaswallaun et Maredud, insuper et Madoci filii G(ri)fud et Owini Brogintun et Elisse et omnium aliorum donatorum suorum vel venditorum. Et illa omnia illis warantizabo et pacificabo secundum fidele posse meum contra omnes homines. Dedi etiam eisdem monachis ad honorem dedicationis ecclesie totam terram illam de Kaledfrud sicut melius et plenius in carta domini Wenunwin quam habent idem continetur. Ut autem hec mea donatio rata sit et firma imperpetuum eam tam sigilli mei impressione quam bonorum virorum attestatione munivi et corroboravi. His testibus: Euelino priore de Pola, Enea, David, Ioab, Madoco et Iervasio monachis eiusdem domus; de secularibus vero Ioh(ann)e archidiacono de Meyuod, Ririd filio Guin, Howel filio Trehaiarn, Ririd filio Enniaun, Madoco filio Goronui et multis aliis. Dat' anno gratie mᵒ ccᵒ xxxiᵒ apud Stradmarchell vi idus marcii.

ᵃ possessioinibus A.

As Thomas has argued (*Ystrad Marchell Charters*, 61, 77), it is likely that Madog was a son of the Caswallon ab Owain Cyfeiliog named in the charter and thus of the grantor of no. 580 above. The land of Caledffrwd has not been located (*Ystrad Marchell Charters*, 126).

GRUFFUDD AP GWENWYNWYN
(d. 1286)

582 Lilleshall Abbey
Grant, with the consent of his mother Lady Margaret, in free and perpetual alms for the salvation of the souls of himself and all his ancestors of all the land called Newland in the fields of Wardlow, from which the men of Longstone used to pay him and his mother 6s. per annum; namely that land which extends in length beyond the bovates pertaining to Longstone to the stream which runs to the ford called Macklesford' *and in breadth between the royal highway which leads from Wardlow to* Macklesford' *and the stream which flows from* Geylmere, *together with common pasture, turbary and sufficient heath according to the quantity of the said land, apart from mining rights, to be held from him and his heirs for ever free of all secular service, custom and exaction pertaining to himself or his heirs. Gruffudd and his heirs warrant all the above with all their appurtenances, liberties and easements within and without the village of Wardlow against all men and women. Sealing clause; witnesses.*

[9 June 1232 × *c*.1245]

A = Shrewsbury, Shropshire Records and Research Centre 972 (Sutherland)/box 220, bundle 4, no. 1. Endorsed: Carta domini Griffini filii Wenunwyn de tota terra sua que dicitur Neulond (s. xiii); early modern endorsements; approx. 212 mm. wide × 114 mm. deep on left, 97 mm. deep on right + 20 mm.; central slit in fold for a tag (*c*.12 mm. wide); sealed on tag. Circular seal, dark green wax, approx. 28 mm. diameter; device of a lion rampant on a triangular shield; legend: + S' GRIFINI FIL' WENVNWEN.

Sciant presentes et futuri quod ego Griffin filius Wennunwen consensu et assensu domine Margarete matris mee dedi et concessi et hac presenti carta mea confirmavi Deo et ecclesie Beate Marie de Lylleshull' et canonicis ibidem Deo servientibus in liberam, puram et perpetuam elemosinam pro salute anime mee et omnium antecessorum meorum totam terram que vocatur Neulond' in campis de Wardelowe, unde homines de Longedon' solebant reddere mihi et matri mee sex solidos per annum; illam scilicet que se extendit extra bovatas que pertinent ad Longedon' usque ad rivulum qui currit usque ad vadum quod vocatur Macklesford' in longitudine, et inter regiam stratam que ducit de Wardelowe ad Macklesford' et rivulum qui exit de Geylmere in latitudine, et communem pasturam et turbariam et brueriam suficientem secundum quantitatem dicte terre salva mineria, habendam et tenendam inperpetuum libere et quiete de me et de heredibus meis sine omni servicio, consuetudine et exactione seculari ad me vel ad heredes meos pertinente. Ego vero et heredes mei dictam terram et omnia supradicta cum omnibus pertinenciis et libertatibus et aisiamentis infra villam de Wardelowe et extra contra omnes homines et feminas warantizabimus. Ut autem hec mea donacio et concessio rata et stabilis inperpetuum permaneat eam presenti scripto et sigilli mei inpressione corroboravi. Hiis testibus: Thom(a) de Endesouere, Iordano de Sinterton', Luca de Beylee, Philipp(o) de Kydermustr', Math(e)o de Reyndon', Ivone de Eyton' clerico, Hug(one) Pekoc, Will(elm)o pincerna, Will(elm)o Scotto et multis aliis.

Wardlow and (Great and Little) Longstone belonged to the manor of Ashford (Derbs.), granted to Gruffudd, apart from the dower of his mother Margaret, on 9 June 1232 (*CR 1231–4*, 70). Margaret appears to have retained interests in Ashford as late as 1251, but the charter must be earlier than that, as the first witness, Sir Thomas of Edensor, seneschal to William Ferrers II, earl of Derby, died *c*.1245 (Turbutt, *History of Derbyshire*, ii. 524). Adam fitz Peter of Great Longstone issued a similar quitclaim to Lilleshall in the fields of Wardlow (Shropshire Records and Research Centre 972 (Sutherland)/box 220, bundle 4, no. 2). Wardlow (SK 181 748) is located about 3 miles north-west of Ashford in the Water.

583 Matthew fitz Thomas of Bakewell

Grant, in return for his homage, of one bovate of land in the vill and territory of Great Longstone, namely that bovate with a toft and croft which Matthew's father Thomas and his ancestors formerly held by enfeoffment of the king and afterwards by confirmation of Gruffudd's father with all its appurtenances, liberties, easements and common rights within and outside the vill of Great Longstone, with sufficient turbaries and heaths in the moor of Longsilowe *and other moors belonging to Great Longstone to be carried to the house of Matthew or his heirs in Little Longstone; to be held by Matthew or his heirs or assigns from Gruffudd or his heirs or assigns. [(?) Matthew is allowed] to give, sell, bequeath or assign the aforesaid bovate freely with all its appurtenances. He and his heirs shall render for it to Gruffudd and his heirs 15d. at two terms, namely 7½d. at Michaelmas [29 September] and 7½d. at the Annunciation of Mary [25 March] for all secular service, custom, exaction and demands, wardships, reliefs, escheats and suits of court and mill. Gruffudd, his heirs and assigns will warrant all the said bovate with all its appurtenances and liberties against all men and women for ever. Sealing clause; witnesses.*

[Probably 9 June 1232 × 1250]

A = Matlock, Derbyshire Record Office, D3580/T1. Early modern endorsement illegible; approx. 169 × 164 + 125 mm.; two central slits in fold for a tag (*c*.19 mm. wide) which exits through a slit in the base of the fold; sealed on tag. Circular seal, dark green wax, imperfect, originally approx. 40 mm. in diameter; worn triangular shield with no device visible; illegible fragments of legend.

Sciant presentes et futuri quod ego Griffin(us) filius Wenunwin de Keuelock dedi, concessi et hac presenti carta mea confirmavi Math(e)o filio Thome clerici de Bauquell et heredibus suis vel cui asignare voluerit pro homagio suo unam bovatam terre in villa et in territorio de Maiori Longisdo(n), scilicet illam bovatam terre cum tofto et crofto quam Thomas pater predicti Math(e)i et eius antecessores quondam de feffamento domini regis et postea de confirmacione patris mei tenuerunt cum omnibus pertinenciis, libertatibus, eisiamentis et communis in villa de Maiori Longisdo(n) et extra cum turbariis fodendis et bruariis evellendis sicuti in mora de Longsilowe et in aliis moris locis ad villam de Maiori Longisdo(n) spectantibus ad mancionem predicti Math(e)i vel suorum heredum in Minori Longisdo(n) sufficienter cariandis, tenendis et habendis predicto M. et heredibus suis vel suis asignatis de me et heredibus meis seu asignatis meis, ᵃ⁻predictam bovatam terre cum pertinentiis dare, vendere, legare et asignare quo, quando et ubi in quo statu fuerit,⁻ᵃ in feodo et hereditate, libere, solute, bene et in pace, iure, quiete, integre, plenarie, in viis, semitis, campis, pratis, moris, boscis, aquis, stangnis, rivariis, communis, saxis, pastis, pasturis sicut aliqua terra infra et extra terram melius vel liberius potuerit teneri; reddendo inde annuatim mihi et heredibus meis ille et heredes sui quindecim denarios ad duos anni terminos, scilicet ad festum Sancti Michael(is) vii denarios et i obolum et ad annuncia-tionem Beate Mar(ie) in marcio vii denarios i obolum pro omni servicio seculari, consuetudine, exaccione et demanda, wardis, releviis, eschaetis, sectis curie mee et molendini mei et pro omnibus aliis que de alliqua terra exiunt vel aliquo casu contingente exire poterunt. Et ego Griffin(us) predictus et heredes mei et asignati mei totam dictam bovatam terre cum omnibus pertinentiis, libertatibus, eisiamentis prenominatis sicut aliqua terra infra et extra terram melius vel liberius poterit teneri et donari dandi, vendendi, legandi aut asignandi cui quando et ubi in omnibus ut predictum est in quocumque statu fuerit sepedicto Math(e)o et heredibus suis vel suis asignatis et eorum heredibus contra omnes homines et feminas imperpetuum warantizabimus ubique aquietabimus semper defendemus. In huius vero donacionis, concessionis, confirmacionis testimonium presentem cartam sigilli mei impressione corroboravi. Hiis testibus: domino Thom(a) de Ednisou(er)e, domino Adamᵇ de H(er)thulle, Luchasᶜ de Beiley, Rob(er)to de Staunton et Rob(er)to filio Ing(ra)m de Noti(n)gha(m), Math(e)o de Reyndon, Nich(ol)o de Ou(er)haddon et Henr(ico) de Hotot et pluribus aliis.

ᵃ⁻ᵃ *sic in* A. | ᵇ *sic in* A *for* Ada. | ᶜ *sic in* A *for* Lucha.

The witness lists of this and the following two charters, each written in a different hand, are identical and the substance of the dispositive clauses is essentially the same. No. 584 is somewhat shorter, with some other minor verbal differences; no. 585 is shorter still, and omits the sub-clause allowing alienation by gift, sale, bequest or assignation. (The syntax of the sub-clause is faulty in the present charter.) The charters are therefore three different records of the same grant, and all were in the possession of the Longsdon family of Little Longstone, descendants of the grantee, before their deposit in the Derbyshire Record Office (see Yeatman *et al.*, *Feudal History*, iv. 340).

Ashford had been held by Gruffudd's father Gwenwynwyn, to whom it was granted by

John in 1200 (*Rot. Chart.*, 44a), and two-thirds of the manor had been assigned to Gruffudd's mother Margaret in dower in 1223 (see notes to nos 579, 582 above). Gruffudd was granted the manor, which included Great Longstone (SK 203 717), situated about 1 mile north-east of Ashford in the Water, except for the dower of his mother, on 9 June 1232, and held it until at least 1262 (no. 599 below). However, his tenure was interrupted at least once, as in May 1260 the sheriff of Derby was ordered to restore Gruffudd to his lands in the county which had been seized into the king's hand on account of trespasses alleged against him by Thomas Corbet (*CR 1259–61*, 49). The manor was presumably confiscated from Gruffudd by the crown following his agreement with Llywelyn ap Gruffudd, finalized on 12 December 1263 (no. 358 above and no. 601 below), and had certainly been granted to the Lord Edward's wife Eleanor of Castile by March 1265 (*CR 1264–8*, 28). It appears that Robert fitz Ingram of Nottingham of the witness list had died by 1250 if, as is likely, he was the same as the person of that name whose heirs were holding the serjeanty of Sandiacre, located between Nottingham and Derby, in that year (*Book of Fees*, ii. 1196). A date no later than 1250 would be consistent with the suggestion that the Richard of Harthill who witnessed charters of 15 February 1250 and 28 October 1252 × 27 October 1253 (Carrington, 'Illustrations of ancient place-names', 49–50; no. 597 below) was the son of the witness Adam of Harthill in the present charter; Adam and Luke of Beeley also occur in a charter datable to the early thirteenth century (Yeatman *et al.*, *Feudal History*, iv. 302; *Great Register of Lichfield*, ed. Savage, 37 (no. 80)). Thomas of Edensor (d. *c*.1245), Luke of Beeley and Matthew of Reyndon witnessed no. 582 above, issued no later than February 1242. Thomas and Luke witnessed a charter dated 29 Henry III (28 October 1244 × 27 October 1245); Matthew also occurs in 1243 (Yeatman *et al.*, *Feudal History*, iv. 354; *Great Register of Lichfield*, ed. Savage, 35, 63 (nos 75, 136)).

584 Matthew fitz Thomas of Bakewell

[Text substantially as no. 583 above.]

[Probably 9 June 1232 × 1250]

A = Matlock, Derbyshire Record Office, D3580/T2. No endorsement; approx. 180 mm. wide × 109 mm. deep on left, 119 mm. deep on right + 14 mm.; central slit in fold for a tag; tag and seal missing.

Sciant presentes et futuri quod ego Griffinus filius Wenunwin dedi, concessi et hac presenti carta mea confirmavi Math(e)o filio Thome de Bauquell' et heredibus suis vel cui asignare voluerit et eorum heredibus pro homagio et servicio suo unam bovatam terre in villa et in territorio de Maiori Longisdon', scilicet illam bovatam terre cum tofto et crofto quam Thom(as) pater predicti Math(e)i quondam de patre meo tenuit cum omnibus pertinentiis et libertatibus et eysiamentis in villa de Maiori Longisdon' et extra cum turbariis fodendis et bruariis evellendis sicuti in mora de Lonsilowe et in omnibus aliis moris ad villam de Maiori Longisdon[a] spectantibus ad mancionem predicti Math(e)i vel suorum heredum in Minori Longisdon' sufficienter cariandis, tenendis et habendis sibi et heredibus suis vel suis asignatis et eorum heredibus de me et heredibus meis dare, vendere, legare et asignare cui, quando et ubi in quo statu fuerit, in feodo, hereditate, libere, solute et quiete, pacifice et integre, bene et plenarie ut predictum est sicut aliqua terra sub et super terram melius vel liberius poterit teneri; reddendo inde annuatim mihi et heredibus meis quindecim denarios ad duos anni terminos, scilicet ad festum Sancti Michael(is)[b] vii denarios et i obolum et ad annunciacionem Beate Mar(ie) in marcio septem denarios et obolum pro omni seculari servicio, consuetudine, demanda et exactione, et sectis curie mee et molendini mei et pro omnibus aliis que de aliqua terra exiunt vel aliquo casu contingente exire possunt. Et ego Griffinus predictus et heredes mei vel mei asignati totam dictam bovatam terre cum omnibus pertinentiis et libertatibus sicut aliqua terra sub et super terram melius vel liberius poterit teneri, dare, vendere, legare vel asignare cui quando et ubi in quo statu fuerit ut predictum est sepedicto Math(e)o et heredibus suis vel suis asignatis et eorum heredibus contra omnes homines et feminas semper warantizabimus, aquietabimus et ubique defendemus. In huius vero donacionis, mee concessionis et confirmacionis testimonio presentem cartam sigilli mei inpressione corroboravi. Hiis testibus: domino Thom(a) de Ednisou(er)e, domino Ada de H(er)thull', Luca de Begeley, Rob(er)to de Sta(n)to(n), Rob(erto) filio Ing(ra)m, Math(e)o de Reidon', Nich(ol)o de Ou(er)haudo(n), Henr(ico) de Hotot et pluribus aliis.

[a] *omitted* A. | [b] Micahel(is) A.

See note to no. 583 above.

585 Matthew fitz Thomas of Bakewell

[Text substantially same as nos *583–4 above, but omits clause permitting alienation by Matthew.]*

[Probably 9 June 1232 × 1250]

A = Matlock, Derbyshire Record Office, D3580/T3. Early modern endorsement illegible; approx. 218 mm. wide at top, 198 mm. wide at bottom × 88 mm. deep + 18 mm.; central slit in fold for a tag (*c.*17 mm. wide); originally sealed on tag. Circular(?) seal unattached to tag, dark grey wax, very imperfect (approx. 25 mm. diameter), possibly originally approx. 35 mm. diameter; fragment of a device of a lion rampant on the left of a triangular shield; no legend survives.

Sciant presentes et futuri quod ego Griffinus filius Wenunwin dedi, concessi et hac presenti carta mea confirmavi Math(e)o filio Thom(e) de Bauquell' et heredibus suis vel cui assignare voluerit et eorum heredibus pro homagio servicio suo unam bovatam terre in villa et in territorio de Magna Longisdon', scilicet illam bovatam terre cum tofto et crofto quam Thom(as) pater predicti Math(e)i quondam de patre meo tenuit cum omnibus pertinenciis suis et libertatibus et eysiamentis in villa de Magna Longisdon' et extra cum turbariis fodendis et bruariis evellendis sicuti in mora de Lonsilowe et in omnibus aliis moris ad villam de Maiori Longisdon' spectantibus ad mancionem predicti Math(e)i vel suorum heredum in Minori Longisdon sufficienter cariandis, tenendis et habendis sibi et heredibus suis vel suis assignatis et eorum heredibus de me et heredibus meis in feodo et hereditate, libere, solute et quiete, pacifice et integre, plenarie ut predictum est sicut aliqua terra melius vel liberius poterit teneri; reddendo[a] inde annuatim mihi et heredibus meis quindecim denarios ad duos anni terminos, scilicet ad festum Sancti Michael(is)[b] vii denarios et obolum et ad annunciacionem Beate Marie in marcio septem denarios et obolum pro omni seculari servicio, consuetudine, demanda et exaccione, et sectis curie et molendini mei. Et ego Griffin(us) predictus et heredes mei vel mei assignati totam dictam bovatam terre cum omnibus pertinenciis et libertatibus ut predictum est sepedicto Math(e)o et heredibus suis vel suis assignatis et eorum heredibus contra omnes homines et feminas semper warantizabimus, aquietabimus et ubique defendemus. In huius vero donacionis mee concessionis et confirmacionis testimonium presentem cartam sigilli mei inpressione corroboravi. Hiis testibus: domino Thom(a) de Ednisou(er)e, domino Ada de Herthull', Luca de Begeley, Rob(erto) de Stanton', Rob(erto) filio Ing(ra)m, Math(e)o de Reyndon', Nich(ol)o de Overhandon, Henr(ico) de Hotot et pluribus aliis.

ᵃ rerddendo A. | ᵇ Micahel(is) A.

See note to no. 583 above.

586 Letter patent concerning the dean and chapter of Lichfield Cathedral

Notification that, since the dean and chapter granted as a special favour his petition to have a chantry for himself, his wife and their free household in the chapel of Ashford until the Purification of the Virgin [2 February] 1257, he gives thanks for this and grants on behalf of himself and his heirs and successors that no injury or prejudice will be caused thereby to the said dean and chapter or to the church of Bakewell. Sealing clause.

[9 June 1232 × 2 February 1258]

B = Lichfield Dean and Chapter Muniments, 'Magnum Registrum Album', fo. 249r. s. xiv¹.
C = BL, MS Harl. 4799 (Cartulary of Lichfield Cathedral), fo. 27v. s. xiv¹. Rubric: Cantaria de Esseford concessa gratiose.
Cd., *Great Register of Lichfield*, ed. Savage, 295 (no. 617); *H*, no. 533.

Universis Cristi fidelibus Griffin(us) filius Wenunwyn' salutem in domino. Cum viri discreti domini decanus et capitulum Lich' ecclesie cantariam in capella de Esseford' nobis et uxori nostre et libere familie nostre usque ad purificationem Beateᵃ Virginis anno domini mᵐᵒ ccᵐᵒ lᵒ viiᵒ ad instantiam et petitionem nostram concesserint ex gratia speciali, nos eis super hoc gratias referentes concedimus tam pro nobis quam pro heredibus et quibuslibet successoribus nostris et presentis scripti testimonio protestamur quod super hoc nec dictis decano et capitulo nec etiam ecclesie de Baucwelleᵇ iniuria vel preiudicium generabitur in hac parte. In cuius rei testimonio presentibus litteris sigillum nostrum fecimus apponi.

ᵃ C *inserts* Mar(ie). | ᵇ Baucwell' C.

Ashford was a chapel of the parish church of Bakewell, granted by King John to the bishop of Coventry and Lichfield and subsequently transferred to the dean and chapter of Lichfield by Bishops William Cornhill (1215–24) and Alexander Stavensby (1224–38) (*VCH Derby*, ii. 3). It is unknown how far in advance of the terminal date of 2 February 1257 (probably 1258 by modern reckoning) the grant of the temporary chantry was made; it can have been no earlier than Gruffudd's acquisition of Ashford in June 1232 (cf. Cox, *Notes*, ii. 47–8, which mistakenly takes the date given in the document to be that of the chantry's foundation). There are no parallels for such a temporary grant in the Great Register of Lichfield. One of Gruffudd's Derbyshire neighbours, Sir Richard of Harthill, had a chantry in his chapel at Harthill by 29 December 1259, when he settled a dispute over his obligations in respect of it to the dean and chapter of Lichfield and the mother church of Bakewell (*Great Register of Lichfield*, ed. Savage, 21–2 (no. 46)).

587 Robert fitz Matthew of Reyndon

Grant of all the land with the meadow which Robert's father Matthew granted to Robert in the vill and territory of Holme with all its appurtenances and liberties, to be held by Robert and his heirs or assigns from Gruffudd and his heirs in fee and inheritance, freely and fully according to the terms of the said Matthew's charter. Sealing clause; witnesses.

[9 June 1232 × 1263]

A = Cardiff, Glamorgan Record Office, CL/DEEDS/1/2384. No endorsement; approx. 231 × 68 + 15 mm.; central slit in fold for a tag (*c.* 11 mm. wide); sealed on tag. Circular seal, green wax, imperfect (about one third missing on left), originally approx. 28 mm. diameter; device of a lion rampant on a triangular shield; legend: .... GRIFINI FIL . W ...
Cd., Jeayes, *Descriptive Catalogue*, 171 (no. 1396); Yeatman *et al.*, *Feudal History*, iv. 411.

Sciant presentes et futuri quod ego Griffinus filius Wenunwini concessi et hac presenti mea carta confirmavi Rob(er)to filio Math(e)i de Reydon' totam terram illam cum prato quam Math(eu)s pater ipsius Rob(er)ti ei dedit et concessit in villa et in territorio de Hulm' cum omnibus pertinentiis et libertatibus suis, tenendam et habendam ipsi Rob(er)to et heredibus suis vel suis inde assignatis de me et heredibus meis in feodo et hereditate, libere, solute et quiete, integre, plenarie, bene et in pace secundum quod carte quas dictus Math(eu)s ei dedit perportant. In huius autem concessionis et confirmacionis mee testimonium huic presenti carte sigillum meum apposui. Hiis testibus: domino Ric(ard)o de Stretton', Yuone persona[a], Math(e)o de Langisdon', Will(elm)o le Wine, Will(elm)o de Langisdon', Nich(ol)o de Winnefeld, Rad(ulfo) Bugge, Will(elm)o de Esseburne, Will(elm)o clerico, Hugon(e) Ponn, Rad(ulfo) de Selladon', Ioh(ann)e de Bathequell' clerico et pluribus aliis.

[a] persone A.

For the dating limits see note to no. 583 above. Robert's father Matthew of Reyndon occurs 1232 × 1250 (nos 583–5 above); it is uncertain whether Matthew was alive when the present confirmation was made. Robert also occurs in two charters datable to after 1254, in the second of which he is called Robert of Reyndon of Bakewell (*Great Register of Lichfield*, ed. Savage, 36–7 (nos 77, 81)). The witness list may indicate a date in the 1250s or early 1260s. Richard of Stretton and Ivo of Eyton, both from Staffordshire, undertook in May 1260 to ensure that Gruffudd would appear before the king in September of that year to answer for trespasses allegedly committed against his uncle Thomas Corbet (*CR 1259–61*, 49). A William of Longstone occurs in April 1252 and, with a Matthew of Longstone, in 1252 × 1253 and 1254 (*Rot. Fin.*, ii. 128; no. 597 below; Yeatman *et al.*, *Feudal History*, iv. 270). William le Wine and William of Ashbourne occur as early as 1243 (*Great Register of Lichfield*, ed. Savage, 35 (no. 75)). However, both also witnessed charters of 25 May 1253 (with Ralph Bugge) and 14 April 1254 (Belvoir Castle, Muniments of the Duke of Rutland, 'Transcripts of Derbyshire Charters at Haddon' by W. A. Carrington, vi. 304–6; ibid., Bakewell Charter 1438; see also Carrington, 'Illustrations of ancient place-names', 43, 49, 50; Cox, 'Ancient documents', 143). William le Wine and Nicholas of Wingfield occur as witnesses in 1262 to no. 599 below. Gruffudd's mother Margaret was assigned dower in a third of Holme, described as a hamlet, on 7 March 1223 (*Rot. Claus.*, i. 536b). According to jurors at a *quo warranto* inquiry at Derby, 10 January 1275, Holme was a manor, whose appurtenances consisted of the townships of Ashford, Great Longstone and Sheldon, which was granted by King John to Gwenwynwyn and descended to Gruffudd, who held it until it was given by Henry III to Eleanor, wife of the Lord Edward (*Rot. Hund.*, ii. 287). Holme (SK 218 692) lay on the edge of Bakewell, just north of the river Wye about 1½ miles south-east of Ashford in the Water.

588 John of Holwell

Grant in return for his homage and service of one acre of land in the fields of Holme, of which half an acre lies below Crakelowebothim *and the other half above* Hathswrthe *next to the land of William Ruffus, to be held by John, his heirs or assigns (excepting religious or Jews) from Gruffudd and his heirs in fee and inheritance, freely with all easements pertaining to the aforesaid land. John shall pay* 6d. *per annum to Gruffudd and his heirs or assigns at two terms, namely* 3d. *at the Annunciation [25 March] and* 3d. *at Michaelmas [29 September], in lieu of all secular service, customs, demands and exactions except for forinsec service. Gruffudd and his heirs will warrant the aforesaid acre against all people for ever. Sealing clause; witnesses.*

[9 June 1232 × 1263]

B = Belvoir Castle, Muniments of the Duke of Rutland, 'Transcripts of Derbyshire Charters at Haddon Hall' by W. A. Carrington, i. 376 (no. 351). 1890. Carrington noted that 'A portion of the right hand side of the Charter, including the six last lines, of a semicircular form has been gnawed away by mice, the missing portion in the widest part would extend about 1½" from the edge of the Charter'. He also described the seal: 'Armorial shield, Heater-shaped, of green wax, bearing a lion rampant and surrounded by the following legend – + S' CRIFINI FIL' WENVNWEN.' A search for the original charter in the muniments room at Belvoir Castle was unsuccessful.

Cd., Yeatman *et al.*, *Feudal History*, iv. 340.

Sciant presentes et futuri quod ego Griff(in)us filius Wenunwen dedi et concessi et hac mea presenti carta confirmavi Ioh(ann)i de Holwell' pro homagio et servitio suo unam acram terre in campis de Hulm, quarum una dimidia acra iacet sub Crakelowebothim et altera dimidia acra iacet super Hathswrthe' iuxta terram Will(elm)i Ruffi, tenendam et habendam ipsi Ioh(ann)i et heredibus suis vel cuicumque assignare voluerit, exceptis viris religiosis et Iudeis, de me et heredibus meis in feodo et hereditate, libere, solute et quiete, bene et honorifice cum omnibus eysiamentis[a] ad predictam terram pertinentibus; reddendo inde annuatim michi et heredibus meis ille et heredes sui vel sui assignati sex denarios ad duos anni terminos, videlicet tres denarios ad annunciationem Beate Marie et tres denarios ad festum Sancti Michaelis pro omni servitio seculari, consuetudine, demanda [et exactione salvo][b] forinseco servitio. Et ego Griffin(us) et heredes mei predictam acram terre cum omnibus pertinentiis suis prenominato Ioh(ann)i et heredibus suis vel suis inde assignatis contra omnes gentes [imperpetuum warantizabimus].[b] In huius vero donationis mee testimonium presentem cartam sigilli mei impressione [corroboravi. Hiis testibus]:[b] Will(elm)o le Wine, Math(e)o de Langesdon', Will(elm)o de eadem, Nic ... de Reydon', Ada filio Pet(ri), Rob(er)to de Fecham tunc servientibus Henr(ici) filii fratris Ric(ar)di, Ioh(ann)e de Baucw(e)ll [et aliis].[b]

^a eysiamentes B. | ^b *written very faintly in pencil, probably to supply missing words in portions of document gnawed by mice* B.

For the dating limits see note to no. 583 above. The witness list may indicate a date in the 1250s or early 1260s: see note to no. 587 above for William le Wine and Matthew and William of Longstone; John of Bakewell witnessed the same charter. John of Holwell issued a charter on 14 April 1254 and, with William le Wine, witnessed charters of 15 February 1250, 25 May 1253, 11 April 1258 and 1262 (Carrington, 'Illustrations of ancient place-names', 50; Belvoir Castle, Muniments of the Duke of Rutland, Bakewell Charter 1438; ibid., 'Transcripts of Derbyshire Charters at Haddon' by W. A. Carrington, v. 16–17; vi. 304–6; no. 599 below). Adam fitz Peter was the grantee of no. 597 below (1252 × 1253).

*589 Agreement with Newstead Priory
Grant of free pasture for 300 sheep and twenty cattle in the moor of Longstone, from the head of the fields of Kalvonere *to the dyke of Blakedon* (Blakedene)*, in return for a quitclaim by the prior and convent of all their rights in the moor, saving the said pasture.*

[9 June 1232 × 1263]

Mention only, in an inquisition ordered in a writ to the bailiff of Peak dated at Westminster, 24 October 1280 (cd., *CIM*, i, no. 1184; *H*, no. 280). The jurors said that the agreement settled a dispute between Gruffudd and the priory over the pasture, which lay in the manor of Ashford. For the dating limits see note to no. 583 above. *Blakedene* may have been at or near Blakedon Hollow, par. Great Longstone (Cameron, *Place-Names of Derbyshire*, i. 139). Newstead Priory (Notts.) was an Augustinian house in Sherwood forest (*VCH Nottinghamshire*, ii. 112–17).

*590 Geoffrey of Pitchford (*Picheforde*)
Grant of the township of Sheldon (villa de Scheladone) *together with 18 marks annually from the mill of Ashford* (Esseforde).

[9 June 1232 × 1263]

Mention only, in a *quo warranto* inquisition at Derby, 10 January 1275 (*Rot. Hund.*, ii. 288a). The jurors declared that Sheldon was a member of the manor of Ashford and was alienated by Gruffudd (*Griphinus filius Wynoneyive*) in the time of Henry III. For the dating limits see note to no. 583 above.

*591 Agreement with Maredudd ap Rhobert
Chirograph, in which Maredudd quitclaims thirteen townships between the Rhiw and the Helygi (inter Reu et Leugy) *to Gruffudd, who in turn grants them to Maredudd to hold for the rest of his life and also remits to him a further nine townships.*

[Probably August 1241 × 1244]

Mention only, in the record of a claim by Gruffudd to the thirteen townships heard before Walter de Hopton at Oswestry, February 1278 (*WAR*, 240; cd., *H*, no. 541). Gruffudd declared that his father Gwenwynwyn had been seised of twenty-two townships until thirteen of them located between the Rhiw and the Helygi were occupied by Maredudd in time of war, probably in 1216 (see note to no. 18 above). After Gwenwynwyn's death (1216) Gruffudd made a claim against Maredudd for the thirteen townships before royal justices, in whose presence the present agreement was made. After Maredudd's death (1244), Gruffudd immediately took seisin of the thirteen townships in accordance with the terms of the chirograph and held them until he was ejected by Llywelyn ap Gruffudd. The hearing before the justices was presumably that referred to by Gruffudd in January 1279 as having occurred at Shewsbury before Ralph Mortimer (d. 1246), the prior of Wenlock and Brian de Brompton, to whom the case had been adjourned after Gruffudd had impleaded Maredudd before Henry III at Reading (*WAR*, 265–6; Morgan, 'Territorial divisions [I]', 12). Although Gruffudd claimed in 1278 that he brought an action against Maredudd after Gwenwynwyn's death, he does not specify how long after. He may well have acted only after his restoration by the king to southern Powys in August 1241 – when Maredudd, with Gruffudd and other Welsh lords, offered charters to the king at Shrewsbury in support of Senana's bid to secure the release of her husband Gruffudd ap Llywelyn (no. 21 above) – as it is unlikely that Maredudd, a close ally of Llywelyn ap Iorwerth, would have agreed to appear before royal justices during Llywelyn's occupation of Gruffudd's lands (cf. Morgan, 'Territorial divisions [I]', 12, which implies a date range of 1241 × 1244). The reference to Reading is inconclusive, as the town featured frequently on the king's itinerary; one possibility, however, is that Gruffudd initiated his plea on 24 February 1242, if he was present when Henry made a grant in his favour at Reading on that day (see no. 595 below). If Brian de Brompton was the same person as the Brian de Brampton named as the first of the jurors who heard the case between Gruffudd and Thomas Corbet in January 1244 (*CRR*, xviii. *1243–5*, 168–9 (no. 829)), this could support a date after August 1241. For the townships (referred to in the sources variously as being thirteen or fourteen in number) and their location in the north of Cedewain and its borders with Arwystli, Caereinion, Swydd Llannerch Hudol and Montgomery, see Lloyd, 'Edward the First's commission', 4–5; *idem*, 'Edward the First's commission … postscript'; Morgan, 'Territorial divisions [I]', 19–21; *idem*, 'Territorial divisions [II]', 35 (Map 1); and no. 605 below.

*592 Strata Marcella Abbey

Grant and confirmation, in free alms, of all their holdings, as set out in the charters of the donors and vendors.

[August 1241 × 1257]

Mention only, in an inspeximus of Edward II dated at Tutbury, 12 March 1322 (*Ystrad Marchell Charters*, no. 74; Jones, 'Abbey of Ystrad Marchell', 313 (from Henry VI's inspeximus, 1450); cd., *CChR 1300–26*, 440; *H*, no. 277). Thomas argued, on the basis of its place in Edward II's inspeximus, that the charter was issued after the charter of Gruffudd's uncle Thomas Corbet, dated 1229, and before that of Owain ap Gruffudd ap Rhys, who died 17 January 1235 (*Ystrad Marchell Charters*, 29, 81 and nos 72, 77). However, it is unlikely that the monks would have sought a confirmation from Gruffudd before he recovered his ancestral lands in Powys in August 1241, lands held by Llywelyn ap Iorwerth and his sons since 1216 (*Rot. Fin.*, i. 350–1; cf. nos 282–3 above for Gruffudd ap Llywelyn's charters for Strata Marcella of 1226). If so, the present charter was probably issued between Gruffudd's restoration and his final expulsion from Powys by Llywelyn ap Gruffudd in the autumn of 1257 (cf. *HW*, ii. 719, 722). The period following Gruffudd's agreement with Llywelyn and recovery of his lands in 1263 (no. 358 above), though not impossible, is also unlikely, as it is difficult to see why the monks would have waited until Gruffudd's power in the region was more precarious than it had been between 1241 and 1257.

593 The burgesses of Welshpool

Grant of a free borough, so that they may be free of all customs and services pertaining to Gruffudd and his heirs throughout all his lands. Further grant of quittance of toll and team, passage, pontage, heriot, relief, tallage and all customs pertaining to him and his heirs. In order that no bailiff of Gruffudd may lay hands on the burgesses and their heirs contrary to the liberties and customs of the law of Breteuil, Gruffudd has freely granted that they may have and keep that law as freely and fully as the citizens of Hereford in all customs [(?)pertaining to it], on condition that no one may trade in the borough unless it be by the said law or by the will of the burgesses. Further grant that they may have a merchant guild with hanse and assize of bread and ale and all liberties pertaining to the guild, so that if any villein from outside comes into the borough and holds land and is in scot and in lot with the burgesses for one year and one day, he may remain there as a freeman and never be handed over to his lord. Further grant that the burgesses may arrest all robbers, murderers and malefactors found in the borough and imprison and judge them. Gruffudd and his heirs will warrant all the above liberties for ever. Sealing clause; witnesses.

[August 1241 × August 1263]

B = Llandrindod Wells, Powys County Archives Office, Welshpool Borough Collection, AA1 (inspeximus of Edward Charlton in his charter for Welshpool, dated at Welshpool, 29 June 1406). Pd. from B, Jones, 'Feudal barons of Powys', 303–4; from Jones, Jones, 'Welsh Pool', 314–15 (trans. only); from Jones, 'Feudal barons of Powys', Morgan, 'Foundation of the borough of Welshpool', 7–8 (trans. only).
Cd., *H*, no. 278.

Gruffinus filius Gwenoynwyn dominus de Keueillyoc omnibus fidelibus hanc presentem cartam inspecturis vel audituris salutem in domino. Noverit universitas vestra me concessisse et hac presenti[a] carta mea confirmasse dilectis et fidelibus burgensibus nostris de la Pole et heredibus suis ut habeant liberum burgum in villa de Pole, ita quod prefati burgenses et eorum heredes sint liberi de omnibus consuetudinibus et servitiis mihi et heredibus meis in omnibus terris meis ubicumque fuerint pertinentibus. Concessi etiam burgensibus eisdem et heredibus suis quod sint quieti de theolonio et *theam*, de passagio, pontagio per omnes terras meas, de herieto, de relevio, de talliagio et de omnibus consuetudinibus mihi et heredibus meis pertinentibus. Et ne aliquis ballivus noster in dictis burgensibus meis et eorum heredibus contra libertates et consuetudines legis Britannie manum (?)impo[nat . . . eis]dem[b] burgensibus et eorum heredibus quiete concessi etiam quod habeant et teneant predictam legem Britanniam tam liberam et integram ut cives Herfordie tenent in omnibus consuetudinibus ad [dictam legem spectantibus],ᶜ ita quod ne aliquis aliquam faciat mercandisam in prefato burgo nisi sit de dicta lege vel per voluntatem predictorum burgensium. Concessi etiam pro me et heredibus meis quod predicti burgenses mei gildam habeant mercandisandi cum hamso et cum assisa panis et cervisie in omnibus libertatibus ad dictam gildam spectantibus, ita quod si aliquis nativus extraneus veniat in prefato burgo et terram teneat et sit in *scott* et in *loth* cum prefatis burgensibus per unum annum et unum diem liber ibidem maneat et nunquam domino suo liberetur. Concessi etiam pro me et heredibus meis predictis burgensibus meis de la Pole et eorum heredibus quod possint omnes latrones, homicidas et malefactores in dicto burgo inventos attachiare et in prisona sua imprisonare et prescriptos iudicare. Ego vero dictus Gruffinus et heredes mei predictis burgensibus et eorum heredibus omnes libertates prescriptas ut prenominatum est pro me et heredibus meis imperpetuum warantizabimus et defendemus. In cuius rei testimonium huic scripto sigillum meum apposui. Hiis testibus: Ioh(ann)e filio Alani, Thoma Corbet, Ioh(ann)e Ext(ra)neo, Madoc filio Gwenoynwyn, Gruff' filio Madoc, Wen' filio Wronev, Gruffino filio Kynvelyn, Eyno(n) filio Adaf et multis aliis.

ᵃ presente B. | ᵇ *letters in square brackets illegible because of staining; Jones, 'Feudal barons of Powys', reads* imposuerit quas eisdem. | ᶜ *letters in square brackets illegible because of staining; suggested reading follows Jones, 'Feudal barons of Powys'.*

Morgan, 'Foundation of the borough', 8–12, argues that the charter is probably datable to between Gruffudd's recovery of southern Powys in August 1241 and the outbreak of disputes with his uncle Thomas Corbet (d. 1274), the second witness, in 1245. However, a broader date range should probably be allowed. To begin with, Gruffudd's conflicts with Thomas seem to have started even before the recovery of southern Powys, for in January 1244 Gruffudd referred to a peace which had settled 'many disputes' between the two sides on 25 March 1241, and further legal action was instigated in September 1243 (*CRR*, xviii. *1243–5*, nos 679, 829). Disputes continued until Thomas's death in 1274 (Stephenson, 'Politics of Powys Wenwynwyn', 55–8; no. 596 below). However, these seem to have been punctuated by occasional agreements or love-days, as in 1241 and also in 1256 (*Roll of the Shropshire Eyre*, ed. Harding, 137–8). The charter could, therefore, have been issued during a respite in the conflicts. However, it is probably no later than the summer of 1263, when Gruffudd invaded and occupied Gorddwr, in Thomas's lordship of Caus, a move followed, in December, by Gruffudd's submission to Llywelyn ap Gruffudd (no. 358 above). Gruffudd remained in his allegiance to Llywelyn until 1274. In any case the charter can be no later than the death of another witness, John fitz Alan, shortly before 10 November 1267 (*CIPM*, i. 216 (no. 684)).

For the 'law of Breteuil', urban customs originating in Breteuil, Normandy, which were adopted in Hereford shortly after the Norman conquest, see Bateson, 'Laws of Breteuil'. *Lex Britannia* is an unusual term for the law, and may reflect a belief that the customs were of early British origin (ibid., 318). Though the charter bears some resemblances to King John's charter for Hereford in 1215 (*Rot. Chart.*, 212b–213a), these are insufficiently close to suggest that the latter – which lacks any reference to the law of Breteuil – influenced Gruffudd's scribe.

I am very grateful to Gordon Reid, Powys County Archivist, for locating Edward Charlton's charter and supplying me with digitally scanned images of it.

*594 Letter patent concerning Henry III
Notification that he will act as a pledge in support of undertakings given by Senana for the release of her husband Gruffudd ap Llywelyn.

[Shrewsbury, 12 August 1241]

Mention only, in an agreement between Senana and the king dated at Shrewsbury, 12 August 1241 (no. 284 above). Presumably the letter patent was similar to that concerning these matters issued on the same occasion by Hywel ap Madog of Bromfield (no. 523 above).

*595 Hawise Lestrange, his wife
Grant of dower in the manor of Ashford.

[Shortly after 24 February 1242]

Mention only, in a charter of Henry III granting royal assent for the grant to be made, dated at Reading, 24 February 1242 (*CChR 1226–57*, 266). Henry allowed Hawise to hold the land as dower for life, even if Gruffudd or his heirs abandoned the service and fealty of the king.

596 Henry III
Letter, stating that because his uncle Thomas Corbet had hanged without judgement or any cause three of Gruffudd's men, who, like Gruffudd and all his men, were under the protection of God and the king, as Gruffudd had previously shown the king, many of the kin of the hanged men had entered Thomas's land and killed certain of his men in revenge . . . though he was very ill in a certain abbey Gruffudd, on hearing of that vengeance, immediately sent his men to find the said malefactors . . . So that nothing . . . or suspect may be suggested to the king by Thomas, Gruffudd informs the king that he would rather suffer all adversities than do or consent to anything contrary to the king's dignity or will. Therefore he throws himself at the king's feet and prays that the king will believe no accusation against Gruffudd . . . and declares himself ready to appear before the king or his men wherever it pleases the king.

[*c.*1247 × 1259]

A = TNA: PRO, SC 1/3, no. 162. No endorsements; approx. 193 mm. wide × 76 mm. deep on left, 60 mm. deep on right; eight sets of double slits for insertion of a tongue or tag; mounted, foot cut away. Parchment badly stained.
Cd., *CAC*, 19–20; *H*, no. 532.

Venerabili domino suo et sibi semper karissimo domino H. Dei gratia illustri regi Angl(ie), domino Hyb(er)n(ie), duci Norm(annie), [Aquit' et] comiti And', suus G. filius Wenunwin' salutem et se ipsum semper ad pedes. Regie serenitati vestre (?)de . . .ᵃ significandum quod quia dominus Thom(as) Corb(er)t avunculus meus tres homines meos in pace et protectione Dei et vestra, sicuti et ego et omnes mei constitutos, sine iudicio et occasione aliqua suspenderat, sicut alias vobis ostendi, plures de progenie dictorum suspensorum se congregaverunt et intraverunt terram domini Thom(e) Corb(er)t et quosdam de hominibus suis occiderunt sumendo de suspensis ultionem. Ego vero minimus (?) . . . cum essem in quadam abbacia valde infirmus, audiens ultionem illam factam, statim misi homines meos ad querendum dictos malefactores ...[b] petuerunt. Ne igitur aliquid ... vel suspiciosum per dominum Thom(am) Corb(er)t avunculum meum serentitati vestre de me vel de meis proponatur, vobis tanquam domino karissimo duxi significandum quod mallem omnia adversa sustinere quam aliquid dignitati vestre et voluntati contrarium ... agere vel consentire. Unde est quod ad pedes vestros provolutus sicut iustum est ... deprecor excellentie vestre quatinus p ... tis Dei intuitu et pro salute anime vestre null[am] de me `a (?)vestris credatis accusacionem ... coram vobis et vestris quandocum[que] volueritis et ubicunque vobis placuerit me exhibebo ... vos quoq ... vestro eo (?)etiam vestram et ... vestra significatis. Semper valeat dominus meus.

[a] *rest of word illegible in* A. | [b] *two words illegible in* A.

The letter is probably no later than December 1259, as the style given to Henry III in the address was abandoned as a result of the Treaty of Paris on 4 December 1259 (though it continued to be used in chancery writs until April 1260 and in exchequer writs until the end of June 1260) (Chaplais, *Essays in Medieval Diplomacy*, I. 248–51). Gruffudd's disputes with his uncle Thomas Corbet, lord of Caus focused on the manors of Buttington, Trewern (Orleton) and Hope, granted from the lordship of Caus in free marriage with Thomas's sister Margaret upon her marriage to Gwenwynwyn (*Reg. Swinfield*, 209; Lloyd, 'Border notes', 51–2). These and other matters were the subjects of litigation between Margaret and her son Gruffudd on the one side and Thomas on the other from at least 1243; indeed, Gruffudd claimed in January 1244 that he had made peace with Thomas in settlement of an earlier dispute on 25 March 1241 (*CRR*, xviii. *1243–5*, 133, 168–9 (nos 679, 829)). The events referred to in the present letter occurred after the inquisition of January 1244, as this does not mention them among the matters in dispute at that time. The earliest references to events comparable to those mentioned in the letter occur in 1247 (cf. Stephenson, 'Politics of Powys Wenwynwyn', 55). At Easter 1247 Thomas accused Gruffudd of ordering his men to rob and kill some of Thomas's men; at the subsequent hearing at Michaelmas in that year Gruffudd's men were accused of killing two of Thomas's men, burning a cart of his corn worth £30 and destroying many of his cattle, all within the county of Shropshire; both parties agreed that arbitrators should be sent to the March to inquire into trespasses committed by each side (*WAR*, 16–17). However, the letter may refer to later disturbances, since disputes between the two parties continued in the mid-1250s (*CPR 1247–58*, 438; *Roll of the Shropshire Eyre*, ed. Harding, 137–8; Morgan, 'Territorial divisions [I]', 41). It is quite possible, as Williams has suggested (*Welsh Cistercians*, 152), that the 'certain abbey' where Gruffudd lay ill was Strata Marcella; if so, the vengeance taken by his men took place no later than autumn 1257, when Gruffudd was expelled from southern Powys by Llywelyn ap Gruffudd (*HW*, ii. 722; Morgan, 'Territorial divisions [I]', 42–3). Yet, even if this is correct, the letter itself could be later, as it was written after the events and Gruffudd had already raised the matter with the king. Nor is it impossible that the events themselves happened after Gruffudd's expulsion: the identification of Strata Marcella is not conclusive and Gruffudd's disputes with Thomas flared up again in 1259 (*CPR 1258–66*, 54; cf. Spurgeon, 'Gwyddgrug castle', 131).

597 Agreement with Adam fitz Peter of Longstone

Gruffudd remits and quitclaims to Adam and his heirs or assigns all secular customs and services due from Adam's fee in Longstone and Wardlow, except for the due services which Adam's predecessors were accustomed to render annually to Gruffudd and his predecessors, namely 13s. per annum to be paid at two terms, namely 6s. 6d. at the Annunciation [25 March] and 6s. 6d. at Michaelmas [29 September], [and] except for three ploughing services and three sowing services for Gruffudd twice a year, suit at the mill of Ashford and help with the pond of the said mill and other repairs to the mill when necessary, and suit at the court of Ashford like the other freemen of the manor of Ashford. Since the king tallages his demesne, let Adam be tallaged in respect of himself and his fee. Sealing clause; witnesses.

28 October 1252 × 27 October 1253

A = half of a bipartite chirograph in possession of the Wright family, made available for examination at Eyam Hall, Eyam, Derbyshire. Modern endorsement; approx. 162 × 107 + 10 mm.; central slit in fold for a tag (*c*.12 mm. wide); sealed on tag. Circular seal, brown wax, imperfect, originally approx. 35 mm. diameter, sewn into a leather bag which encloses nearly all of the seal, hiding both device and legend.

Cd., Yeatman *et al.*, *Feudal History*, iv. 301 (and facsimile, ibid., immediately preceding p. iii).

C   Y   R   O   G   R   A   P   H   V   M [a]

Hec est convencio facta inter dominum Griffinu(m) filium Wenu(n)wini ex una parte et Adam filium Pet(ri) de Langesdon' ex altera anno regni regis Henr(ici) filii regis Ioh(ann)is xxxvii°, videlicet quod dictus dominus Griffin(us) remisit et quietumclamavit predicto Ade filio Pet(ri) de Langesd(on) et heredibus suis vel assignatis suis omnes consuetudines seculares et omnimoda servicia que de feudo prefati A. in Langesd(on) et in Wardlowe exeunt vel aliquo casu contingente exire poterunt, salvis debitis serviciis que antecessores dicti A. predicto domino Griff(ino) et antecessoribus suis de anno in annum facere consueverunt pro tenemento suo de Lang(esdon) et de Wardl(owe), videlicet xiii solidos per annum solvendos ad duos anni terminos, scilicet ad festum Beate Mar(ie) in marcio vi solidos et vi denarios et ad festum Sancti Michael(is) vi solidos et vi denarios, salvis[b] tribus erruris et tribus seuris de prefato A. et hominibus suis predicto domino G. faciendis bis ad cibum per annum, et secta molendini de Essord' de predicto A. et hominibus suis et auxilio eorum ad stagnum dicti molendini et alia que ad dictum molendinum pertinent cum necesse fuerit reficienda, et salva secta curie de Essord' de prefato A. et heredibus suis pro se et pro tenentibus suis de Lang(esdon) et de Wardl(owe) sicut ceteri liberi homines de manerio de Essord' sequntur vel sequi tenentur. Et cum dominus rex dominica sua talliaverit predictus A. pro se et pro feudo suo talliatur. Et quod hec conventio inter illos facta rata et stabilis in posterum permaneat uterque illorum alternatim sigillum suum ad modum cyrographi apponere fecit. Hiis testibus: domino Ricardo de Vernu(n), domino Ricardo de Herthull', Ric(ar)do Daniel de Tydeswell', Will(elm)o de Langesd(on), Math(e)o de Langesd(on), Thom(a) de Langesd(on) et multis aliis.

[a] *top of* A *cut across in a zig-zag fashion with five indents, each c.15 mm. deep, bearing the remains of this word.* | [b] *salvo followed by a space containing two illegible words, followed by* et, *all of which have been erased* A.

The charter is dated 37 Henry III. Adam fitz Peter of Longstone issued a charter probably datable 1232 × 1242 (see note to no. 579 above) and witnessed no. 588 above. The clause concerning tallage seems disingenuous, as on 21 June 1245 the king had ordered Gruffudd to be quit of tallage on Ashford after the barons of the exchequer found that the manor had never been tallaged since Gwenwynwyn was enfeoffed with it by John (*CR 1242–7*, 316; cf. *CR 1237–42*, 449–50).

*598 Henry III

Petition that a pardon be granted to Robert Sais of Shropshire of the outlawry resulting from the death of Philip Sais with which he is charged; Gruffudd undertakes to guarantee Robert's good behaviour in future.

[Shortly before 4 December 1256]

Mention only, in a letter patent of Henry III granting the pardon, dated at Clarendon, 4 December 1256 (*CPR 1247–58*, 532; *H*, no. 542). The king's letter does not explicitly state that the petition was in written form.

599 Agreement with the parishioners of St Giles's chapel, Great Longstone

Grant of two bovates with all their appurtenances in Great Longstone to support a chaplain celebrating divine office in that chapel, namely those two bovates extracted from the bovates of Gruffudd's homage in Great Longstone and previously assigned by the parishioners for that purpose, to be held from Gruffudd and his heirs by the parishioners, or by whoever from that parish to whom they wish to grant them to support that service, freely and in peace for ever, except for multure from those two bovates of up to thirty measures of grain. If the canons of the mother church of Lichfield or the clergy of Bakewell church should wish to appropriate the two bovates in order to support a chaplain in that chapel for ever, or if the parishioners should wish to sell or otherwise alienate them, Gruffudd and his heirs will be permitted to take seisin of them and do with them as he will as his demesne without any hindrance or contradiction from the said parishioners or any other parishioner of the said parish. Gruffudd on behalf of himself and his heirs and, on behalf of all the parish, Thomas le Lewyd' *and Elias fitz William, both of Little Longstone, and Richard fitz Adam, William the clerk, Thomas le* Bond' *and John de* Hul, *all of Great Longstone, and their heirs, have been appointed attorneys and undertaken to keep this agreement for ever and have attached their seals alternately to this chirograph. In return for this grant the parishioners have given Gruffudd 7 marks premium in advance. Witnesses.*

1262

B = Lichfield Dean and Chapter Muniments, 'Magnum Registrum Album', fo. 272r. s. xiv[1].
C = BL, Harl. MS 4799 (Cartulary of Lichfield Cathedral), fos. 47v–48r. s. xiv[1]. Rubric: Assignatio terre pro cantaria de Longedon' in prato.
Cd., *Great Register of Lichfield*, ed. Savage, 333–4 (no. 696).

Anno ab incarnatione domini m^mo cc sexagesimo secundo convenit inter Griffynu(m) filium Wenuwen' ex parte una et omnes parochianos ad capellam Sancti Egidii de^a Magna Longdon' spectantes quod dictus Griffyn(us) concessit pro se et heredibus suis imperpetuum dictis parochianis duas bovatas terre cum omnibus pertinentiis suis in villa et^b in territorio de Magna Longdon' in auxilium sustentationis unius capellani divina in eadem capella celebrantis, videlicet illas duas bovatas terre cum pertinentiis que ^cextracte erant^c de bovatis homagii dicti Griffyni de Magna Longdon' et que prius assignate erant per dictos parochianos ad illud idem servitium sustinendum, habendas et tenendas de dicto Griffyno et heredibus suis dictis parochianis vel cuicumque vel quibuscumque de dicta parochia eas tradere voluerint ad illud idem servitium sustinendum libere, quiete, bene et in pace imperpetuum, salva tamen dicto Griffyno et heredibus suis multura de bladis super dictas duas bovatas terre crescentibus ad tricesimum vas. Sciendum tamen quod si ita contigerit quod canonici matris ecclesie Lich' vel ordinarii ecclesie de Bauqwell'^d se de dictis duabus bovatis terre apropriare voluerint causa unius capellani divina in eadem capella celebrantis imperpetuum sustinendi, vel quod si dicti parochiani dictas duas bovatas alicui vendere vel aliquo modo alienare voluerint, bene licebit dicto Griffyno et heredibus suis dictas duas bovatas terre in manus suas seysire et voluntatem suam sicuti de suo dominico ex eis facere sine aliquo impedimento vel contradictione dictorum parochianorum vel alicuius parochiani de dicta parochia. Ad hanc autem conventionem firmiter et sine fraude imperpetuum tenendum dictus Griffyn(us) pro se et heredibus suis, Thom(as) le Lewyd' de P(ar)va Longesdon', Elias filius Will(elm)i de eadem, Ric(ardus) filius Ade de Magna Longesdon', Will(elm)us clericus de eadem, Tho(mas) le Bond' de eadem, Ioh(ann)e de ^e Hul de eadem et heredibus eorum pro tota parochia atturnati constituti manuceperunt et sigilla sua alternatim in testimonium presenti scripto in modum cirograffi confecto apposuerunt. Pro hac autem concessione dederunt dicti parochiani dicto Griffino^f septem marcas in gersummam^g pre manibus. Hiis testibus: Will(elm)o Wyne, Will(elm)o de Esseburne, Ioh(ann)e de Holewell', Rog(er)o de Scheladon', Will(elm)o de Reyndon', Ioh(ann)e le Wyne, Nich(ol)o de Wynnefeld', Ric(ard)o de Hokelowe clerico et aliis.

^a die C. | ^b C *inserts another* et. | ^{c-c} extraiterant C. | ^d Baucwell' C. | ^e C; dil B. | ^f Griffyno C. ^g gersumana C.

Like the chapel at Ashford, St Giles's chapel at Great Longstone was subject to the mother church of Bakewell and thus to the dean and chapter of Lichfield (see note to no. 586 above). Richard fitz Adam may have been a son of Adam fitz Peter of Longstone, the grantee of no. 597 above (Yeatman *et al.*, *Feudal History*, iv. 331).

600 Henry III

Letter, informing the king that he has diligently enquired about the health of Llywelyn: he was very ill, recovered a little so that he could go about and then twice relapsed into the same illness he had before, so that he is weak, according to some, and may never fully recover as he has heard from the accounts of many. If he had died Gruffudd would have let the king know without delay; he will let him have more certain news concerning Llywelyn's condition if he grows worse.

[22 July × August 1262]

A = TNA: PRO, SC 1/3, no. 163. No endorsements; approx. 188 × 51 mm.; three sets of double slits for insertion of a tongue or tag; mounted, foot cut away. Bottom right-hand corner of parchment torn away.
Cd., *CAC*, 20; *H*, no. 534.

Excellentissimo domino suo domino H. Dei gratia illustri regi Angl(ie), domino Hyb(er)n(ie) et duci[a] Aq(ui)t' suus humilis miles G. filius Wenn' salutem et tam debitam quam devotam in omnibus cum humilitatis subiectione reverentiam. Noverit veneranda excellencia vestra quod diligenter inquisitus veritatem[b] de statu et sanitate Lewelini, et quia nihil vestre regali excellencie constare faciam nisi veritatem scienter, quod ipse valde fuit inf[ir]mus et aliquantulum recuperavit ita quod potuit ire et postea bis rececidit in illam egritudinem quam prius habuit, per quod debilis est ut dicunt quidam, ita quod numquam omnino convalescet prout intellexi ex relatu plurimorum et audivi. Et si mortuus fuisset vobis non esset scelatus[c] quin vobis sine mora scire fecissem, et certiores[d] de statu eius scivero rumores si peioractur[e] vestre excellencie significabo. Valeat regalitas vestra per tempora[f] longiora in domino.

[a] dux A. | [b] veritataem A. | [c] *sic in* A. | [d] A *inserts* scivero. | [e] *sic in* A *for* peioratur. | [f] A *inserts* val *struck through.*

As Edwards argued (*CAC*, 20), the letter was probably sent in the summer of 1262, for Henry III wrote from Amiens on 22 July to the justiciar of England, Philip Basset, thanking him for news of rumours of Llywelyn's death. If the rumours proved to be correct, the justiciar was instructed to send out letters enclosed by the king to various Marcher lords as well as Gruffudd ap Gwenwynwyn ordering them to hinder the succession of Llywelyn's brother Dafydd and dissolve Welsh alliances; he was also to summon a royal army to Shrewsbury by the beginning of September for a campaign against the king's enemies in Wales (*CR 1261–4*, 142–4; Smith, *Llywelyn*, 137–8). The present letter appears to have been written after the king first heard the rumours and is thus probably datable to late July or August 1262.

601 Agreement with Llywelyn ap Gruffudd

[Apart from the difference in the year in the dating clause, correctly given here as 1263, and some minor verbal and orthographical differences, the text is the same as that sealed by Llywelyn ap Gruffudd in no. 358 above.]

Ystumanner, 12 December 1263

B = TNA: PRO, E 36/274 (Liber A), fos. 369r–370r. s. xiii ex.
Pd. from B, *LW*, 111–13 (no. 204); from NLW, Peniarth MS 236, fos. 2v–4v (s. xvii; incomplete), Bridgeman, 'Princes of upper Powys', 117–19.
Cd., *H*, no. 535.

Ad perpetuam rei geste memoriam facta est hec finalis concordia anno domini m[o] cc[o] lxiii[oc] in vigilia Beate Lucie virginis apud Estoim Anneyr inter dominum Lewelinu(m) filium Griffini principem Wallie ex una parte et dominum Griffinu(m) filium Wenwynwyn ex altera, videlicet quod [i] dictus dominus Griffin(us) spontanea voluntate sua fecit homagium pro se et heredibus suis et tactis sacrosanctis iuravit fidelitatem dicto domino Lewelino[a] et heredibus suis coram venerabili patre domino Ricardo episcopo Bangorensi, [fo. 369v] dominis abbatibus de Ab(er)conwe et de Pola, fratre Ieuaf de ordine predicatorum, magistro David archidiacono Bangor', Adaf decano de Ardudwe, David filio Willelmi officiali Deffryncluyd, Goronwe, Tuder, Kynwric filiis Etneued, Ioruerth filio

Grugunan, Enniaun filio[b] Keyriadauc, David filio Enniaun, Keruerth ab Helyn priore de Pola, Adaf ab Meuryc, magistro Iuone, Gruffut filio Gwen, Enniaun filio Edneued et multis aliis.

[ii] Pro dicto autem homagio et fidelitate dicti Griffini dictus L.[a] concessit et restituit eidem G. omnes terras et possessiones suas, videlicet Keueylyauc et Maudwe in terminis suis, Arwistly in terminis suis, Kereynyaun et Mochnant Uch Raeadir in terminis suis, Eteyrswyth cum pertinentiis suis et terminis, totam terram inter Ryw et Helegy cum villa de Lanwydelay.

[iii] Dictus vero G. et heredes sui dictas terras per metas et divisas suas de dicto domino L.[a] et heredibus iure hereditario in perpetuo tenebunt et possidebunt.

[iv] Si vero contigerit, quod absit, dictum G. amittere aliquam partem de dictis terris per gwerram, dicto L.[a] terras suas in integrum possidente idem L.[a] dicto G. restaurabit deperdita in terris ad provisionem subscriptorum virorum, videlicet venerabilium patrum de Bangor' et Sancto Assaph' episcoporum, de Aberco(n)wy et de Pola abbatum, prioris fratrum predicatorum de Bangor', fratris Ieuas eiusdem ordinis, fratrum Ieuas Goch et Ioruerth ab Cadwgaun de ordine minorum de Lanvaes, Goronu, Tudyr et Kenwric filiorum Etneued, Ioruerth filii Grugunan, Enniaun filii Keyircadauc, David filii Will(elm)i et Kefnerth filii Heylyn; si vero contigerit aliquem vel aliquos predictorum virorum deesse vel abesse fiat dicta provisio per eos qui presentes fuerint et superstites.

[v] Si vero contigerit dominum L.[a] aliquam partem suarum terrarum amittere per gwerram, quod absit, sit in provisione dictorum virorum, conpensato utriusque partis dampno, deperdita dicto G. prout melius poterunt restaurare.

[vi] Si vero dictus G. poterit aliquas terras conquirere ultra metas suas a Kemeynaud inferius versus Slosub', dictus G. et heredes sui optineant et gaudeant conquisitis; a Kemeynaud vero superius domino L.[a] remaneant et suis heredibus conquisita.

[vii] Si vero gwerra vel exercitus dicti G. terram invadat, gwerra vel exercitu dictum L.[a] eodem tempore non molestante, prenominatus L.[a] succurret dicto G. pre omnibus aliis suis inprisiis si maiorem habuerit necessitatem.

[viii] Et si ita contigerit, quod absit, quod dictus G. castrum suum de Pola per gwerram amiserit per provisionem suprascriptorum virorum dominus L.[a] eidem assignabit aliud castrum ubi possit res et familiam secure custodire donec castrum suum recuperaverit.

[ix] Omnes enim infeudati per bone memorie L.[a] principem vel per David filium vel per ipsum G. habeant terras suas et quiete possideant nisi postmodum deliquerint ut merito debeant dictis terris privari.

[x] De omnibus vero terris et possessionibus a domino L.[a] quibuscumque collatis in dominio dicti G. sit in voluntate ipsius G. vel ipsas terras auferre vel concedere possidentibus.

[xi] Dominus vero Madocus filius Wenwynwyn commotum et de Maudwy quoad vixerit in capite tenebit de dicto G. et heredibus suis.

[xii] Si vero contigerit dominum G. accusari penes [fo. 370r] dominum L.[a] super aliquo dictus L.[a] non magnificabit dictam accusationem nisi manifeste possit probari; si vero probata fuerit faciat condignam emendam ad arbitrium predictorum virorum, salvis sibi terris et possessionibus, sine corporis incarceratione et hostagio, dummodo taliter satisfacere poterit et voluerit; si vero accusatio contra dictum G. ad plenum probari non poterit dominus L.[a] animadvertet[c] in accusatorem secundum delicti et iniurie quantitatem utrique domino satisfaciendo.

[xiii] Neuter vero dictorum dominorum L.ᵃ et G. receptabit vel defendet contra reliquum delinquentem.

[xiv] Dictus vero G. cum toto posse suo defensabit et succurret terris et possessionibus dicti L.ᵃ et liberis vicinis et a dicto L.ᵃ remotis quotiens necesse habuerint, terra sua sine hostili incursu existente; homines vero dictarum terrarum vice versa tenentur terris dicti G. simili modo succurrere.

[xv] Dictus vero G. tenetur venire in exercitum cum domino L.ᵃ quotiens ab eo fuerit requisitus nisi hostilis incursus tunc immineat terre sue manifeste.

[xvi] Uterque vero dictorum dominorum L. et G. fideliter adinvicem se tenebunt ita quod sint unius pacis et unius gerre et nullis se confederabunt alter sine altero.

[xvii] Quicquid vero homines de Poywys quamdiu fuerunt in dominio dicti L.ᵃ deliquerunt contra dictum G. idem G. eis totaliter condonavit et remisit.

[xviii] Ad plenam vero fidem et securitatem prescriptorum sepedicti L.ᵃ et G. supposuerunt se et heredes suos iurisdictioni venerabilium patrum episcoporum de Bangor' et de Sancto Assaph' necnon et abbatum de Ab(er)conweᵈ et de Pola qui pro tempore fuerint, ipsis in se dictam iurisdictionem assumentibus, quod possint coniunctim et divisim promulgare sententiam excommunicationis in personas L.ᵃ et G. ac heredum suorum et interdicti in terras eorundem si contra aliquem de dictis articulis venire presumpserint. Renuntiant etiam L.ᵃ et G. pro se et heredibus suis omni impetrationi, appellationi, cavillationi et omni remedio iuris canonici vel civilis contra dictas sententias excommunicationis et interdicti valituris; dicti vero episcopi et abbates ad petitionem partis dictas conventiones observantis tenentur coniunctim et divisim dictas sententias promulgare et easdem demandare executioni contra partem a dictis conventionibus resilientem.

In cuius rei testimonium huic parti scripture remanenti penes dominum L.ᵃ dominus G. sigillum suum fecit apponi una cum sigillis dictorum episcoporum et abbatum; parti vero remanenti penes dominum G. sigillum domini L.ᵃ cum ceteris predictis sigillis est appensum.

ᵃ *sic in no. 358*; H. B. | ᵇ filius B. | ᶜ *sic in no. 358*; animadvertit B. | ᵈ *sic in no. 358*; Aber et conwe B.

The sealing clause shows that this text derives from the part of the chirograph sealed by Gruffudd and given to Llywelyn. For the part sealed by Llywelyn and kept by Gruffudd, together with the context of the agreement, see no. 358 and note above.

602 Llywelyn ap Gruffudd ap Gwenwynwyn

Grant, if Llywelyn survives Gruffudd and his wife Hawise, of all his manor of Buttington, namely Buttington, Orleton and Hope with all their appurtenances. Further grant of all the land of Deuddwr with all its appurtenances. Further grant of Llanerfyl, Llysyn and Cnewyll in Caereinion with all their appurtenances. All these lands are to be held after the deaths of Gruffudd and Hawise freely and fully with all their appurtenances, as freely as his mother Margaret ever held them in her lifetime, saving whatever pertains to Gruffudd and his heirs by virtue of chief lordship in those lands. Sealing clause; witnesses.

Pool castle, 1 March 1270 [=1271]

B = TNA: PRO, E 36/274 (Liber A), fo. 383r. s. xiii ex.
Pd. from B, *LW*, 132 (no. 233).
Cd., *H*, no. 259.

[S]ciant presentes et futuri quod ego Griffinus filius Wennunwyny dominus de Keueyloc dedi et concessi et hac presenti carta mea confirmavi Lewelino filio meo, si me et Hawisam uxorem meam matrem suam supravixerit, totum manerium meum de Botinton', videlicet Botintone et Oleretun' et le Hop cum omnibus suis pertinentiis et apendiciis infra terminos suos; concessi etiam eidem Lewelino totam terram de Deudouer cum omnibus suis perti- nentiis et apendiciis infra terminos; preterea concessi eidem Lanneruel et Lessen et Kniwitlle in Creinon cum omnibus suis pertinentiis et apendiciis infra terminos suos; habendas et tenendas omnes predictas terras post mortem meam et post mortem `Hawisie uxoris mee^a de me et heredibus meis sibi et heredibus suis libere, quiete, bene et in pace, plenarie et integre et honorifice, in bosco, in plano, in viis, in semitis, in pratis, in pascuis et pasturis, in aquis, in molendinis et in omnibus aliis locis predictis terris pertinentibus, adeo libere quam Margareta bone memorie mater mea melius, integrius et liberius eas unquam tenuit in vita sua in omnibus, salvo michi et heredibus meis principali dominio in terris predictis quantum pertinet ad principale dominium. Et quia volo quod hec mea donatio, concessio et carte mee confirmatio rata et stabilis permaneat et inviolata presentem cartam sigilli mei munimine roboravi. Hiis testibus: domino Iacobo tunc abbate de Pola, fratre Goronu Puffing tunc priore de Pola, fratre Aniano Du eiusdem domus, viris religiosis; Ada filio Maurici tunc officiali de Powys, Tudur filio Goronov tunc officiali de Keueloc, Griffino filio Wen, Gervasio filio Goronov, Aniano filio Ydeneueth filii Sulien, Aniano filio Ydeneneueth filii Aniani tunc senescallo de Scedst(ra)dmarchel, Griffino filio Meurich *penkenadel* de Kykydua, Ruatllann tunc senescallo de Scedllanharhud(ol), Rob(er)to de Say tunc ballivo de Pola, Will(el)mo de Ekun tunc castri clerico et multis aliis. Datum apud castrum de Pola die Sancti David episcopi anno domini m^o ducentesimo septuagesimo.

^a B *inserts* Hawise *struck through.*

If, as is likely, the beginning of the year was reckoned at the Annunciation (25 March), the letter was dated 1 March 1271 by modern reckoning (as assumed in *LW*, 132). The lands granted to Llywelyn had all belonged to his grandmother Margaret. Buttington, Trewern (Orleton) and Hope were her marriage portion (see note to no. 596 above); the commote of Deuddwr and Llanerfyl, Llysyn and Cnewyll in Caereinion were presumably dower lands conferred on her by her husband Gwenwynwyn. (For the identification of Orleton with Trewern see Morgan, 'Trewern', 122–4.) All the lands named number among those assigned by Gruffudd in May 1277 to his wife Hawise Lestrange (d. 1310) (no. 606 below; see also Lloyd, 'Border notes', 52; *CIPM*, v. 145–6 (no. 269)). Smith, 'Dynastic succession', 226, n. 4, suggests that the present charter is a stray survivor of a group of documents issued at the same time regulating the inheritance of Gruffudd's lands. According to late fifteenth- and early sixteenth-century genealogies, Adda ap Meurig, 'official of Powys' (also named thus in no. 603 below), was a son of the first cousin of Gruffudd ap Meurig, *pencenedl* of Cegidfa (Guilsfield, the centre of the commote of Ystrad Marchell), and both belonged to a kin group descended from an earlier ruling family in Powys that was different from the dynasty of Bleddyn ap Cynfyn to which Gruffudd belonged. The *pencenedl* (chief of kindred) allocated offices among the kindred (Charles-Edwards, *Early Irish and Welsh Kinship*, 203–11, esp. 205–6; see also Bartrum, *WG*, i. 10; iii. 488–9; vi. 207).

603 Trial of Gruffudd and his son Owain

The case brought against Gruffudd and his son Owain was tried as follows. Arbitrators were nominated and approved by the parties, namely the prince's justiciar Tudur ab Ednyfed, his brother Cynwrig, Einion ap Caradog, Dafydd ab Einion prior of Pool [Strata Marcella], Adda ap Meurig official of Powys, Gruffudd's justiciar Gruffudd ap Gwên and Einion ab Ednyfed, before whom Gruffudd and Owain confessed that they had offended against the fealty due to the prince. The arbitrators therefore unanimously adjudged that Gruffudd and Owain should be subject with their lands and possessions to the grace and will of the prince, who could do with them as he willed. Gruffudd, realizing that he had offended greatly against the prince, humbly fell on his knees before the feet of the prince and sought this mercy, namely that the prince should grant him and his heirs the lands of Y Tair Swydd, Caereinion, Cyfeiliog from Arwystli to the Dyfi, Mawddwy and Mochnant Uwch Rhaeadr. The prince mercifully granted these lands on condition that Gruffudd and his heirs would be faithful to him for as long as they lived. In confirmation of this Owain offered himself voluntarily as a hostage for the fealty of his father and himself and was granted as such by his father, together with the homage of twenty-five men chosen from Gruffudd's lands, who swore on relics that they will be faithful to the prince if Gruffudd manifestly offends, and if he is convicted for any manifest offence the twenty-five will totally relinquish the homage and lordship of Gruffudd with his permission and bind themselves inseparably from then on to the prince. If Gruffudd or his heirs are found to have committed any manifest offence against the fidelity sworn to the prince, Gruffudd grants and warrants to the prince that he may seize all the aforenamed lands and possess them for ever. If any wish to bring an action against Gruffudd with respect to the lands granted to him and claim right in them, Gruffudd is bound to answer in the prince's court, where the prince will hear the action and show justice to both parties. If Gruffudd wishes to bring an action against anyone with respect to lands and possessions, he should do so in the prince's court and justice will be done to him there. The names of the twenty-five aforesaid men are: from Caereinion, Einion ab Ednyfed ap Sulien, Madog ab Einion ab Adda, Heilin ab Ednyfed, Madog Crach, Ednyfed Goch, Llywelyn ab Einion ap Gruffudd; from Deuddwr, Rhirid ap Cadwgan, Hywel ap Cadwgan, Griffri ap Iorwerth; from Swydd Ystrad Marchell, Adda ap Meurig, Madog ap Griffri ap Maredudd, Ieuaf Foel ab Einion; from Swydd Llannerch Hudol, Einion ap Dafydd, Madog ap Iorwerth Swlwis, Cynwrig Fychan ap Madog; from Mochnant, Ednyfed ap Gruffudd ab Ednyfed, Madog ab Ithel ap Seisyll; from Cyfeiliog, Tudur ap Goronwy, Iorwerth ap Goronwy, Gruffudd ap Gwên, Dafydd ap Hywel ap Philip, Dafydd ap Meilyr, Meilyr Goch, Tudur ap Maredudd and Llywelyn ap Griffri. The prince's men should have the lands which they hold from Gruffudd in the same liberty in which they used to possess those lands. Sealing clause; witnesses. Maredudd, abbot of Aberconwy and Dafydd, dean of Arllechwedd have seen and inspected the aforesaid account of the trial, in the same words, sealed by Gruffudd and Owain, whose seals were not erased, abolished or damaged in any part, and attached their own seals to this transcript as firm testimony of the above.

Bach-yr-anelau [Dolforwyn], Cedewain, 17 April 1274 (original document); Ardda, 21 July 1278 (transcript)

B = TNA: PRO, E 36/274 (Liber A), fos 368v–369r. s. xiii ex.
Pd. from B, *LW*, 108–10 (no. 203).
Cd., *H*, no. 537.

Sciant tam presentes quam futuri quod in causa accusationum motarum contra dominum Griffinu(m) filium Wenu' et Owenu(m) filium suum primogenitum sic fuit processum: videlicet arbitri fuerunt nominati et numerati ac a partibus approbati, scilicet Tuderus filius Ednyved iusticiarius domini principis, Kynwricus frater suus, Anianus filius Keiriadauc, David filius Einavn prior de Poli, Adam filius Meiric officialis de Powys, Griffin(us) filius Gwen iusticiarius dicti domini Griffini et Enniavn filius Edniued, coram quibus dictus dominus Griffin(us) et Owenus filius suus confessi fuerunt ipsos contra fidelitatem debitam domino principi deliquisse, et secundum confessionem dictorum dominorum Griffini et Oweni predicti arbitri arbitrati fuerunt unanimiter quod ipse dominus Griffin(us) et filius suus predictus corporaliter cum terris et possessionibus suis in gratia et voluntate domini principis deberent devenire, ita scilicet quod dictus dominus princeps posset de ipsis terris et possessionibus suis facere quicquid vellet. Quibus sic actis idem Griffinus sentiens se contra prefatum dominum principem nimium deliquisse humiliter subiciens se pedibus predicti domini principis ad genua provolutus, hanc misericordiam petiit ab eodem, videlicet quod dominus princeps concederet ei et heredibus suis illas terras que vocantur Iteyrswyth, Kereiniavn, Kyueyliavc de Arwystly usque Dyui, Mawdwy et Mochnant Uchraeadyr, cui petitioni dominus princeps predictus misericorditer condescendens dictas terras eidem et heredibus suis concessit sub hac forma, scilicet quod dictus dominus Griffinus et heredes sui fideles existant quoad vixerint prefato domino principi. Et ad dictam fidelitatem conservandam et confirmandam prefatus Owen(us) pro facto suo proprio quod nuper commisit et pro fidelitate patris sui et heredum suorum voluntarie se offerens in obsidem a patre suo fuit datus per assensum et licentiam sui ipsius, et cum hoc homagium viginti quinque virorum electorum de terris predicti Griffini concessis et eorum sacramentum super sanctis reliquiis quod ipsi fideles erunt domino principi si predictus Griffinus manifeste delinquat, vel etiam si fuerit convictus in aliquo delicto manifesto predicti viginti quinque viri homagium et dominium prefati [fo. 369r] domini omnino relinquentes per eius licentiam domino principi extunc inseparabiliter se coniungant. Item si contingat, quod absit, quod dictus dominus Griffinus vel heredes sui inveniantur in aliquo manifesto delicto excessisse contra fidelitatem permissam et iuratam domino principi, dictus dominus Griffinus sano et salvo concedit prefato principi et warentizabit eidem accipere omnes terras superius nominatas et concessas predicto Griffino et earum possessione perpetue gaudere. Ceterum si aliqui velint movere questionem contra dictum dominum Griffinu(m) super terris eidem concessis et dicant se ius habere in eisdem, prefatus dominus Griffinus tenetur respondere in curia prenominati principis, ipso tamen principe dictam causam audiente et examinante ac utrique parti iustitiam exhibente. Ex alia autem parte si dominus Griffin(us) velit movere questionem super terris et possessionibus contra aliquos proponat questionem suam in curia prefati principis et fiet ei iustitia in eadem curia. Nomina autem xx quinque virorum supradictorum sunt hec: de Kerennau, Einiau filius Ednyved ab Sulyen, Maudauc filius Ednavn ab Adaf, Helyn ab Ednyved, Madauc Crach, Ednyved Goch, Lewelin(us) filius Enniavn ab Gruffut; de Deudwyr, Ririd ab Katdogavn, Hywel ab Kadwgavn, Griffri ab Ior'; de Swythystradmarcell, Adaf ab Meuric, Madauc ab Griffri ab Maredut, Ieuas Voel ab Einiavn; de Swythllaynyrchhudwel,

Enniavn ab D(avi)d, Madauc ab Ior' Swlwis, Kynwryc Wychan ab Madauc; de Mochnant, Ednyved ab Gruffut ab Ednyved, Madauc ab Ithael ab Seissyl; de Keueliauc, Tudyr ab Goronw, Ior' filius Goronw, Gruffud ab Gwen, David filius Owel ab Ph', David ᵃ⁻filius ab⁻ᵃ Melyr, Melyr Goch, Tudir ᵃ⁻filius ab⁻ᵃ Mared' et Lewelyn filius Griffri. Preterea homines domini principis debent habere terras suas quas tenent sub dicto Griffino in eadem libertate qua ipsiᵇ easdem terras possidebant in confectione presentis. In cuius rei testimonium sigillum predicti domini Griffini huic scripto est appensum. Hiis testibus: Howelo filio Resi Gric, Madoco Wychan domino de Bro(m)ph', David filio Griffini ab Owein, Ior' filio Mared', Gwrgenv filio Madauc, Rys filio Griffini, Ior' filio Goronw, Tuder filio Goronw, Enniavn filio Ednewed ab Sulyen, Griffin(o) filio Ior' ab Griffri et multis aliis. Datum apud Bachyranneleu in Kedewen anno domini mᵒ ccᵒ lxxiiii xv kalendas maii.

Prefatum autem processum in scriptis redactum sub eadem verborum forma sigillatum predictorum nobilium, videlicet domini Griffini filii Wenu(n)' et Oweni filii sui sigillis non rasum nec abolitum nec in aliqua sui parte vitiatum viderunt et inspexerunt frater Maredwt dictus abbas de Ab(er)cenwy et David decanus de Arllecweth quorum sigilla ad firmum predictorum testimonium huic transcripto sunt apposita anno domini mᵒ ccᵒ lxviii vigilia Beate Marie Magdalene apud Ardev.

ᵃ⁻ᵃ *sic in* B. | ᵇ B *inserts* in.

For differing assessments of the abortive plot by Dafydd ap Gruffudd and Gruffudd ap Gwenwynwyn and his son Owain to assassinate Llywelyn ap Gruffudd on 2 February 1274, and especially of Llywelyn's treatment of Gruffudd and Owain as revealed by the present document, see *LW*, liii–lv; Stephenson, 'Politics of Powys Wenwynwyn', 46–9; Smith, *Llywelyn*, 369–77, esp. 370–3. The significance of the role of arbitrators in the legal process is noticed in Smith, 'Disputes and arbitration', 839. As Edwards argued (*LW*, 110), the list of sureties suggests that Y Tair Swydd referred to Swydd Llannerch Hudol, Swydd Ystrad Marchell and Deuddwr, three commotes located contiguously along the Severn in the region of Welshpool. Lloyd, 'Dolforwyn', 307 showed that Bach-yr-anelau, a name found in only two other documents, likewise dated April 1274 (*LW*, 24 (no. 25); no. 604 below), was an early, apparently experimental, name for Dolforwyn, the site of Llywelyn's new castle in Cedewain. Ardda or Ardda'r Mynach was a grange of Aberconwy Abbey in Nanhwynan (Smith, *Llywelyn*, 322 and n. 182). The transcript was very probably prepared for use in the legal proceedings at Oswestry the following day, 22 July 1278, in order to support Llywelyn's claim to Arwystli and Cyfeiliog between the Dyfi and Dulas by showing that the 1274 conviction still stood (ibid., 470 and n. 78; no. 410 above).

604 Letter patent concerning Llywelyn ap Gruffudd

Notification that Gruffudd and his son Owain grant all their lands and possessions and castle of their free will for ever to Llywelyn, prince of Wales and his heirs whenever Owain, given as a hostage to the prince, seeks by word, deed or writing to escape from the custody of the prince without his permission and is lawfully convicted of this. Whenever Gruffudd and Owain are convicted of transgressing against the above in one or more of the aforesaid ways they place themselves under the sentences of the bishops of St Davids, Llandaff, Bangor and St Asaph, so that the bishops, jointly or separately, may pronounce sentence of excommunication against them; Gruffudd and Owain renounce all appeals, excuses, notification of all claims, acquisition of liberties and all means hindering or abolishing the said obligation in the ecclesiastical and civil courts. They submit themselves freely to the aforesaid obligation so that the prince may permit Owain to follow him and his court in the places and at the times which seem expedient to him in secure custody night and day according to the prince's disposition. Sealing clause; witnesses.

Bach-yr-anelau [Dolforwyn] in Cedewain, 18 April 1274

B = TNA: PRO, E 36/274 (Liber A), fo. 364v. s. xiii ex.
Pd. from B, *LW*, 98–9 (no. 193).
Cd., *H*, no. 538.

Universis Cristi fidelibus presentes litteras visuris vel audituris Griffin(us) filius Wenn' et Owenus filius suus primogenitus salutem in domino. Noverit universitas vestra quod nos pro nobis et heredibus nostris omnes terras et possessiones nostras ac nostrum castrum salvo et sano ex mera et libera volunte nostra perpetuo concedimus et hac presenti carta nostra confirmamus domino Lewelino principi Wallie et eius heredibus quandocumque prefatus Owenus dicto domino principi in obsidem datus quesierit verbo vel facto vel scripto a custodia prefati principis evadere sine dicti domini principis volunte et licentia petita et obtenta et de hoc legitime fuerit convictus. Nos etiam dicti Griffinus et Owen(us) quandocumque convicti fuerimus uno modo vel modis predictis contra predicta excessisse supponimus nos sententiis venerabilium patrum ac dominorum Men', Landaven(sis), Bang' et Ass(av)en(sis) episcoporum extunc, ita videlicet quod predicti domini episcopi coniunctim vel divisim sententiam excommunicationis in nos libere possint promulgare, abrenuntiantes etiam omni appellationi, allegationi, omnium querelarum denuntiationi, libertatis adquisitioni et omnibus modis dictam obligationem impedientibus vel cassantibus qui fieri possunt in foro ecclesiastico vel civili. Prefate autem obligationi libere nos subicimus ut prenominatus princeps sepedictum Owenu(m) sequi permittat ipsum principem et suam curiam in locis temporibusque quibus videbitur prefato principi expedire sub secura custodia die nocteque secundum prefati principis dispositionem. In cuius rei testimonium presentibus litteris sigilla nostra fecimus apponi. Hiis testibus: Madoco, Lewelino, Griffino filiis Grufud ab Madoc, Oweno filio Bledynt, David ab Grufud ab Oweyn, Howelo filio Resi Gric, Tuder filio Edneued, Reso filio Griffud, Kenwrico filio Goronw, David filio Ennyaun Vachan, Iervasio filio M(er)edud, Tuder filio Goronw, Ioru(er)th filio Goronw, Oweno filio David, Griffi parvo filio Ioru(er)th, Ennaun filio Kerudauc, Ke(n)w(ri)c filio Edneued et multis aliis anno domini m° cc° lxxiiii° . Datum apud Bach er Anelev in Kedewig quarto decimo kalendas maii.

See note to no. 603 above.

605 Edward I

Letter, informing the king that he and his predecessors were always in peaceful possession of the fourteen townships when Llywelyn ap Gruffudd deprived him of them, when he wretchedly seized Gruffudd's first-born son and forced Gruffudd into exile for no offence. When the king's council came to the March of Wales and the men of the said townships came into the king's peace and did homage to him, Gruffudd had been in seisin of the townships for a long time; yet

the council disseised him of them. Gruffudd therefore prays the king to order the council to
restore the said seisin to him, since he is ready to show full justice to all claimants against him
wherever and whenever it pleases the king.

[8 April 1277 × February 1278]

B = TNA: PRO, SC 1/18, no. 72. s. xiii². The top left-hand corner of the parchment is missing.
Descenders of letters, presumably originally belonging to another text, are visible on the top of the
parchment, suggesting that the text of this letter is a copy, not an original.
Cd., *CAC*, 79; *H*, no. 539.

... ac sibi semper domino karissimo domino Edwardo Dei gratia regi Anglie, domino
Hybernnie,[a] duci Aquit' suus humilis et fidelis Griffinus filius Wenon' ... honorem et reverentiam. Vestre notum facimus venerande excellentie quod nos et antecessores[b] nostri
semper stetimus in pacifica possessione [quatu]ordecim villarum quando Lewelinus filius
G(ri)ffini nos de eisdem villis[c] deforciavit, cum filium nostrum primogenitum nequiter cepit
et nos similiter sine culpa in exilium redegit. Nunc vero cum consilium vestrum ad
Marchiam Wallie nobiliter accessit et homines de dictis villis ad pacem vestram[d] venientes
vobisque homagium facientes, diu in sesina dictarum stetimus villarum, idem vestrum
consilium nos de dictis villis desesiavit. Quapropter vestre venerande excellentie attentius
supplicamus quatinus dicto consilio vestro in mandatis dare velitis quod nos ad dictam
restituant sesinam, cum parati sumus ubi et quando vestro cedere excellentie omnibus nos
petentibus[e] plenariam exhibere iustitiam. Valete.

[a] *sic in* B. | [b] ancessores B. | [c] B *inserts* nos *struck through.* | [d] B *inserts* vestram *struck through.* | [e] B
inserts parata *struck through.*

The townships referred to were clearly those between the Rhiw and the Helygi, which
Llywelyn confiscated from Gruffudd at his trial at Dolforwyn in April 1274 (*BT, Pen20Tr*,
116; *BT, RBH*, 260–1; nos 591, 603 above). The reference to the men of the townships
coming to the king's peace shows that the letter was written after 8 April 1277, when
Dolforwyn surrendered to Edward I's forces and Gruffudd completed his recovery of
Powys Wenwynwyn (cf. Smith, *Llywelyn*, 415–18; Morgan, 'Territorial divisions [I]',
17–18). As it makes no mention of any legal process other than the disseisin by the royal
council in the spring of 1277, it was probably written before Gruffudd claimed the thirteen
townships in February 1278 before Walter de Hopton at Oswestry, stating that these had
been occupied by Llywelyn ap Gruffudd and were now in the king's hand (*WAR*, 240–1; see
also Morgan, 'Territorial divisions [I]', 19–20, which proposes a similar date range, in
preference to that of 1274 × 1278 suggested by Edwards in *CAC*, 79–80). The accusation
that Llywelyn had driven Gruffudd into exile refers to the latter's flight to England about
the beginning of December 1274, after Llywelyn sent five nobles to Welshpool to confront
him with the full details of the assassination plot against the prince recently revealed to the
bishop of Bangor by Gruffudd's son Owain (*LW*, lv).

606 Hawise, his wife

Grant of all the land of Deuddwr with all its appurtenances within the bounds in which he or
his mother Margaret held it; likewise of three townships in Gorddwr, namely Orleton

[Trewern], Hope and Buttington with all their appurtenances; likewise the township of Argyngroeg within the bounds in which after Hawise's death it will revert to his first-born son Owain; likewise three townships in Caereinion, namely Llysyn, Llanerfyl and Cnewyll with the pasture of Cefn-y-drum; likewise the pastures of Cwmcarnedd Seisyll in Cyfeiliog and Arwystli which Hawise used to have and which after her death will revert to Owain. Further grant of a free burgage in Gruffudd's new market of Trefnant saving his demesne and of the township of Llandybo in Mawddwy with its bounds, appurtenances and easements, to be possessed freely for ever without any exaction, service or demand and especially without cattle tribute or other tallages, and also without the maintenance of gweision bychain *or others on circuit in the country, saving only military service. Sealing clause; witnesses.*

Buttington, 12 May 1277

B = TNA: PRO, C 77/2 (Welsh Rolls), m. 9 (in an inspeximus of Edward I, 11 November 1279). Cd., *CWR*, 179; *H*, no. 260

Universis sancte matris ecclesie filiis presentes litteras visuris vel audituris Griffin(us) filius Wenu(n)wen eternam in domino salutem. Noveritis nos dedisse et concessisse et hac presenti carta confirmasse domine Hawise legitime uxori nostre totam terram de Deudouor cum omnibus pertinentiis suis et terminis melioribus quibus umquam eam possedimus seu pie recordationis mater nostra dominium tenuit vel possedit Margar(eta); similiter tres villas in Coiddour, videlicet Habretun, Hoppe et Bodinton' cum omnibus suis pertinentiis; eodem modo villam de Argegroec in suis omnibus terminis melioribus que quidem villa post mortem dicte Hawis(ie) ad Owenu(m) primogenitum nostrum revertetur; consimili modo tres villas in Kerrenion, scilicet Aessyn, Lanirreuel et Kemwill' cum pastura de Keuenedrum cum omnibus appendiciis et terminis melioribus, similiter et pasturas Cwmkarned Seisill *en*[a] Keueiloc et in Aruistrey quas consuevit habere dicta Hawis(ia), que due pasture post mortem dicte H. ad dictum Owenu(m) revertentur. Insuper concessimus predicte Hawis(ie) unum liberum burgagium in novo mercato nostro apud Treffnam salvo nostro dominio; eodem modo villam de Landebo in Maudoe cum terminis suis melioribus et pertinentiis in bosco et plano sicco et humido, viis, semitis, piscariis et molendinis et omnibus eisiamentis quibus dictas terras umquam possedimus vel possidere debuimus libere, pacifice, quiete, bene et in pace, sine omni exactione, servitio ut demanda et precipue sine tributo vaccarum vel alio tallagio, insuper absque procuratione *wessionbecheyn* seu aliorum in patria discurrentium, salva solummodo expeditione, sibi suo perpetuo possidendam. Et ut nostra donatio robur optineat firmitatis et inconcusse dicte Hawis(ie) ad vitam permaneat presenti carte sigillum nostrum est appensum anno domini m° cc° lxxvii die mercuriis proxima post assumptionem Beate Virginis apud Bodinton'. Hiis testibus: de fratribus minoribus, Hugone de Bolwas, Hug(one) de Salton'; fratre Egidio monacho Cist' tunc capellano domini; de secularibus vero, domino Rog(er)o Ext(ra)neo, Ioh(ann)e Ext(ra)neo, Fulcone filio Warini, David filio Caducani, Aniano filio Heylin et multis aliis, domino Griffino filio Wen' senescallo tunc domini, Mareduco et Gervasio filiis Aniani, Adam filio Meurici, Gervasio tunc *penkenedel'*.

[a] *sic in* B (*?for Mod. W.* yn).

This provision for Hawise was made shortly after Gruffudd's recovery of southern Powys (Smith, 'Dynastic succession', 226, n. 1; see also note to no. 605 above). The market of

Trefnant, subsequently granted to Gruffudd by Edward I in 1279, was probably located in the township of that name about 5 miles north-east of Welshpool in the commote of Gorddwr (Trefnant Hall Farm SJ 303 102): see Barton, 'Gruffudd ap Gwenwynwyn's Trefnant market charter', esp. 74. The procuration for *wessionbecheyn* (Mod. W. *gweision bychain*, 'young servants', possibly denoting youths in fosterage with the territorial lord) was a hospitality due rendered to those on circuit with the lord, or its commutation, and survived as a payment due from tenants in the lordships of Denbigh and Chirk after the Edwardian conquest (*Survey of the Honour of Denbigh*, lxvi; *Extent of Chirkland*, xxiv; Davies, *Lordship and Society*, 135). As there were no Franciscan friaries in Powys, the two Franciscan witnesses probably belonged to the Shropshire friaries of Bridgnorth (founded by 1244) and/or Shrewsbury (founded by 1245) (cf. *VCH Shropshire*, ii. 89). For the office of *pencenedl* see note to no. 602 above.

607 Owain ap Gruffudd ap Gwenwynwyn

(1) Grant, with the assent of his sons Llywelyn, John, Gwilym, Dafydd and Gruffudd, of all his land of Swydd Llannerch Hudol with all its rights, liberties, customs and appurtenances.

(2) Similar grant of all his land of Swydd Ystrad Marchell, except for the township of Argyngroeg which he has assigned to his wife Hawise for her lifetime, so that after her death it shall revert to Owain and his heirs without any hindrance by any of his brothers or their heirs.

(3) Similar grant of all his land of Cyfeiliog, except for the pasture of Cwmcarnedd Seisyll which he has assigned to Hawise for her lifetime, so that it shall revert to Owain and his heirs after her death.

(4) Similar grant of all his cantref of Arwystli.

(5) Similar grant of all his land of Caereinion, except for the three townships of Llanerfyl, Llysyn and Cnewyll with the pasture of Cefn-y-drum, which are to be held by Hawise for her lifetime so that they shall revert to his son Llywelyn and his legitimate heirs after her death; if Llywelyn dies without a legitimate heir the three townships shall revert to Owain.

(6) The townships of Buttington, Orleton and Hope and all the land of Deuddwr with all their appurtenances, which Gruffudd has assigned to Hawise for her lifetime, shall be held by her freely without hindrance from any of his sons or their heirs, so that after her death all these lands will revert to Llywelyn and his legitimate heirs. If Llywelyn dies without a legitimate heir, the lands will revert to Owain.

(7) The four townships assigned to John in Caereinion, namely Llystynwynnan, Blowty, Coetalog and Llangadfan, to be held for his lifetime, shall revert after John's death to Owain.

(8) The four townships of Pen-tyrch, Gelligason, Peniarth and Rhiwhiriarth assigned to Dafydd and his legitimate heirs shall revert to Owain if Dafydd dies without a legitimate heir.

(9) All the land of Mawddwy assigned to Gwilym and his legitimate heirs, except for Llandybo which he has granted to Hawise for her lifetime (so that after her death it shall revert to Gwilym and his legitimate heirs), shall revert to Owain if Gwilym dies without a legitimate heir.

(10) All the land of Mochnant assigned to Gruffudd and his legitimate heirs shall revert to Owain if Gruffudd dies without a legitimate heir.

(11) Further grant to Owain and his heirs of all advowsons of churches in all the lands granted to him and also in all the lands granted to his brothers if they die without legitimate heirs.

(12) All the sons shall hold the lands assigned to them from Owain in chief for ever in fee and by inheritance and shall do homage to Owain and his heirs.

(13) If Owain or his heirs build or repair any castle and their community is called in common to do this, all the community of his brothers' lands shall provide common aid in the same way as Owain's tenants without any hindrance from the brothers or their heirs.

(14) If Owain or his heirs go to war or make any common assembly or pursue any common business, and their community come to do this, all the community of his brothers' lands shall come to the said war or assembly without any hindrance.

(15) If there is a dispute between the brothers, this shall be settled in Owain's court.

(16) If there is a dispute between the tenants of the brothers which cannot be settled in their courts, it shall be settled in Owain's court; but the amercements shall go to the offenders' lord without any contradiction by Owain or his heirs.

(17) If there is any common tallage throughout the said land, all the tenants of both Owain and his brothers shall be tallaged equally according to their number and all of that tallage shall be handed over to Owain and his heirs as their chief lord.

(18) Owain and his heirs shall perform all services due to the king of England for all the aforesaid tenements as the chief lord of the whole fee. Owain shall hold all these lands for ever as freely as Gruffudd held them as his legitimate son and heir.

Sealing clause; witnesses.

[Probably January × 5 February 1278]

B = TNA: PRO, C 77/2 (Welsh Rolls), m. 11d (in an enrolment, 1278).
Pd. from B, *Rotulus Walliae*, 37–9; from B, Bridgeman, 'Princes of upper Powys', 124–8 (and trans., ibid., 38–43).
Cd., *CWR*, 171–3; *H*, no. 261.

[i] Sciant presentes et futuri quod nos Griffinus filius Wennonwen in libera et mera voluntate nostra assensu et consensu Lewelini, Ioh(ann)is, Will(elm)i, David et Griffini filiorum nostrorum dedimus, concessimus, assignavimus et hac presenti carta nostra confirmavimus Owino filio nostro primogenito et fratri filiorum nostrorum predictorum totam terram nostram de Sorlanherchudol cum omnibus suis iuribus, libertatibus, consuetudinibus, pratis, pascuis, viis, semitis, stagnis, vivariis, ripis, aquis, molendinis, nemoribus, exitibus, introiitibus, homagiis, servitiis, escaetis, releviis, herietis, auxiliis et cum omnibus aliis suis pertinentiis que ad dictam terram nostram de Sorlanherchudol pertinent.

[ii] Dedimus etiam et concessimus eidem Owyno filio nostro totam terram nostram de Soyrstradmarghel cum omnibus suis iuribus, libertatibus, consuetudinibus, pratis, pascuis, viis, semitis, stagnis, vivariis, ripis, aquis, molendinis, nemoribus, exitibus, introiitibus, homagiis, servitiis, escaetis, releviis, herietis, auxiliis et cum omnibus aliis suis pertinentiis que ad dictam [terram]ᵃ nostram de Stroyrarradmarghel pertinent, excepta quadam villa nostra que vocatur Hergyngroyk quam assignavimus et tradidimus Hawsie uxori nostre tenendam et hadendam toto tempore vite sue, ita quod post decessum ipsius Hawsie predicta villa de Hergyngroyk cum omnibus suis iuribus, libertatibus et aliis pertinentiis suis que ad dictam villam pertinent revertatur dicto Owyno filio nostro et heredibus suis sine aliqua participatione, contradictione aut impedimento aliquorum fratrum suorum predictorum aut eorum heredum.

[iii] Item dedimus, concessimus et hac presenti carta nostra confirmavimus predicto Owyno filio nostro totam terram nostram de Keuilioc cum omnibus suis iuribus, liber-

tatibus, consuetudinibus, pratis, pascuis, viis, semitis, stagnis, vivariis, ripis, aquis, molen-dinis, nemoribus, exiitibus, introiitibus, homagiis, servitiis, escaetis, releviis, herietis, auxiliis et cum omnibus aliis suis pertinentiis que ad dictam terram nostram de Keuilioc pertinent, excepta quadam pastura nostra que vocatur Cumcarnethapseysil quam dicte Hawys(ie) uxori nostre dedimus et concessimus ad terminum vite sue, ita quod post ipsius Hawys(ie) obitum tota dicta pastura cum omnibus suis iuribus et pertinentiis integraliter revertatur predicto Owyno filio nostro et heredibus suis imperpetuum.

[iv] Item dedimus, concessimus et presenti carta nostra confirmavimus predicto Owyno filio nostro totum cantretum nostrum quod vocatur Aroystly cum omnibus iuribus, liber-tatibus, consuetudinibus, pratis, pascuis, viis, semitis, stagnis, vivariis, ripis, aquis, molendinis, nemoribus, exiitibus, introiitibus, homagiis, servitiis, escaetis, releviis, herietis, auxiliis et cum omnibus aliis suis pertinentiis que ad dictum cantretum nostrum pertinent.

[v] Item dedimus, concessimus et presenti carta nostra confirmavimus predicto Owyno filio nostro totam terram de Keyrhyngnon cum omnibus iuribus, libertatibus, consuetu-dinibus, pratis, pascuis, viis, semitis, stagnis, vivariis, ripis, aquis, molendinis, nemoribus, exiitibus, introiitibus, homagiis, servitiis, escaetis, releviis, herietis, auxiliis et cum omnibus aliis suis pertinentiis que ad dictam terram nostram de Keyrrhyngnon pertinent, preter tres villas, scilicet Lanuruil, Lifrin, Kerewillch cum quadam pastura que vocatur Keuendrun quam [concessimus et dedimus][b] dicte Hawysie uxori nostri habendam et tenendam ad terminum vite sue, ita quod post ipsius decessum predicte tres ville cum omnibus iuribus et pertinentiis suis Lewelino filio nostro et heredibus suis de se legitime procreatis revertantur. Et si contingat dictum Lewelinu(m) filium nostrum sine herede de se legitime procreato in fata decedere, volumus et concedimus quod dicte tres ville cum omnibus iuribus et perti-nentiis suis prefato Owino filio nostro integre revertantur sine aliqua participatione, contradictione aut impedimento dictorum fratrum aut eorum heredum.

[vi] Item volumus et concedimus quod ville nostre de Botington', de Olreton' et de Hop' et etiam totam terram nostram de Deudur cum omnibus villis, libertatibus, iuribus et cum omnibus aliis pertinentiis suis quas assignavimus predicte Hawysie uxori nostre habendas et tenendas toto tempore vite ipsius Hawys(ie) adeo libere et quiete sicut eas unquam habuimus vel habere potuimus vel sicut eas unquam et uberius tenuimus, sine contradic-tione aut impedimento aliquorum filiorum nostrorum et heredum eorum, ita quod post obitum dicte Hawys(ie) quod tota terra predicta cum villis supradictis et omnibus aliis pertinentiis suis predicto Lewelino filio nostro et heredibus de se legitime procreatis rever-tatur. Et si dictus Lewelin(us) decedit in fata sine herede de se legitime procreato, extunc volumus et concedimus quod tota dicta terra cum villis predictis et omnibus aliis perti-nentiis suis dicto Owino filio nostro revertatur sine participatione aliqua, contradictione aut impedimento dictorum fratrum aut eorum heredum.

[vii] Volumus etiam et concedimus quod quatuor villas nostras quas assignavimus Ioh(ann)i filio nostro in predicta terra de Creyngnon, scilicet Lestinwennan, Blaute, Coytalauk, Slangadeuan, toto tempore vite sue habendas et tenendas quod post decessum ipsius Ioh(ann)is dicte quatuor ville dicto Owyno filio nostro et heredibus suis revertantur sine aliqua participatione, contradictione aut impedimento dictorum fratrum aut eorum heredum.

[viii] Item volumus et concedimus quod quatuor ville, scilicet Pentyrigh, Kertlicassan, Pennart, Riwarth, quas assignavimus David filio nostro et heredibus suis de se legitime procreatis predicto Owyno filio nostro revertantur integraliter cum omnibus pertinentiis

suis si contingat dictum David filium nostrum sine herede de se legitime procreato in fata decedere sine aliqua participatione, contradictione aut impedimento dictorum fratrum aut eorum heredum eidem Owino filio nostro et heredibus suis revertantur.

[ix] Item volumus et concedimus quod tota [terra]ª nostra de Mauto cum omnibus iuribus, libertatibus et cum omnibus aliis suis pertinentiis quam assignavimus Will(elm)o filio nostro et heredibus suis de legitime procreatis excepta quadam villa nostra que vocatur Landeboe quam concessimus et dedimus predicte Hawys(ie) uxori nostre habendam et tenendam toto tempore vite sue, ita quod post obitum ipsius Hawys(ie) dicta villa de Landeboe revertatur prefato Will(elm)o filio nostro et heredibus suis de se legitime procreatis. Et si dictus Will(elmu)s filius noster decedat sine herede de se legitime procreato, volumus et concedimus quod tota predicta terra de Mauto una cum predicta villa de Landeboe cum omnibus iuribus, libertatibus et cum omnibus aliis pertinentiis suis prefato Owino filio nostro et heredibus suis revertatur sine aliqua participatione, contradictione aut impedimento dictorum fratrum aut eorum heredum.

[x] Item volumus et concedimus quod tota terra nostra de Mochnand cum omnibus iuribus, libertatibus et cum omnibus aliis pertinentiis suis quam assignavimus Griffino filio nostro et heredibus suis de se legitime procreatis predicto Owino filio nostro et heredibus suis integre revertatur si contingat predictum Griffinu(m) filium nostrum sine herede de se legitime procreato decedere sine participatione, contradictione aut impedimento dictorum fratrum aut eorum heredum.

[xi] Item dedimus, concessimus et hac presenti carta nostra confirmavimus predicto Owino filio nostro et heredibus suis omnes advocationes ecclesiarum omnium terrarum quas eidem Owino imperpetuum contulimus et etiam omnes advocationes ecclesiarum omnium terrarum quas aliis filiis nostris predictis contulimus si ipsos contingat in fata decedere sine herede de ipsis legitime procreatis.

[xii] Item volumus et concedimus quod singuli filiorum nostrorum superius nominati omnes terras et possessiones quas eisdem filiis nostris particulariter assignavimus easdem terras cum suis pertinentiis et iuribus omnibus de dicto Owino filio nostro in feodo, iure et hereditarie ut premittitur imperpetuum capitaliter teneant et eidem Owino et heredibus suis homagia faciant.

[xiii] Volumus etiam et concedimus dicto Owino filio nostro et heredibus suis quod si contingat ipsum Owinu(m) aut heredes suos aliquod castrum suum edificare vel reedificare et communitas eiusdem Owini aut heredum suorum ad hoc fuerit communiter vocata, quod tota communitas terrarum dictorum filiorum nostrorum prestant ad hoc commune auxilium secundum quod tenentes dicti Owini facient et facere tenentur sine omni contra-dictione aut impedimento dictorum fratrum suorum aut eorum heredum.

[xiv] Item si contingat predictum Owinum filium nostrum aut heredes suos adire bellum aut aliquam congregationem facere seu negotium commune prosequi, et communitas predicti Owini aut heredum suorum ad hoc venerit, volumus et concedimus quod tota communitas terrarum dictorum fratrum suorum ad dictum bellum seu congregationem veniat sine omni contradictione aut impedimento eorundem.

[xv] Item si contingat lis vel discordia moveri inter dictos fratres, volumus et concedimus quod dicta lis seu discordia sopiatur et terminatur in curia dicti Owini.

[xvi] Item si emergatur lis vel discordia inter tenentes dictorum fratrum et non possit terminari in curia eorundem, volumus et concedimus quod in curia dicti Owini totaliter

terminatur, ita quod amerciamenta dominis seu domino transgressorum remaneant eisdem seu eidem sine omni contradictione dicti Owini aut heredum suorum.

[xvii] Item si aliquod commune tallagium in tota dicta terra nostra evenerit, volumus et concedimus quod omnes tenentes dictorum fratrum tam dicti Owini quam aliorum pari tallagio secundum vires eorum talliantur et quod totum dictum tallagium plenarie eidem Owino et heredibus suis tradatur sine aliqua diminutione tanquam eorum domino capitali.

[xviii] Item volumus et concedimus quod dictus Owinus filius noster et heredes sui faciant domino regi Angl(ie) omnia servitia de iure debita et consueta pro omnibus tenementis supradictis tanquam dominus capitalis totius feodi, habendas et tenendas dicto Owino et heredibus suis omnes dictas terras cum omnibus suis pertinentiis prenominatis libere, quiete, bene, pacifice, integre, iure et hereditarie imperpetuum adeo libere sicut nos unquam easdem habuimus plenarie tenuimus sicut legitimus filius et heres noster.

Et ut hec donatio, concessio, assignatio et presentis carte nostre confirmatio rata, stabilis et inconcussa imperpetuum permaneat presentem cartam nostram sigilli nostri munimine roboravimus. Hiis testibus: dominis Heynon episcopo Assaven(si), Iacobo abbate de la Pola, Griffino archidiacono Assaven(si), Rog(er)o de Mortuo Mari, Rog(er)o de Clifford', Rog(er)o le Straunge, Rog(er)o Springhose, Griffino Appewen', Yeruoth Appewronn, Tuder Appewronuch et multis aliis.

^a *omitted* B. | ^b *omitted in* B, *but verb(s) required: cf. cc. iii, ix or, for* assignavimus (et tradidimus), *cc. ii, vi.*

The charter is enrolled before a royal letter dated at Dover, 5 February 1278 and was probably drawn up shortly before that date (cf. Smith, 'Dynastic succession', 226, which dates it to early 1278); m. 11r of the roll contains items dated between 4 January and 8 June 1278. The grant was designed to secure the position of Gruffudd's heir Owain as chief lord of southern Powys while making territorial provision for his younger brothers, and was clearly drawn up with reference to Gruffudd's earlier assignation of lands to his wife Hawise on 12 May 1277 (no. 606 above).

608 Robert Burnell, bishop of Bath and Wells

Letter, thanking him for all he has done and will do for Gruffudd; requesting his help in interceding with the king that Gruffudd may have possession of the thirteen vills between the Rhiw and the Helygi, which the king granted to Roger Mortimer without any right and which are now in the king's possession, following Roger's death. If the king's court cannot order that Gruffudd recover his possession, he requests that the king keep them in his hand until the right is settled between Roger's heirs and Gruffudd.

[Shortly after 26 October 1282]

A = TNA: PRO, SC 1/23, no. 121. No endorsements; approx. 152 mm. × 52 mm. deep on left, 36 mm. deep on right; four sets of double slits for insertion of a tongue or tag; mounted, foot cut away.
Cd., *CAC*, 122; *H*, no. 540.

A son cher pere en Deu Rob(er)t par la grace Deu esvek de Ba et de Welles Griffin le fiz Wenu(n)wen saluz et honurs et reverences. Cher sire mout vous merci de touz lé bens ke fet nous aveyt et freyt si vous plest Deu le vous rende . . .[a] nomement vous pri si vous plest ke vous me soet eidaunt vers nostre seynur le rey ke je pusse aver ma poscessioun de xiii viles entre Rew et Elegy, le queles il baila a sire Rog(er) de Mortim(er) saune jekun hi droyt et hore sount en la mein le rey par la mort le avaundist Rog(er) ke Deus asoile. E si la court le rey ne pust agarder ke je reheie ma poscessioun ke le roy les veile `re tener en sa meyn jekes `le dreyt soyt detrié entre les heirs sire Rog(er) et moy. Saluz a Deu ke vous gard cors et alme.

[a] *three letters illegible in* A.

As Edwards argued (*CAC*, 122), this letter to Edward I's chancellor was written shortly after Roger Mortimer's death on 26 October 1282 (*AM*, iv. 481; cf. ibid., 290–1). Gruffudd's brother-in-law Roger Lestrange also wrote to the chancellor in support of Gruffudd's request (*CAC*, 125). For the townships between the Rhiw and the Helygi see nos 591, 605 above.

HAWISE LESTRANGE, WIFE OF GRUFFUDD AP GWENWYNWYN
(d. 1310)

*609 Hamo Lestrange
Promise, with the assent of her husband, that when Hamo returns from the Holy Land he may enter the manor of Stretton (manerium de Strattone) *in Shropshire. Witnesses: Roger Lestrange, Robert his brother, Odo of Hodnet.*

[1270 × January 1271]

Mention only, cited by Eyton from an unidentified 'fragment of a deed' (Eyton, *Shropshire*, x. 274–5; cd., *H*, no. 536). Eyton, *Shropshire*, xii. 25, n. 1, gives the reference as 'Glover's Collect. A. fol. 111', presumably a manuscript written by the antiquary Robert Glover (1544–88), but the fragment does not appear to be contained in any of the manuscripts written by or attributed to Glover in the Bodleian Library or British Library. Le Strange, *Le Strange Records*, 145, notes a reference to what seems to be the same document, namely an undated charter in the exchequer calendared by F. Palgrave: *Carta Hawysie de la Pola de manerio de Strettone concesso Hamoni Extraneo de retinendo manerium predictum.* The document calendared here may have been similar to no. 610 below, which names the three witnesses given in the present text. If so, however, the text printed by Eyton has been heavily abbreviated. Hamo was granted royal protection as a crusader on 25 January 1271 and travelled with the Lord Edmund to join the Lord Edward's crusade in Cyprus early in that year; he died in Syria in 1273, after marrying the heiress of Beirut, Isabella, daughter of John d'Ibelin the younger, in October 1272 (*CPR 1266–72*, 588; Le Strange, *Le Strange Records*, 145–8; Powicke, *Henry III*, ii. 605–6; Lloyd, *English Society and the Crusade*, 100). Both the present document and no. 610 below were presumably drawn up shortly before his departure. Comparison with no. 610 suggests that Hamo had granted Stretton to his sister

Hawise before embarking on crusade. Crusaders commonly granted land to relatives before departing for the east. However, Hamo caused subsequent difficulties for Hawise (and at least one his brothers, Robert) by failing to obtain the royal licence required by tenants-in-chief who wished to alienate land held in chief (Lloyd, *English Society and the Crusade*, 173–4, citing *CFR 1272–1307*, 4; see also Eyton, *Shropshire*, xii. 24–6). Hamo had been granted Church Stretton (and Ellesmere) by the crown in February 1267 (*CPR 1266–72*, 39; cf. Le Strange, *Le Strange Records* (1916), 145; *CIM*, i, no. 966).

LLYWELYN AP GRUFFUDD AP GWENWYNWYN
(d. 1294)

610 Letter patent concerning Hamo Lestrange

Notification, since Hamo had given him the manor of Chirbury with the three townships of Cilcewydd, Ackley and Lletygynfach, that whenever Hamo should return from his journey to the Holy Land, whether or not he has reached the Holy Land, he shall be permitted to enter and peacefully possess the said manor and townships, whoever may have had possession of them in the mean time, without any contradiction, hindrance or claim from Llywelyn or his heirs or assigns, notwithstanding any charter of enfeoffment made for him by Hamo concerning the manor and its townships. Sealing clause; witnesses.

[1270 × January 1271]

B = TNA: PRO, E 36/274 (Liber A), fo. 361r. s. xiii ex.
Pd. from B, *LW*, 87 (no. 169).
Cd., *H*, no. 258.

Omnibus has litteras visuris vel audituris Lewelinus filius Griffini salutem. Noverit universitas vestra quod cum dominus Hamo Ex(tra)neus manerium de Chireburi una cum villatis de Kilkenny, Acle et Lettegynewah cum suis pertinentiis mihi dedisset, concessi eidem pro me et heredibus meis et quibuscumque meis assignatis et presenti scripto confirmavi quod quandocumque contigerit ipsum post iter arreptum versus Terram Sanctam redire, sive terram sanctam adierit sive non, liceat eidem dictum manerium cum villatis predictis ingredi et pacifice[a] possidere, ad cuiuscumque manus medio tempore devenerit, sine contradictione, impedimento vel clamio mei vel heredum seu assignatorum meorum in perpetuum, non obstante aliqua carta feofamenti a dicto domino H. de dicto manerio cum villatis et suis pertinentiis mihi confecta. In cuius rei testimonium presenti scripto sigillum meum apposui. Hiis testibus: dominis Rog(er)o Ex(tra)neo, Rob(er)to fratre suo, Odon(e) de[b] Hodonec, Ioh(ann)e de Chetewind, Ph(ilipp)o fratre suo et aliis.

[a] pascifice B. | [b] et B.

See note to no. 609 above. Ackley, Cilcewydd and Lletygynfach, collectively known as King's Teirtref, were situated in Gorddwr (Morgan, 'Territorial divisions [II]', 30, 39–40, 37 (map 3)).

MECHAIN

LLYWELYN AB OWAIN FYCHAN
(fl. 1187–c.1240)

AND

OWAIN FYCHAN (II) AB OWAIN FYCHAN
(fl. 1187–c.1241)

*611 Valle Crucis Abbey
Grant of Gwernfeifod (Gwarn Mevoc).

[1187 × 1222; possibly 1208 × 1222]

Mention only, in a confirmation of Gruffudd ap Madog dated 1236 (no. 511 above). The grantors' father Owain Fychan died in 1187. Llywelyn and Owain may have recovered Mechain after Llywelyn ap Iorwerth invaded Powys in 1208 or 1216 (Morgan, 'Barony of Powys', 38). The grant was probably earlier than Madog ap Gruffudd's charter for Valle Crucis of 1222 (no. 506 above), which seems to include Gwernfeifod, although this did not refer to the sons of Owain Fychan (or any other previous grantor). The grange of Gwernfeifod lay near Llanrhaeadr-ym-Mochnant (see note to no. 506 above).

OWAIN AP LLYWELYN AB OWAIN FYCHAN
(fl. c.1240–81)

612 Letter patent concerning Llywelyn ap Gruffudd
Notification by Owain and Maredudd sons of Llywelyn, Gruffudd ap Llywelyn, Gruffudd ap Gwên (Guen), Iorwerth and Tudur sons of Goronwy, Einion ab Ednyfed, Gwyn ab Einion, Heilin ab Ednyfed, Madog ap Meilyr of Caereinion, Gruffudd and Llywelyn sons of Owain, the sons of Dafydd ap Maredudd by his lawful wife, Hywel Goch and Dafydd Goch his brother, Maredudd ap Iorwerth Goch (?)o'r Maen (or mein), the son of Madog ap Iorwerth nephew of the aforesaid Maredudd, and the son of Maredudd's brother Llywelyn that they have given themselves, of their own free will, as sureties to their lord Llywelyn ap Gruffudd, prince of Wales and lord of Snowdon, for the fealty and constancy of Gruffudd ap Budr ei hosan ('Dirty-hose') and his sons. If Gruffudd or his sons refuse to go into the presence of the prince when required by him, but rather show themselves to be unfaithful to him, the sureties are bound to pay the prince £120, renouncing all appeal, delay and remedy of all law that could hinder that suretyship. The seals of the aforesaid lords have been attached with those of other nobles who have seals; those who lack seals are bound to perform their suretyship with their own hands before the prince's attorney.

Aber, 16 December 1276

B = TNA: PRO, E 36/274 (Liber A), fo. 342r. s. xiii ex.
Pd. from B, *LW*, 42–3 (no. 63).
Cd., *H*, no. 508.

[O]mnibus Cristi fidelibus presentes litteras visuris vel audituris Owenus et Mared' filii Lewel', Griffin(us) filius Lewel', Griffin(us) filius Guen, Ior' et Tudyr filii Goronv, Enniaun filius Etnyued, Gwyn filius Enniaun, Heilin filius Etniued, Madauc filius Meylyr de Kerenniaun, Gruffin(us) et Lewelinus filii Oweni, filii Dauyd ab Marad' de sua uxore legitima procreatus, Howel Goch et Dauyd Goch suus frater, Maredut filius Ior' Goch ᵃ⁻or mein,⁻ᵃ filius Madauc' ab Ior' nepos predicti Mareduc' et filius Lewelini fratris prefati Mared' salutem. Noverit universitas vestra nos non vi nec metu coactosᵇ sed mera et spontanea voluntate ductosᶜ fideiussionem fecisse domino nostro Lewelino filio Griffini principi Wall(ie), domino Snaudon' pro fidelitate et constantia Griffini filii Budyr Ihossan et suorum filiorum, videlicet quod si dictus Griffin(us) vel filii sui predicti ad presentiam domini principis predicti accedere noluerint cum super hoc fuerint requisiti ab ipso, sed eidem infideles extiterint, nos tenemur solvere prefato domino principi centum et xxᵗⁱ libras bone et legalis monete ex nostra fideiussione, renuntiantes omni appellationi, cavillationi et etiam omni iuris remedio quod possit dictam fideiussionem impedire. In cuius rei testimonium presenti scripto predictorum dominorum sigilla una cum sigillis aliorum optimatum qui sigilla habent sunt appensa; illi autem de nobis qui carent sigillis tenentur suam fideiussionem propriis manibus adimplere coram attornato domini principis memorati. Datum apud Aber anno domini mᵒ cᵒ cᵒ septuagesimo sexto die mercurii proxima post festum Beate Lucie virginis.

ᵃ⁻ᵃ LW *emends to* Owein. | ᵇ coacti B. | ᶜ ducti B.

For brief comment see Stephenson, 'Politics of Powys Wenwynwyn', 49, which identifies, on the basis of late medieval genealogical manuscripts, Budr ei hosan ('Dirty-hose') as Madog Danwr, a noble of Arwystli and former steward of Llywelyn ap Iorwerth. See further Bartrum, *WG*, iv, sub Tudor Trefor, 31, and nos 16–17 above. It is possible, however, that the epithet *Budr ei hosan* was applied to several individuals in thirteenth-century Powys and its surrounding regions: cf. Einion ap Budr ei hosan in no. 16 above, who is unlikely to have been a son of Madog Danwr, since the latter appears under his proper name in the same document.

*613 Edward I
Letter, from the sons of Llywelyn ab Owain, lords of Mechain, stating that they ought to hold their lands from no one other than from the king or from the prince of Wales when he held authority in their parts, and complaining of interference by Gruffudd ap Gwenwynwyn.

[1277, before 21 July]

Mention only, in no. 614 below.

614 Edward I

Letter, from the sons of Llywelyn ab Owain, lords of Mechain, complaining that, though the king, after receiving a letter from the senders informing him that they ought to hold their lands from no one other than from the king or from the prince of Wales when he held authority in their parts, had prohibited Gruffudd ap Gwenwynwyn from interfering in their lands, Gruffudd has, despite the king's letter, molested their lands and unjustly exacted tributes from them and sought other exactions as if from his own men. They pray the king to provide remedy regarding this by again ordering Gruffudd not to interfere with them or their lands in any way, and by recommending them to one of the king's men – be it the justice of Chester, Roger Mortimer or the bailiffs of Perfeddwlad – so that on behalf of the king they may protect the senders from such molestations and not permit them to be troubled by Gruffudd.

[21 July × 3 December 1277]

A = TNA: PRO, SC 1/19, no. 42. Modern endorsement; approx. 180 × 64 mm.; eight slits of double slits for insertion of a tongue or tag; mounted, foot cut away.
Cd., *CAC*, 98; *H*, no. 509.

Excellenti magistro et illustri domino suo domino E. Dei gratia regi Angl(ie), domino Hib(er)n(ie) et duci Aq(ui)tann(ie) sui ligii et devoti filii Lewelini ab Owein domini de Mechein salutem et paratam ad^a obsequia cum honore voluntatem. Quoniam vos vestri gratia, postquam nos per literas nostras vestre maiestatis significavimus de statu et iurisdictione nostra quod de aliquo^b non debemus terras nostras tenere nisi de vobis vel de principe Wallie dum principatum tenuit in partibus nostris, per vestras prohibuistis literas domino G(ri)ffino filio Wenonwyn quod de nobis non intromiteret^c nec nos infestare quoquo modo, presertim non obstantibus vestris literis memoratis nos et terras nostras indebite tractavit ac molestavit, minus iuste tributa de terris nostris exigendo et alias exactiones a nobis petendo prout a suis propriis hominibus exigit atque petit; ideo vestram regiam maiestatem exoramus omni nisu quo possumus et requirimus cum afectu^c quatenus pro Dei amore ac nostra fidelitate nobis remedium in premissis apponatis, dicto G(ri)ffino dantes adhuc in mandatis quod de nobis vel terris nostris non intromitat^c quoquo modo, alicui de vestris nos recommendantes (vel iusticiario Cestr(ie) vel domino Rog(er)o de Mortuo Mari vel ballivis vestris de Beruedwlat) quod nos a talibus molestationibus ex parte vestra defendant nec nos permitant^c a dicto G(ri)ffino perturbari vel etiam molestari. Valeat excellencia vestra diu in [domino].^{d}

^{a} ab A. | ^{b} A *repeats* aliquo. | ^{c} *sic in* A. | ^{d} *word missing in* A, *presumably because originally written on foot which has been cut away*.

The royal mandate to Gruffudd ap Gwenwynwyn referred to in the letter was presumably that dated at Chester, 21 July 1277, which ordered Gruffudd to restore Owain and Maredudd sons of Llywelyn ab Owain and their co-heirs to their lands and other goods in Mechain by which Gruffudd had distrained them to do homage to him; he should leave them in peace until 13 November, so that it could be discussed whether their homage belonged to the king or to Gruffudd (*CCR 1272–9*, 399). Probably it was in response to the present letter that on 3 December Edward ordered Roger Lestrange to permit Maredudd and Owain and their nephew Gruffudd ap Llywelyn Fychan and their brothers to hold the lands of Mechain, seisin of which they had recovered before Master Ralph de

Fremingham, until otherwise ordered, provided that they answered for them to the king as their lord (ibid., 434). It is possible that the letter was sent before the assize held before de Fremingham and his fellow justices at Oswestry on 28 November 1277, which accepted the claim of Maredudd and Owain to half of Mechain Is Coed (*WAR*, 244), as this makes no reference to the assize. See further ibid., 147–8, 199–200, 237; *HW*, ii. 709, n. 93. Four years later, however, on 8 November 1281, the king granted the homage and service of Maredudd and his co-heirs, described as tenants of Mechain, to Gruffudd ap Gwenwynwyn and authorized him to distrain them, if necessary, to do their homages and service to him and to render their arrears (*CWR*, 211).

MAREDUDD AP LLYWELYN AB OWAIN FYCHAN
(*fl. c.*1240–81)

*615 Henry Lacy, earl of Lincoln and constable of Chester
Letter, informing Henry that he is willing to return to the peace and fealty of the king subject to certain conditions concerning the recovery of certain lands.

[April × July 1277]

Mention only, in a letter from Henry to Maredudd, styled lord of Mechain (*domino de Mecheyn*), enrolled on a schedule in the Welsh assize roll which records assizes held at Oswestry on 28 November 1277 (TNA: PRO, JUST 1/1147, m. 4; pd., *WAR*, 244; cd., *H*, no. 511). Henry replied that he would admit Maredudd to the king's peace, but only unconditionally; however, he promised that the king would render justice to Maredudd concerning all his demands if he returned to the king's peace. Presumably Maredudd's letter to the earl, one of Edward I's principal captains in the 1277 war, was sent before he first wrote to the king complaining of Gruffudd ap Gwenwynwyn's interference in his lands, as the king would hardly have responded favourably to that complaint on 21 July 1277 had Maredudd still been at war (see no. 614 above). If so, the letter can be no later than July 1277. Nor is it likely to have been earlier than April of that year, as it implies that Mechain had been occupied by Gruffudd ap Gwenwynwyn, who recovered control of Powys Wenwynwyn and its surrounding districts after the fall of Llywelyn ap Gruffudd's castle of Dolforwyn on 8 April 1277; the earl of Lincoln's forces were active in the region and had taken part in the siege of the castle (Smith, *Llywelyn*, 415–16, 418).

GRUFFUDD AB IFOR
(d. 1211)

*616 Margam Abbey

Grant by the hand of Meilyr Awenydd (per manum fratris Meileri Awenet) *for the making of a hermitage or abbey if possible, namely above [i.e. east of] the river Taff* (super aquam de Taf) *all the land called* Stratvaga, *all Bryn Ceirw [(?) Bryn Caerau]* (Brenkeiru) *and from Bargod Taf* (Berkehu Taf) *to Bargod Rhymni* (Bargau Remni) *and all* Karpdawardmenet *and all (?) Maes Llety* (Maislette) *and from the head of the Mawan [Nant Mafon]* (de Mauhanis capite) *to the Taff* (Taf) *and the fisheries in the Taff* (Taf) *as far as his land extends; furthermore all the land of St Gwladus* (Gladus) *and all pastures from that land to Bochriwgarn* (Bohrukarn) *and from the other part of the land of St Gwladus* (Gladus) *to Henglawdd* (Henglau), *namely the Old Dyke, to Nant Cylla* (usque ad aquam que vocatur Kidliha) *and all Maesmawan [Maes Mafon]* (Masmawan), *to be held in perpetual alms free of all secular service and exaction.*

[1158 × c.1174]

Mention only, in a confirmation by William, earl of Gloucester datable to 1158 × November 1183 (*EGC*, 115 (no. 120)). Gruffudd's father Ifor Bach was still lord of Senghennydd in 1158. Meilyr Awenydd (the epithet denotes an 'inspired person' or 'soothsayer') was very probably the same man as the seer Meilyr, a close confidant of Hywel ap Iorwerth of Caerleon, who died shortly after being wounded at the capture of Usk castle in 1174 by men of Earl Richard fitz Gilbert, lord of Strigoil (Cowley, 'Monastic Order', 35–7, citing *Gir. Camb. Op.*, vi. 57–61 (*IK*, I. 5), and *HW*, ii. 546 and nn. 49–50). The present charter granted lands in northern Senghennydd, including, presumably, the original site of the abortive Cistercian foundation of Pendar, named as the house of 'Brother Meilyr' in no. 121 above and *Cartae*, i. 127–8 (no. 130); like the latter charter, Gruffudd ab Ifor's grant shows that Meilyr's community was somehow linked to Margam Abbey (Williams, *Welsh Cistercians*, 4). *Stratvaga* is possibly identifiable with Ystrad Mynach (former Ystrad Mynach farm at ST 147 936), about 2 miles south-south-east of Gelli-gaer, and the name *Brenkeiru* may be preserved at Bryn Caerau (SO 089 046), a farm near the source of the Bargod Taf and about 1¼ miles west of the Bargod Rhymni. (*Berkehu Taf* and *Bargau Remni*, tributaries of the rivers Taff and Rhymni respectively, are cited as examples of the noun *bargod*, 'edge, border, marches' in *GPC*, s.v. *bargod* 2.) The Mawan is the Mafon, a stream originating in the vicinity of Nelson that flows into the Taff near Craig-y-berth Lwyd at ST 093 957 (Thomas, *Enwau Afonydd*, 76). The land of St Gwladus was in the vicinity of Capel Gwladus (SO 125 993), about 1¼ miles north-east of Gelli-gaer; the lords of Senghennydd retained demesne lands in the area at Maerdy (SO 121 005) (Smith, 'Lordship of Senghennydd', 314, 638, n. 201). Bochrhiwgarn was probably a cairn or rocky outcrop on Mynydd Fochriw (e.g. SO 100 050), about 4 miles north-west of Capel Gwladus (cf. also Fochriw SO 105 055). Nant Cylla flows down through Fforest Gwladus and passes just to the east of Gelli-gaer. See also note to no. 121 above.

617 Margam Abbey

Grant in perpetual alms of 100 acres, of the abbey's choice, of his arable at Leckwith with their appurtenances, 12 acres of meadow of its choice, common pasture in his land of Leckwith and the fisheries of Ely which pertain to that land and common pasture in Senghennydd from below the woodland for as long as his land lasts. If he or his heirs are unable to warrant the aforesaid land, he will give the monks in exchange 100 acres of arable and 12 acres of meadow in his land of Senghennydd where they think fit and the fisheries of the Taff. He has given all this in perpetual alms for the salvation of the souls of himself and of his father, mother, brothers, ancestors and successors, to be held free of all secular service, custom and exaction. When he made this gift he granted his body, and his mother Nest granted her body, to God and the church of Margam, wherever they should die in either England or Wales. Witnesses.

[12 December 1193 × 1211]

B = NLW, Penrice and Margam Roll 290/1. s. xiii. (Right-hand side of roll damaged.)
Pd. from B, *Cartae*, i. 159 (no. 159).
Cd., Birch, *Catalogue*, i. 105; *Episc. Acts*, ii. 698 (L. 308); *H*, no. 281.

Omnibus sancte ecclesie filiis presentibus et futuris Griffin(us) filius Iuor salutem. Sciatis me concessisse et dedisse et hac carta [confirmasse] Deo et ecclesie Sancte Marie de Marg(an) et monachis ibidem Deo servientibus in puram et perpetuam elemosinam centum acras terre arabilis t[erre] mee de Lecwithe cum aisiamentis et pertinentiis suis ad electionem suam, et duodecim acras prati ad electionem suam et communem pasturam terre mee de Lecwithe et piscaturas de Helei que ad ipsam terram pertinent et communem pasturam de Seinhei de subtus boscum quantum terra mea durat in longum et in latum. Et si contigerit quod ego vel heredes mei eis predictam terram de Lecwithe warantizare non possimus, tunc do eis in excambiam terre illius in terra mea de Seinhenic centum acras terre arabilis et xii acras prati ubi sibi viderint expedire et piscationes de Taf. Hec omnia eis dedi in perpetuam elemosinam pro salute anime mee et patris mei et[a] matris mee et fratrum meorum et antecessorum et successorum meorum ut habeant et teneant ea libere et quiete absque omni seculari servitio, consuetudine et exactione sicut ulla elemosina liberius teneri [potest]. Et hoc sciendum quod quando ego G(ri)ffin(us) dedi eis hanc donationem tunc simul cum donatione mea delegavi corpus meum Deo et ecclesie Sancte Marie de Marg(an) et mater mea Nesta corpus suum ubicumque moriamur sive in Anglia sive in Wallia. Testibus: H(e)nrico episcopo, Landavensi capitulo, Iuor sacerdote filio Wrgani, Will(elm)o de Lichefeld et Thom(a) de Brist' monachis de Marg(an), Iordano et Iustino conversis, Gnaithuro Cant(er)el, Iuor P(er)edeu nepote meo, Brugeir Seis.

---

[a] B *inserts* fratris *underlined for deletion*.

The first witness, Bishop Henry, was consecrated to the see of Llandaff on 12 December 1193 (*Llandaff Episcopal Acta*, xv). Gruffudd's mother Nest was a sister of Rhys ap Gruffudd of Deheubarth (*BT, Pen20Tr*, 71). Leckwith (ST 158 744), 2 miles south-west of Cardiff, was one of two demesne manors of the Norman lordship of Glamorgan; it may have been granted to Gruffudd's father Ifor Bach ap Meurig by Earl Robert of Gloucester (Crouch, 'Robert, earl of Gloucester', 230, 242, n. 7). The manor appears in the accounts for the lordship in 1184–5 rendered by its custodian Maurice de Berkeley after Glamorgan reverted to the crown following the death of William, earl of Gloucester in November 1183 (*Pipe Roll 31 Henry II*, 5–6; also *Cartae*, i. 170, 173 (no. 171)). The present grant, with its provision for an exchange for land in Senghennydd, may indicate that Gruffudd claimed, but did not in fact control, Leckwith as part of a wider lordship extending to the lowlands from Senghennydd (Smith, 'Kingdom of Morgannwg', 19, 35; cf. Corbett, *Glamorgan*, 214–15).

RHYS AP GRUFFUDD
(d. 13 July 1256)

618 Margam Abbey

Notification that he has taken the abbey and all its goods and possessions under his protection as if they were his own property. He will not allow any of his men or any men coming to his land to harm the abbey. If any goods or plunder from it are brought to his land, he will compel the malefactors to make full restoration if they wish to have his peace. If any of his men has a claim against the the abbey, he will not allow him to commit any violence against it because of this, but rather the claim will be justly settled before Rhys. He has sworn faithfully to observe all this for ever. Witnesses (not named).

[1211 × 13 July 1256]

B = NLW, Penrice and Margam Roll 290/2. s. xiii.
Pd. from B, *Cartae*, ii. 594–5 (no. 569).
Cd., Birch, *Catalogue*, i. 105; *H*, no. 543.

Sciant omnes presentes et futuri quod ego Resus filius Griffin ab Yuor suscepi in custodiam et protectionem meam domum de Marg(an) et omnes res et possessiones eiusdem domus custodiendas et defendendas sicut res meas proprias et non sustinebo quod aliquis hominum meorum vel aliorum qui in terra mea manere vel ad eam redditum habere voluerit[a] predicte domui molestiam faciat iniuriam vel gravamen. Et si contigerit aliquas res eiusdem domus vel predam in terram meam devenire, ego compellam ipsos malefactores omnes res suas restituere, sicut voluerint pacem meam habere. Et si contigerit aliquem hominum meorum habere querelam erga prefatam domum, non permittam ei propter hoc fieri aliquam violentiam aut gravamen sed ipsa querela coram me iusto iudicio terminabitur. Et ego iuravi et affidavi me fideliter et absque dolo hec omnia servaturum prefate domui in perpetuum. Hiis testibus.

[a] *corrected in* B *from* voluerint *by dotting under* nt *and interlining* t *above.*

This document was evidently issued after Rhys had succeeded his father Gruffudd ab Ifor as lord of Senghennydd.

Concordance
between K. L. Maund, *Handlist of the Acts of Native Welsh Rulers, 1132–1283* (*H*), and the present edition (*AWR*)

H	AWR	H	AWR
1	**2**	41	**62**
2	**1**	42	**34**
3	**3**	43	**61**
4	**4**	44	**59**
5	**11**	45	**60**
6	**12**	46	**69**
7	**13**	47	**64**
8	**—[a]**	48	**482**
9	**16**	49	**121**
10	**17**	50	**131**
11	**18**	51	**132**
12	**14**	52	**152**
13	**15**	53	**133**
14	**82**	54	**134**
15	**71**	55	**188**
16	**78**	56	**150**
17	**22**	57	**129**
18	**26**	58	**136**
19	**28**	59	**124**
20	**27**	60	**139**
21	**46**	61	**142**
22	**35**	62	**138**
23	**50**	63	**154**
24	**55**	64	**155**
25	**56**	65	**170**
26	**57**	66	**144**
27	**63**	67	**143**
28	**84**	68	**141**
29	**68**	69	**148**
30	**90**	70	**127**
31	**49**	71	**135**
32	**96**	72	**130**
33	**58**	73	**122**
34	**23**	74	**137**
35	**24**	75	**128**
36	**47**	76	**145**
37	**29**	77	**146**
38	**33**	78	**160**
39	**32**	79	**168**
40	**41**	80	**159**

H	AWR	H	AWR
81	**171**	126	**225**
82	**151**	127	**226**
83	**164**	128	**227**
84	**162**	129	**231**
85	**172**	130	**229**
86	**161**	131	**233**
87	**169**	132	**239**
88	**163**	133	**250**
89	**157**	134	**256**
90	**176**	135	**282**
91	**158**	136	**286**
92	**166**	137	**260**
93	**167**	138	**258**
94	**186**	139	**259**
95	**183**	140	**272**
96	**185**	141	**288**
97	**184**	142	**289**
98	**179**	143	**292**
99	**180**	144	**317**
100	**165**	145	**318**
101	**173**	146	**283**
102	**175**	147	**320**
103	**177**	148	**321**
104	**178**	149	**322**
105	**189**	150	**313**
106	**153**	151	**441**
107	**174**	152	**367**
108	**119**	153	**397**
109	**182**	154	**447**
110	**125**	155	**423**
111	**156**	156	**424**
112	**126**	157	**457**
113	**197**	158	**460**
114	**198**	159	**217**
115	**199**	160	—[b]
116	**200**	161	**214**
117	**202**	162	**232**
118	**216**	163	**290**
119	**201**	164	**287**
120	**204**	165	**319**
121	**203**	166	**311**
122	**218**	167	**439**
123	**219**	168	**437**
124	**213**	169	**438**
125	**205**	170	**374**

H	AWR	H	AWR
171	**324**	216	**481**
172	**325**	217	**485**
173	—c	218	**484**
174	**462**	219	**543**
175	**463**	220	**490**
176	**464**	221	**491**
177	**465**	222	**497**
178	**467**	223	**498**
179	**473**	224	**500**
180	**474**	225	**499**
181	**469**	226	**501**
182	**471**	227	**503**
183	**470**	228	**504**
184	**472**	229	**522**
185	**475**	230	**506**
186	**477**	231	**508**
187	**468**	232	**509**
188	**479**	233	**511**
189	**108**	234	**510**
190	**9**	235	**515**
191	**113**	236	**516**
192	**103**	237	**514**
193	**104**	238	**526**
194	**109**	239	**529**
195	**115**	240	**519**
196	**114**	241	**531**
197	**206**	242	—d
198	**208**	243	**552**
199	**207**	244	**553**
200	**210**	245	**555**
201	**209**	246	**546**
202	**480**	247	**556**
203	**539**	248	**563**
204	**483**	249	**551**
205	**541**	250	**564**
206	**495**	251	**565**
207	**542**	252	**569**
208	**544**	253	**545**
209	**487**	254	**548**
210	**488**	255	**549**
211	**492**	256	**575**
212	**493**	257	**578**
213	**494**	258	**610**
214	**496**	259	**602**
215	**540**	260	**606**

H	AWR	H	AWR
261	**607**	306	**94**
262	**547**	307	**99**
263	**559**	308	**89**
264	**557**	309	**95**
265	**558**	310	**100**
266	**560**	311	**101**
267	**561**	312	**102**
268	**562**	313	**97**
269	**566**	314	**42**
270	**568**	315	**44**
271	**570**	316	**53**
272	**571**	317	**54**
273	**572**	318	**_e**
274	**573**	319	**67**
275	**574**	320	**190**
276	**580**	321	**123**
277	**592**	322	**147**
278	**593**	323	**181**
279	**595**	324	**187**
280	**589**	325	**192**
281	**617**	326	**195**
282	**616**	327	**193**
283	**19**	328	**194**
284	**79**	329	**196**
285	**80**	330	**221**
286	**72**	331	**220**
287	**73**	332	**230**
288	**70**	333	**234**
289	**74**	334	**235**
290	**75**	335	**240**
291	**81**	336	**241**
292	**76**	337	**242**
293	**77**	338	**244**
294	**83**	339	**243**
295	**52**	340	**280**
296	**43**	341	**246**
297	**20**	342	**247**
298	**85**	343	**245**
299	**66**	344	**248**
300	**86**	345	**249**
301	**87**	346	**252**
302	**88**	347	**254**
303	**92**	348	**255**
304	**93**	349	**261**
305	**98**	350	**262**

H	AWR	H	AWR
351	**266**	396	**361**
352	**238**	397	**362**
353	**267**	398	**363**
354	**268**	399	**366**
355	**269**	400	**369**
356	**271**	401	**370**
357	**274**	402	**368**
358	**291**	403	**375**
359	**296**	404	**458**
360	**298**	405	**376**
361	**294**	406	**377**
362	**284**	407	**378**
363	**299**	408	**380**
364	**301**	409	**383**
365	**302**	410	**444**
366	**303**	411	**384**
367	**304**	412	**385**
368	**305**	413	**386**
369	**309**	414	**387**
370	**310**	415	**389**
371	**307**	416	**390**
372	**308**	417	**391**
373	**312**	418	**392**
374	**314**	419	**393**
375	**315**	420	**394**
376	**323**	421	**400**
377	**440**	422	**398**
378	**316**	423	**401**
379	**327**	424	**445**
380	**328**	425	**402**
381	**329**	426	**403**
382	**330**	427	**404**
383	**331**	428	**405**
384	**335**	429	**407**
385	**336**	430	**406**
386	**342**	431	**410**
387	**346**	432	**411**
388	**347**	433	**450**
389	**351**	434	**422**
390	**349**	435	**446**
391	**353**	436	**449**
392	**354**	437	**453**
393	**355**	438	**452**
394	**356**	439	**414**
395	**357**	440	**433**

H	AWR	H	AWR
441	**415**	486	**365**
442	**418**	487	**371**
443	**434**	488	**372**
444	**416**	489	**373**
445	**417**	490	**379**
446	**435**	491	**395**
447	**413**	492	**396**
448	**419**	493	**408**
449	**420**	494	**409**
450	**421**	495	**432**
451	**459**	496	**426**
452	**451**	497	_h
453	_f	498	**478**
454	**425**	499	**118**
455	**427**	500	**110**
456	**436**	501	**116**
457	**428**	502	_i
458	**429**	503	**111**
459	**454**	504	**112**
460	**430**	505	**106**
461	**455**	506	**107**
462	**456**	507	**117**
463	**222**	508	**612**
464	**276**	509	**614**
465	**277**	510	_j
466	**253**	511	**615**
467	**265**	512	**211**
468	**281**	513	**212**
469	**273**	514	**523**
470	**326**	515	**524**
471	**333**	516	**513**
472	**331**	517	**525**
473	**334**	518	**536**
474	**337**	519	**527**
475	**338**	520	**528**
476	**341**	521	**520**
477	**343**	522	**533**
478	**344**	523	**534**
479	**348**	524	**537**
480	**350**	525	**530**
481	_g	526	**538**
482	**359**	527	**532**
483	**360**	528	**507**
484	**442**	529	**489**
485	**443**	530	_k

H	AWR	H	AWR
531	**576**	538	**604**
532	**596**	539	**605**
533	**586**	540	**608**
534	**600**	541	**591**
535	**358, 601**	542	**598**
536	**609**	543	**618**
537	**603**		

ª Omitted as the identification of the grantor is uncertain. A confirmation of the possessions of Slebech issued by Peter, bishop of St Davids, 7 November 1176 × 16 July 1198, mentions that William de Braose and Meurig ab Addaf granted the church of Llanfihangel Nant Melan with all its appurtenances and liberties to the Hospitallers of Slebech Commandery (*St Davids Episcopal Acta*, 72 (no. 46)). As assumed in *H*, Meurig may have been the same person as the Meurig ab Addaf killed in 1170, who, according to the B-text of *Annales Cambriae*, was the son of Addaf ap Seisyll of Buellt (Builth), a territorial association also given in *Brenhinedd y Saeson* (*BT, Pen20Tr*, 65 and note, 183; *AC*, 52; *BS*, 170–1). If this is correct, Meurig's co-grantor was William II de Braose, who succeeded his father Philip de Braose after the latter's death 1134 × 1155 and died probably in 1175 (Sanders, *Baronies*, 21; Davies, *Conquest*, 277). However, since Llanfihangel Nant Melan, located in the commote of Llythyfnwg about 4 miles south-west of Old Radnor, lay nearer to Maelienydd than to Buellt, it is more likely that the reference is to the Meurig ab Addaf associated with Madog ap Maelgwn of Maelienydd in 1211–12 (*Pipe Roll 13 John*, 233; *Pipe Roll 14 John*, 159). If so, his co-grantor was William III de Braose (d. 1211), whose lands were confiscated by John in 1208 (Sanders, *Baronies*, 108 and n. 3).

ᵇ Omitted as the mention does not necessarily indicate that the grant was the subject of a written act issued by Llywelyn ap Iorwerth (*Rec. Caern.*, 19: *Et nichil inde reddunt per annum quia de dono Leuli(ni) ap Ior' nuper principis Wallie* (orthography and punctuation amended)).

ᶜ Omitted as the mention does not explicitly state that the grant was the subject of a written act issued by Llywelyn ap Gruffudd, and contains an anachronistic reference to the hundred (*Rec. Caern.*, 33: *quia Leuli(n) ap Griffuth nuper princeps Wall(ie) concessit et dedit predictas quattuor bovatas terre antecessoribus predictorum Ior' et Ieu(a)n sine aliquo reddito preter sectam ad commotum et hundredum, et preter quod ibunt cum domino principe in guerra sua ad custagia ipsius domini principis absque aliquibus aliis servitiis* (orthography and punctuation amended)).

ᵈ Omitted as the record on the assize roll merely states that Llywelyn ap Gruffudd ap Madog of Bromfield and his nephews made various quitclaims to Owain ap Gruffudd ap Madog and Gruffudd ap Madog before the justices at Oswestry in February 1278, without making any reference to the quitclaims being the subject of one or more written acts issued by Llywelyn and his nephews (*WAR*, 248).

ᵉ Omitted as the reference in the curia regis roll is to a plea by Maredudd ap Rhys against Bishop Thomas Wallensis of St Davids rather than to a written act issued by Maredudd (*WAR*, 20–1).

ᶠ Omitted as the Welsh roll refers to a petition made, apparently orally, on behalf of Llywelyn ap Gruffudd before Bishop Thomas Bek of St Davids and other appointees of Edward I regarding the legal dispute over Arwystli rather than to an act issued by the prince (*CWR*, 195).

ᵍ Omitted as the text of this letter is extant as no. 356 (*H*, no. 394).

ʰ Omitted as the text of this letter is extant as no. 436 (*H*, no. 456).

[i] Omitted as author of document named erroneously as Hywel ap Maredudd rather than Hywel ap Cadwallon, whose letter patent is already calendared as *H*, no. 499.

[j] *CAP*, 109 (followed by *H*) identified the sender of this petition, named in the text merely as *Oweyn ap Thewelyn* (TNA: PRO, SC 8/75, no. 3731), as Owain ap Llywelyn ab Owain of Mechain and associated it with the claim to Mechain of 1277 attested by nos 613–14. However, it is difficult to see why the justice of South Wales would have been ordered to investigate a claim to lands from this Owain, and it is more likely, therefore, that the petitioner was Owain ap Llywelyn ab Owain of Ceredigion, who succeeded his father on the latter's death in 1309 (see note to no. 83).

[k] Omitted as the reference is to a letter patent of Edward I dated at Cirencester, 26 December 1276, empowering Dafydd ap Gruffudd and Guncelin de Badlesmere, justice of Chester to receive Llywelyn ap Gruffudd ap Madog of Bromfield into the king's peace (*CPR 1272–81*, 186), rather than to an agreement between Dafydd and Guncelin on the one hand and Llywelyn on the other.

INDEX OF PERSONS AND PLACES

Numbers in italic type refer to pages of the introduction, numbers in roman type to the individual documents numbered consecutively. As far as possible, place-names are given in their modern forms, followed by the original spellings in the documents (although variant readings cited in textual notes have not been indexed); original spellings are normally cross-referenced unless their first two letters are the same as those of the modern form. Where identified, Welsh and English place-names are also followed by pre-1974 counties. Further guidance on many place-names is provided in the endnotes to individual documents. W following a number indicates a witness, P following a number a pledge. Additional abbreviations used in the index are abp for archbishop, bp for bishop, gr. for grange and Mr for Master.

A., abbot of Caerleon 76
A., abbot of Enlli 440
A., clerk 509W
A. ab Ithel 43W
Aaron, cellarer of Strata Marcella 552W, 553W
Aaron ap Rhys 43W
Abelauc (unident.) 511
Aber, Caerns. *30*; 379, 612
Aber Call, Aberkall, Caerns. 218
Aber Carrog, Aberkarroc, Caerns. 218
Aber Ceiriog, Abirokeyrok, Denbs. 481
Aber Methen, Abermethen (unident.) 28, 35
Aberaeron, Cards. 28
Aberafan Burrows, *see* Afan, burrows of
Aberalwen, Mer. 400
Aberarth, Cards. 28, 82
Aberbrydwen, Aberbredewen, Aberbredwen, Abrebretwen, Mont. 9–13, 558
Aberbythych, Abirbythich, Carms., church of St Michael 90
Abercain, Aberkeyn, Mer. 229
Abercefail, Aberkeueil, Cards. 68
Abercennen, Aberkennen, Carms., land of church of 90

Abercerdin, Cards. 68
Aberchwiler, Aberwhyler, Denbs. 251, 285
Aberclarach, Aberclaragh', Cards. 82
Abercoil, Abercoill, Abercoyl (unident.) 28, 35, 55, 63, 82
Aberconwy, Abercenwy, Abercon', Aberconeway, Aberconewey, Aberconnewey, Aberconu, Aberconwe, Aberconwey, Aberconwy, Abercunewey, Aberthon', Caerns.
    abbey *26, 28, 30*; 459; abbot of 230, 306n., 342, 349, 358, 391, 601; *see also* Abraham; Anian; Maredudd; seal of 329, 458; grants to 82n., 206, 218–19, 319; monk of 332; princes' archives at *136–7*; prior of, *see* I.
    Treaty of (1277) *31, 33, 40*; 402–5, 407, 426, 429
Abercownen, ecclesia Sancti Michaelis de, *see* Llanfihangel Abercywyn
Abercynllaith, Aberkenllith, Mont. 569
Aberdaron, Caerns., secular canons of 440
Aberdengum, *see* Dengwm
Aberdengy, *see* Dengi
Aberdihonw, Aberdehonoy, Aberde Hony, Brec. 55, 82

INDEX OF SUBJECTS

Numbers in italic type refer to pages of the introduction, numbers in roman type to the individual documents numbered consecutively. Welsh terms are usually given in their Modern Welsh forms, followed (where applicable) by the original spellings in the documents.